The Humanities
Culture, Continuity & Change

THIRD EDITION

Henry M. Sayre
OREGON STATE UNIVERSITY

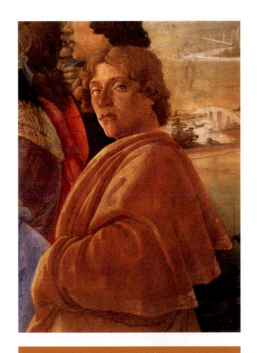

VOLUME I

PREHISTORY TO 1600

PEARSON

Boston   Columbus   Indianapolis   New York   San Francisco
Upper Saddle River   Amsterdam   Cape Town   Dubai   London
Madrid   Milan   Munich   Paris   Montréal   Toronto   Delhi   Mexico City
São Paulo   Sydney   Hong Kong   Seoul   Singapore   Taipei   Tokyo

In memory of my good friend Bud Therien, art publisher and editor par excellence

Editor in Chief: Sarah Touborg
Senior Sponsoring Editor: Helen Ronan
Editorial Assistant: Chris Fegan
Vice-President, Director of Marketing: Brandy Dawson
Executive Marketing Manager: Kate Mitchell
Marketing Assistant: Paige Patunas
Managing Editor: Melissa Feimer
Project Manager: Marlene Gassler
Senior Operations Supervisor: Mary Fischer
Operations Specialist: Diane Peirano
Media Director: Brian Hyland
Senior Media Editor: David Alick
Media Project Manager: Rich Barnes

Pearson Imaging Center: Corin Skidds
Printer/Binder: Courier / Kendallville
Cover Printer: Lehigh Phoenix Color / Hagerstown

Team at Laurence King Publishing:
Commissioning editor: Kara Hattersley-Smith
Senior editor: Felicity Maunder
Production controller: Simon Walsh
Page design: Nick Newton
Cover design: Jo Fernandes
Picture researcher: Emma Brown
Copy editor: Carolyn Jones
Indexer: Barry Campbell

Cover Image: Sandro Botticelli, *Adoration of the Magi* (detail). 1470s. Tempera on panel, 43¾" × 52¾". Galleria degli Uffizi, Florence. © 2013 Photo Scala, Florence – courtesy Ministero per i Beni e le Attività Culturali.

Credits and acknowledgments borrowed from other sources and reproduced, with permission, in this textbook appear on the appropriate page within text or on the credits pages in the back of this book.

Library of Congress Cataloging-in-Publication Data

Sayre, Henry M.
  The humanities : culture, continuity & change / Henry Sayre, Oregon State University. -- Third edition.
    pages cm
  ISBN-13: 978-0-205-97313-2 (volume I student edition)
  ISBN-10: 0-205-97313-2 (volume I student edition)
  ISBN-13: 978-0-205-97772-7 (volume I instructor review copy)
  ISBN-10: 0-205-97772-3 (volume I instructor review copy)
  [etc.]
1. Civilization--History. 2. Humanities--History. 3. Social change--History. I. Title.
  CB69.S29 2014
  909--dc23
                    2013037308

10 9 8 7 6 5 4 3 2 1

Volume I

Student Edition
ISBN 10: 0-205-97313-2
ISBN 13: 978-0-205-97313-2

Instructor's Review Copy
ISBN 10: 0-205-97772-3
ISBN 13: 978-0-205-97772-7

Books à la Carte
ISBN 10: 0-205-98321-9
ISBN 13: 978-0-205-98321-6

PEARSON

BRIEF CONTENTS

CONTENTS

11 Centers of Culture
COURT AND CITY IN THE LARGER WORLD 363

12 The Gothic Style
FAITH AND KNOWLEDGE IN AN AGE OF INQUIRY 405

DEAR READER,

It has been fifteen years since I first sat down to write *The Humanities*, and now, with the publication of this third edition, I'd like to take the opportunity to reflect a moment on this book and the value of the humanities in general.

The great question facing the humanities fifteen years ago was simple and direct: Do we or do we not include the cultures of the world, beyond the West, in the text? Many of us teaching the course felt unequipped to take on the arts and cultures of Asia, Africa, and Central and South America. Others felt that there was already too much to cover in simply addressing the Western world. But as work on the book proceeded, it became evident to me that taking a global perspective was not only important, but essential to the humanistic enterprise in general.

And what, you might well ask, is the humanistic enterprise in the first place? At the most superficial level, a Humanities course is designed to help you identify the significant works of art, architecture, music, theater, philosophy, and literature of distinct cultures and times, and to recognize how these different expressions of the human spirit respond to and reflect their historical contexts. More broadly, you should arrive at some understanding of the creative process, and how what we—and others—have made and continue to value reflects what we all think it means to be human. But in studying other cultures—entering into what the British-born, Ghanian–American philosopher and novelist Kwame Anthony Appiah has described as a "conversation between people from different ways of life"—we learn even more. We turn to other cultures because to empathize with others, to willingly engage in discourse with ideas alien to ourselves, is perhaps the fundamental goal of the humanities. The humanities are, above all, disciplines of openness, inclusion, and respectful interaction. What we see reflected in other cultures is usually something of ourselves: the objects of beauty that delight us, the weapons and the wars that threaten us, the melodies and harmonies that soothe us, the sometimes troubling but often penetrating thoughts that we encounter in the ether of our increasingly digital globe. Through the humanities we learn to seek common ground.

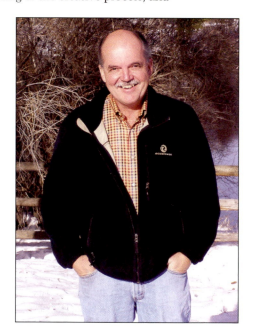

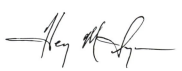

ABOUT THE AUTHOR

Henry M. Sayre is Distinguished Professor of Art History at Oregon State University–Cascades Campus in Bend, Oregon. He earned his Ph.D. in American Literature from the University of Washington. He is producer and creator of the 10-part television series, *A World of Art: Works in Progress*, aired on PBS in the Fall of 1997; and author of seven books, including *A World of Art, The Visual Text of William Carlos Williams, The Object of Performance: The American Avant-Garde since 1970*; and an art history book for children, *Cave Paintings to Picasso*.

What's New

THIS NEW EDITION ENHANCES THE LEARNING EXPERIENCE FOR YOUR STUDENTS:

NEW! Continuing Presence of the Past

This new feature helps students to understand how the arts of the past remain relevant today. Designed to underscore the book's emphasis on continuity and change, the **Continuing Presence of the Past** in each chapter, identified with a special icon, connects an artwork from that period to a contemporary artwork in **MyArtsLab** and demonstrates how the past has informed the present work.

For example, in Chapter 7, **Continuing Presence of the Past** focuses on Cai Guo-Qiang's *Project to Extend the Great Wall of China by 10,000 Meters: Project for Extraterrestrials*, in which the artist detonated a series of explosions from the western end of the Great Wall that slithered in a red line on the horizon to form an ephemeral extension of the Great Wall itself. Gunpowder, originally a force for destruction, had now become an act of creation.

Thinking Ahead and **Thinking Back** questions in each chapter now focus on learning objectives and reflect the larger learning objectives of *The Humanities*. In addition, the **Thinking Back** features pose critical-thinking questions as well as reviewing the material covered in the chapter.

KEY IMPROVEMENTS TO THE ORGANIZATION AND CURRENCY OF THE NEW EDITION:

- **Chapter 1** introduces the new research at Çatalhöyük, with an extended discussion plus three new images.
- **Chapter 4** includes an expanded discussion on the poetry of Sappho, plus material on Greek music and the lyre (with an image of a woman playing a lyre). Solon and Pisistratus are also discussed in more detail.
- **Chapter 5** expands the coverage of Hellenic sculpture, including a third image of the Pergamon frieze and the second sculpture from the "Vanquished Gauls" grouping.
- **Chapter 6** has enhanced coverage of Rome, including a fuller discussion of the Late Roman emperors, new material on the Julio-Claudian emperors, plus new images such as Hadrian's Villa, a second frieze from the Arch of Titus, an image of Stilicho, and a new timeline.
- **Chapter 7**, now entitled **Emerging Empires in the East: Urban Life and Imperial Majesty in China and India**, contains a new discussion on the Chu State in China, reflecting current scholarship.
- **Chapter 9** expands the information on the rise of the Umayyad caliphate and the fall of Ali to help clarify the Shiite/Sunni issues for non-Muslim students.

- **Chapter 12** has significant new coverage of the Limbourg brothers, focusing on *January* and *February* from *Les Très Riches Heures*.
- **Chapter 15**, now called **The High Renaissance in Rome and Venice: Papal Patronage and Civic Pride**, offers more coverage on women in Italian humanist society, with new discussions on Paola Tinagli's *Women in Italian Renaissance Art: Gender, Representation, Identity*, and Titian's *La Bella*. Discussion on Raphael has been expanded, with the addition of more images.
- **Chapter 17** has added discussion of, and an image illustrating, Protestant iconoclasm.
- **Chapter 18** presents significant new coverage on African strategies for cultural survival, accompanied by five images.
- **Chapter 20** further clarifies Mannerism with a new introduction and the addition of Arcimboldo's *Summer*, replacing the discussion of the Escorial, the substitution of Michelangelo's *Pietà* for his *Victory*, and the inclusion of Tintoretto's *Last Supper*.
- The discussion on the English garden has been moved from Chapter 25 into **Chapter 24**, where it is introduced by new coverage on Alexander Pope's villa at Twickenham.
- **Chapter 25** offers a new discussion and image of Wang Hui's *The Colors of Mount Taihang*.
- **Coverage of the American national identity has been significantly reorganized.** Material from Chapters 27, 28, and 29 has been brought into a single chapter: **Chapter 29, Defining a Nation: American National Identity and the Challenge of Civil War**. The chapter includes new coverage of the events leading up to the Civil War. There is expanded coverage of literature with the inclusion of Washington Irving ("Rip Van Winkle" and "The Legend of Sleepy Hollow") and James Fenimore Cooper (an excerpt from *The Pioneers*). Coverage of Rosa Bonheur has been restored to **Chapter 28** from the first edition.
- The material on France in the 1850s and 1860s from Chapters 29 and 30 has now been combined in **Chapter 30, Global Confrontation and Modern Life: The Quest for Cultural Identity**.
- **Chapter 31** expands its coverage of literature with a discussion of and excerpt from John Stuart Mill's *On Liberty*.
- **Chapter 39** includes new material on "low impact" environmental art, with images by Richard Long and Andy Goldsworthy.
- **Chapter 40** adds significantly to its coverage of time-based media with the inclusion of Isaac Julien's *Ten Thousand Waves* and Phil Collins's *the world won't listen*. There is also a new discussion on Takashi Murakami.

Go Digital

The most contextual humanities text now offers students a truly personalized and mobile experience to make learning more affordable and accessible. Here's what Sayre's *The Humanities, Third Edition*, has to offer.

MyArtsLab is an online homework, tutorial, and assessment program that truly engages students in learning. Its interactive eText—with streaming audio, scale figure features, Closer Look tours and panoramas—and personalized study plans help students better prepare for class, quizzes, and exams—resulting in better performance in the course. *All key MyArtsLab learning applications are now available for tablet devices.*

- **Personalized study plan** for each student promotes critical-thinking skills. Assessment tied to videos, applications, and chapters enables both instructors and students to track progress and get immediate feedback.

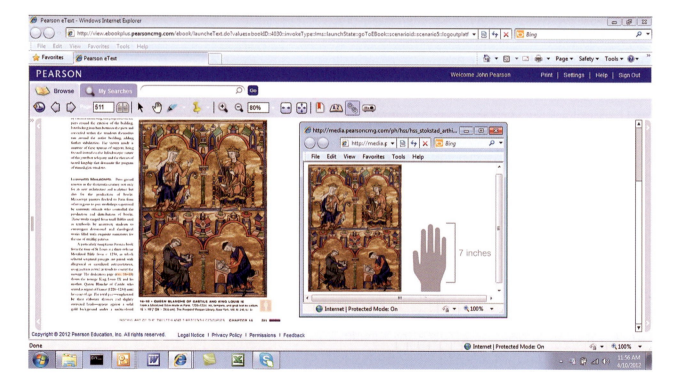

▲ **The Pearson eText** lets students access their textbook anytime, anywhere, and any way they want—including downloading to an iPad or listening to chapter audio read by Henry Sayre and Brian Seymour. Includes a unique scale feature showing students the size of a work in relation to the human figure or the human hand.

New! Introducing Writing Space

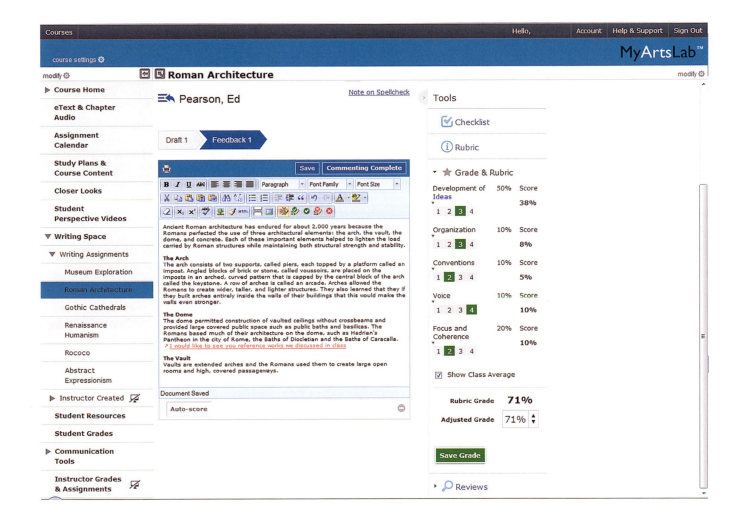

▲ **Writing Space** is the best way to develop and assess critical-thinking skills through writing. It provides a single place within MyArtsLab to create, track, grade writing assignments, access writing resources, and exchange meaningful, personalized feedback quickly and easily. Writing Space can also check students' work for citation and plagiarism by evaluating it against the world's most accurate text comparison database available from Turnitin.

Writing Space helps you keep writing in the classroom and your students thinking critically. Instructors can choose from an assignment and rubric bank, or create their own. The In-line commenting feature helps deliver personalized feedback to every student.

Go Mobile with MyArtsLab

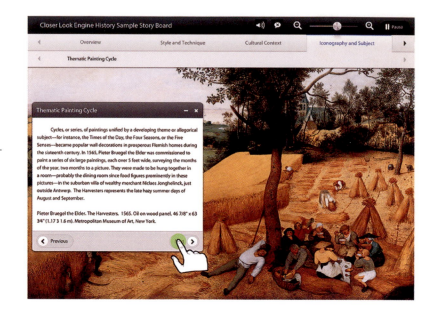

► **New and expanded: Closer Look tours**—interactive walkthroughs featuring expert audio—offer in-depth looks at key works of art. *Over 300 in total, now optimized for tablet.*

● **Listening Guides with Streaming Audio**—available for most of the music selections in the book, these listening guides let students listen to performances and help them connect musical events with cultural context. *Now available for mobile.*

▼ **Studio technique videos** help students understand key techniques like lost-wax casting. *Now available for mobile.*

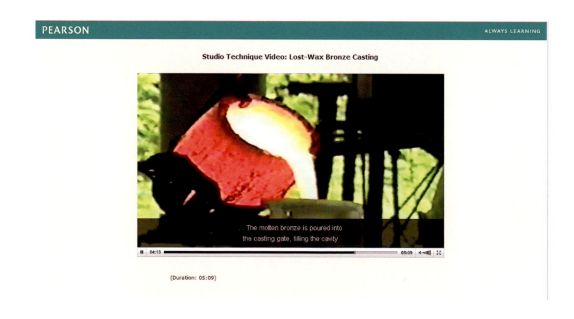

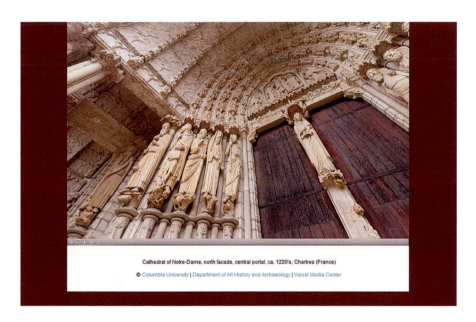

Cathedral of Notre-Dame, north facade, central portal, ca. 1220's, Chartres (France)

© Columbia University | Department of Art History and Archaeology | Visual Media Center

▲ **New and expanded: 360-degree architectural panoramas** and simulations of major monuments help students understand buildings—inside and out. *Over 75 in total, now optimized for mobile.*

▼ **Flashcards,** illustrated with nearly every image in the book, let students review on the go. *Now available for mobile.*

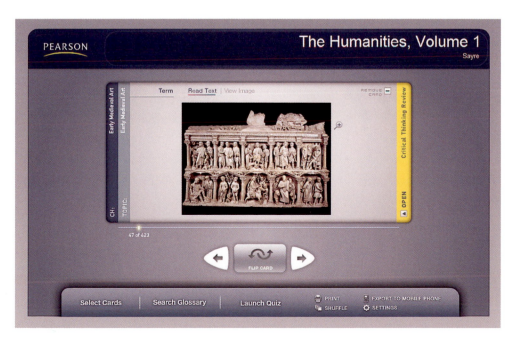

Let Your Students Experience The Humanities

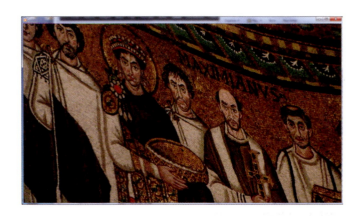

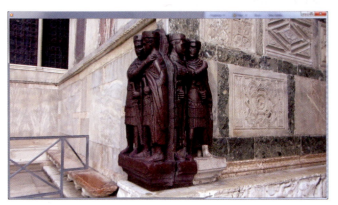

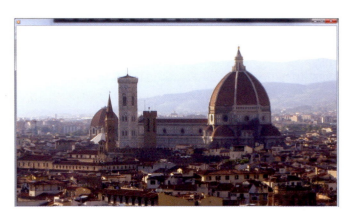

◄ **New: Students on Site videos**—Over 75 in total, produced and edited by students for students, these 2–3 minute videos provide "you are there" impressions of major monuments, reviewed and approved by faculty and students.

WHY USE MYARTSLAB?

MyArtsLab consistently and positively impacts the quality of learning in the classroom. When educators require and integrate MyArtsLab in their course, students and instructors experience success. Join our ever-growing community of 50,000 users across the country giving their students access to the high quality rich media and assessment on MyArtsLab.

"Students who use MyArtsLab perform better on their exams than students who do not."
—*Cynthia Kristan-Graham, Auburn University*

"MyArtsLab also makes students more active learners. They are more engaged with the material."
—*Maya Jiménez, Kingsborough Community College*

"MyArtsLab keeps students connected in another way to the course material. A student could be immersed for hours!"
—*Cindy B. Damschroder, University of Cincinnati*

"I really enjoy using MyArtsLab. At the end of the quarter, I ask students to write a paragraph about their experience with MyArtsLab and 97% of them are positive."
—*Rebecca Trittel, Savannah College of Art and Design*

Give Your Students Choices

ORDERING OPTIONS

Pearson arts titles are available in the following formats to give you and your students more choices—and more ways to save.

The **CourseSmart eTextbook** offers the same content as the printed text in a convenient online format—with highlighting, online search, and printing capabilities. **www.coursesmart.com**

The **Books à la Carte** edition offers a convenient, three-hole-punched, loose-leaf version of the traditional text at a discounted price—allowing students to take only what they need to class. Books à la Carte editions are available both with and without access to MyArtsLab.

Build your own Pearson Custom course material. Work with a dedicated Pearson Custom editor to create your ideal textbook and web material—publishing your own original content or mixing and matching Pearson content. *Contact your Pearson representative to get started.*

MyArtsLibrary: Containing hundreds of primary sources from world civilizations, gives students additional resources for research and writing.

INSTRUCTOR RESOURCES

Instructor's Manual and Test Item File

This is an invaluable professional resource and reference for new and experienced faculty. Each chapter contains the following sections: Chapter Overview, Chapter Objectives, Lecture and Discussion Topics, Resources, and Writing Assignments and Projects. The test bank includes multiple-choice, matching, and essay questions. Available for download from the instructor support section at **www.myartslab.com.**

MyTest

This flexible online test-generating software includes all questions found in the printed Test Item File. Instructors can quickly and easily create customized tests with MyTest. **www.pearsonmytest.com**

PowerPoints featuring nearly every image in the book, with captions and without captions.

NEW! Teaching with MyArtsLab PowerPoints help instructors make their lectures come alive. These slides allow instructors to display the very best interactive features from MyArtsLab in the classroom—quickly and easily.

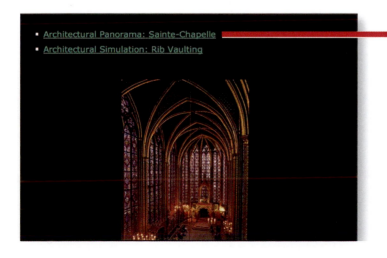

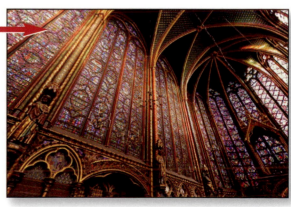

Developing *The Humanities*

The Humanities: Culture, Continuity & Change is the result of an extensive development process involving the contributions of over one hundred instructors and their students. We are grateful to all who participated in shaping the content, clarity, and design of this text. Manuscript reviewers and focus group participants include:

ALABAMA
Cynthia Kristan-Graham, Auburn University

CALIFORNIA
Collette Chattopadhyay, Saddleback College
Laurel Corona, San Diego City College
Cynthia D. Gobatie, Riverside Community College
John Hoskins, San Diego Mesa College
Gwenyth Mapes, Grossmont College
Bradley Nystrom, California State University-Sacramento
Joseph Pak, Saddleback College
John Provost, Monterey Peninsula College
Chad Redwing, Modesto Junior College
Stephanie Robinson, San Diego City College
Alice Taylor, West Los Angeles College
Denise Waszkowski, San Diego Mesa College

COLORADO
Renee Bragg, Arapahoe Community College
Marilyn Smith, Red Rocks Community College

CONNECTICUT
Abdellatif Hissouf, Central Connecticut State University

FLORIDA
Wesley Borucki, Palm Beach Atlantic University
Amber Brock, Tallahassee Community College
Connie Dearmin, Brevard Community College
Kimberly Felos, St. Petersburg College
Katherine Harrell, South Florida Community College
Ira Holmes, College of Central Florida
Dale Hoover, Edison State College
Theresa James, South Florida Community College
Jane Jones, State College of Florida, Manatee-Sarasota
Jennifer Keefe, Valencia Community College
Mansoor Khan, Brevard Community College
Connie LaMarca-Frankel, Pasco-Hernando Community College
Sandi Landis, St. Johns River Community College-Orange Park
Joe Loccisano, State College of Florida
David Luther, Edison College
James Meier, Central Florida Community College
Brandon Montgomery, State College of Florida
Pamela Wood Payne, Palm Beach Atlantic University
Gary Poe, Palm Beach Atlantic University
Frederick Smith, Florida Gateway College
Lynn Spencer, Brevard Community College
Kate Myers de Vega, Palm Beach Atlantic University
Bill Waters, Pensacola State College

GEORGIA
Leslie Harrelson, Dalton State College
Lawrence Hetrick, Georgia Perimeter College
Priscilla Hollingsworth, Augusta State University
Kelley Mahoney, Dalton State College
Andrea Scott Morgan, Georgia Perimeter College

IDAHO
Jennifer Black, Boise State University
Rick Davis, Brigham Young University-Idaho
Derek Jensen, Brigham Young University-Idaho
Christopher Williams, Brigham Young University-Idaho

ILLINOIS
Thomas Christensen, University of Chicago
Timothy J. Clifford, College of DuPage
Leslie Huntress Hopkins, College of Lake County
Judy Kaplow, Harper College
Terry McIntyre, Harper College
Victoria Neubeck O'Connor, Moraine Valley Community College
Sharon Quarcini, Moraine Valley Community College
Paul Van Heuklom, Lincoln Land Community College

INDIANA
Josephina Kiteou, University of Southern Indiana

KENTUCKY
Jonathan Austad, Eastern Kentucky University
Beth Cahaney, Elizabethtown Community and Technical College
Jeremy Killian, University of Louisville
Lynda Mercer, University of Louisville
Sara Northerner, University of Louisville
Elijah Pritchett, University of Louisville

MASSACHUSETTS
Peter R. Kalb, Brandeis University

MICHIGAN
Martha Petry, Jackson Community College
Robert Quist, Ferris State University

MINNESOTA
Mary Johnston, Minnesota State University

NEBRASKA
Michael Hoff, University of Nebraska

NEVADA
Chris Bauer, Sierra College

NEW JERSEY
Jay Braverman, Montclair State University
Sara E. Gil-Ramos, New Jersey City University

NEW MEXICO
Sarah Egelman, Central New Mexico Community College

NEW YORK
Eva Diaz, Pratt Institute
Mary Guzzy, Corning Community College
Thelma Ithier Sterling, Hostos Community College
Elizabeth C. Mansfield, New York University
Clemente Marconi, New York University

NORTH CAROLINA
Melodie Galloway, University of North Carolina at Asheville
Jeanne McGlinn, University of North Carolina at Asheville
Sophie Mills, University of North Carolina at Asheville
Constance Schrader, University of North Carolina at Asheville
Ronald Sousa, University of North Carolina at Asheville
Samer Traboulsi, University of North Carolina at Asheville

NORTH DAKOTA
Robert Kibler, Minot State University

OHIO
Darlene Alberts, Columbus State Community College
Tim Davis, Columbus State Community College
Michael Mangus, The Ohio State University at Newark
Keith Pepperell, Columbus State Community College
Patrice Ross, Columbus State Community College

OKLAHOMA
Amanda H. Blackman, Tulsa Community College-Northeast Campus
Diane Boze, Northeastern State University
Jacklan J. Renee Cox, Rogers State University
Jim Ford, Rogers State University
Diana Lurz, Rogers State University
James W. Mock, University of Central Oklahoma
Gregory Thompson, Rogers State University

PENNSYLVANIA
Elizabeth Pilliod, Rutgers University-Camden
Douglas B. Rosentrater, Bucks County Community College
Debra Thomas, Harrisburg Area Community College

RHODE ISLAND
Mallica Kumbera Landrus, Rhode Island School of Design

TEXAS
Mindi Bailey, Collin County Community College
Peggy Brown, Collin County Community College
Marsha Lindsay, Lone Star College-North Harris
Aditi Samarth, Richland College
Lee Ann Westman, University of Texas at El Paso

UTAH
Matthew Ancell, Brigham Young University
Terre Burton, Dixie College
Nate Kramer, Brigham Young University
Joseph D. Parry, Brigham Young University

Acknowledgments

No project of this scope could ever come into being without the hard work and perseverance of many more people than its author. In fact, this author has been humbled by the teams at Pearson and Laurence King Publishing, who never wavered in their confidence in my ability to finish this third edition of what remains an enormous undertaking. At Laurence King, I am especially grateful to Senior Editor Felicity Maunder for the exceptional care she has taken in moving the project forward. I also want to thank Emma Brown for her sometimes miraculous picture research, Carolyn Jones for her scrupulous copy editing, and Simon Walsh for overseeing matters of production. The overwhelming task of indexing the book has been borne by Barry Campbell, and Nick Newton has patiently worked with me to get the page design as close to perfect as we could manage. For the cover design, the originality of which gets more and more difficult with each edition, I want to express my sincere gratitude to Jo Fernandes. Finally, all of these great people at Laurence King are overseen by the inestimable Kara Hattersley-Smith.

At Pearson, Cory Skidds, senior imaging specialist, has worked on image compositing and color accuracy of the artwork with as much attention to detail as any author could ever hope for. The production of the book was coordinated by Melissa Feimer, managing editor, and Marlene Gassler, project manager, both of whom oversaw with good humor and patience the day-to-day, hour-to-hour crises that arose. Diane Peirano, operations specialist, ensured that this project progressed smoothly through its production route.

And editorial assistant Chris Fegan probably knew more about what was happening when and where than anyone.

The marketing and editorial teams at Pearson are beyond compare. On the marketing side, Brandy Dawson, vice president of marketing, and Kate Mitchell, executive marketing manager, helped us all to understand just what students want and need. On the editorial side, my thanks to Yolanda de Rooy, president of the Social Sciences and the Arts division; to Sarah Touborg, editor-in-chief; Helen Ronan, senior sponsoring editor; and Billy Grieco, editor. The late Bud Therien envisioned this project, saw it through to the first edition, and I am forever grateful for his support, encouragement, and, above all, his friendship. He is everywhere present in these pages. The combined human hours that this group has put into this project are staggering. Billy, Helen, and Sarah have supported me every step of the way in making it as good, or even better, than I envisioned; and Yolanda's over-arching vision is responsible for helping to make Pearson such an extraordinarily good publisher to write for.

Finally, I want to thank, with all my love, my beautiful wife, Sandy Brooke, who has supported this project in every way. I have said this before, but it continues to be true: She has continued to teach, paint, and write, while urging me on, listening to my struggles, humoring me when I didn't deserve it, and being a far better wife than I was a husband. She was, is, and will continue to be, I trust, the source of my strength.

PART ONE

The Ancient World and the Classical Past

PREHISTORY TO 200 CE

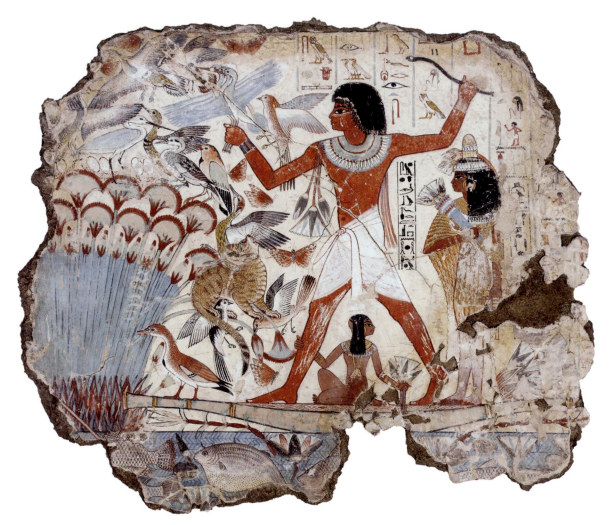

Nebamun Hunting Birds, from the tomb of Nebamun, Thebes, Egypt (detail). ca. 1400 BCE (see Fig 3.2 in Chapter 3).

The history of human beings on this planet is, geologically speaking, very short. The history of their coming together in groups for their common good is even shorter, covering a span of perhaps 25,000 to 50,000 years on a planet that scientists estimate to be between 4 and 5 billion years old. We call these groups, as they become more and more sophisticated, civilizations. A **civilization** is a social, economic, and political entity distinguished by the ability to express itself through images and written language. Civilizations develop when the environment of a region can support a large and productive population. It is no accident that the first civilizations arose in fertile river valleys, where agriculture could take hold: the Tigris and the Euphrates in Mesopotamia, the Nile in Egypt, the Indus on the Indian subcontinent, and the Yellow in China. Civilizations require technologies capable of supporting the principal economy. In the ancient world, agriculture was supported by the technologies related to irrigation.

With the rise of agriculture, and with irrigation, human nature began to assert itself over and against nature as a whole. People increasingly thought of themselves as masters of their own destiny. At the same time, different and dispersed populations began to come into contact with one another as trade developed from the need for raw materials not native to a particular region. Organizing this level of trade and production also required an administrative elite to form and establish cultural priorities. The existence of such an elite is another characteristic of civilization. Finally, as the history of cultures around the world makes abundantly clear, one of the major ways in which societies have acquired the goods they want and simultaneously organized themselves is by means of war.

If a civilization is a system of organization, a **culture** is the set of common values—religious, social, and/or political—that govern that system. Out of such cultures arise scientific and artistic achievements by which we characterize different cultures. Before the invention of writing sometime around the fourth millennium BCE, these cultures created myths and legends that explained their origins and relation to the world. As we do today, ancient peoples experienced the great uncontrollable, and sometimes violent, forces of nature—floods, droughts, earthquakes, and hurricanes. Prehistoric cultures understood these forces as the work of the invisible gods, who could not be approached directly but only through the mediating agency of shamans and priests, or kings and heroes. As cultures became increasingly self-assertive, in the islands between mainland Greece and Asia Minor, in Egypt, in China, on the Indian subcontinent, and on the Greek mainland, these gods seemed increasingly knowable. The gods could still intervene in human affairs, but now they did so in ways that were recognizable. It was suddenly possible to believe that if people could come to understand themselves, they might also understand the gods. The study of the natural world might well shed light on the unknown, on the truth of things.

It is to this moment—it was a long "moment," extending for centuries—that the beginnings of scientific inquiry can be traced. **Humanism**, the study of the human mind and its moral and ethical dimensions, was born. In China, the formalities of social interaction—moderation, personal integrity, self-control, loyalty, altruism, and justice—were codified in the writings of Confucius. In Mesopotamia and Greece, the presentation of a human character working things out (or not) in the face of adversity was the subject of epic and dramatic literature. In Greece, it was also the subject of philosophy—literally, "love of wisdom"—the practice of reasoning that followed from the Greek philosopher Socrates' famous dictum, "Know thyself." Visual artists strove to discover the perfections of human form and thought. By the time of the rise of the Roman Empire, at the end of the first millennium BCE, these traditions were carried on in more practical ways, as the Romans attempted to engineer a society embodying the values they had inherited from the Greeks.

30,000 BCE
Art created in the Chauvet Cave

10,000–8000 BCE
Emergence of agricultural civilizations in Mesopotamia, India, Egypt, China

3200–2000 BCE
Development of pictographic writing systems in Mesopotamia, India, Egypt, China

2500 BCE
Pyramids in Egypt

1792–1750 BCE
Hammurabi's Law Code

1500–322 BCE
Vedic period in India; origins of Hinduism

1300 BCE
Emergence of Olmec culture in Mesoamerica

1200 BCE
Mesopotamia: *Epic of Gilgamesh*

1200 BCE
Earliest use of Phoenician phonetic alphabet

1000 BCE
King David reigns in Israel

800 BCE
Acropolis (citadel) and agora (market)
Homeric epics: *Iliad* and *Odyssey*

800–600 BCE
Etruria: Origins of Roman culture

563–483 BCE
Lifetime of Siddhartha Gautama (Buddha) in India

551–479 BCE
Lifetime of Confucius in Zhou dynasty China

461–429 BCE
Pericles, Socrates, Sophocles
Parthenon on Athens's Acropolis

469–399 BCE
Lifetime of Socrates, Greek philosopher

27 BCE
Octavian becomes Emperor Augustus

20 BCE
Augustus of Primaporta

1

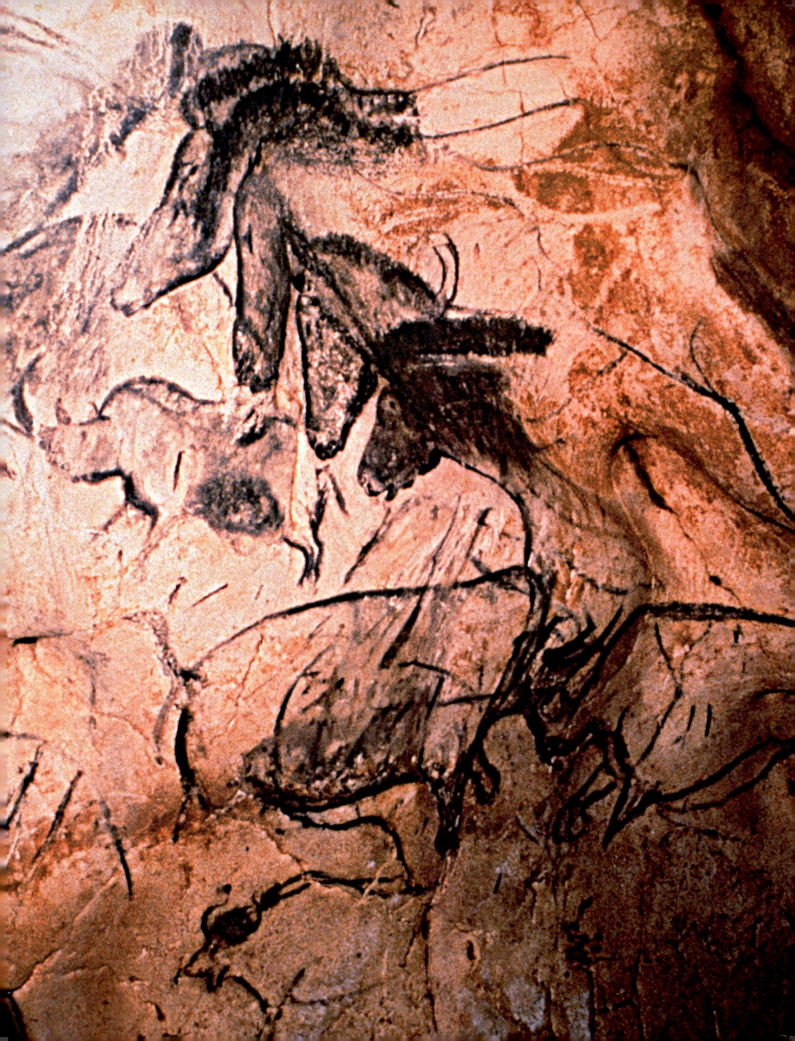

1

The Rise of Culture
From Forest to Farm

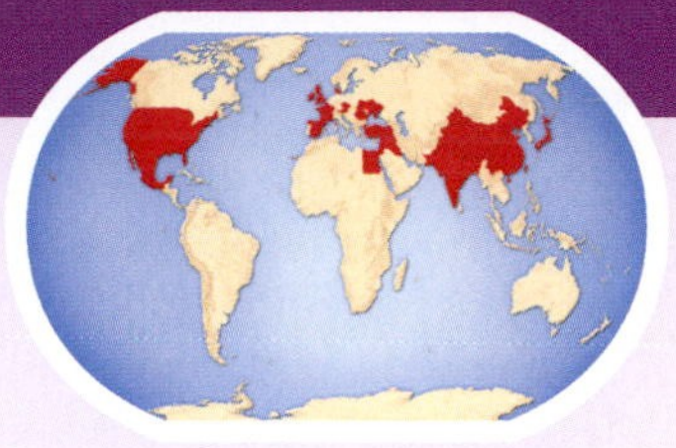

THINKING AHEAD

1.1 Discuss the ways in which cave art and small sculptural figurines in the Paleolithic era have been interpreted.

1.2 Explain how the art and architecture of the Neolithic era reflect changing cultural concerns.

1.3 Understand the function of myth in prehistoric culture.

1.4 Describe the role of sacred sites in prehistoric culture.

On a cold December afternoon in 1994, Jean-Marie Chauvet and two friends were exploring the caves in the steep cliffs along the Ardèche River gorge in southern France. After descending into a series of narrow passages, they entered a large chamber. There, beams from their headlamps lit up a group of drawings that would astonish the three explorers—and the world (Fig. **1.1**).

Since the late nineteenth century, we have known that **prehistoric** peoples, peoples who lived before the time of writing and so of recorded history, drew on the walls of caves. Twenty-seven such caves had already been discovered in the cliffs along the 17 miles of the Ardèche gorge (Map **1.1**). But the cave found by Chauvet and his friends transformed our thinking about prehistoric peoples. Where previously discovered cave paintings had appeared to modern eyes as childlike, this cave contained drawings comparable to those a contemporary artist might have done. We can only speculate that other comparable artworks were produced in prehistoric times but have not survived, perhaps because they were made of wood or other perishable materials. It is even possible that art may have been made earlier than 30,000 years ago, perhaps as people began to inhabit the Near East, between 90,000 and 100,000 years ago.

At first, during the Paleolithic era, or "Old Stone Age," from the Greek *palaios*, "old," and *lithos*, "stone," the cultures of the world sustained themselves on game and wild plants. The cultures themselves were small, scattered, and nomadic, though evidence suggests some interaction among the various groups. We begin this book, then, with the cultures of prehistoric times, evidence of which survives in wall paintings in caves and in small sculptures dating back more than 25,000 years.

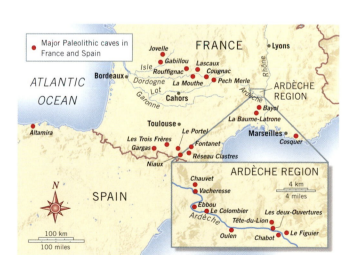

Map 1.1 Major Paleolithic caves in France and Spain.

◀ **Fig. 1.1 Wall painting with horses, Chauvet Cave, Vallon-Pont-d'Arc, Ardèche gorge, France. ca. 30,000 BCE.** Paint on limestone, height approx. 6'. Ministère de la Culture et de la Communication. Direction Régionale des Affaires Culturelles de Rhône-Alpes. Service Régional de l'Archéologie. In the center of this wall are four horses, each behind the other in a startlingly realistic depiction. Below them, two rhinoceroses fight.

Listen to the chapter audio on **MyArtsLab**

THE BEGINNINGS OF CULTURE IN THE PALEOLITHIC ERA

In what ways has the role of art in Paleolithic culture been discussed?

A **culture** encompasses the values and behaviors shared by a group of people, developed over time, and passed down from one generation to the next. Culture manifests itself in the laws, customs, ritual behavior, and artistic production common to the group. The cave paintings at Chauvet suggest that, as early as 30,000 years ago, the Ardèche gorge was a *center of culture*, a focal point of group living in which the values of a community find expression. There were others like it. In northern Spain, the first decorated cave was discovered in 1879 at Altamira. In the Dordogne region of southern France to the west of the Ardèche, schoolchildren discovered the famous Lascaux Cave in 1940 when their dog disappeared down a hole. And in 1991, along the French Mediterranean coast, a diver discovered the entrance to the beautifully decorated Cosquer Cave below the waterline near Marseille.

Agency and Ritual: Cave Art

Ever since cave paintings were first discovered, scholars have marveled at the skill of the people who produced them, but we have been equally fascinated by their very existence. Why were these paintings made? Most scholars believe that they possessed some sort of **agency**—that is, they were created to exert some power or authority over the world of those who came into contact with them. Until recently, it was generally accepted that such works were associated with the hunt. Perhaps the hunter, seeking game in times of scarcity, hoped to conjure it up by depicting it on cave walls. Or perhaps such drawings were magic charms meant to ensure a successful hunt. But at Chauvet, fully 60 percent of the animals painted on its walls were never, or rarely, hunted—such animals as lions, rhinoceroses, bears, panthers, and woolly mammoths. One drawing depicts two rhinoceroses fighting horn-to-horn beneath four horses that appear to be looking on (see Fig. 1.1).

What role, then, did these drawings play in the daily lives of the people who created them? The caves may have served as some sort of **ritual** space. A ritual is a rite or ceremony habitually practiced by a group, often in religious or quasi-religious contexts. The caves, for instance, might be understood as gateways to the underworld and death, as symbols of the womb and birth, or as pathways to the world of dreams experienced in the dark of night, and rites connected with such passage might have been conducted in them. The general arrangement of the animals in the paintings by species or gender, often in distinct chambers of the caves, suggests to some that the paintings may have served as lunar calendars for predicting the seasonal migration of the animals. Whatever the case, surviving human footprints indicate that these caves were ritual gathering places and in some way were intended to serve the common good.

At Chauvet, the use of color suggests that the paintings served some sacred or symbolic function. For instance, almost all of the paintings near the entrance to the cave are painted with natural red pigments derived from ores rich in iron oxide. Deeper in the cave, in areas more difficult to

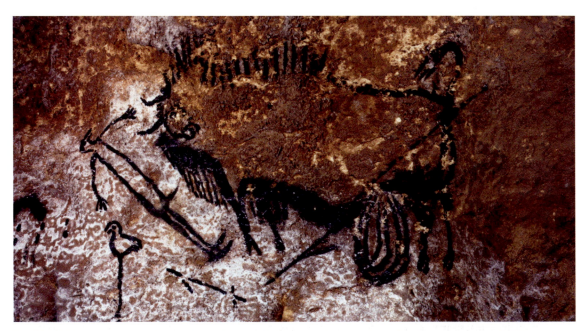

Fig. 1.2 Wall painting with bird-headed man, bison, and rhinoceros, Lascaux Cave, Dordogne, France. ca. 15,000–13,000 BCE. Paint on limestone, length approx. 9'. In 1963, Lascaux was closed to the public so that conservators could fight a fungus attacking the paintings. Most likely, the fungus was caused by carbon dioxide exhaled by visitors. An exact replica called Lascaux II was built and can be visited.

reach, the vast majority of the animals are painted in black pigments derived from ores rich in manganese dioxide. This shift in color appears to be intentional, but we can only guess at its meaning.

The skillfully drawn images at Chauvet raise even more important questions. The artists seem to have understood and practiced a kind of illusionism—that is, they were able to convey a sense of three-dimensional space on a two-dimensional surface. In the painting reproduced at the beginning of this chapter, several horses appear to stand one behind the other (see Fig. 1.1). The head of the top horse overlaps a black line, as if peering over a branch or the back of another animal. In no other cave yet discovered do drawings show the use of shading, or **modeling**, so that the horses' heads seem to have volume and dimension. And yet these cave paintings, rendered over 30,000 years ago, predate other cave paintings by at least 10,000 years, and in some cases by as much as 20,000 years.

One of the few cave paintings that depicts a human figure is found at Lascaux. What appears to be a male wearing a bird's-head mask lies in front of a disemboweled bison (Fig. 1.2). Below him is a bird-headed spear thrower, a device that enabled hunters to throw a spear farther and with greater force. (Several examples of spear throwers have survived.) In the Lascaux painting, the hunter's spear has pierced the bison's hindquarters, and a rhinoceros charges off to the left. We have no way of knowing whether this was an actual event or an imagined scene. One of the painting's most interesting and inexplicable features is the discrepancy between the relatively naturalistic representation of the animals and the highly stylized, almost abstract realization of the human figure. Was the sticklike man added later by a different, less talented artist? Or does this image suggest that man and beast are different orders of being?

Before the discovery of Chauvet, historians divided the history of cave painting into a series of successive styles, each progressively more realistic. But Chauvet's paintings, by far the oldest known, are also the most advanced in their realism, suggesting the artists' conscious quest for visual **naturalism**, that is, for representations that imitate the actual appearance of the animals. Not only were both red and black animals outlined, their shapes were also modeled by spreading paint, either with the hand or a tool, in gradual gradations of color. Such modeling is extremely rare or unknown elsewhere. In addition, the artists further defined many of the animals' contours by scraping the wall behind so that the beasts seem to stand out against a deeper white ground. Three handprints in the cave were evidently made by spitting paint at a hand placed on the cave wall, resulting in a stenciled image.

Art, the Chauvet drawings suggest, does not necessarily evolve in a linear progression from awkward beginnings to more sophisticated representations. On the contrary, already in the earliest artworks, people obtained a very high degree of sophistication. Apparently, even from the earliest

times, human beings could choose to represent the world naturalistically or not, and the choice not to represent the world in naturalistic terms should not necessarily be attributed to lack of skill or sophistication but to other, more culturally driven factors.

Paleolithic Culture and Its Artifacts

Footprints discovered in South Africa in 2000 and fossilized remains uncovered in the forest of Ethiopia in 2001 suggest that, about 5.7 million years ago, the earliest upright humans, or hominins (as distinct from the larger classification of **hominids**, which includes great apes and chimpanzees as well as humans), roamed the continent of Africa. Ethiopian excavations further indicate that sometime around 2.5 or 2.6 million years ago, hominid populations began to make rudimentary stone tools, though long before, between 14 million and 19 million years ago, the *Kenyapithecus* ("Kenyan ape"), a hominin, made stone tools in east central Africa. Nevertheless, the earliest evidence of a culture coming into being are the stone artifacts of *Homo sapiens* (Latin for "one who knows"). *Homo sapiens* evolved about 100,000–120,000 years ago and can be distinguished from earlier hominids by the lighter build of their skeletal structure and larger brain. A 2009 study of genetic diversity among Africans found the San people of Zimbabwe to be the most diverse, suggesting that they are the most likely origin of modern humans from which others gradually spread out of Africa, across Asia, into Europe, and finally to Australia and the Americas.

Homo sapiens were **hunter-gatherers**, whose survival depended on the animals they could kill and the foods they could gather, primarily nuts, berries, roots, and other edible plants. The tools they developed were far more sophisticated than those of their ancestors. They included cleavers, chisels, grinders, hand axes, and arrow- and spearheads made of flint, a material that also provided the spark to create an equally important tool—fire. In 2004, Israeli archeologists working at a site on the banks of the Jordan River reported the earliest evidence yet found of controlled fire created by hominids—cracked and blackened flint chips, presumably used to light a fire, and bits of charcoal dating from 790,000 years ago. Also at the campsite were the bones of elephants, rhinoceroses, hippopotamuses, and small species, demonstrating that these early hominids cut their meat with flint tools and ate steaks and marrow. *Homo sapiens* cooked with fire, wore animal skins as clothing, and used tools as a matter of course. They buried their dead in ritual ceremonies, often laying them to rest accompanied by stone tools and weapons.

The Paleolithic era is the period of *Homo sapiens'* ascendancy. These people carved stone tools and weapons that helped them survive in an inhospitable climate. They carved small sculptural objects as well, which, along with the cave paintings we have already seen, appear to

View the Closer Look for the Lascaux Cave on **MyArtsLab**

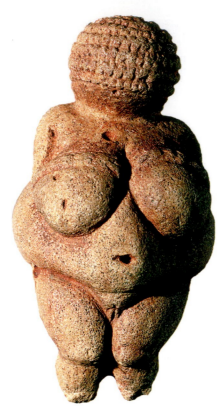

Fig. 1.3 *Woman (Venus of Willendorf)*, **found at Willendorf, Austria. ca. 25,000–20,000 BCE.** Limestone, height 4". Naturhistorisches Museum, Vienna. For many years, modern scholars called this small statue the *Venus of Willendorf*. They assumed that its carvers attributed to it an ideal of female beauty comparable to the Roman ideal of beauty implied by the name Venus.

be the first instances of what we have come to call "art" (see *Materials & Techniques*, page 7). Among the most remarkable of these sculptural artifacts are a large number of female figures, found at various archeological sites across Europe. The most famous of these is *Woman*, the limestone statuette of a woman found at Willendorf, in present-day Austria (Fig. **1.3**), dating from about 22,000 to 21,000 BCE and sometimes called the *Venus of Willendorf*. Markings on *Woman* and other similar figures indicate that they were originally colored, but what these small sculptures meant and what they were used for remains unclear. Most are 4 to 5 inches high and fit neatly into a person's hand. This suggests that they may have had a ritual purpose. Their exaggerated breasts and bellies and their clearly delineated genitals support a connection to fertility and childbearing. We know, too, that the Willendorf *Woman* was originally painted in red ocher, suggestive of menses. And, her navel is not carved; rather, it is a natural indentation in the stone. Whoever carved her seems to have recognized, in the raw stone, a connection to the origins of life. But such figures may have served other purposes as well. Perhaps they were dolls, guardian figures, or images of beauty in a cold, hostile world where having body fat might have made the difference between survival and death.

Female figurines vastly outnumber representations of males in the Paleolithic era, which suggests that women played a central role in Paleolithic culture. Most likely, they had considerable religious and spiritual influence, and their preponderance in the imagery of the era suggests that Paleolithic culture may have been *matrilineal* (in which descent is determined through the female line) and *matrilocal* (in which residence is in the female's tribe or household). Such traditions exist in many primal societies today.

The peoples of the Upper Paleolithic period followed herds northward in summer, though temperatures during the Ice Age rarely exceeded 60 degrees Fahrenheit (16 degrees Celsius). Then, as winter approached, they retreated southward into the cave regions of northern Spain and southern France.

THE RISE OF AGRICULTURE IN THE NEOLITHIC ERA

How do Neolithic art and architecture reflect the era's changing cultural concerns?

As the ice covering the Northern Hemisphere began to recede around 10,000 BCE, the seas rose, covering, for instance, the cave entrance at Cosquer in southern France (see Map 1.1), filling what is now the North Sea and English Channel with water, and inundating the land bridge that had connected Asia and North America. Agriculture began to replace hunting and gathering, and with it, a nomadic lifestyle gave way to a more sedentary way of life. The consequences of this shift were enormous, and ushered in the Neolithic era, or "New Stone Age."

For 2,000 years, from 10,000 to 8000 BCE, the ice covering the Northern Hemisphere receded farther and farther northward. As temperatures warmed, life gradually changed. During this period of transition, areas once covered by vast regions of ice and snow developed into grassy plains and abundant forests. Hunters developed the bow and arrow, which were easier to use at longer range on the open plains. They fashioned dugout boats out of logs to facilitate fishing, which became a major food source. They domesticated dogs to help with the hunt as early as 11,000 BCE, and soon other animals as well—goats and cattle particularly. Perhaps most important, people began to cultivate the more edible grasses. Along the eastern shore of the Mediterranean, they harvested wheat; in Asia, they cultivated millet and rice; and in the Americas, they grew squash, beans, and corn. Gradually, farming replaced hunting as the primary means of sustaining life. A culture of the fields developed—an agri-culture, from the Latin *ager*, "farm," "field," or "productive land."

Agricultural production seems to have originated about 10,000 BCE in the Fertile Crescent, an area arching from southwest Iran, across the foothills of the Taurus Mountains in southeastern Turkey, then southward into Lebanon. By about 8000 BCE, Neolithic agricultural societies began to concentrate in the great river valleys of the Middle East and Asia (Map **1.2**). Here, distinct centers of people

Methods of Carving

Carving is the act of cutting or incising stone, bone, wood, or another material into a desired form. Surviving artifacts of the Paleolithic era were carved from stone or bone. The artist probably held a sharp instrument, such as a stone knife or a chisel, in one hand and drove it into the stone or bone with another stone held in the other hand to remove excess material and realize the figure. Finer details could be scratched into the material with a pointed stone instrument. Artists can carve into any material softer than the instrument they are using. Harder varieties of stone can cut into softer stone as well as bone. The work was probably painstakingly slow.

There are basically two types of sculpture: sculpture-in-the-round and relief sculpture. **Sculpture-in-the-round** is fully three-dimensional; it occupies 360 degrees of space. The Willendorf statuette (see Fig. 1.3) was carved from stone and is an example of sculpture-in-the-round. **Relief sculpture** is

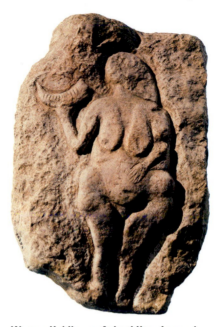

Woman Holding an Animal Horn, Laussel, Dordogne, France. ca. 30,000–15,000 BCE. Limestone, height 17⅜". Musée des Antiquités Nationales, Saint Germain-en-Laye, France.

carved out of a flat background surface; it has a distinct front and no back. Not all relief sculptures are alike. In *high-relief* sculpture, the figure extends more than 180 degrees from the background surface. *Woman Holding an Animal Horn*, found at Laussel, in the Dordogne region of France, is carved in high relief and is one of the earliest relief sculptures known. This sculpture was originally part of a great stone block that stood in front of a Paleolithic rock shelter. In *low* or *bas relief*, the figure extends less than 180 degrees from the surface. In *sunken relief*, the image is carved, or incised, into the surface, so that the image recedes below it. When a light falls on relief sculptures at an angle, the relief casts a shadow. The higher the relief, the larger the shadows and the greater the sense of the figure's three-dimensionality.

👁 **Watch** a video about the technique of relief carving on **MyArtsLab**

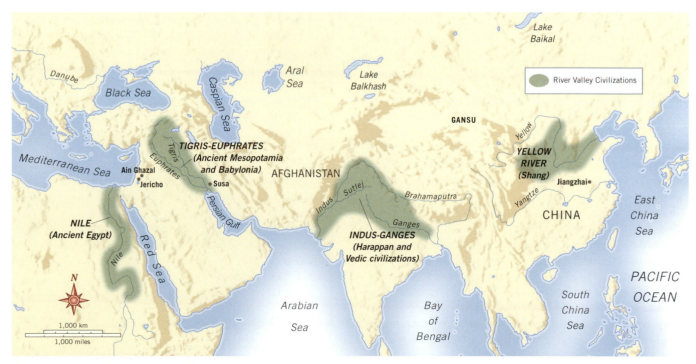

Map 1.2 The great river valley civilizations. ca. 2000 BCE. Agriculture thrived in the great river valleys throughout the Neolithic era, but by the end of the period, urban life had developed there as well, and civilization as we know it had emerged.

involved in a common pursuit began to form. A **civilization** is a social, economic, and political entity distinguished by the ability to express itself through images and written language. Civilizations develop when the environment of a region can support a large and productive population. An increasing population requires increased production of food and other goods, not only to support itself, but to trade for other commodities. Organizing this level of trade and production also requires an administrative elite to form and to establish priorities. The existence of such an elite is another characteristic of civilization. Finally, as the history of cultures around the world makes abundantly clear, one of the major ways that societies have acquired the goods they want and simultaneously organized themselves is by means of war.

Gradually, as the climate warmed, Neolithic culture spread across Europe. By about 5000 BCE, the valleys of Spain and southern France supported agriculture, but there is no evidence of farming in the northern reaches of the European continent and England dating back any earlier than about 4000 BCE. The Neolithic era did not end in these colder climates until about 2000 BCE, and continued in more remote regions, such as Africa and the Americas, well into the first millennium.

Meanwhile, the great rivers of the Middle East and Asia provided a consistent and predictable source of water, and people soon developed irrigation techniques that fostered organized agriculture and animal husbandry. As production outgrew necessity, members of the community were freed to occupy themselves in other endeavors—complex food preparation (bread, cheese, and so on), construction, religion, and even military affairs. Soon, permanent villages began to appear, and villages began to look more and more like cities.

Neolithic Çatalhöyük and Skara Brae

Sometime around 7400 BCE, at Çatalhöyük (also known as Chatal Huyuk) in central Turkey, a permanent village began to take shape that would flourish for nearly 1,200 years. At one point or another, as many as 3,000 people lived in close proximity to one another in rectangular houses made of mud bricks held together with plaster. These houses stood side by side, one wall abutting the next, with entrances through the roof and down a ladder. There were no windows, and the only natural light in the interior came from the entry way. The roof appears to have served as the primary social space, especially in the summer months. Domed ovens were placed both on the roof and in the interior.

The people of Çatalhöyük were apparently traders, principally of obsidian, a black, volcanic, and glasslike stone that can be carved into sharp blades and arrowheads, which they mined at Hasan Dag, a volcano visible from the village. The rows of windowless houses that composed the village, the walls of which rose to as high as 16 feet, must have served a defensive purpose, but they also contained

what archeologists have come to view as an extraordinary sense of communal history. Their interior walls and floors were plastered and replastered, then painted and repainted with a white lime-based paint, again and again over hundreds of years. Beneath the floors of some—but not all—of the houses were burials, averaging about six per house, but sometimes rising to between 30 and 62 bodies. For reasons that are not entirely clear, from time to time, these bodies were exhumed, and the skulls of long-deceased ancestors were removed. The skulls were then reburied in new graves or in the foundations of new houses as they were built and rebuilt. Whatever the rationale for such ceremonies, they could not have helped but create a sense of historical continuity in the community.

Çatalhöyük was first extensively excavated from 1958 by Sir James Mellaart, who concluded that the village's culture was matrilineal, based in no small part on his discovery of a number of female figurines including a clay sculpture of a seated woman (Fig. **1.4**), who represented, he believed, a fertility or mother goddess. Found in a grain bin—evidence of the community's growing agricultural sophistication—she sits enthroned between two felines, perhaps in the process of giving birth. But Ian Hodder of Cambridge University, who took up excavations of the site in 1993, after a nearly 30-year hiatus, has recently concluded that she is something other than a fertility goddess. In 2005, he wrote:

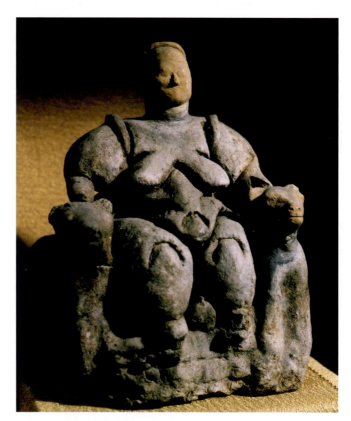

Fig. 1.4 Woman seated between two felines, Çatalhöyük, Turkey. ca. 6850–6300 BCE. Terra cotta, height 4⅝". Museum of Anatolian Civilizations, Ankara. The woman's head in this sculpture is a modern addition.

There are full breasts on which the hands rest and the stomach is extended in the central part. There is a hole in the top for the head which is missing. As one turns the figurine around one notices that the arms are very thin, and then on the back of the figurine one sees a depiction of either a skeleton or the bones of a very thin and depleted human. The ribs and vertebrae are clear, as are the scapulae and the main pelvic bones. The figurine can be interpreted in a number of ways—as a woman turning into an ancestor,

as a woman associated with death, or as death and life conjoined. … Perhaps the importance of female imagery was related to some special role of the female in relation to death as much as to the roles of mother and nurturer.

Supporting Hodder's theories is a burial of a deceased woman who holds in her arms the plastered and painted skull of a male.

Similarly, Mellaart believed that many of the rooms that contained large numbers of bodies were shrines or temples (Fig. **1.5**). The walls of these rooms were decorated with the skulls of cows and the heads and horns of bulls. Found under the floors of some houses were boar tusks, vulture skulls, and fox and weasel teeth. But Hodder has found evidence that these houses—he calls them "history houses"—were not shrines at all, but more or less continually occupied, suggesting that art and decoration were integral to the daily lives of the community's residents. Numerous wall paintings reinforce this idea. In one painting (Fig. **1.6**), small human beings surround a large horned animal, probably a deer, in what has been interpreted as a dangerous game of baiting wild animals. One man appears to be pulling the deer's tongue out of its mouth, while others jump and run around it. The deer itself is depicted with a large erect penis, suggesting that male virility is at least in part at stake in the game. All of this suggests that, by the Neolithic era, the religious and spiritual prominence of the female in Paleolithic culture was gradually diminishing.

Preserved in the cold northern climate of the Orkney Islands off the northeastern coast of Scotland is Skara Brae.

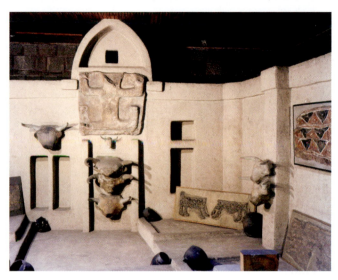

Fig. 1.5 Reconstruction of a "shrine," Çatalhöyük, Turkey. ca. 6850–6300 BCE. Museum of Anatolian Civilizations, Ankara. The relief sculpture below the arch in the center of the room appears to be a decapitated animal or even, possibly, human form.

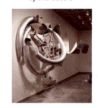
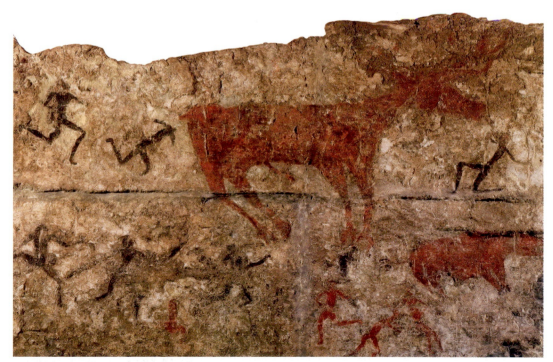

Fig. 1.6 Wall painting showing the capturing or baiting of a deer, Çatalhöyük, Turkey. ca. 6850–6300 BCE. Museum of Anatolian Civilizations, Ankara. The painting, along with many others like it, suggests that the hunt played a significant role in Neolithic culture, as it did in Paleolithic times.

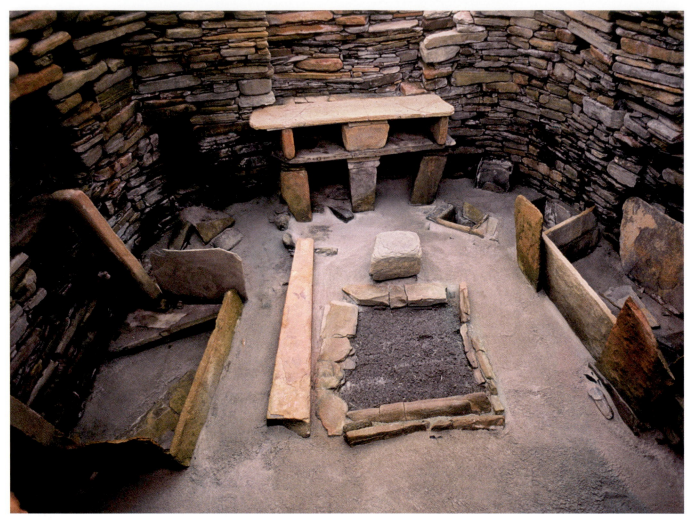

Fig. 1.7 House interior, Skara Brae, Orkney Islands, Scotland. ca. 3100–2600 BCE. This is a view of the interior of house 7 in Fig. 1.8. In this and other houses, archeologists have found stone cooking pots; mortars for grinding grains, including barley and wheat; carved stone balls; bone tools used for fishing and sewing; and pottery. In this view, the corbeled walls are just beginning to curve inward.

Some 4,000 years younger than Çatalhöyük, Skara Brae is a Neolithic village dating from between 3100 and 2600 BCE. The seaside village was apparently buried long ago beneath a layer of sand during a massive storm, and then, in 1850, uncovered when another storm swept the sand away.

The houses of Skara Brae are made entirely of stone— virtually the only building material on the treeless Orkney Islands. The walls are made by **corbeling**, a construction technique (see *Materials & Techniques*, page 18), in which layers of flat stones are piled one upon the other, with each layer projecting slightly inward as the wall rises. As the walls curve inward, they are buttressed, or supported, on the outside by earth. Nothing of the roofs has survived, suggesting that they were constructed of organic matter such as straw thatch or seaweed (seaweed remained a common roofing material in the Orkney Islands into the twentieth century). Furniture was built into the walls—in the house shown here, rectangular stone beds at either side of a central hearth, and a stone bench along the back wall (Fig. 1.7). The bed frames would have been filled with organic

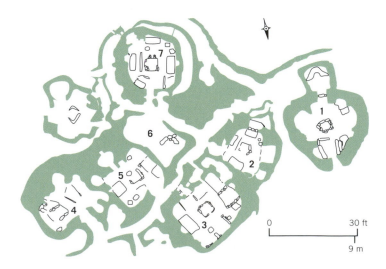

Fig. 1.8 Plan, Village of Skara Brae, Orkney Islands, Scotland. ca. 3100–2600 BCE. The numbers refer to individual houses.

materials such as heather or straw, and covered with furs. Storage spaces have been fashioned into the walls above the beds and in the back left corner. The only light in the house would have come from the smoke hole above the hearth.

The houses in the village were connected by a series of narrow walkways that were probably covered (Fig. **1.8**). Each of the houses is more or less square, with rounded corners. They are relatively spacious, ranging in size from 12 by 14 feet to 20 by 21 feet. That Skara Brae was continually inhabited for 500 years suggests that life in the village was relatively comfortable despite the harsh climate.

Neolithic Pottery Across Cultures

The transition from cultures based on hunting and fishing to cultures based on agriculture led to the increased use of pottery vessels. Ceramic vessels are fragile, so hunter-gatherers would not have found them practical for carrying food, but people living in the more permanent Neolithic settlements could have used them to carry and store water, and to prepare and store certain types of food.

As early as 10,000 BCE, Japanese artisans were making clay pots capable of storing, transporting, and cooking food and water. Over the course of the Neolithic era, called the Jomon period in Japan (12,000–300 BCE), their

work became increasingly decorative. *Jomon* means "cord markings" and refers to the fact that potters decorated many of their wares by pressing cord into the damp clay. As in most Neolithic societies, women made Jomon pottery; their connection to fertility and the life cycle may have become even more important to Neolithic cultures in the transition from hunting and gathering to agricultural food production. Jomon women built their pots up from the bottom with coil upon coil of soft clay. They mixed the clay with a variety of adhesive materials, including mica, lead, fibers, and crushed shells. After forming the vessel, they employed tools to smooth both the outer and interior surfaces. Finally, they decorated the outside with cord markings and fired the pot in an outdoor bonfire at a temperature of about 1650 degrees Fahrenheit (900 degrees Celsius). By the Middle Jomon period, potters had begun to decorate the normal flat-bottomed, straight-sided jars with elaborately ornate and flamelike rims (Fig. **1.9**), distinguished by their asymmetry and their unique characteristics. These rims suggest animal forms, but their significance remains a mystery.

The Neolithic cultures that flourished along the banks of the Yellow River in China beginning in about 5000 BCE also produced pottery. These cultures were based on growing rice and millet (grains from the Near East would not be introduced for another 3,000 years), and this agricultural emphasis spawned towns and villages, such as Jiangzhai, the largest Neolithic site that has been excavated in China. The Jiangzhai community, near present-day Xi'an, in Shaanxi Province, dates to about 4000 BCE and consisted of about 100 dwellings. At its center was a communal gathering place, a cemetery, and, most important, a *kiln*, an oven specifically designed to achieve the high temperatures necessary for firing clay. Indeed, the site yielded many pottery fragments. Farther to the east, in Gansu Province, Neolithic potters began to add painted decoration to their work (Fig. **1.10**). The flowing, curvilinear forms painted

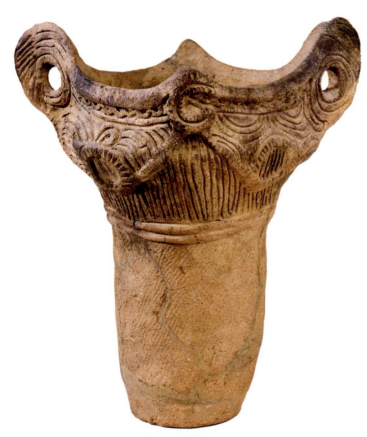

Fig. 1.9 Deep bowl with sculptural rim, late Middle Jomon period (ca. 2500–1600 BCE), Japan. ca. 2000 BCE. Terra cotta, 14½" × 12⅓". Musée des Arts Asiatiques-Guimet, Paris. The motifs incised on this pot may have had some meaning, but most interesting is the potter's freedom of expression. The design of the pot's flamelike rim is anything but practical.

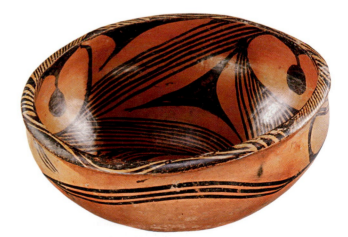

Fig. 1.10 Basin (*pen*), Majiayao culture, Majiayao phase, Gansu Province, China. ca. 3200–2700 BCE. Earthenware with painted decoration, diameter 11". The Metropolitan Museum of Art, New York. Anonymous Loan (L.1996.55.6). The designs on this bowl are examples of the kind of markings that would eventually develop into writing.

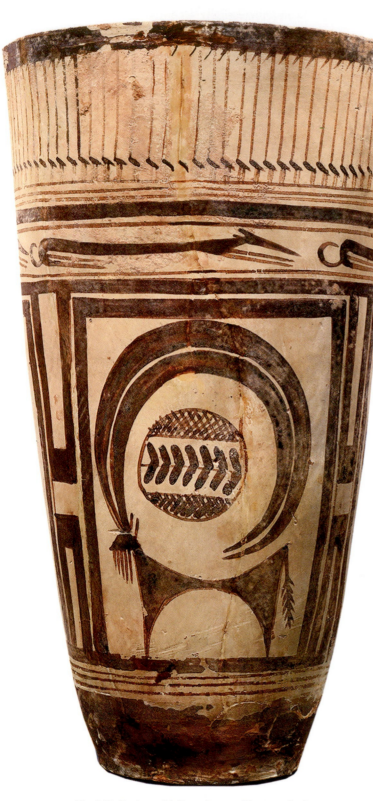

on the shallow basin illustrated here include "hand" motifs on the outside, and round, almost eyelike forms that flow into each other on the inside.

Some of the most remarkable Neolithic painted pottery comes from Susa, on the Iranian plateau. The patterns on one particular beaker (Fig. 1.11) from around 5000 to 4000 BCE are highly stylized animals. The largest of these is an ibex, a popular decorative feature of prehistoric ceramics from Iran. Associated with the hunt, the ibex may have been a symbol of plenty. The front and hind legs of the ibex are rendered by two tri-angles, the tail hangs behind it like a feather, the head is oddly disconnected from the body, and the horns rise in a large, exaggerated arc to encircle a decorative circular form. Hounds race around the band above the ibex, and wading birds form a deco-rative band across the beaker's top.

In Europe, the production of pottery apparently developed some time later, around 3000 BCE. Early pots were made either by molding clay over a round stone or by coiling long ropes of clay on top of one another and then smoothing the seams between them. Then the pots were fired at temperatures high enough to make them watertight—above 700 degrees Fahren-heit (370 degrees Celsius).

By this time, however, artisans in Egypt had begun using the potter's wheel, a revolving platter for forming vessels from clay with the fingers. It allowed artisans to produce a uniformly shaped vessel in a very short time. By 3000 BCE, the potter's wheel was in use in the Mid-dle East as well as China. Because it is a machine created expressly to produce goods, it is in many ways the first mechanical and technological breakthrough in history. As skilled individuals specialized in making and decorating pottery, and traded their wares for other goods and services, the first elemental forms of manufacturing began to emerge.

Neolithic Ceramic Figures

It is a simple step from forming clay pots and firing them to modeling clay sculptural figures and submitting them to the same firing process. Examples of clay modeling can be found in some of the earliest Paleolithic cave sites where, at Altamira, for instance, in Spain, an artist added clay to an existing rock outcropping in order to underscore the rock's natural resemblance to an animal form. At Le Tuc d'Audoubert, south of Lascaux in France, an artist shaped two clay bison, each 2 feet long, as if they were leaning against a rock ridge.

But these Paleolithic sculptures were never fired. One of the most interesting examples of Neolithic fired clay figurines were the work of the so-called Nok people who lived in what is now Nigeria. We do not know what they called themselves—they are identified instead by the name of the place where their artifacts were discovered. In fact,

Fig. 1.11 Beaker with ibex, dogs, and long-necked birds, from Susa, southwestern Iran. ca. 5000–4000 BCE. Baked clay with painted decoration, height 11¼". Musée du Louvre, Paris. The ibex was the most widely hunted game in the ancient Middle East, which probably accounts for its centrality in this design.

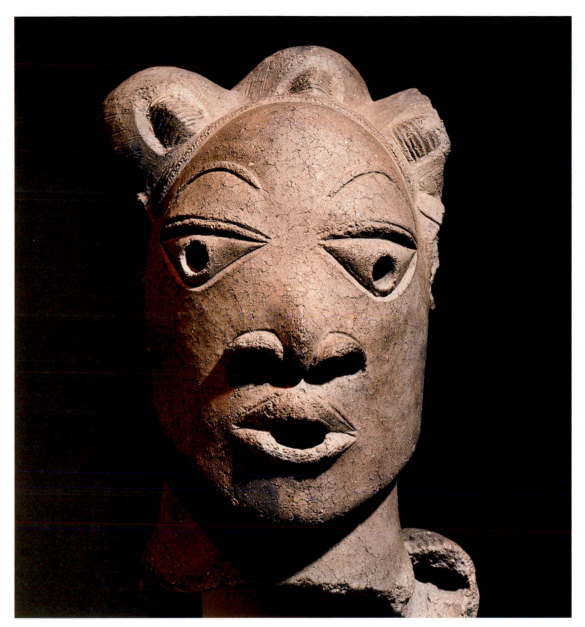

Fig. 1.12 Nok head. ca. 500 BCE–200 CE. Terra cotta, height 14³⁄₁₆". This slightly larger-than-life-size head was probably part of a complete body, and shows the Nok people's interest in abstract geometrical representations of facial features and head shape. Holes in the eyes and nose were probably used to control temperature during firing.

🔎 **View** the Closer Look for the Nok head on **MyArtsLab**

we know almost nothing about the Nok. We do not know how their culture was organized, what their lives were like, or what they believed. But while most Neolithic peoples in Africa worked in materials that were not permanent, the Nok fired clay figures of animals and humans that were approximately life-size.

These figures were first unearthed early in the twentieth century by miners over an area of about 40 square miles. Carbon-14 and other forms of dating revealed that some of these objects had been made as early as 800 BCE and others as late as 600 CE. Little more than the hollow heads have survived intact, revealing an artistry based on abstract geometrical shapes (Fig. 1.12). In some cases, the heads are

represented as ovals, and in others, as cones, cylinders, or spheres. Facial features are combinations of ovals, triangles, graceful arches, and straight lines. These heads were probably shaped with wet clay and then, after firing, finished by carving details into the hardened clay. Some scholars have argued that the technical and artistic sophistication of works by the Nok and other roughly contemporaneous groups suggests that it is likely there are older artistic traditions in West Africa that have not as yet been discovered. Certainly, farther to the east, in the sub-Saharan regions of the Sudan, Egyptian culture had exerted considerable influence for centuries, and it may well be that Egyptian technological sophistication had worked its way westward.

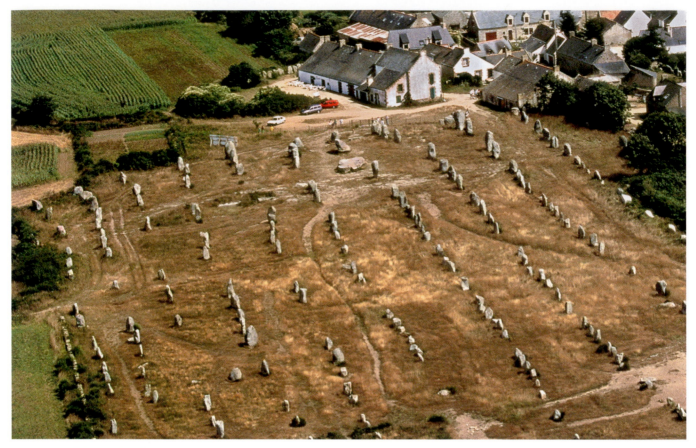

Fig. 1.13 Neolithic menhir alignments at Ménec, Carnac, Brittany, France. ca. 4250–3750 BCE. According to an ancient legend, the Carnac menhirs came into being when a retreating army was driven to the sea. Finding no ships to aid their escape, they turned to face their enemy and were transformed into stone.

The Neolithic Megaliths of Northern Europe

A distinctive kind of monumental stone architecture appears late in the Neolithic period, particularly in what is now Britain and France. Known as **megaliths**, or "big stones," these works were constructed without the use of mortar and represent the most basic form of architectural construction. Sometimes, they consisted merely of posts— upright stones stuck into the ground—called **menhirs**, from the Celtic words *men*, "stone," and *hir*, "long." These single stones occur in isolation or in groups. The largest of the groups is at Carnac, in Brittany (Fig. **1.13**), where some 3,000 menhirs arranged east to west in 13 straight rows, called *alignments*, cover a 2-mile stretch of plain. At the east end, the stones stand about 3 feet tall and gradually get larger and larger until, at the west end, they attain a height of 13 feet. This east–west alignment suggests a connection to the rising and setting of the sun and to fertility rites. Scholars disagree about their significance; some speculate that the stones may have marked out a ritual procession route; others think they symbolized the body and the process of growth and maturation. But there can be no doubt that megaliths were designed to be permanent structures, where domestic architecture was not. Quite possibly the megaliths stood in tribute to the strength of the leaders responsible for assembling and maintaining the considerable labor force required to construct them.

Another megalithic structure, the **dolmen**, consists of two posts roofed with a capstone, or **lintel**. Because it is composed of three stones, the dolmen is a **trilithon**, from Greek *tri*, "three," and *lithos*, "rock," and it formed the basic unit of architectural structure for thousands of years. Today, we call this kind of construction **post-and-lintel** (see *Materials & Techniques*, page 18). Megaliths such as the dolmen in County Clare, Ireland (Fig. **1.14**), were probably once covered with earth to form a fully enclosed burial chamber, or **cairn**.

A third type of megalithic structure is the **cromlech**, from the Celtic *crom*, "circle," and *lech*, "place." Without doubt, the most famous megalithic structure in the world is the cromlech known as Stonehenge (Fig. **1.15**), on Salisbury Plain, about 100 miles west of present-day London. A henge is a special type of cromlech, a circle surrounded by a ditch with built-up embankments, presumably for fortification purposes.

The site at Stonehenge reflects four major building periods, extending from about 2750 to 1500 BCE. By about 2100 BCE, most of the elements visible today were in place. In the middle was a U-shaped arrangement of five post-and-

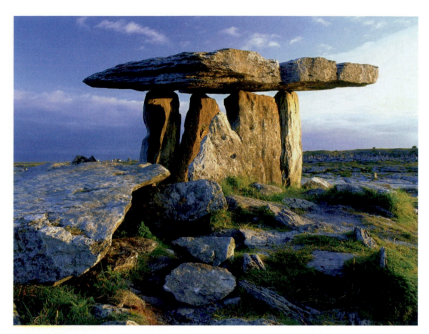

Fig. 1.14 Neolithic dolmen. Poulnabrone Dolmen, on the Burren limestone plateau, County Clare, Ireland. ca. 2500 BCE. A mound of earth probably once covered this structure, an ancient burial chamber.

lintel trilithons. The one at the bottom of the U stands taller than the rest, rising to a height of 24 feet, with a 15-foot lintel 3 feet thick. A continuous circle of sandstone posts, each weighing up to 50 tons and all standing 20 feet high, surrounded the five trilithons. Across their top was a continuous lintel 106 feet in diameter. This is the Sarsen Circle. Just inside the Sarsen Circle was once another circle, made of bluestone—a bluish dolerite—found only in the mountains of southern Wales, some 120 miles away. (See *Closer Look*, pages 16–17.)

Why Stonehenge was constructed remains a mystery, although it seems clear that orientation toward the rising sun at the summer solstice connects it to planting and the harvest. Stonehenge embodies, in fact, the growing importance of agricultural production in the northern reaches of Europe. Perhaps great rituals celebrating the earth's plenty took place here. Together with other megalithic structures

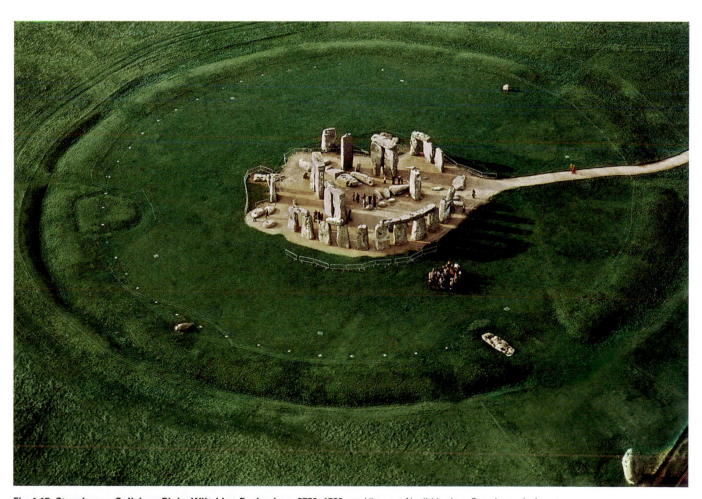

Fig. 1.15 Stonehenge, Salisbury Plain, Wiltshire, England. ca. 2750–1500 BCE. Like most Neolithic sites, Stonehenge invites speculation about its significance. Of this, however, we are certain: At the summer solstice, the longest day of the year, the sun rises directly over the Heel Stone (see page 17). This suggests that the site was intimately connected to the movement of the sun.

How the Neolithic peoples of Britain constructed Stonehenge is uncertain. Scholars believe that the giant stones of the Sarsen Circle, which weigh up to 50 tons, were transported from the Marlborough Downs, roughly 20 miles to the north, by rolling them on logs. Most of the way, the going is relatively easy, but at the steepest part of the route, at Redhorn Hill, modern work studies estimate that it would have taken at least 600 men to push the stones up the hill. A relatively sophisticated understanding of basic physics—the operation of levers and pulleys—was needed to lift the stones, and their lintels, into place.

Recently, archeologists at Stonehenge have uncovered a second cromlech-like circle at Durrington Walls, about 2 miles north of the stone megalith, consisting of a circular ditch surrounding a ring of postholes out of which very large timber posts would have risen. The circle was the center of a village consisting of as many as 300 houses. The site is comparable in scale to Stonehenge itself. These discoveries—together with the ability to carbon date human remains found at Stonehenge with increased accuracy—suggest that Stonehenge was itself a burial ground. Archeologist Mike Parker Pearson of the University of Sheffield speculates that villagers would have transported their dead down an avenue leading to the River Avon, then journeyed downstream, in a ritual symbolizing the passage to the afterlife, finally arriving at an avenue leading up to

Stonehenge from the river. "Stonehenge wasn't set in isolation," Parker Pearson says, "but was actually one half of this monument complex. We are looking at a pairing—one in timber to represent the transience of life, the other in stone marking the eternity of the ancestral dead."

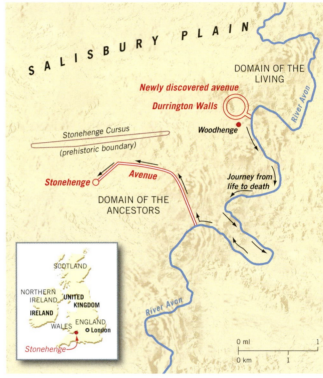

Durrington Walls in relation to Stonehenge. Courtesy of National Geographic.

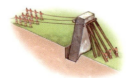

A sarsen stone is raised with a long lever. Logs are placed under the stone, and then it is rolled into place.

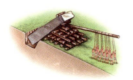

One by one, layers of timber are placed under the lever, both raising the stone and dropping it into the prepared pit.

Something to Think About …

The circle is a geometric form that appears in the earliest manifestations of art and architecture. Can you speculate on its appeal?

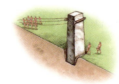

As many as 200 men pull the stone upright on ropes as timbers support it from behind.

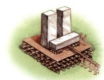

The pit around the stone is filled with stones and chalks to pack it into place.

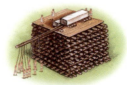

The lintel is raised on successive layers of a timber platform.

Once the platform reaches the top of the posts, the lintel is levered onto the posts.

Finally, the platform is removed, and the trilithon is complete.

The Heel Stone
On Midsummer's Eve, this stone casts a shadow directly into the circle. The stone stands 16 feet high and weighs 35 tons. It was brought from a quarry 23 miles away.

The Avenue
The shadow cast by the Heel Stone on Midsummer's Eve would extend directly down this ceremonial approach.

The Slaughter Stone
It was once believed that humans were sacrificed on this stone, which now lies flat on the ground, but it was originally part of a great portal.

The Sarsen Circle
Erected about 1500 BCE, the circle is capped by lintel stones held in place by mortise-and-tenon joints, similar to those used by woodworkers. The end of the post is narrowed and slotted into a hole in the lintel.

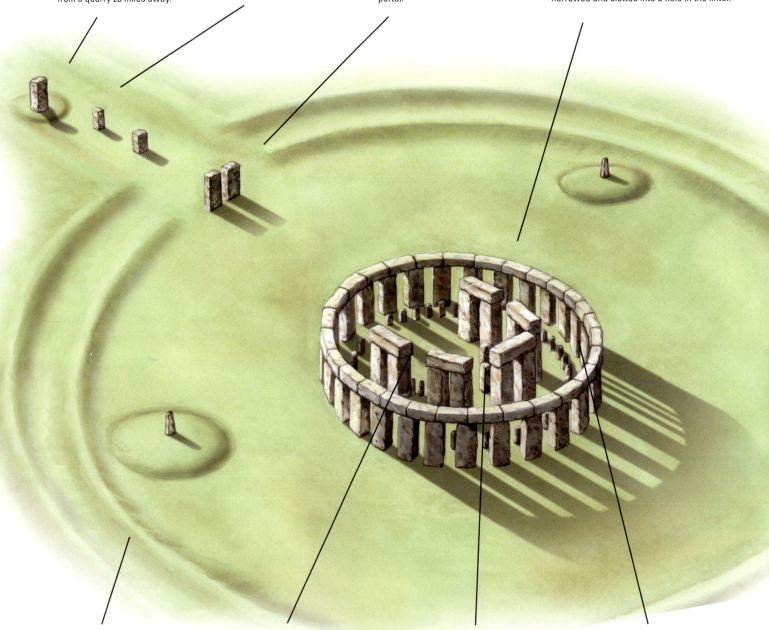

The Outer Bank
This ditch, 330 feet in diameter, is the oldest construction at the site, originally exposing the white limestone beneath the surface soil to form a giant circle.

Five Massive Trilithons
Inside the outer circle stood a horseshoe of trilithons, two on each side and the largest at the closed end at the southwest. Only one of the largest trilithons still stands. It rises 22 feet above ground, with 8 feet more below ground level. The stone weighs about 50 tons.

The Altar Stone
One of the most distinct stones in Stonehenge, the so-called Altar Stone is a 16-foot block of smoothed green sandstone located near the center of the complex.

The Bluestone Circle
This circle of 80 smallish slabs was built in about 2000 BCE from stone quarried in South Wales.

 View the Closer Look for Stonehenge on **MyArtsLab**

Post-and-Lintel and Corbel Construction

Post-and-lintel is the most basic technique for spanning space. In this form of construction two **posts**, or pieces fixed firmly in an upright position, support a lintel, or horizontal span. Two posts and a single lintel, as seen in County Clare and at Stonehenge (see Figs. 1.14, 1.15), constitute a trilithon (from the Greek *tri*, "three," and *lithos*, "rock"). The houses at Skara Brae (see Fig. 1.8) are examples of corbel construction. In corbeling, layers of rock are laid with the edge of each row projecting inward beyond the row below it until the walls almost meet at the top. The rows are buttressed, or supported, by earth piled on the outside. A roof of organic material can cover the top, or a stone can be set over the top to completely enclose the space (to create a tomb, for instance).

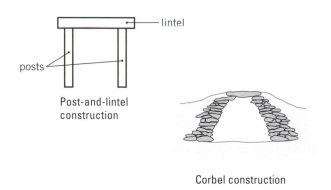

Post-and-lintel construction

Corbel construction

👁 **Watch** an architectural simulation about post-and-lintel on **MyArtsLab**

---

of the era, it suggests that the late Neolithic peoples who built it were extremely social beings, capable of great cooperation. They worked together not only to find the giant stones that stand at the site, but also to quarry, transport, and raise them. In other words, theirs was a culture of some magnitude and no small skill. It was a culture capable of both solving great problems and organizing itself in the name of creating a great social center. For Stonehenge is, above all, a center of culture. Its fascination for us today lies in the fact that we know so little of the culture that left it behind.

THE ROLE OF MYTH IN CULTURAL LIFE

What is the function of myth in prehistoric culture?

Much of our understanding of prehistoric cultures comes from stories that have survived in cultures around the world that developed without writing—that is, **oral cultures**—such as the San cultures of Zimbabwe, and the Oceanic peoples of Tahiti in the South Pacific. These cultures have passed down their myths and histories over the centuries, from generation to generation, by word of mouth. Although, chronologically speaking, many of these cultures are contemporaneous with the medieval, Renaissance, and even modern cultures of the West, they are actually closer to the Neolithic cultures in terms of social practice and organization. Especially in terms of myths and the rituals associated with them, they can help us to understand the outlook of actual Neolithic peoples.

A **myth** is a story that a culture assumes is true. It also embodies the culture's views and beliefs about its world,

often serving to explain otherwise mysterious natural phenomena. Myths stand apart from scientific explanations of the nature of reality, but as a mode of understanding and explanation, myth has been one of the most important forces driving the development of culture. Although myths are speculative, they are not pure fantasy. They are grounded in observed experience. They serve to rationalize the unknown and to explain to people the nature of the universe and their place within it.

Both nineteenth-century and more recent anthropological work among the San people suggests that their belief systems can be traced back for thousands of years. As a result, the meaning of their rock art that survives in open-air caves below the overhanging stone cliffs atop the hills of what is now Matobo National Park in Zimbabwe (Fig. 1.16), some of which dates back as far as 5,000 to 10,000 years ago, is not entirely lost. A giraffe stands above a group of smaller giraffes crossing a series of large, white, lozenge-shaped forms with brown rectangular centers, many of them overlapping one another. To the right, six humanlike figures are joined hand in hand, probably in a trance dance. For the San people, prolonged dancing activates *num*, a concept of personal energy or potency that the entire community can acquire. Led by a **shaman**, a person thought to have special ability to communicate with the spirit world, the dance encourages the *num* to heat up until it boils over and rises up through the spine to explode, causing the dancers to enter into a trance. Sweating and trembling, the dancers variously convulse or become rigid. They might run, jump, or fall. The San believe that in many instances, the dancer's spirit leaves the body, traveling far away, where it might enter into battle with supernatural forces. At any event, the trance imbues the dancer with almost supernatural agency. The dancers' *num* is capable of curing illnesses, managing game, or controlling the weather.

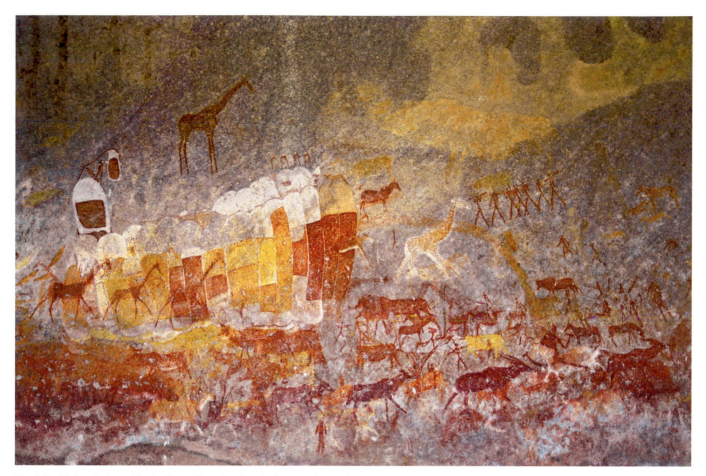

Fig. 1.16 Wall painting with giraffes, zebra, eland, and abstract shapes, San people, Inanke, Matobo National Park, Zimbabwe. Before 1000 CE. Photo: Christopher and Sally Gable © Dorling Kindersley. The animals across the bottom are eland, the largest of antelope, resembling cattle.

Myth in the Native American Cultures of the Southwest

Seventeen thousand years ago, about the time that the hunter-gatherers at Lascaux painted its caves, the Atlantic and Pacific oceans were more than 300 feet below modern levels, exposing a low-lying continental shelf that extended from northeastern Asia to North America. It was a landscape of grasslands and marshes, home to the woolly mammoth, the steppe bison, wild horses, caribou, and antelope. Although recent research has found evidence of migration into North America as early as 25,000 years ago, at some point around 15,000 BCE, large numbers of hunter-gatherers in northeastern Asia followed these animals across the grasslands land bridge into the Americas. By 12,000 BCE, prehistoric hunters had settled across North America and begun to move farther south, through Mesoamerica (the region extending from central Mexico to northern Central America), and on into South America, reaching the southern end of Chile no later than 11,000 BCE.

Around 9000 BCE, for reasons that are still hotly debated—perhaps a combination of overhunting and climatic change—the peoples of the Americas developed agricultural societies. They domesticated animals—turkeys,

guinea pigs, dogs, and llamas, though never a beast of burden, as in the rest of the world—and they cultivated a whole new range of plants, including maize and corn (domesticated in the Valley of Mexico by 8000 BCE), beans, squash, tomatoes, avocados, potatoes, tobacco, and cacao, the source of chocolate. The wheel remained unknown to them, though they learned to adapt to almost every conceivable climate and landscape. A **creation myth**, or story of a people's origin, told by the Maidu tribe of California, characterizes this early time: "For a long time everyone spoke the same language, but suddenly people began to speak in different tongues. Kulsu (the Creator), however, could speak all languages, so he called his people together and told them the names of the animals in their own language, taught them to get food, and gave them their laws and rituals. Then he sent each tribe to a different place to live."

The Anasazi and the Role of Myth The Anasazi people thrived in the American Southwest from about 900 to 1300 CE, a time roughly contemporaneous with the late Middle Ages in Europe. They left us no written record of their culture, only ruins and artifacts. As William M. Ferguson and Arthur H. Rohn, two prominent scholars of

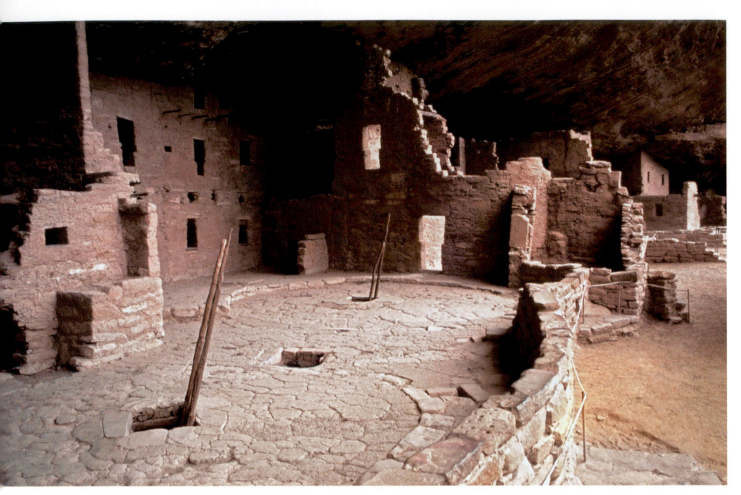

Fig. 1.17 Spruce Tree House, Mesa Verde, Colorado, Anasazi culture. ca. 1200–1300 CE. The courtyard was formed by the restoration of the roofs over two underground kivas.

the Anasazi, have described them: "They were a Neolithic people without a beast of burden, the wheel, metal, or a written language, yet they constructed magnificent masonry housing and ceremonial structures, irrigation works, and water impoundments." At Mesa Verde, in what is today southwestern Colorado, their cliff dwellings (Fig. 1.17) resemble many of the Neolithic cities of the Middle East, such as Ain Ghazal ("spring of the gazelles"), just outside what is now Amman, Jordan. Though Ain Ghazal flourished from about 7200 to 5000 BCE, thousands of years before the Mesa Verde community, both complexes were constructed with stone walls sealed with a layer of mud plaster. Their roofs were made of wooden beams cross-layered with smaller twigs and branches and sealed with mud. Like other Neolithic cultures, the Anasazi were accomplished in pottery-making, decorating their creations with elaborately abstract, largely geometric shapes and patterns.

The Anasazi abandoned their communities in the late thirteenth century, perhaps because of a great drought that lasted from about 1276 to 1299. Their descendants may be the Pueblo peoples of the American Southwest today.

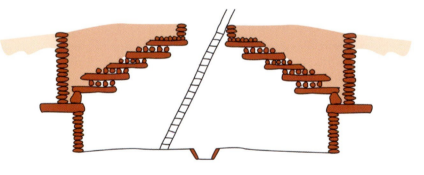

Fig. 1.18 Roof construction of a kiva. After a National Park Service pamphlet.

(*Anasazi* is in fact a Navajo word meaning "enemy ancestors"—we do not know what the Anasazi called themselves.) What is remarkable about the Pueblo peoples, who despite the fact that they speak several different languages share a remarkably common culture, is that many aspects of their culture have survived and are practiced today much as they were in ancient times. For all Pueblo peoples, the village is not just the center of culture but the very center of the world. And the cultural center of village life is the **kiva** (Fig. **1.18**), two of which have been restored at Spruce Tree House to form the plaza visible in Fig. 1.17. They are constructed of horizontally laid logs built up to form a dome with an access hole. The roof area thus created is used as a common area. Down below, in the enclosed kiva floor, was a *sipapu*, a small, round hole symbolic of the Anasazi creation myth, which told of the emergence of the Anasazi's ancestors from the depths of the earth. In the parched Southwestern desert country, it is equally true that water, like life itself, also seeps out of small fissures in the earth. Thus, it is as if the Anasazi community itself, and everything necessary to its survival, had emerged from Mother Earth.

Zuni Pueblo Emergence Tales The Pueblos have maintained the active practice of their ancient religious rites and ceremonies, which they have chosen not to share with outsiders. Most do not allow their ceremonial dances to be photographed. These dance performances tell stories that relate to the experiences of the Pueblo peoples, from planting, hunting, and fishing in daily life to the larger experiences of birth, puberty, maturity, and death. Still other stories explain the origin of the world, the emergence of a particular Pueblo people into the world, and their history. Most Pueblo people believe that they originated in the womb of Mother Earth and, like seeds sprouting from the soil in the springtime, were called out into the daylight by their Sun Father. This belief about origins is embodied in a type of narrative known as an **emergence tale**, a form of creation myth (**Reading 1.1**).

READING 1.1

Zuni Emergence Tale: *Talk Concerning the First Beginning*

Yes, indeed. In this world there was no one at all. Always the sun came up; always he went in. No one in the morning gave him sacred meal; no one gave him prayer sticks; it was very lonely. He said to his two children: "You will go into the fourth womb. Your fathers, your mothers, kä-eto·we, tcu-eto·we, mu-eto·we, le-eto·we, all the society priests, society pekwins, society bow priests, you will bring out yonder into the light of your sun father."

So begins this emergence tale, which embodies the fundamental principles of Zuni religious society. The Zuni, or "Sun People," are organized into groups, each responsible for a particular aspect of the community's well-being, and each group is represented by a particular *-eto·we*, or fetish, connecting it to its spiritual foundation in Earth's womb. The pekwins mentioned here are sun priests, who control the ritual calendar. Bow priests oversee warfare and social behavior. In return for corn and breath given them by the Sun Father, the Zuni offer him cornmeal and downy feathers attached to painted prayer sticks symbolizing both clouds—the source of rain—and breath itself. Later in the tale, the two children of the Sun Father bring everyone out into the daylight for the first time:

Into the daylight of their sun father they came forth standing. Just as early dawn they came forth. After they came forth there they set down their sacred possessions in a row. The two said, "Now after a little while when your sun father comes forth standing to his sacred place you will see him face to face. Do not close your eyes." Thus he said to them. After a little while the sun came out. When he came out they looked at him. From their eyes the tears rolled down. After they had looked at him, in a little while their eyes became strong. "Alas!" Thus they said. They were covered all over with slime. With slimy tails and slimy horns, with webbed fingers, they saw one another. "Oh dear! is this what we look like?" Thus they said.

Then they could not tell which was which of their sacred possessions.

From this point on in the tale, the people and priests, led by the two children, seek to find the sacred "middle place," where things are balanced and orderly. Halona-Itiwana it is called, the sacred name of the Zuni Pueblo, "the Middle Ant Hill of the World." In the process, they are transformed from indeterminate, salamander-like creatures into their ultimate human form, and their world is transformed from chaos to order.

At the heart of the Zuni emergence tale is a moment when, to the dismay of their parents, many children are transformed into water-creatures—turtles, frogs, and the like—and the Hero Twins instruct the parents to throw these children back into the river. Here they become *kachinas* or *katcinas*, deified spirits, who explain:

May you go happily. You will tell our parents, "Do not worry." We have not perished. In order to remain thus forever we stay here. To Itiwana but one day's travel remains. Therefore we stay nearby. … Whenever the waters are exhausted and the seeds are exhausted you will send us prayer sticks. Yonder at the place of our first beginning with them we shall bend over to speak to them. Thus there will not fail to be waters. Therefore we shall stay quietly nearby.

The Pueblo believe that kachina spirits, not unlike the *num* of the San people of Africa, manifest themselves in performance and dance. Masked male dancers impersonate the kachinas, taking on their likeness as well as their supernatural character. Through these dance visits the kachinas, although always "nearby," can exercise their powers for the good of the people. The nearly 250 kachina personalities

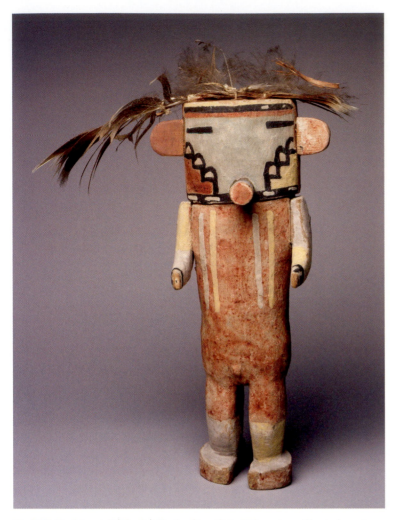

Fig. 1.19 Kachina doll (Maalo), Hopi culture. Late 19th century. Wood, pigment, feathers, fiber, and string, height 11½". Brooklyn Museum of Art. Museum Expedition 1904, Museum Collection Fund, 04.297.5604. The kachina is probably Maalo, an old-style traditional kachina who appears during Angi'wa (a series of Night Dances), and whose dance portrays a prayer for rain and good crop yield.

embody clouds, rain, crops, animals, and even ideas such as growth and fertility. Although kachina figurines (Fig. **1.19**) are made for sale as art objects, particularly by the Hopi, the actual masks worn in ceremonies are not considered art objects by the Pueblo people. Rather, they are thought of as active agents in the transfer of power and knowledge between the gods and the men who wear them in dance, just like the African Baule mask. In fact, kachina dolls made for sale are considered empty of any ritual power or significance.

Pueblo emergence tales, and the ritual practices that accompany them, reflect the general beliefs of most Neolithic peoples. These include the following:

- belief that the forces of nature are inhabited by living spirits, which we call **animism**;
- belief that nature's behavior can be compared to human behavior (we call the practice of investing plants, animals, and natural phenomena with human form or attributes **anthropomorphism**), thus explaining what otherwise would remain inexplicable;
- belief that humans can communicate with the spirits of nature, and that, in return for a sacrificial offering or a prayer, the gods might intercede on their behalf.

Japan and the Role of Myth in the Shinto Religion

A culture's religion—that is, its understanding of the divine—is thus closely tied to and penetrated by mythical elements. Its beliefs, as embodied in its religion, stories, and myths, have always been closely tied to seasonal celebrations and agricultural production—planting and harvest in particular, as well as rain—the success of which was understood to be inextricably linked to the well-being of the community. In a fundamental sense, myths reflect the community's ideals, its history (hence, the preponderance of creation myths in both ancient societies and contemporary religions), and its aspirations. Myths also tend to mirror the culture's moral and political systems, its social organization, and its most fundamental beliefs.

A profound example is the indigenous Japanese religion of Shinto. Before 200 CE, Japan was fragmented; its various regions were separated by sea and mountain, and ruled by numerous competing and often warring states. The *Records of Three Kingdoms*, a classic Chinese text dating from about 297 CE, states that in the first half of the third century CE, many or most of these states were unified under the rule of Queen Himiko. According to the *Records*: "The country formerly had a man as ruler. For some seventy or eighty years after that there were disturbances and warfare. Thereupon the people agreed upon a woman for their ruler. Her name was Himiko." After her rule, Japan was more or less united under the Yamato emperors, who modeled their rule after the Chinese, and whose imperial court ruled from present-day Nara Prefecture, then known as Yamato Province. Its peoples shared a mythology that was finally collected near the end of the Yamato period, in about 700 CE, called the *Kojiki or Chronicles of Japan*. (See **Reading 1.2**, page 29.) According to the *Kojiki*, the islands that constitute Japan were formed by two *kami*, or gods—Izanagi and his consort Izanami. Among their offspring was the sun goddess, Amaterasu Omikami, from whom the Japanese imperial line later claimed to have descended. In other words, Japanese emperors could claim not merely to have been put in position by the gods; they could claim to be direct descendants of the gods, and hence divine themselves.

Amaterasu is the principal goddess of the early indigenous religious practices that came to be known as Shinto. She is housed in a shrine complex at Ise, a sacred site from prehistoric times. In many respects, Shinto shares much

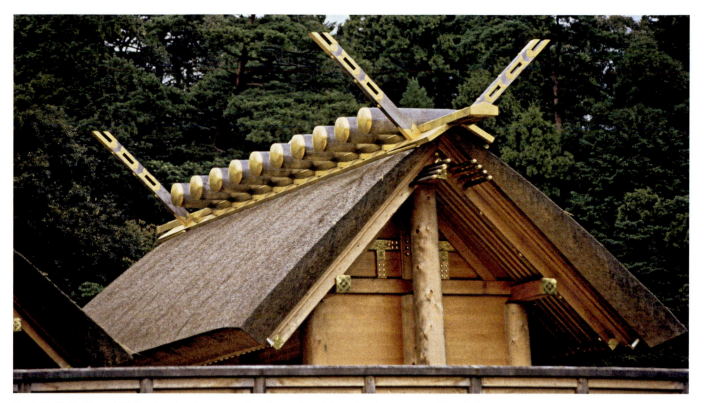

Fig. 1.20 Naiku (Inner) Shrine housing Amaterasu, Ise, Japan. Late 5th–early 6th century CE. Although the site has been sacred to Shinto since prehistoric times, beginning in the reign of the emperor Temmu (r. 673–86 CE), the Shinto shrine at Ise has been rebuilt by the Japanese ruling family, with some inevitable lapses, every 20 years. The most recent reconstruction occurred in 2013 and will occur again in 2033.

View the Closer Look for the Ise Shrine on **MyArtsLab**

with Pueblo religions. In Shinto, trees, rocks, water, and mountains—especially Mount Fuji, the volcano just outside Tokyo which is said to look over the country as its protector—are all manifestations of the *kami*, which, like kachinas, are the spirits that are embodied in the natural world. Even the natural materials with which artists work, such as clay, wood, and stone, are imbued with the *kami* and are to be treated with the respect and reverence due to a god. The *kami* are revered in *matsuri*, festivals that usually occur on an annual basis in which, it is believed, past and present merge into one, everyday reality fades away, and people come face to face with their gods. The *matsuri* serve to purify the territory and community associated with the *kami*, restoring them from the degradation inevitably worked upon them by the passing of time. During the festival, people partake of the original energies of the cosmos, which they will need to restore order to their world. Offerings such as fish, rice, and vegetables, as well as music and dancing, are presented to the *kami*, and the offerings of food are later eaten.

The main sanctuary, or *shoden*, at Ise consists of undecorated wooden beams and a thatched roof (Fig. 1.20). Ise is exceptional in its use of these plain and simple materials, which not only embody the basic tenet of Shinto—reverence for the natural world—but also the continuity and renewal of a tradition where wood, rather

than stone, has always been the principal building material. The most prominent festival at Ise is the *shikinen-sengu* ceremony, which involves the installation of the deity in a new shrine in a celebration of ritual renewal held every 20 years. The shrine buildings are rebuilt on empty ground adjacent to the older shrine, the deity is transferred to the new shrine, and the older shrine is razed, creating empty ground where the next shrine will be erected. The empty site is strewn with large white stones and is left totally bare except for a small wooden hut containing a sacred wooden pole, a practice that scholars believe dates back to very ancient times. This cycle of destruction and renewal connects the past to the present, the human community to its gods and their original energies.

The three sacred treasures of Shinto—a sword, a mirror, and a jewel necklace—were said to be given by Amaterasu to the first emperor, and they are traditionally handed down from emperor to emperor in the enthronement ceremony. The mirror is housed at Ise, the sword at the Atsuta Shrine in Nagoya, and the jewel necklace at the Imperial Palace in Tokyo. These imperial regalia are not considered mere symbols of the divine but "deity-bodies" in which the powers of the gods reside, specifically wisdom in the mirror, valor in the sword, and benevolence in the jewel necklace. To this day, millions of Japanese continue to practice Shinto, and they undertake pilgrimages to Ise each year.

SACRED SITES: THE EXAMPLE OF THE AMERICAS

What role do sacred sites play in prehistoric culture?

In some prehistoric cultures, priests or priestesses were principally responsible for mediating between the human and the divine. In others, as in Shinto, the ruler was the representative of the divine world on earth. But in almost all prehistoric cultures, communication with the spiritual world was conducted in special precincts or places such as Ise. Many scholars believe that caves served this purpose in Paleolithic times. In Neolithic culture, sites such as Stonehenge and the Anasazi kiva served this function.

The Olmec

As early as 1300 BCE, a preliterate group known as the Olmec came to inhabit the area between Veracruz and Tabasco on the southern coast of the Gulf of Mexico (see Map **1.3**), where they built huge ceremonial precincts in the middle of their communities. Many of the characteristic features of later Mesoamerican culture, such as pyramids, ball courts, mirror-making, and the calendar system, originated in the lowland agricultural zones that the Olmec inhabited.

The Olmec built their cities on great earthen platforms, probably designed to protect their ceremonial centers from rain and flood. On these platforms, they erected giant pyramidal mounds, where an elite group of ruler-priests lived, supported by the general population that farmed the rich, sometimes swampy land that surrounded them. These pyramids may have been an architectural reference to the volcanoes that dominate Mexico, or they may have been tombs. Excavations may eventually tell us. At La Venta, very near the present-day city of Villahermosa, three colossal stone heads stood guard over the ceremonial center on the south end of the platform (Fig. **1.21**), and a fourth guarded the north end by itself. Each head weighs between 11 and 24 tons, and each bears a unique emblem on its headgear, which is similar to old-style American leather football helmets. At other Olmec sites—San Lorenzo, for instance—as many as eight of these heads have been found, some up to 12 feet high. They are carved of basalt, although the nearest basalt quarry is 50 miles to the south in the Tuxtla Mountains. They were evidently at least partially carved at the quarry, then loaded onto rafts and floated downriver to the Gulf of Mexico before going back upriver to their final resting places. The stone heads are generally believed to be portraits of Olmec rulers, and they all share the same facial features, including wide, flat noses and thick lips. They suggest that the ruler was the culture's principal mediator with the gods, literally larger than life.

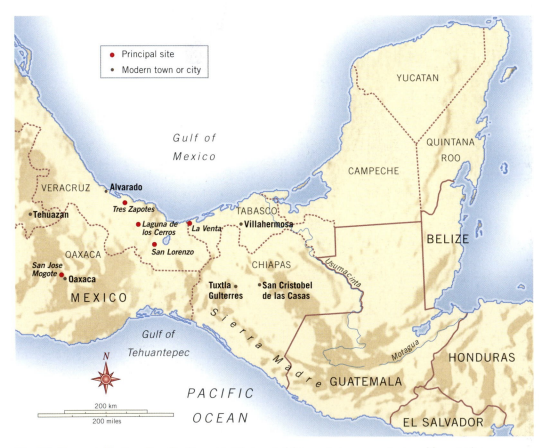

Map 1.3 Olmec civilization sites. The Olmec inhabited most of the area that we now refer to as Mesoamerica from 1300 to 400 BCE.

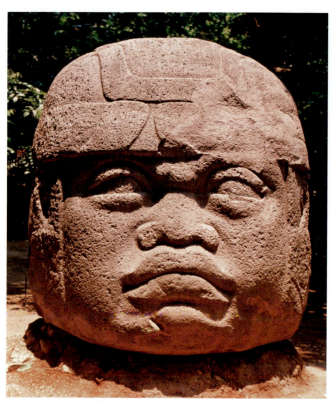

Fig. 1.21 Colossal head, La Venta, Mexico, Olmec culture. ca. 900–500 BCE. Basalt, height 7'50". La Venta Park, Villahermosa, Tabasco, Mexico. Giant heads such as this one faced out from the ceremonial center and evidently served to guard it.

The Mound Builders

Sometime between 1800 and 500 BCE, at about the same time that the Olmec were building the La Venta mound cluster in Mexico, Neolithic hunter-gatherers in eastern North America began building huge ceremonial centers of their own, consisting of large-scale embankments and burial mounds (Map **1.4**). These people, who probably had arrived in North America sometime between 14,000 and 10,000 BCE, are known as the Woodlands peoples because the area where they lived, stretching from the Mississippi River basin in the west to the Atlantic Ocean in the east, was originally forested.

One of these Woodlands peoples, the Hopewell culture in southern Ohio, enveloped the corpses of what we presume were their highest-ranking leaders from head to toe in freshwater pearls, weighted them down with plates of beaten copper, and then surrounded them with jewelry, sculpture, and pottery. These burials give us a fair idea of the extent of Woodlands trade. Their copper came from the Great Lakes, decorative shell from the Gulf coast, alligator and shark teeth from Florida, and mica from the Appalachian Mountains. There are even examples of obsidian that can be traced to what is now Yellowstone National Park, and grizzly bear teeth from the Rocky Mountains.

The most intriguing of the Woodlands mounds is the Great Serpent Mound, near Locust Grove, Ohio

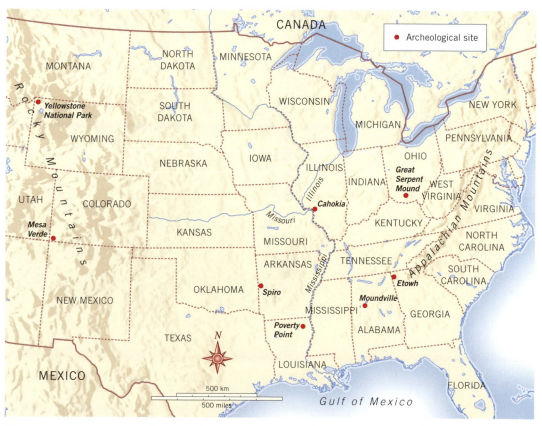

Map 1.4 Archeological sites of the Anasazi and the mound builders' archeological sites in North America.

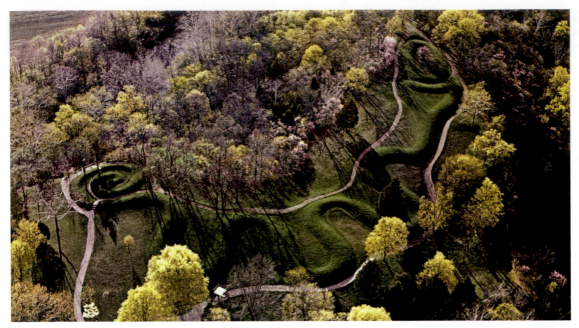

Fig. 1.22 Great Serpent Mound, Adams County, Ohio, possibly Fort Ancient culture. ca. 1000 BCE–1650 CE. Length approx. 1,254'. Recently, archeologists have carbon dated an artifact found at the Great Serpent Mound as late as 1070 CE. Because of this, the mound is believed to be the product of the Fort Ancient people, who were descended from the Hopewell. The late date of the artifact also suggests that the mound may be related to Halley's Comet, which passed by the earth in 1066.

(Fig. 1.22). Nearly a quarter of a mile long, it contains no burial sites. Its "head" consists of an oval enclosure that may have served some ceremonial purpose, and its tail is a spiral. The spiral would, in fact, become a favorite decorative form of the Mississippian culture, which developed out of the Woodlands-era cultures and raised ritual mound building to a new level of achievement. The great mound at Cahokia (Fig. 1.23), near the juncture of the Illinois, Missouri, and Mississippi rivers at present-day East St. Louis, Illinois, required the moving of over 22 million cubic feet of earth and probably three centuries to construct, beginning about 900 CE. It was the focal point of a ritual center that contained as many as 120 mounds, some of which were aligned with the position of the sun at the equinoxes, as well as nearly 400 other platforms, wooden enclosures, and houses. Evidence suggests that the Mississippians worshiped the sun: The Natchez people, one of the Mississippian peoples who survived contact with European culture, called their chief the Great Sun, and their highest social class the Suns.

The Mississippian culture sustained itself primarily by the cultivation of corn, suggesting close connections to Mexico, where cultivation of corn was originally

perfected. As many as 4 million people may have lived in the Mississippi Valley. Cahokia itself thrived, with a population of around 20,000 people within its 6-square-mile area, until just before 1500, when the site was mysteriously abandoned.

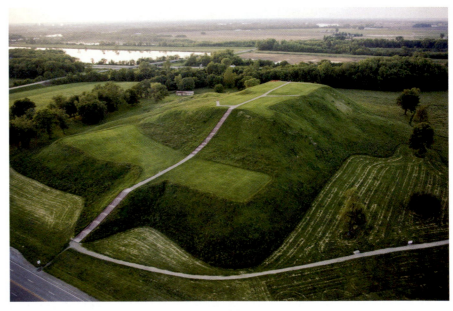

Fig. 1.23 Monks Mound, the centerpiece of Cahokia Mounds State Historic Site, Collinsville, Illinois, Mississippian culture. ca. 1150 CE. East–west length approx. 3 miles; north–south length approx. 2¼ miles; base of great mound, 1,037' × 790'; height approx. 100'. A stockade, or fence, surrounded the mound and a large area in front of it, suggesting that warfare probably played an important role in Mississippian life.

Representing the Power of the Animal World

The two images shown here in some sense bracket the six parts of *The Humanities*. The first (Fig. **1.24**), from the Chauvet Cave, is one of the earliest known drawings of a horse. The second (Fig. **1.25**), a drawing by contemporary American painter Susan Rothenberg (1945–), also represents a horse, though in many ways less realistically than the cave drawing. The body of Rothenberg's horse seems to have disappeared and, eyeless, as if blinded, it leans forward, its mouth open, choking or gagging or gasping for air.

In his catalog essay for a 1993 retrospective exhibition of Rothenberg's painting, Michael Auping, then chief curator at the Albright-Knox Museum in Buffalo, New York, described Rothenberg's kind of drawing: "Relatively spontaneous, the drawings are Rothenberg's psychic energy made imminent. … [They] uncover realms of the psyche that are perhaps not yet fully explicable." The same could be said of the cave drawing executed by a nameless hunter-gatherer more than 30,000 years ago. That artist's work must have seemed just as strange as Rothenberg's, lit by flickering firelight in the dark recesses of the cave, its body disappearing, too, into the darkness that surrounded it.

It seems certain that in some measure both drawings were the expression of a psychic need on the part of the artist—whether derived from the energy of the hunt or of nature itself—to fix upon a surface an image of the power and vulnerability of the animal world. That drive, which we will see in the art of the Bronze Age of the Middle East—for instance, in the haunting image of a dying lion in the palace complex of an Assyrian king at Nineveh (see Fig. 2.12 in Chapter 2)—remains constant from the beginnings of art to the present day. It is the compulsion to express the inexpressible, to visualize the mind as well as the world. ■

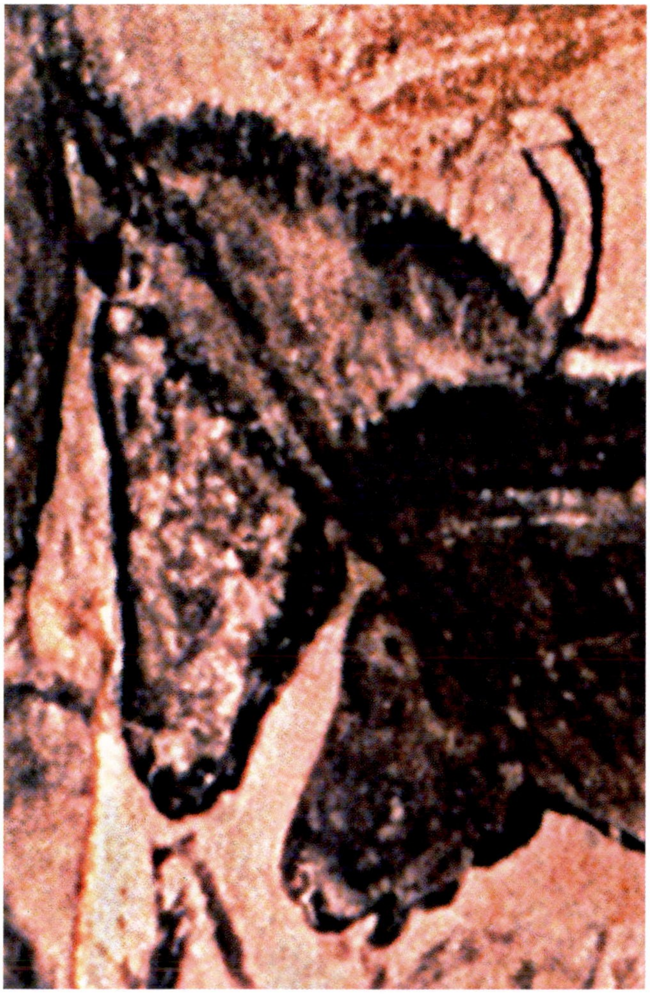

Fig. 1.24 Horse. Detail from the Chauvet Cave, Vallon-Pont-d'Arc, Ardèche gorge, France (Fig. 1.1). ca. 30,000 BCE. Note the realistic shading that defines the volume of the horse's head. It is a realism that artists throughout history have sometimes sought to achieve, and sometimes ignored, in their efforts to express the forces that drive them.

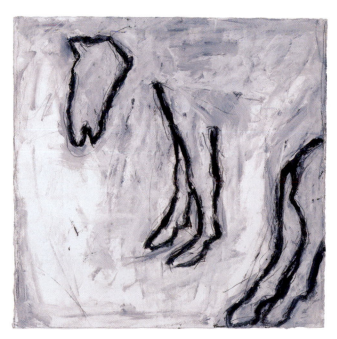

Fig. 1.25 Susan Rothenberg, Untitled. 1978. Acrylic, flashe (vinyl paint), and pencil on paper, 20" × 20". Collection Walker Art Center, Minneapolis. Art Center Acquisition Fund, 1979. © 2014 Susan Rothenberg/Artists Rights Society (ARS), New York. Part of the eeriness of this image comes from Rothenberg's use of flashe, a French vinyl-based color that is clear and so creates a misty, ghostlike surface.

1.1 Discuss the ways in which cave art and small sculptural figurines in the Paleolithic era have been interpreted.

The widespread use of stone tools and weapons by *Homo sapiens*, the hominid species that evolved around 120,000 to 100,000 years ago, gives rise to the name of the earliest era of human development, the Paleolithic era. The peoples of the Paleolithic era made objects and images that we can identify today as works of art. Carvers fashioned stone figures, both in the round and in relief. In cave paintings, such as those discovered at Chauvet Cave, the artists' great skill in rendering animals helps us to understand that the ability to represent the world with naturalistic fidelity is an inherent human skill, unrelated to cultural sophistication. If *culture* can be defined as a way of living—religious, social, and/or political—formed by a group of people and passed on from one generation to the next, what can these earliest works of art tell us about the first human cultures? What questions remain a mystery?

1.2 Explain how the art and architecture of the Neolithic era reflect changing cultural concerns.

As the ice that covered the Northern Hemisphere slowly melted, people began cultivating edible grasses and domesticating animals. Gradually, farming supplanted hunting as the primary means of sustaining life, especially in the great river valleys where water was abundant. The rise of agriculture is the chief characteristic of the Neolithic age. Along with agriculture, permanent villages such as Çatalhöyük and Skara Brae began to appear. What do these villages suggest about the changing nature of cultural life? What does the appearance of fire-baked pottery tell us about life in Neolithic culture?

During the fifth millennium BCE, Neolithic peoples began constructing monumental stone architecture, or megaliths, in France and England. Upright, single stone posts called menhirs were placed in the ground, either individually or in groups, as at Carnac in Brittany. Elementary post-and-lintel construction was employed to create dolmens, two posts roofed with a capstone. The most famous of the third type of monumental construction, the circular cromlech, is Stonehenge, in England. What does the enormous amount of human labor required for the construction of these megaliths suggest about the societies that built them?

1.3 Understand the function of myth in prehistoric culture.

Neolithic culture in the Americas lasted well into the second millennium CE. Much of our understanding of the role of myth in prehistoric cultures derives from the surviving traditions of contemporary Native American tribes such as the Hopi and Zuni, who are the direct descendants of the Anasazi. Their legends, such as the Zuni emergence tale, encapsulate the fundamental religious principles of the culture. Such stories, and the ritual practices that accompany them, reflect the general beliefs of most Neolithic peoples. Can you describe some of these beliefs? What do the myths of the Pueblo peoples have in common with Japanese Shinto mythology?

1.4 Describe the role of sacred sites in prehistoric culture.

In almost all prehistoric cultures, communication with the spiritual world was conducted in special precincts or places. The main sanctuary at Ise in Japan is an example. So are sites such as Stonehenge and the kivas in Anasazi culture. What do the colossal stone heads at La Venta suggest about the ceremonial centers over which they stand guard? Can you speculate, in a general way, about the role of mounds in Woodlands and Mississippian culture?

✓ **Study** and **review** on **MyArtsLab**

READINGS

The Japanese Creation Myth: *The Kojiki*

The following is the beginning of a modern retelling of the *Kojiki* or *Chronicles of Japan*, the oldest surviving account of ancient Japanese history. This creation myth details the origins of Japan and the sacred spirits, or *kami*, which are objects of worship for the indigenous religion of Japan, Shinto.

Before the heavens and the earth came into existence, all was a chaos, unimaginably limitless and without definite shape or form. Eon followed eon: then, lo! out of this boundless, shapeless mass something light and transparent rose up and formed the heaven. This was the Plain of High Heaven, in which materialized a deity called Ame-no-Minaka-Nushi-no-Mikoto (the Deity-of-the-August-Center-of-Heaven). Next the heavens gave birth to a deity named Takami-Musubi-no-Mikoto (the High-August-Producing-Wondrous-Deity), followed by a third called Kammi-Musubi-no-Mikoto (the Divine-Producing-Wondrous-Deity). These three divine beings are called the Three Creating Deities.

In the meantime what was heavy and opaque in the void gradually precipitated and became the earth, but it had taken an immeasurably long time before it condensed sufficiently to form solid ground. In its earliest stages, for millions and millions of years, the earth may be said to have resembled oil floating, medusa-like, upon the face of the waters. Suddenly like the sprouting up of a reed, a pair of immortals were born from its bosom. … Many gods were thus born in succession, and so they increased in number, but as long as the world remained in a chaotic state, there was nothing for them to do. Whereupon, all the Heavenly deities summoned the two divine beings, Izanagi and Izanami, and bade them descend to the nebulous place, and by helping each other, to consolidate it into terra firma. [The heavenly deities] handed them a spear called Ama-no-Nuboko, embellished with costly gems. The divine couple received respectfully and ceremoniously the sacred weapon and then withdrew from the presence of the deities, ready to perform their august commission. Proceeding forthwith to the Floating Bridge of Heaven, which lay between the heaven and the earth, they stood awhile to gaze on that which lay below. What they beheld was a world not yet condensed, but looking like a sea of filmy fog floating to and fro in the air, exhaling the while an inexpressibly fragrant odor. They were, at first, perplexed just how and where to start, but at length Izanagi suggested to his companion that they should try the effect of stirring up the brine with their spear. So saying he pushed down the jeweled shaft and found that it touched something. Then drawing it up, he examined it and observed that the great drops which fell from it almost immediately coagulated into an island, which is, to this day, the Island of Onokoro. Delighted at the result, the two deities descended forthwith from the Floating Bridge to reach the miraculously created island. In this island they thenceforth dwelt and made it the basis of their subsequent task of creating a country. … First, the island of Awaji was born, next, Shikoku, then, the island of Oki, followed by Kyushu; after that, the island Tsushima came into being, and lastly, Honshu, the main island of Japan. The name of Oyashi-ma-kuni (the Country of the Eight Great Islands) was given to these eight islands.

READING CRITICALLY

One of the key moments in this creation myth is when the heavenly deities order Izanagi and Izanami to "descend to the nebulous place, and by helping each other, to consolidate it into terra firma." What does this tell us about Japanese culture?

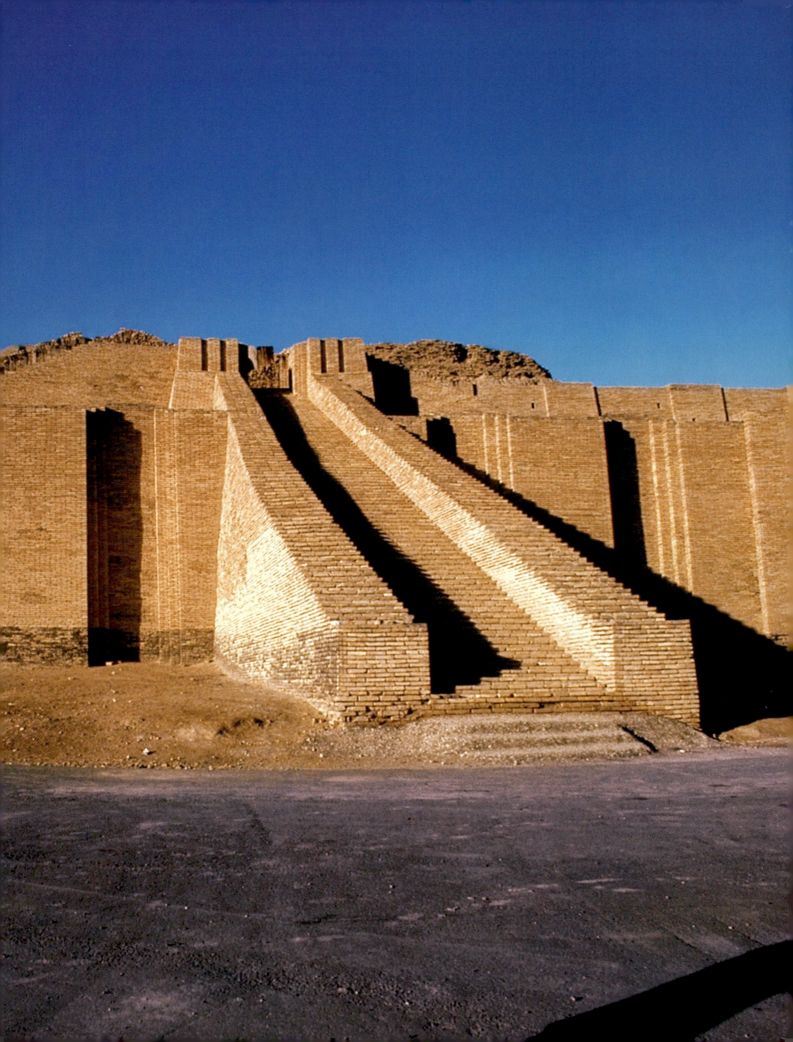

2 The Ancient Near East
Power and Social Order

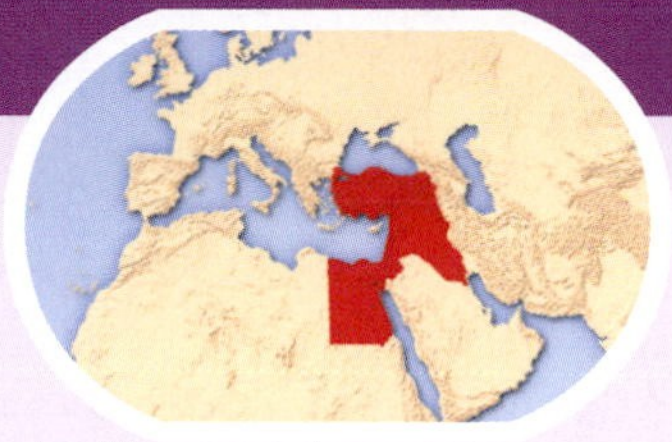

THINKING AHEAD

2.1 Describe the relationship between the gods and the peoples of Sumer, Akkad, Babylon, and Assyria.

2.2 Explain how the *Epic of Gilgamesh* reflects the relationship between the gods and the people.

2.3 Distinguish between the culture of the Hebrews and the other cultures of the ancient Near East.

2.4 Discuss how the art and architecture of Neo-Babylonia and Persia reflect the ambitions of their leaders.

In September 1922, British archeologist C. Leonard Woolley boarded a steamer, beginning a journey that would take him to southern Iraq. There, Woolley and his team would discover one of the richest treasure troves in the history of archeology in the ruins of the ancient city of Ur. Woolley concentrated his energies on the burial grounds surrounding the city's central **ziggurat**, a pyramidal temple structure consisting of successive platforms with outside staircases and a shrine at the top (Fig. **2.1**). Digging there in the winter of 1927, he unearthed a series of tombs with several rooms, many bodies, and masses of golden objects (Fig. **2.2**)—vessels, crowns, necklaces, statues, and weapons—as well as jewelry and lyres made of electrum and the deep-blue stone lapis lazuli. With the same sense of excitement that was felt by Jean-Marie Chauvet and his companions when they first saw the paintings on the wall of Chauvet Cave, Woolley was careful to keep what he called the "royal tombs" secret. On January 4, 1928, Woolley telegrammed his colleagues in Latin. Translated to English, it read:

> *I found the intact tomb, stone built, and vaulted over with bricks of queen Shubad [later known as Puabi] adorned with a dress in which gems, flower crowns and animal figures are woven. Tomb magnificent with jewels and golden cups.*
>
> —Woolley

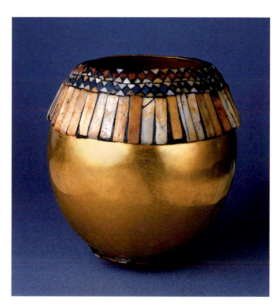

Fig. 2.2 Vessel in the shape of an ostrich egg, from the Royal Cemetery of Ur. ca. 2550 BCE. Gold, lapis lazuli, red limestone, shell, and bitumen, hammered from a single sheet of gold and with geometric mosaics at the top and bottom of the egg. Height 5¾", diameter 5⅛". University of Pennsylvania Museum of Archaeology and Anthropology, Philadelphia. Museum object #152071. The array of materials came from trade with neighbors in Afghanistan, Iran, Anatolia, and perhaps Egypt and Nubia.

◀ **Fig. 2.1 The ziggurat at Ur (present-day Muqaiyir, Iraq). ca. 2100 BCE.** The best preserved and most fully restored of the ancient Sumerian temples, this ziggurat was the center of the city of Ur, in the lower plain between the Tigris and Euphrates rivers.

Listen to the chapter audio on **MyArtsLab**

When Woolley's discovery was made public, it was world-wide news for years.

Archeologists and historians were especially excited by Woolley's discoveries, because they opened a window onto the larger region we call Mesopotamia, the land between the Tigris and Euphrates rivers. Ur was one of 30 or 40 cities that arose in Sumer, the southern portion of Mesopotamia (Map 2.1). In fact, its people abandoned the city more than 2,000 years ago, when the Euphrates changed its course away from the city.

Over the centuries other cultures would vie for control of the region, chief among them the Akkadians, Babylonians, and Assyrians. By 612 BCE, the Assyrian Empire would fall to Nabopolassar, first king of Babylonia, and a second Neo-Babylonian culture would arise, only to fall, in turn, to the Persians. Throughout almost the entire era, a very different culture, that of the Hebrews, coexisted with the major Mesopotamian powers, sometimes peacefully, often not. This chapter outlines the social and political forces that came to define these Mesopotamian cultures.

THE CULTURES OF MESOPOTAMIA, 3200–612 BCE

What was the nature of the relationship between the gods and the peoples of Sumer, Akkad, Babylon, and Assyria?

The peoples of Mesopotamia were almost totally dependent on the Tigris and Euphrates rivers for their livelihoods. By irrigating the lands just outside the marshes on the riverbanks, the conditions necessary for extensive and elaborate communities such as Ur began to arise: People dug canals and ditches and cooperated in regulating the flow of water in them, which eventually resulted in crops that exceeded the needs of the population. These could be transformed into foodstuffs of a more elaborate kind, including beer. Evidence indicates that over half of each grain harvest went into producing beer. Excess crops were also traded by boat with nearby communities or up the great rivers

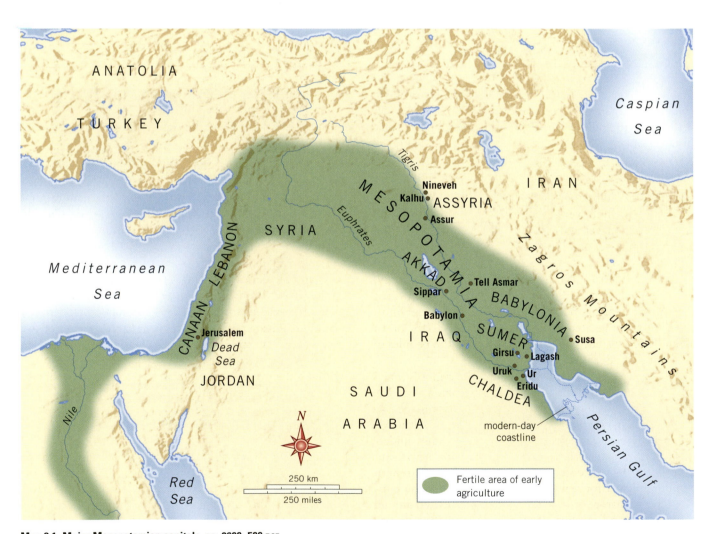

Map 2.1 Major Mesopotamian capitals, ca. 2600–500 BCE.

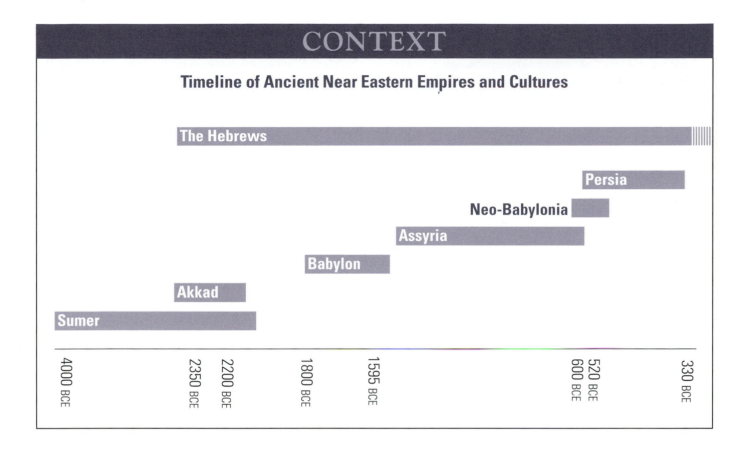

CONTEXT

Timeline of Ancient Near Eastern Empires and Cultures

The Hebrews

Persia

Neo-Babylonia

Assyria

Babylon

Akkad

Sumer

4000 BCE — 2350 BCE — 2200 BCE — 1800 BCE — 1595 BCE — 520 BCE — 600 BCE — 330 BCE

to the north, where stone, wood, and metals were available in exchange. As people congregated in central locations to exchange goods, cities began to form. Cities such as Ur became hubs of great trading networks. With trade came ideas, which were incorporated into local custom and spawned newer and greater ideas in turn. Out of the exchange of goods and ideas, then, the conditions were in place for great cultures to arise.

After agriculture, first among these was **metallurgy**, the science of separating metals from their ores and then working or treating them to create objects. The technology probably originated in the Fertile Crescent to the north about 4000 BCE, but as it spread southward, the peoples of Mesopotamia adopted it as well.

This new technology would change the region's social organization, inaugurating what we have come to call the Bronze Age. Metallurgy required the mining of ores, specialized technological training, and skilled artisans. Although the metallurgical properties of copper were widely understood, technicians discovered that by alloying it with tin they could create bronze, a material of enormous strength and durability. Bronze weapons would transform the military and the nature of warfare. Power consolidated around the control and mastery of weaponry, and thus bronze created a new military elite of soldiers dedicated to protecting the Sumerian **city-states** from one another as they vied for control of produce and trade. The city-states, in turn,

spawned governments ruled by **priest-kings**, who exercised power as intermediaries between the gods and the people. In their secular role, the priest-kings established laws that contributed to the social order necessary for maintaining successful agricultural societies. The arts developed largely as celebrations of the priest-kings' powers. In order to keep track of the production and distribution of goods, the costs of equipping the military, and records relating to enforcing laws and regulations, writing—perhaps the greatest innovation of the Bronze Age—developed. If agricultural production served to stimulate the creation of urban centers, metallurgy made possible the new military cultures of the city-states. The arts served to celebrate these new centers of power, and writing, which arose out of the necessity of tracking the workings of the state, would come to celebrate the state in a literature of its own.

Sumerian Ur

Ur is not the oldest city to occupy the southern plains of Mesopotamia, the region known as Sumer. That distinction belongs to Uruk, just to the north, which by around 3200 BCE was probably the largest settlement in the world. But the temple structure at Ur is of particular note because it is the most fully preserved and restored. It was most likely designed to evoke the mountains surrounding the river valley, which were the source of the water that flowed through

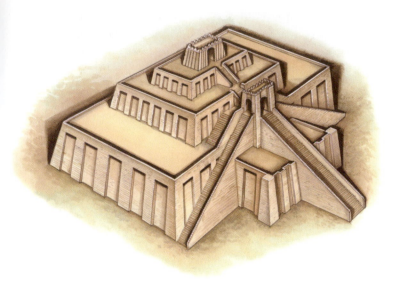

Fig. 2.3 Reconstruction drawing of the ziggurat at Ur (present-day Muqaiyir, Iraq). ca. 2100 BCE. British archeologist Sir Leonard Woolley undertook reconstruction of the ziggurat in the 1930s (see Fig. 2.1). In his reconstruction, a temple on top, which was the home of the patron deity of the city, crowned the three-tiered platform, the base of which measures 140 by 200 feet. The entire structure rose to a height of 85 feet. Woolley's reconstruction was halted before the second and third platforms had been completed.

the two rivers and, so, the source of life. Topped by a sanctuary, the ziggurat might also have symbolized a bridge between heaven and earth. Woolley, who supervised the reconstruction of the first platform and stairway of the ziggurat at Ur (Fig. 2.3), speculated that the platforms of the temple were originally not paved but covered with soil and planted with trees, an idea that modern archeologists no longer accept.

Visitors—almost certainly limited to members of the priesthood—would climb up the stairs to the temple on top. They might bring an offering of food or an animal to be sacrificed to the resident god—at Ur, it was Nanna or Sin, god of the moon. Visitors often placed in the temple a statue that represented themselves in an attitude of perpetual prayer. We know this from the inscriptions on many of the statues. One, dedicated to the goddess Tarsirsir, protector of Girsu, a city-state across the Tigris and not far upstream from Ur, reads:

To Bau, gracious lady, daughter of An, queen of the holy city, her mistress, for the life of Nammahani … has dedicated as an offering this statue of the protective goddess of Tarsirsir which she has introduced to the courtyard of Bau. May the statue, to which let my mistress turn her ear, speak my prayers.

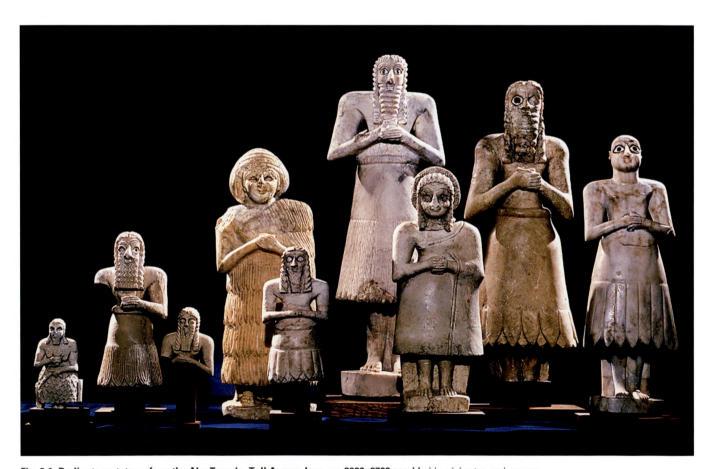

Fig. 2.4 Dedicatory statues, from the Abu Temple, Tell Asmar, Iraq. ca. 2900–2700 BCE. Marble, alabaster, and gypsum, height of tallest figure, approx. 30". Excavated by the Iraq Expedition of the Oriental Institute of the University of Chicago, February 13, 1934. Courtesy of the Oriental Institute of the University of Chicago. The wide-eyed appearance of these figures is probably meant to suggest they are gazing in perpetual awe at the deity.

A group of such statues, found in 1934 in the shrine room of a temple at Tell Asmar, near present-day Baghdad, includes seven men and two women (Fig. 2.4). The men wear belted, fringed skirts. They have huge eyes, inlaid with lapis lazuli (a blue semiprecious stone) or shell set in bitumen. The single arching eyebrow and crimped beard (only the figure at the right is beardless) are typical of Sumerian sculpture. The two women wear robes. All figures clasp their hands in front of them, suggestive of prayer when empty and of making an offering when holding a cup. Some scholars believe that the tallest man represents Abu, god of vegetation, due to his especially large eyes, but all of the figures are probably worshipers.

Religion in Ancient Mesopotamia Although power struggles among the various city-states dominate Mesopotamian history, with one civilization succeeding another, and with each city-state or empire claiming its own particular divinity as chief among the Mesopotamian gods, the nature of Mesopotamian religion remained relatively constant across the centuries. With the exception of the Hebrews, the religion of the Mesopotamian peoples was polytheistic, consisting of multiple gods and goddesses connected to the forces of nature—sun and sky, water and storm, earth and its fertility (see *Context*, page 36). We know many of them by two names, one in Sumerian and the other in the Semitic language of the later, more powerful Akkadians. A famous Akkadian **cylinder seal** (Fig. 2.5), an engraved cylinder used as a signature by rolling it into a wet clay tablet in order to confirm receipt of goods or to identify ownership, represents many of the gods. The figures are recognizably gods because they wear pointed headdresses with multiple horns, though the figure on the left, beside the lion and holding a bow, has not been definitively identified. The figure with two wings standing atop the scaly mountain is Ishtar, goddess of love and war. Weapons rise from her shoulders, and she holds a bunch of dates in her

hand, a symbol of fertility. Beneath her, cutting his way through the mountain so that he can rise at dawn, is the sun god, Shamash. Standing with his foot on the mountain at the right, streams of water with fish in them flowing from his shoulders, is Ea, god of water, wisdom, magic, and art. Behind him is his vizier, or "burden-carrier."

To the Mesopotamians, human society was merely part of the larger society of the universe governed by these gods and a reflection of it. Anu, father of the gods, represents the authority, which the ruler emulates as lawmaker and -giver. Enlil, god of the air—the calming breeze as well as the violent storm—is equally powerful, but he represents force, which the ruler emulates in his role as military leader. The active principles of fertility, birth, and agricultural plenty are those of the goddess Belitili, while water, the life force itself, the creative element, is embodied in the god Ea, or Enki, who is also god of the arts. Both Belitili and Ea are subject to the authority of Anu. Ishtar is subject to Enlil, ruled by his breezes (in the case of love) and by his storm (in the case of war). A host of lesser gods represented natural phenomena, or, in some cases, abstract ideas, such as truth and justice.

The Mesopotamian ruler, often represented as a priest-king, and often believed to possess divine attributes, acts as the intermediary between the gods and humankind. His ultimate responsibility is the behavior of the gods—whether Ea blesses the crop with rains, Ishtar his armies with victory, and so on.

The Royal Tombs of Ur Religion was central to the people of Ur, and the cemetery discovered by Woolley tells us a great deal about the nature of their beliefs. Woolley unearthed some 1,840 graves, most dating from between 2600 and 2000 BCE. The greatest number of graves were individual burials of rich and poor alike. However, some included a built burial chamber rather than just a coffin and contained more than one body, in some cases as many as 80.

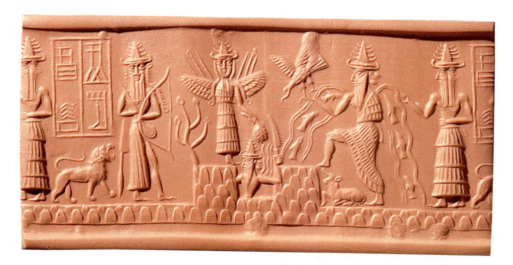
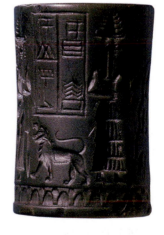

Fig. 2.5 Cylinder seal impression and the Seal of Adda. Akkadian. ca. 2200–2159 BCE. Greenstone, height 1½". © The Trustees of the British Museum. The two-line inscription at the left identifies the seal's owner as Adda, a scribe.

Mesopotamian Gods and Goddesses

Name	Symbol	Role
An/Anu	horned cap	Father of the gods, god of the sky
Enlil	horned cap	God of the air and storm; later replaces Anu as father of the gods
Utu/Shamash	solar disk	Sun god, lord of truth and justice
Inanna/Ishtar	star	Goddess of love and war
Ninhursag /Belitili	'omega'	Mother Earth
Enki/Ea	goat-fish	God of water, lord of wisdom, magic, art
Marduk	spade	Chief god of Babylon

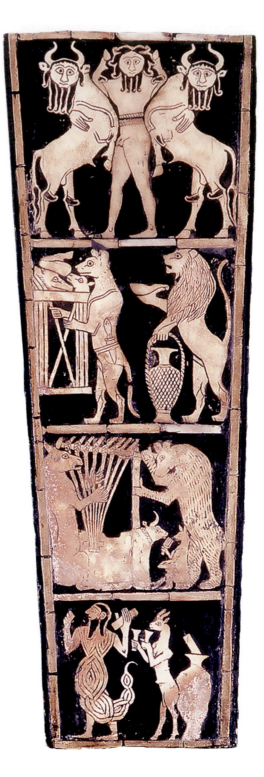

Fig. 2.6 Soundbox panel front of the lyre from Tomb 789 (alternatively identified as the unknown king's or Puabi's tomb), from the cemetery at Ur (present-day Muqaiyir, Iraq). ca. 2600 BCE. Wood with inlaid gold, lapis lazuli, and shell, height approx. 12¼". University of Pennsylvania Museum of Archaeology and Anthropology, Philadelphia. Museum object #B17694 (image #150848). The meaning of the scenes on the front of this lyre has always puzzled scholars. On the bottom, a goat holding two cups attends a man with a scorpion's body. Above that, a donkey plays a bull-headed lyre held by a bear, while a seated jackal plays a small percussion instrument. On the third level, animals walking on their hind legs carry food and drink for a feast. In the top panel, a man with long hair and beard, naked but for his belt, holds two human-headed bulls by the shoulders.

These multiple burials, and the evidence of elaborate burial rituals, suggest that members of a king or queen's court accompanied the ruler to the grave. The two richest burial sites, built one behind the other, are now identified as royal tombs, one belonging to Queen Puabi, the other to an unknown king (but it is not that of her husband, King Meskalamdug, who is buried in a different grave).

In the grave of either the unknown king or Queen Puabi (records are confusing on this point) were two lyres, one of which today is housed in Philadelphia (Fig. **2.6**), the other in London (Fig. **2.7**). Both are decorated with bull's heads and are fronted by a panel of **narrative scenes**—that is, scenes representing a story or event. Although originally made of wood, which rots over time, these objects were able

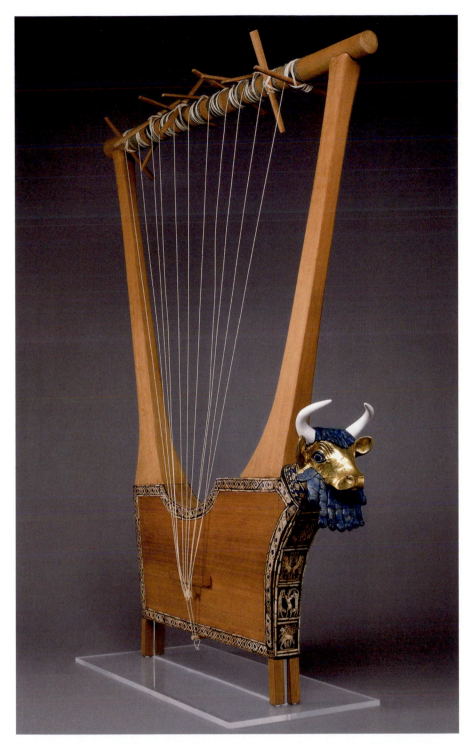

Fig. 2.7 Lyre from Tomb 789 (alternatively identified as the unknown king's or Puabi's tomb), from the cemetery at Ur (present-day Muqaiyir, Iraq). ca. 2600 BCE. Gold leaf and lapis lazuli over a wood core, height 44½". Restored 1971–72. © The Trustees of the British Museum.

forms that decorate these lyres represents a funerary banquet in the realm of the dead. They are related, at least thematically, to events in the Sumerian *Epic of Gilgamesh*, which we will discuss later in the chapter. This suggests that virtually every element of the culture—from its music and literature to its religion and politics—was tied in some way to every other. The women whose bodies were found under the two lyres may have been singers and musicians, and the placement of the lyres over them would indicate that the lyres were put there after the celebrants died.

Such magnificent musical instruments indicate that music was important in Mesopotamian society. Surviving documents tell us that music and song were part of the funeral ritual, and music played a role in worship at the temple, as well as in banquets and festivals. Indeed, a fragment of a poem from the middle of the third millennium BCE found at Lagash indicates

to be saved in their original form due to an innovation of Woolley's during the excavation. He ordered his workers to tell him whenever they came upon an area that sounded hollow. He would fill such hollows (where the original wood had long since rotted away) with wax or plaster, thus preserving, in place, the decorative effects on the object's outside. It seems likely that the mix of animal and human

that Sumerian music was anything but funereal. It is music's duty, the poet says,

> To fill with joy the Temple court
> And chase the city's gloom away
> The heart to still, the passions calm,
> Of weeping eyes the tears to stay.

One of Woolley's most important discoveries in the Royal Cemetery was the so-called *Royal Standard of Ur* (Fig. **2.8**). Music plays a large part here, too. The main panels of this rectangular box of unknown function are called "War" and "Peace," because they illustrate, on one side, a military victory and, on the other, the subsequent banquet celebrating the event, or perhaps a cult ritual. Each panel is composed of three **registers**, or self-contained horizontal bands, within which the figures stand on a **ground line**, or baseline.

At the right side of the top register of the "Peace" panel (the lower half of Fig. 2.8), a musician plays a lyre, and behind him another, apparently female, sings. The king, at the left end, is recognizable because he is taller than the others and wears a tufted skirt, his head breaking the register line on top. In this convention, known as **social perspective**, or **hieratic scale**, the most important figures are represented as larger than the others. In other registers on the "Peace" side of the *Standard*, servants bring cattle, goats,

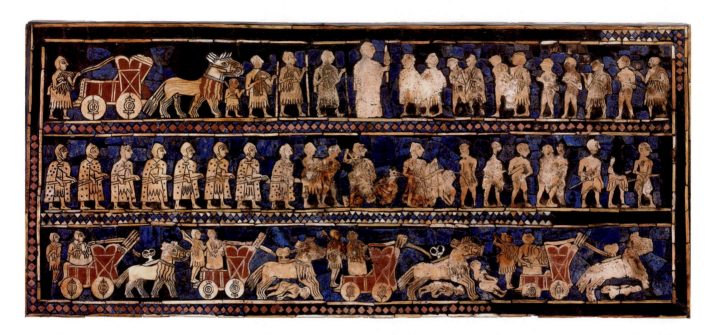

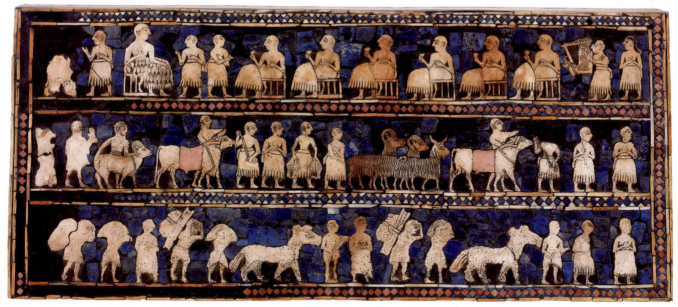

Fig. 2.8 *Royal Standard of Ur*, front ("War") and back ("Peace") sides, from Tomb 779, cemetery at Ur (present-day Muqaiyir, Iraq). ca. 2600 BCE. Shell, lapis lazuli, and red limestone, originally on a wooden framework, height 8", length 19". © The Trustees of the British Museum. For all its complexity of design, this object is not much bigger than a sheet of legal paper. Its function remains a mystery, though it may have served as a pillow or headrest. Woolley's designation of it as a standard was purely conjectural.

View the Closer Look for the *Royal Standard of Ur* on **MyArtsLab**

sheep, and fish to the celebration. These represent the bounty of the land and perhaps even delicacies from lands to the north. (Notice that the costumes and hairstyles of the figures carrying sacks in the lowest register are different from those in the other two.) This display of consumption and the distribution of food may have been intended to dramatize the power of the king by showing his ability to control trade routes.

On the "War" side of the *Standard*, the king stands in the middle of the top register. War chariots trample the enemy on the bottom register. (Note that the chariots have solid wheels; spoked wheels were not invented until approximately 1800 BCE.) In the middle register, soldiers wearing leather cloaks and bronze helmets lead naked, bound prisoners to the king in the top register, who will presumably decide their fate. Many of the bodies found in the royal tombs were wearing similar military garments. The importance of the *Royal Standard of Ur* is not simply as documentary evidence of Sumerian life but as one of the earliest examples we have of historical narrative.

Akkad

At the height of the Sumerians' power in southern Mesopotamia, a people known as the Akkadians arrived from the north and settled in the area around present-day Baghdad. Their capital city, Akkad, has never been discovered and in all likelihood lies under Baghdad itself. Under Sargon I (r. ca. 2332–2279 BCE), the Akkadians conquered virtually all other cities in Mesopotamia, including those in Sumer, to become the region's most powerful city-state. Sargon named himself "King of the Four Quarters of the World" and equated himself with the gods, a status bestowed upon Akkadian rulers from Sargon's time forward. Legends about Sargon's might and power survived in the region for thousands of years. Indeed, the legend of his birth gave rise to what amounts to a **narrative genre** (a class or category of story with a universal theme) that survives to the present day: the boy from humble origins who rises to a position of might and power, the so-called "rags-to-riches" story.

As depicted on surviving clay tablets, Sargon was an illegitimate child whose mother deposited him in the Euphrates River in a basket. There, a man named Akki (after whom Akkad itself is named) found him while drawing water from the river and raised him as his own son. Such stories of abandonment, orphanhood, and being a foundling raised by foster parents were to become a standard feature in the narratives of mythic heroes.

Although the Akkadian language was very different from Sumerian, through most of the third millennium BCE—that is, until Sargon's dynastic ambitions altered the balance of power in the region—the two cultures coexisted peacefully. The Akkadians adopted Sumerian culture and customs (see Fig. 2.5) and their style of **cuneiform writing**, a script made of wedge-shaped characters (see *Closer Look*, pages 40–41), although not their language. In fact,

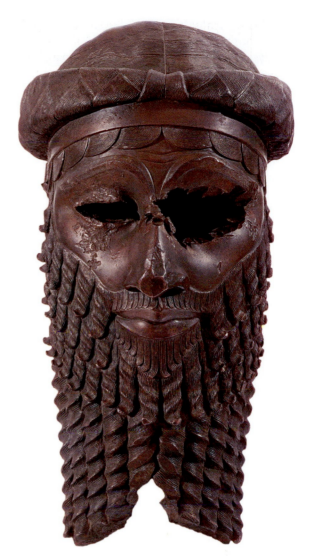

Fig. 2.9 *Head of an Akkadian Man*, from Nineveh (present-day Kuyunjik, Iraq). ca. 2300–2200 BCE. Copper alloy, height 14⅛". Iraq Museum, Baghdad.

many bilingual dictionaries and Sumerian texts with Akkadian translations survive. The Akkadian language was Semitic in origin, having more in common with other languages of the region, particularly Hebrew, Phoenician, and Arabic. It quickly became the common language of Mesopotamia, and peoples of the region spoke Akkadian, or dialects of it, throughout the second millennium BCE and well into the first.

Akkadian Sculpture Although Akkad was arguably the most influential of the Mesopotamian cultures, few Akkadian artifacts survive, perhaps because Akkad and other nearby Akkadian cities have disappeared under Baghdad and the alluvial soils of the Euphrates plain. Two impressive sculptural works do remain, however. The first is the bronze head of an Akkadian man (Fig. **2.9**), found at Nineveh. It was once believed to be Sargon the Great himself, but many modern scholars now think it was part of a statue

Writing first appeared in the middle of the fourth millennium BCE in agricultural records as **pictograms**—pictures that represent things or concepts—etched into clay tablets. For instance, the sign for "woman" is a pubic triangle, and the more complicated idea of "slave" is the sign for "woman" plus the sign for "mountains"—literally, a "woman from over the mountains":

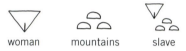

woman   mountains   slave

Pictograms could also represent concepts. For instance, the signs for "hatred" and "friendship" are, respectively, an "X" and a set of parallel lines:

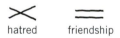

hatred   friendship

Beginning about 2900 BCE, most writing began to look more linear, for it was difficult to draw curves in wet clay. So scribes adopted a straight-line script made with a wedge-shaped **stylus**, or writing tool, cut from reeds. The resulting impressions looked like wedges. Cuneiform writing was named from the Latin *cuneus*, "wedge."

By 2000 BCE, another significant development in the progress of writing had appeared: Signs began to represent not things but sounds. This **phonetic writing** liberated the sign from its picture. Previously, they had been linked, as if, in English, we represented the word *belief* with pictograms for "bee" and "leaf."

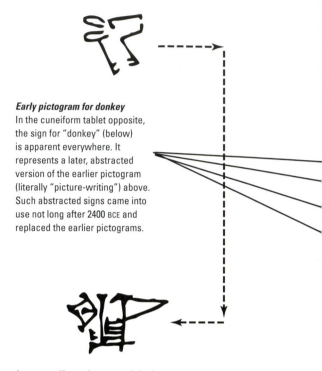

Early pictogram for donkey
In the cuneiform tablet opposite, the sign for "donkey" (below) is apparent everywhere. It represents a later, abstracted version of the earlier pictogram (literally "picture-writing") above. Such abstracted signs came into use not long after 2400 BCE and replaced the earlier pictograms.

Later cuneiform pictogram of donkey

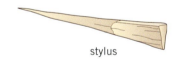

stylus

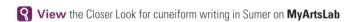 **View** the Closer Look for cuneiform writing in Sumer on **MyArtsLab**

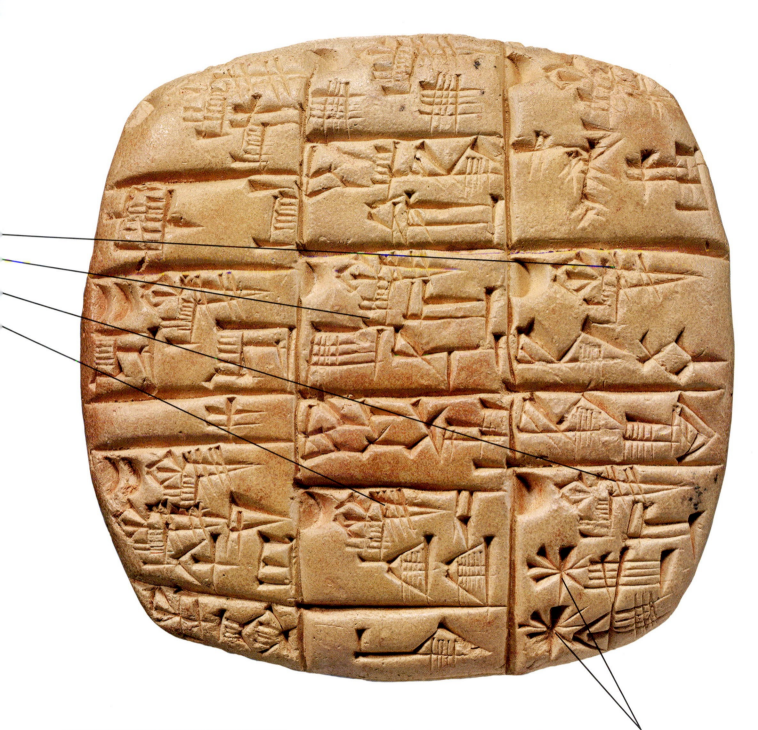

Something to Think About ...

What is it about this "document" that underscores the necessity of writing in the development of a civilization?

Sumerian clay tablet from Lagash (present-day Tello, Iraq). ca. 2360 BCE. Musée du Louvre, Paris. This tablet is an economic document detailing the loan of donkeys to, among others, a farmer, a smith, and a courier.

These stars are the Sumerian sign for "god." They sometimes have many more points than the eight seen here.

Lost-Wax Casting

At about the same time that cuneiform script was adopted, Mesopotamian culture also began to practice metallurgy, the process of mining and smelting ores. At first, copper was used almost exclusively; later, an alloy of copper and tin was melted and combined to make bronze. The resulting material was much stronger and more durable than anything previously known.

Because sources of copper and tin were mined in very different regions of the Middle East, the development of trade routes was a necessary prerequisite to the technology. While solid bronze pieces were made in simple molds as early as 4000 BCE, hollow bronze casts could produce larger pieces and were both more economical and lightweight. The technology for making hollow bronze casts was developed by the time of the Akkadians, in the second millennium BCE. Called **lost-wax casting**, the steps involved in this technique are illustrated below.

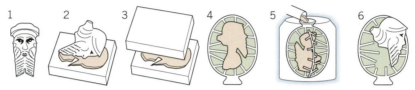

A positive model (1), often created with clay, is used to make a negative mold (2). The mold is coated with wax, the wax shell is filled with a cool fireclay, and the mold is removed (3). Metal rods, to hold the shell in place, and wax rods, to vent the mold, are then added (4). The whole is placed in sand, and the wax is burned out. Molten bronze is poured in where the wax used to be (5). When the bronze has hardened, the whole is removed from the sand and the rods and vents are removed (6).

👁 **Watch** a video about the technique of lost-wax bronze casting on **MyArtsLab**

---

of Sargon's grandson, Naramsin (ca. 2254–2218 BCE). It may be neither, but it is certainly the bust of a king. Highly realistic, it depicts a man who appears both powerful and majestic. In its damaged condition, the head is all that survives of a life-size statue that was destroyed in antiquity. Its original gemstone eyes were removed, perhaps by plundering soldiers, or possibly by a political enemy who recognized the sculpture as an emblem of absolute majesty. In the fine detail surrounding the face—in the beard and elaborate coiffure, with its braid circling the head—it testifies to the Akkadian mastery of the lost-wax casting technique, which originated in Mesopotamia as early as the third millennium BCE (see *Materials & Techniques*, above). It is the earliest monumental work made by that technique that we have.

The second Akkadian sculpture we will look at is the *Stele of Naramsin* (Fig. **2.10**). A stele is an upright stone slab carved with a commemorative design or inscription. (The word is derived from the Greek for "standing block.") This particular stele celebrates the victory of Sargon's grandson over the Lullubi in the Zagros Mountains of eastern Mesopotamia sometime between 2252 and 2218 BCE. The king, as usual, is larger than anyone else (another example of social perspective or hierarchy of scale). The Akkadians, in fact, believed that Naramsin became divine during the course of his reign. In the stele, his divinity is represented by his horned helmet and by the physical perfection of his body. Bow and arrow in hand, he stands atop a mountain pass, dead and wounded Lullubians beneath his feet.

Another Lullubian falls before him, a spear in his neck. Yet another seems to plead for mercy as he flees to the right. Behind Naramsin, his soldiers climb the wooded slopes of the mountain—here represented by actual trees native to the region.

The sculptor abandoned the traditional register system that we saw in the *Royal Standard of Ur* and set the battle scene on a unified landscape. The lack of registers and the use of trees underscore the reality of the scene—and by implication, the reality of Naramsin's divinity. The divine and human worlds are, in fact, united here, for above Naramsin three stars (cuneiform symbols for the gods) look on, protecting both Naramsin, their representative on earth, and his troops. Both the copper head of the Akkadian king and the *Stele of Naramsin* testify to the role of the king in Mesopotamian culture, in general, as both hero and divinity. If the king is not exactly a supreme god, he behaves very much like one, wielding the same awe-inspiring power.

Babylon

The Akkadians dominated Mesopotamia for just 150 years, their rule collapsing not long after 2200 BCE. For the next 400 years, various city-states thrived locally. No one in Mesopotamia matched the Akkadians' power until the first decades of the eighteenth century BCE, when Hammurabi of Babylon (r. 1792–1750 BCE) gained control of most of the region.

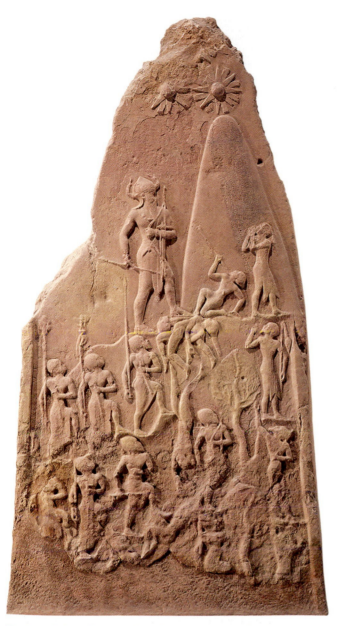

coming from his shoulders. The god is much larger than Hammurabi; in fact, he is to Hammurabi as Hammurabi, the patriarch, is to his people. If Hammurabi is divine, he is still subservient to the greater gods. At the same time, the phallic design of the stele, like such other Mesopotamian steles as the *Stele of Naramsin*, asserts the masculine prowess of the king.

Fig. 2.10 *Stele of Naramsin*, **from Susa (present-day Shush, Iran). ca. 2254–2218 BCE.** Pink sandstone, height approx. 6'6". Chuzeville/Musée du Louvre, Paris. This work, which was stolen by invading Elamites around 1157 BCE, as an inscription on the mountain indicates, was for centuries one of the most influential of all artworks, copied by many rulers to celebrate their own military feats.

View the Closer Look for the *Stele of Naramsin* on **MyArtsLab**

The Law Code of Hammurabi Hammurabi imposed order on Babylon where laxness and disorder, if not chaos, reigned. A giant stele survives, upon which is inscribed the so-called Law Code of Hammurabi (Fig. **2.11**). By no means the first of its kind, though by far the most complete, the stele is a record of decisions and decrees made by Hammurabi over the course of some 40 years of his reign. Its purpose was to celebrate his sense of justice and the wisdom of his rule. Atop the stele, in sculptural relief, Hammurabi receives the blessing of Shamash, the sun god; notice the rays of light

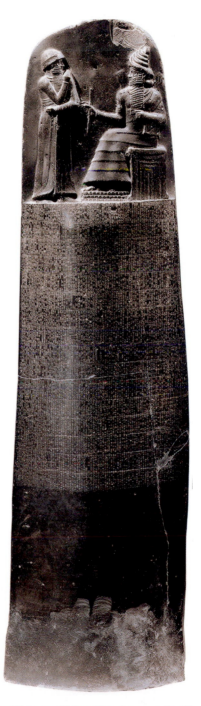

Fig. 2.11 *Stele of Hammurabi*, **from Susa (present-day Shush, Iran). ca. 1760 BCE.** Diorite, height of stele, approx. 7', height of relief, 28". Musée du Louvre, Paris. Like the *Stele of Naramsin*, this stele was stolen by invading Elamites and removed to Susa, where, together with the *Stele of Naramsin*, it was excavated by the French in 1898.

Below the relief, 282 separate "articles" cover both sides of the basalt monument. One of the great debates of legal history is the question of whether these articles actually constitute a code of law. If by *code* we mean a comprehensive, systematic, and methodical compilation of all aspects of Mesopotamian law, then they do not. This code is instead selective, even eccentric, in the issues it addresses. Many of its articles seem to be "reforms" of already existing law, and as such they define new principles of justice.

Chief among these is the principle of *talion*—an eye for an eye, a tooth for a tooth—which Hammurabi introduced to Mesopotamian law. (Sections of earlier codes from Ur compensate victims of crimes with money.) This principle punished the violence or injustice perpetuated by one free person upon another, but violence by an upper-class person on a lower-class person was penalized much less severely. Slaves (who might be either war captives or debtors) enjoyed no legal protection at all—only the protection of their owner.

The code tells us much about the daily lives of Mesopotamian peoples, including conflicts great and small. In rules governing family relations and class divisions in Mesopotamian society, inequalities are sharply drawn. Women are inferior to men, and wives, like slaves, are the personal property of their husbands (although protected from the abuse of neglectful or unjust husbands). Incest is strictly forbidden. Fathers cannot arbitrarily disinherit their sons—a son must have committed some "heavy crime" to justify such treatment. The code's strongest concern is the maintenance and protection of the family, though trade practices and property rights are also of major importance.

The following excerpts from the code, beginning with Hammurabi's assertion of his descent from the gods and his status as their favorite (**Reading 2.1**), give a sense of the code's scope. But the code is, finally, and perhaps above all, the gift of a king to his people, as Hammurabi's epilogue, at the end of the excerpt, makes clear:

READING 2.1

from the Law Code of Hammurabi (ca. 1760 BCE)

When the august god Anu, king of the Anunnaku deities, and the god Enlil, lord of heaven and earth, who determines the destinies of the land, allotted supreme power over all peoples to the god Marduk, the firstborn son of the god Ea, exalted him among the Igigu deities, named the city of Babylon with its august name and made it supreme exalted within the regions of the world, and established for him within it eternal kingship whose foundations are as fixed as heaven and earth, at that time, the gods Anu and Bel, for the enhancement of the well-being of the people, named me by my name, Hammurabi, the pious prince, who venerates the gods, to make justice prevail in the land, to abolish the wicked and the evil, to prevent the strong from oppressing the weak, to rise like the Sun-god Shamash over all humankind, to illuminate the land. …

---

1. If a man accuses another man and charges him with homicide but cannot bring proof against him, his accuser shall be killed. …

8. If a man steals an ox, a sheep, a donkey, a pig, or a boat—if it belongs either to the god or to the palace, he shall give thirtyfold; if it belongs to a commoner, he shall replace it tenfold; if the thief does not have anything to give, he shall be killed. …

32. If there is either a soldier or a fisherman who is taken captive while on a royal campaign, a merchant redeems him, and helps him get back to his city—if there are sufficient in his own estate for the redeeming, he himself shall redeem himself: if there are not sufficient means in his estate to redeem him he shall be redeemed by his city's temple; if there are not sufficient means in his city's temple to redeem him, the palace shall redeem him; but his field, orchard, or house shall not be given for his redemption. …

143. If [a woman] is not circumspect, but is wayward, squanders her household possessions, and disparages her husband, they shall cast that woman into the water. …

195. If a child should strike his father, they shall cut off his hand.

196. If an *awilu* [in general, a person subject to law] should blind the eye of another *awilu*, they shall blind his eye. …

197. If he should break the bone of another *awilu*, they shall break his bone. …

229. If a builder constructs a house for a man but does not make his work sound, and the house he constructs collapses and causes the death of the householder, that builder shall be killed. …

282. If a slave should declare to his master, "You are not my master," he (the master) shall bring charge and proof against him that he is indeed his slave, and his master shall cut off his ear. …

These are the decisions which Hammurabi, the able king, has established, and thereby has directed the land along the course of truth and the correct way of life.

I am Hammurabi, noble king …

May any king who will appear in the land in the future, at any time, observe the pronouncements of justice that I have inscribed upon my stele. May he not alter the judgments that I rendered and verdicts that I gave, nor remove my engraved image. If that man has discernment, and is capable of providing just ways for his land may he heed the pronouncements I have inscribed upon my stele, may the stele reveal for him the traditions, the proper conduct, the judgments of the land that I rendered, the verdicts of the land that I gave and may he, too, provide just ways for all humankind in his care. …

I am Hammurabi, king of justice. …

Consequences of the Code Even if Hammurabi meant only to assert the idea of justice as the basis for his own divine rule, the stele established what amounts to a uniform code throughout Mesopotamia. It was repeatedly copied for over a thousand years, long after it was removed to Susa in 1157

BCE with the Naramsin stele, and it established the rule of law in Mesopotamia for a millennium. From this point on, the authority and power of the ruler could no longer be capricious, subject to the whim, fancy, and subjective interpretation of his singular personality. The law was now, at least ostensibly, more objective and impartial. The ruler was required to follow certain prescribed procedures. But the law, so prescribed in writing, was now also much less flexible, hard to change, and much more impersonal. Exceptions to the rule were few and difficult to justify. Eventually, written law would remove justice from the discretion of the ruler and replace it with a legal establishment of learned judges charged with enacting the king's statutes.

The Assyrian Empire

With the fall of Babylon in 1595 BCE to a sudden invasion of Hittites from Turkey, the entire Middle East appears to have undergone a period of disruption and instability. Only the Assyrians, who lived around the city of Assur in the north, managed to maintain a continuing cultural identity. Over the centuries, they became increasingly powerful until, beginning with the reign of Ashurnasirpal II (r. 883–859 BCE), they dominated the entire region.

Ashurnasirpal II built a magnificent capital at Kalhu (present-day Nimrud), on the Tigris River, surrounded by nearly 5 miles of walls, 120 feet thick and 42 feet high. A surviving inscription tells us that Ashurnasirpal invited 69,574 people to celebrate the city's dedication. The entire population of the region, of all classes, probably did not exceed 100,000, and thus many guests from throughout Mesopotamia and farther away must have been invited.

Assyrian Art Alabaster reliefs decorated many of the walls of Ashurnasirpal's palace complex, including a depiction of *Ashurnasirpal II Killing Lions* (Fig. **2.12**). The scene uses many of the conventions of Assyrian pictorial representation. For instance, to create a sense of deep space, the sculptor used the device of overlapping, which we first encountered in prehistoric cave paintings (see Fig. 1.1 in Chapter 1). This is done convincingly where the king stands in his chariot in front of its driver, but less so in the case of the horses drawing the chariot. For instance, there are three horse heads but only six visible legs—three in front and three in back. Furthermore, Assyrian artists never hid the face of an archer (in this case, the king himself) by realistically having him aim down the shaft of the arrow, which would have the effect of covering his eye with his hand. Instead, they drop the arrow to shoulder level and completely omit the bowstring so that it appears to pass (impossibly) behind the archer's head and back.

The scene is also a **synoptic** view, that is, it depicts several consecutive actions at once: As soldiers drive the lion toward the king from the left, he shoots it; to the right, the same lion lies dying beneath the horses' hooves. If Assyrian artists seem unconcerned about accurately portraying the animals, that is because the focus of the work is on the king himself, whose prowess in combating the lion, traditional symbol of power, underscores his own invincibility. And it is in the artists' careful balance of forms—the relationship between the positive shapes of the relief figures and the negative space between them—that we sense the importance placed on an orderly arrangement of parts. This orderliness reflects, in all probability, their sense of the orderly character of their society.

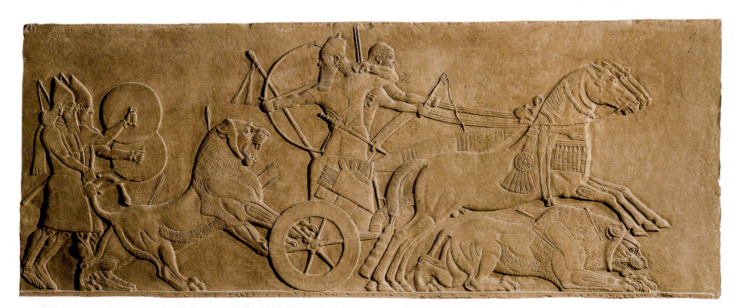

Fig. 2.12 *Ashurnasirpal II Killing Lions*, **from the palace complex of Ashurnasirpal II, Kalhu (present-day Nimrud, Iraq). ca. 850 BCE.** Alabaster, height approx. 39". © The Trustees of the British Museum. The repetition of forms throughout this relief helps create a stunning design. Notice especially how the two shields carried by the soldiers are echoed by the chariot wheel and the king's arched bow.

Cultural Propaganda Rulers in every culture and age have used the visual arts to broadcast their power. These reliefs were designed to celebrate and underscore for all visitors to Ashurnasirpal's palace the military prowess of the Assyrian army and their king. They are thus a form of cultural propaganda, celebrating the kingdom's achievements even as they intimidate its potential adversaries. In fact, the Assyrians were probably the most militant civilization of ancient Mesopotamia, benefactors of the invention of iron weaponry. By 721 BCE, the Assyrians had used their iron weapons to conquer Israel, and by the middle of the seventh century BCE, they controlled most of Asia Minor from the Nile Valley to the Persian Gulf.

The Assyrians also used their power to preserve Mesopotamian culture. Two hundred years after the reign of Ashurnasirpal, Ashurbanipal (r. 668–627 BCE) created the great library where, centuries later, the clay tablets containing the Sumerian *Epic of Gilgamesh*, discussed later in this chapter, were stored. Its still partially intact collection today consists of 20,000 to 30,000 cuneiform tablets containing

approximately 1,200 distinct texts, including a nearly complete list of ancient Mesopotamian rulers. Each of its many rooms was dedicated to individual subjects—history and government, religion and magic, geography, science, poetry, and important government materials.

As late as Ashurbanipal's reign, reliefs of the lion hunt were still a favored form of palace decoration, but those depicted in his palace at Nineveh, in what is now northern Iraq, reveal that the lions were caged and released for the king's hunt, which was now more ritual than real, taking place in an enclosed arena. The lions were sacrificed as an offering to the gods. In one section of the relief, Ashurbanipal, surrounded by musicians, pours a libation, a liquid offering to the gods, over the dead animals as servants bring more bodies to the offering table. This ritual was implicit in all kingly hunts, even Ashurnasirpal's hunt of 200 years earlier, for in his pursuit and defeat of the wild beast, the ruler masters the most elemental force of nature—the cycle of life and death itself.

The Assyrian kings represented their might and power not only through the immense size of their palaces and the decorative programs within, but also through massive gateways that greeted the visitor. Especially impressive are the gateways with giant stone monuments, such as those in Iraq at the Khorsabad palace of Sargon II (r. 721–705 BCE), who named himself after Sargon of Akkad. These monuments (Fig. 2.13) are **composites**, part man, part bull, and part eagle, the bull signifying the king's strength and the eagle his vigilance. The king himself wears the traditional horned crown of Akkad and the beard of Sumer, thus containing within himself all Mesopotamian history. Such composites, especially in monumental size, were probably intended to amaze and terrify the visitor and to underscore the ruler's embodiment of all the forces of nature, which is to say, his embodiment of the very gods.

MESOPOTAMIAN LITERATURE

How does the Epic of Gilgamesh *portray the relationship between the gods and the people?*

Sumerian literature survives on nearly 100,000 clay tablets and fragments. Many deal with religious themes in the form of poems, blessings, and incantations to the gods.

The Blessing of Inanna

One particularly interesting Sumerian religious work is *The Blessing of Inanna* (**Reading 2.2**). It recounts the myth of the goddess Inanna, here depicted as a young girl from Uruk who decides to visit Enki, the god of wisdom. Inanna travels south to Eridu, the chief seaport of Sumer, where Enki lives. Apparently taken with Inanna, Enki offers a series of toasts, each time bestowing upon her one of his special powers, including the highest powers of all:

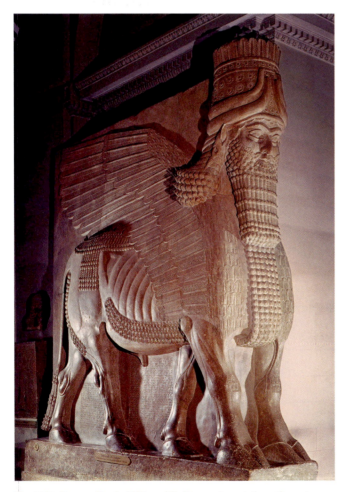

Fig. 2.13 *Human-Headed Winged Bull*, **one of a pair from the entrance to the palace of Sargon II, Khorsabad, Iraq. ca. 720 BCE.** Limestone, height approx. 13'10". Musée du Louvre, Paris. Seen from a three-quarter view, as here, this hybrid beast that guarded the palace entrance has five legs. He stands firmly before you when seen from the front, and seems to stride by you when seen from the side.

Having gathered all 80 of Enki's mighty powers, Inanna piles them all into her boat and sails back upriver. The drunken Enki realizes what he has done and tries to recover his blessings, but Inanna fends him off. She returns to Uruk, blessed as a god, and enters the city triumphantly, bestowing now her own gifts on her people, who subsequently worship her. Enki and the people of Eridu are forced to acknowledge the glory of Inanna and her city of Uruk, assuring peace and harmony between the two competing city-states.

The Sumerians worshiped Inanna as the goddess of fertility and heaven. In this tale, she and Enki probably represent the spirits of their respective cities and the victory of Uruk over Eridu. That Inanna appears in the work first as a mere mortal is a classic example of *anthropomorphism*, endowing the gods and the forces of nature that they represent with humanlike traits. The story has some basis in fact, since Uruk and Eridu are the two oldest Mesopotamian cities, and surviving literary fragments suggest that the two cities were at war sometime after 3400 BCE.

The *Epic of Gilgamesh*

One of the great surviving manuscripts of Mesopotamian culture and the oldest story ever recorded is the *Epic of Gilgamesh*. It consists of some 2,900 lines written in Akkadian cuneiform script on 11 clay tablets, none of them completely whole (Fig. **2.14**). It was composed sometime before Ashurbanipal's reign, possibly as early as 1200 BCE, by Sinleqqiunninni, a scholar-priest of Uruk. This would make Sinleqqiunninni the oldest known author. We know that Gilgamesh was the fourth king of Uruk, ruling sometime between 2700 and 2500 BCE. (The dates of his rule were recorded on a clay tablet, the *Sumerian King List*.) Recovered fragments of his story date back nearly to his actual reign, and the story we have, known as the Standard Version, is a compilation of these earlier versions.

The work is the first example we have of an **epic**, a long, narrative poem in elevated language that follows characters of a high position through a series of adventures, often including a visit to the world of the dead. For many literary scholars, the epic is the most exalted poetic form. The

⊡ **Read** the document *The Epic of Gilgamesh* on **MyArtsLab**

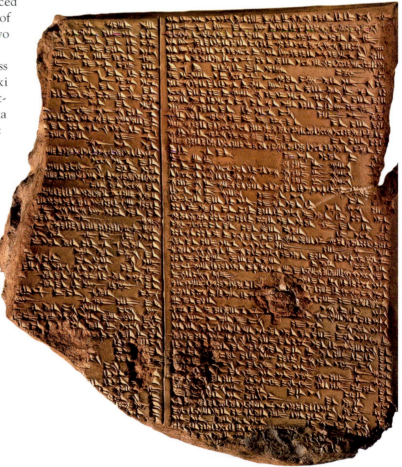

Fig. 2.14 Fragment of Tablet 11 of the *Epic of Gilgamesh*, containing the Flood Story. From the Library of Ashurbanipal, Nineveh (present-day Kuyunjik, Iraq). 2nd millennium BCE. © The Trustees of the British Museum. This example, which is relatively complete, shows how difficult it is to reconstruct the *Gilgamesh* epic in its entirety.

central figure is a legendary or historical figure of heroic proportion, in this case the Sumerian king Gilgamesh. Homer's *Iliad* and *Odyssey* (see Chapter 4) had been considered the earliest epics, until late in the nineteenth century, when *Gilgamesh* was discovered in the library of King Ashurbanipal at Nineveh, believed to be the first library of texts in history systematically collected and organized.

The scope of an epic is large. The supernatural world of gods and goddesses usually plays a role in the story, as do battles in which the hero demonstrates his strength and courage. The poem's language is suitably dignified, often consisting of many long, formal speeches. Lists of various heroes or catalogs of their achievements are frequent.

Epics are often compilations of preexisting myths and tales handed down generation to generation, often orally, and finally unified into a whole by the epic poet. Indeed, the main outline of the story is usually known to its audience. The poet's contribution is the artistry brought to the subject, demonstrated through the use of epithets, metaphors, and similes. **Epithets** are words or phrases that characterize a person (for example, "Enkidu, the protector of herdsmen," or "Enkidu, the son of the mountain"). **Metaphors** are words or phrases used in place of another to suggest a similarity between the two, as when Gilgamesh is described as a "raging flood-wave who destroys even walls of stone." **Similes** compare two unlike things by the use of the word "like" or "as" (for example, "the land shattered like a pot").

Perhaps most important, the epic illuminates the development of a nation or race. It is a national poem, describing a people's common heritage and celebrating its cultural identity. It is hardly surprising, then, that Ashurbanipal preserved the *Epic of Gilgamesh*. Just as Sargon II depicted himself at the gates of Khorsabad in the traditional horned crown of Akkad and the beard of Sumer, containing within himself all Mesopotamian history, the *Epic of Gilgamesh* preserves the historical lineage of all Mesopotamian kings—Sumerian, Akkadian, Assyrian, and Babylonian. The tale embodies their own heroic grandeur, and thus the grandeur of their peoples.

The poem opens with a narrator guiding a visitor (the reader) around Uruk. The narrator explains that the epic was written by Gilgamesh himself and was deposited in the city's walls, where visitors can read it for themselves. Then the narrator introduces Gilgamesh as an epic hero, two parts god and one part human. The style of the following list of his deeds is the same as in hymns to the gods (**Reading 2.3a**):

READING 2.3a

from the *Epic of Gilgamesh*, Tablet I (late 2nd millennium BCE)

Supreme over other kings, lordly in appearance,
he is the hero, born of Uruk, the goring wild bull.

He walks out in front, the leader,
and walks at the rear, trusted by his companions.
Mighty net, protector of his people,
raging flood-wave who destroys even walls of stone! ...
It was he who opened the mountain passes,
who dug wells on the flank of the mountain.
It was he who crossed ocean, the vast seas, to the rising sun,
who explored the world regions, seeking life.
It was he who reached by his own sheer strength the Utnapishtim, the Faraway,
who restored the cities that the Flood had destroyed! ...
Who can compare to him in kingliness?
Who can say like Gilgamesh: "I am King!"?

After a short break in the text, Gilgamesh is described as having originally oppressed his people. Hearing the pleas of the people for relief, the gods create a rival, Enkidu, to challenge Gilgamesh (**Reading 2.3b**):

READING 2.3b

from the *Epic of Gilgamesh*, Tablet I (late 2nd millennium BCE)

Enkidu
born of Silence, endowed with the strength of Ninurta.
His whole body was shaggy with hair,
he had a full head of hair like a woman. ...
He knew neither people nor settled living. ...
He ate grasses with the gazelles,
and jostled at the watering hole with the animals.

Enkidu is, in short, Gilgamesh's opposite, and their confrontation is an example of the classic struggle between nature, represented by Enkidu, and civilization, represented by Gilgamesh. Seduced by a harlot (see **Reading 2.3**, page 63), Enkidu loses his ability to commune with the animals (i.e., he literally loses his innocence), and when he finally wrestles Gilgamesh, the contest ends in a draw. The two become best friends.

Gilgamesh proposes that he and Enkidu undertake a great adventure, a journey to the Cedar Forest (either in present-day southern Iran or Lebanon), where they will kill its guardian, Humbaba the Terrible, and cut down all the forest's trees. Each night on the six-day journey to the forest, Gilgamesh has a terrible dream, which Enkidu manages to interpret in a positive light. As the friends approach the forest, the god Shamash informs Gilgamesh that Humbaba is wearing only one of his seven coats of armor and is thus extremely vulnerable. When Gilgamesh and Enkidu enter the forest and begin cutting down trees, Humbaba comes roaring up to warn them off. An epic battle ensues, and Shamash intervenes to help the two heroes defeat the great guardian. Just before Gilgamesh cuts off Humbaba's head, Humbaba curses Enkidu, promising that he will find no peace in the world and will die before his friend Gilgamesh. In a gesture that clearly evokes the triumph of civilization over nature, Gilgamesh and Enkidu cut down the tallest of the cedar trees to make a great cedar gate for the city of Uruk.

At the center of the poem, in Tablet VI, Ishtar, goddess of both love and war, offers to marry Gilgamesh. Gilgamesh refuses, which unleashes Ishtar's wrath. She sends the Bull of Heaven to destroy them, but Gilgamesh and Enkidu slay it instead (**Reading 2.3c**):

READING 2.3c

from the *Epic of Gilgamesh*, Tablet VI (late 2nd millennium BCE)

A Woman Scorned

... When Gilgamesh placed his crown on his head, Princess Ishtar raised her eyes to the beauty of Gilgamesh.
　"Come along, Gilgamesh, be you my husband,
　to me grant your lusciousness.[1]
　Be you my husband, and I will be your wife.
　I will have harnessed for you a chariot of lapis
　　　lazuli and gold,
　with wheels of gold ...
　Bowed down beneath you will be kings, lords,
　　　and princes.
　The Lullubu people[2] will bring you the produce of the
　　　mountains and countryside as tribute.
　Your she-goats will bear triplets, your ewes twins,
　your donkey under burden will overtake the mule,
　your steed at the chariot will be bristling to gallop,
　your ox at the yoke will have no match."
Gilgamesh addressed Princess Ishtar saying:
　"Do you need oil or garments for your body?
　Do you lack anything for food or drink?
　I would gladly feed you food fit for a god,
　I would gladly give you wine fit for a king ...
　[You are] a half-door that keeps out neither breeze nor
　　　blast,
　a palace that crushes down valiant warriors,
　an elephant who devours its own covering,
　pitch that blackens the hands of its bearer,
　a waterskin that soaks its bearer through,
　limestone that buckles out the stone wall,
　a battering ram that attracts the enemy land,
　a shoe that bites its owner's feet!
　Where are your bridegrooms that you keep forever? ...
　You loved the supremely mighty lion,
　yet you dug for him seven and again seven pits.
　You loved the stallion, famed in battle,
　yet you ordained for him the whip, the goad,
　　　and the lash,

ordained for him to gallop for seven and seven hours,
ordained for him drinking from muddied waters,[3]
you ordained for his mother Silili to wail continually.
You loved the Shepherd, the Master Herder,
who continually presented you with bread
　　　baked in embers,
and who daily slaughtered for you a kid.
Yet you struck him, and turned him into a wolf,
so his own shepherds now chase him
and his own dogs snap at his shins.
You loved Ishullanu, your father's date gardener,
who continually brought you baskets of dates,
and brightened your table daily.
You raised your eyes to him, and you went to him:
　'Oh my Ishullanu, let us taste of your strength,
　stretch out your hand to me, and touch our "vulva."'[4]
Ishullanu said to you:
　'Me? What is it you want from me? ...'
As you listened to these his words
you struck him, turning him into a dwarf(?),[5] ...
And now me! It is me you love, and you will ordain for
me as for them!"

Her Fury

When Ishtar heard this
in a fury she went up to the heavens,
going to Anu, her father, and crying,
going to Antum, her mother, and weeping:
　"Father, Gilgamesh has insulted me over and over,
　Gilgamesh has recounted despicable deeds
　　　about me,
　despicable deeds and curses!"
Anu addressed Princess Ishtar, saying:
　"What is the matter? Was it not you who provoked King
　　　Gilgamesh?
　So Gilgamesh recounted despicable deeds about you,
　despicable deeds and curses!"
Ishtar spoke to her father, Anu, saying:
　"Father, give me the Bull of Heaven,
　so he can kill Gilgamesh in his dwelling.
　If you do not give me the Bull of Heaven,
　I will knock down the Gates of the Netherworld,
　I will smash the door posts, and leave the doors flat
　　　down,
　and will let the dead go up to eat the living!
　And the dead will outnumber the living!"
Anu addressed Princess Ishtar, saying:
　"If you demand the Bull of Heaven from me,
　there will be seven years of empty husks for the land
　　　of Uruk.
　Have you collected grain for the people?
　Have you made grasses grow for the animals?"
Ishtar addressed Anu, her father, saying:
　"I have heaped grain in the granaries for the people,
　I made grasses grow for the animals,

---

[1] Literally "fruit."
[2] The Lullubu were a wild mountain people living in the area of present-day western Iran. The meaning is that even the wildest, least controllable of peoples will recognize Gilgamesh's rule and bring tribute.

[3] Horses put their front feet in the water when drinking, churning up mud.
[4] This line probably contains a word play on *hurdatu* as "vulva" and "date palm," the latter being said (in another unrelated text) to be "like the vulva."
[5] Or "frog"?

in order that they might eat in the seven years of empty
husks.
I have collected grain for the people,
I have made grasses grow for the animals. ..."
When Anu heard her words,
he placed the nose-rope of the Bull of Heaven in her hand.
Ishtar led the Bull of Heaven down to the earth.
When it reached Uruk ...
It climbed down to the Euphrates ...
At the snort of the Bull of Heaven a huge pit opened up,
and 100 Young Men of Uruk fell in.
At his second snort a huge pit opened up,
and 200 Young Men of Uruk fell in.
At his third snort a huge pit opened up,
and Enkidu fell in up to his waist.
Then Enkidu jumped out and seized the Bull of Heaven by
its horns.
The Bull spewed his spittle in front of him,
with his thick tail he flung *his dung behind him* (?).
Enkidu addressed Gilgamesh, saying:
"My friend, we can be bold(?) ...
Between the nape, the horns, and ... thrust your
sword."
Enkidu stalked and *hunted down* the Bull of Heaven.
He grasped it by the thick of its tail
and held onto it with both his hands (?),
while Gilgamesh, like an *expert butcher*,
boldly and *surely approached the Bull of Heaven*.
Between the nape, the horns, and ... he thrust his sword.
...
Ishtar went up onto the top of the Wall of Uruk-Haven,
cast herself into the pose of mourning, and hurled her
woeful curse:
"Woe unto Gilgamesh who slandered me and killed the
Bull of Heaven!"
When Enkidu heard this pronouncement of Ishtar,
he wrenched off the Bull's hindquarter and flung it in her
face:
"If I could only get at you I would do the same to you!
I would drape his innards over your arms!" ...
Gilgamesh said to the palace retainers:
"Who is the bravest of the men?
Who is the boldest of the males?
—Gilgamesh is the bravest of the men,
the boldest of the males!
She at whom we flung the hindquarter of the Bull of
Heaven in anger,
Ishtar has no one that pleases her ..."

But Gilgamesh and Enkidu cannot avoid the wrath of
the gods altogether. One of them, the gods decide, must
die, and so Enkidu suffers a long, painful death, attended by
his friend, Gilgamesh, who is terrified (**Reading 2.3d**):

READING 2.3d

**from the *Epic of Gilgamesh*, Tablet X
(late 2nd millennium BCE)**

My friend ... Enkidu, whom I love deeply, who went
through every hardship with me,
the fate of mankind has overtaken him.
Six days and seven nights I mourned over him
and would not allow him to be buried
until a maggot fell out of his nose.
I was terrified by his appearance,
I began to fear death, and so roam the wilderness.
The issue of Enkidu, my friend, oppresses me,
so I have been roaming long trails through the wilderness.
How can I stay silent, how can I be still?
My friend whom I love has turned to clay.
Am I not like him? Will I lie down, never to get up again?

Dismayed at the prospect of his own mortality, Gilgamesh embarks on a journey to find the secret of eternal
life from the only mortal known to have attained it, Utnapishtim, who tells him the story of the Great Flood. Several
elements of Utnapishtim's story deserve explanation. First
of all, this is the earliest known version of the flood story
that occurs also in the Hebrew Bible, with Utnapishtim in
the role of the biblical Noah. The motif of a single man
and wife surviving a worldwide flood brought about by the
gods occurs in several Middle Eastern cultures, suggesting a
single origin or shared tradition. In the Sumerian version,
Ea (Enki) warns Utnapishtim of the flood by speaking to
the wall, thereby technically keeping the agreement among
the gods not to warn mortals of their upcoming disaster.
The passage in which Ea tells Utnapishtim how to explain
his actions to his people without revealing the secret of the
gods is one of extraordinary complexity and wit (**Reading
2.3e**). The word for "bread" is *kukku*, a pun on the word
for "darkness," *kukkû*. Similarly, the word for "wheat," *kibtu*,
also means "misfortune." Thus, when Ea says, "He will let
loaves of bread shower down, / and in the evening a rain
of wheat," he is also telling the truth: "He will let loaves
of darkness shower down, and in the evening a rain of
misfortune."

READING 2.3e

**from the *Epic of Gilgamesh*, Tablet XI
(late 2nd millennium BCE)**

Utnapishtim spoke to Gilgamesh, saying:
"I will reveal to you, Gilgamesh, a thing that is hidden,
a secret of the gods I will tell you!
Shuruppak, a city that you surely know,
situated on the banks of the Euphrates,
that city was very old, and there were gods inside it.
The hearts of the Great Gods moved them to inflict the
Flood. ...

Ea, the Clever Prince, was under oath with them
so he repeated their talk to the reed house:
'Reed house, reed house! Wall, wall!
Hear, O reed house! Understand, O wall!
O man of Shuruppak, son of Ubartutu:
Tear down the house and build a boat!
Abandon wealth and seek living beings!
Spurn possessions and keep alive human beings!
Make all living beings go up into the boat.
The boat which you are to build,
its dimensions must measure equal to each other:
its length must correspond to its width,
Roof it over like the Apsu.'
I understood and spoke to my lord, Ea:
'My lord, thus is your command.
I will heed and will do it.
But what shall I answer the city, the populace, and the
    Elders?'

Ea spoke, commanding me, his servant:
'... this is what you must say to them:
"It appears that Enlil is rejecting me
so I cannot reside in your city,
nor set foot on Enlil's earth.
I will go ... to live with my lord, Ea,
and upon you he will rain down abundance,
a profusion of fowls, myriad fishes.
He will bring you a harvest of wealth,
in the morning he will let loaves of bread shower down,
and in the evening a rain of wheat."' ...

I butchered oxen for the meat(?),
and day upon day I slaughtered sheep.
I gave the workmen(?) ale, beer, oil, and wine, as if it were
    river water,
so they could make a party like the New Year's Festival. ...
The boat was finished. ...
Whatever I had I loaded on it:
whatever silver I had I loaded on it,
whatever gold I had I loaded on it.
All the living beings that I had I loaded on it,
I had all my kith and kin go up into the boat,
all the beasts and animals of the field and the craftsmen I
    had go up. ...

I watched the appearance of the weather—
the weather was frightful to behold!
I went into the boat and sealed the entry. ...
Just as dawn began to glow
there arose on the horizon a black cloud.
Adad rumbled inside it. ...
Stunned shock over Adad's deeds overtook the heavens,
and turned to blackness all that had been light.
The ... land shattered like a ... pot.
All day long the South Wind blew ...,
blowing fast, submerging the mountain in water,
overwhelming the people like an attack.
No one could see his fellow,
they could not recognize each other in the torrent.
The gods were frightened by the Flood,
and retreated, ascending to the heaven of Anu.
The gods were cowering like dogs, crouching by the outer
    wall.

Ishtar shrieked like a woman in childbirth. ...
Six days and seven nights
came the wind and flood, the storm flattening the land.
When the seventh day arrived, the storm was pounding,
the flood was a war—struggling with itself like a woman
    writhing (in labor).
The sea calmed, fell still, the whirlwind (and) flood stopped
    up.
I looked around all day long—quiet had set in
and all the human beings had turned to clay!
The terrain was flat as a roof.
I opened a vent and fresh air (daylight?) fell upon the side
    of my nose.
I fell to my knees and sat weeping,
tears streaming down the side of my nose.
I looked around for coastlines in the expanse of the sea,
and at twelve leagues there emerged a region (of land).
On Mt. Nimush the boat lodged firm,
Mt. Nimush held the boat, allowing no sway."

When the gods discover Utnapishtim alive, smelling his incense offering, they are outraged. They did not want a single living being to escape. But since he has, they grant him immortality and allow him to live forever in the Faraway. As a reward for Gilgamesh's own efforts, Utnapishtim tells Gilgamesh of a secret plant that will give him perpetual youth. "I will eat it," he tells the boatman who is returning him home, "and I will return to what I was in my youth." But when they stop for the night, Gilgamesh decides to bathe in a cool pool, where the scent of the plant attracts a snake who steals it away, an echo of the biblical story of Adam and Eve, whose own immortality is stolen away by the wiles of a serpent—and their own carelessness. Broken-hearted, Gilgamesh returns home empty-handed.

The *Epic of Gilgamesh* is the first known literary work to confront the idea of death, which is, in many ways, the very embodiment of the unknown. Although the hero goes to the very ends of the earth in his quest, he ultimately leaves with nothing to show for his efforts except an understanding of his own, very human, limitations. He is the first hero in Western literature to yearn for what he can never attain, to seek to understand what must always remain a mystery. And, of course, until the death of his friend Enkidu, Gilgamesh had seemed, in his self-confident confrontation with Ishtar and in the defeat of the Bull of Heaven, as near to a god as a mortal might be. In short, he embodied the Mesopotamian hero-king. Even as the poem asserts the hero-king's divinity—Gilgamesh is, remember, two parts god—it emphasizes his humanity and the mortality that accompanies it. By making literal the first words of the *Sumerian King List*—"After the kingship had descended from heaven"—the *Epic of Gilgamesh* acknowledges what many Mesopotamian kings were unwilling to admit, at least publicly: their own, very human, limitations, and their own powerlessness in the face of the ultimate unknown—death.

THE HEBREWS

What cultural traits distinguish the Hebrews from other cultures in the ancient Near East?

The Hebrews (from *Habiru*, "outcast" or "nomad") were a people forced out of their homeland in the Mesopotamian basin in about 2000 BCE. According to their tradition, it was in the delta of the Tigris and Euphrates rivers that God created Adam and Eve in the Garden of Eden. It was there that Noah survived the same great flood that Utnapishtim survived in the *Epic of Gilgamesh*. And it was out of there that Abraham of Ur led his people into Canaan, in order to escape the warlike Akkadians and the increasingly powerful Babylonians. There is no actual historical evidence to support these stories. We know them only from the Hebrew Bible—a word that derives from the Greek, *biblia*, "books"—a compilation of hymns, prophecies, and laws transcribed by its authors between 800 and 400 BCE, some 1,000 years after the events the Hebrew Bible describes. Although the archeological record in the Near East confirms some of what these scribes and priests wrote, especially about more contemporaneous events, the stories themselves were edited and collated into the stories we know today. They recount the Assyrian conquest of Israel, the Jews' later exile to Babylon after the destruction of Jerusalem by the Babylonian king Nebuchadnezzar in 587 BCE, and their eventual return to Jerusalem after the Persians conquered the Babylonians in 538 BCE. The stories represent the Hebrews' attempt to maintain their sense of their own history and destiny. But it would be a mistake to succumb to the temptation to read the Hebrew Bible as an accurate account of the historical record. Like all ancient histories, passed down orally through generation upon generation, it contains its fair share of mythologizing.

The Hebrews differed from other Near Eastern cultures in that their religion was *monotheistic*—they worshiped a single god, whereas others in the region tended to have gods for their clans and cities, among other things. According to Hebrew tradition, God made an agreement with the Hebrews, first with Noah after the flood, later renewed with Abraham and each of the subsequent **patriarchs** (scriptural fathers of the Hebrew people): "I am God Almighty; be fruitful and multiply; a nation and a company of nations shall come from you. The land which I gave to Abraham and Isaac I will give to you, and I will give the land to your descendants after you" (Genesis 35: 11–12). In return for this promise, the Hebrews, the "chosen people," agreed to obey God's will. "Chosen people" means that the Jews were chosen to set an example of a higher moral standard (a light unto the nations), not chosen in the sense of favored, which is a common misunderstanding of the term.

Genesis, the first book of the Hebrew Bible, tells the story of the creation of the world out of a "formless void."

It describes God's creation of the world and all its creatures, and his continuing interest in the workings of the world, an interest that would lead, in the story of Noah, to God's near-destruction of all things. It also posits humankind as easily tempted by evil. It documents the moment of the introduction of sin (and shame) into the cosmos, associating these with the single characteristic separating humans from animals—knowledge. And it shows, in the example of Noah, the reward for having "walked with God," the basis of the covenant. (See **Reading 2.4**, pages 63–65, for two selections from Genesis, the story of Adam and Eve and the story of Noah.)

Moses and the Ten Commandments

The biblical story of Moses and the Ten Commandments embodies the centrality of the written word to Jewish culture. The Hebrew Bible claims that in about 1600 BCE, drought forced the Hebrew people to leave Canaan for Egypt, where they prospered until the Egyptians enslaved them in about 1300 BCE. Defying the rule of the pharaohs, the Jewish patriarch Moses led his people out of Egypt. According to tradition, Moses led the Jews across the Red Sea (which miraculously parted to facilitate the escape) and into the desert of the Sinai peninsula. (The story became the basis for the book of Exodus.) Most likely, they crossed a large tidal flat, called the Sea of Reeds; subsequently, that body of water was misidentified as the Red Sea. Unable to return to Canaan, which was now occupied by local tribes of considerable military strength, the Jews settled in an arid region of the Sinai desert near the Dead Sea for a period of 40 years, which archeologists date to sometime between 1300 and 1150 BCE.

In the Sinai desert, the Hebrews forged the principal tenets of a new religion that would eventually be based on the worship of a single god. There, too, the Hebrew god supposedly revealed a new name for himself—YHWH, a name so sacred that it could neither be spoken nor written. The name is not known and YHWH is a cipher for it. There are, however, many other names for God in the Hebrew Bible, among them Elohim, which is plural in Hebrew, meaning "gods, deities"; Adonai ("Lord"); and El Shaddai, literally "God of the fields" but usually translated "God Almighty." Some scholars believe that this demonstrates the multiple authorship of the Bible. Others argue that the Hebrews originally worshiped many gods, like other Near Eastern peoples. Still other scholars suggest that God has been given different names to reflect different aspects of his divinity, or the different roles that he might assume—the guardian of the flocks in the fields, or the powerful master of all. Translated into Latin as "Jehovah" in the Middle Ages, the name is now rendered in English as "Yahweh." This God also gave Moses the Ten Commandments, carved onto stone tablets, as recorded in Deuteronomy 5:6–21. Subsequently, the Hebrews carried the commandments in a sacred chest, called the Ark of the Covenant (Fig. **2.15**), which was lit by seven-branched candelabras known as

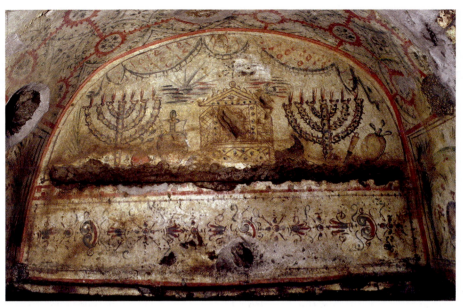

Fig. 2.15 *Menorahs and Ark of the Covenant*, **wall painting in a Jewish catacomb, Villa Torlonia, Rome. 3rd century CE.** 3'11" × 5'9". Two *menorahs* (seven-branched candelabras) flank each side of the Ark. The *menorah* is considered a symbol of the nation of Israel and its mission to be "a light unto the nations" (Isaiah 42:6). Instructions for making it are outlined in Exodus 25:31–40. Relatively little ancient Jewish art remains. Most of it was destroyed as the Jewish people were conquered, persecuted, and exiled.

menorahs. The centrality to Hebrew culture of these written words is even more apparent in the words of God that follow the commandments (**Reading 2.4a**):

READING 2.4a

from the Hebrew Bible, Deuteronomy 6:6–9

6 Keep these words that I am commanding you today in your heart.
7 Recite them to your children and talk about them when you are at home and when you are away, when you lie down and when you rise.
8 Bind them as a sign on your hand, fix them as an emblem on your forehead,
9 and write them on the doorposts of your house and on your gates.

Whenever the Hebrews talked, wherever they looked, wherever they went, they focused on the commandments of their God. Their monotheistic religion was thus also an ethical and moral system derived from an omnipotent God. The Ten Commandments were the centerpiece of the Torah, or Law (literally "instructions"), consisting of the books of Genesis, Exodus, Leviticus, Numbers, and Deuteronomy. (Christians would later incorporate these books into their Bible as the first five books of the Old Testament.) The Hebrews considered these five books divinely inspired and attributed their original authorship to Moses himself, although, as we have noted, the texts as we know them were written much later.

The body of laws outlined in the Torah is quite different from the code of Hammurabi. The code was essentially a list of punishments for offenses; it is not an *ethical* code (see Fig. 2.11 and Reading 2.1). Hebraic and Mesopotamian laws are distinctly different. Perhaps because the Hebrews were once themselves aliens and slaves, their law treats the lowest members of society as human beings. As Yahweh declares in Exodus 23:6: "You will not cheat the poor among you of their rights at law." At least under the law, class distinctions, with the exceptions of slaves, did not exist in Hebrew society, and punishment was levied equally. Above all else, rich and poor alike were united for the common good in a common enterprise, to follow the instructions for living as God provided.

After 40 years in the Sinai had passed, it is believed that the patriarch Joshua led the Jews back to Canaan, the Promised Land, as Yahweh had pledged in the covenant. Over the next 200 years, they gradually gained control of the region through a protracted series of wars described in the books of Joshua, Judges, Samuel, and Kings in the Bible, which together make up a theological history of the early Jewish peoples. The Jews named themselves the Israelites, after Israel, the name that was given by God to Jacob. The nation consisted of 12 tribes, each descending from one of Jacob's 12 sons. By about 1000 BCE, Saul had established himself as King of Israel, followed by David, who as a boy rescued the Israelites from the Philistines by killing the giant Goliath with a stone thrown from a sling, as described in First Samuel, and later united Israel and Judah into a single state.

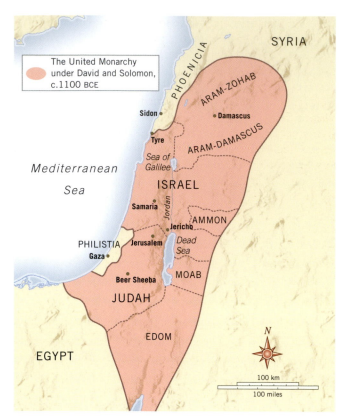

Map 2.2 **The United Monarchy of Israel under David and Solomon, ca. 1100 BCE.**

Although women were their husbands' possessions, the Hebrew Scriptures provide evidence that women may have had greater influence in Hebrew society than this patriarchal structure would suggest. In one of the many texts later incorporated into the Hebrew Bible and written during Solomon's reign, the "The Song of Songs, which is Solomon's" (as Chapter 1, Verse 1 of this short book reads), the woman's voice is particularly strong. It is now agreed that the book is not the work of Solomon himself, but rather a work of secular poetry, probably written during his reign. It is a love poem, a dialogue between a man (whose words are reproduced here in regular type) and a younger female lover, a Shulamite, or "daughter of Jerusalem" (whose voice is in italics) (**Reading 2.4b**). This poem of sexual awakening takes place in a garden atmosphere reminiscent of Eden, but there is no Original Sin here, only fulfillment:

READING 2.4b

from the Hebrew Bible, Song of Solomon 4:1–6, 7:13–14

**The Song of Songs
(translated by Ariel and Chana Bloch)**

How beautiful you are, my love,
My friend! The doves of your eyes
looking out
from the thicket of your hair.

Your hair
like a flock of goats
bounding down Mount Gilead. …

Your breasts are two fauns
twins of a gazelle,
grazing in a field of lilies.

An enclosed garden is my sister, my bride,
A hidden well, a sealed spring. …

*Awake, north wind! O south wind, come,
breathe upon my garden,
let its spices stream out.
Let my lover come into his garden
and taste its delicious fruit. …*

*Let us go early to the vineyards
to see if the vine has budded,
if the blossoms have opened
and the pomegranate is in flower.*

*There I will give you my love …
rare fruit of every kind, my love,
I have stored away for you.*

Kings David and Solomon, and Hebrew Society

King David reigned until 961 BCE. It was he who captured Jerusalem from the Canaanites and made it the capital of Israel (Map **2.2**). As represented in the books of Samuel, David is one of the most complex and interesting individuals in ancient literature. A poet and musician, he is author of some of the Psalms. Although he was capable of the most deceitful treachery—sending one of his soldiers, Uriah, to certain death in battle so that he could marry his widow, Bathsheba—he also suffered the greatest sorrow, being forced to endure the betrayal and death of his son Absalom. David was succeeded by his other son, Solomon, famous for his fairness in meting out justice, who ruled until 933 BCE.

Solomon undertook to complete the building campaign begun by his father, and by the end of his reign, Jerusalem was, by all reports, one of the most beautiful cities in the Near East. A magnificent palace and, most especially, a splendid temple dominated the city. First Kings claims that Yahweh himself saw the temple and approved of it.

The rule of the Hebrew kings was based on the model of the scriptural covenant between God and the Hebrews. This covenant was the model for the relationship between the king and his people. Each provided protection in return for obedience and fidelity. The same relationship existed between the family patriarch and his household. His wife and children were his possessions, whom he protected in return for their unerring faith in him.

So vivid are the poem's sexual metaphors that many people have wondered how the poem found its way into the Scriptures. But the Bible is frank enough about the attractions of sex. Consider Psalms 30:18–19: "Three things I marvel at, four I cannot fathom: the way of an eagle in the sky, the way of a snake on a rock, the way of a ship in the heart of the sea, the way of a man with a woman." The

Song of Songs is full of **double-entendres**, expressions that can be understood in two ways, one of them often sexual or risqué. Although the implications of such language are almost unavoidable, embarrassed Christian interpreters of the Bible for centuries worked hard to avoid the obvious and assert a higher purpose for the poem, reading it, especially, as a description of the relation between Christ and his "Bride," the Church.

Generations of translators also sought to obscure the powerful voice of the female protagonist in the poem by presenting the young woman as chaste and submissive, but of the two voices, hers is the more active and authoritative. In a world in which history is traced through the patriarchs, and genealogies are generally written in the form of the father "begetting" his sons, the young woman asserts herself here in a way that suggests that if in Hebrew society the records of lineage were in the hands of its men, the traditions of love-making—and by extension, the ability to propagate the lineage itself—were controlled by its women. It is even possible that a woman composed all or large parts of the poem, since women traditionally sang songs of victory and mourning in the Bible, and the daughters of Jerusalem actually function as a chorus in the poem, asking questions of the Shulamite.

The Prophets and the Diaspora

After Solomon's death, the United Monarchy of Israel split into two separate states. To the north was Israel, with its capital in Samaria, and to the south, Judah, with its capital in Jerusalem. In this era of the two kingdoms, Hebrew culture was dominated by **prophets**, men who were prophetic not in the sense of foretelling the future, but rather in the sense of serving as mouthpieces and interpreters of Yahweh's purposes, which they claimed to understand through visions. The prophets instructed the people in the ways of living according to the laws of the Torah, and they more or less freely confronted anyone guilty of wrongful actions, even the Hebrew kings. They attacked, particularly, the wealthy Hebrews whose commercial ventures had brought them unprecedented material comfort and who were inclined to stray from monotheism and worship Canaanite fertility gods and goddesses. The moral laxity of these wealthy Hebrews troubled the prophets, who urged the Hebrew nation to reform spiritually.

In 722 BCE, Assyrians attacked the northern kingdom of Israel and scattered its people, who were thereafter known as the Lost Tribes of Israel. The southern kingdom of Judah survived another 140 years, until Nebuchadnezzar and the Babylonians overwhelmed it in 587 BCE, destroying the Temple of Solomon in Jerusalem and deporting the Hebrews to Babylon (Fig. **2.16**). Not only had the Hebrews lost their homeland and their temple, but the Ark of the Covenant itself had also disappeared. For nearly 60 years, the Hebrews endured what is known as the Babylonian Captivity. As recorded in Psalm 137: "By the rivers of Babylon, there we sat down, yea we wept, when we remembered Zion."

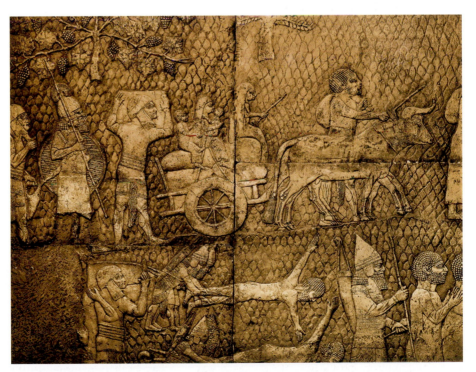

Fig. 2.16 *Exile of the Israelites*, **detail of a limestone relief from the palace of Sennacherib, Nineveh, Assyria. Late 8th century BCE.** This relief shows a family of Israelites, their cattle yoked to a cart carrying their household into exile after being defeated by the Assyrians in 722 BCE. The relief seems to depict three generations of a family: the father in front with the cattle, the son behind carrying baggage, the wife of the father seated on the front of the cart, the son's wife and children seated behind her.

Finally, invading Persians, whom they believed had been sent by Yahweh, freed them from the Babylonians in 520 BCE. They returned to Judah, known now, for the first time, as the Jews (after the name of their homeland). They rebuilt a Second Temple of Jerusalem, with an empty chamber at its center, meant for the Ark of the Covenant should it ever return. And they welcomed back other Jews from around the Mediterranean, including many whose families had left the northern kingdom almost 200 years earlier. Many others, however, were by now permanently settled elsewhere, and they became known as the Jews of the Diaspora, or the "dispersion."

Hebrew culture would have a profound impact on Western civilization. The Jews provided the essential ethical and moral foundation for religion in the West, including Christianity and Islam, both of which incorporate Jewish teachings into their own thought and practice. In the Torah, we find the basis of the law as we understand and practice it today. So moving and universal are the stories recorded in the Torah that over the centuries they have inspired—and continue to inspire—countless works of art, music, and literature. Most important, the Hebrews introduced to the world the concept of ethical monotheism, the idea that there is only one God, and that God demands that humans behave in a certain way, and rewards and punishes accordingly. Few, if any, concepts have had a more far-reaching effect on history and culture.

THE LATE EMPIRES: NEO-BABYLONIA AND PERSIA

How do the art and architecture of Neo-Babylonia and Persia reflect the aspirations of the two cultures?

As noted earlier in this chapter, the Assyrians had begun to conquer neighboring peoples in about 1000 BCE, and they controlled most of Mesopotamia by the end of the ninth century BCE, eventually extending their dominance as far west as the Nile Valley by the seventh century BCE. The Assyrians modeled a kind of military and cultural prowess that others envied and aspired to attain. The most successful of these new imperial adventurers were the Babylonians and the Persians.

Neo-Babylonia

From the eighth through the seventh century BCE, Babylon fell in and out of Assyrian rule, until Nabopolassar (r. 626–604 BCE), the first king of Babylonia, defeated the Assyrians, sacking Nineveh in 612 BCE. The Assyrian Empire collapsed completely in 609 BCE. Nabopolassar was followed by his son and heir, Nebuchadnezzar (r. 604–562 BCE), who continued on with his father's plan to restore Babylon's palace as the center of Mesopotamian civilization. It was here that the Hebrews lived in exile for nearly

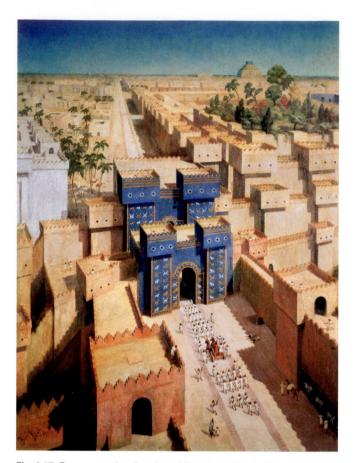

Fig. 2.17 Reconstruction drawing of Babylon with the Processional Way and the Ishtar Gate as it might have appeared in the 6th century BCE. Courtesy of the Oriental Institute of the University of Chicago. In the distance is the Marduk ziggurat, and between the ziggurat and the Ishtar Gate are the famous Hanging Gardens in the palace of Nebuchadnezzar II.

50 years (586–538 BCE) after Nebuchadnezzar captured the people of Jerusalem.

Nebuchadnezzar wished to remake Babylon as the most remarkable and beautiful city in the world. It was laid out on both sides of the Euphrates River, joined together by a single bridge. Through the middle of the older, eastern sector, ran the Processional Way, an avenue also called "May the Enemy Not Have Victory" (Fig. **2.17**). It ran from the Euphrates bridge eastward through the temple district, past the Marduk ziggurat. (Many believe this ziggurat was the legendary Tower of Babel, described in Genesis 11 as the place where God, confronted with the prospect of "one people … one language," chose instead to "confuse the language of all the earth," and scatter people "abroad over the face of the earth.") Then it turned north, ending at the Ishtar Gate (Fig. **2.18**), the northern entrance to the city. Processions honoring Marduk, the god celebrated above all others in Babylonian lore and considered the founder of Babylon itself, regularly filled the street, which was as much as 65 feet wide at some points and paved with large stone slabs. Marduk's might is celebrated in the *Hymn to Marduk* (**Reading 2.5**), found in Ashurbanipal's library:

READING 2.5

from the *Hymn to Marduk* (1000–700 BCE)

Lord Marduk, Supreme god, with unsurpassed
  wisdom. …
When you leave for battle the Heavens shake,
  when you raise your voice, the Sea is wild!
When you brandish your sword, the gods turn
  back.
There is none who can resist your furious blow!
Terrifying lord, in the Assembly of the gods no
  one equals you! …
Your weapons flare in the tempest!
Your flame annihilates the steepest mountain.

No trace survives of the city's famous Hanging Gardens, once considered among the Seven Wonders of the World, and only the base and parts of the lower stairs of the Marduk ziggurat still remain. But in the fifth century BCE, the Greek historian Herodotus (ca. 484–430/420 BCE) described the ziggurat as follows:

There was a tower of solid masonry, a furlong in length and breadth, on which was raised a second tower, and on that a third, and so on up to eight. The ascent to the top is on the outside, by a path which winds round all the towers. … On the topmost tower, there is a spacious temple, and inside the temple stands a couch of unusual size, richly adorned with a golden table by its side. … They also declare that the

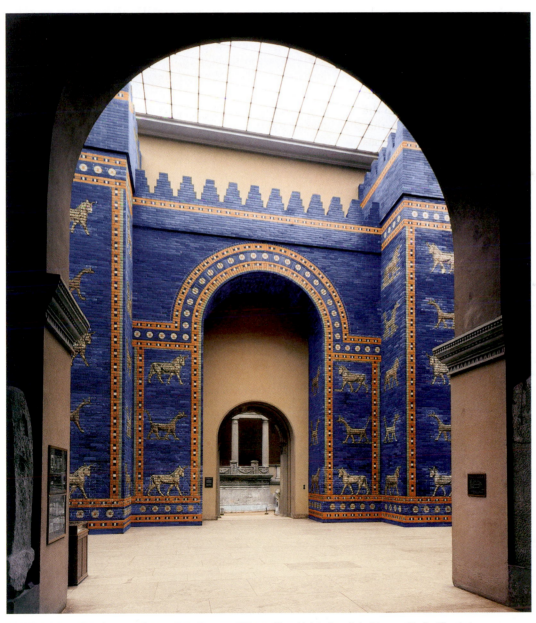

Fig. 2.18 Ishtar Gate (restored), from Babylon. ca. 575 BCE. Glazed brick. Staatliche Museen, Berlin. The dark blue bricks are glazed—that is, covered with a film of glass—and they would have shone brilliantly in the sun.

View the Closer Look for the Ishtar Gate on **MyArtsLab**

god comes down in person into this chamber, and sleeps on the couch, but I do not believe it.

Although the ziggurat has disappeared, we can glean some sense of the city's magnificence from the Ishtar Gate, named after the Babylonian goddess of fertility. Today, the gate is restored and reconstructed inside one of the Berlin State Museums. It was made of glazed and unglazed bricks, and decorated with animal forms. The entire length of the Processional Way was similarly decorated on both sides, so the ensemble must have been a wondrous sight. The gate's striding lions are particularly interesting. They are traditional symbols of Ishtar herself. Alternating with rows of bulls with blue horns and tails, associated with deities such as Adad, god of the weather, are fantastic dragons with long necks, the forelegs of a lion, and the rear legs of a bird of prey, an animal form sacred to the god Marduk. Like so much other Mesopotamian art, it is at once a monument to the power of Nebuchadnezzar, an affirmation of his close relation to the gods, and a testament to his kingdom's wealth and well-being.

The Persian Empire

In 520 BCE, the Persians, formerly a minor nomadic tribe that occupied the plateau of Iran, defeated the Babylonians and freed the Jews. Their imperial adventuring had begun in 559 BCE with the ascension of Cyrus II (called the Great, r. 559–530 BCE), the first ruler of the Achaemenid dynasty, named after Achaemenes, a warrior-king whom Persian legend says ruled on the Iranian plateau around 700 BCE. By the time of Cyrus's death, the Persians had taken control of the Greek cities in Ionia on the west coast of Anatolia. Under King Darius (r. 522–486 BCE), they soon ruled a vast empire that stretched from Egypt in the south, around Asia Minor, to the Ukraine in the north. The capital of the Empire was Parsa, which the Greeks called Persepolis, or city of the Persians, located in the Zagros highlands of present-day Iran (Fig. **2.19**). Built by artisans and workers from all over the Persian Empire, including Greeks from Ionia, it reflected Darius's multicultural ambitions. If he was, as he said, "King of Kings, King of countries, King of the earth," his palace should reflect the diversity of his peoples.

The columns reflect Egyptian influence, and, especially in their **fluting**, the vertical channels that exaggerate their height and lend them a feeling of lightness, they reflect the influence of the Greeks (see Chapter 4). Rulers are depicted in relief sculptures with Assyrian beards and headdresses (Fig. **2.20**). In typical Mesopotamian fashion, they are larger than other people in the works. These decorations further reflect the Persians' sense that all the peoples of the region owed them allegiance. The relief from the stairway to the audience hall, where Darius and his son Xerxes received visitors, is covered with images of their subjects bringing gifts to the palace—23 subject nations in all, including Ionian, Babylonian, Syrian, and Susian, each culture recognizable by its beards and costumes. Darius can be seen receiving tribute as Xerxes stands

👁 **Watch** the video about Persepolis on **MyArtsLab**

The CONTINUING PRESENCE of the PAST

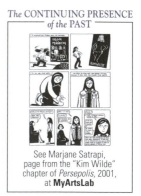

See Marjane Satrapi, page from the "Kim Wilde" chapter of *Persepolis*, 2001, at **MyArtsLab**

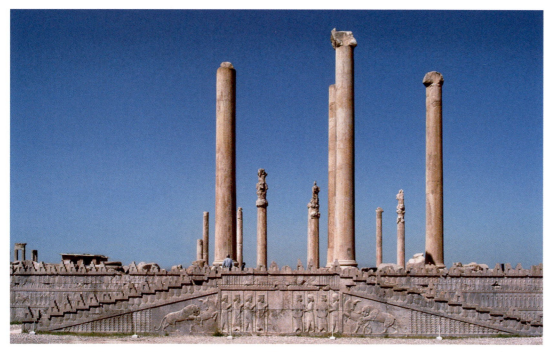

Fig. 2.19 Palace of Darius and Xerxes, Persepolis, Iran. 518–ca. 460 BCE. The palace stands on a rock terrace 545 yards deep and 330 yards wide. Its centerpiece was the Hall of One Hundred Columns, a forest of stone comprised of ten rows of ten columns, each rising to a height of 40 feet. The Hall was approached by a broad staircase decorated with reliefs of men carrying gifts (see Fig. 2.20).

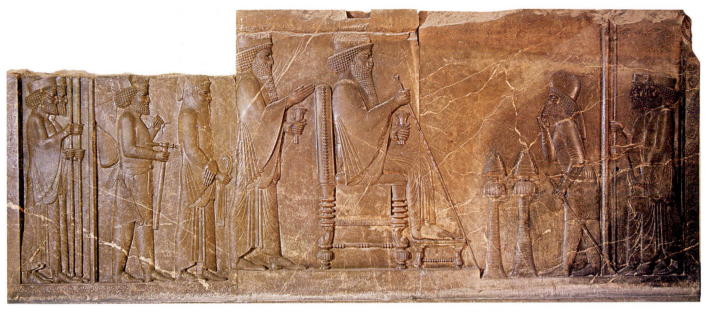

Fig. 2.20 *Darius and Xerxes Receiving Tribute*, **detail of a relief from a stairway leading to the Hall of One Hundred Columns, ceremonial complex, Persepolis, Iran. 491–486 BCE.** Limestone, height 8'4". Iranbastan Museum, Teheran. This panel was originally painted in blue, scarlet, green, purple, and turquoise. Objects such as Darius's necklace and crown were covered in gold.

behind him, as if waiting to take his place as the Persian ruler. Huge winged bulls with the heads of bearded kings, reminiscent of the human-headed winged bulls that guard the Khorsabad palace of the Assyrian king Sargon II (see Fig. 2.13), dominated the approach to the south gateway. Thus, Mesopotamian, Assyrian, Egyptian, and Greek styles all intermingle in the palace's architecture and decoration.

The Persians also perfected the art of metalwork. The rhyton, or ritual cup, illustrated here (Fig. 2.21), is related to the many mythological creatures that can be found throughout Mesopotamian art—the hybrid human and bull creature that guarded the palace gate at Parsa, for instance, or the dragon with lion's feet decorating the Ishtar Gate in Babylon. This gold rhyton has been fashioned into a *simurgh*, a mythical creature with the body of a lion, the head of a dog, the wings of a griffin, and a peacock's tail.

The rhyton would have been used in rituals connected to the Zoroastrian religion practiced by the Persians. Zoroaster (the Greek name for the Iranian Zarathustra) was a Persian prophet who according to tradition

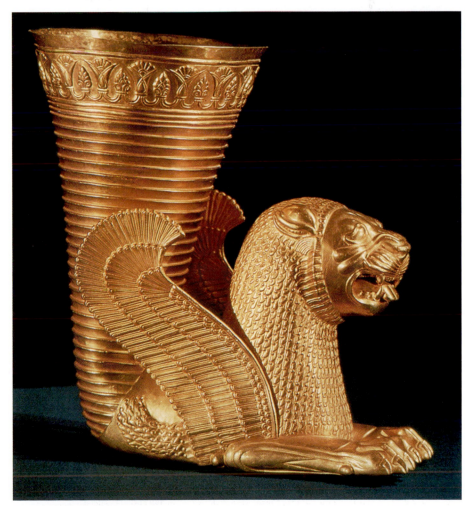

Fig. 2.21 Rhyton. Achaemenid, 5th–3rd centuries BCE. Gold. Archaeological Museum, Teheran, Iran. This elaborate gold vessel would have probably served as both a drinking cup and a wine decanter.

lived in the sixth century BCE. However, linguistic analysis of the writings that are attributed to him places him around 1000 BCE. Whatever the case, his writings and other ritual hymns, prayers, and laws associated with the religion were collected in the sixth century into the *Zend-Avesta*, or Book of Knowledge, the holy book of the Zoroastrian faith. Ahura Mazda, "the Wise Lord," is its supreme deity, creator of heaven and earth, and in almost all inscriptions, the one and only god. It was he, Darius would proclaim, who lent Darius his very power: "A great God is Ahura Mazda, who created this earth, who created yonder sky, who created man, who created happiness for man, who made Darius king, one king over many, one lord over many." Zoroastrianism is only semi-monotheistic: there are lesser gods—many of them remnants of earlier religious practices—but all of them were created by Ahura Mazda himself. He rules over these gods as Darius rules over his people. The *Zend-Avesta* sets up a dualistic universe in which *asha* (literally, "truth") is opposed to *druj* ("lie" or "deceit"). The physical order of the universe is the chief manifestation of *asha* and is wholly the work of Ahura Mazda. *Druj* manifests itself as anything that is opposed to this physical order—chaos, natural decay, evil deeds. Perhaps Zoroaster's greatest contribution to religious thought is his emphasis on free will. As the *Zend-Avesta* says, Ahura Mazda "has left it to men's wills" to choose for themselves whether to lead a life of "good thoughts, good words, good deeds." Those who do—thus helping Ahura Mazda to maintain the order of the universe—will be admitted to heaven. Those who choose to follow the path of evil will be condemned to hell.

In Zoroastrian tradition, the *simurgh* whose image is invoked on the rhyton lives on Mount Alburz, the highest mountain in the world, around which circled the sun, moon, and stars. From the summit of the mountain, the legendary Chinwad bridge, the "bridge of judgment," extended to heaven. There, the souls of the good men and women are greeted by a beautiful maiden and led across an ever-widening pathway to *pairidaeza*, from which the English word "paradise" derives, and the souls of the bad are greeted by an ugly old hag and led across an ever-narrowing bridge until they fall into hell. The bridge is described at some length in the *Zend-Avesta* (**Reading 2.6**):

27. O Maker of the material world, thou Holy One! Where are the rewards given? Where does the rewarding take place? Where is the rewarding fulfilled? Whereto do men come to take the reward that, during their life in the material world, they have won for their souls?

28. Ahura Mazda answered: "When the man is dead, when his time is over, then the wicked, evil-doing Daevas[1] cut off his eyesight. On the third night, when the dawn appears and brightens up, when Mithra, the god with beautiful weapons, reaches the all-happy mountains, and the sun is rising.

29. "Then the fiend, named Vizaresha[2], O Spitama[3] Zoroaster, carries off in bonds the souls of the wicked Daeva-worshippers who live in sin. The soul enters the way made by Time, and open both to the wicked and to the righteous. At the head of the Chinwad bridge, the holy bridge made by Mazda, they ask for their spirits and souls the reward for the worldly goods which they gave away here below.

30. "Then comes the beautiful, well-shapen, strong and well-formed maid, with the dogs at her sides, one who can distinguish, who has many children, happy, and of high understanding. She makes the soul of the righteous one go up above … the Chinwad bridge; she places it in the presence of the heavenly gods themselves."

[1] **Daevas**: supernatural entities with variously disagreeable characteristics; in the oldest Zoroastrian works they are "wrong" or "false" gods that are to be rejected in favor of the worship of the one God, Ahura Mazda.
[2] **Vizaresha**: a demon who, during that struggle of three days and three nights with the souls of the departed, wages terror on them and beats them. He sits at the gate of hell.
[3] **Spitama**: the original name of Zoroaster, who as a prince gave up his royal duties to meditate, spending 15 years searching for enlightenment before a vision of Ahura Mazda gave him the answers to his many questions.

In this context, it is worth recalling that the *Zend-Avesta* was compiled at about the same time as the Hebrew Bible. Its teachings would, in fact, influence all three of the great religions of the Western world—Judaism, Christianity, and Islam.

Mesopotamia and Egypt: A Comparison

Civilization in Mesopotamia developed across the last three millennia BCE almost simultaneously with civilization in Egypt, a region on the northeastern corner of the African continent in close proximity to Mesopotamian and Mediterranean cultures. The civilizations of Egypt and Mesopotamia had much in common. Both formed around river systems—the Tigris and Euphrates in Mesopotamia; the Nile in Egypt. Both were agrarian societies that depended on irrigation, and their economies were hostage to the sometimes fickle, sometimes violent flow of their respective river systems. As in Mesopotamia, Egyptians learned to control the river's flow by constructing dams and irrigation canals, and it was probably the need to cooperate with one another in such endeavors that helped Mesopotamia to thrive and Egypt to create the civilization that would eventually arise in the Nile Valley.

The Mesopotamians and the Egyptians built massive architectural structures dedicated to their gods—the ziggurat in Mesopotamia and the pyramid in Egypt (see Fig. 2.1, and Fig. 3.6 in Chapter 3). Both unite the earth and the heavens in a single architectural form, although the Mesopotamian ziggurat is topped by a temple and is considered the house of the city-state's god, and the Egyptian pyramid is funerary in nature with a royal burial within. Both cultures developed forms of writing, although the cuneiform script of Mesopotamian culture and the hieroglyphic script of Egyptian society were very different. There is ample evidence that the two civilizations traded with one another, and to a certain degree influenced one another.

What most distinguishes Mesopotamian from Egyptian culture, however, is the relative stability of the latter. Mesopotamia was rarely, if ever, united as a single entity. Whenever it was united, it was through force, the power of an army, not the free will of a people striving for the common good. In contrast, political transition in Egypt was *dynastic*—that is, rule was inherited by members of the same family, sometimes for generations. As in Mesopotamia, however, the ruler's authority was cemented by his association with divine authority. He was, indeed, the manifestation of the gods on earth. As a result, the dynastic rulers of Egypt sought to immortalize themselves through art and architecture. In fact, there is clear reason to believe that the sculptural image of a ruler was believed to be, in some sense, the ruler himself.

Embodying the ruler's sense of his own permanence is an **obelisk**—a four-sided stone shaft topped by a pyramid-shaped block—which once marked the entrance to the Amun Temple at Luxor during the reigns of the pharaohs Ramses II and Ramses III (Fig. **2.22**). Some 3,300 years old, it stands today at the center of the Place de la Concorde in

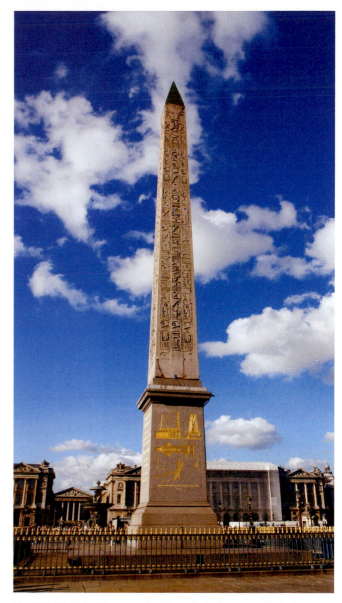

Fig. 2.22 Obelisk of Luxor in the Place de la Concorde, Paris. Dynasty 19, Egypt, ca. 1279–1213 BCE. Height 75'. The obelisk was a gift of the Egyptian government to the French, presented to them in 1829 by the Egyptian viceroy, Mehemet Ali. Gilded images on the pedestal portray the monumental task of transporting the monolith to Paris and erecting it in the city's most central square.

Paris, a gift to the French from the Egyptian government in the nineteenth century. The inscription, carved in hieroglyphs, says it all: "Son of Ra [the sun god]: Ramses-Meryamun ["Beloved of Amun"]. As long as the skies exist, your monuments shall exist, your name shall exist, firm as the skies." ∎

THINKING BACK

2.1 Describe the relationship between the gods and the peoples of Sumer, Akkad, Babylon, and Assyria.

The royal tombs at the Sumerian city of Ur reveal a highly developed Bronze Age culture, based on the social order of the city-state, which was ruled by a priest-king acting as the intermediary between the gods and the people. The rulers also established laws and encouraged record-keeping, which in turn required the development of a system of writing—cuneiform script. In Sumer and subsequent Mesopotamian cultures, monumental architecture such as ziggurats were dedicated to the gods, and in each city-state, one of the gods rose to prominence as the city's protector. Under the rule of Hammurabi of Babylon, Mesopotamian law was codified, specifically in the stele that records the Law Code of Hammurabi. How would you characterize the general relationship between Mesopotamian rulers and the gods?

2.2 Explain how the *Epic of Gilgamesh* reflects the relationship between the gods and the people.

Preserved in the library of the Assyrian king Ashurbanipal, the *Epic of Gilgamesh* remains one of the greatest expressions of world literature. The sense of cultural continuity in Mesopotamia is underscored by the fact that the *Epic of Gilgamesh* preserves the historical lineage of all Mesopotamian kings—Sumerian, Akkadian, Babylonian, and Assyrian. While asserting the king's divinity, the story also admits the king's human mortality. What are the characteristics of its epic form? What are its principal themes? In particular, how do Gilgamesh and Enkidu relate to the gods?

2.3 Distinguish between the culture of the Hebrews and the other cultures of the ancient Near East.

The Hebrews practiced a monotheistic religion. They considered themselves the "chosen people" of God, for whom they used the cipher YHWH ("Yahweh" in modern English). The written word is central to their culture, and it is embodied in a body of law, the Torah, and more specifically in the Ten Commandments. What does the Torah have in common with the Law Code of Hammurabi? How does it differ? How do the stories in Genesis, the first book of the Hebrew Bible, compare to the *Epic of Gilgamesh*?

2.4 Discuss how the art and architecture of Neo-Babylonia and Persia reflect the ambitions of their leaders.

The last of the great Mesopotamian empires appeared after the fall of the Assyrians in 612 BCE. First in Neo-Babylonia, then in Persia, city-states arose that aspired to control the entire eastern Mediterranean and Mesopotamia. Each built magnificent capitals, Nebuchadnezzar remaking Babylon into the most magnificent city in the world, and then, after the Persians defeated the Babylonians in 520 BCE, Darius constructing his new capital of Parsa, or Persepolis, in the highlands of western Iran. What features of these cities suggest the imperial aspirations of their leaders?

The Persian kings practiced the Zoroastrian religion. Like the Jews, the Persians' beliefs were collected in a single holy book, compiled at about the same time as the Hebrew Bible. However, the Persian religion was only semi-monotheistic. Their supreme deity, Ahura Mazda, was the creator of many lesser gods. How did the Zoroastrian religion lend authority to the Persian kings? In what way was Zoroastrian religion dualistic?

✔ **Study** and **review** on **MyArtsLab**

READINGS

from the *Epic of Gilgamesh*, Tablet I (late 2nd millennium BCE) (translated by Maureen Gallery Kovacs)

The *Epic of Gilgamesh* describes the exploits of the Sumerian ruler Gilgamesh and his friend Enkidu. The following passage, from the first of the epic's 12 tablets, recounts how Enkidu, the primal man raised beyond the reach of civilization and fully at home with wild animals, loses his animal powers, and with them his innocence, when a trapper, tired of Enkidu freeing animals from his traps, arranges for a harlot from Uruk to seduce him. The story resonates in interesting ways with the biblical tale of Adam and Eve and their loss of innocence in the Garden of Eden.

TABLET I

The Harlot

The trapper went, bringing the harlot, Shamhat, with him,
they set off on the journey, making direct way.
On the third day they arrived at the appointed place,
and the trapper and the harlot sat down at their posts(?).
A first day and a second they sat opposite the watering hole.
The animals arrived and drank at the watering hole,
the wild beasts arrived and slaked their thirst with water.
Then he, Enkidu, offspring of the mountains,
who eats grasses with the gazelles,
came to drink at the watering hole with the animals, 10
with the wild beasts he slaked his thirst with water.
Then Shamhat saw him—a primitive,
a savage fellow from the depths of the wilderness!
  "That is he, Shamhat! Release your clenched arms,
  expose your sex so he can take in your voluptuousness.
  Do not be restrained—take his energy!
  When he sees you he will draw near to you.
  Spread out your robe so he can lie upon you,
  and perform for this primitive the task of womanhood!
  His animals, who grew up in his wilderness, will become 20
    alien to him,
    and his lust will groan over you."

Shamhat unclutched her bosom, exposed her sex, and he
    took in her voluptuousness.
She was not restrained, but took his energy.
She spread out her robe and he lay upon her,
she performed for the primitive the task of womankind.
His lust groaned over her;
for six days and seven nights Enkidu stayed aroused,
and had intercourse with the harlot 30
until he was sated with her charms.
But when he turned his attention to his animals,
the gazelles saw Enkidu and darted off,
the wild animals distanced themselves from his body.
Enkidu … his utterly depleted (?) body,
his knees that wanted to go off with his animals went rigid;
Enkidu was diminished, his running was not as before.
But then he drew himself up, for his understanding had
    broadened.

READING CRITICALLY

In giving in to the temptation of the harlot Shamhat, Enkidu loses much here, but he also gains something. What is it that he comes to understand? How does it differ from the physical prowess that he has evidently lost?

from the Hebrew Bible, Genesis, Chapters 2–3, 6–7

The following excerpts from the first book of both the Hebrew Torah and the Christian Old Testament describe the story of Adam and Eve and the story of Noah. Together they demonstrate some of the characteristics of Hebrew monotheism—belief in the direct agency of their God in the workings of the world and his creation of a universe that is systematically planned and imbued with a moral order that derives from him. The passages also demonstrate the power and authority the Hebrews invested in their God.

CHAPTER 2

1 Thus the heavens and the earth were finished, and all their multitude.

2 And on the seventh day God finished the work that he had done, and he rested on the seventh day from all the work that he had done.

3 So God blessed the seventh day and hallowed it, because on it God rested from all the work that he had done in creation …

7 then the LORD God formed man from the dust of the ground, and breathed into his nostrils the breath of life; and 10 the man became a living being.

8 And the LORD God planted a garden in Eden, in the east; and there he put the man whom he had formed.

9 Out of the ground the LORD God made to grow every tree that is pleasant to the sight and good for food, the tree of life also in the midst of the garden, and the tree of the knowledge of good and evil.

10 A river flows out of Eden to water the garden, and from there it divides and becomes four branches.

11 The name of the first is Pishon; it is the one that flows around the whole land of Havilah, where there is gold;

12 and the gold of that land is good; odellium and onyx stone are there.

13 The name of the second river is Gihon; it is the one that flows around the whole land of Cush.

14 The name of the third river is Tigris, which flows east of Assyria. And the fourth river is the Euphrates.

15 The LORD God took the man and put him in the garden of Eden to till it and keep it.

16 And the LORD God commanded the man, "You may freely eat of every tree of the garden;

17 but of the tree of the knowledge of good and evil you shall not eat, for in the day that you eat of it you shall die."

18 Then the LORD God said, "It is not good that the man should be alone; I will make him a helper as his partner."

19 So out of the ground the LORD God formed every animal of the field and every bird of the air, and brought them to the man to see what he would call them; and whatever the man called every living creature, that was its name.

20 The man gave names to all cattle, and to the birds of the air, and to every animal of the field; but for the man there was not found a helper as his partner.

21 So the LORD God caused a deep sleep to fall upon the man, and he slept; then he took one of his ribs and closed up its place with flesh.

22 And the rib that the LORD God had taken from the man he made into a woman and brought her to the man.

23 Then the man said, "This at last is bone of my bones and flesh of my flesh; this one shall be called Woman, for out of Man this one was taken."

24 Therefore a man leaves his father and his mother and clings to his wife, and they become one flesh.

25 And the man and his wife were both naked, and were not ashamed.

THE TEMPTATION AND EXPULSION

CHAPTER 3

1 Now the serpent was more crafty than any other wild animal that the LORD God had made. He said to the woman, "Did God say, 'You shall not eat from any tree in the garden'?"

2 The woman said to the serpent, "We may eat of the fruit of the trees in the garden;

3 but God said, 'You shall not eat of the fruit of the tree that is in the middle of the garden, nor shall you touch it, or you shall die.'"

4 But the serpent said to the woman, "You will not die;

5 for God knows that when you eat of it your eyes will be opened, and you will be like God, knowing good and evil."

6 So when the woman saw that the tree was good for food, and that it was a delight to the eyes, and that the tree was to be desired to make one wise, she took of its fruit and ate; and she also gave some to her husband, who was with her, and he ate.

7 Then the eyes of both were opened, and they knew that they were naked; and they sewed fig leaves together and made loincloths for themselves.

8 They heard the sound of the LORD God walking in the garden at the time of the evening breeze, and the man and his wife hid themselves from the presence of the LORD God among the trees of the garden.

9 But the LORD God called to the man, and said to him, "Where are you?"

10 He said, "I heard the sound of you in the garden, and I was afraid, because I was naked; and I hid myself."

11 He said, "Who told you that you were naked? Have you eaten from the tree of which I commanded you not to eat?"

12 The man said, "The woman whom you gave to be with me, she gave me fruit from the tree, and I ate."

13 Then the LORD God said to the woman, "What is this that you have done?" The woman said, "The serpent tricked me, and I ate."

14 The LORD God said to the serpent, "Because you have done this, cursed are you among all animals and among all wild creatures; upon your belly you shall go, and dust you shall eat all the days of your life.

15 I will put enmity between you and the woman, and between your offspring and hers; he will strike your head, and you will strike his heel."

16 To the woman he said, "I will greatly increase your pangs in childbearing; in pain you shall bring forth children, yet your desire shall be for your husband, and he shall rule over you."

17 And to the man he said, "Because you have listened to the voice of your wife, and have eaten of the tree about which I commanded you, 'You shall not eat of it,' cursed is the ground because of you; in toil you shall eat of it all the days of your life;

18 thorns and thistles it shall bring forth for you; and you shall eat the plants of the field.

19 By the sweat of your face you shall eat bread until you return to the ground, for out of it you were taken; you are dust, and to dust you shall return."

20 The man named his wife Eve, because she was the mother of all living.

21 And the LORD God made garments of skins for the man and for his wife, and clothed them.

22 Then the LORD God said, "See, the man has become like one of us, knowing good and evil; and now, he might reach out his hand and take also from the tree of life, and eat, and live forever"—

23 therefore the LORD God sent him forth from the garden of Eden, to till the ground from which he was taken.

24 He drove out the man; and at the east of the garden of Eden he placed the cherubim, and a sword flaming and turning to guard the way to the tree of life.

THE STORY OF NOAH

CHAPTER 6

5 The LORD saw that the wickedness of humankind was great in the earth, and that every inclination of the thoughts of their hearts was only evil continually.

6 And the LORD was sorry that he had made humankind on the earth, and it grieved him to his heart.

7 So the LORD said, "I will blot out from the earth the human beings I have created—people together with animals and creeping things and birds of the air, for I am sorry that I have made them." 130

8 But Noah found favor in the sight of the LORD. …

13 And God said to Noah, "I have determined to make an end of all flesh, for the earth is filled with violence because of them; now I am going to destroy them along with the earth.

14 Make yourself an ark of cypress wood; make rooms in the ark, and cover it inside and out with pitch. …

17 For my part, I am going to bring a flood of waters on the earth, to destroy from under heaven all flesh in which is the 140 breath of life; everything that is on the earth shall die.

18 But I will establish my covenant with you; and you shall come into the ark, you, your sons, your wife, and your sons' wives with you.

19 And of every living thing, of all flesh, you shall bring two of every kind into the ark, to keep them alive with you; they shall be male and female.

20 Of the birds according to their kinds, and of the animals according to their kinds, of every creeping thing of the ground according to its kind, two of every kind shall come in to you, to keep them alive. 150

21 Also take with you every kind of food that is eaten, and store it up; and it shall serve as food for you and for them."

22 Noah did this; he did all that God commanded him.

CHAPTER 7

6 Noah was six hundred years old when the flood of waters came on the earth.

7 And Noah with his sons and his wife and his sons' wives went into the ark to escape the waters of the flood.

8 Of clean animals, and of animals that are not clean, and of birds, and of everything that creeps on the ground, 160

9 two and two, male and female, went into the ark with Noah, as God had commanded Noah.

10 And after seven days the waters of the flood came on the earth. …

11 … on that day all the fountains of the great deep burst forth, and the windows of the heavens were opened.

12 The rain fell on the earth forty days and forty nights. …

18 The waters swelled and increased greatly on the earth; and the ark floated on the face of the waters.

19 The waters swelled so mightily on the earth that all the 170 high mountains under the whole heaven were covered; …

21 And all flesh died that moved on the earth, birds, domestic animals, wild animals, all swarming creatures that swarm on the earth, and all human beings;

22 everything on dry land in whose nostrils was the breath of life died.

23 He blotted out every living thing that was on the face of the ground, human beings and animals and creeping things and birds of the air; they were blotted out from the earth. Only Noah was left, and those that were with him in the 180 ark. …

READING CRITICALLY

The story of Noah is, in some sense, a parable of the value of choosing to "walk with God." How does it reflect, then, the idea of the covenant, God's agreement with the Hebrews?

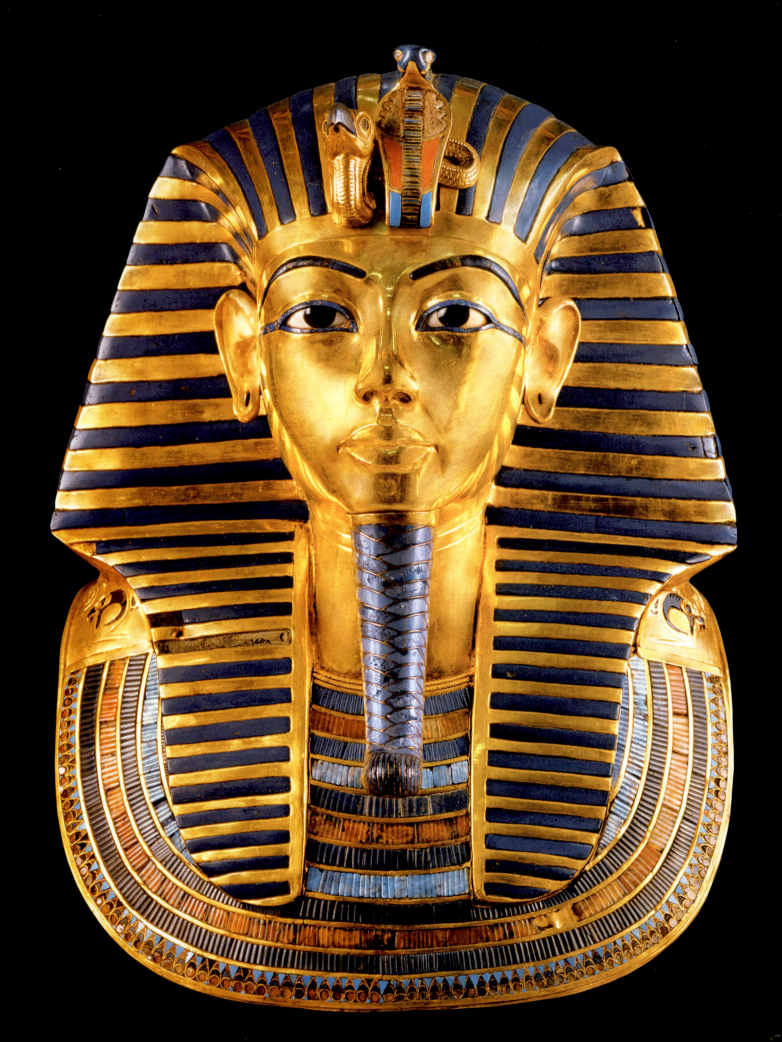

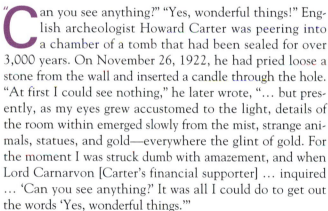

3

The Stability of Ancient Egypt

Flood and Sun

THINKING AHEAD

3.1 Describe how the idea of cyclical return shaped Egyptian civilization.

3.2 Analyze how religious beliefs are reflected in the funerary art and architecture of the Old Kingdom.

3.3 Compare and contrast Middle Kingdom art and literature to that of the Old Kingdom.

3.4 Characterize New Kingdom worship of Amun and contrast it to the major transformation of Egyptian tradition under the rule of Akhenaten.

3.5 Discuss Egypt's relations with its African neighbors to the south and with the Mediterranean powers to the north during the Late Period.

"Can you see anything?" "Yes, wonderful things!" English archeologist Howard Carter was peering into a chamber of a tomb that had been sealed for over 3,000 years. On November 26, 1922, he had pried loose a stone from the wall and inserted a candle through the hole. "At first I could see nothing," he later wrote, "… but presently, as my eyes grew accustomed to the light, details of the room within emerged slowly from the mist, strange animals, statues, and gold—everywhere the glint of gold. For the moment I was struck dumb with amazement, and when Lord Carnarvon [Carter's financial supporter] … inquired … 'Can you see anything?' It was all I could do to get out the words 'Yes, wonderful things.'"

The tomb was that of Tutankhamun, and among the most spectacular of the "wonderful things" Carter and Carnarvon would find inside was a coffin consisting of three separate coffins placed one inside the other. These were in turn encased in a quartzite **sarcophagus**, a rectangular stone coffin that was encased in four gilded, boxlike wooden shrines, also nestled one inside the other. Inside the innermost coffin, itself made of solid gold, a gold funerary mask had been placed over the upper body of the young king's mummified body (Fig. **3.1**). As news of Carter's discovery leaked out, the world press could hardly contain its enthusiasm. "This has been, perhaps, the most extraordinary day in the whole history of Egyptian excavation," *The Times* of London wired *The New York Times* on February 18, 1922, the day that the sealed door to the burial chamber was finally opened. "Whatever one may have guessed or imagined of the secret of Tut-ankh-Amen's tomb, they [sic] surely cannot have dreamed the truth that is now revealed. The entrance today was made into the sealed chamber of the tomb of Tut-ankh-Amen, and yet another door opened beyond that. No eyes have seen the King, but to practical certainty we know that he lies there close at hand in all his original state, undisturbed." It would be another year until the quartzite lid to Tutankhamun's coffin, weighing nearly 1.25 tons, was hoisted off, and yet another nine months before the inner coffins were removed to reveal the king's body. Carter's discovery revealed the wealth that defined the Egyptian kingship, as well as the elaborate rituals surrounding the burial of the king himself.

The Egyptian kingship was deeply connected to the life-blood and heart of Egyptian culture, the Nile River. Like

◀ **Fig. 3.1 Funerary mask of Tutankhamun. Dynasty 18, ca. 1327 BCE.** Gold inlaid with glass and semiprecious stones, height 21¼". Egyptian Museum, Cairo. So many items of extraordinary value were found in Tutankhamun's tomb—furniture, perfumes, chariots, weapons, jewelry, clothing, utensils, cups, and on and on—that it took Carter ten years to empty it and inventory its contents.

 Listen to the chapter audio on **MyArtsLab**

the Tigris and Euphrates in Mesopotamia, the Nile could be said to have made Egypt possible. The river begins in central eastern Africa, one tributary in the mountains of Ethiopia and another at Lake Victoria in Uganda, from which it flows north for nearly 4,000 miles. Egyptian civilization developed along the last 750 miles of the river's banks, extending from the granite cliffs at Aswan, north to the Mediterranean Sea (see Map **3.1**).

Nearly every year, torrential rains caused the river to rise dramatically. Most years, from July to November, the Egyptians could count on the Nile flooding their land. When the river receded, deep deposits of fertile silt covered the valley floor. Fields would then be tilled, and crops planted and tended. If the flooding was either too great or too minor, especially over a period of years, famine could result. The cycle of flood and sun made Egypt one of the most productive cultures in the ancient world and one of the most stable. For 3,000 years, from 3100 BCE

until the defeat of Mark Antony and Cleopatra by the Roman general Octavian in 31 BCE, Egypt's institutions and culture remained remarkably unchanged. Its stability contrasted sharply with the conflicts and shifts in power that occurred in Mesopotamia. The constancy and achievements of Egypt's culture are the subject of this chapter.

THE NILE AND ITS CULTURE

How does the idea of cyclical return inform Egyptian culture?

As a result of the Nile's annual floods, Egypt called itself Kemet, meaning "Black Land." In Upper Egypt, from Aswan to the Delta, the black, fertile deposits of the river covered an extremely narrow strip of land. Surrounding the river's alluvial plain was the "Red Land," the desert

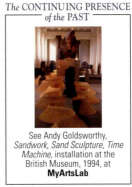

The CONTINUING PRESENCE
of the PAST

See Andy Goldsworthy,
Sandwork, Sand Sculpture, Time Machine, installation at the British Museum, 1994, at
MyArtsLab

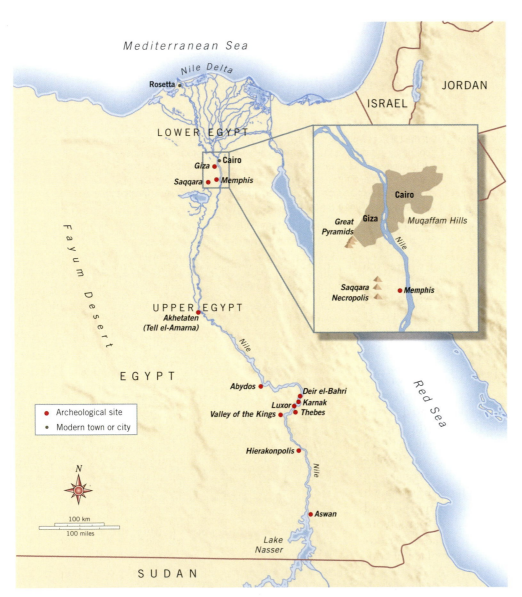

Map 3.1 Nile River basin with archeological sites in relation to present-day Cairo. The broad expanse of the Lower Nile Delta was crisscrossed by canals, allowing for easy transport of produce and supplies.

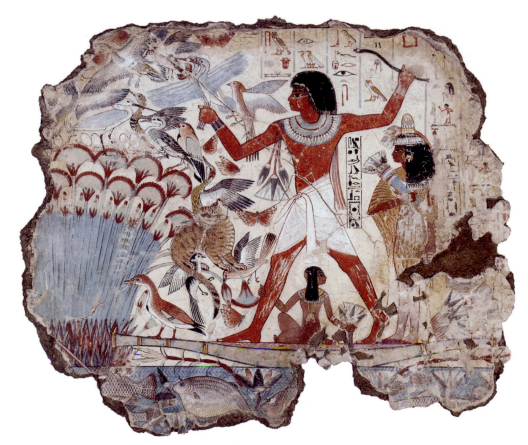

Fig. 3.2 *Nebamun Hunting Birds,* **from the tomb of Nebamun, Thebes. Dynasty 18, ca. 1400** BCE. Fresco on dry plaster, height approx. 2'8". © The Trustees of the British Museum. The fish and the birds, and the cat, are completely realistic, but this is not a realistic scene. It is a conventional representation of the deceased, in this case Nebamun, spearing fish or hunting fowl, almost obligatory for the decoration of a tomb. The pigments were applied directly to a dry wall, a technique that has come to be known as ***fresco secco***, dry fresco. Such paintings are extremely fragile and susceptible to moisture damage, but Egypt's arid climate has preserved them.

👁 **Watch** a Students on Site video about the tomb of Nebamun on **MyArtsLab**

environment that could not support life, but where rich deposits of minerals and stone could be mined and quarried. Lower Egypt consists of the Delta itself, which today begins some 13 miles north of Giza, the site of the largest pyramids, across the river from what is present-day Cairo. But in ancient times, it began 18 miles south of Giza, near the city of Memphis.

In this land of plenty, great farms flourished, and wildlife abounded in the marshes. In fact, the Egyptians linked the marsh to the creation of the world and represented it that way in the famous hunting scene that decorates the tomb of Nebamun at Thebes (Fig. **3.2**). Nebamun is about to hurl a snake-shaped throwing stick into a flock of birds as his wife and daughter look on. The painting is a sort of visual pun, referring directly to sexual procreation. The verb "to launch a throwing stick" also means "to ejaculate," and the word for "throwing stick" itself, to "create." The hieroglyphs written between Nebamun and his wife translate as "enjoying oneself, viewing the beautiful, … at the place of constant renewal of life."

Scholars divide Egyptian history into three main periods of achievement. Almost all of the conventions of Egyptian art were established during the first period, the *Old*

Kingdom. During the *Middle Kingdom,* the "classical" literary language that would survive through the remainder of Egyptian history was first produced. The *New Kingdom* was a period of prosperity that saw a renewed interest in art and architecture. During each of these periods, successive dynasties—or royal houses—brought peace and stability to the country. Between them were "Intermediate Periods" of relative instability (see *Context,* page 70).

Egypt's continuous cultural tradition—lasting over 3,000 years—is history's clearest example of how peace and prosperity go hand in hand with cultural stability. As opposed to the warring cultures of Mesopotamia, where city-state vied with city-state and empire with successive empire, Egyptian culture was predicated on unity. It was a **theocracy**, a state ruled by a god or by the god's representative —in this case a king (and very occasionally a queen), who ruled as the living representative of the sun god, Re. Egypt's government was indistinguishable from its religion, and its religion manifested itself in nature, in the flow of the Nile, the heat of the sun, and in the journey of the sun through the day and night and through the seasons. In the last judgment of the soul after death, Egyptians believed that the heart was weighed to determine whether it was "found

Major Periods of Ancient Egyptian History

The dates of the periods of Egyptian history, as well as the kingships within them, should be regarded as approximate. Each king numbered his own regnal years, and insufficient information about the reign of each king results in dates that sometimes vary, especially in the earlier periods, by as much as 100 years. Although there is general consensus on the duration of most individual reigns and dynasties, there is none concerning starting and ending points.

5500–2972 BCE	**Predynastic Period** *No formal dynasties*	Reign of Narmer and unification of Upper and Lower Egypt
2972–2647 BCE	**Early Dynastic Period** *Dynasties 1–2*	A unified Egypt ruled from Memphis
2647–2124 BCE	**Old Kingdom** *Dynasties 3–8*	The stepped pyramid at Saqqara in Dynasty 3; Pyramids at Giza in Dynasty 4
2124–2040 BCE	**First Intermediate Period** *Dynasties 9–10*	Egypt divided between a Northern power center at Hierakonpolis and a Southern one at Thebes
2040–1648 BCE	**Middle Kingdom** *Dynasties 11–16*	Reunification of Upper and Lower Egypt
1648–1540 BCE	**Second Intermediate Period** *Dynasty 17*	Syro-Palestinian invaders, the Hyksos, hold Lower Egypt and much of Upper Egypt until the Thebans defeat them
1540–1069 BCE	**New Kingdom** *Dynasties 18–20*	Reunification of Egypt; an extended period of prosperity and artistic excellence
1069–715 BCE	**Third Intermediate Period** *Dynasties 21–24*	More political volatility
715–332 BCE	**Late Period** *Dynasties 25–31*	Foreign invasions, beginning with the Kushites from the south and ending with Alexander the Great from the north

true by trial of the Great Balance." Balance in all things—in nature, in social life, in art, and in rule—this was the constant aim of the individual, the state, and, Egyptians believed, the gods.

Whereas in Mesopotamia the flood was largely a destructive force (recall the flood in the *Epic of Gilgamesh*; see Chapter 2), in Egypt it had a more complex meaning. It could, indeed, be destructive, sometimes rising so high that great devastation resulted. But without it, the Egyptians knew, their culture could not endure. So, in Egyptian art and culture, a more complex way of thinking about nature, and about life itself, developed. Every aspect of Egyptian life is countered by an opposite and equal force, which contradicts and negates it, and every act of negation gives rise to its opposite again. As a result, events are cyclical, as abundance is born of devastation and devastation closely follows abundance. Likewise, just as the floods brought the Nile Valley back to life each year, the Egyptians believed that rebirth necessarily followed death. So their religion, which played a large part in their lives, reflected the cycle of the river itself.

Egyptian Religion: Cyclical Harmony

The religion of ancient Egypt, like that of Mesopotamia, was *polytheistic*, consisting of many gods and goddesses who were associated with natural forces and realms (see *Context*, page 71). When represented, gods and goddesses have human bodies and human or animal heads, and wear crowns or other headgear that identifies them by their attributes. The religion reflected an ordered universe in which the stars and planets, the various gods, and basic human activities were thought to be part of a grand and harmonious design. A person who did not disrupt this harmony did not fear death because his or her spirit would live on forever.

At the heart of this religion were creation stories that explained how the gods and the world came into being. Chief among the Egyptian gods was Re, god of the sun. According to these stories, at the beginning of time, the Nile created a great mound of silt, out of which Re was born. It was understood that Re had a close personal relationship with the king, who was considered the son of Re. But the king could also identify closely with other gods. The king was simultaneously believed to be the personification of the sky god, Horus, and was identified with deities associated with places like Thebes or Memphis when his power resided in those cities. Though not a full-fledged god, the king was *netjer nefer*, literally, a "junior god." That made him the representative of the people to the gods, whom he contacted through statues of divine beings placed in all temples. Through these statues, Egyptians believed, the gods manifested themselves on earth. Not only did the orderly functioning of social and political events depend upon the king's successful communication with the gods, but so did events of nature—the ebb and flow of the river chief among them.

Like the king, all the other Egyptian gods descend from Re, as if part of a family. As we have said, many can be traced back to local deities of predynastic times who later assumed greater significance at a given place—at Thebes, for instance, the trinity of Osiris, Horus, and Isis gained a special significance. Osiris, ruler of the underworld and god of the dead, was at first a local deity in the eastern Delta. According to myth, he was murdered by his wicked brother Seth, god of storms and violence, who chopped his brother into pieces and threw them into the Nile. But Osiris's wife and sister, Isis, the goddess of fertility, collected what parts she could find, put the god back together, and restored him to life. Osiris was therefore identified with the Nile itself, with its annual flood and renewal. The child of Osiris and Isis was Horus, who defeated Seth and became the mythical first king of Egypt. The actual, living king was considered the earthly manifestation of Horus (as well as the son of Re). When the living king died, he became Osiris, and his son took the throne as Horus. Thus, even the kingship was cyclical.

At Memphis, the triad of Ptah, Sakhmet, and Nefertum held sway. A stone inscription at Memphis describes Ptah as the supreme artisan and creator of all things (**Reading 3.1**):

READING 3.1

from Memphis, "This It Is Said of Ptah" (ca. 2300 BCE)

This it is said of Ptah: "He who made all and created the gods." And he is Ta-tenen, who gave birth to the gods, and from whom every thing came forth, foods, provisions, divine offerings, all good things. This it is recognized and understood that he is the mightiest of the gods. Thus Ptah was satisfied after he had made all things and all divine words.

He gave birth to the gods, He made the towns,
He established the nomes [provinces],
He placed the gods in their shrines,
He settled their offerings,
He established their shrines,
He made their bodies according to their wishes,
Thus the gods entered into their bodies,
Of every wood, every stone, every clay,
Every thing that grows upon him
In which they came to be.

Sekhmet is Ptah's female companion. Depicted as a lioness, she served as protector of the king in peace and war. She is also the mother of Nefertum, a beautiful young man whose name means "perfection," small statues of whom were often carried by Egyptians for good luck.

The cyclical movement through opposing forces, embodied in stories such as that of Osiris and Isis, is one of the

CONTEXT

Some of the Principal Egyptian Gods

A Horus, son of Osiris, a sky god closely linked with the king; pictured as a hawk, or hawk-headed man.
B Seth, enemy of Horus and Osiris, god of storms; pictured as an unidentifiable creature (some believe a wild donkey), or a man with this animal's head.
C Thoth, a moon deity and god of writing, counting, and wisdom; pictured as an ibis, or ibis-headed man, often with a crescent moon on his head.
D Khnum, originally the god of the source of the Nile, pictured as a bull who shaped men out of clay on his potter's wheel; later, god of pottery.
E Hathor, goddess of love, birth, and death; pictured as a woman with cow horns and a sun disk on her head.
F Sobek, the crocodile god, associated both with the fertility of the Nile, and, because of the ferocity of the crocodile, with the army's power and strength.
G Re, the sun god in his many forms; pictured as a hawk-headed man with a sun disk on his head.

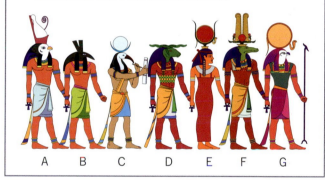

A   B   C   D   E   F   G

earliest instances of a system of religious and philosophic thought that survives even in contemporary thought. Life and death, flood and sun, even desert and oasis were part of a larger harmony of nature, one that was predictable in both the diurnal cycle of day and night but also in its seasonal patterns of repetition. A good deity like Osiris was necessarily balanced by a bad deity like Seth. The fertile Nile Valley was balanced by the harsh desert surrounding it. The narrow reaches of the upper Nile were balanced by the broad marshes of the Delta. All things were predicated upon the return of their opposite, which negates them, but which in the process completes the whole and regenerates the cycle of being and becoming once again.

Pictorial Formulas in Egyptian Art

This sense of duality, of opposites, informs even the earliest Egyptian artifacts, such as the Palette of Narmer, found at Hierakonpolis, in Upper Egypt (see *Closer Look*, pages 72–73). A palette is technically an everyday object used for grinding pigments and making body- or eye-paint.

CLOSER LOOK

The Egyptians created a style of writing very different from that of their northern neighbors in Mesopotamia. It consists of **hieroglyphs**, "writing of the gods," from the Greek *hieros*, meaning "holy," and *gluphein*, "to engrave." Although the number of signs increased over the centuries from about 700 to nearly 5,000, the system of symbolic communication underwent almost no major changes from its advent in the fourth millennium BCE until 395 CE, when Egypt was conquered by the Roman Empire. It consists of three kinds of signs: **pictograms**, or stylized drawings that represent objects or beings, which can be combined to express ideas; **phonograms**, which are pictograms used to represent sounds; and **determinatives**, signs used to indicate which category of objects or beings is in question. The Palette of Narmer is an early example of the then-developing hieroglyphic style. It consists largely of pictograms, though in the top center of each side, Narmer's name is represented as a phonogram.

The circle formed by the two elongated lions' necks intertwined on the recto, or front, of the palette is a bowl for mixing pigments. The palette celebrates the defeat by Narmer (r. ca. 3000 BCE) of his enemies and his unification of both Upper and Lower Egypt, which before this time had been at odds. So on the recto side, Narmer wears the red cobra crown of Lower Egypt, associated with the cobra goddess Wadjit of Buto in the Delta, and on the verso, or back, he wears the white crown of Upper Egypt, associated with Wadjit's sister, the vulture goddess Nekhbet of Nekheb in southern Egypt—representing his ability (and duty) to harmonize antagonistic elements.

Flanking the top of each side of the palette is a goddess wearing cow's horns; such headdresses represent the divine attributes of the figure. Later, **Hathor**, the Sky Mother, a goddess embodying all female qualities, would possess these attributes, but this early image probably represents the cow-goddess, **Bat**.

The **mace** was the chief weapon used by the king to strike down enemies, and the scene here is emblematic of his power.

As on the other side of the palette, the king is here accompanied by his sandal-bearer, who stands on his own ground-line. He carries the king's sandals to indicate that the king, who is barefoot, stands on **sacred ground**, and that his acts are themselves sacred.

Narmer, wearing the white crown of Upper Egypt, strikes down his enemy, probably the embodiment of **Lower Egypt** itself, especially since he is, in size, comparable to Narmer himself, suggesting he is likewise a leader.

Two more figures represent the defeated enemy. Behind the one on the left is a small aerial view of a **fortified city**; behind the one on the right, a **gazelle trap**. Perhaps together they represent Narmer's victory over both city and countryside.

The hawk is a symbolic representation of the god **Horus**. The king was regarded as the earthly embodiment of Horus. Here, Horus has a human hand with which he holds a rope tied to a symbolic representation of a conquered land and people.

A human head grows from the same ground as six **papyrus** blossoms, possibly the symbol of Lower Egypt.

This hieroglyph identifies the man that Narmer is about to kill, a name otherwise unknown.

Palette of Narmer, verso side, from Hierakonpolis. Dynasty 1, ca. 3000 BCE. Schist, height 25¼". Egyptian Museum, Cairo.

View the Closer Look for the Palette of Narmer on **MyArtsLab**

The Palette of Narmer was not meant for actual use. Rather, it is a **votive**, or ritual object, a gift to a god or goddess that was placed in a temple to ensure that the king, or perhaps some temple official, would have access to a palette throughout eternity. It may or may not register actual historical events, although, in fact, Egypt marks its beginnings with the unification of its Upper and Lower territories. Subsequent kings, at any rate, presented themselves in almost identical terms, as triumphing over their enemies, mace in hand, even though they had played no role in a similar military campaign. It is even possible that by the time of Narmer such conventions were already in place, although our system of numbering Egyptian dynasties begins with him. Whether the scene depicted is symbolic, the **pictorial formulas**, or conventions of representation, that Egyptian culture used for the rest of its history are fully developed in this piece.

Something to Think About ...

Do you see any connection between the Egyptian hieroglyphs, as seen on the Palette of Narmer, and Sumerian cuneiform writing?

These are two instances of the hieroglyphic sign for **Narmer**, consisting of a catfish above a chisel. Each individual hieroglyph is a pictogram but is utilized here for its phonetic sound. *Nar* is the word for "catfish," and *mer* is the word for "chisel" (or, perhaps, "sickly")—hence "Narmer." In the lower instance, the hieroglyph identifies the king. In the instance at the top, the king's name is inside a depiction of his palace seen simultaneously from above, as a ground plan, and from the front, as a facade. This device, called a *serekh*, is traditionally used to hold the king's name.

We are able to identify **Narmer** not only from his hieroglyphic name, next to him, but by his relative size. As befits the king, he is larger than anyone else.

Similarly positioned on the other side of the palette and identified by the accompanying hieroglyph, this is the king's **sandal-bearer**.

The **bull** here strikes down his victim and is another representation of the king's might and power. Note that in the depictions of Narmer striking down his victim and in procession, a bull's tail hangs from his waistband.

The defeated **dead** lie in two rows, their decapitated heads between their feet. Narmer in sacred procession reviews them, while above them, a tiny Horus (the hawk) looks on.

This is the **mixing bowl** of the palette. The lions may represent competing forces brought under control by the king. Each is held in check by one of the king's **lion-tamers**, figures that in some sense represent state authority.

This is a representation of a **fortified city** as seen both from above, as a floor plan, and from the front, as a facade. It is meant to represent the actual site of Narmer's victory.

Palette of Narmer, recto side, from Hierakonpolis. Dynasty 1, ca. 3000 BCE. Schist, height 25¼". Egyptian Museum, Cairo.

The scenes on the Palette of Narmer are in low relief. Like those on the *Royal Standard of Ur* (see Fig. 2.8 in Chapter 2), they are arranged in registers that provide a ground line upon which the figures stand (the two lion-tamers are an exception). The figures typically face to the right, though often, as is the case here, the design is balanced left and right. The artist represents the various parts of the human figure in what the Egyptians thought was their most characteristic view. So, the face, arms, legs, and feet are in profile, with the left foot advanced in front of the right. The eye and shoulders are in front view. The mouth, navel and hips, and knees are in three-quarter view. As a result, the viewer sees each person in a **composite view**, the integration of multiple perspectives into a single unified image.

In Egyptian art, not only the figures but the scenes themselves unite two contradictory points of view into a single image. In the Palette of Narmer, the king approaches his dead enemies from the side, but they lie beheaded on the ground before him as seen from above. Egyptian art often represents architecture in the same terms. At the top middle of the Palette of Narmer, the external facade of the palace is depicted simultaneously from above, in a kind of ground plan, with its niched facade at the bottom. The design contains Narmer's Horus-name, consisting of a catfish and a chisel. The hieroglyphic signs for Narmer could not be interpreted until the Rosetta Stone was discovered (see *Context*, page 77), but we are still not sure whether it is to be read "Narmer," which are the later phonetic values of the signs. In fact, later meanings of these signs suggest that it might be read "sick catfish," which seems rather unlikely.

THE OLD KINGDOM

In what ways do the art and architecture of the Old Kingdom reflect religious beliefs?

Although the Palette of Narmer probably commemorates an event in life, as a votive object it is devoted, like most surviving Egyptian art and architecture, to burial and the afterlife. The Egyptians buried their dead on the west side of the Nile, where the sun sets, a symbolic reference to death and rebirth, since the sun always rises again. The pyramid was the first monumental royal tomb. A massive physical manifestation of the reality of the king's death, it was also the symbolic embodiment of his eternal life. It would endure for generations as, Egyptians believed, would the king's *ka*. This idea is comparable to an enduring "soul" or "life force," a concept found in many other religions. The *ka*, which all persons possessed, was created at the same time as the physical body, itself essential for the person's existence since it provided the *ka* with an individual identity in which its personality, or *ba*, might also manifest itself. This meant that it was necessary to preserve the body after death so that the *ba* and *ka* might still

recognize it for eternity. All the necessities of the afterlife, from food to furniture to entertainment, were placed in the pyramid's burial chamber with the king's body.

Funerary temples and grounds surrounded the temple so that priests could continuously replenish these offerings in order to guarantee the king's continued existence after death. Pyramids are the massive architectural product of what is known as the Old Kingdom, which dates from 2647 to 2124 BCE, a period of unprecedented achievement that solidified the accomplishments of the Early Dynastic Period initiated by Narmer.

The Stepped Pyramid at Saqqara

The first great pyramid was the stepped pyramid of Djoser (r. ca. 2628–2609 BCE), who ruled at Saqqara, just south of present-day Cairo (Figs. **3.3**, **3.4**). It predates the ziggurat at Ur, the great temple of ancient Sumer in Mesopotamia (see Fig. 2.1 in Chapter 2), by nearly 500 years and is therefore the first great monumental architecture in human history to have survived. It consists of a series of stepped platforms rising to a height of 197 feet, but since it sits on an elevated piece of ground, it appears even taller to the approaching visitor.

Above ground level, the pyramid of Djoser contains no rooms or cavities. The king's body rested below the first

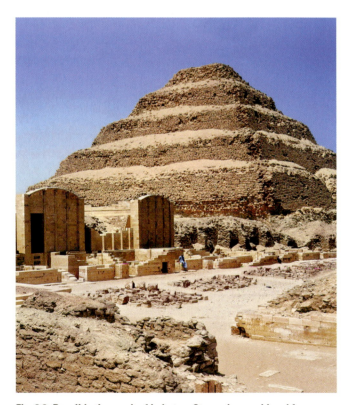

Fig. 3.3 Possibly the work of Imhotep, Stepped pyramid and funerary complex of Djoser, Saqqara. Dynasty 3, 2610 BCE. Limestone, height of pyramid 197'. The base of this enormous structure measures 460 feet east to west, and 388 feet north to south. It is the earliest known use of cut stone for architecture. The architect, Imhotep, was Djoser's prime minister. He is the first architect in history known to us by name.

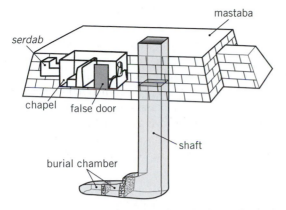

Fig. 3.4 Section and restored view of a typical mastaba tomb. The mastaba is a brick or stone structure with a sloping (or "battered") wall. The *serdab* is a chamber for a statue of the deceased.

level of the pyramid, in a chamber some 90 feet beneath the original **mastaba**—a trapezoidal tomb structure that derives its name from the Arabic word for "bench." Such mastabas predate Djoser's pyramid but continued to be used for the burial of figures of lesser importance for centuries. The pyramid is situated in a much larger, ritual area than this earlier form of tomb. The total enclosure of this enormous complex originally measured 1,800 by 900 feet—or six football fields by three.

The idea of stacking six increasingly smaller mastabas on top of one another to create a monumental symbol of the everlasting spirit of the king was apparently the brainchild

of Imhotep, Djoser's chief architect. He is the first artist or architect whose name survives, and his reputation continued to grow for centuries after his death. Graffiti written on the side of the pyramid a thousand years after Djoser's death praises Imhotep for a building that seems "as if heaven were within it" and as though "heaven rained myrrh and dripped incense upon it."

Three Pyramids at Giza

From Djoser's time forward, the tomb of the king was dramatically distinguished from those of other members of the royal family. But within 50 years, the stepped form of Djoser's pyramid was abandoned and replaced with a smooth-sided, starkly geometric monument consisting of four triangular sides slanting upward from a square base to an apex directly over the center of the square. The most magnificent examples of this form are found at Giza, just north of Djoser's tomb at Saqqara.

Khufu's Pyramid Of the three pyramids at Giza, Khufu's (r. 2549–2526 BCE) is both the earliest and the grandest one (Fig. 3.5), measuring 479 feet high on a base measuring 755 feet square, built from an estimated 2.3 million stone blocks, weighing between 2 and 5 tons each. Historians speculate that the stones were dragged up inclined ramps made of compacted rubble bonded and made slippery with a kind of lime-clay, called *tafl*, although they may well have been raised from tier to tier up the side of the pyramid by means of levers not unlike those used by the workers at

● **Watch** an architectural simulation about the pyramid on **MyArtsLab**

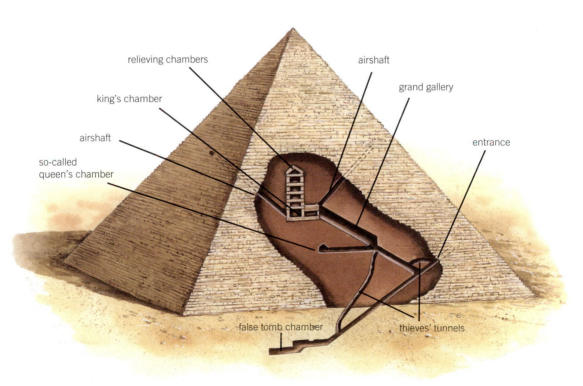

Fig. 3.5 Cutaway elevation of the pyramid of Khufu.

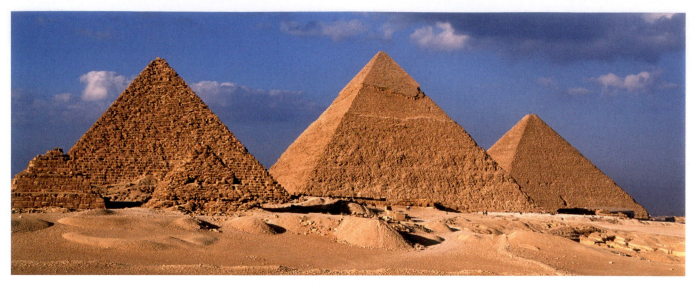

Fig. 3.6 The pyramids of Menkaure (ca. 2470 BCE), Khafre (ca. 2500 BCE), and Khufu (ca. 2530 BCE). Giza was an elaborate complex of ritual temples, shrines, and ceremonial causeways, all leading to one or another of the three giant pyramids.

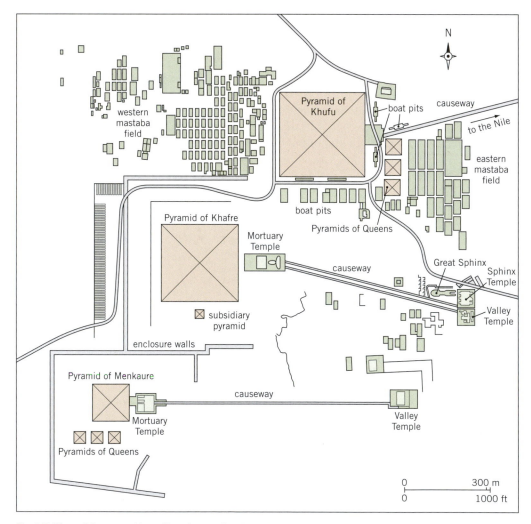

Fig. 3.7 Plan of the pyramids at Giza. Surrounding the northernmost pyramid of Khufu were mastaba fields, a royal cemetery in which were buried various officials, priests, and nobility of the king's court. When a king died in the royal palaces on the east bank of the Nile, his body was transported across the river to a valley temple on the west bank. After a ritual ceremony, it was carried up the causeway to the temple in front of the pyramid where another ritual was performed—the "opening of the mouth," in which priests "fed" the deceased's *ka* a special meal. The body was then sealed in a relatively small tomb deep in the heart of the pyramid (see Fig. 3.5).

The Rosetta Stone

Until the nineteenth century, Egyptian hieroglyphs remained untranslated. The key to finally deciphering them was the Rosetta Stone, a discovery made by Napoleon's army in 1799 and named for the town in the Egyptian Delta near where it was found. On the stone was a decree issued in 196 BCE by the priests of Memphis honoring the ruler Ptolemy V, recorded in two different languages and three separate scripts—Greek, demotic Egyptian (an informal and stylized form of writing used by the people—the "*demos*"), which first came into use in the eighth century BCE, and finally hieroglyphs, the high formal writing used exclusively by priests and scribes.

The stone was almost immediately understood to be a key to deciphering hieroglyphs, but its significance was not fully realized until years later. French linguist Jean-François Champollion began an intensive study of the stone in 1808 and concluded that the pictures and symbols in hieroglyphic writing stood for specific phonetic sounds, or, as he described it, constituted a "phonetic alphabet." A key to unlocking the code was a **cartouche**, an ornamental and symbolic frame reserved for the names of rulers. Champollion noticed that the cartouche surrounded a name, and deciphered the phonetic symbols for P, O, L, and T—four of the letters in the name Ptolemy. In another cartouche, he found the symbols for Cleopatra's name. By 1822, he had worked out enough of the writing system and the language to translate two texts, but Egyptologists have continued to improve and refine our understanding of the language to this day.

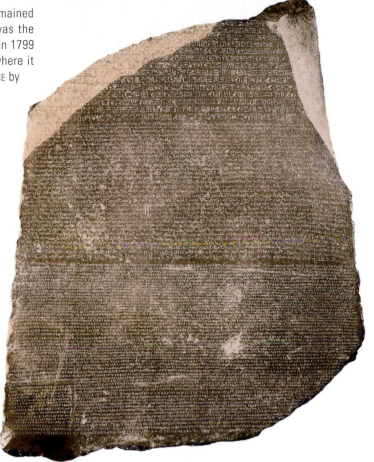

The Rosetta Stone. 196 BCE. Basalt, 46½" × 30⅛". © The Trustees of the British Museum. The top, parts of which have been lost, contains the formal hieroglyphs; the middle, demotic Egyptian; and the bottom, the Greek text of the decree.

Stonehenge (see *Closer Look*, Chapter 1, pages 16–17). Whatever feats of engineering accomplished the transport of so much stone into such an enormous configuration, what still dazzles us is this pyramid's astronomical and mathematical precision. It is perfectly oriented to the four cardinal points of the compass (as are the other two pyramids, which were positioned later, probably using Khufu's alignment as a reference point).

The two airshafts that run from the two top chambers seem oriented to specific stars, including Sirius, the brightest star in the night sky. The relationship between the various sides of the structure suggests that the Egyptians understood and made use of the mathematical value π (pi). All of this has led to considerable theorizing about "the secret of the pyramids," the other two of which are Khafre's (r. 2518–2493 BCE), and Menkaure's (r. 2488–2460 BCE)

(Figs. **3.6** and **3.7**). Most convincing is the theory that the pyramid's sides represented the descending rays of the sun god Re, whose cult was particularly powerful at the time the pyramids were built. Because they were covered in a polished limestone sheath (the only remnant survives atop Khafre's pyramid), the sun must have glistened off them. And one convincing text survives: "I have trodden these rays as ramps under my feet where I mount up to my mother Uraeus on the brow of Re." Whatever their symbolic significance, the pyramids of Giza are above all extraordinary feats of human construction.

The Great Sphinx In front of the pyramid dedicated to Khufu's son Khafre, and near the head of the causeway leading from the valley temple to the mortuary temple (see Fig. 3.7), is the largest statue ever made in the ancient

Monumental Royal Sculpture: Perfection and Eternity

The Sphinx's monumentality indicates the growing importance of sculpture to the Egyptian funerary tradition. The word for sculpture in Egyptian is, in fact, the same as for giving birth, and funerary sculpture served the same purpose as the pyramids themselves—to preserve and guarantee the king's existence after death, thereby providing a kind of rebirth. Although there are thousands of limestone and not a few sandstone funerary monuments, the materials of choice were diorite, schist, and granite, stones as durable and enduring as the *ka* itself. These stones can also take on a high polish and, because they are not prone to fracture, can be finely detailed when carved. These stones were carved into three main types of male statue: (1) a seated

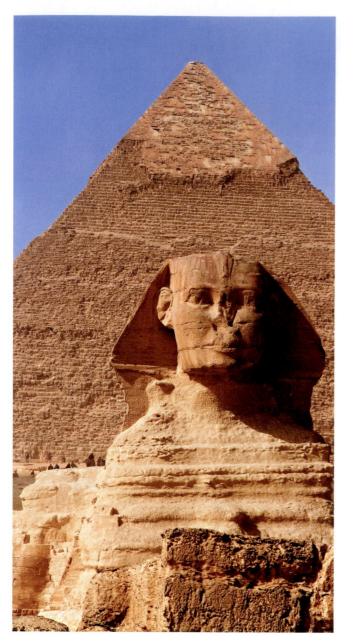

Fig. 3.8 The Great Sphinx (with the pyramid of Khafre in the background), Giza. Dynasty 4, ca. 2500 BCE. Limestone, height approx. 65'. Over the years, legend has had it that the artillery forces of Napoleon's invading army shot off the Sphinx's nose and ears. In truth, a fanatical Muslim cleric from Cairo severely damaged the statue in an attack in 1378.

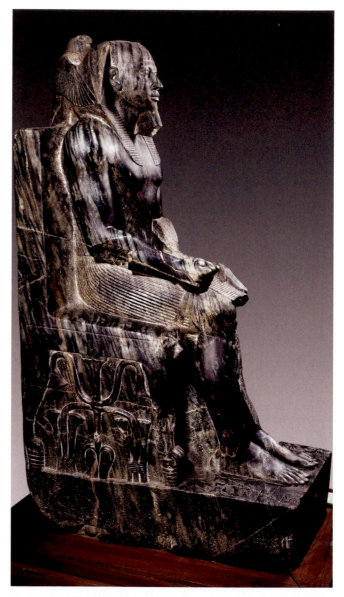

Fig. 3.9 Seated statue of Khafre, from the valley temple of Khafre, Giza. Dynasty 4, ca. 2500 BCE. Diorite, height 66". Egyptian Museum, Cairo. On the side of Khafre's throne, intertwining lotus and papyrus blossoms signify his rule of both Upper and Lower Egypt.

world, the Great Sphinx, carved out of an existing limestone knoll (Fig. 3.8). As in Egyptian depictions of the gods, the Sphinx is half man and half animal. But where the gods are normally depicted with an animal's head and a human body, the Sphinx is just the opposite: a lion's body supports the head of a king wearing the royal headcloth. The sculpture probably represents Khafre himself protecting the approach to his own funerary complex, and thus it requires Khafre's physical likeness, but its combination of animal and human forms also suggests the king's connection to the gods.

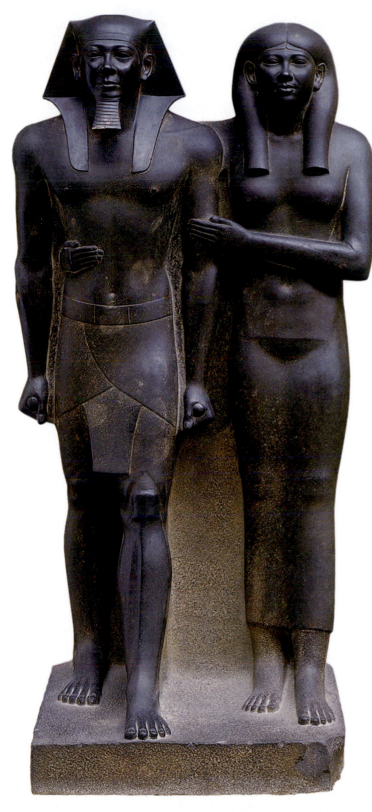

Fig. 3.10 *Menkaure with a Queen*, probably Khamerernebty, from the valley temple of Menkaure, Giza. Dynasty 4, ca. 2460 BCE. Schist, height 54¼". Museum of Fine Arts, Boston. Harvard University–Boston Museum of Fine Arts Expedition, 11.1738. Photograph © 2014 Museum of Fine Arts, Boston. Note that the woman's close-fitting attire is nearly transparent, indicating a very fine weave of linen.

figure, looking directly ahead, his feet side by side, one hand resting flat on the knee, the other clenched in a fist; (2) a standing figure, his gaze fixed into the distance, left foot forward, both hands alongside the body with fists clenched; and (3) a figure seated on the ground with legs crossed. The first two types were used for kings as well as important officials. The third was used for royal scribes. Also popular were statue pairs of husband and wife, either seated or standing.

The statue of Khafre from his valley temple at Giza (see Fig. 3.7) is an example of the first type (Fig. **3.9**). The king sits rigidly upright and frontal, wearing a simple kilt and the same royal headdress as the Great Sphinx outside the valley temple. His throne is formed of the bodies of two stylized lions. Behind him, as if caressing his head, is a hawk, a manifestation of the god Horus, extending its wings in a protective gesture. In Egyptian society, the strong care for and protect the weak; so too Horus watches over Khafre as Khafre watches over his people. Because Khafre is a king and a divinity, he is shown with a smooth, perfectly proportioned face and a flawless, well-muscled body. This idealized anatomy was used in Egyptian sculpture regardless of the actual age and body of the king portrayed, its perfection mirroring the perfection of the gods themselves. Most Egyptian statues were *monolithic*, or carved out of a single piece of stone, even those depicting more than a single figure.

The same effect is apparent in the statue of Menkaure with a woman—perhaps his queen, his mother, or even a goddess—that was also found at his valley temple at Giza (Fig. **3.10**). Here, the deep space created by carving away the side of the stone to expose fully the king's right side seems to free him from the stone. He stands with one foot ahead of the other in the second traditional pose, the conventional depiction of a standing figure. He is not walking. Both feet are planted firmly on the ground (and so his left leg is, of necessity, slightly longer than his right). His back is firmly implanted in the stone panel behind him, but he seems to have emerged farther from it than the female figure who accompanies him, as if to underscore his power and might. Although the woman is almost the same size as the man, her stride is markedly shorter than his. She embraces him, her arm reaching round his back, in a gesture that reminds us of Horus's protective embrace of Khafre, but suggests also the simple marital affection of husband and wife. The ultimate effect of both of these sculptures—their solidity and unity, their sense of resolution—testifies finally to their purpose, which is to endure for eternity.

The Sculpture of the Everyday

Idealized athletic physiques, austere dignity, and grand scale were for royalty and officials only. Lesser figures were depicted more naturally, with flabby physiques or rounded shoulders, and on a more human scale. The third traditional type of male figure in Egyptian sculpture was the royal scribe, and in one such, we can see that a soft,

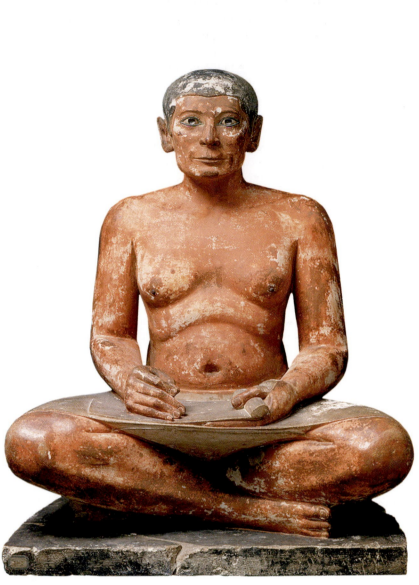

Fig. 3.11 *Seated Scribe*, from his mastaba, Saqqara. Dynasty 5, ca. 2400 BCE. Painted limestone, height 21". Musée du Louvre, Paris. Scribes were the most educated of Egyptians—not only able to read and write but accomplished in arithmetic, algebra, religion, and law. Their *ka* statues necessarily accompanied those of their kings into the afterlife.

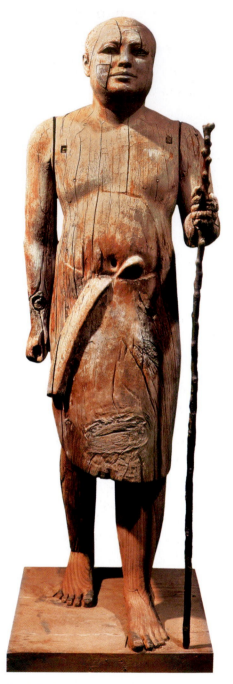

Fig. 3.12 *Priest Ka-aper* (also known as the "*Sheikh el-Beled*"), from his mastaba, Saqqara. Dynasty 5, ca. 2450 BCE. Plaster and painted wood, height 3'7". Egyptian Museum, Cairo. This paunchy priest lacks the idealized physique reserved for more eminent nobility.

flabby body replaces the hardened chest of a king (Fig. 3.11). But the scribe's pose, seated cross-legged on the floor, marks him as literate and a valuable official of the king. The stone was carved out around his arms and head so that, instead of the monumental space of the king's sculpture, which derives from its compactness and its attachment to the slab of stone behind it, the scribe seems to occupy real space. The scribe's task was important: His statue would serve the king through eternity as he had served the king in life.

Statues of lesser persons were often made of less permanent materials, such as wood. Carved from separate pieces, with the arms attached to the body at the shoulders, such statues as that of the priest Ka-aper, found in his own tomb at Saqqara, could assume a more natural pose (Fig. 3.12). The eyes, made of rock crystal, seem vital and lively. Originally, the statue was covered with plaster and painted (men were usually red-brown, like the seated scribe in Fig. 3.11, and women yellow). Small statues of servants, especially those who made food, have also been found in the tombs of officials.

THE MIDDLE KINGDOM AT THEBES

How do the art and architecture of the Middle Kingdom differ from those of the Old Kingdom?

The Old Kingdom collapsed for a variety of reasons—drought, a weakened kingship, greater autonomy of local administrators—all of which led to an Egypt divided between competing power centers in the North and South. After over 150 years of tension, Nebhepetre Mentuhotep II (r. 2040–1999 BCE) assumed the rule of the Southern capital at Thebes, defeated the Northern kings, and reunited the country. The Middle Kingdom begins with his reign.

Thebes, on the west bank of the Nile, was the primary capital of the Middle Kingdom and included within its outer limits Karnak, Luxor, and other sites on the east bank (see Map 3.1). Although certain traditions remained in place from the Old Kingdom, change was beginning to occur.

Middle Kingdom Literature

One of the greatest changes took place in literature. Earlier, most writing and literature served a sacred purpose. But, during the Middle Kingdom, writers produced stories, instructive literature, satires, poems, biography, history, and scientific writings. Much of the surviving writing is highly imaginative, including tales of encounters with the supernatural. Among the most interesting texts is *The Teachings of Khety*, a satiric example of instructive literature in which a scribe tries to convince his son to follow him into the profession. He begins by extolling the virtues of the scribe's life: "I shall make you love books more than your mother, and I shall place their excellence before you. It is greater than any office. There is nothing like it on earth." But he goes on to defend his own work by detailing all that is wrong with every other profession available to him:

> I have seen a coppersmith at his work at the door of his furnace. His fingers were like the claws of the crocodile, and he stank more than fish excrement. …
>
> I shall also describe to you the bricklayer. His kidneys are painful. When he must be outside in the wind, he lays bricks without a garment. His belt is a cord for his back, a string for his buttocks. His strength has vanished through fatigue and stiffness. …
>
> The sandal maker is utterly wretched carrying his tubs of oil. His stores are provided with carcasses, and what he bites is hides.

The work provides us with a broad survey of daily life in the Middle Kingdom. It ends in a series of admonitions about how a young scribe must behave—advice that parents have been giving children for millennia (see **Reading 3.2**, page 95 for more of the text).

Middle Kingdom Sculpture

Although a new brand of literature began to appear in the Middle Kingdom, sculpture remained firmly rooted in tradition. The only innovation in the traditional seated king funerary statue of Nebhepetre Mentuhotep II is that the pose has been slightly modified (Fig. **3.13**). Most noticeably, the king crosses his arms tightly across his chest. The pose is reminiscent of a **mummy**, an embalmed body wrapped for burial (see *Materials & Techniques*, page 86). The king's mummylike pose probably refers to the growing cult of the god Osiris, discussed earlier. As early as the late Fifth Dynasty, the dead king was called "Osiris [King's Name]." By the time of the Middle Kingdom, ordinary, non-royal people were beginning to be identified with Osiris as well. Osiris, god of the underworld, overseer of the judgment of souls, is usually depicted wrapped in white linen, but unlike Nebhepetre Mentuhotep II, whose legs and hands are exposed, Osiris is usually completely wrapped.

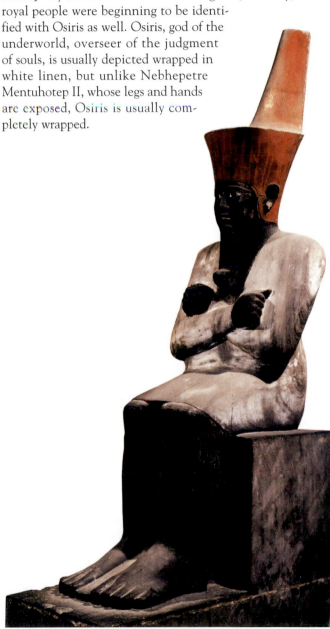

Fig. 3.13 *Nebhepetre Mentuhotep II*, **from his funerary temple at Deir el-Bahri, western Thebes. Dynasty 11, ca. 2000 BCE.** Painted sandstone, height 72". Egyptian Museum, Cairo. The king's dark color here may refer to the "black land" of the Nile Valley, another symbol of the cycle of death and resurrection that is embodied in the Osiris myth.

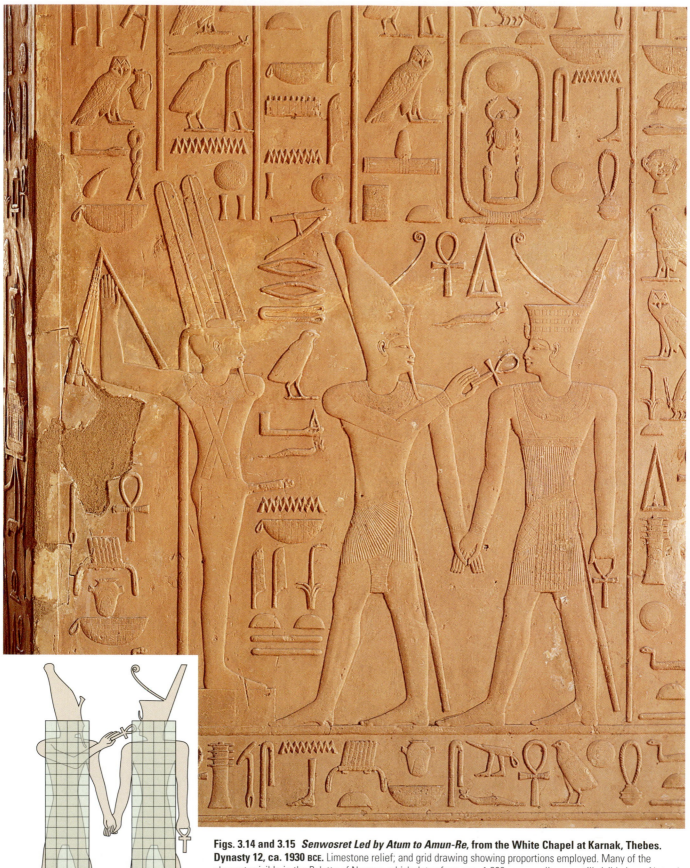

Figs. 3.14 and 3.15 *Senwosret Led by Atum to Amun-Re,* **from the White Chapel at Karnak, Thebes. Dynasty 12, ca. 1930 BCE.** Limestone relief; and grid drawing showing proportions employed. Many of the elements visible in the Palette of Narmer, which dates from over 1,000 years earlier, are still visible here. Not only are the bodies depicted in the conventional poses, but note the two figures on the right: King Senwosret wears the white crown of Upper Egypt, and the god Atum wears the double crown of both Upper and Lower Egypt. Note also that, just like Narmer, Senwosret and Atum each wear a bull's tail draped from their waist.

In relief carvings found in the temples of the Middle Kingdom, the traditional pose of the figure, which dates back to Narmer's time, still survives. The figures in a Twelfth Dynasty relief from the White Chapel at Karnak are depicted with right foot forward, feet and face in profile, and the shoulders and hips frontal (Fig. 3.14). But we have learned that figures were now conceived according to a *grid*. Much like a piece of graph paper, a grid is a system of regularly spaced horizontally and vertically crossed lines. Used in the initial design process, it enables the artist to transfer a design or enlarge it easily (Fig. 3.15). In the Egyptian system, the height of the figure from the top of the forehead (where it disappears beneath the headdress) to the soles of the feet is 18 squares. The top of the knee is 6 squares high, the waist, 11. The elbows are at the twelfth square, the armpits at the fourteenth, and the shoulders at the sixteenth. Each square also relates to the human body as a measure, representing the equivalent of one clenched fist.

This particular relief depicts the rise of yet another god in the Middle Kingdom—Amun, or, to associate him more closely with the sun, Amun-Re. He was originally the chief god of Thebes, but as the city became more prominent, Amun became the chief deity of all of Egypt. His name would appear (sometimes as "Amen") in many subsequent royal names—such as Amenhotep ("Amun is Satisfied") or, most famously, Tutankhamun ("The Living Image of Amun"). In the relief from the White Chapel, Atum, the god of the city of Heliopolis, just north of Memphis, that Nebhepetre Mentuhotep II had defeated four generations earlier, leads King Senwosret I (r. 1960–1916 BCE) to Amun, who stands at the left on a pedestal with an erect penis, signifying fertility. Atum turns to Senwosret and holds the hieroglyph **ankh**, signifying life, to his nose. The king is depicted as having received the gift, since he holds it in his left hand.

The continuity and stability implied by this relief ended abruptly in 1648 BCE, when a Hyksos king declared himself King of Egypt. The Hyksos were foreigners who had apparently lived in Egypt for some time. They made local alliances, introduced the horse-drawn chariot (which may well have helped them achieve their military dominance), and led Egypt into another "intermediate" period of disunity and disarray. Dissatisfaction with Hyksos rule originated, once again, in Thebes, and finally, in 1540 BCE, the Theban king Ahmose defeated the last Hyksos ruler and inaugurated the New Kingdom.

THE NEW KINGDOM

How did Akhenaten transform the New Kingdom's traditional worship of Amun?

The worship of Amun that developed in the Twelfth Dynasty continued though the Middle Kingdom and into the Eighteenth Dynasty of the New Kingdom, 500 years later. In fact, there is clear evidence that the rulers of the Eighteenth Dynasty sought to align themselves closely with the aims and aspirations of the Middle Kingdom. The funerary temple of Hatshepsut in western Thebes is an interesting case in point.

Temple and Tomb Architecture and Their Rituals

Hatshepsut (r. ca. 1479–1457 BCE) was the daughter of Thutmose I (r. ca. 1504–1492 BCE) and married her half-brother Thutmose II. When her husband died, she became regent for their young son, Thutmose III, and ruled for 20 years as king (priests of Amun, in fact, declared her king). As her reign continued, sculptures of Hatshepsut increasingly lost many of their female characteristics until she is barely distinguishable, given family resemblances, from later sculptures of her son, Thutmose III (Fig. 3.16). Her breasts are barely visible, and she wears the false beard of

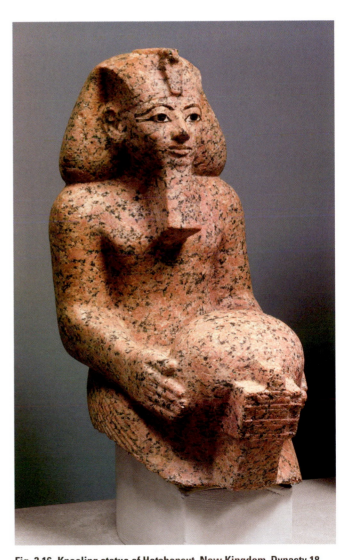

Fig. 3.16 Kneeling statue of Hatshepsut. New Kingdom, Dynasty 18, Joint reign of Hatshepsut and Thutmose III. ca. 1473–1458 BCE. Granite, paint; height 34¼", width 12¹³⁄₁₆", diameter 20¼". The Metropolitan Museum of Art, New York. This is one of at least 8, perhaps 12, small kneeling statues of Hatshepsut believed to have lined the processional way of her temple at Deir el-Bahri.

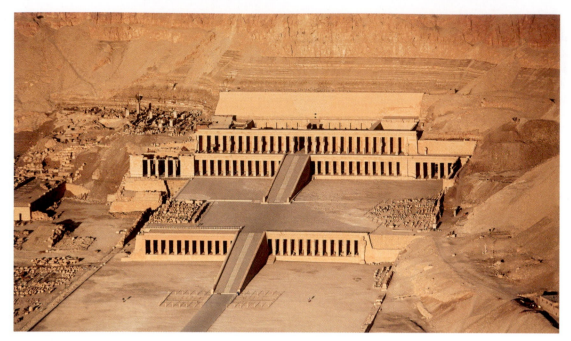

Fig. 3.17 **Senenmut, Funerary temple of Hatshepsut, Deir el-Bahri, western Thebes. Dynasty 18, ca. 1460 BCE. At the far left is the ramp and funerary temple of Nebhepetre Mentuhotep II. Dynasty 11 (Middle Kingdom), ca. 2000 BCE.** Senenmut's name is associated with the temple because he has titles that suggest he oversaw the project, and he had little images of himself carved behind doors, where they would not be seen. But he may or may not have been the actual architect.

View the Closer Look for the funerary temple of Hatshepsut on **MyArtsLab**

the Egyptian kings, the traditional symbol of the king's power and majesty.

Hatshepsut's temple, built on three levels, is modeled precisely on the two-level funerary temple of Nebhepetre Mentuhotep II, next to which it stands. Hatshepsut's temple is partly freestanding and partly cut into the rock cliffs of the hill (Fig. **3.17**). The first level consisted of a large open plaza backed by a long **colonnade**, a sequence or row of columns supporting a lintel and roof. A long ramp led up to a second court that housed shrines to Anubis (god of embalming and agent of Osiris) and Hathor (the Sky Mother, probably a reference to Hatshepsut's gender). Another ramp led to another colonnade fronted with colossal royal statues, two more colonnades, a series of chapels, and behind them, cut into the cliff, a central shrine to Amun-Re.

The Great Temple of Amun at Karnak Directly across the valley from Hatshepsut's temple, and parallel to it, is the Great Temple of Amun at Karnak. It is a product of the age in which the Egyptian king came to be known as **pharaoh**, from Egyptian *per-aa*, "great house," meaning the palace of the king. In the same way that we refer to the presidency as "the White House," or the government of England as "10 Downing Street," so the Egyptians, beginning in the Eighteenth Dynasty, came to speak of their rulers by invoking their place of residence. (The modern practice of referring to all Egyptian kings as "pharaoh," incidentally, can probably be attributed to its use in the Hebrew Bible to refer to both earlier and later Egyptian kings.)

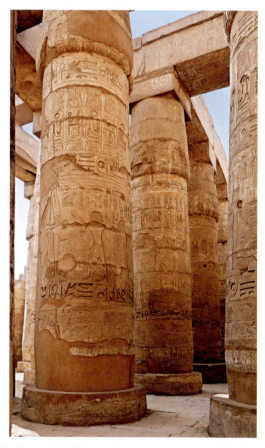

Fig. 3.18 **Hypostyle hall, Great Temple of Amun, Karnak, Thebes. Dynasty 19, ca. 1294–1212 BCE.** It is difficult to sense the massive scale of these columns from a photo. Dozens of people could easily stand on the top of one of them, and it takes at least eight people, holding hands, to span the circumference of a given column near its base. An average person is no taller than the base and first drum, or circular disk of stone, forming the column.

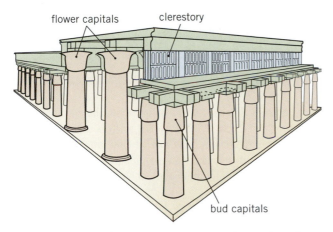

flower capitals   clerestory

bud capitals

Fig. 3.19 Reconstruction drawing of the hypostyle hall, Great Temple of Amun, Karnak. Dynasty 19, ca. 1294–1212 BCE. The foreground columns have bud capitals, and the hall's central columns are taller with flower capitals. The center columns are taller than the outer ones, to admit light into the hall through windows along the upper walls. (Note that here the first five rows of columns in the front have been omitted for clarity. There are seven rows of columns on each side of the center rows.)

The pharaohs engaged in massive building programs during the New Kingdom, lavishing as much attention on their temples as their tombs. Not only was Amun a focus of worship, but so was his wife, Mut, and their son Khonsu. Although each temple is unique, all of the New Kingdom temples share a number of common architectural premises. They were fronted by a **pylon**, or massive gateway with sloping walls, which served to separate the disorderly world of everyday existence from the orderly world of the temple.

Behind the pylon was one or more open courtyards leading to a roofed **hypostyle hall**, a vast space filled with the many massive columns required to hold up the stone slabs forming the roof. The columns in the hypostyle hall of the Great Temple of Amun at Karnak have flower and bud capitals (Figs. **3.18**, **3.19**). Behind the hypostyle hall was the **sanctuary**, in which the statue of the deity was placed. To proceed into the temple was to proceed out of the light of the outside world and into a darker and more spiritual space. The temple was therefore a metaphor for birth and creation.

Each day, priests washed the deity statue, clothed it with a clean garment, and offered it two meals of delicious food. It was the "spirit" of the food that the gods enjoyed, and after the offering, the priests themselves ate the meals. Only kings and priests were admitted to the sanctuary, but

at festival times, the cult statue of the deity was removed to lead processions—perhaps across the Nile to the funerary temples of the kings or to visit other deities in their temples (Mut regularly "visited" Amun, for instance).

The Great Temple of Amun at Karnak was the largest temple in Egypt. Although the temple was begun in the Middle Kingdom period, throughout the New Kingdom period pharaohs strove to contribute to its majesty and glory by adding to it or rebuilding its parts. The pharaohs built other temples to Amun as well. Each year, in an elaborate festival, the image of Amun from Karnak would travel south to visit his temple at Luxor. The most monumental aspects of both temples were the work of the Nineteenth Dynasty pharaoh Ramses II (1279–1213 BCE), whose 66-year rule was longer than that of all but one other Egyptian king. It was he who, with his father, was responsible for decorating the enormous hypostyle hall at Karnak, and it was he who built the massive pylon gate at Luxor (Fig. **3.20**).

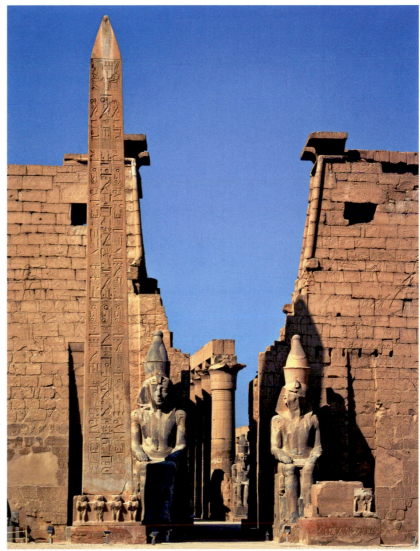

Fig. 3.20 Pylon gate of Ramses II with obelisk in the foreground, at Luxor, Thebes. Dynasty 19, ca. 1279–1212 BCE. The inscriptions on the pylon celebrate Ramses II's victory at the Battle of Qadesh over the Hittites as the two empires fought for control of Syria.

Mummification

In the belief that the physical body was essential to the *ka's* survival in the afterlife, the Egyptians developed a sophisticated process to preserve the body, **mummification**. This was a multistaged, highly ritualized process.

The oldest evidence of mummification was found near Saqqara and dates from 3100 to 2890 BCE. Mummification methods changed over time, and the techniques used between 1085 and 945 BCE were the most elaborate. Upon death, the body was carried across to the west bank of the Nile, symbolically "going into the west" like the setting sun. There it was taken to "the place of purification," where it was washed with natron. (Natron is a hydrated form of sodium carbonate used to absorb the body's fluids; it also turned the body black.) After this first step in its symbolic rebirth, the body was transferred to the House of Beauty, where it was properly embalmed, its inner organs removed, dried, coated in resin, and either preserved in their own special containers, now called canopic jars, or wrapped in linen and put back inside the body. The body itself was stuffed with linen and other materials in order to maintain its shape and was surrounded by bags of natron for 40 days. The entire process was overseen by an Overseer of Mysteries, God's Seal-Bearer, who served as chief surgeon, and a lector priest who recited the required texts and incantations.

After 40 days, the body was cleaned with spices and perfumes, rubbed with oils to restore some of its suppleness, and then coated with resin to waterproof it. Its nails were sewn back on and artificial eyes put into its eye sockets. Cosmetics were applied to the face and a wig put on its head. Dressed and decked out in jewels, the body was, finally, wrapped in a shroud of bandages from head to foot, along with small figurines and amulets as protection on the journey through the underworld. Finally, a mask was placed on the head and shoulders. The wrapping process involved several stages: First the head and neck were wrapped, then fingers and toes individually, and the same for the arms and legs, which were then tied together. The embalmers also placed a papyrus scroll with spells from the Book of the Dead (see pages 90–91) between the wrapped hands (**a**). After several more layers of wrapping impregnated with liquid resin to glue the bandages together, the embalmers painted a picture of the god Osiris on the wrapping surface, did a final bandaging of the entire mummy with a large cloth attached by strips of linen (**b**), and then placed a board of painted wood on top. The mummy was now ready for its final ritual burial. The entire process took 70 days!

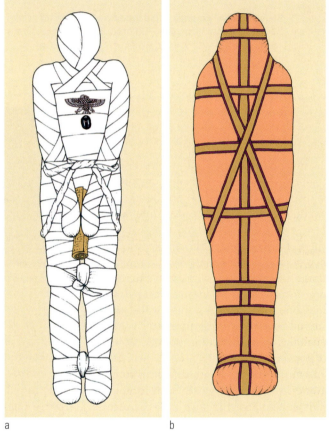

a   b

Two stages in the wrapping of a mummy. © The Trustees of the British Museum.

Ramses's Pylon Gate at Luxor In front of the pylon stand two enormous statues of the king and, originally, a pair of **obelisks**—square, tapered stone columns topped by a pyramid shape—although only the eastern one remains in place; the other is in the Place de la Concorde in Paris (see Fig. 2.22 in Chapter 2). The outside of the pylon was decorated with reliefs and texts describing the king's victory over the Hittites, at a battle fought on the river separating present-day Syria and Lebanon. The battle was not the unqualified military success depicted by the reliefs, so these may be an early example of art used as propaganda, a theme that continues up to the present. It may be better to think of these reliefs as symbolic rather than historical, as images of the king restoring order to the land. Inside the pylon, around the walls of the courtyard, were complex reliefs depicting the king, in the company of deities, together with his chief wife, 17 of his sons, and some of the nearly 100 other royal children whom he fathered with eight other official wives.

Such complexity typifies New Kingdom decoration. We see it clearly in the many surviving wall paintings in the rock-cut tombs across the river from Thebes. Earlier, we discussed the variety of fish and bird life in the painting of *Nebamun Hunting Birds* (see Fig. 3.2). In a feast scene from the same tomb, the guests receive food from a servant in the top register, while below them, musicians and dancers entertain the group (Fig. **3.21**). Very little is known

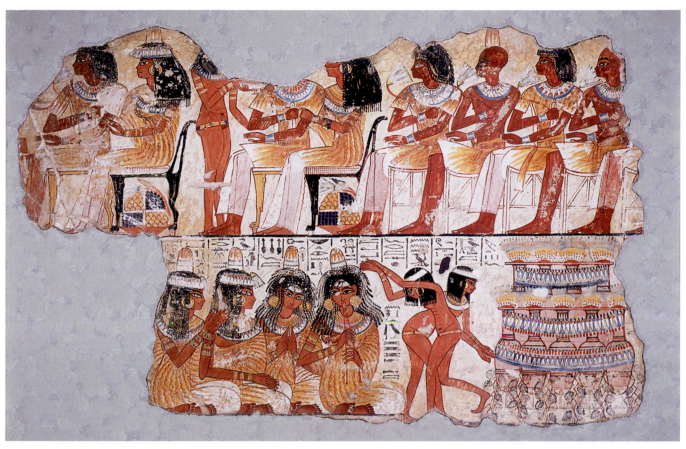

Fig. 3.21 *Female Musicians and Dancers Entertaining Guests at a Meal*, detail of a fresco from the tomb of Nebamun, western Thebes. Dynasty 18, ca. 1360 BCE. Paint on plaster, height of fragment 24". © The Trustees of the British Museum. The inclusion of such a scene in a tomb suggests that, in the New Kingdom, the dead demanded not only that they be accompanied by the usual necessities into the afterlife, but that they be entertained there as well.

about how Egyptian music actually sounded. Evidently, hymns were chanted at religious festivals, and song was a popular part of daily life. As in Mesopotamia, musical instruments—flutes, harps, lyres, trumpets, and metal rattles called *sistrums*—were often found in Egyptian tombs. In this wall painting, the two nude dancers are posed in a complex intertwining of limbs. Furthermore, of the four seated figures on the left—one of whom plays a double flute while the others appear to be clapping and, perhaps, chanting—two are depicted frontally, a rarity in Egyptian art. The soles of the womens' feet are turned toward us, and they are depicted wearing cones of a scented fatty substance on their heads, which when melted would bathe the women in its perfume. It is believed to be unlikely that they really wore such cones and that the cones are instead a visual metaphor for their scent. In this luxurious atmosphere, a new informality seems to have introduced itself into Egyptian art.

Akhenaten and the Politics of Religion

Toward the end of the Eighteenth Dynasty, Egypt experienced one of the few real crises of its entire history when, in 1353 BCE, Amenhotep IV (r. 1353–1337 BCE) assumed the throne of his father Amenhotep III (r. 1391–1353 BCE). It was

the father who had originally begun construction of the greater (southern) part of the Temple of Amun-Mut-Khonsu at Luxor and who built the third and tenth pylons at the Temple of Amun at Karnak. The great additions to these temples undertaken by Ramses II some 70 years later may have been a conscious return to the style—and traditions—of Amenhotep III. Certainly, they represent a massive, even overstated rejection of the ways of the son, for Amenhotep IV had forsaken not only the traditional conventions of Egyptian representation but the very gods themselves.

Although previous Egyptian kings may have associated themselves with a single god whom they represented in human form, Egyptian religion supported a large number of gods. Even the Nile was worshiped as a god. Amenhotep IV abolished the pantheon of Egyptian gods and established a religion in which the sun disk Aten was worshiped exclusively. Other gods were still acknowledged, but they were considered to be too inferior to Aten to be worth worshiping. Whether Amenhotep's religion was *henotheistic*—the belief and worship of a single god while accepting that other deities might also exist and be worshiped, as we have seen before, in the Zoroastrian worship of Ahura Mazda in Persia (see Chapter 2)—or truly monotheistic, is a matter of some debate.

Amenhotep IV believed the sun was the creator of all life, and he may have composed the *Hymn to the Sun*, inscribed on the west wall of the tomb of Ay (r. 1327–1323 BCE) at Tell el-Amarna and in many other tombs as well (**Reading 3.3**):

READING 3.3

**from *Akhenaten's Hymn to the Sun*
(14th century BCE)**

Let your holy Light shine from the height of heaven,
    O living Aten, source of all life!
From eastern horizon risen and streaming,
    you have flooded the world with your beauty.
You are majestic, awesome, bedazzling, exalted,
      overlord over all earth,
    yet your rays, they touch lightly, compass the lands
      to the limits of all your creation.
There in the Sun, you reach to the farthest of those
    you would gather in for your Son,
      whom you love;
Though you are far, your light is wide upon earth;
    and you shine in the faces of all
      who turn to follow your journeying.
When you sink to rest below western horizon
    earth lies in darkness like death,
Sleepers are still in bedchambers, heads veiled,
    eye cannot spy a companion;
All their goods could be stolen away,
    heads heavy there, and they never knowing!
Lions come out from the deeps of their caves,
    snakes bite and sting;
Darkness muffles, and earth is silent:
    he who created all things lies low in his tomb.
Earth-dawning mounts the horizon,
    glows in the sun-disk as day:
You drive away darkness, offer your arrows of shining,
    and the Two Lands are lively with morningsong.
Sun's children awaken and stand,
    for you, golden light, have upraised the sleepers;
Bathed are their bodies, who dress in clean linen,
    their arms held high to praise your Return.
Across the face of the earth
    they go to their crafts and professions.
The herds are at peace in their pastures,
    trees and the vegetation grow green;
Birds start from their nests,
    wings wide spread to worship your Person;
Small beasts frisk and gambol, and all
    who mount into flight or settle to rest
      live, once you have shone upon them;
Ships float downstream or sail for the south,
    each path lies open because of your rising;
Fish in the River leap in your sight,
    and your rays strike deep in the Great Green Sea.
It is you create the new creature in Woman,
    shape the life-giving drops into Man,
Foster the son in the womb of his mother,
    soothe him, ending his tears. …

Aten is clearly the life force and source of all good, the very origin of creation itself.

Amenhotep IV was so dedicated to Aten that he changed his own name to Akhenaten ("The Shining Spirit of Aten") and moved the capital of Egypt from Thebes to a site many miles north that he named Akhetaten (present-day Tell el-Amarna). This move transformed Egypt's political and cultural as well as religious life. At this new capital he presided over the worship of Aten as a divine priest with his queen as a divine priestess. Temples to Aten were open courtyards, where the altar received the sun's direct rays.

Why would Amenhotep IV/Akhenaten have substituted monotheism for Egypt's traditional polytheistic religion? Many Egyptologists argue that the switch had to do with enhancing the power of the pharaoh. With the pharaoh representing the one god who mattered, all religious justification for the power held by a priesthood dedicated to the traditional gods was gone. As we have seen, the pharaoh was traditionally associated with the sun god Re. Now in the form of the sun disk Aten, Re was the supreme deity, embodying the characteristics of all the other gods, therefore rendering them superfluous. By analogy, Amenhotep IV/Akhenaten was now supreme priest, rendering all other priests superfluous as well. Simultaneously, the temples dedicated to the other gods lost prestige and influence. These changes also converted the priests into dissidents.

A New Art: The Amarna Style Such significant changes had a powerful effect on the visual arts as well. Previously, Egyptian art had been remarkably stable because its principles were considered a gift of the gods—thus perfect and eternal. But now, the perfection of the gods was in question, and the principles of art were open to re-examination as well. A new art replaced the traditional canon of proportion—the familiar poses of king and queen—with realism, and a sense of immediacy, even intimacy. So Akhenaten allowed himself and his family to be portrayed with startling realism, in what has become known, from the modern name for the new capital, as the Amarna style.

An example is a small relief from Akhenaten's new capital: The king is depicted with a skinny, weak upper body, his belly protruding over his skirt; his skull is elongated behind an extremely long, narrow facial structure; and he sits in a slumped, almost casual position (Fig. **3.22**). (One theory holds that Akhenaten had Marfan syndrome, a genetic disorder that leads to skeletal abnormalities.) This depiction contrasts sharply with the idealized depictions of the pharaohs in earlier periods. Akhenaten holds one of his children in his arms and seems to have just kissed her. His two other children sit with the queen across from him, one turning to speak with her mother, the other touching the queen's cheek. The queen herself, Nefertiti, sits only slightly below her husband and appears to share his position and authority. In fact, one of the most striking features of the Amarna style is Nefertiti's prominence in the decoration of the king's temples. In one, for example, she is shown slaughtering prisoners, an image traditionally reserved for

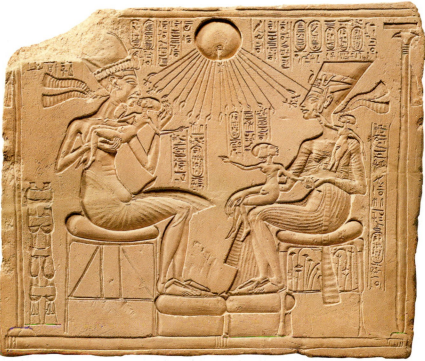

Fig. 3.22 *Akhenaten and His Family*, **from Akhetaten (present-day Tell el-Amarna). Dynasty 18, ca. 1345 BCE.** Painted limestone relief, 12¾" × 14⅞". Staatliche Museen, Berlin, Preussischer Kulturbesitz, Ägyptisches Museum. Between Akhenaten and his queen Nefertiti, the sun disk Aten shines down beneficently. Its rays end in small hands, which hold the *ankh* symbol for life before both the king and queen.

View the Closer Look for *Akhenaten and His Family* on **MyArtsLab**

the king himself. It is likely that her prominence was part of Akhenaten's attempt to substitute the veneration of his own family (who, after all, represented Aten on earth) for the traditional Amun-Mut-Khonsu family group.

In a house in the southern part of Akhenaten's new city at Amarna, the famous bust of Queen Nefertiti was discovered along with drawings and sculptures of the royal family (Fig. **3.23**). This was the workshop of Thutmose, one of the king's royal artists. It seems likely that many other sculptures and reliefs were modeled on the bust of Nefertiti. At any rate, the queen's beauty cannot be denied, and this image of her has become famous worldwide. Even in her own time, she was known by such epitaphs as "Fair of Face" and "Great in Love."

The Return to Thebes and to Tradition

Akhenaten's revolution was short-lived. Upon his death, Tutankhaten (r. 1336–1327 BCE) assumed the throne and changed his name to Tutankhamun (indicating a return to the more traditional gods, in this case Amun). The new king abandoned Tell el-Amarna, moved the royal family to Memphis in the north, and reaffirmed Thebes as the nation's religious center. He died shortly after and was buried on the west bank of the Nile at Thebes, near the tomb of Hatshepsut.

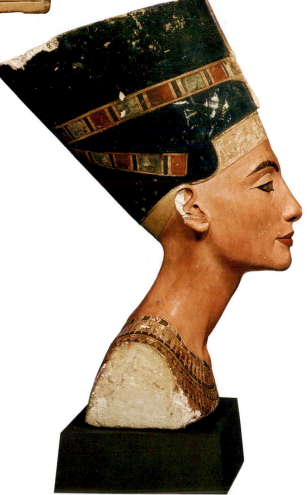

Fig. 3.23 *Nefertiti*, **from Akhetaten (present-day Tell el-Amarna). Dynasty 18, ca. 1348–1336 BCE.** Painted limestone, 19". Staatliche Museen, Berlin, Preussischer Kulturbesitz, Ägyptisches Museum. Some scholars theorize that Nefertiti's long neck may not be so much her own as a reflection of the king's—so that the reality of the king takes precedence over her own.

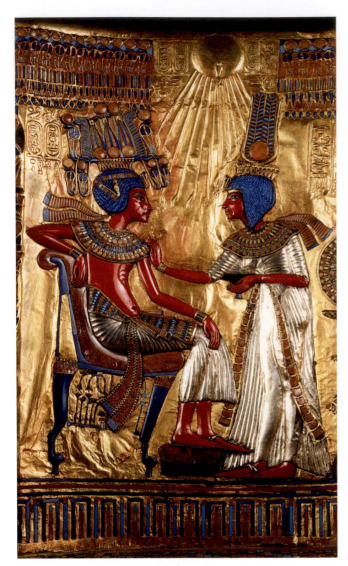

Fig. 3.24 Back of Tutankhamun's "Golden Throne," from his tomb, Valley of the Kings, western Thebes. Dynasty 18, ca. 1335 BCE. Wood, gold, faience, and semiprecious stones, height of entire throne 41", height of detail approx. 12¼". Egyptian Museum, Cairo. This throne shows that early in his life, at least, Tutankhamun was still portrayed in the Amarna style.

The Tomb of Tutankhamun Tutankhamun's is the only royal tomb in Egypt to have escaped the total pillaging of looters. In addition to the royal sarcophagus discovered by Carter (see Fig. 3.1), there were also vast quantities of beautiful furniture in the tomb, including a golden throne that dates from early in the king's rule and still bears the indelible stamp of the Amarna style, with Aten shining down on both the king and queen (Fig. **3.24**). Jewelry of exquisite quality abounded, as did textiles—rarest of all archeological finds because they deteriorate over time. Carter and his team also found a golden canopic chest—which held the king's embalmed internal organs—a shrine-shaped box of alabaster, carved with four compartments, each of which had a carved and gilded stopper depicting the king. It had an alabaster

lid that covered the stoppers, and it was set in a larger shrine of gilded wood, protected by three gilded statues of goddesses, and covered by a shroud covered with gold rosettes.

The Final Judgment The elaborate burial process was not meant solely to guarantee survival of the king's *ka* and *ba*. It also prepared him for a "last judgment," a belief system that would find expression in the Hebrew faith as well. In this two-part ritual, deities first questioned the deceased about their behavior in life. Then their hearts, the seat of the *ka*, were weighed against an ostrich feather, symbol of Maat, the goddess of truth, justice, and order. Egyptians believed the heart contained all the emotions, intellect, and character of the individual, and so represented both the good and bad aspects of a person's life. If the heart did not balance with the feather, then the dead person was condemned to nonexistence, to be eaten by a creature called Ammit, the vile "Eater of the Dead," part crocodile, part lion, and part hippopotamus. Osiris, wrapped in his mummy robes, oversaw this moment of judgment. Tutankhamun himself, depicted on his sarcophagus with his crossed arms holding crook and flail, was clearly identified with Osiris.

Books of Going Forth by Day At the time of Tutankhamun's death, the last judgment was routinely illustrated in Books of Going Forth by Day (now also called Books of the Dead), collections of magical texts or spells buried with the deceased to help them survive the ritual of judgment. One such magical text was the "Negative Confession" (**Reading 3.4**), which the deceased would utter upon entering the judgment hall:

READING 3.4

from a *Book of Going Forth by Day*

I have come unto you; I have committed no faults; I have not sinned; I have done no evil; I have accused no man falsely; therefore let nothing be done against me. I live in right and truth, and I feed my heart upon right and truth. That which men have bidden I have done, and the gods are satisfied thereat. I have pacified the god, for I have done his will. I have given bread unto the hungry and water unto those who thirst, clothing unto the naked, and a boat unto the shipwrecked mariner. I have made holy offerings unto the gods; and I have given meals of the tomb to the sainted dead. O, then, deliver ye me, and protect me; accuse me not before the great god. I am pure of mouth, and I am pure of hands …

I offer up prayers in the presence of the gods, knowing that which concerneth them. I have come forward to make a declaration of right and truth, and to place the balance upon its supports within the groves of amaranth. Hail, thou who art exalted upon thy resting place, thou lord of the atef crown,[1] who declarest thy name as the lord of the winds,

[1] A conical headdress decorated with two ostrich feathers, joined with ram's horns and a sun disk, and associated particularly with Osiris.

Read the document related to the Egyptian Book of the Dead on **MyArtsLab**

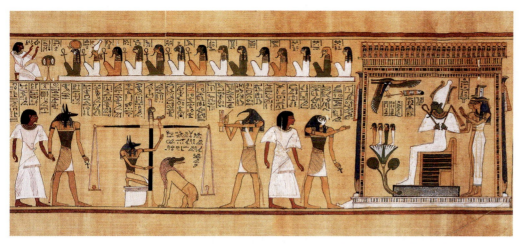

Fig. 3.25 *Last Judgment of Hunefer by Osiris*, from a Book of Going Forth by Day in his tomb at Thebes. Dynasty 19, ca. 1285 BCE. Painted papyrus scroll, height 15⅝". © The Trustees of the British Museum. At the top, Hunefer, having passed into eternity, is shown adoring a row of deities.

deliver thou me from thine angels of destruction, who make dire deeds to happen and calamities to arise, and who have no covering upon their faces, because I have done right and truth, O thou Lord of right and truth. I am pure, in my fore-parts have I been made clean, and in my hinder parts have I been purified; my reins [kidneys] have been bathed in the Pool of right and truth, and no member of my body was wanting. I have been purified in the pool of the south …

The following moment of judgment is depicted in one such Book of Going Forth by Day, a papyrus scroll created for an otherwise anonymous man known as Hunefer (Fig. **3.25**). The scene reads from left to right in a continuous pictorial narrative. To the left, Anubis, overseer of funerals and cemeteries, brings Hunefer into the judgment area. Hunefer's heart, represented as a pot, is being weighed against the ostrich feather. In this image, Hunefer passes the test—not surprising, given that the work is dedicated to ensuring that Hunefer's *ka* survive, in the afterlife. Horus brings Hunefer to Osiris, seated under a canopy, with Isis and her sister Nephthys behind.

THE LATE PERIOD, THE KUSHITES, AND THE FALL OF EGYPT

What was the nature of Egypt's relations with its African neighbors to the south and with the Mediterranean powers to the north?

From Tutankhamun's time through the Late Period (715–332 BCE) and until the fall of Egypt to the Romans in 30 BCE, the conventions of traditional representation remained in place. For example, the pose we saw in Menkaure's funerary sculpture of 2460 BCE (see Fig. 3.10) is repeated in the seventh-century BCE statue of *Mentuemhet*, the governor

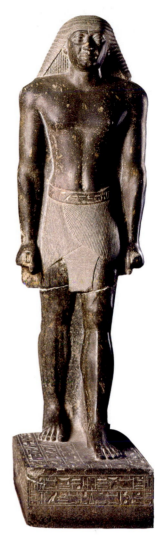

Fig.3.26 *Mentuemhet*, from Karnak, Thebes. Dynasty 25, ca. 660 BCE. Granite, height 54". Egyptian Museum, Cairo. The only concession to naturalistic representation in this sculpture is in the governor's facial features.

(Fig. **3.26**). Mentuemhet strides forward into eternal life, nearly 2,000 years after that Old Kingdom pharaoh, a strong visual signal of the stability of Egyptian culture.

Mentuemhet was probably the most influential official of the Twenty-fifth Dynasty (ca. 715–656 BCE). He was appointed governor of Thebes by the Kushites (from Kush, the Egyptian name for the southern region of Nubia, in today's Sudan). Nubia had long been an important neighbor, appearing in Egyptian records as far back as the Old Kingdom. Nubia served as a corridor for trade between Egypt and sub-Saharan Africa and was the main means by which Egypt procured gold and incense, as well as ivory, ebony, and other valuable items (Fig. **3.27**). Because of its links with tropical Africa, over time, the population of Nubia became a diverse mixture of ethnicities.

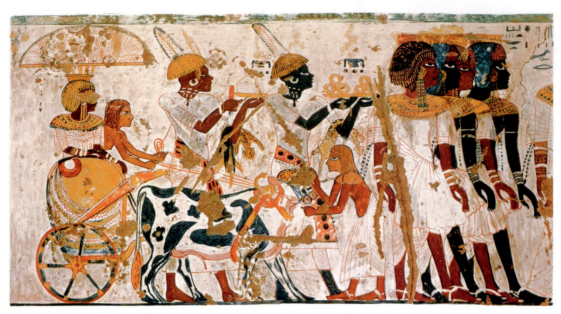

Fig. 3.27 *Nubians Bringing Tribute*, from the tomb of Amenhotep Huy, the Nubian viceroy under Tutankhamun, Qurnet Murai, western Thebes. Dynasty 18, ca. 1330 BCE. Painting on plaster. Editions Gallimard, Paris. This painting represents the kind of goods that Egypt might have traded with Nubia and Kush.

Nubia had been the location of several wealthy urban centers, including Kerma, whose walls, mud-brick buildings, and lavish tombs were financed and built by indigenous Nubian rulers around 1650 BCE. Napata was built during an Egyptian annexation of the area in approximately 1500 BCE, during the reign of Thutmose I. Napata became the provincial capital of Kush.

The Kushites

The Kushites had an immense appetite for assimilating Egyptian culture. They adopted Egyptian religion and practices, worshiping Egyptian gods, particularly Amun, the Egyptian state god. The main religious center of Kush was at Jebel Barkal, a mountain near the fourth cataract of the Nile where the Kushites believed Amun dwelled. Their adoption of Egyptian ways nevertheless retained their distinctly Nubian identity. The Kushites developed hieroglyphs to express their own language, continued to worship many of their own gods, and though they also began to erect pyramids over their royal tombs, theirs started from smaller bases and were distinctly steeper and more needle-like than their Egyptian counterparts. There are nearly 300 of these pyramids in present-day Sudan, more than in Egypt itself. Although annexed to Egypt, Kush was essentially an independent state toward the end of the New Kingdom. Egypt relied upon Kush to supply gold and other resources (including Nubian soldiers, among the most feared warriors in the region), but as Egypt struggled with its own enemies to the east, the rulers of Kush eventually found themselves in a position to take control of Egypt themselves. In the eighth century BCE, the Egyptians turned to Kush for the leadership they needed to help hold off the mounting threat of an Assyrian invasion, and the Egyptianized African rulers of Kush became the Twenty-fifth Dynasty of pharaohs. As pharaohs, the Kushite kings ruled an empire that stretched from the borders of Palestine possibly as far upstream as the Blue and White Niles, uniting the Nile Valley from Khartoum to the Mediterranean. They were expelled from Egypt by the Assyrians after a rule of close to 100 years.

Egypt Loses Its Independence

The Assyrians left rule of Egypt to a family of local princes at Saïs, in the western portion of the Nile Delta, inaugurating the Twenty-sixth, or Saite, Dynasty (664–525 BCE). With Memphis as their administrative center, they emphasized Mediterranean trade, which in turn produced over 100 years of economic prosperity. But Egypt was anything but secure in power struggles that dominated the larger political climate of the region. In 525 BCE, the Persians invaded from the north, satisfying their own imperial ambitions, capturing the Egyptian treasury, and reducing the country to a mere province in the Persian Empire. For the next 200 years, Egypt enjoyed brief periods of independence, until the Persians invaded again in 343 BCE. They had ruled for not much more than a decade when the Macedonian conqueror Alexander the Great drove them out and asserted his own authority. According to legend, the god Amun spoke to Alexander through an oracle, acknowledging him as his son and therefore legitimate ruler of Egypt. Its independence as a state had come to an end. When Alexander died, the country fell to the rule of one of his generals, Ptolemy, and beginning in 304 BCE, the final Ptolemaic Dynasty was under way. A kingdom in the Greek constellation, Egypt would finally fall to an invading Roman army in 30 BCE. But remarkably, until this moment, its artistic and religious traditions, as well as its daily customs, remained largely in place, practiced as they had been for 3,000 years.

Mutual Influence through Trade

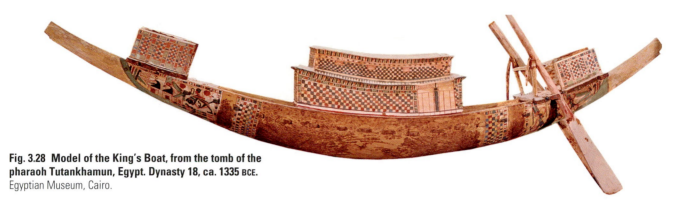

Fig. 3.28 Model of the King's Boat, from the tomb of the pharaoh Tutankhamun, Egypt. Dynasty 18, ca. 1335 BCE. Egyptian Museum, Cairo.

Although Egyptian art and culture remained extraordinarily stable for over 3,000 years, it would be a mistake to assume that this was because the region was isolated. In fact, Egypt was a center of trade for the entire Mediterranean basin. Spiral and geometric designs on Egyptian pottery from as early as the Twelfth Dynasty (1980–1801 BCE) suggest the influence of Aegean civilizations, and during the reign of Hatshepsut's young son, Thutmose III, connections with Aegean cultures appear to have been extremely close. Evidence from surviving images of both cultures' ship designs—ships that would have facilitated Aegean trade—suggests a mutual influence. A small-scale model of the king's boat from the tomb of King Tutankhamun shows a stern cabin, decorated with images of the king, where the steersmen would have guided the boat (Fig. **3.28**). Ships such as this were equipped with a mast that could be raised and fitted with a sail to catch the Nile winds from astern.

Egypt's influence in the Mediterranean was far-flung, although it is unlikely that its ships set out to sea. Rather, their boats would have generally hugged the coast. But Egypt was a port of call, and traders from around the Mediterranean visited there. Archeologists excavating at Mycenae, a center of culture that was firmly established on the Greek Peloponnese

by 1500 BCE, have discovered Egyptian scarabs at the site, including one bearing the name of Queen Tiy, mother of Akhenaten. Scarabs are amulets in the shape of a beetle, and since the Egyptian word for beetle, *kheprer*, is derived from the word *kheper*, "to come into being," scarabs were associated with rebirth in the afterlife. Those displaying names were generally used as official seals. A shipwreck discovered off the coast of southern Turkey in 1982 gives us some sense of the extent of Mediterranean trade (Fig. **3.29**). Carbon dating of firewood found on board suggests the ship sank in about 1316 BCE. Its cargo included gold from Egypt, weapons from Greece, a scarab bearing Nefertiti's name, amber from northern Europe, hippopotamus and elephant ivory, and tin from Afghanistan. Such trade resulted not only in the transfer of goods between various regions, but in a broader cultural diffusion as well, for ideas, styles, religions, and technologies spread from one culture to another throughout the region. Much work remains to be done on the interconnections and lines of continuity and change among the peoples of the Aegean, the broader Mediterranean, Mesopotamia, and Egypt, but it is clear that they knew of one another, traded with one another, and were stimulated by one another's presence. ∎

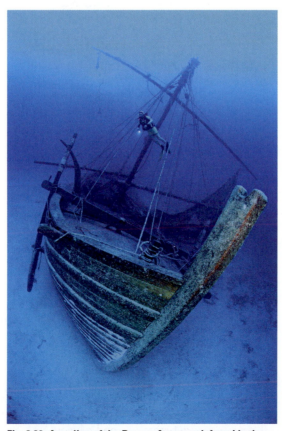

Fig. 3.29 A replica of the Bronze Age wreck found in the Mediterranean at Uluburun, off the coast of Turkey.

3.1 Describe how the idea of cyclical return shaped Egyptian civilization.

The annual cycle of flood and sun, the inundation of the Nile River Valley that annually deposited deep layers of silt, followed by months of sun in which crops could grow in the fertile soil, helped to define Egyptian culture. This predictable cycle helped to create a cultural belief in the stability and balance of all things that lasted for over 3,000 years. Can you describe this belief in terms of cyclical harmony? How does the Egyptian religion reflect this belief system?

3.2 Analyze how religious beliefs are reflected in the funerary art and architecture of the Old Kingdom.

Most surviving Egyptian art and architecture was devoted to burial and the afterlife, the cycle of life, death, and rebirth. The pyramids at Saqqara and Giza and the statuary of kings and queens were especially dedicated to this cycle. What particular aspect of Egyptian spiritual life do they embody? How do sculptures of lesser figures serve the same ends?

3.3 Compare and contrast Middle Kingdom art and literature to those of the Old Kingdom.

Whereas in the Old Kingdom, writing had been used almost exclusively in a religious context, in the Middle Kingdom a vast secular literature developed. What does the rise of this secular literature tell us about Egyptian society? Except for slight modification of the pose of seated kings in funerary statues, sculpture remained firmly rooted in tradition. Still, Middle Kingdom artists seem to have conceived of a new way of organizing their compositions. Describe this new grid system.

3.4 Characterize New Kingdom worship of Amun and contrast it with the major transformation of Egyptian tradition under the rule of Akhenaten.

The New Kingdom kings, now called "pharaoh," undertook massive, elaborately decorated building projects at Karnak and Thebes. Toward the end of the Eighteenth Dynasty, Amenhotep IV forsook traditional conventions of Egyptian representation, abolished the pantheon of Egyptian gods, established a monotheistic religion in which the sun disk Aten was worshiped exclusively, and changed his own name to Akhenaten. How does Amenhotep IV's religion differ from Egyptian religion in general? What other changes to Egyptian tradition occurred during his reign?

Funeral practices soon included the incantation of texts and spells collected in Books of Going Forth by Day, which accompanied the deceased as they underwent a last judgment. What significance do you attach to the title of these books?

3.5 Discuss Egypt's relations with its African neighbors to the south and with the Mediterranean powers to the north during the Late Period.

After the end of the New Kingdom, traditional representational practices remained in place, even when Kushite kings from the south in present-day Sudan ruled the country. How did the Nubians and Kushites contribute to Egyptian culture? How did the political climate of the Mediterranean basin affect the country? After Egypt fell to Alexander the Great in 332 BCE, its independence as a state came to an end, even though the new Greek Ptolemaic Dynasty continued traditional Egyptian ways until Rome conquered the country in 30 BCE.

✔ **Study** and **review** on **MyArtsLab**

READINGS

The Teachings of Khety (ca. 2040–1648 BCE)

In the following example of instructive literature, dating from the Middle Kingdom, a royal scribe tries to convince his son to follow him into the profession by debunking virtually every other career path the young man might choose to follow. The work is as instructive as it is amusing, since it presents a wonderfully complete picture of daily life in the Middle Kingdom.

The beginning of the teaching which the man of Tjel named Khety made for his son named Pepy, while he sailed southwards to the Residence to place him in the school of writings among the children of the magistrates, the most eminent men of the Residence.

So he spoke to him: Since I have seen those who have been beaten, it is to writings that you must set your mind. Observe the man who has been carried off to a work force. Behold, there is nothing that surpasses writings! They are a boat upon the water. Read then at the end of the Book of Kemyet this statement in it saying: 10

As for a scribe in any office in the Residence, he will not suffer want in it. When he fulfills the bidding of another, he does not come forth satisfied. I do not see an office to be compared with it, to which this maxim could relate. I shall make you love books more than your mother, and I shall place their excellence before you. It is greater than any office. There is nothing like it on earth. When he began to become sturdy but was still a child, he was greeted (respectfully). When he was sent to carry out a task, before he returned he was dressed in 20 adult garments.

I do not see a stoneworker on an important errand or a goldsmith in a place to which he has been sent, but I have seen a coppersmith at his work at the door of his furnace. His fingers were like the claws of the crocodile, and he stank more than fish excrement.

Every carpenter who bears the adze is wearier than a field-hand. His field is his wood, his hoe is the axe. There is no end to his work, and he must labor excessively in his activity. At nighttime he still must light his lamp. … 30

The barber shaves until the end of the evening. But he must be up early, crying out, his bowl upon his arm. He takes himself from street to street to seek out someone to shave. He wears out his arms to fill his belly, like bees who eat (only) according to their work.

The reed-cutter goes downstream to the Delta to fetch himself arrows. He must work excessively in his activity. When the gnats sting him and the sand fleas bite him as well, then he is judged.

The potter is covered with earth, although his lifetime is still 40 among the living. He burrows in the field more than swine to bake his cooking vessels. His clothes being stiff with mud, his head cloth consists only of rags, so that the air which comes forth from his burning furnace enters his nose. He operates a pestle with his feet with which he himself is pounded, penetrating the courtyard of every house and driving earth into every open place.

I shall also describe to you the bricklayer. His kidneys are painful. When he must be outside in the wind, he lays bricks without a garment. His belt is a cord for his back, a string for 50 his buttocks. His strength has vanished through fatigue and stiffness, kneading all his excrement. He eats bread with his fingers, although he washes himself but once a day. …

The weaver inside the weaving house is more wretched than a woman. His knees are drawn up against his belly. He cannot breathe the air. If he wastes a single day without weaving, he is beaten with 50 whip lashes. He has to give food to the doorkeeper to allow him to come out to the daylight …

See, there is no office free from supervisors, except the scribe's. He is the supervisor! 60

But if you understand writings, then it will be better for you than the professions which I have set before you. … What I have done in journeying southward to the Residence is what I have done through love of you. A day at school is advantageous to you. …

Be serious, and great as to your worth. Do not speak secret matters. For he who hides his innermost thoughts is one who makes a shield for himself. Do not utter thoughtless words when you sit down with an angry man.

When you come forth from school after midday recess has 70 been announced to you, go into the courtyard and discuss the last part of your lesson book.

When an official sends you as a messenger, then say what he said. Neither take away nor add to it. …

See, I have placed you on the path of God. … See, there is no scribe lacking sustenance, (or) the provisions of the royal house. … Honour your father and mother who have placed you on the path of the living.

READING CRITICALLY

Although the scribe Khety spends much time describing the shortcomings of other lines of work, he also reminds his son how he should behave at school. What do the father's words of advice tell us about the values of Egyptian society?

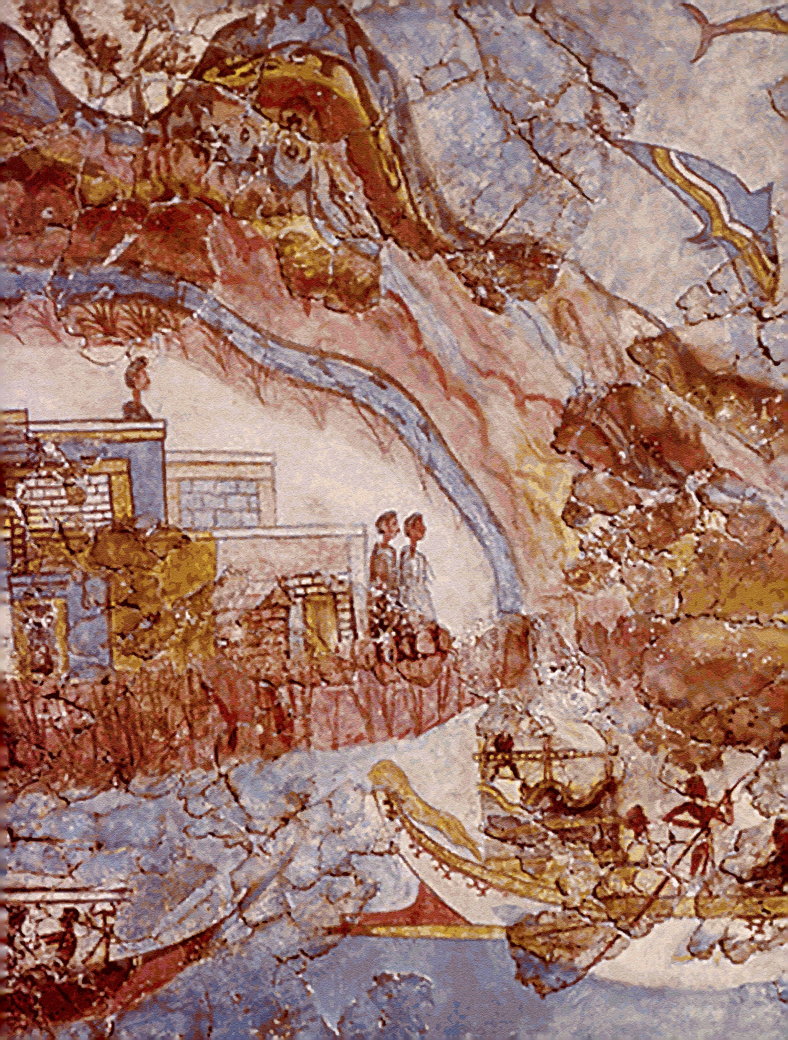

4

The Aegean World and the Rise of Greece

Trade, War, and Victory

THINKING AHEAD

4.1 Compare and contrast the Cycladic, Minoan, and Mycenaean cultures.

4.2 Define the formal features of the Homeric epic, and compare and contrast the *Iliad* and the *Odyssey*.

4.3 Discuss the ways in which the values of the Greek polis shaped Greek culture.

4.4 Describe the rise of democracy in Athens.

The Aegean Sea, in the eastern Mediterranean, is filled with islands. Here, beginning in about 3000 BCE, seafaring cultures took hold. So many were the islands, and so close to one another, that navigators were always within sight of land. In the natural harbors where seafarers came ashore, port communities developed and trade began to flourish. A house from approximately 1650 BCE was excavated at Akrotiri on Thera, one of these islands. The *Miniature Ship Fresco*, a frieze that extended across the top of at least three walls in a second-story room, suggests a prosperous, seafaring community engaged in a celebration of the sea (Fig. **4.1**). People lounge on terraces and rooftops as boats glide by, accompanied by leaping dolphins.

THE CULTURES OF THE AEGEAN

How do the Cycladic, Minoan, and Mycenaean cultures differ?

The later Greeks thought of the Bronze Age Aegean peoples as their ancestors—particularly those who inhabited the islands of the Cyclades, the island of Crete, and Mycenae, on the Peloponnese—and considered their activities and culture part of their own prehistory. They even had a word for the way they knew them—*archaiologia*, "knowing the past." They did not practice archeology as we do today, excavating ancient sites and scientifically analyzing

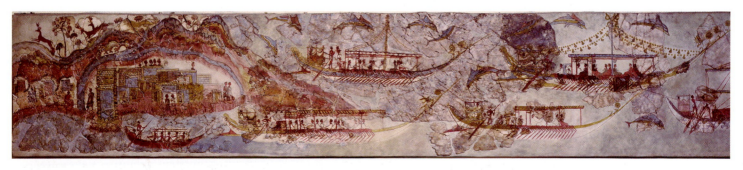

◄ **Fig. 4.1 (left and above)** *Miniature Ship Fresco* **(detail and larger view from the left section), from Room 5, West House, Akrotiri, Thera. Before 1623 BCE.** Height 14⁵⁄₁₆". National Archeological Museum, Athens. The total length of this fresco is over 24 feet. Harbors such as this one provided shelter to traders who sailed between the islands of the Aegean Sea as early as 3000 BCE.

Listen to the chapter audio on **MyArtsLab**

the artifacts discovered there. Rather, they learned of their past through legends passed down, at first orally and then in writing, from generation to generation. Interestingly, the modern practice of archeology has confirmed much of what was legendary to the Greeks.

The Cyclades

The Cyclades are a group of more than 100 islands in the Aegean Sea between mainland Greece and the island of Crete (Map **4.1**). They form a roughly circular shape, giving them their name, from the Greek word *kyklos*, "circle" (also the origin of our word "cycle"). No written records of the early Cycladic people remain, although archeologists have found a good deal of art in and around hillside burial chambers. Marble was abundant in the islands, especially on Naxos and Paros, and these figures were carved with obsidian scrapers—abundant in these volcanic islands— and then polished with crushed emery, mined on Naxos. The most famous of these artifacts are marble figurines in a highly simplified and abstract style that appeals to the modern eye (Fig. **4.2**). In fact, Cycladic figurines have deeply influenced modern sculptors. The Cycladic figures originally looked quite different because they were painted. Most of the figurines depict females, but male figures, including seated harpists and acrobats, also exist. The figurines range in height from a few inches to life-size, but anatomical detail in all of them is reduced to essentials. With their toes pointed down, their heads tilted back, and their arms crossed across their chests, the fully extended figures are corpselike. Their function remains unknown, but since most of these figures were found in graves, it seems likely that they were created for a mortuary purpose.

By about 2200 BCE, trade with the larger island of Crete to the south brought the Cyclades into Crete's political orbit and radically altered Cycladic life. Evidence of this influence survives in the form of wall paintings discovered

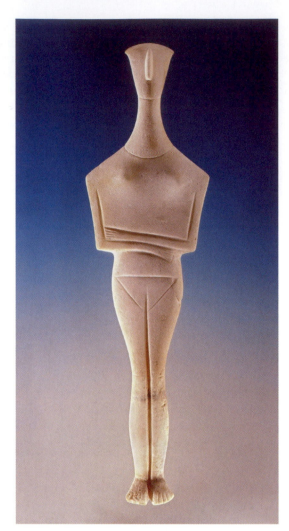

Fig. 4.2 Figurine of a woman from the Cyclades. ca. **2400–2100 BCE.** Marble, height 17". Antikensammlung, Staatliche Museen, Berlin. *Larger examples of such figurines may have been objects of worship.*

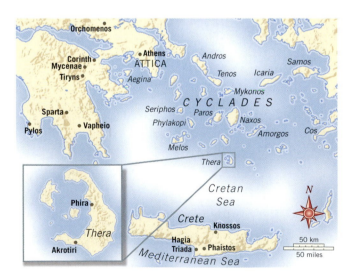

Map 4.1 Crete, the Cyclades, and the island of Thera. Thera lies just north of Crete. Evidence suggests Cretan influence was felt here by about 2000 BCE.

in 1967 on the island of Thera (also commonly known as Santorini), at Akrotiri, a community that had been buried beneath one of the largest volcanic eruptions in the last 10,000 years. About 7 cubic miles of magma spewed forth, and the ash cloud that resulted during the first phase of the eruption was about 23 miles high. The enormous size of the eruption caused the volcano at the center of Thera to collapse, producing a caldera, a large basin or depression that filled with seawater. The island of Thera is actually the eastern rim of the original volcano (small volcanoes are still active in the center of Thera's crescent sea).

The eruption was so great that it left evidence worldwide—in the stunted growth of tree rings as far away as Ireland and California, and in ash taken from ice core samples in Greenland. With this evidence, scientists have dated the eruption to 1623 BCE. In burying the city of Akrotiri, it also preserved it. Not only were the homes of Akrotiri elaborately decorated—with mural paintings such as the *Miniature Ship Fresco* (see Fig. 4.1), made with water-based pigments on wet plaster—but residents also enjoyed a level of personal hygiene unknown elsewhere in Western culture until Roman times. Clay pipes led from interior toilets and baths to sewers built under winding, paved streets. Straw reinforced the walls of their homes, protecting them against earthquakes and insulating them from the heat of the Mediterranean sun.

Minoan Culture in Crete

Just to the south of the Cyclades lies Crete, the largest of the Aegean islands. Bronze Age civilization developed there as early as 3000 BCE. Trade routes from Crete established communication with such diverse areas as Turkey, Cyprus, Egypt, Afghanistan, and Scandinavia, from which the island imported copper, ivory, amethyst, lapis lazuli, carnelian, gold, and amber. From Britain, Crete imported the tin necessary to produce bronze. A distinctive culture called Minoan flourished on Crete from about 1900 to 1375 BCE. The name comes from the legendary king Minos, who was said to have ruled the island's ancient capital of Knossos.

Minoan Painting Many of the motifs in the frescoes at Akrotiri, in the Cyclades, also appear in the art decorating Minoan palaces on Crete, including the palace at Knossos. This suggests the mutual influence of Cycladic and Minoan cultures by the start of the second millennium BCE. Unique

to Crete, however, is emphasis on the bull, the central element of one of the best-preserved frescoes at Knossos, the *Toreador Fresco* (Fig. **4.3**). Three almost-nude figures appear to toy with a charging bull. (As in Egyptian art, women are traditionally depicted with light skin, men with a darker complexion.) The woman on the left holds the bull by the horns, the man vaults over its back, and the woman on the right seems to have either just finished a vault or to have positioned herself to catch the man. It is unclear whether this is a ritual activity, perhaps part of a rite of passage. What we do know is that the Minoans regularly sacrificed bulls, as well as other animals, and that the bull was at least symbolically associated with male virility and strength.

Minoan frescoes, as well as those on Thera, differ from ancient Egyptian frescoes in several ways. The most obvious is that they were painted not in tombs but on the walls of homes and palaces, where they could be enjoyed by the living. The two kinds of frescoes were made differently as well. Rather than applying pigment to a dry wall in the *fresco secco* technique of the Egyptians, Minoan artists employed a **buon fresco** technique similar to that used by Renaissance artists nearly 3,000 years later (see Chapter 13). In *buon fresco*, pigment is mixed with water and then applied to a wall that has been coated with wet lime plaster. As the wall dries, the painting literally becomes part of it. *Buon fresco* is far more durable than *fresco secco*, for the paint will not flake off as easily (though all walls will eventually crumble).

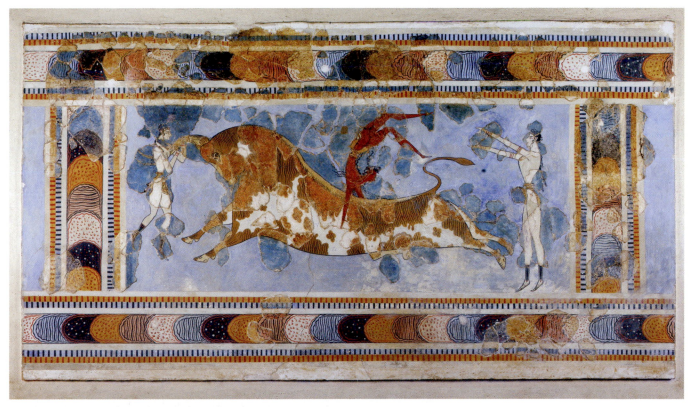

Fig. 4.3 ***Bull Leaping*** (***Toreador Fresco***), **from the palace complex at Knossos, Crete. ca. 1450–1375 BCE.** Fresco, height approx. 24½". Archeological Museum, Iráklion, Crete. The darker patches of the fresco are original fragments. The lighter areas are modern restorations.

Minoan Religion The people of Thera and Crete seem to have shared the same religion as well as similar artistic motifs. Ample archeological evidence tells us that the Minoans in Crete worshiped female deities. We do not know much more than that, but some students of ancient religions have proposed that the Minoan worship of one or more female deities is evidence that in very early cultures the principal deity was a goddess rather than a god.

It has long been believed that one of the Minoan female deities was a snake goddess, but recently, scholars have questioned the authenticity of most of the existing snake goddess figurines. Sir Arthur Evans (1851–1941), who first excavated at the Palace of Minos on Crete, identified images of the Cretan goddess as "Mountain Goddess," "Snake Goddess," "Dove Goddess," "Goddess of the Caves," "Goddess of the Double Axes," "Goddess of the Sports," and "Mother Goddess." He saw all of these as different aspects of a single deity, or Great Goddess. A century after Evans introduced the Snake Goddess (Fig. **4.4**) to the world, scholars are still debating its authenticity. In his book *Mysteries of the Snake Goddess* (2002), Kenneth Lapatin

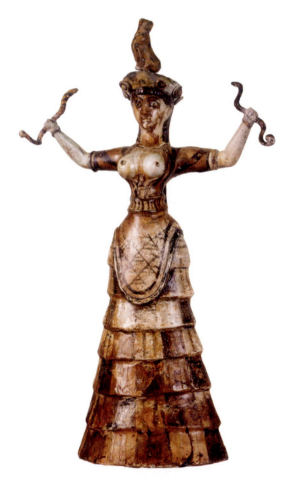

Fig. 4.4 *Snake Goddess* or *Priestess*, from the palace at Knossos, **Crete. ca. 1500 BCE.** Faience, height 11⅝". Archeological Museum, Iráklion, Crete. **Faience** is a kind of earthenware ceramic decorated with glazes. Modern faience is easily distinguishable from ancient because it is markedly lighter in tone.

🔍 **View** the Closer Look for the *Snake Goddess* on **MyArtsLab**

makes a convincing case that craftspeople employed by Evans manufactured artifacts for the antiquities market. He believes that the body of the statue is an authentic antiquity, but the form in which we see it is largely the imaginative fabrication of Evans's restorers. Many parts were missing when the figure was unearthed, and so an artist working for Evans fashioned new parts and attached them to the figure. The snake in the goddess's right hand lacked a head, leaving its identity as a snake open to question. Most of the goddess's left arm, including the snake in her hand, was absent and later fabricated. When the figure was discovered, it lacked a head, and this one is completely fabricated. The cat on the goddess's head is original, although it was not found with the statue. Lapatin believes that Evans, eager to advance his own theory that Minoan religion was dedicated to the worship of a Great Goddess, never questioned the manner in which the figures were restored. As interesting as the figure is, its identity as a snake goddess is at best questionable. We cannot even say with certainty that the principal deity of the Minoan culture was female, let alone that she was a snake goddess. There are no images of snake goddesses in surviving Minoan frescoes, engraved gems, or seals, and almost all of the statues depicting her are fakes or imaginative reconstructions.

It is likely, though, that Minoan female goddesses were closely associated with a cult of vegetation and fertility, and the snake is an almost universal symbol of rebirth and fertility. We do know that the Minoans worshiped on mountaintops, closely associated with life-giving rains, and deep in caves, another nearly universal symbol of the womb in particular and origin in general. And in early cultures, the undulations of the earth itself—its hills and ravines, caves and riverbeds—were (and often still are) associated with the curves of the female body and genitalia. But until early Minoan writing is deciphered, the exact nature of Minoan religion will remain a mystery.

The Palace of Minos The *Snake Goddess* was discovered along with other ritual objects in a storage pit in the Palace of Minos at Knossos. The palace as Evans found it is enormous, covering over 6 acres. There were originally two palaces at the site—an "old palace," dating from 1900 BCE, and a "new palace," built over the old one after an enormous earthquake in 1750 BCE. This "new palace" was the focus of Evans's attention.

It was one of three principal palace sites on Crete (see Map 4.1), and although Knossos is the largest, they are laid out along similar lines, with a central court surrounded by a labyrinth of rooms. They served as administrative, commercial, and religious centers ruled by a king, similar to the way palaces functioned in the civilizations of Mesopotamia and Egypt. The complexity of these unfortified palaces and the richness of the artifacts uncovered there testify to the power and prosperity of Minoan culture.

As its floor plan and reconstruction drawing make clear, the palace at Knossos was only loosely organized around a central, open courtyard (Fig. **4.5**). Leading from

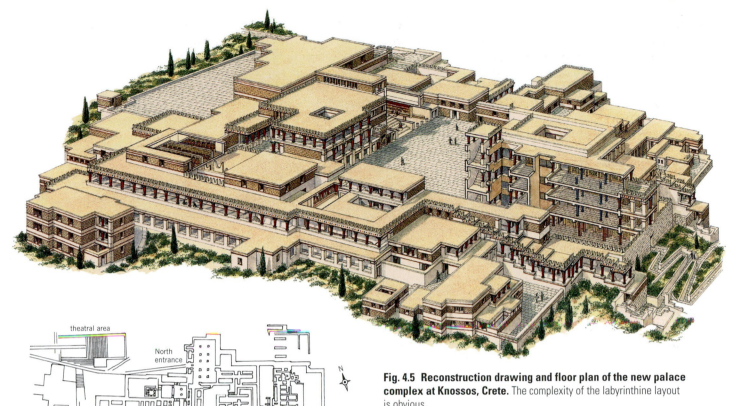

theatral area

North entrance

corridor access to magazines

temple repositories

West entrance

altars

throne room

staircase

main shrine

pillar crypt

grand staircase

East entrance

lapidary's workshop

Hall of the Double Axes

bathroom storeroom

Corridor of the Procession

South entrance

staircase

lavatory

Queen's Hall

0 10 20 30 meters

0 20 40 60 80 100 feet

Fig. 4.5 Reconstruction drawing and floor plan of the new palace complex at Knossos, Crete. The complexity of the labyrinthine layout is obvious.

the courtyard were corridors, staircases, and passageways that connected living quarters, ritual spaces, baths, and administrative offices, in no discernible order or design. Workshops surrounded the complex, and vast storerooms could easily provide for the needs of both the palace population and the population of the surrounding countryside. In just one storeroom, excavators discovered enough ceramic jars to hold 20,000 gallons of olive oil.

Hundreds of wooden columns decorated the palace. Only fragments have survived, but we know from paintings and ceramic house models how they must have looked. Evans created concrete replicas displayed today at the West Portico and the Grand Staircase (Fig. 4.6). The originals were made of huge timbers cut on Crete and then turned upside down so that the top of each is broader than the base.

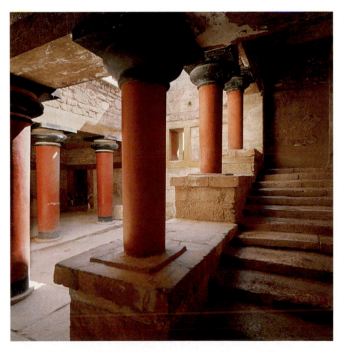

Fig. 4.6 Grand Staircase, east wing, palace complex at Knossos, Crete. ca. 1500 BCE. As reconstructed by Sir Arthur Evans. The staircase served as a light well and linked all five stories of the palace.

The columns were painted bright red with black **capitals**, the sculpted blocks that top them. The capitals are shaped like pillows or cushions. (In fact, they are very close to the shape of an evergreen's root ball, as if the original design were suggested by trees felled in a storm.) Over time, as the columns rotted or were destroyed by earthquakes or possibly burned by invaders, they must have become increasingly difficult to replace, for Minoan builders gradually deforested the island. This may be one reason why the palace complex was abandoned sometime around 1450 BCE.

Representations of double axes decorated the palace at every turn, and indeed the Palace of Minos was known in Greek times as the House of the Double Axes. In fact, the Greek word for the palace was *labyrinth*, from *labrys*, "double ax." Over time, the Greeks came to associate the House of the Double Axes with its inordinately complex layout, and *labyrinth* came to mean "maze."

The Legend of Minos and the Minotaur The Greeks solidified the meaning of the labyrinth in a powerful legend. King Minos boasted that the gods would grant him anything he wished, so he prayed that a bull might emerge from the sea that he might sacrifice to the god of the sea, Poseidon. A white bull did emerge from the sea, one so beautiful that Minos decided to keep it for himself and sacrifice a different one from his herd instead. This angered Poseidon, who took revenge by causing Minos' queen, Pasiphae, to fall in love with the bull. To consummate her passion, she convinced Minos' chief craftsperson, Daedalus, to construct a hollow wooden cow into which she might place herself and attract the bull. The result of this union was a horrid creature, half man, half bull: the Minotaur.

To appease the monster's appetite for human flesh, Minos ordered the city of Athens, which he also ruled, to send him 14 young men and women each year as sacrificial victims. Theseus, son of King Aegeus of Athens, vowed to kill the Minotaur. As he set sail for Crete with 13 others, he promised his father that he would return under white sails (instead of the black sails of the sacrificial ship) to announce his victory. At Crete, he seduced Ariadne, daughter of Minos. Wishing to help Theseus, she gave him a sword with which to kill the Minotaur and a spindle of thread to lead himself out of the maze in which the Minotaur lived. Victorious, Theseus sailed home with Ariadne but abandoned her on the island of Naxos, where she was discovered by the god of wine, Dionysus, who married her and made her his queen. Theseus, sailing into the harbor at Athens, neglected to raise the white sails, perhaps intentionally. When his father, King Aegeus, saw the ship still sailing under black sails, he threw himself into the sea, which from then on took his name, the Aegean. Theseus, of course, then became king.

The story is a creation or origin myth, like the Zuni emergence tale (see Reading 1.1 in Chapter 1) or the Hebrew story of Adam and Eve in Genesis. But it differs from them on one important point: Rather than narrating the origin of humankind in general, it tells the story of the birth of one culture out of another. It is the Athenian Greeks' way of knowing their past, their *archaiologia*. The tale of the labyrinth explained to the later Greeks where and how their culture came to be. It correctly suggests a close link to Crete, but it also emphasizes Greek independence from that powerful island. It tells us, furthermore, much about the emerging Greek character, for Theseus would, by the fifth century BCE, achieve the status of a national hero. The great tragedies of Greek theater represent Theseus as wily, ambitious, and strong. He stops at nothing to achieve what he thinks he must. If he is not altogether admirable, he mirrors behavior the Greeks attributed to their gods. Nevertheless, he is anything but idealized or godlike. He is, almost to a fault, completely human.

It was precisely this search for the origins of Greek culture that led Sir Arthur Evans to the discovery of the Palace of Minos in Crete. He confirmed "the truth" in the legend of the Minotaur. If there was no actual monster, there was indeed a labyrinth. And that labyrinth was the palace itself.

Mycenaean Culture on the Mainland

When the Minoans abandoned the palace at Knossos in about 1450 BCE, warriors from the mainland culture of Mycenae, on the Greek mainland, quickly occupied Crete (see Map 4.1). One reason for the abandonment of Knossos was suggested earlier—the deforestation of the island. Another might be that Minoan culture was severely weakened in the aftermath of the volcanic eruption on Thera, and therefore susceptible to invasion or internal revolution. A third might be that the Mycenaean army simply

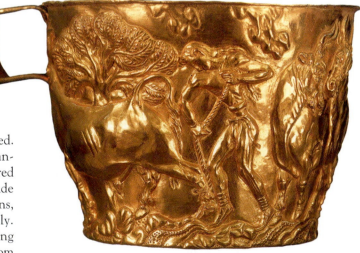

Fig. 4.7 ***Vaphio Cup*, from a tomb at Vaphio, south of Sparta, Greece. ca. 1650–1450 BCE.** Gold, height 3½". National Archeological Museum, Iráklion, Crete. Mycenaean invaders used Crete as a base for operations for several centuries, and probably acquired the cup there.

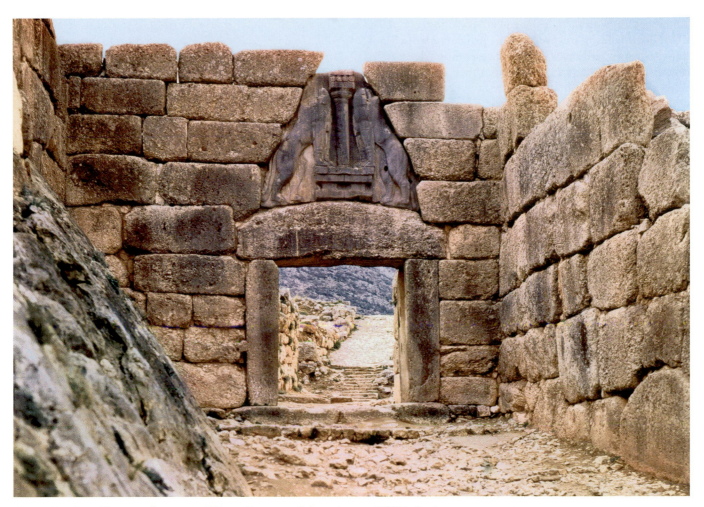

Fig. 4.8 Lion Gate, Mycenae, Greece. ca. 1300 BCE. Limestone relief, panel approx. 9'6" high. The lionesses are carved on a triangle of stone that relieves the weight of the massive doorway from the lintel. The original heads, which have never been found, were attached to the bodies with dowels.

overwhelmed the island. The Mycenaeans were certainly acquainted with the Minoan culture some 92 miles to their south, across the Aegean.

Minoan metalwork was prized on the mainland. Its fine quality is very evident in the *Vaphio Cup*, one of two golden cups found in the nineteenth century in a tomb at Vaphio, just south of Sparta, on the Peloponnese (Fig. **4.7**). This cup was executed in **repoussé**, a technique in which the artist hammers out the design from the inside. It depicts a man in an olive grove capturing a bull by tethering its hind legs. The bull motif is classically Minoan. The Mycenaeans, however, could not have been more different from the Minoans. Whereas Minoan towns were unfortified, and battle scenes were virtually nonexistent in their art, the Mycenaeans lived in communities surrounding fortified hilltops, and battle and hunting scenes dominate their art. Minoan culture appears to have been peaceful, while the warlike Mycenaeans lived and died by the sword.

The ancient city of Mycenae, which gave its name to the larger Mycenaean culture, was discovered by German archeologist Heinrich Schliemann (1822–90) in the late nineteenth century, before Sir Arthur Evans discovered

Knossos. Its citadel looks down across a broad plain to the sea. Its walls—20 feet thick and 50 feet high—were built from huge blocks of rough-hewn stone, in a technique called **cyclopean masonry** because it was believed by later Greeks that only a race of monsters known as the Cyclopes could have managed them. Visitors to the city entered through a massive Lion Gate at the top of a steep path that led from the valley below (Fig. **4.8**). The lionesses that stood above the gate's lintel were themselves 9 feet high. It is likely that their missing heads originally turned in the direction of approaching visitors, as if to ward off evil or, perhaps, humble them in their tracks, like Sargon's human-headed bull gates at Khorsabad (see Fig. 2.13 in Chapter 2). They were probably made of a different stone than the bodies and may have been plundered at a later time. From the gate, a long, stone street wound up the hill to the citadel itself. Here, overseeing all, was the king's palace.

Mycenae was only one of several fortified cities on mainland Greece that were flourishing by 1500 BCE and that have come to be called Mycenaean. Mycenaean culture was the forerunner of ancient Greek culture and was essentially **feudal** in nature—that is, a system of political organization held together by ties of allegiance between a lord and those who relied on him for protection. Kings controlled not only their own cities but also the surrounding countryside. Merchants, farmers, and artisans owed their own prosperity to the king and paid high taxes for the privilege of living under his protection. More powerful kings, such as those at Mycenae itself, also expected the loyalty (and financial support) of other cities and nobles over whom they exercised authority. A large bureaucracy of tax collectors, civil servants, and military personnel ensured the state's continued prosperity. Like the Minoans, they engaged in trade, especially for the copper and tin required to make bronze.

The feudal system allowed Mycenae's kings to amass enormous wealth, as Schliemann's excavations confirmed. He discovered gold and silver death masks of fallen heroes (Fig. **4.9**), as well as swords and daggers inlaid with imagery of events such as a royal lion hunt. He also found delicately carved ivory, from the tusks of hippopotamuses and elephants, suggesting if not the breadth of Mycenae's power, then the extent of its trade, which clearly included Africa. It seems likely, in fact, that the Mycenaean taste for war, and certainly their occupation of Crete, was motivated by the desire to control trade routes throughout the region.

Schliemann discovered most of this wealth in **shaft graves**, vertical pits some 20 or 25 feet deep enclosed in a circle of stone slabs. These all date from the early years of Mycenaean civilization, about 1500 BCE. Beginning in about 1300 BCE, the Mycenaeans used a new architectural

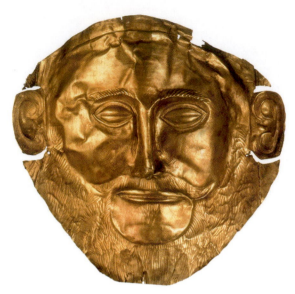

Fig. 4.9 Funerary mask (*Mask of Agamemnon*), from Grave Circle A, Mycenae, Greece. ca. 1600–1550 BCE. Gold, height approx. 12". National Archeological Museum, Athens. When Schliemann discovered this mask, he believed it was the death mask of King Agamemnon, but it predates the Trojan War by some 300 years. Recent scholarship suggests that Schliemann may have added the handlebar mustache and large ears, perhaps to make the mask appear more "heroic."

form, the *tholos*, to bury their kings. A *tholos* is a round building often called a *beehive* because of its shape. The most famous of these tombs is the Treasury of Atreus,

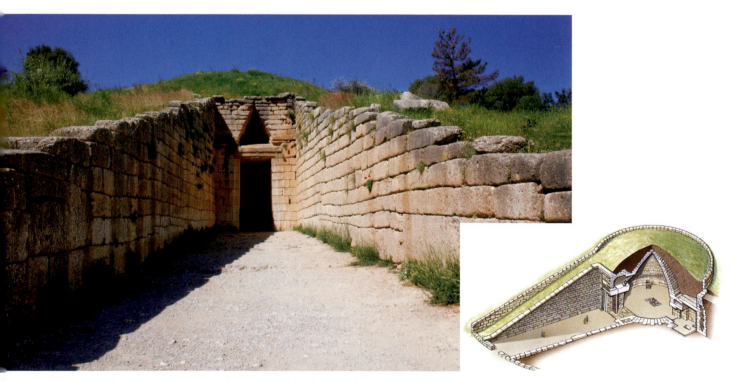

Fig. 4.10 and Fig. 4.11 Facade and sectioned view of the *tholos* of the Treasury of Atreus, Mycenae, Greece. ca. 1250 BCE. Interior vault height, 43', diameter 47'6". The interior space of this *tholos*—a round building—remained the largest uninterrupted space in Europe until the Pantheon was built in Rome 1,000 years later. The dome is an example of corbeled construction: As the roof's squared stones curve inward toward the top, they were buttressed, or supported, on the outside by earth. Because of the conical shape of such burial chambers, they are known as *beehive tombs*.

the name Schliemann attributed to it (Figs. **4.10, 4.11**). Atreus was the father of Agamemnon, an early king of Mycenae known to us from the literature of later Greeks. However, no evidence supports Schliemann's attribution except the structure's extraordinary size, which was befitting of a legendary king, and the fact that it dates from approximately the time of the Trojan War. (Agamemnon led the Greeks in the ten-year war against Trojans that would form the background for Homer's epic poems, the *Iliad* and the *Odyssey*, discussed next.) The approach to the Treasury of Atreus is by way of a long, open-air passage nearly 115 feet long and 20 feet wide leading to a 16-foot-high door. Over the door is a **relieving triangle**, a triangular opening above the lintel designed to relieve some of the weight the lintel has to bear. (See the discussions of lintels in Chapter 1.) Surviving fragments reveal that a pair of green marble columns topped by two red marble columns originally adorned the facade of the Treasury of Atreus. The columns were **engaged**—that is, they projected in relief from the wall but served no structural purpose. Behind the door lay the burial chamber, a giant domed space, in which the dead would have been laid out together with gold and silver artifacts, ceremonial weapons, helmets, armor, and other items that would indicate power, wealth, and prestige.

THE HOMERIC EPICS

What is an epic, and how do Homer's epics the Iliad *and the* Odyssey *differ?*

One of the most fascinating aspects of the eastern Mediterranean in the Bronze Age is the development of written language. First, around the middle of the second millennium BCE, as trade increasingly flourished between and among the Greek islands and the mainland, a linear Minoan script began to appear on tablets and objects across the region. Then, 600 to 700 years later, the Phoenicians, the great traders of the area, began to spread a distinctly new writing system, based on an alphabet (apparently of their own invention), across the entire Mediterranean basin.

But if the Greeks plundered Phoenician traders, they also were quick to take advantage of their writing system. Their alphabet allowed the Phoenicians to keep records more easily and succinctly than their competitors. It could be quickly taught to others, which facilitated communication in the far-flung regions where their ships sailed, and, written on papyrus, it was much more portable than the clay tablets used in Mesopotamia.

Once the ancient Greeks adopted the Phoenician alphabet in about 800 BCE, they began to write down the stories from and about their past—their *archaiologia*—that had been passed down, generation to generation, by word of mouth. The most important of these stories were composed

by an author whom history calls Homer. Homer was most likely a **bard**, a singer of songs about the deeds of heroes and the ways of the gods. His stories were part of a long-standing oral tradition that dated back to the time of the Trojan War, which we believe occurred sometime around 1200 BCE. Out of the oral materials he inherited, Homer composed two great epic poems, the *Iliad* and the *Odyssey*. The first narrates an episode in the ten-year Trojan War, which, according to Homer, began when the Greeks launched a large fleet of ships under King Agamemnon of Mycenae to bring back Helen, the wife of his brother King Menelaus of Sparta, who had eloped with Paris, son of King Priam of Troy. The *Odyssey* narrates the adventures of one of the principal Greek leaders, Odysseus (also known as Ulysses), on his return home from the fighting.

Most scholars believed that these Homeric epics were pure fiction until the discovery by Heinrich Schliemann in the 1870s of the actual site of Troy, a multilayered site near modern-day Hissarlik, in northwestern Turkey. The Troy of Homer's epic was discovered at the sixth layer. (Schliemann also believed that the shaft graves at Mycenae, where he found so much treasure, were those of Agamemnon and his royal family, but modern dating techniques have ruled that out.) Suddenly, the *Iliad* assumed, if not the authority, then the aura of historical fact. Scholars studying both the poem and a Mycenaean vase known as the *Warrior Vase* have been struck by the similarity of many passages in the *Iliad* and scenes depicted on the vase. Those similarities testify to the accuracy of many of the poem's descriptions of Bronze Age Greece (Fig. **4.12**).

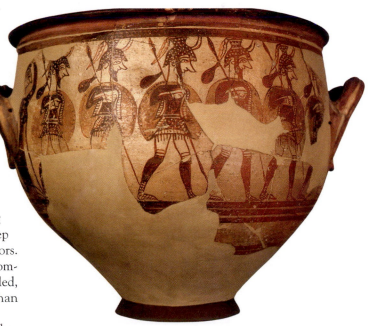

Fig. 4.12 ***Warrior Vase*****, from Mycenae, Greece. ca. 1300–1100 BCE.** Ceramic, height 16". National Archeological Museum, Athens. Dating from the time of the Trojan War, the vase depicts a woman, on the left, waving goodbye to departing troops.

How Homer came to compose two works as long as the *Iliad* and the *Odyssey* has been the subject of much debate. Did he improvise each oral performance from memory, or did he rely on written texts? There is clear evidence that **formulaic epithets**—descriptive phrases applied to a person or thing—helped him, suggesting that improvisation played an important part in the poem's composition. Common epithets in the *Iliad* include such phrases as "fleet-footed Achilles" and "bronze-armed Achaeans." (*Achaean* is the term Homer uses to designate the Greeks whom we associate with the Mycenaeans.) These epithets appear to have been chosen to allow the performing poet to fit a given name easily into the **hexameter** structure of the verse line—what we today call "epic" meter. Each hexameter line

of Homer's verse is composed of six metrical units, which can be made up of either **dactyls** (a long syllable plus two short ones) or **spondees** (two long syllables). "Fleet-footed" is a dactyl; "bronze-armed" a spondee. The first four units of the line can be either dactyls or spondees; the last two must be dactyl and spondee, in that order. This regular meter, and the insertion of stock phrases into it, undoubtedly helped the poet to memorize and repeat the poem.

In order to perform the 15,693 lines of the *Iliad*, it became increasingly necessary to write the poem down. By the sixth century BCE, it was recited every four years in Athens (without omission, according to law), and many copies of it circulated around Greece in the fifth and fourth centuries BCE. Finally, in Alexandria, Egypt, in the

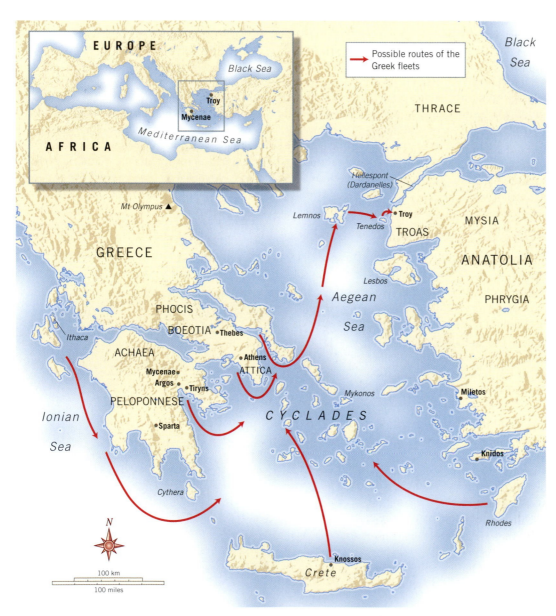

Map 4.2 Possible routes of the Greek fleets as they gathered and then sailed to Troy. At the end of Book 2 of the *Iliad*, Homer catalogs the participating parties in the Trojan War. He lists kings and their followers from more than 150 places. It seems doubtful that the conflict was truly precipitated by the abduction of Helen from Sparta. More likely, the Greeks wanted to wrest control of the Hellespont (today known as the Dardanelles) from the Trojans, in order to gain access to trading opportunities in the Black Sea and Asia.

late fourth century BCE, scribes wrote the poem on papyrus scrolls, perhaps dividing it into the 24 manageable units we refer to today as the poem's books.

The poem was so influential that it established certain **epic conventions**, standard ways of composing an epic that were followed for centuries to come. Examples include starting the poem *in medias res*, Latin for "in the middle of things," that is, in the middle of the story; invoking the muse at the poem's outset; and stating the poem's subject at the outset.

The *Iliad*

The *Iliad* tells but a small fraction of the story of the Trojan War, which was launched by Agamemnon of Mycenae and his allies to attack Troy around 1200 BCE (Map **4.2**). The tale begins after the war is under way and narrates what is commonly called "the rage of Achilles," a phrase drawn from the first line of the poem. Already encamped on the Trojan plain, Agamemnon has been forced to give up a girl that he has taken in one of his raids, but he takes the beautiful Briseis from Achilles as compensation. Achilles, by far the greatest of the Greek warriors, is outraged, suppresses his urge to kill Agamemnon, but withdraws from the war. He knows that the Greeks cannot succeed without him, and in his rage he believes they deserve their fate. Indeed, Hector, the great Trojan prince, soon drives the Greeks back to their ships, and Agamemnon sends ambassadors to Achilles to offer him gifts and beg him to return to the battle. Achilles refuses: "His gifts, I loathe his gifts … I wouldn't give you a splinter for that man! Not if he gave me ten times as much, twenty times over." When the battle resumes, things become desperate for the Greeks. Achilles partially relents, permitting Patroclus, his close friend and perhaps his lover, to wear his armor in order to put fear into the Trojans. Led by Patroclus, the Achaeans drive the Trojans back.

An excerpt from Book 16 of the *Iliad* narrates the fall of the Trojan warrior Sarpedon at the hands of Patroclus (see **Reading 4.1**, page 128). The passage opens with one of the scene's many Homeric similes: The charging Trojan forces described as "an onrush dark as autumn days / when the whole earth flattens black beneath a gale." Most notable, however, is the unflinching verbal picture Homer paints of the realities of war, not only its cowardice, panic, and brutality, but its compelling attraction as well. In this arena, the Greek soldier is able to demonstrate one of the most important values in Greek culture, his *areté*, often translated as "virtue," but actually meaning something closer to "being the best you can be" or "reaching your highest human potential." Homer uses the term to describe both Greek and Trojan heroes, and it refers not only to their bravery but to their effectiveness in battle.

The sixth-century BCE painting on the side of the *Botkin Class Amphora*—an **amphora** is a Greek jar, with an egg-shaped body and two curved handles, used for storing oil or wine—embodies the concept of *areté* (Fig. **4.13**). Here, two warriors, one armed with a sword, the other with a spear,

confront each other with unwavering determination and purpose. At one point in the *Iliad*, Homer describes two such warriors, holding their own against one another, as "rejoicing in the joy of battle." They rejoice because they find themselves in a place where they can demonstrate their *areté*.

The following passage, from Book 24, the final section of the *Iliad*, shows the other side of war and the other side of the poem, the compassion and humanity that distinguish Homer's narration (**Reading 4.1a**). Soon after Patroclus kills Sarpedon, Hector, son of the king of Troy, strikes down Patroclus with the aid of the god Apollo. On hearing the news, Achilles is devastated and finally enters the fray. Until now, fuming over Agamemnon's insult, he has sat out the battle, refusing, in effect, to demonstrate his own *areté*. But now, he redirects his rage from Agamemnon to the Trojan warrior Hector, whom he meets and kills. He then ties Hector's body to his chariot and drags it to his tent. The act is pure sacrilege, a violation of the dignity due the great Trojan warrior and an insult to his memory. Late that night, Priam, the king of Troy, steals across enemy lines to Achilles' tent and begs for the body of his son:

View the Closer Look for red-figure and black-figure vessels on **MyArtsLab**

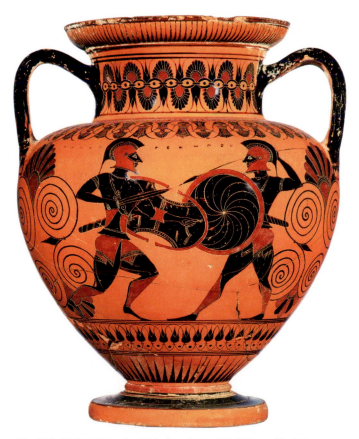

Fig. 4.13 *Botkin Class Amphora*, Greek. ca. 540–530 BCE. Black-figure decoration on ceramic, height 11⁹⁄₁₆", diameter 9½". Museum of Fine Arts, Boston, Henry Lillie Pierce Fund, 98.923. Photograph © 2014 Museum of Fine Arts, Boston. On the other side of this vase are two heavily armed warriors, one pursuing the other.

READING 4.1a

from Homer, *Iliad*, Book 24
(ca. 750 BCE)

"Remember your own father, great godlike Achilles—
as old as I am, past the threshold of deadly old age!
No doubt the countrymen round about him plague him now,
with no one there to defend him, beat away disaster.
No one—but at least he hears you're still alive
and his old heart rejoices, hopes rising, day by day,
to see his beloved son come sailing home from Troy.
But I—dear god, my life so cursed by fate …
I fathered hero sons in the wide realm of Troy
and now not a single one is left, I tell you.
Fifty sons I had when the sons of Achaea came,
nineteen born to me from a single mother's womb
and the rest by other women in the palace. Many,
most of them violent Ares cut the knees from under.
But one, one was left me, to guard my wall, my people—
the one you killed the other day, defending his fatherland,
my Hector! It's all for him I've come to the ships now,
to win him back from you—I bring a priceless ransom.
Revere the gods, Achilles! Pity me in my own right,
remember your own father! I deserve more pity …
I have endured what no one on earth has ever done
     before—
I put to my lips the hands of the man who killed my son."

Those words stirred within Achilles a deep desire
to grieve for his own father. Taking the old man's hand
he gently moved him back. And overpowered by memory
both men gave way to grief. Priam wept freely
for man-killing Hector, throbbing, crouching
before Achilles' feet as Achilles wept himself,
now for his father, now for Patroclus once again,
and their sobbing rose and fell throughout the house. …
Then Achilles called the serving-women out:
"Bathe and anoint the body—
bear it aside first. Priam must not see his son."
He feared that, overwhelmed by the sight of Hector,
wild with grief, Priam might let his anger flare
and Achilles might fly into fresh rage himself,
cut the old man down and break the laws of Zeus.
So when the maids had bathed and anointed the body
sleek with olive oil and wrapped it round and round
in a braided battle-shirt and handsome battle-cape,
then Achilles lifted Hector up in his own arms
and laid him down on a bier, and comrades helped him
raise the bier and body onto a sturdy wagon …
Then with a groan he called his dear friend by name:
"Feel no anger at me, Patroclus, if you learn—
ever there in the House of Death—I let his father
have Prince Hector back. He gave me worthy ransom
and you shall have your share from me, as always,
your fitting, lordly share."

Homer clearly recognizes the ability of these warriors to exceed their mere humanity, to raise themselves not only to a level of great military achievement, but to a state of compassion, nobility, and honor. It is this exploration of the "doubleness" of the human spirit, its cruelty and its humanity, its blindness and its insight, that perhaps best defines the power and vision of the Homeric epic.

The *Odyssey*

The fall of Troy to the Greek army after the famous ruse of the Trojan Horse (Fig. **4.14**) is actually described in Book 4 of the *Odyssey*, the *Iliad*'s 24-book sequel. In **Reading 4.2a**, Menelaus, now returned home with Helen, addresses her, while Telemachus, son of the Greek commander Odysseus, listens:

READING 4.2a

from Homer, *Odyssey*, Book 4
(ca. 725 BCE)

… never have I seen one like Odysseus
for steadiness and stout heart. Here, for instance,
is what he did—had the cold nerve to do—
inside the hollow horse, where we were waiting,
picked men all of us, for the Trojan slaughter,
when all of a sudden, you [Helen] came by—I dare say
drawn by some superhuman
power that planned an exploit for the Trojans;
and Deïphobos, that handsome man, came with you.
Three times you walked around it, patting it everywhere,
and called by name the flower of our fighters,
making your voice sound like their wives, calling.
Diomêdês and I crouched in the center
Along with Odysseus; we could hear you plainly;
and listening, we two were swept
by waves of longing—to reply, or go.
Odysseus fought us down, despite our craving,
and all the Akhaians kept their lips shut tight,
all but Antiklos. Desire moved his throat
to hail you, but Odysseus' great hands clamped
over his jaws, and held. So he saved us all,
till Pallas Athena led you away at last.

Many of the themes of Homer's second epic are embedded in this short reminiscence. For although the poem narrates the adventures of Odysseus on his ten-year journey home from the war in Troy—his encounters with monsters, giants, and a seductive enchantress, and a sojourn on a floating island and in the underworld—its subject is, above all, Odysseus' passionate desire to once more see his wife, Penelope, and Penelope's fidelity to him. Where anger and lust drive the *Iliad*—remember Achilles' angry sulk and Helen's fickleness—love and familial affection drive the *Odyssey*. Penelope is gifted with *areté* in her own right, since for the 20 years of her husband's absence, she uses all the cunning in her power to ward off the many suitors who flock to marry her, convinced that Odysseus is never coming home.

A second important theme taken up by Menelaus is the role of the gods in determining the outcome of human

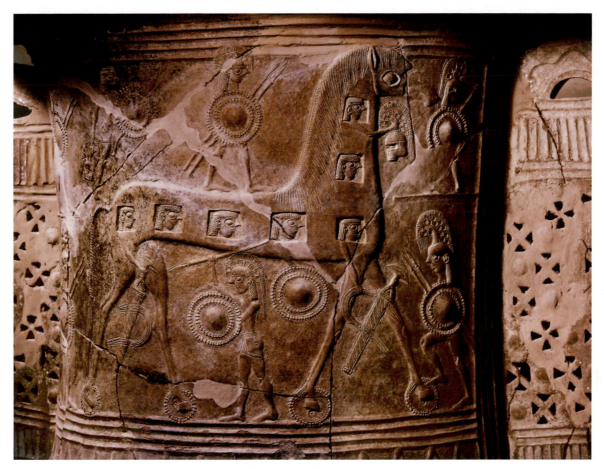

Fig. 4.14 *The Trojan Horse,* **detail from a storage jar from Chora, Mykonos. ca. 650 BCE.** Total height of jar 5", detail as shown approx. 1". Archeological Museum, Mykonos. This is the earliest known depiction of the Trojan Horse, the hollow "gift" that the supposedly departing Greeks left to King Priam and his followers. The artist has opened little windows in its side, showing the Greeks hiding within, ready to attack.

Read the document related to Homer on **MyArtsLab**

events. Helen, he says, must have been drawn to the Trojan Horse "by some superhuman / power that planned an exploit for the Trojans"—some god, in other words, on the Trojans' side. And, indeed, Pallas Athena, goddess of war and wisdom and protectress of the Achaeans, leads Helen away from the horse. But in both the *Iliad* and the *Odyssey,* Homer is careful to distinguish between how people believe the gods exercise control over events (**Reading 4.2b**) and what control they actually exercise. In fact, early on in Book 1 of the *Odyssey,* Zeus, king of the gods, exclaims:

READING 4.2b

from Homer, *Odyssey,* Book 1
(ca. 725 BCE)

My word, how mortals take the gods to task!
All their afflictions come from us, we hear.
And what of their own failings? Greed and folly
double the suffering in the lot of man.

The Greek view of the universe contrasts dramatically with that of the Hebrews. If the Greek gods exercise some authority over the lives of human beings—they do control their ultimate fate—human beings are in complete control of how they live. By exercising selflessness and wisdom, as opposed to greed and folly, they could at least halve their suffering, Zeus implies. In the *Iliad,* the crimes that Paris and Achilles commit do not violate a divine code of ethics like the Ten Commandments but, rather, a code of behavior defined by their fellow Greeks. In the Greek world, humans are ultimately responsible for their own actions.

This is the real point of the fantastic episode of Odysseus' cunning trickery of the Cyclops Polyphemus in Book 9 of the *Odyssey,* related by Odysseus himself to Alkinoös, King of Phaeacia (see **Reading 4.2**, pages 130–133 for the full tale). It is Odysseus' craftiness—his wit and his intelligence—not the intervention of the gods, that saves him and his men. Compared to the stories that have come down to us from other Bronze Age cultures such as Egypt or Mesopotamia, Homer is less concerned with what happened than *how* it happened. We encounter Odysseus' trickery, his skill at making weapons, and his wordplay (Odysseus

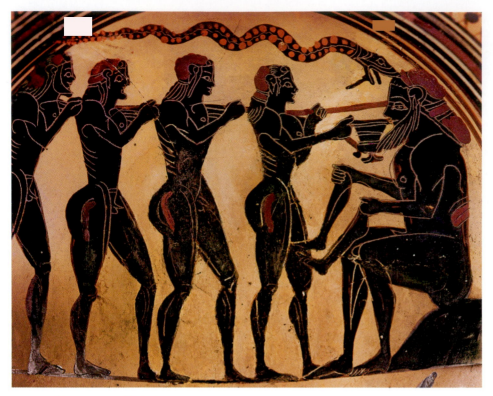

Fig. 4.15 *The Blinding of Polyphemus*, **inside of drinking cup from Sparta. ca. 550 BCE.** Ceramic, diameter 8¼". Cabinet des Médailles, Bibliothèque nationale de France. At the same time that Odysseus and his companions blind Polyphemus with the pointed pole, they offer him the drink that inebriates him sufficiently to allow them to complete their task, and he finishes eating one of their companions, whose two legs he holds in his hands.

calling himself "Nobody" in anticipation of Polyphemus being asked by the other Cyclopes who has blinded him and Polyphemus replying, "Nobody").

Greek artists shared this concern. They would try to refer to as many of Odysseus' talents as they could in a single work, depicting successive actions around the diameter of a vase or, as in the case of a drinking cup from Sparta, packing more than one action into a single scene (Fig. **4.15**). We saw this form of synoptic pictorial narrative in Mesopotamia, in the sculptural relief of *Ashurnasirpal II Killing Lions* (see Fig. 2.12 in Chapter 2). It is also similar to the pictorial narrative used in the *Last Judgment of Hunefer* in an Egyptian Book of Going Forth by Day, where instead of reading left to right, the actions are compounded one upon the other (see Fig. 3.25 in Chapter 3).

In later Greek culture, the *Iliad* and the *Odyssey* were the basis of Greek education. Every schoolchild learned the two poems by heart. They were the principal vehicles through which the Greeks came to know the past, and through the past, they came to know themselves. The poems embodied what might be called the Greeks' own cultural, as opposed to purely personal, *areté*, their desire to achieve a place of preeminence among all states. But in defining this larger cultural ambition, the *Iliad* and *Odyssey* laid out the individual values and responsibilities that all Greeks understood to be their personal obligations and duties if the state were ever to realize its goals.

THE GREEK POLIS

How are the values of the Greek polis reflected in its art and architecture?

After the fall of Mycenae in about 1100 BCE, some 100 years after the Trojan War, Greece endured a long period of cultural decline that many refer to as the Dark Ages. Greek legend has it that a tribe from the north, the Dorians, overran the Greek mainland and the Peloponnese (Map **4.3**), but there is little historical evidence to support this story. Whatever caused the decline, the Greek people almost forgot the rudiments of culture, and reading and writing fell into disuse. For the most part, the Greeks lived in small rural communities that often warred with one another. But despite these conditions, which hardly favored the development of art and architecture, the Greeks managed to sustain a sense of identity and even, as the survival of the Trojan War legends suggests, some idea of their cultural heritage.

The Greek **polis**—or city-state—arose during the eighth century BCE, around the time of Homer. Colonists set sail from cities on the Greek mainland to establish new settlements. Eventually, there were as many as 1,500 Greek poleis (plural of polis) scattered around the Mediterranean and the Black Sea from Spain to the Crimea, including large colonies in Italy (Fig. **4.16**). This process of

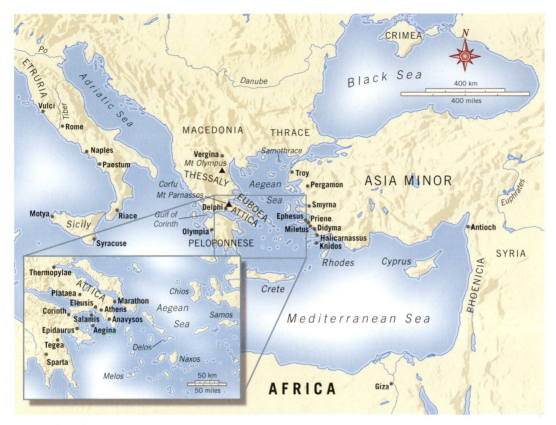

Map 4.3 **The city-states of ancient Greece.**

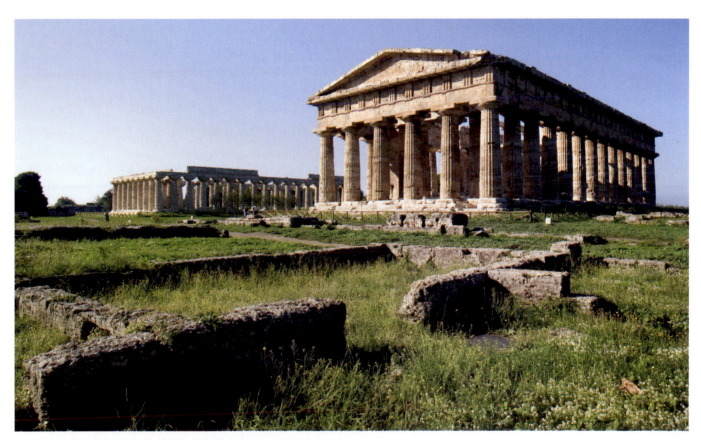

Fig. 4.16 **The Temple of Hera I (background), ca. 540 BCE, and the Temple of Hera II (foreground), ca. 460 BCE, Paestum, Italy.** Two of the best-preserved Greek temples can be found in Italy, at Paestum, south of Naples, in a place the Greeks called Poseidonia, after the god of the sea, Poseidon.

colonization occurred gradually. First, across Greece, communities began to organize themselves and exercise authority over their own limited geographical regions, which were defined by natural boundaries—mountains, rivers, and plains. The population of even the largest communities was largely dedicated to agriculture, and agricultural values—a life of hard, honest work and self-reliance—predominated. The great pastoral poem of the poet Hesiod (flourished ca. 700 BCE), *Works and Days*, testifies to this. *Works and Days* was written at about the same time as the Homeric epics in Boeotia, the region of Greece dominated by the city-state of Thebes. Particularly interesting is Hesiod's narration of the duties of the farmer as the seasons progress. Here are his words regarding the farmer's obligation to plow his fields (**Reading 4.3**):

READING 4.3

from Hesiod, *Works and Days* (ca. 700 BCE)

Autumn

Mind now, when you hear the call of the crane
Coming from the clouds, as it does year by year:
That's the sign for plowing, and the onset of winter
And the rainy season. That cry bites the heart
Of the man with no ox.

      Time then to feed your oxen
In their stall. You know it's easy to say,
"Loan me a wagon and a team of oxen."
And it's easy to answer, "Got work for my oxen."
It takes a good imagination for a man to think
He'll just peg together a wagon. Damn fool,
Doesn't realize there's a hundred timbers make up a wagon
And you have to have 'em laid up beforehand at home.
Soon as you get the first signs for plowing
Get a move on, yourself and your workers,
And plow straight through wet weather and dry,
Getting a good start at dawn, so your fields
Will fill up. Work the land in spring, too,
But fallow turned in summer won't let you down.
Sow your fallow land while the soil's still light.
Fallow's the charm that keeps wee-uns well-fed.
Pray to Zeus-in-the-ground and to Demeter sacred
For Demeter's holy grain to grow thick and full.
Pray when you first start plowing, when you
Take hold of the handle and come down with your stick
On the backs of the oxen straining at the yoke-pins.
A little behind, have a slave follow with a hoe
To make trouble for the birds by covering the seeds.
Doing things right is the best thing in the world,
Just like doing 'em wrong is the absolute worst.
This way you'll have ears of grain bending
Clear to the ground …

In this extract, Hesiod gives us a clear insight not only into many of the details of Greek agricultural production, but into social conditions as well. He mentions slaves twice in this short passage, and, indeed, all landowners possessed slaves (taken in warfare), who comprised over half the population. He also mentions the Greek gods Zeus, king of the gods and master of the sky, and Demeter, goddess of agriculture and grain (see *Context*, page 114). In fact, it was Hesiod, in his *Theogony* (*The Birth of the Gods*), who first detailed the Greek **pantheon** (literally, "all the gods"). The story of the creation of the world that he tells in this work (**Reading 4.4**) resembles the origin myths from the Zuni emergence tale (see Reading 1.1 in Chapter 1) and the Japanese Shinto *Kojiki* (see Reading 1.2 in Chapter 1):

READING 4.4

from Hesiod, *Theogony* (ca. 700 BCE)

First of all the Void[1] came into being, next broad-bosomed Earth, the solid and eternal home of all,[2] and Eros [Desire], the most beautiful of the immortal gods, who in every man and every god softens the sinews and overpowers the prudent purpose of the mind. Out of the Void came Darkness and black Night, and out of Night came Light and day, her children conceived after union in love with Darkness. Earth first produced starry Sky, equal in size with herself.

[1] The Greek word is *Chaos;* but this has a misleading connotation in English.
[2] Omitting lines 118–19: "the immortals who live on the peaks of snowy Olympus, and gloomy Tartarus in a hole underneath the highways of the earth."

Behavior of the Gods

Of particular interest here—as in Homer's *Iliad*—is that the gods are as susceptible to Eros, or Desire, as is humankind. In fact, the Greek gods are sometimes more human than humans—susceptible to every human foible. Like many a family on earth, the father, Zeus, is an all-powerful philanderer, whose wife, Hera, is watchful, jealous, and capable of inflicting great pain upon rivals for her husband's affections. Their children are scheming and self-serving in their competition for their parents' attention. The gods think like humans, act like humans, and speak like humans. They sometimes seem to differ from humans only in the fact that they are immortal. Unlike the Hebrew God, who is sometimes portrayed as arbitrary, the Greek gods present humans with no clear principles of behavior, and the priests and priestesses who oversaw the rituals dedicated to them produced no scriptures or doctrines. The gods were capricious, capable of changing their minds, susceptible to argument and persuasion, alternately obstinate and malleable. If these qualities created a kind of cosmic uncertainty, they also embodied the intellectual freedom and the spirit of philosophical inquiry that would come to define the Greek state.

The Competing Poleis

Although Greece was an agricultural society, the polis—not the farm—was the focal point of cultural life. It consisted of an urban center, small by modern standards, often surrounding some form of natural citadel, which could serve as a fortification, but which usually functioned as the city-state's religious center. The Greeks called this citadel an **acropolis**—literally, the "top of the city." On lower ground, at the foot of the acropolis, was the **agora**, a large open area that served as public meeting place, marketplace, and civic center (see the beginning of Chapter 5).

Athens led the way, perhaps because it had become something of a safe haven during the Dark Ages, even flourishing as a result, and it thus maintained something of a civic identity. Gradually, the polis came to describe less a place and more a cultural and communal identity. The citizens of the polis, including the rural population of the region—the polis of Sparta, for instance, comprised some 3,000 square miles of the Peloponnese, while Athens controlled the 1,000 square miles of the region known as Attica—owed allegiance and loyalty to it. They depended upon and served in its military. They worshiped and trusted in its gods. And they asserted their identity, first of all, by participating in the affairs of the city-state, next by their family (*genos*) involvement, and, probably least of all, by any sense of being Greek.

In fact, the Greek poleis were distinguished by their isolation from one another and their fierce independence. For the most part, Greece is a very rugged country of mountains separating small areas of arable plains. The Greek historian Thucydides attributed the independence of the poleis to the historical competition in earlier times for these fertile regions of the country. His *History of the Peloponnesian Wars*, written in the last decades of the fifth century BCE and begun during the wars (he served as a general in the Athenian army), opens with an account of these earlier times, tracing the conflict in his own time to that historical situation (**Reading 4.5**):

READING 4.5

Thucydides, *History of the Peloponnesian Wars*

[I]t is evident that the country now called Hellas had in ancient times no settled population; on the contrary, migrations were of frequent occurrence, the several tribes readily abandoning their homes under the pressure of superior numbers. Without commerce, without freedom of communication either by land or sea, cultivating no more of their territory than the exigencies of life required, destitute of capital, never planting their land (for they could not tell when an invader might not come and take it all away, and when he did come they had no walls to stop him), thinking that the necessities of daily sustenance could be supplied at one place as well as another, they cared little for shifting their habitation, and consequently neither built large cities nor attained to any other form of greatness. The richest soils were always most subject to this change of masters; such as the district now called Thessaly, Boeotia, most of the Peloponnese, Arcadia excepted, and the most fertile parts of the rest of Hellas. The goodness of the land favored the aggrandizement of particular individuals, and thus created faction which proved a fertile source of ruin. It also invited invasion.

While Greek poleis might form temporary alliances, almost always in league against other poleis, few of the invasions Thucydides speaks of resulted in the domination of one polis over another, at least not for long. Rather, each polis maintained its own identity and resisted domination.

But inevitably, certain city-states became more powerful than others. During the Dark Ages, many Athenians had migrated to Ionia in southwestern Anatolia (present-day Turkey), and relations with the Near East helped Athens to flourish. Corinth, situated on the isthmus between the Greek mainland and the Peloponnese, controlled north–south trade routes from early times, but after it built a towpath to drag ships over the isthmus on rollers, it soon controlled the sea routes east and west as well.

Life in Sparta Of all the early city-states, Sparta was perhaps the most powerful. The Spartans traced their ancestry back to the legendary Dorians, whose legacy was military might. The rule of the city-state fell to the *homoioi*, or "equals," who comprised roughly 10 percent of the population. The population consisted largely of farm laborers, or *helots*, essentially slaves who worked the land held by the *homoioi*. (A third class of people, those who had inhabited the area before the arrival of the Spartans, enjoyed limited freedom but were subject to Spartan rule.)

Political power resided with five overseers who were elected annually by all *homoioi*—excluding women—over the age of 30. At age 7, males were taken from their parents to live under military discipline in barracks until age 30 (though they could marry at age 20). Men ate in the military mess until age 60. Women were given strenuous physical training so that they might bear strong sons. Weak-looking babies were left to die. The city-state, in short, controlled every aspect of the Spartans' lives. If the other Greek poleis were less militaristic, they nevertheless exercised the same authority in some fashion. They exercised power more often through political rather than militaristic means, though most could be as militaristic as Sparta when the need arose.

The Greek Gods

The religion of the Greeks informed almost every aspect of daily life. The gods watched over the individual at birth, nurtured the family, and protected the city-state. They controlled the weather, the seasons, health, marriage, longevity, and the future, which they could foresee. Each polis traced its origins to a particular founding god—Athena for Athens, Zeus for Sparta. Sacred sanctuaries were dedicated to others.

The Greeks believed that the 12 major gods lived on Mount Olympus, in northeastern Greece. There they ruled over the Greeks in a completely human fashion—they quarreled and meddled, loved and lost, exercised justice or not—and they were depicted by the Greeks in human form. There was nothing special about them except their power, which was enormous, sometimes frighteningly so. But the Greeks believed that as long as they did not overstep their bounds and try to compete with the gods—the sin of **hubris**, or pride—that the gods would protect them.

Among the major gods (with their later Roman names in parentheses) are:

Zeus (Jupiter): King of the gods, usually bearded, and associated with the eagle and thunderbolt.

Hera (Juno): Wife and sister to Zeus, the goddess of marriage and maternity.

Athena (Minerva): Goddess of war, but also, through her association with Athens, of civilization; the daughter of Zeus, born from his head; often helmeted, shield and spear in hand, the owl (wisdom) and the olive tree (peace) are sacred to her.

Ares (Mars): God of war, and son of Zeus and Hera, usually armored.

Aphrodite (Venus): Goddess of love and beauty; Hesiod says she was born when the severed genitals of Uranus, the Greek personification of the sky, were cast into the sea and his sperm mingled with sea foam to create her. Eros is her son.

Apollo (Phoebus): God of the sun, light, truth, prophecy, music, and medicine; he carries a bow and arrow, sometimes a lyre; often depicted riding a chariot across the sky.

Artemis (Diana): Goddess of the hunt and the moon; Apollo's sister, she carries bow and arrow, and is accompanied by hunting dogs.

Demeter (Ceres): Goddess of agriculture and grain.

Dionysus (Bacchus): God of wine and inspiration, closely aligned to myths of fertility and sexuality.

Hermes (Mercury): Messenger of the gods, but also god of fertility, theft, dreams, commerce, and the marketplace; usually wearing winged sandals and a winged hat, he carries a wand with two snakes entwined around it.

Hades (Pluto): God of the underworld, accompanied by his monstrous dog, Cerberus.

Hephaestus (Vulcan): God of the forge and fire; son of Zeus and Hera and husband of Aphrodite; wears a blacksmith's apron and carries a hammer.

Hestia (Vesta): Goddess of the hearth and sister of Zeus.

Poseidon (Neptune): Brother of Zeus and god of the sea; carries a trident (a three-pronged spear); the horse is sacred to him.

Persephone (Proserpina): Goddess of fertility, Demeter's daughter, carted off each winter to the underworld by her husband Hades, but released each spring to restore the world to plenty.

The Sacred Sanctuaries

Although rival poleis were often at war with one another, they also increasingly came to understand their common heritage. As early as the eighth century BCE, they created sanctuaries where they could come together to share music, religion, poetry, and athletics. The sanctuary was a large-scale reflection of another Greek invention, the **symposium**, literally "drinking together" by men (originally of the same military unit) meeting to share poetry, food, and wine. At the sanctuaries, people from different poleis came together to honor their gods and, by extension, to celebrate, in the presence of their rivals, their own accomplishments.

Delphi The sanctuaries were sacred religious sites. They inspired the poleis, which were always trying to outdo one another, to create the first monumental architecture since Mycenaean times. At Delphi, high in the mountains above the Gulf of Corinth, and home to the Sanctuary of Apollo, the poleis, in their usual competitive spirit, built monuments and statues dedicated to the god, and elaborate treasuries to store offerings. Here, the Greeks believed, Earth was attached to the sky by its navel. Here, too, through a deep crack in the ground, Apollo spoke, through the medium of a woman called the Pythia. Priests interpreted the cryptic omens and messages she delivered. The Greek author Plutarch, writing in the first century CE, said that the Pythia entered a small chamber beneath the temple, smelled sweet-smelling fumes, and went into a trance. Modern scholars dismissed the story as fiction until recently, when geologists discovered that two faults intersect directly below the Delphic temple, allowing hallucinogenic gases to rise through the fissures, specifically ethylene, which has a sweet smell and produces a narcotic effect described as a floating or disembodied euphoria.

The facade of the Athenian Treasury at Delphi consisted of two columns standing *in antis* (that is, between two squared stone pilasters, called **antae**). Behind them is the

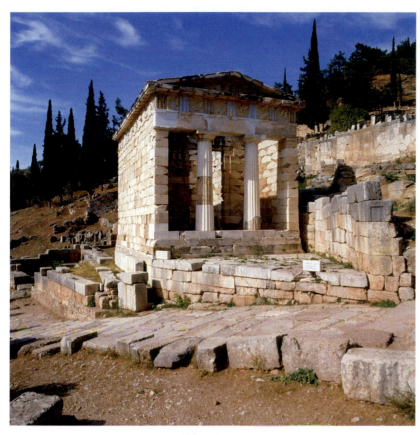

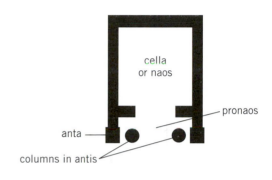

cella
or naos

pronaos

anta

columns in antis

Fig. 4.17 The Athenian Treasury, Delphi, and plan. ca. 510 BCE. The sculptural program around the Treasury, just below the roof line, depicts the adventures of two great Greek mythological heroes, Theseus and Heracles.

pronaos, or enclosed vestibule, at the front of the building, with its doorway leading into the **cella** (or naos), the principal interior space of the building (see the floor plan, Fig. **4.17**).

We can see the antecedents of this building type in a small ceramic model of an early Greek temple dating from the eighth century BCE and found at the Sanctuary of Hera near Argos (Fig. **4.18**). Its projecting porch supported by two columns anticipates the *in antis* columns and pronaos of the Athenian Treasury. The triangular area over the porch created by the pitch of the roof, called the **pediment**, is not as steep in the Treasury.

The Temples of Hera at Paestum From this basic form, surviving in the small treasuries at Delphi, the larger temples of the Greeks would develop. Two distinctive **orders**— systems of proportion that include the building's plan, its **elevation** (the arrangement and appearance of the temple's foundation, columns, and lintels), and decorative scheme—developed before 500 BCE, the **Doric order** and the **Ionic order**. Later, a third **Corinthian order** would emerge (see *Closer Look*, pages 116–117). Among the earliest surviving examples of a Greek temple of the Doric order are the Temples of Hera I and II in the Sanctuary of Hera at Paestum, a Greek colony established in the seventh century BCE in Italy, about 50 miles south of present-day

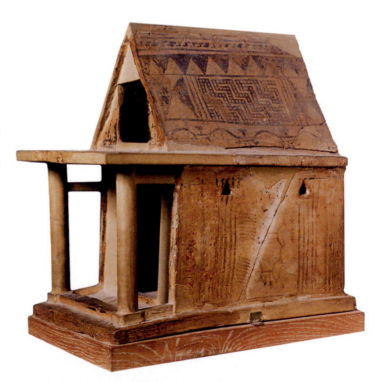

Fig. 4.18 Model of a temple, found in the Sanctuary of Hera, Argos. Mid-8th century BCE. Terra cotta, length 4½". National Archeological Museum, Athens. We do not know if later temples were painted like the model here.

Classical Greek architecture is composed of three vertical elements—the **platform**, the **column**, and the **entablature**—which comprise its elevation. The relationship of these three units is referred to as the elevation's order. There are three orders: Doric, Ionic, and Corinthian, each distinguished by its specific design.

The Classical Greek orders became the basic design elements for architecture from ancient Greek times to the present day. A major source of their power is the sense of order, predictability, and proportion that they embody. Notice how the upper elements of each order—the elements comprising the entablature—change as the column supporting them becomes narrower and taller. In the Doric order, the **architrave** (the bottom layer of the entablature), and the frieze (the flat band just above the architrave decorated with sculpture, painting, or moldings), are comparatively massive. The Doric is the heaviest of the columns. The Ionic is lighter and noticeably smaller. The Corinthian is smaller yet, seemingly supported by mere leaves.

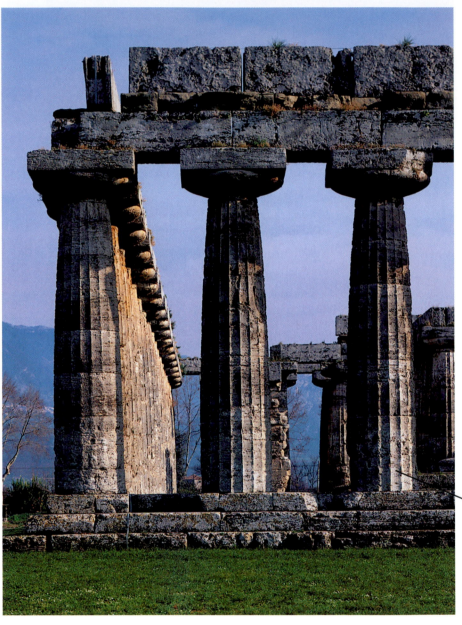

Doric columns at the Temple of Hera I, and plan. Paestum, Italy. ca. 540 BCE.
The floor plan of all three orders is essentially the same, although in the Doric order, the last two columns were set slightly closer together—corner contraction, as it is known—resulting in the corner gaining a subtle visual strength and allowing for regular spacing of sculptural elements in the entablature above.

Something to Think About ...

The base, shaft, and capital of a Greek column have often been compared to the feet, body, and head of the human figure. How would you compare the Doric, Ionic, and Corinthian orders to Figs. 4.20, 4.21, and 4.30?

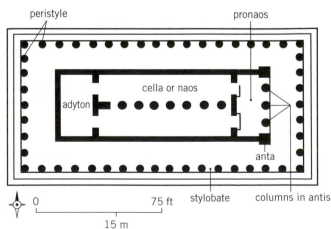

peristyle   pronaos

cella or naos

adyton

anta

0   75 ft

15 m

stylobate   columns in antis

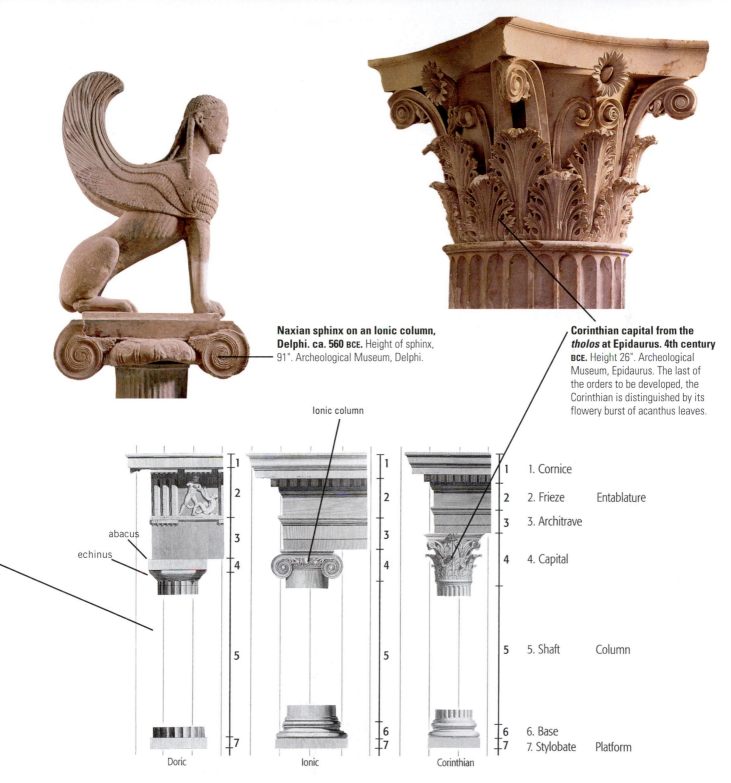

Naxian sphinx on an Ionic column, Delphi. ca. 560 BCE. Height of sphinx, 91". Archeological Museum, Delphi.

Ionic column

Corinthian capital from the *tholos* at Epidaurus. 4th century BCE. Height 26". Archeological Museum, Epidaurus. The last of the orders to be developed, the Corinthian is distinguished by its flowery burst of acanthus leaves.

abacus

echinus

Doric

Ionic

Corinthian

1. Cornice

2. Frieze   Entablature

3. Architrave

4. Capital

5. Shaft   Column

6. Base

7. Stylobate   Platform

The Classical orders, from James Stuart, *The Antiquities of Athens*, London 1794. An architectural order lends a sense of unity and structural integrity to a building as a whole. By the sixth century BCE, the Greeks had developed the Doric and the Ionic orders. The former is sturdy and simple. The latter is lighter in proportion and more elegant in detail, its capital characterized by a scroll-like motif called a **volute**. The Corinthian order, which originated in the last half of the fifth century BCE, is the most elaborate of all. It would become a favorite of the Romans.

👁 **Watch** an architectural simulation about the Greek orders on **MyArtsLab**

Naples (see Fig. 4.16). As the plan of the Temple of Hera I makes clear (see *Closer Look*, page 116), the earlier of the two temples was a large, rectangular structure, with a pronaos containing three (as opposed to two) columns and an elongated cella, behind which is an **adyton**, the innermost sanctuary housing the place where, in a temple with an oracle, the oracle's message was delivered. Surrounding this inner structure was the **peristyle**, a row of columns that stands on the **stylobate**, the top step of the platform on which the temple rests. The columns swell about one-third of the way up and contract again at the top, a characteristic known as **entasis**, and are topped by the two-part capital of the Doric order with its rounded **echinus** and tablelike **abacus**.

Olympia and the Olympic Games The Greeks date the beginning of their history to the first formal Panhellenic ("all-Greece") athletic competition, held in 776 BCE. These first Olympic Games were held at Olympia. There, a sanctuary dedicated to Hera and Zeus also housed an elaborate athletic facility. The first contest of the first games was a 200-yard dash the length of the Olympia stadium, a race called the *stadion* (Fig. **4.19**). Over time, other events of solo performance were added, including chariot-racing, boxing, and the *pentathlon* (from Greek *penta*, "five," and *athlon*, "contest"), consisting of discus, javelin, long jump, sprinting, and wrestling. There were no second or third prizes. Winning was all. The contests were conducted every four years during the summer months and were open only to men (married women were forbidden to attend, and unmarried women probably did not attend). The Olympic Games were held for more than 1,000 years, until the Christian Byzantine emperor Theodosius banned them in 394 CE. The Games were revived in 1896 to promote international understanding and friendship.

The Olympic Games were only one of numerous athletic festivals held in various locations. These games comprised a defining characteristic of the developing Greek national identity. As a people, the Greeks believed in *agonizesthai*, a verb meaning "to contend for the prize." They were driven by competition. Potters bragged that their work was better than any other's. Playwrights competed for best play, poets for best recitation, athletes for best performance. As the poleis themselves competed for supremacy, they began to understand the spirit of competition as a trait shared by all.

Male Sculpture and the Cult of the Body

Greek athletes performed nude, so it is not surprising that athletic contests gave rise to what may be called a "cult of the body." The physically fit male not only won accolades in athletic contests, he also represented the conditioning and strength of the military forces of a particular polis. The male body was also celebrated in a widespread genre of sculpture known as the *kouros*, meaning "young man" (Figs. **4.20**, **4.21**). This celebration of the body was uniquely Greek. No other Mediterranean culture so emphasized depiction of the male nude.

Several thousand *kouroi* (plural of *kouros*) appear to have been carved in the sixth century BCE alone. They could be found in sanctuaries and cemeteries, most often serving as votive offerings to the gods or as commemorative grave markers, embodying the best characteristics of the aristocracy.

Egyptian Influences Although we would never mistake an early Greek figure for the work of an Egyptian sculptor—its nudity and much more fully realized anatomical features are clear differences—still, its Egyptian influences are obvious. In fact, as early as 650 BCE, the Greeks were in Egypt, and by the early sixth century BCE, 12 cooperating poleis had

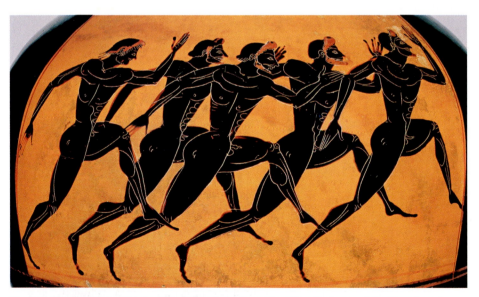

Fig. 4.19 The Euphiletos Painter, Black-figure amphora showing a foot-race at the Panathenaic Games in Athens (detail). ca. 530 BCE. Terra cotta, height 24½". The Metropolitan Museum of Art, New York. Rogers Fund, 1914 (14.130.12). Greek athletes competed nude. In fact, our word *gymnasium* derives from the Greek word for "naked," *gymnos*.

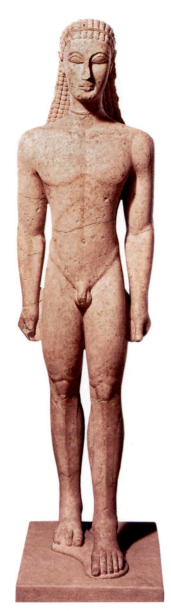

Fig. 4.20 *New York Kouros.* **ca. 600 BCE.** Marble, height 6'4". The Metropolitan Museum of Art, New York. Fletcher Fund, 1932 (32.11.1).

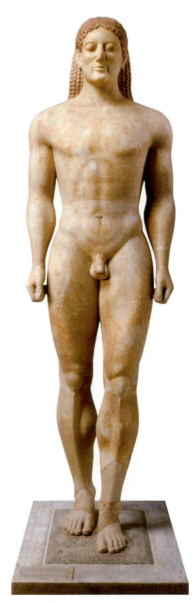

Fig. 4.21 *Anavysos Kouros,* **from Anavysos cemetery, near Athens. ca. 525 BCE.** Marble with remnants of paint, height 6'4". National Archeological Museum, Athens. The sculpture on the left is one of the earliest known life-size standing sculptures of a male in Greek art. The one on the right represents 75 years of Greek experimentation with the form. Note its closed-lip "Archaic smile," a symbol of liveliness and vitality.

established a trading outpost in the Nile Delta. The Greek sculpture serves much the same funerary function as its Egyptian ancestors. The young man's arms drop stiffly to his side. His fists are clenched in the Egyptian manner. His left foot strides forward, though both heels remain unnaturally cemented to the ground, altogether like the Old Kingdom Egyptian *ka* statue of Menkaure with his queen (see Fig. 3.10 in Chapter 3), which is nearly 2,000 years older. The facial features of the *kouros*, with its wide, oval eyes, sharply delineated brow, and carefully knotted hair, are also reminiscent of third-millennium BCE Sumerian votive statues (see Fig. 2.4 in Chapter 2).

Increasing Naturalism During the course of the sixth century, *kouroi* became distinguished by **naturalism**. That is, they increasingly reflect the artist's desire to represent the human body as it appears in nature. This in turn probably reflects the growing role of the individual in Greek political life.

We see more stylistic change between the first *kouros* and the second, a span of just 75 years, than between the first *kouros* and its Egyptian and Sumerian ancestors, created over 2,000 years earlier. The musculature of the later figure, with its highly developed thighs and calves, the naturalistic curve delineating the waist and hips, the collarbone and tendons

CONTINUITY & CHANGE

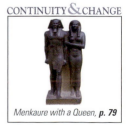

Menkaure with a Queen, **p. 79**

in the neck, the muscles of the ribcage and belly, the precisely rendered feet and toes, all suggest that this is a representation of a real person. In fact, an inscription on the base of the sculpture reads, "Stop and grieve at the dead Kroisos, slain by wild Ares [the god of war] in the front rank of battle." This is a monument to a fallen hero, killed in the prime of youth.

Both sculptures are examples of the developing **Archaic style**, the name given to art produced from 600 to 480 BCE. We do not know why sculptors wanted to realize the human form more naturalistically, but we can surmise that the reason must be related to *agonizesthai*, the spirit of competition so dominant in Greek society. Sculptors must have competed against one another in their attempts to realize the human form. Furthermore, since it was believed that the god Apollo manifested himself as a well-endowed athlete, the more lifelike and natural the sculpture, the more nearly it could be understood to resemble the god himself.

Female Sculpture and the Worship of Athena

At the center of Athenian life was the worship, on the Acropolis, of the goddess Athena, the city's protector. Just as the *kouros* statue seems related to Apollo, statues of *korai*, or "maidens" (singular *kore*) appear to have been votive offerings to Athena and were apparently conceived as gifts to the goddess. Male citizens dedicated *korai* to her as a gesture of both piety and evident pleasure in the beauty of the sculpture itself. From the mid-sixth century BCE on, the sculptural production of *korai* flourished in Athens.

As with the *kouroi* statues, the *korai* also became more naturalistic during the century. This trend is especially

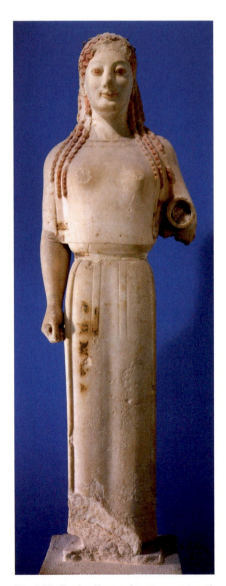
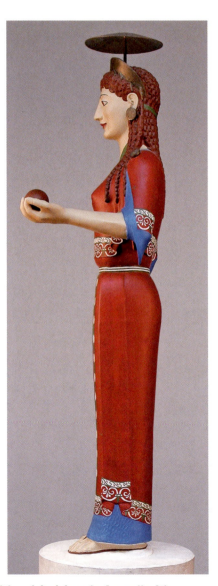

Fig. 4.22 *Peplos Kore* **and cast reconstruction of the original, from the Acropolis, Athens. Dedicated 530 BCE.** Polychromed marble, height 47½". Acropolis Museum, Athens (original), and Museum of Classical Archaeology, University of Cambridge, UK (cast). The extended arm, probably bearing a gift, was originally a separate piece, inserted in the round socket at her elbow. Note the small size of this sculpture, more than two feet shorter than the male *kouros* sculptures (Figs. 4.20, 4.21).

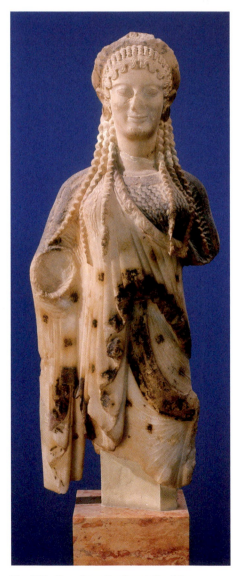

Fig. 4.23 *Kore,* **from the Acropolis, Athens. ca. 520 BCE.** Polychromed marble, height 21". Acropolis Museum, Athens. Although missing half its height, the sculpture gives us a clear example of the elaborate dress of the last years of the sixth century BCE.

obvious in their dress. In the sculpture known as the *Peplos Kore* (Fig. **4.22**), anatomical realism is suppressed by the straight lines of the sturdy garment known as a *peplos*. Usually made of wool, the peplos is essentially a rectangle of cloth folded down at the neck, pinned at the shoulders, and belted. Another *kore*, also remarkable for the amount of original paint on it, is the *Kore* dating from 520 BCE, found on the Athenian Acropolis (Fig. **4.23**). This one wears a *chiton*, a garment that by the last decades of the century had become much more popular than the peplos. Made of linen, the chiton clings more closely to the body and is gathered to create pleats and folds that allow the artist to show off his virtuosity. On top of it, a gathered mantle called a *himation* is draped diagonally from one shoulder. These sculptures, dedicated to Athena, give us some idea of the richness of decoration that adorned sixth-century Athens.

Athenian Pottery

As early as the tenth century BCE, elaborate ceramic manufactories had been established in Athens at the Kerameikos cemetery (the origin of the word *ceramics*) on the outskirts of the city. Athenian artisans invented a new, much faster potter's wheel that allowed them to control more reliably the shapes of their vases. They also created new kilns, with far greater capacity to control heat,

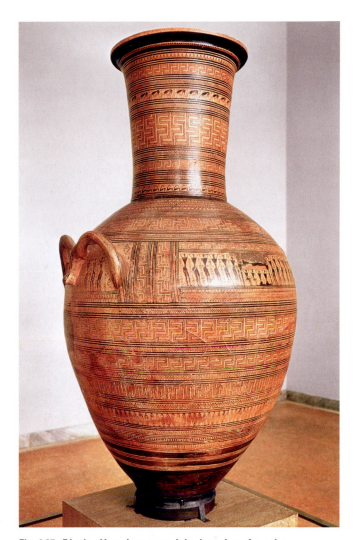

Fig. 4.25 *Dipylon Vase*, large sepulchral amphora from the Kerameikos cemetery, Athens, with *prothesis* (ritual mourning) scene. ca. **760** BCE. Height 5'1". National Archeological Museum, Athens. This monumental vase was placed above a grave as a memorial.

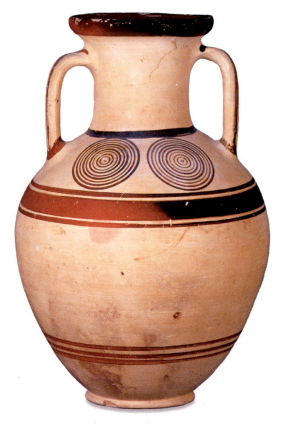

Fig. 4.24 Protogeometric *skyphos* from the Kerameikos cemetery, Athens. 10th century BCE. © The Trustees of the British Museum. A *skyphos* is a two-handled drinking cup.

resulting in richer, more lustrous glazes. Because the human figure is largely absent from the pots produced, which favor abstract geometric patterns, some see this work as unsophisticated, especially when compared to the great figurative tradition of later Greek art. But when we consider the Greek genius for mathematics, the abstract design and patterning of these ceramics begin to seem complex and sophisticated. Concentric circles, made with a new tool—a compass with multiple brushes—decorate even the earliest pots (Fig. **4.24**).

By the middle of the ninth century BCE, an elaborate **geometric style** dominates the pottery's surface (Fig. **4.25**), characterized by circles, rectangles, and triangles in parallel bands around the vase. This represents an extremely elaborate and highly stylized approach to decoration, one that echoes the Homeric epic in the submission of its detail to the unity of the whole. Layered band upon band, these geometric designs hint at what the Greeks believed to be the structure of the cosmos as a whole, a structure they tirelessly sought to understand. Soon, the physical philosopher Pythagoras (ca. 570–490 BCE), who studied the mathematical differences in the lengths of strings needed to produce various notes on the lyre, would develop his famous theorem. The Pythagorean theorem states that in a right-angled triangle, the square of the hypotenuse (the longest side) is equal to the sum of the squares of the other two sides of the triangle. And by 300 BCE, Euclid, a Greek philosopher (flourished early third century BCE) working in Alexandria, Egypt, would formulate his definitive geometry of two- and three-dimensional space.

Athenian potters were helped along by the extremely high quality of the clay available in Athens, which turned a deep orange color when fired. As with Athenian sculpture, the decorations on Athenian vases grew increasingly naturalistic and detailed until, generally, only one scene

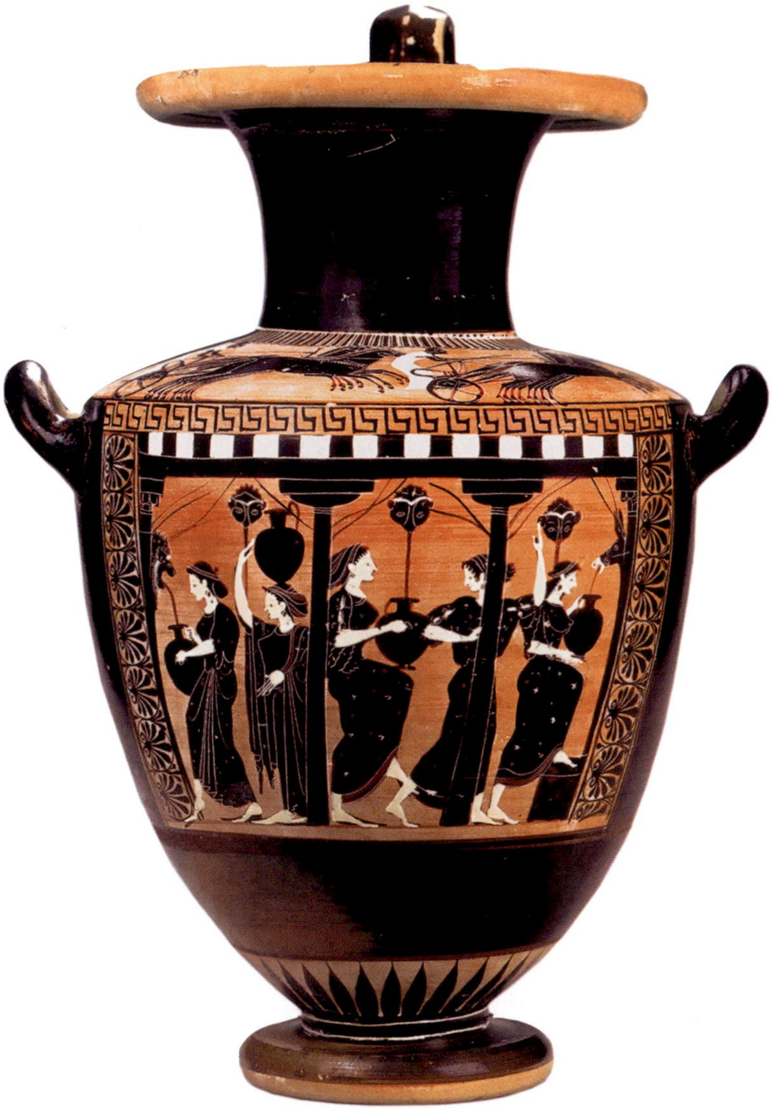

Fig. 4.26 The Priam Painter, *Women at a Fountain House*. ca. 520–510 BCE.
Black-figure decoration on a *hydria* (water jug), height 20⅞". Museum of Fine Arts, Boston. Reproduced with permission. Photograph © 2014 Museum of Fine Arts, Boston. All rights reserved. The convention of depicting women's skin as white is also found in Egyptian and Minoan art.

filled each side of the vase. The Greeks soon developed two types of vases characterized by the relationship of figure to ground: black- and red-figure vases. The figures on **black-figure** vases are painted with slip, a mixture of clay and water, so that after firing they remain black against an unslipped red background. *Women at a Fountain House* (Fig. **4.26**) is an example. Here the artist, whom scholars have dubbed the Priam Painter, has added touches of white by mixing white pigment into the slip. By the second half of the sixth century, new motifs, showing scenes of everyday life, became increasingly popular. This *hydria*, or water jug, shows women carrying similar jugs as they chat at a fountain house of the kind built by the tyrant Pisistratus in the sixth century at the ends of the aqueducts that brought water into the city. Such fountain houses were extremely popular spots, offering women, who were for the most part confined to their homes, a rare opportunity to gather socially. Water flows from animal-head spigots at both the sides and across the back of the scene. The composition's strong vertical and horizontal framework, with its Doric columns, is softened by the rounded contours of the women's bodies and the vases they carry. This vase underscores the growing Greek taste for realistic scenes and naturalistic representation.

Many pots depict gods and heroes, including representations inspired by the *Iliad* and *Odyssey* (see Figs. 4.14 and 4.15). An example of this tendency is a *krater*, or vessel in which wine and water were mixed, that shows the *Death of Sarpedon*. It was made by the potter Euxitheos by 515 BCE and painted by Euphronius (Fig. **4.27**). Euphronius was praised especially for his ability to render human anatomy accurately. Here, Sarpedon has just been killed by Patroclus (see Reading 4.1). Blood pours from his leg, shoulder, and carefully drawn abdomen. The winged figures of Hypnos (Sleep) and Thanatos (Death) are about to carry off his body as Hermes, messenger of the gods who guides the dead to the underworld, looks on. But the naturalism of the scene is not the source of its appeal. Rather, its perfectly balanced composition transforms the tragedy into a rare depiction of death as an instance of dignity and order. The spears of the two warriors left and right mirror the edge of the vase, the design formed by Sarpedon's stomach muscles is echoed in the decorative bands both top and bottom, and the handles of the vase mirror the arching backs of Hypnos and Thanatos.

The *Death of Sarpedon* is an example of a **red-figure** vase. The process is the reverse of the black-figure process, and more complicated. Here, the slip is used to paint the background, outlining the figures. Using the same slip, Euphronius also drew details on the figure (such as Sarpedon's abdomen) with a brush. The

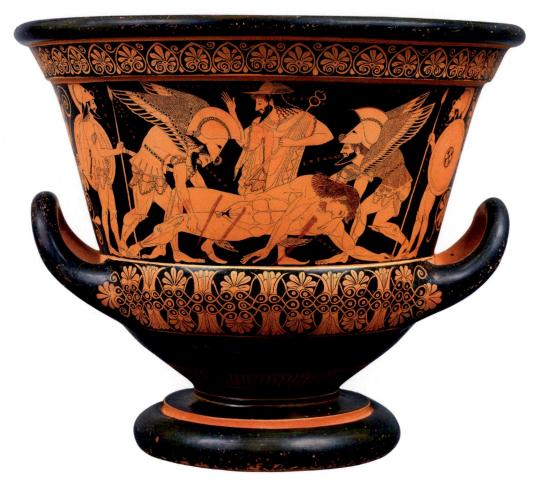

Fig. 4.27 Euphronius (painter) and Euxitheos (potter), *Death of Sarpedon*. CA. 515 BCE. Red-figure decoration on a calyx krater. Ceramic, height of krater 18". Museo Nazionale di Villa Giulia, Rome. This type of krater is called a *calyx krater* because its handles curve up like the calyx of a flower. The krater was housed in the collection of the Metropolitan Museum of Art in New York until it became clear that it was illegally excavated in Italy in the early 1970s. The Museum returned the piece to Italy in 2008.

View the Closer Look for the *Euphronius Krater* on **MyArtsLab**

vase was then fired in three stages, each one varying the amount of oxygen allowed into the kiln. In the first stage, oxygen was allowed into the kiln, which "fixed" the whole vase in one overall shade of red. Then, oxygen in the kiln was reduced to the absolute minimum, turning the vessel black. At this point, as the temperature rose, the slip became vitrified, or glassy. Finally, oxygen entered the kiln again, turning the unslipped areas—in this case, the red figures—back into a shade of red. The areas painted with the vitrified slip were not exposed to oxygen, so that they remained black.

The Poetry of Sappho

The poet Sappho (ca. 610–ca. 580 BCE) was hailed throughout antiquity as "the tenth Muse" and her poetry celebrated as a shining example of female creativity. We know little of Sappho's somewhat extraordinary life. She was born on the island of Lesbos, and probably married. She mentions both a brother and a daughter, Cleis, in her poetry. As an adult poet, she surrounded herself with a group of young women who together engaged in the celebration of Aphrodite (love), the Graces (beauty), and the Muses (poetry). Her own poetry gives rise to the suggestion that her relation to these women was erotic. It seems clear that most of her circle shared their lives with one another only for a brief period before marriage. As we will see later, Plato's *Symposium* suggests that homoeroticism was institutionalized for young men at this stage of life; it may have been institutionalized for young women as well.

Sappho wrote **lyric poems** on themes of love and personal relationships, often with other women. Only fragments of Sappho's poetry have survived. It is impossible to convey the subtlety and beauty of her poems in translation, but their astonishing economy of feeling does come across. In the following poem (**Reading 4.6a**), one of the longest surviving fragments, she expresses her love for a married woman:

Poems such as this one were sung to the accompaniment of a lyre, as depicted in a red-figure vase by Polygnotus (Fig. **4.28**). We have little knowledge of what Greek music actually sounded like. The only complete work of music to have survived is a *skiolion*, or drinking song, by Seikolos, found chiseled on the first-century BCE gravestone of his wife

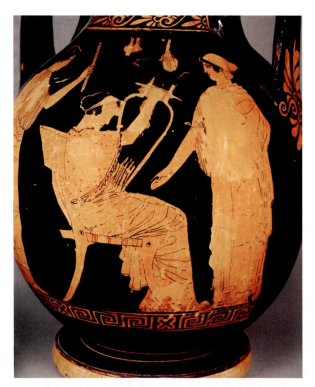

Fig. 4.28 Polygnotus (vase painter), *Two women, one playing a lyre*. 5th century BCE. Red-figure decoration on a *pelike*. Musée du Louvre, Paris. Most of Sappho's poems were written to be sung by a performer accompanying herself on the lyre.

Euterpe. The Greek system of musical notation, apparently borrowed from the Phoenicians, marked the position of the fingers on the strings of the instrument.

Sappho's talent is the ability to condense the intensity of her feelings into a single breath, a breath that, as the following poem suggests, lives on (**Reading 4.6b**). Even in so short a poem, Sappho realizes concretely the Greek belief that we can achieve immortality through our words and deeds:

Sappho's work was collected into nine volumes (arranged according to meter) by the Library of Alexandria, but these are now lost, like most of the rest of the library's 700,000 volumes (see Chapter 5). After Homer, she was probably the most admired poet in antiquity, but where Homer's poetry was concerned with creating a national, Hellenic identity, Sappho's lyrics were more personal, establishing her own, individual sense of self.

THE RISE OF ATHENIAN DEMOCRACY

How did democracy develop in Athens?

The growing naturalism of sixth-century BCE sculpture, to say nothing of the highly personal poetry of Sappho, coincided with the rise of democratic institutions in Athens and reflects this important development. Both bear witness to a growing Greek spirit of innovation and accomplishment. And both testify to a growing belief in the dignity and worth of the individual.

Toward Democracy: Solon and Pisistratus

Early in the sixth century BCE, a reformer statesman named Solon (ca. 630–ca. 560 BCE) overturned a severe code of law that had been instituted about one century earlier by an official named Draco. Draco's law was especially hard on debtors, and from his name comes our use of the term "Draconian" to describe particularly harsh punishments or laws. A bankrupt member of the polis could not sell or mortgage his land, but was required to mortgage the produce of the land to his creditor, effectively enslaving himself and his family to the creditor forever. Similarly, a bankrupt merchant was obliged to become the slave of his creditor.

Solon addressed the most painful of these provisions. He canceled all current debts, freed both peasants who found themselves in a state of servitude and landowners and merchants enslaved through debt, and published a new code of law. He deemphasized the agricultural basis of the polis and encouraged trade and commerce, granting citizenship to anyone who would come and work in Athens. He also formed the Council of Four Hundred, which was comprised of landowners selected by Solon himself. This group recommended policy, which a general assembly of all citizens voted on. Only the council could formulate policy, but the citizens could veto it. By the end of the fifth century, Athenians had come to view Solon as the founding father of Athenian **democracy**—from the Greek *demokratia*, "the rule" (*kratia*) of "the people" (*demes*).

Solon was a poet, and in his poems it is clear that he was intent on finding some common ground between the rich and privileged and the poor and unprivileged. The aristocratic landowners from the plains thought that Solon had overstepped his authority. The much poorer hill people living on the mountainsides thought he had not gone far enough; only the coastal and urban people felt satisfied with his reforms. But in freeing the enslaved, weakening the aristocracy, and strengthening the legal system, Solon laid the groundwork for Athenian democracy.

But when Pisistratus (r. 560–527 BCE) assumed power in the polis, any further advance toward democracy was stymied. A tyrant, Pisistratus ruled as a dictator, without consulting the people. But he was successful in moderating the conflict among the three factions—the landowners on the plains, the hill people, and the urban and coastal dwellers—thus establishing a period of lasting peace in the polis. The hill people in particular supported him, because he advanced money to help them sustain themselves and thereby agricultural production in the polis. Two centuries later, the philosopher Aristotle would tell a story that reflects Pisistratus' rule (**Reading 4.7**):

READING 4.7

from Aristotle's *Athenian Constitution*

His revenues were increased by the thorough cultivation of the country, since he imposed a tax of one tenth on all the produce. For the same reasons he instituted the local justices, and often made expeditions in person into the country to inspect it and to settle disputes between individuals, that they might not come into the city and neglect their farms. It was in one of these progresses that, as the story goes, Pisistratus had his adventure with the man of Hymettus, who was cultivating the spot afterwards known as "Tax-free Farm." He saw a man digging and working at a very stony piece of ground, and being surprised he sent his attendant to ask what he got out of this plot of land. "Aches and pains," said the man; "and that's what Pisistratus ought to have his tenth of." The man spoke without knowing who his questioner was; but Pisistratus was so pleased with his frank speech and his industry that he granted him exemption from all taxes. And so in matters in general he burdened the people as little as possible with government, but always cultivated peace and kept them in all quietness.

Pisistratus was, by and large, a benevolent tyrant. He recognized the wisdom of Solon's economic policies and encouraged the development of trade. Perhaps most important of all, he initiated a lavish program of public works in order to provide jobs for the entire populace. He built roads and drainage systems and provided running water to most of the city. He was also a patron of the arts. Evidence suggests that in the agora he built the first Athenian space for dramatic performances. On the Acropolis, he built several temples, though only fragmentary evidence remains.

Cleisthenes and the First Athenian Democracy

Pisistratus' son Hippias became the ruler of Athens in 527 BCE. Pisistratus had been a tyrant, exiling aristocrats who did not support him, and often keeping a son of a noble family as a personal hostage to guarantee the family's loyalty. Hippias was harsher still, exiling more nobles and executing many others. In 510, the exiled nobles led a revolt, with aid from Sparta, and Hippias escaped to Persia.

In 508 BCE, Cleisthenes instituted the first Athenian democracy, an innovation in self-government that might not have been possible until the Athenians had experienced the tyranny of Hippias. Cleisthenes reorganized the Athenian political system into *demes*, small local areas comparable to precincts or wards in a modern city. Because all citizens—remember, only males were citizens—registered in their given *deme*, landowners and merchants had equal political rights. Cleisthenes then grouped the *demes* into ten political "tribes," whose membership cut across all family, class, and regional lines, thus effectively diminishing the power and influence of the noble families. Each tribe appointed 50 of its members to a Council of Five Hundred, which served for 36 days. There were thus ten separate councils per year, and no citizen could serve on the council more than twice in his lifetime. With so many citizens serving on the council for such short times, it is likely that nearly every Athenian citizen participated in the government at some point during his lifetime.

The new Greek democracy was immediately threatened by the rise of the Persian Empire in the east. These were the same Persians who had defeated the Babylonians and freed the Jews in 520 BCE (see Chapter 2). In 499 BCE, probably aware of the newfound political freedoms in Athens and certainly chafing at the tyrannical rule of the Persians, Persian-controlled cities in Ionia rebelled, burning down the city of Sardis, the Persian headquarters in Asia Minor. In 495 BCE, the Persian ruler Darius struck back. He burned down the most important Ionian city, Miletus, slaughtering the men and taking its women and children into slavery. Then, probably influenced by Hippias, who lived in exile in his court, Darius turned his sights on Athens, which had sent a force to Ionia to aid the rebellion. But if the Greek democracy was threatened—and it was, to the point of destruction—it would respond by creating a new Golden Age.

Egyptian and Greek Sculpture

Freestanding Greek sculpture of the Archaic period—that is, sculpture dating from about 600 to 480 BCE—is notable for its stylistic connections to 2,000 years of Egyptian tradition. The Late Period statue of *Mentuemhet* (Fig. **4.29**), from Thebes, dating from around 660 BCE, differs hardly at all from Old Kingdom sculpture at Giza (see Figs. 3.9 and 3.10 in Chapter 3), and even though the *Anavysos Kouros* (Fig. **4.30**), from a cemetery near Athens, represents a significant advance in relative naturalism over the Greek sculpture of just a few years before, it still resembles its Egyptian ancestors. Remarkably, since it follows upon the *Anavysos Kouros* by only 75 years, the *Doryphoros* (*Spear Bearer*) (Fig. **4.31**) is significantly more naturalistic. Although

this is a Roman copy of a lost fifth-century BCE bronze Greek statue, we can assume it reflects the original's naturalism, since the original's sculptor, Polyclitus, was renowned for his ability to render the human body realistically. But this advance, characteristic of Golden Age Athens, represents more than just a cultural taste for naturalism. It also represents a heightened cultural sensitivity to the worth of the individual, a belief that as much as we value what we have in common with one another—the bond that creates the city-state—our *individual* contributions are at least of equal value (see Chapter 5). By the fifth century BCE, the Greeks clearly understood that individual genius and achievement could be a matter of civic pride. ■

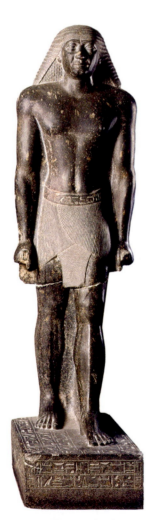

Fig. 4.29 *Mentuemhet*, from Karnak, Thebes, Egypt. ca. 660 BCE. Granite, height 54". Egyptian Museum, Cairo.

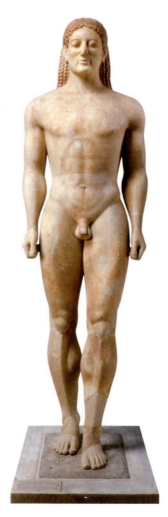

Fig. 4.30 *Anavysos Kouros*, from a cemetery at Anavysos, near Athens. ca. 525 BCE. Marble with remnants of paint, height 6'4". National Archeological Museum, Athens.

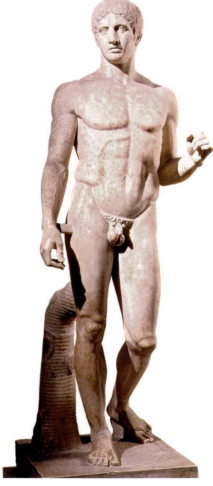

Fig. 4.31 *Doryphoros* (*Spear Bearer*), Roman copy after the original bronze by Polyclitus of ca. 450–440 BCE. Marble, height 6'6". Museo Archeologico Nazionale, Naples.

THINKING BACK

4.1 Compare and contrast the Cycladic, Minoan, and Mycenaean cultures.

The later Greeks traced their ancestry to the cultures that arose in the islands of the Aegean Sea. The art of the Cyclades consisted of highly simplified Neolithic figurines and, later, probably under the influence of Minoan culture to the south, elaborate wall frescoes depicting everyday events. Unique to Minoan culture is an emphasis on the bull, associated with the legend of King Minos and the Minotaur, and the double ax, symbol of the Palace of Minos at Knossos, the complex layout of which gave rise to the word "labyrinth." Mycenaean warriors from the Greek mainland invaded Crete in about 1450 BCE. There is abundant archeological evidence that they had valued Minoan artistry long before and had traded with the Minoans. But from all appearances their two cultures could not have been more different. In what ways did Minoan and Mycenaean cultures differ most dramatically?

4.2 Define the formal features of the Homeric epic and compare and contrast the *Iliad* and the *Odyssey*.

Around 800 BCE, Homer's great epics, the *Iliad* and the *Odyssey*, were transcribed. The stories had been passed down orally for generations, and it is evident that formulaic epithets helped in remembering the story. These epithets helped the performing poet to fit a given name into the verse. What is "epic" meter? The *Iliad* tells of the anger of the Greek hero Achilles and its consequences during a war between the Achaeans and Troy, which occurred sometime between 1800 and 1300 BCE. The *Odyssey* follows the Greek commander Odysseus on his adventure-laden journey home to his faithful wife, Penelope. These stories, and legends such as the myth of the Minotaur, comprised for the Greeks their *archaiologia*, their way of knowing their past. How do the *Iliad* and the *Odyssey* differ from each other in their depictions of Greek culture and values?

4.3 Discuss the ways in which the values of the Greek polis shaped Greek culture.

Each of the rural areas of Greece, separated from one another by mountainous geography, gradually began to form into a community—the polis, or city-state—that exercised authority over its region. Inevitably, certain of these poleis became more powerful than the others. Corinth's central location allowed it to control sea traffic, and trade with the Near East inspired its thriving pottery industry. Sparta was the most powerful of the early Greek city-states, and it exercised extreme authoritarian rule over its people. At Delos, Delphi, Olympia, and even in colonies such as Paestum on the Italian peninsula, the city-states came together to honor their gods at sanctuaries. What role did these sanctuaries play in the development of Greek culture?

The Greeks were unique among Mediterranean cultures in portraying the male nude, especially in the widespread genre of *kouros* sculpture, ideal male nude statues found in sanctuaries and cemeteries, most often serving as votive offerings to the gods or as commemorative grave markers. How would you describe the evolution of the *kouros* in the sixth century BCE? Why did sculptures of robed females, or *korai*, evolve in Athens in particular? Why do you think paintings of scenes from the *Iliad* and the *Odyssey* were particularly popular decorative additions to Greek pottery? How does the poetry of Sappho reflect the growing Greek concern with the individual?

4.4 Describe the rise of democracy in Athens.

In the early sixth century BCE, the statesman and poet Solon eliminated Draconian slavery, weakened the aristocracy, and strengthened the legal system. Later generations thus saw him as the father of Athenian democracy. But the rise of democratic institutions in Athens was inspired in no small part by the reaction to the tyranny of Pisistratus and his son and successor, Hippias. Pisistratus was by and large a benevolent tyrant who championed the arts, while Hippias was almost his opposite. After Hippias was overthrown, Cleisthenes instituted the first Athenian democracy in 508 BCE. The power and influence of noble families was diminished under the rule of the Council of Five Hundred, the membership of which changed every 36 days. What almost immediately threatened this new-found democracy?

✔ **Study** and **review** on **MyArtsLab**

READINGS

from Homer, *Iliad*, Book 16 (ca. 750 BCE)

Homer's epic poem the *Iliad* begins after the Trojan War has begun. It narrates, in 24 books, what it describes in the first line as "the rage of Achilles," the Greeks' greatest warrior. Achilles has withdrawn from combat in anger at the Greek leader Agamemnon for taking the beautiful Briseis from him. Finally, in Book 16, with the Greeks in desperate straits, Achilles partially relents and allows his close friend Patroclus to don his armor and lead the Greeks into combat. The following excerpts from Book 16 describe scenes from the battle in which Patroclus defeats the Trojan warrior Sarpedon. It is a stunning portrayal of the horrible realities of war.

… And Hector? Hector's speeding horses swept him away
armor and all, leaving his men to face their fate,
Trojans trapped but struggling on in the deep trench.
Hundreds of plunging war-teams dragging chariots down,
snapping the yoke-poles, ditched their masters' cars
and Patroclus charged them, heart afire for the kill,
shouting his Argives forward—"Slaughter Trojans!"
Cries of terror breaking as Trojans choked all roads,
their lines ripped to pieces, up from under the hoofs
a dust storm swirling into the clouds as rearing horses   10
broke into stride again and galloped back to Troy,
leaving ships and shelters in their wake. Patroclus—
wherever he saw the biggest masses dashing before him,
there he steered, plowing ahead with savage cries
and fighters tumbled out of their chariots headfirst,
crushed under their axles, war-cars crashing over, yes,
but straight across the trench went his own careering team
at a superhuman bound. Magnificent racing stallions,
gifts of the gods to Peleus, shining immortal gifts,
straining breakneck on as Patroclus' high courage   20
urged him against Prince Hector, keen for the kill
but Hector's veering horses swept him clear.
And all in an onrush dark as autumn days
when the whole earth flattens black beneath a gale,
when Zeus flings down his pelting, punishing rains—
up in arms, furious, storming against those men
who brawl in the courts and render crooked judgments,
men who throw all rights to the winds with no regard
for the vengeful eyes of the gods—so all their rivers
crest into flood spate, ravines overflowing cut the hilltops   30
off into lonely islands, the roaring flood tide rolling down
to the storm-torn sea, headlong down from the foothills
washes away the good plowed work of men—
        Rampaging so,
the gasping Trojan war-teams hurtled on.
        Patroclus—
soon as the fighter cut their front battalions off
he swerved back to pin them against the warships,
never letting the Trojans stream back up to Troy
as they struggled madly on—but there mid-field   40
between the ships, the river and beetling wall
Patroclus kept on sweeping in, hacking them down,
making them pay the price for Argives slaughtered.
There, Pronous first to fall—a glint of the spear
and Patroclus tore his chest left bare by the shield-rim,
loosed his knees and the man went crashing down.

And next he went for Thestor the son of Enops
cowering, crouched in his fine polished chariot,
crazed with fear, and the reins flew from his grip—
Patroclus rising beside him stabbed his right jawbone,   50
ramming the spearhead over the chariot-rail,
hoisted, dragged the Trojan out as an angler perched
on a jutting rock ledge drags some fish from the sea,
some noble catch, with line and glittering bronze hook.
So with the spear Patroclus gaffed him off his car,
his mouth gaping round the glittering point
and flipped him down facefirst,
dead as he fell, his life breath blown away.
And next he caught Erylaus closing, lunging in—
he flung a rock and it struck between the eyes   60
and the man's whole skull split in his heavy helmet,
down the Trojan slammed on the ground, head-down
and courage-shattering Death engulfed his corpse.
Then in a blur of kills, Amphoterus, Erymas, Epaltes,
Tiepolemus son of Damastor, and Echius and Pyris,
Ipheus and Euippus and Polymelus the son of Argeas—
he crowded corpse on corpse on the earth that rears us all.

But now Sarpedon watching his comrades drop and die,
war-shirts billowing free as Patroclus killed them,
dressed his godlike Lycians down with a harsh shout: 70
"Lycians, where's your pride? Where are you running?
Now be fast to attack! I'll take him on myself,
see who he is who routs us, wreaking havoc against us—
cutting the legs from under squads of good brave men."

With that he leapt up from his chariot fully armed
and hit the ground and Patroclus straight across,
as soon as he saw him, leapt from his car too.
As a pair of crook-clawed, hook-beaked vultures
swoop to fight, screaming above some jagged rock—
so with their battle cries they rushed each other there.   80
And Zeus the son of Cronus with Cronus' twisting ways,
filling with pity now to see the two great fighters,
said to Hera, his sister and his wife, "My cruel fate . . .
my Sarpedon, the man I love the most, my own son—
doomed to die at the hands of Menoetius' son Patroclus.
My heart is torn in two as I try to weigh all this.
Shall I pluck him up, now, while he's still alive
and set him down in the rich green land of Lycia,
far from the war at Troy and all its tears?
Or beat him down at Patroclus' hands at last?"   90
        But Queen Hera, her eyes wide, protested strongly:

"Dread majesty, son of Cronus—what are you saying?
A man, a mere mortal, his doom sealed long ago?
You'd set him free from all the pains of death?
Do as you please, Zeus …
but none of the deathless gods will ever praise you.
And I tell you this—take it to heart, I urge you—
if you send Sarpedon home, living still, beware!
Then surely some other god will want to sweep
his own son clear of the heavy fighting too.   100
Look down. Many who battle round King Priam's
mighty walls are sons of the deathless gods—
you will inspire lethal anger in them all.

                              No,
dear as he is to you, and your head grieves for him,
leave Sarpedon there to die in the brutal onslaught,
beaten down at the hands of Menoetius' son Patroclus.
But once his soul and the life force have left him,
send Death to carry him home, send soothing Sleep,
all the way till they reach the broad land of Lycia.   110
There his brothers and countrymen will bury the prince
with full royal rites, with mounded tomb and pillar.
These are the solemn honors owed the dead.

                              So she pressed
and Zeus the father of men and gods complied at once.
But he showered tears of blood that drenched the earth,
showers in praise of him, his own dear son,
the man Patroclus was just about to kill
on Troy's fertile soil, far from his fatherland.

      Now as the two came closing on each other   120
Patroclus suddenly picked off Thrasymelus
the famous driver, the aide who flanked Sarpedon—
he speared him down the guts and loosed his limbs.
But Sarpedon hurled next with a flashing lance
and missed his man but he hit the horse Bold Dancer,
stabbing his right shoulder and down the stallion went,
screaming his life out, shrieking down in the dust
as his life breath winged away. And the paired horses
reared apart—a raspy creak of the yoke, the reins flying,
fouled as the trace horse thrashed the dust in death-throes. 130
But the fine spearman Automedon found a cure for that—
drawing his long sharp sword from his sturdy thigh
he leapt with a stroke to cut the trace horse free—
it worked. The team righted, pulled at the reins
and again both fighters closed with savage frenzy,
dueling now to the death.

                        Again Sarpedon missed—
over Patroclus' left shoulder his spearhead streaked,
it never touched his body. Patroclus hurled next,
the bronze launched from his hand—no miss, a mortal hit. 140
He struck him right where the midriff packs the pounding
    heart
and down Sarpedon fell as an oak or white poplar falls
or towering pine that shipwrights up on a mountain
hew down with whetted axes for sturdy ship timber—
so he stretched in front of his team and chariot,
sprawled and roaring, clawing the bloody dust.
As the bull a marauding lion cuts from the herd,
tawny and greathearted among the shambling cattle,
dies bellowing under the lion's killing jaws—   150

so now Sarpedon, captain of Lycia's shieldsmen,
died at Patroclus' hands and died raging still,
crying out his beloved comrade's name: "Glaucus—
oh dear friend, dear fighter, soldier's soldier!
Now is the time to prove yourself a spearman,
a daring man of war—now, if you are brave,
make grueling battle your one consuming passion.
First find Lycia's captains, range the ranks,
spur them to fight and shield Sarpedon's body.
Then you, Glaucus, you fight for me with bronze!   160
You'll hang your head in shame—every day of your life—
if the Argives strip my armor here at the anchored ships
where I have gone down fighting. Hold on, full force—
spur all our men to battle!"
      Death cut him short.
The end closed in around him, swirling down his eyes,
choking off his breath. Patroclus planted a heel
against his chest, wrenched the spear from his wound
and the midriff came out with it—so he dragged out both
the man's life breath and the weapon's point together.   170

      … …

So veteran troops kept swarming round that corpse,
never pausing—nor did mighty Zeus for a moment
turn his shining eyes from the clash of battle.
He kept them fixed on the struggling mass forever,
the Father's spirit churning, thrashing out the ways
the numberless ways to cause Patroclus' slaughter …
To kill him too in this present bloody rampage
over Sarpedon's splendid body? Hector in glory
cutting Patroclus down with hacking bronze   180
then tearing the handsome war-gear off his back?
Or let him take still more, piling up his kills? …
And storming Zeus was stirring up Apollo: "On with it now—
sweep Sarpedon clear of the weapons, Phoebus, my friend,
and once you wipe the dark blood from his body,
bear him far from the fighting, off and away,
and bathe him well in a river's running tides
and anoint him with deathless oils …
dress his body in deathless, ambrosial robes.
Then send him on his way with the wind-swift escorts,   190
twin brother Sleep and Death, who with all good speed
will set him down in the broad green land of Lycia,
There his brothers and countrymen will bury the prince
with full royal rites, with mounded tomb and pillar.
These are the solemn honors owed the dead."
                        So he decreed
and Phoebus did not neglect the Father's strong desires.
Down from Ida's slopes he dove to the bloody field
and lifting Prince Sarpedon clear of the weapons,
bore him far from the fighting, off and away. …   200

READING CRITICALLY

The scene described is full of Homeric similes. Two of the
most effective follow each other in short order directly after
Patroclus hurls his spear into Sarpedon's midriff. How do
these similes contribute to the power of the poem? How
might they either contribute to or diminish our sense of the
warriors' *areté*?

from Homer, *Odyssey*, Book 9 (ca. 725 BCE)

The sequel to Homer's *Iliad*, the *Odyssey* is a second epic poem by Homer that narrates the adventures of the Greek warrior Odysseus on his 20-year journey home from the Trojan War. The following passage, from Book 9, recounts Odysseus' confrontation with the Cyclops Polyphemus. In this confrontation Odysseus displays the cunning and skill that make him a great leader.

In the next land we found were Kyklopês,[1]
giants, louts, without a law to bless them.
In ignorance leaving the fruitage of the earth in mystery
to the immortal gods, they neither plow
nor sow by hand, nor till the ground, though grain—
wild wheat and barley—grows untended, and
wine-grapes, in clusters, ripen in heaven's rain.
Kyklopês have no muster and no meeting,
no consultation or old tribal ways,
but each one dwells in his own mountain cave   10
dealing out rough justice to wife and child,
indifferent to what the others do. ...
[Camped on a desert island across from the mainland home
of the Kyklopes, Odysseus announces his intention to explore
   the mainland itself.]
"Old shipmates, friends,
the rest of you stand by; I'll make the crossing
in my own ship, with my own company,
and find out what the mainland natives are—
for they may be wild savages, and lawless,   20
or hospitable and god fearing men."
At this I went aboard, and gave the word
to cast off by the stern. My oarsmen followed,
filing in to their benches by the rowlocks,
and all in line dipped oars in the grey sea.
As we rowed on, and nearer to the mainland,
at one end of the bay, we saw a cavern
yawning above the water, screened with laurel,
and many rams and goats about the place
inside a sheepfold—made from slabs of stone   30
earthfast between tall trunks of pine and rugged
towering oak trees.
A prodigious man
slept in this cave alone, and took his flocks
to graze afield—remote from all companions,
knowing none but savage ways, a brute
so huge, he seemed no man at all of those
who eat good wheaten bread; but he seemed rather
a shaggy mountain reared in solitude.
We beached there, and I told the crew   40
to stand by and keep watch over the ship;
as for myself I took my twelve best fighters
and went ahead. I had a goatskin full
of that sweet liquor that Euanthês' son,
Maron, had given me. ...
   No man turned away
when cups of this came round.

A wineskin full
I brought along, and victuals in a bag,
for in my bones I knew some towering brute   50
would be upon us soon—all outward power,
a wild man, ignorant of civility.
We climbed, then, briskly to the cave. But Kyklops
had gone afield, to pasture his fat sheep,
so we looked round at everything inside. ...
My men came pressing round me, pleading:
"Why not
take these cheeses, get them stowed, come back,
throw open all the pens, and make a run for it?
We'll drive the kids and lambs aboard. We say   60
put out again on good salt water!"
Ah,
how sound that was! Yet I refused. I wished
to see the caveman, what he had to offer—
no pretty sight, it turned out, for my friends.
We lit a fire, burnt an offering,
and took some cheese to eat; then sat in silence
around the embers, waiting. When he came
he had a load of dry boughs on his shoulder
to stoke his fire at suppertime. He dumped it   70
with a great crash into that hollow cave,
and we all scattered fast to the far wall. ...
"Strangers," he said, "who are you? And where from?
What brings you here by sea ways—a fair traffic?
Or are you wandering rogues, who cast your lives
like dice, and ravage other folk by sea?"
We felt a pressure on our hearts, in dread
of that deep rumble and that mighty man.
But all the same I spoke up in reply:
"We are from Troy, Akhaians, blown off course   80
by shifting gales on the Great South Sea;
homeward bound, but taking routes and ways
uncommon; so the will of Zeus would have it. ...
It was our luck to come here; here we stand,
beholden for your help, or any gifts
you give—as custom is to honor strangers.
We would entreat you, great Sir, have a care
for the gods' courtesy; Zeus will avenge
the unoffending guest."[2]
He answered this   90
from his brute chest, unmoved:
"You are a ninny,
or else you come from the other end of nowhere,
telling me, mind the gods! We Kyklopês

---

[1]One-eyed giants, inhabitants of Sicily. Also spelled *Cyclops*.

[2]Zeus was the protector and guarantor of the laws of hospitality.

care not a whistle for your thundering Zeus
or all the gods in bliss; we have more force by far.
I would not let you go for fear of Zeus—
you or your friends—unless I had a whim to.
Tell me, where was it, now, you left your ship—
around the point, or down the shore, I wonder?"   100
He thought he'd find out, but I saw through this,
and answered with a ready lie:
"My ship?
Poseidon Lord, who sets the earth a-tremble,
broke it up on the rocks at your land's end.
A wind from seaward served him, drove us there.
We are survivors, these good men and I."
Neither reply nor pity came from him,
but in one stride he clutched at my companions
and caught two in his hands like squirming puppies   110
to beat their brains out, spattering the floor.
Then he dismembered them and made his meal,
gaping and crunching like a mountain lion—
everything: innards, flesh, and marrow bones.
We cried aloud, lifting our hands to Zeus,
powerless, looking on at this, appalled;
but Kyklops[3] went on filling up his belly
with manflesh and great gulps of whey,
then lay down like a mast among his sheep.
My heart beat high now at the chance of action,   120
and drawing the sharp sword from my hip I went
along his flank to stab him where the midriff
holds the liver. I had touched the spot
when sudden fear stayed me: if I killed him
we perished there as well, for we could never
move his ponderous doorway slab aside.
So we were left to groan and wait for morning.
When the young Dawn with finger tips of rose
lit up the world, the Kyklops built a fire
and milked his handsome ewes, all in due order,   130
putting the sucklings to the mothers. Then,
his chores being all dispatched, he caught
another brace of men to make his breakfast,
and whisked away his great door slab
to let his sheep go through—but he, behind,
reset the stone as one would cap a quiver.
There was a din of whistling as the Kyklops
rounded his flock to higher ground, then stillness.
And now I pondered how to hurt him worst,
if but Athena granted what I prayed for.   140
Here are the means I thought would serve my turn:
a club, or staff, lay there along the fold—
an olive tree, felled green and left to season
for Kyklops' hand. And it was like a mast
a lugger of twenty oars, broad in the beam—
a deep-sea-going craft—might carry:
so long, so big around, it seemed. Now I
chopped out a six foot section of this pole
and set it down before my men, who scraped it;
and when they had it smooth, I hewed again   150

to make a stake with pointed end. I held this
in the fire's heart and turned it, toughening it,
then hid it, well back in the cavern, under
one of the dung piles in profusion there.
Now came the time to toss for it: who ventured
along with me? whose hand could bear to thrust
and grind that spike in Kyklops' eye, when mild
sleep had mastered him? As luck would have it,
the men I would have chosen won the toss—
four strong men, and I made five as captain.   160
At evening came the shepherd with his flock,
his woolly flock. The rams as well, this time,
entered the cave: by some sheep-herding whim—
or a god's bidding—none were left outside.
He hefted his great boulder into place
and sat him down to milk the bleating ewes
in proper order, put the lambs to suck,
and swiftly ran through all his evening chores.
Then he caught two more men and feasted on them.
My moment was at hand, and I went forward   170
holding an ivy bowl of my dark drink,
looking up, saying:
"Kyklops, try some wine.
Here's liquor to wash down your scraps of men.
Taste it, and see the kind of drink we carried
under our planks. I meant it for an offering
if you would help us home. But you are mad,
unbearable, a bloody monster! After this,
will any other traveller come to see you?"
He seized and drained the bowl, and it went down   180
so fiery and smooth he called for more:
"Give me another, thank you kindly. Tell me,
how are you called? I'll make a gift will please you. ..."
I saw the fuddle and flush come over him,
then I sang out in cordial tones:
"Kyklops,
you ask my honorable name? ...
My name is Nohbdy: mother, father, and friends,
everyone calls me Nohbdy."
And he said: 190
"Nohbdy's my meat, then, after I eat his friends.
Others come first. There's a noble gift, now."
Even as he spoke, he reeled and tumbled backward,
his great head lolling to one side; and sleep
took him like any creature. Drunk, hiccuping,
he dribbled streams of liquor and bits of men.
Now, by the gods, I drove my big hand spike
deep in the embers, charring it again,
and cheered my men along with battle talk
to keep their courage up: no quitting now.   200
The pike of olive, green though it had been,
reddened and glowed as if about to catch.
I drew it from the coals and my four fellows
gave me a hand, lugging it near the Kyklops
as more than natural force nerved them; straight
forward they sprinted, lifted it, and rammed it

[3]Here used as a singular; his name, we learn later, is Polyphemus.

deep in his crater eye, and I leaned on it
turning it as a shipwright turns a drill
in planking, having men below to swing
the two-handled strap that spins it in the groove.   210
So with our brand we bored that great eye socket
while blood ran out around the red hot bar.
Eyelid and lash were seared; the pierced ball
hissed broiling, and the roots popped.
In a smithy
one sees a white-hot axehead or an adze
plunged and wrung in a cold tub, screeching steam—
the way they make soft iron hale and hard—
just so that eyeball hissed around the spike.
The Kyklops bellowed and the rock roared round him,   220
and we fell back in fear. Clawing his face
he tugged the bloody spike out of his eye,
threw it away, and his wild hands went groping;
then he set up a howl for Kyklopês
who lived in caves on windy peaks nearby.
Some heard him; and they came by divers ways
to clump around outside and call:
"What ails you,
Polyphêmos? Why do you cry so sore
in the starry night? You will not let us sleep.   230
Sure no man's driving off your flock? No man
has tricked you, ruined you?"
Out of the cave
the mammoth Polyphêmos roared in answer:
"Nohbdy, Nohbdy's tricked me, Nohbdy's ruined me!"
To this rough shout they made a sage reply:
"Ah well, if nobody has played you foul
there in your lonely bed, we are no use in pain
given by great Zeus. Let it be your father,
Poseidon Lord, to whom you pray."   240
So saying
they trailed away. And I was filled with laughter
to see how like a charm the name deceived them.
Now Kyklops, wheezing as the pain came on him,
fumbled to wrench away the great doorstone
and squatted in the breach with arms thrown wide
for any silly beast or man who bolted—
hoping somehow I might be such a fool.
But I kept thinking how to win the game:
death sat there huge; how could we slip away?   250
I drew on all my wits, and ran through tactics,
reasoning as a man will for dear life,
until a trick came—and it pleased me well.
The Kyklops' rams were handsome, fat, with heavy
fleeces, a dark violet.
Three abreast
I tied them silently together, twining
cords of willow from the ogre's bed;
then slung a man under each middle one
to ride there safely, shielded left and right.   260
So three sheep could convey each man. I took
the woolliest ram, the choicest of the flock,

and hung myself under his kinky belly,
pulled up tight, with fingers twisted deep
in sheepskin ringlets for an iron grip.
So, breathing hard, we waited until morning.
When Dawn spread out her finger tips of rose
the rams began to stir, moving for pasture,
and peals of bleating echoed round the pens
where dams with udders full called for a milking.   270
Blinded, and sick with pain from his head wound,
the master stroked each ram, then let it pass,
but my men riding on the pectoral fleece
the giant's blind hands blundering never found.
Last of them all my ram, the leader, came,
weighted by wool and me with my meditations.
The Kyklops patted him, and then he said:
"Sweet cousin ram, why lag behind the rest
in the night cave? You never linger so,
but graze before them all, and go afar   280
to crop sweet grass, and take your stately way
leading along the streams, until at evening
you run to be the first one in the fold.
Why, now, so far behind? Can you be grieving
over your Master's eye? That carrion rogue
and his accurst companions burnt it out
when he had conquered all my wits with wine.
Nohbdy will not get out alive, I swear.
Oh, had you brain and voice to tell
where he may be now, dodging all my fury!   290
Bashed by this hand and bashed on this rock wall
his brains would strew the floor, and I should have
rest from the outrage Nohbdy worked upon me."
He sent us into the open, then. Close by,
I dropped and rolled clear of the ram's belly,
going this way and that to untie the men.
With many glances back, we rounded up
his fat, stiff-legged sheep to take aboard,
and drove them down to where the good ship lay.
We saw, as we came near, our fellows' faces   300
shining; then we saw them turn to grief
tallying those who had not fled from death.
I hushed them, jerking head and eyebrows up,
and in a low voice told them: "Load this herd;
move fast, and put the ship's head toward the breakers."
They all pitched in at loading, then embarked
and struck their oars into the sea. Far out,
as far off shore as shouted words would carry,
I sent a few back to the adversary:
"O Kyklops! Would you feast on my companions?   310
Puny, am I, in a Caveman's hands?
How do you like the beating that we gave you,
you damned cannibal? Eater of guests
under your roof! Zeus and the gods have paid you!"
The blind thing in his doubled fury broke
a hilltop in his hands and heaved it after us.
Ahead of our black prow it struck and sank
whelmed in a spuming geyser, a giant wave

that washed the ship stern foremost back to shore.
I got the longest boathook out and stood   320
fending us off, with furious nods to all
to put their backs into a racing stroke—
row, row, or perish. So the long oars bent
kicking the foam sternward, making head
until we drew away, and twice as far.
Now when I cupped my hands I heard the crew
in low voices protesting:
"Godsake, Captain!
Why bait the beast again? Let him alone!"
"That tidal wave he made on the first throw   330
all but beached us."
"All but stove us in!"
"Give him our bearing with your trumpeting,
he'll get the range and lob a boulder."
"Aye
He'll smash our timbers and our heads together!"
I would not heed them in my glorying spirit,
but let my anger flare and yelled:

"Kyklops,
if ever mortal man inquire   340
how you were put to shame and blinded, tell him
Odysseus, raider of cities, took your eye:
Laërtês' son, whose home's on Ithaka!" …
Now he laid hands upon a bigger stone
and wheeled around, titanic for the cast,
to let it fly in the black-prowed vessel's track.
But it fell short, just aft the steering oar,
and whelming seas rose giant above the stone
to bear us onward toward the island. …

READING CRITICALLY

One of the features that distinguishes this particular tale in the *Odyssey* from Homer's narration in the *Iliad* is that Odysseus tells it himself, in his own voice. How does this first-person narrative technique help us to understand Homer's hero better than we might if Homer narrated the events himself?

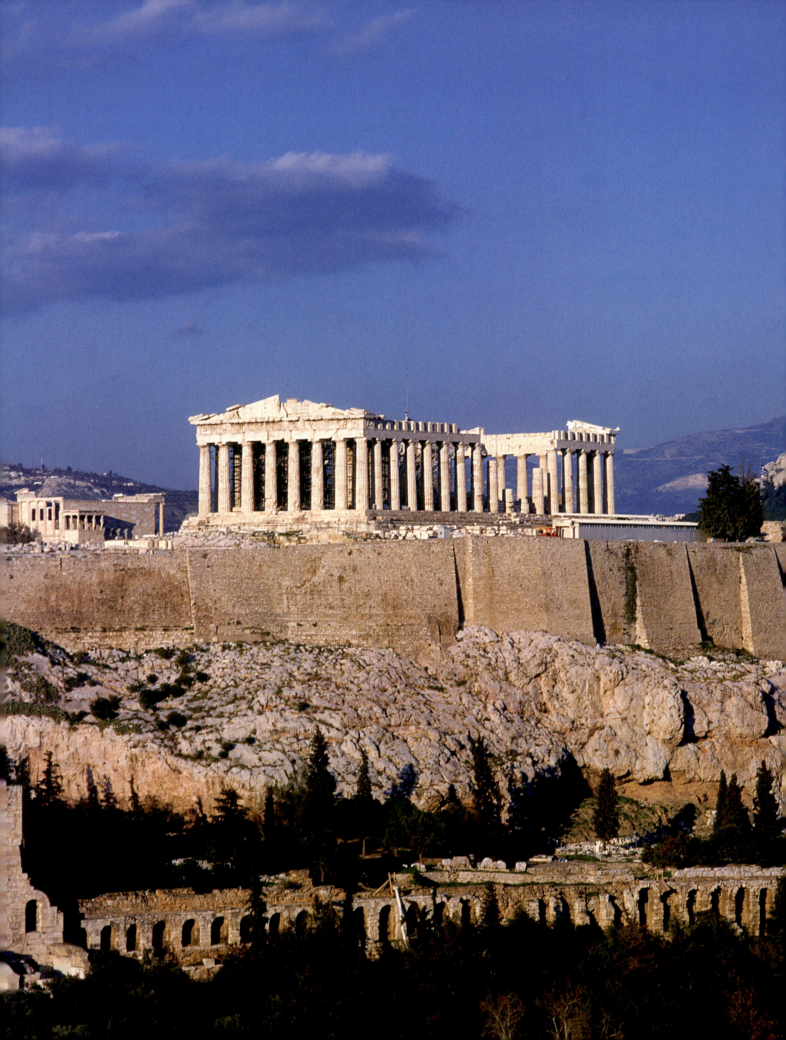

5

Golden Age Athens and the Hellenic World

The School of Hellas

THINKING AHEAD

5.1 Explain the role of *eudaimonia* in Athenian life and contrast it with the role of women.

5.2 Describe Pericles' sense of Athenian greatness and how it is reflected in the art of the Golden Age.

5.3 Compare and contrast the philosophical positions of the pre-Socratics, the Sophists, Socrates, and Plato.

5.4 Outline the chief characteristics of both Greek comedy and Greek tragedy.

5.5 Describe the gradual shift in sculptural style from the Classical art of Phidias to the art of the Hellenic world, and discuss how Aristotle's philosophy reflects this stylistic change.

In 490 BCE, a huge Persian army, estimated at 90,000, landed at Marathon, on the northern plains of Attica. They were met by a mere 10,000 Greeks, led by a professional soldier named Miltiades, who had once served under the Persian king, Darius, in Persia, and who understood Darius's vulnerability to sudden attack. Miltiades struck Darius's forces at dawn, killing 6,000 Persians and suffering minimal losses himself. The Persians were routed. The anxious citizens of Athens heard news of the victory from Phidippides, who ran the 26 miles between Marathon and Athens, thus completing the original marathon, a run that the Greeks would soon incorporate into their Olympic Games. (Contrary to popular belief, Phidippides did not die in the effort.)

Darius may have been defeated, but the Persians were not done. In 480 BCE, Darius's son Xerxes led a huge army into Greece. Modern estimates suggest it was composed of at least 150,000 men. The Greek leader Themistocles (ca. 524–ca. 460 BCE), who had been anticipating the invasion for a decade, knew that the Persians had to be delayed so that the Athenians would have time to abandon the city and take to the sea. At a narrow pass between the sea and

the mountains called Thermopylae, a band of 300 Spartans, led by their king, Leonidas, gave their lives so that the Athenians could escape.

The Greeks abandoned Athens, and Xerxes soon sacked the city, laying its sacred precinct, the Acropolis, to waste (Fig. **5.1**). But as Xerxes pursued them to Salamis, off the Athenian coast, the Greeks, led by Themistocles, set a trap. The Persian fleet, numbering about 800 galleys, faced the Greek fleet of about 370 smaller and more maneuverable *triremes*, galleys with three tiers of oars on each side. Themistocles lured the Persian fleet into the narrow waters of the strait at Salamis. The Greek triremes then attacked the crowded Persian fleet and used the great curved prows of their galleys to ram and sink about 300 Persian vessels. The Greeks lost only about 40 of their own fleet, and Xerxes was forced to retreat, never to threaten the Greek mainland again. Athens lay in ruins, and the Greeks were faced with the task of rebuilding it.

This chapter traces the rise and fall of Athens as a political power from the time of its victory over the Persians at Salamis until its defeat by Sparta in the Peloponnesian Wars in 404 BCE, the years of Athens's Golden Age. It

◄ **Fig. 5.1 The Acropolis, Athens, Greece. Rebuilt in the second half of the 5th century BCE.** After the Persians destroyed Athens in 479 BCE, the entire city, including the Acropolis, had to be rebuilt. This afforded the Athenians a unique opportunity to create one of the greatest monumental spaces in the history of Western architecture.

 Listen to the chapter audio on **MyArtsLab**

continues by surveying the subsequent **Hellenistic** period of Greek history, which began with the rise to power of Alexander the Great (356–323 BCE) and extended to the Roman defeat of Cleopatra in Egypt in 30 BCE. (*Hellenes* is what the Greeks called, and still call, themselves, and Alexander was understood to have made the world over in the image of Greece.) In the Hellenistic age, as Alexander conquered region after region, cities were built on the model of the Athenian polis, many of which became great centers of culture and learning in their own right. Soon, the accomplishments of Greek culture had spread throughout the Mediterranean, across North Africa and the Middle East, and even into the Indian subcontinent.

THE GOOD LIFE AND THE POLITICS OF ATHENS

What role did eudaimonia *play in Athenian life?*

When the Athenians returned to a devastated Athens after their victory at Salamis, they turned their attention first to the **agora**, an open place used for congregating or as a market (Map **5.1**). The principal architectural feature of the agora was the **stoa** (Fig. **5.2**), a long, open arcade supported by **colonnades**, rows of columns. While Athenians could shop for grapes, figs, flowers, and lambs in the agora, it was far more than just a shopping center. It was the place where

citizens congregated, debated the issues of the day, argued points of law, settled disputes, and presented philosophical discourse. In short, it was the place where they practiced their politics.

In his *Politics*, the Greek philosopher Aristotle (384–322 BCE) described the politics and the Athenian polis like

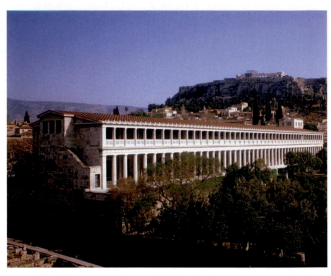

Fig. 5.2 The Stoa of Attalus, Athens, Greece. 150 BCE. This stoa, reconstructed at the eastern edge of the modern agora, retains traditional form. The broad causeway on the right was the Panathenaic Way, the route of the ritual processions to the Acropolis in the distance. The original agora buildings lie farther to the right and overlook the Panathenaic Way.

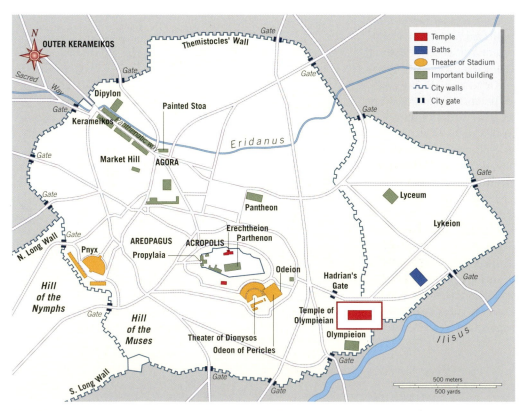

Map 5.1 Athens as it appeared in the late 5th century BCE. The map shows a modern artist's rendering of the city.

this: "The partnership finally composed of several villages is the polis; it has at last attained the limit of virtually complete self-sufficiency, and thus while it comes into existence for the sake of mere life, it exists for the sake of the good life." For Aristotle, the essential purpose of the polis was to guarantee, barring catastrophe, that each of its citizens might flourish. Writing in the fourth century BCE, Aristotle is thinking back to the Athens of the fifth century BCE, the so-called Golden Age. During these years, the pursuit of what Aristotle called *eudaimonia*, "the good or flourishing life," resulted in a culture of astonishing sophistication and diversity. For *eudaimonia* is not simply a happy or pleasurable existence; rather, the polis provides the conditions in which each individual may pursue an "activity of soul in accordance with complete excellence." For Aristotle, this striving to "complete excellence" defines Athens in the Golden Age.

A politics such as Aristotle describes depends upon at least a limited democracy. In a tyranny, there can be no politics because there can be no debate. Whatever their diverging views, the citizens of the polis were free to debate the issues, to speak their minds. They spoke as individuals, and they cherished the freedom to think as they pleased. But they spoke out of a concern for the common good, for the good of the polis, which, after all, gave them the freedom to speak in the first place. When Aristotle says, in his *Politics*, that "man is a political animal," he means that man is a creature of the polis, bound to it, dedicated to it, determined by it, and, somewhat paradoxically, liberated by it as well.

The Council of Five Hundred was elected annually, and met in the Bouleuterion in the agora. Its executive committee dined, at public expense, in the nearby Tholos, a round building with six columns supporting a conical roof. In the Metroon, the polis housed its weights and measures as well as its official archives. A special place honored the laws of Solon. Carved into the hill in the southwestern part of the city was a giant bowl, the Pnyx, where as many as 10,000 citizens could gather. Here the polis convened four times each month (the Greek calendar consisted of ten months), to vote on the resolutions of its governing council.

The chief occupation of Athenian citizens was to gather in the agora to exercise their political duties. This purpose explains several seemingly contradictory aspects of the Athenian polis. Most citizens lived, by modern standards, in relatively humble circumstances. Homes were tiny and hygiene practically nonexistent. Furniture was basic and minimal. Bread was the staple of life, eaten with olives or relish made from fish (though wine, at least, was plentiful). Wood for fire and heat was scarce, and the water supply was inadequate. This is not to say that the Athenians had no wealth. They were richer than most. And they acquired leisure, the free time necessary to perform the responsibilities of citizenship.

Slaves and Metics

The limited Athenian democracy was based on its citizens' ability to have others do its manual work. This marks a radical departure from the culture of Hesiod's *Works and Days*, in which one advanced oneself by "work with work upon work." To the Athenian citizen, work was something to be avoided. Typically, working fell to slaves or to *metics*, free men who were not citizens because they came from some other polis in Greece or from a Greek colony.

By the middle of the Golden Age, the population of Athens was approximately 275,000, of which only 40,000 were citizens. Between 80,000 and 100,000 residents of Athens were slaves. The rest were metics and women. The practice of slavery came naturally to the Greeks, since most slaves were "barbarians" (the word Greeks used to describe non-Greek-speaking people) and hence by definition inferior. Almost every citizen had at least one slave attendant and a female domestic servant. As for the metics, one contemporary reported that "They do everything. ... [They] do the removal of rubbish, mason's work, and plastering, they capture the wood trade, timber construction, and rough carpentry, metal work and all subsidiary occupations are in their hands, and they hold the clothing industries, the sale of colors and varnishes, and in short every small trade."

Metics were equally central to the development of the arts and philosophy in the Golden Age. Most of the sculptors, potters, and painters came from abroad and thus were metics. Almost all of the city's philosophers—except, most notably, Socrates and Plato—were also metics. By the fourth century, so were all the leading comic playwrights, with the important exception of Aristophanes.

The Women of Athens

Like the metics, the women of Athens were not citizens and did not enjoy any of the privileges of citizenship. In 431 BCE, the playwright Euripides put these words into the mouth of Medea, a woman believed to be of divine origin who punished the mortal Jason for abandoning her. Medea kills Jason's new bride as well as her own children (**Reading 5.1**):

READING 5.1

from Euripides, *Medea* (431 BCE)

Of all things which are living and can form a judgment
We women are the most unfortunate creatures.
Firstly, with an excess of wealth it is required
For us to buy a husband and take for our bodies
A master; for not to take one is even worse. ...
A man, when he's tired of the company in his home,
Goes out of the house and puts an end to his boredom
And turns to a friend or companion of his own age.
But we are forced to keep our eyes on one alone [i.e., the
 husband].
What they say of us is that we have a peaceful time
Living at home, while they do the fighting in war.
How wrong they are! I would very much rather stand
Three times in front of battle than bear one child.

As Medea suggests, women in Athens were excluded from most aspects of social life. In general, they married before they were 15 years old, at an age when they were considered to be still educable by husbands who averaged about 30 years of age. Athenian women were not educated. Near the beginning of the third century BCE, the comic playwright Menander explained the reason this way: "Teach a woman to read and write? What a terrible thing to do! Like feeding a vile snake on more poison." Neither were women expected to participate in conversation, which was the male's prerogative. Their role was largely domestic, even though their household obligations were sometimes minimal given the number of slaves and maids. Above all, the wife's primary duty was to produce male offspring for her husband's household.

Women did, in fact, serve another important role in Athenian social life—they took part in religious rituals and public festivals. They were also, as Euripides' *Medea* suggests, central figures in much of Greek culture, from its mythology, to its painting and sculpture, and, perhaps above all, its theater. Plays such as Euripides' *Medea* and Sophocles' *Antigone*, and especially Aristophanes' comedy *Lysistrata*, in which the women of Athens and Sparta unite to withhold sexual favors from their husbands until they agree to make peace, suggest that Athenian society was deeply torn by the tension between the reality of female power and the insistence on male authority.

Nevertheless, we know that some women exerted real power in Greek culture. A particularly powerful woman was Aspasia (ca. 469–ca. 406 BCE), mistress of the statesman and leader Pericles (whose rule is discussed below). Aspasia was a *hetaira*, one of a class of Greek courtesans distinguished by their beauty and, as opposed to most women in Athenian society, their often high level of education. After Pericles divorced his wife around 445 BCE, Aspasia lived with him openly as if they were married. (Since she was both foreign-born and a *hetaira*, actual marriage was forbidden by Athenian law.) She is said to have taught rhetoric with such skill that some scholars believe it was actually she who invented the "dialectical method" (see page 148). And she evidently exerted enough political influence on Pericles that their relationship was the target of attacks and jokes in Greek comedy.

Some Hellenic city-states treated their women better than the Athenians. Spartan women were taught to read and write, and they were encouraged to develop the same physical prowess as Spartan men, participating in athletic events such as javelin, discus, and foot races, as well as fighting in staged battles. Spartan women met with their husbands only for procreative purposes and had little to do with their children, who were raised by the community. A woman's property was her own to keep and manage, and if her husband was away too long at war, she was even free to remarry.

PERICLES AND THE SCHOOL OF HELLAS

What did Pericles believe to be the source of Athenian greatness and how is that greatness reflected in the art of the Golden Age?

No person dominated Athenian political life during the Golden Age more than the statesman Pericles (ca. 495–429 BCE), who served for nearly 30 years on the Board of Ten Generals, which was elected annually rather than chosen by lot, and was thus truly representative of the people. An aristocrat by birth, he was nonetheless democracy's strongest advocate. Late in his career, in 431 BCE, he delivered a speech honoring soldiers who had fallen in early battles of the Peloponnesian War, a struggle for power between Sparta and Athens that would eventually result in Athens's defeat in 404 BCE, long after Pericles' own death. Although Athens and Sparta had united to form the Delian League in the face of the Persian threat in 478 BCE, by 450 BCE, Persia was no longer a threat, and Sparta sought to foment a large-scale revolt against Athenian control of the Delian League. Sparta formed its own Peloponnesian League, motivated at least partly by Athens's use of Delian League funds to rebuild its acropolis. Pericles resisted the rebellion vigorously, as Athenian preeminence among the Greeks was at stake. The Greek historian Thucydides recorded Pericles' speech in honor of his soldiers in its entirety in his *History of the Peloponnesian Wars* (**Readings 5.2a**, **5.2b**, and **5.2c**). Although Thucydides, considered the greatest historian of antiquity, tried to achieve objectivity—to the point that he claimed, rather too humbly, that he was so true to the facts that the reader might find him boring—he did admit that he had substituted his own phrasings when he could not remember the exact words of his subjects. Thus, Pericles' speech may be more Thucydides than Pericles. Furthermore, gossip at the time suggests that the speech was in large part the work of Aspasia, Pericles' mistress and partner. So the speech may, in fact, be more Aspasia than Pericles, and more Thucydides than Aspasia. Nevertheless, it reflects what the Athenians thought of themselves.

Pericles begins his speech by saying that, in order to properly honor the dead, he would like "to point out by what principles of action we rose to power, and under what institutions and through what manner of life our empire became great." First and foremost in his mind is Athenian democracy:

READING 5.2a

from Thucydides, *History of the Peloponnesian Wars*, Pericles' Funeral Speech (ca. 410 BCE)

Our form of government does not enter into rivalry with the institutions of others. We do not copy our neighbors, but are an example to them. It is true that we are called a democracy, for the administration is in the hands of the many not the few. But while the law secures equal justice to all alike in their private disputes, the claim of excellence is also recognized; and when a citizen is in any way distinguished, he is preferred to the public service, not as a matter of privilege, but as the reward of merit. Neither is poverty a bar, but a man may benefit his country whatever be the obscurity of his condition. There is no exclusiveness in our public life, and in our private intercourse we are not suspicious of one another, nor angry with our neighbor if he does what he likes, we do not put on sour looks at him which, though harmless, are not pleasant. We are thus unconstrained in our private intercourse, a spirit of reverence pervades our public acts; we are prevented from doing wrong by respect for authority and for the laws. ...

This "claim of excellence" defines Athenians' political, social, and cultural life. It is the hallmark not only of their political system but also of their military might. It explains their spirited competitions in the arts and in their athletic contests, which the citizens regularly enjoyed. All true Athenians, Pericles suggests, seek excellence through the conscientious pursuit of the beautiful and the good:

READING 5.2b

from Pericles' Funeral Speech

For we are lovers of the beautiful, yet with economy, and we cultivate the mind without loss of manliness. Wealth we employ, not for talk and ostentation, but when there is a real use for it. To avow poverty with us is no disgrace; the true disgrace is in doing nothing to avoid it. An Athenian citizen does not neglect the state because he takes care of his own household; and even those who are engaged in business have a very fair idea of politics. We alone regard a man who takes no interest in public affairs, not as a harmless, but as a useless character; and if few of us are originators, we are all sound judges of policy. The great impediment to action is, in our opinion, not discussion, but the want of that knowledge which is gained by discussion preparatory to action. For we have a peculiar power of thinking before we act and of acting too, whereas other men are courageous from ignorance but hesitate upon reflection.

Pericles is not concerned with politics alone. He praises the Athenians' "many relaxations from toil." He acknowledges that life in Athens is as good as it is because "the fruits of the whole earth flow in upon us." And, he insists, Athenians are "lovers of the beautiful" who seek to "cultivate the mind." "To sum up," he concludes:

READING 5.2c

from Pericles' Funeral Speech

I say that Athens is the school of Hellas, and that the individual Athenian in his own person seems to have the power of adapting himself to the most varied forms of action with the utmost versatility and grace. This is no passing and idle word, but truth and fact; and the assertion is verified by the position to which these qualities have raised the state. ... I have dwelt upon the greatness of Athens because I want to show you that we are contending for a higher prize than those who enjoy none of these privileges, and to establish by manifest proof the merit of these men whom I am now commemorating. Their loftiest praise has been already spoken. For in magnifying the city, I magnify them, and men like them whose virtues made her glorious.

When Pericles says that Athens is "the school of Hellas," he means that it teaches all of Greece by its example. He insists that the greatness of the state is a function of the greatness of its individuals. The quality of Athenian life depends upon this link between individual freedom and civic responsibility—which most of us in the Western world recognize as the foundation of our own political idealism (if, too often, not our political reality).

Beautiful Mind, Beautiful Body

One of the most interesting aspects of Pericles' oration is his sense that the greatness of the Athenians is expressed in both the love of beauty and the cultivation of intellectual inquiry. We find this particularly in the development of scientific inquiry. In fact, one of the more remarkable features of fifth-century Greek culture is that it spawned a way of thinking that transformed the way human beings see themselves in relation to the natural world. Most people in the ancient world saw themselves at the mercy of flood and sun, subject to the wiles of gods beyond their control. They faced the unknown through the agency of priests, shamans, kings, mythologies, and rituals.

In contrast, the Greeks argued that the forces that governed the natural world were knowable. The causes of natural disasters—flood, earthquake, drought—could be understood as something other than the punishment of an angry god. As early as 600 BCE, for instance, Thales of Miletus (ca. 625–547 BCE) accurately described the causes of a solar eclipse—an event that had periodically terrorized ancient peoples. His conclusions came from objective observation and rigorous analysis of the facts. Observing that water could change from solid to liquid to gas, Thales also argued that water was the primary substance of the universe. Many disagreed, opting for air or fire as the fundamental substance. Nevertheless, the debate inaugurated a tradition of dialogue that fostered increasingly sophisticated thinking. Intellectuals challenged one another to ever more demonstrable and reasonable explanations of natural phenomena.

In this light, the cult of the human body developed in the Golden Age. The writings attributed to Hippocrates (ca. 470–390 BCE), the so-called "father of medicine," insist on the relationship between cause and effect in physical illness, the mind's ability to influence the physical body for good or ill, and the influence of diet and environment on physical health. In fact, in the Golden Age, the beautiful body comes to reflect not only physical but also mental superiority.

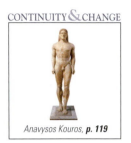

CONTINUITY & CHANGE

Anavysos Kouros, p. 119

In a pile of debris on the Acropolis, pushed aside by Athenians cleaning up after the Persian sack of Athens in 479 BCE, a sculpture of a nude young man, markedly more naturalistic than its *kouros* predecessors, was uncovered in 1865 (its head was discovered 23 years later, in a separate location). Attributed by those who found it to the sculptor Kritios, the so-called *Kritios Boy* (Fig. 5.3) demonstrates the increasing naturalism of Greek sculpture during the first 20 years of the fifth century BCE.

Compare the *Kritios Boy* with the earlier stiff-looking *kouros* figures (see Figs. 4.20 and 4.21 in Chapter 4). The boy's head is turned slightly to the side. His weight rests on the left leg, and the right leg extends forward, bent slightly at the knee. The figure seems to twist around its **axis**, or imaginary central line, the natural result of balancing the body over one supporting leg. The term for this stance, coined during the Italian Renaissance, is **contrapposto** ("counterpoise"), or weight-shift. The inspiration for this development seems to have been a growing desire by Greek sculptors to dramatize the stories narrated in the decorative programs of temples and sanctuaries. Liveliness of posture and gesture and a sense of capturing the body in action became their primary sculptural aim and the very definition of beauty in the Classical world.

An even more developed version of the *contrapposto* pose can be seen in the *Doryphoros*, or *Spear Bearer* (Fig. **5.4**), whose weight falls on the forward right leg. An idealized portrait of a warrior, originally done in bronze, the *Doryphoros* is a Roman copy of the work of Polyclitus, one of the great artists of the Golden Age. The sculpture was famous throughout the ancient world as a demonstration of Polyclitus' treatise on proportion, known as *The Canon* (from the Greek *kanon*, meaning "measure" or "rule"). In Polyclitus' system, the ideal human form was determined by the height of the head from the crown to the chin. The head was one-eighth the total height, the width of the shoulders was one-quarter the total height, and so on, each measurement reflecting these ideal proportions. For Polyclitus, these relations resulted in the work's *symmetria*, the origin of our word *symmetry*, but meaning, in Polyclitus' usage, "commensurability," or "having a common measure." Thus, the figure, beautifully realized in great detail, right down to the veins on the back of the hand, reflects a higher mathematical order and embodies the ideal harmony between the natural world and the intellectual or spiritual realm.

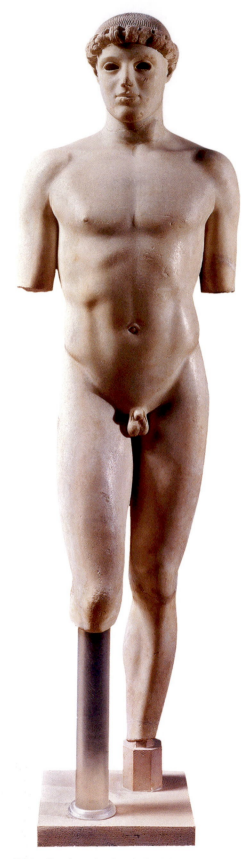

Fig. 5.3 *Kritios Boy*, from the Acropolis, Athens. ca. 480 BCE. Marble, height 46". Acropolis Museum, Athens. The growing naturalism of Greek sculpture is clear when one compares the *Kritios Boy* to the earlier *kouros* figures (see Chapter 4). Although more naturalistic, this figure still served a votive function.

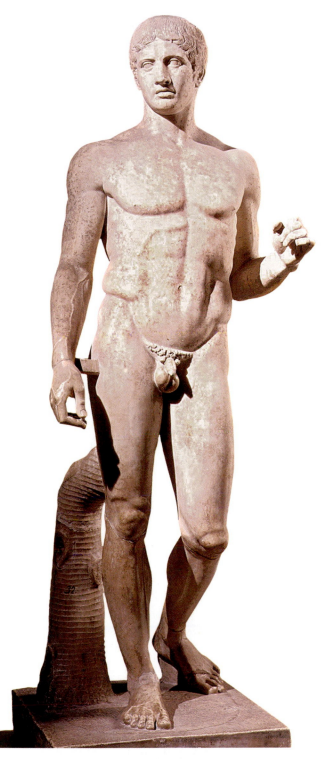

Fig. 5.4 *Doryphoros* (*Spear Bearer*), **Roman copy after the original bronze by Polyclitus of ca. 450–440 BCE.** Marble, height 6'4". Museo Archeologico Nazionale, Naples. There is some debate about just what "measure" Polyclitus employed to achieve his ideal figure. Some argue that his system of proportions is based on the length of the figure's index finger or the width of the figure's hand across the knuckles. The idea that it is based on the distance between the chin and the crown derives from a much later discussion of proportion by the Roman writer Vitruvius, who lived in the first century CE. It is possible that Vitruvius had firsthand knowledge of Polyclitus' *Canon*, which was lost long ago.

👁 **Watch** a Students on Site video about the *Doryphoros* on **MyArtsLab**

Rebuilding the Acropolis

After the Persian invasion in 480 BCE, the Athenians had initially vowed to keep the Acropolis in a state of ruin as a reminder of the horrible price of war; however, Pericles convinced them to rebuild it. Richly decorated with elaborate architecture and sculpture, it would become, Pericles argued, a fitting memorial not only to the war but especially to Athena's role in protecting the Athenian people. Furthermore, at Persepolis, the defeated Xerxes and then his son and successor Artaxerxes I (r. 465–424 BCE), were busy expanding their palace, and Athens was not about to be outdone.

Pericles placed the sculptor Phidias in charge of the sculptural program for the new buildings on the Acropolis, and Phidias may have been responsible for the architectural project as well. The centerpiece of the project was the Parthenon, a temple to honor Athena, which was completed in 432 BCE after 15 years of construction. The monumental entryway to the complex, the Propylaia, was completed the same year. Two other temples, completed later, the Erechtheion (430s–406 BCE) and the Temple of Athena Nike (420s BCE), also may have been part of the original scheme. The chief architects of the Acropolis project were Ictinus, Callicrates, and Mnesicles.

The Architectural Program at the Acropolis The cost of rebuilding the Acropolis was enormous, but despite the reservations expressed by many over such an extravagant expenditure—financed mostly by tributes that Athens levied upon its allies in the Delian League—the project had the virtue of employing thousands of Athenians—citizens, metics, and slaves alike—thus guaranteeing its general popularity. Writing a *Life of Pericles* five centuries later, the Greek-born biographer Plutarch (ca. 46–after 119 CE) gives us some idea of the scope of the rebuilding project and its effects (**Reading 5.3**):

READING 5.3

from Plutarch, *Life of Pericles* (75 CE)

The raw materials were stone, bronze, ivory, gold, ebony, and cypress wood. To fashion them were a host of craftsmen: carpenters, molders, coppersmiths, stonemasons, goldsmiths, ivory-specialists, painters, textile-designers, and sculptors in relief. Then there were the men detailed for transport and haulage: merchants, sailors, and helmsmen at sea; on land, cartwrights, drovers, and keepers of traction animals. There were also the rope-makers, the flax-workers, cobblers, roadmakers, and miners. Each craft, like a commander with his own army, had its own attachments of hired labourers and individual specialists organized like a machine for the service required. So it was that the various commissions spread a ripple of prosperity throughout the citizen body.

The Parthenon (see *Closer Look*, pages 142–143) was of course the centerpiece of the project, but there were several

CLOSER LOOK

The Parthenon is famous both for its architectural perfection and for the sculptural decoration that is so carefully integrated into the structure. The decorative sculptures were in three main areas—in the pediments at each end of the building, on the **metopes**, or the square panels between the beam ends under the roof, and on the frieze that runs across the top of the outer wall of the cella. Brightly painted, these sculptures must have appeared strikingly lifelike. In the clarity of its parts, the harmony among them, and its overall sense of proportion and balance, it represents the epitome of Classical architecture. Built to give thanks to Athena for the salvation of Athens and Greece in the Persian Wars, it was a tangible sign of the power and might of the Athenian state, designed to impress all who visited the city. It was built on the foundations and platform of an earlier structure, but the architects Ictinus and Callicrates clearly intended it to represent the Doric order in its most perfect form. It has 8 columns at the ends and 17 on the sides. Each column swells out about one-third of the way up, a device called **entasis**, to counter the eye's tendency to see the uninterrupted parallel columns as narrowing as they rise and to give a sense of "breath" or liveliness to the stone. The columns also slant slightly inward, so that they appear to the eye to rise straight up. And since horizontal lines appear to sink in the middle, the platform beneath them rises nearly 5 inches from each corner to the middle. There are no true verticals or horizontals in the building, a fact that lends its apparently rigid geometry a sense of liveliness and animation.

The building's Classical sense of beauty manifests itself in the architects' use of a system of proportionality in order to coordinate the construction process in a way that resulted in a harmonious design. The ratio controlling the Parthenon's design can be expressed in the algebraic formula $x = 2y + 1$. The temple's columns, for instance, reflect this formula: there are 8 columns on the short ends and 17 on the sides, because $17 = (2 \times 8) + 1$. The ratio of the stylobate's length to width is 9:4, because $9 = (2 \times 4) + 1$. This mathematical regularity is central to the overall harmony of the building.

✷ **Explore** the architectural panoramas of the Parthenon on **MyArtsLab**

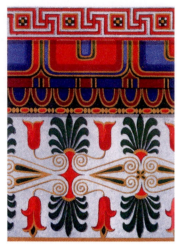

The interior decoration of the Parthenon ceiling, as reconstructed and published by Gottfried Semper, 1878. Paint traces provided clues to the original decorative design that once adorned the ceiling of the temple.

Something to Think About …

Athena, to whom the Parthenon is dedicated, is not only goddess of war, but also goddess of wisdom. How does the Parthenon reflect both of her roles?

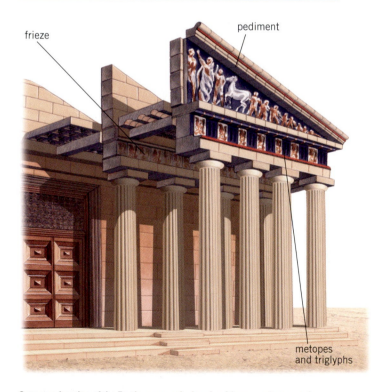

frieze

pediment

metopes and triglyphs

Cutaway drawing of the Parthenon porch showing friezes, metopes, and pediment. Evident here is the architect Ictinus' juxtaposition of the Doric order, used for the columns with their capitals and the entablature on the outside, with the lighter Ionic order of its continuous frieze, used for the entablature inside the colonnade.

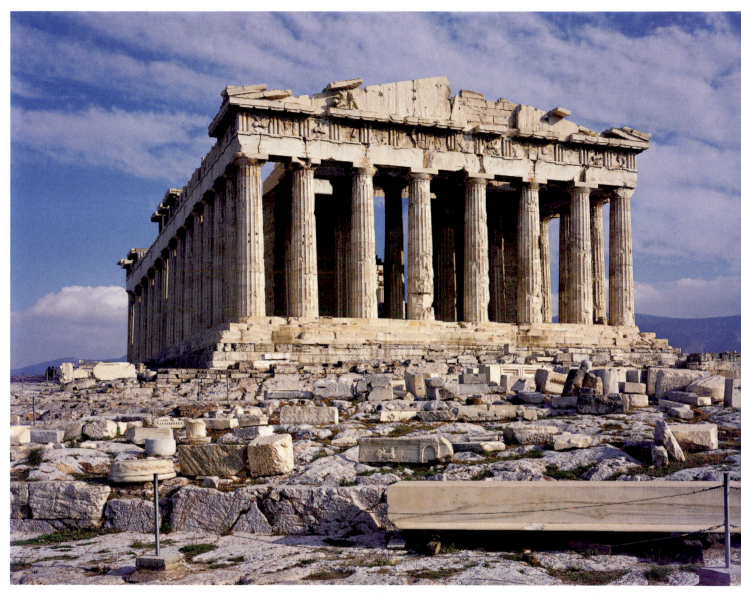

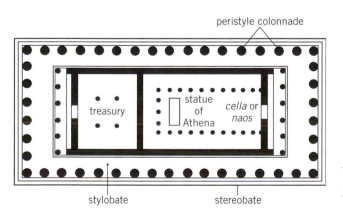

peristyle colonnade

treasury

statue
of
Athena

cella or
naos

stylobate

stereobate

Ictinus, with contributions by Callicrates, The Parthenon and its plan, Acropolis, Athens. 447–438 BCE. Sculptural program completed 432 BCE. The temple measures about 228' × 101' on the top step. The temple remained almost wholly intact (though it served variously as a church and then a mosque) until 1687, when attacking Venetians exploded a Turkish powder magazine housed in it.

The giant, 40-foot-high sculpture of Athena Parthenos was located in the Parthenon's cella, or naos, the central interior room of a temple in which the cult statue was traditionally housed.

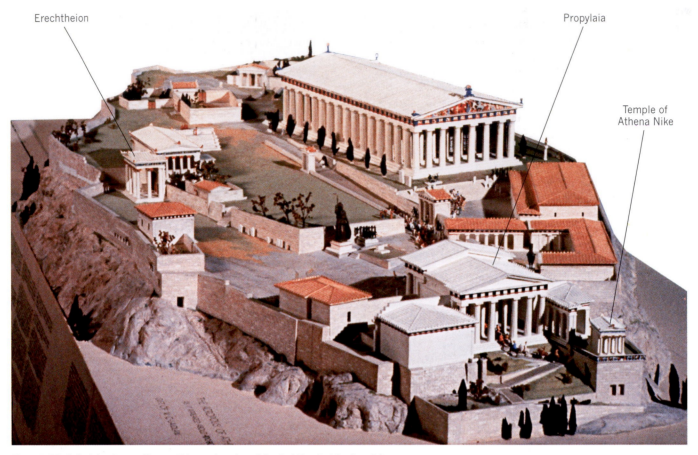

Erechtheion

Propylaia

Temple of
Athena Nike

Fig. 5.5 Model of the Acropolis. ca. 400 BCE. American School of Classical Studies, Athens.

other important structures built on the Acropolis as well (Fig. **5.5**).

One of the architects employed in the project, Mnesicles, was charged with designing the **propylon**, or large entryway, where the Panathenaic Way approached the Acropolis from below. Instead of a single gate, he created five, an architectural tour de force named the Propylaia (the plural of *propylon*), flanked with porches and colonnades of Doric columns. The north wing eventually included a picture gallery featuring paintings of Greek history and myth, none of which survive. Contrasting with the towering mass of the Propylaia was the far more delicate Temple of Athena Nike (Fig. **5.6**), situated on the promontory just to the west and overlooking the entrance way. Graced by slender Ionic columns, the diminutive structure (it measures a mere 27 by 19 feet) was built in 425 BCE, not long after the death of Pericles. It was probably meant to celebrate what the Athenians hoped would be their victory in the Peloponnesian Wars, as *nike* is Greek for "victory." Before the end of the wars, between 410 and 407 BCE, it was surrounded by a **parapet**, or low wall, faced with panels depicting Athena together with her winged companions, the Victories.

After passing through the Propylaia into the sacred precinct at the top of the Acropolis, the visitor would confront not only the massive spectacle of the Parthenon, but also an imposing statue of Athena Promachus, Athena the Defender, executed by Phidias between 465 and 455 BCE. Twenty feet high, it was tall enough that sailors landing at the port of Piraeus several miles away could see the sun reflected off Athena's helmet. And just to the left of the statue they would have seen the Erechtheion (Fig. **5.7**). Its asymmetrical and multileveled structure is unique, resulting from the rocky site on which it is situated. Flatter areas were available on the Acropolis, so its demanding position is clearly intentional. The building surrounds a sacred spring dedicated to Erechtheus, the first legendary king of Athens, after whom the building is named. Work on the building began after the completion of the Parthenon, in the 430s BCE, and took 25 years. Among its unique characteristics is the famous Porch of the Maidens, facing the Parthenon. It is supported by six **caryatids**, female figures serving as columns. These figures illustrate the idea of the temple column as a kind of human figure, and the idea that the stability of the polis depends upon the conduct of its womenfolk. All assume a classic *contrapposto* pose, the three on the left with their weight over the right leg, the three on the right with their weight over the left. Although each figure is unique—the folds on their chitons fall differently, and their breasts are different sizes and shapes—together they create a sense of balance and harmony.

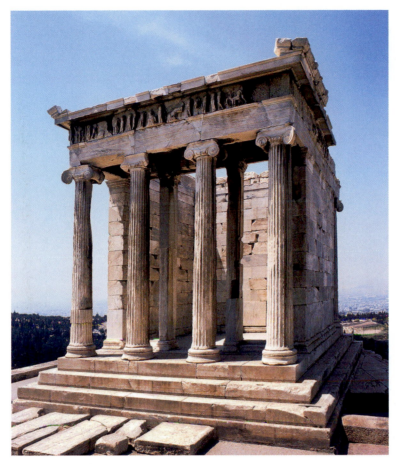

Fig. 5.6 Temple of Athena Nike, Acropolis, Athens. ca. 425 BCE. Overlooking the approach to the Propylaia, the temple's lighter Ionic columns contrast dramatically with the heavier, more robust Doric columns of the gateway.

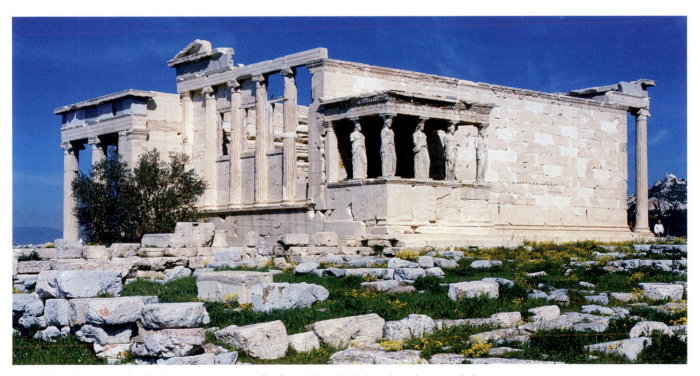

Fig. 5.7 Erechtheion, Acropolis, Athens. 430s–405 BCE. The Erechtheion, with its irregular and asymmetrical design, slender Ionic columns, and delicate Porch of the Maidens, contrasts dramatically and purposefully with the more orthodox and highly regular Parthenon across the Acropolis to the south.

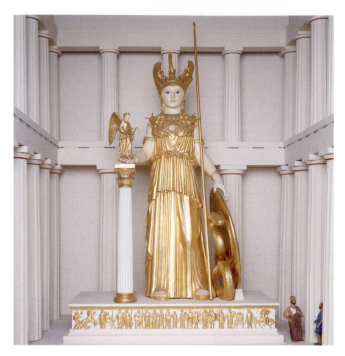

Fig. 5.8 **Model of the Athena Parthenos, original by Phidias, ca. 440** BCE. Royal Ontario Museum, Toronto. Surviving "souvenir" copies of Phidias' original give us some idea of how it must have originally appeared, and this model is based on those.

The Sculptural Program at the Parthenon If Phidias' hand was not directly involved in carving the sculpture decorating the Parthenon, most of the decoration is probably his design. We know for certain that he designed the giant statue of Athena Parthenos housed in the Parthenon (Fig. 5.8). Though long since destroyed, we know its general characteristics through literary descriptions and miniature copies. It stood 40 feet high and was supported by a ship's

mast. Its skin was made of ivory and its dress and armor of gold. Its spectacular presence was meant to celebrate not only the goddess's religious power but also the political power of the city she protected. She is at once a warrior, with spear and shield, and the model of Greek womanhood, the *parthenos*, or maiden, dressed in the standard Doric peplos. And since the gold that formed the surface of the statue was removable, she was, in essence, an actual treasury.

The 3-foot-high frieze that originally ran at a height of nearly 27 feet around the central block of the building depicts a ceremonial procession (Fig. 5.9). Traditionally, the frieze has been interpreted as a depiction of the Panathenaic procession, a civic festival occurring every four years in honor of Athena. Some 525 feet long, the frieze consists of horsemen, musicians, water carriers, maidens, and sacrificial beasts. All the human figures have the ideal proportions of the *Doryphoros* (see Fig. 5.4).

The sculptural program in the west pediment depicts Athena battling with Poseidon to determine who was to be patron of Athens. Scholars debate the identity of the figures in the east pediment, but it seems certain that overall it portrays the birth of Athena with gods and goddesses in attendance (Fig. 5.10). The 92 metopes on the four sides of the temple, each separated from the next by **triglyphs**, square blocks divided by grooves into three sections, narrate battles between the Greeks and four enemies—the Trojans on one side, and on the other three, giants, Amazons (perhaps symbolizing the recently defeated Persians), and centaurs, mythological beasts with the legs and bodies of horses and the trunks and heads of humans. Executed in high relief (Fig. 5.11), these metopes represent the clash between the forces of civilization—the Greeks—and their barbarian, even bestial, opponents. The male nude reflects not only physical but mental superiority, a theme particularly appropriate for a temple to Athena, goddess of both war and wisdom.

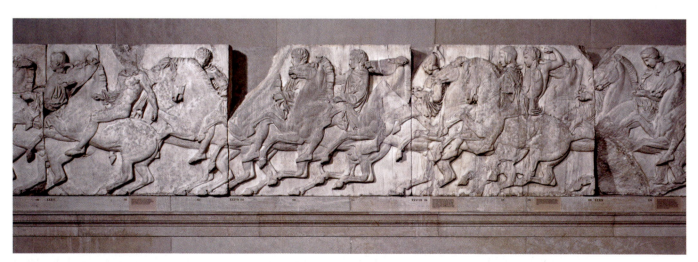

Fig. 5.9 *Young Men on Horseback*, **segment of the north frieze of the Parthenon. ca. 440** BCE. Marble, height 41". © The Trustees of the British Museum. This is just a small section of the entire procession, which extends completely around the Parthenon.

👁 **Watch** a studio video about carving on **MyArtsLab**

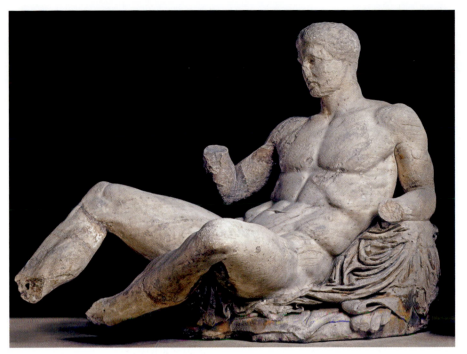

Fig. 5.10 *A Recumbent God* (Dionysus or Heracles), east pediment of the Parthenon. ca. 435 BCE. © The Trustees of the British Museum. In 1801, Thomas Bruce, Earl of Elgin and British ambassador to Constantinople, brought the marbles from the east pediment, as well as some from the west pediment and the south metopes, and a large part of the frieze, back to England—the source of their name, the *Elgin Marbles*. The identities of the figures are much disputed, but the greatness of their execution is not. Now exhibited in the round, in their original position on the pediment they were carved in high relief. As the sun passed over the three-dimensional relief on the east and west pediments, the sculptures would have appeared almost animated by the changing light and the movement of their cast shadows.

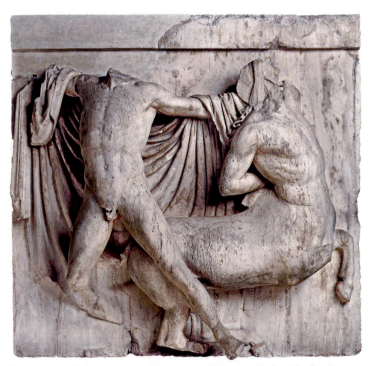

Fig. 5.11 *Lapith Overcoming a Centaur*, south metope 27, from the Parthenon. 447–438 BCE. Marble relief, height 4'5". © The Trustees of the British Museum. The Lapiths are a people in Greek myth who defeated drunken centaurs at the wedding of their king, Pirithous. The Greeks identified centaurs with the Persians, whom they considered the embodiment of chaos, possessing centaur-like forces of irrationality.

PHILOSOPHY AND THE POLIS

How do the philosophies of Socrates and Plato compare?

The extraordinary architectural achievement of the Acropolis is matched by the philosophical achievement of the great Athenian philosopher Socrates, born in 469 BCE, a decade after the Greek defeat of the Persians. His death in 399 BCE arguably marks the end of Athens's Golden Age. Socrates' death was not a natural one. His execution was ordered by a polis in turmoil after its defeat by the Spartans in 404 BCE. The city had submitted to the rule of the oligarchic government installed by the victorious Spartans, the so-called Thirty Tyrants, whose power was ensured by a gang of "whip-bearers." They deprived the courts of their power and initiated a set of trials against rich men, especially metics, and democrats who opposed their tyranny. Over 1,500 Athenians were subsequently executed. Socrates was brought to trial, accused of subversive behavior, corrupting young men, and introducing new gods, though these charges may have been politically motivated. He antagonized his jury of citizens by insisting that his life had been as good as anyone's and that far from committing any wrongs, he had greatly benefited Athens. He was convicted by a narrow majority and condemned to death by drinking poisonous hemlock. His refusal to flee and his willingness to submit to the will of the polis and drink the potion testify to his belief in the very polis that condemned him. His eloquent defense of his decision to submit is recorded in the *Crito* (see **Reading 5.4** on pages 168–169), a dialogue between Socrates and his friend Crito, actually written by Plato, Socrates' student and fellow philosopher. Although the Athenians would continue to enjoy relative freedom for many years to come, the death of Socrates marks the end of their great experiment with democracy. Although Socrates was no defender of democracy—he did not believe that most people were really capable of exercising good government—he became the model of good citizenship and right thinking for centuries to come.

The Philosophical Context

To understand Socrates' position, it is important to recognize that the crisis confronting Athens in 404 BCE was not merely political, but deeply philosophical. And furthermore, a deep division existed between the philosophers and the polis. Plato, Socrates' student, through whose writings we know Socrates' teachings, believed good government was unattainable "unless either philosophers become kings in our cities or those whom we now call kings and rulers take to the pursuit of philosophy." He well understood that neither was likely to happen, and good government was, therefore, something of a dream. To further complicate matters, there were two distinct traditions of Greek *philosophia*—literally, "love of wisdom"—pre-Socratic and Sophist.

The Pre-Socratic Tradition The oldest philosophical tradition, that of the **pre-Socratics**, referring to Greek philosophers who preceded Socrates, was chiefly concerned with describing the natural universe—the tradition inaugurated by Thales of Miletus. "What," the pre-Socratics asked, "lies behind the world of appearance? What is everything made of? How does it work? Is there an essential truth or core at the heart of the physical universe?" In some sense, then, they were scientists who investigated the nature of things, and they arrived at some extraordinary insights. Pythagoras (ca. 570–490 BCE) was one such pre-Socratic thinker. He conceived of the notion that the heavenly bodies appear to move in accordance with the mathematical ratios and that these ratios also govern musical intervals, producing what was later called "the harmony of the spheres." Leucippus (fifth century BCE) was another. He conceived of an atomic theory in which everything is made up of small, indivisible particles and the empty space, or void, between them (the Greek word for "indivisible" is *atom*). Democritus of Thrace (ca. 460–ca. 370 BCE) furthered the theory by applying it to the mind. Democritus taught that everything from feelings and ideas

to the physical sensations of taste, sight, and smell could be explained by the movements of atoms in the brain. Heraclitus of Ephesus (535–475 BCE) argued for the impermanence of all things. Change, or flux, he said, is the basis of reality, although an underlying Form or Guiding Force (*logos*) guides the process, a concept that later informs the Gospel of John in the Christian Bible, where *logos* is often mistranslated as "word."

The Sophist Tradition Socrates was heir to the second tradition of Greek philosophy, that of the **Sophists**, literally "wise men." The Sophists no longer asked, "What do we know?" but, instead, "How do we know what we think we know?" and, crucially, "How can we trust what we think we know?" In other words, the Sophists concentrated not on the natural world but on the human mind, fully acknowledging the mind's many weaknesses. The Sophists were committed to what we have come to call **humanism**—that is, a focus on the actions of human beings, political action being one of the most important.

Protagoras (ca. 485–410 BCE), a leading Sophist, was responsible for one of the most famous of all Greek dictums: "Man is the measure of all things." By this he meant that each individual human, not the gods, not some divine or all-encompassing force, defines reality. All sensory appearances and all beliefs are true for the person whose appearances or beliefs they are. The Sophists believed that there were two sides to every argument. Protagoras' attitude toward the gods is typical: "I do not know that they exist or that they do not exist."

The Sophists were teachers who traveled about, imparting their wisdom for pay. Pericles championed them, encouraging the best to come to Athens, where they enjoyed considerable prestige despite their status as metics. Their ultimate aim was to teach political virtue—*areté*—emphasizing skills useful in political life, especially rhetorical persuasion, the art of speaking eloquently and persuasively. Their emphasis on rhetoric—their apparent willingness to assume either side of any argument merely for the sake of debate—as well as their critical examination of myths, traditions, and conventions, gave them a reputation for cynicism. Thus, their brand of argumentation came to be known as *sophistry*—subtle, tricky, superficially plausible, but ultimately false and deceitful reasoning.

Socrates and the Sophists Socrates despised everything the Sophists stood for, except their penchant for rhetorical debate, which was his chief occupation. He roamed the streets of Athens, engaging his fellow citizens in dialogue, wittily and often bitingly attacking them for the illogic of their positions. He employed the **dialectical method**—a process of inquiry and instruction characterized by continuous question-and-answer dialogue intent on disclosing the unexamined premises held implicitly by all reasonable beings. Unlike the Sophists, he refused to demand payment for his teaching, but like them, he urged his fellow men not to mistake their personal opinions for truth. Our beliefs, he knew, are built mostly on a foundation of prejudice and historical conditioning. He differed from the Sophists most crucially in his emphasis on virtuous behavior. For the Sophists, the true, the good, and the just were relative things. Depending on the situation or one's point of view, anything might be true, good, or just—the point, as will become evident in the next section of this chapter, of many a Greek tragedy.

For Socrates, understanding the true meaning of the good, the true, and the just was prerequisite for acting virtuously, and the meaning of these things was not relative. Rather, true meaning resided in the **psyche**, the seat of both intelligence and character. Through **inductive reasoning**—moving from specific instances to general principles, and from particular to universal truths—it was possible, he believed, to understand the ideals to which human endeavor should aspire. Neither Socrates nor the Sophists could have existed without the democracy of the polis and the freedom of speech that accompanied it. Even during the reign of Pericles, Athenian conservatives had charged the Sophists with the crime of impiety. In questioning everything, from the authority of the gods to the rule of law, they challenged the stability of the very democracy that protected them. It is thus easy to understand how, when democracy ended, Athens condemned Socrates. He was democracy's greatest defender, and if he believed that the polis had forsaken its greatest invention, he himself could never betray it. Thus, he chose to die.

Plato's *Republic* and Idealism

So far as we know, Socrates himself never wrote a single word. We know his thinking only through the writings of his greatest student, Plato (ca. 428–348 BCE). Thus, it may be true that the Socrates we know is the one Plato wanted us to have, and that when we read Socrates' words, we are encountering Plato's thought more than Socrates'.

As Plato presents Socrates to us, the two philosophers, master and pupil, have much in common. They share the premise that the psyche is immortal and immutable. They also share the notion that we are all capable of remembering the psyche's pure state. But Plato advances Socrates' thought in several important ways. Plato's philosophy is a brand of **idealism**—it seeks the eternal perfection of pure ideas, untainted by material reality. He believes that there is an invisible world of eternal Forms, or Ideas, beyond everyday experience, and that the psyche, trapped in the material world and the physical body, can only catch glimpses of this higher order. Through a series of mental exercises, beginning with the study of mathematics and then moving on to the contemplation of the Forms of Justice, Beauty, and Love, the student can arrive at a level of understanding that amounts to superior knowledge.

Socrates' death deeply troubled Plato—not because he disagreed with Socrates' decision, but because of the injustice of his condemnation. The result of Plato's thinking is *The Republic*. In this treatise, Plato outlines his model of the ideal state. Only an elite cadre of the most highly educated men were to rule—those who had glimpsed Plato's ultimate Form, or Idea—the Good. In *The Republic*, in a section known as the "Allegory of the Cave" (Fig. **5.12**),

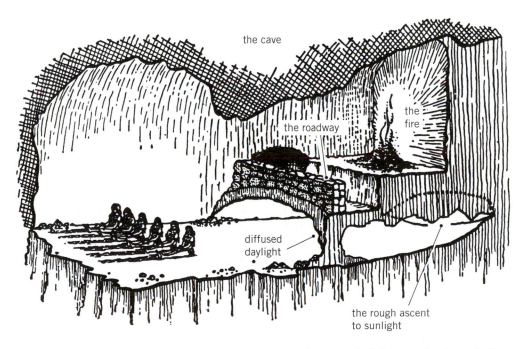

Fig. 5.12 "Allegory of the Cave," from *The Great Dialogues of Plato*, trans. W.H.D. Rouse. Translation © 1956, renewed 1984 by J.C.G. Rouse. Used by permission of Dutton Signet, a division of Penguin Books USA Inc. The scene imaged here is fully described by Plato in Reading 5.5, page 169.

Socrates addresses Plato's older brother, Glaucon, in an attempt to describe the difficulties the psyche encounters in its attempt to understand the higher Forms (see **Reading 5.5** on pages 169–171). The Form of Goodness, Socrates says, is "the universal author of all things beautiful and right, parent of light and of the lord of light in this visible world, and the immediate source of reason and truth in the intellectual; and … this is the power upon which he who would act rationally, either in public or private life must have his eye fixed." The Form of Goodness, then, is something akin to God (though not God, from whom imperfect objects such as human beings descended, but more like an aspect of the Ideal, of which, one supposes, God must have some superior knowledge). The difficulty is that, once having attained an understanding of the Good, the wise individual will appear foolish to the people, who understand not at all. And yet, as Plato argues, it is precisely these individuals, blessed with wisdom, who must rule the commonwealth.

In many ways, Plato's ideal state is reactionary—it certainly opposes the individualistic and self-aggrandizing world of the Sophists. Plato is indifferent to the fact that his wise souls will find themselves ruling what amounts to a totalitarian regime. He believes their own sense of Goodness will prevail over their potentially despotic position. Moreover, rule by an intellectual philosopher king is superior to rule by any person whose chief desire is to satisfy his own material appetites.

To live in Plato's *Republic* would have been dreary indeed. Sex was to be permitted only for purposes of procreation. Everyone would undergo physical and mental training reminiscent of Sparta in the sixth century BCE. Although he believed in the intellectual pursuit of the Form or Idea of Beauty, Plato did not champion the arts. He condemned certain kinds of lively music because they affected not the reasonable mind of their audience but the emotional and sensory tendencies of the body. (But even

for Plato, a man who did not know how to dance was uneducated—Plato simply preferred more restrained forms of music.) He also condemned sculptors and painters, whose works, he believed, were mere representations of representations—for if an actual bed is once removed from the Idea of Bed, a painting of a bed is twice removed, the faintest shadow. Furthermore, the images created by painters and sculptors appealed only to the senses. Thus he banished them from his ideal republic. Because they gave voice to tensions within the state, poets were banned as well.

Plato's *Symposium*

If Plato banned sex in his *Republic*, he did not ban it in his life. Indeed, one of the most remarkable of his dialogues is *The Symposium*. A symposium is literally a drinking party, exclusively for men, except for a few slaves and a nude female flute player or two. Dinner was served first, followed by ritualized drinking. Wine was poured to honor the "good spirit," hymns were sung, a member of the group was elected to decide the strength of the wine, which was mixed with water (usually five parts water to two of wine), and then host and guests, seated usually two to a couch around a square room, took turns in song or speech, one after another around the room.

Plato's *Symposium* recounts just such an evening. At the outset, the female flute player provided by the host is sent away, indicating the special nature of the event, which turns out to be a series of speeches on the nature of love, homoerotic love in particular. To the Greeks, it was considered normal for males to direct their sexual appetites toward both males and females, generally without particular preference for one or the other. Since the symposium was an all-male environment (Fig. **5.13**), it is hardly surprising that homoerotic behavior was commonplace, or at least commonly discussed.

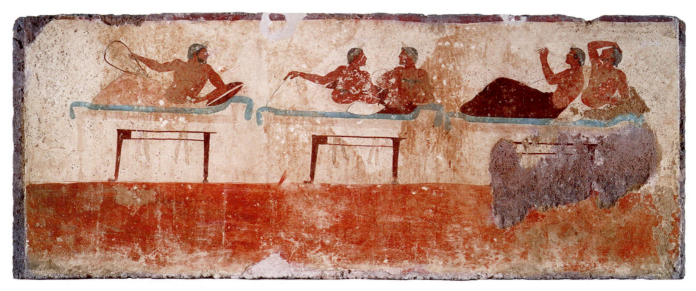

Fig. 5.13 *Banqueting Scene,* **panel from the Tomb of the Diver, Paestum, Italy. Early 5th century** BCE. Fresco. Museo Archeologico Nazionale, Paestum. Part of a painted tomb, this is a rare surviving example of Greek painting.

In *The Symposium*, each member of the party makes a speech about the nature of Love—or more precisely Eros, the god of love *and* desire—culminating with Socrates, whose presentation is by far the most sophisticated. Phaedrus makes clear, and all agree, that the loved one becomes virtuous by being loved. Pausanius contributes an important distinction between Common Love, which is simply physical, and Heavenly Love, which is also physical but is generated only in those who are capable of rational and ethical development. Thus, he suggests, an older man contributes to the ethical education of a youth through his love for him. No one disagrees, though the question remains whether *physical* love is necessary to the relationship.

Since Plato was himself a bachelor who led an essentially monastic existence, it is hardly surprising that by the time Socrates contributes to this discussion, Eros comes to be defined as more than just interpersonal love; it is also desire, desire for something it *lacks*. What Eros lacks and needs is beauty. The purpose of love, then, according to Socrates, and by extension Plato, is to give birth to beauty "in both body and mind," and, finally, to attain insight into the ultimate Form of Beauty. These are lessons, Socrates claims, that he learned from a woman named Diotima, who "was wise about this and many other things," a character many believe to be modeled on Aspasia, Pericles' mistress and partner. In our excerpt, Socrates quotes Diotima at length (see **Reading 5.6** on page 171).

The high philosophical tone of Socrates' speech comes to an abrupt end when the drunken politician Alcibiades crashes the party, regaling all with a speech in praise of Socrates, including an account of his own physical attraction to the older philosopher, his desire for an erotic-educational relationship with him, and the surprising denouement, a description of a time when he succeeded in getting into bed with him (**Reading 5.6a**).

READING 5.6a

from Plato, *The Symposium*

I threw my arms round this really god-like and amazing man, and lay there with him all night long. And you can't say this is a lie, Socrates. After I'd done all this he completely triumphed over my good looks—and despised, scorned and insulted them—although I placed a very high value on these looks, gentlemen of the jury. ... I swear to you by the gods, and by the goddesses, that when I got up the next morning I had no more slept with Socrates than if I'd been sleeping with my father or elder brother.

Socrates, Plato finally shows us, knows a higher form of Love than the physical and is an example to all present at the symposium.

📖 **Read** the document related to Plato on **MyArtsLab**

THE THEATER OF THE PEOPLE

How do Greek comedy and tragedy compare?

The Dionysian aspects of the symposium—the drinking, the philosophical dialogue, and sexual license—tell us something about the origins of Greek drama. The drama was originally a participatory ritual, tied to the cult of Dionysus. A chorus of people participating in the ritual would address and respond to another chorus or to a leader, such as a priest, perhaps representing (thus "acting the part" of) Dionysus. These dialogues usually occurred in the context of riotous dance and song—befitting revels dedicated to the god of wine. By the sixth century BCE, groups of men regularly celebrated Dionysus, coming together for the enjoyment of dance, music, and wine. Sexual license was the rule of the day. On a mid-sixth-century amphora used as a wine container (Fig. **5.14**) we see five **satyrs**, minor deities with characteristics of goats or horses, making wine, including one playing pipes. Depicted in the band across the top is Dionysus himself, sitting in the midst of a rollicking band of satyrs and **maenads**—the frenzied women with whom he cavorted.

This kind of behavior gave rise to one of the three major forms of Greek drama, the **satyr play**. Always the last event of the daylong performances, the satyr play was **farce**, that is, broadly satirical comedy, in which actors disguised themselves as satyrs, replete with extravagant genitalia, and generally honored the "lord of misrule," Dionysus, by misbehaving themselves. One whole satyr play survives, the *Cyclops* of Euripides, and half of another, Sophocles' *Trackers*. The spirit of these plays can perhaps be summed up best

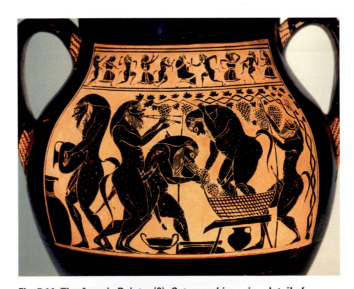

Fig. 5.14 The Amasis Painter (?), *Satyrs making wine*, detail of Athenian black-figure amphora. ca. 540–530 BCE. Martin von Wagner Museum, University of Würzburg. The entire ritual of wine production is depicted here, from harvesting the grapes, to stomping them to render their juice, to pouring the juice into large vats for fermentation. All lead to the state of ecstasy (*ekstasis*) painted across the top band.

by Odysseus' first words in the *Cyclops* as he comes ashore on the island of Polyphemus (compare Homer's description of the same event in the *Odyssey*; see Reading 4.2, page 130, and Fig. 4.15 in Chapter 4): "What? Do I see right? We must have come to the city of Bacchus. These are satyrs I see around the cave." The play, in other words, spoofs or lampoons traditional Greek legend by setting it in a world that has been turned topsy-turvy, a world in which Polyphemus is stronger than Zeus because his farts are louder than Zeus' thunder.

Comedy

Closely related to the satyr plays was **comedy**, an amusing or lighthearted play designed to make its audience laugh. The word itself is derived from the *komos*, a phallic dance, and nothing was sacred to comedy. It freely slandered, buffooned, and ridiculed politicians, generals, public figures, and especially the gods. Foreigners, as always in Greek culture, are subject to particular abuse, as are women; in fact, by our standards, the plays are racist and sexist. Most of what we know about Greek comedies comes from two sources: vase painting and the plays of the playwright Aristophanes.

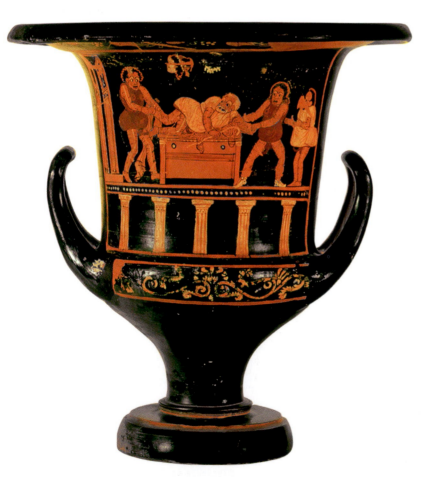

Fig. 5.15 Assteas, red-figure krater depicting a comedy, from Paestum, Italy. ca. 350 BCE. Staatliche Museen, Berlin. On a stage supported by columns, with a scenic backdrop to the left, robbers try to separate a man from his strongbox.

Comedic action was a favorite subject of vase painters working at Paestum in Italy in the fourth century BCE. They depict actors wearing masks and grotesque costumes distinguished by padded bellies, buttocks, and enlarged genitalia. These vases show a theater of burlesque and slapstick that relied heavily on visual gags (Fig. **5.15**).

The works of Aristophanes (ca. 445–388 BCE) are the only comedies to have survived, and only 11 of his 44 plays have come down to us. *Lysistrata* is the most famous. Sexually explicit to a degree that can still shock a modern audience, it takes place during the Peloponnesian Wars and tells the story of an Athenian matron who convinces the women of Athens and Sparta to withhold sex from their husbands until they sign a peace treaty. First performed in 411 BCE, seven years before Sparta's victory over Athens, it has its serious side, begging both Athenians and Spartans to remember their common traditions and put down their arms. Against this dark background, the play's action must have seemed absurd and hilarious to its Athenian audience, ignorant of what the future would hold for them.

Tragedy

It was at **tragedy** that the Greek playwrights truly excelled. As with comedy, the basis for tragedy is conflict, but the tensions at work in tragedy—murder and revenge, crime and retribution, pride and humility, courage and cowardice—have far more serious consequences. Tragedies often explore the physical and moral depths to which human life can descend. The form also has its origins in the Dionysian rites—the name itself derives from *tragoidos*, the "goat song" of the half-goat, half-man satyrs, and tragedy's seriousness of purpose is not at odds with its origins. Dionysus was also the god of immortality, and an important aspect of his cult's influence is that he promised his followers life after death, just as the grapevine regenerates itself year after year. If tragedy can be said to have a subject, it is death—and the lessons the living can learn from the dead.

The original chorus structure of the Dionysian rites survives as an important element in tragedy. Thespis, a playwright from whom we derive the word *thespian*, "actor," first assumed the conscious role of an actor in the mid-sixth century BCE and apparently redefined the role of the **chorus**. At first, the actor asked questions of the chorus, perhaps of the "tell me what happened next" variety, but when two, three, and sometimes four actors were introduced to the stage, the chorus began to comment on their interaction. In this way, the chorus assumed its classic function as an intermediary between actors and audience. Although the chorus's role diminished noticeably in the fourth century BCE, it remained the symbolic voice of the people, asserting the importance of the action to the community as a whole.

Greek tragedy often focused on the friction between the individual and his or her community, and, at a higher level, between the community and the will of the gods. This conflict manifests itself in the weakness or "tragic flaw" of the play's **protagonist**, or leading character, which brings the character into conflict with the community, the gods, or some **antagonist** who represents an opposing will. The action occurs in a single day, the result of a single incident that precipitates the unfolding crisis. Thus the audience feels that it is experiencing the action in real time, that it is directly involved in and affected by the play's action.

During the reign of the tyrant Pisistratus, the performance of all plays was regularized. An annual competitive festival for the performance of tragedies called the City Dionysia was celebrated for a week every March as the vines came back to life, and a separate festival for comedies occurred in January. At the City Dionysia, plays were performed in sets of four—**tetralogies**—all by the same author, three of which were tragedies, performed during the day, and the fourth a satyr play, performed in the evening. The audiences were as large as 14,000, and audience response determined which plays were awarded prizes. Slaves, metics, and women judged the performances alongside citizens.

Aeschylus Although many Greek playwrights composed tragedies, only those of Aeschylus, Sophocles, and Euripides have come down to us. Aeschylus (ca. 525–ca. 456 BCE), the oldest of the three, is reputed to have served in the Athenian armies during the Persian Wars and fought in the battles at Marathon and Salamis. He won the City Dionysia 13 times. It was Aeschylus who introduced a third actor to the tragic stage, and his chorus plays a substantial role in drawing attention to the underlying moral principles that define or determine the action. He also was a master of the visual presentation of his drama, taking full advantage of stage design and costume. Three of his plays, known as the *Oresteia*, form the only complete set of tragedies from a tetralogy that we have.

The plays narrate the story of the Mycenaean king Agamemnon, murdered by his adulterous wife Clytemnestra and mourned and revenged by their children, Orestes and Electra. In the first play, *Agamemnon*, Clytemnestra murders her husband, partly in revenge for his having sacrificed their daughter Iphigenia to ensure good weather for the invasion of Troy, and partly to marry her lover, Aegisthus. In the second play, *The Libation Bearers*, Orestes murders Aegisthus and Clytemnestra, his mother, to avenge his father's death. Orestes is subsequently pursued by the Furies, a band of *chthonian gods* (literally "gods of the earth," a branch of the Greek pantheon that is distinguished from the Olympian, or "heavenly" gods), whose function is to seek retribution for wrongs and blood-guilt among family members. The Furies form the chorus of the last play in the cycle, the *Eumenides*, in which the seemingly endless cycle of murder comes to an end. In this play, Athens institutes a court to hear Orestes' case. The court absolves him of the crime of matricide, with Athena herself casting the deciding vote.

None of the violence in the plays occurs on stage—either the chorus or a messenger describes it. And in fact, the ethical dimension of Aeschylus' trilogy is underscored by the triumph of civilization and law, mirrored by the transformation of the Furies—the blind forces of revenge—into the Eumenides, or "Kindly Ones," whose dark powers have been neutralized.

Sophocles Playwright, treasurer for the Athenian polis, a general under Pericles, and advisor to Athens on financial matters during the Peloponnesian Wars, Sophocles (ca. 496–406 BCE) was an almost legendary figure in fifth-century BCE Athens. He wrote over 125 plays, of which only 7 survive, and he won the City Dionysia 18 times. In *Oedipus the King*, Sophocles dramatizes how the king of Thebes, a polis in east central Greece, mistakenly kills his father and marries his mother, then finally blinds himself to atone for his crimes of patricide and incest. In *Antigone*, he dramatizes the struggle of Oedipus' daughter, Antigone, with her uncle, Creon, the tyrannical king who inherited Oedipus' throne. Antigone struggles for what amounts to her democratic rights as an individual to fulfill her familial duties, even when this opposes what Creon argues is the interest of the polis. Her predicament is doubly complicated by her status as a woman.

As the play opens, Antigone's brothers, Polynices and Eteocles, have killed each other in a dispute over their father's throne. Creon, Oedipus' brother-in-law, who has inherited the throne, has forbidden the burial of Polynices, believing Eteocles to have been the rightful heir. Antigone, in the opening scene, defends her right to bury her brother, and this willful act, which she then performs in defiance of Creon's authority, leads to the tragedy that follows. She considers the burial her duty, since no unburied body can enjoy an afterlife. The play begins as Antigone explains her action to her sister, Ismene, who thoroughly disapproves of what she has done (**Reading 5.7a**).

READING 5.7a

from Sophocles, *Antigone*

ISMENE Oh my sister, think—
think how our own father died, hated,
his reputation in ruins, driven on
by the crimes he brought to light himself
to gouge out his eyes with his own hands—
then mother … his mother and wife, both in one,
mutilating her life in the twisted noose—
and last, our two brothers dead in a single day,
both shedding their own blood, poor suffering boys,
battling out their common destiny hand-to-hand.
Now look at the two of us, left so alone. …
think what a death we'll die, the worst of all
if we violate the laws and override
the fixed decree of the throne, its power—
we must be sensible. Remember we are women,

> we're not born to contend with men. Then too,
> we're underlings, ruled by much stronger hands,
> so we must submit in this, and things still worse.
> I, for one, I'll beg the dead to forgive me—
> I'm forced, I have no choice—I must obey
> the ones who stand in power. Why rush to extremes?
> It's madness, madness.

The conflict between Antigone and Creon is exacerbated by their gender difference. The Greek male would expect a female to submit to his will. But it is, in the end, Antigone's "rush to extremes" that forces the play's action—that, and Creon's refusal to give in. Creon's "fatal flaw"—his pride (hubris)—leads to the destruction of all whom he loves, and Antigone herself is blindly dedicated to her duty to honor her family. Her actions in the play have been the subject of endless debate. Some readers feel that she is far too hard on Ismene, and certainly a Greek audience would have found her defiance of male authority shocking. Nevertheless, her strength of conviction seems to many—especially modern audiences—wholly admirable.

But beyond the complexities of Antigone's personality, one of Sophocles' greatest achievements, the play really pits two forms of idealism against one another: Antigone's uncompromising belief in herself plays off Creon's equally uncompromising infatuation with his own power and his dedication to his political duty, which he puts above devotion even to family.

The philosophical basis of the play is clearly evident in the essentially Sophist debate between Creon and his son Haemon, as Haemon attempts to point out the wrong in his father's action (**Reading 5.7b**):

READING 5.7b

from Sophocles, *Antigone*

HAEMON Father, the gods implant reason in men, the highest of all things that we call our own. Not mine the skill—far from me be the quest!—to say wherein thou speakest not aright; and yet another man, too, might have some useful thought. ... No, though a man be wise, 'tis no shame for him to learn many things, and to bend in season. Seest thou, beside the wintry torrent's course, how the trees that yield to it save every twig, while the stiff-necked perish root and branch? And even thus he who keeps the sheet of his sail taut, and never slackens it, upsets his boat, and finishes his voyage with keel uppermost.

Nay, forego thy wrath; permit thyself to change. For if I, a younger man, may offer my thought, it were far best, I ween, that men should be all-wise by nature; but, otherwise—and oft the scale inclines not so—'tis good also to learn from those who speak aright. ...

CREON Men of my age are we indeed to be schooled, then, by men of his?

HAEMON In nothing that is not right; but if I am young, thou shouldest look to my merits, not to my years.

CREON Is it a merit to honour the unruly?

HAEMON I could wish no one to show respect for evil-doers.

CREON Then is not she tainted with that malady?

HAEMON Our Theban folk, with one voice, denies it. ...

CREON Am I to rule this land by other judgment than mine own?

HAEMON That is no city which belongs to one man.

CREON Is not the city held to be the ruler's?

HAEMON Thou wouldst make a good monarch of a desert.

CREON This boy, it seems, is the woman's champion.

HAEMON If thou art a woman; indeed, my care is for thee.

CREON Shameless, at open feud with thy father!

HAEMON Nay, I see thee offending against justice.

CREON Do I offend, when I respect mine own prerogatives?

HAEMON Thou dost not respect them, when thou tramplest on the gods' honours . ...

CREON Thou shalt rue thy witless teaching of wisdom.

HAEMON Wert thou not my father, I would have called thee unwise.

CREON Thou woman's slave, use not wheedling speech with me.

HAEMON Thou wouldest speak, and then hear no reply?

CREON Sayest thou so? Now, by the heaven above us— be sure of it—thou shalt smart for taunting me in this opprobrious strain. Bring forth that hated thing, that she may die forthwith in his presence—before his eyes—at her bridegroom's side!

Finally, the play demonstrates the extreme difficulty of reconciling the private and public spheres—one of Greek philosophy's most troubling and troubled themes—even as it cries out for the rational action and sound judgment that might have spared its characters their tragedy.

Euripides The youngest of the three playwrights, Euripides (ca. 480–406 BCE), writing during the Peloponnesian Wars, brought a level of measured skepticism to the stage. Eighteen of his 90 works survive, but Euripides won the City Dionysia only four times. His plays probably angered more conservative Athenians, which may be why he moved from Athens to Macedonia in 408 BCE. In *The Trojan Women*, for instance, performed in 415 BCE, he describes, disapprovingly, the Greek enslavement of the women of Troy, drawing an unmistakable analogy to the contemporary Athenian victory at Melos, where women were subjected to Athenian abuse.

His darkest play, and his masterpiece, is *The Bacchae*, which describes the introduction to Thebes of the worship

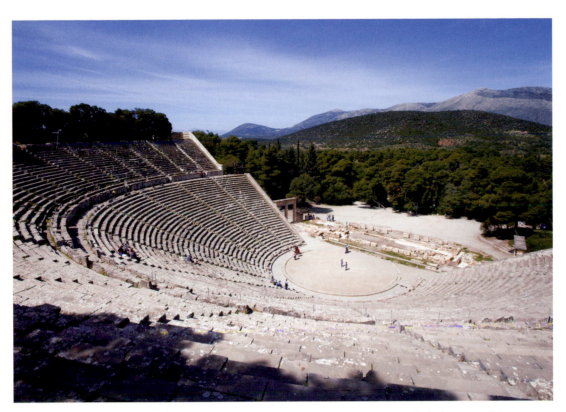

Fig. 5.16 Theater, Epidaurus. Early 3rd century BCE. This theater is renowned for its democratic design—not only is every viewer equally well situated, but the acoustics of the space are unparalleled. A person sitting in the very top row can hear a pin drop on the *orchestra* floor.

of Dionysus by the god himself, disguised as a mortal. Pentheus, the young king of the city, opposes the Dionysian rites both because all the city's women have given themselves up to Dionysian ecstasy and because the new religion disturbs the larger social order. Performed at a festival honoring Dionysus, the play warns of the dangers of Dionysian excess as the frenzied celebrants, including Pentheus' own mother, mistake their king for a wild animal and murder him. Euripides' play underscores the fact that the rational mind is unable to comprehend, let alone control, all human impulses.

Greek theater itself, particularly the tragedies of Aeschylus, Sophocles, and Euripides, would become the object of study in the fourth century BCE, when the philosopher Aristotle, Plato's student, attempted to account for tragedy's power in his *Poetics*. And despite the fact that the tragedies were largely forgotten in the Western world until the sixteenth century, they have had a lasting impact upon Western literature, deeply influencing writers ranging from William Shakespeare to the modern American novelist William Faulkner.

The Performance Space

During the tyranny of Pisistratus, plays were performed in an open area of the agora called the **orchestra**, or "dancing space." Spectators sat on wooden planks laid on portable scaffolding. Sometime in the fifth century BCE, the

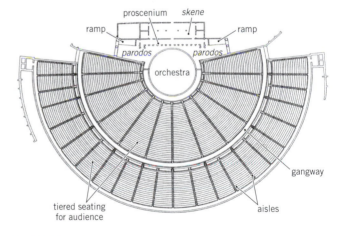

Fig. 5.17 Plan of the theater at Epidaurus. Early 3rd century BCE.

scaffolding collapsed, and many people were injured. The Athenians built a new theater (*theatron*, meaning "viewing space"), dedicated to Dionysus, into the hillside on the side of the Acropolis away from the agora and below the Parthenon. Architecturally, it was very similar to the best preserved of all Greek theaters, the one at Epidaurus (Figs. **5.16** and **5.17**), built in the early third century BCE. The *orchestra* here was transformed into a circular performance space, approached on each side by an entryway called a **parodos**, through which the chorus would enter the *orchestra* area. Behind this was an elevated platform, the **proscenium**, the stage on which the actors performed and where painted backdrops could be hung. Behind the proscenium was the *skene*, literally a "tent," and originally a changing room for the actors. Over time, it was transformed into a building, often two stories tall. Actors on the roof could portray the gods, looking down on the action below. By the time of Euripides, it housed a rolling or rotating platform that could suddenly reveal an interior space.

Artists were regularly employed to paint stage sets, and evidence suggests that they had at least a basic knowledge of perspective (although the geometry necessary for a fully realized perspectival space would not be developed until around 300 BCE, in Euclid's *Optics*). Their aim was, as in sculpture, to approximate reality as closely as possible. We know from literary sources that the painter Zeuxis "invented" ways to shade or model the figure in the fifth century BCE. Legend also has it that he once painted grapes so realistically that birds tried to eat them. The theatrical sets would have at least aimed at this degree of naturalism.

THE HELLENISTIC WORLD

How does Greek sculpture change between the Classical and Hellenistic periods, and how does Aristotle's philosophy reflect this shift?

Both the emotional drama of Greek theater and the sensory appeal of its music reveal a growing tendency in the culture to value emotional expression at least as much as, and sometimes more than, the balanced harmonies of Classical art. During the Hellenistic age in the fourth and third centuries BCE, the truths that the culture increasingly sought to understand were less idealistic and universal, and more and more empirical and personal. This shift is especially evident in the new empirical philosophy of Aristotle (384–322 BCE), whose investigation into the workings of the real world supplanted, or at least challenged, Plato's idealism. In many ways, however, the ascendancy of this new aesthetic standard can be attributed to the daring, the audacity, and the sheer awe-inspiring power of a single figure, Alexander of Macedonia, known as Alexander the Great (356–323 BCE). Alexander aroused the emotions and captured the imagination of not just a theatrical audience, but an entire people—perhaps even the entire Western world—and created a legacy that established Hellenic Greece as the model against which all other cultures in the West had to measure themselves.

The Empire of Alexander the Great

Alexander was the son of Philip II (382–336 BCE) of Macedonia, a relatively undeveloped state to the north whose inhabitants spoke a Greek dialect unintelligible to Athenians. Macedonia was ruled loosely by a king whose power was checked by a council of nobles. Philip had been a hostage in the polis of Thebes early in his life, and while there

he had learned to love Greek civilization, but he also recognized that, after the Peloponnesian Wars, the Greek poleis were in disarray. In 338 BCE, at the Battle of Chaeronea, on the plains near Delphi, he defeated the combined forces of southern Greece, led by Athens and Thebes, and unified all of Greece, with the exception of Sparta, in the League of Corinth.

In the process of mounting a military campaign to subdue the Persians, Philip was assassinated in 336 BCE, possibly on the order of Alexander himself. (Philip had just divorced the 19-year-old's mother and removed him from any role in the government.) Although the Thebans immediately revolted, Alexander quickly took control, burning Thebes to the ground and selling its entire population into slavery. He then turned his sights on the rest of the world, and henceforth representations of him would proliferate. Even during his lifetime, but especially after his death, sculptures celebrating the youthful hero abounded, almost all of them modeled on originals sculpted by Lysippus (flourished fourth century BCE) whom Alexander hired to do all his portraits. Alexander is easily recognizable—his disheveled hair long and flowing, his gaze intense and melting, his mouth slightly open, his head alertly turned

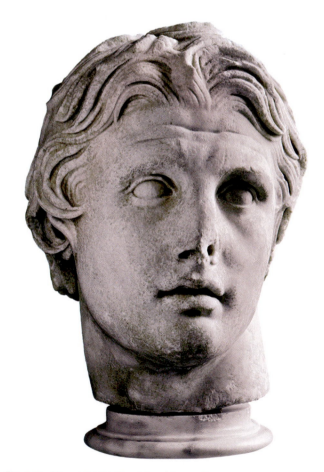

Fig. 5.18 *Alexander the Great,* **head from a Pergamene copy (ca. 200 BCE) of a statue, possibly after a 4th-century BCE original by Lysippus.** Marble, height 16⅛". Archeological Museum, Istanbul. Alexander is traditionally portrayed as if looking beyond his present circumstances to greater things.

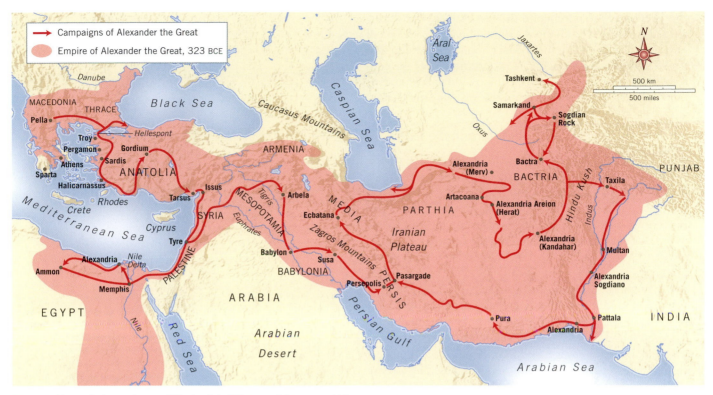

Map 5.2 Alexander's empire as of his death in 323 BCE and the route of his conquests.
Alexander founded over 70 cities throughout his empire, naming many after himself.

on a slightly tilted neck (Fig. **5.18**). Lysippus dramatized his hero. That is, he did not merely represent Alexander as naturalistically as possible, he also animated him, showing him in the midst of action. In all likelihood, he idealized him as well. The creation of Alexander's likeness was a conscious act of propaganda. Early in his conquests, the young hero referred to himself as "Alexander the Great," and Lysippus' job was to embody that greatness.

Within two years of conquering Thebes, Alexander had crossed the Hellespont into Asia and defeated Darius III of Persia at the Battle of Issus (just north of present-day Iskenderon, Turkey). The victory continued Philip's plan to repay the Persians for their role in the Peloponnesian Wars and to conquer Asia as well. By 332 BCE, Alexander had conquered Egypt, founding the great city of Alexandria (named, of course, after himself) in the Nile Delta (Map **5.2**). Then he marched back into Mesopotamia, where he again defeated Darius III and then marched into both Babylon and Susa without resistance. After making the proper sacrifices to the Akkadian god Marduk (see Chapter 2)—and thus gaining the admiration of the locals—he advanced on Persepolis, the Persian capital, which he burned after seizing its royal treasures. Then he entered present-day Pakistan.

Alexander's object was India, which he believed was relatively small. He thought if he crossed it, he would find what he called Ocean, and an easy sea route home. Finally, in 326 BCE, his army reached the Indian Punjab. Under Alexander's leadership, it had marched over 11,000 miles without a defeat. It had destroyed ancient empires, founded

many cities (in the 320s BCE, Alexandrias proliferated across Alexander's world), and created the largest empire the world had ever known.

When Alexander and his army reached the banks of the Indus River in 326 BCE, he encountered a culture that had long fascinated him. His teacher Aristotle had described it, wholly on hearsay, as had Herodotus before him, as the farthest land mass to the east, beyond which lay an Endless Ocean that encircled the world. Alexander stopped first at Taxila (20 miles north of present-day Islamabad, Pakistan; see Map 5.2), where King Omphis greeted him with a gift of 200 silver talents, 3,000 oxen, 10,000 sheep, and 30 elephants, and bolstered Alexander's army by giving him 700 Indian cavalry and 5,000 infantry.

While Alexander was in Taxila, he became acquainted with the Hindu philosopher Calanus. Alexander recognized in Calanus and his fellow Hindu philosophers a level of wisdom and learning that he valued highly, one clearly reminiscent of Greek philosophy, and his encounters with them represent the first steps in a long history of the cross-fertilization of Eastern and Western cultures.

But in India the army encountered elephants, whose formidable size proved problematic. East of Taxila, Alexander's troops managed to defeat King Porus, whose army was equipped with 200 elephants. Rumor had it that farther to the east, the kingdom of the Ganges, their next logical opponent, had a force of 5,000 elephants. Alexander pleaded with his troops: "Dionysus, divine from birth, faced terrible tasks—and we have outstripped him! ... Onward, then: let us add to our empire the rest of Asia!" The army refused to budge. His conquests thus concluded, Alexander himself sailed down the Indus River, founding the city that would later become Karachi. As he returned home, he contracted fever in Babylon and died in 323 BCE. Alexander's life was brief, but his influence on the arts was long-lasting.

Toward Hellenistic Art: Sculpture in the Late Classical Period

During Alexander's time, sculpture flourished. Ever since the fall of Athens to Sparta in 404 BCE, Greek artists had continued to develop the **Classical** style of Phidias and Polyclitus, but they modified it in subtle yet innovative ways. Especially notable was a growing taste for images of men and women in quiet, sometimes dreamy and contemplative moods, which increasingly replaced the sense of nobility and detachment characteristic of fifth-century Classicism and found its way even into depictions of the gods. The most admired sculptors of the day were Lysippus, Praxiteles, and Skopas. Very little of the latter's work has survived, though he was noted for high-relief sculpture featuring highly energized and emotional scenes. The work of the first two is far better known.

The Heroic Sculpture of Lysippus In sculpting a full-length standing figure of Alexander, which we know only from descriptions, Lysippus also challenged the Classical *kanon* of proportion created by Polyclitus—smaller heads and slenderer bodies lent his heroic sculptures a sense of greater height. In fact, he transformed the Classical tradition in sculpture and began to explore new possibilities that, eventually, would define Hellenistic art, with its sense of animation, drama, and psychological complexity. In a Roman copy of a lost original by Lysippus known as the *Apoxyomenos* (Fig. **5.19**), or *The Scraper*, an athlete removes oil and dirt from his body with an instrument called a strigil. Compared to the *Doryphoros* (*Spear Bearer*) of Polyclitus (see Fig. 5.4), *The Scraper* is much slenderer, his legs much longer, his torso shorter. *The Scraper* seems much taller, though, in fact, the sculptures are very nearly the same height. The arms of *The Scraper* break free of his frontal form and invite the viewer to look at the sculpture from the sides as well as the front. He seems detached from his circumstances, as if recalling his athletic performance. All in all, he seems both physically and mentally uncontained by the space in which he stands.

The Sensuous Sculpture of Praxiteles Competing with Lysippus for the title of greatest sculptor of the fourth century BCE was the Athenian Praxiteles (flourished 370–330 BCE). Praxiteles was one of the 300 wealthiest men in Athens, thanks to his skill, but he also had a reputation as a womanizer. The people of the port city of Knidos, a Spartan colony in Asia Minor, asked him to provide them with an image of their patron goddess, Aphrodite, in her role as the protectress of sailors and merchants. Praxiteles responded with a sculpture of Aphrodite as the goddess of

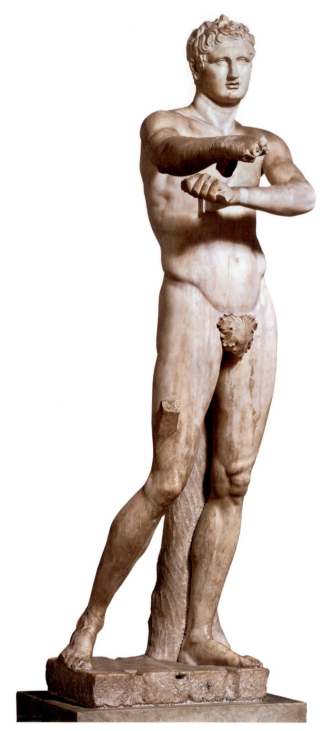

Fig. 5.19 Lysippus, *Apoxyomenos* (*The Scraper*), Roman copy of an original Greek bronze of ca. 350–325 BCE. Museo Pio Clementino, Vatican Museums, Vatican State. Marble, height 6'8". According to the Roman scholar Pliny the Elder, writing in his *Natural History* in the first century CE, Lysippus "made the heads of his figures smaller than the old sculptors used to do." In fact, the ratio of the head size to the body in Lysippus' sculpture is 1:9, as compared to Polyclitus' Classical proportions of 1:8.

love, here reproduced in a later Roman copy (Fig. **5.20**). She stands at her bath, holding her cloak in her left hand. The sculpture is a frank celebration of the body—reflecting in the female form the humanistic appreciation for the dignity of the human body in its own right. (Images of it on

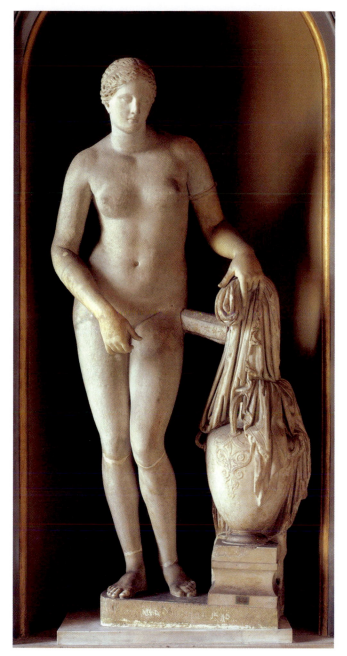

Fig. 5.20 Praxiteles, *Aphrodite of Knidos*, Roman copy of an original of ca. 350 BCE. Marble, height 6'8". Vatican Museums, Vatican State. The head of this figure is from one Roman copy, the body from another. The right forearm and hand, the left arm, and the lower legs of the *Aphrodite* are all seventeenth- and eighteenth-century restorations. There is reason to believe that her hand was not so modestly positioned in the original.

Praxiteles' *Aphrodite of Knidos* may be the first fully nude depiction of a woman in Greek sculpture, which may be why it caused such a sensation. Its fame elevated female nudity from a sign of low moral character to the embodiment of beauty, even truth itself. Paradoxically, it is also one of the earliest examples of artwork designed to appeal to what some art historians describe as the **male gaze**, which regards woman as a sexual object. Praxiteles' canon for depicting the female nude—wide hips, small breasts, oval face, and centrally parted hair—remained the standard throughout antiquity.

Aristotle: Observing the Natural World

We can only guess what motivated Lysippus and Praxiteles to so dramatize and humanize their sculptures, but it is likely that the aesthetic philosophy of Aristotle (384–322 BCE) played a role. Aristotle was a student of Plato's. Recall that, for Plato, all reality is a mere reflection of a higher, spiritual truth, a higher dimension of Ideal Forms that we glimpse only through philosophical contemplation (see Fig. 5.12).

Aristotle disagreed. Reality was not a reflection of an ideal form, but existed in the material world itself, and by observing the material world, one could come to know universal truths. So Aristotle observed and described all aspects of the world in order to arrive at the essence of things. His methods of observation came to be known as *empirical investigation*. And though he did not create a formal **scientific method**, he and other early empiricists did create procedures for testing their theories about the nature of the world that, over time, would lead to the great scientific discoveries of Bacon, Galileo, and Newton. Aristotle studied biology, zoology, physics, astronomy, politics, logic, ethics, and the various genres of literary expression. Based on his observations of lunar eclipses, he concluded as early as 350 BCE that the Earth was spherical, an observation that may have motivated Alexander to cross India in order to sail back to Greece. He described over 500 animals in his *Historia Animalium*, including many that he dissected himself. In fact, Aristotle's observations of marine life were unequaled until the seventeenth century and were still much admired by Charles Darwin in the nineteenth.

He also understood the importance of formulating a reasonable hypothesis to explain phenomena. His *Physics* is an attempt to define the first principles governing the behavior of matter—the nature of weight, motion, physical existence, and variety in nature. At the heart of Aristotle's philosophy is a question about the relation of *identity* and *change* (not far removed, incidentally, from one of the governing principles of this text, the idea of continuity and change in the humanities). To discuss the world coherently, we must be able to say what it is about a thing that makes it the thing it is, that separates it from all the other things in the world. In other words, what is the attribute that we would call its material identity or *essence*? What it means to be human, for instance, does not depend on whether one's

local coins suggest that her original pose was far less modest than that of the Roman copy, her right hand not shielding her genitals.) The statue made Knidos famous, and many people traveled there to see it. She was enshrined in a circular temple, easily viewed from every angle, the Roman scholar Pliny the Elder (23–79 CE) tells us, and she quickly became an object of religious attention—and openly sexual adoration. The reason for this is difficult to assess in the rather mechanical Roman copies of the lost original.

hair turns gray. Such "accidental" changes matter not at all. At the same time, our experience of the natural world suggests that any coherent account requires us to acknowledge process and change—the change of seasons, the changes in our understanding associated with gaining knowledge in the process of aging, and so on. For Aristotle, any account of a thing must accommodate both aspects: We must be able to say what changes a thing undergoes while still retaining its essential nature, and Aristotle thus approached all manner of things—from politics to the human condition—with an eye toward determining what constituted its essence.

Aristotle's *Poetics* What constitutes the essential nature of literary art, and the theater in particular, especially fascinated him. Like all Greeks, Aristotle was well acquainted with the theater of Aeschylus, Euripides, and Sophocles, and in his *Poetics* he defined their literary art as "the imitation of an action that is complete and whole." Including a whole action, or a series of events that ends with a crisis, gives a play a sense of unity. Furthermore, he argued (against Plato, who regarded imitation as inevitably degrading and diminishing) that such imitation elevates the mind ever closer to the universal.

One of the most important ideas that Aristotle expressed in the *Poetics* is **catharsis**, the cleansing, purification, or purgation of the soul (see **Reading 5.8** on pages 172–173). As applied to drama, it is not the tragic hero who undergoes catharsis, but the audience. The audience's experience of catharsis is an experience of change, just as change always accompanies understanding. In the theater, what moves the audience to change is its experience of the universality of the human condition—what it is that makes us human, our weaknesses as well as our strengths. At the sight of the action onstage, they are struck with "fear and pity." Plato believed that both of these emotions were pernicious. But Aristotle argued that the audience's emotional response to the plight of the characters on stage clarified for them the fragility and mutability of human life. What happens in tragedy is universal—the audience understands that the action could happen to anyone at any time.

The Golden Mean In Aristotle's philosophy, such Classical aesthetic elements as unity of action and time, orderly arrangement of the parts, and proper proportion all have ethical ramifications. He argued for them by means of a philosophical method based on the **syllogism**, two premises from which a conclusion can be drawn. The most famous of all syllogisms is this:

All men are mortal;
Socrates is a man;
Therefore, Socrates is mortal.

In the *Nicomachean Ethics*, written for and edited by his son Nicomachus, Aristotle attempts to define, once and for all, what Greek society had striven for since the beginning of the polis—the good life. The operative syllogism goes something like this:

The way to happiness is through the pursuit of moral virtue;
The pursuit of the good life is the way to happiness;
Therefore, the good life consists in the pursuit of moral virtue.

The good life, Aristotle argued, is attainable only through balanced action. Tradition has come to call this the **Golden Mean**—not Aristotle's phrase but that of the Roman poet Horace—the middle ground between any two extremes of behavior. Thus, in a formulation that was particularly applicable to his student Alexander the Great, the Golden Mean between cowardice and recklessness is courage. Like the arts, which imitate an action, human beings are defined by their actions: "As with a flute-player, a statuary, or any artisan, or in fact anybody who has a definite function, so it would seem to be with humans. … The function of humans is an *activity* of soul in accordance with reason." This activity of soul seeks out the moral mean, just as "good artists … have an eye to the mean in their works."

Despite the measure and moderation of Aristotle's thinking, Greek culture did not necessarily reflect the balanced approach of its leading philosopher. In his emphasis on catharsis—the value of experiencing "fear and pity," the emotions that move us to change—Aristotle introduced the values that would go on to define the age of Hellenism, the period lasting from 323 to 31 BCE, that is, from the death of Alexander to the Battle of Actium, the event that marks in the minds of many the beginning of the Roman Empire.

Pergamon: Hellenistic Capital

Upon his death, Alexander left no designated successor, and his three chief generals divided his empire into three successor states: the kingdom of Macedonia (including all of Greece), the kingdom of the Ptolemies (Egypt), and the kingdom of the Seleucids (Syria and what is now Iraq). But a fourth, smaller kingdom in western Anatolia, Pergamon (present-day Bergama, Turkey), soon rose to prominence and became a center of Hellenistic culture. Ruled by the Attalids—descendants of a Macedonian general named Attalus—Pergamon was founded as a sort of treasury for the huge fortunes Alexander had accumulated in his conquests. It was technically under the control of the Seleucid kingdom. However, under the leadership of Eumenes I (r. 263–241 BCE), Pergamon achieved virtual independence.

The Library at Pergamon The Attalids created a huge library filled with over 200,000 Classical Athenian texts. These were copied onto parchment, a word that derives from the Greek *pergamene*, meaning "from Pergamon," and refers to sheets of tanned leather. Pergamon's vast treasury allowed the Attalids the luxury of investing enormous sums of money in decorating their acropolis with art and architecture. Especially under the rule of Eumenes II (r. 197–160 BCE), the building program flourished. It was Eumenes II who built the library, as well as the theater and a gymnasium. And he was probably responsible for the Altar of Zeus (Fig. **5.21**), which is today housed in Berlin.

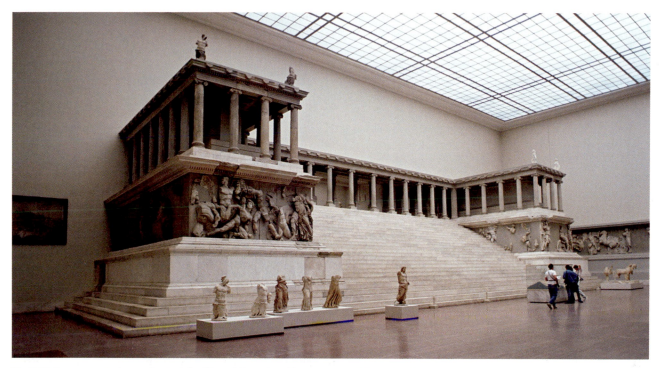

Fig. 5.21 Reconstructed west front of the Altar of Zeus, from Pergamon. ca. 165 BCE. Marble. Staatliche Museen, Berlin, Antikensammlung, Pergamonmuseum. The Pergamon altar was exported to Germany with the permission of the Ottoman authorities in 1899, but in recent years, Turkish authorities have expressed interest in its return with ever increasing insistence.

The staircase entrance to the altar is 68 feet wide and nearly 30 feet deep. It rises to an Ionic colonnade. As opposed to the Parthenon, where the frieze is elevated above the colonnade, the first thing the viewer confronts at the Altar of Zeus is the frieze itself, a placement that draws attention to its interlace of nearly 200 separate twisted, turning, and animated figures. Notice how, as the frieze narrows and rises up the stairs (Fig. **5.22**), the figures seem to break free of the architectural space that confines them and crawl out onto the steps of the altar. As the

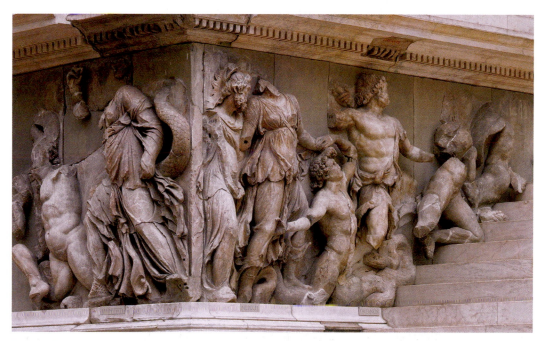

Fig. 5.22 Reconstructed west staircase frieze of the Altar of Zeus, from Pergamon. ca. 165 BCE. Marble. Staatliche Museen, Berlin, Antikensammlung, Pergamonmuseum. Particularly notable here is the extended arm of the kneeling warrior in the center, which reaches several feet into the viewer's space.

The CONTINUING PRESENCE
of the PAST

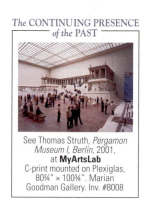

See Thomas Struth, *Pergamon Museum I, Berlin,* 2001, at **MyArtsLab**
C-print mounted on Plexiglas, 80¾" × 100¾". Marian Goodman Gallery. Inv. #8008

figures come to occupy real space, they simultaneously gain a theatrical reality, as if they were live stage presences in the visitor's space.

A New Sculptural Style The altar is decorated with the most ambitious sculptural program since the Parthenon, but unlike the Parthenon, its frieze is at eye level and is 7½ feet high. Its subject is the mythical battle of the gods and the giants for control of the world. The giants are depicted with snakelike bodies that coil beneath the feet of the triumphant gods (Fig. **5.23**). These figures represent one of the greatest examples of the Hellenistic style of sculpture that depends for its effects on its **expressionism**, that is, the attempt to elicit an emotional response in the viewer. The theatrical effects of Lysippus are magnified into a heightened sense of drama. Where Classical artists sought balance, order, and proportion, this frieze, with its figures twisting, thrusting, and striding in motion, stresses diagonal forces that seem to pull each other apart. Swirling bodies and draperies weave in and out of the sculpture's space, and the relief is so three-dimensional that contrasts of light and shade add to the dramatic effects. Above all, the frieze is an attempt to evoke the emotions of fear and pity that Aristotle argued led to catharsis in his *Poetics* (see Reading 5.8, page 172), not the intellectual order of Classical tradition.

The relief was designed to celebrate Pergamon's role as the new center of Hellenism, its stature as the "new Athens." To that end, most authorities agree that the relief depicts the Attalid victory over the Gauls, a group of non-Greek-speaking and therefore "barbarian" central European Celts who had begun to migrate south through Macedonia as early as 300 BCE, and who had eventually settled in Galatia, just east of Pergamon. Sometime around 240–230 BCE, Attalus I (r. 241–197 BCE) defeated the Gauls in battle. Just as the Athenians had alluded to the battle between the forces of civilization and inhuman, barbarian aggressors in the metopes of the Parthenon (see Fig. 5.11), so too the Pergamenes suggested the nonhumanity of the Gauls by depicting the giants as snakelike and legless, unable to even begin to rise to the level of the Attalid victors.

When Attalus I defeated the Gauls, he commissioned a group of three life-size figures to decorate the sanctuary of Athena Nikephoros (the "Victory-bringer") on the acropolis of Pergamon. Possibly the work of the sculptor

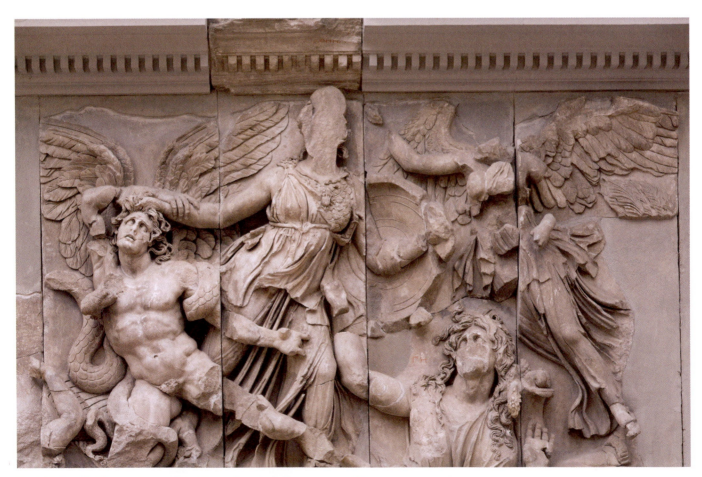

Fig. 5.23 Detail of the east frieze of the Altar of Zeus, from Pergamon. ca. 165 BCE. In this image, Athena grabs the hair of a winged, serpent-tailed monster, who is identified on the base of the monument as Alkyoneos, son of the earth goddess Ge. Ge herself rises up from the ground on the right to avenge her son. Behind Ge, a winged Nike flies to Athena's rescue.

Epigonus, the original bronze versions of these sculptures, which represent the vanquished Gauls, no longer exist, and how they related to each other is not clear. Nevertheless, the drama of their presentation and their appeal to the emotions of the viewer is unmistakable. In what was probably the centerpiece of the installation (Fig. 5.24), a Gallic chieftain, having just killed his wife, in order to prevent her capture, possible abuse at the hands of the Pergamenes, and almost certain sale into slavery, now turns his sword on himself. He twists in an expressive theatricality, his arms and body rising to the task in marked contrast to the limp collapse of his wife beside him. A second sculpture, which probably flanked the suicide in the center of the installation, depicts a wounded Gallic trumpeter (Fig. 5.25). The Gaul's identity is established by the horn that lies at his feet, by his tousled hair and moustache (uncharacteristic of Greeks), and by his golden Celtic torc, or choker, the only item of clothing the Gauls wore in combat. He is dying from a chest wound that bleeds profusely below his right breast. The brutal realism together with the nobility and heroism of the defeated Gaul places this work among the earliest examples of Hellenistic expressionism.

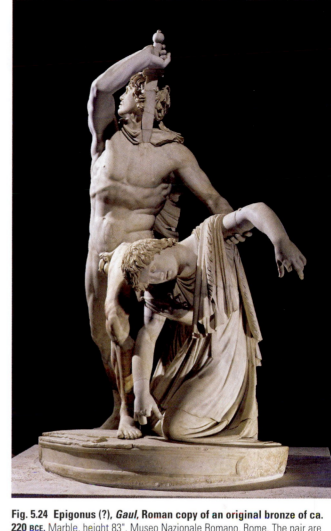

Fig. 5.24 Epigonus (?), *Gaul*, Roman copy of an original bronze of ca. 220 BCE. Marble, height 83". Museo Nazionale Romano, Rome. The pair are a study in contrast: the wife clothed, her husband nude; she dropping to the ground, he looking heavenward; her body falling limp, his torqued in action. Such contrast is yet another characteristic of Hellenistic expressionism.

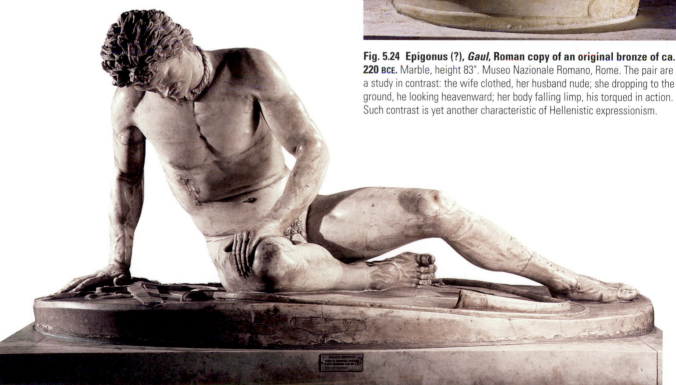

Fig. 5.25 Epigonus (?), *Dying Gaul*, Roman copy of an original bronze of ca. 220 BCE. Marble, height 37". Museo Capitolino, Rome. The Gaul seems both resigned to his fate—pressing against the ground to support himself as if pushing futilely against death—and also determined to show his valor and strength to the end—holding himself up as long as he can. Such emotional ambiguity is an integral aspect of Hellenistic art.

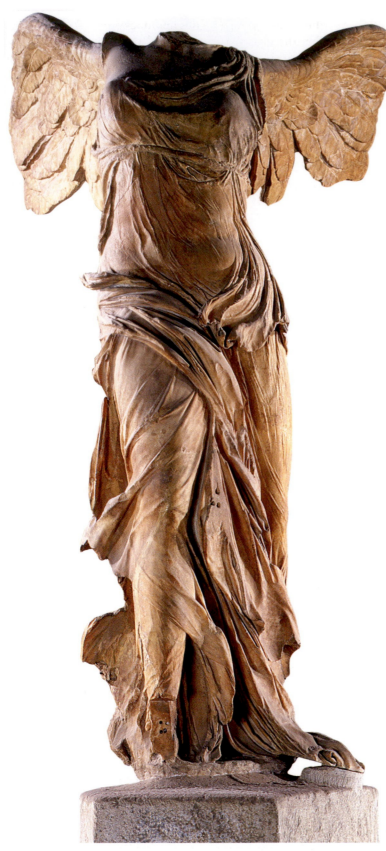

Fig. 5.26 *Nike* (*Victory*) *of Samothrace*, from the Sanctuary of the Great Gods, Samothrace. ca. 300–190 BCE. Marble, height 8'1". Musée du Louvre, Paris. Discovered by French explorers in 1863, the *Nike* appears so immediate and alive that the viewer can almost feel the gust of wind that blows across her body.

Watch a video about the *Nike* (*Victory*) *of Samothrace* on **MyArtsLab**

One other Hellenistic sculpture deserves particular attention—the *Nike of Samothrace*. Convincing arguments date the *Nike of Samothrace* (Fig. **5.26**) anywhere from 300 BCE to as late as 31 BCE, though most agree that it was probably commissioned to celebrate a naval victory. It originally stood (with head and arms that have not survived, except for a single hand) upon the sculpted prow of a ship that was dramatically set in a pool of water at the top of a cliff on the island of Samothrace in the north Aegean. The dynamic forward movement of the striding figure is balanced dramatically by the open gesture of her extended wings and the powerful directional lines of her windblown gown across her body. When light rakes across the deeply sculpted forms of this figure, it emphasizes the contrasting textures of feathers, fabric, and flesh. With the Altar of Zeus and the *Dying Gaul*, this sculpture reflects a new direction in art. Not only is this new art more interested in non-Greek subjects (Gauls and Trojans, for instance), but the calm and restraint of Classical art have disappeared, replaced by the freedom to explore the emotional extremes of the human experience.

Alexandria

If Pergamon was a spectacular Hellenistic city, it paled beside Alexandria in Egypt. Alexander had conceived of all the cities he founded as centers of culture. They would be hubs of trade and learning, and Greek culture would radiate out from them to the surrounding countryside. But Alexandria exceeded even Alexander's expectations.

The city's ruling family, the Ptolemies (heirs of Alexander's close friend and general, Ptolemy I), built the world's first museum—from the Greek *mouseion*, literally, "temple to the **muses**"—conceived as a meeting place for scholars and students. Nearby was the largest library in the world, exceeding even Pergamon's. It contained over 700,000 volumes. Plutarch later claimed that it was destroyed in 47 BCE, after Julius Caesar ordered his troops to set fire to the Ptolemaic fleet and winds spread

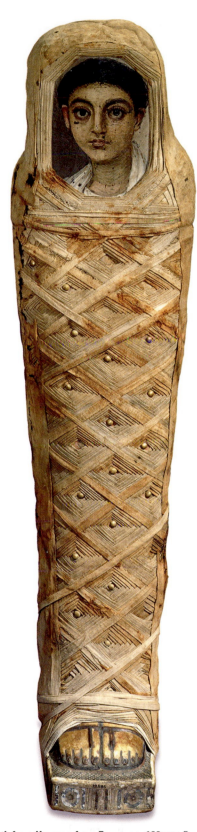

Fig. 5.27 *Youth from Hawara*, from Egypt. ca. 100 BCE. Encaustic on wood, height of entire coffin, 52". © The Trustees of the British Museum. Mummy portraits were executed in encaustic, a medium composed of beeswax and pigment. Applied in molten form, it fuses to the surface to create a lustrous enamel effect of intense color. It is the most durable of all artists' paints, since wax is impervious to moisture. As the Egyptian mummy portraits attest, over time, encaustic retains all the freshness of a newly finished work.

the flames to warehouses and dockyards. We now know that the library survived—the Roman geographer Strabo worked there in the 20s BCE. But here were collected the great works of Greek civilization, the writings of Plato and Aristotle, the plays of the great tragedians Aeschylus, Sophocles, and Euripides, as well as the comedies of Aristophanes. Stimulated by the intellectual activity in the city, the great mathematician Euclid formulated the theorems of plane and solid geometry here. And, when Ptolemy I (r. 323–285 BCE) diverted the funeral train of Alexander the Great from its Macedonian destination to Egypt, burying him either in Memphis or Alexandria (his tomb has never been found), the city was inevitably associated with the cult of Alexander himself. Tomb decorations at Luxor depict Alexander in the traditional role and style of an Egyptian pharaoh.

The city was designed by Alexander's personal architect, Dinocrates of Rhodes (flourished fourth century BCE), laid out in a grid, enclosed by a wall, and accessible by four gates at the ends of its major avenues. It was blessed by three extraordinary harbors. One was connected to the Nile, allowing for the transfer of the Nile's enormous agricultural wealth. Two others opened onto the Mediterranean, the Western Port and the Great Port, both protected by the island of Pharos, upon which was erected a giant lighthouse. Atop its 440-foot structure, a beam of light from a lantern was magnified by a system of reflectors so that approaching sailors could see the harbor from far off at sea. With the Hanging Gardens of Babylon and the Pyramids at Giza, the lighthouse at Pharos was considered one of the Seven Wonders of the World. (Its remains have been discovered in the harbor.)

Alexandria was a cosmopolitan city, exceeding even Golden Age Athens in the diversity of its inhabitants. As its population approached 1 million at the end of the first century BCE, commerce was its primary activity. Banks performed transactions. Markets bustled. Inhabitants traded with others from all parts of the known world. Peoples of different ethnic backgrounds—Jews, black Africans, Greeks, Egyptians, various races and tribes from Asia Minor—all came together with the single purpose of making money. Gradually, Hellenistic and Egyptian cultures merged. The most striking evidence of this are the large number of mummy coffins decorated with startlingly realistic portraits of the deceased (Fig. **5.27**). These give us some idea of Hellenistic portrait painting, almost none of which otherwise survives. They are **encaustic**, done with pigment mixed with heated wax, and the artists, in keeping with the Hellenistic style, were evidently intent on conveying something of the deceased's personality and emotional makeup. No more dramatic or moving approach to coffin decoration could be conceived, nor one more traditional in terms of preserving the tradition of the Egyptian *ka*.

Rome and Its Hellenistic Heritage

Rome traced its origins back to the Trojan warrior Aeneas, who at the end of the Trojan War sailed off to found a new homeland for his people. The Roman poet Virgil (70–19 BCE) would celebrate Aeneas' journey in his epic poem, the *Aeneid*, written in the last decade of his life. There, he describes how the gods who supported the Greeks punished the Trojan priest Laocoön for warning his countrymen not to accept the "gift" of a wooden horse from the Greeks:

> I shudder even now,
> Recalling it—there came a pair of serpents
> With monstrous coils, abreast the sea, and aiming
> Together for the shore. ...
> Straight toward Laocoön, and first each serpent
> Seized in its coils his two young sons, and fastened
> The fangs in those poor bodies. And the priest
> Struggled to help them, weapons in his hand.
> They seized him, bound him with the mighty coils,
> Twice round his waist, twice round his neck, they
>   squeezed
> With scaly pressure, and still towered above him
> Straining his hands to tear the knots apart,
> His chaplets[1] stained with blood and the black poison,
> He uttered horrible cries, not even human,
> More like the bellowing of a bull when, wounded,
> It flees the altar, shaking from the shoulder
> The ill-aimed axe.

> [1] chaplets: Garlands for the head.

It is likely that as he wrote the *Aeneid*, Virgil had seen the sculpture of *Laocoön and His Sons* (Fig. **5.28**), carved in about 150 BCE. (Some argue that the sculpture, discovered in 1506 in the ruins of a palace belonging to the emperor Titus [r. 79–81 CE] in Rome, is a copy of the now-lost original.) Whatever the case, the drama and expressionism of the sculpture are purely Hellenic. So too are its complex interweaving of elements and diagonal movements reminiscent of Athena's struggle with the giants on the frieze of the Altar of Zeus at Pergamon (see Fig. 5.23).

In fact, even though Rome conquered Greece in 146 BCE (at about the time that the *Laocoön* was carved), Greece could be said to have "ruled" Rome, at least culturally. Rome was a fully Hellenized culture—it fashioned itself in the image of Greece almost from its beginnings. Indeed, many of the works of Greek art reproduced in this book are not Greek at all but later Roman copies of Greek originals. The emperor Augustus (r. 27 BCE–14 CE) sought to transform Rome into the image of Pericles' Athens. A sculpture by Lysippus was a favorite of the emperor Tiberius (r. 14–57 CE), who had it removed from public display and placed in his bedroom. So outraged was the public, who considered

the sculpture theirs and not the emperor's, that he was forced to return it to its public place. Later Roman emperors, notably Caligula and Nero, raided Delphi and Olympia for works of art.

It was not, in the end, its art in which Rome most prided itself. "Others," Virgil would write in his poem, "no doubt, will better mold the bronze." He concludes:

> ... remember, Roman,
> To rule the people under law, to establish
> The way of peace, to battle down the haughty,
> To spare the meek. Our fine arts, these, forever. ∎

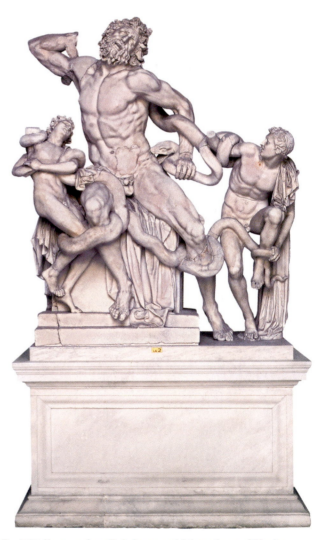

Fig. 5.28 Hagesandros, Polydoros, and Athanadoros of Rhodes, *Laocoön and His Sons,* **Hellenistic, 2nd–1st century BCE, or marble copy of an original, Rome, 1st century CE.** Marble, height 8'. Museo Pio Clementino, Vatican Museums, Vatican State. Pliny the Elder attributes the sculpture to the three artists from Rhodes. If this is a copy of a lost original (and scholars debate the issue), it was probably inspired by Virgil's poem.

THINKING BACK

5.1 Explain the role of *eudaimonia* in Athenian life and contrast it with the role of women.

In their politics, the Athenians sought to strike a balance between the rights of the individual and the needs of the state. They collectively pursued what Aristotle called *eudaimonia*, "the good or flourishing life" in the agora, the secular center of the city. Slaves and metics, as well as women, were excluded from governance. Women were, however, given greater privileges in other city-states, particularly in Sparta. The place of women in Greek society is dramatized in Sophocles' play *Antigone*. How does that play depict the predicament of the Greek woman's place in society?

5.2 Describe Pericles' sense of Athenian greatness and how it is reflected in the art of the Golden Age.

In the fifth century, the statesman Pericles dominated Athenian political life. In his funeral speech honoring the war dead, delivered early in the Peloponnesian Wars, he claimed "excellence" for Athenians in all aspects of endeavor, leading Greece by its example.

The Athenians realized the excellence of their sculpture, which became increasingly naturalistic even as they embodied an increasingly perfect sense of proportion. They realized it even more dramatically on the Acropolis, where Pericles instituted a massive architectural program that included what is perhaps the highest expression of the Doric order, the Parthenon. How would you explain the Idea of Beauty as reflected in Greek sculpture? How is it exemplified by the Parthenon? Why have we come to call this work "Classical"?

5.3 Compare and contrast the philosophical positions of the pre-Socratics, the Sophists, Socrates, and Plato.

Pericles also championed the practice of philosophy in Athens. His Athens inherited two distinct philosophical traditions, that of the Pre-Socratics, who were chiefly concerned with describing the natural universe, and that of the Sophists, who were primarily concerned with understanding the nature of human "knowing" itself. Pericles was particularly interested in the Sophists. Why? The Sophist philosophy was, however, questioned by Socrates. A stonemason by training, he practiced philosophy by engaging all comers in conversation in the agora. Socrates never wrote a word himself, but his student Plato recorded his thoughts. How does Plato extend Socratic thought in the *Republic* and the *Symposium*?

5.4 Outline the chief characteristics of both Greek comedy and Greek tragedy.

Greek theatrical practice arose out of rites connected with Dionysus, god of wine. In what ways do both Greek comedy and Greek tragedy reflect this common origin? What is the role of the chorus in tragedy? What tension does tragedy most often exploit?

5.5 Describe the gradual shift in sculptural style from the Classical art of Phidias to the art of the Hellenic world, and discuss how Aristotle's philosophy reflects this stylistic change.

The influence of Alexander the Great extended across North Africa and Egypt, the Middle East, as far as the Indian subcontinent, creating the largest empire the world had ever known. During his reign, sculpture flourished as a medium, the two masters of the period being Lysippus and his chief competitor, Praxiteles. What new direction in sculpture did they introduce and how did later Hellenistic sculptors exploit that direction?

Alexander's tutor, the philosopher Aristotle, emphasized the importance of empirical observation in understanding the world, distinguishing between a thing's identity, its essence, and the changes that inevitably occur to it over time. How would you compare Aristotle's philosophy to Plato's? How does Aristotle's *Poetics* inform later Hellenistic sculpture?

✔ **Study** and **review** on **MyArtsLab**

READINGS

from Plato, *Crito*

The *Crito* is a dialogue between Socrates and his friend, the rich Athenian citizen Crito, about the source and nature of political obligation. Crito tries to persuade Socrates to escape his imprisonment and go into exile after he is sentenced to death on the charges of impiety and corrupting the youth of Athens. But Socrates counters each of Crito's arguments.

SOCRATES Why have you come at this hour, Crito? Is it not still early?

CRITO. Yes, very early.

SOCR. About what time is it?

CRITO. It is just daybreak.

SOCR. I wonder that the jailer was willing to let you in.

CRITO. He knows me now, Socrates; I come here so often, and besides, I have given him a tip.

SOCR. Have you been here long?

CRITO. Yes, some time. 10

SOCR. Then why did you sit down without speaking? Why did you not wake me at once?

CRITO. Indeed, Socrates, I wish that I myself were not so sleepless and sorrowful. But I have been wondering to see how soundly you sleep. And I purposely did not wake you, for I was anxious not to disturb your repose. Often before, all through your life, I have thought that your temperament was a happy one; and I think so more than ever now when I see how easily and calmly you bear the calamity that has come to you. … But, O my good Socrates, I beg you for the last time to lis- 20 ten to me and save yourself. For to me your death will be more than a single disaster; not only shall I lose a friend the like of whom I shall never find again, but many persons who do not know you and me well will think that I might have saved you if I had been willing to spend money, but that I neglected to do so. And what reputation could be more disgraceful than the reputation of caring more for money than for one's friends? The public will never believe that we were anxious to save you, but that you yourself refused to escape.

SOCR. But, my dear Crito, why should we care so much about 30 public opinion? Reasonable men, of whose opinion it is worth our while to think, will believe that we acted as we really did.

CRITO. But you see, Socrates, that it is necessary to care about public opinion, too. This very thing that has happened to you proves that the multitude can do a man not the least, but almost the greatest harm, if he is falsely accused to them.

SOCR. I wish that the multitude were able to do a man the greatest harm, Crito, for then they would be able to do him the greatest good, too. That would have been fine. But, as it is, they can do neither. They cannot make a man either wise or 40 foolish: they act wholly at random. … Consider it in this way. Suppose the laws and the commonwealth were to come and appear to me as I was preparing to run away (if that is the right phrase to describe my escape) and were to ask, "Tell us, Socrates, what have you in your mind to do? What do you mean by trying to escape but to destroy us, the laws and the whole state, so far as you are able? Do you think that a state can exist and not be overthrown, in which the decisions of law are of no force, and are disregarded and undermined by private individuals?" How shall we answer questions like that, Crito? 50 Much might be said, especially by an orator, in defense of the law which makes judicial decisions supreme. Shall I reply, "But the state has injured me by judging my case unjustly?" Shall we say that?

CRITO. Certainly we will, Socrates.

SOCR. And suppose the laws were to reply, "Was that our agreement? Or was it that you would abide by whatever judgments the state should pronounce?" And if we were surprised by their words, perhaps they would say, "Socrates, don't be surprised by our words, but answer us; you yourself are 60 accustomed to ask questions and to answer them. What complaint have you against us and the state, that you are trying to destroy us? Are we not, first of all, your parents? Through us your father took your mother and brought you into the world. Tell us, have you any fault to find with those of us that are the laws of marriage?" "I have none," I should reply. … "Well, then, since you were brought into the world and raised and educated by us, how, in the first place, can you deny that you are our child and our slave, as your fathers were before you? And if this be so, do you think that your rights are on a level 70 with ours? Do you think that you have a right to retaliate if we should try to do anything to you? … And do you think that you may retaliate in the case of your country and its laws? If we try to destroy you, because we think it just, will you in return do all that you can to destroy us, the laws, and your country, and say that in so doing you are acting justly—you, the man who really thinks so much of excellence? Or are you too wise to see that your country is worthier, more to be revered, more sacred, and held in higher honor both by the gods and by all men of understanding, than your father and 80 your mother and all your other ancestors; and that you ought to reverence it, and to submit to it, and to approach it more humbly when it is angry with you than you would approach your father; and either to do whatever it tells you to do or to persuade it to excuse you; and to obey in silence if it orders you to endure flogging or imprisonment, or if it sends you to battle to be wounded or to die? … But it is impious to use violence against your father or your mother; and much more impious to use violence against your country." What answer shall we make, Crito? Shall we say that the laws speak the truth, 90 or not?

CRITO. I think that they do.

SOCR. "Then consider, Socrates," perhaps they would say, "if we are right in saying that by attempting to escape you are attempting an injustice. We brought you into the world, we raised you, we educated you, we gave you and every other citizen a share of all the good things we could. Yet we proclaim that if any man of the Athenians is dissatisfied with us, he may take his goods and go away wherever he pleases; we give that privilege to every man who chooses to avail himself of it, so soon as he has reached manhood, and sees us, the laws, and the administration of our state. No one of us stands in his way or forbids him to take his goods and go wherever he likes, whether it be to an Athenian colony or to any foreign country, if he is dissatisfied with us and with the state. But we say that every man of you who remains here, seeing how we administer justice, and how we govern the state in other matters, has agreed, by the very fact of remaining here, to do whatsoever we tell him. And, we say, he who disobeys us acts unjustly on three counts: he disobeys us who are his parents, and he disobeys us who reared him, and he disobeys us after he has agreed to obey us, without persuading us that we are wrong. Yet we did not tell him sternly to do whatever we told him. We offered him an alternative; we gave him his choice either to obey us or to convince us that we were wrong; but he does neither. ...

They would say, "Socrates, we have very strong evidence that you were satisfied with us and with the state. You would not have been content to stay at home in it more than other Athenians unless you had been satisfied with it more than they. You never went away from Athens to the festivals, nor elsewhere except on military service; you never made other journeys like other men; you had no desire to see other states or other laws; you were contented with us and our state; so strongly did you prefer us, and agree to be governed by us. And what is more, you had children in this city, you found it so satisfactory. Besides, if you had wished, you might at your trial have offered to go into exile. At that time you could have done with the state's consent what you are trying now to do without it. But then you gloried in being willing to die. You said that you preferred death to exile. And now you do not honor those words: you do not respect us, the laws, for you are trying to destroy us; and you are acting just as a miserable slave would act, trying to run away, and breaking the contracts and agreement which you made to live as our citizen. First, therefore, answer this question. Are we right, or are we wrong, in saying that you have agreed not in mere words, but in your actions, to live under our government?" What are we to say, Crito? Must we not admit that it is true?

CRITO. We must, Socrates.

READING CRITICALLY

What is the "implicit contract" Socrates speaks about, and why does it follow that, having entered this contract, Socrates must accept his punishment?

READING 5.5

from Plato, *The Republic*, "Allegory of the Cave"

The Republic is an inquiry into the nature of justice, which in turn leads logically to a discussion about the nature of the ideal state (where justice would, naturally, be meted out to perfection). The work takes the form of a dialogue between Socrates and six other speakers. The passage here is from Book 7, the famous "Allegory of the Cave," in which Socrates addresses an older brother of Plato named Glaucon. Socrates distinguishes between unenlightened people and enlightened philosophers such as himself, even as he demonstrates how difficult it is for the enlightened to reenter the sphere of everyday affairs—which they must, of course, since it is their duty to rule.

And now, I [Socrates] said, let me show in a figure how far our nature is enlightened or unenlightened:—Behold! human beings living in an underground den, which has a mouth open towards the light and reaching all along the den; here they have been from their childhood, and have their legs and necks chained so that they cannot move, and can only see before them, being prevented by the chains from turning round their heads. Above and behind them a fire is blazing at a distance, and between the fire and the prisoners there is a raised way; and you will see, if you look, a low wall built along the way, like the screen which marionette players have in front of them, over which they show the puppets.

I see [replied Glaucon].

And do you see, I said, men passing along the wall carrying all sorts of vessels, and statues and figures of animals made of wood and stone and various materials, which appear over the wall? Some of them are talking, others silent.

You have shown me a strange image, and they are strange prisoners.

Like ourselves, I replied; and they see only their own shadows, or the shadows of one another, which the fire throws on the opposite wall of the cave?

True, he said; how could they see anything but the shadows if they were never allowed to move their heads?

And of the objects which are being carried in like manner they would only see the shadows?

Yes, he said.

And if they were able to converse with one another, would they not suppose that they were naming what was actually before them?

Very true.

And suppose further that the prison had an echo which came from the other side, would they not be sure to fancy when one of the passers-by spoke that the voice which they heard came from the passing shadow?

No question, he replied.

To them, I said, the truth would be literally nothing but the shadows of the images.

That is certain.

And now look again, and see what will naturally follow it: the prisoners are released and disabused of their error. At first, when any of them is liberated and compelled suddenly to stand up and turn his neck round and walk and look towards the light, he will suffer sharp pains; the glare will distress him, and he will be unable to see the realities of which in his former state he had seen the shadows; and then conceive some one saying to him, that what he saw before was an illusion, but that now, when he is approaching nearer to being and his eye is turned towards more real existence, he has a clearer vision—what will be his reply? And you may further imagine that his instructor is pointing to the objects as they pass and requiring him to name them—will he not be perplexed? Will he not fancy that the shadows which he formerly saw are truer than the objects which are now shown to him?

Far truer.

And if he is compelled to look straight at the light, will he not have a pain in his eyes which will make him turn away to take refuge in the objects of vision which he can see, and which he will conceive to be in reality clearer than the things which are now being shown to him?

True.

And suppose once more, that he is reluctantly dragged up a steep and rugged ascent, and held fast until he's forced into the presence of the sun himself, is he not likely to be pained and irritated? When he approaches the light his eyes will be dazzled, and he will not be able to see anything at all of what are now called realities.

Not all in a moment, he said.

He will require to grow accustomed to the sight of the upper world. And first he will see the shadows best, next the reflections of men and other objects in the water, and then the objects themselves; then he will gaze upon the light of the moon and the stars and the spangled heaven; and he will see the sky and the stars by night better than the sun or the light of the sun by day?

Certainly.

Last of all he will be able to see the sun, and not mere reflections of him in the water, but he will see him in his own proper place, and not in another; and he will contemplate him as he is. ... And when he remembered his old habitation, and the wisdom of the den and his fellow-prisoners, do you not suppose that he would felicitate himself on the change, and pity them?

Certainly, he would. ...

Would he not say with Homer, Better to be the poor servant of a poor master, and to endure anything, rather than think as they do and live after their manner?

Yes, he said, I think that he would rather suffer anything than entertain these false notions and live in this miserable manner. Imagine once more, I said, such a one coming suddenly out of the sun to be replaced in his old situation; would he not be certain to have his eyes full of darkness?

To be sure, he said. ...

This entire allegory, I said, you may now append, dear Glaucon, to the previous argument; the prison-house is the world of sight, the light of the fire is the sun, and you will not misapprehend me if you interpret the journey upwards to be the ascent of the soul into the intellectual world according to my poor belief, which, at your desire, I have expressed whether rightly or wrongly God knows. But, whether true or false, my opinion is that in the world of knowledge the idea of good appears last of all, and is seen only with an effort; and, when seen, is also inferred to be the universal author of all things beautiful and right, parent of light and of the lord of light in this visible world, and the immediate source of reason and truth in the intellectual; and that this is the power upon which he who would act rationally, either in public or private life must have his eye fixed.

I agree, he said, as far as I am able to understand you.

Moreover, I said, you must not wonder that those who attain to this beatific vision are unwilling to descend to human affairs; for their souls are ever hastening into the upper world where they desire to dwell; which desire of theirs is very natural, if our allegory may be trusted. ...

[A]nd there is another thing which is likely, or rather a necessary inference from what has preceded, that neither the uneducated and uninformed of the truth, nor yet those who never make an end of their education, will be able ministers of State; not the former, because they have no single aim of duty which is the rule of all their actions, private as well as public; nor the latter, because they will not act at all except upon compulsion, fancying that they are already dwelling apart in the islands of the blest.

Very true, he replied.

Then, I said, the business of us who are the founders of the State will be to compel the best minds to attain that knowledge which we have already shown to be the greatest of all—they must continue to ascend until they arrive at the good; but when they have ascended and seen enough we must not allow them to do as they do now.

What do you mean?

I mean that they remain in the upper world: but this must not be allowed; they must be made to descend again among the prisoners in the den, and partake of their labours and honours, whether they are worth having or not.

But is not this unjust? he said; ought we to give them a worse life, when they might have a better? ...

Observe, Glaucon, that there will be no injustice in compelling our philosophers to have a care and providence of others; we shall explain to them that in other States, men of their class are not obliged to share in the toils of politics: and this is reasonable, for they grow up at their own sweet will, and the government would rather not have them. Being self-taught, they cannot be expected to show any gratitude for a culture which they have never received. But we have brought you into the world to be rulers of the hive, kings of yourselves and of the other citizens, and have educated you far better and more perfectly than they have been educated, and you are better 150 able to share in the double duty. Wherefore each of you, when his turn comes, must go down to the general underground abode, and get the habit of seeing in the dark. When you have acquired the habit, you will see ten thousand times better than the inhabitants of the den, and you will know what the several images are, and what they represent, because you have seen the beautiful and just and good in their truth. And thus our

State which is also yours will be a reality, and not a dream only, and will be administered in a spirit unlike that of other States, in which men fight with one another about shadows only and 160 are distracted in the struggle for power, which in their eyes is a great good. Whereas the truth is that the State in which the rulers are most reluctant to govern is always the best and most quietly governed, and the State in which they are most eager, the worst. ...

READING CRITICALLY

In what way does Glaucon's experience, as Socrates' student, mirror Socrates' allegory?

READING 5.6

from Plato, *The Symposium*

The Symposium recounts a discussion about the nature of Love among members of a drinking party in Athens at which Plato and Socrates were in attendance. Their homosexual love for young boys, commonplace in Athens, is the starting point, but the essay quickly moves beyond discussion of mere physical love. In the excerpt below, Socrates quotes a woman named Diotima who has taught him, he says, that the purpose of love is to give birth to beauty, which in turn allows the philosopher to attain insight into the ultimate Form of Beauty. His speech is addressed to one Phaedrus, who has already made an important distinction between common physical love and a higher heavenly love.

"Even you, Socrates, could perhaps be initiated in the rites of love I've described so far. But the purpose of these rites, if they are performed correctly, is to reach the final vision of the mysteries; and I'm not sure you could manage this. But I'll tell you about them," she said, "and make every effort in doing so; try to follow, as far as you can."

"The correct way," she said, "for someone to approach this business is to begin when he's young by being drawn towards beautiful bodies. At first, if his guide leads him correctly, he should love just one body and in that relationship 10 produce beautiful discourses. Next he should realize that the beauty of any one body is closely related to that of another, and that, if he is to pursue beauty of form, it's very foolish not to regard the beauty of all bodies as one and the same. Once he's seen this, he'll become a lover of all beautiful bodies, and will relax his intense passion for just one body, despising this passion and regarding it as petty. After this, he should regard the beauty of minds as more valuable than that of the body, so that, if someone has goodness of mind even if he has little of the bloom of beauty, he will be content with him, and will 20 love and care for him, and give birth to the kinds of discourse that help young men to become better. As a result, he will be forced to observe the beauty in practices and laws and to see that every type of beauty is closely related to every other, so that he will regard beauty of body as something petty. After practices, the guide must lead him towards forms of knowledge, so that he sees their beauty too. Looking now at beauty in general and not just at individual instances, he will no longer be slavishly attached to the beauty of a boy, or of any particular person at all, or of a specific practice. Instead of this low and 30 small-minded slavery, he will be turned towards the great sea of beauty and gazing on it he'll give birth, through a boundless

love of knowledge, to many beautiful and magnificent discourses and ideas. At last, when he has been developed and strengthened in this way, he catches sight of one special type of knowledge, whose object is the kind of beauty I shall now describe.

"Now try," she said, "to concentrate as hard as you can. Anyone who has been educated this far in the ways of love, viewing beautiful things in the right order and way, will now 40 reach the goal of love's ways. He will suddenly catch sight of something amazingly beautiful in its nature; this, Socrates, is the ultimate objective of all the previous efforts. First, this beauty always is, and doesn't come into being or cease; it doesn't increase or diminish. Second, it's not beautiful in one respect but ugly in another, or beautiful at one time but not at another, or beautiful in relation to this but ugly in relation to that; nor beautiful here and ugly there because it is beautiful for some people but ugly for others. Nor will beauty appear to him in the form of a face or hands or any part of the body; 50 or as a specific account or piece of knowledge; or as being anywhere in something else, for instance in a living creature or earth or heaven or anything else. It will appear as in itself and by itself, always single in form; all other beautiful things share its character, but do so in such a way that, when other things come to be or cease, it is not increased or decreased in any way nor does it undergo any change. ..."

READING CRITICALLY

How does the process of coming to a higher understanding of the nature of love compare to Socrates' description of arriving at enlightenment in "Allegory of the Cave"?

from Aristotle, *Poetics*

Aristotle's *Poetics* is an attempt to account for the power of tragedy by defining the chief attributes of Greek theater. In it, Aristotle contributed a number of key ideas to literary criticism, most especially the idea of the imitation of an action, the definition of plot as "an arrangement of incidents," and the concept of catharsis, translated in the first passage below, from Book 6 of the *Poetics*, as "purification." Catharsis is an effect of the "feat and pity" aroused in the spectator, discussed by Aristotle in the second passage quoted below, from Book 14.

BOOK 6

Tragedy, then, is an imitation of an action that is serious, complete, and of a certain magnitude; in language embellished with every kind of artistic ornament, the several kinds being found in separate parts of the play; in the form of dramatic action, not of narrative; through pity and fear effecting the proper purification of these emotions.[1] By "language embellished," I mean language into which rhythm, harmony, and song enter. By "the several kinds in separate parts," I mean that some parts are rendered through the medium of verse alone, others again with the aid of song. 10

Now as tragic imitation implies persons acting, it necessarily follows, in the first place, that spectacular equipment will be a part of tragedy. Next, song and diction, for these are the medium of imitation. By diction, I mean the metrical arrangement of the words: as for song, it is a term whose sense everyone understands.

Again, tragedy is the imitation of an action, and an action implies personal actors, who necessarily possess certain distinctive qualities of character and thought; for it is by these that we form our estimate of their actions and these two— 20 thought and character—are the natural causes from which their actions spring, and on their actions all success or failure depends. Now, the imitation of the action is the plot; by plot I here mean the arrangement of the incidents. By character I mean that because of which we ascribe certain qualities to the actors. Thought is needed whenever they speak to prove a statement or declare a general truth. Every tragedy, therefore, must have six parts, which parts determine its quality—namely, plot, character, diction, thought, spectacle, song. ...

But most important of all is the structure of the incidents. 30 For tragedy is an imitation, not of men, but of action and life, of happiness and misery. And life consists of action, and its end is a mode of activity, not a quality. Now character determines men's qualities, but it is their actions that make them happy or wretched. The purpose of action in the tragedy, therefore, is not the representation of character: character comes in as contributing to the action. Hence the incidents and the plot are the end of the tragedy; and the end is the chief thing of all. So without action there cannot be a tragedy; there may be one without character. ... 40

Again, you may string together a set of speeches expressive of character, and well finished in point of diction and thought, and not produce the essential tragic effect nearly so well as with a play which, however deficient in these respects, yet has a plot and artistically constructed incidents. Besides which, the most powerful elements of emotional interest in tragedy—reversal of the situation and recognition scenes—are parts of the plot. A further proof is that novices in the art attain to finish of diction and precision of portraiture before they can construct the plot. It is the same with almost all the early poets. 50

The plot, then, is the first principle, and, as it were, the soul of a tragedy: character holds the second place. A similar statement is true of painting. The most beautiful colors, laid on confusedly, will not give as much pleasure as a simple chalk outline of a portrait. Thus tragedy is the imitation of an action, and of actors mainly with a view to the action. ...

The spectacle is, indeed, an attraction in itself, but of all the parts it is the least artistic, and connected least with the art of poetry. For the power of tragedy is felt even apart from representation and actors. Besides, the production of scenic effects 60 is more a matter for the property man than for the poet.

BOOK 14

Fear and pity may be aroused by spectacular means; but they may also result from the inner structure of the piece, which is the better way, and indicates a superior poet. For the plot ought to be so constructed that, even without the aid of the eye, he who hears the tale told will thrill with horror and melt to pity at what takes place. This is the impression we should receive from hearing the story of Oedipus. But to produce this effect by the mere spectacle is a less artistic method, and dependent on extraneous aids. Those who employ spec- 70 tacular means to create a sense not of the terrible but of the merely monstrous are strangers to the purpose of tragedy; for we must not demand of tragedy any and every kind of pleasure, but only that which is proper to it. And since the pleasure the tragic poet should offer is that which comes from pity and fear through imitation, it is evident that this quality must be impressed on the incidents.

Let us then determine what circumstances strike us as terrible or pitiful.

---

[1] Note that an unhappy or what we call a tragic ending was not one of the Greek requirements for a tragedy, though Aristotle thought it the perfect ending. Many tragedies ended with a solemn reconciliation after a conflict or quiet after pain, to please the audience, Aristotle says.

Actions of this sort must happen between persons who are either friends or enemies or indifferent to one another. If an enemy kills an enemy, there is nothing to excite pity either in the act or the intention—except in so far as the suffering itself is pitiful. So too with indifferent persons. But when the tragic incident occurs between those who are near or dear to one another—if, for example, a brother kills, or intends to kill, a brother, a son his father, a mother her son, a son his mother, or any other deed of the kind is done—these are situations to be looked for by the poet. He may not indeed destroy the framework of the received legends—the fact, for instance, that Clytemnestra was slain by Orestes ... but he ought to show invention of his own, and skillfully handle the traditional material. ...

Enough has now been said concerning the structure of the incidents and the right kind of plot.

READING CRITICALLY

Can you say what actions in Sophocles' *Antigone* might lead, in Aristotle's view, to the catharsis of the play's audience?

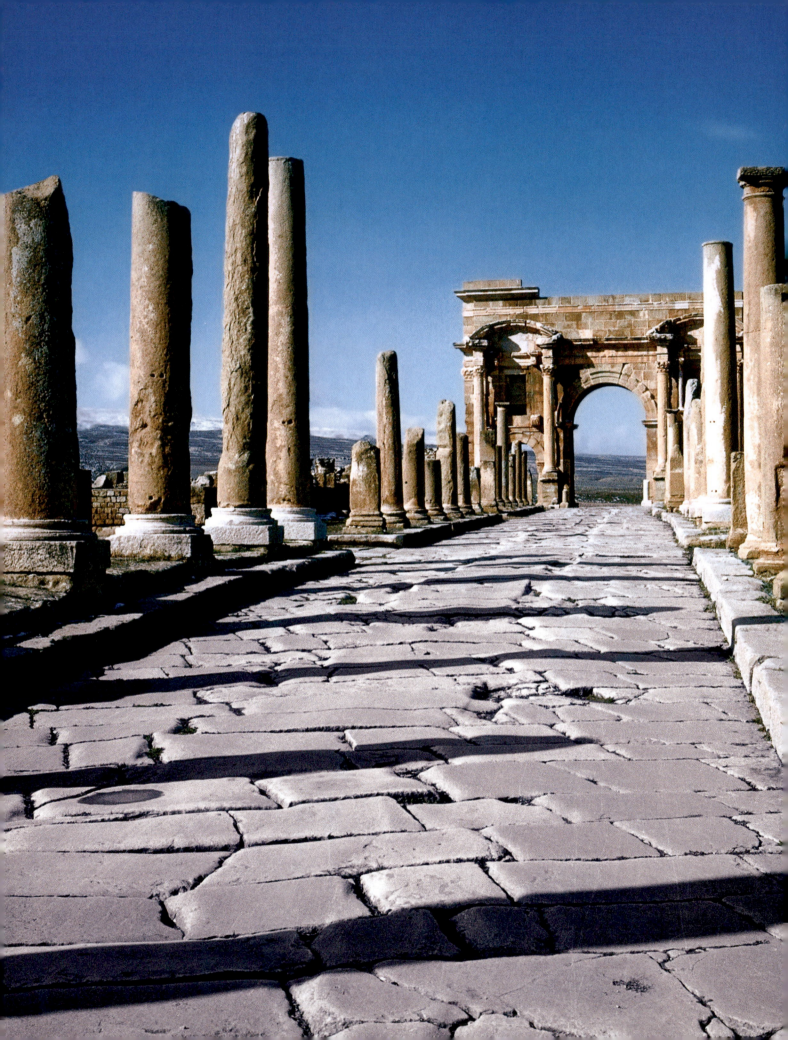

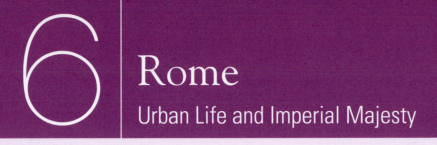

6 Rome
Urban Life and Imperial Majesty

THINKING AHEAD

6.1 Describe the dual origins of Roman culture.

6.2 Outline the patronage system of the Roman Republic and explain how it is reflected in its art and literature.

6.3 Discuss the imperial aspirations of Rome and their manifestation in art, architecture, and literature.

6.4 Examine the factors that led to Rome's decline.

Thamugadi, present-day Timgad, Algeria, is one of the few totally excavated towns of the Roman Empire, and its ruins tell us as much or more about Roman civilization as any other Roman city, including Rome itself. It was founded during the reign of Trajan in about 100 CE as a colony for retired soldiers of the Roman legions who had served the Empire as it constantly expanded its borders in Africa. Whereas Rome had grown haphazardly over hundreds of years and under many rulers, Thamugadi was an entirely new city and a model, if not of Rome itself, then of the Roman sense of order. It was based on the rigid grid of a Roman military camp and was divided into four quarters defined by east–west and north–south arteries, broad avenues lined with columns (Fig. 6.1), with a forum, or public square, at their crossing. The town had 111 *insulae* (apartment blocks), and all the amenities of Roman life were available: 14 public baths, a library, a theater, and several markets, including one that sold only clothes (Fig. 6.2).

Thamugadi is the product of the conscious Roman decision to "Romanize" the world, a symbol of empire itself. By the middle of the third century BCE, it had begun to seek control of the entire Mediterranean basin and its attendant wealth. The Roman military campaigns led to the building of these cities, with their amphitheaters, temples, arches,

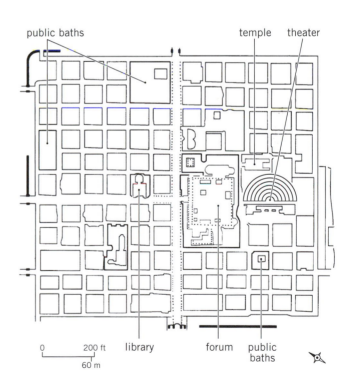

Fig. 6.2 City plan of Thamugadi. ca. 200 CE. The layout of Thamugadi is a symbol of Roman reason and planning—efficient and highly organized.

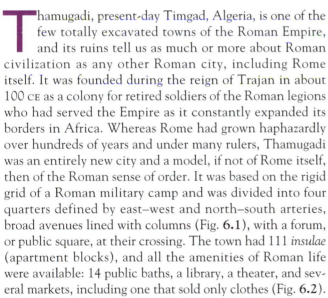

◀ **Fig. 6.1 Colonnaded street in Thamugadi, North Africa. View toward the Arch of Trajan. Late 2nd century CE.** Thamugadi was established in about 100 CE as a colony for retired soldiers of the Roman Third Legion. It represents the deep imprint Rome left upon its entire empire.

 Listen to the chapter audio on **MyArtsLab**

roads, fortresses, aqueducts, bridges, and monuments of every description. From Scotland in the north to the oases of the Sahara desert in the south, from the Iberian peninsula in the west to Asia Minor as far as the Tigris River in the east, local aristocrats took up Roman customs (Map 6.1). Roman law governed each region. Rome remained the center of culture all others at the periphery imitated.

Rome admired Greece for its cultural achievements, from its philosophy to its sculpture, and, as we have seen, its own art developed from Greek–Hellenic models. But Rome admired its own achievements as well, and its art differed from that of its Hellenic predecessors in certain key respects. Instead of depicting mythological events and heroes, Roman artists depicted current events and real people, from generals and their military exploits to portraits of their leaders and recently deceased citizens. They celebrated the achievements of a state that was their chief patron so that all the world might stand in awe of the state's accomplishments.

Nowhere was this identity more fully expressed than in Roman architecture. Though the structural principles of the arch had long been known, the Romans mastered the form. They also invented concrete, the structural strength of which, when combined with the arch, made possible the vault, and the vault in turn made possible the soaring and expansive interior spaces for which Roman architecture is known. The Romans were great engineers, and public works were fundamental to the Roman sense of identity, propagandistic tools that symbolized Roman power.

This chapter traces the rise of Roman civilization from its Greek and Etruscan origins in the sixth century BCE to about 313 CE, when the Empire was Christianized. Based on values developed in Republican Rome and extended to the imperial state, the Roman citizen owed the state dutiful respect. As the rhetorician and orator Marcus Tullius Cicero put it in his first-century BCE essay, *On Duty*, "It is our duty, then, to be more ready to endanger our own than the public welfare." This sense of duty was mirrored in

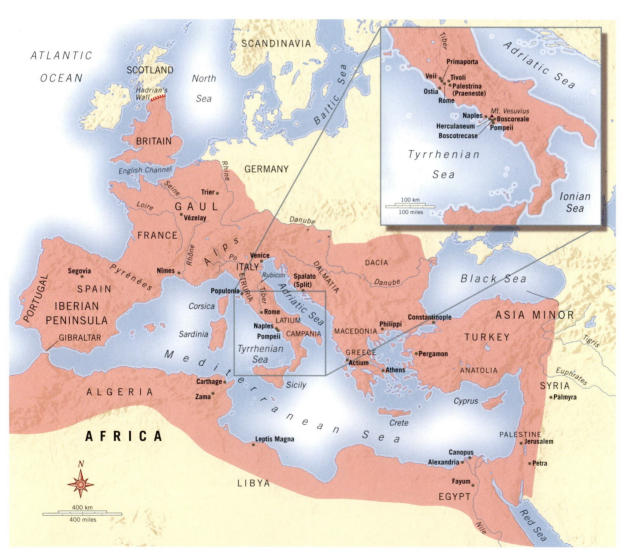

Map 6.1 The Roman Empire at its greatest extent, ca. 180 CE. By 180 CE, the Roman Empire extended from the Atlantic Ocean in the west to Asia Minor, Syria, and Palestine in the east, and from Scotland in the north to the Sahara desert in North Africa.

family life, where reverence for one's ancestors was reflected in the profusion of portrait busts that decorated Roman households. One was obliged to honor one's father as one honored Rome itself. The family became one of the focuses of the first Roman emperor, Augustus, and his dedication to it was reflected in his public works and statuary, and in the work of the artists and writers he supported. But the lasting legacy of Augustus was his transformation of Rome into what he called "a city of marble." Subsequent emperors in the first two centuries CE would continue to transform Rome until it was arguably the most magnificent center of culture ever built.

ORIGINS OF ROMAN CULTURE

From what two sources did Roman culture spring?

The origins of Roman culture are twofold. On the one hand, there were the Greeks, who as early as the eighth century BCE colonized the southern coastal regions of the Italian peninsula and Sicily, and whose Hellenic culture the Romans adopted for their own. On the other hand, there were the Etruscans.

The Etruscan Roots

The Etruscan homeland, Etruria, occupied the part of the Italian peninsula that is roughly the same as modern-day Tuscany. It was bordered by the Arno River to the north (which runs through Florence) and the Tiber River to the south (which runs through Rome). No Etruscan literature survives, although around 9,000 short texts do, enough to make clear that even though the alphabet was related to Greek, the language itself was unrelated to any other in Europe. Scholars know how to pronounce most of its words, although only several hundred words have been translated with any certainty. By the seventh and sixth centuries BCE, the Etruscans were major exporters of fine painted pottery, a black ceramic ware known as *bucchero*, bronze-work, jewelry, oil, and wine. By the fifth century BCE, they were known throughout the Mediterranean for their skill as sculptors in both bronze and terra cotta.

Tombs: Clues to Etruscan Life The Etruscans buried their dead in cemeteries removed from their cities. The tombs were arranged like a town with a network of streets winding through them. They used a type of tomb called a **tumulus**, a round structure partially below ground and partially above ground, covered with earth. Inside, the burial chambers are rectangular and resemble domestic architecture. In fact, they may resemble actual Etruscan homes—only the foundations of their homes survive, so we cannot be sure—since entire families were buried together. Plaster reliefs on the walls include kitchen implements, tools, and, in general, the necessities for everyday life, suggesting that the Etruscan sense of the afterlife was in some ways similar to that of the Egyptians, with whom, incidentally, they traded.

Most of what we know about the Etruscans comes from the sculptures and paintings that have survived in tombs. Women evidently played a far more important role in Etruscan culture than in Greek, and Roman culture would later reflect the Etruscan sense of women's equality. On Etruscan **sarcophagi**, or coffins, many of which are made of terra cotta, there are many examples of husbands and wives reclining together. One of the most famous examples comes from Cerveteri, on the coast north of Rome (Fig. **6.3**). Husband and wife are depicted reclining on a dining couch, and they are given equal status. Their hands are

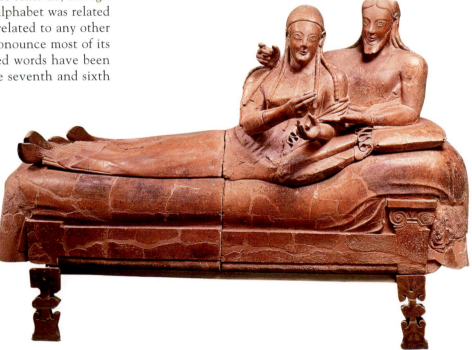

Fig. 6.3 Sarcophagus, from Cerveteri, Italy. ca. 520 BCE. Terra cotta, length 6'7". Museo Nazionale di Villa Giulia, Rome. The entire sarcophagus was once painted in bright colors.

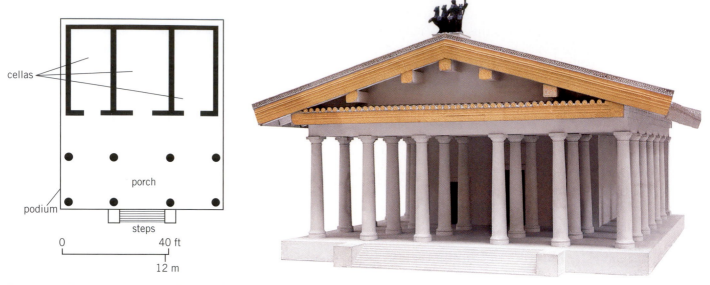

Figs. 6.4 and 6.5 Plan and reconstruction model of an Etruscan temple. Istituto di Etruscologia e Antichità Italiche, University of Rome. Note the sculptures adorning the roof, an innovation in Etruscan architecture very different from the relief sculptures decorating the pediments and entablatures of the Greek temple.

animated, their smiles full, and they seem engaged in a lively dinner conversation. Their smiles, in fact, are reminiscent of those found on Greek Archaic sculptures such as the nearly contemporary *Anavysos Kouros* (see Fig. 4.21 in Chapter 4), suggesting that the Etruscans were acquainted with Greek art.

Architectural Influences Because of their mud-brick wall and wooden-column construction, only the foundations of Etruscan temples survive, but we know something of what they looked like from surviving votive terra-cotta models and from written descriptions. The first-century BCE Roman architect Vitruvius described Etruscan temples in writings that date from between 46 and 39 BCE, 700 years after the Etruscans built them. Vitruvius describes temples constructed on a platform, or **podium**, with a single set of steps up to a porch or portico in front of three interior cellas (modern archeological evidence demonstrates that there were many other arrangements as well, including one- and two-cella temples). The ground plan was almost square, and the space was divided about equally between the porch and three interior cellas which probably housed cult statues (Figs. **6.4** and **6.5**).

The Etruscans also adapted the Greek Doric order to their own ends, creating what Vitruvius called the **Tuscan order** (Fig. **6.6**). The Tuscan order used an unfluted, or smooth, shaft and a pedestal base. Overall, the Tuscan order shares with the Doric a sense of geometric simplicity. But the Etruscan temples were also heavily decorated with brightly colored paintings, probably similar to those that survive in the tombs, and their roofs were decorated with sculptural groups. Both of these features must have lent them an air of visual richness and complexity.

The later Romans modified the Tuscan order by adding a much more elaborate pedestal, but their debt to Etruscan temples is especially evident if we compare the Etruscan

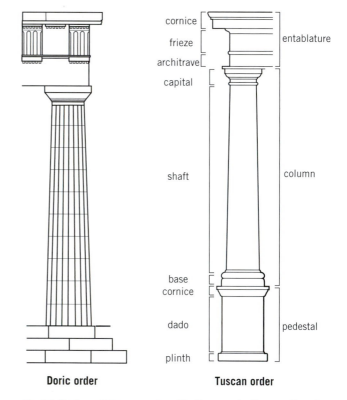

Fig. 6.6 Doric and Tuscan orders. The Tuscan order illustrated here is a later Roman version of the early Tuscan order. The simple base of the column, evident in the temple model in Fig. 6.5 but never found in the Doric order, was elaborated by the Romans into a pedestal composed of a plinth, a dado, and a base cornice.

model and its plan to a Roman temple from the late second century BCE (Figs. **6.7** and **6.8**), the Temple of Portunus (also known as the Temple of Fortuna Virilis). Dedicated to Portunus, the god of harbors and ports, the temple stands beside the Tiber River and represents a mixture of Etruscan and Greek influences. Like the Etruscan temple, it is

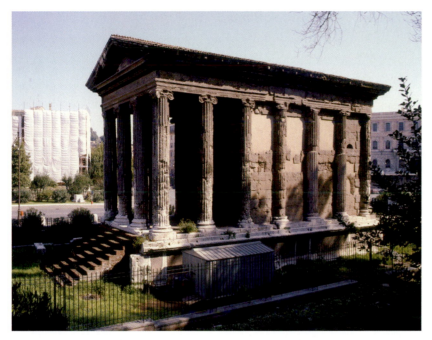

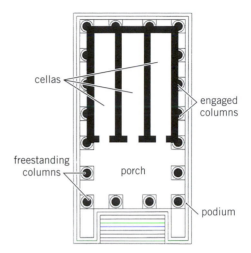

cellas

engaged columns

freestanding columns

porch

podium

Figs. 6.7 and 6.8 Plan and Temple of Fortuna Virilis (Temple of Portunus), Forum Boarium (cattle market), Rome. Late 2nd century BCE. This temple stood next to the Bridge of Aemilius, remnants of which still survive. The bridge crossed the River Tiber just below Tiber Island.

elevated on a podium and approached by a set of stairs at the front. Although more rectangular than its Etruscan ancestor, its floor plan is similarly divided between exterior porch and interior space. But it uses the Greek Ionic order, and its Ionic columns represent a new direction in exterior design. Though freestanding on the porch, they are *engaged* around the cella. That is, they serve no real support function, but rather are decorative additions that give the effect of a continuous colonnade surrounding the entire structure.

The double ancestry of the Temple of Portunus, both Etruscan and Greek, is reflected in almost every aspect of early Roman culture. Even geographically, Rome lies between the two cultures, with the Greek colonies to the south and the Etruscan settlements to the north. Its situation, in fact, is geographically improbable. Rome was built on a hilly site (seven hills to be precise) on the east bank of the Tiber. Its low-lying areas were swampy and subject to flooding, while the higher elevations of the hillsides did not easily lend themselves to building. The River Tiber itself provides a sensible explanation for the city's original siting, since it gave the city a trade route to the north and access to the sea at its port of Ostia to the south. And so does Tiber Island, next to the Temple of Portunus, which was one of the river's primary crossings from the very earliest times. Thus, Rome was physically and literally the crossing place of Etruscan and Greek cultures.

The Etruscan Founding Myth The city also had competing foundation myths. One was Etruscan. Legend had it that twin infants named Romulus and Remus were left to die on the banks of the Tiber but were rescued by a she-wolf who suckled them (Fig. **6.9**). Raised by a shepherd, the twins decided to build a city on the Palatine Hill above the spot where they had been saved (accounting, in the manner of foundation myths, for the unlikely location of the

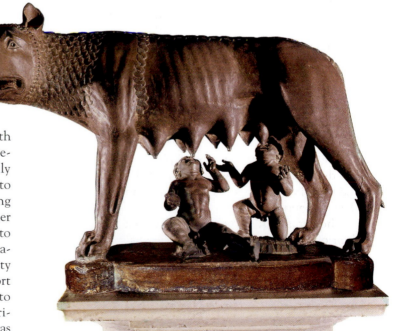

Fig. 6.9 *She-Wolf*. ca. 500–480 BCE. Bronze, with glass-paste eyes, height 33". Museo Capitolino, Rome. Scholars have recently suggested that the sculpture dates from medieval times. The two suckling figures representing Romulus and Remus are Renaissance additions. This Etruscan bronze, which became a symbol of Rome, combines a ferocious realism with the stylized portrayal of, for instance, the wolf's geometrically regular mane.

city). Soon, the two boys feuded over who would rule the new city. In his *History of Rome*, the Roman historian Livy (59 BCE–17 CE) briefly describes the ensuing conflict:

> Then followed an angry altercation; heated passions led to bloodshed; in the tumult Remus was killed. The more common report is that Remus contemptuously jumped over the newly raised walls and was forthwith killed by the enraged Romulus, who exclaimed, "So shall it be henceforth with every one who leaps over my walls." Romulus thus became sole ruler, and the city was called after him, its founder.

The date, legend has it, was 753 BCE.

It has long been known that the figures of Romulus and Remus in the she-wolf sculpture are Renaissance additions, but scholars now believe the work itself is of medieval origin. Results of carbon dating of its bronze conducted at the University of Salerno in 2008 have resulted in a very precise indication that it was cast in the thirteenth century CE. In addition, it appears as if the method used to cast the bronze was unknown in Classical times. Nevertheless, the centrality of the she-wolf to Roman legend is indisputable.

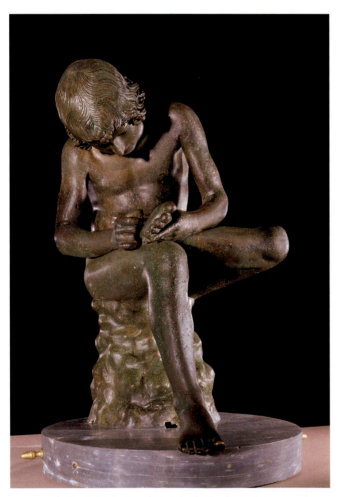

Fig. 6.10 *Thorn-Puller.* **Late 1st century** BCE. Bronze, height 33". Museo Capitolino, Rome. The statue is one of the few large-scale bronze sculptures to survive from antiquity.

The Greek Roots

The second founding myth, as told by the poet Virgil (70–19 BCE) in his epic poem the *Aeneid*, was Greek in its inspiration. By the second and first centuries BCE, Rome had achieved political control of the entire Mediterranean. But even after Rome conquered Greece in 146 BCE, Greece dominated Rome culturally. The Romans loved Greek art (see Chapter 5, *Continuity & Change*). Even works of art that may be original to Rome, like the first-century CE bronze *Thorn-Puller* (Fig. **6.10**), reveal strong Hellenistic influence. Depicting a young boy pulling a thorn from his foot, this statue is derived from Hellenistic models of the third century BCE for the body, with a head derived from Greek works of the fifth century BCE. The boy is probably a slave—masters rarely provided shoes for their slaves—or, given the rock he is sitting on, he might be a boy from the countryside. The realistic portrayal of his self-absorbed and intense concentration combined with the beauty of his physique both suggest the Roman attraction to Hellenistic precedents.

Rome's sense of its Greek origins is nowhere more forcefully stated than in the story of its founding by the Trojan warrior Aeneas, who at the end of the Trojan War sailed off to found a new homeland for his people. Aeneas' story is recounted by Virgil in the *Aeneid*, which was written around 30–19 BCE. In the following extract from Book 2, Virgil recounts Laocoön's warning to his countrymen not to accept the "gift" of a wooden horse from the Greeks (**Reading 6.1a**):

READING 6.1a

from Virgil, *Aeneid*, Book 2

"Are you crazy wretched people?
Do you think they have gone, the foe? Do you think that any
Gifts of the Greeks lack treachery? Ulysses,[1]—
What was his reputation? Let me tell you,
Either the Greeks are hiding in this monster,
Or it's some trick of war, a spy, or engine,
To come down on the city. Tricky business
Is hiding in it. Do not trust it, Trojans,
Do not believe this horse. Whatever it may be,
I fear the Greeks even when bringing presents."
With that, he hurled the great spear at the side
With all the strength he had. I hastened, trembling,
And the struck womb rang hollow, a moaning sound.

[1] **Ulysses:** the Roman name for Odysseus.

Laocoön's warning is ignored (see Chapter 5, *Continuity & Change*), and a few pages later, Aeneas describes how the gods (probably Athena) who supported the Greeks punished Laocoön, entangling him in the coiled snakes, which crush him together with his sons—the subject of the famous sculpture that belonged to the Roman emperor Titus (r. 79–81 CE) in Rome (see Fig. 5.28 in Chapter 5).

And yet Virgil's poem Romanizes the story. Virgil incorporates Greek culture as part and parcel of Roman tradition even as he rejects it, a fact that becomes apparent in comparing Virgil's version to Homer's description of the same scene in the *Odyssey*. At the end of Book 8, Odysseus asks a minstrel to sing the story of the wooden horse:

READING 6.1b

from Homer, *Odyssey*, Book 8

The minstrel stirred, murmuring to the god, and soon
clear words and notes came one by one, a vision
of the Akhaians in their graceful ships
drawing away from shore: the torches flung
and shelters flaring: Argive soldiers crouched
in the close dark around Odysseus: and
the horse, tall on the assembly ground of Troy.
For when the Trojans pulled it in, themselves,
up to the citadel, they say nearby
with long-drawn-out and hapless argument—
favoring, in the end, one course of three:
either to stave the vault with brazen axes,
or to haul it to a cliff and pitch it down,
or else to save it for the gods, a votive glory—
the plan that could not but prevail.
For Troy must perish, as ordained, that day. ...

Though Laocoön's position on the wooden horse is articulated, no mention is made of him—nor in the entire *Odyssey*—let alone his terrible fate. Virgil's debt to Homer is clear. In fact, the first six books of the *Aeneid*, in which Aeneas' wanderings through the Mediterranean are narrated, could be said to mirror the *Odyssey*, while the last six books are a war story similar to the *Iliad*. But Laocoön is not a Homeric character (Virgil probably knew him through a Greek epic cycle dating from the seventh and sixth centuries BCE, of which only a few fragments survive). He is, by and large, a Roman invention.

If the Romans trace their origins to the Trojans, Laocoön functions in Virgil's poem as almost the sole embodiment of wisdom among their ancestors and as Rome's first martyr, sacrificed together with his children to the gods. Virgil's poem celebrates this martyrdom. But Laocoön's warning against Greeks bearing gifts had clear cultural implications for Virgil. In Book 6, the ghost of Aeneas' father Anchises tells his son (see also Chapter 5, *Continuity & Change*):

READING 6.1c

from Virgil, *Aeneid*, Book 6

Others, no doubt, will better mold the bronze
To the semblance of soft breathing, draw, from marble,
The living countenance; and others plead

With greater eloquence, or learn to measure,
Better than we, the pathways of the heaven,
The risings of the stars: remember, Roman,
To rule the people under law, to establish
The way of peace, to battle down the haughty,
To spare the meek. Our fine arts, these, forever.

If the Greeks brought to Rome the gifts of art, rhetoric, and scientific knowledge, it remained for Rome to rule wisely—this was the art it practiced best. Good governance would become, Virgil's *Aeneid* argued, Rome's historical destiny.

REPUBLICAN ROME

How is the Roman patronage system reflected in the art and literature of the Republic?

By the time of Virgil, the Greek and Etruscan myths had merged. Accordingly, Aeneas' son founded the city of Alba Longa, just to the south of Rome, which was ruled by a succession of kings until Romulus brought it under Roman control.

According to legend, Romulus inaugurated the traditional Roman distinction between **patricians**, the land-owning aristocrats who served as priests, magistrates, lawyers, and judges, and **plebians**, the poorer class who were craftspeople, merchants, and laborers. When, in 510 BCE, the Romans expelled the last of the Etruscan kings and decided to rule themselves without a monarch, the patrician/plebian distinction became very similar to the situation in fifth-century BCE Athens. There, a small aristocracy who owned the good land and large estates shared citizenship with a much larger working class (see Chapter 5).

In Rome, as in the Greek model, every free male was a citizen, but in the Etruscan manner, not every citizen enjoyed equal privileges. The Senate, the political assembly in charge of creating law, was exclusively patrician. In reaction, the plebians formed their own legislative assembly, the Consilium Plebis (Council of Plebians), to protect themselves from the patricians, but the patricians were immune from any laws the plebians passed, known as *plebiscites*. Finally, in 287 BCE, the plebiscite became binding law on all citizens, and something resembling equality of citizenship was assured.

The expulsion of the Etruscan kings and the dedication of the Temple of Jupiter on the Capitoline Hill in 509 BCE mark the beginning of actual historical records documenting the development of Rome. They also mark the beginning of the Roman Republic, a state whose political organization rested on the principle that the citizens were the ultimate source of legitimacy and sovereignty. Many people believe that the Etruscan bronze

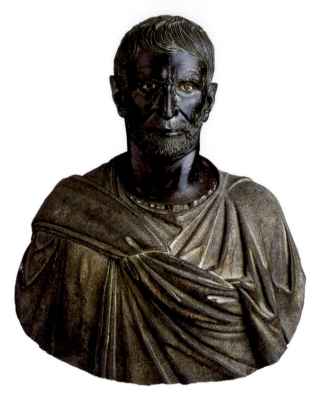

Fig. 6.11 *Head of a Man* **(possibly a portrait of Lucius Junius Brutus). ca. 300 BCE.** Bronze, height 27½". Museo Capitolino, Palazzo dei Conservatori, Rome. The eyes, which look slightly past the viewer, and the intensely furrowed brow, give the figure an almost visionary force and suggest the influence of Lysippus (compare Fig. 5.18 in Chapter 5).

head of a man (Fig. **6.11**) is a portrait of Lucius Junius Brutus, the founder and first consul of the Roman Republic. However, it dates from approximately 100 to 200 years after Brutus' life, and it more likely represents a noble "type," an imaginary portrait of a Roman founding father, or *pater*, the root of the word *patrician*. This role is conveyed through the figure's strong character and strength of purpose.

In republican Rome, every plebian chose a patrician as his patron—and, indeed, most patricians were themselves clients of some other patrician of higher status—whose duty it was to represent the plebian in any matter of law and provide an assortment of assistance in other matters, primarily economic. This paternalistic relationship—which we call *patronage*—reflected the family's central role in Roman culture. The *pater*, "father," protected not only his wife and family but also his clients, who submitted to his patronage. In return for the *pater*'s protection, family and client equally owed the *pater* their total obedience—which the Romans referred to as *pietas*, "dutifulness." So embedded was this attitude that when toward the end of the first century BCE the Republic declared itself an empire, the emperor was called *pater patriae*, "father of the fatherland."

Roman Rule

By the middle of the third century BCE, the Republic had embarked on a series of military exploits known as the Punic

Wars that recall Alexander's imperial adventuring of the century before. For over 100 years, beginning in 264 BCE, the Republic advanced against Carthage, the Phoenician state in present-day Tunisia (see Map 6.1). Carthage controlled most of the wealth of the western Mediterranean, including the vast agricultural and commercial resources of Sicily, Sardinia, Corsica, and the eastern portion of the Iberian peninsula.

In his *History of Rome*, Livy immortalized the Carthaginian general Hannibal's march, from what is now Spain, over the Pyrenees, across the Rhône River, and through the Alps with his army of nearly 100,000 men—including a contingent of elephants. (Perhaps this was meant to imitate the armies of India that had terrorized Alexander's troops.) Hannibal laid waste to most of northern Italy, defeating an army of 80,000 men in 216 BCE, the worst defeat in Roman history. But Rome eventually defeated him by adopting a policy of cutting off supplies from the Iberian peninsula, and counterattacking back home in Carthage. When Hannibal returned to defend his homeland, in 202 BCE, without ever having lost a battle to the Romans in Italy, he was defeated by the general Scipio Africanus (236–ca. 184 BCE) in northern Africa. Despite the fact that Hannibal had occupied Italy for 15 years, marching to the very gates of Rome in 211 BCE, his eventual defeat led the Romans (and their potential adversaries) to believe Rome was invincible.

Meanwhile, in the eastern Mediterranean, Philip V of Macedonia (r. 221–179 BCE), Alexander's heir, had made an alliance with Hannibal and threatened to overrun the Greek peninsula. With Greek help, the Romans defeated him in the northern Greek region of Thessaly in 197 BCE, then pressed on into Asia Minor, which they controlled by 189 BCE. (Just over 50 years later, in 133 BCE, Attalus III of Pergamon would deed his city and all its wealth to Rome.) Finally, in the Third Punic War (149–146 BCE), the Romans took advantage of a weakened Carthage and destroyed the city, plowing it under and sprinkling salt in the furrows to symbolize the city's permanent demise. Its citizens were sold into slavery. When all was said and done, Rome controlled almost the entire Mediterranean world (see Map 6.1).

The Aftermath of Conquest Whenever Rome conquered a region, it established permanent colonies of veteran soldiers who received allotments of land, virtually guaranteeing them a certain level of wealth and status. These soldiers were citizens. If the conquered people proved loyal to Rome, they could gain full Roman citizenship. Furthermore, when not involved in combat, the local Roman soldiery transformed themselves into engineers, building roads, bridges, and civic projects of all types, significantly improving the region. In this way, the Republic diminished the adversarial status of its colonies and gained their loyalty.

The prosperity brought about by Roman expansion soon created a new kind of citizen in Rome. They called themselves *equites* ("equestrians") to connect them to the cavalry, the elite part of the military, since only the wealthy could afford the necessary horses. The *equites* were wealthy businessmen, but not often landowners and therefore not patricians. The patricians considered the commercial exploits of the *equites* crass and their wealth ill-gotten. Soon the two groups were in open conflict, the *equites* joining ranks with the plebians.

The Senate was the patrician stronghold, and it feared any loss of power and authority. When the general Pompey the Great (106–48 BCE) returned from a victorious campaign against rebels in Asia Minor in 62 BCE, the Senate refused to ratify the treaties he had made in the region and refused to grant the land allotments he had given his soldiers. Outraged, Pompey joined forces with two other successful military leaders. One had put down the slave revolt of Spartacus in 71 BCE. The other was Gaius Julius Caesar (100–44 BCE), a military leader from a prestigious patrician family that claimed descent from Aeneas and Venus. The union of these three leaders became known as the First Triumvirate.

A Divided Empire Wielding the threat of civil war, the First Triumvirate soon dominated the Republic's political life, but theirs was a fragile relationship. Caesar accepted a five-year appointment as governor of Gaul, present-day France. By 49 BCE, he had brought all of Gaul under his control. He summed up this conquest in his *Commentaries* in the famous phrase "*Veni, vidi, vici*"—"I came, I saw, I conquered"—a statement that captures, perhaps better than any other, the militaristic nature of the Roman state as a whole. He was preparing to return home when Pompey joined forces with the Senate. They reminded Caesar of a long-standing tradition that required a returning commander to leave his army behind, in this case on the Gallic side of the Rubicon River, but Caesar refused. Pompey fled to Greece, where Caesar defeated him a year later. Again Pompey fled, this time to Egypt, where he was murdered. The third member of the Triumvirate had been captured and executed several years earlier.

Now unimpeded, Caesar assumed dictatorial control over Rome. Caesar treated the Senate with disdain, and most of its membership counted themselves as his enemies. On March 15, 44 BCE, the Ides of March, he was stabbed 23 times by a group of 60 senators at the foot of a sculpture honoring Pompey on the floor of the Senate. This scene was memorialized in English by Shakespeare's great play *Julius Caesar* and Caesar's famous line, as he sees his ally Marcus Junius Brutus (85–42 BCE) among the assassins, "*Et tu, Brute?*"—"You also, Brutus?" Brutus and the others believed they had freed Rome of a tyrant, but the people were outraged, the Senate disgraced, and Caesar considered a martyr.

Caesar had recognized that his position was precarious, and he had prepared a member of his own family to assume power in his place, his grandnephew, Gaius Octavius, known as Octavian (63 BCE–14 CE), whom he adopted as son and heir. Although only 18 years old when Caesar died,

Octavian quickly defeated his main rival, Marcus Antonius (ca. 82–30 BCE), known to most English speakers as Mark Antony. Octavian then adroitly formed an alliance with the defeated Marcus Antonius and Marcus Emilius Lepidus (died ca. 12 BCE), another of Caesar's officers, known as the Second Triumvirate. Octavian and Antonius pursued Cassius and Brutus into Macedonia and defeated them at the Battle of Philippi. Octavian, Antonius, and Lepidus then divided up the Empire, which was larger than any one person could control and govern: Lepidus got Africa, Antonius the eastern provinces including Egypt, and Octavian the west, including Rome. Lepidus soon plotted against Octavian, but Octavian persuaded Lepidus' troops to desert him. Antonius, meanwhile, had formed an alliance with Cleopatra VII, the queen of Egypt (r. 51–31 BCE). When Octavian defeated Antonius at the Battle of Actium in 31 BCE, Antonius and Cleopatra committed suicide. Octavian was left the sole ruler of the Empire. He assumed power as a monarch in everything but actual title.

Cicero and the Politics of Rhetoric

In times of such political upheaval, it is not surprising that one of the most powerful figures of the day would be someone who specialized in the art of political persuasion. In pre-Augustan Rome, that person was the **rhetorician** (writer and public speaker, or orator) Marcus Tullius Cicero (106–43 BCE). First and foremost, Cicero recognized the power of the Latin language to communicate with the people. Although originally used almost exclusively as the language of commerce, Latin, by the first century CE, was understood to be potentially a more powerful tool of persuasion than Greek, still the literary language of the upper classes. The clarity and eloquence of Cicero's style can be quickly discerned, even in translation, as an excerpt (**Reading 6.2**) from his essay *On Duty* demonstrates.

READING 6.2

from Cicero, *On Duty*

That moral goodness which we look for in a lofty, high-minded spirit is secured, of course, by moral, not physical strength. And yet the body must be trained and so disciplined that it can obey the dictates of judgment and reason in attending to business and in enduring toil. But that moral goodness which is our theme depends wholly upon the thought and attention given to it by the mind. And, in this way, the men who in a civil capacity direct the affairs of the nation render no less important service than they who conduct its wars: by their statesmanship oftentimes wars are either averted or terminated; sometimes also they are declared. … And so diplomacy in the friendly settlement of controversies is more desirable than courage in settling them on the battlefield; but we must be careful not to take that course merely for the sake of avoiding war rather than for the sake of public expediency. War, however, should be undertaken in such a way as to make it evident that it has no other object than to secure peace.

But it takes a brave and resolute spirit not to be disconcerted in times of difficulty or ruffled and thrown off one's feet, as the saying is, but to keep one's presence of mind and one's self-possession and not to swerve from the path of reason.

Now all this requires great personal courage; but it also calls for great intellectual ability by reflection to anticipate the future, to discover some time in advance what may happen whether for good or for ill, and what must be done in any possible event, and never to be reduced to having to say "I had not thought of that."

The dangers attending great affairs of state fall sometimes on those who undertake them, sometimes upon the state. In carrying out such enterprises, some run the risk of losing their lives, others their reputation and the good-will of their fellow-citizens. It is our duty, then, to be more ready to endanger our own than the public welfare and to hazard honor and glory more readily than other advantages. ...

Philosophically, Cicero's argument extends back to Plato and Aristotle, but rhetorically—that is, in the structure of its argument—it is purely Roman. It is purposefully deliberative in tone—that is, its chief concern is to give sage advice rather than to engage in a Socratic dialogue to evolve that advice.

In his speeches and his letters, Cicero was particularly effective. His speeches were notoriously powerful. He understood, as he wrote in *De Oratore* (*Concerning Oratory*), that "Nature has assigned to each emotion a particular look and tone of voice and bearing of its own; and the whole of a person's frame and every look on his face and utterance of his voice are like strings of a harp, and sound according as they are struck by each successive emotion." In his letters, he could be disarmingly frank. After having invited Julius Caesar to dinner—in the struggle between Pompey and Caesar, Cicero had backed Pompey, and he hardly trusted the new dictator—he described the great man in a letter to his friend Atticus (**Reading 6.3**):

nothing serious, a lot about literature: he seemed to enjoy it and have a good time. So now you know about how I entertained him—or rather had him billeted on me. It was a nuisance, as I said, but not unpleasant.

His ambivalence about Caesar notwithstanding, the "dangers attending great affairs of state" that concerned Cicero in his *On Duty* would come back to haunt him. Fearing Cicero's power, and angry that he had called Antonius a tyrant in his speeches, the Second Triumvirate sent troops to hunt him down at his country estate in 43 BCE. Laena, their leader, severed Cicero's head, then presented it, in Rome, to Antonius himself.

Portrait Busts, *Pietas*, and Politics

This historical context helps us understand a major Roman art form of the second and first centuries BCE, the portrait bust. These are generally portraits of patricians (and upper-middle-class citizens wishing to emulate them) rather than

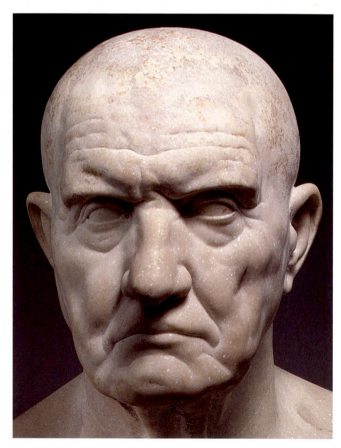

Fig. 6.12 *A Roman Man.* ca. 80 BCE. Marble, life-size. The Metropolitan Museum of Art, New York. Rogers Fund, 1912 (12.233). His face creased by the wrinkles of age, this man is the very image of the *pater*, the man of *gravitas* (literally "weight," but also, "presence" or "influence"), *dignitas* ("dignity," "worth," and "character"), and *fides* ("honesty" and "conscientiousness").

📖 **Read** the document related to Cicero on **MyArtsLab**

equites. Roman portrait busts share with their Greek ancestors an affinity for naturalistic representation, but they are even more realistic, revealing their subjects' every wrinkle and wart (Fig. **6.12**). This form of realism is known as **verism** (from the Latin *veritas*, "truth"). Indeed, the high level of naturalism may have resulted from their original form, wax ancestral masks, usually made at the peak of the subject's power, called *imagines*, which were then transferred to stone.

CONTINUITY&CHANGE

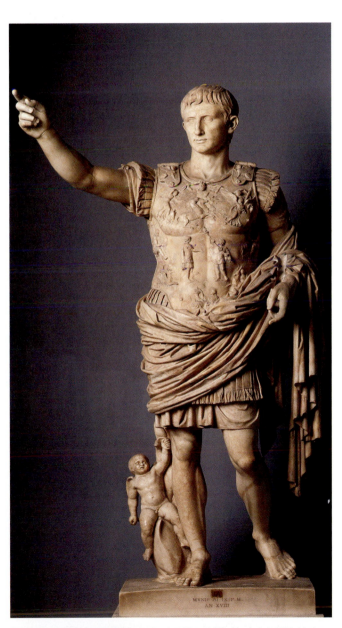

Alexander the Great, p. 156

Compared to the Greek Hellenistic portrait bust—recall Lysippus' portrait of Alexander (see Fig. 5.18 in Chapter 5), copies of which proliferated throughout the Mediterranean in the third century BCE—the Roman portrait differs particularly in the age of the sitter. Both the Greek and Roman busts are essentially propagandistic in intent, designed to extol the virtues of the sitter, but where Alexander is portrayed as a young man at the height of his powers, the usual Roman portrait bust depicts its subject at or near the end of life. The Greek portrait bust, in other words, signifies youthful possibility and ambition, while the Roman version claims for its subject the wisdom and experience of age. These images celebrate *pietas*, the deep-seated Roman virtue of dutiful respect toward the gods, fatherland, and parents. To respect one's parents was tantamount, for the Romans, to respecting one's moral obligations to the gods. The respect one owed one's parents was, in effect, a religious obligation.

If the connection to Alexander—especially the emphasis in both on the power of the gaze—is worth considering, the Roman portrait busts depict a class under attack, a class whose virtues and leadership were being threatened by upstart generals and *equites*. They are, in other words, the very picture of conservative politics. Their furrowed brows represent their wisdom, their wrinkles their experience, their extraordinarily naturalistic representation their character. They represent the Senate itself, which should be honored, not disdained.

IMPERIAL ROME

How do the art and architecture of imperial Rome reflect the aspirations of its emperors?

On January 13, 27 BCE, Octavian came before the Senate and gave up all his powers and provinces. It was a rehearsed event. The Senate begged him to reconsider and take Syria, Gaul, and the Iberian peninsula for his own (these provinces just happened to contain 20 of the 26 Roman legions, guaranteeing him military support). They also asked him to retain his title as Consul of Rome, with the supreme authority of *imperium*, the power to give orders and exact obedience, over all of Italy and subsequently all Roman-controlled territory. He agreed "reluctantly"

to these terms, and the Senate, in gratitude, granted him the semidivine title Augustus, "the revered one." Augustus (r. 27 BCE–14 CE) thereafter portrayed himself as a near-deity. The *Augustus of Primaporta* (Fig. **6.13**) is the slightly larger-than-life-size sculpture named for its location at the home of Augustus' wife, Livia, at Primaporta, on the outskirts of Rome. Augustus is represented as the embodiment of the famous admonition given to Aeneas by his dead father (*Aeneid*, Book 6), "To rule the people under law, to establish / The way of peace."

Augustus, like Aeneas, is duty-bound to exhibit *pietas*, the obligation to his ancestor "to rule earth's peoples."

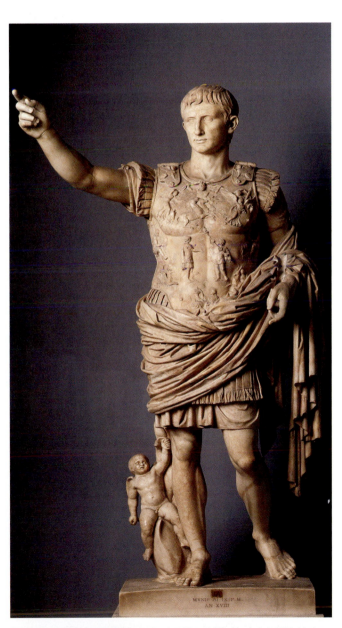

Fig. 6.13 *Augustus of Primaporta.* **CA. 20 BCE.** Marble, height 6'8". Vatican Museums, Vatican State. On the breastplate, a bearded Parthian from Asia Minor hands over Roman standards that had been lost in a battle of 53 BCE. In 20 BCE, when the original version of this statue was carved—most scholars believe this is actually a later copy—Augustus had won them back.

The sculpture, though recognizably Augustus, is nevertheless idealized. It adopts the pose and ideal proportions of Polyclitus' *Doryphoros* (see Fig. 5.4 in Chapter 5). The gaze, reminiscent of the look of Alexander the Great, purposefully recalls the visionary hero of Greece who died 300 years earlier. The right arm is extended in the gesture of *ad locutio*—he is giving a (military) address. The military garb announces his role as commander-in-chief. Riding a dolphin at his feet is a small Cupid, son of the goddess Venus, laying claim to the Julian family's divine descent from Venus and Aeneas. Though Augustus was over 70 years old when he died, he was always depicted as young and vigorous, choosing to portray himself, apparently, as the ideal leader rather than the wise, older *pater*.

CONTINUITY & CHANGE

Doryphoros, **p. 141**

Augustus was careful to maintain at least the trappings of the Republic. The Senate stayed in place, but Augustus soon eliminated the distinction between patricians and *equites* and fostered the careers of all capable individuals, whatever their origin. Some he made provincial governors, others administrators in the city, and he encouraged still others to enter political life. Soon the Senate was populated with many men who had never dreamed of political power. All of them—governors, administrators, and politicians—owed everything to Augustus. Their loyalty further solidified his power.

Family Life

Augustus also quickly addressed what he considered to be another crisis in Roman society—the demise of family life. Adultery and divorce were commonplace. There were more slaves and freed slaves in the city than citizens, let alone aristocrats. And family size, given the cost of living in the city, was diminishing. He reacted by criminalizing adultery and passed several other laws to promote family life. Men between the ages of 20 and 60 and women between the ages of 20 and 50 were required to marry. A divorced woman was required to remarry within six months, a widow within a year. Childless adults were punished with high taxes or deprived of inheritance. The larger an aristocrat's family, the greater his political advantage. It is no coincidence that when Augustus commissioned a large monument to commemorate his triumphal return after establishing Roman rule in Gaul and restoring peace to Rome, the *Ara Pacis Augustae* (Altar of Augustan Peace), he had its

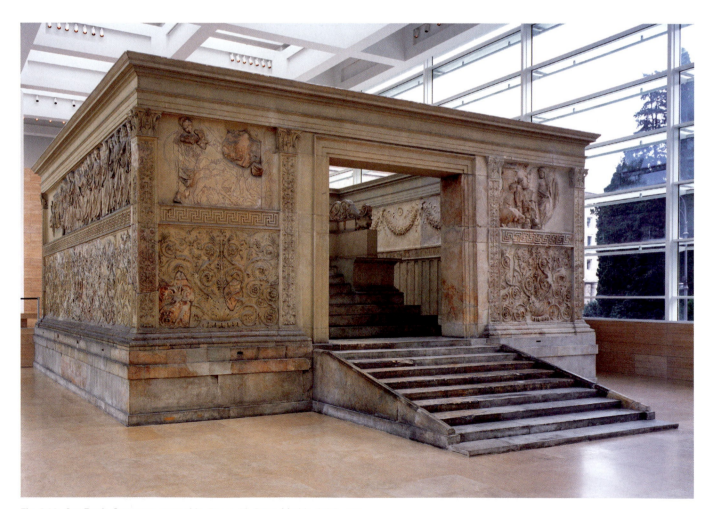

Fig. 6.14 *Ara Pacis Augustae*, **west side. Rome. 13–9 BCE.** Marble, 34'5" × 38'.

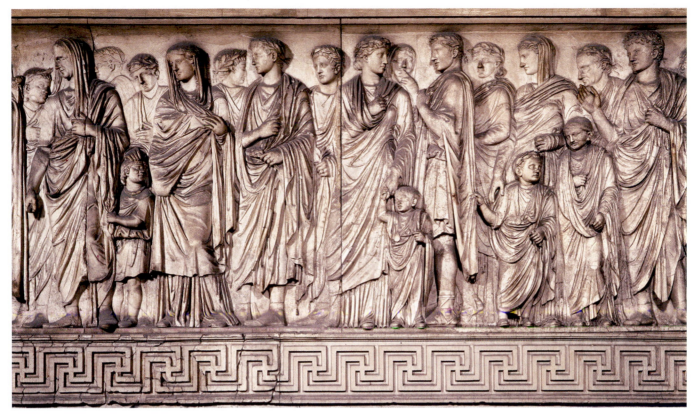

Fig. 6.15 *Ara Pacis Augustae*, **detail of Imperial Procession, south frieze. Rome. 13–9 BCE.** Marble, width approx. 35'. At the left is Marcus Agrippa, Augustus' son-in-law, married to his daughter Julia. The identities of the other figures are not secure, but scholars speculate that clinging to Agrippa's robe is either a foreign child belonging to Agrippa's household or Augustus' grandson, Gaius Caesar, who with his brother Lucius often traveled with their grandfather and whom Augustus taught to imitate his own handwriting. The child looks backward and up at Augustus' wife, Livia, one of the most powerful people in Rome. Behind Livia is her son by an earlier marriage, Tiberius, who would succeed Augustus as emperor.

exterior walls on the south decorated with a retinue of his own large family, a model for all Roman citizens, in a procession of lictors (the class of citizens charged with guarding and attending to the needs of magistrates), priests, magistrates, senators, and other representatives of the Roman people (Figs. **6.14** and **6.15**).

Art historians believe that the *Ara Pacis Augustae* represents a real event, perhaps a public rejoicing for Augustus' reign (it was begun in 13 BCE when he was 50), or the dedication of the altar itself, which occurred on Livia's fiftieth birthday in 9 BCE. The realism of the scene is typically Roman. A sense of spatial depth is created by depicting figures farther away from us in low relief and those closest to us in high relief, so high in fact that the feet of the nearest figures project over the architectural frame into our space (visible in the detail, Fig. 6.15). This technique would have encouraged viewers—the Roman public—to feel that they were part of the same space as the figures in the sculpture itself. The Augustan peace is the peace enjoyed by the average Roman citizen, the Augustan family a metaphor for the larger family of Roman citizens.

The *Ara Pacis Augustae* is preeminently a celebration of family. Three generations of Augustus' family are depicted in the relief. It also demonstrates the growing prominence of women in Roman society. Augustus' wife, Livia, is depicted holding Augustus' family together, standing between her stepson-in-law, Marcus Agrippa, and her own sons, Tiberius and Drusus.

Livia became a figure of idealized womanhood in Rome. She was the "female leader" of Augustus' programs of reform, a sponsor of architectural projects, and a trusted advisor to both her husband and son. While Livia enjoyed greater power and influence than most, Roman women possessed the rights of citizenship, although they could not vote or hold public office. Still, married women retained their legal identity. They controlled their own property and managed their own legal affairs. Elite women modeled themselves after Livia, wielding power through their husbands and sons.

Education of the Sexes

The Romans educated their girls like their boys. Patricians probably hired tutors for their daughters, but the middle classes sent both their boys and girls to school until they were 12 years old, where they learned to read, write, and

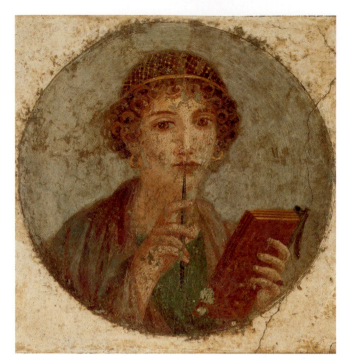

Fig. 6.16 *Young Woman Writing*, **detail of a wall painting from Pompeii. Late 1st century CE.** Diameter 14⅝". Museo Archeologico Nazionale, Naples. Women at all levels of society, except the very poorest, apparently learned to read and write.

READING 6.4

from Juvenal, *Satires*

Exasperating is the woman who begs as soon as she sits down to dinner to discourse on poets and poetry. ... She rattles on at such a pitch that you'd think that all the pots and pans in the kitchen were crashing to the floor and that every bell in town was clanging. ... She should learn the philosopher's lesson: "moderation is necessary even for intellectuals." And if she still wants to appear educated and eloquent, let her dress as a man, sacrifice to men's gods, and bathe in men's baths. Wives shouldn't try to be public speakers; they shouldn't use rhetorical devices; they shouldn't read the classics—there should be some things women don't understand. I myself cannot understand a woman who can quote the rules of grammar and never make a mistake and cite obscure, long-forgotten poets—as if men cared for such things.

calculate. Education as a whole was left largely to Greeks, who came to Rome in Republican times to teach language, literature, and philosophy, as well as what the Romans called *humanitas*. *Humanitas* was considered the equivalent of the Greek *paideia*, the process of educating a person into his or her true and genuine form. It developed from Plato's insistence on the four sciences—arithmetic, geometry, astronomy, and music—as well as grammar and rhetoric. Both formed the core of the curriculum from Roman times through the Middle Ages. Through the study of Classical Greek literature, a student possessing true *humanitas* should be able to find beauty in the equilibrium and harmony of a work of art, which should in turn inspire the student to search for such beauty in his or her own way of life.

Most Romans learned Greek from a teacher called a *grammaticus*, who taught not only rhetoric and grammar but also Greek literature, especially Homer. As a result, most Romans were bilingual. As Latin began to establish a literature of its own—it was initially the language of politics, law, and commerce—translation became a course of study, and the great Greek classics were soon available in Latin.

In a wall painting from Pompeii (Fig. **6.16**), a young woman bites on her stylus, as if contemplating her next words. Perhaps she is a poet. There were notable women poets in Roman times, including Julia Balbilla and Sulpicia, an elegist who was accepted into male literary circles. Women were, at any rate, sufficiently well educated that the satirist Juvenal would complain about it in his *Satires*, written in the early second century CE (**Reading 6.4**).

For all the misogyny in Juvenal's diatribe, one thing is clear: Women understand most everything that men do—and maybe better. His is a world in which women have attained an education at least comparable to that of men.

The Philosophy of the City: Chance and Reason

Many wealthier Romans hired Greek philosophers to teach their children in their own homes, and as a result Roman philosophy is almost wholly borrowed from the Greeks. Two of the most attractive philosophical systems to the Romans were Epicureanism and Stoicism.

Epicureanism Epicurus (341–270 BCE) was a Greek philosopher who taught in Athens. His ideas were promoted in Rome, particularly by the poet Lucretius (ca. 99–ca. 55 BCE) in his treatise *On the Nature of Things*. **Epicureanism** is based on the theory of Epicurus, who believed that fear, particularly fear of death, was responsible for all human misery, and that the gods played no part in human affairs. All things, he argued, are driven by the random movement of atoms swirling through space. There are no first causes or final explanations, only chance. Thus, life can be enjoyed with complete serenity, and pleasure is the object of human life. At death, he concluded, our atoms simply disperse. Epicurus' philosophy might seem hedonistic, but, in fact, he argued that pleasure of the soul, attained through the quiet contemplation of philosophy, was far preferable to bodily pleasure. He stressed clarity and simplicity of thought, and "sober reasoning." In Lucretius' version of the philosophy, love is but a mental delusion.

Stoicism Most Romans rejected Epicureanism because they associated it with self-indulgence and debauchery, despite Lucretius' efforts to emphasize its more moderate and intellectual aspects. **Stoicism**, a hardheaded, practical philosophy that had developed in the Athenian stoa during the late fourth and early third centuries BCE, was far more popular. In the first century CE, as the population of Rome approached 1 million and the Empire expanded almost unimaginably, the rational detachment and practical common-sense principles of Stoicism appealed to a citizenry confronting a host of problems related to the sheer size of city and Empire. By submitting one's emotions to the practice of reason, one could achieve what the playwright and essayist Lucius Annaeus Seneca (ca. 8 BCE–65 CE) called "tranquility of mind." In his most famous essay, *Tranquility of Mind*, Seneca argues that the best way to achieve peace of mind is to avoid responsibilities, especially those associated with excessive wealth (**Reading 6.5**):

READING 6.5

from Seneca, *Tranquility of Mind*

Our question, then, is how the mind can maintain a consistent and advantageous course, be kind to itself and take pleasure in its attributes, never interrupt this satisfaction but abide in its serenity, without excitement or depression. This amounts to tranquility. We shall inquire how it may be attained. …

A correct estimate of self is prerequisite, for we are generally inclined to overrate our capacities. One man is tripped by confidence in his eloquence, another makes greater demands upon his estate than it can stand, another burdens a frail body with an exhausting office. Some are too bashful for politics, which require aggressiveness; some are too headstrong for court; some do not control their temper and break into unguarded language at the slightest provocation; some cannot restrain their wit or resist making risky jokes. For all such people retirement is better than a career; an assertive and intolerant temperament should avoid incitements to outspokenness that will prove harmful. …

We pass now to property, the greatest source of affliction to humanity. If you balance all our other troubles—deaths, diseases, fears, longings, subjection to labor and pain—with the miseries in which our money involves us, the latter will far weigh the former. Reflect, then, how much less a grief it is not to have money than to lose it, and then you will realize that poverty has less to torment us with in the degree that it has less to lose. If you suppose that rich men take their losses with greater equanimity you are mistaken; a wound hurts a big man as much as it does a little. …

All life is bondage. Man must therefore habituate himself to his condition, complain of it as little as possible, and grasp whatever good lies with his reach. No situation is so harsh that a dispassionate mind cannot find some consolation in it. If a man lays even a very small area out skillfully it will provide ample space for many uses, and even a foothold can be made livable by deft arrangement. Apply good sense to your problems; the hard can be softened, the narrow widened, and the heavy made lighter by the skillful bearer. …

Seneca's message was especially appealing to many Romans who were struggling for survival in the city. If we are all slaves to our situation, he seemed to argue, then like slaves, we must make of life the best we can. Tragically, Seneca would not get the opportunity to practice what he preached. When his student, the emperor Nero, ordered him to commit suicide, a practice sanctioned by his Stoic philosophy, Seneca obliged.

Literary Rome: Catullus, Virgil, Horace, and Ovid

Perhaps the most influential poet in Rome before the Augustan age was Gaius Valerius Catullus (ca. 84–54 BCE). In his short life, Catullus wrote only 114 poems, many of them very short, but in their insistence on revealing the details of his personal emotional life, they reflect the Roman taste for the kind of verism we see in the ancestral masks and sculptures that dominate Roman portraiture (see Fig. 6.12). Particularly popular were a series of poems written to a woman many believe to be one Clodia, sister of a Roman patrician and senator, and wife of another, with whom he had a passionate if short-lived affair. In the poems, he addresses her as Lesbia, a clear reference to the poems of Sappho (see Readings 4.6a and 4.6b in Chapter 4), and a testament to the Greek poet's lasting influence on Roman literature. Catullus' poems to Lesbia move from the passion of his early infatuation to a growing sense of despair that their love will not last (see **Reading 6.6** on page 213).

Catullus' work influenced virtually all subsequent Roman poets, but where Catullus worked independently, after Augustus took control of Rome, all artistic patronage passed through his office. During the civil wars, the two major poets of the day, Virgil and Horace, had lost all their property, but Augustus' patronage allowed them to keep on with their writings. Because the themes they pursued were subject to Augustus' approval, they tended to glorify both the emperor and his causes. He was far less supportive of the poet Ovid, whom he permanently banished from Rome.

Virgil and the *Aeneid* After Augustus' triumph over Antony and Cleopatra at the Battle of Actium in 31 BCE, Virgil retired to Naples, where he began work on an epic poem designed to rival Homer's *Iliad* and to provide the Roman state—and Augustus in particular—with a suitably grand founding myth. Previously he had been engaged with two series of pastoral idylls, the *Eclogues* (or *Bucolics*) and the *Georgics*. The latter poems (**Reading 6.7**) are modeled after Hesiod's *Works and Days* (see Chapter 4). They extol the importance of hard work, the necessity of forging order in the face of a hostile natural world, and, perhaps above all, the virtues of agrarian life.

CONTINUITY & CHANGE
Works and Days, **p. 112**

READING 6.7

from Virgil, *Georgics*

In early spring-tide, when the icy drip
Melts from the mountains hoar, and Zephyr's breath
Unbinds the crumbling clod, even then 'tis time;
Press deep your plow behind the groaning ox,

And teach the furrow-burnished share to shine.
That land the craving farmer's prayer fulfils,
Which twice the sunshine, twice the frost has felt;
Ay, that's the land whose boundless harvest-crops
Burst, see! the barns.

The political point of the *Georgics* was to celebrate Augustus' gift of farmlands to veterans of the civil wars, but in its exaltation of the myths and traditions of Italy, it served as a precursor to the *Aeneid*. It was written in **dactylic hexameter**, the verse form that Homer had used in the *Iliad* and *Odyssey* (the metrical form of the translation above, however, is iambic pentameter—five rhythmic units, each short long, as in *dee-dum*—a meter much more natural to English than the Latin dactylic hexameter). In dactylic hexameter, each line consists of six rhythmic units, or **feet**, and each foot is either a **dactyl** (long, short, short, as in *dum-diddy*) or a **spondee** (long, long, as in *dum-dum*). Virgil reportedly wrote the *Georgics* at a pace of less than one line a day, perfecting his understanding of the metrical scheme in preparation for the longer poem.

The *Aeneid* opens in Carthage, where, after the Trojan War, Aeneas and his men have been driven by a storm, and where they are hosted by the Phoenician queen Dido. During a rainstorm, Aeneas and Dido take refuge in a cave, where the queen, having fallen in love with the Trojan hero, gives herself willingly to him. She now assumes that she is married, but Aeneas, reminded by his father's ghost of his duty to accomplish what the gods have predetermined—a classic instance of *pietas*—knows he must resume his destined journey (see **Reading 6.8** on pages 213–215). An angry and accusing Dido begs him to stay. When Aeneas rejects her pleas, Dido vows to haunt him after her death and to bring enmity between Carthage and his descendants forever (a direct reference on Virgil's part to the Punic Wars). As his boat sails away, she commits suicide by climbing a funeral pyre and falling upon a sword. The goddesses of the underworld are surprised to see her. Her death, in their eyes, is neither deserved nor destined, but simply tragic. Virgil's point is almost coldly hard-hearted: All personal feelings and desires must be sacrificed to one's responsibilities to the state. Civic duty takes precedence over private life.

The poem is, on one level, an account of Rome's founding by Aeneas, but it is also a profoundly moving essay on human destiny and the great cost involved in achieving and sustaining the values and principles upon which culture—Roman culture in particular, but all cultures by extension—must be based. Augustus, as Virgil well knew, claimed direct descent from Aeneas, and it is particularly important that the poem presents war, at which Augustus excelled, as a moral tragedy, however necessary.

In Book 7, Venus gives Aeneas a shield made by the god Vulcan. The shield displays the important events in the future history of Rome, including Augustus at the Battle of Actium. Aeneas is, Virgil writes, "without understanding … proud and happy … [at] the fame and glory of his children's children." But in the senseless slaughter that ends the poem, as Aeneas and the Trojans battle Turnus and the Italians, Virgil demonstrates that the only thing worse than not avenging the death of one's friends and family is, perhaps, avenging them. In this sense the poem is a profound plea for peace, a peace that Augustus would dedicate himself to pursuing.

The Horatian *Odes* Quintus Horatius Flaccus, known as Horace (65–8 BCE), was a close friend of Virgil. Impressed by Augustus' reforms, and probably moved by his patronage, Horace was won over to the emperor's cause, which he celebrated directly in two of his many **odes**, lyric poems of elaborate and irregular meter. Horace's odes imitated Greek precedents. The following lines open the fifth ode of Book 3 of the collected poems, known simply as the *Odes*:

Jove [the Roman Zeus, also called Jupiter] rules in
    heaven, his thunder shows;
Henceforth Augustus earth shall own
Her present god, now Briton foes
And Persians bow before his throne.

The subject matter of the *Odes* ranges from these patriotic pronouncements to private incidents in the poet's own life, the joys of the countryside (Fig. 6.17), the pleasures of wine, and so on. His villa offered him an escape from the trials of daily life in Rome itself. In Ode 13 of Book 2, for instance, Horace addresses a tree that had unexpectedly crashed down, nearly killing him (see **Reading 6.9** on page 215). He begins by cursing the man who planted the tree but then concludes that we all fail to pay attention to the real dangers in life. Apparently lost in thought, he begins to imagine the underworld, the abode of departed souls, where he sees the Greek love poet Sappho (see Chapter 4) and the political poet Alcaeus both writing poetry. Their lyrics give comfort to the dead, just as Horace's own poem has comforted him and allowed him to forget his near-death experience. No Roman poet more gracefully harmonized the Greek reverence for beauty with the Roman concern with duty and obligation.

Ovid's *Art of Love* and *Metamorphoses* Augustus' support for poets did not extend to Publius Ovidius Naso, known as Ovid (43 BCE–17 CE). Ovid's talent was for love songs designed to satisfy the notoriously loose sexual mores of the Roman aristocrats, who lived in somewhat open disregard of Augustus and Livia's family-centered lifestyle. His *Ars Amatoria* (*Art of Love*) angered Augustus, as did some undisclosed indiscretion by Ovid. As punishment—probably more for the indiscretion than the poem—Augustus permanently exiled him to the town of Tomis on the Black Sea, the remotest part of the Empire, famous for its wretched weather. The *Metamorphoses*, composed in the years just before his exile, is a collection of stories describing or revolving around one sort of supernatural change of shape

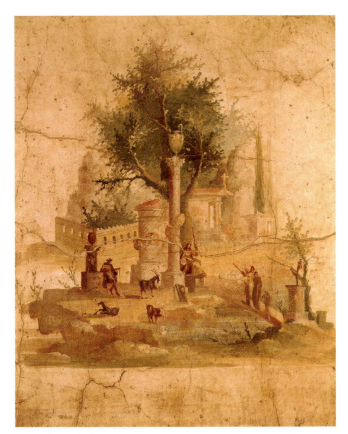

Fig. 6.17 *Idyllic Landscape,* **wall painting from a villa at Boscotrecase, near Pompeii. 1st century BCE.** Museo Archeologico Nazionale, Naples. This landscape depicts the love of country life and the idealizing of nature that is characteristic of the Horatian *Odes.* It contrasts dramatically with urban life in Rome.

or another, from the divine to the human, the animate to the inanimate, the human to the vegetal.

In the *Ars Amatoria,* the poet describes his desire for the fictional Corinna. Ovid outlines the kinds of places in Rome where one can meet women, from porticoes to gaming houses, from horse races to parties, and especially anywhere wine, that great banisher of inhibition, can be had. Women, he says, love clandestine affairs as much as men; they simply do not chase after men, "as a mousetrap does not chase after mice." Become friends with the husband of a woman you desire, he advises. Lie to her—tell her that you only want to be her friend. Nevertheless, he says, "If you want a woman to love you, be a lovable man."

Ovid probably aspired to Virgil's fame, though he could admit, "My life is respectable, but my Muse is full of jesting." His earliest major work, the *Amores* (*Loves*), begins with many self-deprecating references to Virgil's epic, which begins with the famous phrase, "Arms and the man I sing":

> Arms, warfare, violence—I was winding up to produce
> A regular epic, with verse-form to match—
> Hexameters, naturally. But Cupid (they say) with
>   a snicker
> Lopped off one foot from each alternate line.

"Nasty young brat," I told him, "who made *you*
    Inspector of Metres?"

Nevertheless, Ovid uses dactylic hexameter for the *Metamorphoses* and stakes out an epic scope for the poem in its opening lines:

> My intention is to tell of bodies changed
> To different forms; the gods, who made the changes,
> Will help me—or I hope so—with a poem
> That runs from the world's beginning to our
>   own days!

If the *Metamorphoses* is superficially more a collection of stories than an epic, few poems in any language have contributed so importantly to later literature. It is so complete in its survey of the best-known Classical myths, plus stories from Egypt, Persia, and Italy, that it remains a standard reference work. At the same time, it tells its stories in an utterly moving and memorable way. The story of Actaeon, for instance, is a cautionary tale about the power of the gods. Actaeon happens to see the virgin goddess Diana bathing one day when he is out hunting with his dogs. She turns him into a stag to prevent him from ever telling what he has seen. As his own dogs turn on him and savagely tear him apart, his friends call out for him, lamenting his absence from the kill. But he is all too present:

> Well might he wish not to be there, but he was there, and well
>   might he wish to see
> And not to feel the cruel deeds of his dogs.

In the story of Narcissus, Echo falls in love with the beautiful youth Narcissus, but when Narcissus spurns her, she fades away. He in turn is doomed to fall in love with his own image reflected in a pool, according to Ovid, the spring at Clitumnus. So consumed, he finally dies beside the pool, his body transformed into the narcissus flower. In such stories, the duality of identity and change, Aristotle's definition of the essence of a thing, becomes deeply problematic. Ovid seems to deny that any human characteristic is essential, asserting that all is susceptible to change. To subsequent generations of readers, from Shakespeare to Freud, Ovid's versions of myths would raise the fundamental questions that lie at the heart of human identity and psychology.

Augustus and the City of Marble

Of all the problems facing Augustus when he assumed power, the most overwhelming was the infrastructure of Rome. The city was, quite simply, a mess. Seneca reacted by preaching Stoicism. He argued that it was what it was, and one should move on as best one can. Augustus reacted by calling for a series of public works, which would serve the people of Rome and, he well understood, himself. The grand civic improvements Augustus planned would be a kind of imperial propaganda, underscoring not only his power but also his care for the people in his role as *pater patriae*. Public works could—and indeed did—elicit the public's loyalty.

Rome had developed haphazardly, without any central plan, spilling down the seven hills it originally occupied into the valleys along the Tiber. By contrast, all of the Empire's provincial capitals were conceived on a strict grid plan, with colonnaded main roads leading to an administrative center, and adorned with public works like baths, theaters, and triumphal arches. In comparison, Rome was pitiable. Housing conditions were dreadful, water was scarce, food was in short supply. Because the city was confined by geography to a small area, space was at a premium.

Urban Housing: The Apartment At least as early as the third century BCE, the ancient Romans created a new type of living space in response to overcrowding—the multistoried apartment block, or *insula* (Fig. **6.18**). In Augustus' time, the city was increasingly composed of such *insulae*, in which 90 percent of the population of Rome lived.

The typical apartment consisted of two private rooms—a bedroom and a living room—that opened onto a shared central space. The poor lived in kitchenless apartments, cooking and eating in the shared space.

The *insulae* were essentially tenements, with shops on the ground floor and living quarters above. They rose to a height of 60 or 70 feet (five or six stories), were built with inadequate wood frames, and often collapsed. Fire was an even greater danger. Richer apartment dwellers—and there were many, buildable land being scarce—often employed slaves as their own private fire brigades. In 6 CE, Augustus introduced *vigils* to the city, professional firefighters (and policemen) who patrolled the city at night.

In the *insulae*, noise was a constant problem, and hygiene an even worse issue. Occupants of the upper stories typically dumped the contents of their chamber pots into the streets rather than carry them down to the cesspool. As the satirist Juvenal described the situation: "You can suffer as many deaths as there are open windows to pass under. So offer up a prayer that people will be content with just emptying out their slop bowls."

Augustus could not do much about the housing situation, although he did build aqueducts to bring more water into the city. He created a far larger administrative bureaucracy than before and oversaw it closely, guaranteeing its efficiency. But most of all he implemented an ambitious building program designed to provide elegant public spaces where city dwellers could escape from their cramped apartments. He once claimed that he had restored 82 temples in one year. But if he could boast, "I found a city of brick, and left it a city of marble," that was largely because he had put a lot of marble veneer over brick wall. By the second century CE, the city would be one of the most beautiful in the world, but the beauty was only skin-deep. The housing situation that Augustus inherited had barely improved at all.

Public Works and Monuments Augustus inaugurated what amounted to an ongoing competition among the emperors to outdo their predecessors in the construction of public works and monuments. His ambitions are reflected in the work of the architect Vitruvius (flourished late first century BCE to early first century CE). A military engineer for Julius Caesar, under Augustus' patronage, Vitruvius wrote the ten-volume *On Architecture*. The only work of its kind to have survived from antiquity, it would become extremely

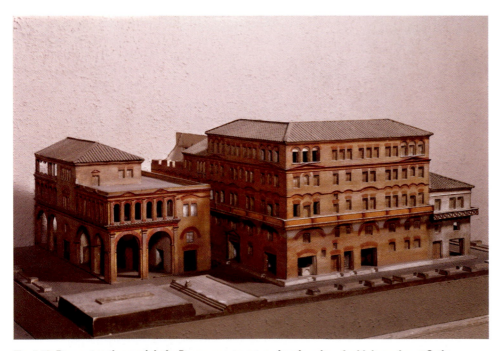

Fig. 6.18 Reconstruction model of a Roman apartment, or *insula*, ruins of which survive at Ostia, Rome's port, ca. 150 CE. The ground floor of this *insula* contained shops. Above these were many apartments. There were also single-room living quarters behind the shops.

CONTEXT

The Roman Emperors 27 BCE–337 CE

Julio-Claudian dynasty

27 BCE–14 CE	Augustus
14–37	Tiberius (Augustus' adopted son and husband to Augustus' daughter Julia)
37–41	Gaius Caligula (son of Germanicus, nephew and adopted son of Tiberius)
41–54	Claudius (his paternal grandparents were Livia, Augustus' third wife, and Tiberius Claudius Nero, the emperor Tiberius' father)
54–68	Nero (son of Caligula's sister and adopted by his great-uncle Claudius as his heir)

Civil War

68–69	Galba
69	Otho
69	Vitellius

Flavian dynasty

69–79	Vespasian
79–81	Titus (Vespasian's elder son)
81–96	Domitian (Vespasian's younger son)

The Five Good Emperors

96–98	Nerva (appointed by the Senate after Domitian's murder in a palace coup)
98–117	Trajan (adoptive heir of Nerva)
117–38	Hadrian (Trajan's cousin, ostensibly adopted on Trajan's deathbed)
138–61	Antonius Pius (adoptive heir of Hadrian)
161–80	Marcus Aurelius (adoptive heir of Pius; from 161–169 served as co-emperor with his adoptive brother Lucius Verus)
180–92	Commodus (son of Marcus Aurelius)
193	Helvius Pertinax (appointed by Senate after murder of Commodus; rules three months)
193	Didius Julianus (wins emperorship by outbidding Pertinax's father-in-law at "auction" held by the Senate's bodyguards; rules two months)

Severan dynasty

193–211	Septimus Severus (wins the Empire after civil war)
211–17	Caracalla and Geta (co-emperors and sons of Septimus Severus; Geta murdered by Caracalla in December 211, making Caracalla sole emperor)
217–18	Macrinus (appointed emperor by his troops after Caracalla's death; captured in battle in Asia Minor and put to death)
218–22	Elagabalus (said to be the son of Caracalla, his mother's cousin and thus heir of the Severan house)
222–35	Alexander Severus (adopted cousin of Elagabalus; assumes power after the latter's murder)

Period of Anarchy

235–84	18 "legitimate" emperors (and many more usurpers), most meeting violent deaths after short reigns

Diocletian and the Tetrarchy

284–305	Diocletian (in 286 adopts Maximian and installs him as emperor in the west, while he is emperor in the east; from 293, each rules with a junior colleague – the Tetrarchy or "rule of four")
306–37	Constantine (rules first as junior emperor in the west, then as emperor in the west, and then finally, beginning in 324, as sole ruler)

influential over 1,000 years later, when Renaissance artists became interested in Classical design. In its large scale, the work matches its patron's architectural ambitions, dealing with town planning, building materials and construction methods, the construction of temples, the Classical orders, and the rules of proportion. Vitruvius also wrote extensively about one of Rome's most pressing problems—how to satisfy the city's needs for water. In fact, one of the most significant contributions of the Julio-Claudian dynasty, which extends from Augustus through Nero (r. 54–68 CE), was an enormous aqueduct, the Aqua Claudia. Such aqueducts depended on Roman ingenuity in perfecting the arch and vault so that river gorges could be successfully spanned to carry the pipes bringing water to a city miles away. The Aqua Claudia delivered water from 40 miles away into the very heart of the city, not so much for private use as for the fountains, pools, and public baths. (See *Materials & Techniques*, page 198.)

Such grand works, which made the Rome of the *insulae* more livable, at least in its public spaces, masked other, more deeply intractable political problems. Many in Rome continued to mourn the loss of Republican values. The question of imperial succession was a major concern. None of the Julio-Claudian emperors had sons themselves,

and so the family maintained power by resorting to other relationships for legitimacy. Most notably a great-nephew might inherit power from his great-uncle, a nephew from his uncle, or a stepson from his stepfather, including combinations of these. In this situation, virtually any male connected in any way by blood or marriage to the imperial family could be considered a legitimate contender for power, and every sitting emperor from Tiberius to Nero understood that these family members constituted a threat. Treason trials and executions became something of a hallmark of the era. Tiberius, in fact, instituted a series of trials before the Senate for *maiestas minuta populi Romani*, "diminishing the majesty of the Roman people." The vagueness of the term made it adaptable to almost any situation, and under Tiberius' rule it came to cover libel, slander, and even adultery with his daughter. So tyrannical had Tiberius' rule become that upon his death Gaius Caligula's accession was met with rejoicing. But within two years Caligula was fighting with the Senate, and he announced that slandering the emperor was, once again, a treasonable offense. His cruelty so offended the Senate that the threat of assassination was constant, and in fact he was murdered in the palace, along with his wife and daughter, in January 41.

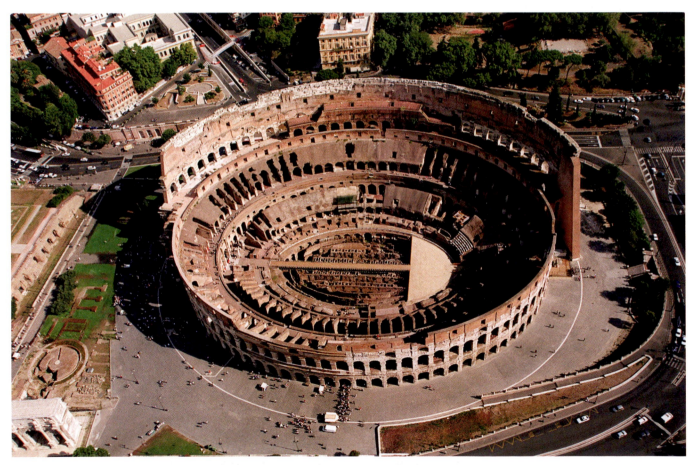

Fig. 6.19 Aerial view of the Colosseum, Rome. Constructed 72–80 CE. The opening performance at the Colosseum in 80 CE lasted 100 days. During that time, 9,000 wild animals—lions, bears, snakes, boars, even elephants, imported from all over the Empire—were killed, and so were 2,000 gladiators.

✳ **Explore** the architectural panorama of the Colosseum on **MyArtsLab**

His successor, Claudius, while preaching civil relations with the Senate, so distrusted the institution that he constantly put its members on trial, for real offenses occasionally, but often for imaginary ill deeds, the product of his own paranoia, or, just as often, the political machinations of his advisors. When Claudius himself died in 54, his stepson, Nero, ascended to power. Son of Claudius' fourth wife and married, the year before Claudius' death, to his daughter, Claudia Octavia, Nero had at best a dubious claim to the throne. He was only 16 years of age, but, at least initially, he ruled well. The turning point seems to have been his mother's resistance to his adulterous affair with Poppaea Sabina, a native of Pompeii. Nero arranged for his mother's murder (when his efforts to have her drowned in the Bay of Naples failed, he had her stabbed to death at her villa). In short order he divorced, banished, then executed Claudia Octavia and married Poppaea Sabina. From this point forward, paranoid prosecutions followed each other in rapid succession. In fact, such prosecutions had become so routine that the later emperor Domitian would observe that "the only time that anybody believed an emperor's statement that he had detected a conspiracy was when the conspiracy had succeeded and he was dead."

The Colosseum The end of Nero's rule was increasingly tumultuous. First, fire destroyed a large portion of the *insulae* in 64 CE. When Nero revealed that, in taking the opportunity to institute a new code of building safety to protect against future fires, he would also confiscate a large piece of land previously in private occupation for an enormous new house (the Golden House, as it became known) and spacious parks in the center of the city, rumors quickly circulated that he had set the fire himself and recited his own poems as the city burned. Nero claimed, however, that Christians had set the blaze, and publicly burned them alive, to the horror, particularly, of the upper classes. Taxes levied to support the new construction met with the disfavor of this same elite; assassination attempts followed, Nero was declared a public enemy, and he subsequently committed suicide. He was succeeded by one of his own generals, Vespasian (r. 69–79 CE), the former commander in Palestine. Across from Nero's Golden House, Vespasian built the Colosseum (Fig. **6.19**), so named in the Middle Ages after the Colossus, a 120-foot-high statue of Nero as sun god that stood in front of it. The Colosseum formed a giant oval, 615 feet long, 510 feet wide, and 159 feet high, and audiences of as many as 50,000 could enter or exit through its 76 vaulted arcades in a matter of minutes.

These vaults were made possible by the perfection of concrete, which the Romans had increasingly used in their buildings since the second century BCE. Mixed with volcanic aggregate from nearby Naples and Pompeii, it set more quickly and was stronger than any building material yet known. The Colosseum's wooden floor, the *arena* (Latin for "sand," which covered the floor), lay over a maze of rooms and tunnels that housed the gladiators, athletes, and wild animals that

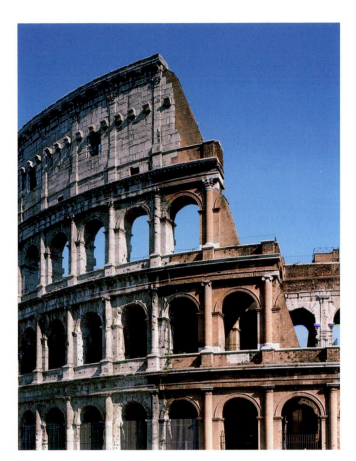

Fig. 6.20 Detail of outer wall of the Colosseum, Rome. 72–80 CE.
Behind the archways of the facade at ground level, barrel vaults ringed the oval arena, providing entrance into this central area. See *Materials & Techniques*, page 198.

entertained the masses. The top story of the building housed an awning system that could be extended on an array of pulleys and ropes to shield part of the audience from the hot Roman sun. Each level employed a different architectural order: the Tuscan order on the ground floor, the Ionic on the second, and the Corinthian, the Romans' favorite, on the third (Fig. **6.20**). All of the columns are engaged and purely decorative, serving no structural purpose. The facade thus moves from the heaviest and sturdiest elements at the base of the building to the lightest, most decorative at the top, a logic that seems both structurally and visually satisfying.

The Imperial Roman Forum The Colosseum stands at the eastern end of the imperial Roman Forum. (See *Closer Look*, pages 196–197.) This vast building project was among the most ambitious to be undertaken in Rome by the Five Good Emperors.

Rome thrived under the rule of the Five Good Emperors: Nerva (r. 96–98 CE), Trajan (r. 98–117 CE), Hadrian (r. 117–38 CE), Antonius Pius (r. 138–61 CE), and Marcus Aurelius (r. 161–80 CE). The stability and prosperity of the city was due, at least in part, to the fact that none of these men except Marcus Aurelius had a son to whom he could

CLOSER LOOK

The Forum Romanum, or Roman Forum, was the chief public square of Rome, the center of Roman religious, ceremonial, political, and commercial life. Originally, a Roman forum was comparable to a Greek agora, a meeting place in the heart of the city. Gradually, the forum took on a symbolic function as well, becoming representative of the imperial power that testified to the prosperity—and peace—that the emperor bestowed upon Rome's citizenry. Julius Caesar was the first to build a forum of his own in 46 BCE, just to the north of the Forum Romanum. Augustus subsequently paved it over, restored its Temple of Venus, and proceeded to build his own forum with its Temple of Mars the Avenger. Thus began what amounted to a competition among successive emperors to outdo their predecessors by creating their own more spectacular forums. These imperial forums lined up north of and parallel to the great Roman Forum, which over the years was itself subjected to new construction. Stretched out along the Via dei Fori Imperiali (Street of Imperial Forums) were Vespasian's Forum of Peace (laid out after the Jewish War in 70 CE), the Forum of Nerva (completed in 97 CE), the Forum of Augustus, the Forum of Caesar, and the Forum of Trajan (completed by Hadrian, ca. 117 CE). The result was an extremely densely built city center. Trajan's was the last, largest, and most splendid forum. It

Something to Think About …

The shopping center at Caesar's Palace Hotel and Casino in Las Vegas, Nevada, is called The Forum. In what ways is a modern shopping mall comparable to the Roman Forum? In what important ways do they differ?

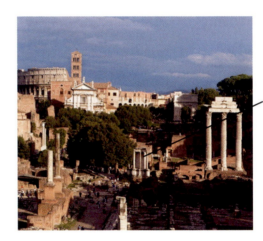

Contemporary view of the Forum Romanum. Little remains of the Forum Romanum but a field of ruins in the heart of the city. The rounded white columns are the ruins of the Temple of Vesta, one of the earliest buildings erected there.

sheltered the Column of Trajan, Trajan's Market, and the Basilica Ulpia—the largest basilica in the Empire (see the discussion of the basilica in Chapter 8, page 264).

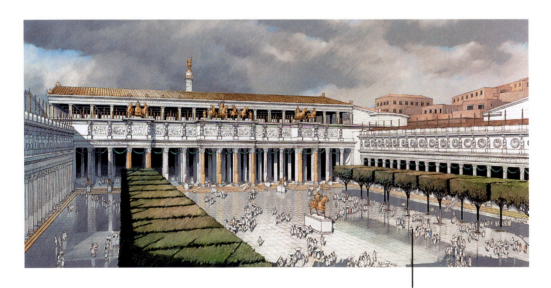

Model of the Roman Forum and the imperial forums, Rome. ca. 46 BCE–117 CE. This model emphasizes the dense building plan of ancient Rome.

Forum of Trajan, Rome. 110–12 CE. Restored view by Gilbert Gorski. To make up for the destruction of a major commercial district that was required to construct his forum, Trajan commissioned a large marketplace. Like a contemporary mall, the market had 150 different shops on several levels.

View the Closer Look for the Roman Forum on **MyArtsLab**

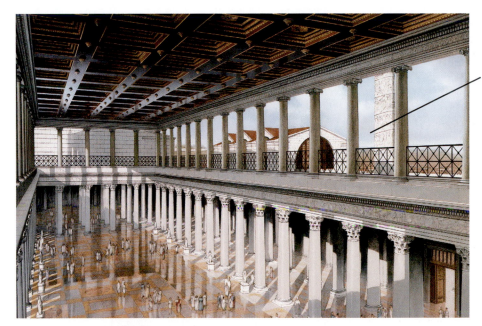

Reconstruction drawing of the central hall, Basilica Ulpia, Forum of Trajan, Rome. 113 CE. A basilica is a large, rectangular building with a rounded extension, called an apse, at one or both ends, and easy access in and out. It was a general-purpose building that could be adapted to many uses. Designed by Trajan's favorite architect, the Greek Apollodorus of Damascus, the Basilica Ulpia was 200 feet wide and 400 feet long. In a courtyard outside a door in the middle of the colonnade to the right stood the Column of Trajan. Relatively plain and massive on the outside, the basilica is distinguished by its vast interior space, which would later serve as the model for some Christian churches.

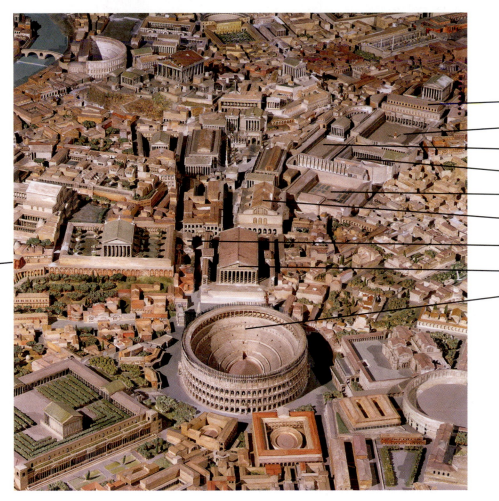

Basilica Ulpia

Forum of Trajan

Forum of Julius Caesar

Forum of Augustus

Forum of Vespasian (Peace)

Basilica of Maxentius and Constantine

Arch of Titus

Temple of Venus and Mars

Colosseum

Arches and Vaults

While the arch was known to cultures such as the Mesopotamians, the Egyptians, and the Greeks, it was the Romans who perfected it, evidently learning its principles from the Etruscans but developing those principles further. The Pont du Gard, a beautiful Roman aqueduct in southern France near the city of Nîmes, is a good example.

The Romans understood that much wider spans could be achieved with the **round arch** than with post-and-lintel construction, and they bridged wider spans than the Etruscans. The weight of the masonry above the arch is displaced to the supporting upright elements (**piers** or **jambs**). The arch is constructed on a temporary supporting scaffolding and is formed with wedge-shaped blocks, called **voussoirs**, capped by a large, wedge-shaped stone, called the **keystone**, the last element put in place. The space inside the arch is called a **bay**. And the wall areas between the arches of an **arcade** (a succession of arches, such as seen on the Pont du Gard) are called **spandrels**.

When a round arch is extended, it forms a **barrel vault**. To ensure that the downward pressure from the arches does not collapse the walls, a **buttress** support is often added. When two barrel vaults meet one another at a right angle, they form a **groin vault**. The interior corridors of the Colosseum in Rome use both barrel and groin vaulting. Since all the stones in a vault must be in place to support the arched structure, the vault cannot be penetrated by windows.

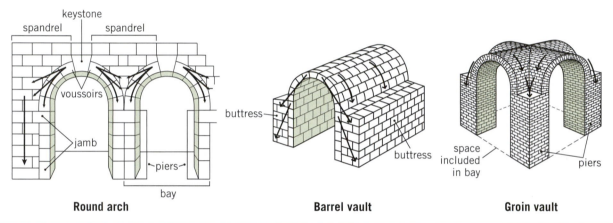

Round arch   **Barrel vault**   **Groin vault**

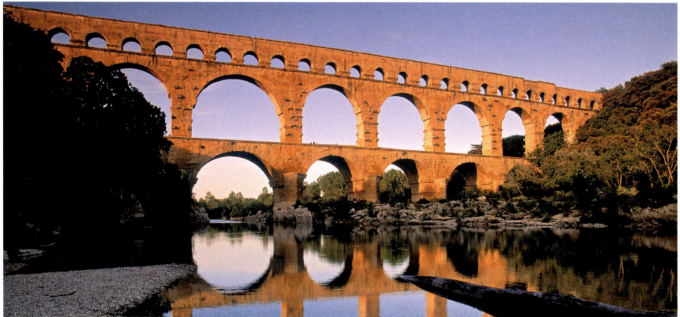

Pont du Gard, near Nîmes, France. Late 1st century BCE–early 1st century CE. Height 180'.
The Roman city of Nîmes received 8,000 to 12,000 gallons of water a day from this aqueduct.

👁 **Watch** an architectural simulation about the round arch on **MyArtsLab**

👁 **Watch** an architectural simulation about barrel and groin vaults on **MyArtsLab** pass on the Empire. Thus, each was handpicked by his predecessor from among the ablest men in the Senate. When, in 180 CE, Marcus Aurelius' decadent and probably insane son, Commodus (r. 180–92 CE), took control, the Empire quickly learned that the transfer of power from father to son was not necessarily a good thing.

Triumphal Arches and Columns During Vespasian's reign, his son Titus (r. 79–81 CE) defeated the Jews in Judea, who were rebelling against Roman interference with their religious practices. Titus' army sacked the Second Temple of Jerusalem in 70 CE. To honor this victory and the death of Titus 11 years later, a memorial arch was constructed on the Sacred Way. Originally, the Arch of Titus was topped by a statue of a four-horse chariot and driver. Such arches, known as *triumphal arches* because triumphant armies marched through them, were composed of a simple barrel vault enclosed within a rectangle, and enlivened with sculpture and decorative engaged columns (Fig. 6.21). They would deeply influence later architecture, especially the facades of Renaissance cathedrals. Hundreds of arches of similar form were built throughout the Roman Empire. Most were not technically triumphal, but like all Roman monumental architecture, they were intended to symbolize Rome's political power and military might.

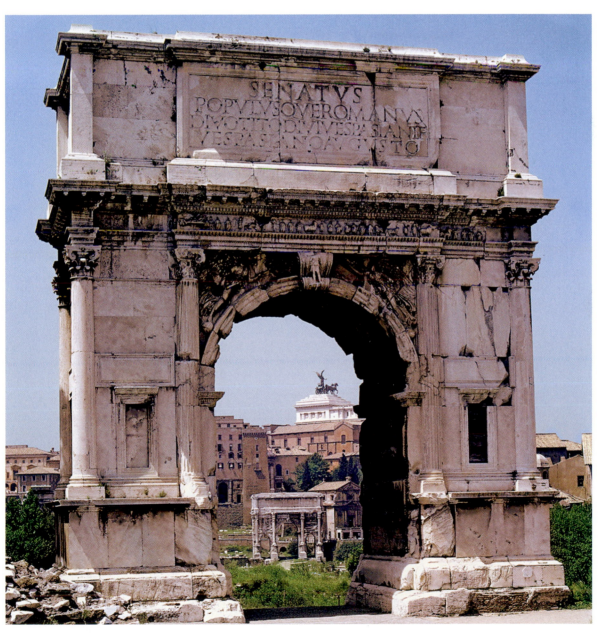

Fig. 6.21 Arch of Titus, Rome. ca. 81 CE. The inscription at the top of the arch, which reads "The Senate and the Roman people to the Deified Titus Vespasian Augustus, son of the Deified Vespasian," was chiseled deeply into the stone so that it might catch the light, allowing it to be read from a great distance.

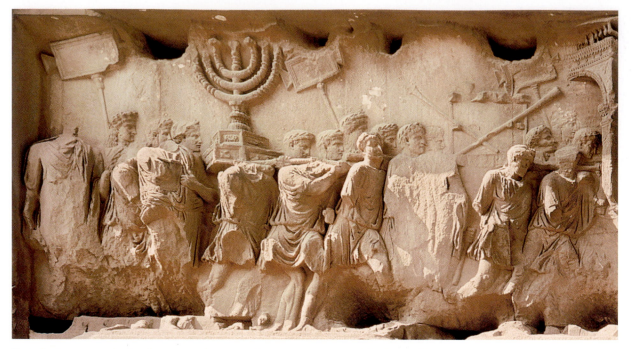

Fig 6.22 *Spoils from the Temple in Jerusalem,* **a detail of the interior relief of the Arch of Titus.**
ca. 81 CE. Height of relief, approx. 7'10". The figures in the relief are nearly life-size. The relief has been badly
damaged, largely because in the Middle Ages a Roman family used the arch as a fortress, constructing a
second story in the vault. Holes for the floor beams appear at the top of the relief.

The Arch of Titus was constructed of concrete and
faced with marble, its inside walls decorated with two
narrative reliefs. One of them shows Titus' soldiers marching with the treasures of the Second Temple in Jerusalem
(Fig. **6.22**). In the foreground, the soldiers carry what some
speculate might be the golden Ark of the Covenant, and
behind that a menorah, the sacred Jewish candelabrum,
also made of gold. They bend under the weight of the gold

and stride forward convincingly. The carving is extremely
deep, with nearer figures and elements rendered with
undercutting and in higher relief than more distant ones.
This creates a sense of real space and, when light and
shadow play over the sculptural relief, even a sense of real
movement.

The second relief (Fig. **6.23**), directly across the arch
from the procession of spoils, shows Titus in a *quadriga* (a

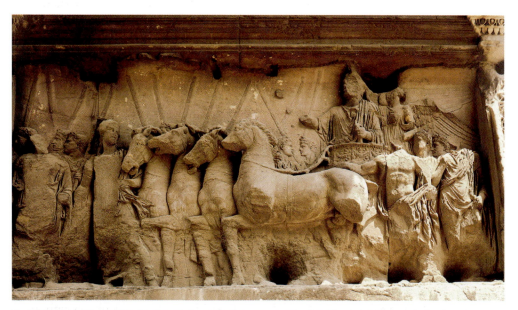

Fig 6.23 *Imperial quadriga in triumphal procession commemorating Titus' victory over Judea,* **interior
relief of the Arch of Titus. ca. 81 CE.** Height of relief, approx. 7'10". Scholars speculate that the figures to the
right of the chariot may represent Honor and Virtue, or, perhaps, Rome herself.

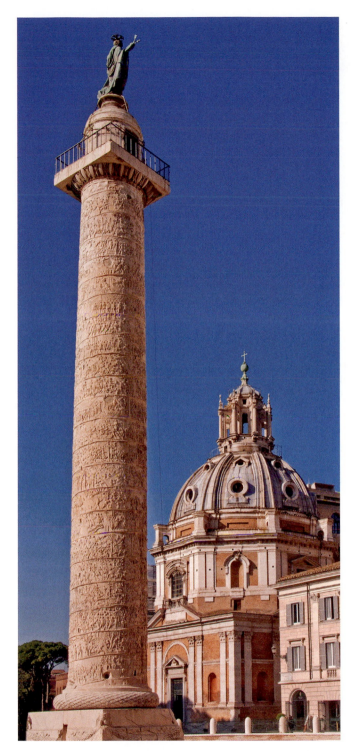

Fig. 6.24 Column of Trajan, Forum of Trajan, Rome. 106–13 CE. Marble, overall height with base, 125'. Winding through the interior of the shaft is a staircase leading to a viewing platform on the top.

View the Closer Look for the Column of Trajan on **MyArtsLab**

chariot drawn by four horses) riding in triumph into Rome. The horses are depicted in profile, but the chariot is frontal, as if the horses have just turned a sharp corner. A winged Victory crowns the general with a wreath. As in the other

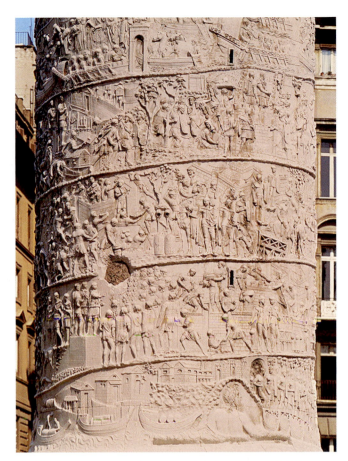

Fig. 6.25 Lower portion of the Column of Trajan, Rome. 106–13 CE. To the left of the second band, Trajan addresses his troops. To the right of that scene, his troops build a fortification.

relief, nearer figures and elements are rendered with undercutting and in higher relief than more distant ones.

Another type of monument favored by the Romans and with similar symbolic meaning—suggestive not only of power but also of male virility—is the ceremonial column. Like the triumphal arch, it was a masonry and concrete platform for narrative reliefs. Two of the so-called Five Good Emperors who ruled Rome after the Flavian dynasty—Trajan and Marcus Aurelius—built columns to celebrate their military victories. The Column of Trajan, perhaps the most complete artistic statement of Rome's militaristic character, consists of a spiral of 150 separate scenes from his military campaign in Dacia, across the Danube River in what is now Hungary and Romania. If laid out end to end, the complete narrative would be 625 feet long (Fig. **6.24**). At the bottom of the column, the band is 36 inches wide, at the top 50 inches, so that the higher elements might be more readily visible. In order to eliminate shadow and increase the legibility of the whole, the carving is in very low relief. At the bottom of the column, the story begins with Roman troops crossing the Danube on a pontoon bridge (Fig. **6.25**). A river god looks on with some interest. Battle scenes constitute less than a quarter of the entire narrative. Instead, we witness the Romans building

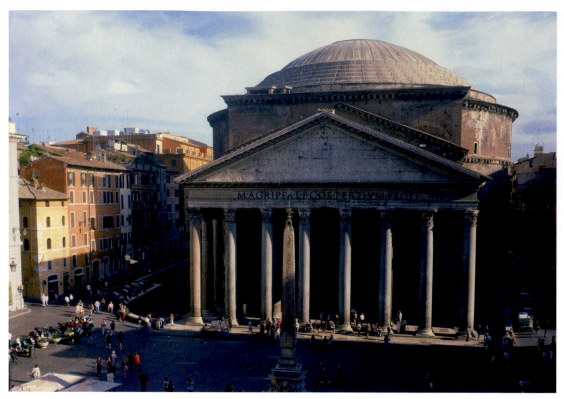

Fig. 6.26 The Pantheon, Rome. 118–25 CE. The Pantheon is an impressive feat of architectural engineering, and it would inspire architects for centuries to come. However, Hadrian humbly (and politically) refused to accept credit for it. He passed off the building as a "restoration" of a temple constructed on the same site by Augustus' closest friend, colleague, and son-in-law, Marcus Agrippa, in 27 to 25 BCE. Across the architrave (the bottom element in an entablature above the columns) of the facade is an inscription that serves both propagandistic and decorative purposes: "Marcus Agrippa, son of Lucius, three times consul, made this."

✳ **Explore** the architectural panorama of the Pantheon on **MyArtsLab**

fortifications, harvesting crops, participating in religious rituals. All in all, the column's 2,500 figures are carrying out what Romans believed to be their destiny—they are bringing the fruits of civilization to the world.

The Pantheon Hadrian's Pantheon ranks with the Forum of Trajan as one of the most ambitious building projects undertaken by the Good Emperors. The Pantheon (from the Greek *pan*, "all," and *theoi*, "gods") is a temple to "all the gods," and sculptures representing all the Roman gods were set in recesses around its interior. The facade is a Roman temple, originally set on a high podium, with its eight massive Corinthian columns and deep portico, behind which are massive bronze doors (Fig. **6.26**). Photography presents little evidence of its monumental presence, once elevated above a long forecourt (Fig. **6.27**). Today, both the forecourt and the elevation have disappeared beneath the streets of present-day Rome. Fig. 6.26 shows the Pantheon as it looks today.

The facade gives no hint of what lies beyond the doors. The interior of the Pantheon consists of a cylindrical space topped by a dome, the largest built in Europe before the twentieth century (Fig. **6.28**). The whole is a perfect hemisphere—the diameter of the rotunda is 144 feet, as is the height from floor to ceiling. The weight of the

dome rests on eight massive supports, each more than 20 feet thick. The dome itself is 20 feet thick at the bottom but narrows to only 6 feet thick at the **oculus**, the circular opening at the top. The oculus is 30 feet in diameter. Recessed panels, called **coffers**, further lighten the weight of the roof. The oculus, or "eye," admits light, which forms a round spotlight that moves around the building during

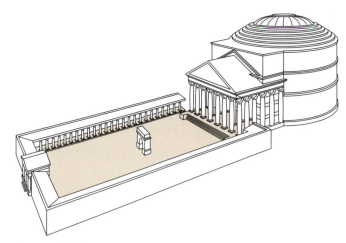

Fig. 6.27 The Pantheon, Rome. Schematic drawing showing the original forecourt.

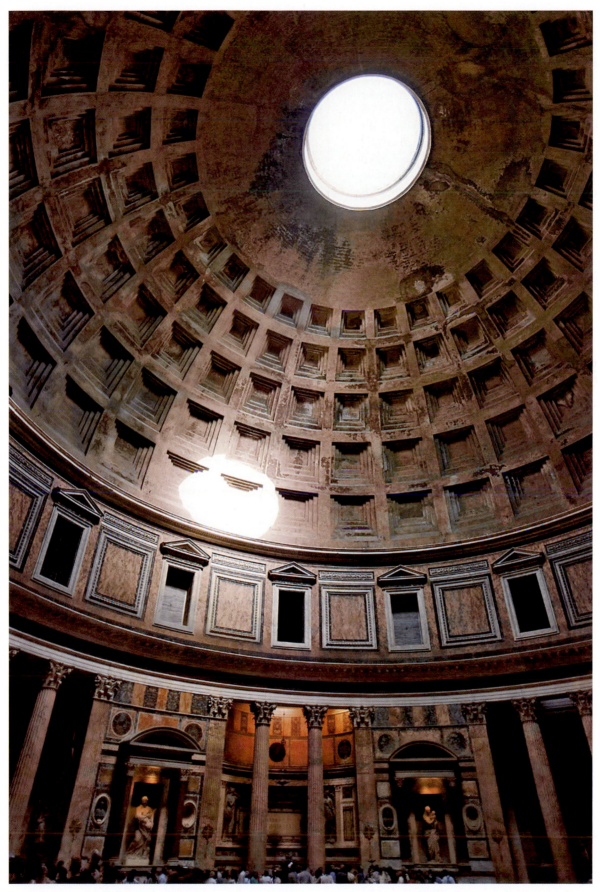

Fig. 6.28 Interior of the Pantheon, Rome. The sun's rays entering through the oculus form a spotlight on the Pantheon's interior, moving and changing intensity with the time of day.

the course of a day (it admits rain as well, which is drained out by small openings in the floor). For the Romans, this light may well have symbolized Jupiter's ever-watchful eye cast over the affairs of state, illuminating the way.

In the vast openness of its interior, the Pantheon mirrors the cosmos, the vault of the heavens. Mesopotamian and Egyptian architecture had created monuments with exterior mass. Greek architecture was a kind of sculptural event, built up of parts that harmonized. But the Romans concentrated on sheer size, including the vastness of interior space. Like the Basilica Ulpia (see *Closer Look*, pages 196–197) in the Forum of Trajan, the Pantheon is concerned primarily with realizing a single, whole, uninterrupted interior space.

In this sense, the Pantheon mirrors the Empire. It, too, was a single, uninterrupted space, stretching from Hadrian's Wall in the north of England to the Rock of Gibraltar in the south, across North Africa and Asia Minor, and encompassing all of Europe except what is now northern Germany and Scandinavia (see Map 6.1). Like Roman architecture, the Empire was built up of parts that were meant to harmonize in a unified whole, governed by rules of proportion and order. And if the monuments the Empire built to celebrate itself were grand, the Empire was grander still.

Pompeii

In 79 CE, during the rule of the emperor Titus, the volcano Vesuvius erupted southeast of Naples, burying the seaside town of Pompeii in 13 feet of volcanic ash and rock. Its neighbor city Herculaneum was covered in 75 feet of a ground-hugging avalanche of hot ash that later solidified. Living in retirement nearby was Pliny the Elder, a commander in the Roman navy and the author of *The Natural History*, an encyclopedia of all contemporary knowledge. At the time of the eruption, his nephew, Pliny the Younger (ca. 61–ca. 113 CE), was staying with him. This is his eyewitness account (**Reading 6.10**):

READING 6.10

from *Letters of Pliny the Younger*

On 24 August, in the early afternoon, my mother drew his attention to a cloud of unusual size and appearance. He had been out in the sun, had taken a cold bath, and lunched while lying down, and was then working at his books. He called for his shoes and climbed up to a place which would give him the best view of the phenomenon. It was not clear at that distance from which mountain the cloud was rising (it was afterwards known to be Vesuvius); its general appearance can best be expressed as being like an umbrella pine, for it rose to a great height on a sort of trunk and then split off into branches, I imagine because it was thrust upwards by the first blast and then left unsupported as the pressure subsided, or else it was borne down by its own weight so that it spread out and gradually dispersed. ...

They debated whether to stay indoors or take their chance in the open, for the buildings were now shaking with violent shocks, and seemed to be swaying to and fro as if they were torn from their foundations. Outside on the other hand, there was the danger of falling pumice-stones, even though these were light and porous; however, after comparing the risks they chose the latter. In my uncle's case one reason outweighed the other, but for the others it was a choice of fears. As a protection against falling objects they put pillows on their heads tied down with cloths. ...

We also saw the sea sucked away and apparently forced back by the earthquake: at any rate it receded from the shore so that quantities of sea creatures were left stranded on dry sand. On the landward side a fearful black cloud was rent by forked and quivering bursts of flame, and parted to reveal great tongues of fire, like flashes of lightning magnified in size. ...

You could hear the shrieks of women, the wailing of infants, and the shouting of men; some were calling their parents, others their children or their wives, trying to recognize them by their voices. People bewailed their own fate or that of their relatives, and there were some who prayed for death in their terror of dying. Many besought the aid of the gods, but still more imagined there were no gods left, and that the universe was plunged into eternal darkness for evermore. ...

Pliny's uncle, Pliny the Elder, interested in what was happening, made his way toward Vesuvius, where he died, suffocated by the poisonous fumes. Pliny the Younger, together with his mother, survived. Of the 20,000 inhabitants of Pompeii, 2,000 died, mostly slaves and the poor left behind by the rich who escaped the city after early warning shocks.

Much of what we know today about everyday Roman life is the direct result of the Vesuvius eruption. Those who survived left their homes in a hurry, and were unable to recover anything they left behind. Buried under the ashes were not only homes and buildings but also food and paintings, furniture and garden statuary, even pornography and graffiti. The latter include the expected—"Successus was here," "Marcus loves Spendusa"—but also the unexpected and perceptive—"I am amazed, O wall, that you have not collapsed and fallen, since you must bear the tedious stupidities of so many scrawlers." When Pompeii was excavated, beginning in the eighteenth century, many of the homes and artifacts were found to be relatively well preserved. The hardened lava and ash had protected them from the ravages of time. But eighteenth-century excavators also discovered something unexpected. By filling the hollows where the bodies of those caught in the eruption had decomposed, they captured images of horrific death.

Domestic Architecture: The *Domus* Although by no means the most prosperous town in Roman Italy, Pompeii was something of a resort, and, together with villas from other nearby towns, the surviving architecture gives us a good sense of the Roman ***domus***—the townhouse

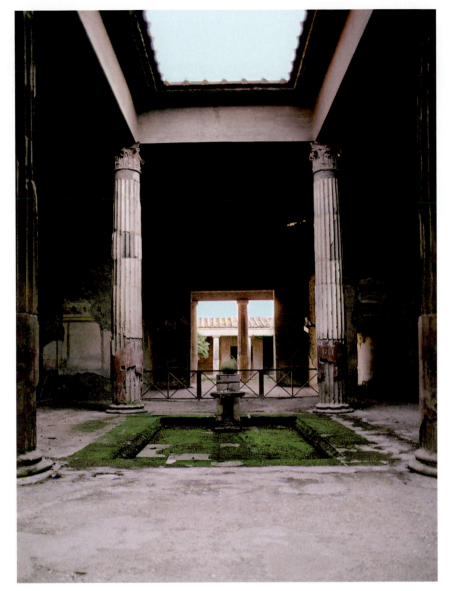

Fig. 6.29 Atrium, House of the Silver Wedding, Pompeii. 1st century BCE. Erich Lessing/akg-images. This view looks through the atrium to the main reception area and the peristyle courtyard. The house gets its name from the silver wedding anniversary of Italy's King Humbert and his queen, Margaret of Savoy, in 1893, the year it was excavated. They actively supported archeological fieldwork at Pompeii, which began in the mid-eighteenth century.

of the wealthier class of citizen. The *domus* was oriented to the street along a central axis that extended from the front entrance to the rear of the house. The House of the Silver Wedding at Pompeii is typical in its design (Figs. **6.29** and **6.30**). An **atrium**, a large space with a shallow pool for catching rainwater below its open roof, extends directly behind the vestibule. The atrium was the symbolic heart of the house: the location for the *imagines*, the wax masks from which portrait busts were later made (see Fig. 6.12), and the main reception area. *Imagines* were also housed in the reception rooms just off the main one, which in turn opens onto a central **peristyle courtyard**, surrounded by a colonnaded walkway. The dining room faces into the courtyard, as do a number of *cubicula*, small general-purpose rooms often used for sleeping quarters. At

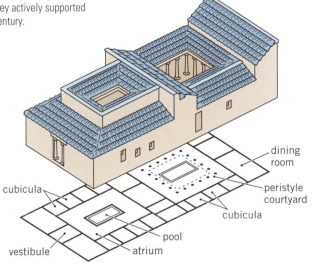

Fig. 6.30 Plan of the House of the Silver Wedding, Pompeii. 1st century BCE.

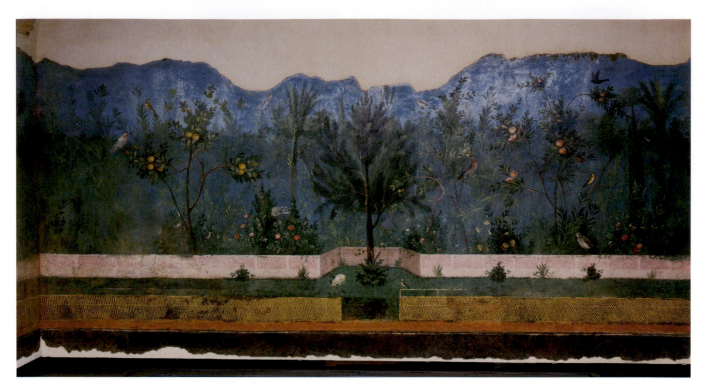

Fig. 6.31 *Garden Scene*, detail of a wall painting from the Villa of Livia at Primaporta, near Rome. **Late 1st century** BCE. Museo Nazionale Romano, Rome. The artist created a sense of depth by setting a wall behind a fence with an open gate.

the back of the house, facing into the courtyard, is a hall furnished with seats for discussion. Servants probably lived upstairs at the rear of the house.

The *domus* was a measure of a Roman's social standing, as the vast majority lived in apartment blocks or *insulae*. The house itself was designed to underscore the owner's reputation. Each morning, the front door was opened and left open. Gradually, the atrium would fill with clients—remember, the head of a Roman household was patron to many—who came to show their respect in a ritual known as the *salutatio*. Passersby could look in to see the crowded atrium, and the patron himself was generally seated in the open area between the atrium and the peristyle courtyard, silhouetted by the light from the peristyle court behind. Surrounded by the busts of his ancestors, the symbol of his social position and prestige, he watched over all who entrusted themselves to his patronage.

At the center of the Roman *domus* was the garden of the peristyle courtyard, with a fountain or pond in the middle. Thanks to the long-term research of the archeologist Wilhelmina Jashemski, we know a great deal about these courtyard gardens. At the House of G. Polybius in Pompeii, excavators carefully removed ash down to the level of the soil on the summer day of the eruption in 79 CE, when the garden would have been in full bloom. They were able to collect pollen, seeds, and other evidence, including root systems (obtained by pouring plaster into the surviving cavities) and thus determine what plants and trees were cultivated in it. Polybius' garden was lined, at one end, with

lemon trees in pots, which were apparently trained and pruned to cover the wall in an *espalier*—a geometric trellis. Cherry, pear, and fig trees filled the rest of the space. Gardens at other homes suggest that most were planted with nut- and fruit-bearing trees, including olive, which would provide the family with a summer harvest. Vegetable gardens are sometimes found at the rear of the *domus*, a source of more fresh produce.

The garden also provided visual pleasure for the family. In the relatively temperate south Italian seaside climate, the garden was in bloom for almost three-quarters of the year. It was the focus of many rooms in the *domus*, which opened onto it. And it was evidently a symbol for the fertility, fecundity, and plenty of the household itself, for many a Roman garden was decorated with statuary referencing the cult of Dionysus.

Wall Painting

Mosaics decorated many floors of the *domus*, and paintings adorned the walls of the atrium, the hall, the dining room, and other reception rooms throughout the villa. Artists worked with pigments in a solution of lime and soap, sometimes mixed with a little wax, polished with a special metal or glass, and then buffed with a cloth. Even the *cubicula* bedrooms were richly painted.

Writing in the second century CE, the satirist and rhetorician Lucian (ca. 120–after 180 CE) describes what he takes to be the perfect house—"lavish, but only in such degree as

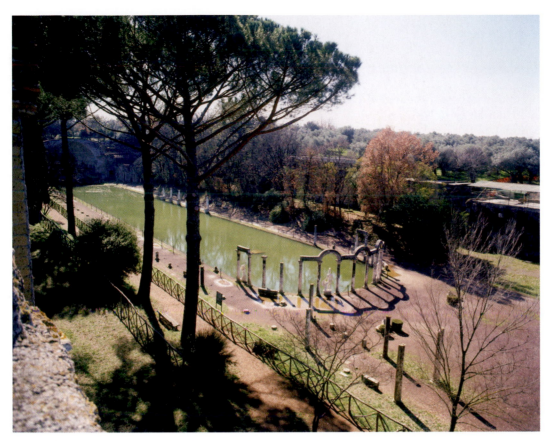

Fig. 6.32 The Canal (reflecting pool) at Hadrian's Villa, Tivoli. ca. 125–35 CE. At the far end of the pool is an outdoor dining room, with concrete benches facing the pool. These would have been covered with cushions for comfort.

would suffice a modest and beautiful woman to set off her beauty." He continues, describing the wall paintings:

> The … decoration—the frescoes on the walls, the beauty of their colors, and the beauty, exactitude and truth of each detail—might well be compared with the face of spring and with a flowery field, except that those things fade and wither and change and cast their beauty, while this is spring eternal, field unfading, bloom undying.

Just outside Rome, at the Villa of Livia at Primaporta, a wall painting depicting a garden full of fresh fruit, songbirds, and flowers reflects this sensibility (Fig. **6.31**). It is rendered as if it were an extension of the room itself, as if Livia and Augustus and their visitors could, at any time, step through the wall into their "undying" garden. Thus, although naturalistically rendered, it is an idealistic representation.

Hadrian's Villa at Tivoli

If the *domus* was the urban townhouse of Rome's wealthier class of citizen, the **villa**, or country residence, was often far more luxurious, and among the most luxurious ever constructed was the emperor Hadrian's at Tivoli, some 18 miles east of Rome at the edge of the Sabine Hills. Situated on over 300 acres on a slope overlooking the surrounding countryside, it was a masterful blending of inventive buildings, waterworks, and gardens. At the turning of almost every corner, a surprising new vista reveals itself. The buildings themselves were copies of Hadrian's favorite places throughout the entire Empire, including the Stoa from the Athenian agora (see Fig. 5.2 in Chapter 5), the Ptolemaic capital of Egypt, Alexandria, and the Academia in Athens, where Plato conversed with his students in the shade of an olive grove. One of the complex's most attractive features is a long reflecting pool, called the Canal (Fig. **6.32**). It was surrounded by a colonnade with alternating arched and linteled entablatures. Between the columns, Hadrian set copies of the most famous sculptures of ancient Greece, including a marble copy of the *Discobolus*, or *Discus Thrower*, originally cast in bronze by the Greek sculptor Myron in the middle of the fifth century BCE. Hadrian was so enamored of Greek sculpture that he had the caryatids from the Erechtheion on the Athenian Acropolis (see Fig. 5.7 in Chapter 5) copied for the villa. In its architectural and sculptural scope, the villa embodied the imperial reach of Rome itself.

The CONTINUING PRESENCE of the PAST

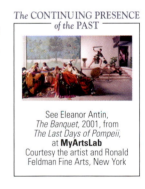

See Eleanor Antin, *The Banquet*, 2001, from *The Last Days of Pompeii*, at **MyArtsLab** Courtesy the artist and Ronald Feldman Fine Arts, New York

THE LATE ROMAN EMPIRE: MORAL AND SOCIAL DECLINE

What factors contributed to Rome's decline?

Most of the late emperors were themselves "Romanized" provincials. Both Trajan and Hadrian were born on the Iberian peninsula, near present-day Seville, and during his reign, Hadrian had the city redesigned with colonnaded streets and an amphitheater. Septimius Severus (r. 193–211 CE), the founder of the Severan dynasty which came to power in the civil war following the emperor Commodus' murder in 192 CE, was African, and two of his successors were Syrian. Septimius Severus lavished an elaborate public works project on his hometown of Leptis Magna, on the coast just east of Tripoli in present-day Libya, giving the city a new harbor, a colonnaded forum, and an aisled basilica, the Roman meeting hall that would develop into the earliest architectural form of the Christian church.

Septimus Severus' building campaign at Leptis Magna was, in no small part, a way to secure the African frontier. However, Rome was threatened, in the east, by the Persians along the frontier demarcated by the Euphrates; to the north, by Germanic barbarians along the frontier defined by the Rhine–Danube; and, in England, by Hadrian's Wall. Much of the fortification of the wall still stands, running just south of the current Scottish border. By Hadrian's time, the majority of the Roman army was, however, deployed in defense of the Danube area, where 12 legions were stationed, and the Euphrates, where 6 legions were in place.

By the mid-third century, the major threat was, in fact, from the Goths, who launched massive attacks on the Roman Balkans and Asia Minor. It was a period of considerable unrest in the Empire, as in rapid succession emperor after emperor vied for power, resulting in near political anarchy. By the end of the next century, between 395 and 418 CE, the Visigoths, or Western Goths, streamed across the Empire by the hundreds of thousands, sacking Rome in 410 CE. Even more ferocious invaders from the Eurasians steppelands would arrive later, in the mid- and late fourth century. These were the Huns, whose fierce appearance many Roman writers felt was the result of self-mutilation, and whose cruelty was matched only by their raw indifference to hygiene. Under threat from these hordes, the Empire's borders were becoming increasingly indefensible.

Of course, a large number of these barbarian invaders were Romanized, especially the mercenary soldiers whom the Empire increasingly relied on to defend its borders. One of the most famous of these was Stilicho, an East Germanic Vandal, who rose to a position of extraordinary power, as can be inferred from a set of ivory panels of a kind usually reserved for the commemoration of Roman consuls, depicting himself, his son, Eucherius, and his wife, Serena (Fig. **6.33**). An advisor to the emperor Theodosius I (r. 379–95 CE), Stilicho would, upon the emperor's death, serve as regent to the emperor's young son, Honorius (r. 395–423 CE), who was but 11 years old. Thus Stilicho effectively ruled the Western Empire from 395 to 408 CE. He dreamed of making his own son, Eucherius, emperor, and his daughter, Maria, did in fact marry Honorius. Accused of treason—in the tradition of Roman emperors, it is hard to say whether Honorius' charges were true or false—he was executed in 408 CE.

Under pressure from invading hordes, as well as the growing popularity of Christianity, maintaining the loyalty of the masses was ever more important for Roman rulers. Public works, as ever, remained the primary way to accomplish this. In the third century CE, during the Severan dynasty (193–235 CE), Rome's every amenity was imitated at its outposts, especially baths, like those begun by Septimius Severus, and dedicated in 217 by his son and successor, Caracalla (Fig. **6.34**). The baths were set within a 50-acre walled park on the south side of Rome and were fed by an aqueduct dedicated exclusively to this purpose. Although no ceilings survive, the vaulted central hall appears to have been 140 feet high. There were three bathing halls with a combined capacity of 1,600 bathers: the *frigidarium* (cold bath), the *tepidarium* (lukewarm bath), and

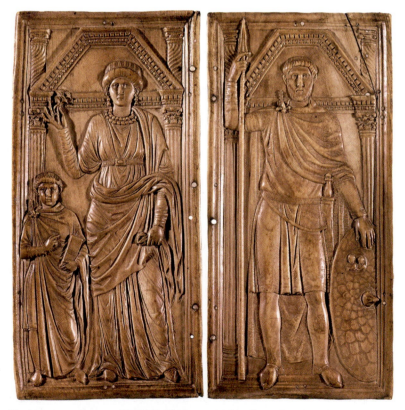

Fig. 6.33 *Ivory Diptych of Stilicho, Serena, and Son.* **400** CE. Treasury of Monza Cathedral, Italy. These portraits are executed in a fully Byzantine style, as discussed in Chapter 8. Compare, particularly, Figs. 8.28 and 8.29 in Chapter 8.

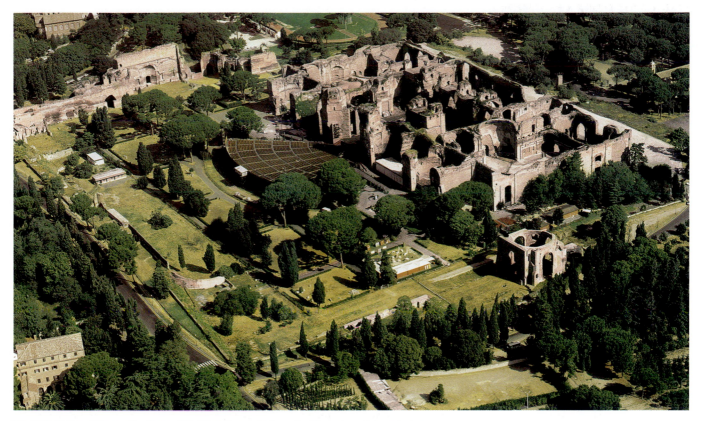

Fig. 6.34 Baths of Caracalla, Rome. 211–17 CE. Rome's baths and public waterworks required enormous amounts of water. The city's 14 aqueducts brought 220 million gallons of pure spring water per day from the Apennines, the mountain chain that extends the length of the Italian peninsula. This water supplied 11 public baths, 856 private smaller baths, and 1,352 fountains and cisterns.

the *caldarium* (hot bath). There were two *gymnasia* (exercise rooms) on either side of the pools, as well a barbershop and a hair salon, sauna-like moist- and dry-heat chambers, and outdoor areas for sunbathing or exercising in the nude. Other amenities of the baths included libraries, a painting gallery, auditoriums, and, possibly, a stadium. Early in the fourth century, the emperor Diocletian would build even more enormous and sumptuous baths at the northern end of the city. Although dedicated to public health and hygiene, the baths came to signal a general decline in the values that had defined Rome. Writing as early as the mid-first century CE, in his *Moral Epistles*, Seneca complained that no one in his day could bathe in the simple way of the great Republican general Scipio Africanus, who had defeated Hannibal in 202 BCE (**Reading 6.11**):

READING 6.11

Seneca, *Moral Epistles*, Epistle 86

Who today could bear to bathe in such a fashion? We think ourselves poor and mean if our walls are not resplendent with large and costly mirrors; if our marbles from Alexandria are not set off by mosaics of Numidian stone, if their borders are not faced over on all sides with difficult patterns, arranged in many colors like paintings; if our vaulted ceilings are not buried in glass; if our swimming pools are not lined with Thasian marble, once a rare and wonderful sight in any temple. ... What a vast number of statues, of columns that support nothing, but are built for decoration, merely in order to spend money! And what masses of water that fall crashing from level to level! We have become so luxurious that we will have nothing but precious stones to walk upon.

To many citizens at the time, such material excess, embodied perhaps most of all in the self-indulgent lifestyle of Nero, signaled an atmosphere of moral depravity, inevitably associated with the public nudity practiced at the baths. In Carthage, the Christian writer Tertullian (ca. 160–ca. 240 CE) had argued against the worldly pleasures of secular culture, as early as 197 CE, going so far as to propose the "rule of faith" over the rule of Roman law. By the early fourth century CE, Christians across the Empire forbade visitation to the baths, arguing that bathing might be practiced for cleanliness but not for pleasure. Thus would the Empire find itself defined in moral opposition to a growing religious community throughout its territories, even as it was threatened from without by Germanic invaders.

Christian Rome

Throughout its history, the Roman Empire had been a polytheistic state in which literally dozens of religions were tolerated. But as Christianity became a more and more dominant force in the Empire, it threatened the political and cultural identity of the Roman citizen. No longer was a Roman Christian first and foremost Roman. Increasingly, that citizen was first and foremost Christian.

In reaction to this threat to imperial authority, during the chaotic years after the fall of the Severan emperors in 235 CE, Christians were blamed, as their religion spread across the Empire (see Map 8.1 in Chapter 8), for most of Rome's troubles. By the end of the third century, there were about 5 million Christians in the Roman Empire, nearly a tenth of the population. Rome had a particularly large Christian congregation with considerable influence, since its leadership was believed to have descended from Jesus' original disciples, Peter and Paul. In 303 CE, the emperor Diocletian (r. 284–305 CE) unleashed a furious persecution of Christians that lasted for eight years.

Diocletian saw the Roman Church as a direct threat to his own authority, recognizing that it had achieved an almost monarchical control over the other dioceses, or Church territories, in the Empire. He forbade Christian worship, ordered churches destroyed, burned books, and had all bishops arrested. Under penalty of death, Christians were compelled to make sacrifices to the emperor, whom non-Christian Romans considered divine. Thousands refused, and the martyrdom they thus achieved fueled rather than diminished the Church's strength.

In 305, Diocletian retired due to bad health, ushering in a period of instability. Finally, Constantine I, known as "Constantine the Great" (r. 306–37 CE), won a decisive battle at the Milvian Bridge, at the entrance to Rome, on October 28, 312, establishing himself as emperor. Two years earlier, as Constantine was advancing on Rome from Gaul, the story had circulated that he had seen a vision of the sun god Apollo accompanied by Victory (Nike) and the Roman numeral XXX, symbolizing the 30 years he would reign. By the end of his life, he claimed to have seen, instead, above the sun, a single cross, by then an increasingly common symbol of Christ, together with the legend, "In this sign you shall conquer." At any rate, it seems certain that at the Battle of the Milvian Bridge, Constantine ordered that his troops decorate their shields with crosses, and perhaps the Greek letters *chi* and *rho* as well. These letters stood for *Christos*, although *chi* and *rho* had long meant *chrestos*,

Figs. 6.35 and 6.36 The Basilica of Maxentius and Constantine, also known as the Basilica Nova (right), and plan (below), Rome. 306–13 CE. Constantine added an imposing entrance on the southwest side of Maxentius' basilica and another apse across from it, perhaps to accommodate crowds.

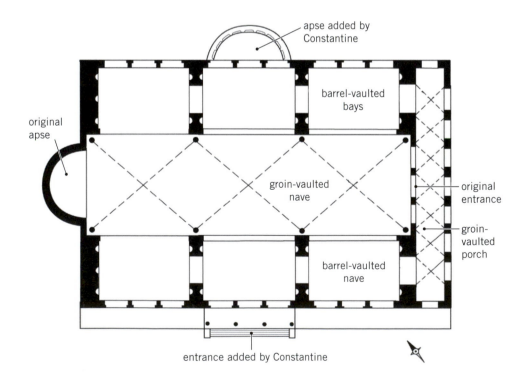

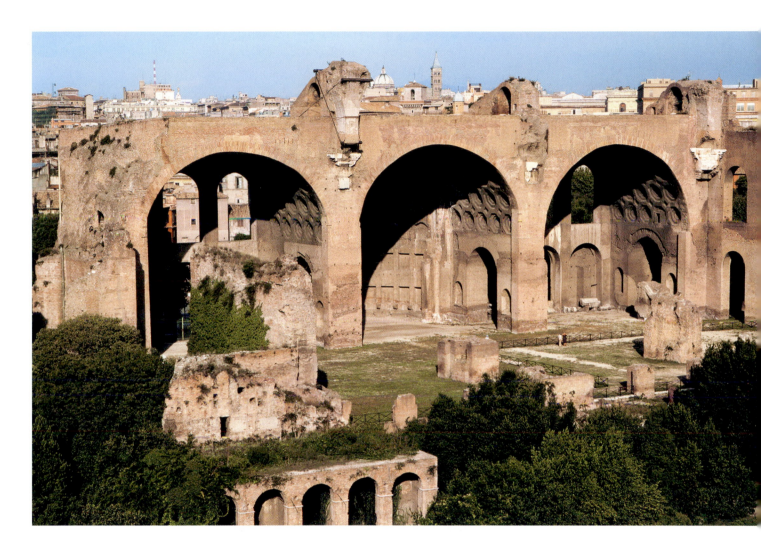

"auspicious," and Constantine probably meant only this and not Jesus Christ. While Constantine himself reasserted his devotion to the Roman state religion, within a year, in 313, he issued the Edict of Milan, which granted religious freedom to all, ending religious persecution in the Empire.

Constantine's architectural program in Rome would leave a lasting mark on subsequent Christian architecture, particularly his work on a basilica at the southern end of the line of imperial forums (see *Closer Look*, pages 196–197). Originally built by Maxentius, it was the last of the great imperial buildings erected in Rome (Figs. **6.35** and **6.36**). Like all Roman basilicas, the Basilica of Maxentius and Constantine (also known as the Basilica Nova) was a large rectangular building with a rounded extension, called an apse, at one or both ends, and easy access in and out. It was, similarly, an administrative center—courthouse, council chamber, and meeting hall—and its high vaulted ceilings were purposefully constructed on the model of the Baths of Caracalla (see Fig. 6.34). Its **nave**, the large central area, rose to an elevation of 114 feet. One entered through a triple portico at the southeast end and looked down the nave some 300 feet to the original semicircular apse at the other end of the building, which acted as a focal point. The basilica plan, with the apse as its focal point, would exert considerable influence on later Christian churches. These later churches would transform the massive interiors from administrative purposes to religious sanctuaries, whose vast interior spaces elicited religious awe. ■

✸ **Explore** the architectural panorama of the Basilica Nova on **MyArtsLab**

THINKING BACK

6.1 Describe the dual origins of Roman culture.

Roman culture developed out of both Greek and indigenous Etruscan roots. Most of what we know of the Etruscans comes from sculptures and paintings that survive in tombs. How does a Roman temple, such as the Temple of Fortuna Virilis, differ from a Greek temple, such as the Parthenon?

The Etruscans also provided the Romans with one of their founding myths, the legend of Romulus and Remus. What was Rome's other founding myth?

6.2 Outline the patronage system of the Roman Republic and explain how it is reflected in its art and literature.

According to legend, it was Romulus who inaugurated the traditional Roman distinction between patricians and plebians, with its system of patronage and *pietas*. Describe this system. During the Republic, Rome embarked on a series of military exploits culminating in the Punic Wars, which began in 264 BCE and lasted for over 100 years. Subsequently, whenever Rome conquered a region, it established permanent colonies and gave land to the victorious citizen-soldiers. During the first century, the powerfully eloquent and persuasive writing of the rhetorician Cicero helped to make Latin the chief language of the Empire. His essay *On Duty* helped to define *pietas* as a Roman value. How is this value evidenced in the portrait busts of the era? How does Cicero's essay argue against the political state of affairs in Rome itself?

6.3 Discuss the imperial aspirations of Rome and their manifestation in art, architecture, and literature.

In 27 BCE, the Senate granted Octavian the imperial name Augustus and the authority of *imperium* over all the Empire. Why was Augustus idealized in the monumental statues dedicated to him? How did he present his wife Livia and his family to the public, and what values did he wish his family to embody?

Two Greek philosophical systems gained considerable Roman following—Epicureanism and, especially, Stoicism. How would you describe these philosophies? How does each, in its way, reflect the values of the state? Under Augustus, Roman literature also thrived. Although the poetry of Catullus, Virgil, Horace, and Ovid are very different in character, their work could all be described as exploring the nature of Roman identity. Using their work as examples, can you describe that Roman identity?

But Augustus' greatest achievement, and that of the emperors who followed him, was the transformation of Rome into, in Augustus' words, "a city of marble." Why did the Roman emperors build so many public works? What did they symbolize or represent? In the private sphere, how does the architecture of the *domus* reflect Roman values?

6.4 Examine the factors that led to Rome's decline.

Rome faced its greatest threat at its far-flung frontiers, where Germanic tribes—first, as the Empire itself endured political near-anarchy, the Goths, and then a century later, the Huns—taxed the ability of the military to defend the Empire. By the third century, the Empire's material excess produced an atmosphere of decadence and depravity. Christianity posed an internal threat to Roman values. What was the appeal of Christianity as it came to supplant the rule of Roman law?

✓ **Study** and **review** on **MyArtsLab**

READINGS

READING 6.6

Catullus, Poems 5 and 43

Born in Verona, Catullus apparently arrived in Rome as a very young man. His poems were inspired directly by Greek Hellenistic models, as well as more Classical Greek writers such as Sappho. The most famous of his works are the so-called Lesbia poems, written to a lover whom many believe to be Clodia, sister of a Roman patrician and senator, and notoriously adulterous wife of yet another Roman patrician. Poem 5 is the most famous of the Lesbia series, and Poem 43 is a good example of Catullus' wit, as he compares a prostitute to his beloved.

POEM 5

Lesbia,
    live with me
& love me so
we'll laugh at all
the sour-faced strict-
ures of the wise.
This sun once set
will rise again,
when our sun sets,
follows night &   10
an endless sleep.
Kiss me now a
thousand times &
now a hundred
more & then a
hundred & a
thousand more again
till with so many
hundred thousand
kisses you & I   20
shall both lose count
nor any can
from envy of
so much kissing
put his finger
on the number
of sweet kisses

you of me &
I of you
darling, have had.   30

POEM 43

O elegant whore!
    with remarkably long nose
unshapely feet
    lack lustre eyes
fat fingers
    wet mouth
and language not the choicest,
you are I believe the mistress
of the hell-rake Formianus.

And the Province calls you beautiful;   10
they set you up beside my Lesbia.
O generation witless and uncouth!

READING CRITICALLY

How does Catullus' Poem 43 compare to Roman statuary portraiture? What do his poems share with the poetry of Sappho? If the poems are addressed to other people, what do they reveal about Catullus himself? In other words, are they in some sense confessional?

READING 6.8

from Virgil, the *Aeneid*, Book 4

Modeled on the epics of Homer, Virgil's *Aeneid* opens in Carthage, where Aeneas and his men have been the guests of the Phoenician queen Dido. She has fallen in love with Aeneas, but he must, he knows, forge ahead to meet his destiny. The following passage opens as Dido begins to realize that he is preparing to desert her.

He is more than eager
To flee that pleasant land, awed by the warning
Of the divine command. But how to do it?
How get around that passionate queen? What opening
Try first? His mind runs out in all directions,
Shifting and veering. Finally, he has it,
Or thinks he has: he calls his comrades to him,
    The leaders, bids them quietly prepare
The fleet for voyage, meanwhile saying nothing

About the new activity; since Dido   10
Is unaware, has no idea that passion
As strong as theirs is on the verge of breaking,
He will see what he can do, find the right moment
To let her know, all in good time. Rejoicing,
The captains move to carry out the orders.
Who can deceive a woman in love? The queen
Anticipates each move, is fearful even
While everything is safe, foresees this cunning,

And the same trouble-making goddess, Rumor,
Tells her the fleet is being armed, made ready   20
For voyaging. She rages through the city
Like a woman mad. ...
She waits no explanation from Aeneas;
She is the first to speak: "And so, betrayer,
You hoped to hide your wickedness, go sneaking
Out of my land without a word? Our love
Means nothing to you, our exchange of vows,
And even the death of Dido could not hold you.
The season is dead of winter, and you labor
Over the fleet; the northern gales are nothing—   30
You must be cruel, must you not? Why, even,
If ancient Troy remained, and you were seeking
Not unknown homes and lands, but Troy again,
Would you be venturing Troyward in this weather?
I am the one you flee from: true? I beg you
By my own tears, and your right hand—(I have nothing
Else left my wretchedness)—by the beginnings
Of marriage, wedlock, what we had, if ever
I served you well, if anything of mine
Was ever sweet to you, I beg you, pity   40
A falling house; if there is room for pleading
As late as this, I plead, put off that purpose. ..."
There was nothing he could say. Jove bade him keep
Affection from his eyes, and grief in his heart
With never a sign. At last, he managed something:—
"Never, O Queen, will I deny you merit
Whatever you have strength to claim; I will not
Regret remembering Dido, while I have
Breath in my body, or consciousness of spirit.
I have a point or two to make. I did not,   50
Believe me, hope to hide my flight by cunning;
I did not, ever, claim to be a husband,
Made no such vows. If I had fate's permission
To live my life my way, to settle my troubles
At my own will, I would be watching over
The city of Troy, and caring for my people,
Those whom the Greeks had spared, and Priam's palace
Would still be standing; for the vanquished people
I would have built the town again. But now
It is Italy I must seek, great Italy,   60
Apollo orders, and his oracles
Call me to Italy. There is my love,
There is my country. ..."
Out of the corner of her eye she watched him
During the first of this, and her gaze was turning
Now here, now there; and then, in bitter silence,
She looked him up and down; then blazed out at him:—
"You treacherous liar! No goddess was your mother,
No Dardanus the founder of your tribe,
Son of the stony mountain-crags, begotten   70
On cruel rocks, with a tigress for a wet-nurse!
Why fool myself, why make pretense? What is there

To save myself for now? When I was weeping
Did he so much as sigh? Did he turn his eyes,
Ever so little, toward me? Did he break at all,
Or weep, or give his lover a word of pity?
What first, what next? Neither Jupiter nor Juno
Looks at these things with any sense of fairness.
Faith has no haven anywhere in the world.
He was an outcast on my shore, a beggar,   80
I took him in, and, like a fool, I gave him
Part of my kingdom; his fleet was lost, I found it,
His comrades dying, I brought them back to life.
I am maddened, burning, burning: now Apollo
The prophesying god, the oracles
Of Lycia, and Jove's herald, sent from heaven,
Come flying through the air with fearful orders,—
Fine business for the gods, the kind of trouble
That keeps them from their sleep. I do not hold you,
I do not argue, either. Go. And follow   90
Italy on the wind, and seek the kingdom
Across the water. But if any gods
Who care for decency have any power,
They will land you on the rocks; I hope for vengeance,
I hope to hear you calling the name of Dido
Over and over, in vain. Oh, I will follow
In blackest fire, and when cold death has taken
Spirit from body, I will be there to haunt you,
A shade, all over the world. I will have vengeance,
And hear about it; the news will be my comfort   100
In the deep world below." She broke it off,
Leaving the words unfinished; even light
Was unendurable; sick at heart, she turned
And left him, stammering, afraid, attempting
To make some kind of answer. And her servants
Support her to her room, that bower of marble,
A marriage-chamber once; here they attend her,
Help her lie down.
                            And good Aeneas, longing
To ease her grief with comfort, to say something   110
To turn her pain and hurt away, sighs often,
His heart being moved by this great love, most deeply,
And still—the gods give orders, he obeys them;
He goes back to the fleet. And then the Trojans
Bend, really, to their work, launching the vessels
All down the shore. The tarred keel swims in the water,
The green wood comes from the forest, the poles are
    lopped
For oars, with leaves still on them. All are eager
For flight; all over the city you see them streaming,   120
Bustling about their business, a black line moving
The way ants do when they remember winter
And raid a hill of grain, to haul and store it
At home, across the plain, the column moving
In thin black line through grass, part of them shoving
Great seeds on little shoulders, and part bossing

The job, rebuking laggards, and all the pathway
Hot with the stream of work.
And Dido saw them
With who knows what emotion: there she stood   130
On the high citadel, and saw, below her,
The whole beach boiling, and the water littered
With one ship after another, and men yelling,
Excited over their work, and there was nothing
For her to do but sob or choke with anguish.
There is nothing to which the hearts of men and women
Cannot be driven by love. Break into tears,

Try prayers again, humble the pride, leave nothing
Untried, and die in vain. ...

READING CRITICALLY

The tragedy here lies in the conflict between personal desire
and civic duty. What metaphor does Virgil use to underscore
the power of civic duty and responsibility to overcome the
demands of human love? What does Dido do that demonstrates the opposite? How, for Virgil, do these alternatives
seem to be driven by gender?

READING 6.9

from Horace, the *Odes*, Ode 13

Horace's *Odes* are lyric poems of elaborate and complex meter. Although they often extol the virtues of life on his rural
estate outside Rome, in the following example Horace curses a tree that has unexpectedly crashed down, nearly killing
him. It is an instance, among many others that he mentions, of the unanticipated but nevertheless real dangers of life.
In the last half of the poem, he imagines that he has been killed, finding himself in the underworld with other lyric poets
who give comfort to the dead with their verses.

The man who first planted thee did it upon an
evil day and reared thee with a sacrilegious
hand, O tree, for the destruction of posterity
and the countryside's disgrace.
I could believe that he actually strangled his
own father and spattered his hearthstone with
a guest's blood at dead of night; he too has
dabbled in Colchic poisons
and whatever crime is anywhere
conceived—the man that set thee out on my   10
estate, thou miserable stump, to fall upon the
head of thy unoffending master.
Man never heeds enough from hour to hour
what he should shun. The Punic sailor dreads
the Bosphorus,[1] but fears not the unseen fates
beyond that threaten from other quarters.
The soldier dreads the arrows of the Parthians and their swift
retreat; the Parthian fears the chains and rugged strength of
Italy; but the fatal violence that has snatched away, and again
will snatch away, the tribes of men, is something unforeseen.   20
How narrowly did I escape beholding the realms
of dusky Proserpine[2] and Aeacus[3] on his
judgment-seat, and the abodes set apart

for the righteous,
and Sappho complaining on Aeolian lyre of her
countrywomen, and thee, Aleaeus, rehearsing in fuller
strain with golden plectrum[4] the woes of a seaman's
life, the cruel woes of exile, and the woes of war.
The shades[5] marvel at both as they utter words worthy
of reverent silence; but the dense throng, shoulder   30
to shoulder packed, drinks in more eagerly with
listening ear stories of battles and of tyrants banished.
What wonder, when lulled by such strains,
the hundred-headed monster lowers his
black ears, and the serpents writhing in the
locks of the Furies stop for rest!
Yea, even Prometheus and Pelops' sire[6] are
beguiled of their sufferings by the soothing
sound, nor does Orion[7] care to chase the lions
or the wary lynxes.   40

READING CRITICALLY

Why do you suppose this poem has been described as
"a defense of poetry"?

---

[1] **Punic sailor dreads the Bosphorus, etc. (lines 14–19):** each person fears the
danger near at hand.
[2] **Proserpine:** wife of Pluto and queen of the underworld.
[3] **Aeacus:** a righteous king who, after his death, judges the souls who arrive in the
underworld.

[4] **plectrum:** a device for plucking a stringed instrument, such as a lyre.
[5] **shades:** souls of the dead in the underworld.
[6] **Prometheus and Pelops' sire:** Prometheus and Tantalus, both of whom received
especially terrible punishments.
[7] **Orion:** a mighty hunter.

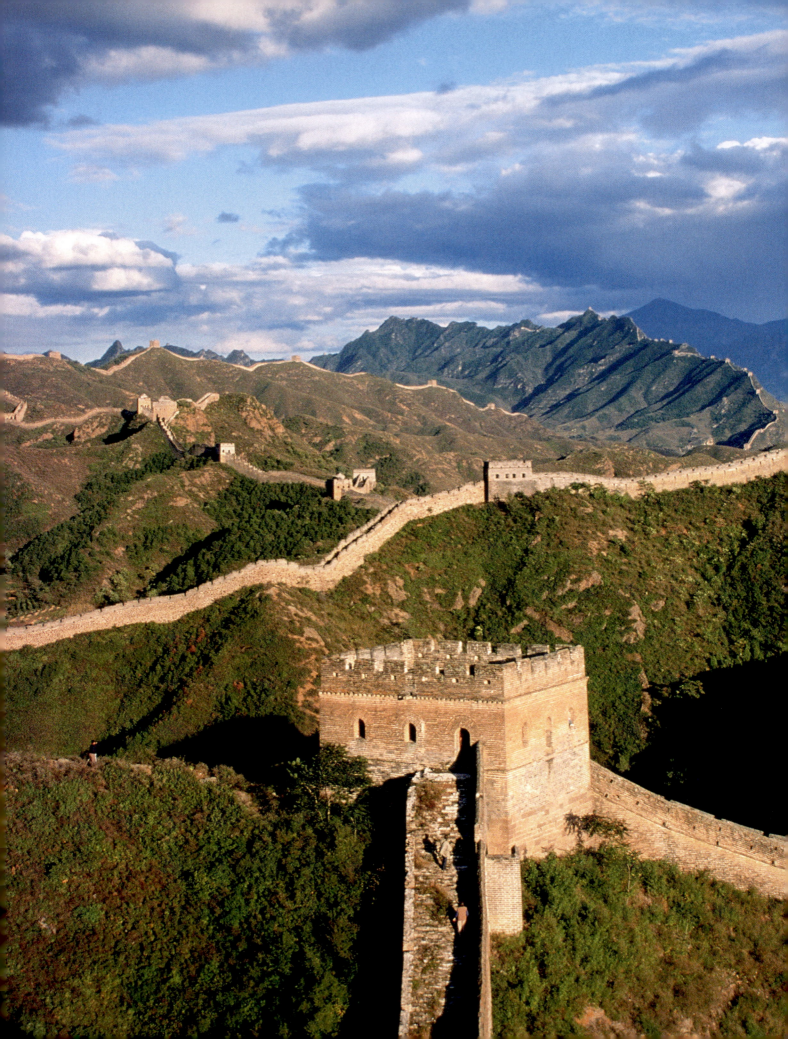

7

Emerging Empires in the East

Urban Life and Imperial Majesty in China and India

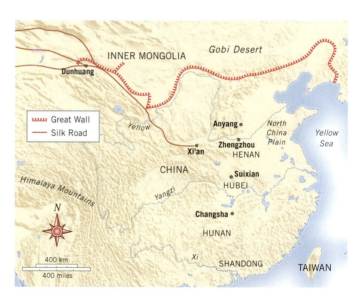

THINKING AHEAD

7.1 Identify the enduring artistic, literary, and philosophical directions that developed early in Chinese history.

7.2 Understand how the art and literature of the Qin and Han dynasties reflect the values of the imperial court.

7.3 Describe the Hindu and Buddhist faiths and how they helped to shape the cultures of ancient India.

The North China plain lies in the large, fertile valley of the Yellow River (Map **7.1**). Around 7000 BCE, when the valley's climate was much milder and the land more forested than it is today, the peoples inhabiting this fertile region began to cultivate the soil, growing primarily millet. Archeologists recognize at least three separate cultural groups in this region during this period, distinguished by their different pottery styles and works in jade. As Neolithic tribal people, they used stone tools, and although they domesticated animals very early on, they maintained the shamanistic practices of their hunter-gatherer heritage. Later inhabitants of this region would call this area the "Central Plain" because they believed it was the center of their country. During the ensuing millennia, Chinese culture in the Central Plain coalesced in ways that parallel developments in the Middle East and Greece during the same period, as China transformed itself from an agricultural society into a more urban-centered state.

By the third century BCE, at about the same time that Rome began establishing its imperial authority over the Mediterranean world, the government of China was sufficiently unified that it could build a Great Wall (Fig. **7.1**) across the hills north of the Central Plain to protect the realm from the intruding Central Asians who lived beyond

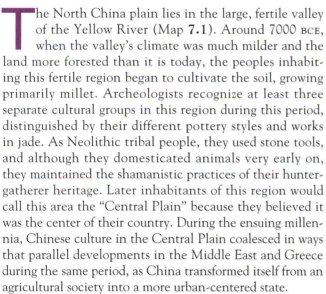

Map 7.1 Map of China, 1000–200 BCE.

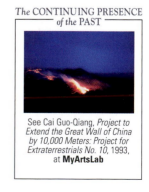

The CONTINUING PRESENCE of the PAST

See Cai Guo-Qiang, *Project to Extend the Great Wall of China by 10,000 Meters: Project for Extraterrestrials No. 10*, 1993, at **MyArtsLab**

◀ **Fig. 7.1 The Great Wall, near Beijing, China. Begun late 3rd century BCE.** Length approx. 4,100 miles, average height 25'. In the third century BCE, Qin Shihuangdi, the first emperor of China, ordered his army to reconstruct, link, and augment walls on the northern frontier of China in order to form a continuous barrier protecting his young country from northern Mongol "barbarians."

((• **Listen** to the chapter audio on **MyArtsLab**

its northern borders. Some sections of the wall were already in place, built in previous centuries to protect local areas. These were rebuilt and connected to define a frontier stretching some 1,500 miles from northeast to northwest China. New roads and canal systems were built linking the entire nation, a large salaried bureaucracy was established, and a new imperial government headed by an emperor collected taxes, codified the law, and exerted control over a domain of formerly rival territories. Unification—first achieved here by the Qin dynasty—has remained a preeminent problem throughout China's long history.

This ritual jade disk, or *bi*, made sometime in the fourth or third century BCE (Fig. **7.2**), is emblematic of the continuity of Chinese historical traditions and ethnic identity. The earliest *bi* disks are found in burials dating from around 4000 BCE, and are thought to be part of the archaic paraphernalia of the shaman. While their original significance is unknown, by the time this one was made they were said to symbolize heaven. This example is decorated with a dragon and two tigers, auspicious symbols likewise emerging from China's prehistoric past. The first part of this chapter surveys the rise of the Chinese culture into a unified state capable of such an enormous undertaking as the Great Wall, as well as the artistic refinement of the jade *bi* disk seen here.

At the same time, another culture was developing in the river valleys of the Asian subcontinent of India. In both China and India, national literatures arose, as did religious and philosophical practices that continue to this day and are influential worldwide. But in the ancient world, East and West had not yet met. The peoples of the Mediterranean world and those living in the Yellow and Indus River valleys were isolated from one another. As trade routes stretched across the Asian continent, these cultures would eventually cross paths. Gradually, Indian thought, especially Buddhism, would find its way into China, and Chinese goods would find their way to the West. Even more gradually, intellectual developments in ancient China and India, from Daoism to the teachings of Confucius and Buddha, would come to influence cultural practice in the Western world. But throughout the period studied in this chapter, up until roughly 200 CE, the cultures of China and India developed independently of those in the West.

EARLY CHINESE CULTURE

What early Chinese artistic, literary, and philosophical developments would have a lasting impact on Chinese culture?

Very few of the built edifices of ancient Chinese civilization have been found. We know that by the middle of the second millennium BCE, Chinese leaders ruled from large capitals, rivaling those in the West in their size and splendor. Beneath present-day Zhengzhou, for instance, lies an early metropolitan center with massive earthen walls. Stone was scarce in this area, but abundant forests made wood plentiful, so it was used to build cities. As impressive as they were, cities built of wood were vulnerable to fire and military attack, and no sign of them remains. Nevertheless, we know a fair amount about early Chinese culture from the remains of its written language and the tombs of its rulers. Even the most ancient Chinese writing—found on oracle bones and ceremonial bronze vessels—is closely related to modern Chinese. And archeologists discovered that royal Chinese tombs, like Egyptian burial sites, contain furnishings, implements, luxury goods, and clothing that—together with the written record—give us a remarkably vivid picture of ancient China.

Chinese Calligraphy

Sometime during the Bronze Age, the Chinese developed a writing system that used individual pictographic characters to stand for distinct ideas and specific spoken words. According to Chinese legend, this writing system was invented by the culture-hero Fu Xi (who also taught the clans to hunt and fish), inspired by both the constellations and bird and animal footprints. Abundant surviving examples

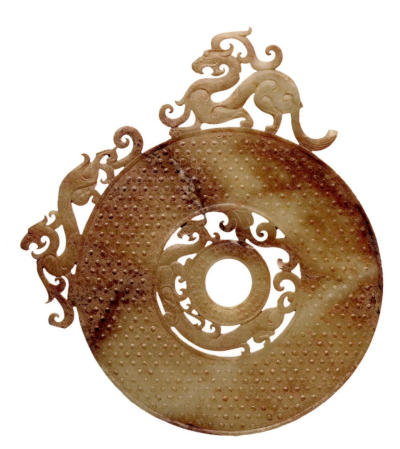

Fig. 7.2 Ritual disk (*bi*) with dragon and phoenix motif. Eastern Zhou dynasty, Warring States period, 4th–3rd century BCE. Jade, diameter 6¼". The Nelson-Atkins Museum of Art, Kansas City, Missouri. Purchase: Nelson Trust 33-81. This disk was discovered in a tomb, probably placed there because the Chinese believed that jade preserved the body from decay.

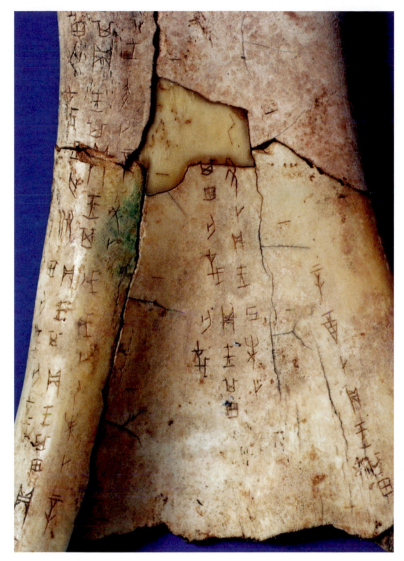

Fig. 7.3 Inscribed oracle bone. Shang period, ca. 1765–1122 BCE. The priests inscribed the characters representing the question from top to bottom in columns.

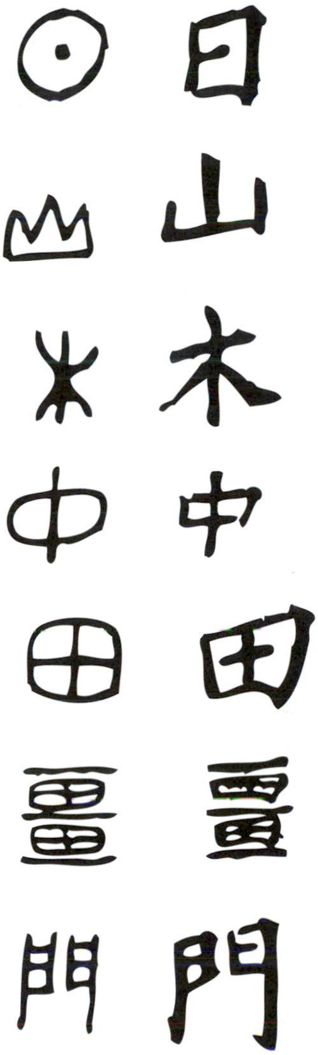

Fig. 7.4 Chinese characters. Shown are ancient characters (left) and modern ones (right). From top to bottom, they mean "sun," "mountain," "tree," "middle," "field," "frontier," and "door."

of writing from around 1400 to 1200 BCE—engraved with a sharp point on oracle bones made of turtle plastrons and ox scapulae—record answers received from the spirit world during rituals asking about the future. We know as much as we do about the day-to-day concerns of the early Chinese rulers from these oracular fragments, on which a special order of priests, or diviners, posed questions of importance and concern (Fig. 7.3). They might ask about the harvest, the outcome of a war, the threat of flood, the course of an illness, or the wisdom of an administrative decision. To find answers, bones were heated with hot pokers, causing fissures to form with a loud crack. The patterns of these fissures were interpreted, and the bones were then inscribed. The first Chinese signs were pictograms, which, as with the development of cuneiform in Mesopotamia (see Chapter 2, *Closer Look*, pages 40–41), soon became stylized, particularly after the brush became the principal writing instrument. The essence of Chinese written language is that

a single written character has a fairly fixed significance, no matter how its pronunciation might vary over time or from place to place. This stability of meaning has allowed the Chinese language to remain remarkably constant through the ages. In the figure above right, 3,000 years separate the characters on the right from those on the left (Fig. 7.4).

The Shang Dynasty (ca. 1700–1045 BCE)

Chinese records say that King Tang established the Shang dynasty. The Shang state was a linked collection of villages, stretching across the plains of the lower Yellow River valley. But it was not a contiguous state with distinct borders; other villages separated some of the Shang villages from one another, and were frequently at war with the Shang. The royal family surrounded itself with shamans, who soon developed into a kind of nobility and, in turn, walled urban centers formed around the nobles' palaces or temples. The proliferation of bronze vessels, finely carved jades, and luxury goods produced for the Shang elite suggests that well-organized centers of craft production were located nearby. The Shang nobility organized itself into armies—surviving inscriptions describe forces as large as 13,000 men—that controlled the countryside and protected the king.

The *Book of Changes*: The First Classic Chinese Text The Shang priests were avid interpreters of oracle bones. From a modern Western perspective, cracks in burned bones are a matter of pure chance, but to the Shang, no event was merely random. The belief that the cosmos is pervaded by a greater logic and order lies at the heart of Chinese culture. In other words, there is no such thing as chance, and no transformation is without significance, not even a crack in a bone. The challenge lies in conducting one's affairs in accordance with the transformations of the cosmos.

The first classic of Chinese literature, the *Book of Changes*, or *Yi Jing*, compiled later from ideas that developed in the Shang era, is a guide to interpreting the workings of the universe. A person seeking to understand some aspect of his or her life or situation poses a question and tosses a set of straws or coins. The arrangement they make when they fall leads to one of 64 readings (or hexagrams) in the *Yi Jing*. (Fu Xi, the culture-hero who invented writing, is also said to have invented the 8 trigrams that combine in pairs to form the 64 hexagrams.) Each hexagram describes the circumstances of the specific moment, which is, as the title suggests, always a moment of transition, a movement from one set of circumstances to the next. The *Yi Jing* prescribes certain behaviors appropriate to the moment. Thus, it is a book of wisdom.

This wisdom is based on a simple principle—that order derives from balance, a concept that the Chinese share with the ancient Egyptians. The Chinese believe that over time, through a series of changes, all things work toward a condition of balance. Thus, when things are out of balance, diviners might reliably predict the future by understanding that the universe tends to right itself. For example the eleventh hexagram, entitled *T'ai*, or "Peace," indicated the unification of heaven and earth. The image reads:

> Heaven and earth unite: the image of PEACE.
> Thus the ruler
> Divides and completes the course of heaven and earth,
> And so aids the people.

In fact, according to the Shang rulers, "the foundation of the universe" is based on the marriage of *Qian* (at once heaven and the creative male principle) and *Kun* (the earth, or receptive female principle), symbolized by the Chinese symbol of *yin-yang* (Fig. 7.5). *Yin* is soft, dark, moist, and cool; *yang* is hard, bright, dry, and warm. The two combine to create the endless cycles of change, from night to

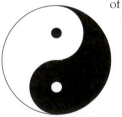

Fig. 7.5 Yin-yang symbol.

day, across the four seasons of the year. They balance the five elements (wood, fire, earth, metal, and water) and the five powers of creation (cold, heat, dryness, moisture, and wind). The yin-yang sign, then, is a symbol of harmonious integration, the perpetual interplay and mutual relation among all things. And note that each side contains a circle of the same values as its opposite—neither side can exist without the other.

Shang Bronze The interlocking of opposites illustrated by the yin-yang motif is also present in the greatest artistic achievement of the Shang, their bronze casting. In order to cast bronze, a negative shape must be perfected first, into which the molten metal is then poured to make a positive shape. Through the manufacture of ritual vessels, the Shang developed an extremely sophisticated bronze-casting technology, as advanced as any ever used. Made for offerings of food, water, and wine during ceremonies of ancestor worship, these bronze vessels were kept in an ancestral hall and brought out for banquets. Like formal dinnerware, each type of vessel had a specific shape and purpose; the *guang* (Fig. 7.6), for example, was a wine vessel.

The conduct of the ancestral rites was the most solemn duty of a family head, with explicit religious and political significance. While the vessel shapes derived from the shapes of Neolithic pottery, in bronze they gradually became decorated with fantastic, supernatural creatures, especially dragons. For the Shang, the bronzes came to symbolize political power and authority. Leaders made gifts of bronze as tokens of political patronage, and strict rules governed the number of bronzes a family might possess according to rank. Like the oracle bones, many of these bronzes are inscribed with written characters.

At the last Shang capital and royal burial center, Yinxu (present-day Anyang), archeologists have unearthed the undisturbed royal tomb of Lady Fu Hao (died ca. 1250 BCE), consort to the king Wu Ding. Consisting of a deep pit over which walled buildings were constructed as ritual sites to honor the dead, Lady Fu Hao's grave contained the skeletons of horses and dogs; about 440 cast and decorated bronzes, which probably originally held food and drink; 600 jade objects; chariots; lacquered items; weapons; gold and silver ornaments; and about 7,000 cowrie shells, which the Shang used as money. Though geographically separate, the Bronze Age tombs of the Sumerians, Egyptians, Mycenaeans, and Shang demonstrate the widespread belief in life after death. They also testify to the enormous wealth that Bronze Age rulers were capable of accumulating.

The Zhou Dynasty (1027–256 BCE)

The Shang believed that their leaders were the sole conduit to the heavenly ancestors. However, in 1027 BCE, a rebel tribe known as the Zhou overthrew the Shang dynasty, claiming that the Shang had lost the Mandate of Heaven by not ruling virtuously. The Zhou asserted that the legitimacy of a ruler derived from divine approval, and that the Shang had lost this favor because of their decadent

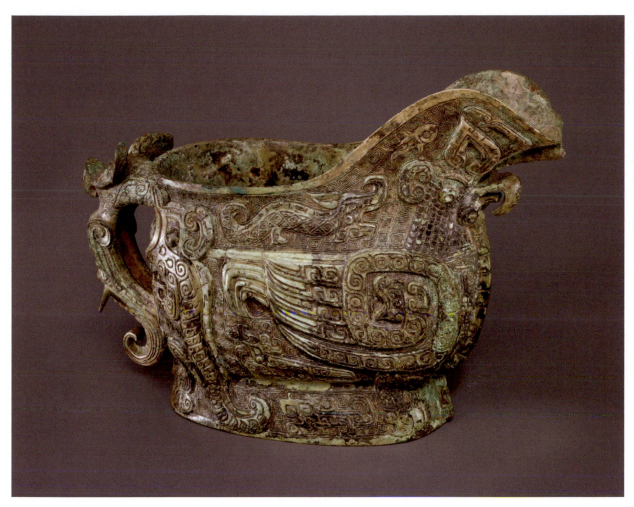

Fig. 7.6 Spouted ritual wine vessel (*guang*). Shang dynasty, early Anyang period, 13th century BCE. Bronze, height 8½".
The Metropolitan Museum of Art, New York. Rogers Fund, 1943 (43.25.4). Coiled serpents emerge from the wings and roaring tiger-dragons decorate the sides. Serving as a handle is a horned bird that is transformed into a dragon-serpent.

extravagances. Even so, the Zhou took measures to intermarry with the elite whom they had overthrown and took pains to conserve and restore what they admired of Shang culture. In fact, both the *Book of Changes* and the yin-yang symbol were originated by the Shang but codified and written down by the Zhou.

The Zhou ushered in an era of cultural refinement and philosophical accomplishment. One example is the oldest collection of Chinese poetry, the *Book of Songs* (*Shi Jing*), still taught in Chinese schools today. According to tradition, government officials were sent into the countryside to record the lyrics of songs that expressed the feelings of the people. The collection that survives, first compiled by the Zhou, consists of 305 poems from between the eleventh and seventh centuries BCE. The poems address almost every aspect of life. There are love poems, songs celebrating the king's rule, sacrificial hymns, and folk songs. Descriptions of nature abound—over 100 kinds of plant are mentioned, as well as 90 kinds of animal and insect. Marriage practices, family life, clothing, and food are all subjects of poems. One of the oldest celebrates the harvest as an expression of the family's harmony with nature,

the symbol that the family's ancestors are part of the same natural cycle of life and death, planting and harvest, as the universe as a whole (**Reading 7.1a**; for more selections from the *Book of Songs*, see **Reading 7.1**, page 241):

> ### READING 7.1a
>
> #### from the *Book of Songs*
>
> Abundant is the year, with much millet, much rice;
> But we have tall granaries,
> To hold myriads, many myriads and millions of grain.
> We make wine, make sweet liquor,
> We offer it to ancestor, to ancestress,
> We use it to fulfill all the rites,
> To bring down blessings upon each and all.

Zhou Music The *Book of Songs* lists 29 different types of percussion, wind, and stringed instrument. The Chinese classified their instruments according to which of eight different materials they were made from: bronze (bells),

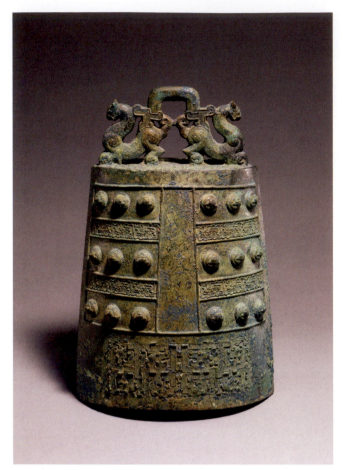

Fig. 7.7 Bell, Eastern Zhou dynasty, late Spring and Autumn period (770–ca. 475 BCE). Early 5th century BCE. Bronze, height 15". The Metropolitan Museum of Art, New York. Charlotte C. and John C. Weber Collection, Gift of Charlotte C. and John C. Weber through the Live Oak Foundation, 1988 (1988.20.7). Each face of the bell has three rows of rounded ornamental projections in the form of coiled serpents, further divided by trapezoidal panels with faint dragon motifs.

embedded in nature, and to attain it, the individual must practice the art of "not-doing." (It is said that those who speak about the Dao, do not know of it, and those who know about the Dao, do not speak of it.) The book, probably composed in the third century BCE, is traditionally ascribed to Lao Zi ("the Old One"), who lived during the sixth century BCE. In essence, it argues for a unifying principle in all nature, the interchangeability of energy and matter, a principle the Chinese call *qi*. The *qi* can be understood only by those who live in total simplicity, and to this end the Daoist engages in strict dietary practices, breathing exercises, and meditation. In considering such images as the one expressed in the following poem, the first in the volume, the Daoist finds his or her way to enlightenment (**Reading 7.2**):

READING 7.2

from the *Dao De Jing*

There are ways but the Way is uncharted;
There are names but not nature in words:
Nameless indeed is the source of creation
But things have a mother and she has a name.

The secret waits for the insight
Of eyes unclouded by longing;
Those who are bound by desire
See only the outward container.

These two come paired but distinct
By their names.
Of all things profound,
Say that their pairing is deepest,
The gate to the root of the world.

The final stanza seems to be a direct reference to the principle of yin-yang, itself a symbol of the *qi*. But the chief argument here, and the outlook of Daoism as a whole, is that enlightenment lies neither in the visible world nor in language, although to find the "way" one must, paradoxically, pass through or use both. Daoism thus represents a spiritual desire to transcend the material world.

If Daoism sought to leave the world behind, another great canon of teachings developed during the second half of the Zhou dynasty which sought to define the proper way to behave *in* the world. The Zhou controlled most of China until internal feuding and a coup d'état forced them to move their capital east in 771 BCE. From that point on, the power of the Zhou rulers gradually declined. For 550 years, until the final collapse of the Zhou in 221 BCE, China was subjected to ever greater political turmoil as warring political factions, with at best only nominal allegiance to the emperor, struggled for power. Reacting to this state of affairs was the man many consider China's greatest philosopher and teacher, Kong Fuzi, or, as he is known in the West, Confucius.

bamboo (flutes), bone (flutes), clay (simple wind instruments), animal skin (drums), calabash (mouth-organs), wood (percussion), and silk (zithers and lutes with silk strings). Like the Shang, the Zhou were masterful bronze artisans, and they carried this mastery into crafting bells (Fig. **7.7**) capable of producing two accurately tuned tones, one when struck in the center and another when struck on the side. Large sets of these bells have been discovered capable of producing 130 different pitches or notes (compared with 88 on a modern piano) available in octaves of up to 10 notes. Along with stone chimes, bells were the primary instrument of Chinese ritual music until the end of imperial rule in 1911.

Spiritual Beliefs: Daoism and Confucianism The songs in the *Shi Jing* are contemporary with the poems that make up the *Dao De Jing* (*The Way and Its Power*), the primary philosophical treatise, written in verse, of Daoism, the Chinese mystical school of thought. The *Dao* ("the way") is deeply

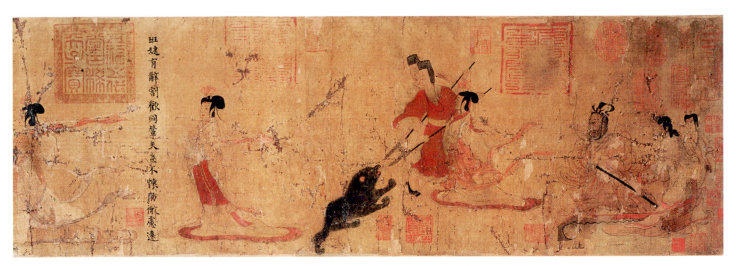

Fig. 7.8 Attributed to Gu Kaizhi, *Admonitions of the Imperial Instructress to Court Ladies* (detail). Six Dynasties period, ca. 344–464 CE. Handscroll, ink and colors on silk, 9¾" × 11'6". © The Trustees of the British Museum. This handscroll, painted nearly 900 years after the death of Confucius, shows his impact on Chinese culture.

Confucius was born to aristocratic parents in the province of Shandong in 551 BCE, the year before Pisistratus came to power in Athens. By his early twenties, Confucius had begun to teach a way of life, now referred to as Confucianism, based on self-discipline and proper relations among people. If each individual led a virtuous life, then the family would live in harmony. If the family lived in harmony, then the village would follow its moral leadership. If the village exercised proper behavior toward its neighbor villages, then the country would live in peace and thrive.

Traditional Chinese values—values that Confucius believed had once guided the Zhou, such as self-control, propriety, reverence for one's elders, and virtuous behavior—lie at the core of this system. Tradition has it that Confucius compiled and edited the *Book of Changes*, the *Book of Songs* (which he edited down to 305 verses), and four other "classic" Chinese texts: the *Book of History*, containing speeches and pronouncements of historical rulers; the *Book of Rites*, which is essentially a code of conduct; the *Spring and Autumn Annals*, a history of China up to the fifth century BCE; and a lost treatise on music.

Confucius particularly valued the *Book of Songs*. "My little ones," he told his followers, "why don't you study the *Songs*? Poetry will exalt you, make you observant, enable you to mix with others, provide an outlet for your vexations; you learn from it immediately to serve your parents and ultimately to serve your prince. It also provides wide acquaintance with the names of birds, beasts, and plants."

After his death in 479 BCE, Confucius's followers transcribed their conversations with him in a book known in English as the *Analects*. (For a selection, see **Reading 7.3** on page 242.) Where the *Dao De Jing* is a spiritual work, the *Analects* is a practical one. At the heart of Confucius's teaching is the principle of *li*—propriety in the conduct of the rites of ancestor worship. The courtesy and dignity required when performing the rites lead to the second principle, *ren*, or benevolent compassion and fellow feeling, the ideal relationship that should exist among all people. Based on respect for oneself, *ren* extends this respect to all others, manifesting itself as charity, courtesy, and above all, justice. *De*, or virtue, is the power of moral example that an individual, especially a ruler, can exert through a life dedicated to the exercise of *li* and *ren*. Finally, *wen*, or culture, will result. Poetry, music, painting, and the other arts will all reveal an inherent order and harmony reflecting the inherent order and harmony of the state. Like an excellent leader, brilliance in the arts illuminates virtue. The Chinese moral order depended not upon divine decree or authority, but instead upon the people's own right actions. A scene from a painted handscroll of a later period, known as *Admonitions of the Imperial Instructress to Court Ladies* (Fig. **7.8**), illustrates a Confucian story of wifely virtue and proper behavior. As the viewer unrolled the scroll (handscrolls were not meant to be viewed all at once, as displayed in modern museums, but to be unrolled right to left a foot or two at a time, as a tabletop might allow), he or she would observe a bear, who having escaped from his cage threatens the emperor, seated at the right. Until two guards arrive to try to keep the bear at bay, Lady Feng has stepped forward, courageously placing herself between the bear and her lord. She illustrates the fifth rule of Confucian philosophy—*yi*, or duty, the obligation of the wife to her husband and of the subject to her ruler.

Its emphasis on respect for age, authority, and morality made Confucianism extremely popular among Chinese leaders and the artists they patronized. It embraced the emperor, the state, and the family in a single ethical system with a hierarchy that was believed to mirror the structure of the cosmos. As a result, the Han dynasty (206 BCE–220 CE) adopted Confucianism as the Chinese state religion, and a thorough knowledge of the

Confucian classics was subsequently required of any politically ambitious person. Despite the later ascendancy among intellectuals of Daoism and Buddhism (which would begin to flourish in China after the collapse of the Han dynasty), Confucianism continued to be the core of civil service training in China until 1911, when the Chinese Republic ended the dynastic system. Even though Mao Zedong, chairman of the Chinese Communist Party from 1945 until his death in 1976, conducted a virulent campaign against Confucian thought, many in China now believe that Confucianism offers the most viable alternative to the nation's political status quo. In fact, the noncommunist "Little Dragons" of East Asia—Hong Kong, Singapore, Taiwan, and South Korea—would all attribute their economic success in the 1980s to their Confucian heritage.

The Chu State

When Chinese historian Sima Qian wrote the *Shiji*, or *Historical Records*, in 100 BCE, he regarded Confucianism as the product of the northern Chinese dynasties—the Shang and the Zhou—and Daoism as a product of the southern state of Chu, which occupied most of present-day Hubei and Hunan provinces. He considered the people of Chu barbarians—shiftless, uneducated, living off the abundance of a land that knew nothing of the cold, harsh reality of winters in the north, and indifferent to government. They were, from this later point of view, an exotic people who worshiped fantastical ghosts and

spirits (dragons, from the northern point of view, were not woven of the same fiber) through the agency of shamans and priests who led them in dancing, singing, and *yinsi*—excessive, even lewd, rites.

It can be argued that this view of the Chu people represents a later, Confucian, desire to repress shamanistic cult religious practices in the imperial court, but surviving sculptures, such as a carved wooden guardian figure with a long protruding tongue and wearing antlers made of dry lacquer (Fig. **7.9**), do suggest a unique ritual practice. Such figures were placed in tombs, often centered at the head of the coffin, presumably to intercede on the deceased's behalf with the spirit world. However much it might have challenged Confucian logic and authority, this southern Chu spirituality would remain firmly lodged in Chinese culture.

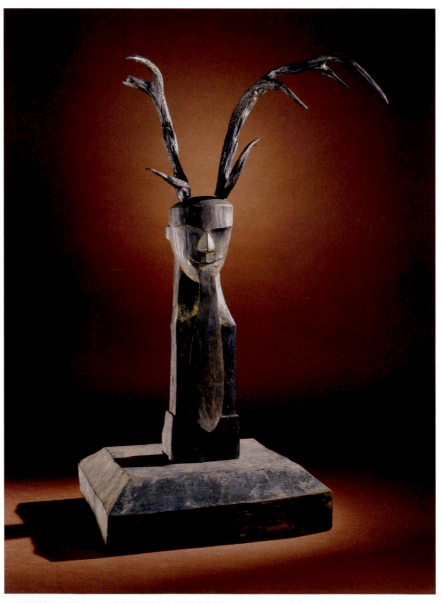

Fig. 7.9 Wooden guardian figure crowned by antlers made of dry lacquer. China, Eastern Zhou dynasty, 4th–3rd centuries BCE. Height (from base) 17¼". © The Trustees of the British Museum. This is one of the very few wooden sculptures of this period to have survived.

IMPERIAL CHINA

How do the art and literature of the Qin and Han dynasties reflect the values of the imperial court?

At the same time that Rome rose to dominance in the West (see Chapter 6), a similar empire arose in China. But whereas Rome's empire derived from outward expansion, China's empire arose from consolidation at the center. From about the time of Confucius onward, seven states vied for control. They mobilized armies to battle one another; iron weapons replaced bronze; they organized bureaucracies and established legal systems; merchants gained political power; and a "hundred schools of thought" flowered.

The Qin Dynasty (221–206 BCE): Organization and Control

This period of warring states culminated when the western state Qin (the origin of our name for China) conquered the other states and unified them under the Qin Empire in 221 BCE. Under the leadership of Qin Shihuangdi (r. 221–210 BCE), who declared himself "First Emperor," the Qin worked very quickly to achieve a stable society. To discourage nomadic invaders from the north, they built a wall from the Yellow Sea east of present-day Beijing far into Inner Mongolia, known today as the Great Wall of China (see Fig. 7.1).

The wall was constructed by soldiers, augmented by accused criminals, civil servants who found themselves in disfavor, and conscripts from across the countryside. Each family was required to provide one able-bodied adult male to work on the wall each year. It was made of rammed earth, reinforced by continuous, horizontal courses of brushwood, and faced with stone. Watchtowers were constructed at high points, and military barracks were built in the valleys below. At the same time, the Chinese constructed nearly 4,350 miles of roads, linking even the furthest reaches of the country to the Central Plain. By the end of the second century CE, China had some 22,000 miles of roads serving a country of nearly 1.5 million square miles.

Such massive undertakings could only have been accomplished by an administrative bureaucracy of extraordinary organizational skill. Indeed, in the 15 years that the Qin ruled China, the written language was standardized, a uniform coinage was introduced, all wagon axles were required to be the same width so that they would uniformly fit in the existing ruts on the Chinese roads (thus accommodating trade and travel), a system of weights and measures was introduced, and the country was divided into the administrative and bureaucratic provinces much as they exist to the present day.

Perhaps nothing tells us more about Qin organization and control than the tomb of its first emperor, Qin Shihuangdi (see *Closer Look*, pages 226–227). When he died, battalions of life-size earthenware guards in military formation were buried in pits beside his tomb. (Nearly 8,000 have been excavated so far.) Like the Great Wall, this monumental undertaking required an enormous workforce, and we know that the Qin enlisted huge numbers of workers in this and its other projects.

The Philosophy of Han Feizi To maintain control, in fact, the Qin suppressed free speech, persecuted scholars, burned classical texts, and otherwise exerted absolute power. They based their thinking on the writings of Han Feizi, who had died in 233 BCE, just before the Qin took power. Orthodox Confucianism had been codified by Meng-zi, known as Mencius (ca. 370–300 BCE), an itinerant philosopher and sage who argued for the innate goodness of the individual. He believed that bad character was a result of society's inability to provide a positive, cultivating atmosphere in which individuals might realize their capacity for goodness. Han Feizi, on the other hand, argued that human beings were inherently evil and innately selfish (exactly the opposite of Mencius's point of view). **Legalism**, as Han Feizi's philosophy came to be called, required that the state exercise its power over the individual, because no agency other than the state could instill enough fear in the individual to elicit proper conduct. The Qin Legalist bureaucracy, coupled with an oppressive tax structure imposed to pay for their massive civil projects, soon led to rebellion, and after only 15 years in power, the Qin collapsed.

The Han Dynasty (206 BCE–220 CE): The Flowering of Culture

In place of the Qin, the Han dynasty came to power, inaugurating over 400 years of intellectual and cultural growth. The Han emperors installed Confucianism as the official state philosophy and established an academy to train civil servants. Where the Qin had disenfranchised scholars, the Han honored them, even going so far as to give them an essential role in governing the country.

Han prosperity was constantly threatened by incursions of nomadic peoples to the north, chiefly the Huns, whom the Chinese called Xiongnu, and whose impact would later be felt as far away as Rome. In 138 BCE, Emperor Wu (r. 141–87 BCE) attempted to forge military alliances with the Huns, sending General Zhang Qian with 100 of his best fighting men into the northern territories. The Huns held General Zhang captive for ten years. When he returned, he spoke of horses that were far stronger and faster than those in China. Any army using them, he believed, would be unbeatable. In fact, horses could not be bred successfully in China owing to a lack of calcium in the region's water and vegetation, and until General Zhang's report, the Chinese had known horses only as small, shaggy creatures of Mongolian origin. To meet the Huns on their own terms, with cavalry instead of infantry, China needed horses from the steppes of western Asia.

CLOSER LOOK

One day in 1974, peasants digging a well on the flat plain 1,300 yards east of the huge Qin dynasty burial mound of the emperor Qin Shihuangdi, in the northern Chinese province of Shaanxi, unearthed parts of a life-size clay soldier—a head, hands, and body. Archeologists soon discovered an enormous subterranean pit beneath the fields containing an estimated 6,000 infantrymen, most standing 4 abreast in 11 parallel trenches paved with bricks. In 1976 and 1977, two smaller but equally spectacular sites were discovered north of the first one, containing another 1,400 individual warriors and horses, complete with metal weaponry.

Qin Shihuangdi's actual tomb has never been excavated. The burial mound rises 140 feet above the plain. Historical records indicate that below the mound is a subterranean palace estimated to be about 400 feet by 525 feet. According to the *Shiji* (*Historical Records*) of Sima Qian, the emperor was buried there in a bronze casket surrounded by

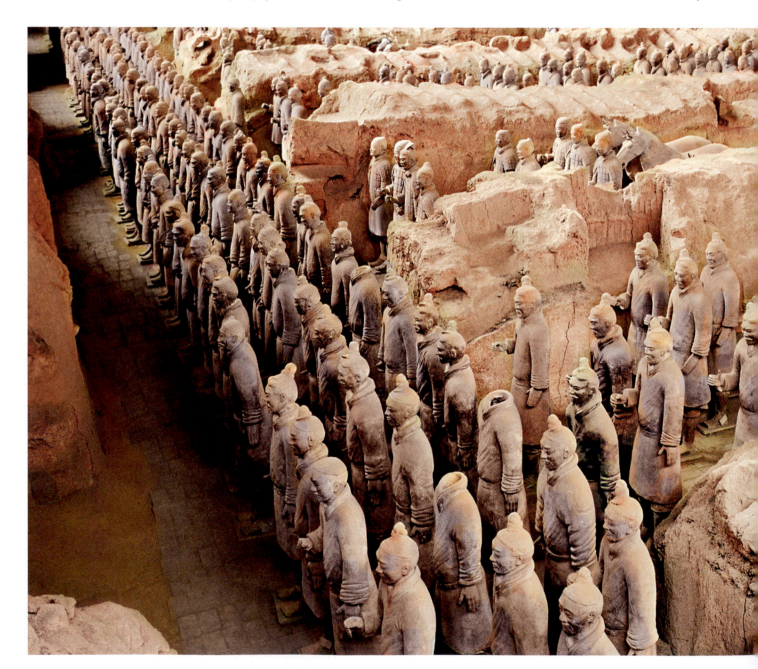

a river of mercury. Scientific tests conducted by Chinese archeologists confirm the presence of large quantities of mercury in the soil of the burial mound. Magnetic scans of the tomb have also revealed large numbers of coins, suggesting the emperor was buried with his treasury.

Something to Think About …

Why do you suppose this ceramic army was deployed outside the tomb of Qin Shihuangdi and not in it?

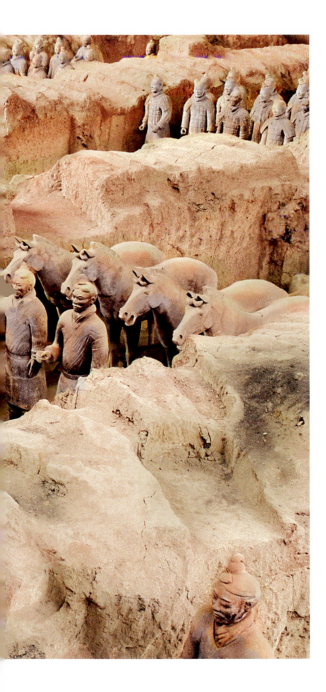

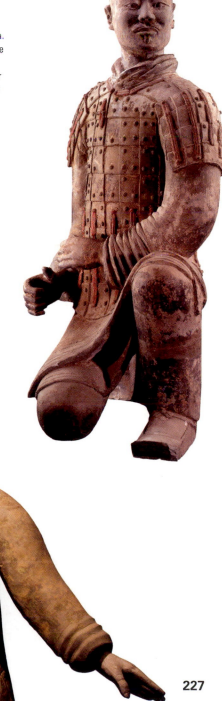

Left: Soldiers and horses, from the pits near the tomb of Qin Shihuangdi, Shaanxi Province, China. Qin dynasty, ca. 210 BCE. Terra cotta, life-size. The practice of fashioning clay replicas of humans for burial at mausoleum sites replaced an earlier practice of actual human sacrifice. Over 700,000 people were employed in preparing the tomb.

Right and below: Two terra-cotta soldiers from the burial mound of Qin Shihuangdi, Shaanxi Province, China. Both ca. 210 BCE. On the right, a kneeling archer, height 48"; below, an infantryman poised for hand-to-hand combat, height 70". The bodies of most of the soldiers in the tomb appear to have been mass-produced in molds. After each stylized body was baked, head and hands were added. No two heads are alike. Many seem to possess unique, individual facial features, and they exhibit a variety of hairstyles. They were subsequently painted in vivid colors, and most carried actual weapons. Knives, spears, swords, and arrowheads have been found at the site.

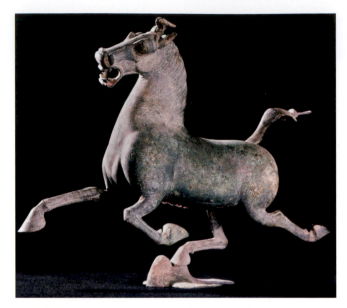

Fig. 7.10 *Flying Horse Poised on One Leg on a Swallow*, from the tomb of Governor-General Zhang at Wuwei, Gansu. Late Han dynasty, **2nd century CE.** Bronze, 13½" × 17¾". Gansu Provincial Museum, Lanzhou. According to Chinese tradition, these horses sweated blood, perhaps the result of a parasitic infection. The Chinese, incidentally, also imported grass seed to feed these horses.

"The Heavenly Horses" A small bronze horse found in the tomb of General Zhang at Wuwei in Gansu represents the kind of horse to which the Chinese aspired (Fig. **7.10**). Its power is captured in the energetic lines of its composition, its flaring nostrils and barreled chest. But it is, simultaneously, perfectly, almost impossibly, balanced on one leg, as if defying gravity, having stolen the ability to fly from the bird beneath its hoof. In 101 BCE, the emperor Wu, awaiting delivery of 30 such horses in the Chinese capital of Chang'an, composed a hymn in their honor (**Reading 7.4**):

READING 7.4

from Emperor Wu's "Heavenly Horses"

The Heavenly Horses are coming,
Coming from the Far West …
The Heavenly Horses are coming
Across the pastureless wilds
A thousand leagues at a stretch,
Following the eastern road …
Should they choose to soar aloft,
Who could keep pace with them?
The Heavenly Horses are coming …

Han Poetry Under Emperor Wu, Chinese literary arts flourished. In 120 BCE, he established the *Yue fu*, the so-called Music Bureau, which would come to employ some 829 people charged with collecting the songs of the common people. The folk style of the *yuefu* songs was widely imitated, both by court poets during the Han and throughout the history of Chinese poetry. The lines are of uneven length, although often of five characters, and emphasize the joys and vicissitudes of daily life. A case in point is a poem by Liu Xijun, a Chinese princess who, around 110 BCE, was married for political reasons to the chief of the Wusun, a band of nomads who lived in the steppes of northwest China. Her husband, as it turned out when she arrived, was old and decrepit, spoke almost no Chinese, and by and large had nothing to do with her, seeing her every six months or so. This is her "Lament" (**Reading 7.5**):

READING 7.5

Liu Xijun, "Lament"

My family married me off
to the King of the Wusun.
and I live in an alien land
a million miles from nowhere.
My house is a tent,
My walls are of felt.
Raw flesh is all I eat,
with horse milk to drink.
I always think of home
and my heart strings,
O to be a yellow snow-goose
floating home again!

The poem's last two lines—what might be called the flight of Liu Xijun's imagination—are typical of Chinese poetry, where time and again the tragic circumstances of life are overcome through an image of almost transcendent natural beauty.

As Liu Xijun's poem suggests, women poets and scholars were common—and respected—during the Han dynasty. But as the circumstances surrounding Liu Xijun's poem also suggest, women did not enjoy great power in society. The traditional Chinese family was organized around basic Confucian principles: Elder family members were wiser, and therefore superior to the younger, and males were superior to females. Thus, while a grandmother might hold sway over her grandson, a wife owed unquestioning obedience to her husband. The unenviable plight of women is the subject of a poem by Fu Xuan, a male poet of the late Han dynasty, who apparently was one of the most prolific poets of his day, although only 63 of his poems survive (**Reading 7.6**):

READING 7.6

Fu Xuan, "To Be A Woman"

It is bitter to be a woman,
the cheapest thing on earth.
A boy stands commanding in the doorway
like a god descended from the sky.
His heart hazards the four seas,
thousands of miles of wind and dust,

---

but no one laughs when a girl is born.
The family doesn't cherish her.
When she's a woman she hides in back rooms,
scared to look a man in the face.
They cry when she leaves to marry—
a brief rain, then mere clouds.
Head bowed she tries to compose her face,
her white teeth stabbing red lips.
She bows and kneels endlessly,
even before concubines and servants.
If their love is strong as two stars
she is like a sunflower in the sun,
but when their hearts are water and fire
a hundred evils descend on her.
The years change her jade face
and her lord will find new lovers.
Who were close like body and shadow
will be remote as Chinese and Mongols.
Sometimes even Chinese and Mongols meet
but they'll be far as polar stars.

The poem is notable for the acuity and intensity of its imagery—her "white teeth stabbing red lips," the description of a close relationship as "like body and shadow," and, in the last lines, the estrangement of their relationship to a point as far apart as "polar stars," farther apart even than the Chinese and Mongols. (And who, one must ask, is more like the barbarian hordes, the male or the female?)

Han Architecture What we know about the domestic setting of Han dynasty society we can gather mostly from surviving poetic images describing everyday life in the home, but our understanding of domestic architecture derives from ceramic models. A model of a house found in a tomb, presumably provided for the use of the departed in the afterlife, is four stories high and topped by a watchtower (Fig. 7.11). The family lived in the middle two stories, while livestock, probably pigs and oxen, were kept in the gated lower level with its courtyard extending in front of the house.

Architecturally, the basic form of the house is commonly found across the world—rectangular halls with columns supporting the roof or the floor above. The walls serve no weight-bearing function. Rather, they serve as screens separating the inside from the outside, or one interior room from another. Distinctive to Chinese architecture are the broad eaves of the roof, which would become a standard feature of East Asian construction. Adding playful charm is the elaborate decoration of the facade, including painted trees flanking the courtyard.

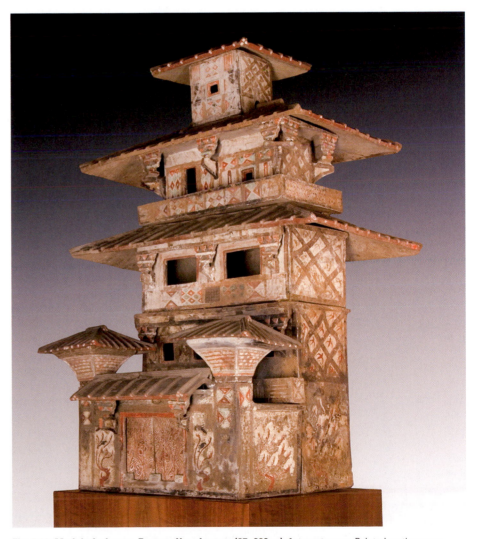

Fig. 7.11 Model of a house. Eastern Han dynasty (25–200 CE), 1st century CE. Painted earthenware with unfired coloring, 52" × 33½" × 27". The Nelson-Atkins Museum of Art, Kansas City, Missouri. This is one of the largest and most complete models of a Han house known.

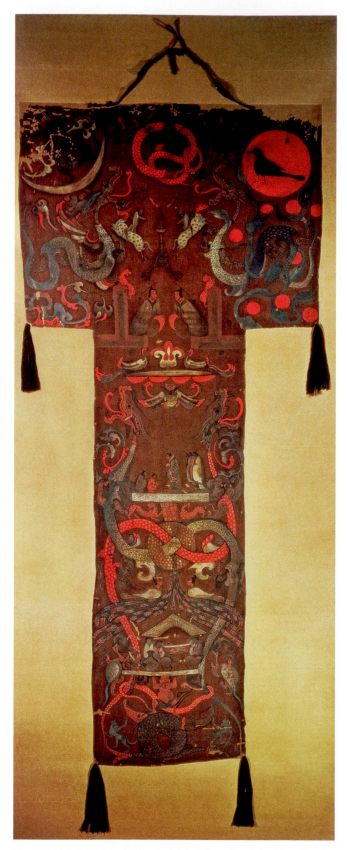

Fig. 7.12 Painted banner from the tomb of the wife of the Marquis of Dai, Mawangdui, Changsha, Hunan. Han dynasty, ca. 160 BCE. Colors on silk, height 6'8½". Hunan Provincial Museum, Changsha. The banner was found in the innermost of the nested coffins opened in 1972.

Han Silk Aside from their military value, horses advanced the growth of trade along the Silk Road. Nearly 5,000 miles long, this trade route led from the Yellow River valley to the Mediterranean, and along it, the Chinese traded their most exclusive commodity, silk. (See *Continuity & Change*, page 239.) The quality of Han silk is evident in a silk banner from the tomb of the wife of the Marquis of Dai, discovered on the outskirts of present-day Changsha in Hunan (Fig. **7.12**). Painted with scenes representing the underworld, the earthly realm, and the heavens, it represents the Han conception of the cosmos. Long, sinuous lines representing dragons' tails, coiling serpents, long-tailed birds, and flowing draperies unify the three realms. In the right corner of the heavenly realm, above the crossbar of the T, is an image of the sun containing a crow, and in the other corner is a crescent moon supporting a toad. Between them is a deity entwined within his own long, red serpent tail. The deceased noblewoman herself stands on the white platform in the middle region of the banner. Three attendants stand behind her and two figures kneel before her, bearing gifts. On a white platform in the lower realm, bronze vessels contain food and wine for the deceased.

Papermaking and Other Han Technologies One of the important characteristics of Han poetry is that, as opposed to the poems in the *Book of Songs*, many poems did not emerge out of oral traditions but originated as written works. In the West, the limitations of papyrus as a writing medium had led to the invention of parchment at Pergamon (see Chapter 5), but the Chinese invention of cellulose-based paper in 105 CE by Cai Lun, a eunuch and attendant to the imperial court who held a post responsible for manufacturing instruments and weapons, enabled China to develop widespread literacy much more rapidly than the West. Paper made of hemp had already been produced by the Han for over 200 years, but Cai Lun improved both the techniques used and its quality while using a variety of materials, such as tree bark, hemp, and rags. Although modern technologies have simplified the process, his method remains basically unchanged—the suspension in water of softened plant fibers that are formed in molds into thin sheets, couched (pressed), drained, and then dried.

The Han were especially inventive. Motivated by trade, they began to make maps, becoming the world's first cartographers. They invented important agricultural technologies such as the wheelbarrow and horse collar. They learned to measure the magnitude of earthquakes with a crude but functional seismograph. But persistent warring with the Huns required money to support military and bureaucratic initiatives. Unable to keep up with increased taxes, many peasants were forced off the land and popular rebellion ensued. By the third century CE, the Han dynasty had collapsed. China reentered a period of political chaos lasting from 220 until 589 CE, when imperial rule finally regained its strength.

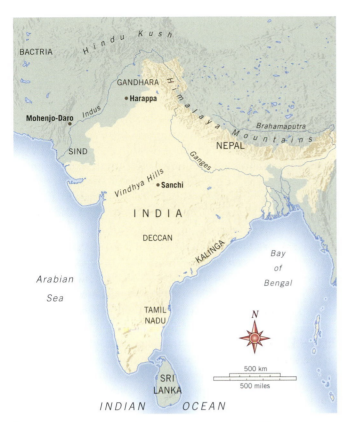

Map 7.2 **India around 1500 BCE.** Cut off from the rest of Asia by high mountains to the north, India was nevertheless a center of trade by virtue of its prominent maritime presence.

ANCIENT INDIA

How did the Hindu and Buddhist faiths help to shape the cultures of ancient India?

Indian civilization was born along the Indus River in the northwest corner of the Indian subcontinent in present-day Pakistan, somewhere around 2700 BCE in an area known as Sind—from which the words *India* and *Hindu* originate (see Map **7.2**). The earliest Indian peoples lived in at least two great cities in the Indus Valley, Mohenjo-Daro, on the banks of the Indus, and Harappa, on the River Ravi, downstream from present-day Lahore. These great cities thrived until around 1900 BCE and were roughly contemporaneous with Sumerian Ur, the Old Kingdom of Egypt, and Minoan civilization in the Aegean.

The cities were discovered by chance in the early 1920s, and excavations have continued since. The best preserved of the sites is Mohenjo-Daro. Built atop a citadel is a complex of buildings, presumably a governmental or religious center, surrounded by a wall 50 feet high. Set among the buildings on the citadel is a giant pool (Fig. **7.13**). Perhaps a public bath or a ritual space, its finely fitted bricks, laid on edge and bound together with gypsum plaster, made it watertight. The bricks on the side walls of the tank were covered with a thick layer of bitumen (natural tar) to keep water from seeping through the walls and up into the superstructure.

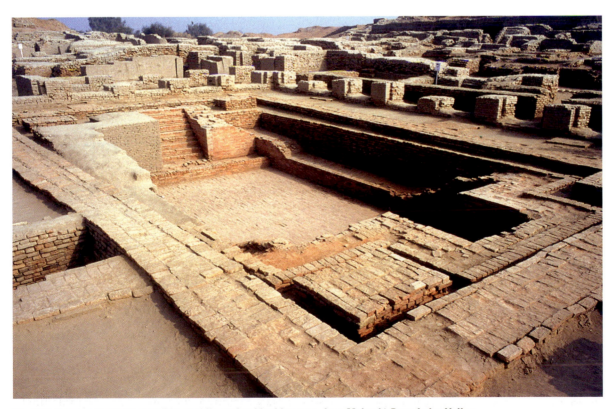

Fig. 7.13 **Large water tank, possibly a public or ritual bathing area, from Mohenjo-Daro, Indus Valley civilization. ca. 2600–1900 BCE.** It measures approximately 39½ feet north–south and 23 feet wide, with a maximum depth of almost 8 feet.

The pool was open to the air and originally surrounded by a brick colonnade.

Outside the wall and below the citadel, a city of approximately 6 to 7 square miles, with broad avenues and narrow side streets, was laid out in a rough grid. It appears to have been home to a population of between 20,000 and 50,000. Most of the houses were two stories tall and built around a central courtyard. A network of covered drainage systems ran through the streets, channeling waste and rainwater into the river. The houses were built with standard sizes of baked brick, each measuring 2¾ × 5½ × 11 inches, a ratio of 1:2:4. A brick of identical ratio but larger—4 × 8 × 16 inches—was used in the building of platforms

and city walls. Unlike the sun-dried bricks used in other cultures at the time, Mohenjo-Daro's bricks were fired, which made them much more durable. All of this suggests a civilization of considerable technological know-how and sophistication.

The arts of the Indus civilizations include human figurines and animal figurines made of stone, terra cotta, bronze, and other materials—including the so-called "priest-king" found at Mohenjo-Daro (Fig. **7.14**)—terracotta pottery, and various styles of decorative ornaments for human wear, including beads and stoneware bangles. Over 2,000 small seals have been unearthed. Carved from steatite stone, coated with alkali, and then fired to produce a luminous white surface, many depict animals with an extraordinary naturalism, especially considering that they are rendered in such miniature detail (Fig. **7.15**). Depictions of warfare or conquered enemies are strikingly absent in representational art. As the top of this seal indicates, the peoples of the valley had a written language, although it remains undeciphered.

Sometime around 1500 BCE the Aryans, nomads from the north, invaded the Indus River valley and conquered its inhabitants, making them slaves. Thus began the longest-lasting set of rigid, class-based societal divisions in world history, the Indian caste system. By the beginning of the first millennium BCE, these castes consisted of five principal groups, based on occupation: At the bottom of the ladder was a group considered "untouchable," people so scorned by society that they were not even considered a caste. Next in line were the Shudras, unskilled workers. Then came

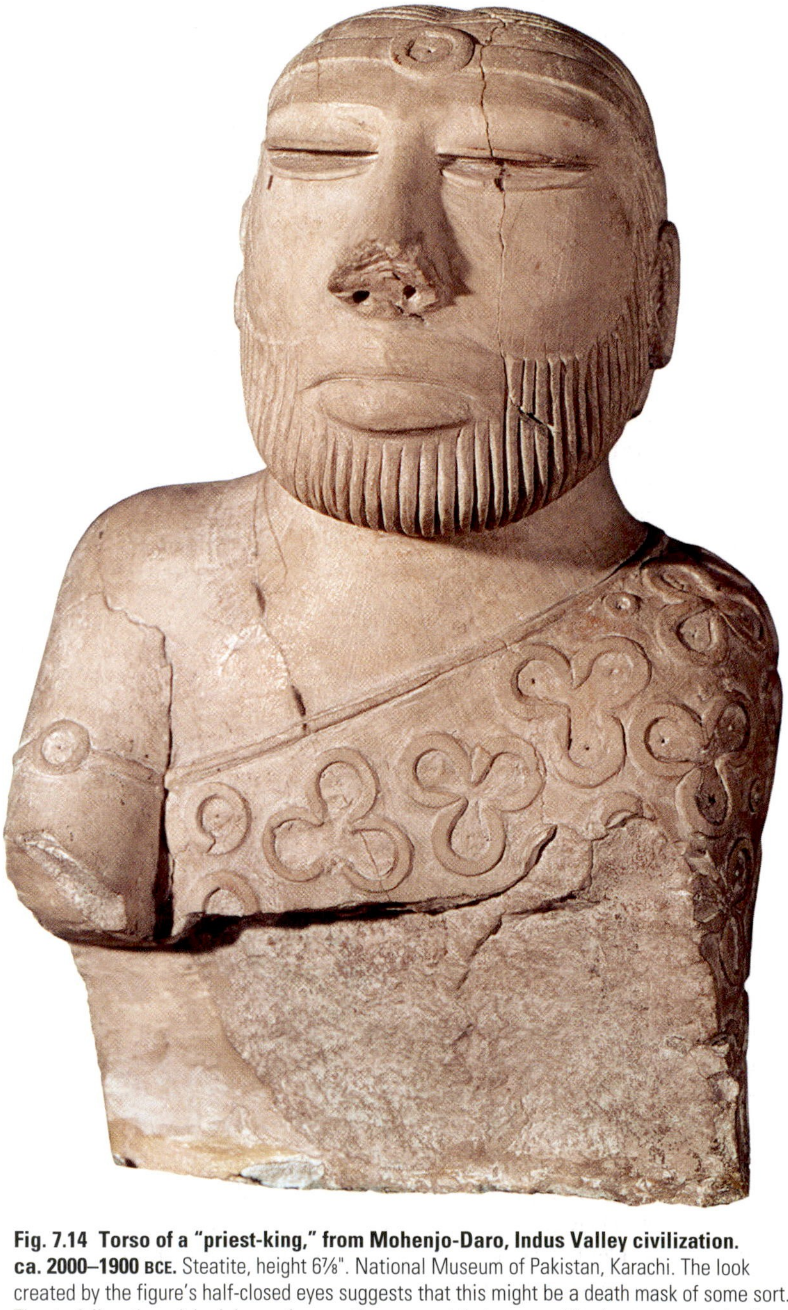

Fig. 7.14 Torso of a "priest-king," from Mohenjo-Daro, Indus Valley civilization. ca. 2000–1900 BCE. Steatite, height 6⅞". National Museum of Pakistan, Karachi. The look created by the figure's half-closed eyes suggests that this might be a death mask of some sort. The *trefoil*, or three-lobed decorations on the garment that crosses his chest, were originally filled with red paint.

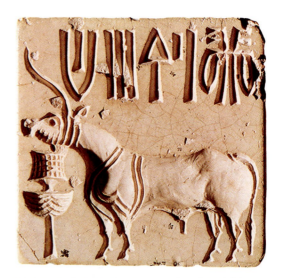

Fig. 7.15 Seal depicting a horned animal, Indus Valley civilization. ca. 2500–1900 BCE. Steatite, approx. 1¼" × 1¼". National Museum of Pakistan, Karachi. The function of seals like this remains unknown.

the Vaishyas, artisans and merchants. They were followed by the Kshatriyas, rulers and warriors. At the highest level were the Brahmins, priests and scholars.

Hinduism and the Vedic Tradition

The social castes were sanctioned by the religion the Aryans brought with them, a religion based on a set of sacred hymns to the Aryan gods. These hymns, called *Vedas*, were written in the Aryan language, Sanskrit, and they gave their name to an entire period of Indian civilization, the Vedic period (ca. 1500–322 BCE). From the *Vedas* in turn came the *Upanishads*, a book of mystical and philosophical texts that date from sometime after 800 BCE. Taken together, the *Vedas* and the *Upanishads* form the basis of the Hindu religion, with Brahman, the universal soul, at its center. The religion has no single body of doctrine, nor any standard set of practices. It is defined above all by the diversity of its beliefs and deities. Indeed, several images of mother goddesses, stones in the phallic form, as well as a seal with an image that resembles the Hindu god Shiva, have been excavated at various Indus sites, leading scholars to believe that certain aspects and concepts of Hinduism survived from the Indus civilizations and were incorporated into the Vedic religion.

The *Upanishads* argue that all existence is a fabric of false appearances. What appears to the senses is entirely illusory. Only Brahman is real. Thus, in a famous story illustrating the point, a tiger, orphaned as a cub, is raised by goats. It learns, as a matter of course, to eat grass and make goat sounds. But one day it meets another tiger, who takes it to a pool to look at itself. There, in its reflection in the water, it discovers its true nature. The individual soul needs to discover the same truth, a truth that will free it from the endless cycle of birth, death, and rebirth and unite it with the Brahman in **nirvana**, a place or state free from worry, pain, and the external world.

Brahma, Vishnu, and Shiva As Hinduism developed, the functions of Brahman, the divine source of all being, were split among three gods: Brahma, the creator; Vishnu, the preserver; and Shiva, the destroyer. Vishnu was one of the most popular of the Hindu deities. In his role as preserver, he is the god of benevolence, forgiveness, and love, and like the other two main Hindu gods, he was believed capable of assuming human form, which he did more often than the other gods due to his great love for humankind. Among Vishnu's most famous incarnations is his appearance as Rama in the oldest of the Hindu epics, the *Ramayana* (*Way of Rama*), written by Valmiki in about 550 BCE. Like Homer in ancient Greece, Valmiki gathered together many existing legends and myths into a single story, in this case narrating the lives of Prince Rama and his queen, Sita. The two serve as models of Hindu life. Rama is the ideal son, brother, husband, warrior, and king, and Sita loves, honors, and serves her husband with absolute and unquestioning fidelity. These characters face moral dilemmas to which they must react according to **dharma**, good and righteous conduct reflecting the cosmic moral order that underlies all existence. For Hindus, correct actions can lead to cosmic harmony; bad actions, violating dharma, can trigger cosmic tragedies such as floods and earthquakes.

An equally important incarnation of Vishnu is as the charioteer Krishna in the later Indian epic the *Mahabharata*, composed between 400 BCE and 400 CE. In the sixth book of the *Mahabharata*, titled the *Bhagavad Gita* (see **Reading 7.7**, pages 242–244), Krishna comes to the aid of Arjuna, a warrior who is tormented by the conflict between his duty to fight and kill his kinsmen in battle and the Hindu prohibition against killing. Krishna explains to Arjuna that as a member of the Kshatriya caste—that is, as a warrior—he is freed from the Hindu sanction against killing. In fact, by fighting well and doing his duty, he can free himself from the endless cycle of birth, death, and reincarnation, and move toward spiritual union with the Brahman.

But Vishnu's popularity is probably most attributable to his celebration of erotic love, which to Hindus symbolizes the mingling of the self and the absolute spirit of Brahman. In the *Vishnu Puranas* (the "old stories" of Vishnu), collected about 500 CE, Vishnu, in his incarnation as Krishna, is depicted as seducing one after another of his devotees. In one story of the *Vishnu Puranas*, he seduces an entire band of milkmaids: "They considered every instant without him a myriad of years; and prohibited (in vain) by husbands, fathers, brothers, they went forth at night to sport with Krishna, the object of their affection." Allowing themselves to be seduced does not suggest that the milkmaids were immoral, but shows an almost inevitable manifestation of their souls' quest for union with divinity.

If Brahma is the creator of the world, Shiva takes what Brahma has made and embodies the world's cyclic rhythms. Since in Hinduism the destruction of the old world is followed by the creation of a new world, Shiva's role as destroyer is both positive and necessary. In this sense, he possesses reproductive powers, and in this part of his being, he is represented as a *linga* ("phallus"), often carved in stone on temple grounds or at shrines.

The Goddess Devi Goddess worship is fundamental to Hindu religion. Villages usually recognize goddesses as their protectors, and the goddess Devi is worshiped in many forms throughout India. She is the female aspect without whom the male aspect, which represents consciousness or discrimination, remains impotent and void. For instance, in the *Devi Mahatmayam*, another of the Puranas, composed like the *Vishnu Puranas* around 500 CE, Vishnu was asleep on the great cosmic ocean, and due to his slumber, Brahma was unable to create. Devi intervenes, kills the demons responsible for Vishnu's slumber, and helps wake up Vishnu. Thus continues the cycle of life.

Devi is synonymous with Shakti, the primordial cosmic energy, and represents the dynamic forces that move through the entire universe. Shaktism, a particular brand of Hindu faith that regards Devi as the Supreme Brahman

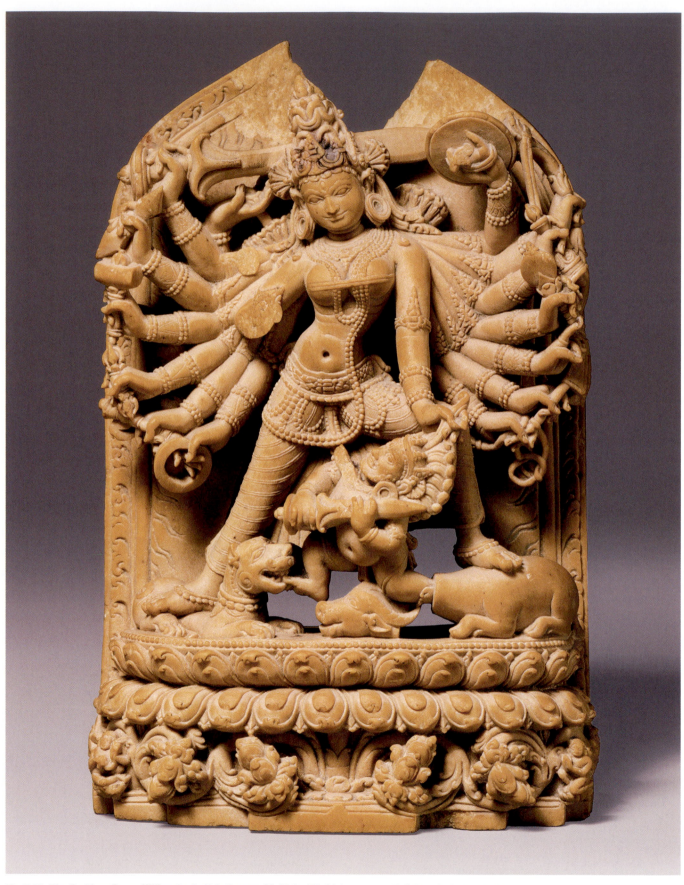

Fig. 7.16 *The Goddess Durga Killing the Buffalo Demon, Mahisha (**Mahishasuramardini**), Bangladesh or India.*
Pala period, 12th century CE. Argillite, height. 5⅚". The Metropolitan Museum of Art, New York. Durga represents the warrior aspect of Devi.

itself, believes that all other forms of divinity, female or male, are themselves simply forms of Devi's diverse manifestations. But she has a number of particular manifestations. In an extraordinary miniature carving from the twelfth century, Devi is seen in her manifestation as Durga (Fig. 7.16), portrayed as the 16-armed slayer of a buffalo inhabited by the fierce demon Mahisha. Considered invincible, Mahisha threatens to destroy the world, but Durga comes to the rescue. In this image, she has just severed the buffalo's head and Mahisha, in the form of a tiny, chubby man, his hair composed of snake heads, emerges from the buffalo's decapitated body and looks up admiringly at Durga even as his toes are being bitten by her lion. Durga smiles serenely as she hoists Mahisha up by his hair and treads gracefully on the buffalo's body.

Buddhism: "The Path of Truth"

Because free thought and practice mark the Hindu religion, it is hardly surprising that other religious movements drew on it and developed from it. Buddhism is one of those. Its founder, Shakyamuni Buddha, lived from about 563 to 483 BCE. He was born Prince Siddhartha Gautama, child of a ruler of the Shakya clan—Shakyamuni means "sage of the Shakyas"—and was raised to be a ruler himself. Troubled by what he perceived to be the suffering of all human beings, he abandoned the luxurious lifestyle of his father's palace to live in the wilderness. For six years he meditated, finally attaining complete enlightenment while sitting under a banyan tree at Bodh Gaya. Shortly thereafter he gave his first teaching, at the Deer Park at Sarnath, expounding the Four Noble Truths:

1. Life is suffering.
2. This suffering has a cause, which is ignorance.
3. Ignorance can be overcome and eliminated.
4. The way to overcome this ignorance is by following the Eightfold Path of right view, right resolve, right speech, right action, right livelihood, right effort, right mindfulness, and right concentration.

Living with these truths in mind, one might overcome what Buddha believed to be the source of all human suffering—the desire for material things, which is the primary form of ignorance. In doing so, one would find release from the illusions of the world, from the cycle of birth, death, and rebirth, and ultimately reach nirvana. These principles are summed up in the *Dhammapada*, the most popular canonical text of Buddhism, which consists of 423 aphorisms, or sayings, attributed to Buddha and arranged by subject into 26 chapters (see **Reading 7.8**, pages 244–245). Its name is a compound consisting of *dhamma*, the vernacular form of the formal Sanskrit word *dharma*, mortal truth, and *pada*, meaning "foot" or "step"—hence it is "the path of truth." The aphorisms are widely admired for their wisdom and their sometimes stunning beauty of expression.

The Buddha (which means "Enlightened One") taught for 40 years until his death at age 80. His followers preached that anyone could achieve buddhahood, the ability to see the ultimate nature of the world. Persons of very near total enlightenment, but who have vowed to help others achieve buddhahood before crossing over to nirvana, came to be known as **bodhisattvas**, meaning "those whose essence is wisdom." In art, bodhisattvas wear the princely garb of India, while Buddhas wear a monk's robe.

The Maurya Empire Buddhism would become the official state religion of the Maurya Empire, which ruled India from 321 to 185 BCE. The Empire was founded by Chandragupta Maurya (r. ca. 321–297 BCE) in eastern India. Its capital was Pataliputra (present-day Patna) on the Ganges River, but Chandragupta rapidly expanded the Empire westward, taking advantage of the vacuum of power in the Indus Valley that followed in the wake of Alexander the Great's invasion of 326 BCE (see Chapter 5). In 305 BCE, the Hellenistic Greek ruler Seleucus I, ruler of one of the three states that succeeded Alexander's empire, the kingdom of the Seleucids, tried to reconquer India once again. He and Chandragupta eventually signed a peace treaty, and diplomatic relations between Seleucid Greece and the Maurya Empire were established. Several Greek ambassadors were soon residing in the Mauryan court, the beginning of substantial relations between East and West. Chandragupta was succeeded by his son Bindusara (r. ca. 297–273 BCE), who also had a Greek ambassador at his court, and who extended the Empire southward, conquering almost all of the Indian peninsula and establishing the Maurya Empire as the largest empire of its time. He was in turn succeeded by his son Ashoka (r. ca. 273–232 BCE).

It was Ashoka who established Buddhism as the official state religion. On a battlefield in 261 BCE, Ashoka was appalled by the carnage he had inflicted in his role as a warrior-king. As he watched a monk walking slowly among the dead, Ashoka was moved to decry violence and force of arms, and to spread the teachings of Buddha. From that point, Ashoka, who had been described as "the cruel Ashoka," began to be known as "the pious Ashoka." At a time when Rome was engaged in the Punic Wars, Ashoka pursued an official policy of nonviolence. The unnecessary slaughter or mutilation of animals was forbidden. Sport hunting was banned, and although the limited hunting of game for the purpose of consumption was tolerated, Ashoka promoted vegetarianism. He built hospitals for people and animals alike, preached the humane treatment of all living things, and regarded all his subjects as equals, regardless of politics, religion, or caste. He also embarked on a massive Buddhist architectural campaign, erecting as many as 8,400 shrines and monuments to Buddha throughout the Empire. Soon, Buddhism would spread beyond India, and Buddhist monks from China would travel to India to observe Buddhist practices.

📖 **Read** the document related to the Buddha on **MyArtsLab**

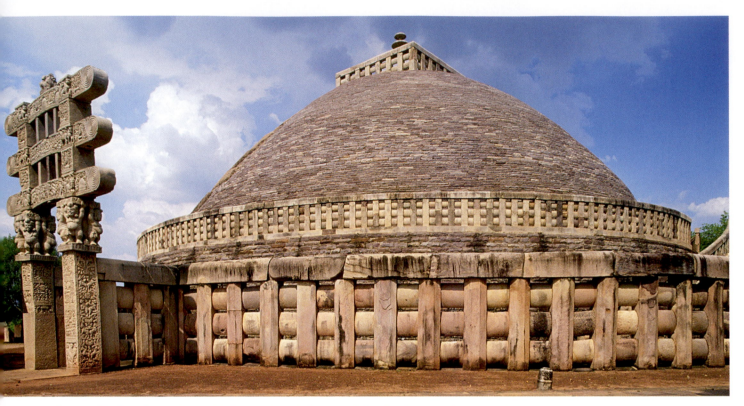

Fig. 7.17 The Great Stupa, Sanchi, Madhya Pradesh, India, view of the West Gateway. Founded 3rd century BCE, enlarged ca. 150–50 BCE. Shrine height 50', diameter 105'. In India, the stupa is the principal monument to Buddha. The stupa symbolizes, at once, the World Mountain, the Dome of Heaven, and the Womb of the Universe.

View the Closer Look for the Great Stupa at Sanchi on **MyArtsLab**

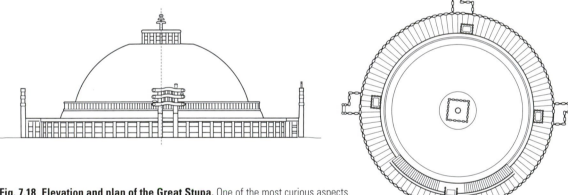

Fig. 7.18 Elevation and plan of the Great Stupa. One of the most curious aspects of the Great Stupa is that its four gates are not aligned on an axis with the four openings in the railing. Some scholars believe that this arrangement is derived from gates on farms, which were designed to keep cattle out of the fields.

Buddhist Monuments: The Great Stupa Among the most famous of the Buddhist monuments that Ashoka erected is the Great Stupa at Sanchi (Fig. 7.17), which was enlarged in the second century BCE. A **stupa** is a kind of burial mound. The earliest eight of them were built around 483 BCE as reliquaries for Buddha's remains, which were themselves divided into eight parts. In the third century, Ashoka opened the original eight stupas and further divided Buddha's relics, scattering them among a great many other stupas, probably including Sanchi.

The stupa as a form is deeply symbolic, consisting first and foremost of a hemispheric dome, built of rubble and dirt and faced with stone, evoking the Dome of Heaven (see the plan, Fig. 7.18). Perched on top of the dome is a small square platform, in the center of which is a mast supporting three circular disks or "umbrellas," called *chatras*. These signify both the banyan tree beneath which Buddha achieved enlightenment and the three levels of Buddhist consciousness—desire, form, formlessness—through which the soul ascends to enlightenment. The dome is set on a

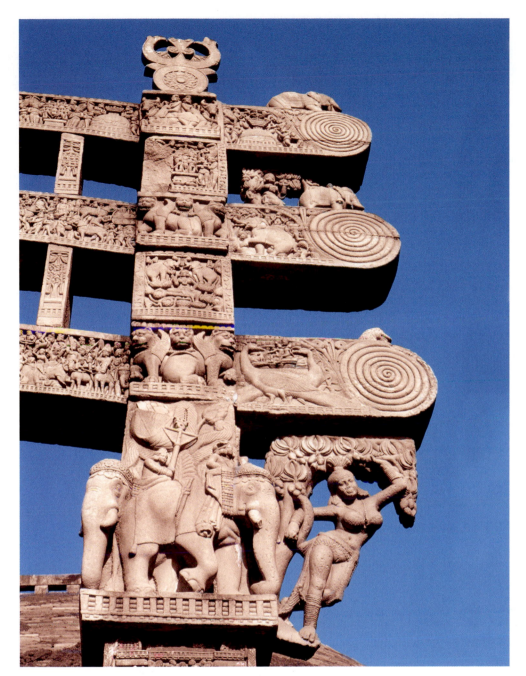

Fig. 7.19 Column capital on the East Gate of the Great Stupa, Sanchi. Stone, height of gate, 32'. The carved elephants that serve as the capital to the gateway column are traditional symbols of Buddha, signs of his authority and spiritual strength. A *yakshi* figure serves as a bracket at the right front of the elephant.

raised base, around the top of which is a circumambulatory walkway. As pilgrims to the stupa circle the walkway, they symbolically follow Buddha's path, awakening to enlightenment. The whole is a **mandala** (literally "circle"), the Buddhist diagram of the cosmos.

Leading out from the circular center of the stupa are four gates, positioned at the cardinal points, that create directional "rays," or beams of teaching, emanating from the "light" of the central mandala. They are 32 feet high and decorated with stories from the life of Buddha, as well as other sculptural elements including vines, lotuses, peacocks, and elephants (Fig. **7.19**). Extending as a sort of

bracket from the sides of the gateways are *yakshis*—some 24 in all—female spirit figures that probably derive from Vedic tradition. The *yakshi* symbolizes the productive forces of nature. As in Hinduism, sexuality and spirituality are visually represented here as forms of an identical cosmic energy, and the sensuous curves of the *yakshi* illustrated above emphasize her deep connection to the creative force. In fact, here she seems to cause the fruit in the tree above her head to ripen, as if she is the source of its nourishment.

The *yakshi* and the gate she decorates embody the distinctive sense of beauty that is characteristic of Indian art. Both are images of abundance that reflect a belief in the generosity of spirit that both Buddha and the Hindu gods share. Sensuous form, vibrant color, and a profusion of ornament dominate Indian art as a whole, and the rich textures of this art are meant to capture the very essence of the divine.

Buddhist Monuments: The Pillar Ashoka also erected a series of pillars across the Empire, primarily at sites related to Buddha's life. These pillars, made of sandstone, usually rested on a stone foundation sunk more than 10 feet into the ground. They rose to a height of about 50 feet. They were inscribed with inscriptions relating to dharma, the rules of good conduct that Vedic kings such as Rama were required to uphold in the *Ramayana*. But Buddhists quickly interpreted the writings as referring to Buddhist teachings. At the top of each pillar was a capital carved in the shape of an animal.

The pillar at Sarnath, the site of Buddha's first sermon, was crowned with a sculpture of four lions facing in the cardinal directions and standing back to back on a slab decorated with four low-relief sculptures of wheels and, between each wheel, four different animals—lion, horse, bull, and elephant (Fig. **7.20**). Beneath these features are the turned-down petals of a lotus flower, which, since the lotus emerges from dirty water without blemish, traditionally symbolized the presence of divine purity (which is to say, Buddha and his teachings) in an imperfect world. All of the other elements on the capital have similar symbolic significance. The lions probably refer to Buddha himself, who was known "the lion of the Shakya," the clan into which he was born as prince, and whose teachings spread in all directions like the roar of the lions. The wheels, too, are a universal symbol of Buddha's teachings at Sarnath, where, it is said, "he set the wheel of the law in motion." In fact, the lions originally supported a large copper wheel, now lost.

Ashoka's missionary ambition matched his father's and grandfather's military zeal, and he sent Buddhist emissaries as far west as Syria, Egypt, and Greece. No Western historical record of these missions survives, and their impact on Western thought remains a matter of speculation.

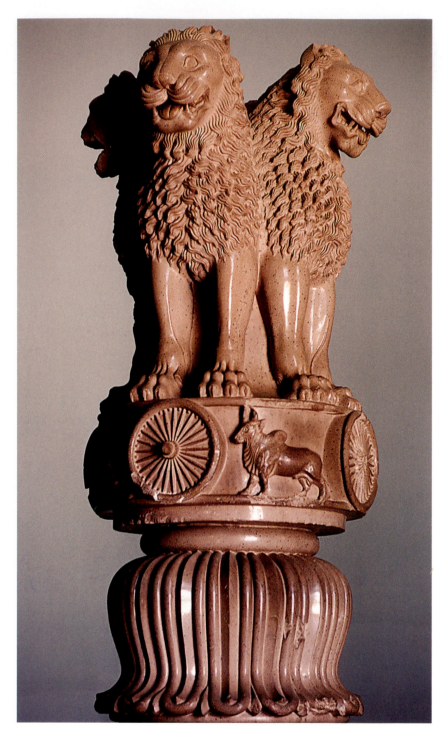

Fig. 7.20 Lion capital, Ashokan pillar at Sarnath, Uttar Pradesh, India. Maurya period, ca. 250 BCE. Polished sandstone, height 7'. Archeological Museum, Sarnath. Some scholars speculate that the pillars upon which such capitals rested represent the *axis mundi*, or "axis of the world," joining the earth with the heavens.

CONTINUITY & CHANGE

The Silk Road

Under the Han (206 BCE–220 CE), Chinese trade flourished. Western linen, wool, glass, and gold, Persian pistachios, and mustard originating in the Mediterranean, were imported in exchange for the silk, ceramics, fur, lacquered goods, and spices that made their way west along the "Silk Road" that stretched from the Yellow River across Asia to the Mediterranean (see Map **7.3**). The road followed the westernmost spur of the Great Wall to the oasis town of Dunhuang, where it split into northern and southern routes, passing through smaller oasis towns until converging again at Kashgar on the western edge of the western Chinese deserts. From there, traders could proceed into present-day Afghanistan, south into India, or westward through present-day Uzbekistan, Iran, and Iraq into Syria and the port city of Antioch. Goods passed through many hands, trader to trader, before reaching the Mediterranean, and according to an official history of the Han dynasty compiled in the fifth century CE, it was not until 97 CE that one Gan Ying went "all the way to the Western sea and back." According to Gan Ying, there he encountered an empire with "over four hundred walled cities" to which "tens of small states are subject"—some of them probably outposts of the Roman Empire, but others, like the city of Bam, with its towering

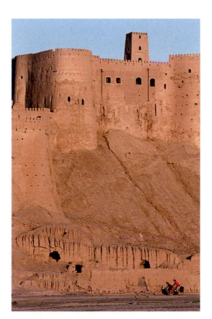

Fig. 7.21 The Arg-é Bam ("Bam Citadel"), Iran. The citadel was the largest adobe structure in the world until approximately 80 percent of it was destroyed in a massive earthquake in 2003. The Iranian government has undertaken its reconstruction.

citadel—first constructed in about 55 BCE (Fig. **7.21**)—Persian strongholds.

Goods and ideas spread along the Silk Road, as trade spurred the cultural interchange between East and West, India and China. As early as the first century BCE, silk from China reached Rome, where it captured the Western imagination, but the secret of its manufacture remained a mystery in the West until the sixth century CE. Between the first and third centuries CE, Buddhist missionaries from India carried their religion over the Silk Road into Southeast Asia and north into China and Korea, where it quickly became the dominant religion. By the last half of the first millennium, the Chinese capital of Chang'an, at the eastern terminus of the Silk Road, hosted Korean, Japanese, Jewish, and Christian communities, and Chinese emperors maintained diplomatic relations with Persia. Finally, the Venetian merchant Marco Polo (ca. 1254–1324), bearing a letter of introduction from Pope Gregory X, crossed the Asian continent on the Silk Road in 1275. He arrived at the new Chinese capital of Beijing, and served in the imperial court for nearly two decades. His *Travels*, written after his return to Italy in 1292, constitute the first eyewitness account of China available in Europe. ■

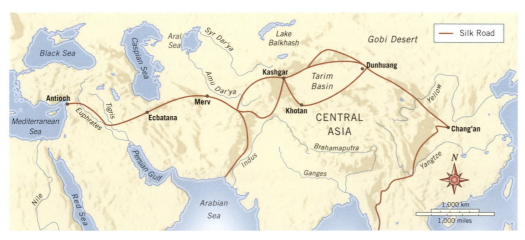

Map 7.3 The Silk Road, the trading route between the East and West and between Southeast Asia and China.

7.1 Identify the enduring artistic, literary, and philosophical directions that developed early in Chinese history.

As inscribed on oracle bones and bronze vessels, the earliest Chinese written language is so closely related to modern Chinese written language that it remains legible. During the Shang (ca. 1700–1045 BCE) and Zhou (1045–221 BCE) dynasties, with the production of the *Book of Changes*, or *Yi Jing*, and the collection of a national poetry in the *Book of Songs*, or *Shi Jing*, a lasting national literature began to arise. The two great strains of Chinese philosophy—Daoism, a mystical quietism based on harmony with nature, and Confucianism, a pragmatic political philosophy based on personal cultivation—came into full flower at this time as well. The philosophical symbol of the yin-yang was devised during this early period too. Can you detect the workings of the yin-yang philosophy in the poetry of the *Book of Songs*? In the *Dao De Jing*? In Confucianism? How did Confucianism contribute to the workings of the Chinese state? Why is Daoism less suitable as a political philosophy? Why did later Chinese historians think of Daoism as originating in the state of Chu?

7.2 Understand how the art and literature of the Qin and Han dynasties reflect the values of the imperial court.

Under the leadership of the first emperor, Qin Shihuangdi, the Qin dynasty (221–206 BCE) unified China and undertook massive building projects, including the 4,000-mile-long Great Wall, enormous networks of roads, and the emperor's own tomb, guarded by nearly 8,000 life-size ceramic soldiers, projects that required the almost complete reorganization of Chinese society. This reorganization was made possible by placing totalitarian authority in the hands of a ruthless dictator. What philosophy supported the emperor's approach? How do the massive building projects of the Qin dynasty compare to those of the Roman Empire in the West?

During the Han dynasty (206 BCE–220 CE), the scholars and writers disenfranchised by the Qin were restored to respectability, but women remained disenfranchised. How does *yuefu* poetry reflect women's lot? How does it compare to the poetry of the *Book of Songs*? Paper was invented during the Han dynasty. What effect did this invention have on Chinese culture? How did trade come to serve the aspirations of the Empire?

7.3 Describe the Hindu and Buddhist faiths and how they helped to shape the cultures of ancient India.

Before 2000 BCE, in the Indus Valley, sophisticated cultures arose at cities such as Mohenjo-Daro and Harappa. What archeological evidence gives credence to the idea that these were indeed sophisticated cultures?

After the invasion of the Aryans in about 1500 BCE, the Hindu religion took hold in India. The *Vedas* and *Upanishads* were its two basic texts. Its three major gods were Brahma, the creator; Vishnu, the preserver, and god of benevolence, forgiveness, and love; and Shiva, the destroyer, who is also a great dancer, embodying the sacred rhythms of creation and destruction, birth, death, and rebirth. Vishnu was an especially popular god, who appeared in human form as Rama in the epic *Ramayana*, and as Krishna in the epic *Mahabharata*. What place do female divinities hold in Hindu religion? What does this religion share with the official Indian state religion adopted by the Maurya emperor Ashoka, Buddhism? In what ways did Ashoka seek to spread Buddhism as the dominant Indian faith?

✔ **Study** and **review** on **MyArtsLab**

READINGS

from the *Book of Songs*

The *Book of Songs* is the earliest collection of Chinese poetry. Like all subsequent Chinese poetry, for which these poems, not coincidentally, provide the tradition, the poems provide a telling glimpse into everyday Chinese life. But they also demonstrate the centrality of the natural world and its rhythms and cycles to Chinese thought and feeling.

In the Wilds Is a Dead River-Deer

In the wilds is a dead river-deer
wrapped in white rushes.
A lady yearned for spring
and a fine man seduced her.

In the woods are clusters of bushes
and in the wilds a dead river-deer
wrapped in white rushes.
There was a lady fine as jade.

Oh! Slow down, don't be so rough,
let go of my girdle sash.
Shhh! You'll make the dog bark.

READING CRITICALLY

The poem contrasts the dead deer to the lady's desire. What is the point? How does time, the sense of human urgency versus the natural rhythm of nature, play into this theme?

When the Gourd Has Dried Leaves

When the gourd has dried leaves,
you can wade the deep river.
Keep your clothes on if the water's deep;
hitch up your dress when it's shallow.

The river is rising,
pheasants are chirping.
The water is just half a wheel deep,
and the hen is chirping for the cock.

Wild geese are trilling,
the rising sun starts dawn.
If you want to marry me,
come before the river is frozen.

The ferryman is gesturing,
other people are going, but not me,
other people are going, but not me,
I'm waiting for you.

READING CRITICALLY

Who is the speaker? How does the cycle of the seasons play into the poem's argument? Are there any double-entendres at work in this argument?

All the Grasslands Are Yellow

All the grasslands are yellow
and all the days we march
and all the men are conscripts
sent off in four directions.

All the grasslands are black
and all the men like widowers.
So much grief! Are soldiers
not men like other men?

We aren't bison! We aren't tigers
crossing the wilderness,
but our sorrows
roam from dawn till dusk.

Hairy-tailed foxes slink
through the dark grass
as we ride tall chariots
along the wide rutted roads.

READING CRITICALLY

Clearly, the speaker of this poem is very different from the speakers of the first two. But in what ways are the themes of the first two poems reiterated here?

READING 7.3

from Confucius, the *Analects*

The *Analects* of Confucius are a collection of his dialogues and utterances, probably recorded by his disciples after his death. They reflect Confucius's dream of an ideal society of hardworking, loyal people governed by wise, benevolent, and morally upright officials—a government based on moral principles that would be reflected in the behavior of its populace.

2-1 The Master said, "He who exercises government by means of his virtue may be compared to the north polar star, which keeps its place and all the stars turn towards it."

2-2 The Master said, "In the Book of Poetry are three hundred pieces, but the design of them all may be embraced in one sentence 'Having no depraved thoughts.'"

2-3 The Master said, "If the people be led by laws, and uniformity sought to be given them by punishments, they will try to avoid the punishment, but have no sense of shame."

"If they be led by virtue, and uniformity sought to be given them by the rules of propriety, they will have the sense of shame, and moreover will become good." ... 10

4-3 The Master said, "It is only the truly virtuous man, who can love, or who can hate, others."

4-4 The Master said, "If the will be set on virtue, there will be no practice of wickedness."

4-5 The Master said, "Riches and honors are what men desire. If they cannot be obtained in the proper way, they should not be held. Poverty and meanness are what men dislike. If they cannot be avoided in the proper way, they should not be avoided." ... 20

4-6 The Master said, "I have not seen a person who loved virtue, or one who hated what was not virtuous. He who loved virtue, would esteem nothing above it. He who hated what is not virtuous, would practice virtue in such a way that he would not allow anything that is not virtuous to approach his person." ...

4-9 The Master said, "A scholar, whose mind is set on truth, and who is ashamed of bad clothes and bad food, is not fit to be discoursed with." 30

4-10 The Master said, "The superior man, in the world, does not set his mind either for anything, or against anything; what is right he will follow."

4-11 The Master said, "The superior man thinks of virtue; the small man thinks of comfort. The superior man thinks of the sanctions of law; the small man thinks of favors which he may receive."

4-12 The Master said, "He who acts with a constant view to his own advantage will be much murmured against." ...

4-17 The Master said, "When we see men of worth, we 40 should think of equaling them; when we see men of a contrary character, we should turn inwards and examine ourselves."

4-18 The Master said, "In serving his parents, a son may remonstrate with them, but gently; when he sees that they do not incline to follow his advice, he shows an increased degree of reverence, but does not abandon his purpose; and should they punish him, he does not allow himself to murmur." ...

4-22 The Master said, "The reason why the ancients did not readily give utterance to their words, was that they feared lest their actions should not come up to them." 50

4-23 The Master said, "The cautious seldom err."

4-24 The Master said, "The superior man wishes to be slow in his speech and earnest in his conduct." ...

READING CRITICALLY

Give two or three examples, from the previous passages, of the principle of *li* at work, and explain how *li* leads to *ren* (these terms are defined in the chapter).

READING 7.7

from the *Bhagavad Gita: Krishna's Counsel in Time of War*

The *Bhagavad Gita* constitutes the sixth book of the first-century CE epic Sanskrit poem, the *Mahabharata*. It represents, in many ways, a summation of Hindu thought and philosophy. The bulk of the poem consists of the reply of Krishna, an avatar, or incarnation, of Vishnu, to Arjuna, leader of the Pandavas, who on the battlefield has decided to lay down his arms. In the following passage, Arjuna declares his unwillingness to fight. The charioteer Sanjaya, the narrator of the entire *Mahabharata*, then introduces Krishna, who replies to Arjuna's decision and goes on to describe, at Arjuna's request, the characteristics of a man of "firm concentration and pure insight."

from "The Second Teaching"

Sanjaya:

Arjuna sat dejected,
filled with pity,
his sad eyes blurred by tears.
Krishna gave him counsel.

Lord Krishna:

Why this cowardice
in time of crisis, Arjuna?
The coward is ignoble, shameful,
foreign to the ways of heaven.
Don't yield to impotence!
It is unnatural in you! 10
Banish this petty weakness from your heart.
Rise to the fight, Arjuna!

Arjuna:

Krishna, how can I fight
against Bhishma and Drona
with arrows
when they deserve my worship?
It is better in this world
to beg for scraps of food
than to eat meals
smeared with the blood   20
of elders I killed
at the height of their power
while their goals
were still desires.
We don't know which weight
is worse to bear—
our conquering them
or their conquering us.
We will not want to live
if we kill   30
the sons of Dhritarashtra
assembled before us.
The flaw of pity
blights my very being
conflicting sacred duties
confound my reason.
I ask you to tell me
decisively—Which is better?
I am your pupil.
Teach me what I seek!   40
I see nothing
that could drive away
the grief
that withers my senses;
even if I won kingdoms
of unrivaled wealth
on earth
and sovereignty over gods.

Sanjaya:

Arjuna told this
To Krishna—then saying,   50
"I shall not fight,"
he fell silent.
Mocking him gently,
Krishna gave this counsel
as Arjuna sat dejected,
between the two armies.

Lord Krishna:

You grieve for those beyond grief,
and you speak words of insight;
but learned men do not grieve
for the dead or the living.   60
Never have I not existed,
nor you, nor these kings;
and never in the future
shall we cease to exist.
Just as the embodied self
enters childhood, youth, and old age,

so does it enter another body:
this does not confound a steadfast man.
Contacts with matter make us feel
heat and cold, pleasure and pain.   70
Arjuna, you must learn to endure
fleeting things—they come and go!
When these cannot torment a man,
when suffering and joy are equal
for him and he has courage,
he is fit for immortality.
Nothing of nonbeing comes to be,
nor does being cease to exist;
the boundary between these two
is seen by men who see reality.   80
Indestructible is the presence
that pervades all this;
no one can destroy
this unchanging reality.
Our bodies are known to end,
but the embodied self is enduring,
indestructible, and immeasurable;
therefore, Arjuna, fight the battle!
He who thinks this self a killer
and he who thinks it killed,   90
both fail to understand;
it does not kill, nor is it killed. …

Arjuna:

Krishna, what defines a man
deep in contemplation whose insight
and thought are sure? How would he speak?
How would he sit? How would he move?

Lord Krishna:

When he gives up desires in his mind,
is content with the self within himself,
then he is said to be a man
whose insight is sure, Arjuna.   100

When suffering does not disturb his mind,
when his craving for pleasures has vanished,
when attraction, fear, and anger are gone,
he is called a sage whose thought is sure.

When he shows no preference
in fortune or misfortune
and neither exults nor hates,
his insight is sure.

When, like a tortoise retracting its limbs
he withdraws his senses   110
completely from sensuous objects,
his insight is sure.

So, Great Warrior, when withdrawal
of the senses
from sense objects is complete,
discernment is firm.

When it is night for all creatures,
a master of restraint is awake;
when they are awake, it is night
for the sage who sees reality.   120

As the mountainous depths
of the ocean
are unmoved when waters
rush into it,
so the man unmoved
when desires enter him
attains a peace that eludes
the man of many desires.

When he renounces all desires
and acts without craving,   130
possessiveness,
or individuality, he finds peace.

This is the place of the infinite spirit;
achieving it, one is freed from delusion;
abiding in it even at the time of death,
one finds the pure calm of infinity.

READING CRITICALLY

What does Krishna mean when he says, "Nothing of non-being comes to be / nor does being cease to exist; / the boundary between these two / is seen by men who see reality"?

READING 7.8

from the *Dhammapada*

The *Dhammapada*, or "path of truth," consists of 423 sayings, or aphorisms, of Buddha divided by subject into 26 books. They are commonly thought to be the answers to questions put to Buddha on various occasions, and as such they constitute a summation of Buddhist thought. The following passages, consisting of different aphorisms from five different books, emphasize the Buddhist doctrine of self-denial and the wisdom inherent in pursuing the "path."

from 5. *The Fool*

… Should a traveler fail to find a companion
Equal or better,
Rather than suffer the company of a fool,
He should resolutely walk alone.
"I have children; I have wealth."
These are the empty claims of an unwise man.
If he cannot call himself his own,
How can he then claim children and wealth as his own?
To the extent that a fool knows his foolishness,
He may be deemed wise.   10
A fool who considers himself wise
Is indeed a fool. …

from 6. *The Wise*

Irrigators contain the flowing waters.
Arrowsmiths fashion arrows.
Carpenters shape wood to their design.
Wise men mold their characters. …

from 11. *Old Age*

Can there be joy and laughter
When always the world is ablaze?
Enshrouded in darkness
Should you not seek a light?   20
Look at the body adorned,
A mass of wounds, draped upon a heap of bones,
A sickly thing, this subject of sensual thoughts!
Neither permanent, nor enduring!
The body wears out,
A nest of disease,
Fragile, disintegrating,
Ending in death.
What delight is there in seeing the bleached bones,
Like gourds thrown away,   30

Dried and scattered in the autumn sun?
A citadel is this structure of bones,
Blood and flesh, within which dwell
Decay, death, conceit, and malice.
The royal chariots surely come to decay
Just as the body, too, comes to decay.
But the shining truth and loving kindness live on.
So speak the virtuous to the virtuous.

from 18. *Blemishes*

… The wise man, carefully, moment by moment,
One by one,   40
Eliminates the stains of his mind,
As a silversmith separates the dross from the silver.
Just as rust produced by iron
Corrodes the iron,
So is the violator of moral law
Destroyed by his own wrong action.
Disconnection from scripture is learning's taint,
Neglect is the taint of houses,
Uncared-for beauty withers,
Negligence is the taint of one who keeps watch.   50
A woman behaving badly loses her femininity.
A giver sharing grudgingly loses his generosity.
Deeds done from bad motives remain everlastingly tainted.
But there is nothing more tainted than ignorance.
Eliminate ignorance, O disciples,
And purity follows. …
Be aware, everyone, that those flawed in their nature
Have no control of themselves.
Do not let greed and anger cause you suffering
By holding you in their grasp.   60
Men give for different reasons,
Such as devotion or appreciation.
Whoever finds fault with the food or drink given by others

Will have no peace, day or night.
However, whoever gives up this habit of finding fault
With others' offerings
Will know peace, day and night.
There is no fire like lust,
No vice like hatred,
No trap like delusion,   70
And no galloping river like craving.

from 24. *Craving*

… Unchecked craving strangles the careless man,
Like a creeper growing in the jungle.
He leaps from lifetime to lifetime,
Like a monkey seeking fruit.
This craving, this clinging,
Overpowers the man caught in it,
And his sorrows multiply,
Like prairie grass fed by rain.
Although it is hard to gain this freedom,   80
Sorrow leaves the man who overcomes this toxic craving,
This clinging to the world,
Just as drops of water fall from a lotus leaf.
Therefore, I admonish you all who are here assembled.
You have my blessings.
Eradicate craving at the root, as you would weeds.
Find the sweet root.
Do not succumb to temptation over and over again.
The tree may be cut down but the roots remain,
Uninjured and strong,   90
And it springs up again.
Likewise, suffering returns, again and again,
If the dormant craving is not completely eradicated. …
Craving grows in the man aroused by worldly thoughts.

Tied to his senses, he makes his fetters strong.
Taking delight in calming sensual thoughts,
Ever mindful, meditating on the impurities of the body and so on,
One will certainly get rid of craving.
Such a one will cut off Mara's bond.
The diligent monk   100
Has reached the summit,
Fearless, free of passion.
This is the final birth of such a man.
Free of craving and grasping,
Skilled in the knowledge of the meanings within meanings,
The significance of terms, the order of things.
This great man, greatly wise,
Need return no more.
I have conquered all, I know all,
I am detached from all, I have renounced all,   110
I am freed through destruction of craving.
Having myself realized all,
Whom shall I call my teacher?
The gift of truth is the highest gift.
The taste of truth is the sweetest taste.
The joy of truth is the greatest joy.
The extinction of craving is the end of suffering.

READING CRITICALLY

The *Dhammapada* is rich in metaphors, figures of speech that draw direct comparison between two seemingly unrelated things (from "Craving," for instance, the comparison of a craving to an entangling creeper). How does Buddha's use of metaphor reflect his status as the "Enlightened One"?

PART TWO

The Medieval World and the Shaping of Culture

200 CE–1400

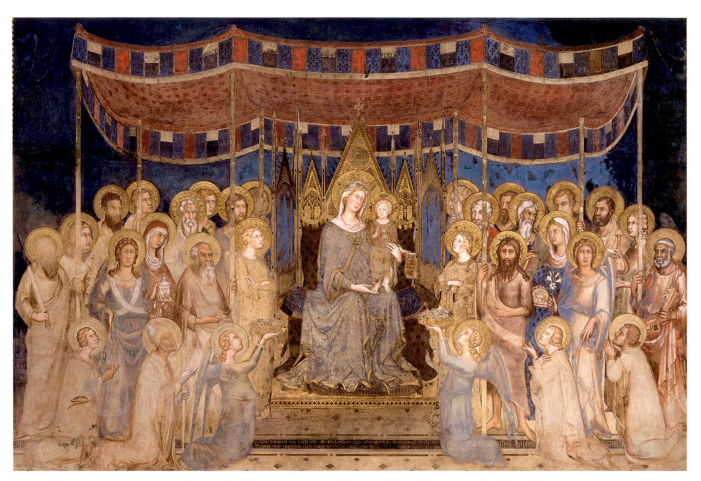

Simone Martini, *Maestà*, Council Chamber, Palazzo Pubblico, Siena. ca. 1311–17, repaired 1321 (see Fig 13.6 in Chapter 13).

During the last 300 years of the Roman Empire, Christianity gained a stronger and stronger foothold, until the Western Roman Empire collapsed in about 500 CE. The following Middle Ages span a period of about 1,000 years of European history, up to the beginning of the fifteenth century. Its opening centuries, until about 800 CE, were once commonly referred to as the "Dark Ages." During this time, the great cultural achievements of the Greeks and Romans were forgotten, so-called barbarian tribes from the north overran the Continent, and ignorance reigned. But this era was followed by an age of remarkable innovation and achievement, marked by the ascendancy of three great religions—Christianity, Buddhism, and newborn Islam. Because of the way these three religions dominated their respective cultures, the centuries covered in Part Two might be best thought of as the Age of Faith.

This was the age of the monastery, the religious pilgrimage, the cathedral, the mosque, and the spread of Buddhism across Asia. By the sixth century, a new Christian mode of representation, reflecting a new ideal of beauty, had asserted itself in Byzantium, the Eastern Roman Empire.

Unlike the Romans and Greeks, Byzantine artists showed little interest in depicting the visual appearance of the material world. They abandoned perspectival depth and rendered figures as highly stylized, almost geometric configurations. In other words, they depicted a spiritual rather than physical ideal.

In the first half of the seventh century, after the death of the prophet Muhammad, Islam began its rapid spread from Arabia across the Middle East to North Africa and into Spain. At the same time, in the rest of Europe, Christian and feudal traditions gradually merged. By the time Charlemagne was crowned emperor by Pope Leo III in the year 800, fidelity to one's chief could be understood as analogous to fidelity to one's God. By the late twelfth century, this brand of loyalty had found its way into the social habits of court life, where it took the form known as courtly love. In the love songs of the troubadour poets, the loyalty that a knight or nobleman had once conferred upon his lord was now transferred to a lady.

Charlemagne's passionate interest in education and the arts was broadcast across Europe through the development first of monastic schools and later of universities, which were themselves made possible by a resurgence of economic activity and trade. The Christian Crusades to recapture the Holy Land, principally Jerusalem, from Muslim control contributed to this economic revitalization, as did the practice of pilgrimage journeys to the Holy Land and to churches that housed sacred relics. The art of creating monumental stone sculpture was revived to decorate these churches, which grew ever larger to accommodate the throngs that visited them. The culmination of this trend was the Gothic cathedral, adorned with stained glass and rising to formerly unachieved heights. The sacred music of the liturgy became more complex and ornate as well, reflecting the architecture of the buildings in which it was played. To appeal to the masses of worshipers, the sculpture and painting that decorated these churches became increasingly naturalistic. Similarly, poetry and prose were more frequently written in the **vernacular**—the everyday language of the people—and less often in Latin. In both literature and art, the depiction of universal types, or generalized characters, gave way to the depiction of real characters and actual personalities.

We can begin to account for this shift by recognizing that, by the late Middle Ages, the center of intellectual life had shifted from the monastery to the town. From the great metropolis of Hangzhou, China, which Marco Polo visited in 1271, to the cities of Teotihuacán and Palenque in Mesoamerica, daily life was an increasingly urban experience. In Asia and the Americas, these centers reflected the aspirations and power of the ruling nobility. But in Europe, towns such as Florence and Siena flourished as a result of ever-enlarging trade networks. Now, suddenly, merchants and bankers began to assert themselves with as much or more power than either pope or king, ruling local governments and commissioning civic and religious works of architecture and art.

4 BCE–30 CE
Lifetime of Jesus

300 CE
Buddha carvings at Bamiyan, Silk Road

313
Pyramid of the Sun at Teotihuacán, Mesoamerica

313
Emperor Constantine grants religious freedom to all

410
Visigoths sack Rome

610–32
Prophet Muhammad transcribes the *Qur'an*

752
Todaiji Temple, Nara, Japan

768–814
Reign of Charlemagne

700–1000
Epic English poem *Beowulf* composed from Anglo-Saxon myths

937/8–after 1014
Lifetime of Murasaki Shikibu, author of *Tale of Genji*, world's first novel, Japan

1066
Norman invasion of England at Hastings, depicted in the *Bayeux Tapestry*

1100
Ife culture, Africa, develops brass casting

1150
Chartres cathedral, first phase

1187
Muslim Saladin conquers Jerusalem

1279
Kublai Khan conquers China

1300–1450
Inca granite construction at Machu Picchu

1304–74
Lifetime of Petrarch, author of *Canzoniere* (1349)

1338
Allegory of Good Government, Ambrogio Lorenzetti, Palazzo Pubblico, Siena

1354–91
Alhambra palace at Granada, Spain

1364–ca. 1430
Lifetime of Christine de Pizan, author of *The Book of the City of Ladies* and *Tale of Joan of Arc*

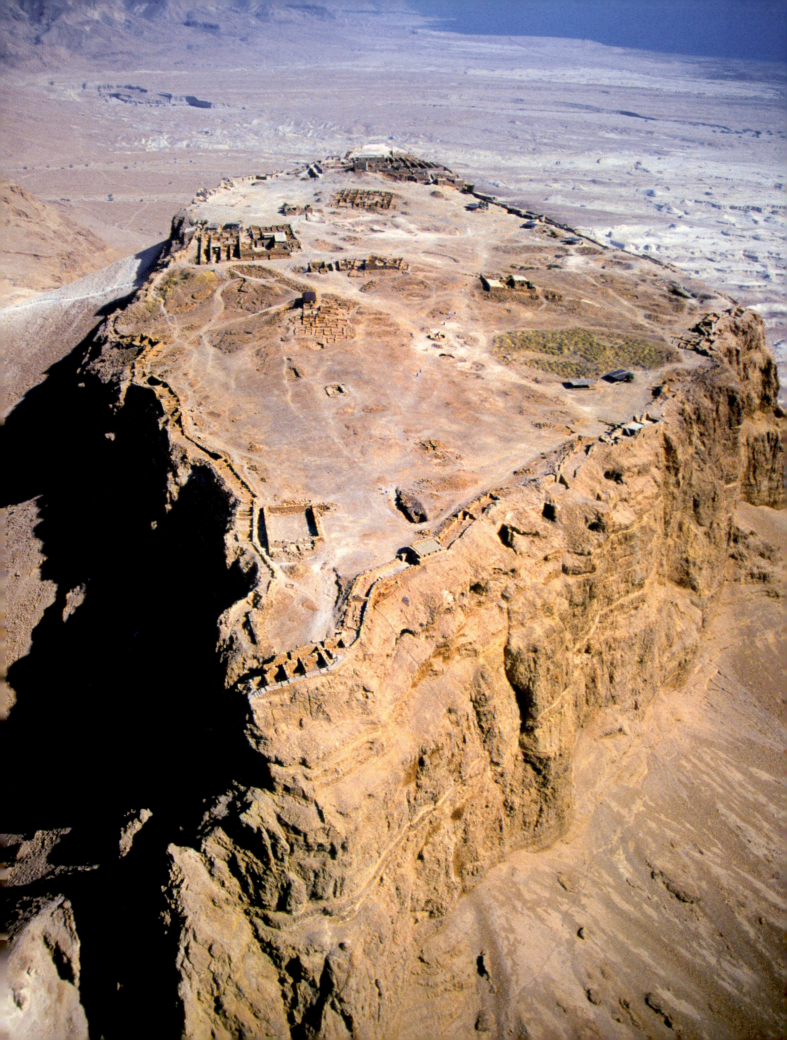

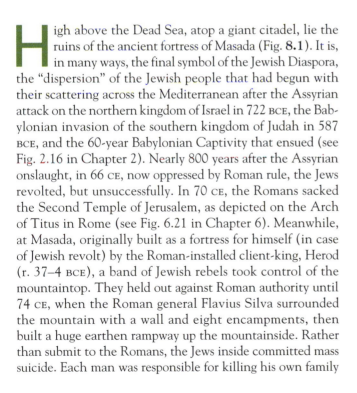

The Flowering of Christianity

Faith and the Power of Belief in the Early First Millennium

THINKING AHEAD

8.1 Outline the development of Judaic culture after the destruction of the Second Temple.

8.2 Identify the forces at work in the spread of Christianity and differentiate between the new religion's use of typology, symbolism, and iconography.

8.3 Describe the Roman reaction to Christianity and explore the ways in which Roman traditions may have impacted the religion's development.

8.4 Characterize the new Byzantine style of art and discuss how it reflects the values of the Byzantine emperors, especially Justinian.

8.5 Explain the role of images in Byzantine art and why they were subject to iconoclast attack.

High above the Dead Sea, atop a giant citadel, lie the ruins of the ancient fortress of Masada (Fig. **8.1**). It is, in many ways, the final symbol of the Jewish Diaspora, the "dispersion" of the Jewish people that had begun with their scattering across the Mediterranean after the Assyrian attack on the northern kingdom of Israel in 722 BCE, the Babylonian invasion of the southern kingdom of Judah in 587 BCE, and the 60-year Babylonian Captivity that ensued (see Fig. 2.16 in Chapter 2). Nearly 800 years after the Assyrian onslaught, in 66 CE, now oppressed by Roman rule, the Jews revolted, but unsuccessfully. In 70 CE, the Romans sacked the Second Temple of Jerusalem, as depicted on the Arch of Titus in Rome (see Fig. 6.21 in Chapter 6). Meanwhile, at Masada, originally built as a fortress for himself (in case of Jewish revolt) by the Roman-installed client-king, Herod (r. 37–4 BCE), a band of Jewish rebels took control of the mountaintop. They held out against Roman authority until 74 CE, when the Roman general Flavius Silva surrounded the mountain with a wall and eight encampments, then built a huge earthen rampway up the mountainside. Rather than submit to the Romans, the Jews inside committed mass suicide. Each man was responsible for killing his own family and then, because suicide is strongly discouraged by the Jewish faith, the rebels drew lots and killed each other in turn, down to the last man standing, who would be the only one to actually have to take his own life. Masada today is one of the most symbolic sites in all of Israel. There Israeli soldiers swear an oath: "Masada shall not fall again."

After the fall of Jerusalem and Masada, the Romans changed the name of the province from Judea, "land of the Jews," to Palestine, "land of the Philistines"—the ancient enemy of the Jews, but a culture that had disappeared long before Herod's time (the giant Goliath, slain by David, as told in the Book of Samuel, had been a Philistine). It was as if the history of the Jewish presence in the region were to be permanently erased. Finally, in 135 CE, after yet another Jewish revolt, the emperor Hadrian rebuilt Jerusalem as a Roman city named Aelia Capitolina, which Jews were forbidden to enter. Many Jews were sold into slavery; others fled throughout the Mediterranean and Middle East. But the Diaspora that had begun with the Assyrian invasion of Israel 900 years earlier was now complete. Not until 1948, when the state of Israel was established by the United Nations, would Jews see their original homeland again.

◀ **Fig. 8.1 Masada, the fortress of King Herod on the Dead Sea. Late 1st century CE.** Herod built a magnificent palace here, on three terraces at the point of the promontory. A steep ramp built by the Roman army commander Flavius Silva in 73 CE, as part of the Roman effort to take the palace back from Jewish rebels, is visible on the left.

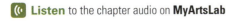 **Listen** to the chapter audio on **MyArtsLab**

DEVELOPMENTS IN JUDAIC CULTURE

How did Judaic culture evolve after the destruction of the Second Temple?

From the time of the Babylonian Captivity to the rise of rabbinic Judaism (the Judaism of the rabbis, the scholars and teachers of the Jewish faith), at about the time of the Roman destruction of the Second Temple, the Jewish religion had become increasingly **messianic**—that is, it prophesied that the world would end in apocalypse, the coming of God on the day of judgment, and that the postapocalyptic world would be led by a **Messiah**, or Anointed One, in everlasting peace. These feelings were first fueled in 168 BCE, when the Seleucid king Antiochus IV tried to impose worship of the Greek gods on the Jews, placing a statue of Zeus in the Second Temple of Jerusalem and allowing pigs to be sacrificed there. The Jews were outraged. From their point of view, the Greek conquerors had not merely transformed the sacred temple into a pagan shrine, but had replaced the Ark with a "graven image." The slaughter of pigs rendered the temple impure. Still worse, Antiochus made observance of the Hebrew law punishable by death. Led by Judas Maccabeus, a priest of the Maccabean family, the Jews revolted, defeating Antiochus, purifying the temple, and reestablishing Jewish control of the region for the period 142–63 BCE. In 63 BCE, the Romans, led by their great general Pompey, conquered Judea (present-day Israel).

Sectarianism and Revolt

It was a deeply unsettled time and place. In the early first century CE, large numbers of people claiming to be the Messiah and larger numbers of apocalyptic preachers roamed Judea. This situation was complicated by the growing sectarianism of Judaism itself. Much of what we know about this time comes from the writings of Josephus, a Jewish historian (ca. 37–ca. 100 CE). Josephus' *Jewish War*, completed in the early 80s CE, outlines Jewish history from the rise of the Maccabees to the destruction of the temple in 70 CE and the subsequent fall of Masada. "There are three philosophical sects among the Jews," Josephus writes. "The followers of the first of which are the Pharisees, a scribal group associated with the masses; of the second, the Sadducees, priests and high priests associated with the aristocracy; and the third sect, which pretends to a severer discipline, are called Essenes." (For Josephus' extended description of these sects, see **Reading 8.1**, pages 284–285.)

A **sect** is a small, organized group that separates itself from a larger religious movement because it asserts that it alone understands God's will and therefore it alone embodies the ideals of the religion. As a result, a sect generally creates strongly enforced social boundaries between its members and all others. Finally, members of a sect often view themselves as good and all others as evil. Of the three sects Josephus described (there were many more), the Essenes were the most conservative, going so far as to ban

women from their community so that they might live in celibacy and purity. The Essenes are generally identified with the group of Jews who lived at Qumran, on the Dead Sea, southeast of Jerusalem, where in 1947 a Bedouin shepherd discovered the oldest extant version of the Hebrew Scriptures, dating from around the time of Jesus—the so-called Dead Sea Scrolls. These documents are the richest source of our knowledge of Jewish sectarianism, for they include the Hebrew Scriptures—the Torah (the five books of Moses), *Nevi'im* (the Prophets), and *Ketubim* (the Writings), what Christians call the "Old Testament"—as well as other works originating in sectarian circles within and outside the Qumran community.

The Jews of Qumran abandoned their coreligionists to seek salvation on their own. Unlike the Pharisees and Sadducees, they never engaged in the Jewish political struggle with the Romans or with the other sects. The Pharisees and Sadducees argued, sometimes violently, over questions of philosophy, the temple, and purity. Philosophically, the Sadducees denied the resurrection of the dead, while the Pharisees affirmed it.

The purity laws were a point of special contention with far-reaching implications for the temple. According to Leviticus and Numbers (two books of the Hebrew Bible), the house of God (the temple) must be pure, and that which is impure must be expelled. In practice, the laws of purity prevented normal social relations between those who observed them and those who did not, to the point that even routine physical contact (a handshake, for instance) with a nonobserver was forbidden. Since all the sects developed their own purity laws, they were in essence forbidding contact with one another. The Qumran Essenes withdrew completely from Jewish society. Furthermore, the sectarian communities, especially the Pharisees, considered the Jerusalem Temple, the traditional center of Jewish worship, to be polluted, its priests—particularly the Sadducees—corrupt, and its rituals debased. The Pharisees, and perhaps the Sadducees as well, considered the house of God to be the larger state of Judea rather than just the temple in Jerusalem, and they felt compelled to expel the "impure" Romans from their midst.

The Romans had been careful not to make the same mistake as Antiochus IV. They installed the same Herod who built the fortress at Masada as their client-king. Herod claimed to be Jewish, but was not according to Jewish law. He tried, nevertheless, to reconcile Jews and Romans, primarily through religious tolerance and a massive building program. During his reign (37–4 BCE), he rebuilt the city of Jerusalem, constructing a large palace and enlarging the Second Temple (Fig. 8.2). We can see the Hellenistic influence in its tall, engaged Corinthian columns and its decorative frieze, and its Roman roots in its triple-arched gateway. Herod also engaged in other massive building programs, including a port at Caesarea and the fortress at Masada. Though Herod's three sons ruled briefly after their father's death, Rome became less and less tolerant of the Jewish faith—the laws of Rome often coming into conflict

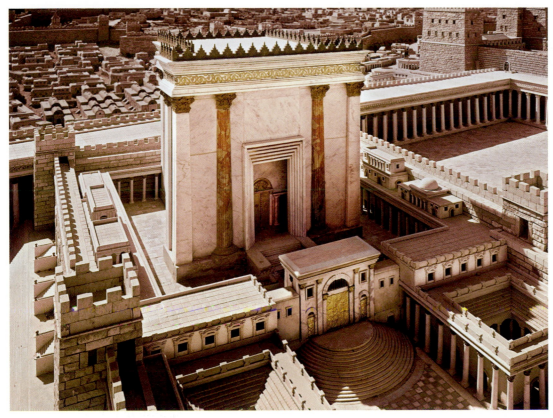

Fig. 8.2 Model of the Second Temple of Jerusalem. ca. 20 BCE. Only the Western Wall of Herod's temple survives today, and for Jews it remains the most sacred site in Jerusalem. It serves as a reminder of both the First Temple, totally destroyed by the Babylonians in 586 BCE, and, of course, the destruction of the Second Temple by the Romans. As a result of the sense of loss associated with the site and the lamentations it provokes, for centuries it has been known as the Wailing Wall.

with the Law of the Book—and so direct Roman rule was soon imposed.

The Rabbis and the Mishnah

With the destruction of the Second Temple in 70 CE and the subsequent Diaspora, the center and focal point of Jewish faith evaporated. From then on, Judaism developed as a religion in a sectarian manner. The sects, after all, had viewed the temple and temple rituals with deep skepticism and had practiced their religion outside the temple, in localized **synagogues**, or "houses of assembly," engaging in daily prayer, studying the Torah, and observing the laws of purity more or less independently of priests. Yet despite growing sectarianism, a community of scholars known as Sanhedrin, who had met for centuries to discuss and interpret the Torah, continued to provide a strong intellectual center for the Jews. In the town of Yavneh, where the group had moved after the destruction of the First Temple by the Babylonians, ongoing study of the Torah and other traditional teachings known as the Oral Torah had been sufficient to maintain continuity about what it meant to live and think properly as Jews. After the Diaspora of the second century CE, however, it seemed likely that the Jews would be living

for generations in many different places under widely varying circumstances, and without an institution such as the Sanhedrin, maintaining a strong, collective Jewish identity was unlikely.

The solution to this problem came from the rabbis, to whom, in the second to the sixth centuries CE, Jewish communities throughout the Mediterranean world turned for guidance and instruction. The rabbis, who were scholars functioning as both teachers and scribes, realized the importance of writing down the Oral Torah, a massive body of explanations and interpretations of the covenant, as well as traditional stories told to each new generation. In the early years of the third century CE, under the leadership of Rabbi Judah haNasi (ca. 165–220 CE), the Oral Torah was recorded in a work called the Mishnah.

Almost immediately, the work was viewed as inadequate. The Oral Torah was part of a dynamic intellectual tradition of applying what was perceived as the perfect and unchanging word of God to the circumstances and demands of the changing times. The Mishnah seemed too permanent, too dry, too incomplete. To capture some of the stimulating discussion characteristic of the Sanhedrin, as well as its traditional respect for well-reasoned but differing points of view, a commentary known as the Gemara began to surround the text of each passage of the Mishnah. The Gemara was a record of what had been debated, preserving disagreements as well as consensus. Commentaries on the commentaries continued to be added by successive generations of rabbis, and the Gemara did not take its final shape until around 700 CE. The combined Mishnah and Gemara came to be known as the Talmud.

THE RISE OF CHRISTIANITY

What forces contributed to the spread of the Christian religion and how did Christians make use of typology, symbolism, and iconography?

The development of Christianity, the religion that would have such a profound effect upon the history of the Western world, can only be understood in the context of Jewish history. It developed as one among many other minor sects of Judaism, at first so inconsequential that Josephus only briefly mentions it. Later theological writings, as opposed to actual historical accounts written at the time, tell us that in Judea's sectarian climate, Jesus of Nazareth was born to Mary and Joseph of Judea in about 4 BCE. At about the age of 30, Jesus began to lead the life of an itinerant rabbi. He preached repentance, compassion for the poor and meek, love of God and neighbor, and the imminence of the apocalypse, which he called the coming of the kingdom of God.

Although his teachings were steeped in the wisdom of the Jewish tradition, they antagonized both Jewish and Roman leaders. Jesus, in the spirit of reform, had challenged the commercialization of the Jewish Temple in Jerusalem, especially the practice of money-changing within its sacred precincts, alienating the Sadducee sect that managed it. After his followers identified him as the Messiah, or Savior—he did not make the claim for himself—both conservative Jewish leaders and Roman rulers were threatened. The proclamation by his followers that he was the son of God amounted to a crime against the Roman state, since the emperor was considered to be the only divine human on earth. In fact, since Jews were monotheistic and refused to worship other gods, including the emperor, their beliefs were a political threat to the Romans. The Christian sect's belief in the divinity of Jesus posed a special problem.

An enemy of the state, denounced by the other Jews that he had antagonized, betrayed by his disciple Judas (a betrayal now called into question with the publication of the Gospel of Judas), Jesus was crucified in about 30 CE, a degrading fate reserved for criminals and non-Roman citizens. Christian tradition has it—we possess no actual historical account—that the Crucifixion occurred outside the city walls on a hillside known as Golgotha, now the site of the Church of the Holy Sepulchre (Fig. **8.3**), and that Jesus was buried in a rock tomb just behind the site. Three days later, his followers reported that he rose from the dead and reappeared among them. The promise of resurrection, already a fundamental tenet of the Pharisee and Essene sects, became the foundation of Christian faith.

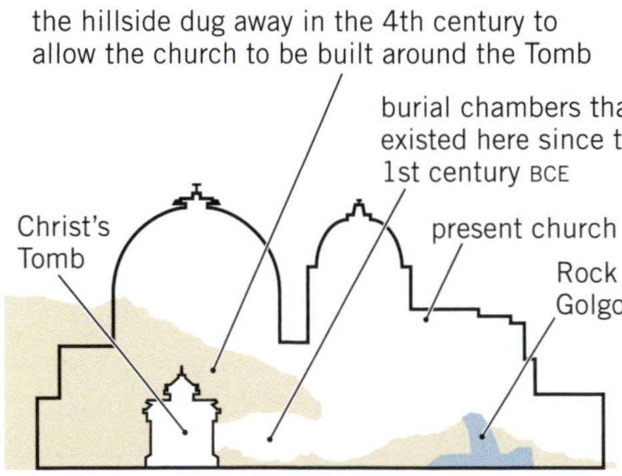

The Evangelists

Upon his death, Jesus' reputation grew as his **evangelists** spread the word of his life and resurrection (the word *evangelist* comes from the Greek *evangelos*, meaning "bearer of good"—and note the root *angel* in the word as well). Preeminent among these was Paul, who had persecuted Jews in Judea before converting to the new faith in Damascus (in present-day Syria) in 35 CE. Paul's epistles, or letters, are the earliest writings of the new Christian faith. In letters written to churches he founded or visited in Asia Minor, Greece, Macedonia, and Rome, which comprise 14 books of the Christian Scriptures, he argues the nature of religious truth and interprets the life of Christ—his preferred name for Jesus, one that he coined. *Christ* means, literally, "the Anointed One." It refers to the Jewish tradition of anointing priests, kings, and prophets with oil, and the fact that by Jesus' time Jews had come to expect a savior who embodied all the qualities of priest, king, and prophet. In true sectarian tradition, for Paul, the only correct expression of Judaism included faith in Christ. Paul conflated Jewish tradition, then, with his belief that Jesus' Crucifixion was the act of his salvation of humankind. He argued that Christ was blameless and suffered on the cross to pay for the sins of humanity. Resurrection, he believed, was at the heart of the Christian faith, but redemption was by no means automatic—sinners had to show their faith in Christ and his salvation. Faith, he argues in his Epistle to the Church in Rome, ensures salvation (**Reading 8.2**):

the hillside dug away in the 4th century to allow the church to be built around the Tomb

burial chambers that had existed here since the 1st century BCE

Christ's Tomb

present church

Rock of Golgotha

Fig. 8.3 Cutaway drawing of the Church of the Holy Sepulchre, Jerusalem, showing site of Christ's Tomb. This site was originally a small rocky hill, Golgotha, upon which Jesus was crucified, and an unused stone quarry in which tombs had been cut. The first basilica on the site was built by the emperor Constantine between 326 and 335 CE.

> ### READING 8.2
>
> **from the Bible, Romans 5:1–11**
>
> [1]Therefore, since we are justified by faith, we have peace with God through our Lord Jesus Christ, [2]through whom we have obtained access to this grace in which we stand;

and we boast in our hope of sharing the glory of God. ³And not only that, but we also boast in our sufferings, knowing that suffering produces endurance, ⁴and endurance produces character, and character produces hope, ⁵and hope does not disappoint us, because God's love has been poured into our hearts through the Holy Spirit that has been given to us.

⁶For while we were still weak, at the right time Christ died for the ungodly. ... ⁸But God proves his love for us in that while we still were sinners Christ died for us. ⁹Much more surely then, now that we have been justified by his blood, will we be saved through him from the wrath of God. ¹⁰For if while we were enemies, we were reconciled to God through the death of his Son, much more surely, having been reconciled, will we be saved by his life. ¹¹But more than that, we even boast in God through our Lord Jesus Christ, through whom we have now received reconciliation.

Fifteen centuries after Paul wrote these words, the Church would find itself divided between those who believed that salvation was determined by faith alone, as Paul argues, and those who believed in the necessity of good works to gain entry to heaven, a tradition that survives in the Epistle of James—"What use is it, my brethren, if a man says he has faith, but he has no works?" (2:14). Other aspects of Paul's writings would also have lasting significance, particularly his emphasis, like that of the Essene sect, on sexual chastity. Although it was better to marry than engage in sexual activity out of marriage, it was better still to live chastely. In later years, the celibate lives of priests, monks, and nuns, as well as the Church's teaching that sexuality was sinful except for the purposes of procreation, were directly inspired by Paul's position.

Not long after Paul's death, as the religion spread rapidly through Asia Minor and Greece, other evangelists began to write gospels, or "good news," specifically narrating the story of Jesus' life. What would become the first three books of the Christian New Testament, the gospels of Matthew, Mark, and Luke, are believed by scholars to have been written between 70 and 90 CE. Each emphasizes slightly different aspects of Jesus' life, though all focus particularly on his last days. It is important to recognize that many early Christian documents do not describe a virgin birth or a resurrection, a difference from Paul that reflects sectarian differences already present in the Jewish community. Evidence suggests that both the virgin birth and the Resurrection were Matthew and Luke's additions to Mark's Gospel. Luke also wrote the Acts of the Apostles, narrating the activities of Jesus' apostles, literally "those who have been sent" by God as his witness, immediately after the Resurrection. The apostles were originally those who had seen or lived with Jesus, and the book contains descriptions of miraculous events, signs from God that validate the apostles' teachings.

The Gnostic Gospels Many New Testament scholars say that the actions and sayings attributed to Jesus in the gospels cannot be factually traced to him, and that since they were written many decades after his death, they are composites of hearsay, legends, and theological interpolations, reflecting the hopes and beliefs of the early Christian community. There are, furthermore, other versions of Jesus' life than those contained in the Bible, especially among the 52 texts dating from the fourth century buried in a jar discovered by an Arab peasant in 1945 in Naj Hammadi, Upper Egypt. These texts are Gnostic (from the Greek *gnosis*, "knowledge" in the sense of "insight"), written by Christians who claimed special, even secret, knowledge of Jesus' life.

The Gospel of Thomas claims that Jesus had a twin. Other relationships are suggested in these books as well; among the most controversial was the implication in the Gospel of Philip that Christ had a sexual relationship with Mary Magdalene. At other points in the Gnostic texts, common Christian beliefs, such as the virgin birth and the bodily Resurrection, are criticized as naïve misunderstandings. In the late 1970s, another batch of Gnostic gospels was discovered near El Minya in Egypt. These contained the Gospel of Judas, in which, unlike the accounts in the canonical Gospels of Matthew, Mark, Luke, and John, where Judas is portrayed as a reviled traitor, Judas is described as acting at Jesus' request in handing him over to the authorities.

As the Church developed, it banned the Gnostic books (and other texts like them) as **heresy**, opinion or doctrine at odds with what would become normative belief. Although extremely diverse in their beliefs, with opinions at least as various as the Jewish sects, Gnostics tended to believe that a transcendent and impersonal God rules the heavens, while Christianity, as it developed, came to believe that God resided in Jesus, in the human realm. John's insistence that "Jesus Christ has come in the flesh" (1 John 4:2) suggests that his gospel is aimed directly at refuting Gnostic gospels. Gnostics believed that the material world in which humankind finds itself is evil and ruled by darkness, while the heavenly world is good and ruled by light.

In contrast, Christianity as it developed would come to argue that humankind is inherently good, and although fallen in sin, is capable of repentance. Normative Christians would argue that salvation is acquired through faith, not knowledge, but Gnostics would cite the example of Jesus himself, who, they believed, was sent to earth to open humanity's eyes, offering them enlightenment or *gnosis*. Finally, the Gnostics believed that only those with great intellectual strength might, through the acquisition of *gnosis*, regain the spiritual condition lost in the material world. The normative Christian position was that salvation was available to all believers.

It seems possible, perhaps even likely, that the Gnostics were influenced by Indian philosophy. Gnostic doctrine is decidedly Eastern in spirit (see Chapter 7). Alexander the Great had introduced the teachings of the Brahmins, and the Christian bishop Hippolytus, writing in approximately 225 CE in Rome, directly attributed Gnostic belief to Indian thought:

There is … among the Indians a heresy of those who philosophize among the Brahmins, who live a self-sufficient life, abstaining from (eating) living creatures and all cooked food. … They say that God is light, not like the light one sees, nor like the sun nor fire, but to them God is discourse, not that which finds expression in articulate sounds, but that of knowledge (*gnosis*) through which the secret mysteries of nature are perceived by the wise.

Brahmins and Gnostics share one important trait—their common belief that spiritual ascendancy is acquired through knowledge, not mere faith. Gnosticism was eventually rejected as sectarian and nonauthoritative as the Church developed.

The Gospels of Matthew, Mark, and Luke Particularly important to the normative view of Jesus' life is the recording in the Gospel of Matthew of the so-called Sermon on the Mount. The gospel was probably written in the last decades of the first century CE. So many of the principles of Jesus' message are included in this sermon that some scholars believe it is more an anthology of many sermons than a single address. In fact, it incorporates many traditional Jewish teachings, and Jesus' primary source is his Judaism. The sermon contains Jesus' most famous sayings, and his most famous metaphors. It includes the famous Lord's Prayer—itself a kind of collage of passages from the Hebrew Scriptures—and it differentiates, particularly, between accepted wisdom ("You have heard that it was said, 'You shall love your neighbor and hate your enemy …'") and the compassionate wisdom of the new faith ("But I say to you, Love your enemies and pray for those who persecute you, so that you may be children of your Father in heaven"). It is, furthermore, a masterpiece of rhetorical persuasion.

Consider the famous "lilies of the field" section (6:25–34) (**Reading 8.3**):

READING 8.3

from the Bible, Matthew 6:25–33

[25]Therefore I tell you, do not worry about your life, what you will eat or what you will drink, or about your body, what you will wear. Is not life more than food, and the body more than clothing? [26]Look at the birds of the air; they neither sow nor reap nor gather into barns, and yet your heavenly Father feeds them. Are you not of more value than they? [27]And can any of you by worrying add a single hour to your span of life? [28]And why do you worry about clothing? Consider the lilies of the field, how they grow; they neither toil nor spin, [29]yet I tell you, even Solomon in all his glory was not clothed like one of these. [30]But if God so clothes the grass of the field, which is alive today and tomorrow is thrown into the oven, will he not much more clothe you—you of little faith? [31]Therefore do not worry, saying, "What will we eat?" or "What will we drink?" or "What will we wear?" [32]For it is the Gentiles who strive for all these things; and indeed your heavenly Father knows

---

that you need all these things. [33]But strive first for the kingdom of God and his righteousness, and all these things will be given to you as well.

Jesus employs the natural metaphor of lilies clothing the landscape more richly than even Solomon in all his glory to convince his listeners that God will provide for them, thus creating an analogy between what they cannot know for sure and what they can see for themselves with certainty. This is one of 36 times in his gospel that Matthew refers to the "kingdom of God," which, it is important to understand, is not "heaven" but a spiritual kingdom on earth that people willingly enter through belief, spiritual rebirth, and carrying out the will of God. Thus, Matthew argues that God's promise is available to all through the agency of faith.

The gospels of Matthew, Mark, and Luke are known as the **synoptic gospels**—literally, "seeing together." That is, they tell the same stories, in the same sequence, often using the same words, although they differ in their details. Sometime between 90 and 100 CE, the apostle John gave a different picture of Jesus. John's Gospel omits materials found in the first three books, including the temptation of Jesus and the story of the Last Supper, and provides new material, including Jesus' early ministry in Galilee, his several visits to Jerusalem prior to the final one (the only one mentioned in the first three books), and the raising of Lazarus from the dead.

One of its most notable features is its prologue, which consciously echoes the opening motif of the Hebrew Scriptures in Genesis: "In the beginning," John begins, "was the Word, and the Word was with God, and the Word was God" (John 1:1). Where Genesis 1 focuses on God's creation, John 1 focuses on the Word of God (*logos* in Greek) and its significance in the already created world. The term *logos* was widely used by the Greek Stoics, who in turn had adopted it from the sixth-century BCE writings of Heraclitus. They believed that the universe is pervaded by *logos*, or ultimate rationality, which permeates and directs all things. Thus, John begins his gospel by appealing directly to a Greek audience in terms that would be familiar to them.

Symbols and Iconography in Christian Thinking and Art

The new Christian faith did not immediately abandon its traditions as a Jewish sect. Jesus, for instance, never thought of himself as anything other than a Jew. All of his associates and disciples were Jews. He regularly worshiped in Jewish communal worship and he preached from the Torah, the authority of which he never denied. The major distinction was that Christian Jews believed in Jesus' Resurrection and status as Messiah, while non-Christian Jews did not. Christian Jews regarded the failure of the larger Jewish community to recognize the importance of Jesus as reason to separate themselves from that community to pursue what they believed to be the true will of God. Not until sometime in the early second century CE did Christianity cease to be a Jewish sect. By then, Christians had abandoned Jewish rituals, including circumcision, but even as it slowly distinguished itself from its Jewish roots, Christianity had to come to terms with those roots. In doing so, it found a distinctive way to accept the Hebrew Scriptures.

Christians believed the stories in the Hebrew Scriptures prefigured the life of Jesus. For example, Adam and Eve's fall from grace in the Garden of Eden—the original sin that was believed to doom all of humanity—was seen as anticipating the necessity of God's sacrifice of his son, Jesus, to atone for the sins of humankind. Similarly, Christians interpreted Abraham's willingness to sacrifice his son, Isaac, as prefiguring God's sacrifice of his son. This view of history is called **typology**, from the Greek *tupos* meaning "example" or "figure." Thus Solomon, in his wisdom, is a **type** for Christ.

Very little early Christian art survives, and most of what we have dates from the third and fourth centuries. In paintings decorating catacombs, underground cemeteries, and a few sculptures, certain themes and elements are so prevalent that we can assume they reflect relatively long-standing representational traditions. In almost all of these works, it is not so much the literal meaning of the image that matters, but rather its symbolic significance. Likewise, the aesthetic dimension of the work is clearly less important than its message. A very common image is that of Christ as the Good Shepherd, which derives from Jesus' promise, "I am the good shepherd. A good shepherd lays down his life for the sheep" (John 10:11). The overwhelming message of this symbolism involves the desire of the departed to join Jesus' flock in heaven, to be miraculously reborn like Jonah. As the Lamb of God, a reference to the age-old role of the lamb in sacrificial offerings, Jesus is, of course, both shepherd and sheep—guardian of his flock and God the Father's sacrificial lamb. In fact, it is unclear whether images such as the freestanding representation of *The Good Shepherd* (Fig. **8.4**) represent Christ or symbolize a more general concept of God caring for his flock, perhaps even capturing a sheep for sacrifice. The naturalism of the sculpture echoes Classical and Hellenistic traditions. We see this too in monumental funerary sculpture, such as the sarcophagus of Junius Bassus (see *Closer Look*, pages 256–257). The shepherd adopts a *contrapposto* pose, reminiscent of Polyclitus' *Doryphoros* of the fifth century BCE (see Fig. 5.4 in Chapter 5). His body is confidently modeled beneath the drapery of his clothing. He turns as if engaged with some other person or object outside the scope of the sculpture itself, animating the space around him. And the sheep he carries on his back seems to struggle to set itself free.

CONTINUITY & CHANGE

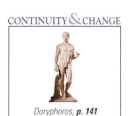

Doryphoros, p. 141

These examples make clear the importance of symbolism to Christian thinking. Over the course of the first 200 years of Christianity, before freedom of worship was legalized,

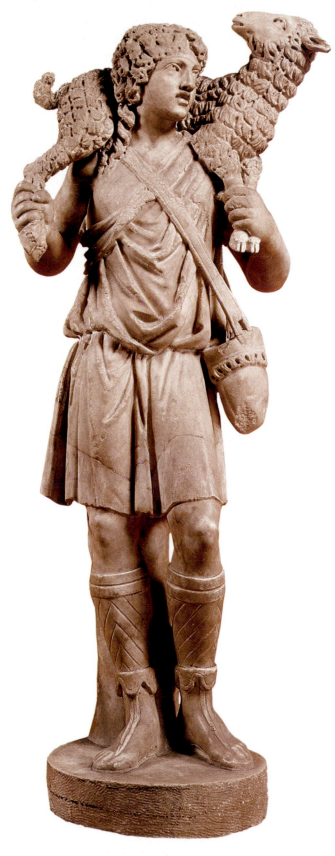

Fig. 8.4 ***The Good Shepherd.*** **ca. 300 CE.** Marble, height 39". Vatican Museums, Vatican State. The legs of this figure have been restored. Freestanding sculptures such as this one are rare in the early Christian period. Much more common are wall paintings.

CLOSER LOOK

The stone coffin known as the sarcophagus of Junius Bassus is one of the most extraordinary pieces of sculpture of the late Roman Empire. It consists of ten individual scenes on two tiers, each separated from the next by a column (in fact, the two top right-hand scenes are one, representing Christ's confrontation with Pontius Pilate). The columns framing the central two scenes are decorated with *putti*, plump, naked boys who in Classical art are usually cupids and in Christian art are called *cherubs*. They can be seen here harvesting grapes, symbolic of the blood of Christ and his sacrifice. This element underscores the importance of these two central panels, which depict Christ in his glory. The bottom panel represents Christ's triumphal entry into Jerusalem on Palm Sunday, the top his presentation of the Christian law to Peter and Paul after his Resurrection. In the top panel, Christ's feet rest on what is generally taken to be a symbolic personification of the sky, the figure of Aeolus, suggesting Christ's position in heaven.

Across the top of the sarcophagus these words are written: "Junius Bassus, a man of highest rank, who lived 42 years, 2 months, in his own prefecture of the city, went to God, the 8th day from the Kalends of September, Eusebius and Hypatius being consuls [25 August 359]." Thus, the sarcophagus collapses the "present" time of Junius Bassus' death into historical time. Four scenes from the Old Testament prophesy the story of Christ, itself represented in four panels, as well as the arrest and persecution of two Roman martyrs, Paul and Peter, who represent the fate of all Roman Christians up until the Edict of Milan, which Constantine endorsed just four years before Junius Bassus' birth. In his sarcophagus, Bassus assumes his place in Christian history.

Something to Think About …

Although the drapery, poses, and deep relief of this sculpture demonstrate the continued influence of Classical tradition, the heads of the figures appear disproportionately large. How does this relate to the colossal portrait sculpture of Constantine the Great in Rome (see Fig. 8.10)?

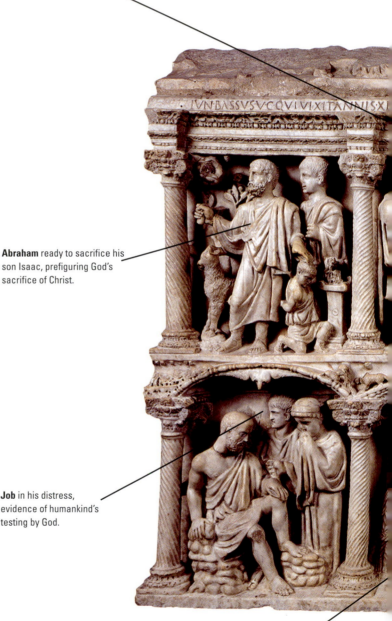

The arrest of **Saint Peter**, who would be crucified in Rome in imitation of Christ. At his own insistence, Peter was crucified upside down, to emphasize his status as lesser than his Saviour's.

Abraham ready to sacrifice his son Isaac, prefiguring God's sacrifice of Christ.

Job in his distress, evidence of humankind's testing by God.

Adam and Eve in the Garden of Eden, at the moment when they succumbed to the Temptation of Satan, who is shown wrapped around the Tree of the Knowledge of Good and Evil in his guise as a serpent.

Sarcophagus of Junius Bassus. 359 CE. Marble, Museo Storico del Tesoro della Basilica di San Pietro, Vatican City.

View the Closer Look for the sarcophagus of Junius Bassus on **MyArtsLab**

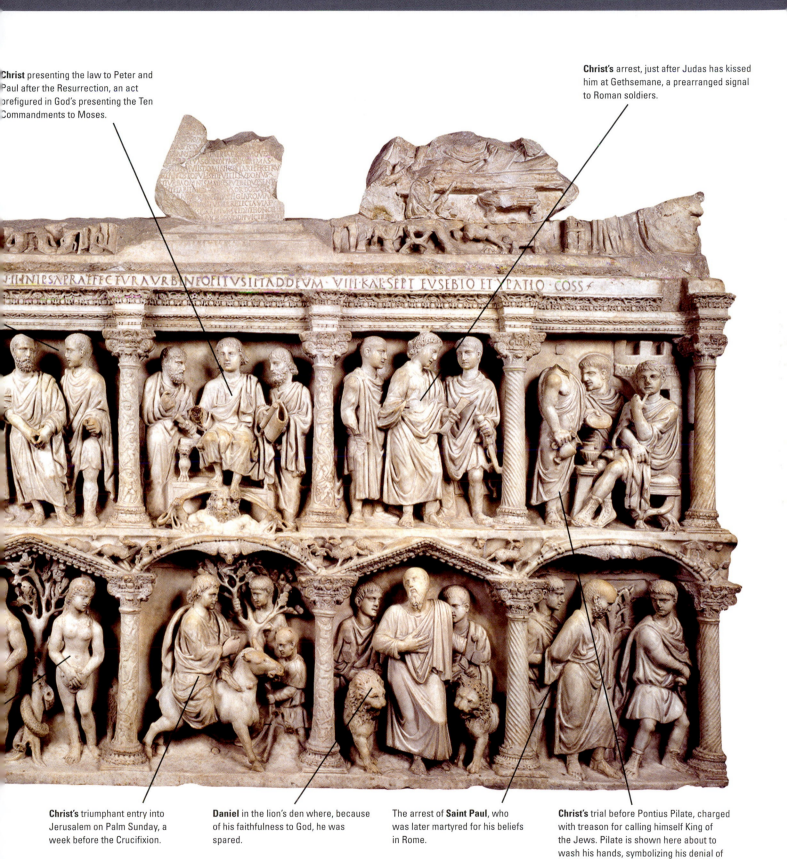

Christ presenting the law to Peter and Paul after the Resurrection, an act prefigured in God's presenting the Ten Commandments to Moses.

Christ's arrest, just after Judas has kissed him at Gethsemane, a prearranged signal to Roman soldiers.

Christ's triumphant entry into Jerusalem on Palm Sunday, a week before the Crucifixion.

Daniel in the lion's den where, because of his faithfulness to God, he was spared.

The arrest of **Saint Paul**, who was later martyred for his beliefs in Rome.

Christ's trial before Pontius Pilate, charged with treason for calling himself King of the Jews. Pilate is shown here about to wash his hands, symbolizing his denial of responsibility for Jesus' death.

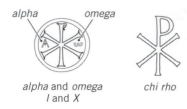

alpha   *omega*

alpha and *omega*
I and *X*

chi rho

Fig. 8.5 Traditional Christian symbols.

Christians developed many symbols that served to identify them to each other and to mark the articles of their faith. Their symbols allowed them to represent their faith in full view of a general populace that largely rejected it. They adopted the symbol of the fish, for instance, because the Greek word for fish, *ichthys*, is a form of acronym, a combination of the first letters of the Greek words for "Jesus Christ, Son of God, Saviour." The first and last letters of the Greek alphabet, *alpha* and *omega*, symbolize Christ's presence from the beginning to the end of time. The *alpha* and *omega* often flank the initials *I* and *X*, the first letters of Jesus and Christ in Greek, and the initials *XP* were the first two letters of the word *Christos* (Fig. **8.5**).

Over the years, Christians developed a consistent **ico-nography**—the subject matter of a work, both literal (factual) and figurative (symbolic)—in their art and literature. A story or person might be a type for some other story or person. A figure might symbolize something else, as particular figures symbolized each of the four evangelists—a man with wings for Matthew, symbolizing his humanity; a lion for Mark; an ox for Luke; an eagle for John. And the

stories surrounding Jesus' life coalesced into distinct story "cycles," each part in some sense signifying the whole, and all of them becoming standard themes in the arts throughout the history of the West.

CHRISTIAN ROME

What was the Roman reaction to Christianity and in what ways did Roman tradition influence the religion's development?

Christianity spread rapidly across the Roman Empire (Map **8.1**). As the map indicates, Christian areas of the Empire increased dramatically from 200 to 400 CE, and as Christian authority increased, Roman authority naturally waned. The emperor Constantine's predecessor, Diocletian (see Chapter 6, *Continuity & Change*), had unleashed a furious persecution of Christians that lasted for eight years beginning in 303, but he also moved to cement Roman authority by implementing a scheme of government known as the **tetrarchy**, a four-part monarchy. Diocletian ruled from Solana, a city on the Adriatic near present-day Split, Croatia, and controlled the East, with the other regions of the Empire governed by monarchs in Milan, the Balkans, and Gaul. In a sculpture representing the four (Fig. **8.6**), they are almost indistinguishable from one another, except that the two senior Tetrarchs are bearded and their juniors clean-shaven. They hold identical bird-headed swords and wear flat caps from Pannonia. This Roman province

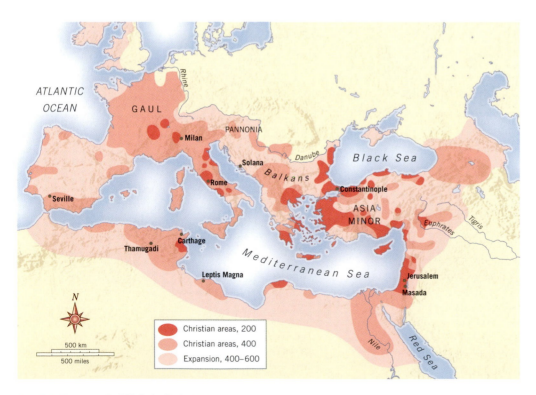

Map 8.1 The spread of Christianity by 600 CE.

The Nicene Creed

Constantine recognized that Diocletian's scheme for controlling the Empire was, in most respects, sound. Particularly important was an imperial presence near the eastern and Danubian frontiers of the Empire. To provide this imperial presence in the East, in 324 CE, Constantine founded the city of Constantinople, present-day Istanbul, on the site of the Greek city of Byzantium. The city was dedicated with both pagan rites and Christian ceremonies on May 11, 330. Constantine's own Christianity became more and more pronounced in his new eastern capital. Though he did not persecute pagans, he officially rejected pagan practices, openly favored Christians as officials, and admitted Church clergy to his court. Perhaps his most important act was to convene the first **ecumenical**, or worldwide, **council** of Church leaders in 325 CE at Nicea (present-day Iznik), a site just southeast of Constantinople, in order to address, particularly, the claims of Bishop Arius of Alexandria. Arius argued that Father and Son were not of the same substance, and therefore not coequal and not coeternal. The council rejected the Arian position and produced a document, the Nicene Creed, that unified the Church behind a prescribed doctrine, or **dogma**, creating, in effect, an orthodox faith. Church leaders believed that by memorizing the Creed, laypeople would be able to easily identify deviations from orthodox Christianity.

The Creed was revised and extended in 381 by a Second Ecumenical Council in Constantinople, quoted here (**Reading 8.4**):

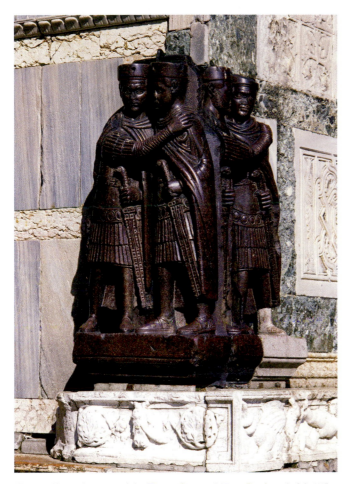

Fig. 8.6 Portrait group of the Tetrarchs. ca. 305 CE. Porphyry, height 51". Basilica of San Marco, Venice. Originally decorating a crossroads square in Constantinople known as the Philadelphion, this sculpture was probably the base of a porphyry column. It was removed to Venice after 1204.

was bordered on the north and east by the Danube River in present-day Central Europe, which was the meeting place of the Eastern and Western empires. Their sameness symbolizes their equality, just as their embrace symbolizes their solidarity. Even the sculpture's material is symbolic: Porphyry is a deep-purple Egyptian stone traditionally reserved for imperial portraits.

This shift of the Empire's administration from Rome to its provincial capitals had dramatic implications for Rome itself. Perhaps most important was Diocletian's removal to Asia Minor (present-day Turkey). There, he almost completely deified the role of the emperor, presenting himself more as the divine manifestation of the gods than as a leader of a citizen-state. He dressed in robes of blue- and gold-threaded silk, glittering with jewels, to symbolize sky and sun. He had his fingernails gilded and gold dust sprinkled in his hair to create the sense of a halo or nimbus encircling his head. When he entered the throne room, servants sprinkled perfume behind him and fan-bearers spread the scent through the room. All kneeled in his presence. He was addressed as *dominus*, "lord," and his right to rule, he claimed, was derived not from the people but from God.

READING 8.4

The Nicene Creed

We believe in one God the Father All-Sovereign, maker of heaven and earth, and of all things visible and invisible;

And in one Lord Jesus Christ, the only-begotten Son of God, Begotten of the Father before all the ages, Light of Light, true God of true God, begotten not made, of one essence with the Father, through whom all things were made; who for us men and for our salvation came down from the heavens, and was made flesh of the Holy Spirit and the Virgin Mary, and became man, and was crucified for us under Pontius Pilate, and suffered and was buried, and rose again on the third day according to the Scriptures, and ascended into the heavens, and sitteth on the right hand of the Father, and cometh again with glory to judge living and dead, of whose kingdom there shall be no end;

And [we believe] in the Holy Spirit, the Lord and the Life-giver, that proceedeth from the Father, who with Father and Son is worshiped together and glorified together, who spake through the prophets;

In one holy catholic and apostolic Church: We acknowledge one baptism unto remission of sins. We look for a resurrection of the dead, and the life of the age to come.

The Creed is an article of mystical faith, not a doctrine of rational or empirical observation. In its very first line, it states its belief in the invisible. It argues for the virgin birth of Jesus, for a holy "spirit," for the resurrection of the dead. It imagines what cannot be rationally known: Jesus in heaven at the right hand of God (perhaps not coincidentally an image evocative of Diocletian modeling himself as *dominus*, "lord," ruling at the will of and beside God). Nothing could be further from the Aristotelian drive to describe the knowable world and to represent it in naturalistic terms. (See Chapter 5.)

But perhaps most important, the Nicene Creed establishes "the one holy catholic and apostolic Church," that is, a united church that is universal ("catholic") and based on the teachings of the apostles ("apostolic"). The Church was organized around the administrative divisions of the Roman state—archbishops oversaw the provinces, bishops the dioceses, and priests the parishes—an organization that provided Constantine with the means to impose the Creed throughout the Empire, eliminate rivalries within the Empire, and rule over both church and state. Finally, the Church's **liturgy**, the rites prescribed for public worship, was established. In Rome, Saint Jerome (ca. 342–420 CE) translated the Hebrew Bible and the Greek books of the New Testament into Latin. The resulting **Vulgate**, meaning "common" or "popular," became the official Bible of the Roman Catholic Church. As the version of the Bible known by the faithful for over a thousand years, from about 400 CE to 1530, it would exert an influence over Western culture, which came to consider it virtually infallible.

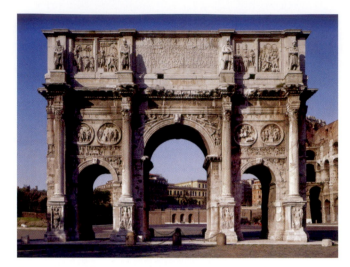

Fig. 8.7 Arch of Constantine (south side), Rome. 312–15 CE. Constantine built the arch to celebrate his victory over Maxentius.

View the Closer Look for the Arch of Constantine on **MyArtsLab**

The Abandonment of Classicism in Art

Roman art was transformed in this period as well. For instance, one of Constantine's first projects after his victory over his rival Maxentius at the Milvian Bridge in Rome was to construct an impressive triple arch in celebration (Fig. 8.7), for which he raided the artworks of other Roman monuments. Comparing the reliefs made for Constantine's arch, particularly the horizontal panel that shows *Constantine Addressing the People*, with the circular **roundels** (round reliefs) above it, provides insight into the changes

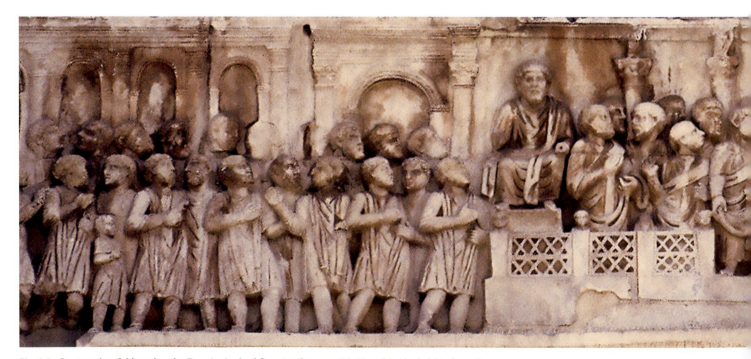

Fig. 8.9 *Constantine Addressing the People*, Arch of Constantine. ca. 130–38 CE. Marble, height of panel approx. 40". Compared to Fig. 8.8, the lack of spatial complexity in this relief is striking.

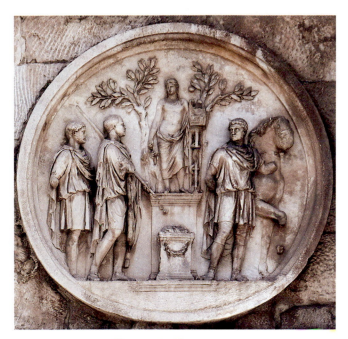

Apollo. The space is illusionistic, rendered realistically so that the figures seem to stand well in front of the sculpture. The horse on the right emerges from behind its master on a diagonal that emphasizes a logical progression from background to foreground. The draperies of the figures fall naturalistically.

The relief depicting *Constantine Addressing the People* is quite different (Fig. **8.9**). No real sense of illusionistic space exists. Constantine stands in the middle (his head has not survived), surrounded by a linear arrangement of mostly frontally posed attendants whose clothing is rendered merely by lines cut into the flat surface of the stone—they are not really sculpted at all. All of the figures are the same height, their heads abutting on a line dividing the upper piece of marble from the bottom. But the real difference between the two pieces becomes apparent when we realize that the two seated figures on either side of the podium are themselves sculptures—statues of Hadrian and Marcus Aurelius. These statues signal Constantine's dedication to them and his identification with their imperial majesty. Unlike the statue of the deity in the Hadrian roundel, they are undistinguishable from the other figures. This comparison indicates that by the fourth century CE, naturalism is no longer an important aim of art, and the Classical heritage of the Greek and Roman tradition has been abandoned. How large a role Christianity played in this transition is difficult to say, but the symbolic function of art has supplanted its illusionistic purposes; the spiritual has replaced the physical. Additionally, the standards of beauty that defined Classical art, specifically those defining the beauty of the human body, have been replaced by a more abstract standard

Fig. 8.8 *Hadrian Sacrificing to Apollo,* roundel imported from a monument to Hadrian (ca. 130–38 CE) and reused over the left arch on the Arch of Constantine. Diameter of roundel 40". Constantine recycled many works from other monuments as well, including reliefs taken from a monument celebrating Marcus Aurelius' victory over the Germans in 174 CE.

in the art and culture of this period that the Christian faith inspired. The roundels come from a monument to Hadrian made almost 200 years earlier. In one roundel (Fig. **8.8**), Hadrian and two companions stand before the statue of

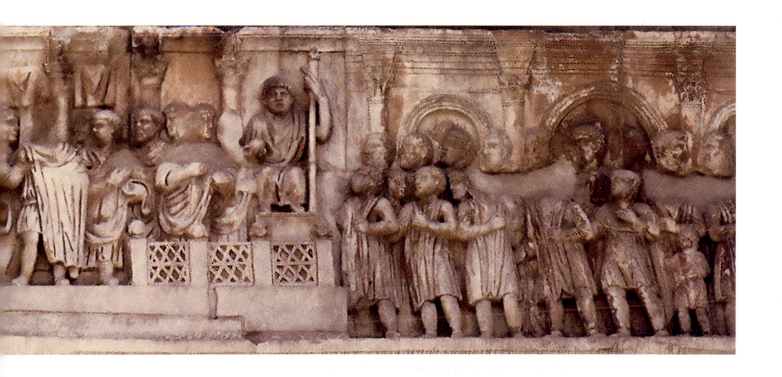

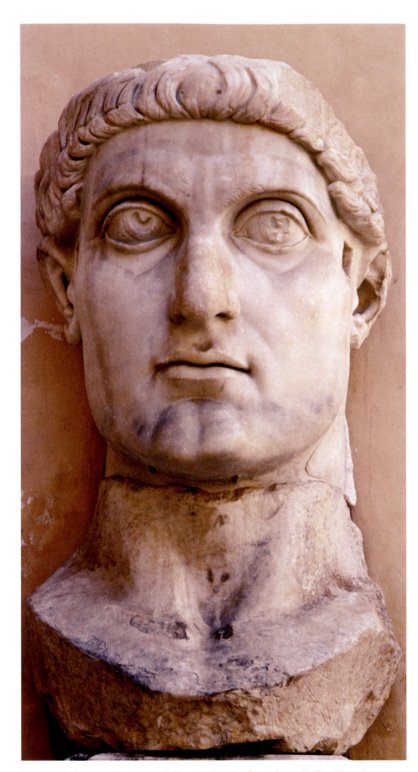

Fig. 8.10 Fragment of a statue of _Constantine the Great_, from the Basilica of Maxentius and Constantine, Rome. ca. 315–30 CE. Marble, height of bust approx. 8½'. Palazzo dei Conservatori, Rome. The flesh of Constantine's body, wherever revealed beneath its bronze armor, was sculpted in marble. Fragments of the right hand, the upper right arm, the lower left leg, and both feet also survive.

of beauty. The new standard still depends on visual balance and order, but it has little or no interest in the body, since it is in the symbolism of an image that true beauty is believed to lie.

A giant portrait of Constantine erected at the Basilica Nova in Rome offers a different example of the increasing tendency of Roman-Christian art to capture the spiritual rather than physical beauty of its subject (Fig. **8.10**). The head alone is 8½ feet high, composed entirely of marble, and the entire seated figure was approximately 30 feet in height. The emperor's hair is composed of repeated geometric arcs. His eyes are disproportionately large, symbolizing contact with the divine. He looks both serene and imposing, appearing to gaze into the far distance, as if symbolically contemplating spiritual things beyond the material world itself. Even if the jutting chin and hawklike nose reflect his actual appearance, the totality has been transformed into a godlike presence, more an abstract image of imperial majesty and power than a realistic representation of the human emperor.

Roman Influences on Christian Churches

The community that developed around the new Christian liturgy embodied in the Nicene Creed required a physical church, and Constantine obliged with a building that became a model for many subsequent churches: Saint Peter's Basilica, begun in 320 on the site of Peter's tomb in Rome (Figs. **8.11** and **8.12**). Its original dimensions are difficult to fathom, but an eighteenth-century print of a nearly contemporary church in Rome, Saint Paul's Outside the Walls, gives us a fair idea (Fig. **8.13**). The church was as long, as high,

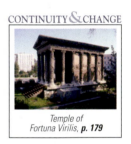

CONTINUITY & CHANGE

Temple of Fortuna Virilis, **p. 179**

and as wide as the Roman **basilicas** upon which it was modeled (see Figs. 6.35 and 6.36 in Chapter 6). It was approached by a set of stairs to a podium, reminiscent of the Roman Temple of Fortuna Virilis (see Figs. 6.7 and 6.8 in Chapter 6). Entering through a triple-arched gateway (again reminiscent of Roman triumphal arches), visitors found themselves in a colonnaded atrium with a fountain in the center (reminiscent of the Roman _domus_—perhaps suggesting the "House of God"; see Fig. 6.29 in Chapter 6).

The church proper consisted of a **narthex**, or entrance hall, and a **nave**, with two aisles on each side. At the eastern end was an **apse**, housing the altar framed by a giant triumphal

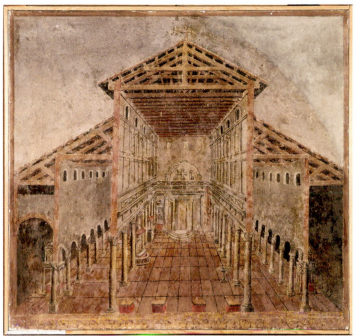

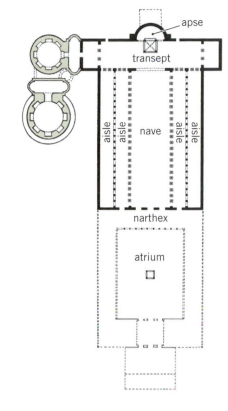

Figs. 8.11 and 8.12 Domenico Tasselli, *The Nave and Aisles of the Ancient Basilica of Constantine in Rome Looking Toward the Entrance Wall*. 319–26 CE. Fresco. Sacristy, Saint Peter's Basilica, Vatican State, Rome. What we know of Old Saint Peter's (a "new" Saint Peter's replaced it in the sixteenth century) comes from modern archeological finds, written descriptions, drawings made both before and during its destruction, and the surviving churches it inspired.

Fig. 8.13 *Interior of Saint Paul's Outside the Walls, Rome*. Begun 386 CE. Etching by Gianbattista Piranesi, 1749. Note the wooden tresses of the ceiling and the spaciousness of the interior, reminiscent of the Roman baths.

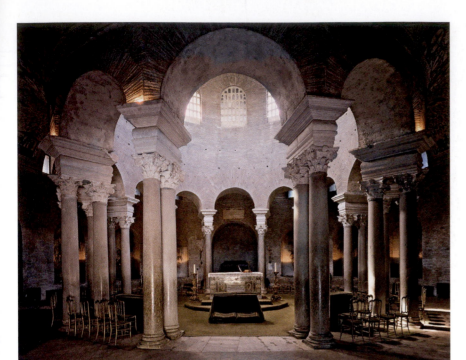

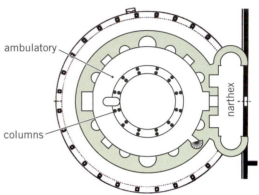

ambulatory

columns

narthex

Figs. 8.14 and 8.15 Interior view and plan of the Church of Santa Costanza, Rome. ca. 350 CE. The view on the left is from the ambulatory into the central space. This is the earliest surviving central-plan building in the world. Originally, the central plan was used for mausoleums or shrines. Another central-plan church very much like this one originally covered Christ's tomb in Jerusalem, but it was later incorporated into the basilica. The Church of Santa Costanza was originally attached to the now-destroyed basilica of Saint Agnes Outside the Walls.

arch, where the sacrament of Holy Communion was performed. A transverse aisle, or **transept**, crossed between the nave and the apse; in other church plans, it could be extended north and south to form a **Latin cross** (a long arm, the nave, with three shorter arms—the apse and the arms of the transept). The nave was two stories high, the aisles one story, allowing for a **clerestory**, a zone with windows that lit the length of the church. Open timberwork tresses supported the roof (making the structure particularly susceptible to fire).

All in all, the basilica church was far more than an assembly hall. It was a richly decorated spiritual performance space, designed to elicit awe and wonder in worshipers. As the liturgy was performed, as the congregation—consisting of literally thousands—raised their voices together in song and then fell silent in prayer, the effect would have been stunning. No one, it was hoped, could leave without their faith reenergized.

A second type of Christian church also first developed in Rome, although it was initially conceived as a mausoleum for the daughter of Constantine, Constantia, a devout Christian who died in 354. Santa Costanza is a **central-plan** church, so called because of its circular structure, topped by a dome (Figs. **8.14** and **8.15**). The architectural forerunners of this type of church include the high domed space of the Pantheon (see Fig. 6.28 in Chapter 6).

A double ring of paired columns separates the circular central space from the barrel-vaulted **ambulatory**, the walkway or passage encircling the domed interior. (Later Christian churches would adapt this ambulatory to encircle the apse.) This ambulatory is elaborately decorated with mosaics (Fig. **8.16**), consisting of an overall vine pattern interspersed with small scenes, such as laborers picking grapes and putting them into carts, transporting them to a press, and then crushing them underfoot.

One of the Christian references here is to the use of wine in the Eucharist, symbolizing the blood of Christ. But the Dionysian implications of the scene, with its unruly swirls of undulating lines—the very opposite of the Roman (and Classical) sense of order and proportion—are unmistakable. Used to decorate a church, these lines imply the very nature of faith—that is, the abandonment by faith of reason and logic, the very principles of Classical balance and proportion.

Greek and Roman Myths in Christianity

The design makes clear, in fact, the ways in which Christianity incorporated into itself many Greek and Roman mythic traditions—a practice known as **syncretism**, the reconciliation of different rites and practices into a single philosophy or religion. This occurred not only in the design of Christian churches but also in the symbolism of its art and literature—and it makes perfect sense. How better to convert pagan peoples than to present your religious program in their own terms? After all, the Greek wine god Dionysus had, like Christ, promised human immortality in the manner of the grapevine itself, which appears to die each

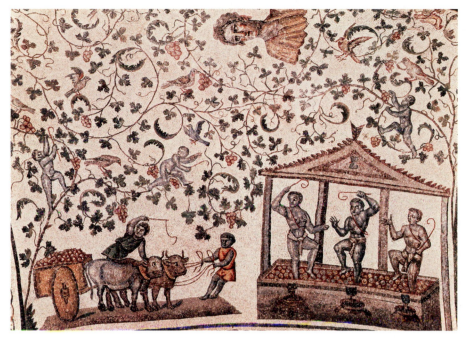

Fig. 8.16 Ambulatory vault mosaic, Church of Santa Costanza, Rome. ca. 350 CE. The figure at the top of this reproduction (which is actually positioned in the center of the grapevine motif) is probably Constantine's daughter, Constantia herself.

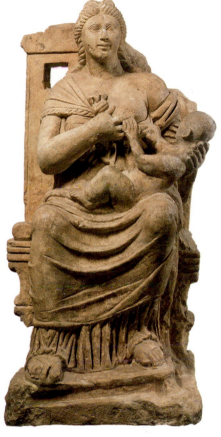

Fig. 8.17 *Isis Lactans,* **Isis giving the breast to the infant Horus, from Antinoe, Egypt. Late 4th or early 5th century.** Limestone, height 35". Staatliche Museen, Berlin. This is one example of a Greco-Egyptian motif that was popular in the first four or five centuries CE.

fall only to be reborn in the spring. Just as Christians had found prefigurings of Christ in the Hebrew Bible, it was possible to argue that Dionysus was a pagan type of Christ.

The cult of Bacchus, as the Romans referred to Dionysus, was extremely popular in Rome. So high-spirited were the drunken orgies engaged in by the cult of Dionysus that the Roman Senate had restricted its activities in 186 BCE. Other cults, known as **mystery cults** because their initiation rites were secret, were also popular among the Romans, and Christianity borrowed freely from these as well. In fact, the evidence suggests a remarkable process of cross-fertilization, each cult adapting elements from the others that were attractive or popular as they competed for followers. By the second century CE, in Rome, the *taurobolium,* or sacrifice of a bull, usually associated with the Great Mother of the Gods, was performed annually on March 24. The bull's blood would run over a person beneath the sacrificial altar, who received the blood on his face, tongue, and palate, and who was said to be "reborn for eternity," as a consequence of the ceremony. Note that the *taurobolium*'s date is near the beginning of the Christian Easter season, which celebrates rebirth and resurrection. And it resonates as well with the practice of the Eucharist, or Communion, the part of the liturgy when Christians, in taking bread and wine, are believed to partake of the body and blood of Christ.

The cult of Isis in Rome had originated in Egypt and was based on the ebb and flow of the Nile. Each summer, Isis would see Egypt's arid desert landscape and she would be moved to tears of compassion for the Egyptian people. Her tears, in turn, would cause the Nile to flood, bringing the land back to life—regarded by the Isis cult as an act of resurrection, not unlike the return of the vines in the

Dionysian cult. In Egypt, in the late fourth and early fifth centuries, a new representation of Isis suckling the baby Horus began to appear (Fig. 8.17). (Remember, too, Horus is the son of Osiris, just as, in Christian tradition, Jesus is the son of God.) In a Christian context, an image of a mother with a child at her breast could easily be mistaken for Mary and Jesus, and it is entirely possible that the Isis cult was the inspiration for the Virgin and Child theme in Christian art.

Finally, the secret cult of Mithras, which originated in Persia perhaps as far back as Neolithic times, became very popular among the Roman troops stationed in Palestine at the time of Christ. In the second through fourth centuries, it spread across the Empire, and examples of its iconography can be found in Mithraic temples from Syria to Britain. Almost no texts explaining the cult survive; its rites and traditions were likely passed down orally among initiates. What we know of it comes from wall paintings and relief sculptures in its sanctuaries. It appears to have derived from a Persian religion, based on the teachings of Zoroaster (born between 1000 BCE and the early seventh century BCE). The *Zend-Avesta*, the Zoroastrian sacred book, teaches that life is a battlefield between the forces of good and evil, truth and deceit. Free to choose between these forces, humans await a Last Judgment consigning those who choose evil to eternal darkness, and those who choose good to a place of eternal luxury and light—the Persian *pairidaeza*, the origin of the English word "paradise." In Zoroastrian tradition, Mithras appears as a judge at the Last Judgment.

In the most widespread of his representations, Mithras is depicted killing a bull by stabbing him in the neck, as a snake and dog lap up the bull's blood and a scorpion clutches the bull's testicles (Fig. 8.18). The end of the bull's tail is metamorphosed into an ear of wheat. At the top left and right are busts of the sun and moon. Zoroastrian sources suggest that Mithras was sent to earth by a divine bull, and all living things sprang from the bull's blood. The story can be read as a reverse version of God's sacrifice of Jesus. Mithras sacrifices his "father"—or, at least, his divine ruler, the bull—in order to create life itself. The cult had seven stages of initiation, one of which was baptism. We also know that the birthday of Mithras was celebrated each year on December 25. When this date was adopted in about 350 CE as the traditional birth date of Jesus, the choice was most likely an attempt to appropriate the rites of Mithraic cults, then still active throughout the Roman Empire, to Christianity.

Mithraism shares many ritual practices with Christianity—baptism, periods of fasting, a communal meal of bread and wine representing the flesh and blood of the bull, reminiscent of the Christian Eucharist (in which bread and wine are believed to be transformed into the flesh and blood of Christ)—as well as many themes, especially sacrifice for the good of humanity. And it was Christianity's chief rival among the Roman people through the first four centuries CE. Christianity's ability to supplant the various mystery cults probably had several related causes. The new religion's advocates labeled the cults "pagan" and "heretical," at the same time as they codified and promoted their own rituals, beliefs, and sacred texts.

Augustine and Early Christian Philosophy

There is one other aspect of Mithras' cult that we also know—he was the god of truth and light. How much the Mithras cult influenced the Church Fathers is unclear, but light played an important role in their writing, and images of light appear often in the writings of early Christians. For instance, the Roman prelate Ambrose (339–397), Bishop of Milan, refers to God as the "Light of light, light's living spring" in his "Ancient Morning Hymn." Perhaps the most important of the early Church Fathers, Augustine of Hippo (present-day Annaba, Algeria), describes the moment of his conversion to Christianity as one in which he was infused with "the light of full certainty."

Confessions* and *The City of God Augustine, who lived from 354 to 430 CE, was in his forties and had recently been made Bishop of Hippo when he felt the need to come to terms with his past. He did this in the form of a prose work, the *Confessions*, the first Western autobiography. Though addressed to God, it was intended to be read by fellow Christians. Augustine had enjoyed an apparently wild adolescence. He describes it as a kind of "overcast" and "shadowy" atmosphere in which he gave up the "bright path" of friendship for carnal pleasure (**Reading 8.5a**):

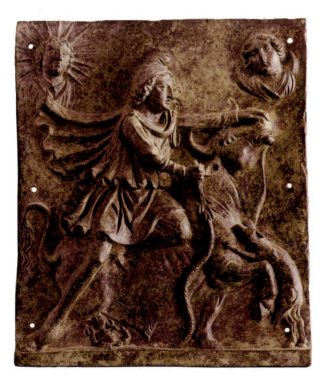

Fig. 8.18 Mithraic relief. Early 3rd century CE. The Metropolitan Museum of Art, New York. Gift of Mr. and Mrs. Klaus G. Peris, 1997 (1997.145.3). Similar versions of this image have been found throughout the Roman Empire.

READING 8.5a

from Augustine, *Confessions*

As I became a youth, I longed to be satisfied with worldly things, and I dared to grow wild in a succession of various and shadowy loves. ... But what was it that delighted me save to love and to be loved? Still I did not keep the moderate way of the love of mind to mind—the bright path of friendship. Instead, the mists of passion steamed up out of the puddly concupiscence of the flesh, and the hot imagination of puberty, and they so obscured and overcast my heart that I was unable to distinguish pure affection from unholy desire. Both boiled confusedly within me, and dragged my unstable youth down over the cliffs of unchaste desires and plunged me into a gulf of infamy.

Such thinking about the dangers of sexuality has exercised enormous influence over Western thought. For Augustine, sexuality is not so much an act, but an inferior state of mind, and all sensual pleasure represents a triumph of the carnal will over the spiritual. Sex is the means of transmission of original sin, and sexual desire is evidence of humanity's inability to resist it. The exercise of the carnal inevitably led, in his mind, to the famous episode of "The Pear Tree" in Book 2, where he describes his darkest moment: his theft of a neighbor's pears when he was 16. Later, in Book 8, still leading a dissolute life as a student, but despairing of his lifestyle, he describes his conversion to Christianity in a garden near Carthage (see **Reading 8.5**, page 285, for both episodes).

Augustine's storytelling is so compelling that the *Confessions* became one of the most influential books of the Middle Ages. The frankness of Augustine's autobiographical self-assessment—for instance, he is not proud of the follies of his youth though he is clearly still fascinated by them—would also make it influential later, in the context of the general rediscovery of the self that defines the great awakening to awareness of the human body known as the Renaissance.

But the *Confessions* is also a profoundly religious treatise that became influential on the merits of its religious arguments as well as its narrative power. For Augustine, humankind is capable of understanding true ideas only when they are illuminated by the soul of God. He adds to the Platonic emphasis on pure ideas a Christian belief in the sacred word of God, in which God's "light" is understood to shine. In the *Confessions*, too, Augustine codified the idea of typological readings of the Bible, proposing, for example, Eve, the biological mother of humanity, as a type for Mary, the spiritual mother. Similarly, he saw the deliverance of the Israelites from Egypt as a prefiguration of the redemption of Jesus.

Augustine was a prolific writer and thinker and a renowned teacher. One of his most important works is *The City of God*, written between 413 and 425. It is a reinterpretation of history from a theological point of view. In many ways, the book was a response to the sack of Rome by the Visigoths in 410. What had happened to the once powerful empire that had controlled the world, in a common phrase, "to its very edge"? How had such a disaster come to pass? Augustine attempts to answer these questions.

Many Romans blamed the Christians for the city's downfall, but Augustine argued, to the contrary, that pagan religion and philosophy, and particularly the hubris, or arrogance, of the emperors in assuming to be divine had doomed Rome from the beginning. Even more to the point, Augustine argued that the fall of Rome had been inevitable, since the city had been a product of humankind, and thus corrupt and mortal. Even a Christian Rome would inevitably have been doomed. As described in *The City of God*, history is a forward movement—at least in a spiritual sense—to the Day of Judgment, a movement from the earthly city, with its secular ways, to the heavenly city, untouched by worldly concerns (**Reading 8.6a**):

READING 8.6a

from Augustine, *The City of God*

The two cities were created by two kinds of love: the earthly city by a love of self even to the point of contempt for God, the heavenly city by a love of God carried even to the point of contempt for self. Consequently, the earthly city glories in itself while the heavenly city glories in the Lord. ... In the one, the lust for dominion has dominion over its princes as well as over the nations it subdues; in the other, both those put in charge and those placed under them serve one another in love, the former by their counsel, the latter by their obedience. ...

Thus, in the earthly city ... if any of [its wise men] were able to know God, "they did not honor him as God, or give thanks to him, but they became futile in their thinking and their senseless minds were darkened ... [and] they became fools, and exchanged the glory of the immortal God for images resembling mortal man or birds or beasts or reptiles," for in adoration of idols of this sort they were either leaders or followers of the populace, "and worshiped and served the creature rather than the creator, who is blessed forever."

The quotations at the end of this excerpt from *The City of God* are from Romans 1:21–25, Paul's first epistle to the Romans. The Romans are portrayed here as Stoics, "futile in their thinking," and worshipers of pagan images, but they are not necessarily lost souls. Paul, after all, is preaching to them. For Augustine, as for Paul, evil is a deficiency of good, the result of incorrect choices, as prefigured by Adam and Eve's choice to eat the forbidden fruit in the Garden of Eden, not something that exists in its own right. The Romans can be saved, then, but only if they give up the earthly city and accept the City of God. And if history was the progress of humankind from the earthly city to the heavenly one, then the church was "the mediator between God and men," between one city and the other.

Augustine's world view is essentially dualistic, composed of two parts. In his writings, the movement of history (and of life itself) follows a linear progression from darkness to light, from body to soul, from evil to goodness, from doubt to faith, and from blindness to understanding. His own life story, as described in *Confessions*, revealed him as the sinner saved. He saw himself, in fact, as a type for all Christians, whose ultimate place, he believed, would one day be the City of God.

He reads the Bible in much the same terms, seeing its characters and stories as symbolic of larger abstract and universal qualities—that is, he reads the Bible as a kind of **allegory**, the representation of abstract or spiritual meanings through concrete or material forms. In this way, not only does Noah become a type for all men on the path toward salvation, but his ark is symbolic, at once, of the body of Christ, the Church itself, and the City of God (see **Reading 8.6**, page 286, for Augustine's allegorical interpretation of the story of Noah's ark). Augustine's symbolic readings of the scripture provide the foundation of biblical interpretation down to the present day.

Augustine, Ambrose, and Music in the Liturgy In his *Confessions*, Saint Augustine declared that "the practice and singing of hymns and psalms ... was established so that the people [of Milan] would not become weak as a result of boredom or sorrow. It has been retained from that day to this; many, in fact, nearly all of God's flocks now do likewise throughout the rest of the world." These hymns and songs, Augustine says, represented a "kind of consolation and exhortation, in which the voice and the hearts of the brethren joined in zealous harmony." The bishop of Milan, Ambrose, wrote hymns to be sung by the congregation, recognizing them, like Augustine, to be an important part of the new liturgy. Recognizing that common people, with no musical training, were to sing along with the clergy, Ambrose composed simple, melodic songs or psalms, generally characterized by one syllable for each note of the hymn. His description of them, as evidenced in the most famous of them, the "Ancient Morning Hymn" (**Reading 8.7**, pages 286–287), again reflects the importance of the image of light in the early Christian liturgy. "The psalm is our armor by night," he wrote, "our instructor by day. The dawn of the day resounds with the psalm, and the psalm re-echoes at sunset."

Ambrose's authorship is certain for only four hymns, all attributed to him by Augustine. The melodies survive only in tenth- and eleventh-century versions, and their authenticity is disputed. Each hymn is composed of eight four-line stanzas, each written in a strict **iambic tetrameter** (short-long, short-long, short-long, short-long). Ambrose also seems to have introduced an **antiphonal** method of chanting, where one side of the choir responds to the other. What is certain, however, is that music was now employed as a way of bringing the community of worshipers together in common practice.

THE BYZANTINE EMPIRE AND ITS CHURCH

How does Byzantine art differ from earlier, Classical models and how does it reflect the values of the empire and its church?

Constantine had built his new capital at Constantinople in 325 CE in no small part because Rome was too vulnerable to attack from Germanic tribes. Located on a highly defensible peninsula, Constantinople was far less susceptible to threat, and indeed, while Rome finally collapsed after successive Germanic invasions in 476, Constantinople would serve as the center of Christian culture throughout the early Middle Ages, surviving until 1453 when Ottoman Turks finally succeeded in overrunning it.

In Constantine's Constantinople, Christian basilicas stood next to Roman baths, across from a Roman palace and Senate, the former connected to a Roman hippodrome, all but the basilicas elaborately decorated with pagan art and sculpture gathered from across the Empire (Map **8.2**).

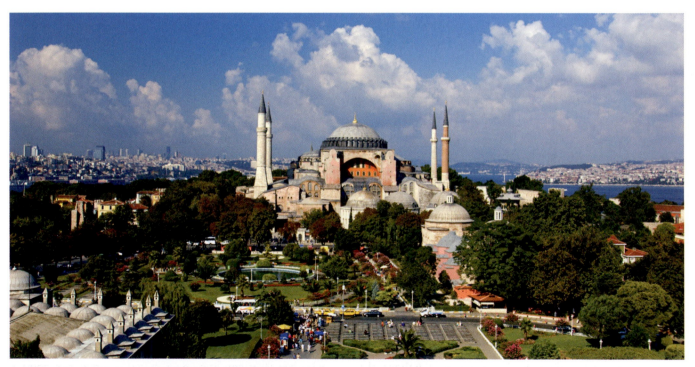

Fig. 8.19 Hagia Sophia, Istanbul (formerly Constantinople). 532–37. Originally dedicated to Christ as the personification of Holy (*hagia*) Wisdom (*sophia*), the church was transformed into a mosque by Muslim conquerors in 1453. Today, it serves as a museum, although it remains one of the oldest religious sanctuaries in the world.

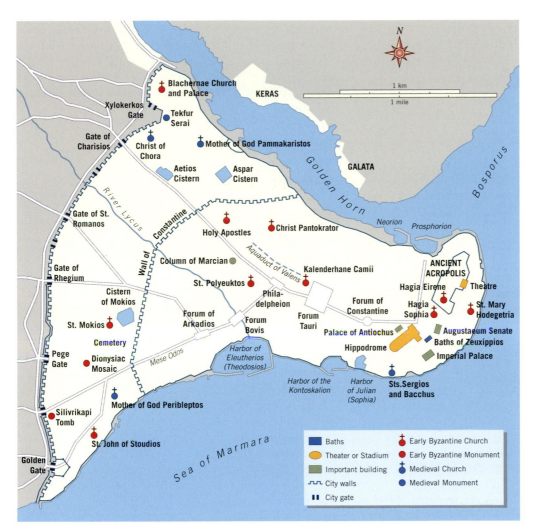

Map 8.2 Early Byzantine and medieval Constantinople.

Christians soon developed an important new understanding of these pagan works: They could ignore their pagan elements and think of them simply as *art*. This was the argument of Basil the Great (ca. 329–79), the major theologian of the day. In his twenties, he had studied the classics of Greek literature in Athens and had fallen in love with them. He believed it was possible to understand them as literature, not theology, as great works of art, not as arguments for the existence of pagan gods.

Nonetheless, Roman pagan ways soon gave way to Christian doctrine. Constantine himself outlawed pagan sacrifices, and though the emperor Julian the Apostate (r. 361–63) briefly attempted to reinstate paganism, by the time of Theodosius I's rule (379–95), all pagan temples were closed throughout the Empire, and Christianity was the official religion. However, Roman law, not Biblical law, remained the norm in Byzantine culture, schools taught Classical Greek texts, especially Homer's *Iliad*, and important writers still modeled their work on Classical precedents. Nevertheless, by the middle of the sixth century, the emperor Justinian had closed the Academy of Athens, the last pagan school of philosophy in the Empire, and over 100 churches and monasteries stood in Constantinople alone.

Justinian's Empire

After Rome collapsed in 476, Odoacer, a Germanic leader, named himself King of Italy (r. 476–93), which he governed from the northern Italian city of Ravenna. When the Ostrogoth ("Eastern Goth") king Theodoric the Great overthrew Odoacer in 493 (he would rule Italy until 526), the Byzantine emperors tolerated him, largely because he was Christian and had been raised in the imperial palace in Constantinople. But after a new, young emperor, Justinian (r. 527–65), assumed the Byzantine throne, things quickly changed. Justinian launched a massive campaign to rebuild Constantinople, including the construction of a giant new Hagia Sophia (Fig. **8.19**) at the site of the old one when the latter was burned to the ground in 532 by rioting civic "clubs"—that probably were more like modern "gangs." The riots briefly caused Justinian to consider abandoning Constantinople, but his queen, Theodora, persuaded him to stay: "If you wish to save yourself, O Emperor," she is reported to have counseled, "that is easy. For we have much money, there is the sea, here are the boats. But think whether after you have been saved you may not come to feel that you would have preferred to die." Justinian may well have begun construction of the new Hagia Sophia to

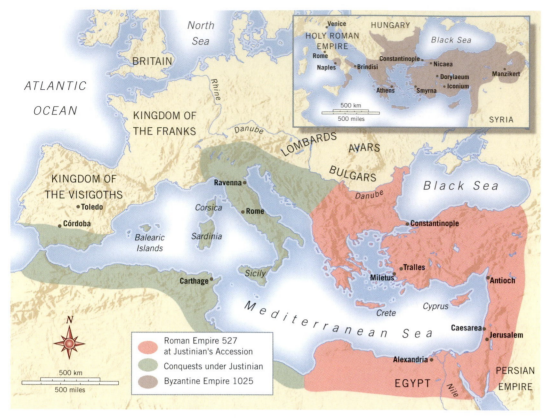

Map 8.3 The Byzantine Empire at the death of Justinian in 565 and in 1025. The insert shows the Empire nearly 500 years after Justinian's reign, in 1025. Although it had shrunk in size, the Byzantine Empire remained a powerful force in the eastern Mediterranean throughout the Middle Ages.

divert attention from the domestic turmoil stirred up by the warring gangs. And he may have conceived his imperial adventuring to serve the same end (Map **8.3**). In 535, he retook North Africa from the Visigoths, and a year later, he launched a campaign, headed by his general Belisarius, to retake Italy from the successors of Theodoric. But through his massive building program, in particular, Justinian aimed to assert not only his political leadership but his spiritual authority as well. His rule was divine, as his divine works underscored.

Hagia Sophia At the emperor's request, Procopius of Caesarea (ca. 490–ca. 560), Justinian's official court historian, wrote a treatise, *On Justinian's Buildings*, celebrating the emperor's building campaign. Book 1 is dedicated to the new Hagia Sophia (Figs. **8.19** and **8.20**) that Justinian erected on the site of the one that had burned down. As a result of Procopius' writings, we know a great deal about the building itself, including the identity of its architects, two mathematicians named Isidorus of Miletus and Anthemius of Tralles. Isidorus had edited the works of Archimedes, the third-century BCE geometrician who established the theory of the lever in mechanics, and both Isidorus and Anthemius had made studies of parabolas

and curved surfaces. Their deep understanding of mathematics and physics is evident in their plan for Hagia Sophia.

Their completely original design (Fig. **8.21**) consisted of a giant dome on a square base, the thrust of the dome carried on four giant arches that make up each side of the square. Between these arches are triangular curving vault sections, called **pendentives**, that spring from the corners of the base. The dome that rises from these pendentives has around its base 40 windows, creating a circle of light that makes the dome appear to float above the naos, underscoring its symbolic function as the Dome of Heaven. The sheer height of the dome adds to this effect—it is 184 feet high (41 feet higher than the Pantheon), and 112 feet in diameter. In his treatise *On Justinian's Buildings*, Procopius describes the central domed section of the church (**Reading 8.8**):

READING 8.8

from Procopius, *On Justinian's Buildings* (ca. 537)

So the church has been made a spectacle of great beauty, stupendous to those who see it and altogether incredible to those who hear of it. ... It abounds

📖 **Read** the document related to Procopius of Caesarea on **MyArtsLab** exceedingly in gleaming sunlight. You might say that the [interior] space is not illuminated by the sun from the outside, but that the radiance is generated within, so great an abundance of light bathes this shrine all round. In the middle of the church there rise four man-made eminences which are called piers, two on the north and two on the south, each pair having between them exactly four columns. The eminences are built to a great height. As you see them, you could suppose them to be precipitous mountain peaks. Upon these are placed four arches so as to form a square, their ends coming together in pairs and made fast at the summit of those piers, while the rest of them rise to an immense height. Two of the arches, namely those facing the rising and setting sun, are suspended over empty air, while the others have beneath them some kind of structure and rather tall columns. Above the arches the construction rises in a circle. Rising above this circle is an enormous spherical dome which makes the building exceptionally beautiful. It seems not to be founded on solid masonry, but to be suspended from heaven by that golden chain and so covers the space.

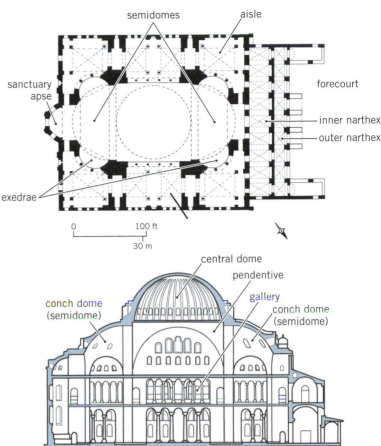

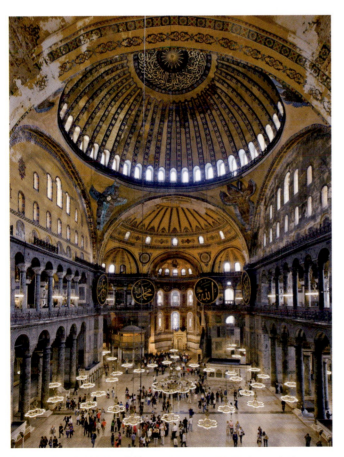

Fig. 8.20 Interior of Hagia Sophia, Istanbul. 532–37. So vast is the central dome of the church that it was likened, in its own time, to the Dome of Heaven. It was said that to look up at the dome from below was akin to experiencing the divine order of the cosmos.

Fig. 8.21 Anthemius of Tralles and Isidorus of Miletus, Plan and section of Hagia Sophia, Istanbul. 532–37.

Procopius does not mention that to the east and west, beneath the arches, are conch domes, or half-domes, semi-circular structures that spread out from a central dome, extending the space, and that these in turn are punctuated by yet smaller conch domes. Thus, a succession of curving spaces draw the visitor's eyes both upward to the symbolically heavenly space of the dome and forward to the sanctuary apse, seat of the altar and the liturgy. The intricate and lacy carving on the lower levels lends the stonework an almost immaterial lightness. The domes above are believed to have been covered with mosaics, probably consisting in the sixth century of plain gold grounds ornamented with crosses. Light from the windows around the base of the dome and conch domes would have ricocheted around the gold-covered interior, creating the magical, even celestial light that Procopius describes.

Saint Catherine's Monastery Justinian was not content merely to rebuild Constantinople. Bridges, roads, aqueducts, monuments, churches, and monasteries sprang up around the Empire. Not the least important of these sixth-century works was the fortress and monastery known as

👁 **Watch** an architectural simulation about pendentives on **MyArtsLab**

Byzantine mural mosaics were made by embedding into a soft cement or plaster more or less regular squares of naturally colored stone, together with squares of opaque glass, which offered an even greater variety of color. These squares are called *tesserae* (singular *tessera*), from the Greek word meaning "squares" or "groupings of four." Gold tesserae could be made by sandwiching gold leaf between two layers of glass, a practice widely used in Byzantine mosaics. Artists first outlined the image on the wall, then covered successive areas with cement or plaster, filling in the tesserae as they went. Each tessera was set at a slight angle to the one adjacent to it, so that as light struck the squares, the changing angle of refraction would create a shimmering, almost heavenly radiance, both mystical and spiritual. In contrast, Greek, Roman, and earlier floor mosaics were usually laid with flat tesserae in a perfectly even surface so as not to impede walking. And the tesserae were usually limited to pebble, stone, and shell.

Saint Catherine's (Fig. **8.22**), at the foot of Mount Sinai, in the desert near the tip of the Sinai peninsula, in present-day Egypt. It was at Mount Sinai that, according to the Old Testament, God gave Moses the Ten Commandments. The monastery was sited on the spot of the burning bush, where tradition held that God had first addressed Moses and instructed him to go to Egypt and lead the Jews to the Promised Land. Thus, the monastery had great symbolic significance.

Justinian decorated the monastery church with marble imported from quarries on an island in the Sea of Marmara, approximately 112 miles southwest of Constantinople. On the east end of the monastery, above these marble panels, in the conch dome of the apse, artisans created an extraordinary mosaic of the *Transfiguration of Christ* (Fig. **8.23**). The scene depicts the moment described in Matthew 17:1–6 when Jesus becomes a dazzling vision on Mount Tabor and a heavenly voice proclaims him to be God's son. In the center of the mosaic, Jesus appears within a **mandorla**, the light encircling or emanating from the entire figure of a sacred person, here an almond-shaped halo that signifies his glory. At his sides are the Old Testament prophets Elijah and Moses, and the disciples John, Peter, and James cower beneath his feet in amazement. Mount Tabor seems to be represented by the layered bands of greens and yellows at the bottom of the image—each of the figures except Christ seems to stand, kneel, or lie on it—but there is no real sense of space here. Rather, the entire scene is bathed in the celestial gold light that emanates in rays from Christ's white tunic. This effect is heightened by the way light reflects off the irregular surface of the *tesserae*, the small pieces of stone or glass that make up the mosaic (see *Materials & Techniques*, above).

The Abandonment of Naturalism The naturalism that dominates Greek and Roman Classical art is not apparent in the Saint Catherine mosaics. The artists evidently had no interest in depicting the visual appearance of the material world; instead, they turned their attention to the supernatural event of the Transfiguration. There is no perspectival depth—as if the vision of Christ's transformation obliterates the possibility of even thinking in terms of real space. Although the event depicted is highly dramatic, the participants' gestures are stiff, lacking the natural drama of Hellenistic sculpture (compare Epigonus' *Dying Gaul* of ca. 220 BCE; see Fig. 5.25 in Chapter 5). The figures are highly stylized and realized in a uniform geometric configuration. Notice the repeated use of a lozenge shape to depict the thighs of the disciples. And despite being bathed in light, these figures cast no shadows. The robes of both John, on the left, and James, on the right, blow backward in identical but improbable folds. The feet of the two prophets and Christ not only look alike but are similarly positioned. The sandaled feet of the three disciples could be transferred one to the other without a problem.

The artists, in other words, employed a standardized shorthand to depict the events. It is as if their artistic vocabulary consisted of a limited repertoire of feet, hands, robes, and faces, all of which could be used over and over again in any context, the most important figure being the largest. We call this style, which is at once formally abstract and priestly, **hieratic**. In retrospect, we can see the abstraction developing in earlier Christian art, in the reliefs, for instance, on Constantine's triumphal arch in Rome (see Fig. 8.7). But whereas the figures on Constantine's relief are squat and blocky, now, 300 years later, they are tall, thin, and elegant. These priestly figures float weightlessly in an ethereal space, as if, in witnessing the supernatural mystery of the Transfiguration, they have been transfigured themselves. But the differences between these figures and earlier ones are not just stylistic—they extend to meaning as well. Constantine had built and decorated his triumphant arch to celebrate his temporal power, but the mosaic at Saint Catherine's celebrates a power that is otherworldly, just as Christ stands wholly disconnected from the ground.

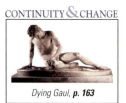

CONTINUITY & CHANGE

Dying Gaul, **p. 163**

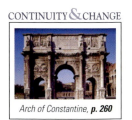

CONTINUITY & CHANGE

Arch of Constantine, **p. 260**

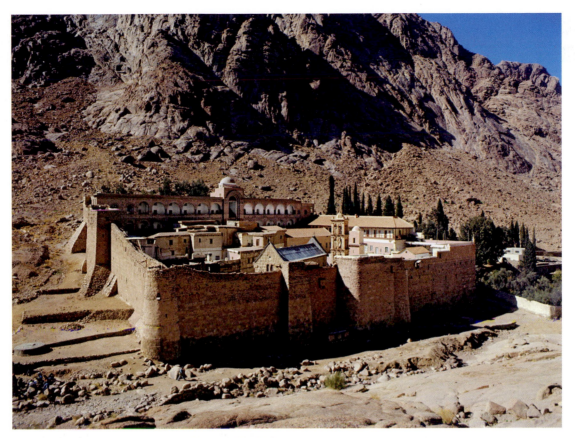

Fig. 8.22 Saint Catherine's Monastery, Sinai. ca. 548–65. The fortress around the monastery was built to protect pilgrims and monks from marauding "Saracens" (i.e., Arabs).

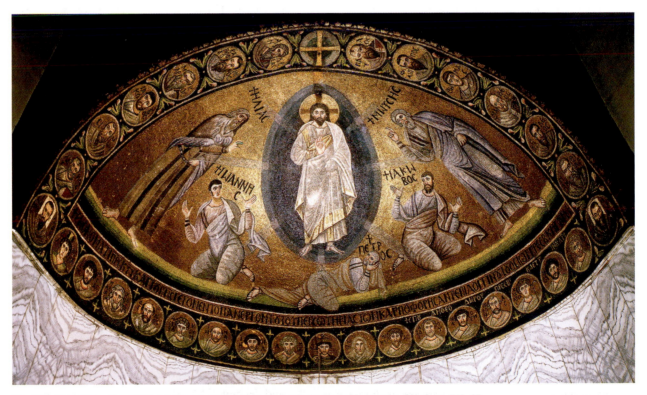

Fig. 8.23 *Transfiguration of Christ*, Church of the Virgin, Saint Catherine's Monastery, Sinai. ca. 548–65. Mosaic. The marble panels, below the mosaic, must have been brought to the relatively remote site at great expense. The creators of the mosaic were probably also from elsewhere, though an inscription attributes the work to "the zeal" of Theodoros the Priest. He may have cultivated Justinian's patronage of the monastery.

Ravenna and the Western Empire

The most extensive examples of Byzantine art survive in Ravenna, a relatively small city in northern Italy near the Adriatic Sea. (In the Eastern Empire, conquering Muslims were not nearly so interested in preserving Christian art and architecture as their Christian counterparts in the West.) Ravenna's art was the result of over 250 years of Byzantine rule, beginning in 402 when Honorius, son of Theodosius I, made it the capital of the Western Empire. Surrounded by marshes and easily defended from the waves of Germanic invasion that struck at Rome, by the fifth and sixth centuries, Ravenna was the most prosperous city in the West, the economic, political, and religious center of Western culture. Its art reflected its stature.

Honorius was succeeded by the first of several women to rise to positions of power in the Byzantine world, the empress Galla Placidia, whose name means "the gentle, or mild, woman of Gaul." Galla Placidia was Honorius' half-sister. The Goths captured her in Rome in 410, where she became the wife of the Goth ruler. By 416, her Goth husband dead, she returned to Ravenna and married the consul Constantius, who apparently tried to usurp the throne. Ultimately, she ruled as Galla Placidia Augusta until 450.

In Ravenna, Galla Placidia built a large basilica dedicated to Saint John the Evangelist. (Only the columns, capitals, and bases of the original church survive in the present San Giovanni Evangelista.) The story goes that on her return to Ravenna, while caught in a severe storm at sea, she prayed to Saint John for deliverance, promising to build him a church if she survived. She also built a second large, cross-shaped church, Santa Croce, which reputedly contained a relic of the True Cross, the one upon which Christ had been sacrificed.

Church Building under Theodoric A period of turmoil followed Galla Placidia's death and the murder of her son and successor. It culminated in the capture of Ravenna by the Germanic leader Odoacer in 476 and Theodoric's defeat of Odoacer in 493. Like Galla Placidia, Theodoric soon constructed his own basilica, now called Sant'Apollinare Nuovo (Fig. **8.24**), one of the best-preserved sixth-century Byzantine churches. On both sides of the nave, there are three tiers of mosaic decoration. At the top, in the clerestory, 26 scenes depict the life of Christ, 13 on each side (Fig. **8.25**). Below these rather small scenes, between the clerestory windows, are 16 figures on each side, possibly representing the prophets of the Hebrew Bible on one side and the apostles and evangelists of the New Testament on the other. The bottom tier of mosaics was radically altered under Justinian, whose general Belisarius conquered Ravenna in 540. Ostrogothian Ravenna had followed the theological position of Bishop Arius of Alexandria. The Arians denied that Christ and God could be of the same essence, nature, or substance. Christ is therefore not like God, not equal in dignity with God, nor even coeternal with God. In contrast, Orthodox Christians, like Justinian, argued that God and his Son were one and the same. Justinian could thus justify his military campaign on the grounds that he was overthrowing a heretical Christian state.

But Justinian had other motives as well. Theodoric's Ravenna was not only the center of both civic and Church

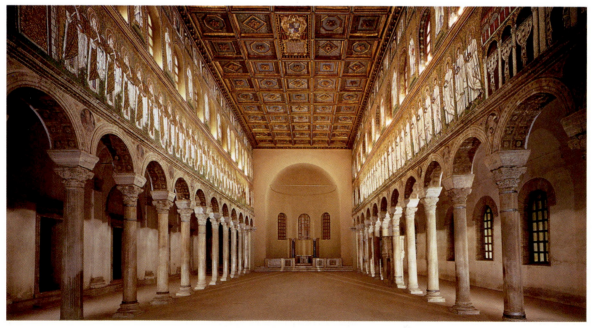

Fig. 8.24 Nave of Sant'Apollinare Nuovo, looking east, Ravenna. ca. 500 and later. The rising water table in Ravenna has caused the floor of the church to be raised 4 feet since the sixth century. In the process, a fourth tier of mosaics has been lost, cut out of the wall to accommodate the higher floor. It is not clear what was represented in this tier of mosaic, nor do we know what originally decorated the apse, which was also destroyed.

✳ **Explore** the architectural panorama of Sant'Apollinare Nuovo on **MyArtsLab**

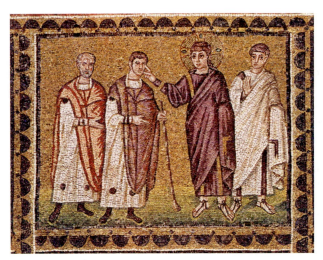

Fig. 8.25 *The Healing of the Blind*, wall mosaic, Sant'Apollinare Nuovo, Ravenna. ca. 500. This is one of the 26 scenes that depict the life of Christ at the top of the nave mosaics above the clerestory windows. The series as a whole is the earliest surviving example of such a complete iconography. It has survived unaltered from Theodoric's time. The Crucifixion, which is not included, may have decorated at least part of the original apse, which has been destroyed.

authority in the West, it was also a thriving trade center, connected to the nearby port of Classis, on the Adriatic, by canal. The luxurious decoration of the port's many churches—as many as 60 churches may have been built in the city between 400 and 750—is the result of its trade with the Eastern Empire and the importance the Eastern emperors attached to the city as their seat of power in the West. The emperor Justinian's decision to send Belisarius to seize Ravenna in 540 is at least partly attributable to the city's wealth and reputation.

San Vitale In Ravenna, Justinian's new Orthodox clergy oversaw the construction of the church of San Vitale, a unique central-plan building, similar to Santa Costanza in Rome (see Figs. 8.14 and 8.15), but octagonal in design rather than circular (Figs. **8.26** and **8.27**). On seven of its eight sides, the central space opens out into semicircular bays or niches called **exedrae**, which themselves open, through a triple arcade, to the ambulatory. On the eighth side, the bay extends into a rectangular sanctuary and apse. The narthex (entrance hall), which has long since disappeared, was a lozenge-shaped space set

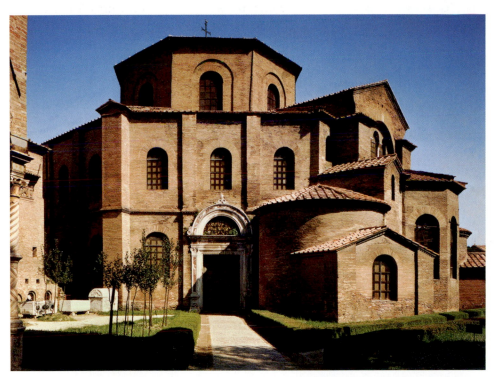

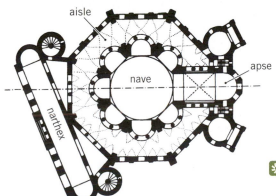

Figs. 8.26 and 8.27 Exterior and plan of San Vitale, Ravenna. Dedicated 547. Like most Byzantine churches, San Vitale is a study in contrasts. The exterior is exceedingly plain. (The decorated doorway is a later addition.) But inside, the elaborate decoration symbolizes the richness of the spiritual world.

✳ **Explore** the architectural panorama of the Church of San Vitale on **MyArtsLab** at an angle to the church itself. Entering from the double doors, the visitor has two options. One is to look directly across into the exedrae spaces, seeing a complex pattern of curves, niches, columns, and mosaics. The other is to glance directly across the central space to the sanctuary and apse, which rise two stories to a gorgeously decorated conch dome, decorated with intricately interwoven vines and animals in a predominantly gold and green mosaic.

On the side walls of the apse, level with the windows, are two mosaics, one featuring the emperor Justinian (Fig. 8.28) and the other the empress Theodora (Fig. 8.29). Perhaps inspired by the as yet unaltered processions in Sant'Apollinare Nuovo, which, as we have seen, probably featured Theodoric and his court, the artist has the emperor and empress lead retinues of courtiers toward the back of the apse. Possibly they proceeded toward reunion with Christ in paradise, as depicted in the conch-dome mosaic of the apse. A haloed Justinian carries a paten, the plate on which the bread is placed in the celebration of the Eucharist. On the other side of the apse, the empress holds a chalice of wine for the Eucharist, and on the bottom of her robe are the Three Magi, who, like her, come bearing gifts to the Virgin and Child. These mosaics possess a distinct political agenda, serving as propaganda to remind the faithful of the emperor's divine authority—the union of the political and spiritual spheres.

The most intriguing aspect of the two mosaics, however, is their composition. Even though Theodora, for instance, stands before a scalloped half-dome niche and the attendant to her right pulls back a curtain as if to reveal the space beyond, these mosaics do not represent a view into a natural world extending back toward a distant horizon (compare Fig. 6.31 in Chapter 6). Rather, Byzantine artists conceived of space as extending forward from the picture plane, with parallel lines converging on the eye of the beholder. This technique, known as **reverse perspective**, makes objects appear to tip upward—note the top of the fountain to Theodora's right—and elongates and heightens figures. Human eyesight, Byzantine artists believed, is imperfect and untrustworthy, a fact demonstrated by the apparent decrease in the size of objects as they recede in the distance. By depicting objects in reverse perspective and in shallow space, Byzantine artists rejected earthly illusion, privileging the sacred space of the image over the mundane space of the viewer.

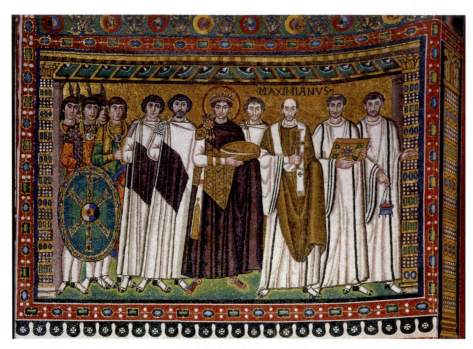

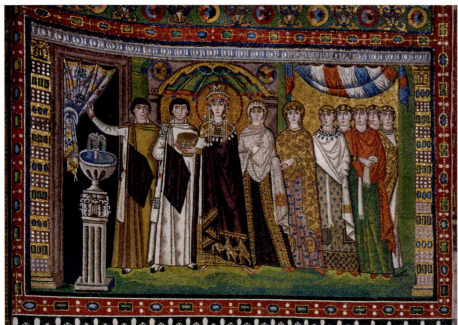

Figs. 8.28 and 8.29 (top) *Emperor Justinian with Maximian, Clergy, Courtiers, and Soldiers*, and (bottom) *Empress Theodora with Courtiers and Ladies of Her Court*, **wall mosaics, San Vitale, Ravenna. ca. 547.** Standing between and behind Justinian and Maximian is Julianus Argentarius, the benefactor of the church.

Watch a video about the technique of mosaic on **MyArtsLab**

Music in Ravenna We know about the music of the Church in Ravenna almost exclusively at a theoretical level. Music was considered a branch of mathematics and studied as such, and no medieval manuscripts of musical notation have survived from before the late ninth century. Yet as early as the fifth century, in Augustine of Hippo's *Confessions*, the role of music in the Church liturgy was a topic of much discussion. Augustine was himself ambivalent about it:

> I realize that when they are sung … sacred words stir my mind to greater religious fervor and kindle in me a more ardent flame of piety than they would if they were not sung. … But I ought not to allow my mind to be paralyzed by the gratification of my senses, which often leads it astray. … Sometimes, too, from over-anxiety to avoid this particular trap I make the mistake of being too strict. When this happens, I have no wish but to exclude from my ears, and from the ears of the Church as well, all the melody of those lovely chants to which the Psalms of David are habitually sung. … But I remember the tears that I shed on hearing the songs of the Church in the early days, soon after I had recovered my faith … so I waver between the danger that lies in gratifying the senses and the benefits which, as I know from experience, can accrue from singing.

Thus, we know that as early as the late fourth century, not long after Augustine's revelation in the garden (see Reading 8.5), "lovely chants" based on the Psalms of David were habitually sung in Christian churches. Just what they sounded like is another question entirely, although Ambrose's surviving hymns give us some clue.

Among the ministers who served Theodoric in Ravenna was Boethius, author of *De Institutione Musica* (*The Fundamentals of Music*), which would remain in obscurity until the late ninth century. There are, Boethius argues, three classes of music: *musica mundana*, *musica humana*, and *musica instrumentalis*. These are illustrated in the twelfth-century frontispiece to one of the earliest compilations of medieval music for the liturgy, the *Magnus Liber Organi*, or *Great Book of Polyphony* (Fig. **8.30**), showing Boethius's continuing influence throughout the medieval period. In the top register of the frontispiece, the allegorical figure of Musica points her baton at a sphere containing the four elements—earth, water, air, and fire (represented by the stars). This is *musica mundana*, the highest form of music, created by planetary motion, the classical "harmony of the spheres." Below, in the second register, she lifts her baton for *musica humana*, the music humans create through the harmonious attunement of mind and body, reason and spirit. Finally, at the bottom, she shakes her finger, somewhat disapprovingly, at *musica instrumentalis*, the music of sound, the only one of the three that can be heard by mortals. Likewise, for Boethius, there were three classes of musician—those who play instruments, those who sing, and those who judge performance and song. These last, persons grounded in reason and thought, are the most musical, he argues, once again demonstrating the medieval emphasis on music as a form of philosophical thought.

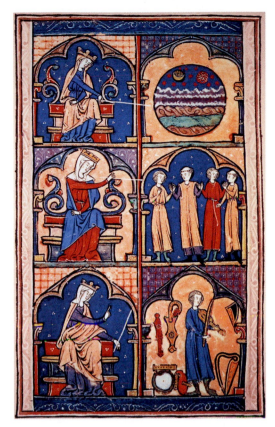

Fig. 8.30 *The Three Varieties of Music,* **frontispiece to** *Magnus Liber Organi F.* **ca. 1245–55, probably in Paris.** Florence, Biblioteca Medicea Laurenziana MS. Laur. Plut. 29.1, c. 1v. By concession of the Ministero per i Beni e le Attività Culturali. Further reproduction by any means is prohibited. Photo: Donato Pineider. There are four surviving manuscripts of the *Magnus Liber Organi*. This one is referred to as "F" because it is housed in Florence, Italy. It is the largest and the oldest of the four.

THE LATER BYZANTINE EMPIRE

What is the role of the image in Byzantine art and why did iconoclasts attack it?

Strange as it may seem, Justinian and Theodora never actually set foot in Ravenna, let alone San Vitale, and their depiction on its walls is probably best understood as a symbol of the relations between Church and State in the Byzantine Empire. Intimately interrelated and mutually dependent, the two balanced one another. Thus, while Maximian, the bishop of Ravenna, stands a little forward of Justinian in the San Vitale mosaic, Justinian's arm and the paten it holds lie (somewhat improbably) in front of Maximian. It is easy to understand, then, how the century and a half of military and political setbacks that followed Justinian's rule were interpreted in Byzantium as Church-related. Germanic tribes overran Italy and the Balkans. Persian forces sacked Jerusalem in 614. But even more important was the rise of Islam after the death of Muhammad in 632 (see Chapter 9). Although the Byzantine emperor Heraclius (r. 610–41) recaptured Jerusalem in 620, the Muslim Arabs took it in 638. Within two years, the Muslim Arabs had conquered Syria, Palestine, and Iraq. In 642, the Byzantine army abandoned Alexandria, and Islam in effect controlled all of what once had been Byzantine Asia Minor. Constantinople itself did not fall, but it was besieged twice, from 674 to 678 and from 717 to 718. Only its invincible walls held the Muslim invaders at bay.

The Iconoclast Controversy

The sudden rise of Islam as a powerful military force had a chilling effect on Byzantine art. The Byzantine emperor Leo III (r. 717–41), who came to power during the second Muslim siege of Constantinople, began to formulate a position opposing the use of holy images. He understood that the Muslims, who were still regarded as Christian heretics, had barred images from their mosques and, so the logic went, their military successes against the Byzantine Empire were a sign both of God's approval of their religious practice and disapproval of Byzantium's. Like the Muslims, Leo argued that God had prohibited religious images in the Ten Commandments—"Thou shalt not make any graven image, or any likeness of any thing that is in heaven above, or that is in the earth beneath, or that is in the water under the earth: Thou shalt not bow down thyself to them nor serve them" (Exodus 20:4–5). Therefore, anyone worshiping such images was an idolater and was offending God. The solution was to ban images.

Thus was inaugurated a program of **iconoclasm**, from the Greek *eikon* ("icon" or "image") and *klao* (to "break" or "destroy"), the practice of destroying religious images. By the eighth century, the icon had a rich history in Byzantium. Mosaic icons decorated all churches, and most homes had an icon stand at the front door which visitors greeted even before greeting their host. Among the earliest examples of icons are a set of paintings on wooden panels from Saint Catherine's monastery, Mount Sinai, among them a *Theotokos and Child* (Fig. **8.31**). *Theotokos* means "God-bearing," an epithet defining Mary as the Mother of God, an official Orthodox Church view after 431. If Mary is the mother of Jesus, the Church argued, and if Jesus is God, then Mary is the Mother of God. Such images, and the doctrine associated with them, were expected to stir the viewer to prayer. Mary's eyes are averted from the viewer's, but the Christ Child, like the two military saints, Theodore (left) and George, who flank the central pair, looks straight out. The two angels behind raise their eyes to the sky, down from which God's hand descends in blessing. The words of the sixth-century Byzantine poet Agathias (ca. 536–82) are useful here: "The mortal man who beholds the image directs his mind to a higher contemplation. ... The eyes encourage deep thoughts, and art is able by means of colors to ferry over the prayer of the mind." Thus, the icon was in some sense a vessel of prayer directed to the saint, and, given Mary's military escort, must have offered the viewer her protection.

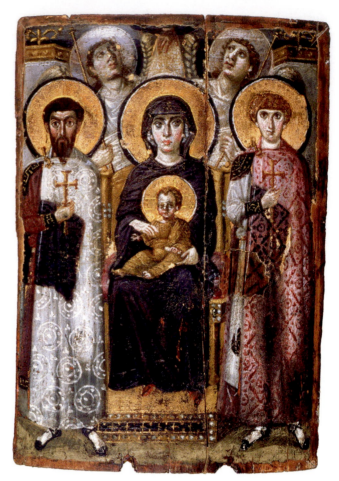

Fig. 8.31 *Theotokos and Child with Saint Theodore and Saint George.* **6th century.** Encaustic on board, 27" × 19¾". Saint Catherine's Monastery, Mount Sinai. Byzantine culture rarely, if ever, referred to Mary as "the Virgin." Instead she was the *Theotokos*, the "Mother of God."

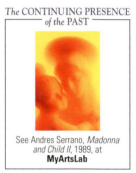

The CONTINUING PRESENCE of the PAST

See Andres Serrano, *Madonna and Child II*, 1989, at **MyArtsLab**

Leo would have none of this. In 726, he removed the image of Christ above the Chalke (Bronze) Gate of the Imperial Palace, resulting in a pitched battle between his soldiers and iconophiles ("lovers of icons") in which several soldiers died. In 730, he issued an edict requiring the removal of all religious images from all churches. The righteousness of his position was established, Leo believed, by a quick succession of military victories over the Muslims and cemented by the length of his reign—25 years, longer than the reigns of his five predecessors combined.

As the incident at the Chalke Gate suggests, not everyone was happy with the iconoclast position. John of Damascus (ca. 675–749) led the Orthodox defense of icons. He argued that the Incarnation itself justified the icon: "When he who is bodiless and without form, immeasurable in the boundlessness of his own nature, existing in the form of God, empties himself and is found in a body of flesh, then you may draw his image and show it to anyone willing to

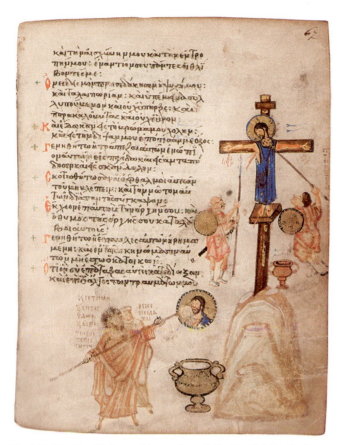

Fig. 8.32 *The Crucifixion and Iconoclasts,* folio 67r, *Chludov Psalter.* **ca. 850–75.** 7¾" × 6". State Historical Museum, Moscow. The psalter gets its name from its nineteenth-century Russian owner.

gaze upon it." The iconophiles furthermore argued that the honor that worshipers bestow upon an image passes on to whomever the image represents.

A page from a Russian Psalter (Book of Psalms) showing *The Crucifixion and Iconoclasts* sums up the iconophile position toward iconoclasts (Fig. **8.32**). The passage quoted on this page is from Psalm 21, which is interpreted as a prophecy of the Crucifixion: "They gave me also gall for my meat; and in my thirst they gave me vinegar to drink." On the right, a soldier offers Jesus a drink from a vinegar-soaked sponge, stuck on the end of a long stick. At the bottom of the page, two iconoclasts raise a sponge, just dipped in a vase of lime whitewash, to an icon of Christ and begin to paint it over. The image suggests that to destroy an image of Christ is tantamount to crucifying Jesus.

The importance of the iconoclast controversy to the history of Western art cannot be overstated. Iconoclasm would reappear several hundred years later during the Renaissance, but more important, the controversy affirmed the centrality of visual imagery to Western culture. In the debate over the function of the image—ranging from the artist's motives for creating it to the viewer's understanding of it to the patron's support of it—attention focused on the role of the visual not only in religion but also in communication, learning, and understanding. The iconoclast controversy could be said to have instigated the very

notion of "visual literacy"—the idea that understanding certain images is central to cultural literacy. It also contributed to the radical division, or schism, between the Roman Catholic and Eastern Orthodox churches that developed especially in the last half of the first millennium. The two churches disputed papal authority—from the Eastern point of view the pope's rule of the Eastern Church was merely nominal. There were huge cultural differences as well, for few in the West spoke Greek, few in the East, Latin. Doctrinal issues having to do with the Catholic position that the Holy Spirit proceeded from both the Father *and* the Son, an idea wholly unknown in the East, also played a part.

In terms of iconography, most Roman Catholics believed that images of God the Father, Christ, and the Virgin served to inspire reverence and piety, while, as we have seen, a very large segment of the Eastern Church did not. The iconoclast controversy in the East was settled in 843, when the widow of the iconoclast emperor Theophilus restored icon veneration, an event still celebrated in the Eastern Orthodox Church on the first Sunday of Lent as the Feast of Orthodoxy. The theological conservatism of the Eastern Orthodox Church discouraged innovation to the point that its art remained remarkably consistent right down to modern times. In contrast, the Church in the West was consistently open to artistic innovation, especially after the twelfth and thirteenth centuries. Any visitor to a Greek or Russian Orthodox church today would be struck by the similarity of its art to that of early medieval Constantinople. When Russia accepted Christianity in 988, Byzantine artists were dispatched to Kiev and other artistic centers in order to pass on the traditions of icon painting to Russian monks. While an individual painter might interpret tradition in an individual way—in the manner, for instance, that a musician might interpret a score—tradition dominates the art of Eastern Orthodoxy.

Tradition and Innovation: The Icon in the Second Golden Age

When the Macedonian dynasty (867–1056) initiated by Basil I came to power, the Empire enjoyed a cultural rebirth of art and architecture, often referred to as the Second Golden Age. Although the Empire's reach was somewhat reduced, its wealthy autocracy could claim control of present-day Turkey and other areas around the Black Sea, the Balkan peninsula including Greece, and southern Italy, including Sicily. It also exerted influence over Russia, Ukraine, and Venice, its major trading partner in the Adriatic.

The artists of the Macedonian era turned to both Classical and Justinian models for their church decoration, lending the traditional icon a more naturalistic air and an almost Hellenistic emotional appeal. While images of Christ on the cross had occasionally appeared in earlier centuries, after the iconoclast controversy, they appeared with greater frequency. A particularly fine example survives at Daphni, near Athens, Greece, in the Church of the Dormition (from the Latin word for "sleep" and referring to the assumption

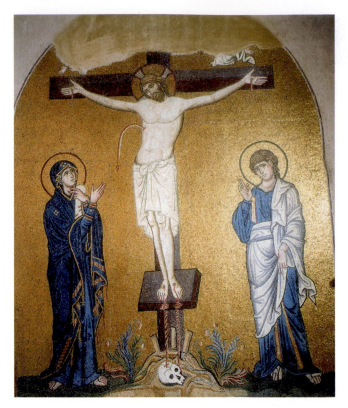

Fig. 8.33 *Crucifixion*, **mosaic in the north arm of the east wall, Church of the Dormition, Daphni, Greece. Late 11th century.** The skull at the foot of the cross symbolizes Golgotha, the "place of the skull," a hill outside Jerusalem. Many believed it was the site of Adam's burial and of the Crucifixion.

into heaven of the Virgin Mary at the moment of her death) (Fig. 8.33). The image remains completely traditional in its reverse perspective (noticeable particularly on the platform at Christ's feet) and in its refusal to create a realistic spatial setting, opting instead for the spiritual space of its golden background. But the nudity of Christ and the graceful gestures of the Virgin and Saint John, the draperies of their clothing falling almost softly in comparison to the stiff folds of the Justinian and Theodora mosaics at San Vitale, are clearly inspired by Classical antecedents. Even more Classical is the pure human emotion that the figures convey. Where early Christian art had emphasized the Saviour's power, wisdom, and personal strength, this image hints at his vulnerability, the human pathos of his sacrifice. The arc of blood and water springing from his side, referring to both the Eucharist and the Baptism, connects his "passion" to our own.

No single image underscores the role of the Theotokos as protectress more than the tenth-century mosaic *Theotokos and Child with Justinian and Constantine* that decorates the vestibule to Hagia Sophia (Fig. 8.34). To the right of the Theotokos and Child at the center stands "Justinian the Glorious King," as his inscription calls him, holding an architectural model of Hagia Sophia. To their left is "Constantine the Great, numbered among the saints," holding a model of the walled city of Constantinople. The city, the mosaic suggests, has been under the protection of the Mother of God since its inception. The implication is that such protection will continue, as indeed it would, until the year 1453, when Constantinople would finally fall to the Turks.

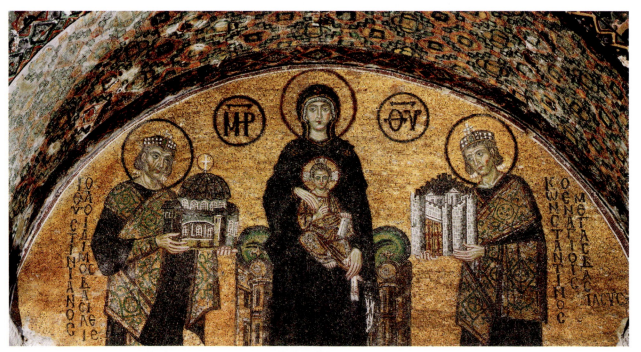

Fig. 8.34 *Theotokos and Child with Justinian and Constantine*, **vestibule mosaic, Hagia Sophia, Istanbul. Early 10th century.** Constantine and Justinian are beardless, which distinguished them from contemporary emperors, all of whom wore beards and had long hair. Note the reverse perspective, so typical of Byzantine art, of the throne upon which the Theotokos Mary sits.

Byzantine Influences

Located at the crossroads of Europe and Asia and serving as the focal point of a vast trade network that stretched as far east as China, Constantinople was the economic center of first the Roman Empire and then the entire Mediterranean for nearly a thousand years. Only Venice would ever rival it as a center of trade, and Venice would finally conquer Constantinople during the Fourth Crusade in 1204 in order to draw the city into its own sphere of influence. Venetian mercenaries looted the city in the process, taking back to Italy art and artifacts representing over 900 years of accumulated wealth and artistic tradition. In the early years of the twelfth century, Venetian artists copied more than 110 scenes for the atrium of Saint Mark's Basilica from Byzantine originals. And Saint Mark's itself was directly inspired by Byzantine architecture and decoration (Fig. **8.35**).

The wealth of Constantinople in artifacts would spread to the north as well. In 1238, Venetian merchants purchased from Byzantine officials one of the most precious relics of Western Christendom, the Crown of Thorns, supposedly worn by Jesus during the Crucifixion. The same year, King Louis IX of France paid the Venetians 13,304 gold coins to take the crown to Paris and place it in his newly dedicated Gothic church, Sainte-Chappelle.

Throughout its history, Byzantine Constantinople was constantly under attack, not only by the rest of Christendom but also by Islam, the new religion that had originated to the south (see Chapter 9). Many in Constantinople attributed the Muslims' success to their refusal to allow images in their mosques, and this belief fed the iconoclast controversy in Byzantine political and religious life, as we have seen. The Christian West, in turn, would come to see the Muslim world not merely as barbarian, but as a direct threat to Christian dominance—political, economic, and religious—of the Mediterranean world. Increasingly, the region's two competing empires, East and West, would cease to be Byzantine and Catholic, but instead would become Muslim and Christian. The traditions of Byzantine art lived on, however, especially in Greece and Russia, where in the thirteenth through sixteenth centuries especially, Byzantine art continued to flourish. ∎

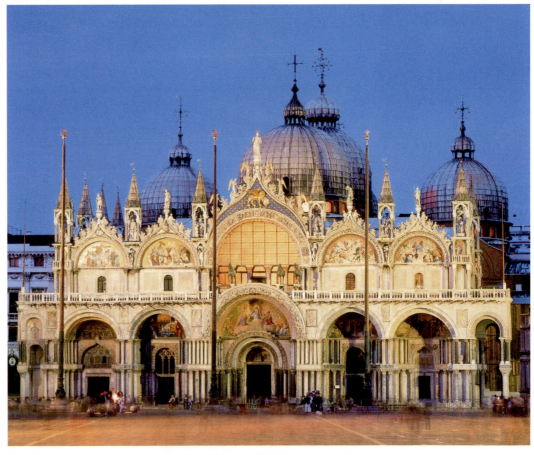

Fig. 8.35 Saint Mark's Basilica, Venice, west facade. 1063–94, with decorations added for centuries after. The original brick front of the basilica is inlaid with marble slabs and carvings, much of it looted from Constantinople in 1204.

8.1 Outline the development of Judaic culture after the destruction of the Second Temple.

By the first century CE, Judaism had become increasingly sectarian in nature, each sect believing that it possessed the one true understanding of God's will. It had also become increasingly messianic and apocalyptic. The destruction of the Second Temple of Jerusalem in 70 CE resulted in a general Jewish Diaspora. What replaced the Temple as a site of worship? With the Jewish people scattered, Jewish rabbis realized that they could not rely on the Oral Torah, and that its explanations and interpretations of the covenant needed to be written down. This eventually resulted in the Talmud. What two components of Jewish tradition make up the Talmud? How do they differ?

8.2 Identify the forces at work in the spread of Christianity, and differentiate between the new religion's use of typology, symbolism, and iconography.

Christianity developed out of the increasing sectarianism of Jewish culture, and spread across the Roman Empire. Who were the evangelists? The apostles? Both orthodox and Gnostic versions of Christ's life developed. How do they differ? To incorporate its Jewish heritage, early Christianity viewed its history as a typology. How does typology work? Early Christian art is clearly indebted to Classical and Hellenistic precedents, but it includes many symbols designed to indicate the Christian content of the image. What are some of the iconographic features of these symbols?

8.3 Describe the Roman reaction to Christianity and explore the ways in which Roman traditions may have impacted the religion's development.

Christians were consistently blamed for the troubles that beset Rome. Diocletian unleashed a furious persecution in 303 and divided the Empire into four areas of rule—the Tetrarchy. Diocletian ruled in Asia Minor, where he presented himself as the divine manifestation of the Roman gods on earth. Thus Christians, who were monotheistic and worshiped their own god, were a direct threat to his own authority. In 312, Constantine I ("Constantine the Great") assumed total authority. Constantine became increasingly supportive of Christianity, convening the first ecumenical council of Church leaders in 325 at Nicea, near his new capital at Constantinople. What are the basic tenets of the resulting Nicene Creed? How does it serve to define the nature of Christian belief?

Like so many Roman emperors before him, the victorious Constantine celebrated with a campaign of public works. How does the traditional style of Roman art compare to the relief *Constantine Addressing the People*? What new standards of beauty began to define Christian art? Constantine erected the last great imperial building in Rome, the Basilica Nova. Its architectural features anticipate the first great Christian church, Saint Peter's Basilica. A second type of Christian church was built as a mausoleum for Constantine's daughter, Constantia. How would you describe the principal features of this church? It was decorated with mosaics of a vine pattern. How do these mosaics suggest the ways in which Christianity incorporated Greek and Roman mythic traditions? What features of the mystery cults of Isis and Mithras can be seen to surface in Christian practice?

Two important early Roman converts to the Christian religion are Ambrose, Bishop of Milan, and Augustine of Hippo. Augustine's *Confessions* are the first Western autobiography, describing his conversion to Christianity. What temptations does he find most difficult to overcome and how do you think these difficulties have impacted Western theology? His *City of God* argues that the demise of the Roman Empire was caused by the arrogance of its emperors and the worldly concerns of the citizens of the earthly city. Romans, he argues, might have been saved if they had turned their attention to the heavenly City of God. Much of the argument is based on an allegorical reading of the Bible. How do you see allegory developing out of the tradition of typological reading in Christian thought? Augustine began to realize that music might play a meaningful role in the liturgy, and he was drawn, particularly, to the hymns of the bishop of Milan, Ambrose. What value do Augustine and Ambrose see in music? How does the imagery of Ambrose's "Ancient Morning Hymn" recall the Mithraic mystery cult?

8.4 Characterize the new Byzantine style of art and discuss how it reflects the values of the Byzantine emperors, especially Justinian.

When in 325 the emperor Constantine began to build his new capital at Byzantium (in present-day Istanbul), he modeled it on Rome, but instead of temples dedicated to the Roman gods, he erected Christian basilicas. By the sixth century, when the emperor Justinian closed the last pagan school of philosophy in the Empire, there were over 100 churches and monasteries in the city. Justinian ordered the mammoth new church Hagia Sophia to be built and oversaw construction of bridges, roads, aqueducts, monuments, churches, and monasteries all around the Empire, including Saint Catherine's Monastery on the Sinai peninsula with its extraordinary mosaic of the *Transfiguration of Christ*. The naturalism that marks Classical art disappears here. What replaces it? Why?

A small city in northern Italy near the Adriatic Sea, Ravenna contains the most extensive survivals of Byzantine Christian art and architecture. What motivated Justinian to conquer Ravenna? The clergy installed in Ravenna by Justinian constructed a new central-plan church, San Vitale, decorated with two mosaics featuring Justinian and Theodora. How do these compare to the mosaic *Transfiguration of Christ* at Saint Catherine's

Monastery in the Sinai? Music played a role in the liturgy, and, although we have little surviving music from the period, we do have an important treatise on the topic, Boethius's *The Fundamentals of Music*. What are the three forms of music as outlined by Boethius? What is their relationship to Byzantine beliefs about art?

8.5 Explain the role of images in Byzantine art and why they were subject to iconoclast attack.

The rise of Islam motivated the emperor Leo III to inaugurate a program of iconoclasm in 726, requiring the removal of all religious images from all churches. Muslims barred images from their mosques, and like them Leo suspected that religious images fostered idolatry. What were the arguments against iconoclasm? Later Macedonian emperors brought about a cultural revival, a Second Golden Age of Byzantine art, reinvigorating the traditional icon. Along with differences in language and doctrine, however, the iconoclast controversy contributed to the radical division, or schism, between the Roman Catholic and Eastern Orthodox churches.

✓ **Study** and **review** on **MyArtsLab**

READINGS

from Josephus, *The Jewish War*, Book 2, "The Three Sects"

At the beginning of *The Jewish War*, its author introduces himself as "Joseph, son of Matthias, an ethnic Hebrew, a priest from Jerusalem." He had fought the Romans in the First Jewish-Roman War beginning in 66 CE, as a commander in Galilee, but after the destruction of the Second Temple in 70 CE, he apparently joined Titus' entourage when it returned to Rome with all its spoils. Despite living rather comfortably under the patronage of the Flavian emperors, he remained, in his own eyes at least, a loyal and observant Jew, intent on advocating for the Jewish people in the hostile atmosphere of the Roman Empire.

Josephus wrote all his works, including *The Jewish War*, in Rome. His is the most thorough account we have of Roman-Jewish relations in the first century CE. It also provides much information about Jewish sectarian thought, since he blamed the Jewish War on "unrepresentative and over-zealous fanatics" among the Jews—sects, that is, other than the aristocratic Pharisees to which he belonged. The passage from *The Jewish War* excerpted here concentrates on one of the "overzealous" sects, the Essenes.

2 For there are three philosophical sects among the Jews. The followers of the first of which are the Pharisees; of the second, the Sadducees; and the third sect, which pretends to a severer discipline, are called Essenes. These last are Jews by birth, and seem to have a greater affection for one another than the other sects have. These Essenes reject pleasures as an evil, but esteem continence, and the conquest over our passions, to be virtue. They neglect wedlock, but choose out other persons' children, while they are pliable, and fit for learning, and esteem them to be of their kindred, and form them according to their own manners. They do not absolutely deny the fitness of marriage, and the succession of mankind thereby continued; but they guard against the lascivious behavior of women, and are persuaded that none of them preserve their fidelity to one man. [10]

3 These men are despisers of riches, and so very communicative as raises our admiration. Nor is there any one to be found among them who hath more than another; for it is a law among them, that those who come to them must let what they have be common to the whole order—insomuch that among them all there is no appearance of poverty, or excess of riches, but every one's possessions are intermingled with every other's possessions; and so there is, as it were, one patrimony among all the brethren. They think that oil is a defilement; and if any one of them be anointed without his own approbation, it is wiped off his body; for they think to be sweaty is a good thing, as they do also to be clothed in white garments. They also have stewards appointed to take care of their common affairs, who every one of them have no separate business for any, but what is for the uses of them all. ... [30]

5 And as for their piety towards God, it is very extraordinary; for before sun-rising they speak not a word about profane matters, but put up certain prayers which they have received from their forefathers, as if they made a supplication for its rising. After this every one of them are sent away by their curators, to exercise some of those arts wherein they are skilled, in which they labor with great diligence till the fifth hour. After which they assemble themselves together again into one place; and when they have clothed themselves in white veils, they then bathe their bodies in cold water. And after this purification is [40] over, they every one meet together in an apartment of their own, into which it is not permitted to any of another sect to enter; while they go, after a pure manner, into the dining-room, as into a certain holy temple, and quietly set themselves down; upon which the baker lays them loaves in order; the cook also brings a single plate of one sort of food, and sets it before every one of them; but a priest says grace before meat; and it is unlawful for any one to taste of the food before grace be said. The same priest, when he hath dined, says grace again after meat; and when they begin, and when they end, they [50] praise God, as he that bestows their food upon them; after which they lay aside their [white] garments, and betake themselves to their labors again till the evening; then they return home to supper, after the same manner; and if there be any strangers there, they sit down with them. Nor is there ever any clamor or disturbance to pollute their house, but they give every one leave to speak in their turn; which silence thus kept in their house appears to foreigners like some tremendous mystery; the cause of which is that perpetual sobriety they exercise, and the same settled measure of meat and drink that [60] is allotted them, and that such as is abundantly sufficient for them. ...

11 For their doctrine is this: That bodies are corruptible, and that the matter they are made of is not permanent; but that the souls are immortal, and continue for ever; and that they come out of the most subtle air, and are united to their bodies as to prisons, into which they are drawn by a certain natural enticement; but that when they are set free from the bonds of the flesh, they then, as released from a long bondage, rejoice and mount upward. And this is like the opinions of the Greeks, [70] that good souls have their habitations beyond the ocean, in a region that is neither oppressed with storms of rain or snow, or with intense heat, but that this place is such as is refreshed by the gentle breathing of a west wind, that is perpetually blowing from the ocean; while they allot to bad souls a dark and tempestuous den, full of neverceasing punishments. ...

14 But then as to the two other orders at first mentioned, the Pharisees are those who are esteemed most skillful in the exact explication of their laws, and introduce the first sect. These ascribe all to fate [or providence], and to God, and 80 yet allow, that to act what is right, or the contrary, is principally in the power of men, although fate does co-operate in every action. They say that all souls are incorruptible, but that the souls of good men only are removed into other bodies—but that the souls of bad men are subject to eternal punishment. But the Sadducees are those that compose the second order, and take away fate entirely, and suppose that God is not concerned in our doing or not doing what is evil; and they say, that to act what is good, or what is evil, is at men's own choice, and that the one or the other belongs so 90 to every one, that they may act as they please. They also take away the belief of the immortal duration of the soul, and the punishments and rewards in Hades. Moreover, the Pharisees are friendly to one another, and are for the exercise of concord, and regard for the public; but the behavior of the Sadducees one towards another is in some degree wild, and their conversation with those that are of their own party is as barbarous as if they were strangers to them. And this is what I had to say concerning the philosophic sects among the Jews.

READING CRITICALLY

Is there any correspondence between the doctrines of the Essene sect and Christianity, which was also developing as a sect of Judaism in Josephus' time? In terms of their relations with others, both Jewish and non-Jewish, Essenes and Christians differed dramatically. How do they differ, and what do you think are the consequences of those differences?

READING 8.5

from Augustine's *Confessions*

Of all the Latin Church fathers, Augustine of Hippo was the most influential. His *Confessions* are unique in the history of early Christianity because they represent the personal struggle of an individual to overcome his love of worldly pleasures and come, instead, to love God. The distinction he draws between the rewards of the physical appetites as opposed to those of spiritual knowledge, between the demands of the body and those of the soul, are fundamental to the development of Christian doctrine. In the first of the two passages excerpted below, the famous episode of "The Pear Tree" in Book 2, he describes what can only be called his darkest moment, when, in his sixteenth year, he stole a neighbor's pears. Later, in Book 8, still leading a dissolute life as a student but despairing of his lifestyle, he describes his conversion to Christianity in a garden near Carthage at the age of 33.

from Book 2:

There was a pear tree close to our own vineyard, heavily laden with fruit, which was not tempting either for its color or for its flavor. Late one night—having prolonged our games in the streets until then, as our bad habit was—a group of young scoundrels, and I among them, went to shake and rob this tree. We carried off a huge load of pears, not to eat ourselves, but to dump out to the hogs, after barely tasting some of them ourselves. Doing this pleased us all the more because it was forbidden. Such was my heart, O God, such was my heart—which thou didst pity even in that bottomless pit. Behold, now 10 let my heart confess to thee what it was seeking there, when I was being gratuitously wanton, having no inducement to evil but the evil itself. It was foul, and I loved it. I loved my own undoing. I loved my error—not that for which I erred but the error itself. A depraved soul, falling away from security in thee to destruction in itself, seeking nothing from the shameful deed but shame itself.

from Book 8:

The streams of my eyes gushed out. ... And, not indeed in these words, but to this effect, I cried to thee: "And thou, O Lord, how long? How long, O Lord? Wilt thou be angry forever? ... How long, how long? Tomorrow and tomorrow? Why not now? Why not this very hour make an end to my uncleanness?"

I was saying these things and weeping in the most bitter contrition of my heart, when suddenly I heard the voice of a boy or a girl I know not which—coming from the neighboring house, chanting over and over again, "Pick it up, read it; pick 10 it up, read it." Immediately I ceased weeping and began most earnestly to think whether it was usual for children in some kind of game to sing such a song, but I could not remember ever having heard the like. So, damming the torrent of my tears, I got to my feet, for I could not but think that this was a divine command to open the Bible and read the first passage I should light upon. So I quickly returned to the bench where ... I had put down the apostle's book when I had left there. I snatched it up, opened it, and in silence read the paragraph on which my eyes first fell: "Not in rioting and drunkenness, not in 20 chambering and wantonness, not in strife and envying, but put on the Lord Jesus Christ, and make no provision for the flesh to fulfill the lusts thereof" [Romans 13:13]. I wanted to read no further, nor did I need to. For instantly, as the sentence ended, there was infused in my heart something like the light of full certainty and all the gloom of doubt vanished away.

READING CRITICALLY

What do you believe motivated Augustine to write his *Confessions*?

from Augustine's *The City of God*

The following passage is representative of Augustine's use of allegory in *The City of God*. In allegory, meanings of an abstract or spiritual nature are revealed in material and concrete forms. Thus, here, Augustine sees Noah's ark as an allegorical figure for, first, the wooden cross upon which Christ was crucified, then the lives of the saints, and then the Church itself.

Now God, as we know, enjoined the building of an ark upon Noah, a man who was righteous and according to the true testimony of Scripture, perfect in his generation [see Genesis 6:9], that is, perfect, not as the citizens of the City of God are to become in that immortal state where they will be made equal with the angels of God, but as they can be during their sojourn here on earth. In this ark he was to be rescued from the devastation of the flood with his family, that is, his wife, sons and daughters-in-law, as well as with the animals that came to him in the ark at God's direction. We doubtless have 10 here a symbolic representation of the City of God sojourning as an alien in this world, that is, of the church which wins salvation by virtue of the wood on which the mediator between God and men, the man Christ Jesus, was suspended.

The very measurements of the ark's length, height and breadth symbolize the human body, in the reality of which it was prophesied that Christ would come to mankind, as, in fact, he did come. For the length of the human body from top to toe is six times its breadth from one side to the other and ten times its thickness measured on a side from back to belly. 20 Thus if you measure a man lying on his back or face down, his length from head to foot is six times his breadth from right to left or from left to right and ten times his elevation from the ground. This is why the ark was made three hundred cubits in length, fifty in breadth and thirty in height. And as for the door that it received on its side, that surely is the wound that was made when the side of the crucified one was pierced by the spear. This is the way by which those who come to him enter, because from this opening flowed the sacraments with which believers are initiated. Moreover, that order that it should be 30 made of squared beams contains an allusion to the foursquare stability of saints' lives, for in whatever direction you turn a squared object, it will stand firm. In similar fashion, everything else mentioned in the construction of this ark symbolizes some aspect of the church. ...

READING CRITICALLY

Augustine's allegory is based on the fact that both the ark and the cross were made of wood. How does he extend and expand on this analogy?

Ambrose's "Ancient Morning Hymn"

Ambrose was a Roman aristocrat, a generation older than Augustine, who became the bishop of Milan in 374, about 13 years before Augustine's conversion to Christianity in a garden near Carthage. A great mediator between different factions of the Church, he was also the first to compose hymns to be sung by the entire congregation. The simplicity of his diction and the direct optimism embodied in his imagery go a long way toward accounting for the popularity of his hymns—to say nothing of their survival in the liturgy. In short, the crowds could both enjoy singing his verses and identify with his vision.

O Splendor of God's glory bright,
O Thou who bringest light from light,
O Light of light, light's living spring,
O Day, all days illumining!

O Thou true Sun, on us Thy glance
Let fall in royal radiance;
The Spirit's sanctifying beam
Upon our earthly senses stream.

The Father, too, our prayers implore,
Father of glory evermore. 10
The Father of all grace and might,
To banish sin from our delight.

To guide whate'er we nobly do,
With love all envy to subdue,
To make ill-fortune turn to fair,
And give us grace our wrongs to bear.

Rejoicing may this day go hence,
Like virgin dawn our innocence,
Like fiery noon our faith appear,
Nor know the gloom of twilight clear. 20

Morn in her rosy car is borne;
Let him come forth, our perfect morn,
The Word in God the Father one,
The Father perfect in the Son.

All laud to God the Father be;
All praise, eternal Son, to Thee;
All glory, as is ever meet,
To God the holy Paraclete.[1]

[1] Holy Spirit; the Comforter

READING CRITICALLY

Both Ambrose's hymn and the Egyptian *Akhenaten's Hymn to the Sun* (see Reading 3.3 in Chapter 3) are addressed to the sun. How do they otherwise compare?

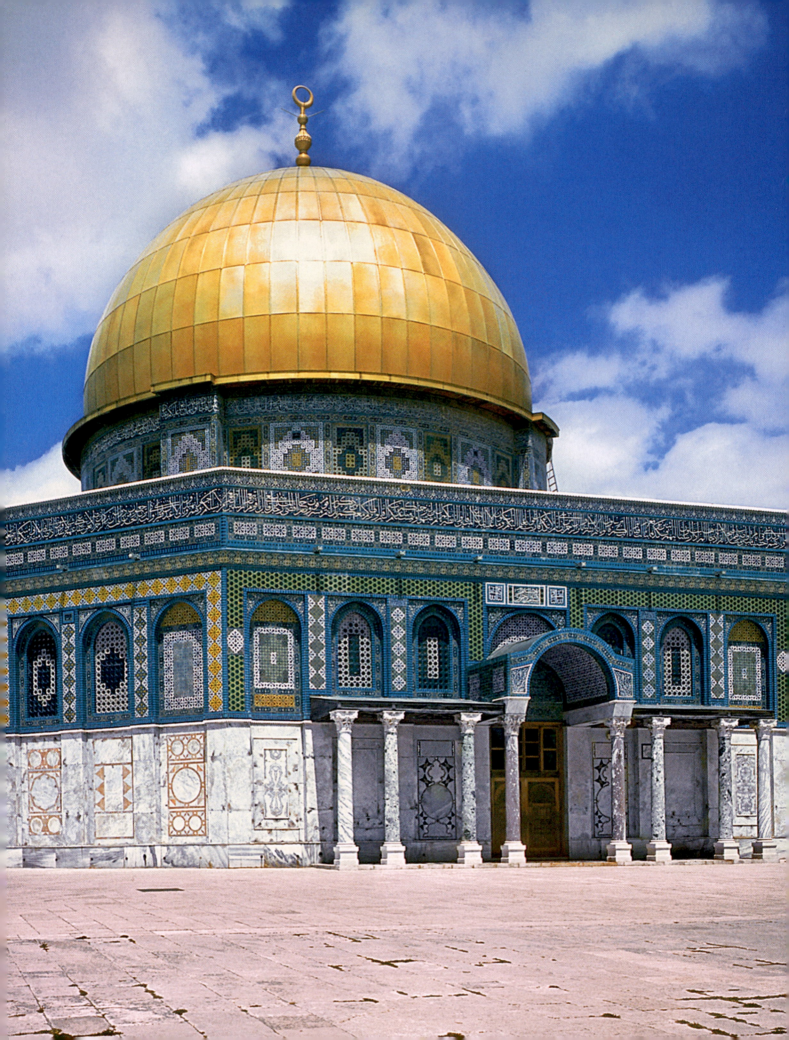

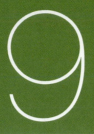

9 The Rise and Spread of Islam

A New Religion

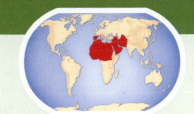

THINKING AHEAD

9.1 Outline the principal tenets of the Muslim faith.

9.2 Explain the rapid spread of the Muslim faith.

9.3 Describe Islamic culture in both Africa and Spain.

9.4 Explore the importance of calligraphy in Islamic art and explain how the other arts reflect its emphasis on abstract rhythms of pattern and repetition.

The Dome of the Rock (Fig. **9.1**) stands atop the Temple Mount in Jerusalem, on the site where, in Jewish tradition, Abraham prepared to sacrifice his son Isaac. The Jewish Temple of Solomon originally stood here, and the site is further associated—by Jews, Christians, and Muslims alike—with God's creation of Adam. The Second Temple of Jerusalem also stood on this spot until it was destroyed by Roman soldiers when they sacked the city in 70 CE to put down a Jewish revolt, an event commemorated on the Arch of Titus in Rome (see Fig. 6.21 in Chapter 6). Only the Wailing Wall remains, part of the original retaining wall for the platform supporting the Temple Mount and for Jews the most sacred site in Jerusalem. To this day, the plaza in front of the wall functions as an open-air synagogue where daily prayers are recited and other Jewish rituals are performed. On Tisha B'Av, the ninth day of the month of Av, which occurs either in July or August, a fast is held commemorating the destruction of the successive temples on this site, and people sit on the ground before the wall reciting the Book of Lamentations.

One of the earliest examples of Muslim architecture, built in the 680s, the Dome's ambulatory—its circular,

colonnaded walkway—encloses a projecting rock that lies directly beneath its golden dome. By the sixteenth century, the Islamic faithful claimed that the Prophet Muhammad ascended to heaven from this spot, on a winged horse named Buraq, but there is no evidence that this story was in circulation when the Dome was originally built. Others thought that it represents the ascendancy of Islam over Christianity in the Holy Land. Still others believed the rock is the center of the world, or that it could refer to the Temple of Solomon, the importance of which is fully acknowledged by Muslims, who consider Solomon a founding father of their own faith. All of this suggests that the Dome was meant to proselytize, or convert, both Jews and Christians to the Muslim faith.

The sanctity of this spot, then, at the heart of Jerusalem, is recognized equally by the three great faiths of the Western world—Judaism, Christianity, and Islam—but it is the rise of Islam that is the subject of this chapter, and if the Dome of the Rock is one of Islam's most venerated sites, its holiest city is Mecca, located 760 miles to the south, about 50 miles inland from the Red Sea in present-day Saudi Arabia (Map **9.1**). Its natural spring originally

◀ **Fig. 9.1 The Dome of the Rock, Jerusalem. Late 680s–691.** The golden dome of the building rises above a projecting rock that is surrounded by an ambulatory. The building's function remains unclear. It is not a mosque, although it is certainly some kind of religious memorial. Inscriptions from the Qur'an decorate its interior. These are the oldest excerpts from the text to have survived.

 View the Closer Look for the Dome of the Rock on **MyArtsLab**

 Listen to the chapter audio on **MyArtsLab**

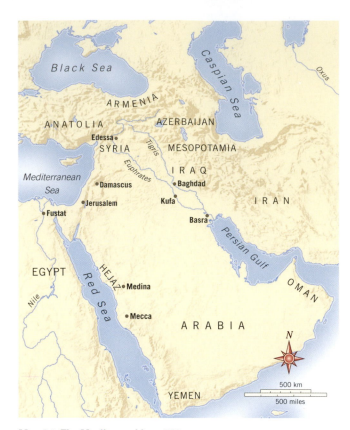

Map 9.1 **The Muslim world. ca. 700 CE.**

honor. That passerby turned out to be the Muslim prophet Muhammad (ca. 570–632), who placed the stone on his cloak and then gave a corner of the cloak to the head of each tribe to carry into the building (Fig. **9.3**). The story establishes Muhammad as a political as well as spiritual leader, and, perhaps more important, as a prophet capable of uniting the diverse elements of Arab culture.

Today, practitioners of the Muslim faith from all over the world face toward the Kaaba when they pray. They believe it is their place of origin, the site of the first "house of God," built at God's command by the biblical Abraham and his son Ismael, the ancestors of all Muslims, on the spot where, in Muslim tradition, Abraham prepared to sacrifice Ismael (not Isaac, as in the Jewish tradition, at the Dome of the Rock). Thus, walking around the Kaaba is a key ritual in the Muslim pilgrimage to Mecca, for the cube represents the physical center of the planet and the universe. It is the physical center of Muslim life, around which all things turn and to which all things in the universe are connected, symbolic of the cosmos itself. The Islamic transformation of Middle Eastern and Western culture, which began in Mecca in the seventh century and spread outward from that city, is the subject of this chapter.

Just as Muslims physically turn toward Mecca when they pray, they turn their thoughts toward the teachings of their prophet Muhammad. Wherever Muslims found themselves—and Islam rapidly spread across the Middle East, North Africa, and even into Spain—they built places of worship modeled on Muhammad's home in Medina, the city on the Arabian peninsula where Muhammad moved when he was driven from Mecca (see Map 9.1). And, as

made it an important stopping point for nomadic Arabs, known as Bedouins, who traded along caravan routes across the arid peninsula. Until the seventh century CE, they worshiped more than one god. They stored images of those gods in a square structure in the center of the city that came to be known as the *Kaaba*, literally "cube" (Fig. **9.2**). Scholars believe that the original Kaaba was linked to the astronomical year, containing an array of 360 idols, each associated with seasonal rituals and the passing of the days and months. Built with a bluish-gray stone from the hills surrounding Mecca, it is now usually covered with a black curtain. The Kaaba also held a sacred Black Stone, probably a meteorite, which reportedly "fell from heaven." Legend has it that when workers who had been rebuilding the Kaaba were ready to place the sacred stone inside, a quarrel broke out among the principal Arab tribes regarding who would have the privilege of laying the stone. Everyone agreed that the first passerby would do the

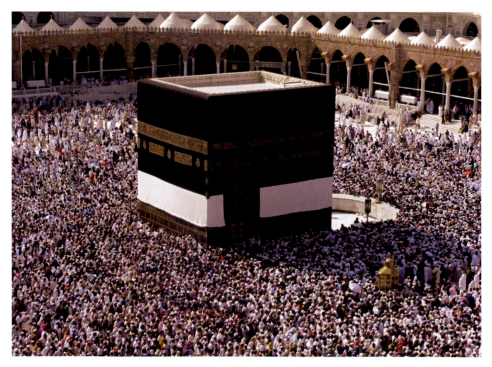

Fig. 9.2 **The Kaaba, center of the Haram Mosque, Mecca, Saudi Arabia.** Traditionally, all Muslims must make a pilgrimage to Mecca at least once in their lives. Once there, they must walk around the Kaaba seven times. The Kaaba has been rebuilt many times over the years, the last time in 1631.

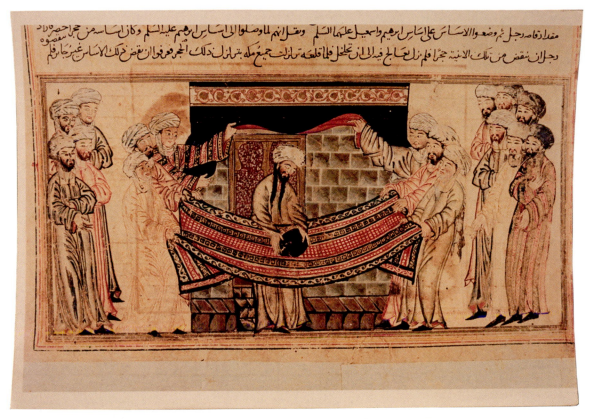

مقدار ذلك رجل ثم وضعه والاساس على اساس ابراهيم واسماعيل عليهما السلام وقل انهم ما وصلوا الى الاساس علىهم وهم عليهم السلام وكان الاساس من حجر احكم يقضوه
رجل ان ينقض من تلك الامانة حجرا لم نزل بعالم حجرا فلا ان نخلل ذلك براتله فلا قلعة مكه جميع تراسلت فيدا نزل ذلك رجل وقول ان نقض ذلك الاساس غيرنا بأرملا فلم

Fig. 9.3 *Muhammad Placing the Black Stone on His Cloak*, from Rashid al-Din's *Jami al-Tawarikh* (*Universal History*), **copied and illustrated at Tabriz, Iran. 1315.** Illuminated manuscript, 5⅛" × 10¼". University Library, Edinburgh. Notice that the figures in the back of the central section are lifting a veil that covers the Kaaba. Today, the veil, the meaning of which is obscure, is black, with quotations from the Qur'an woven across it in gold thread.

individuals, they submitted themselves to the authority of their faith, so much so that the Muslim religion quickly became synonymous with the Islamic state itself. Because Arabic, as the language of divine revelation, was believed to have a sacred nature, writing too was revered, and **calligraphy** developed into the preeminent form of visual art in Islam, creating an almost wholly abstract standard of beauty devoid of figurative elements. As a faith that considered sensory satisfaction, love, luxury, sensuality, and enjoyment to be manifestations of divine grace, the Muslim religion enveloped Islamic culture, its art, music, and literature, in the pursuit of beauty.

THE PROPHET MUHAMMAD

What are the principal tenets of the Muslim faith?

Born in Mecca in about 570 to a prominent family that traced its ancestry back to Ismael, son of Abraham, Muhammad was orphaned at age six and received little formal education. He worked in the desert caravan trade, first as a camel driver for his uncle, and then, after marrying a wealthy widow 15 years his senior, as head of his wife's flourishing caravan firm. At the age of 40, in 610, he heard

a voice in Arabic—the archangel Gabriel's, as the story goes—urging him, "Recite!" He responded, "What shall I recite?" And for the next 22 years, he claimed to receive messages, or "recitations," from God through the agency of Gabriel. These he memorized and dictated to scribes, who collected them to form the scriptures of Islam, the **Qur'an** (or Koran), which means "recitations." Muhammad also claimed that Gabriel commanded him to declare himself the "Seal of the Prophets," that is, the messenger of the one and only Allah (the Arab word for God) and the final prophet in a series of prophets extending from Abraham and Moses to Jesus.

At the core of Muhammad's revelations is the concept of submission to God—the word *Islam*, in fact, means "submission" or "surrender." God, or Allah, is all— all-powerful, all-seeing, all-merciful. Because the universe is his creation, it is necessarily good and beautiful, and the natural world reflects Allah's own goodness and beauty. To immerse oneself in nature is thus to be at one with God. But the most beautiful creation of Allah is human-kind, which God made in his own image. Like Christians, Muslims believe that human beings possess immortal souls and that they can live eternally in heaven if they surrender to Allah and accept him as the one and only God.

Muslims, or practitioners of Islam, dedicate themselves to the "five pillars" of the religion:

1. **Witness (Shahadah):** The repetition of the *shahadah*, or "witness," which consists of a single sentence, "There is no God but Allah; Muhammad is the messenger of Allah."
2. **Prayer (Salat):** The practice of daily prayer, recited facing Mecca, five times each day, at dawn, midday, mid-afternoon, sunset, and nightfall, and the additional requirement for all men to gather for a noon prayer and sermon on Fridays.
3. **Alms (Zakat):** The habit of giving alms to the poor and needy, consisting of at least one-fortieth of a Muslim's assets and income.
4. **Fasting (Sawm):** During the lunar month of Ramadan (which, over a 33-year period, will occur in every season of the year), the ritual obligation to fast by abstaining from food, drink, medicine, tobacco, and sexual intercourse from sunrise to sundown each day.
5. **Pilgrimage (Hajj):** At least once in every Muslim's life, in the twelfth month of the Muslim calendar, the undertaking of a pilgrimage to Mecca.

The five pillars are supported by the teachings of the Qur'an, which, slightly shorter than the New Testament, consists of 114 surahs, or chapters, each numbered but more commonly referred to by their titles. Each begins, as do most Muslim texts, with the **bismillah**, the first word of the sacred invocation *bismillah al-rahman al-rahim*, which can be translated "In the name of Allah, the Beneficent, Ever-Merciful" (see *Closer Look*, pages 294–295). When, after Muhammad's death in 632, the Qur'an's text was established in its definitive form, the 114 surahs were arranged from the longest to the shortest. Thus, the first surah contains 287 *ayas*, or verses, while the last consists of only 3. The mandatory ritual prayer (*salat*) that is performed five times a day consists of verses from Surahs 2, 4, and 17.

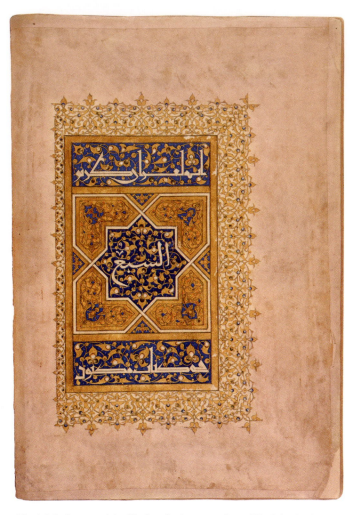

Fig. 9.4 Left page of double frontispiece to volume VII of the Qur'an of Baybars al-Jashnagir, from Egypt. 1304–06. Illuminated manuscript, 18½" × 12½". British Library, London. The most elaborate Qur'ans, such as this one, were financed by endowments created by wealthy individuals in support of a mosque and attendant buildings.

The Qur'an

As the direct word of God, the beauty of the Qur'an's poetry rises above what any worldly poet might create, even though in pre-Islamic Arabia, poetry was considered the highest form of art. The beauty of the poetry inspired the creation of many beautiful editions of the work (Fig. **9.4**) and, as we shall see, the art of calligraphy. But unfortunately, the beautiful, melodic qualities of the Arabic language are completely lost in translation, a fact that has helped to inspire generations of non-Arabic-speaking Muslims to learn the language. Almost all Muslims regularly read the Qur'an in Arabic, and many have memorized it completely. Translations of the Qur'an are problematic on another, more important level. Since the Qur'an is believed to be the direct word of God, it cannot be modified, let alone translated—a translation of the Qur'an is no longer the Qur'an. Nevertheless, something of the power of the poem's imagery can be understood in translation. Consider a passage describing paradise from the Surah 76, known as "Time" (**Reading 9.1a**):

This vision of paradise addresses all the senses—touch, taste, and smell (the fruit so "easy to reach," the drink of ginger), sight ("when you see there, you shall see blessings"), and sound (in the very melody of the verse itself). All is transformed into riches. Even the young people in attendance will appear to be "scattered pearls."

The promise of heaven, so richly described here, is balanced by a moral dimension reminiscent of both the Old and New Testaments of the Christian Bible. Note particularly the call for believers to "let not hatred of a people incite you not to act equitably." Other parts of the Qur'an explicitly appeal to Jews and Christians to accept the teachings of Islam (**Reading 9.1b**):

READING 9.1b

from the Qur'an, Surah 5

5.8 O you who believe! Be upright for Allah, bearers of witness with justice, and let not hatred of a people incite you not to act equitably; act equitably, that is nearer to piety, and be careful of (your duty to) Allah; surely Allah is Aware of what you do.

5.9 Allah has promised to those who believe and do good deeds (that) they shall have forgiveness and a mighty reward. ...

5.68 Say: O followers of the Book! ...

5.69 Surely those who believe and those who are Jews and the Sabians and the Christians whoever believes in Allah and the last day and does good—they shall have no fear nor shall they grieve. ...

5.75 The Messiah,[1] son of Marium, is but an apostle; apostles before him have indeed passed away; and his mother was a truthful woman; they both used to eat food. See how we make the communications clear to them, then behold, how they are turned away.

[1] **Messiah:** Jesus.

In the context of the present-day political climate in the Middle East, it is worth remembering that such moral positioning—and apparent tolerance—is fundamental to the Islamic tradition. However, like both Christianity and Judaism, the Qur'an also contains less tolerant messages. In the surah "Muhammad," the Prophet calls for his followers to "smite the necks" of those "who disbelieve" (for excerpts from the surah, see **Reading 9.1**, page 315). In other words, as is the case with the Bible, what one takes from the Qur'an depends on what one chooses to emphasize.

The Hadith

In addition to the Qur'an, another important source of Islamic tradition are collections of **hadith**, meaning "narratives" or "reports," which consist of sayings of Muhammad and anecdotes about his life. The story of Muhammad and the Black Rock of the Kaaba comes from the hadith. The hadith literature was handed down orally, as was common in Arab society until about 100 years after Muhammad's death, when followers began to write the sayings down (**Reading 9.2**).

READING 9.2

From the hadith

"Actions are but by intention and every man shall have but that which he intended."

"None of you [truly] believes until he wishes for his brother what he wishes for himself."

"Get to know Allah in prosperity and He will know you in adversity. Know that what has passed you by was not going to befall you; and that what has befallen you was not going to pass you by. And know that victory comes with patience, relief with affliction, and ease with hardship."

"If you feel no shame, then do as you wish."

"Everyone starts his day and is a vendor of his soul, either freeing it or bringing about its ruin."

"O My servants, it is but your deeds that I reckon up for you and then recompense you for, so let him who finds good [i.e., in the hereafter] praise Allah, and let him who finds other than that blame no one but himself."

"Renounce the world and Allah will love you, and renounce what people possess and people will love you."

The *Hijra* and Muslim Practice

In 622, Muhammad was forced to flee Mecca when its polytheistic leadership became irritated at his insistence on the worship of only one God. In a journey known as the *hijra* (or *hegira*, "emigration"), he and his followers fled to the oasis of Yathrib, 200 miles north, which they

📖 **Read** the document related to the Qur'an on **MyArtsLab**

The *bismillah* consists of the phrase "In the name of Allah, the Beneficent, Ever-Merciful." Every pious Muslim begins any statement or activity with it, and it inaugurates each chapter of the Qur'an. For Arab calligraphers, to write the *bismillah* in as beautiful a form as possible brings the scribe forgiveness for sins, and the phrase appears in the Islamic world in many different forms—even in the shape of a parrot. By 700 it had become an important part of architectural practice as well. It first appears in written form on a band of mosaic script around the interior walls and above the entrance of the Dome of the Rock in Jerusalem (see Fig. 9.1). The fourteenth-century ceramic tile decoration on a *mihrab* niche (see page 295), a design feature in all Islamic mosques commemorating the spot at Medina where Muhammad planted his lance to indicate the direction in which people should pray, gives some indication of how the calligraphic script could blend with floral motifs and geometric designs to create an elaborate ornamental surface.

The importance of writing in spreading the new faith suggests one reason that Muslim calligraphers were held in such high esteem. Most Westerners think of handwriting

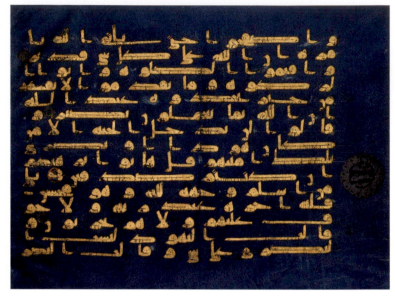

Page from a Qur'an manuscript, probably Tunisia. Late 9th–early 10th century. Gold on blue vellum, 9¾" × 13⅝". *Surah al-Baqarah* (Chapter 2), part of verse 109 through part of verse 114. Seattle Art Museum, Eugene Fuller Memorial Collection, 69.37. From a luxurious Qur'an known as the "Blue Qur'an," this manuscript page was written in ink made of gold dust mixed with emulsion (glair or gum), applied to animal-skin vellum dyed indigo. The dye was itself harvested from tiny sea-shells.

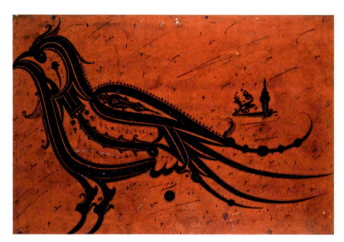

***Bismillah* in the form of a parrot, from Iran. 1834–35.** Ink on paper under wax coating. Cincinnati Art Museum, Franny Bryce Lehmer Fund. 1977.65. The parrot reads right to left, beginning over the large dot beneath its tail. The word *Allah* appears at the back of its head. The parrot is to humankind as humankind is to Allah. That is, it mimics human language without understanding it, just as humans recite the words of Allah without fully understanding them.

as a form of self-expression. But the Muslim calligrapher's style has a much more important role to play: to attract the attention of the reader, eliciting admiration for the beauty of the script, and in turn reflecting the beauty of the Muslim faith. The Muslim calligrapher is considered the medium through which Allah expresses himself. The more beautiful the calligraphic script, the more fully Allah's beauty is realized. Hence, over time, many styles of elaborate cursive script developed, as illustrated on the next page. At the same time, everyday affairs required the development of simpler, less artistic forms, and the *riq'a* script is an example.

Mastering the art of calligraphy was, in this sense, a form of prayer, and it was practiced with total dedication. A famous story about an incident that happened in the city of Tabriz, in northern Iran, during the great earthquake of 1776–77, illustrates this. The quake struck in the middle of the night and buried many in the rubble. Survivors stumbled through the debris looking for signs of life. In the

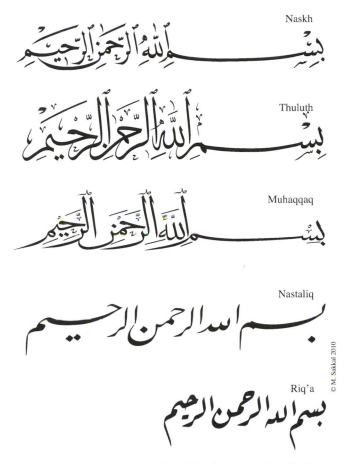

Naskh

Thuluth

Muhaqqaq

Nastaliq

Riq'a

© M. Sakkal 2010

Five examples of the *bismillah* in different Islamic cursive scripts. *Naskh*, literally "copying," was developed in the tenth century, and refined into a fine art form in Turkey in the sixteenth century. *Thuluth* evolved over the centuries into a more impressive, stately calligraphic style, often used for titles or epigrams rather than lengthy texts, and often found in many variations on architectural monuments, as well as on glass, metalwork, textiles, and wood. It is the script employed on the *mihrab* niche on the right. *Muhaqqaq* emerged in the eleventh century in the art of making manuscripts of the Qur'an. *Nastaliq* developed in Iran in the fourteenth and fifteenth centuries. It is the most fluid and expressive of the scripts presented here, and is used extensively in copying romantic and mystical epics in Persian. *Riq'a*, the simpler style of everyday writing, is very economical and easy to write.

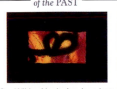

The CONTINUING PRESENCE
of the PAST

See Wijdan (Jordanian, born Iraq, 1939), *Karbala Series: Hussein*, 1993, at **MyArtsLab**
© Wijdan/ © The Trustees of the British Museum

Something to Think About …

How might modern technologies—from type to the Internet—pose a challenge to the calligraphic tradition in Islam?

basement of a ruined house, rescuers discovered a man sitting on the floor absolutely absorbed in his work. He did not respond to their yells for him to hurry out before an aftershock buried him. Finally, he looked up and complained that they were disturbing him. They told him that thousands had been killed in an earthquake, and if he did not hurry up, he would be next. "What is all that to me?" he replied. "After many thousands of attempts I have finally made a perfect 'waw' [meaning 'and']." He showed them the letter, indeed a very difficult letter to make. "Such a perfect letter," he exclaimed, "is worth more than the whole city!"

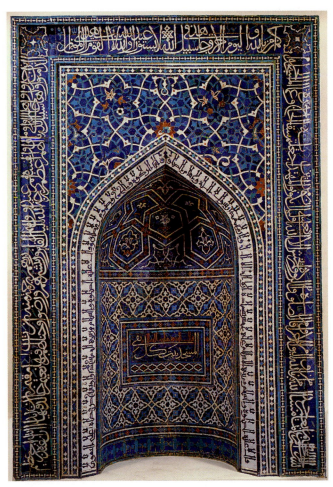

***Mihrab* niche, Isfahan, Iran. ca. 1354–55.** Mosaic of polychrome-glazed cut tiles on fritware body; set into plaster, 135¹⁄₁₆" × 113¹¹⁄₁₆". The Metropolitan Museum of Art, New York. Harris Brisbane Dick Fund, 1939 (39.20). The words in the rectangle in the center of the niche read, "The Prophet, peace be upon him, said, 'The mosque is the house of every person.'"

View the Closer Look for tile mosaic on **MyArtsLab**

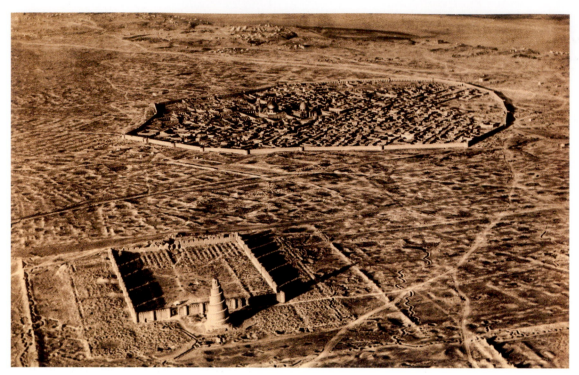

Fig. 9.5 The Mosque of al-Mutawakkil, Samarra, Iraq. 848–52. The huge dimensions of the mosque can be accounted for by the fact that all worshipers must face the same direction—that is, toward Mecca—arranging themselves in parallel lines to kneel prostrate. Thus, each worshiper requires a good deal of individual space. As early as 670, many mosques were large enough to accommodate as many as 3,000 worshipers.

renamed al-Medina, meaning "the city of the Prophet." Here Muhammad created a community based not on kinship, the traditional basis of Arab society, but on common submission to the will of God. Such submission did not need to be entirely voluntary. Muslims were obligated to pursue the spread of their religion, and they did so by means of the **jihad**, the impassioned religious struggle that could take either of two forms: a lesser form, holy war; or a greater form, self-control over the baser human appetites. In order to enforce submission, Muhammad raised an army of some 10,000 men and returned to Mecca, conquering the city and destroying the idols in the Kaaba, with the exception of the Black Stone. Confronted by a Muslim army defined by both piety and zealotry, soon the entire western region of Arabia came under Muslim sway.

The community of all Muslims would come to be known as the *Umma*. This represented such a departure from tradition that its creation required a new calendar. Based on lunar cycles, the Muslim year is about 11 days shorter than the Christian year, resulting in a difference of about three years per century. The calendar began in 622 CE. Thus, in the year 2013, the Muslims celebrated the start of their year 1434.

The Mosque At Medina, Muhammad built a house that surrounded a large, open courtyard, which served as a community gathering place. There the men of the community would gather on Fridays to pray and listen to a sermon delivered by Muhammad. It thus inspired the **masjid**, the

Arabic word for **mosque**, or "place of prostration." On the north and south ends of the courtyard, covered porches supported by palm tree trunks and roofed by thatched palm fronds protected the community from the hot Arabian sun. This many-columned covered area, known as a **hypostyle** space (from the Greek *hupostulos*, "resting upon pillars"), would later become a feature of many Muslim mosques. An important feature was the **qibla**, a wall that indicated the direction of Mecca. On this wall were both the **minbar**, or stepped pulpit for the preacher, and the **mihrab**, a niche commemorating the spot at Medina where Muhammad planted his lance to indicate the direction in which people should pray.

The Prophet's Mosque in Medina has been rebuilt so many times that its original character has long since been lost. But at Samarra, some 60 miles north of Baghdad on the Tigris River in present-day Iraq, the remnants of the Mosque of al-Mutawakkil, built in the mid-ninth century, as well as a similar floor plan from a relatively contemporary mosque in Muslim Spain, show how large the mosque would soon become (Figs. **9.5** and **9.6**). Built between 848 and 852, the mosque measures 800 by 500 feet, an area of over 10 acres. For centuries, it was the largest mosque in the world. It demonstrates the extraordinary popularity of the Muslim religion, since its central courtyard and hypostyle spaces would have been filled with many thousands of worshipers each Friday. About half the site was covered with a wooden roof on 464 supports, under which worshipers could pray. Although in a state of ruin today, the walls of

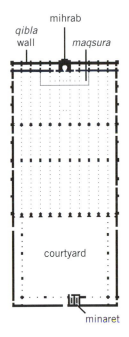

Hypostyle mosque
Great Mosque, Córdoba, Spain,
after extension by
al-Hakam II

Fig. 9.6 Plan of the Great Mosque, Córdoba, Spain. After its extension, ca. 961–76. See Fig. 9.13.

the mosque were originally richly decorated with glass mosaic and marble panels.

The most remarkable feature of the surviving mosque at Samarra is the spiral tower opposite the *mihrab*. Some speculate that this tower, originally 165 feet tall, is a minaret, the tower from which the *muezzin* ("crier") calls the faithful to prayer. But none of the earliest mosques had minarets, and although the call to prayer has become standard Muslim practice, even the earliest minarets may have been modeled on lighthouses (the root of *minaret* is *nur*, meaning "light"), serving as sentinels to guide the faithful across the desert to the mosque. Others theorize that the tower was inspired by the ziggurats of ancient Mesopotamia (see Fig. 2.1 in Chapter 2).

Women in Islam Although Muslim practice today varies widely, in Muhammad's time, women were welcome in the mosque. In the Qur'an, Muhammad teaches that women and men are equal partners: "The faithful men and the faithful women are protecting friends for each other" (Surah 9:7). The husband's honor becomes an integral part of his wife's honor, and vice versa. They share equally in each other's prosperity and adversity. But Muhammad further allowed for Muslim men to have up to four wives, provided that they treated all justly and gave each equal attention. (Polygamy was widely practiced in the Arab world at the time, and marrying the widow of a deceased comrade, for instance, was understood to be an act of protective charity.) Muhammad himself—and subsequently other leaders as well—was exempt from the four-wife limitation. Although he had only one wife for 28 years, after she died when he was 53, he married at least 10 other women. The Qur'an describes the wives of Muhammad—and by extension, the wives of all Muslim men—as "Mothers of the Faithful" whose duty was the education of the *Umma*'s children. They helped them along their spiritual path, transmitting and explaining the teaching of Muhammad in all spheres of life.

One of the most discussed and most controversial aspects of Muslim faith (even among Muslims) is the **hijab**, literally "curtain," the requirement that women be covered or veiled. Its origins can be traced to Islam's Jewish heritage and the principle of *tzenuit*, which in Hebrew means

"modesty" in both dress and behavior and which requires, among other strictures, that all married women cover their hair whenever nonfamily members are present. Islamic covering ranges from a simple scarf covering the hair to the **chador**, which covers the wearer from head to toe, leaving only her hands and her face (or part of her face) exposed. This full covering is currently popular, especially in Iran. Interestingly, the Qur'an is not explicit about the covering. Women are advised to dress in a way that enables them to avoid harassment by not drawing attention to their beauty, or *zinat*, a word that means both physical beauty and material adornment in Arabic. The basic message and instruction expressed in the Qur'an is for Muslims to act modestly and dress modestly, a rule that applies to men and women.

Both men and women are entitled to equal treatment before the law, and justice is considered to be genderless. Both have the right to have disputes settled by an arbiter of *shari'a*, the divine law that governs crime, politics, and economics, and sets standards of personal conduct. In the manuscript page showing a husband complaining about his wife before a state-appointed judge, or *qadi* (Fig. **9.7**), the wife, accompanied by two other women who serve as witnesses, points an accusing finger at her husband. In such disputes, the first duty of the *qadi* is to reconcile the couple

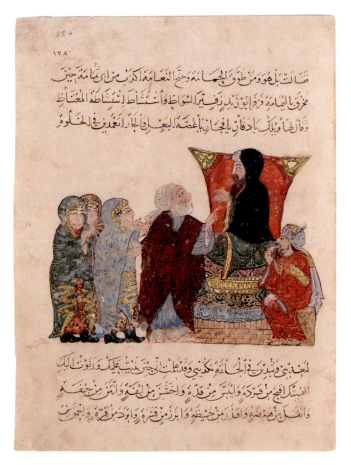

Fig. 9.7 *A Qadi Sits in Judgment*, Baghdad. 1327. Illuminated manuscript, 14½" × 11". Bibliothèque nationale de France. The women wear the *hijab*, in this instance, a full-length scarf.

and avoid divorce, which, though legal in Islam, is discouraged. But all in all, the *shari'a* regulated gender relations in ways that favored males. It defined marriage as a reciprocal relationship in which a man owed his wife material support, and a wife owed her husband unwavering obedience. It asserted the male right of polygamy and outlined the terms in which males were to treat their multiple wives equally. A man could unilaterally repudiate a wife, but a woman could only bargain with her husband to end a marriage. And the *shari'a* affirmed the patrilineal structure of Muslim society by granting mothers only temporary custody of their children after the termination of a marriage, giving ultimate custody to the father or father's family.

Many modern scholars see the *shari'a* as a social revolution, providing new rights and security for women in the cultures of the Middle East. But others regard the rules and regulations of the *shari'a* as a stifling suppression of the marriage practices of pre-Islamic Arab society, which was far less patriarchal. Traditional Arab society provided, among other things, for unilateral divorce by women and a woman's right to remain in her own clan and keep her children after divorce. It seems clear as well, that as Islam spread across the Middle East in the eighth and ninth centuries, the *shari'a* was adapted to and modified by local customs and practices. A clear example is the *shari'a*'s stated punishment for adultery. The Qur'an ordains that adulterers be given 100 lashes. But the standard punishment outlined in the *shari'a* by the early ninth century is death by stoning, justified by a hadith attributed to the Prophet but probably originating in pre-Islamic tribal practices.

THE SPREAD OF ISLAM

Why did Islam spread so rapidly?

Following the death of the Prophet in 632, the **caliphs**, or successors to Muhammad, assumed political and religious authority. The first two caliphs were Abu Bakr (r. 632–34) and Umar (r. 634–44), both of whom were fathers to two of Muhammad's wives. Waiting in the wings was Ali, the Prophet's cousin, second convert to Islam (after the prophet's wife Khadija), and husband of Fatima, Muhammad and Khadija's daughter. But when Umar died in 644, disciples responsible for choosing the new caliph, among them the two leading candidates for caliph, Ali and Uthman, a member of the Ummayad clan of Mecca, passed over Ali and selected the 70-year-old Uthman (r. 644–56). When Uthman was assassinated in 656, victim of an Egyptian revolt, Ali (r. 656–61) was finally named caliph, but over the objections of the Umayyad clan. In 661, Ali was assassinated by a rival faction, led by Muawiya, Uthman's cousin, that opposed Ali's rise to power, blaming him for refusing to avenge Uthman's death. A more conservative group, the Kharijites, supported the assassination of Ali on grounds of his moral weakness. Muawiya (r. 661–80) became caliph, establishing the Umayyad dynasty, and moving the Caliphate from Medina in Arabia to Damascus in Syria. (This tension between Ali's followers and the Ummayad caliphs exists to this day. Those who believe that only descendants of Ali should rule are known as Shiites [*Shi'a*, or "followers of Ali"], and they live largely in Iran and Iraq. Another

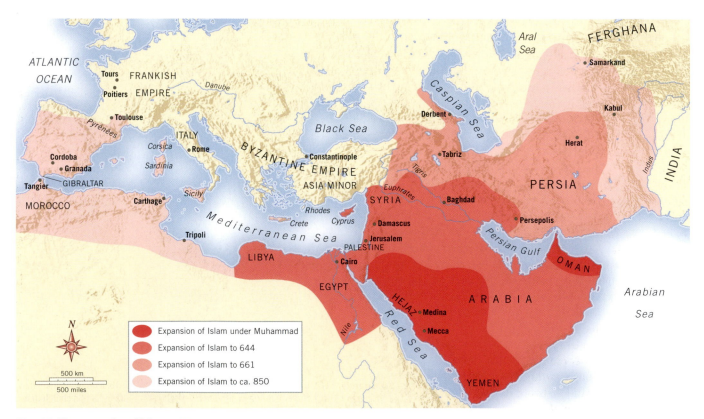

Map 9.2 The expansion of Islam to 850.

group, known as Sunnis, who today represent the vast majority of Muslims, believe that religious leaders should be chosen by the faithful. These two groups continue to vie for power in present-day Islam, especially in Iraq. The more conservative Kharijites still survive in Oman and North Africa.)

Despite this turmoil, Islam spread with a rapidity that is almost unimaginable (Map **9.2**). Damascus fell to the caliphs in 634, Persia in 636, Jerusalem in 638, and Egypt in 640. By 710, all of North Africa and Spain were under Muslim rule. The speed of the conquest can be partially accounted for by the fact that the Byzantine and Persian Empires were exhausted by a long war. Soon after the Byzantine emperor Heraclius (r. 610–40) captured Egypt, Palestine, Syria, and Asia Minor from the Persians, Muslim armies struck, driving the Byzantine armies out of their newly acquired territories and overrunning most of the Persian Empire as well. Most of the peoples in these territories, although Christian, were of the same linguistic and ethnic background as their new Muslim conquerors. Furthermore, the brand of Greek Orthodox Christianity that the Byzantine rulers had imposed on them was far too conservative for many. From Persia to Egypt, many peoples accepted their Muslim conquerors as preferable to the Byzantine rulers who had preceded them.

The successes of Islam must also be attributed to its appeal both as a religion and as a form of social organization. It denied neither Judaism nor Christianity, but merely superseded them. As opposed to the Jewish faith, which was founded on a common ethnic identity, Islam opened its arms to any and all comers—a feature it shared with Christianity. But unlike Christianity, it did not draw any special distinction between the clergy and the laity. It brought people together in the mosque, which served as a community meetinghouse, courthouse, council chamber, military complex, and administrative center. Traders naturally migrated to it, as did poets, artists, and scholars. In fact, the mosque was closer in function to the Classical agora than to the Christian tabernacle. The sense of community that the mosque inspired played a central role in the spread of Islam.

By the eleventh century, a *madrasa*, or teaching college, was attached to mosques, and mosques became centers of learning as well. Here students studied the Qur'an, the hadith, and Islamic law, as well as mathematics, poetry, and astronomy. The madrasas eventually contributed to the rise of an intellectual elite, the *ulama* (people possessing "correct knowledge"), a group that functioned more or less in the manner of Christian priests or Jewish rabbis. Yet any man of great religious learning could serve as an *alim* (the singular form of *ulama*), and *ulama* had the singular role of overseeing the rulers of Islam, guaranteeing that they followed the letter of the law as stated in the Qur'an.

Works of the Umayyad Caliphs: The Great Mosque of Damascus

The departure of the Umayyad caliphs from Medina to Damascus required them to build a new mosque in Damascus (Fig. **9.8**). Originally, the Muslim community in Damascus shared the site with the Christian community, who worshiped in a Byzantine church enclosed inside a walled compound. But by 705, the Muslim community had grown so large that radical steps had to be taken to accommodate it. During the reign of Abd al-Malik (r. 685–705), the Dome of the Rock (see Fig. 9.1) had been completed, and his son, al-Walid (r. 705–15), was responsible for the construction and decoration of the Great Mosque in Damascus. One large section of the original interior decoration survives—a glass mosaic landscape in the covered walkway surrounding the courtyard. The mosaics were probably the work of Christian Byzantine artisans brought to Damascus by al-Walid. Rising in improbable scale above the walkway is an expanse of colonnaded pavilions, towering trees, and

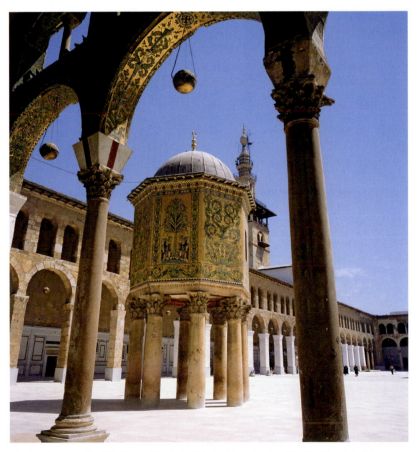

Fig. 9.8 Courtyard of the Great Mosque of Damascus, Syria. 706–15. Muslim builders may have considered the site of this mosque to possess mystical powers. The Byzantine church that had stood here was dedicated to John the Baptist. It had supplanted a Roman temple of Jupiter, which had earlier supplanted a temple dedicated to Haddad, the ancient Ammonite storm god.

arched bridges (Fig. **9.9**). It has been suggested that this is the Paradise promised by the Prophet in Surah 76 of the Qur'an (see Reading 9.1a, pages 292–293), but it may be, instead, that this landscape was designed as simply an attractive decorative addition.

Images in Muslim Art

It is worth noting that human figures are notably absent in the Great Mosque's mosaic decoration. Neither are there any animals. In fact, Muslim religious architecture is so notably free of figurative decoration that many people, even some Muslims, assume that representations of "living beings" are forbidden in Islam. The Byzantine emperor Leo III (see Chapter 8) attributed the successes of the Muslim armies to their ban on human figures in their mosques. The following admonition from the Qur'an (5:92) is often cited by Muslims who worry about the role of image-making in Muslim art and decoration: "O believers, wine and arrow-shuffling idols and divining arrows are an abomination, / some of Satan's work; then avoid it." But, it can be argued, "idols" here refers to pagan idols of the kind the Prophet eliminated from the Kaaba in Mecca. Also, at the time, Muhammad had allowed a painting of Mary and the infant Jesus to remain in the building. The had-iths, however, also supported those who opposed image-making. There the Prophet is reported to have warned, "An angel will not enter a house where there is a dog or a painting." Likewise, the Prophet claimed that "those who make these pictures will be punished on the Day of Judgment by being told: Make alive what you have created."

Some religious scholars believed that the ban on representation applied only to "living" things. Thus, the depiction of Paradise, as on the walls of the Great Mosque of Damascus, was acceptable, because Paradise is "beyond the living." Such thinking would also lead the Muslim owner of a Persian miniature representing a prince feasting in the countryside to erase the heads of all those depicted (Fig. **9.10**). Such an act is closely related to Byzantine iconoclasm, as no one could presume to think that figures without heads could possibly be "alive." In fact, as we will see, Muslim artists in Persia took great delight in illustrating literary texts, creating scene after scene depicting people in various forms of action, including lovemaking. Their freedom to do so is partly explained by their distance from more conservative brands of Arabian Islam, but also by their belief that they were not illustrating "living beings" so much as fictive characters.

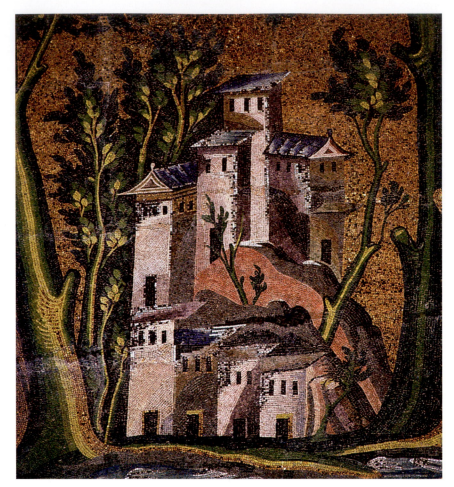

Fig. 9.9 Detail of mosaic decoration, Great Mosque of Damascus. 715. The decorative scheme of such panels reflects Byzantine influence, as well as the Roman love of landscape mosaic.

Whatever an individual Muslim's feelings about image-making might be, all Muslims recognized that it posed a problem. The practical solution to the problem was to decorate without images, and this was especially true for the decoration of both the Qur'an and religious architecture. At the heart of Islamic culture was the word, in the form of the recitations that make up the Qur'an. In fact, those who transcribed the Qur'an enjoyed a status higher than that of artists and architects and at least equal to that of poets, whose largely oral works had, from pre-Islamic times, been considered the highest form of art. It is also important to remember that the Qur'an is itself a work of oral poetry.

ISLAM IN AFRICA AND SPAIN

How would you characterize Islam in both Africa and Spain?

Scholars once believed that the rapid expansion of Islam was entirely due to the determination of the faithful to convert new followers to the faith, but overpopulation of the Arabian peninsula probably also played a role. If faith

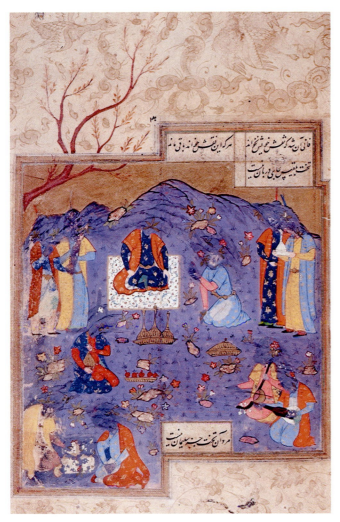

Fig. 9.10 Page from a copy of Nezami's *Khamseh* (the "Quintet"), illustrating a princely country feast, from Persia (present-day Iran). 1574–75. Illuminated manuscript, 9¾" × 6". India Office, London. Nezami's poem, written in the twelfth century, consists of five romantic epics in 30,000 couplets. It became one of the most widely illustrated poems in Persian literature.

resulted in a series of military crusades to free the Holy Land, and Jerusalem in particular, of Muslim influence (discussed in Chapter 10). However, the Arabs maintained a dominant presence in Spain, particularly in the southern region of Andalusia (al-Andalus, in Arabic). There Muslim culture flourished until Christian armies finally expelled the Muslims in 1492, the same year that Columbus set sail for America.

Islamic Africa

The Muslim impact on the culture of North Africa cannot be overstated. Beginning in about 750, not long after Muslim armies had conquered most of North Africa, Muslim traders, following the trade routes created by the Saharan Berber peoples, began trading for salt, copper, dates, and especially gold with the sub-Saharan peoples of the Niger River drainage. Gradually they came to dominate the trans-Saharan trade routes (Map 9.3), and Islam became the dominant faith of West Africa. By the ninth century, a number of African states existed in the broad savanna south of the Sahara desert known as the Sudan (which literally means "land of the blacks"). These states seemed to have formed in response to the prospects of trade with the Muslim and Arab world. Ghana, which means "war chief," is an early example, and its name suggests that a single chieftain, and later his family, exerted control over the material goods of the region, including gold, salt, ivory, iron, and particularly slaves. Muhammad accepted slavery as the just spoils of war, although no Muslim was ever to enslave another Muslim. Between the ninth and twelfth centuries, the slave trade grew from 300,000 enslaved to over a million, and it was so lucrative that the peoples of the Sudan, all eager to enslave each other for profit, were constantly at war. (There is some reason to believe that many African converts to Islam were initially attracted to the religion as a way to avoid becoming slaves, since the

offered the excuse, the practical result of Islamic expansion was the acquisition of new territories and the wealth they brought with them.

After gaining control of virtually all of the Middle East, the Arabic Muslim armies moved into North Africa in 639. After gaining control of the port of Alexandria, they launched a navy that seized Cyprus and Rhodes and began attacking Italy and Sicily. They moved across North Africa and took Carthage in 698, defeating the native Berber tribes. In 711, Muslim armies, under the command of a freed Berber slave, Tariq, crossed into Spain at the Strait of Gibraltar (*Gibraltar* is a corruption of the Arabic words meaning "Rock of Tariq") and moved quickly northward, deep into France. They were finally defeated in 732 at the Battle of Poitiers, also known as the Battle of Tours, by the king of the Franks, Charles Martel, and pushed back south of the Pyrenees. In the succeeding centuries, most of Europe became increasingly united in its opposition to Islam. This

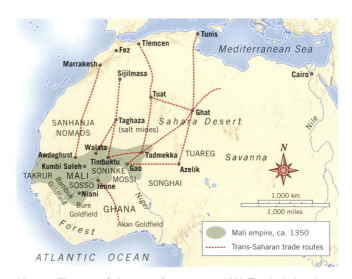

Map 9.3 The trans-Saharan trade routes. ca. 1350. The shaded portion indicates the empire of Mali in the fourteenth century. The dashed lines trace the main trans-Saharan routes of the period.

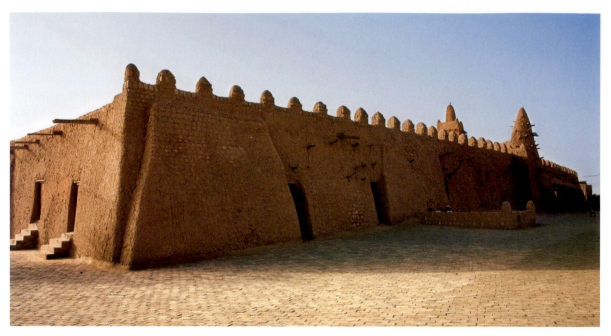

Fig. 9.11 Djingareyber Mosque, Timbuktu, Mali. ca. 1312. Today the mosque—and the entire city of Timbuktu—is in danger of becoming a desert, as the sands from the Sahara overtake what once was the Mali savanna.

faithful were exempt from servitude.) Finally, the empire of the Mali people subsumed Ghana under the leadership of the warrior-king Sunjata (r. 1230–55) and gained control of the great trade routes north out of the savanna, through Timbuktu, the leading trading center of the era.

In 1312, Mansa Moussa (*mansa* is the equivalent of the term "emperor") came to the Malian throne. A devout Muslim, he built magnificent mosques throughout his empire, including the Djingareyber Mosque in Timbuktu (Fig. **9.11**). Still standing today and made of burned brick and mud, it dominates the city. Under Moussa's patronage, Timbuktu grew in wealth and prestige and became a cultural focal point for the finest poets, scholars, and artists of Africa and the Middle East. To draw further attention to Timbuktu, and to attract more scholars and poets to it, Mansa Moussa embarked on a pilgrimage to Mecca in 1334. He arrived in Cairo at the head of a huge caravan of 60,000 people, including 12,000 servants, with 80 camels carrying more than two tons of gold to be distributed among the poor. Five hundred of the servants carried staffs of pure gold. In fact, Moussa distributed so much gold in Egypt that the value of the precious metal fell dramatically and did not recover for a number of years. When Moussa returned from the holy cities of Mecca and Medina, he built mosques, libraries, and madrasas throughout his kingdom. He convinced the Arab poet and architect Abu-Ishaq Ibrahim-es-Saheli to return with him, and it was Ibrahim-es-Saheli who devised the burned brick and many of the construction techniques for the Djingareyber Mosque.

Such was Mansa Moussa's fame that the Jewish mapmaker Abraham Cresques prominently represented him in his *Catalan Atlas*, made in 1375 for Charles V of France (Fig. **9.12**). Crowned in gold and enthroned above his capital of Timbuktu, Mansa Moussa holds a golden orb in one hand and a golden scepter in the other. Cresques depicts a river of gold flowing out of Mali eastward to Cairo and Alexandria. The caption to the king's right reads, "So abundant is the gold which is found in his country that he is the richest and most noble king in the land."

Islamic traditions meanwhile continued to exist alongside indigenous African art and music. For instance, the military exploits of the first Malian *mansa*, Sunjata, still survive in an epic poem, the *Sunjata*. The poem was passed down through the generations, much in the way that the Homeric epics must have been passed down in prehistoric Greece. Its transmitters were Malian griots, professional poet/storytellers who chant or sing traditional narratives from memory, generally accompanying themselves on a harp, either a three- or four-stringed **bolon**, or a 21-stringed *kora*. The *Sunjata* was not transcribed until the twentieth century. The poem opens with the griot identifying himself (**Reading 9.3a**):

> **READING 9.3a**
>
> **from the *Sunjata* (12th century)**
>
> I am a griot. … We are vessels of speech, we are the repositories which harbor secrets many centuries old. The art of eloquence has no secrets for us; without us the names of kings would vanish into oblivion, we are the memory of mankind; by the spoken word we bring to life the deeds and exploits of kings for younger generations. … Listen to my word, you who want to know; by my mouth you will learn the history of Mali.

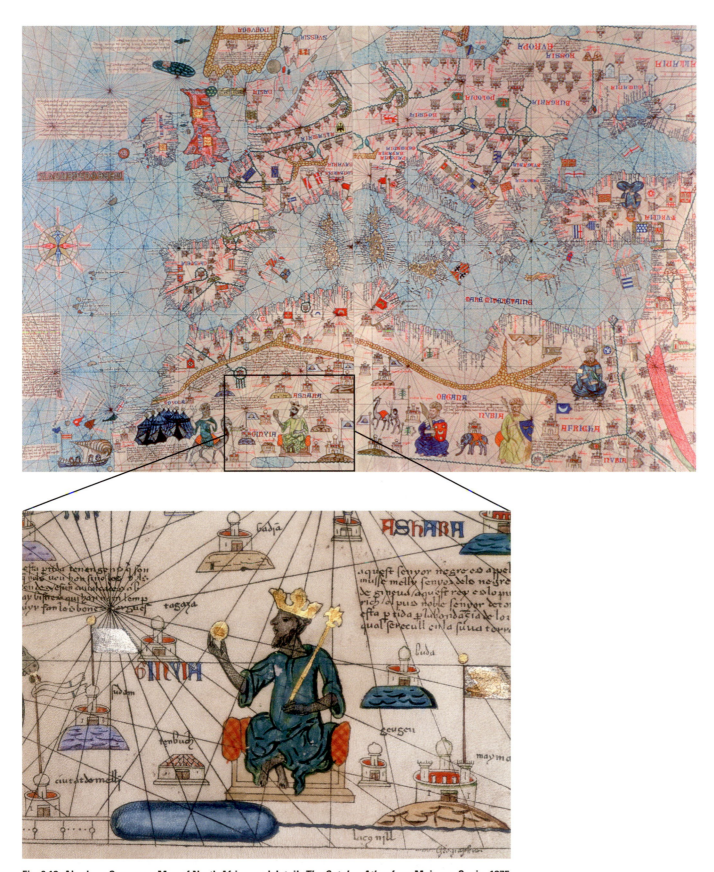

Fig. 9.12 Abraham Cresques, Map of North Africa, and detail, *The Catalan Atlas*, from Majorca, Spain. 1375.
Bibliothèque nationale de France. The map features the Atlas Mountains, Mansa Moussa of Mali, the king of Organa, the king of Nubia, the king of Babylon, and the Red Sea. Note the "River of Gold" that flows across North Africa to Egypt. The mapmaker, Cresques, lived on the Catalan island of Majorca, where a school of nautical mapmakers thrived, their work based on the experience of Mediterranean sailors. The gold used in the map is actual gold leaf.

Later in the poem, Sunjata oversees a festival in celebration of his military exploits, a description that creates a vivid picture of Malian tradition (**Reading 9.3b**):

READING 9.3b

from the *Sunjata* (12th century)

The festival began. The musicians of all the countries were there. Each people in turn came forward to the dais under Sunjata's impassive gaze. Then the war dances began. The sofas [soldiers] of all the countries had lined themselves up in six ranks amid a great clatter of bows and spears knocking together. The war chiefs were on horseback. The warriors faced the enormous dais and at a signal from Balla Fasséké [Sunjata's griot], the musicians, massed on the right of the dais, struck up. The heavy war drums thundered, the bolons gave off muted notes while the griot's voice gave the throng the pitch for the "Hymn to the Bow." The spearmen, advancing like hyenas in the night, held their spears above their heads; the archers of Wagadou and Tabon, walking with a noiseless tread, seemed to be lying in ambush behind bushes. They rose suddenly to their feet and let fly their arrows at imaginary enemies. In front of the great dais the Kéké-Tigui, or war chiefs, made their horse perform dance steps under the eyes of the Mansa. The horses whinnied and reared, then, overmastered by the spurs, knelt, got up and cut little capers, or else scraped ground with their hooves.

The rapturous people shouted the "Hymn to the Bow" and clapped their hands. The sweating bodies of the warriors glistened in the sun while the exhausting rhythm of the tam-tams [large circular gongs] wrenched from them shrill cries.

To this day, griots in West Africa perform the *Sunjata* (track **9.1**). The performance features many of the characteristics common to West African music. These include polyrhythmic percussion, featuring as many as five to ten different rhythms simultaneously played on a variety of instruments (such as drums, rattles, and, here, bows and spears knocking together), communal performance, responsive chants, and what in another context might be considered "noise"— shrill cries, for instance—adding to the tonal richness of the whole.

Islamic Spain

Like Islamic Africa, Islamic Spain maintained its own indigenous traditions while it absorbed Muslim ones, thus creating a distinctive cultural and political life. In 750, the Abbasids, a large family that claimed descent from Abbas, an uncle of Muhammad, overthrew the Umayyad caliphs. The Abbasids shifted the center of Islamic power from Damascus, where the Umayyads had centered their power, to a magnificent new capital in Iraq popularly known as Baghdad. In the middle of the ninth century, they moved

again, to the complex at Samarra (see Fig. 9.5), 60 miles farther up the Tigris, probably in an attempt to seek more space to build palaces and mosques. Meanwhile, Spain remained under Umayyad control, initially under the leadership of Abd ar-Rahman (r. 756–88), who had escaped the Abbasid massacre of Umayyads in Syria in 750, arriving in Córdoba in 756. For over three centuries, the Spain he encountered had been controlled politically by a Germanic tribe from the north, the Visigoths, who had become Christian. But some 45 years earlier, in about 711 or 712, these Christian Visigoths had been defeated in southern Spain by a force of invading Muslim Arabs and Berbers. Gradually, Abd ar-Rahman solidified Muslim control of the region, first in Córdoba, then in Seville, Toledo (the former Visigothic capital), and Granada.

The Great Mosque of Córdoba In the last years of his reign, secure in his position, Abd ar-Rahman built a magnificent new mosque in Córdoba, tearing down an existing Visigothic church and building his new mosque in its place, for which the Christian church was handsomely reimbursed. Abd ar-Rahman's original design included a double-tiered system of reused Roman and Visigothic columns and capitals supporting horseshoe-shaped double arches, all topped by a wooden roof (Fig. **9.13**). The double arches may have served a practical function. The Visigoths tended to build with relatively short, stubby columns. To create the loftier space for the mosque, the architects superimposed another set of columns on top, creating the double tier. But the design also echoes the same double-tiered design found at the Great Mosque at Damascus, which also reuses Roman columns, and the architects may have simply copied the Damascus model. The arches also employ a distinctive design of alternating stone and red brick voussoirs, the wedge-shaped stones used to build an arch (see *Materials & Techniques*, Chapter 6, page 198). The use of two different materials is functional as well, combining the flexibility of brick with the strength of stone. The hypostyle plan of the mosque was infinitely expandable, and subsequent Umayyad caliphs enlarged the mosque in 852, 950, 961–76, and 987, until it was more than four times the size of Abd ar-Rahman's original mosque and incorporated 1,200 columns.

Under the Umayyad caliphs, Muslim Spain thrived intellectually. Religious tolerance was extended to all. (It is worth noting that Muslims were exempt from taxes, while Christians and Jews were not—a practice that encouraged conversion.) Spanish Jews, who had been persecuted under the Visigoths, welcomed the Muslim invasion and served as scientists, scholars, and even administrators in the caliphate. Classical Greek literature and philosophy had already been translated into Arabic in Abbasid Baghdad. The new School of Translation established by the Umayyads in Toledo soon was responsible for spreading the nearly forgotten texts throughout the West. Muslim mathematicians in Spain invented algebra and introduced the concept of zero to the West, and soon their Arabic numerals

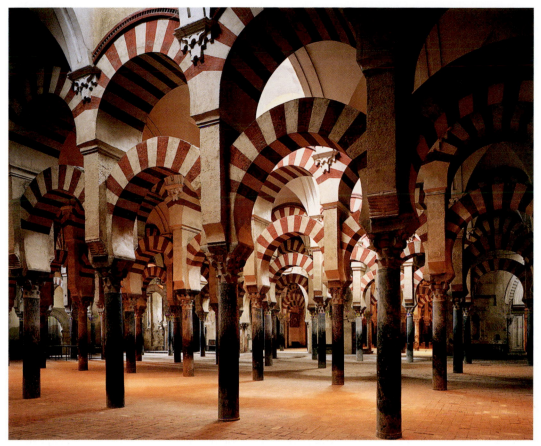

Fig. 9.13 Great Mosque of Córdoba. Begun 785; extensions 852, 950, 961–76, and 987. The caliphs of Spain intended their mosque to rival those in Jerusalem, Damascus, and Iraq. The forestlike expanse of the interior is a result of these aspirations. Even though only 80 of the original 1,200 columns survive, the space appears infinite, like some giant hall of mirrors.

👁 **Watch** an architectural simulation about Islamic arches on **MyArtsLab**

replaced the unwieldy Roman system. By the time of Abd ar-Rahman III (r. 912–61), Córdoba was renowned for its medicine, science, literature, and commercial wealth, and it became the most important center of learning in Europe. The elegance of Abd ar-Rahman III's court was unmatched, and his tolerance and benevolence extended to all, as Muslim students from across the Mediterranean soon found their way to the mosque-affiliated madrasa that he founded—the earliest example of an institution of higher learning in the Western world.

Outside of Córdoba, Abd ar-Rahman III built a huge palace complex, Madinat al-Zahra, to honor his wife. (Its extensive remains are still being excavated.) Its staff included 13,750 male servants along with another 3,500 pages, slaves, and eunuchs. Its roof required the support of 4,300 columns, and elaborate gardens surrounded the site. As many as 1,200 loaves of bread were required daily just to feed the fish in the garden ponds.

The decorative arts of the era are equally impressive. A famous example is a **pyxis**, a small, cylindrical box with a lid, made for Prince al-Mughira, Abd ar-Rahman III's son (Fig. **9.14**), in ca. 968. Carved in ivory by artisans at

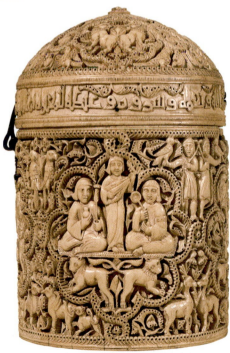

Fig. 9.14 Royal workshop of Madinat al-Zahra, Pyxis of al-Mughira. ca. 968. Elephant ivory, carved and engraved decoration, trace of black inlay, possibly jade, height 6". Musée du Louvre, Paris, former Riano Collection, purchased 1898. OA 4068. The Arabic inscription around the base of the lid reads: "God's blessing, favors, joy, beatitude to al-Mughira son of the Commander of the faithful, may God have mercy upon him, in the year 357 [of the Hegira]."

Madinat al-Zahra, perhaps to hold the prince's jewelry or toiletries, each of its four sides is decorated with a medallion linked to the others by borders of delicately pierced foliage of an oriental palm. In one of these medallions, a lutist stands between two cross-legged figures, one holding a fan, the other a bottle of a kind associated particularly with the Umayyad caliph. Above them to the right two falconers stand back to back—the falcon being the traditional symbol of the Umayyad dynasty. Almost every element in the design has symbolic meaning, especially the oriental palm tree, which symbolizes the exile of the dynasty, banished to the distant land of Spain by the Abbasids.

The city of Córdoba reflected the splendor of its palace. Writers at the time, visiting the caliphate, testify that its population was about 500,000 (compared to 40,000 in Paris at about the same time). There were 1,600 mosques, 900 public baths, and more than 80,000 shops. About half the population had running water and lavatories in their homes. And the main city streets were lighted by torchlight at night.

Jews in Muslim Spain Jews had settled in Spain as early as 586 BCE, when Nebuchadnezzar II conquered Jerusalem and destroyed the First Temple in Jerusalem. The Hebrew word for Spain was *Sepharad*, and the Spanish Jews were thus known as Sephardim. Under Umayyad rule, the Jewish population flourished to such an extent that some scholars refer to the period as the Golden Age of Jewish Culture. Jews served at the highest levels of government and participated in the social and intellectual fervor that marked the Umayyad court. They dedicated themselves to the study of science and medicine. In fact, Abd ar-Rahman III's court physician was the Jewish Hasdai ibn Shaprut (ca. 915–ca. 990). Jewish scholars also devoted themselves, under Hasdai ibn Shaprut's patronage, to the art of poetry and the study of Hebrew grammar. He was also instrumental in making Córdoba the new center of Jewish theological studies.

The Umayyad caliphate in Spain ultimately collapsed in the eleventh century, when internal politics caused it to break up into small competing states called *taifas*. *Taifa* Spain was far less tolerant of Judaism than the Umayyads, and persecutions began. The first one was on December 30, 1066, when the Jews were expelled from Granada and 1,500 families who refused to leave were killed. Nevertheless, Jewish culture still thrived, especially in Toledo and Córdoba. It was in Córdoba that Moses Maimonides (1138–1204), one of the greatest Jewish scholars, was born, although he and his family were driven out of the country in 1148 by the Almoravids, a Muslim Berber dynasty that had been called into Spain in 1085 from its capital in Marrakesh, in present-day Morocco, in order to help the *taifas* drive Christian armies from northern Spain. Maimonides is renowned for being the first person to write a systematic summary of Jewish law, the *Mishneh Torah*. He also produced one of the great philosophical works of Judaism, *Guide to the Perplexed*, a work about the nature of God in general that would influence later Christian thinkers such as Thomas Aquinas (see Chapter 12).

One of the great Jewish poets of the era is Judah Halevi (ca. 1075–1141). In Córdoba, he wrote one of the best-known books of the era, *The Book of Argument and Proof in Defense of the Despised Faith*, later known as *The Book of the Kuzari*. This dialogue between a Jewish scholar and the pagan king of the Khazars, a seminomadic Turkish people, is considered by many to be one of the most important works of Jewish philosophy. The book argues, among other things, that the Hebrew language is itself divine, that the Torah is supernatural—not just a "gift from God" but the very "presence of God"—and that the special function of the Jewish people in God's plan is to bring about the redemption of the world.

Halevi was a poet of both secular and religious verse, including love songs, drinking songs, and autobiographical lyric poems concerning his faith. One of the most moving of the latter is "My Heart Is in the East." It embodies feelings shared by all Jews of the Diaspora (**Reading 9.4**):

READING 9.4

Judah Halevi, "My Heart Is in the East"

My heart is in the East, and I live at the edge of the West.
I eat. I taste nothing. How can I enjoy it?
How can I fulfill my word to leave
While Zion is locked up in red Edom[1]
and I stand in the ropes of Arabia?
Easily I could give up
all the good wonders of Spain.
Glory would be to see the dust of the Temple,
our ravaged shrine.

[1] **Edom:** a Hebrew word meaning "red" but referring to Esau in the Hebrew Scriptures, as well as to the nation tracing its ancestry to him.

Before the end of his life, Halevi did leave his native Spain for Zion, perhaps driven out by the Berbers. He reached Alexandria, where he continued to write, but died six months later.

The Alhambra The collapse of the Umayyad caliphate and the subsequent rise and fall of the various Islamic dynasties was the inspiration for a pioneering work of sociology, the *Muqaddimah* (literally "Introduction") of Ibn Khaldun (1332–1406), the first volume of a universal history that comprises six books. Originally conceived by its Tunisian-born author as a history of the North African Berber dynasties that rose to power in Spain after the Almoravid arrival in 1085, the work is based on Ibn Khaldun's central concept of *asabiyah*, or "group feeling." *Asabiyah* is the source of cohesion within a community, and although it occurs almost naturally in small groups, such as families or tribes, religion can greatly expand its effects. Khaldun analyzes how *asabiyah* can carry groups to power, but he also

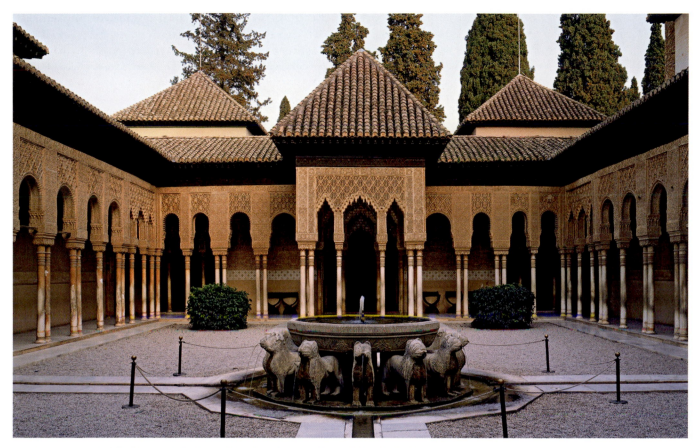

Fig. 9.15 Courtyard of the Palace of the Lions, Alhambra, Granada, Spain. 1354–91. The 12 stone lions supporting the fountain were salvaged from an earlier complex that stood on the Alhambra hill overlooking Granada.

✳ **Explore** the architectural panorama of the Alhambra on **MyArtsLab**

demonstrates how, over time, the power of *asabiyah* dissipates in a group, causing its downfall and its eventual replacement by a new group with a more vital or contemporary sense of itself as a coherent power.

Of all the Berber dynasties in Spain, the Nasrid dynasty (r. 1230–1492) represented this new, stronger power, and their architecture embodied their sense of *asabiyah*. On a hill above Granada they erected a magnificent palace and fortress, which flourished as a center for the arts. Named the Alhambra—from the Arabic word for "red citadel"— after the reddish tone of its walls, it gives us some sense of what Abd ar-Rahman III's palace complex in Córdoba must have been like.

Within the walls of the Alhambra are palaces, mosques, gardens, quarters for artisans, baths, and tombs. The Palace of the Myrtles served as the official chambers for receiving and hosting visitors. Named after the shrubs planted in its courtyard, it was based on the plan of an urban dwelling in the Arab heartland, where life centered around a sheltered outdoor patio surrounded by doorways leading to the bedrooms, sitting rooms, and storage areas. The Palace of the Lions, named after the fountain in its courtyard surrounded by 12 stone lions, served as a private residence (Fig. **9.15**). The various rooms of the palaces opened into their central courtyards. Poetic texts adorn the palaces, carved into the capitals of their colonnades and inscribed on their walls and **miradors**, projecting rooms with windows on three sides. On a mirador overlooking the gardens of one palace are the words "I am a garden adorned with beauty. Gaze upon my loveliness and you will know this to be true." On another is the poignant phrase "I believe that the full moon has its home here." On the walls beneath the decorated ceilings of the Palace of the Lions, the fourteenth-century court poet Ibn Zamrak outlined the spiritual essence of the architectural traceries and grilles of the palace's arches and domes:

And how many arches rise up in its vault supported by columns which at night are embellished by light!

You would think that they are heavenly spheres whose orbits revolve, overshadowing the pillar of dawn when it barely begins to appear after having passed through the night.

The play of light and shadow, and the airy lightness of the stone- and plasterwork that adorn the Alhambra, symbolize the celestial heavens. The ceiling of the Hall of the Abencerrajes is decorated with **muqarnas**, small nichelike components unique to Islamic architecture that are combined in successive layers to enclose a space and produce surfaces rich in three-dimensional geometric compositions

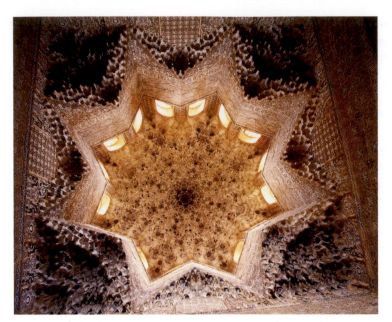

Fig. 9.16 *Muqarnas* **dome (plaster ceiling), Hall of the Abencerrajes, Palace of the Lions, Alhambra, Granada. 1354–91.** The Hall of the Abencerrajes may have been used as a music room, the elaborate ceiling contributing to its nearly perfect acoustics.

(Fig. **9.16**). Here they are used to catch the changing light as it moves from window to window across the top of the dome drum. The inescapable conclusion is that the Alhambra was meant to be something akin to heaven on earth, or paradise (from the Arabic word for an enclosed park, *faradis*), the literal embodiment of what, in the Great Mosque of Damascus, could only be imaged in mosaic (see Fig. 9.9).

The visitor to the Alhambra is struck by one other inescapable reality—there is water everywhere, in gardens, courtyards, and patios. Inscribed on the wall of one courtyard are the words, "The water in the basin in my center is like the soul of a believer who rests in the remembrance of God." But the water in the Alhambra is not merely passive. It flows, gurgles, and bubbles. Everywhere there is the *sound* of water, the essential *melody* of nature.

THE ARTS OF THE ISLAMIC WORLD

How do Islamic music, book design, narrative, and poetry reflect calligraphy's emphasis on abstract rhythms of pattern and repetition?

Between the eighth and thirteenth centuries, the Islamic world, from Baghdad in the east to Córdoba in the west, developed artistic traditions and practices compared to which the arts in Western Europe simply paled. With the same technical virtuosity that the architects at the Alhambra employed, Islam's musicians, bookmakers, illustrators, and poets crafted beautiful works of complex abstract design. Calligraphy, as we have seen (see *Closer Look*, pages

294–295), was perhaps the highest form of artistic expression, but by its very emphasis on abstract rhythms of pattern and repetition, it greatly influenced music, book design, narrative, and poetry.

Music in the Islamic World

Music was central to Islamic culture. Though Muhammad and his followers initially viewed music with some skepticism, believing that it distracted the faithful from their true purpose, within a century of his death, Muslim worship had become a highly musical event. In the call to prayer, each of the call's seven phrases is sung, with a long pause between each phrase and each phrase becoming more melodic than the last. In the daily prayer service and on holy days, verses from the Qur'an are chanted and special songs are sung.

Traditional Arabic music is based on intonations and rhythms closely related to the inflections of words. It uses many more pitch intervals than Western music, breaking what we think of as a given pitch into fractions of semitones and microtones. In addition, Arabic song is "voiced" through the nose as well as the mouth, resulting in a range of distinctly nasal pitches, as in the Andalusian song from the "Nuba 'al'istihlal'", "Songs to be sung after sunset" (track **9.2**). These songs were often accompanied, at least outside the mosque, by a range of instruments, including drums, tambourine, flute, oboe, and lute—or oud, from the Arabic for "wood"—a bent-necked, pear-shaped string instrument. As Islam spread, the oud became known, throughout North Africa, as the *qitara*—the guitar—which achieved its modern form in Islamic Spain. Like Arabic music in general, the *qitara* was believed to be closely connected to nature. Its four strings variously represented the four seasons, the four phases of the moon, the four alchemical elements (hotness, coldness, dryness, and moistness), or the four bodily humors (in the medieval world, the four elemental fluids of the body—blood, phlegm, choler or yellow bile, and melancholy or black bile).

During the Abbasid era (750–1258), only an accomplished musician could be considered a truly educated person. Al-Kindi (790–874) studied the effects of music on people's feelings and behavior and developed a system of modes, or scales, corresponding to the emotions that the music was meant to evoke. In effect, the Arabs were the first to put into writing the concepts of scale that would become second nature in European theory. (Their notation, like European chant, lacked rhythmic notation until the twelfth to thirteenth centuries.) Many theorize that the new instruments were introduced into Europe from the Middle East, and may have been accompanied by the theoretical ideas behind them. By the ninth century, the renowned musician Ziryab (789–857) arrived in Córdoba from Baghdad and founded the first conservatory of music in Spain. Here, musicians began to experiment with ensemble compositions

Listen on MyArtsLab

divided into five or more movements performed by string, wind, and percussion instruments, and often accompanied by a vocal chorus. New instruments were invented—trumpets, viols, and kettledrums. In essence, the elements of the Western orchestra were now in place.

The Art of the Book

Sometime in the eighth century, the art of papermaking was introduced into the Arabic world from China. The process involved extracting cellulose pulp from any of a number of plants, suspending the pulp in water, catching it on a fine screen, and then drying it into sheets. By the first years of the ninth century, most official documents in Baghdad were executed on paper, and soon afterward books, which were more affordable than parchment manuscripts, began to increase in number. Calligraphers and artists created not only scholarly treatises but also romances, epics, and lyric poetry, and most Abbasid cities soon boasted special booksellers' markets. As Jonathan M. Bloom notes in his history of papermaking in the Islamic world, *Paper Before Print*, "Paper ... became the prime medium of memory." Bloom suggests that although scholars have long recognized "the major achievements of intellectual life under the Abbasids ... these achievements were not accidental. Rather, they were tied to the introduction of paper: they were a product of both increased intellectual curiosity—itself fostered by the growth of learning made possible by the explosion of books—and attempts to exploit the potential applications of paper." It is likely that the West did not produce paper in any sufficient quantity for another 500 years—until the invention of the printing press—because of its comparative lack of interest in the written word. The richest library in the West by the mid-fourteenth century, for instance, was the college library of the Sorbonne in Paris, which boasted some 2,000 volumes. By contrast, a single tenth-century Andalusian scholar, Ibn Hani al-Andalusi, reputedly owned a private library of some 400,000 volumes. Muslim culture, in turn, was slow to adopt the printing press because it so valued the art of calligraphy.

As a result of its book production, Abbasid Baghdad at the height of its influence, from the ninth to the twelfth centuries, was the center of world culture. Trade flourished as silk and porcelain from China, horses from Arabia, cotton from Egypt, and minerals from throughout Europe overflowed its markets. As one late ninth-century visitor remarked, "Goods are brought from India, Sind [i.e., Pakistan], China, Tibet, the lands of the Turks ... the Ethiopians, and others to such an extent that [the goods] are more plentiful in Baghdad than in the countries from which they come. They can be procured so readily and so certainly that it is as if all the good things of the world are sent there, all the treasures of the earth assembled there, and all the blessings of creation perfected there." There are, he commented further, "none more learned than their scholars, better informed than their traditionists, more cogent than their

theologians ... more literate than their scribes, more lucid than their logicians ... more eloquent than their preachers, more poetic than their poets." The book made this cultural eloquence manifest and transportable. Islamic learning—and with it, Islamic faith—spread throughout the world.

Nezami's *Haft Paykar* One of the most widely illustrated poems of the Middle Ages is the *Haft Paykar* ("Seven Beauties"). It is one of five romantic epics in 30,000 couplets that make up *Khamseh* ("Quintet") by the Persian poet considered to be the master of the genre, Nezami (ca. 1141–1203 or 1217), whose full name is Elyas Yusof Nezami Ganjavi. A romantic epic is a poem that celebrates love between a man and woman as a cosmic force for harmony and justice. Thus, the love stories that form the epic's core narrative are also vehicles for treating broader philosophical issues such as just rule, human perfection, and spiritual growth. The *Haft Paykar*, Nezami's masterpiece, narrates how, one day, the legendary Persian prince Bahram Gur discovers a mysterious pavilion with portraits of seven beautiful princesses decorating its walls (Fig. **9.17**). He falls in love with all of them, marries them, sets up each princess in a separate pavilion of her own, and visits them one by one. Each

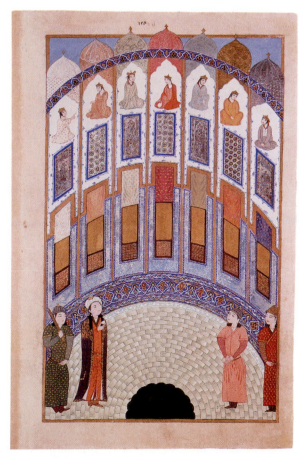

Fig. 9.17 *Prince Bahram Gur Introduced into the Hall of Seven Images,* **from a copy of Nezami's poem** *Haft Paykar* **("Seven Beauties"), from** *Nezami's Khamseh,* **in the Anthology of Iskandar Sultan. From Shiraz, Iran. 1410.** Illuminated manuscript, 9⅞" × 5⅞". Calouste Gulbenkian Foundation Museum, Lisbon. Another illustration of Nezami's poem is reproduced in Fig. 9.10, but defaced by its owner.

princess tells him a story—each of about 1,000 couplets, two-line rhymed stanzas—that is meant to instruct him in the art of love and the love of beauty. **Reading 9.5** includes the first 29 couplets of "The Tale of the Black Princess."

READING 9.5

from Nezami, *Haft Paykar*, "The Tale of the Black Princess" (1197)

When Bahram pleasure sought, he set
his eyes on those seven fair portraits;
On Saturday, from Shammasi temple[1] went
in Abbasid black[2] to pitch his tent,
Entered the musk-hued dome, and gave
his greetings to the Indian maid.
Til night he there made merry sport,
burnt aloes-wood,[3] and scattered scent.
When Night in kingly fashion spilled
black grains of musk on whitest silk,
The king from that Kashmiri spring[4]
sought perfume like the dawn breeze brings:
That she might loose some women's words,
sweet stories from her store of pearls,
Those tales for which all hearers long,
and soothe to sleep the drunken man.
That Turk-eyed, Hindu-born gazelle
loosed fragrant musk, her tale to tell.
She said, "May the king's fanfare play
above the moon's high throne; and may
He live as long as turns the world;
may all heads at his threshold bow.
May he gain all his wishes; may
his fortune never flag." This prayer
Concluded, she bowed low, and loosed
from sugared lips sweet aloes-wood.
She told (her eyes cast down in shame)
a tale unmatched by anyone. ...

[1] **Shammasi temple:** the temple of fire, served by white-robed priests.
[2] **Abbasid black:** the color of the Abbasid caliphs.
[3] **aloes-wood:** incense made of aloe.
[4] **Kashmiri spring:** a reference to the "black princess," who is from India.

The story of Bahram and his seven wives is a narrative device known as a **framing tale**. This form allows the poet to unite different tales—in this case seven—under an overarching narrative umbrella. The Western reader is probably most familiar with the framing tale in *The Thousand and One Nights*, also known as *The Arabian Nights*.

The Thousand and One Nights *The Thousand and One Nights* is a compilation of prose tales from various sources—Persian, Arabic, and Indian—that were united into a single narrative between the eighth and tenth centuries in Baghdad. It is likely that Nezami knew it well. The framing tale derives from the Indian story of Scheherazade (Shahrasad, in Persian), who chooses to marry King Shahryar, who so fears the prospect of female infidelity that he kills each new wife on the morning after their wedding night. In a conscious defense of womankind, Scheherazade knows that if she can tell a story each night and carefully construct it so as to reach its climax just after dawn, the king must let her live until the next evening in order to hear the tale's ending. After a thousand nights—and some 250 tales—the king comes to appreciate Scheherazade's beauty, wit, and civilizing power, and so spares her the fate of all his previous wives.

Both the *Haft Paykar* and *The Thousand and One Nights* show the centrality of love and sexuality in Islamic culture. In Islam, erotic sensory satisfaction, love, luxury, sensuality, and enjoyment were manifestations of divine grace. And although both framing tales portray women in almost total subservience to the ruler/husband, the women in each tale assert a certain real authority. In the *Haft Paykar*, women bring the prince Bahram Gur to a state of wisdom and spiritual wholeness. In *The Thousand and One Nights*, women's intelligence, wit, and reason at least equal and sometimes surpass that of their male counterparts.

The Thousand and One Nights was extremely popular in the West from the eighteenth century onward, and it exercised a considerable influence on the development of the novel in Western literature. It contains a wealth of stories popular to the present day—the adventures of Sinbad the Sailor, Ali Baba, and Aladdin, to name just a few—but its eroticism and ribald humor have often been sanitized in Western retellings. The stories wind in and out of one another in a seemingly endless pattern of repetition. The famous "Tale of the Fisherman and the Genie" (see **Reading 9.6**, pages 315–317) is a sequence of stories within stories that mirrors the framing technique of the whole, the fisherman telling tales to outwit an angry genie just as Scheherazade tells her tales to outwit the king. The sequence is repeatedly interrupted as dawn approaches and Scheherazade's stories must end for the night.

The Thousand and One Nights embodies a tension that pervades Islamic culture to this day and, it is fair to say, Western culture as a whole. That tension is between the exercise of authoritarian power over women in patriarchal society and the need for women to free themselves of that power—in Scheherazade's case, in order to survive. Related to this is the tendency of patriarchal society to reduce women to sexual objects even as it recognizes their great intellectual capacity. Scheherazade's tales must be understood in this context: They allow her to resist the king whom she entertains nightly, a man who is empowered by the *shari'a* or a like set of laws, who feels no compunction about executing wife after wife, day after day.

The Sufi Tradition

After the 1258 fall of Baghdad to Mongol invaders—the conquering Mongols would themselves become Muslim—the art of bookmaking shifted to Persia, where a thriving literary culture, exemplified by the poetry of Nezami, already existed. Particularly at the provincial capitals of Shiraz and Herat, home to a number of important Persian poets and

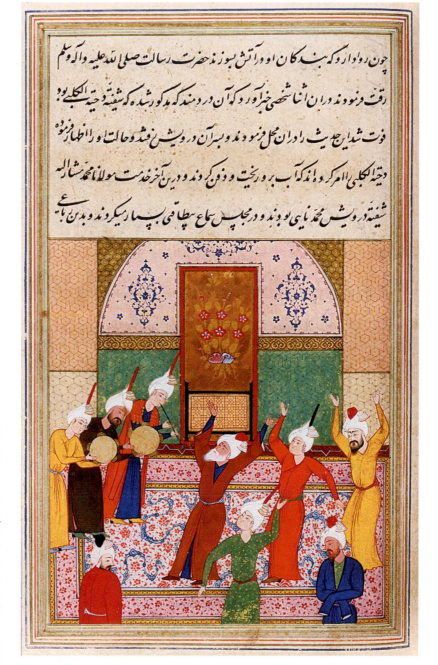

painters, the art of the book became associated with the mystical practices of the Sufi orders. Sufism (from the Arabic word for "wool," *suf*, a reference to the coarse woolen garments worn by Sufi practitioners) embraces a wide range of mystical practices. All of them share a belief in attaining visionary experience and divine inspiration by means of trances achieved in the intense experience of music, poetry, and dance. Thus, the ecstasy of the wild, whirling dervish dance (the Persian word for a Sufi or Muslim mystic is *darvish*) represents the path of the soul as it moves closer to God (Fig. 9.18). The great Sufi poets—Sa'di (ca. 1213–92), Rumi (ca. 1207–73), and Jami (1414–92) among them—emphasize the pursuit of the beautiful, often in the form of a beautiful woman or, in the case of Rumi, a beautiful man. However, such a pursuit is an allegory for, or figurative representation of, the pursuit of the beauty that is God.

For instance, Jami's version of the "Seduction of Yusuf and Zulaykha" (**Readings 9.7a** and **9.7b**), a story celebrated by several Sufi writers, retells, in elaborate fashion, the biblical story of Joseph and the wife of Potiphar, Zuleika, which is also included in the Qur'an as the story of Yusuf and Zulaykha. Yusuf protests that his love is not sexual but divinely inspired:

Fig. 9.18 *Dervishes Dancing*, from a copy of *Sessions of the Lovers*, from Turkey. **16th century.** Illuminated manuscript, approx. 9" × 6". Bodleian Library, Oxford. The Sufi's goal was to achieve direct contact with God through mystical trance, and the ecstatic whirling dance could, the Sufis believed, induce such a trance. In this miniature, the dervishes dance to the accompaniment of flutes and tambourines.

READING 9.7a

from Jami, "Seduction of Yusuf and Zulaykha" (1483)

I would not passion's victim be,
And turned from sin—but not from thee.
My love was pure, no plant of earth
From my rapt being sprung to birth:
I loved as angels might adore. …

His pure adoration leads Yusuf to understand "the great lesson"—"That vice and bliss are wide apart." His love for his lady leads him to the love of God.

In Jami's poem, Zulaykha builds a palace with seven rooms, each decorated with an erotic painting of herself and Yusuf, in order to seduce the beautiful youth. As she leads the unsuspecting Yusuf from room to room, she locks each door behind her. When they reach the last room, she throws herself on Yusuf, who flees as each of the seven doors miraculously opens before him. In Jami's poem, the palace and its decorations stand for the temptations of the material world with its seven climes, the habitable climatic regions of the earth (Fig. **9.19**). Yusuf's beauty, which Zulaykha mistakenly sees as physical rather than spiritual, is comparable to the beauty of God, and his faith in the all-seeing God unlocks the doors to allow his escape. Recalling Yusuf's power over her, Zulaykha then bemoans her loss:

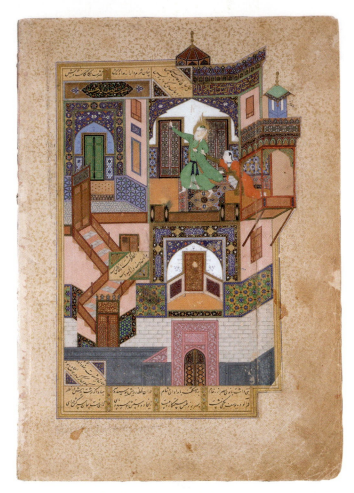

Fig. 9.19 Bihzad, *The Seduction of Yusuf,* **from a copy of Sadi's** *Bustan* **("Orchard"), prepared for Sultan Husayn Mirza at Herat, Persia (present-day Afghanistan). 1488.** Ink and color on paper, 11⅞" × 8⅔". National Library, Cairo. Bihzad is one of the most renowned illustrators of the fifteenth century. In illustrating this manuscript, he worked together with Sultan Ali Mashhadi, who was himself the greatest calligrapher of the day. The text of Sadi's version of the Yusuf story is in the cream-colored panels at the top, middle, and bottom of the page.

READING 9.7b

from Jami, "Seduction of Yusuf and Zulaykha" (1483)

Let me look back to that dark hour
That bound my spirit to thy power—
Thy grateful words, thy glance recall,
My hopes, my love—and curse them all;
Let me thy tender looks retrace,
The glories of thy heavenly face;
Thy brow, where Aden's[1] splendor lies,
And the mild luster of thine eyes:
Yet let my heart no weakness prove,
But hate thee as I once could love.
What fearful eloquence was thine,
What awful anger—just—divine!
Shuddering, I saw my heart displayed
And knew all this I should have said!
'Twas mine to shrink, withstand, in time,
For, while I sinned, I knew my crime.
O wretched, wavering heart!—as vain
Thy wild resentment as thy pain:
One thought alone expels the rest,
One sole regret distracts my breast,
O'ermastering and subduing all—
More than my crime, more than my fall:
Are not shame, fear, remorse, forgot,
In that one thought—he loves me not?

[1] **Aden:** the Garden of Eden.

Zulaykha's point of view, and, more powerfully, Yusuf's understanding of love itself, would soon make its way to Europe, particularly in the tradition of "courtly love" championed by the troubadour poets (see Chapter 10).

Rumi's poetry, especially the *Mathnavi* ("Rhymed Discourses"), an epic-length verse collection of mystical stories composed of some 27,000 verse couplets, is considered the masterwork of the Sufi tradition—"the Qur'an in Persian," Jami called it. The stories, which invariably end happily,

illustrate God's limitless mercy toward humankind, and Rumi invokes the Qur'an's message of hope repeatedly. Indeed, for him hope is virtually synonymous with faith. The stories continually cite the Qur'an and interpret it in terms of human potential for mystical union with God, a potential hinted at in physical union with a lover. This hinted potential is the subject of Rumi's collection of about 30,000 verses entitled *The Divan of Shams of Tabriz.* Rumi thought of Shams (meaning "Sun") of Tabriz as the "Divine Beloved," the physical incarnation of spiritual love. Rumi met him in 1244, and when Shams disappeared 15 months later, Rumi wrote poems describing the loss of his lover in terms of abandonment by God. Poems like "Love's Body," "Caring for My Lover," and "The Clear Bead at the Center" (see **Reading 9.8**, page 317) are at once carnal and spiritual, erotic and mystical, and they speak of the rebirth of the human spirit through love.

The Islamic Heritage

Islam is often considered outside the Western tradition, but it is a fundamental part of the Western heritage. As we have seen, Western music—indeed, the Western orchestra—originated in Muslim musical traditions. The spiritual depth of the love poem, as it comes to fruition in the work of the medieval troubadour poets and the poets of the Renaissance, was first developed in the Muslim world. Many of the decorative effects achieved in medieval architecture and design reflect the interlace and arabesques that inform Islamic architecture. See, for example, the portal of Saint Michel d'Aiguilhe, in Le-Puy-en-Venay, France (Fig. **9.20**), the first stop on a Christian pilgrimage route to Santiago de Compostela, where the body of the apostle Saint James the Greater lay at rest, a pilgrimage itself modeled in many ways on the Muslim **hajj** to Mecca.

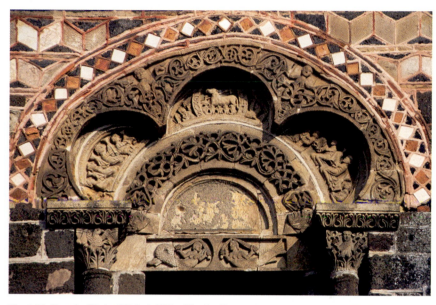

Fig. 9.20 Portal of Saint Michel d'Aiguilhe, Le-Puy-en-Venay, France. ca. 1162–80. Charles Martel stopped the Arab invasion of France at Poitiers in 792, but decorative work such as this underscores the lasting Islamic influence in Europe (see Chapter 13).

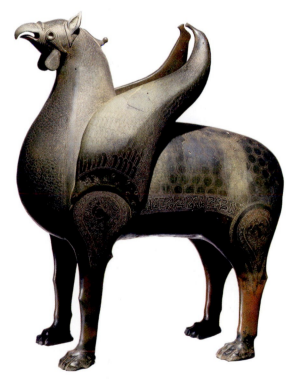

Fig. 9.21 Griffin, from the Islamic Mediterranean, probably Fatimid Egypt. 11th century. Bronze, height 3'6⅛". Museo dell'Opera del Duomo, Pisa. The griffin was moved into the museum in 1828 to protect it from the elements.

The portal incorporates the colored stonework and double arches of the mosque at Córdoba and the intricate design of a *mihrab* niche.

But in its insistence that Jesus was a "mere" prophet and not the son of God, and in its belief that the Qur'an superseded both the Hebrew and Christian Scriptures, Islam inevitably came into conflict with the Christian West. By the time that Pope Urban II (papacy 1088–99) launched the First Crusade in 1095, gathering over 100,000 people to march on Jerusalem, Islam represented the forces of darkness to European Christians. Their determination to liberate the Holy Land from Muslim domination became a key factor in the history of the late Middle Ages.

A notable symbol of this determination is an Islamic bronze griffin that, from 1100 to 1828, sat atop Pisa Cathedral, itself built to celebrate the victory in 1063 of this Italian city-state over Muslim forces in the western Mediterranean (Fig. **9.21**). Decorated with incised feathers, its back designed to suggest silk drapery, the griffin symbolized to Muslims eaglelike vigilance, lionlike courage, and, perhaps most of all, the rich history of Mesopotamia and Persia. But the Catholic Church appropriated this bronze griffin to different ends and transformed its meaning. From its perch atop Pisa Cathedral it symbolized the dual nature of Christ, his divinity (the eagle) and his humanity (the lion). The composite creature was, in the Church's mind, the image of the Christian victory over Islam. ∎

THINKING BACK

9.1 Outline the principal tenets of the Muslim faith.

According to tradition, beginning in 610 the Muslim prophet Muhammad began to recite messages from God, which he dictated to scribes who collected them to form the scriptures of Islam, the Qur'an. At the core of the Qur'an is the concept of "submission" or "surrender" to Allah, the all-merciful, all-seeing, all-powerful God. Other than the Qur'an, what other work forms the basis of Islamic faith? How is the idea of community reflected in the mosque and its attendant rituals? How is it reflected in the idea of the jihad? What are the "lesser" and "greater" forms of the jihad? What is the *shari'a*, and how would you describe traditional relations between men and women as outlined in the *shari'a*?

9.2 Explain the rapid spread of the Muslim faith.

Islam spread rapidly throughout the Middle East. It was appealing both as a religion that welcomed all converts and as a form of social organization that drew no distinction between clergy and congregation. As the center of the religious community, the mosque serves as meeting-house, courthouse, and administrative center. What role do the madrasas, or teaching colleges, built at mosques, play?

9.3 Describe Islamic culture in both Africa and Spain.

In the eighth and ninth centuries, Muslims came to dominate the trans-Saharan trade routes, and Islam became the dominant faith of North and West Africa. Muslims especially traded in salt, gold, and slaves (Muhammad had expressly authorized the practice of enslaving conquered peoples). By 1334, the Malian ruler Mansa Moussa, a devout Muslim, had built the Djingareyber Mosque in Timbuktu and led a pilgrimage to Mecca. The epic of *Sunjata*, detailing the exploits of the first Malian king, reflects this world and is still sung by Malian griots, or professional poets, to this day.

In Spain, the Umayyad caliph Abd ar-Rahman built a magnificent new mosque in Córdoba, and by the middle of the tenth century, under the leadership of Abd ar-Rahman III, Córdoba was the most important center of learning in Europe. How did the Jewish population of Spain fit into this culture? What cultural priorities are reflected in such Spanish Muslim works as the Alhambra in Granada?

9.4 Explore the importance of calligraphy in Islamic art and explain how the other arts reflect its emphasis on abstract rhythms of pattern and repetition.

Many faithful believed that Muhammad had opposed image-making in the hadith. As a result, the art of calligraphy assumed a central place in Islamic visual culture, especially the *bismillah*, consisting of the phrase "In the name of Allah, the Beneficent, Ever-Merciful," with which every pious Muslim begins any statement or activity. How does iconoclasm manifest itself in Islam? By its very emphasis on abstract rhythms of pattern and repetition, calligraphy greatly influenced music, book design, narrative, and poetry.

Traditional Arabic music is based on intonations and rhythms closely related to the inflections of words, and it uses many more pitch intervals than Western music, but how does it contribute to the development of Western music? The art of papermaking transformed Islamic culture, as the book became the prime medium of memory and Baghdad became a major publishing center. One of the most widely illustrated poems of the Middle Ages is Nezami's *Haft Paykar* ("Seven Beauties"), a romantic epic. What is the primary narrative device that it employs? How is this device central to *The Thousand and One Nights*, a prose compilation of Persian, Arabic, and Indian stories told by Scheherazade? After the fall of Baghdad to invading Mongols in 1258, book publishing moved to Persia, where we find the mystical poetry of Sufi poets such as Jami and Rumi. What is the central theme of their work, and how does it reflect larger cultural values, both secular and religious?

✓ **Study** and **review** on **MyArtsLab**

READINGS

from the Qur'an, Surah 47

The Qur'an consists of the revelations said to have been made to Muhammad and preserved in oral traditions by his followers, who used them in ritual prayers. The core of Islamic faith, they were written down and gathered into a single book in 651–52 at the order of Uthman, the third caliph, or successor to the Prophet. Divided into 114 chapters, or surahs ("units of revelation"), the Qur'an is, very often, a book of remarkable beauty, but in the surah reproduced here, it reveals itself to be less than tolerant of those who do not accept the Muslim faith.

Surah 47 Muhammad

In the name of Allah, most benevolent, ever-merciful.

1. (As for) those who disbelieve and turn away from Allah's way, He shall render their works ineffective.

2. And (as for) those who believe and do good, and believe in what has been revealed to Muhammad, and it is the very truth from their Lord, He will remove their evil from them and improve their condition.

3. That is because those who disbelieve follow falsehood, and those who believe follow the truth from their Lord; thus does Allah set forth to men their examples.

4. So when you meet in battle those who disbelieve, then 10 smite the necks until when you have overcome them, then make (them) prisoners, and afterwards either set them free as a favor or let them ransom (themselves) until the war terminates. That (shall be so); and if Allah had been pleased He would certainly have exacted what is due from them, but that He may try some of you by means of others; and (as for) those who are slain in the way of Allah, He will by no means allow their deeds to perish.

5. He will guide them and improve their condition.

6. And cause them to enter the garden which He has made 20 known to them.

7. O you who believe if you help (the cause of) Allah, He will help you and make firm your feet.

8. And (as for) those who disbelieve, for them is destruction, and He has made their deeds ineffective.

9. That is because they hated what Allah revealed, so He rendered their deeds null.

10. Have they not then journeyed in the land and seen how was the end of those before them: Allah brought down destruction upon them, and the unbelievers shall have the like of it. 30

11. That is because Allah is the Protector of those who believe, and because the unbelievers shall have no protector for them.

READING CRITICALLY

Despite its apparent intolerance for non-Muslims, this surah also contains many passages that could be called compassionate and caring. How are the two opposing sentiments reconciled?

"Tale of the Fisherman and the Genie" from *The Thousand and One Nights* (ca. 800–1300)

The Thousand and One Nights was assembled sometime between the eighth and tenth centuries from stories of Persian, Arabic, and Indian origin that had circulated orally for hundreds of years. The work itself, consisting of some 250 tales, exists in many versions—often sanitized in English translation, reducing this adult masterpiece to a collection of children's stories. It is a framed tale in which Scheherazade, a woman of great wit and beauty, tells a story each night to her king and husband. He is a man so obsessed with the possibility of female adultery that, until he marries Scheherazade, he has killed each of his new brides the morning after their wedding night. To forestall her own death, Scheherazade cleverly stops her stories each morning before they reach their conclusion. "The Tale of the Fisherman and the Genie," the opening of which is excerpted here, is itself a sequence of tales within a tale, mirroring the structure of the whole, as the fisherman tells his stories in order to forestall the anger of a genie.

I have heard, Oh worthy King, that there was once a poor, old Fisherman who had a wife and three children to support. Each day, it was his custom to cast his fishing-net into the ocean exactly four times, and no more. One day, at about noon, he went towards the seashore, where he set his basket down in the sand. Tucking up his shirt and plunging into the water, he cast his net and waited until it settled to the bottom of the sea. Then, he gathered the cords of the net together, and tried to haul it away. But its heaviness overpowered him, and no matter how hard he tried, he could not pull it up. So he carried the 10 ends of the cords to the shore, drove a stake into the sand, and bound the cords tightly to the stake. Then he stripped his clothes from his body and dove into the water, working hard until he finally raised the net from the sea.

Rejoicing, he put his clothes back on and went to examine the net and found a dead jackass inside of it, which had torn all the net's meshes. As he saw this, the Fisherman sadly exclaimed, "There is no majesty, and there is no might except

Allah the glorious, the great! But, well, this is a strange sort of daily bread." He paused, considering, and then murmured to himself, "Well, up and at it! I'll finish my fishing now, for I'm very sure of Allah's goodness." 20

So the Fisherman gazed at the dead ass for a moment, and then pulled it free from the netting. He wrung out the net, and spread it over the sand. Calling out "In Allah's name!" he plunged back into the sea. He cast the net a second time. …

[*He casts his net three times, pulling a large earthen pitcher out of the sea the second time, and shards of pottery and glass the third, blessing Allah each time although he catches no fish. On the fourth cast he pulls out …*] a cucumber-shaped 30 copper jar, brimming with something mysterious. The mouth of the jar was sealed with lead, and stamped with the seal of our Lord Solomon, David's son, Allah praise them! Seeing this the Fisherman rejoiced and said, "If I sell this in the brass bazaar, I could get ten golden dinars for it!" He shook the jar, and finding it heavy, murmured, "I wish I knew what was in it. I feel as if I must find out—so I'll open it and look inside, and then I'll store it in my bag, to sell at the brass market." Taking out a knife, he pried the lead until he had loosened it from the jar. He set the seal on the ground, and turned the vase 40 upside-down, shaking it and trying to pour out whatever could be inside. Surprisingly, nothing emerged, and the Fisherman stood in wonder.

But suddenly, a spiral of smoke burst from the jar, rising toward the heavens. The Fisherman marvelled as it was drawn into the air, ascending far above him. As it reached its full height, the thick, vaporous smoke condensed and formed a Genie, so huge that his head brushed the sky, and his feet touched the ground. The Genie's head curved as large as a dome; his hands dangled, big as pitchforks. His legs were long 50 as masts, his mouth as wide as a cave, his teeth like large stones, and his nostrils flared like pitchers' spouts. His eyes shone like two lamps, and his face proved fierce and threatening.

Now, when the Fisherman saw the Genie, his muscles quivered, his teeth chattered, and his throat grew too dry to swallow. Paralyzed, clenched with fear, he could do nothing.

The Genie looked at him and cried, "There is no god but *the* God, and Solomon is the prophet of God." He added, "Oh Apostle of Allah, do not slay me. Never again will I oppose you 60 or sin against you."

The Fisherman replied, "Oh Genie, did you say, 'Solomon the Apostle of Allah?' Solomon has been dead for nearly eighteen hundred years, and now we're in the last days of the world! Where have you come from? What's happened to you? Why have you been in that jar?"

When the Evil Spirit heard the Fisherman's words, he answered, "There is no god but *the* God. Be happy, Fisherman!"

"Why should I be happy?" asked the Fisherman. 70

"Because," replied the Genie, "you must die a terrible death this very hour."

"You deserve heaven's abandonment for your good tidings!" cried the Fisherman. "For what reason should you kill me? What have I done to deserve death? I, who freed you

from the jar, dragged you from the depths of the sea, and brought you up to dry land?"

"Ask me only in which way you will die, how I will slaughter you," said the Genie.

"What's my crime?" the Fisherman persisted. "Why such 80 retribution?"

"Hear my story, Oh Fisherman!" cried the Genie.

The Fisherman swiftly answered, "Tell it, but tell it briefly. My heart is in my mouth."

And so, the Genie began his tale. "I am one of the heretical Genie," he explained. "I, along with the famous Sakhr al Jinni, sinned against Solomon, David's son. After this, the Prophet Solomon sent his minister, Asaf son of Barkhiya, to seize me. This minister bound me and took me against my will, bringing me to stand before the Prophet Solomon like a supplicant. 90 When Solomon saw me, he appealed to Allah, and demanded that I embrace the True Faith and obey Allah's commands. I refused; and so he sent for this jar and imprisoned me in it, sealing it with lead and stamping it with the Most High Name. He ordered another spirit to carry me off, and cast me into the center of the ocean. I lived there for a hundred years, and during this time I said in my heart, 'I'll forever reward whoever releases me with the greatest of riches.' But an entire century passed, and when no one set me free, I began the second century saying, 'I'll reveal the secret treasures of the earth to 100 whoever will release me.' Still, no one set me free, and soon four hundred years passed. Then I said, 'I'll grant three wishes to whoever will release me.' Yet again, no one set me free. Then I became angry, so furious, I said to myself, 'From now on, I'll kill whoever releases me, and I'll let him choose what type of death he will die.' And now, as you're the one who's released me, I give you the choice of your death."

The Fisherman, hearing the words of the Genie; exclaimed, "Oh Allah! How could it be that I didn't come to free him before this? Spare my life, Genie, and Allah will spare yours; 110 don't kill me, and Allah will never send anyone to kill you!"

"There is no help for you. You must die," the Genie obstinately explained. …

As the Genie spoke, the Fisherman said to himself, "This is a Genie, but I'm a man to whom Allah has given a cunning wit. So now, as he uses his malice to destroy me, I'll use my intelligence and cunning to stop *him*." He turned to the Genie and said, "Have you really resolved to kill me?"

"Of course."

"Even so," exclaimed the Fisherman, "if I ask you a question about a certain matter, will you swear by the Most Great 120 Name, engraved on the seal-ring of Solomon, Son of David, that you'll answer it truthfully?"

The Genie trembled as he heard the Fisherman mention the Most Great Name. "Yes," he promised the Fisherman, though his mind grew troubled. "Yes, ask, but be brief."

The Fisherman said, "How did you fit into this bottle, which doesn't even look big enough to hold your hand, or even your foot? How could it have been big enough to contain all of you?" 130

"What!" replied the Genie. "You don't believe my whole body was in there?"

"No!" cried the Fisherman. "I'll never believe it until I see all of you inside of it, with my own eyes."

And then Scheherazade saw that dawn crept over the edge of the horizon, and so she stopped telling her story. But the next day, when the fourth night came, her sister said to her, "Please finish the story. None of us are sleepy." And so, Scheherazade resumed her storytelling. ...

READING CRITICALLY

In what way does the genie mirror the king in both action and attitude?

READING 9.8

from Rumi, *The Divan of Shams of Tabriz* (ca. 1250)

Jalal ad-Din Rumi was born in the Persian province of Khorasan in 1207. After the Mongol invasion of central and western Asia, he settled in Anatolia, a region of Asia Minor known as Rum (Rome in Turkish). Jalal ad-Din means, literally, "Glory of Religion." His entire name means, then, "Roman Glory of Religion." Rumi became a leader of the Sufi community, named sheik, or elder, and received the title "Mevlana," meaning "our master." He is still known by that name throughout the Middle East and India. The four poems below are from a collection of lyrics entitled *The Divan of Shams of Tabriz*, which contains about 30,000 verses celebrating the poet's physical love for Shams ad-din of Tabriz, who represented for him the physical incarnation on earth of the spiritual love of God.

Love's Body

The moon and a battalion of stars came
and the sun, a lonely horseman, dissolved.
The moon lives beyond the night, beyond the day.
What eye can see him?
The sightless eye is a minaret.
How can it make out the bird on the minaret?
Sometimes the cloud in our heart is tight
because we love the moon.
Sometimes it falls away.
When you began to love your passion died   10
and though you had a thousand things to do,
you did nothing,
but since one day granite becomes a ruby,
it isn't lazy.
If in the market of love you see decapitated heads
hanging from butcher hooks,
don't run off. Come in. Look closely.
The dead are alive again.

Caring for My Lover

Friends, last night I carefully watched my love
sleeping by a spring circled with eglantine.[1]

The houris[2] of paradise stood around him,
    their hands cupped together
between a tulip field and jasmines.
Wind tugged softly in his hair.
His curls smelled of musk and ambergris.[3]
Wind turned mad and tore the hair right off
    his face
like a flaming oil lamp in a gale.   10
From the beginning of this dream I told myself
    go slowly, wait
for the break into consciousness. Don't breathe.

The Clear Bead at the Center

The clear bead at the center changes everything.
There are no edges to my loving now.
I've heard it said there's a window that opens
from one mind to another,
but if there's no wall, there's no need
for fitting the window, or the latch.

READING CRITICALLY

Explain, in your own words, the argument of "The Clear Bead at the Center."

---

[1] **eglantine:** sweetbrier, a fragrant pink climbing rose.
[2] **houris:** beautiful virgins provided in paradise to faithful Muslims.

[3] **musk and ambergris:** perfumes.

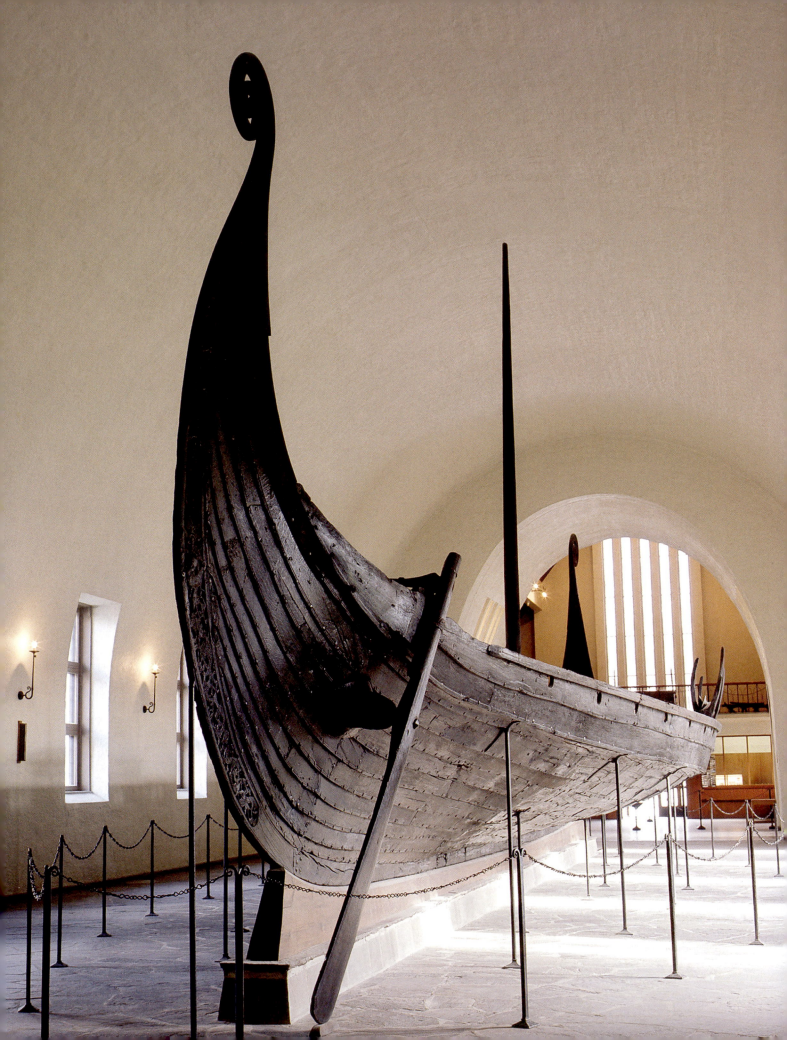

10 Fiefdom and Monastery, Pilgrimage and Crusade

The Early Medieval World in Europe

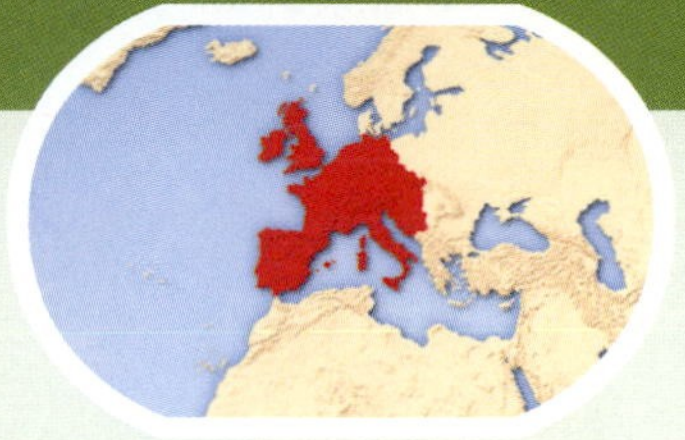

THINKING AHEAD

10.1 Describe what Anglo-Saxon art and literature tell us about Anglo-Saxon culture.

10.2 Discuss Charlemagne's impact on medieval culture and the legacy of his rule.

10.3 Define the Romanesque and its relation to both pilgrimage churches and the Cluniac abbey.

10.4 Examine the motivations for the Crusades and appraise their outcome.

10.5 Explain the courtly love tradition as it manifests itself in the literature of the period.

Sutton Hoo lies near the modern city of Ipswich, England, in the county of Suffolk, East Anglia (Map 10.1). There, a burial mound contains the remains of a wealthy and powerful Anglo-Saxon man, probably a seventh-century king. (Coins found at the site date to the late 630s.) The burial mound concealed a ship, 90 feet long and 14 feet wide, a little larger than a similar burial ship excavated in 1904 at Oseberg, just outside Oslo, Norway (Fig. 10.1). The burial ship at Sutton Hoo had been dragged up a 100-foot hill—or "hoo"—above the River Deben and laid in a trench. Midway between the ship's bow and stern, a house had been constructed. Inside the house was the coffin, accompanied by a treasure hoard of richly decorative ornaments and armor, gold coins from France, silver spoons and bowls from the eastern Mediterranean, and a wooden harp. The trench was filled in and a mound was raised over it. For 1,300 years it remained untouched, high above the Deben estuary, as if the dead warrior were standing perpetual guard over East Anglia, looking eternally out to sea.

The site was first excavated in 1939. Only two objects discovered there show any evidence of Christian culture— two silver spoons inscribed with the names Saulos and Paulos in Greek lettering. The names might refer to the biblical king Saul of the Hebrew Bible and Saint Paul of the New Testament. Christianity had, in fact, almost completely disappeared in England shortly after the Romans left in 406. Over the next 200 years, Germanic and Norse tribes—Angles, Saxons, Jutes, and Frisians—invited in as mercenaries by Romanized British leaders, began to operate on their own. Their Anglo-Saxon culture, steeped in Germanic and Norse values and traditions, soon came to dominate cultural life in Britain. Nevertheless, at the time of the Sutton Hoo burial, in the late 630s, Christianity had begun to reassert itself in England. There is some speculation that the elaborate Sutton Hoo burial ceremony, which included cremation—forbidden by Christianity—and apparent human and animal sacrifice, represented an open defiance of Christian practices.

At the time of its seventh-century burials, Sutton Hoo was, at best, a remote outpost of Anglo-Saxon culture, but no other archeological site has revealed more about the Anglo-Saxons. Whoever was buried there was a lord or chief to whom his followers owed absolute loyalty; this was the basis of the feudal societies that would later dominate European life in the Middle Ages. **Feudalism** is related to

◀ **Fig. 10.1 Burial ship, from Oseberg, Norway. ca. 800.** Wood, length 75′6″. Vikingskiphuset, Universitetets Oldsaksamling, Oslo. This ship served as a burial chamber for two women. They were laid out on separate beds in a cabin containing wooden chests (empty, but probably once filled with precious objects) and several wooden, animal-head posts.

 Listen to the chapter audio on **MyArtsLab**

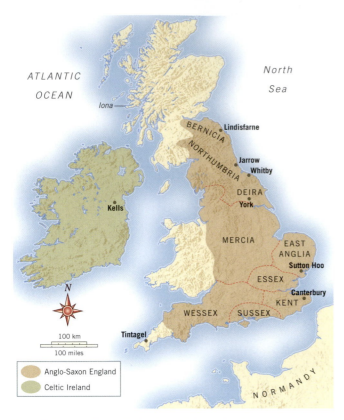

Map 10.1 Anglo-Saxon England and Celtic Ireland.

the Roman custom of patronage (see Chapter 6), under which a patron, usually a lord or nobleman, provided protection to a person who worked for him in exchange for his loyalty. In the Middle Ages, this relationship developed into an agriculturally based economic system, in which the tenant was obligated to serve the nobleman (often militarily) and pay him with goods or produce in exchange for use of a piece of land—called a **fief**—and the nobleman's protection.

The rudiments of this system were in place in sixth-century England. The Anglo-Saxons comprised only about one-tenth of a total population of roughly 1 million; the remainder were Britons. The Anglo-Saxons controlled the land while the Britons largely worked it, and the wealth the Anglo-Saxons extracted from this relationship is everywhere apparent in the treasures discovered at Sutton Hoo. The nobles in control of their various fiefdoms in turn owed allegiance to their king, who was overlord of all the fiefdoms in his kingdom. In return for their loyalty, the king rewarded his nobles with gold, weaponry, and elaborately decorated items of personal adornment, like the artifacts buried at Sutton Hoo.

When Christianity was reintroduced to Anglo-Saxon England, the Church adapted the principles of feudalism. Instead of the tenant owing allegiance to his nobleman and the nobleman to his king, all owed allegiance to the Christian God. Briton and Anglo-Saxon alike might make gifts to the Church, and in return the Church offered them not

protection, but salvation. As a result, the Church quickly became wealthy. To decorate its sanctuaries, the Church promoted the same refined and elaborate handiwork as the feudal lords had commissioned for their personal use, incorporating Christian themes and imagery into the animal and interlace styles of Germanic and Norse culture. And it acquired large parcels of property overseen by a clergy who were feudal lords themselves. These properties soon developed into large working monasteries, where like-minded individuals gathered in the pursuit of religious perfection. The monasteries in turn became great centers of learning.

These monasteries soon began to promote the idea of doing penance for one's sins by embarking on religious pilgrimages. Part of the reason that pilgrims undertook these journeys is that pilgrimage sites housed sacred **relics** (venerated objects associated with a saint or martyr), in which, they believed, the spirit and authority of the deceased continued to reside. The miraculous properties of such relics, it was thought, could result in physical as well as spiritual healing. Political and religious motives also played a role in the monasteries' promotion of the practice. The pilgrimage to Mecca had played an important role in Islamic tradition, and the economic benefits realized by that relatively remote city on the Arabian peninsula were not lost on Rome. But more important, the religious value of a Christian pilgrimage to Jerusalem—the most difficult and hence potentially most rewarding of Christian pilgrimages—demanded that the Western Church eliminate Muslim control of the region, a prospect the Church frankly relished. By 1100, thousands of pilgrims annually were making their way to Jerusalem, which Christian forces retook in 1099 in the First Crusade, and to Rome, where the remains of Saints Peter and Paul were housed. Large numbers of pilgrims traveled across Europe to Santiago de Compostela, in the northwest corner of present-day Spain, where the body of the apostle Saint James the Greater lay at rest, and in England, pilgrims would soon journey to Canterbury to worship at the shrine of Saint Thomas à Becket, the Archbishop of Canterbury, who had staunchly defended the authority of the Church over that of the English throne, resulting, in 1170, in his assassination.

This chapter outlines the rise to power of feudal society and the adaptation of feudal practices by the medieval kings and emperors and by the Christian Church. Perhaps the most important ruler to codify and adopt these practices was Charlemagne, who dreamed not only of unifying Europe under his rule, but also of unifying Church and State in a single administrative and political bureaucracy. Although Charlemagne's empire dissolved with his death in 843, subsequent rulers, such as the Ottonian kings in Germany, followed his example by building a tightly knit political bureaucracy and championing the arts. But the Church competed with the kings for the loyalty of the people, and in its architecture, in its art, and in the music of its liturgy, the Church sought to appeal to the emotions of the people, calling on them to reject the worldly aspirations of the court and seek the rewards of heaven.

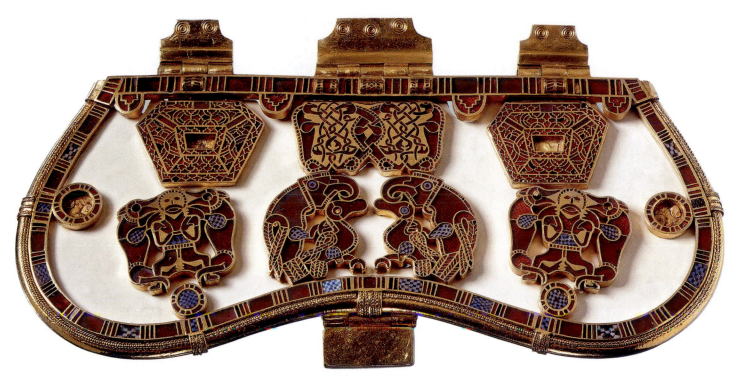

Fig. 10.2 Purse cover, from the Sutton Hoo burial ship. ca. 625. Gold with Indian garnets and cloisonné enamels, originally on an ivory or bone background (now lost), length 8". © The Trustees of the British Museum. This elaborate purse lid would have been attached to the owner's belt by hinges. In the Sutton Hoo burial mound, the purse contained gold coins and ingots.

ANGLO-SAXON ARTISTIC STYLE AND CULTURE

What can we learn about Anglo-Saxon culture from its art and literature?

A purse cover from the Sutton Hoo site (Fig. 10.2) is a fine example of the artistic style of this non-Christian Germanic culture. It is a work of **cloisonné**, a technique in which strips of gold are set on edge to form small cells. The cells are then filled with a colored enamel glass paste and fitted with thin slices of semiprecious stones (in this case, garnet). At the top of the purse cover shown here, two hexagons flank a central motif of **animal interlace**. In this design, two pairs of animals and birds, facing each other, are elongated into serpentine ribbons of decoration, a common Scandinavian motif. Below this, two Swedish hawks with curved beaks attack a pair of ducks. On each side of this design, a male figure stands between two animals. This **animal style** was used in jewelry design throughout the Germanic and Scandinavian world in the era before Christianity. Notice its symmetrical design, its combination of interlaced organic and geometric shapes, and, of course, its animal motifs. Throughout the early Middle Ages, this style was imitated in manuscripts, stone sculpture, church masonry, and wood sculpture.

In many ways, the English language was shaped by Anglo-Saxon traditions. Our days of the week are derived from the names of Saxon gods: Tuesday and Wednesday are named after two Saxon gods of war, Tiw and Woden. Thursday is named after Thor, the god of thunder, and Friday after Frigg, Woden's wife. Similarly, most English place-names have Saxon origins. *Bury* means fort, and Canterbury means the fort of the Cantii tribe. *Ings* means tribe or family; Hastings is where the family of chief Haesta lived. *Strat* refers to a Roman road; Stratford-on-Avon designates the place where the Roman road fords the River Avon. *Chester* means Roman camp, as in Dorchester; *minster* means monastery, as in Westminster; and *ham* means home, as in Nottingham.

Society, Law, and Family Life

The survival of Anglo-Saxon names in modern English suggests the degree to which this culture dominated even medieval English life. Earlier Anglo-Saxon culture revolved around the king and his thanes (lords). The king possessed his own large estate, as did each of his thanes, and the king and his retinue moved continually among the estates of the thanes, who owed hospitality and loyalty to the throne. Aside from these few powerful persons, feudal society was composed of peasants. Some were *ceorls*, or churls, free men who owned farms of 90 to 100 acres. Others rented land

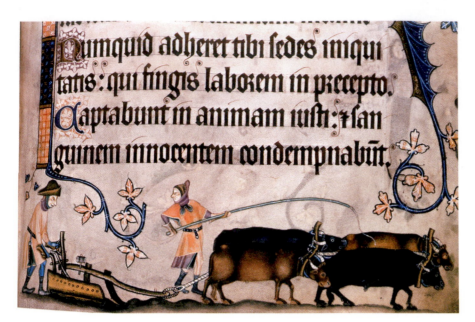

Fig. 10.3 **Farmers using a moulboard plow and harnessed oxen, from the Luttrell Psalter. ca. 1325–40.** British Library, London. Add. MS 42130. The Luttrell Psalter is a decorated (illuminated) manuscript from the Middle Ages. It was written and illuminated from about 1325 for a landowner and knight, Sir Geoffrey Luttrell of Irnham in Lincolnshire (England).

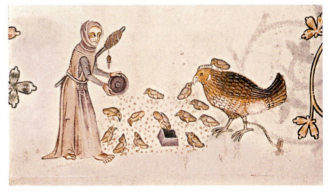

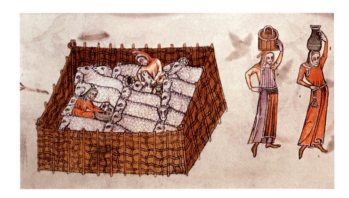

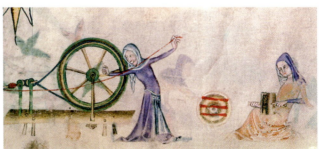

Fig. 10.4 **Details from the Luttrell Psalter. ca. 1325–40.** British Library, London. These illustrations show women at their daily tasks: carrying jugs of milk from the sheep pen, feeding the chickens, carding and spinning wool.

from the thanes, usually in lots of 20 acres. They paid their lords in goods—sheep or grain—and worked his fields two or three days per week. All employed serfs (day laborers) and thralls (slaves), often captives of wars. (Evidence suggests that by the eighth century, the Anglo-Saxons were routinely marketing slaves abroad, in France and Rome particularly.) Runaway slaves were punished by death, as were those convicted of disloyalty to their thanes.

Anglo-Saxon law was based on the idea of the *wergeld*, or "life-price" of an individual. A thane's value was roughly six times that of a churl, and a thrall had no value at all. If a thane were killed (or injured), his family (or in the case of injury, he himself) was entitled to be compensated at the highest fixed rate. But a thane could kill or injure a thrall with no *wergeld* due at all. The *wergeld* for men and women was identical, although a pregnant woman was worth as much as three times the usual rate, and a woman's potential as a bearer of children could raise her value even if she were not pregnant.

The medieval fief averaged from 3,000 to 5,000 acres and included one or more manor houses occupied by the lord. The manor house was surrounded by a small village that included as many as 50 families, a common mill, a wine press, an oven, and a church. Surrounding the village were fields and pasture. Oats, corn, barley, wheat, and rye were the largest crops, and over time, serfs developed the heavy-wheeled plow for cultivating sandy soil and the moulboard plow for plowing clay soils. The tandem four-oxen harness helped them in their work (Fig. **10.3**). They also learned to offset soil depletion by crop rotation, allowing one-third of their fields to lie fallow each year to recover their fertility.

They made beer from barley and kept pigs, cattle, goats, and sheep.

Anglo-Saxon law provided women with considerable legal status, including the right to own property and the right to sell it or even give it away without male consent. They could act in their own defense in a court of law and testify to another person's truthfulness, male or female. Women could not be forced to marry against their will, nor could they be sold for money. Most of these rights would be lost after the 1066 invasion of England by the Normans, who believed that in marrying a woman they acquired her property as well. Under the Normans, women themselves became property; their function was to serve their husbands.

Family life in Anglo-Saxon England consisted largely of work, though there seems to have been a clear division of labor between men and women. In Anglo-Saxon wills, the male line was referred to as the *wœpnedhealf*, "weapon half" or *sperehealf*, "spear half," and the female line the *wifhealf*, "wife half" or *spinlhealf*, "spindle half." Whether this division of labor between warrior and housekeeper extended into the peasant classes is debatable. It seems likely that among the lower classes, all household members worked in the fields, although food preparation and cloth-making remained women's work as well (Fig. **10.4**). In fact, the Anglo-Saxon *lorg*, or weaver's beam, later known as the distaff, became the universal symbol of women's side of the family.

Beowulf, the Oldest English Epic Poem

This rigidly hierarchical society is celebrated in the oldest English epic poem, *Beowulf*. In the poem, a young hero, Beowulf, comes from afar to rid a community of monsters that have been ravaging it. A treasure very much like that found in the Sutton Hoo ship burial is described just 26 lines into the poem, when the death of the Danish king Shild is described (**Reading 10.1a**).

READING 10.1a

Beowulf, trans. Burton Raffel

When his time was come the old king died,
Still strong but called to the Lord's hands.
His comrades carried him down to the shore,
Bore him as their leader had asked, their lord
And companion, while words could move on his tongue.
Shild's reign had been long; he'd ruled them well.
There in the harbor was a ring-prowed fighting
Ship, its timbers icy, waiting,
And there they brought the belovèd body
Of their ring-giving lord, and laid him near
The mast. Next to that noble corpse
They heaped up treasures, jeweled helmets,
Hooked swords and coats of mail, armor
Carried from the ends of the earth: no ship
Had ever sailed so brightly fitted,

No king sent forth more deeply mourned.
Forced to set him adrift, floating
As far as the tide might run, they refused
To give him less from their hordes of gold
Than those who'd shipped him away, an orphan
And a beggar, to cross the waves alone.
High up over his head they flew
His shining banner, then sadly let
The water pull at the ship, watched it
Slowly sliding to where neither rulers
Nor heroes nor anyone can say whose hands
Opened to take that motionless cargo.

The ship described here probably looked very much like the one excavated in 1904 from Oseberg, just outside Oslo, Norway (see Fig. 10.1). Its prow rises to a spiral that corresponds to the "ring-prowed fighting ship" described above. A thick layer of blue clay, nearly impenetrable by water or air and topped with turf, preserved the ship and the other objects of wood, leather, and textiles discovered in it. As *Beowulf* suggests ("Nor heroes nor anyone can say whose hands / Opened to take that motionless cargo"), it seems likely that burial mounds were commonly looted and that the Oseberg mound was plundered in ancient times. No jewelry, gold, or silver was found in the grave.

The findings at Sutton Hoo and Oseberg suggest that *Beowulf* accurately reflects many aspects of life in the northern climates of Europe in the Middle Ages. The poem was composed in Anglo-Saxon, or Old English, sometime between 700 and 1000 CE, handed down first as an oral narrative and later transcribed. Its 3,000 lines represent a language that predates the merging of French and English tongues after 1066, when William the Conqueror, a Norman duke, invaded England. The poem survived in a unique tenth-century manuscript, copied from an earlier manuscript and itself badly damaged by fire in the eighteenth century. It owes its current reputation largely to J.R.R. Tolkien, author of *The Lord of the Rings*, who in the 1930s argued for the poem's literary value. The source of Tolkien's attraction to the poem will be obvious to anyone who knows his own great trilogy.

Beowulf is an English poem, but the events it describes take place in Scandinavia. One of its most notable literary features, common to Old English literature, is its reliance on compound phrases, or **kennings**, substituted for the usual name of a person or thing. Consider, for instance, the following line:

Hwæt we Gar-Dena in gear-dagum
Hear me! We've heard of Danish heroes,

The translation's use of the past tense—"We've heard"—appears in the original as the kenning *gear-dagum*, which literally means "year-days." *Gar-Dena*, rendered here as "Danish heroes," is literally "Spear-Danes," implying their warrior attributes. The poet calls the sea the *fifelstréam*, literally the "sea-monster stream," or "whale-path," and the king, the "ring-giver." A particularly poetic example is *beado-leoma*, "battle-light," referring to a flashing sword. In a sense, then, these compound phrases are metaphoric riddles that context helps to explain. *Beowulf* contains many such compounds that occur only once in all Anglo-Saxon literature—*hapax legomena*, as they are called, literally, "said or counted once"—and context is our only clue to their meaning.

The poem opens with Beowulf's arrival among the Danes to rid them of the monster Grendel. The monsters in the poem, it becomes clear, are in some sense metaphors for fate and the destructive forces of nature. When Beowulf and his troops meet a Dane guarding the coast, they are undaunted by the prospect of confronting these forces (**Reading 10.1b**):

READING 10.1b

***Beowulf*, trans. Burton Raffel**

... "You know (if we've heard
The truth, and been told honestly) that your country
Is cursed with some strange, vicious creature [Grendel]
That hunts only at night and that no one
Has seen. It's said, watchman, that he has slaughtered
Your people, brought terror to the darkness. Perhaps
Hrothgar can hunt, here in my heart,
For some way to drive this devil out—
If anything will ever end the evils
Afflicting your wise and famous lord.
Here he can cool his burning sorrow.
Or else he may see his suffering go on
Forever, for as long as Herot towers
High on your hills."
    The mounted officer
Answered him bluntly, the brave watchman:
    "A soldier should know the difference between words
And deeds, and keep that knowledge clear
In his brain. I believe your words, I trust in
Your friendship. Go forward, weapons and armor
And all, on into Denmark. I'll guide you
Myself ..."
    Then they moved on. Their boat lay moored,
Tied tight to its anchor. Glittering at the top
Of their golden helmets wild boar heads gleamed,
Shining decorations, swinging as they marched,
Erect like guards, like sentinels, as though ready
To fight. They marched, Beowulf and his men
And their guide, until they could see the gables
Of Herot, covered with hammered gold
And glowing in the sun—that most famous of all dwellings,
Towering majestic, its glittering roofs
Visible far across the land.

The Danish king Hrothgar is described elsewhere in *Beowulf* as "the best of Denmark's rulers, the wisest ring-giver Danish warriors had ever known." Like all Anglo-Saxon rulers, he relied on his wealth to guarantee the loyalty of his followers—and, interestingly, a gold boar-shaped helmet crest like the ones described above has been unearthed in England (Fig. **10.5**).

Beowulf keeps his word and kills Grendel. Subsequently, Grendel's mother attacks in an even more fearsome battle, which again Beowulf wins. But Hrothgar reminds him of life's fragility (**Reading 10.1c**):

READING 10.1c

***Beowulf*, trans. Burton Raffel**

Belovèd Beowulf, best of warriors, ...
Push away pride! Your strength, your power,
Are yours for how many years? Soon
You'll return them where they came from, sickness
        or a sword's edge
Will end them, or a grasping fire, or the flight
Of a spear, or surging waves, or a knife's
Bite, or the terror of old age, or your eyes
Darkening over. It will come, death
Comes faster than you think, no one can flee it.

With these words in mind, Beowulf returns home to Sweden with his men and rules well, but 50 years later, he meets the dragon, who teaches him Hrothgar's lesson. Resigned to the fact that only he of all warriors can defeat the dragon that is menacing his loyal people, he exhibits the courage and loyalty to his vassals that define the warrior's world in the Middle Ages (**Reading 10.1d**).

READING 10.1d

***Beowulf*, trans. Burton Raffel**

    "I'd use no sword, no weapon, if this beast
Could be killed without it, crushed to death
Like Grendel, gripped in my hands and torn
Limb from limb. But his breath will be burning
Hot, poison will pour from his tongue.
I feel no shame, with shield and sword
And armor, against this monster: when he comes to me
I mean to stand, not run from his shooting
Flames, stand till fate decides
Which of us wins. ..."
    Then Beowulf rose, still brave, still strong,
And with his shield at his side, and a mail shirt
        on his breast,
Strode calmly, confidently, toward the tower, under
The rocky cliffs: no coward could have walked there!
And then he who'd endured dozens of desperate
Battles, who'd stood boldly while swords and shields
Clashed, the best of kings, saw
Huge stone arches and felt the heat
Of the dragon's breath, flooding down
Through the hidden entrance, too hot for anyone
To stand, a streaming current of fire
And smoke that blocked all passage. And the Geats'
Lord and leader, angry, lowered
His sword and roared out a battle cry,

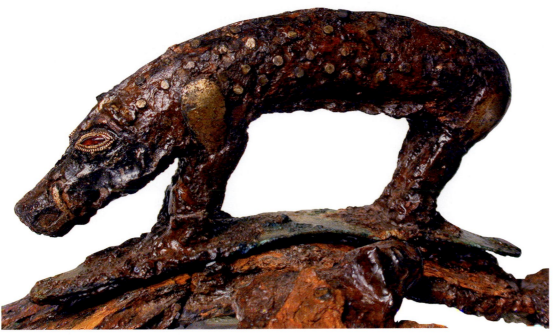

Fig. 10.5 Crest of the Benty Grange Helmet, Derbyshire. Late 7th century. Hollow bronze, approx. length of crest 3½". Courtesy of Sheffield Galleries & Museums Trust. Boar-crested helmets such as this are described in *Beowulf*. The boar evidently symbolized both ferocity and courage.

A call so loud and clear that it reached through
The hoary rock, hung in the dragon's
Ear. The beast rose, angry,
Knowing a man had come—and then nothing
But war could have followed. Its breath came first,
A steaming cloud pouring from the stone,
Then the earth itself shook. Beowulf
Swung his shield into place, held it
In front of him, facing the entrance. The dragon
Coiled and uncoiled, its heart urging it
Into battle. Beowulf's ancient sword
Was waiting, unsheathed, his sharp and gleaming
Blade. The beast came closer; both of them
Were ready, each set on slaughter. …
And for the first time in his life that famous prince
Fought with fate against him, with glory
Denied him. …
And the Geats' ring-giver did not boast of glorious
Victories in other wars: his weapon
Had failed him, deserted him, now when he needed it
Most, that excellent sword. Edgetho's
Famous son stared at death,
Unwilling to leave this world, to exchange it
For a dwelling in some distant place—a journey
Into darkness that all men must make, as death
Ends their few brief hours on earth.

Some have interpreted the poem as a Christian allegory, but these last lines suggest otherwise. And although Hrothgar does indeed exclaim "let God be thanked!" after Beowulf kills Grendel, adding that "the Almighty makes miracles / When He pleases," there is nothing in the poem to suggest that this is the Christian God. There are no overtly Christian references in the work. If, at the beginning of the poem, Shild is "called to the Lord's hands," it is also true that no one "can say whose hands / Opened to take" him. The poem teaches its audience that power, strength, fame, and life itself are fleeting—a theme consonant with Christian values, but by no means necessarily Christian. And although Beowulf, in his arguably foolhardy courage at the end of the poem, displays a Christ-like willingness to sacrifice himself for the greater good, the honor and courage he exhibits are fully in keeping with the values of feudal warrior culture.

The Merging of Pagan and Christian Styles

Whatever *Beowulf*'s relation to Christian tradition, it is easy to see how the poem might have been read, even in its own time, in Christian terms. Other clearly Christian poems survive from the era, among them *The Dream of the Rood*, in which a poet recounts his dream of a conversation with the wooden cross (the *rood*) upon which Jesus was crucified. Jesus is portrayed as if he were a Germanic king willing to die, like Beowulf, for the greater good. Another is the short poem known as *Caedmon's Hymn*, written by the Anglo-Saxon monk, Caedmon, probably in the 670s or 680s (**Reading 10.2**). It is the only surviving text of what was reportedly a large body of vernacular religious poetry by Caedmon. Tradition holds that the monk was unable to sing, but one night he heard himself singing his poem in a dream, and he miraculously awoke with the ability to sing it. So that you can see how remote the Anglo-Saxon is from the English translation, here is the original text following the translation.

The poem makes traditional use of kennings—*modgidanc*, "mind-plans," for instance, means wisdom. But perhaps what is most notable is that Caedmon's word for "Lord," *dryctin*, is the West Saxon version of the secular and military Germanic word, *truhtin*, "warlord." In Caedmon's use of this word we see the merging of Christian and pagan traditions.

Caedmon's Hymn is the product of a gradual re-Christianization of the British Isles that had begun in the fifth century. After the Romans withdrew from Britain in 406, Christianity had survived only in the westernmost reaches of the British Isles—in Cornwall, in Wales, and in Ireland, where Saint Patrick had converted the population between his arrival in 432 and his death in 461. Around 563, an Irish monk, Columba, founded a monastery on the Scottish island of Iona. He traveled widely through Scotland and converted many northern Picts, a Scottish tribe, to Christianity. In about 635, almost simultaneous with the pagan burial at Sutton Hoo, in which only a few if any Christian artifacts were discovered, a monk from Iona built another monastery at Lindisfarne, an island off the coast of Northumbria in northeast England. The "re-Christianization" of Britain was under way.

The Celtic Christian Church differed from Roman Christianity in several important ways. It celebrated Easter on the vernal equinox and believed that Mary, mother of Jesus, was exempt from original sin. It invented private confession. The office of bishop was a ceremonial position, and authority rested instead with abbots and abbesses, giving women an important role in the Church. And the Celtic cross is itself unique, symmetrical and superimposed upon a circle.

These differences would later cause considerable difficulty, but meanwhile, in 597, Pope Gregory I (papacy 590–604) sent a mission to England of 40 monks, headed by the Benedictine prior Augustine (d. 604)—not the same Augustine who had written *Confessions* and *The City of God*—to convert the pagan Anglo-Saxons. Augustine met with the Anglo-Saxon king Aethelberht (r. 560–616) on the island of Thanet, in Kent. The encounter is described by the eighth-century historian Bede (ca. 672–735) in his *History of the English Church and People*, written in 731:

> After some days, the king came to the island and, sitting down in the open air, summoned Augustine and his companions to an audience. But he took precautions that they should not approach him in a house; for he held an ancient superstition that, if they were practicers of magic, they

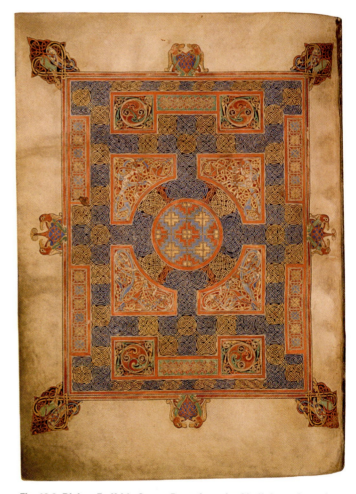

Fig. 10.6 Bishop Eadfrith, Carpet Page, from the *Lindisfarne Gospels*, Northumbria, England. ca. 698. Tempera on vellum, 13½" × 9¾". British Library, London. An inscription on the manuscript identifies Eadfrith as its scribe and decorator, Ethelwald as its binder, Billfrith as the monk who adorned it with gems, and Aldred as its translator into Anglo-Saxon: "Thou living God be mindful of Eadfrith, Ethelwald, Billfrith, and Aldred a sinner; these four have, with God's help, been engaged upon this book."

🔎 **View** the Closer Look for the Carpet Page from the *Lindisfarne Gospels* on **MyArtsLab** might have opportunity to deceive and master him. But the monks were endowed with power from God, not from the devil, and approached the king carrying a silver cross as their standard and the likeness of our Lord and Saviour painted on a board.

The story narrates the confrontation, in other words, of two distinct styles of thought and art—the animal style, with which Aethelberht was at home, and the Christian icon (see Chapter 8); pagan superstition and Christian faith; an oral, illiterate culture and a text-based one. Although Aethelberht was slow to convert, he allowed Augustine to build a cathedral at Canterbury on the site of an old Roman church and, soon after, a church in London dedicated to Saint Paul.

Manuscript Illustration: Blending of Anglo-Saxon and Christian Traditions

In 601, Gregory sent Augustine a letter urging him not to eliminate pagan traditions overnight, but to incorporate them into Christian practice: "For it is certainly impossible to eradicate all errors from obstinate minds at one stroke, and whoever wishes to climb a mountain top climbs gradually step by step, and not in one leap." This is one reason that the basic elements of the animal style, evident in the purse cover from Sutton Hoo (see Fig. 10.2), appear in a manuscript page from the *Lindisfarne Gospels*, designed by Bishop Eadfrith of Lindisfarne in 698 (Fig. **10.6**). Notice particularly how the geometric grids in the border decoration of the purse cover are elaborated in the central circle of the Lindisfarne **carpet page** (a descriptive term, not used in the Middle Ages, that refers to the resemblance between such pages and Turkish or Islamic carpets). The animal interlace of the purse cover reappears in the corner designs that frame the central circle of the carpet page, where two birds face outward and two inward. And the beasts that turn to face one another in the middle of the purse cover are echoed in the border figures of the carpet page, top and bottom, left and right. The pre-Christian decorative vocabulary of the Sutton Hoo treasure, created to honor a pagan king, has been transformed to honor the Christian conception of God.

This carpet page is an example of a Celtic cross. Legend has it that while preaching to a group of the soon-to-be converted, Saint Patrick had been shown an ancient standing stone monument with a circle carved onto it, symbolic, he was told, of the moon goddess. Patrick reportedly made the mark of a Latin cross through the circle and blessed the stone, thereby making the first Celtic cross. The story is probably only a legend—the circle with a cross through it antedates

Patrick's arrival in Ireland, where it probably symbolized, in pagan culture, the sun and moon, male and female, unity and balance in all things—but the legend speaks to the *syncretism* (the combining of different practices and principles) of the age.

The syncretic style of art that flourished in England and Ireland during the early Middle Ages is called *Hiberno-Saxon* (*Hibernia* is the Latin name for Ireland). Hiberno-Saxon manuscript illustration is notable particularly for its unification of Anglo-Saxon visual culture with the textual tradition of Christianity. In the monastic *scriptoria* (singular *scriptorium*)—the halls in which monks worked to copy and decorate biblical texts—artists soon began to decorate the letterforms themselves, creating elaborate capitals at the beginning of important sections of a document. One of the most beautiful capitals is a page from the *Book of Kells*, made at Iona in the late eighth century (Fig. **10.7**). The basis of the design consists of the Greek letters *chi*, *rho*, and *iota* (*X*,

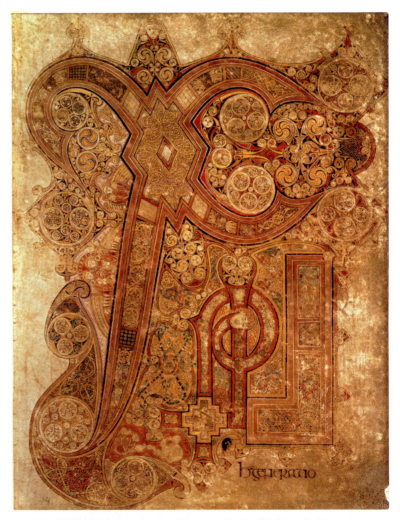

Fig. 10.7 *Chi Rho Iota* page, *Book of Matthew*, *Book of Kells*, **probably made at Iona, Scotland. Late 8th or early 9th century.** Tempera on vellum, 13″ × 9½″. Trinity College Library, Dublin. MS 58 (A.1.6.), fol. 34v. While the abbreviation for *Christi—XPI* or *Chri*—dominates the page, the remainder of the verse from Matthew is at the bottom right. *Autem* appears as an abbreviation resembling the letter *h*, followed by *generatio*, which is fully written out. So common were abbreviations in manuscript illumination, saving both time and space, that the scribes were often given the title of official court "abbreviator."

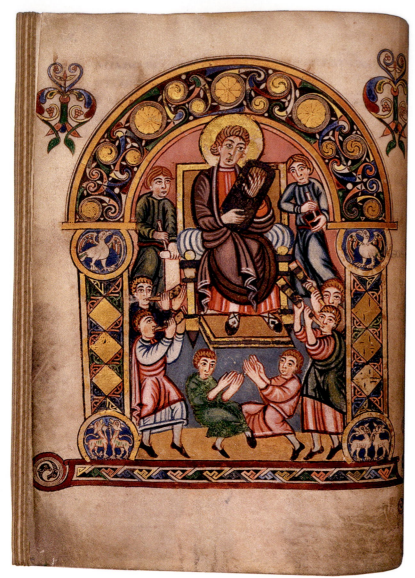

Fig. 10.8 Page with *David and Court Musicians*, now fol. 30b, but likely once the frontispiece of the *Vespasian Psalter*, Canterbury, England. First half of 8th century. British Library, MS Cotton Vespasian A.i. A psalter is a book of psalms. One of the most interesting aspects of this illustration is that it suggests that instrumental music may have played a role in Christian liturgy long before the twelfth century, when instrumentation is usually thought to have been introduced.

thane, to God. They could not offer gold, or material wealth, but only salvation, or spiritual fulfillment. They had to substitute for the great treasure at Sutton Hoo the more subtle treasures of faith and hope. The missionaries' tactic was simple—they bathed the spiritual in material splendor. They illuminated their manuscripts with a rich decorative vocabulary. They adorned Christianity in gold and silver, jewels and enamel, and placed it within an architecture of the most magnificent kind. And they transplanted pagan celebrations to the context of the Christian worship service.

A manuscript page probably created at Canterbury in the first half of the eighth century is revealing on this last point (Fig. **10.8**). It depicts an enthroned David, author of the Psalms, surrounded by court musicians. The scene could as easily illustrate an episode in *Beowulf* when a great celebration takes place in Hrothgar's hall after Beowulf defeats the monster Grendel:

> Hrothgar's hall resounded with the harp's
> High call, with songs and laughter and the telling
> Of tales, stories sung by the court
> Poet as the joyful Danes drank
> And listened, seated along their mead-benches.
>
> *Beowulf*, lines 1063–67

David, indeed, is a Judeo-Christian version of "the king's poet," only his king is the Christian God. More to the point, the harp that David plays in the manuscript illustration is very like the six-stringed wooden harp discovered at Sutton Hoo. As the animal-style frames and borders of the scene suggest, this is a celebration any Anglo-Saxon noble would have recognized. In the centuries to come, Christianity would create its own treasure trove, its own celebratory music, its own great halls (the cathedrals), and its own armored warriors fighting their own heroic battles (the Crusades). Beowulf's Grendel would become the infidel Muslim, and his king, his Lord God.

CAROLINGIAN CULTURE AND THE FRANKISH KINGS

How did Charlemagne change medieval culture and what was his legacy to the Frankish kings?

Although England was slow to Christianize, the European continent was not. Christianity was firmly established in 732, at Poitiers, France, just south of Tours in the

P, and *I*, or *chri*), an abbreviation of *Christi*. In this instance, the text begins *Christi autem generatio*, "Now this is how the birth of Jesus Christ came about," quoting Matthew 1:18. The dominant letterform is *chi*, a giant unbalanced X much larger on the left than on the right. Below the right side of the *chi* is *rho*, which curves around and ends with the head of a red-haired youth, possibly a depiction of Christ, which also dots the *I*. Not long after Ionan monks completed this manuscript, Vikings began to threaten the Scottish coast, and the monks retreated to Kells in the interior of Ireland. So great was the renown of the book they had created that in 1006 it was referred to as "the chief relic of the Western world."

The task of Christian missionaries in England was to transfer the allegiance of the people from their king, or

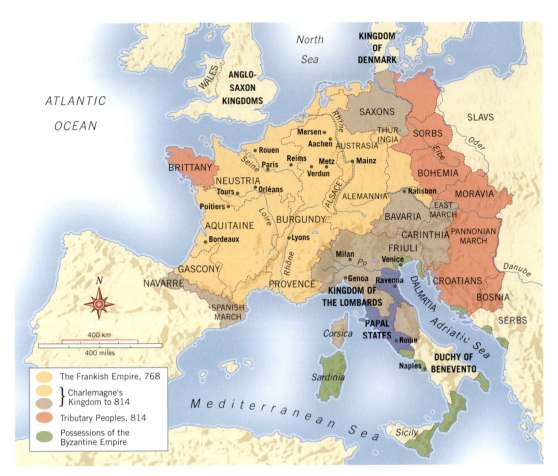

Map 10.2 The empire of Charlemagne to 814.

Loire Valley. There Charles Martel, king of the Franks, defeated the advancing Muslim army, which had entered Spain in 711 and had been pushing northward ever since. The Arabs retreated south, beyond the Pyrenees, and settled into Spain. The Franks were one of many Germanic tribes—like the Angles and Saxons in England—that had moved westward beginning in the fourth century CE. Most of these tribes adopted most of the Christian beliefs of the Roman culture they conquered, most notably the Ostrogoths in Italy, the Visigoths in southern Gaul (France) and Spain, the Vandals in North Africa, and the Franks, who controlled most of present-day France. Unlike the other Germanic tribes, the Franks were Orthodox, or Catholic, Christians, the result of the conversion in 496 of Clovis (ca. 466–511). Clovis was the founder of the first Frankish dynasty, the Merovingians. Within a hundred years, the Franks would come to control most of western Europe.

During the Merovingian era, the Franks attempted to establish order across a broad area that included three major regions: Neustria (western France), Austrasia (roughly comparable to central Germany), and Burgundy (Map **10.2**). They did this by making pacts with the local noble landowners and creating a new royal office, the count. Frankish kings gave land to the counts in return for their loyalty. But by the seventh century, counts and noblemen alike ruled their small territories like petty tyrants, paying little or no heed to the king. Real power rested instead with the head of each of the three regions, who held the office of mayor of the palace.

With the rise of Pepin I (d. 639) to the position of mayor of the palace in Austrasia, the family which would come to be known as the Carolingians gradually assumed complete power. Pepin II's son, Charles Martel (r. 714–41), not only defeated the Muslim army at Poitiers, but also bestowed more property on already landed gentry. These parcels of land, or fiefdoms, were confiscated from the Church, which depended on the Franks for protection and so had little choice in the matter.

In 751, with the pope's blessing, the Carolingian nobility elected Martel's son, Pepin the Short, as their king. Three years later, a new pope traveled to Saint-Denis, near Paris, where he anointed Pepin protector of the Church and the Carolingians "kings by the grace of God." In return, Pepin led an army south into Italy and crushed the Lombards, a Germanic people who had invaded Italy nearly 200 years earlier and established a kingdom in the Po Valley. Pepin turned the territory over to the pope; the land became known as the Papal States.

Pepin the Short's son, Charlemagne, "Charles the Great" (r. 768–814), had even greater imperial ambitions than his

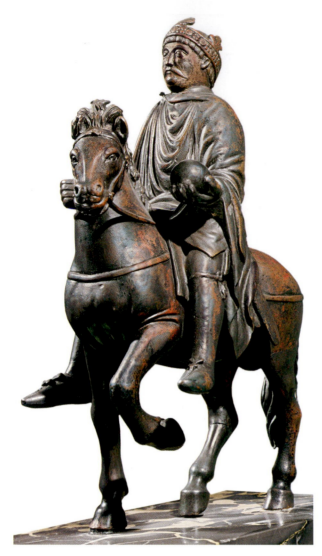

Fig. 10.9 Equestrian statue of Charlemagne. Early 9th century. Bronze with traces of gilt, height 9½". Musée du Louvre, Paris. The real Charlemagne stood 6'3½" tall, remarkably tall for the time.

court to court and performed ***chansons de geste*** ("songs of heroic deeds"). The oldest of these, and the most famous, is the *Song of Roland*, a poem built around a kernel of historical truth transformed into legend and eventually embellished into an epic. Four thousand lines long, composed of ten-syllable lines grouped in stanzas, it was transmitted orally for three centuries and finally written down in about 1100, by which time the story of a military defeat of little consequence had become an epic drama of ideological importance. The *jongleurs* sang the poem accompanied by a lyre. The only surviving musical notations to the poem are the letters *AOI* that end some verses. The exact meaning of this phrase is unclear, but it probably indicates a musical refrain, repeated throughout the performance. Most likely, the poem was sung in a **syllabic** setting, one note per syllable, in the manner of most folk songs even today. Its melody was probably also **strophic**—that is, the same music repeated for each stanza of the poem.

The *Song of Roland* tells the story of an event that occurred in 778, when Charlemagne's rear guard, led by his nephew Roland, Roland's friend Oliver, and other peers, was ambushed by Muslim forces as Charlemagne's army returned from his invasion of Spain. (In fact, it was Basque Christians who ambushed Charlemagne, and he had actually been invited into Spain by Muslim Saracens to help them fight other Muslims. However, over time, the story's villains were transformed from Basque Christians into Muslims for political and propagandistic purposes, as armies were organized to fight in the Middle East for the liberation of Jerusalem from Islam.)

The story is a simple one: The heroic Roland's army is betrayed by Ganelon, who tells the Saracen Muslim army of Roland's route through Roncevaux, where his 20,000 soldiers are attacked by 400,000 Muslims. Roland sounds his ivory horn, alerting Charlemagne to the Saracen presence, but by then the Frankish guard has been defeated. Discovering Roland and his army dead, Charlemagne executes the treacherous Ganelon, and an epic battle between Charlemagne and the Muslims ensues. Charlemagne is victorious—but not without divine intervention. Charlemagne's prayer keeps the sun from setting, allowing his army time to defeat the Saracens.

Roland as the Ideal Feudal Hero The poem embodies the values of feudalism, celebrating courage and loyalty to one's ruler above all else, in this case Roland's loyalty to Charlemagne. Although the feudal obligation of the vassal to his lord had long been established in Germanic culture—among the Anglo-Saxons, for instance—its purest form was probably Carolingian. Roland is an ideal feudal hero, courageous and loyal, but he possesses—or is possessed by—a sense of pride that inevitably leads to his demise, just as Beowulf's self-confidence leads to his. In the following reading (**Reading 10.3**), Roland's companion, Oliver, counsels Roland that the Muslim (Saracen) army is so great that he ought to use his horn, Oliphant, to call Charlemagne to help him, but Roland's pride prevails.

father (Fig. **10.9**). (It is for him that historians have labeled this the Carolingian era, from *Carolus*, Latin for Charles.) Charlemagne brought one after another pagan tribe to submission, forcing them to give up their brand of Christianity and submit to Rome's Nicene Creed. Charlemagne's kingdom grew to include all of modern-day France, Holland, Belgium, Switzerland, almost all of Germany, northern Italy and Corsica, and Navarre, in northern Spain. Even larger areas paid him tribute. In return for his Christianization of this vast area, Pope Leo III crowned him emperor on Christmas Day, 800, creating what would later be known as the Holy Roman Empire.

The *Song of Roland*: Feudal and Chivalric Values

Charlemagne's military might was the stuff of legend. For centuries after his rule, tales of his exploits circulated throughout Europe in cycles of poems sung by *jongleurs*, professional entertainers or minstrels who moved from

Song of Roland

81 Count Oliver has climbed up on a hill;
From there he sees the Spanish lands below,
And Saracens assembled in great force.
Their helmets gleam with gold and precious stones,
Their shields are shining, their hauberks[1] burnished gold,
Their long sharp spears with battle flags unfurled.
He tries to see how many men there are:
Even battalions are more than he can count.
And in his heart Oliver is dismayed;
Quick as he can, he comes down from the height,
And tells the Franks what they will have to fight.

82 Oliver says, "Here come the Saracens—
A greater number no man has ever seen!
The first host carries a hundred thousand shields,
Their helms are laced, their hauberks shining white,
From straight wood handles rise ranks of burnished spears.
You'll have a battle like none on earth before!
Frenchmen, my lords, now God give you the strength
To stand your ground, and keep us from defeat."
They say, "God's curse on those who quit the field!
We're yours till death—not one of us will yield." AOI

83 Oliver says, "The pagan might is great—
It seems to me, our Franks are very few!
Roland, my friend, it's time to sound your horn;
King Charles will hear, and bring his army back."
Roland replies, "You must think I've gone mad!
In all sweet France I'd forfeit my good name!
No! I will strike great blows with Durendal,[2]
Crimson the blade up to the gilt of gold.
To those foul pagans I promise bitter woe—
They are all doomed to die at Roncevaux." AOI

84 "Roland, my friend, let the Oliphant[3] sound!
King Charles will hear it, his host will all turn back,
His valiant barons will help us in this fight."
Roland replies, "Almighty God forbid
That I bring shame upon my family,
And cause sweet France to fall into disgrace!
I'll strike that horde with my good Durendal;
My sword is ready, girdled here at my side,
And soon you'll see its keen blade dripping blood.
The Saracens will curse the evil day
They challenged us, for we will make them pay." AOI

85 "Roland, my friend, I pray you, sound your horn!
King Charlemagne, crossing the mountain pass,
Won't fail, I swear it, to bring back all his Franks."
"May God forbid!" Count Roland answers then.
"No man on earth shall have the right to say
That I for pagans sounded the Oliphant!
I will not bring my family to shame.
I'll fight this battle; my Durendal shall strike
A thousand blows and seven hundred more.

[1] **hauberks:** long coats of chain mail.
[2] **Durendal:** Roland's sword.
[3] **Oliphant:** Roland's horn, made of elephant tusk.

You'll see bright blood flow from the blade's keen steel,
We have good men; their prowess will prevail,
And not one Saracen shall live to tell the tale."

86 Oliver says, "Never would you be blamed;
I've seen the pagans, the Saracens of Spain.
They fill the valleys, cover the mountain peaks;
On every hill, and every wide spread plain,
Vast hosts assemble from that alien race;
Our company numbers but a few."
Roland replies, "The better, then, we'll fight!
If it please God and His angelic host,
I won't betray the glory of sweet France!
Better to die than learn to live with shame—
Charles loves us more as our keen swords win fame."

87 Roland is brave, and Oliver is wise;
Both are so brave men marvel at their deeds.
When they mount chargers, take up their swords and
  shields,
Not death itself could drive them from the field.
They are good men; their words are fierce and proud.

The loyalty of the Franks—and of Roland and Oliver in particular—to Charlemagne is expressed in these words, uttered by Roland a moment later:

"In his lord's service, a man must suffer pain,
Bitterest cold and burning heat endure;
He must be willing to lose his flesh and blood. …
And if I die, whoever takes my sword
Can say its master has nobly served his lord."

It is out of a sense of duty that Roland turns to face the Saracens—duty to Charlemagne, his lord, and by extension, duty to the Christian God in the battle against Islam. Roland's insistence that he "will strike great blows with Durendal" (his sword is itself a gift from Charlemagne) expresses the Christian nature of the combat. Durendal's golden hilt conceals four relics, including hairs of Saint Denis, the patron saint of France whose name the Franks shout as a battle cry. Thus, each blow is a blow for Christendom. The reward for such dutiful combat is, as he says, the love of his king. But it is also the love of the whole Christian world, demonstrated by the many visual retellings of episodes from the epic in church art and in manuscripts. Indeed, Roland ultimately sacrifices all for his king and his God. Mortally wounded in combat, he "knows that death is very near / His ears give way, he feels his brain gush out." Explicit and vivid language heightens the intensity of the moment, and the directness lends credence to characters who are otherwise reduced to stereotypes ("Roland is brave, and Oliver is wise"). But, finally, in his slow and painful death—"Count Roland feels the very grip of death / Which from his head is reaching for his heart"— he becomes a type for Jesus, sacrificing himself for all of Christendom.

The Chivalric Code The *Song of Roland* is one of the earliest expressions of feudalism's **chivalric code**. The term *chivalry* (from the French *chevalier*, "horseman") expressed the qualities of an ideal knight, and may in fact more nearly reflect the values of the eleventh century (when the poem was written down) than the eighth-century practices of Charlemagne's day. Nevertheless, something very like this set of values already exists in *Beowulf*. The chevalier was a **knight** (from the German *knecht*, "young soldier"), and he was guided by a strict, though unwritten, code of conduct: courage in battle, loyalty to his lord and peers, and a courtesy verging on reverence toward women. Although in practice these values often broke down, feudalism and chivalry were powerful mechanisms for maintaining social order and political harmony throughout medieval Europe.

Promoting Literacy

Across Europe, the Church had traditionally served as the chief guardian of culture. In its monastic centers, the Roman love of learning had been maintained, especially in the manuscripts transcribed by monastic copyists. But literacy was anything but widespread. Charlemagne sought to remedy this situation at his court at Aachen (present-day Aix-la-Chapelle), which soon attracted leading scholars and artists, whose efforts Charlemagne rewarded handsomely. Chief among these was an Englishman, perhaps even of Anglo-Saxon origin, Alcuin of York (735–804), who in 782 became head of Charlemagne's court school. One of the foremost grammarians and theologians of the period, Alcuin served as Charlemagne's personal tutor.

Alcuin's main purpose in Aachen was to create a curriculum to promote literacy that could be disseminated throughout the Carolingian Empire. Schools designed to teach children basic skills in reading and writing and some further study in the liberal arts and theology were established in Lyon, Orléans, Mainz, Tours, Laon, and Metz, which was a center for singing and liturgy (see Map 10.2). By 798, a decree from Aachen ordered prelates and country clergy throughout the Empire to start schools for children. The emphasis was on educating males. The work of the state bureaucracy would fall to them, and by receiving a Christian education, they would lead in accordance with Church principles. But there is evidence that girls, especially those of noble birth, were also admitted to the local schools created by Alcuin.

There was also a religious purpose in educating the people. Charlemagne believed that to spread the gospel, people should be able to read aloud and sing in church, to say nothing of grasping the fundamental truth believed to be revealed in the Bible. Education thus furthered the traditional role of the Church. It provided a means for the Church—and Charlemagne's state as agent of the Church—to insert itself into the lives of every individual. Alcuin published a book of Old and New Testament passages to be read during Mass, as well as a book of prayers and rites that was made obligatory for all churches in the Empire in 785. The last eight years of Alcuin's life were dedicated to producing a corrected version of the Latin Vulgate Bible that would become the standard text throughout the Middle Ages.

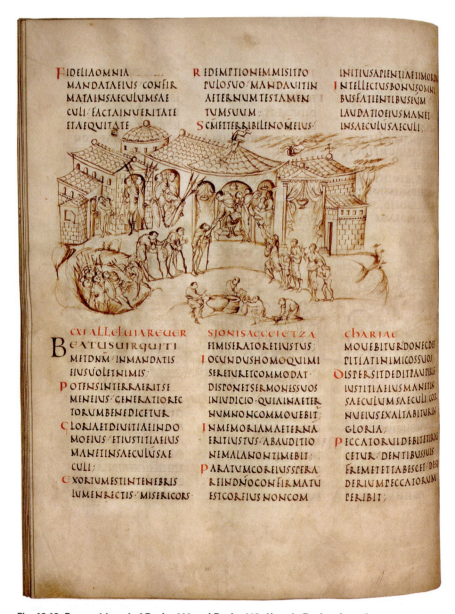

Fig. 10.10 Page with end of Psalm 111 and Psalm 112, *Utrecht Psalter*, from the Benedictine Abbey at Hautvilliers, France. ca. 825–50. Ink on vellum or parchment, 13" × 9⅛". Bibliotheek der Rijksuniversiteit, Utrecht, MS. 32, f. 65 v.

A New Style of Writing All of this was made possible by one of the less heralded but most important accomplishments of Charlemagne's court—a standardized, legible style of writing. Until this time, manuscripts had employed a Roman script made up entirely of capital letters with no space between the words, a style still evident in the famous *Utrecht Psalter*, made in Reims during Carolingian times (Fig. **10.10**). But Charlemagne, who demanded written documentation of his holdings by his vassals, required a more uniform and legible writing style, and Alcuin helped him develop it. The new style, known as *Carolingian minuscule*, was characterized by clearly formed lowercase letters, linked into individual words, with clearly delineated spaces between each word, and capital letters beginning each sentence. The page from the *Harley Psalter* (Fig. **10.11**) is an example of Carolingian minuscule, and except for the writing style, it is a direct copy of the text from the *Utrecht Psalter* shown in Figure 10.10.

The importance of this script to our cultural history cannot be overstated: It is the ancestor of the modern alphabet. All subsequent writing and type fonts derive from this model, and it made written material accessible not only to generations of learned scholars and teachers, but eventually, in the print era, to laypeople throughout Europe.

The Medieval Monastery

The monastery was a central part of Carolingian culture, arguably its most important institution. Before the Carolingian era, monastic life varied widely across Europe. In Italy, the rule of solitude (the Greek word *monos*, from which *monasticism* derives, means "alone") was barely enforced, and life in a monastery could be positively entertaining. If, in Ireland, more austere conditions prevailed, still the lively intellectual climate of the monastery attracted men and women seeking a vocation. Even from monastery to monastery, different conditions and rules prevailed.

Charlemagne imposed on all monasteries in the Frankish kingdom the rule of Benedict of Nursia, an Italian monk who had lived two centuries earlier (ca. 480–547). The Rule of Saint Benedict defined monastic life as a community of like-minded individuals, all seeking religious perfection, under the direction of an abbot elected by the monks. Monks were to live a family life in the pursuit of religious perfection. They were to possess nothing of their own, accepting worldly poverty. They were to live in one place and not wander, guaranteeing the community's stability. And they were never to marry, acknowledging their chastity. Each day was divided into eight parts, the *horarium* (from the Latin *hora*, "hour"). The *horarium* is the daily prayer schedule of liturgical praise called the **Divine Office** (the word *Office* comes from the Latin *officium*, meaning "duty"), marked by recitations of the psalms and the chanting of hymns and prayers at eight specific times of the day, from early morning until bedtime. Between services, the monks studied, worked, and ate a light breakfast and heartier dinner. They lived by the motto of their order: "Pray and work."

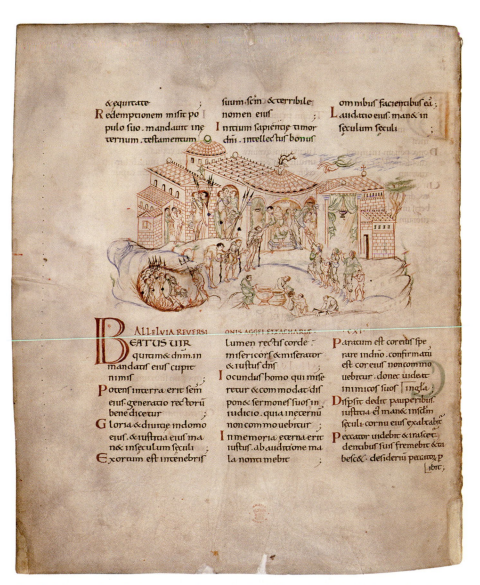

Fig. 10.11 Page in Carolingian minuscule with Psalm 111, from the *Harley Psalter*, written in Christ Church, Canterbury, England. 1010–30. Ink on vellum, 15" × 12¼". 73 fols. British Library, London. In the late tenth century, the *Utrecht Psalter* (see Fig. 10.10) made its way to Canterbury, where scribes copied it in the new writing style developed at Charlemagne's court.

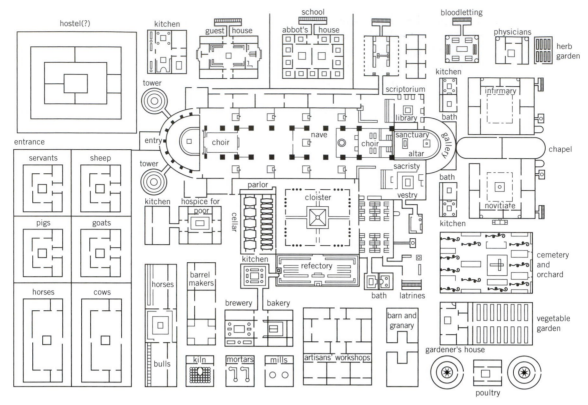

Fig. 10.12 Plan for a monastery at Saint Gall, Switzerland. ca. 820. Redrawn from an original in red ink on parchment (inscriptions translated into English from Latin). 28" × 44⅛". Stiftsbibliothek, Saint Gall.

The Ideal Monastery: Saint Gall The Swiss monastery of Saint Gall, near Lake Constance, was Charlemagne's ideal monastery (Fig. **10.12**); its functional, orderly plan was used in many Benedictine monasteries. As medieval historian Walter Horn pointed out in the 1970s, the original plan was laid out in modules, or standard units, of 2½ feet, and the entire complex was composed of multiples or parts of this standard unit. The nave and the transept of the church, each 40 feet wide, are composed of 16 modules. The area where they cross is a perfect square with 16 modules on a side. Each arm of the transept is equal to the crossing square—that is, 16 modules square. The area between the transept and the apse is also one crossing square. And the nave is 4½ crossing squares long—or 56 modules. The rest of the monastery is built on this rational and orderly plan. The length of each monk's bed was to be 2½ modules, the width of each garden path 1¼ modules, and so on. This systematic arrangement reflects an increasing tendency in medieval thinking to regard Christianity as a logical and rational philosophy of life, based on carefully constructed arguments and precise definition of parts as orderly as the "rule" of the day in the *horarium*.

Adjacent to the church, with its imposing western facade, is a **cloister**, or rectangular courtyard, typically arcaded and dedicated to contemplation and reflection. Beside it, on the east side, are the monks' dormitories, latrines, and baths, and on the west, storage cellars. To the south of the cloister is the **refectory**, or dining hall. Further to the south, and to the west and east, behind and adjacent

to the refectory are outbuildings housing all the facilities necessary to support a community of approximately 100 monks—a kitchen, a brewery, a bakery, a mill, workshops for artisans, barns for various animals, a vegetable garden (with its own gardener), and an orchard that doubles as a cemetery. Surrounding the entire complex were fields in which the brothers worked. This side of the monastery was reserved for the members of the community.

The general public could enter the north side of the monastery. Here, beside the entrance to the church, we find a hostel, or inn, for housing less-well-to-do visitors, as well as a guesthouse for nobility, and between them a special kitchen (Saint Benedict had directed that monasteries extend hospitality to all visitors). Directly to the north of the church is the monastery school, dedicated, by imperial decree, to educating the youth of local nobility. Another school, the novitiate, to the east of the church, was dedicated to the education and housing of young novices—those hoping to take vows and become brothers. In the northeast corner of the monastery was a public hospital, including an herb garden for remedies, the physician's quarters, and a facility for bloodletting—in the Middle Ages and until the nineteenth century the most common means of curing severe illness.

Women in Monastic Life Although the religious life offered women an alternative to life as housewife or worker, life in the convent or nunnery was generally available only to the daughters of aristocrats. Within the monastic system, women could achieve significant prestige. Saint Benedict himself had a sister, Scholastica (d. ca. 543), who headed a monastery not far from his own. Hilda, Abbess of Whitby (614–80), ran one of the most prominent Anglo-Saxon monasteries, a community of both monks and nuns. One of her most important acts was to host a Council at Whitby in an attempt to reconcile Celtic and Latin factions of the Church in England. It was to Hilda that the poet Caedmon first sang his *Hymn* (see Reading 10.2). She was one of the first women who rose to a prominent position within the largely male medieval Church.

Roswitha of Gandersheim (ca. 935–75) never achieved Hilda's political prominence, but she was one of the notable playwrights of her day. Forgotten until the late fifteenth century, her plays concentrate on women heroines whose personal strength and sense of self-worth allow them to persevere in the face of adversity and challenges to their modesty and chastity.

One of the foremost women of the age was Hildegard of Bingen (1098–1179), who ran the monastery at Bingen, near Frankfurt, Germany. She entered the convent at the age of eight and eventually became its abbess. Extraordinarily accomplished—she wrote tracts on natural science, medicine, and the treatment of disease, an allegorical dialogue between the vices and virtues, as well as a significant body of devotional songs (see the next section on monastic music)—she is best known as the first in a long line of female Christian visionaries and mystics, a role anticipated in Western culture by the Delphic priestesses (see Chapter 4). Her visions are recorded in the *Scivias*, a work whose title derives from the Latin *Scite vias domini*, "Know the ways of the Lord" (**Reading 10.4a**). The *Scivias* was officially designated by the pope as divinely inspired. A zealous advocate for Church reform, Hildegard understood that this recognition lent her the authority to criticize her secular and Church superiors, including the pope himself, and she did not hesitate to do so.

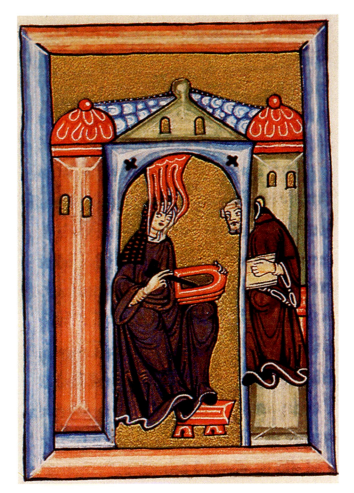

Fig. 10.13 Facsimile of page with *Hildegard's Vision, Liber Scivias*. ca. 1150–1200. Hildegard wrote 33 visionary tracts, collected in *Liber Scivias*, which were acknowledged by the Church as divine. The original manuscript was lost during World War II.

READING 10.4a

from Hildegard of Bingen, *Scivias*

In the year 1141 of the incarnation of Jesus Christ the Son of God, when I was forty-two years and seven months of age, a fiery light, flashing intensely, came from the open vault of heaven and poured through my whole brain. ... And suddenly I could understand what such books as the psalter, the gospel and the other catholic volumes of the Old and New Testament actually set forth.

Indeed, from the age of girlhood, from the time that I was fifteen until the present, I had perceived in myself, just as until this moment, a power of mysterious, secret, and marvelous visions of a miraculous sort. ... I have not perceived these visions in dreams, or asleep, or in a delirium, or with my bodily eyes, or with my external mortal ears, or in secreted places, but I received them awake and looking attentively about me with an unclouded mind, in open places, according to God's will.

The page from the *Scivias* reproduced here (Fig. **10.13**) illustrates this passage. Hildegard is shown recording her divine revelation, as her copyist waits to transcribe her words. Such images were directly supervised by Hildegard herself.

Later in the *Scivias*, Hildegard has a vision of the devil (**Reading 10.4** on pages 357–358), embodied as a monstrous worm who oversees a marketplace full of material goods. After describing her vision, she interprets some of the key images. Hildegard's impulse to interpret her own words is typical of religious literature in the Middle Ages: Its primary purpose was to teach and instruct. But, more than that, Hildegard's *Scivias* shares with other visionary and mystical writing of the period an impulse to make the unknowable vividly present in the mind's eye of her audience. Like the Delphic priestess, she directly encounters the divine through revelation and vision.

Monastic Music Hildegard is responsible for more surviving compositions than any other musician, male or female, who worked before the early fourteenth century. Her *Ordo virtutum* ("Play of the Virtues") is a composition of texts and 82 melodies that dramatizes the conflict between good and evil. In it the devil, who never sings but shouts all his lines, confronts a personification of each of the 16 Virtues. Hildegard collected all of her liturgical works in a *Symphonia armonie electium revelationum* ("Symphony of the Harmony of Celestial Revelations"). Like her *Scivias*, Hildegard's music is designed to illuminate spiritual truths. She believed that in singing and playing music, the mind, heart, and body become one, that discord among celebrants is healed, and the harmony of the heavens is realized on earth.

By the time that Hildegard was composing, the liturgy, and particularly its music, had become remarkably unified. This had been accomplished at Charlemagne's insistence. Although we have no written melodies from Charlemagne's time, most scholars agree that he adopted a form that later became known as **Gregorian chant**—named after Pope Gregory I, the same pope who sent Augustine to England in 597. Called *cantus planus*, plainsong or **plainchant**, it consisted of **monophonic** songs (that is, songs for one or many voices singing a single melodic line with no harmony). The style of Gregorian chant probably originated in the way that ancient Jews sang the Psalms. In its simplest form, the chant is sung **a capella** (that is, without musical accompaniment) and performed in a syllabic style (a single note for each syllable). Often the final word of each phrase is emphasized by the addition of one or two other notes:

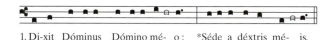

1. Di-xit Dóminus Dómino mé- o : *Séde a déxtris mé- is.

Dixit dominus from Psalm 109

This is the opening line of Psalm 109 ("The Lord said to my Lord: sit on my right hand"). Its four-line staff would become the traditional Gregorian notation, with each note, or **neume**, indicated by a small square. Neumatic chant derives its name from these notes. In **neumatic** chant, the syllabic style gives way to a form in which each syllable is sung to two or three notes (track **10.1**). In later medieval chant, a single syllable may be sung to many notes, a practice known as **melismatic** chant (track **10.2**):

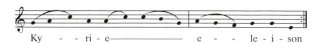

Ky - - ri - e——— e - - le - i - son

Kyrie Eleison from opening of Mass

The Mass Since the earliest times, the celebration of the Mass was a central rite of the Christian Church. It is a celebration of the Eucharist, the fulfillment of Jesus' instruction (recorded in 1 Corinthians 11:24–25) to do in memory of him what he did for his disciples at the Last Supper—that is, Jesus gave his disciples bread, saying, "This is my body," and wine, saying "This is my blood." Christians generally recognized, in its celebration, the presence of Christ. In the medieval Mass, the *Kyrie*, which is either the first or second element in every Mass, consists of three phrases: *Kyrie eleison* ("Lord, have mercy") is sung three times, followed by *Christe eleison* ("Christ, have mercy"), likewise sung three times, and then another *Kyrie eleison*, set to different music, repeated three times again. The repetition of three phrases three times each is deeply symbolic, the number 3 referring to the Trinity, and the 3 squared (3 times 3) signifying absolute perfection.

The plainchant composed by Hildegard of Bingen is unique in the range of musical effects it employs. In contrast to the rather narrow scope of most chants of her day, she uses extremes of register to create "soaring arches" that, she believed, brought heaven and earth together. Although traditional plainchant rarely employed intervals, greater than a second or third (one or two notes apart on a keyboard), Hildegard regularly used wider intervals such as fourths and fifths, again to create a sense of moving between the divine and mundane. Her melodies ascend rapidly upward as if toward the heavens. She combines neumatic and melismatic passages; the former seem grounded in the everyday, while the latter suggest the joy of salvation. Her unique style can be more readily appreciated by comparing track **10.3** to the more traditional approaches to plainchant represented in tracks **10.1** and **10.2**.

The most important single element in determining the nature of a given plainchant melody is its function in the liturgy, which remained consistent from the time of Charlemagne through the sixteenth century. Certain chants, focusing on the Psalms, were composed specifically for the eight *horarium* ("hours") of the Divine Office and sung exclusively by cloistered monks and nuns. The Rule of Saint Benedict required that the entire 150 Psalms be recited each week.

The Mass had its own repertoire of plainchant. It was celebrated once each day, between 6 AM and 9 AM in every church, convent, and monastery, and was open to any baptized member of the community or congregation. Some elements were performed at every Mass, including the Credo, a musical setting of the Nicene Creed (see Chapter 8), while others were sung only on special Sundays or feast days of the liturgical year. The liturgical year revolves around two major feast days, Christmas and Easter; each is preceded by a season of penitence.

Charlemagne standardized the liturgy by creating several singing schools, including one at Saint Gall, where plainchant was taught to choirmasters from throughout the Empire. "In every bishop's see," he ordered in the Law of 789, "instruction shall be given in the psalms, musical notation, chant, the computation of the years and seasons, and grammar."

The Ottonian Empire

Charlemagne's empire dissolved in 843 when his son Louis the Pious (r. 814–40) divided the kingdom among his own feuding sons: Lothar, the eldest of the three; Louis the German; and their half-brother, Charles the Bald. To the east, Louis the German ruled most of what is today Germany and Austria. To the west, Charles the Bald ruled most of what is now France. And between the two was Lothar, whose kingdom extended in a narrow band from the North Sea to Italy. When Lothar died in 855, his kingdom was partitioned among his three sons. With this middle territory thus weakened, Charles the Bald to the west and Louis the German to the east began to fight over it, a contest between the German and French Frankish kingdoms. By the end of the tenth century, two powerful kingdoms—one German, the other French—had emerged.

The German kingdom was led by Duke Otto I (r. 936–73). Otto came to the rescue of Pope John XII in 961, and in return, the pope crowned Otto emperor on February 2, 962. Nevertheless, the pope lost control of the Church, as Otto made it clear that the Church depended on his military support. When John refused to accept the situation, Otto deposed him and proclaimed that the pope ruled at the pleasure of the emperor. Although the Ottonian Empire was a conscious reinvention of the Carolingian dream, unifying Church and State in a single administrative and political bureaucracy, it was built on the exercise of power, not consensus, and it collapsed in the eleventh century, as the Church retaliated against secular power.

The art created under the five Ottonian rulers (936–1024) is distinguished by its spiritual expressiveness. The so-called *Gero Crucifix*—the oldest surviving large-scale crucifix in carved wood—was commissioned by Archbishop Gero of Cologne, in 970 (Fig. **10.14**). It is intensely emotional, focusing on Christ's suffering, not his triumph. The tendons in his chest are drawn tight, and his abdomen protrudes as the weight of his body sags downward in death. That the *Gero Crucifix* is slightly larger than life size adds to its expressive force. It seems less sculpture than real flesh, an object designed to inspire pity and awe in the viewer. Sagging, emaciated, and bloodied, Christ seems the very opposite of the triumphant Christ of the Resurrection—

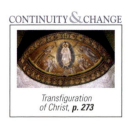

CONTINUITY & CHANGE

Transfiguration of Christ, **p. 273**

compare, for instance, the *Transfiguration of Christ* mosaic from Saint Catherine's Monastery, Sinai, ca. 548–65 (see Fig. 8.23 in Chapter 8). It announces a new, powerful expressiveness that would be passed on to the artists of the Romanesque period, discussed in the following pages.

Capetian France and the Norman Conquest

To the west of the Ottonian Empire, the Frankish territory formerly controlled by Charles the Bald was invaded in the

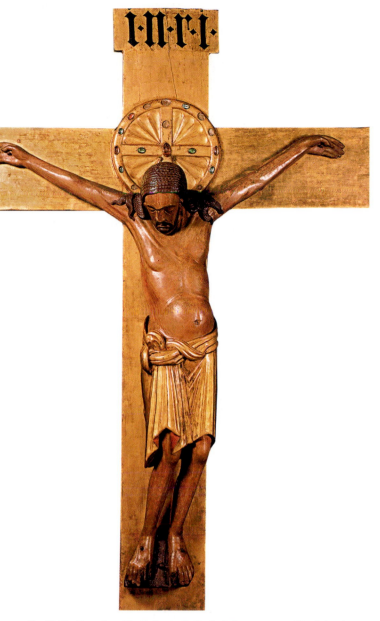

Fig. 10.14 *Gero Crucifix*, **Cologne Cathedral, Germany. ca. 970.** Painted and gilded oak, height of figure 6'2". This is one of the few surviving pieces of wooden sculpture from the period and certainly one of the largest. It is the most powerful representation of Christ as a tortured martyr in the early Middle Ages. A cavity in the back of the head was made to hold a piece of communion bread, the Host. Thus, the crucifix not only represents the body of the dying Jesus, but contains within it the body of Christ obtained through the sacrament of the Eucharist.

middle of the ninth century by Normans—that is, "Northmen"—Viking warriors from Scandinavia. The Viking onslaught was devastating, as they plundered and looted across the north European seas, targeting especially isolated but wealthy monasteries such as Lindisfarne, which they had attacked even earlier, in 793. The Viking invasions fragmented the former empire and caused nobility, commoners, and peasants alike to attach themselves to anyone who might provide military protection—thus cementing the feudal system. By the tenth century, they had raided, explored, and settled territories from North America, which the explorer Leif Eriksson reached in about the year 1000, to Iceland, Greenland, the British Isles, and France. In France, they besieged Paris in 845 and gained control of the lower Seine Valley. In 915, the Frankish king Charles III (r. 893–923) was forced to grant the Norse leader Rolf, or Rollo, permanent control of the region. Rollo became the first duke of Normandy.

The rest of the western Carolingian Empire, now called France, remained fragmented, with various counts and dukes competing for power. Finally, in 987, Hugh Capet, lord of the Île-de-France, a relatively small domain stretching from Paris and its environs south to Orléans in the Loire Valley, was selected to serve as king. Hugh began a dynasty of Capetian kings that ruled for the next 350 years. From the beginning, the Capetians concentrated their energies on building a tightly knit administrative bureaucracy. Their most contentious relationship was with the dukes of Normandy, who were fiercely independent, going so far as to claim England for themselves, independent of Capetian influence.

The Normans invaded England in 1066, a story narrated in the famous *Bayeux Tapestry* (see *Closer Look*, pages 340–341). England and northern France thus became one country, with one king, William I, the Conqueror, and a small group of barons who owned estates on both sides of the English Channel. To both pacify and defend themselves against the Saxons, the Normans constructed **motte and bailey** castles (Fig. 10.15). A motte is a raised earth

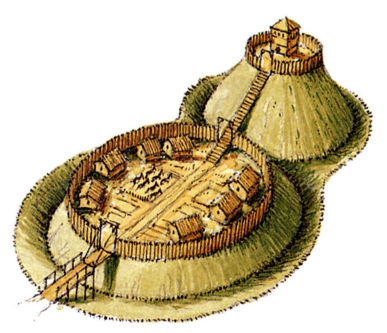

Fig. 10.15 Motte and bailey castle. When Normans first landed in England, they constructed mounds, called *mottes*, upon which they built a square wooden tower called a *keep*. First used as a lookout tower and elevated fighting point, the keep later became an accommodation for the lord of the castle. At the foot of the motte was a flat area called a *bailey*, surrounded by a wooden stockade. Domestic buildings, including stables, kitchens, and servants' quarters, were located in the bailey. A moat, or trench filled with water, often surrounded the castle—a natural result of digging dirt for the motte.

mound, and a bailey is the enclosed courtyard at its base. Archeologists estimate that the Normans built about 500 of them between 1066 and 1086, or one every two weeks. Such fortifications could be built in as little as eight days. In time, elaborate stone castles would replace these fire-prone wooden fortifications.

Fearing an invasion from Denmark, William I ordered a complete survey of the country so that he could more accurately determine how much tax he could raise to provide a new army. Known as the *Domesday* (or "Judgment") *Book*, it measured the population of England at about 1 million, with fully three-quarters of the country's wealth resting in the hands of the king and 300 landowners. Two hundred of these were French nobles, and only two were English. The other hundred were archbishops, bishops, and the heads of monasteries. The rest of the land was in the hands of small farmers, and 90 percent of the population worked on the land. Some were freemen, but most owed at least partial allegiance to a local lord. Ten percent of the people were serfs, who owned no land at all. The *Domesday Book* gives us a remarkable view of medieval society and of the great gulf between rich and poor upon which it was based.

THE ROMANESQUE: THE PILGRIMAGE CHURCH AND THE MONASTIC ABBEY

How does the Romanesque style manifest itself in both pilgrimage churches and the Cluniac abbey?

Throughout the Middle Ages, it was customary for Christians to go on religious pilgrimages to holy places or sites containing sacred objects. People believed that their prayers for forgiveness, healing, fertility, or anything else would have a better chance of being fulfilled if they were able to get physically close to a holy object, person, or site. The pilgrimage was also an act of piety, demonstrating the pilgrim's faith, and, in part, an act of penance. As Europe became increasingly urbanized, worsening hygienic conditions spread disease. Believing that disease was related to sinfulness, pilgrims sought to atone for their sins, saving themselves from sickness and contagion on earth and perpetual damnation in the afterlife.

Perhaps because it was closer to northern Europeans than either Jerusalem or Rome, Santiago de Compostela was by far the most popular site of pilgrimages in the eleventh through thirteenth centuries. It had also developed a reputation for repeated miracles, and by the mid-twelfth century, a *Pilgrim's Guide to Santiago de Compostela* had appeared. Written in Latin, probably by monks in southern France, it describes and illustrates the towns and monuments on the major pilgrimage routes through France and Spain (Map 10.3).

Specific routes soon developed that allowed pilgrims to visit other sacred sites along the way. These sites housed the relics—bones, clothing, or other possessions—of Christian saints and martyrs. Relics arrived, virtually by the boatload, from the Middle East, where Crusaders, fighting the Muslims for control of Jerusalem and other sites sacred to Christianity, purchased them for resale in the West. The resale of these artifacts, whose authenticity was often questionable, helped to finance the Crusades. What was reputed to be the tunic that the Virgin Mary wore when she gave birth to Christ was housed at Chartres. At Vézelay, the starting point of one of the four routes to Santiago de Compostela, pilgrims could pray to what were asserted to be the bones of Mary Magdalene.

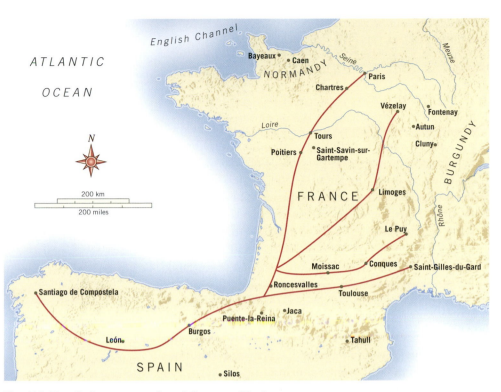

Map 10.3 The pilgrimage routes through France and Spain.

The Abbey Church of Sainte-Foy at Conques is the oldest of the major pilgrimage churches (Fig. **10.16**). The Abbey Church is one of the earliest examples of a style that art historians have come to call the **Romanesque**, "in the manner of the Romans," because it revives elements of Roman architectural tradition. The basilica tradition that extends back to the Roman

Basilica Nova (see Fig. 6.36 in Chapter 6) became the model for the Romanesque church floor plan, although the wooden ceilings of churches like Old Saint Peter's (see Figs. 8.11 and 8.12 in Chapter 8) were replaced by much more fire-resistant barrel vaults.

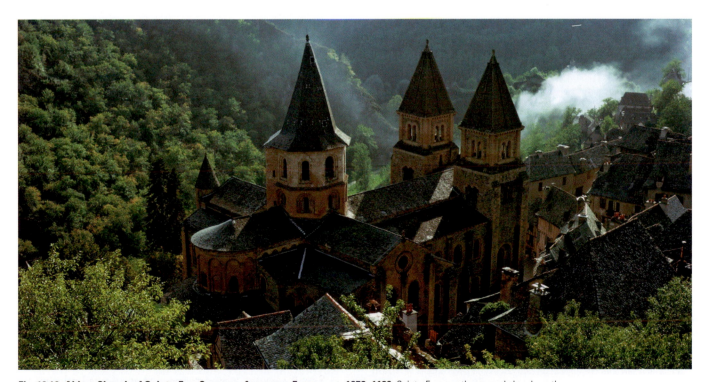

Fig. 10.16 Abbey Church of Sainte-Foy, Conques, Auvergne, France. ca. 1050–1120. Sainte-Foy was the second church on the route to Santiago de Compostela that began at the church of Saint Michel d'Aiguilhe at Le-Puy-en-Venay (see Fig. 9.20 in Chapter 9).

The *Bayeux Tapestry*—actually a 231-foot-long embroidery—was sewn between 1070 and 1080, almost certainly by women at the School of Embroidery at Canterbury, in Kent, England—one of the few surviving works by women we have from the period. The embroiderers of the *Bayeux Tapestry* worked with twisted wool, dyed in eight colors, and used only two basic stitches. It was commissioned by Bishop Odo of Bayeux, half-brother of William, Duke of Normandy, whose conquest of England in 1066 it narrates in both pictures and words (in Latin). Like the Column of Trajan in Rome (see Figs. 6.24 and 6.25 in Chapter 6), its story is both historical and biased. The tapestry was designed to be hung around the choir of Odo's Bayeux Cathedral—an unabashed act of self-promoting propaganda on the part of the Normans.

When the English king Edward the Confessor died on January 5, 1066, without an heir, William, Duke of Normandy, claimed the throne, swearing that Edward had promised him the English throne when he died. But on his deathbed, Edward named Harold of Wessex king, while two other contenders, Harold Hardrada of Norway and Tostig, Earl of Northumbria, also laid their claims. Battle was inevitable.

William was particularly unhappy with Harold of Wessex's claim to the throne. Harold had visited Normandy, sometime between 1064 and the end of 1065, at the insistence of King Edward. In fact, the *Bayeux Tapestry* begins at this point. The tapestry narrates the Norman point of view, so its reliability is uncertain, but according to both the tapestry and other Norman sources, during his stay, Harold recognized William as Edward's heir. Whether Harold did so willingly is debatable—even the tapestry shows Harold being taken prisoner by a vassal of William.

Harold was back in England before Edward died in 1066, and he became king, abrogating whatever oath he may have sworn to William. The tapestry shows him in February with Halley's Comet in the sky—interpreted by the Anglo-Saxons as a portent of disaster and resulting, the tapestry implies, from his having broken his oath. Ghost ships, perhaps from a dream, decorate the border below the troubled king, foreshadowing the invasion to come.

As William prepared to invade England from the south, Harold Hardrada and the Norwegians prepared to press their own claims from the north. The weather determined the course of battle. Strong northerly winds kept William docked in Normandy, but the same winds favored the Norwegians, who soon landed on the north coast. Harold met

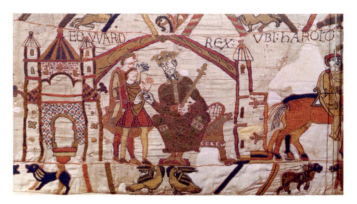

The *Bayeux Tapestry*. 1070–80. Embroidered wool on linen, height 6'. Entire length of fabric, 231'. Musée de la Tapisserie, Bayeux, France/With special authorization of the city of Bayeux/The Bridgeman Art Library. This, the first section of the tapestry, depicts King Edward the Confessor talking to Harold, earl of Wessex, his wife's brother. He is sending Harold on a mission to France, ostensibly to tell William, Duke of Normandy, that he will be Edward's successor.

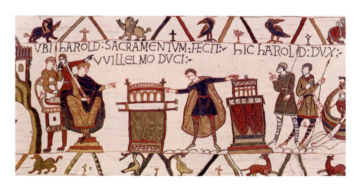

The *Bayeux Tapestry*. 1070–80. Musée de la Tapisserie, Bayeux, France/With special authorization of the city of Bayeux/The Bridgeman Art Library. Harold swears allegiance to William, his right hand on the altar between them, and his left on a chest presumably housing sacred objects from the Cathedral at Bayeux.

them at Stamford Bridge, near York, on September 25, 1066, and defeated them. By then, the winds had changed, and William sailed from the south, landing in Sussex. Harold turned his troops southward, but exhausted from both battle and the hurried march, they were defeated by William's army at Hastings on October 14, 1066. Harold died in the battle. The embroidery ends with a simple statement—"and the English turned and fled"—as if there is nothing more to say.

For seven centuries, the tapestry was cared for at Bayeux Cathedral, where it was hung round the nave on feast days and special occasions. It escaped destruction in the French Revolution in 1789, and was taken to Paris in the early eighteenth century when Napoleon exhibited it in his own propaganda campaign as he prepared to invade England.

The *Bayeux Tapestry*

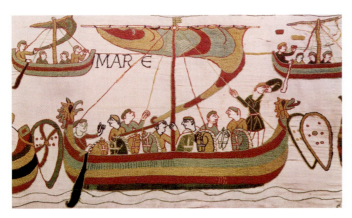

The *Bayeux Tapestry*. **1070–80.** Musée de la Tapisserie, Bayeux, France/With special authorization of the city of Bayeux. Giraudon/The Bridgeman Art Library. The Normans sail for England. Note the animal-head prow of the ship, which underscores the Norse origins of the Normans.

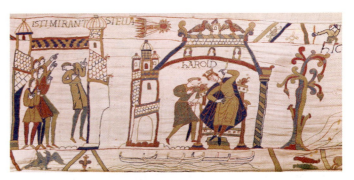

The *Bayeux Tapestry*. **1070–80.** Musée de la Tapisserie, Bayeux, France/With special authorization of the city of Bayeux/The Bridgeman Art Library. Having returned to England just before Edward's death and having assumed the throne, Harold is disturbed by the arrival of a comet with a fiery tail, visible here in the top border.

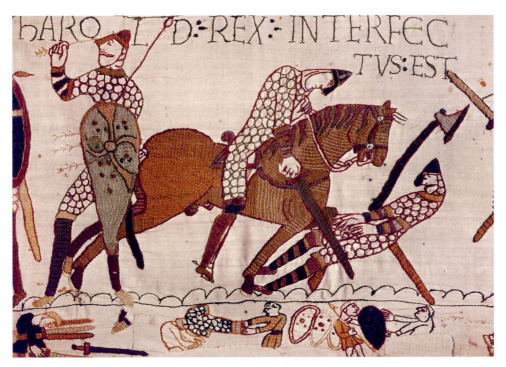

The *Bayeux Tapestry*. **1070–80.** Erich Lessing/Art Resource, New York. Harold, with the green shield, receives an arrow to the eye at the Battle of Hastings. Immediately to the right, a Norman soldier slays him. Note the soldiers stripping armor from the dead in the tapestry's bottom border.

Something to Think About ...

Looking more closely at the sections of the narrative reproduced here, in what ways does the tapestry reveal itself to be a work of propaganda?

View the Closer Look for the *Bayeux Tapestry* on **MyArtsLab**

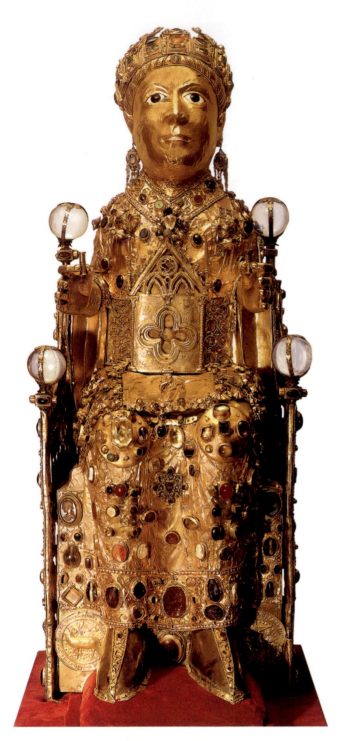

Fig. 10.17 Reliquary effigy of Saint Foy. Made in the Auvergne region, France, for the Abbey Church of Sainte-Foy, Conques, France. Mostly 983–1013 with later additions.
Gold and silver over a wooden core, studded with precious stones and cameos, height 34". Church Treasury, Conques. This jewel-encrusted reliquary survived because monks hid it in the wall of the church when Protestants burned the abbey in 1568. It was not discovered until restoration of the church in the 1860s.

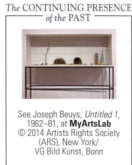

The CONTINUING PRESENCE *of the* PAST

See Joseph Beuys, *Untitled 1,* 1962–81, at **MyArtsLab**
© 2014 Artists Rights Society (ARS), New York/ VG Bild Kunst, Bonn

The portals of new pilgrimage churches were modeled after the triumphal arches of Rome, but they celebrate the triumph of the Christian God, not a worldly leader. Such a revival of architectural tradition, reaching back for almost an entire millennium, represents in part a lack of technological innovation rather than a philosophical return to Roman traditions. However, the Christian adoption of Roman architectural styles also underscores the long-standing Christian rejection of its Judaic heritage—the Temple and the synagogue—as well as a growing identification with the Greco-Roman West. As this identification took hold, religious fervor came to define the age.

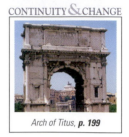

CONTINUITY & CHANGE

Arch of Titus, p. 199

The Abbey Church at Conques housed the relics of Saint Foy ("Saint Faith" in English), a child who was martyred in 303 for refusing to worship pagan gods. Her remains were contained in an elaborate jeweled **reliquary** (Fig. 10.17), a container used to protect and display sacred relics. It stood in the choir of the church, where pilgrims could view it from the ambulatory. The head of the reliquary, which is disproportionately large, was salvaged from a late Roman wooden mask and covered with gold foil. Many of the precious stones that decorate the reliquary were gifts from pilgrims. The actual remains of the saint were housed in a recess carved into the back of the reliquary, and below it, on the back of her throne, was an engraving of the Crucifixion, indicating the connection between Saint Foy's martyrdom and Christ's.

Like the largest of the pilgrimage churches, Sainte-Foy was constructed to accommodate large numbers of visitors. Its west portal was large and opened directly into the nave (Figs. 10.18 and 10.19). Wide aisles skirted the nave and continued around the transept, choir, and apse, creating the ambulatory. A second-story gallery was built over the side aisles; it both accommodated still more people and served structurally to support the extra weight of the arched stone ceilings.

The **barrel vault** that rises above the nave of Sainte-Foy is one of the distinctive features of Romanesque architecture. Barrel vaults are elongated arched masonry structures spanning an interior space and shaped like a half-cylinder. They had been used in the Roman Empire (see Chapter 6, *Materials & Techniques*). In Romanesque churches, the space created by such vaults was designed to raise the worshiping pilgrims' eyes and thus direct their thoughts to heaven. An especially interesting example of this effect can be seen in the groin vaults of the Romanesque church of Sainte-Madeleine at Vézelay (Fig. 10.20). As at Sainte-Foy, the nave is divided into sections, called **bays**, by the round arches of the vault. But at Vézelay, these arches are constructed of alternating pink

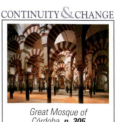

CONTINUITY & CHANGE

Great Mosque of Córdoba, p. 305

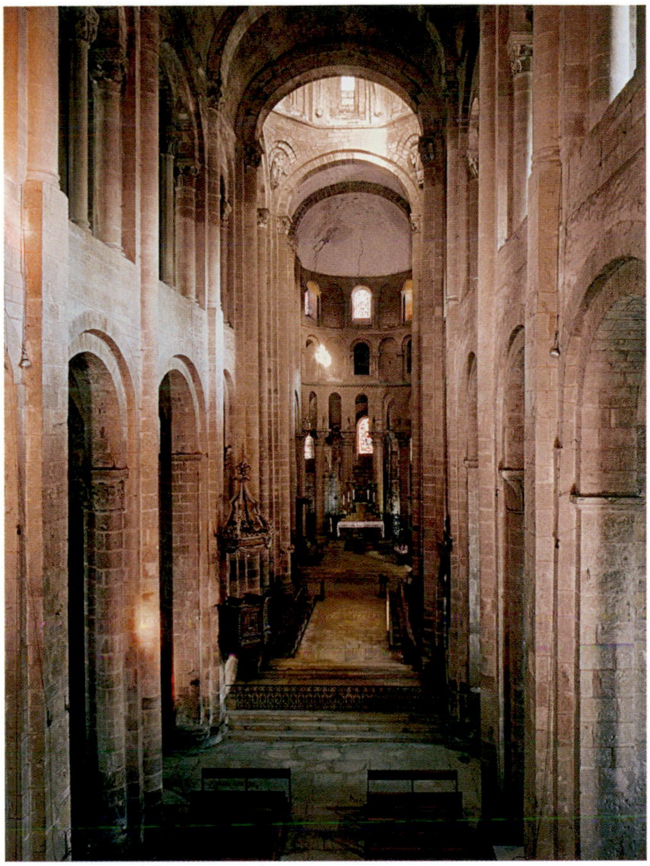

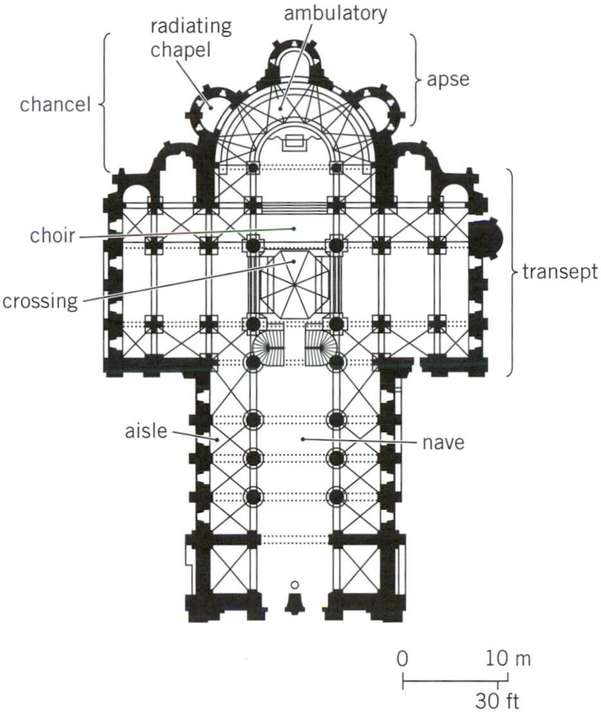

Figs. 10.18 and 10.19 Floor plan and interior of the nave, Abbey Church of Sainte-Foy, Conques. ca. 1050–1120. Some of the innovations of the Romanesque cathedral can be explained, at least in part, by the need to allow pilgrims to pass through the church without disturbing the monks as they attended to their affairs at the main altar in the choir. Thus, an ambulatory extended around the transept and the apse where pilgrims could walk.

and gray stone voussoirs, the wedge-shaped stones that form the arch, quarried locally. The effect is similar to the interior of the Great Mosque at Córdoba (see Fig. 9.13 in Chapter 9), built 300 years earlier, although it remains uncertain if they were influenced by the Islamic mosque. This alternation of brick and stone is a fairly common building technique in Roman architecture, and in fact it may be the case that the architects at Córdoba were themselves imitating Roman models. The effect of the alternating voussoirs at Vézelay, as at Córdoba, is to lighten the visual impact of the arches, giving them an almost airy height.

The pilgrimage churches evidently competed with one another in decorating their basilicas. Writing in the eleventh century, the French Benedictine monk Raoul Glaber noted, "throughout the world, especially in Italy and Gaul, a rebuilding of church basilicas [is occurring], ... each Christian people striving against the others to erect nobler ones." The portals to the churches were of special importance. Not only was the portal the first thing the visitor would see, it also marked the boundary between secular and sacred space. The space created under the portal arch, called the **tympanum**, was filled with sculptural relief.

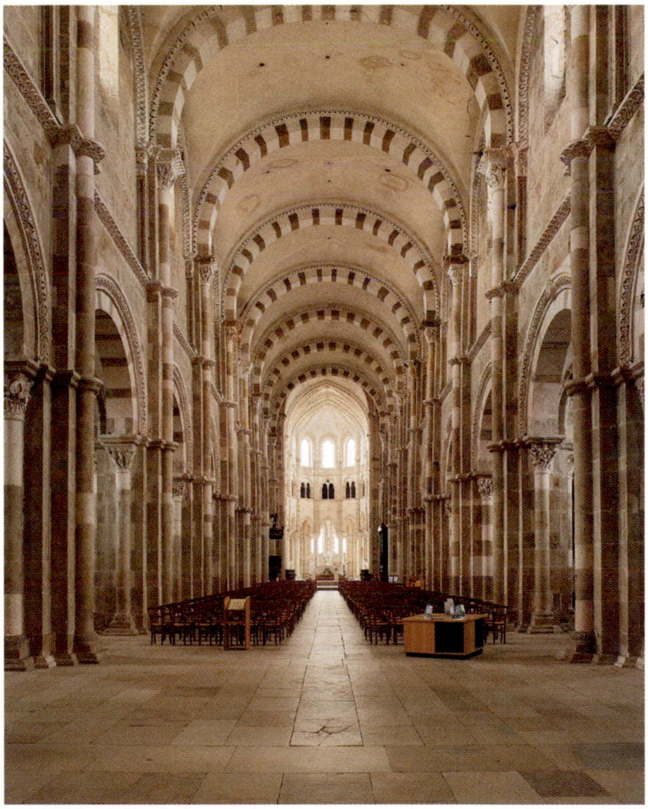

Fig. 10.20 Interior of the nave, Church of Sainte-Madeleine, Vézelay, France. ca. 1089–1206. The nave of this church is extremely long—nearly 200 feet—giving pilgrims a sense of ever-increasing majesty as they moved from the portal at the western, "dark" end of the church toward the choir and reliquary at the eastern end, toward the light of salvation. Vézelay was extensively restored in the nineteenth century.

Explore the architectural panorama of the Church of Sainte-Madeleine, Vézelay, on **MyArtsLab**

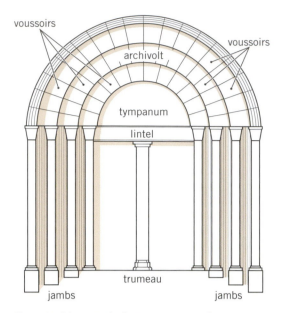

Fig. 10.21 **Diagram of a Romanesque portal.**

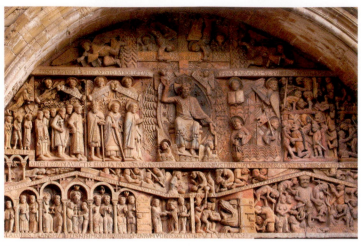

Fig. 10.22 *Last Judgment*, **tympanum and detail of west portal, Sainte-Foy, Conques. ca. 1065.** This depiction of the Last Judgment uses composition subtly and effectively to distinguish the saved from the damned. To Christ's left, the action is chaotic—figures twist and turn in often unpredictable directions. To his right, on the other hand, everyone stands upright under orderly arrangements of arches.

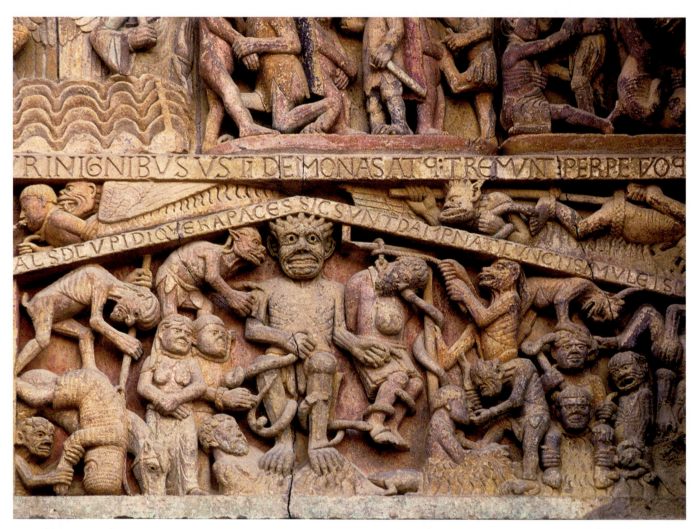

Fig. 10.23 **Detail of west portal tympanum, Sainte-Foy, Conques.** Showing, in the lower register, Satan meting out punishments and torture.

👁 **Watch** an architectural simulation about the Romanesque portal on **MyArtsLab**

All of the elements of Romanesque portals were equally subject to decorative relief (see diagram, Fig. **10.21**): the lintel, **jambs** (the vertical elements on both sides of door supporting the lintel or arch), **trumeau** (the column or post in the middle of a large door helping to support the lintel), and the **archivolt** (the curved molding formed by the voussoirs making up the arch). The tympanum of Sainte-Foy at Conques depicts the Last Judgment (Figs. **10.22** and **10.23**). At the center of the tympanum, Christ raises his right arm to welcome those who are saved. His lowered left hand points to hell, the destination of the damned. He sits enthroned in a **mandorla**, an almond-shaped oval of light signifying divinity, a motif imported to the Western world from the Far East, through Byzantium (see Fig. 8.23 in Chapter 8), and one widely used by Romanesque artists. Below Christ's feet, the weighing of souls is depicted as a contest between the archangel Michael and a desperate demon who cheats by pressing his forefinger onto the pan, nevertheless failing to overcome the goodness of the soul in question.

The lintel is divided into two parts: on the left, heaven, and on the right, hell. The two are divided by a partition: An angel welcomes the saved, while on the other side, a demon armed with a bludgeon shoves the damned into hell's monstrous jaws. Situated frontally under the arches of heaven, the saved give the appearance of order and serenity, while all is confusion and chaos on hell's side. Satan stands in the center of the right lintel (see Fig. 10.23), presiding over an astonishing array of tortures. On Satan's left, a figure symbolizing Pride is thrown from his high horse, stabbed through with a pitchfork. Next to them, a bare-breasted adulteress and her lover await Satan's wrath. A figure symbolizing Greed is hung from on high with his purse round his neck and a toad at his feet. A demon tears the tongue out of Slander. In the small triangular space at the right above Satan, two fiendish-looking rabbits roast a poacher on a spit. In the corresponding triangular space to the left, a devil devours the brain of a damned soul who commits suicide by plunging a knife into his throat. Close by, another hunchbacked devil has just grabbed the harp of a damned soul and tears his tongue with a hook. Such images were designed to move the pilgrim to the right hand of Christ, not the left.

These themes are the focus of perhaps the most famous sermon of the Middle Ages, *On the Misery of the Human Condition*. Pope Innocent III (papacy 1198–1216) wrote this tract before his ascension to the papacy; on his election, the Church cardinals unanimously approved it as official Church doctrine. In the sermon, Innocent rails at length on the wretchedness and worthlessness of human beings, their weaknesses, folly, selfishness, vileness, their crimes, and their sins. He describes the human body as putrid in both life and death: "In life, [man] produced dung and vomit; in death he produces rottenness and stench." But perhaps most dramatically, he catalogs the fate that awaits them in hell (**Reading 10.5**):

READING 10.5

from Pope Innocent III, *On the Misery of the Human Condition*

There shall be weeping and gnashing of teeth, there shall be groaning, wailing, shrieking, and flailing of arms and screaming, screeching, and shouting; there shall be fear and trembling, toil and trouble, holocaust and dreadful stench, and everywhere darkness and anguish; there shall be asperity, cruelty, calamity, poverty, distress, and utter wretchedness; they will feel an oblivion of loneliness and namelessness; there shall be twistings and piercings, bitterness, terror, hunger and thirst, cold and hot, brimstone and fire burning, forever and ever world without end …

Such imagery is meant to strike terror into the soul of listeners by serving as a **memento mori**, a "reminder of death." Faced with such prospects, pilgrims were willing to endure the physical hardship and considerable danger their journeys entailed. Some brought great sums of money with them—gold, silver, jewelry, at least enough money to pay for their lodging and meals. If they inaugurated a new economy of hospitality in their travels, they also invited larceny, even murder, and bandits plagued the pilgrimage routes.

Cluny and the Monastic Tradition

One of the most influential of the Romanesque pilgrimage churches was the Abbey of Cluny. Like Charlemagne's Saint Gall (see Fig. 10.12), Cluny, founded in about 910, was a reformed Benedictine monastery. The Cluniac order enjoyed a special status in the Church hierarchy, reporting directly to the pope and bypassing all feudal or ecclesiastic control. No secular ruler could exercise any control over the monastery (the origin of our modern insistence on the separation of Church and State). Furthermore, the Cluniac order insisted on the celibacy of its monks and nuns—the Church was to be their only lord and spouse. Celibacy was not the rule elsewhere, and was not officially imposed on Catholic priests until 1139.

Perhaps the most important role of the Cluniac order was its sense of culture as something wider than local traditions. Its monks preserved and translated Classical texts. They rediscovered, particularly, Greek and Roman antecedents. The plan of their church mimicked Old Saint Peter's in Rome. They were lovers of knowledge and of beauty (both considered chief attributes of the Almighty), and of Classical means of representation. The naturalism we associate with Greek and Roman art gradually began to find favor once again.

Cluny's abbot was among the most powerful men in Europe; Abbot Hugh de Semur, who ruled the abbey from 1049 to 1109, was the most influential of these. In 1088, Hugh began work on a new church for the abbey, supported financially by King Alfonso VI of León and Castile, in

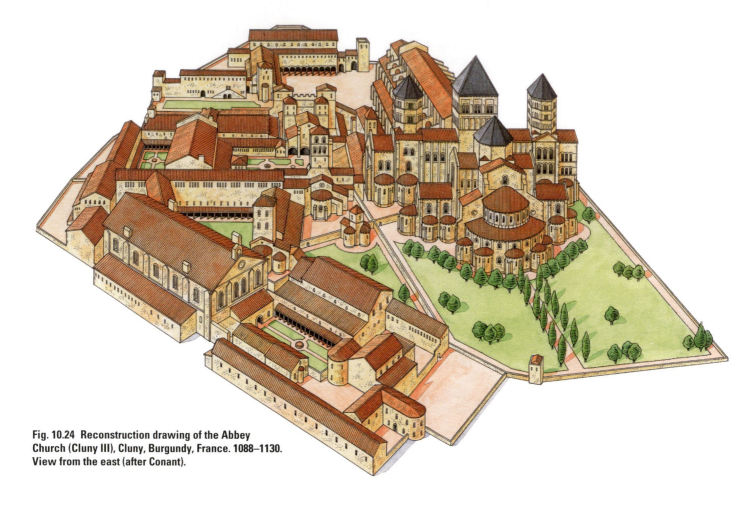

Fig. 10.24 **Reconstruction drawing of the Abbey Church (Cluny III), Cluny, Burgundy, France. 1088–1130. View from the east (after Conant).**

northern Spain. Known as Cluny III (Fig. **10.24**) because it was the third church built on the site, it was described by a contemporary as "shining on the earth like a second sun." Today only a portion of its south transept and tower remain—the rest was destroyed in the late eighteenth century by French revolutionaries.

The entire arrangement reflects the ideal Carolingian monastery at Saint Gall. Originally, the barrel-vaulted ceiling of Cluny III soared to a height of nearly 100 feet. It had a five-aisled nave and a double transept. From the portal to the end of the apse, the interior space stretched 415 feet—twice as long as Vézelay's impressive nave. The interior of the church was richly decorated. The floor was paved with mosaic, and an elaborate sculpture scheme, most of which was painted in brilliant colors, lined the walls. Over 1,200 carved capitals topped the interior columns. Of these, some of the most interesting crowned a semicircular group surrounding the high altar, among them a pair that depicts the eight tones of the sacred psalmody (Fig. **10.25**). They indicate the importance of the liturgy to the Cluniac order and the centrality of music to that liturgy. The rich decoration, the soaring space of the stone architecture (which naturally enhanced the sound of the monks' chants), and music itself showed the faithful, according to the monk Theophilus, writing in the first decades of the twelfth century, "something of the likeness of the paradise of God."

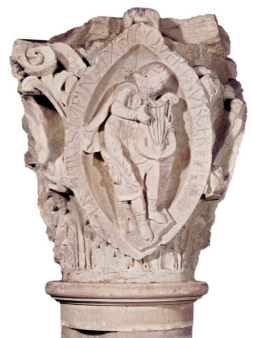

Fig. 10.25 *The Third Tone of the Sacred Psalmody,* **ambulatory capital from the Abbey Church (Cluny III), Cluny, Burgundy, France. 1088–1130.** Musée du Farinier, Ancienne Abbaye, Cluny. The inscription reads: "The third [tone] strikes, and represents the Resurrection of Christ." The lyre, with its strings stretching upward to the horizontal frame, was thought to resemble the cross.

Choral Music Benedictine monks at Cluny introduced choral music into the liturgy sometime in the first half of the tenth century. Odo of Cluny (879–942), the monastery's second abbot, was an important musical theorist. He is often credited with developing one of the first effective systems of musical notation, used to teach choral music to other monasteries in the Cluniac fold. The method used the letters A through G to name the seven notes of the Western scale. Working from Odo's example, 100 years later Guido of Arezzo (ca. 990–ca. 1050) introduced the idea of depicting notes on a staff of lines so that the same note always appears on the same line. With this innovation, modern musical notation was born.

Choral music introduces the possibility of **polyphony**—two or more lines of melody—as opposed to the monophonic quality of Gregorian chant. The earliest form of this new polyphonic music was called **organum**. It simply consists of voices singing note-to-note in parallel. Probably the first instance of this would have been adult monks singing a monophonic chant in parallel with boys' voices singing the same melody at a higher pitch. Soon the second voice began to move in contrary motion to the bass chant (**free organum**), or to add numerous notes to individual syllables above the bass chant (**melismatic organum**). An excellent example of melismatic organum is the "Alleluia, dies sanctificatus" by the composer Léonin, who worked from 1163 to 1190 at Notre-Dame Cathedral in Paris (track 10.4). The movement of the two voices could be diagrammed as shown here:

Listen on MyArtsLab

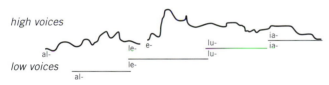

Diagram of melismatic organum from Léonin's "Alleluia, dies sanctificatus."

The lower voices hold unusually long notes, while the upper voices move more rapidly and freely, creating two independent musical lines. One can only imagine how music like this, performed by as many as 100 voices, might have sounded in Cluny III, which was renowned for its acoustics.

The Cistercian Challenge

Not everyone supported the richness of the Cluniac liturgy and its accompanying music, art, and architecture. From the point of view of Bernard, abbot of Clairvaux, such artistic excess—in other words, beauty—was an affront to the monastic mission. Chief spokesperson for a new order of Cistercian monks, Bernard of Clairvaux (1091–1153) advocated a rigorous application of the Rule of Saint Benedict.

Cistercians were to be self-sufficient, living off their own cultivation of the land (this proved impossible in practice). They were to live a simple life of self-imposed poverty symbolized by the undyed wool of their habits. And their plain, undecorated churches stand in stark contrast to the grandeur and opulence of the rest of Romanesque architecture. Can it be, Bernard asks in his *Apologia for Abbot William*, that the riches of such large and sumptuous churches as Cluny and others are meant to stimulate financial donations to the Church? Is it really true, he asks, that if "their eyes are feasted with relics … their purse strings are loosed"? Bernard is denouncing not beauty itself, but the use of beauty for monetary profit. He also objects to the fact that it distracts attention from prayer. The Cistercians belong to a long tradition of thought that challenges the role of art in religion, extending back to the early years of Islam and the iconoclasts in Byzantium, although they do not oppose the use of imagery. They simply discourage using imagery in an ostentatious way.

THE CRUSADES

Why did the Crusades occur and what, if anything, did they accomplish?

On November 25, 1095, at the Council of Clermont (present-day Clermont-Ferrand), Pope Urban II (papacy 1088–99) preached the First Crusade. The pope had received his training as a monk at Cluny, under the direct tutelage of Hugh de Semur. What motivated the First Crusade is difficult to say. We know that throughout Christendom there was a widespread desire to regain free access to Jerusalem, which had been captured by the Arabs in 638. In part, however, the aim was to bring peace to Europe. Because of the feudal **primogeniture** system, by which the eldest son in a family inherited all of its property, large numbers of aristocratic younger brothers were disinherited and left to their own devices. They had taken to feuding with one another (and with their elder brothers) and raiding other people's land. The Crusades organized these disenfranchised men with the promise of reward, both monetary and spiritual: "Jerusalem," Urban preached, "is the navel of the world; the land is fruitful above all others, like another paradise of delights. … Undertake the journey [also] for the remission of your sins, with the assurance of the imperishable glory of the kingdom of heaven." The pope also presented the Crusades as a Holy War:

> A race from the kingdom of the Persians, an accursed race, a race utterly alienated from God … has invaded the lands of the Christians and has depopulated them by the sword, pillage and fire. … They destroy the altars, after having defiled them with their uncleanness. … When they wish to torture people by a base death, they perforate their navels, and dragging forth the extremity of the intestines, bind it to a stake; then with flogging they lead the victim around

until the viscera having gushed forth the victim falls prostrate upon the ground. … What shall I say of the abominable rape of the women? … On whom therefore is the labor of avenging these wrongs and of recovering this territory, if not upon you?

It was convincing rhetoric. Nearly 100,000 young men signed on.

The First Crusade was thus motivated by several forces: religious zeal, the desire to reduce conflict at home by sending off Europe's feuding aristocrats, defending Christendom from barbarity, the promise of monetary reward otherwise unavailable to the disenfranchised young nobility, and, not least of all, that nobility's own hot blood and sense of adventure. The First Crusade was a low point in Christian culture. Late in the year 1098, having destroyed the city of Antioch, the Frankish army (called the *Franj* by the Muslims) attacked the city of Ma'arra (present-day Ma'arrat an Nu'man in Syria). "For three days they put people to the sword," the Arab historian Ibn al-Athïr wrote, "killing more than a hundred thousand people and taking many prisoners." This is undoubtedly an exaggeration, since the city's population was then something under 10,000,

but the horror of what happened next somewhat justifies Ibn al-Athïr's numbers. As reported by Frankish chronicler Radulph of Caen, "In Ma'arra our troops boiled pagan adults in cooking pots; they impaled children on spits and devoured them grilled." In an official letter to the pope, the commanders explained: "A terrible famine racked the army in Ma'arra, and placed it in the cruel necessity of feeding itself upon the bodies of the Saracens." An anonymous poet of Ma'arra lamented: "I know not whether my native land be a grazing ground for wild beasts or yet my home!" Descriptions of the slaughter of the citizens of Jerusalem, when the Crusaders finally took that city on July 15, 1099, are no less gruesome. One important account of the First Crusade is the *Deeds of the Franks*, a history written anonymously about 1100–1101 (**Reading 10.6**, pages 358–359).

The Muslim peoples of the Middle East were not the only victims of the Crusades. During the early days of the First Crusade in 1096, Count Emicho of Leiningen, in present-day Germany, making his way down the Rhine to embark for Jerusalem, robbed and murdered all the Jews he could find, killing 800 in Worms and wiping out the entire Jewish population of both Mainz and Cologne. Emicho seems to have been motivated by the need for funds

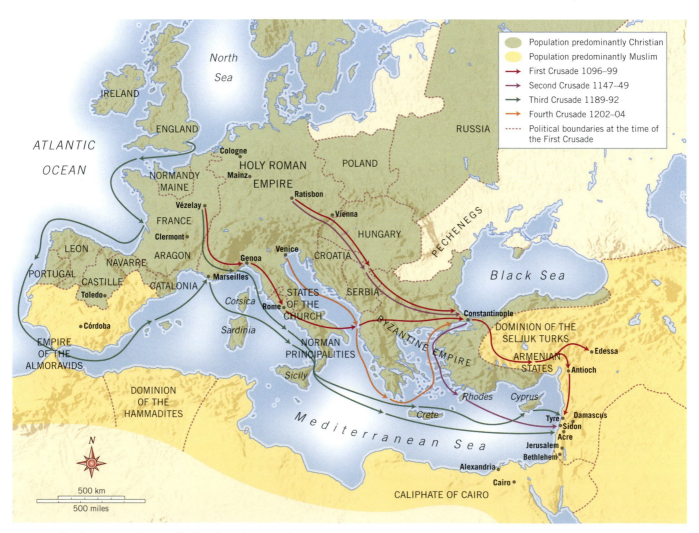

Map 10.4 The Crusades. 1096–1204. The First Crusade was predominantly over land, but the subsequent efforts were all by sea.

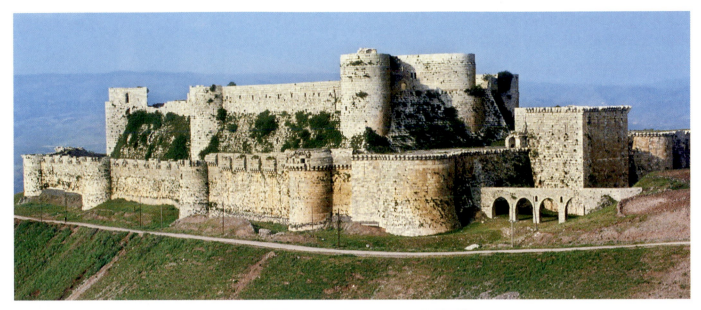

Fig. 10.26 Krak des Chevaliers, Syria. First occupied 1109. Two lines of defense made the castle virtually impenetrable. An aqueduct brought water to the castle. Water was stored in huge cisterns beneath the outer ward. If during siege the water supply was cut off, the knights could hold out for several months.

View the Closer Look for Krak des Chevaliers on **MyArtsLab**

to support his army, but his was a religious war as well. In his eyes, the Jews, like the Muslims, were the enemies of Christ. Local bishops, to their credit, attempted to stop the carnage, and Bernard of Clairvaux would later preach against the persecution of Jews, but in the Middle East, once Jerusalem was taken, Jews were burned alive or sold into slavery. The small number who survived did so by converting to Christianity.

The First Crusade was militarily successful. But by the middle of the eleventh century, Islamic armies had recaptured much of the Middle East, prompting a Second Crusade from 1147 to 1149, and then a Third in 1189 (see Map **10.4**). Politically and religiously, the first three Crusades were failures. Rather than freeing the Holy Land from Muslim influence, they cemented it more firmly than ever. But they did succeed in stimulating Western trade with the East. Merchants from Venice, Genoa, and Pisa followed the Crusaders into the region, and soon new wealth, generated by these new markets, flowed into Europe. The Fourth Crusade in 1202 was motivated almost entirely by profit as Venice agreed to transport some 30,000 Crusaders in return for their destroying its commercial rivals in the Adriatic and Aegean, particularly Constantinople.

Krak des Chevaliers and the Medieval Castle

Krak des Chevaliers (Fig. **10.26**), in northern Syria, was first occupied by Crusaders in 1109, and, beginning in 1142, it was occupied by the Knights Hospitaller, whose mission was to care for the sick and wounded. During the Crusades, it was besieged 12 times, finally falling to Berber invaders in 1271.

Krak des Chevaliers was modeled on the castle-fortresses built by the Normans in England and northern France.

When the Normans arrived in England in the twelfth century, they needed defenses against the Saxons. To provide protection, they built mounds, or mottes, topped with a wooden tower, or keep (see Fig. 10.15). Beginning in 1078, stone castles gradually replaced these wooden fortifications (Fig. **10.27**). The sheer weight of the stone keep required that it be built on solid ground. So, unless a natural hill presented itself, the motte (the mound on which the older wooden towers had been built) was eliminated. Now the keep served as the main residence of the lord and included a main hall, a chapel, and a dungeon. Workshops, kitchens, and storehouses surrounded the bailey. Most stone castles had a well for fresh water in case of siege, a great advantage over the aqueduct supplying Krak des Chevaliers.

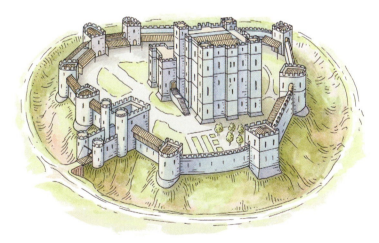

Fig. 10.27 Stone castle. Surrounded by a moat, a trench filled with water, the stone castles that replaced motte and bailey castles were eminently defensible, comparatively immune from fire, and, rising as high as 100 feet, imposing symbols of Norman power.

ELEANOR OF AQUITAINE AND THE ART OF COURTLY LOVE

What is courtly love and how does it manifest itself in the literature of the period?

In the Second Crusade, Eleanor of Aquitaine (ca. 1122–1204) accompanied her husband, King Louis VII, into battle in the Middle East, along with 300 ladies of similar mind, all dressed in armor and carrying lances. Her intent was to help the sick and wounded. The women, most of whom eventually returned safely to Europe, never engaged in battle, but theirs was an act of uncommon personal and social bravery. They were widely chided by contemporary commentators, but their actions underscore the changing role of women in medieval society.

Eleanor was, by all accounts, fiercely independent, so much so that, in March 1152, Louis had his marriage to her annulled, technically on the grounds that they were related by blood, but in reality because he suspected her of adultery. Eleanor lost no time in reestablishing her position—just eight weeks after the annulment from Louis, she married Henry of Anjou, soon to be King Henry II of England. Together they had eight children, including the future English kings, Richard the Lion-Hearted and John, but Eleanor's relationship with Henry was anything but easy. Henry cheated on her and treated her abusively, until she finally abandoned England for France in 1170. From Poitiers, in 1173, she encouraged her three surviving sons, Richard, John, and Geoffrey, to rebel against their father, and Henry ultimately responded to her meddling by bringing her back to England in 1179 and keeping her under house arrest until his death in 1189.

In the decade that she lived at Poitiers, Eleanor and her daughter by Louis VII, Marie, countess of Champagne, established that city as the center of a secular culture and literary movement that celebrated the art of courtly love. This was the time in which the great oral poems of the first millennium—poems like *Beowulf* and *Song of Roland*—were first written down. Furthermore, over 2,600 poems survive as texts composed by the **troubadour** poets of Eleanor's own day, and some of these survive with the accompanying music for the poems as well.

Troubadour Poetry

Troubadour poetry originated in the south of France, in Provence, the area around the lower Rhone Valley, and slightly later spread north (the Northern poets are sometimes called *trouvère* poets to distinguish from their Southern forebears—and far more *trouvère* music survives than troubadour). The troubadour poets, most of them men, though a few were women, usually accompanied themselves on a lyre or lute, and in their poems they can be said to have "invented" romantic love as we know it today—not

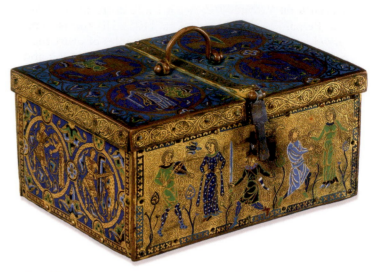

Fig. 10.28 Casket with scenes of courtly love, from Limoges. ca. 1180. Champlevé enamel, 3⅝" × 8½" × 6⅜". © The Trustees of the British Museum. At the left, a lady listens, rather sternly, as a troubadour poet expresses his love for her. In the center is a knight, sword in one hand and key to the lady's heart in the other. On the right, the knight kneels before the lady, his hands shaped in a heart; a rope around his neck, held by the lady, signifies his fidelity to her.

the feelings and emotions associated with love, but the conventions and vocabulary that we use to describe it. The primary feeling is one of longing, of a knight or nobleman for a woman (usually unattainable because married or of a higher status), or, when the troubadour was a woman—a **trobairitz**—the reverse. Thus, to love is to suffer, to wander aimlessly, unable to concentrate on anything but the mental image of the beloved, to lose one's appetite, to lie sleepless at night—in short, to give up life for a dream. There was, in addition, a quasi-religious aspect to courtly love. Recognizing that he is beset by earthly desires, the lover sees his ability to resist these temptations and rise above his own base humanity as evidence of his spiritual purity. Finally, in the courtly love tradition, the smitten knight or nobleman must be willing to perform any deed to win his lady's favor. In fact, the loyalty that he once conferred upon his lord in the feudal system is, in courtly love, transferred to his lady (who is often, in fact, his lord's wife), as the scenes on a jeweled twelfth-century casket make clear (Fig. **10.28**). If the courtly love tradition reduced women to little more than objects of male desire, in some measure it also allowed them to share in the power enjoyed by their husbands. The thirteenth-century poet Guiraut Requier wrote that four ranks of musicians existed. The lowest was the *jongleurs*, musicians who not only sang but also engaged in acrobatics, animal tricks, and other like entertainments. *Minstrels* were next on the ladder, full-time musicians of lesser station than troubadours because they did not write their own material. The *troubadours* composed their own music and lyrics and performed their own songs, most often at court. The highest rank of musician was *doctores de trobar* (*trobar* means "to invent" and is the root of *troubadour*), the most outstanding composers of the day.

Bernard de Ventadour One of these *doctores de trobar* was Bernard de Ventadour (d. ca. 1195). His poems, composed in honor of Eleanor, became staples of court society. Bernard apparently first met Eleanor at Anjou and accompanied her to England after she became queen. Thus, it is likely that his music influenced English song as well as French. Bernard's work is remarkable in that 41 of his surviving songs are musically notated, so that they can be performed today more or less as they were originally. "The Skylark" is typical (track **10.5**, **Reading 10.7**).

Listen on MyArtsLab

READING 10.7

Bernard de Ventadour, "The Skylark," verses 1–4 and 7

Now when I see the skylark lift
His wings for joy in dawn's first ray
Then let himself, oblivious, drift
For all his heart is glad and gay,
Ay! such great envies seize my thought
To see the rapture others find,
I marvel that desire does not
Consume away this heart of mine.
Alas, I thought I'd grown so wise;
In love I had so much to learn:
I can't control this heart that flies
To her who pays love no return.
Ay! now she steals, through love's sweet theft,
My heart, my self, my world entire;
She steals herself and I am left
Only this longing and desire.

Losing control, I've lost all right
To rule my life; my life's her prize
Since first she showed me true delight
In those bright mirrors, her two eyes.
Ay! once I'd caught myself inside
Her glances, I've been drowned in sighs,
Dying as fair Narcissus died
In streams that mirror captive skies.

Deep in despair, I'll place no trust
In women though I did before;
I've been their champion so it's just
That I renounce them evermore;
When none will lift me from my fall
When she has cast me down in shame,
Now I distrust them, one and all,
I've learned too well they're all the same.

Since she, my Lady, shows no care
To earn my thanks, nor pays Love's rights
Since she'll not hear my constant prayer
And my love yields her no delights,
I say no more; I silent go;
She gives me death; let death reply.
My Lady won't embrace me so
I leave, exiled to pain for aye.

Beatriz de Dia We know of 12 or so *trobairitz*, or woman troubadour poets. Of these, one of the best is Beatriz de Dia, wife of William, count of Poitiers. While married, Beatriz fell in love with a knight and, according to a contemporary chronicler, wrote "many good songs" dedicated to him. Of the four of these late twelfth- or early thirteenth-century songs that survive, only one, "A chantar" ("Song"), still has its music (track **10.6**). Each line of the poem has its own musical phrase, and, as is true for most secular song, the music is strophic—the same music repeats in each stanza.

Listen on MyArtsLab

Beatriz's "Cruel Are the Pains I've Suffered" is an example of the remarkable freedom of expression that a *trobairitz* could enjoy. She clearly regrets her choice to remain true to her husband, and in fact the poem reads as a frank invitation to adultery (**Reading 10.8**):

READING 10.8

Comtessa de Dia's "Cruel Are the Pains I've Suffered," from *Lark in the Morning: The Verses of the Troubadours*

Cruel are the pains I've suffered
For a certain cavalier
Whom I have had. I declare
I love him—let it be known forever.
But now I see that I was deceived:
When I'm dressed or when I languish
In bed, I suffer a great anguish—
I should have given him my love.

One night I'd like to take my swain
To bed and hug him, wearing no clothes—
I'd give him reason to suppose
He was in heaven, if I deigned
To be his pillow! For I've been more
In love with him than Floris was
With Blanchefleur: my mind, my eyes
I give to him; my life, *mon cor.*[1]

When will I have you in my power,
Dearest friend, charming and good?
Lying with you one night I would
Kiss you so you could feel my ardor.
I want to have you in my husband's
Place, of that you can rest assured—
Provided you give your solemn word
That you'll obey my every command.

[1] Mon cor means "my heart" and alludes to a popular French romance, *Floris et Blanchefleur*.

That poems such as this survived, let alone that they became well known, underscores the remarkable personal freedom of court women of the age. In fact, we know that aristocratic women, particularly in France, gained many rights during the period, among them the right to hold property, administer estates, and create wills—all at least partially attributable to the need for women to manage their husbands' estates while the men were fighting in the Crusades

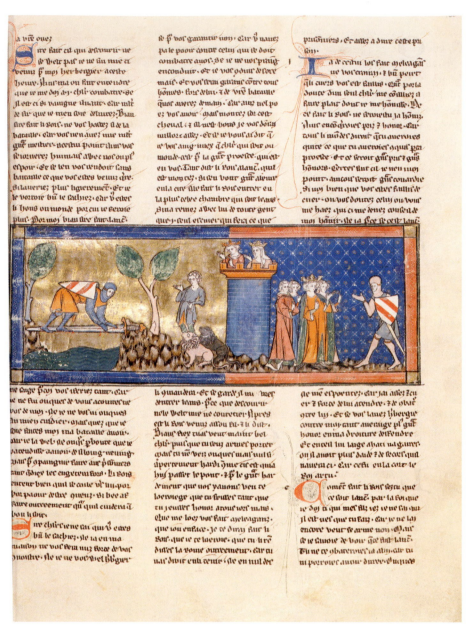

Fig. 10.29 Page with *Lancelot Crossing the Sword Bridge and Guinevere in the Tower,* from *Romance of Lancelot.* **ca. 1300.** Illuminated manuscript, 13¼" × 10". © The Pierpont Morgan Library/Art Resource, New York. In this trial, Lancelot crosses a raging stream, cutting himself on a long, sharpened sword, but "even his suffering is sweet to him" with Guinevere in sight.

or other wars. That they also felt free to confess to loving men other than their husbands suggests that Eleanor's notorious relationship with Henry II was hardly unique.

The Romance: Chrétien de Troyes's *Lancelot*

Because the poetry of the courtly love tradition was written in the **vernacular**—the common language of everyday life—and not in the Latin of the highly educated, a broader audience was able to enjoy it. And longer forms, like the *Song of Roland*, also began to circulate widely, some of them in prose. A remarkable example is the work of Marie de France. Though born in France, she wrote in the English court, and in the late twelfth century, she published a

collection of over 100 *Fables*, many of which were her own. Marie also published another collection of 12 *Lais*, folktales that deal, in a variety of forms and lengths, with matters of love. A *lai* was technically a short romance that combined supernatural elements and the courtly love tradition; typically they were sung by minstrels, accompanied by a harp or lyre. In *Bisclavret* (see **Reading 10.9,** pages 359–361), she tells the story of a werewolf who is unjustly betrayed by his "loving" wife but ultimately saved by a more loving king.

One of the most popular works of the day, Chrétien de Troyes's *Lancelot,* appeared around 1170. Centered on the adventures of Lancelot, a knight in the court of the legendary King Arthur of Britain, and focusing particularly on his courtly love-inspired relationship with Guinevere, Arthur's wife, the poem is an example of the **medieval romance**. The term "romance" derives from the Old French term *romans*, which referred to the vernacular, everyday language of the people as opposed to Latin. The medieval romance was designed to entertain a broad audience with stories of adventure and love, while it pretended to be an actual historical account of Charlemagne, King Arthur, or Roman legend.

Lancelot, subtitled *The Knight of the Cart*, opens with a challenge offered to King Arthur and his court on Ascension Day by a knight named Sir Meleagant of Gorre. Sir Meleagant claims to hold many of Arthur's knights in prison, but offers to free them if any knight dares to escort the beautiful Queen Guinevere into the forest and defend her against him. Arthur's brother Kay asks to take on the mission, and Arthur agrees. Knowing Kay to be a poor knight, Sir Gawain and the other knights of the Round Table quickly chase after him into the forest. Too late, they come upon Kay's riderless horse, all that remains of a scene of recent combat. Lancelot takes one of Gawain's horses and charges off after Meleagant, who has abducted Guinevere. Gawain catches up to Lancelot, finds the horse he has lent him dead, the victim of a fierce battle, and then discovers Lancelot on foot, having overtaken a cart of the kind used to take criminals to their execution. The cart is driven by a dwarf, who has told Lancelot that if he boards the cart, he will soon know Guinevere's fate. To board such a cart is a great dishonor, but Lancelot reluctantly agrees, and the next day, Lancelot and Gawain learn the way to Meleagant's kingdom of Gorre from a damsel standing at a fork in the road.

Both forks lead to Gorre, one by way of the perilous Underwater Bridge, the other by the even more perilous Sword Bridge. Gawain takes the first, Lancelot the second. Lancelot faces many challenges and temptations but finally arrives at the Sword Bridge, which he crosses by virtue of his love for Guinevere (Fig. **10.29**). He subsequently defeats Meleagant but spares his life at Guinevere's behest. Guinevere, to his dismay, behaves coldly toward him, offended at his earlier hesitation to enter the cart. He should not have put his own honor before love, she explains. After reuniting with Gawain, who was preparing to take on Meleagant himself in Lancelot's absence, Lancelot overcomes Meleagant once and for all, and he and Guinevere are reconciled. Guinevere agrees to meet Lancelot in Meleagant's castle secretly at night. There he kneels before her, "holding her more dear than the relic of any saint," a scene in which the "religion of love"—so marvelous in its physical joy that the narrator cannot tell of it, "for in a story it has no place"—is confounded with spiritual ecstasy. This feature is surely indebted to Islamic notions of physical love as a metaphor for the love of God, as found in Sufi poetry (see Chapter 9) and in the love songs popular in the Islamic Spanish courts, where the bilingual minstrels who inaugurated the troubadour tradition first flourished.

CONTINUITY & CHANGE

Sufi poetry, **p. 310**

The love of woman celebrated in medieval romance and troubadour poetry was equated in the Christian mind with love for the Virgin Mary. As Mother of Heaven and of Christ, as the all-compassionate mediator between the Judgment seat and the horrors of hell, Mary was increasingly recognized as the spiritual equivalent of the lady of chivalry, crowned the Queen of Heaven, overseeing her heavenly court. Songs were sung to her, cathedrals built in her honor (all cathedrals named Notre-Dame, "Our Lady," are dedicated to her), and a Cult of the Virgin developed around her.

Lancelot was written at the request of Eleanor of Aquitaine's daughter, Marie—herself named after the Virgin—as its laudatory prologue, a standard feature of the form, attests (**Reading 10.10**):

READING 10.10

from Chrétien de Troyes, *Lancelot*

Since my lady of Champagne wishes me to undertake to write a romance, I shall very gladly do so, being so devoted to her service as to do anything in the world for her, without any intention of flattery. But if one were to introduce any flattery upon such an occasion, he might say, and I would subscribe to it, that this lady surpasses all others who are alive, just as the south wind which blows in May or April is more lovely than any other wind. But upon my word, I am not one to wish to flatter my lady. I will simply say: "The Countess is worth as many queens as a gem is worth of pearls and sards." Nay I shall make no comparison, and yet it is true in spite of me; I will say, however, that her command has more to do with this work than any thought or pains that I may expend upon it. Here Chrétien begins his book. … The material and the treatment of it are given and furnished to him by the Countess, and he is simply trying to carry out her concern and intention.

Chrétien presents himself as the servant of Marie who devotes his writer's skill to doing her bidding, just as the knight Lancelot serves Queen Guinevere with his knightly skill, and as the Christian serves the Virgin Mary. Similarly, Chrétien's story transforms the heroism of the *Song of Roland*, which is motivated by feudal loyalty to king and country, to a form of chivalry based on the allegiance of the knight to his lady. In a medieval romance, the knight is driven to heroic action not so much by the lure of greater glory as by his own desire for his lady. To the knight, the lady is a prize to be won, an object to be possessed. Beyond the drama of his exploits and his lady's distress, the conflict between the sexual desires of both knight and lady and the hypothetical purity of their "spiritual" love gives the story its narrative power. In a medieval romance, as well as in the troubadour poem, perhaps the greatest test the lovers face is their own sexuality—an almost sure-fire guarantor of the form's popularity.

Toward a New Urban Style: The Gothic

Romanesque art and architecture thrived, especially along the pilgrimage routes in the south of France, from roughly 1050 to 1200. But in the 1140s, a new style began to emerge in the north that today we call Gothic. New cathedrals—at Saint-Denis, just outside Paris, and at Chartres—were dominated by soaring spires and stained-glass windows. Decorative sculpture proliferated. Pointed arches, as opposed to the rounded arches of the Romanesque barrel vault, lifted interior spaces to new heights. All of these new elements were anticipated in the Romanesque, in the magnificent stained glass at Poitiers, in the sculpture of the pilgrimage-route church portals, and in the pointed arches of Fontenay Abbey. And like their Romanesque forebears, most of the new Gothic cathedrals were built to house precious relics and to accommodate large crowds of pilgrims.

The Romanesque style was a product of rural monastic life, separated from worldly events and interactions, but the Gothic style was a creation of the emerging city—of the craft guilds and artisans, merchants, lawyers, and bankers who gathered there. It represents the first step in a gradual shift in the West from a spiritually centered culture to one with a more secular focus. No longer was religion—worshiping at a pilgrimage church or fighting a Crusade—the dominant motive for travel. Instead, trade was. Merchants and bankers grew in importance. Craftsmen flourished. Secular rulers became more ambitious. In fact, personal ambition and success would increasingly be defined in worldly, rather than spiritual, terms.

The Gothic does not, however, abandon the spiritual. The new masonry architecture that developed resulted in intricate stonework that was almost skeletal in its lightness, soaring ever higher to create lofty interior spaces

that inevitably caused the viewers' eyes, upon entering the space, to raise heavenward. These extraordinarily high spaces were lit, furthermore, by stained glass that purposefully evoked the miraculous light of the Creator himself. Although the architecture was intended to invoke intensely spiritual feelings, we also see the beginning of a renewed interest in worldly things. This shift is evident in two images of angels. The flattened, distorted features of the angel on the Romanesque capital from Vézelay (Fig. **10.30**) contrast dramatically with the heightened naturalism of the

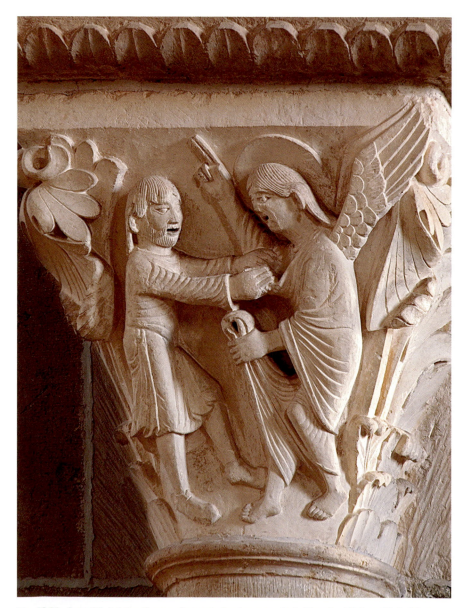

Fig. 10.30 *Angel Subduing Demon*, decorated column capital, Church of Sainte-Madeleine, Vézelay, France. ca. 1089–1206.

angel from the portal at Reims (Fig. **10.31**). The Romanesque angel is depicted in profile, its wings flattened behind it. The folds of the drapery covering its body are realized by parallel bands of shallowly incised lines. But freed from the stone backdrop of relief sculpture, the Gothic angel steps forward with an amazingly lifelike gesture. Where the gender of the Romanesque angel is indeterminate, the Reims sculpture is so lifelike—and clearly feminine—that it seems to have been modeled on a real person. Nothing of the formulaic vocabulary of Romanesque sculpture remains. The winsome smile and delicate figure of the Gothic angel are, finally, more worldly than angelic. In fact, she seems so much a part of our world that we hardly miss the halo that identifies her Romanesque forebear. ∎

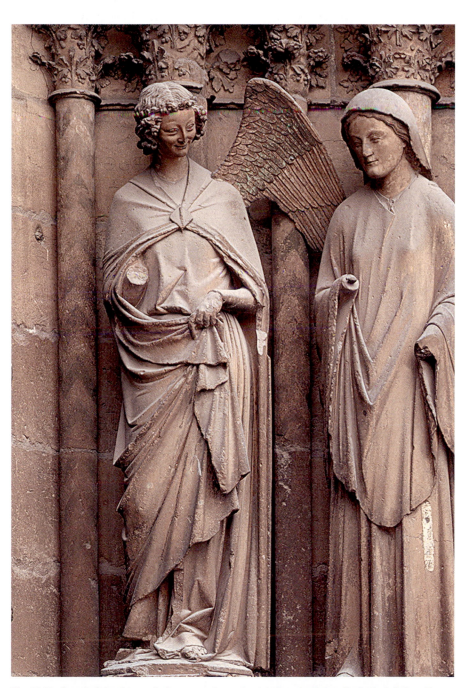

Fig. 10.31 *Angel of the Annunciation*, **central portal, west facade, Reims Cathedral, Reims, France. ca. 1245–55** (detail of Fig. 12.16 in Chapter 12).

10.1 Describe what Anglo-Saxon art and literature tell us about Anglo-Saxon culture.

The burial mound at Sutton Hoo has revealed more about the art and culture of Anglo-Saxon England than any other archeological site. Buried in the mound was a lord or chief to whom his followers owed absolute loyalty. Can you describe the nature of the economic relationship between the lord and his followers? How is this relationship reflected in the epic poem *Beowulf*? How does it compare to the Roman system of patronage?

Although by no means a Christian poem, *Beowulf's* themes are consonant with Christian values, teaching its audience that power, strength, fame, and life itself are transitory. Christianity survived the end of Roman control over Britain only in the farthest reaches of the British islands—in Cornwall, Wales, and Ireland. But in 597, Pope Gregory I sent a mission to England, headed by the Benedictine prior Augustine, to convert the pagan Anglo-Saxons. The pope urged Augustine not to try to eliminate pagan traditions but to incorporate them into Christian practice. How is this reflected in the manuscripts produced in the monasteries?

10.2 Discuss Charlemagne's impact on medieval culture and the legacy of his rule.

Charlemagne gained control of most of the European continent, creating what would later be known as the Holy Roman Empire. Charlemagne's exploits were celebrated in many poems, chief among them the *Song of Roland*. What feudal values are reflected in this poem? How do they differ from those of *Beowulf*? Why do we call the *Song of Roland*'s values system a "chivalric code"?

In keeping with his stature as head of the largest feudal empire since Roman times, Charlemagne charged the scholars working in his capital of Aachen, chief among them Alcuin of York, with creating a curriculum that would promote literacy throughout the Empire. How did writing contribute to this aim? Arguably the most important institution of the Carolingian era was the monastery. Charlemagne imposed the Rule of Saint Benedict on all monasteries and created what he believed to be the ideal monastery at Saint Gall. What is the Rule of Saint Benedict? What role does music play in monastic life? What role did women have in monastic life, and how was Hildegard of Bingen unique among them?

Although the Ottonian Empire was a conscious reinvention of the Carolingian dream, unifying Church and State in a single administrative and political bureaucracy, it was built on the exercise of power, not consensus, and it eventually collapsed in the eleventh century. How would you characterize the art created in this period?

When Viking warriors from Scandinavia invaded the Frankish territory to the west of the Ottonian Empire in the tenth century, the Carolingian Empire effectively dissolved. As illustrated in the famous *Bayeux Tapestry*, the Normans subsequently also invaded England from their stronghold in northern France, defeating the English at the Battle of Hastings on October 14, 1066. England and northern France thus became one country, with one king, William I, the Conqueror. Why did William immediately order a survey of the country, called the Domesday Book?

10.3 Define the Romanesque and its relation to both pilgrimage churches and the Cluniac abbey.

Churches such as the Abbey Church of Sainte-Foy in Conques, France, became the focus of Western culture in the Middle Ages as Christians began to do penance for their sins by undertaking pilgrimages to churches housing the relics of venerated saints. The churches were Romanesque. How would you define this architectural style?

Most of the pilgrimage churches were controlled by the Abbey of Cluny. Cluny's abbot was among the most powerful men in Europe, and the church at Cluny was a model for all pilgrimage churches. Music was central to the Cluniac liturgy. Can you describe the musical practices at Cluny? How do they differ from those of Charlemagne's time? Why did Bernard, abbot of the Cistercian monastery at Clairvaux, object to Cluniac practice?

10.4 Examine the motivations for the Crusades and appraise their outcome.

On November 25, 1095, Pope Urban II, who had been trained at Cluny, preached the First Crusade, pleading with Christians to retake Jerusalem from the Muslims. Nearly 100,000 young men signed on out of religious zeal, and for the sake of adventure and a chance to get away from troubles at home. How did the feudal primogeniture system play a role? In the Middle East the Crusaders built giant fortresses such as the Krak des Chevaliers, modeled on the fortresses built by the Normans in England. In general, how would you describe the outcome of the first and the three subsequent Crusades?

10.5 Explain the courtly love tradition as it manifests itself in the literature of the period.

Eleanor of Aquitaine accompanied her husband, King Louis VII of France, on the Second Crusade. At Poitiers, Eleanor and her daughter, Marie de Champagne, championed a literary movement that celebrated the art of courtly love. These values are reflected in medieval romances and in the work of troubadour poets like Bernard de Ventadour and Beatriz de Dia. How does courtly love reflect feudal traditions? How does it also reflect certain religious ideals? How does the medieval romance reflect the same traditions and ideals?

✔ **Study** and **review** on **MyArtsLab**

READINGS

from Hildegard of Bingen, *Scivias*

Hildegard of Bingen's remarkable *Scivias* ("Know the Ways of the Lord") is a compilation of her visions and her analyses of them. The following is her vision of the devil. After describing her vision, she analyzes it line by line, and in so doing creates a vision of hell sufficient to frighten any soul into accepting a Christian calling. Such visions of the devil would become commonplace in the art of her time (see Fig. 10.23), but hers is one of the earliest and most powerful presentations.

Then I saw a burning light, as large and as high as a mountain, divided at its summit as if into many tongues. And there stood in the presence of this light a multitude of white-clad people, before whom what seemed like a screen of translucent crystal had been placed, reaching from their breasts to their feet. And before that multitude, as if in a road, there lay on its back a monster shaped like a worm, wondrously large and long, which aroused an indescribable sense of horror and rage. On its left stood a kind of marketplace, which displayed human wealth and worldly delights and various sorts of merchandise; and some people were running through it very fast and not buying anything, while others were walking slowly and stopping both to sell and to buy. Now that worm was black and bristly, covered with ulcers and pustules, and it was divided into five regions from the head down through the belly to its feet, like stripes. One was green, one white, one red, one yellow and one black; and they were full of deadly poison. But its head had been so crushed that the left side of its jawbone was dislocated. Its eyes were bloody on the surface and burning within; its ears were round and bristly: its nose and mouth were those of a viper, its hands human, its feet a viper's feet, and its tail short and horrible.

And around its neck a chain was riveted, which also bound its hands and feet and this chain was firmly fastened to a rock in the abyss, confining it so that it could not move about as its wicked will desired. Many flames came forth from its mouth, dividing into four parts: One part ascended to the clouds, another breathed forth among secular people, another among spiritual people, and the last descended into the abyss. And the flame that sought the clouds was opposing the people who wanted to get to Heaven. And I saw three groups of these. One was close to the clouds, one in the middle space between the clouds and the earth, and one moved along near the earth; and all were shouting repeatedly, "Let us get to Heaven!" But they were whirled hither and thither by that flame; some did not waver, some barely kept their balance and some fell to the earth but then rose again and started toward Heaven. The flame that breathed forth among secular people burned some of them so that they were hideously blackened and others it transfixed so that it could move them anywhere it wanted. Some escaped from the flame and moved toward those who sought Heaven, reiterating shouts of "O you faithful, give us help!" But others remained transfixed. Meanwhile, the flame that breathed forth among spiritual people concealed them in obscurity; but I saw them in six categories. For some of them were cruelly injured by the flame's fury; but when it could not

injure one of them, it burningly breathed on them the deadly poison that flowed from the worm's head to its feet, either green or white or red or yellow or black. But the flame that sought the abyss contained in itself diverse torments for those who had worshiped Satan in place of God, not washed by the font of baptism or knowing the light of truth and faith. And I saw sharp arrows whistling loudly from its mouth, and black smoke exhaling from its breast, and a burning fluid boiling up from its loins, and a hot whirlwind blowing from its navel, and the uncleanness of frogs issuing from its bowels; all of which affected human beings with grave disquiet. And the hideous and foul-smelling vapor that came out of it infected many people with its own perversity. But behold, a great multitude of people came, shining brightly; they forcefully trod the worm underfoot and severely tormented it, but could not be injured by its flames or its poison. And I heard again the voice from Heaven, saying to me …:

3. The deceptions of the Devil lie in the path humans take in this world

    And before that multitude, as if in a road, there lies on its back a monster shaped like a worm, wondrously large and long. This means that the ancient serpent is well-known to humanity in the course of the pilgrimage of the good and the bad through the world, not in that visible form but in its inner meaning. Its mouth is gaping upward in order to pull down by deception those who are tending toward the celestial regions; but it is lying down, because the Son of God destroyed so much of its strength that it cannot stand up. **And it arouses an indescribable sense of horror and rage;** for the mental capacity of mortal humans is insufficient to understand the manifold variations of its poisonous fury and malicious exertions.

4. The Devil offers fraudulent riches and delights, and some buy them

    On its left stands a kind of marketplace, which displays human wealth and worldly delights and various sorts of merchandise. For the left hand of the destroyer signifies death, and there is seen a marketplace composed of Death's evil works: pride and vainglory in corruptible riches, licentiousness and lust for transitory pleasures, and trafficking in all kinds of earthly desires. Thus those who would be terrified by the horror of the Devil if they met it openly are deceived by these things; they are lightly offered persuasions to vice as a merchant displays his diverse wares to people, and delighted by the display so that they buy what is offered. So the Devil offers humanity his lying arts; and those who desire them buy them. How? They throw away a good conscience as if selling it, and they collect deadly wounds in their souls as if buying them. ...

6. The Devil labors to deceive the five senses of humanity

But you see that **that worm is black and gristly, covered with ulcers and pustules.** This shows that the ancient serpent is full of the darkness of black betrayal, and the bristles of concealed deception, and the ulcers of 100 impure pollution, and the pustules of repressed fury. **And it is divided into five sections from the head down through the belly to its feet, like stripes;** for from the time of his first deception when he tried to put himself forward until the final time when his madness will end, he does not cease to inspire the five human senses with the desire for vices. Simulating a deceitful rectitude he draws people to the downward slopes of his unclean arts. One is green, one white, one red, one yellow, and one black and they are full of deadly poison. The green indicates worldly melancholy; 110 the white, improper irreverence; the red, deceptive glory; the yellow, biting envy; and the black, shameful deceit, with all other perversities that bring death to the souls of those who consent to them. ...

8. What the eyes and ears and nostrils of the serpent signify

Its eyes are bloody on the surface and burning within; because his wicked intent outwardly inflicts harm on human bodies and inwardly drives a fiery dart into their souls. **Its ears are round and bristly;** for the bristles of his arts pierce a person all around, so that if he finds anything 120 that is his in that person, he may quickly throw him down. **Its nose and mouth are those of a viper;** for he shows people unbridled and vile behavior, through which transfixing them with many vices, he may cruelly slay them.

9. Its hands and feet and tail and what they signify

Its hands are human, for he practices his arts in human deeds; its feet a viper's feet, because he ceaselessly ambushes people when they are journeying and inflicts devilish lacerations on them; **and its tail short and horrible,** for it signifies his power in the short but most evil time 130 of the son of perdition, whose desire to run wild exceeds his power to do it.

READING CRITICALLY

In her third point of analysis, Hildegard says that "the mental capacity of mortal humans is insufficient to understand the manifold variations of its poisonous fury and malicious exertions." What is her rhetorical strategy here? In other words, why does she say this, and what effect does she think it will have on the reader?

READING 10.6

from the *Gesta Francorum* (*Deeds of the Franks*), "The Fall of Jerusalem"

The *Gesta Francorum* is an anonymous account of the First Crusade (1096–99). It is an extraordinary account not only of military matters—tactical operations, supply and provision operations, and so on—but also of the psychological mood of the Crusaders. The knight who wrote it was, apparently, an average soldier, and he gives us something of the unprejudiced point of view of the army as a whole.

At length, our leaders decided to beleaguer the city with siege machines, so that we might enter and worship the Saviour at the Holy Sepulchre.[1] They constructed wooden towers and many other siege machines. Duke Godfrey made a wooden tower and other siege devices, and Count Raymond did the same, although it was necessary to bring wood from a considerable distance. However, when the Saracens saw our men engaged in this work, they greatly strengthened the fortifications of the city and increased the height of the turrets at night. On a certain Sabbath night, the leaders, after having decided which parts of the wall were weakest, dragged the tower and the machines to the eastern side of the city. Moreover, we set up the tower at earliest dawn and equipped and covered it on the first, second, and third days of the week. The Count of St. Gilles erected his tower on the plain to the south of the city.

While all this was going on, our water supply was so limited that no one could buy enough water for one denarius[2] to satisfy or quench his thirst. ... Early on the sixth day of the week we again attacked the city on all sides, but as the assault was unsuccessful, we were all astounded and fearful. However, when the hour approached on which our Lord Jesus Christ deigned to suffer on the Cross for us, our knights began to fight bravely in one of the towers—namely, the party with Duke Godfrey and his brother, Count Eustace. One of our knights, named Lethold, clambered up the wall of the city, and no sooner had he ascended than the defenders fled from the walls and through the city. Our men followed, killing and slaying even to the Temple of Solomon, where the slaughter was so great that our men waded in blood up to their ankles. ...

[Finally] the pilgrims entered the city, pursuing and killing the Saracens up to the Temple of Solomon, where the enemy gathered in force. The battle raged throughout the day, so that the Temple was covered with their blood. When the pagans had been overcome, our men seized great numbers, both men and women, either killing them or keeping them captive, as they wished. ... Afterward, the army scattered throughout the city and took possession of the gold and silver, the horses and mules, and the houses filled with goods of all kinds.

[1] **Holy Sepulchre:** the church built at the site where Jesus was believed to be buried and where he rose from the dead.
[2] ***Denarius*:** a silver coin of the Roman Empire.

Rejoicing and weeping for joy, our people came to the Sepulchre of Jesus our Saviour to worship and pay their debt [i.e., fulfill crusading vows by worshiping at the Sepulchre]. At dawn our men cautiously went up to the roof of the Temple and attacked Saracen men and women, beheading them with naked swords. Some of the Saracens, however, leaped from the Temple roof. …

Then our leaders in council decided that each one should offer alms with prayers, that the Lord might choose for Himself whom He wanted to reign over the others and rule the city. They also ordered all the Saracen dead to be cast outside because of the great stench, since the whole city was filled with their corpses; and so the living Saracens dragged the dead before the exits of the gates and arranged them in heaps, as if they were houses. No one ever saw or heard of such slaughter of pagan people, for funeral pyres were formed from them like pyramids, and no one knows their number except God alone.

READING CRITICALLY

This account of the fall of Jerusalem amounts to a description of what might be called, from a contemporary point of view, a war crime. Why does the writer not see it in those terms?

READING 10.9

from Marie de France, *Bisclavret* (*The Werewolf*)

We actually know almost nothing about Marie de France, except that she was a marvelous storyteller. At the end of her collection of *Fables*, she tells us, "I'll give my name, for memory: / I am from France, my name's Marie"—and that about sums up what we know of her. Some speculate that she worked in Henry II's court, and that she was Henry II's half-sister, since Henry's father had an illegitimate daughter named Marie who subsequently became abbess of Shaftesbury about 1180.

The following *lai* represents one of the darker of the 12 she wrote. Combining the stuff of medieval folk superstition and the chivalric tradition, it is a perfect example of the growing popular appeal of literary works in the Romanesque world.

Since I am undertaking to compose *lais*,
I don't want to forget Bisclavret;
In Breton, the *lai's* name is *Bisclavret*—
the Normans call it *Garwaf* [The Werewolf].
In the old days, people used to say—
and it often actually happened—
that some men turned into werewolves
and lived in the woods.
A werewolf is a savage beast;
while his fury is on him   10
he eats men, does much harm,
goes deep in the forest to live.
But that's enough of this for now:
I want to tell you about the Bisclavret.
In Brittany there lived a nobleman
whom I've heard marvelously praised;
a fine, handsome knight
who behaved nobly.
He was close to his lord,
and loved by all his neighbors.   20
He had an estimable wife,
one of lovely appearance;
he loved her and she him,
but one thing was very vexing to her:
during the week he would be missing
for three whole days, and she didn't know
what happened to him or where he went.
Nor did any of his men know anything about it.
One day he returned home
happy and delighted;   30
she asked him about it.
"My lord," she said, "and dear love,

I'd very much like to ask you one thing—
if I dared;
but I'm so afraid of your anger
that nothing frightens me more."
When he heard that, he embraced her,
drew her to him and kissed her.
"My lady," he said, "go ahead and ask!
There's nothing you could want to know,   40
that, if I knew the answer, I wouldn't tell you."
"By God," she replied, "now I'm cured!
My lord, on the days when you go away from me
I'm in such a state—
so sad at heart,
so afraid I'll lose you—
that if I don't get quick relief
I could die of this very soon.
Please, tell me where you go,
where you have been staying.   50
I think you must have a lover,
and if that's so, you're doing wrong."
"My dear," he said, "have mercy on me, for God's sake!
Harm will come to me if I tell you about this,
because I'd lose your love
and even my very self."
When the lady heard this
she didn't take it lightly;
she kept asking him,
coaxed and flattered him so much,   60
that he finally told her what happened to him—
he hid nothing from her.
"My dear, I become a werewolf:
I go off into the great forest,

in the thickest part of the woods,
and I live on the prey I hunt down."
When he had told her everything,
she asked further
whether he undressed or kept his clothes on [when he
    became a werewolf]. 70
"Wife," he replied, "I go stark naked."
"Tell me, then, for God's sake, where your clothes are."
"That I won't tell you;
for if I were to lose them,
and then be discovered,
I'd stay a werewolf forever.
I'd be helpless
until I got them back.
That's why I don't want their hiding place to be known."
"My lord," the lady answered, 80
"I love you more than all the world;
you mustn't hide anything from me
or fear me in any way:
that doesn't seem like love to me.
What wrong have I done? For what sin of mine
do you mistrust me about anything?
Do the right thing and tell me!"
She harassed and bedeviled him so,
that he had no choice but to tell her.
"Lady," he said, "near the woods, 90
beside the road that I use to get there,
there's an old chapel
that has often done me good service;
under a bush there is a big stone,
hollowed out inside;
I hide my clothes right there
until I'm ready to come home."
The lady heard this wonder
and turned scarlet from fear;
she was terrified of the whole adventure. 100
Over and over she considered
how she might get rid of him;
she never wanted to sleep with him again …
[The lady asks a knight who has always loved her to find
    Bisclavret and steal her husband's clothing. When, as a
    result, Bisclavret fails to return, she marries the knight. But
    one day some hunters find Bisclavret in the woods.]
[T]he hunters and the dogs
chased him all day,
until they were just about to take him 110
and tear him apart,
at which point he saw the king
and ran to him, pleading for mercy.
He took hold of the king's stirrup,
kissed his leg and his foot.
The king saw this and was terrified;
he called his companions.
"My lords," he said, "come quickly!
Look at this marvel—
this beast is humbling itself to me. 120
It has the mind of a man, and it's begging me for mercy!
Chase the dogs away,
and make sure no one strikes it.

This beast is rational—he has a mind.
Hurry up: let's get out of here.
I'll extend my peace to the creature;
indeed, I'll hunt no more today!"
Thereupon the king turned away.
Bisclavret followed him;
he stayed close to the king, and wouldn't go away; 130
he'd no intention of leaving him.
The king led him to his castle;
he was delighted with this turn of events,
for he'd never seen anything like it.
He considered the beast a great wonder
and held him very dear.
He commanded all his followers,
for the sake of their love for him, to guard Bisclavret well,
and under no circumstances to do him harm;
none of them should strike him; 140
rather, he should be well fed and watered.
They willingly guarded the creature;
every day he went to sleep
among the knights, near the king.
Everyone was fond of him;
he was so noble and well behaved
that he never wished to do anything wrong.
Regardless of where the king might go,
Bisclavret never wanted to be separated from him;
he always accompanied the king. 150
The king became very much aware that the creature loved
    him.
Now listen to what happened next.
The king held a court;
to help him celebrate his feast
and to serve him as handsomely as possible,
he summoned all the barons
who held fiefs from him.
Among the knights who went,
and all dressed up in his best attire, 160
was the one who had married Bisclavret's wife.
He neither knew nor suspected
that he would find Bisclavret so close by.
As soon as he came to the palace
Bisclavret saw him,
ran toward him at full speed,
sank his teeth into him, and started to drag him down.
He would have done him great damage
if the king hadn't called him off,
and threatened him with a stick. 170
Twice that day he tried to bite the knight.
Everyone was extremely surprised,
since the beast had never acted that way
toward any other man he had seen.
All over the palace people said
that he wouldn't act that way without a reason:
that somehow or other, the knight had mistreated Bisclavret,
and now he wanted his revenge.
And so the matter rested
until the feast was over 180
and until the barons took their leave of the king
and started home.

The very first to leave,
to the best of my knowledge,
was the knight whom Bisclavret had attacked.
It's no wonder the creature hated him.
Not long afterward,
as the story leads me to believe,
the king, who was so wise and noble,
went back to the forest   190
where he had found Bisclavret,
and the creature went with him.
That night, when he finished hunting,
he sought lodging out in the countryside.
The wife of Bisclavret heard about it,
dressed herself elegantly,
and went the next day to speak with the king,
bringing rich presents for him.
When Bisclavret saw her coming,
no one could hold him back;   200
he ran toward her in a rage.
Now listen to how well he avenged himself!
He tore the nose off her face.
What worse thing could he have done to her?
Now men closed in on him from all sides;
they were about to tear him apart,
when a wise man said to the king,
"My lord, listen to me!
This beast has stayed with you,
and there's not one of us   210
who hasn't watched him closely,
hasn't traveled with him often.
He's never touched anyone,
or shown any wickedness,
except to this woman.
By the faith that I owe you,
he has some grudge against her,
and against her husband as well.
This is the wife of the knight
whom you used to like so much,   220
and who's been missing for so long—
we don't know what became of him.
Why not put this woman to torture
and see if she'll tell you
why the beast hates her?
Make her tell what she knows!
We've seen many strange things
happen in Brittany!"
The king took his advice;
he detained the knight.   230
At the same time he took the wife
and subjected her to torture;
out of fear and pain
she told all about her husband:
how she had betrayed him
and taken away his clothes;
the story he had told her

about what happened to him and where he went;
and how after she had taken his clothes
he'd never been seen in his land again.   240
She was quite certain
that this beast was Bisclavret.
The king demanded the clothes;
whether she wanted to or not
she sent home for them,
and had them brought to Bisclavret.
When they were put down in front of him
he didn't even seem to notice them;
the king's wise man—
the one who had advised him earlier—   250
said to him, "My lord, you're not doing it right.
This beast wouldn't, under any circumstances,
in order to get rid of his animal form,
put on his clothes in front of you;
you don't understand what this means:
he's just too ashamed to do it here.
Have him led to your chambers
and bring the clothes with him;
then we'll leave him alone for a while.
If he turns into a man, we'll know about it."   260
The king himself led the way
and closed all the doors on him.
After a while he went back,
taking two barons with him;
all three entered the king's chamber.
On the king's royal bed
they found the knight asleep.
The king ran to embrace him.
He hugged and kissed him again and again.
As soon as he had the chance,   270
the king gave him back all his lands;
he gave him more than I can tell.
He banished his wife,
chased her out of the country.
She went into exile with the knight
with whom she had betrayed her lord.
She had several children
who were widely known
for their appearance:
several women of the family   280
were actually born without noses,
and lived out their lives noseless.
The adventure that you have heard
really happened, no doubt about it.
The *lai* of Bisclavret[1] was made
so it would be remembered forever.

READING CRITICALLY

How does Marie's story suggest the conflict between bestiality and civilization in human behavior? What values does it most uphold?

[1] Until this point, "Bisclavret" is a common noun; hereafter it is used as the werewolf's name.

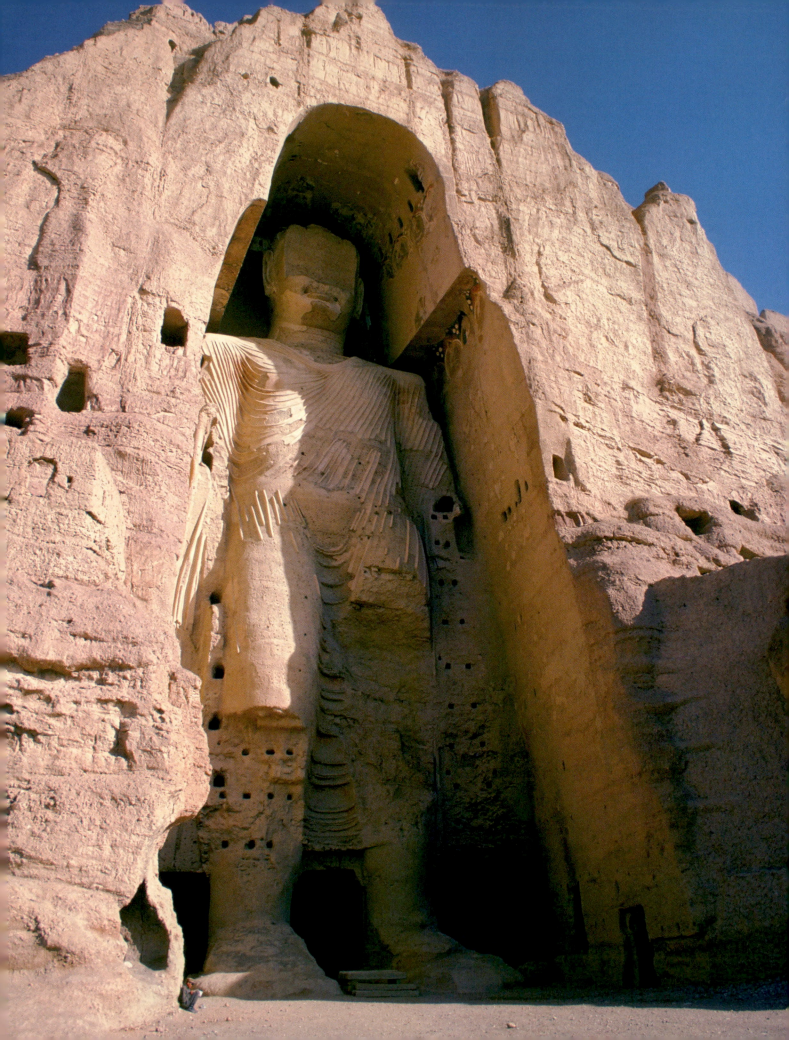

11 Centers of Culture
Court and City in the Larger World

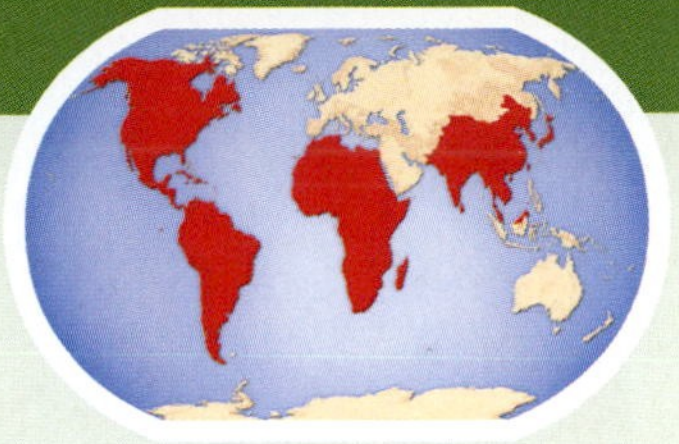

THINKING AHEAD

11.1 Describe how the literature, art, and architecture of the Tang and Song dynasties reflect the values of Chinese society.

11.2 Compare and contrast the ways in which Buddhist and Hindu art and architecture embody the presence of, respectively, Buddha and the Hindu gods.

11.3 Describe the complex relationship between court life and spiritual practice in Heian and Kamakura Japan.

11.4 Discuss the ways in which African arts serve as bridges between the temporal and supernatural worlds.

11.5 Understand how Mesoamerican and South American art and architecture reflect the relationship of the various cultures of the region to their gods.

Buddhism lies at the heart of culture in Asia during the period that in the West we call the Middle Ages. Between the first and third centuries CE, Buddhist missionaries from India had carried the religion along the Silk Road (see Chapter 7, *Continuity & Change*, page 239) into Southeast Asia and north into China and Korea. By 600 CE, Buddhism had reached all the way to Japan (Map **11.1**).

The first Chinese Buddhist monk to set out on the Silk Road in search of Buddhist scripture to translate into Chinese was Zhu Shixing of Hunan province. His journey dates from about 260 CE. At the same time, far away on the Silk Road, a resident of Dunhuang began his life's work as a translator of Buddhist texts. One of the most telling manifestations of the religion's spread is the appearance everywhere of images of Buddha (Fig. **11.1**). In early Buddhist art, the Buddha was never shown in figural form. It was believed to be impossible to represent the Buddha, since he had already passed to nirvana. Instead, his presence was symbolized by such things as his footprints, the banyan tree (see Chapter 7), the wheel (representing dharma, or the Wheel of Law), or elephants (see Fig. 7.19 in Chapter 7).

By the fourth century, during the reign of the Gupta rulers in India, the Buddha was commonly represented in human form. Typically his head is oval, framed by a halo. Atop his head is a mound, symbolizing his spiritual wisdom, and on his forehead is a "third eye," symbolizing his spiritual vision. His demeanor is gentle, reposed, and meditative. His elongated ears refer to his royal origins, and his hands are set in one of several symbolic gestures, called **mudra**. At Bamiyan, on the Silk Road in present-day Afghanistan, two massive Buddhas, 175 and 120 feet tall, were carved into a cliff face in the third century CE. These figures were completely destroyed by the fundamentalist Islamic Taliban in 2001. However, many surviving replicas from the Silk Road era suggest that the hands of these Buddhas, which succumbed to natural forces long ago, were held up in the *Dharmachakra* mudra, the teaching pose. This mudra symbolizes intellectual debate and is often associated with Buddhist centers of learning. Painted gold and studded with jewels, and surrounded by caves decorated

◀ **Fig. 11.1 Colossal Buddha, Bamiyan, Afghanistan. ca. 3rd century CE.** Stone, height 175′. This sculpture embodies the spread of ideas across Asia during the period of the European Middle Ages. Buddhism would spread, through China, to Japan by 600 CE. Indian Hinduism would, in turn, spread across Southeast Asia. This and another colossal sculpture of Buddha nearby were destroyed in February 2001 by the fundamentalist Islamic Taliban, who evidently felt that as false idols they were an affront to Muhammad.

((‹ **Listen** to the chapter audio on **MyArtsLab**

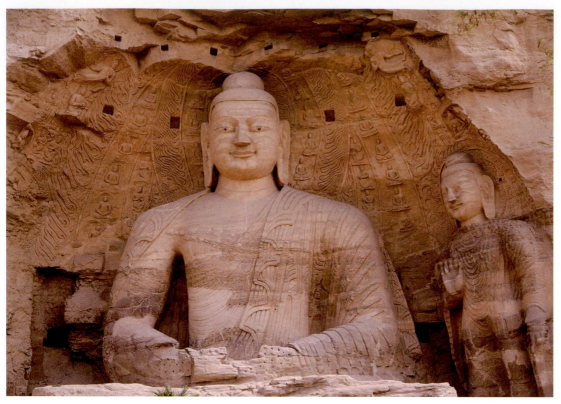

Fig. 11.2 *Large Seated Buddha with Standing Bodhisattva*, from cave 20, Ungang, Shaanxi, China, Northern Wei dynasty. ca. 460–70 CE. Stone, height 44'. By the last half of the fifth century, when this sculpture was carved, the Chinese Wei rulers, who lived near the eastern end of the Silk Road, had become acquainted with the Indian Buddhist religion.

View the Closer Look for the *Large Seated Buddha* on **MyArtsLab**

with Buddhist wall paintings, these enormous images reflect the magnitude of Buddha's eternal form, at which the earthly body can barely hint.

A seated Buddha from another cave, in Ungang, Shaanxi, China (Fig. **11.2**), exhibits the *Dhyana* mudra, a gesture of meditation and balance. The lower hand represents the physical world of illusion, the upper, nirvana. Together they symbolize the path to enlightenment. The bodhisattva—a person of near total enlightenment who has vowed to help others achieve it—standing next to him is exhibiting the *Abhaya* mudra, a gesture of reassurance, blessing, and protection.

This chapter traces the development of five great centers of culture during the period that coincides with Europe's Middle Ages: China, India, Japan, Africa, and the Americas. It was a period of great cross-fertilization in Asia, as the example of Buddhism demonstrates. Chinese technological innovation was unrivaled in the world, and Chinese art and literature flourished as well. In India, Buddhists, threatened by invading Muslims from Persia, retreated into the Himalayan Mountains, even as the Hindu religion regained prominence and spread across Southeast Asia. In Japan, a feudal, military society vied with Buddhist teaching for preeminence. Across the African continent, sophisticated peoples rose to dominate their regions. Similarly, in the Americas, cultures in Mesoamerica and Peru achieved

similar levels of complexity and sophistication without the kind of contact with other great cultures that marked development in Asia. This chapter's overview of these cultures puts the Western Middle Ages in a broader perspective. During these years, the growing globalization of culture was just beginning to assert itself on the Silk Road. As we will see, the world's centers of culture were never again to be isolated from each other.

DEVELOPMENTS IN CHINA

How are the values of the Tang and Song dynasties reflected in their art, architecture, and literature?

After the fall of the Han dynasty in 220 CE (see Chapter 7), China entered an uneasy period. Warring factions vied for control of greater or lesser territories, governments rose to power and fell again, civil wars erupted, and tribes from Central Asia continuously invaded. During this time, Buddhism began to spread through the culture. The ethical system based on the teachings of Confucius, which stressed self-discipline, propriety, reverence for elders, and virtuous behavior (see Chapter 7), seemed to have resulted in civil and cultural dysfunction. In contrast, Buddhism offered an

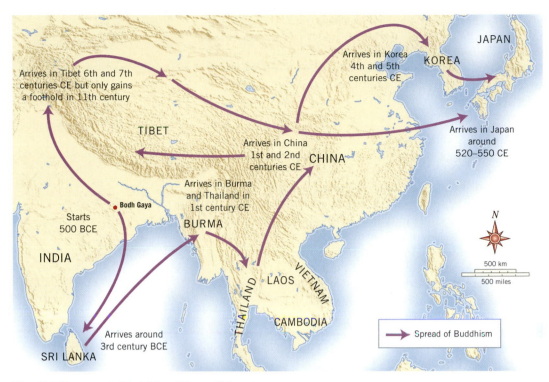

Map 11.1 The spread of Buddhism, 500 BCE–11th century CE.

ethical system based less on social and civic duty and more on each person's responsibility for his or her actions. Especially in its emphasis on meditation and enlightenment, Buddhism was compatible with Daoism and its emphasis on mysticism and harmony with nature (also discussed in Chapter 7). By the seventh century CE, Chinese leaders had learned to take the best from all three—Confucianism, Buddhism, and Daoism—and the culture was once again unified.

The Tang Dynasty in Chang'an, "The City of Enduring Peace" (618–907 CE)

In 618, the Tang dynasty reestablished a period of peace and prosperity in China that, except for a brief period of turmoil in the tenth century, would last for 660 years. The Tang dynasty was the largest and most organized government in the world in the second half of the first millennium CE. Its capital was the eastern terminus of the Silk Road, Chang'an, "City of Enduring Peace" (present-day Xi'an, which is about one-seventh the size of the Tang capital). The city had served as the capital of the Han dynasty as well, but as the Tang restored trade along the Silk Road, they created elaborate plans to restore the city, too. By the eighth century, its population was well over 1 million, living inside a walled perimeter nearly 26 miles in length and enclosing almost 42 square miles. Outside the walls lived perhaps as many as another million people. Among its inhabitants were Korean, Japanese, Jewish, and Christian populations, and its emperors maintained diplomatic relations with Persia.

Chang'an was the largest city in the world, laid out in a carefully conceived grid that dramatized the Tang commitment to social order and mirrored, they believed, the order of the cosmos (Fig. 11.3). Each of the city's 108 blocks was itself a miniature walled city, with its own interior streets and gates that locked at night. Astronomers laid out the streets by aligning them with the shadow of the sun at noon and the position of the North Star at night, thereby orienting the city to the four cardinal directions. The imperial palace

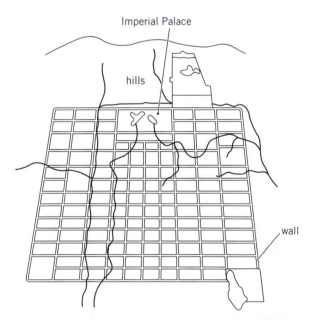

Fig. 11.3 Plan of the Tang capital of Chang'an, China. ca. 600. The location of the capital had been determined in Han times by the practice of *feng shui*, literally "wind and water," which assesses the primal energy that flows through a particular landscape. In this case, the hills to the north of the city and the streams running through it were understood to protect the precinct. *Feng shui* is still practiced to this day.

was located at the north end, facing south, thus symbolizing the emperor looking out over his city and, by extension, his empire. Traditionally, Chinese emperors turned their backs to the north, from where, it was believed, evil spirits (not to mention Huns) came. Government buildings occupied the space in front of the imperial palace. A 500-foot-wide avenue led from these directly to the southern gate.

Tang Art and Architecture Like all major Chinese dynasties, the Tang were great builders. One of their most important accomplishments was to build the Grand Canal from the Yellow River, just downstream from Chang'an, to the Hangzhou Bay, at the mouth of the Yangzi River, thus uniting northern and southern China. The Chinese had developed iron- and steel-casting during the Han dynasty in the third century BCE, and by the sixth or seventh century CE, the technique had become commonplace, used to construct not only suspension bridges but also **pagodas**. (Equally sophisticated iron- and steel-casting would not develop in the West until the eighteenth century.) The pagoda is a multistoried structure of successively smaller, repeated stories, with projecting roofs at each story. The design derives from Han watchtowers and Indian stupas such as the Great Stupa at Sanchi (see Fig. 7.17 in Chapter 7), which had become more and more towerlike in the sixth century CE. The pagoda was understood to offer the temple a certain protection. Of the few surviving buildings in China that predate 1400, the Great Wild Goose Pagoda at Ci'en Temple in Xi'an is one of the most magnificent (Fig. **11.4**). It was built—entirely of masonry, not iron or steel—in 645 for the monk Xuanzang, who taught and translated the materials he brought back with him from a 16-year pilgrimage to India. In its simplicity and symmetry, it represents the essence of Tang architecture.

Tang Poetry The Tang valued education above all. The imperial college at Chang'an trained all civil servants (women were excluded), and intellectual achievement was held in high esteem. Confucian and Daoist philosophy dominated the arts, particularly poetry, where two Tang poets, the Daoist Li Bai (701–62) and the Confucian Du Fu (712–70), achieved special prominence. Both relied for inspiration on the *Book of Songs*, an anthology of poems from all over China collected in the Zhou dynasty (see Chapter 7), but extended its range considerably. Their different temperaments are expressed in two short poems (**Reading 11.1a**):

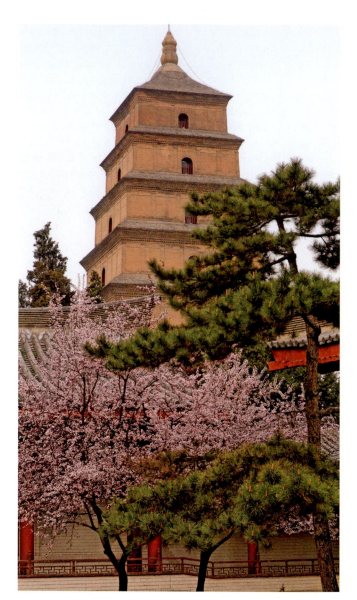

Fig. 11.4 Great Wild Goose Pagoda at Ci'en Temple, Xi'an, Shanxi. Tang dynasty, first erected 645 CE. The Temple was rebuilt in the eighth century, when two stories were added to the original five.

> **"Broken Lines" by Du Fu**
>
> River so blue the birds seem to whiten.
> Flowers almost flame on the green mountainside.
> Spring is dying yet again.
> Will I ever go home?

Li Bai is famous for the self-examination in his poems, his colloquial speech, and his frank celebration of his own sensuality. We see these characteristics, too, in his poem, "Drinking Alone by Midnight," addressed to the moon (see **Reading 11.1** on page 401).

The poems of Du Fu are sometimes full of pathos. He wrote "Dreaming of Li Bai" when his friend was in exile in the south. The two belonged to a group called the Eight

> ### READING 11.1a
>
> **Poems by Li Bai and Du Fu**
>
> **"Summer Day in the Mountains" by Li Bai**
>
> Lazy today, I wave my white feather fan.
> Then I strip naked in the green forest,
> untie my hatband and hang it on a stone wall.
> Pine wind sprinkles my bare head.

Immortals of the Wine Cup, famous for gathering in a garden of peach and plum trees on moonlit spring nights, where they drank wine to unleash their poetic temperaments. Like all the Immortals of the Wine Cup, Li Bai and Du Fu were equally expert in poetry, calligraphy, and painting—as well as statesmanship and philosophy. They present a model of what 500 years later the West would come to call the "Renaissance Man," the perfectly rounded individual, at home in any arena. They also embody the complex characteristics of Tang culture—at once strong and vigorous as well as passionate and sympathetic, simultaneously realistic and idealistic, intensely personal even while dedicated to public service.

The Song Dynasty and Hangzhou, "The City of Heaven" (960–1279 CE)

"The most splendid city in the world"—so the Venetian explorer Marco Polo (1254–1324) described Hangzhou, the capital of China's Southern Song dynasty (1127–1279) when Polo first visited it in 1274. Although Hangzhou was then the world's largest city—home to about 2 million people—no other Westerner had ever seen it. Marco Polo's father and uncle had a successful trading business with the East, and Polo lived with them in China for 17 years.

He wrote at length about his journey to Hangzhou in his *Travels*, first published in 1299. He claimed that he first visited the city as the ambassador of Kublai Khan. Northern Song China was already in Kublai Khan's hands, conquered in 1271, but he would not conquer the Southern Song on the Yangzi River until 1279. So when Polo first saw Hangzhou, it was still a Song city. Its lakes and parks were so beautiful, filled with floating teahouses from which passengers could view the palaces, pagodas, and temples that dotted the shore, that the city was known as Kinsai, or the "City of Heaven." The entire city, some 200 square miles in area, was protected by a 30-foot-high wall, with even higher watchtowers rising above it. Inside the walls, a system of canals, which must have reminded Polo of his native Venice, was crisscrossed by some 12,000 bridges. These canals were fed by the most famous and probably most beautiful lake in China, the so-called West Lake, a popular resort. Beautiful women and pleasure-seekers gathered on houseboats on its waters, and writers and artists congregated in the tranquil libraries and monasteries on its shores.

"In this city," Polo would write, "there are 12 guilds of different crafts, and each guild has 12,000 houses in the occupation of its workmen. Each of these houses contains at least 12 men, while some contain 20 and some 40, including the apprentices who work under the masters. All these craftsmen had full employment since many other cities of the kingdom are supplied by this city." In fact, each guild was formed around people from the same province. In Hangzhou, tea and cloth merchants hailed from the eastern province of Anhui, carpenters and cabinetmakers from the city of Ningbo, and so on. All came together to enjoy the benefits of trade and commerce in the capital. Foodstuffs, silks, spices, flowers, and books filled the markets (**Reading 11.2**):

READING 11.2

from Marco Polo, *Travels*

Those markets make a daily display of every kind of vegetable and fruit; and among the latter there are in particular certain pears of enormous size, weighing as much as ten pounds apiece, and the pulp of which is white and fragrant like a confection, besides peaches in their season both yellow and white, of every delicate flavor. … From the Ocean Sea also come daily supplies of fish in great quantity, brought 25 miles up river, and there is also great store of fish from the lake, which is the constant resort of fishermen, who have no other business. Their fish is of sundry kinds, changing with the season; and it is remarkably fat and tasty. Anyone who should see the supply of fish in the market would suppose it impossible that such a quantity could ever be sold; and yet in a few hours the whole shall be cleared away; so great is the number of inhabitants who are accustomed to delicate living.

These citizens "accustomed to delicate living" apparently lived remarkably well: "The houses of the citizens are well built and elaborately finished," Polo claims, "and the delight they take in decoration, in painting and in architecture, leads them to spend in this way sums of money that would astonish you." In other words, Hangzhou was a center of Asian culture that no one in the West, save Marco Polo, could even dream existed, in many ways exceeding anything the West had realized.

The Song dynasty enjoyed tremendous prosperity. It was the world's greatest producer of iron, and its flourishing merchant class traded not only along the Silk Road (see Chapter 7) but also throughout the Southeast Asian seas by boat. The government was increasingly controlled by this wealthy merchant class. Crucial to their rise was the development of movable type, which allowed the Song to begin printing books on paper. The printing press revolutionized the transmission of knowledge in China. (Gutenberg's movable-type printing press, which, in the West, we commonly credit with revolutionizing the transmission of knowledge, was 400 years in the future.) The children of the thriving merchant class attended public, private, and religious schools, where they could study the newly printed books—including the *Book of Songs*, required reading for all Chinese civil servants, and various encyclopedias—as they prepared for government examinations. This new class of highly educated government officials restored Confucianism to dominance and strengthened it with relevant additions from Daoism and Buddhism. Buddhism was officially rejected as foreign, but its explanation of the universe provided an invaluable metaphysical element to

Confucianism. As a result, these new officials brought to government a deep belief, based on neo-Confucian teaching, that the well-run society mirrored the unchanging moral order of the cosmos.

Chan Buddhism Especially important to artists and literati in the Song era was the development of Chan Buddhism. "Chan" (better known in the West as "Zen," as it is pronounced in Japanese) derives from the Sanskrit word *dhyana*, meaning "meditation." Like Daoism, Chan Buddhism teaches that one can find happiness by achieving harmony with nature. By using yoga techniques and sitting meditation, the Chan Buddhist strives for oneness with the Dao ("the Way") and the Confucian *li*, the principle or inner structure of nature. The Chan Buddhists thought that the traditional scriptures, rituals, and monastic rules of classical Buddhism were essentially beside the point, because Buddha's spirit was innate in everyone, waiting to be discovered through meditation. Thus, the poets and artists who practiced Chan Buddhism considered themselves instruments through which the spirit of nature expressed itself.

Song Painting This essential "rightness" of the Song world is manifested especially in Chinese painting of the Song era, when landscape painting became the principal and most esteemed means of personal and philosophic expression in the arts. The landscape was believed to embody the underlying principle behind all things, made manifest in the world through its material presence. Closely akin to the spiritual quest of the Dao, the task of the artist was to reveal the unifying principle of the natural world, the eternal essence of mountain, waterfall, pine tree, rock, reed, cloud, and sky. Human figures are dwarfed by the landscape, insignificant in the face of nature. Over and over again, the paintings of the period rise from foreground valleys to high mountaintops, the eye following paths, cascading waterfalls, rocky crags, and tall pines pointing ever higher in imitation of "the Way," the path by which one leaves behind the human world and attains the great unifying principle (see *Closer Look*, pages 370–371).

The Yuan Dynasty (1279–1368)

Throughout the period known as the medieval era in the West, China was threatened from the north by nomadic tribes. The Northern Song capital of Bianjing had fallen to tribes from Manchuria in 1126, forcing the Song to retreat south to Hangzhou. Finally, the Song dynasty succumbed to the Mongol leader Kublai Khan in 1279. Kublai Khan ruled from a new capital at present-day Beijing, transforming it into a walled city constructed on a grid plan and extending the Grand Canal to provision the city.

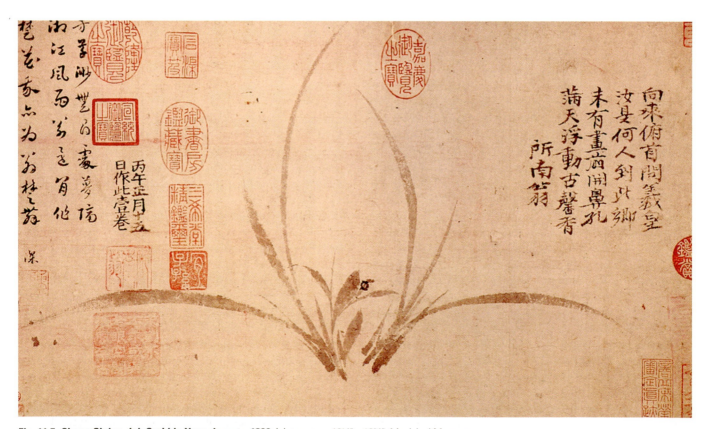

Fig. 11.5 Cheng Sixiao, *Ink Orchids*. Yuan dynasty, 1306. Ink on paper, 10⅛" × 16¾". Municipal Museum of Fine Art, Osaka, Japan. Artists of the Yuan dynasty such as Cheng Sixiao painted for their fellow artists and friends, not for the public. Thus, Cheng Sixiao could feel comfortable describing his political intentions in the text accompanying this painting.

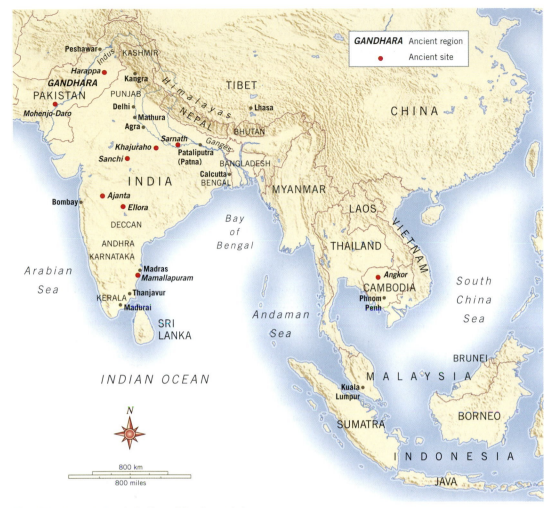

Map 11.2 Ancient sites in India and Southeast Asia.

Calling themselves the Yuan dynasty, the Mongols under Kublai Khan and his descendants controlled the highest posts in the government, but they depended on Chinese officials to collect taxes and maintain order. The Chinese understood the need to cooperate with the Mongols, but they viewed the Mongols as foreigners occupying their homeland.

Not long after Marco Polo's arrival in China, the scholar-painters of the Chinese court, unwilling to serve under foreign domination, were retreating from public life. But while in exile, they created an art symbolic of their resistance. Paintings of bamboo, for instance, abound, because bamboo is a plant that might bend, like the Chinese themselves, but never break. Painted in 1306, Cheng Sixiao's *Ink Orchids* (Fig. **11.5**), according to its inscription, is meant to protest the "theft of Chinese soil by the invaders." Orchids, in fact, can live without soil, in rocks or in trees, sustained by the moisture in the air around them, even as Sixiao the painter thrives. The Mongols were finally overthrown in 1368, when Zhu Yuanzhang (r. 1368–98) drove the last Yuan emperor north into the Gobi desert and declared himself first emperor of the new Ming dynasty. China was once again ruled by the Chinese.

INDIAN AND SOUTHEAST ASIAN CIVILIZATIONS

How do Buddhist and Hindu art and architecture make manifest the living presence of Buddha and the Hindu gods?

By 1200, Indian civilization was among the world's oldest, and it asserted broad influence over all of Southeast Asia (Map **11.2**). Its history during the centuries before and after 1200 was largely determined by competing religious forces, especially Buddhism, Islam, and Hinduism. Buddhism, which flourished in India from about 100 to 600 CE, had steadily waned in influence. It was further diminished when Muslim invaders entered northern India in the eleventh and twelfth centuries, destroying centers of worship in their path. Many of the Buddhist monks fled north into Nepal and across the Himalayas into Tibet or eastward into present-day Myanmar (formerly Burma). The Muslim invaders, who established their capital at Delhi, brought with them new forms of art and architecture rooted in Persian court traditions. Meanwhile, Hinduism became

The human presence in nature goes almost unnoticed in Guo Xi's hanging scroll, *Early Spring*. Nature, embodied by the mountain, is all-embracing, a powerful and imposing symbol of eternity. The composition of Guo Xi's painting is based on the Chinese written character for mountain. The fluid gestures of the calligrapher's hand are mirrored in Guo Xi's painting, both in the organization of the whole and in the individual brush-and-ink strokes that render this ideal landscape. Like the calligrapher, Guo Xi is interested in the balance, rhythm, and movement of his line.

A court painter during the reign of the emperor Shenzong (r. 1068–85), Guo Xi was given the task of painting all the murals in the Forbidden City, the imperial compound in Beijing that foreigners were prohibited from entering. His ideas about landscape painting were recorded by his son, Guo Si, in a book entitled *The Lofty Message of the Forests and Streams*. According to this book, the central peak here symbolizes the emperor himself and its tall pines the gentlemanly ideals of the court. Around the emperor the masses assume their natural place, as around this mountain the trees and hills fall into the order and rhythms of nature.

Guo Xi, *Early Spring*. Song dynasty, 1072. Hanging scroll, ink and slight color on silk, length 5'. Collection of the National Palace Museum, Taipei, Taiwan, Republic of China. Everything has its proper place in the Chinese universe, and thus the painting possesses multiple points of view. Accordingly, each part of this painting is constructed at the appropriate "distance."

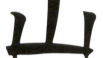

Chinese character for "mountain."

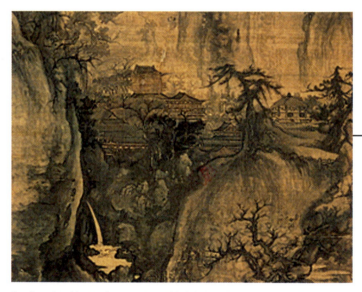

Barely noticeable, two figures get out of their boat at the bottom left, and another figure stands on the shoreline at the right. Two waterfalls cascade down the hillside behind this second figure, and a small village can be seen nestled on the mountainside above the falls.

Something to Think About …

In the West, landscape painting did not become a popular genre until the eighteenth century. What differences in attitude between East and West during the Middle Ages might account for this?

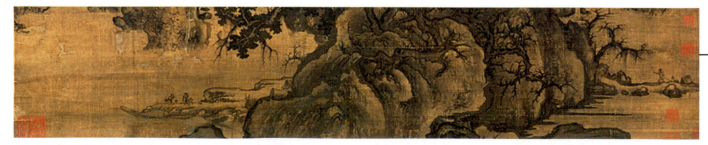

View the Closer Look for Guo Xi's *Early Spring* on **MyArtsLab**

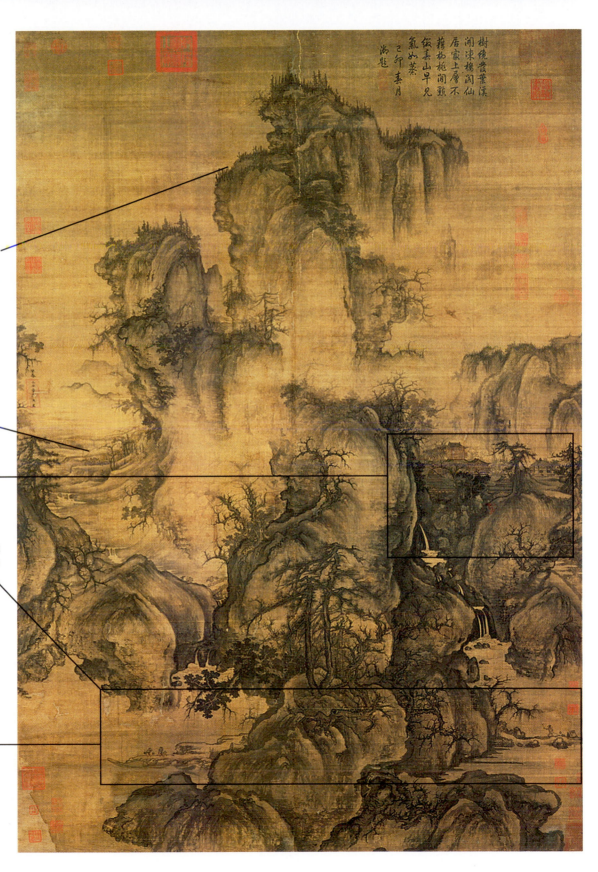

The central mountain is painted so that we gaze up to it in the "high distance," as we would gaze up at the emperor.

On the left side of the painting, we gaze far off into a "level distance," creating a sense of limitless, eternal space.

In the humbling "deep distance" of the foreground, far below our point of view, we see images that reflect our own insignificance in nature.

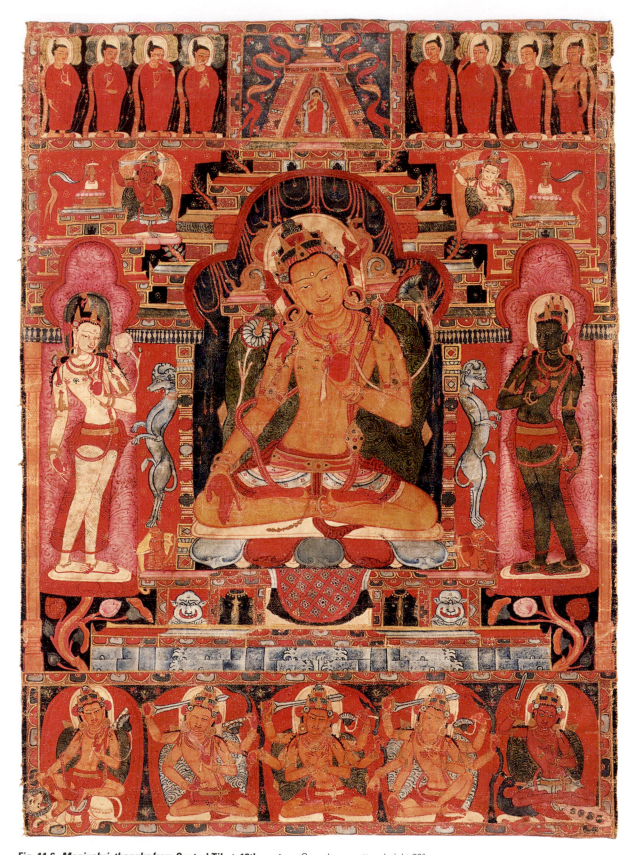

Fig. 11.6 *Manjushri, thangka* **from Central Tibet. 13th century.** Gouache on cotton, height 22".
Private collection. At the base of the *thangka* are three images of Manjushri wielding swords with four arms,
representing his ability to cut through ignorance.

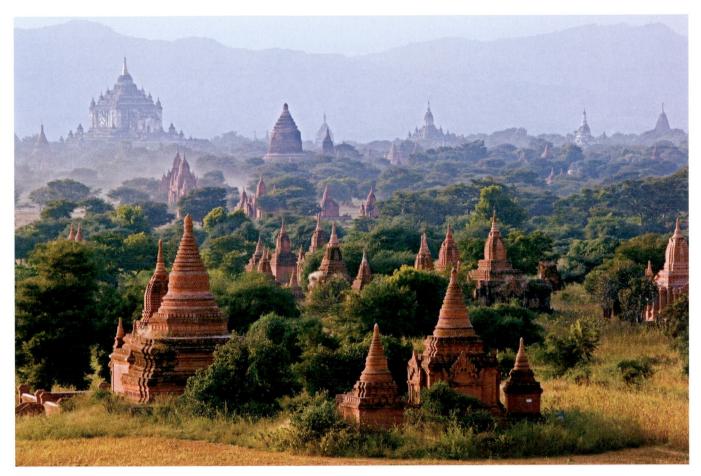

Fig. 11.7 Jungle filled with ancient temples and pagodas, Bagan, Myanmar (formerly Burma).
1057–1287. The temple complex at Bagan covers an area of approximately 16 square miles. © Keren Su/ Corbis. All rights reserved.

increasingly popular, and it gradually asserted itself as the dominant Indian religion. Well into the fifteenth and sixteenth centuries, India was ruled by Hindu dynasties, especially in the south, where the culture was relatively isolated from the influence of the Delhi sultans. Hinduism spread throughout Southeast Asia, where Cambodian monarchs constructed magnificent temples inspired by Indian prototypes.

Buddhist Art and Architecture

High in the isolated valleys of the Himalayas in Nepal and Tibet, Buddhist monks adapted Buddhism to the native Tibetan mystical religion known as Bon. The local religious leaders, known as *lamas* (meaning "none superior"), considered themselves the reincarnation of earlier deceased lamas and Buddhist bodhisattvas. The chief lama, the Dalai (meaning "ocean"), was believed to be the reincarnation of the bodhisattva Avalokiteshvara, the embodiment of compassion in this new form of Buddhism. Enlightenment, not simply nirvana, is the goal of this version of Buddhism, generally known as Mahayana, and the vow of every bodhisattva is to help others achieve enlightenment before they themselves cross over into paradise.

Among the artistic expressions of this faith were rolled-up cloth paintings, known as *thangkas*. As monks traveled from one monastery to another, they would unroll *thangkas* as aids to instruction. Painted on the *thangkas* were images representing Buddhist figures of authority, including lamas, bodhisattvas, and the Buddha himself, which, the Tibetans believed, were manifest in their images. The *thangka* reproduced here (Fig. **11.6**) represents Manjushri, a bodhisattva associated with a great historical teacher. Thus, the *thangka* not only symbolizes wisdom, it makes Manjushri's wisdom present.

In Myanmar, Anawratha, the first king of the Bagan Empire (r. 1044–77), was a devout Buddhist. His capital at Bagan became a center of Buddhist learning, attracting monks from across Southeast Asia, especially from India, as Muslims gained control of the subcontinent. There he built the Shwesandaw Paya, or "Sunset Pagoda," in 1057 (visible in the far distance at the middle right, Fig. **11.7**), a five-terraced structure topped by a circular bell-shaped stupa that, legend has it, contains the hairs of Buddha. Here, Buddha was manifest, present to the pilgrim circling the stupa in search of enlightenment. For the next two centuries, until Bagan was overrun by the army of Kublai Khan in 1287, Anawratha's heirs built more than 13,000 temples, pagodas, and other religious structures, of which some 2,200 temples remain standing.

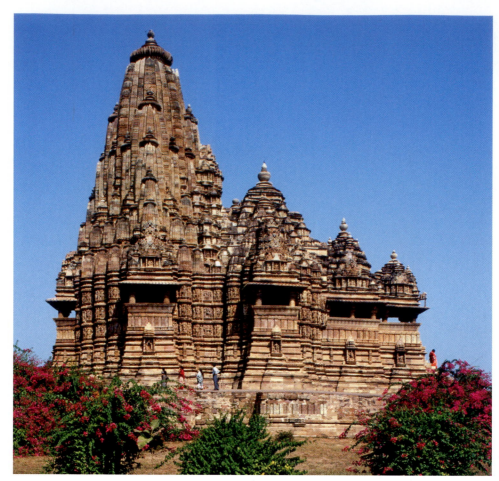

Fig. 11.8 Kandarya Mahadeva Temple, Khajuraho, Madhya Pradesh, India. Chandella dynasty, ca. 1025–50. The temple's formal design, like that of all Hindu temples, was prescribed in the *shastras*, a body of ancient Hindu writing that sets out the principles of poetry, music, dance, and the other arts. By the second millennium, most temples followed the *shastras* only loosely, freely elaborating on the basic plan.

Hindu Art and Architecture

Hindu religion and art are infused with a deep respect for sexuality, evident even in the architecture (see Chapter 7). The Kandarya Mahadeva Temple (Fig. **11.8**) at Khajuraho, the capital of the Chandella dynasty, represents the epitome of northern Indian Hindu architecture. Its rising towers are meant to suggest the peaks of the Himalayas, home of the Hindu gods, and this analogy would have been even clearer when the temple was painted in its original white gesso. The plan (Fig. **11.9**) is a double cross, with arms extending north and south from the east–west axis. At the first crossing is the *mandapa*, the columned assembly hall. At the second crossing is the *garbhagriha*, or "womb chamber," the symbolic sacred cavern at the heart of the sacred mountain/temple. Here rests the cult image of the Brahman, in this case the *lingam*, or symbol of male sexuality, of Shiva, the first, or formless emanation of the Brahman. (The Brahman is the creator and the universal soul; see Chapter 7.) Although it is actually almost completely dark, the *garbhagriha* is considered by Hindu worshipers to

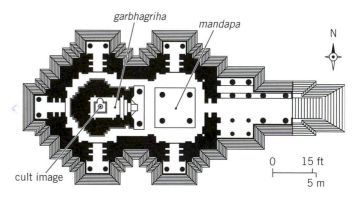

Fig. 11.9 Plan of Kandarya Mahadeva Temple, Khajurabo, India. ca. 1025–50. The temple's main features are the *garbhagriha*, the cult image, and the *mandapa*.

be filled with the pure light of the Brahman. The towers of the temple rise from east to west, as if gathering around the central tower, known as the *sikhara*, that rises to a height of over 100 feet above the *garbhagriha*. As the height increases, the temple seems to gather the energy of the

👁 **Watch** an architectural simulation about stupas and temples on **MyArtsLab**

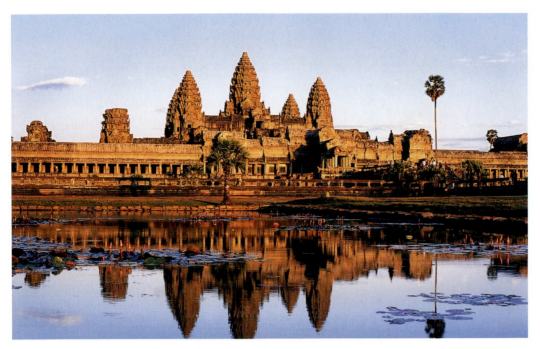

Fig. 11.10 Angkor Wat, Cambodia. Early 12th century. The entire complex was constructed in the short span of about 30 years.

✳ **Explore** an architectural panorama about Angkor Wat on **MyArtsLab**

Hindu religion to a single rising point, soaring with the spirit of the worshiper.

By the twelfth century, Hinduism had spread from India southeast into present-day Cambodia, where Hindu art achieved a monumental imperial grandeur. In Cambodia, the Khmer monarchy established its capital at Angkor, about 150 miles northwest of present-day Phnom Penh. Covering about 70 square miles, the city was crossed by broad avenues and canals and filled with royal palaces and temples. The largest of these temples, Angkor Wat (Fig. **11.10**), was created by Suryavarman II (r. 1113–ca. 1150). Five central towers, representing the five peaks of Mount Meru, the center of the Hindu cosmos, rise above a moat surrounding the complex. The approach to the galleries at the towers' base is from the west, crossing a long bridge over the moat, which symbolizes the oceans surrounding the known world. On June 21, the summer solstice and the beginning of the Cambodian solar year, a visitor to the temple arriving through the western gate would see the sun rise directly over the central tower. In this way, the symbolic evocation of the cosmos, so fundamental to Hindu temple architecture, is further elaborated in astronomical terms.

There are literally miles of relief sculptures decorating the walls of Angkor Wat, including images of the *apsaras*, mythological goddesses whose dances were used by the gods to seduce mortals, and *devatas*, guardian spirits who stand individually or in groups with an air of refined elegance (Fig. **11.11**). They are uniformly bare-breasted and wear both a crown and a pleated *sampot* (a wrapped skirt), rolled at the top below the belly to open like a flower. The

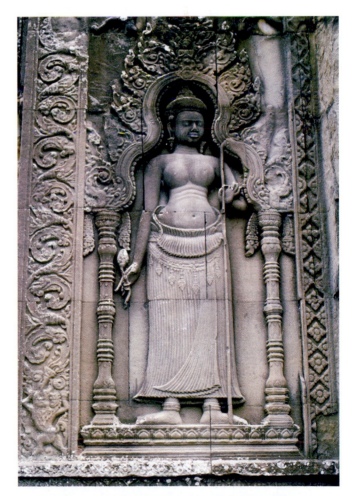

Fig. 11.11 *Devata*, Angkor Wat, Cambodia. Early 12th century. There are over 2,000 *devatas* at Angkor Wat.

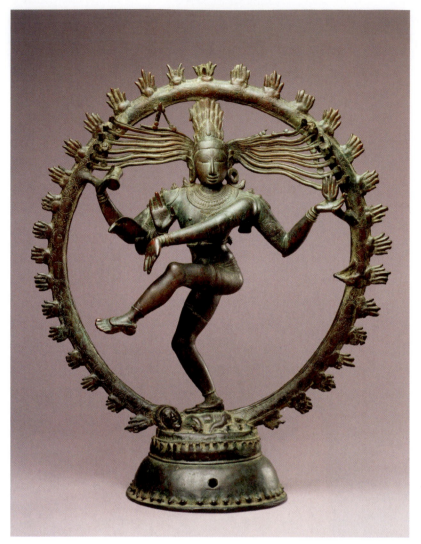

Fig. 11.12 *Shiva as Lord of the Dance (Nataraja)*, **Tamil Nadu, India. Chola period (880–1279), ca. 11th century.** Copper alloy, height 26⅛", diameter 22¼". The Metropolitan Museum of Art, New York. Gift of R.H. Ellsworth Ltd., in honor of Susan Dillon, 1987 (1987.80.1). In his back left hand, Shiva carries fire, representing the destructive energy of his dance at the end of each cosmic age, which cleanses sins and removes illusion from the world. In his back right hand, he holds an hourglass-shaped drum, which represents the rhythmic sound of his dance as he ceaselessly re-creates the universe.

ubiquity of such figures underscores the important role of goddess worship in Hindu culture (see Chapter 7).

Hindu artists also mastered the art of bronze-casting. In the Tamil Nadu region of southern India, artists began making large bronze editions of Shiva in his manifestation as Shiva Nataraja, Lord of the Dance, as early as the tenth and eleventh centuries. Such images were commissioned as icons for the region's many temples. Since Shiva embodies the rhythms of the universe, he is also a great dancer. All the gods were present when Shiva first danced, and they begged him to dance again. Shiva promised to do so in the hearts of his devotees as well as in a sacred grove in Tamil Nadu itself. As he dances, he is framed in a circle of fire, symbolic of both creation and destruction, the endless cycle of birth, death, and reincarnation (Fig. 11.12).

JAPAN: THE COURT, THE MILITARY, AND SPIRITUAL LIFE

What was the relationship between court and spiritual life in the Heian and Kamakura periods?

Although Buddhism may have been known in Japan earlier, it is commonly believed that it arrived in the Yamato period (before 700 BCE; see Chapter 1) from Korea and China. According to the *Chronicles of Japan*, a statue of Buddha and a collection of sacred Buddhist texts were given to Japanese rulers by the king of the Baekje region of Korea in 552. Chinese calligraphy was already the basis of the Japanese written language, and to some, Buddhism seemed equally amenable to Japanese adaptation. But Buddhism was by no means welcomed by all. Of the three rival clans then most powerful in Yamato Japan—the Soga, Mononobe, and Nakatomi, each tied to the imperial family through marriage to the emperor—both the Mononobe, who were in charge of the emperor's military, and the Nakatomi, in charge of Shinto ritual, opposed the introduction of Buddhism into the country. But the Soga, managers of imperial estates who were in constant contact with the Koreans and Chinese, were deeply attracted to the religion, and the Yamato emperor allowed them to practice it within their own clan.

The Rise of Court Life in Japan and the Coming of the Fujiwara

As the Soga gained more and more power over the last decades of the sixth century, they eventually defeated the Mononobe and Nakatomi in a civil war, and the head of the Soga clan, Umako, installed his 39-year-old daughter, Suiko, as empress and declared her 29-year-old nephew, Shotoku (r. 593–622), her regent and crown prince. The capital was moved inland from Osaka on the coast to the Soga homeland in the Asuka Valley in the central Yamato plain.

Shotoku, whose name means "Wise and Virtuous," emphasized the importance of the Chinese model of civil administration, and introduced Confucianism to the court. When he built a new palace at Ikaruga, in the central Asuka plain, he constructed a Buddhist temple next to it. Others were built during his administration, and over 1,300 Buddhist monks and nuns were ordained. But Buddhism was in fact practiced only by a small number of the aristocracy around the Asuka capital.

In 645, the Nakatomi, who had been forced to tolerate Buddhism even as they continued to maintain Shinto ritual at court, rebelled, executing the Soga clan. Anyone else who showed resistance to their rule was executed as well. Nakatomi no Kamatari (614–69) was awarded the surname of Fujiwara by Emperor Tenji for his part in crushing the Soga and placing Tenji on the throne. The Fujiwara clan, thus directly descended from the Nakatomi, would become the greatest noble clan of classical Japan, ruling it for 500 years.

In 708, the Fujiwara oversaw the construction of a new capital at Hojeikyo, commonly called Nara after its location in the Nara plain, some 15 miles to the northwest of Asuka (see Map **11.3**). It was laid out according to the principles of Chinese city planning as a walled city on the model of Chang-an (see Fig. 11.3), 2.7 miles from east to west and about 3.1 miles from north to south, with a broad avenue running north and south in its center culminating at the Heijo Palace. And although the Nakatomi/Fujiwara clan had despised the Buddhist-leaning Soga the century before, at Nara, they officially accepted Buddhism as the state religion. Magnificent temples and monasteries were constructed, including what would remain, for a thousand years, the largest wooden structure in the world, the Todaiji Temple (Fig. **11.13**). It houses a giant bronze, known as the Great Buddha, over 49 feet high and weighing approximately 380 tons. According to ancient records, as many as 2.6 million people were required to aid in its construction, although that number represents approximately half of Japan's population at the time and is probably a gross exaggeration. The original temple was twice destroyed by

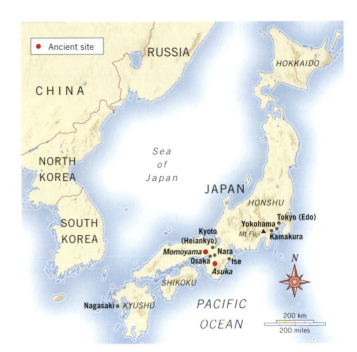

Map 11.3 Japan. Isolated from the Asian mainland, Japan was both slow to develop and susceptible to the influence of the more advanced cultures once it became aware of them.

warring factions, in 1180 and again in 1567. The current Buddha is in fact a 1691 reconstruction of the original, and the Todaiji Temple is itself a reconstruction of 1709. The restored temple is considerably smaller than the original, approximately two-thirds its size, and now stands 188 feet in width and 156 feet in height.

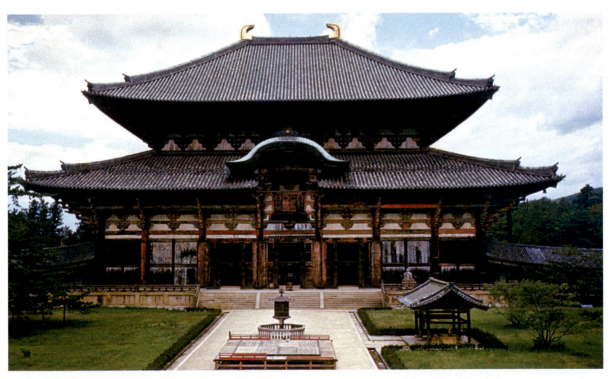

Fig. 11.13 Todaiji Temple, Nara, Japan. 752. The temple's sweeping horned roof is typical of Japanese architecture.

The Heian Period: Courtly Refinement

The acceptance of Buddhism by the Fujiwara clan at Nara suggests that the conflict between the clans in the earlier Yamato period was probably as much about power as it was religion. But it is also true that by the seventh century Buddhist doctrine and Shinto had begun to influence each other. The Great Buddha at Nara became identified with the Shinto goddess Amaterasu (see Chapter 1), and Buddhist ceremonies were incorporated into Shinto court ritual. But between 784 and 794, the capital of Japan was moved to Heian-kyo—present-day Kyoto—which quickly became the most densely populated city in the world. According to records, the move occurred because the secular court needed to distance itself from the religious influence of the Buddhist monks at Nara. Indeed, one of these monks had risen to power as the lover of the empress Koken (r. 749–59, 765–70).

Like Nara, Heian-kyo was modeled on Chang'an, the capital of the Tang dynasty, and, also as at Nara, the ordered grid of its streets was a conscious bow to Chinese philosophy and its reflection in the workings of government. Between the late eleventh and the middle of the twelfth century at Heian-kyo, scholars estimate that the royal family regularly dedicated new Shinto shrines and new Buddhist temples.

Life of the Nobility At Heian-kyo, the arts flourished in an atmosphere of elegance and refinement. The nobility numbered around 100,000, and they lived in residential complexes that extended across several acres with multiple single-story pavilions and secondary halls tied together by covered walkways. The entire complex usually encircled a garden with a pond and small streams crossed by bridges, the whole surrounded by an earthen wall (Fig. **11.14**).

As in traditional Shinto shrines, the roofs of the complex were made of cypress-bark shingles. This style of architecture is known as *shinden-zukuri*, after its main hall, or *shinden*, and *zukuri*, "style." Following Chinese tradition, it was oriented to the south. It was large enough to accommodate the nobleman's several wives—limited polygamy was practiced by the high aristocracy, permitting a nobleman to have one or two lesser wives who could bear him fully recognized children. Theoretically at least, these lesser wives enjoyed less prestige in the court. Behind the *shinden*, in a separate hall to the north, lived the main wife, known as the *kita no kata*, "the person to the north." Secondary wives lived in pavilions to the east and west. Each hall could open into the gardens by means of latticed shutters that could be raised to take advantage of good weather.

Life in the Heian court was determined by gender. Men lived public lives, women much more private ones. In fact, women were rarely visible. An aristocratic woman might make a public excursion to a Buddhist temple, but she would remain out of public view. She might receive a male visitor, but the two would converse through a portable set of curtain panels. Women were, however, highly educated, and they were expected to contribute to the aesthetic of the Heian court. They were judged on their looks—although it is striking to note that there are almost no detailed descriptions of a woman's face or body in Heian writing—on the arrangement of their many layers of silk robes, on their perfumes, on the beauty of their calligraphy, and on their ability to compose poetry at a moment's notice. As opposed to a man's identity, which was regularly displayed in public settings, a woman's identity was defined particularly by her speech, her correspondence, and her poetry and other writings.

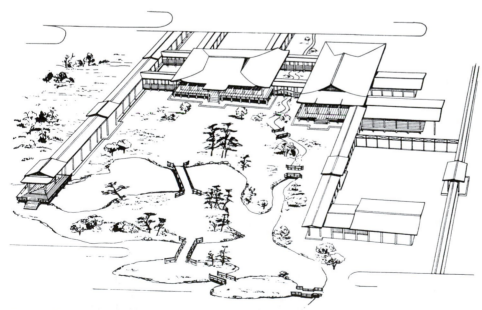

Fig. 11.14 Reconstruction drawing of a *shinden-zukuri* mansion. No original mansions of the nobility survive in present-day Kyoto. Drawings such as this one are based on the ample literary descriptions of these elaborate residences, as well as their representations in illustrated scrolls.

Literature and Calligraphy Although many court gatherings took place for the purpose of poetry competitions, in which both men and women participated, poems were generally composed for a single recipient—a friend or lover—and a reply was expected. In her *Diaries*—or *Nikki* in Japanese—Murasaki Shikibu (973/8–after 1014), one of the most accomplished women of the Heian court, a lady-in-waiting to the empress Shoshi (988–1074), describes just such an exchange (**Reading 11.3**):

READING 11.3

from Murasaki Shikibu, *Diaries*

I can see the garden from my room beside the entrance to the gallery. The air is misty, the dew is still on the leaves. The Lord Prime Minister is walking there; he orders his men to cleanse the brook. He breaks off a stalk of omenaishi[1], which is in full bloom by the south end of the bridge. He peeps in over my screen! His noble appearance embarrasses us, and I am ashamed of my morning face.[2] He says, "Your poem on this! If you delay so much the fun is gone!" and I seize the chance to run away to the writing-box, hiding my face:

> Flower-maiden in bloom—
> Even more beautiful for the bright dew,
> Which is partial, and never favors me.

"So prompt!" said he, smiling, and ordered a writing-box to be brought [for himself].
His answer:

> The silver dew is never partial.
> From her heart
> The flower-maiden's beauty.

[1] **omenaishi:** a flowering plant.
[2] **morning face:** a face without powder or makeup.

Something of the flavor of court life is captured in this brief passage, in the private space of the gentlewoman's world, her relation to the gentlemen of the court, the attention of the two poets to natural beauty, and the expression of that beauty as a means of capturing personal feeling.

Diaries comprised an important literary form that tell us much about court life in the Heian period. Murasaki's poems—indeed her entire text—are written in a new, purely Japanese writing system, known as **hiragana**. Beginning in the early ninth century, *hiragana* gradually replaced the use of Chinese characters and enabled writers to spell out the Japanese language phonetically. The university curriculum, however, remained based on Chinese classics and history, and the formal workings of state and government still required the use of Chinese. Chinese was the language of the world of men. Since the Heian court strongly discouraged displays of education in Chinese by women, they were taught the *hiragana* script, even though many court women actually knew Chinese quite well.

The popularity of *hiragana*, even among men, who recognized its convenience, encouraged the development of new Japanese forms of poetry, especially the **waka** (literally the "poetry of Wa," or Japan). A *waka* consists of 31 syllables in 5 lines on a theme drawn from nature and the changing of seasons. Here is a *waka* by one of the great poets of the Heian period, Ki no Tomonori (act. 850–904) (**Reading 11.4**):

READING 11.4

Ki no Tomonori, "This Perfectly Still"

This perfectly still
Spring day bathed in the soft light
From the spread-out sky.
Why do the cherry blossoms
So restlessly scatter down?

The tension here, between the calm of the day and the restlessness of the cherry blossoms, is meant to mirror a similar tension in the poet's mind, suggesting a certain sense of anticipation or premonition. The *waka* serves as a model for other Japanese poetic forms, particularly the famous **haiku**, the 3-line, 17-syllable form that developed out of the first three lines of the *waka*.

Sei Shonagon's *Pillow Book* Aside from poetry and diaries, the women of the Japanese court also created a new literary form, the *zuihitsu* (literally, "by the line of the brush"), random notes or occasional writings. The first of these was the *Pillow Book* by Sei Shonagon (ca. 965–aft. 1000), lady-in-waiting to the imperial consort Teishi (970–1001) and head of a literary salon that openly competed against that of Murasaki Shikibu, a rivalry that helped to inspire the literary innovation of the period. The clarity of Sei Shonagon's observation in the *Pillow Book* is captured in her short list of "Elegant Things" (**Reading 11.5a**):

READING 11.5a

from Sei Shonagon, *Pillow Book*, "Elegant Things"

A white coat worn over a violet waistcoat.
Duck eggs.
Shaved-ice mixed with liana syrup[1] and put in a new
  silver bowl.
A rosary[2] of rock crystal.
Wisteria blossoms. Plum blossoms covered with snow.
A pretty child eating strawberries.

[1] **liana syrup:** a light, sweet syrup made from the fruit of a climbing vine.
[2] **rosary:** not the series of prayers practiced by Roman Catholics, but rather a miniature sculpture of a rose garden made of rock crystal.

Another, longer list, entitled "Hateful Things" (see **Reading 11.5** on pages 402–403), gives the reader a remarkable overview of daily life in the Heian court. Sei Shonagon looks at the entirety of her world, from its insects to the palace dog.

The First Novel: *The Tale of Genji* Murasaki Shikibu, whose *Diaries* we discussed previously, is more famous as the author of a long book of prose and poetry (over 1,000 pages in English translation), including many exchanges of poetry of the type recorded in her *Diaries*. Many consider it the world's first novel—certainly no fiction in the Western world matches its scope until the eighteenth century. Called *The Tale of Genji*, it tells the story of Genji, an imperial prince, born to the favorite wife of the emperor, though she is too low in rank for her son to be an heir to the throne. Much of the action takes place in the homes and gardens of Heian-kyo, and besides being a moving romantic story covering 75 years of the hero's life, from his birth to his death, the novel presents us with a vivid picture of life in Japanese society at the turn of the millennium. As opposed to the *Diaries*, the stories related in *The Tale of Genji* are, of course, fiction, but, as Genji says at one point in the *Tale*: "Among these lies there certainly are some plausible touching scenes, convincingly told; and yes, we know they are fictions, but even so we are moved."

Soon after it was written, *The Tale of Genji* was illustrated in a handscroll that was an ensemble of more than 100 excerpts from the *Tale*, written in elegant calligraphy on decorative paper, probably at court. The paintings, of which only 20 of the original 100 survive, have been attributed to Takayoshi (Fig. **11.15**). Most are focused on intimate episodes of high narrative tension, and of the 20 paintings that survive, 17 depict events happening either in the outer corridor or on the veranda or outer corridor of a *shinden*.

As the scroll was unwound, the viewer would have first seen the right side of Fig. 11.15, the courtyard (now brown but originally silver), and then, at a sharp angle, the veranda and curtain wall of a house in which a deeply moving scene is unfolding in the outer corridor. As a young man, Genji had fallen in love with his father's youngest wife, Fujitsubo, and fathered a son by her. Genji's own father, the emperor, acknowledged the child as his own, and the boy eventually became emperor himself. Genji came to understand the human consequences of his youthful actions only when his own youngest wife bore a son by another man and Genji was forced to acknowledge the child as his own, just as his father had accepted Genji's son. Depicted here is the moment of Genji's acceptance of his wife's son.

The scene is depicted from an aerial perspective just above the roof, which has been "blown off" (a technique known as *fakinaki yatai*) in order to provide a view of the interior. The result is a highly chaotic composition in which geometrical lines of the architecture play off against the figures and their clothing. Genji holds the child in his arms. Beside him to the right, half hidden by the curtains, bowls of food are placed for the ritual celebration. Ladies-in-waiting, one dressed in black, sit below, and at the extreme upper left, the child's mother is indicated by a heap of fabric. Genji knows that the attendants understand that he is not the child's father, and yet he fully understands his duty.

Although Genji is the hero of the book, Murasaki Shikibu gives the women of the Heian court full treatment, chief among them the tellingly named Murasaki, whose own life, from childhood to death, is fully narrated. She is Genji's greatest love, and she receives his lavish attentions. And yet, given the polygamous nature of Japanese society, she suffers much. She is unable to bear Genji a child, and Genji must turn elsewhere for an heir. Likewise, her social status is not high enough to qualify her as his principal wife. Thus, despite her wit and intelligence, her beauty and charm, she is condemned to second-class status.

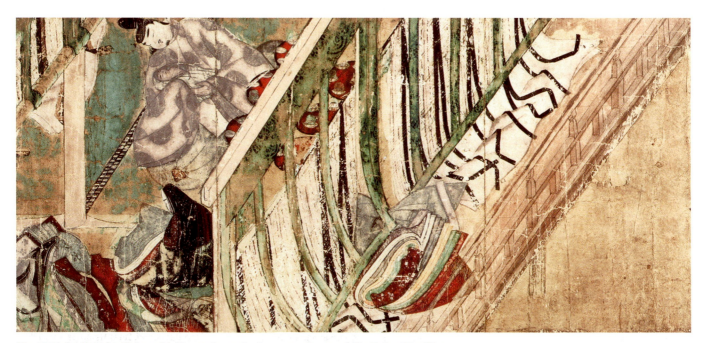

Fig. 11.15 Attributed to Takayoshi, Illustration to the Azumaya chapter of *The Tale of Genji* by Murasaki Shikibu. Late Heian period, 12th century. Handscroll, ink and color on paper, height 8½". Tokugawa Art Museum, Nagoya, Japan. Of the original illustrations of *The Tale of Genji*, only 20 pictures survive.

Yamato-e and ***Omna-e*** **Painting** The *Genji* scroll has often been described as an example of *yamato-e* painting, a term coined during the Heian period to distinguish between Japanese and Chinese (*kara-e*) painting styles. This distinction announces a movement away from traditional Chinese styles to one characterized by Japanese literary themes, native subject matter, and landscapes evocative of traditional poetry. But recently scholars have suggested that *yamato-e* refers more specifically to large-scale landscape paintings generally executed on walls, sliding doors, and folding screens, and that the *Genji* illustrations are, rather, examples of *omna-e* paintings, "women's pictures." *Omna-e* pictures are not necessarily works done exclusively by women, but are rather pictures appropriate to the space of women's lives at court. By the time of the *Genji* scroll, *omna-e* paintings were executed by professional artisans at court.

The Kamakura Period (ca. 1185–1392): Samurai and Shogunate

During the Heian period, the emperors had increasingly relied on regional warrior clans—**samurai** (literally, "those who serve")—to exercise military control, especially in the countryside. Over time these clans became more and more powerful, until, by 1100, they had begun to emerge as a major force in Japanese military and political life, inaugurating the Kamakura period, which takes its name from the capital city of the most prominent of these clans, the Minamoto. Their newfound power in many ways represented a resurgence of the familial clan-based system of authority that had been deeply engrained in Japanese society since at least the time of the Yamato emperors, but almost inevitably, their rise also resulted, as it had among the Yamato clans, in intense rivalry and, eventually, warfare.

Pure Land Buddhist Art As war spread across the country, many Japanese felt that it announced the coming of *Mappo*, the so-called Third Age of Buddha, often translated as the "Age of Dharma Decline." Prophesied to begin 2,000 years after the death of Sakyamuni Buddha, it would last, so it was believed, for 10,000 years. During this period no one would be able to attain enlightenment and society would descend into a condition of degeneracy and corruption. Pure Land Buddhism seemed to offer a way out. Pure Land Buddhism had originated in the late sixth century in China as a particular form of Mahayana Buddhism. The Mahayana Buddhists believed that compassion for all beings is the foundation of faith and that not nirvana but buddhahood is one's ultimate goal. They recognized Buddhas other than Sakyamuni, among them Amitabha Buddha, the Buddha of Infinite Light and Life who dwells in a paradise known as the Western Pure Land. This Pure Land Buddhism had been introduced to Japan as early as the seventh century, the Chinese Amitabha Buddha becoming Buddha Amida.

Particularly attractive to the Japanese was the Pure Land belief that by chanting *Namu Amida Butsu* ("Hail to the Buddha Amida"), the faithful would be reborn into the Western Pure Land paradise, where the enlightenment impossible to achieve in the world might finally be attained.

It was commonly believed that if even the most vile sinner uttered one sincere chant, he might be led to the Western Paradise, and one of the most popular expressions of the Paradise's availability was the **raigo** (or "welcoming approach") painting (Fig. 11.16). Amida is seen descending on a white cloud, surrounded by 25 bodhisattvas, toward the veranda of a nobleman's house. One of ten thematically related paintings on the doors of Phoenix Hall (Hoodo) at the Byodin Temple in Kyoto, the painting is particularly remarkable for its rendering of the landscape. There is no trace of the craggy peaks that distinguish Chinese landscape paintings. Instead, in what is one of the earliest examples of *yamato-e* painting, we see the gently rolling, pine-capped slopes of what is recognizably the Heian countryside. It is probably no accident that Shinto paintings depicting the Japanese landscape first appear in the mid-eleventh century, contemporaneously with this door painting, and it is no surprise that the Shinto reverence for nature should find expression in Pure Land Buddhist art.

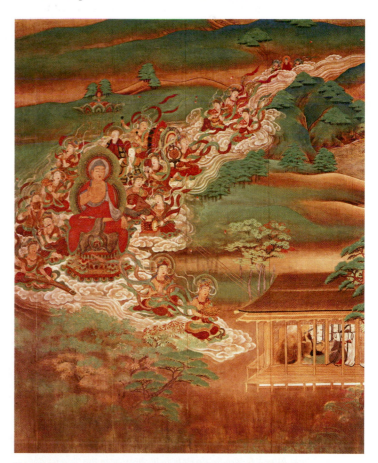

Fig. 11.16 Tamenari, ***The Descent of Amida and the Twenty-Five Bodhisattvas to Collect the Soul of the Deceased.*** **Later Heian period, 1053.** Byodin Temple, Uji, Kyoto Prefecture, Japan. This and the other paintings at Byodin originally surrounded a golden sculpture of Amida on a tall, lotus-blossom pedestal that is still in place.

The Arts of Military Culture The Kamakura period actually began when the Minamoto clan defeated its chief rival, the Taira, in 1185, but the contest for power between the two dominated the last years of the Heian period. The complex relationship between the Fujiwara of the Heian era and the samurai clans of the Kamakura is embodied in a long hand-scroll narration of an important battle of 1160, from the *Scrolls of Events of the Heiji Period*, painted by an unknown artist in the thirteenth century, perhaps 100 years after the events themselves (Fig. **11.17**). In 1156, Go Shirakawa (1127–92; r. 1156–58) ascended to the throne, with the Fujiwara to serve in what had become their traditional role as regent to the emperor, the highest position in the government. But Go Shirakawa resisted the Fujiwara attempt to take control of the government, and in 1157, they recruited one of the two most powerful samurai clans, the Minamoto, to help them stage a coup and imprison the emperor. *Night Attack on the Sanjo Palace* depicts the moment troops led by Fujiwara Nobuyori attacked the emperor's palace in the middle of the night, taking him prisoner and burning his palace to the ground. The chaos and violence of the events are captured by the sweeping linear ribbons of flame and

smoke rising to the upper right and the confusion of horsemen, warriors, fleeing ladies, the dead, and the dying in the foreground, all framed by an architecture that falls at a steep diagonal to the bottom left. The samurai warriors, dressed in elaborate iron armor, were master horsemen and archers. In this scene, many hold their bows, the lower portions of which are smaller than the top in order that they might pass over a horse's neck. As it turned out, this was a brief moment of triumph for the Minamoto. The rebellion was quickly quashed by the second of the powerful clans, the Taira, and for the next 20 years, the Taira managed to control the Japanese imperial court with the abdicated emperor Go Shirakawa's blessing. But in 1185, the Minamoto samurai army, led by Minamoto Yoshitusune (1159–89), defeated the Taira, killing virtually all male members of the Taira clan and large numbers of their wives and children.

Yoshitusune's brother, Yoritomo (1147–99), had sat out the war in Kamakura, and as soon as the war was ended, he quickly disposed of all samurai rivals in the region, including his own brother, whom he hunted down, but who managed to commit suicide rather than be captured. Yoritomo demanded that all other samurai lords pledge allegiance to

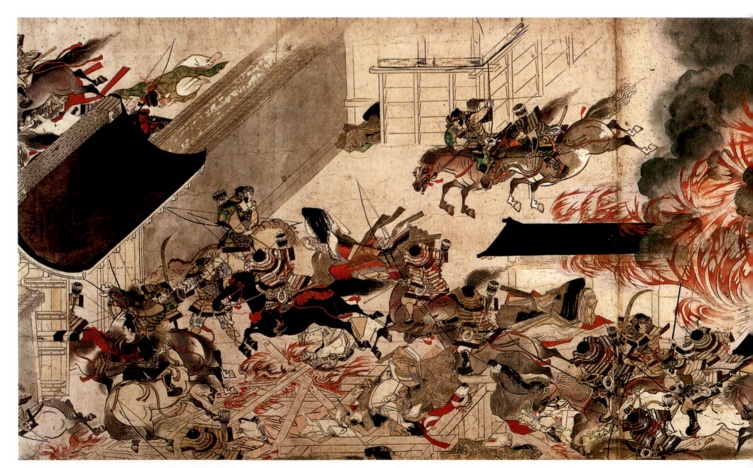

Fig. 11.17 *Night Attack on the Sanjo Palace* (detail), from the *Scrolls of Events of the Heiji Period*. **Kamakura period, late 13th century.** Handscroll, ink and colors on paper, 16¼" × 275½". Courtesy Museum of Fine Arts, Boston. Fenollosa-Weld Collection (11.4000). Reproduced with permission. Photograph © 2013 Museum of Fine Arts, Boston. All rights reserved. This is the central scene of the scroll, which begins with the army moving toward the palace from the right and ends with it leaving in triumph to the left.

View the Closer Look for *Night Attack on the Sanjo Palace* on **MyArtsLab**

him or risk the fate of his brother, and he soon controlled most of the Japanese archipelago. He established his rule at Kamakura, and thus removed Japanese government from the influence of both the aristocratic court at Heian-kyo and the Buddhist stronghold at Nara. Interestingly, Yoritomo never tried to assume the imperial throne, and neither did any of the subsequent samurai rulers. Instead, he considered himself the emperor's servant, much as the Fujiwara had served the Heian emperors. But, in 1192, the imperial court granted him the title of Seiitai Shogun, literally "Barbarian-subduing General," and as **shogun**—that is, general-in-chief of the samurais—his military form of government, known as the shogunate, ruled the country for 150 years.

Yoritomo's shogunate was, in many ways, defined by land reforms that he immediately instituted. In essence, he granted the country estates that had belonged formerly to his enemies as gifts to his followers. These new landholders came to be officially known as *daimyo*, literally "great name," by the fifteenth century. They defined themselves first by their absolute allegiance to the shogun, and then by their devotion to military arts and their concern for their "great name"—by extension, their honor, their fame, and

their pride in their family or clan. Eventually, when Japan enjoyed an extended period of peace, from 1600 until the mid-nineteenth century, these values were codified and expanded upon by a *daimyo* class—whose militarism seemed increasingly irrelevant—into a well-defined code of conduct, **bushido**, "the way of the warrior," which continues to influence many aspects of Japanese society to this day.

THE CULTURES OF AFRICA

In what ways does African art seek to bridge the gap between the temporal and spiritual worlds?

Just as in Europe and Asia, all over Africa, powerful kingdoms arose during this period. Several large kingdoms dominated the western African region known as the Sahel, the grasslands that serve as a transition between the Sahara desert and the more temperate zones to the west and south. Among the most important is the kingdom of Mali (see Chapter 9), which shows the great influence Islam had

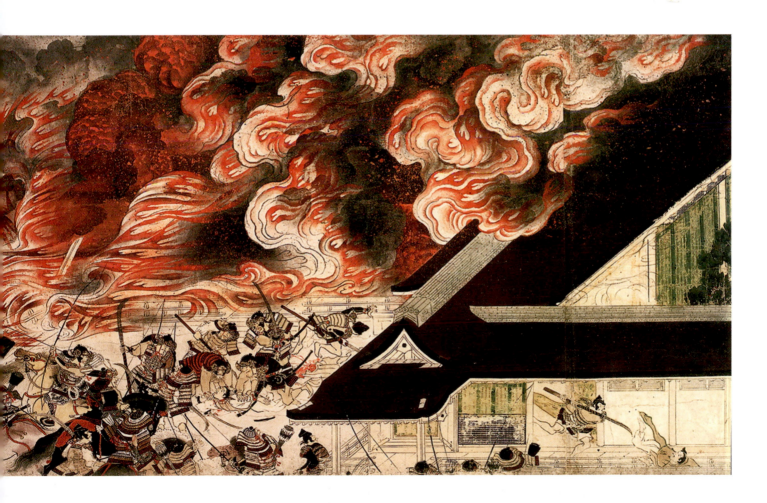

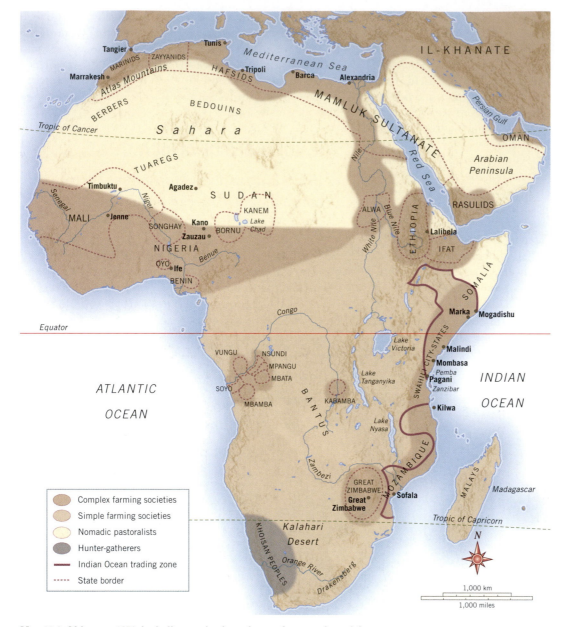

Map 11.4 Africa, ca. 1350, including predominant forms of economic activity.

come to have on much of North Africa long before the end of the first millennium CE. Farther south, along the western coast of central Africa, were the powerful Yoruba state of Ife and the kingdom of Benin. On the eastern side of Africa, the Zagwe dynasty continued long Christian traditions in the Horn of Africa, while the Arab Swahili culture thrived along the central east coast. Farther south, near the southeastern tip of Africa, the ancient Shona civilization produced urban centers represented today by the ruins of "Great Zimbabwe" (Map **11.4**).

Ife Culture

The Ife culture is one of the oldest in West Africa. It developed beginning around the eighth century along the Niger River, in what is now Nigeria. It was centered in

the city of Ife. By 1100, it was producing highly naturalistic, sculptural, commemorative portraits in clay and stone, probably depicting its rulers, and not long after, elegant brass sculptures as well.

An example of Ife brasswork is the *Head of a King* (or *Oni*) (Fig. **11.18**). The parallel lines that run down the face represent decorative effects made by scarring—**scarification**. A hole in the lower neck suggests that the head may have been attached to a wooden mannequin, and in memorial services, the mannequin may have worn the royal robes of the Ife court. Small holes along the scalp line suggest that hair, or perhaps a veil of some sort, also adorned the head. But the head itself was, for the Ife, of supreme importance. It was the home of the spirit, the symbol of the king's capacity to organize the world and to prosper. Ife culture depended on its kings' heads for its own welfare.

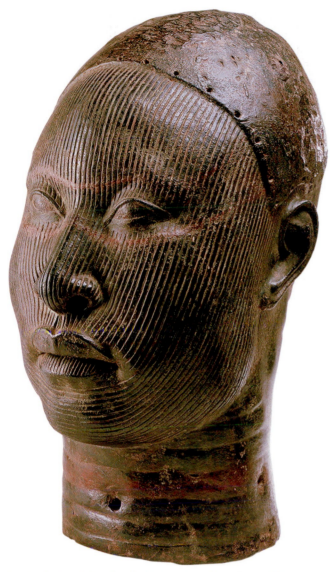

Fig. 11.18 *Head of an Oni (King).* **Ife culture, Nigeria. ca. 13th century.** Brass, height 11⁷⁄₁₆". Museum of Ife Antiquities, Ife, Nigeria. The metal used to cast this head is an alloy of copper and zinc, and therefore not technically bronze, but brass.

Since the Ife did not leave a written record of their cultural beliefs, we can best understand their ancient culture by looking at their contemporary descendants.

Yoruba Origin Myths The Yoruba people, whose population today is about 11 million, trace their ancestry directly to Ife culture. The Yoruba cosmos consists of the world of the living (*aye*) and the realm of the gods (*orun*). The gods are themselves called *orisha* and among them are the primordial deities, who created the world, as well as forces of nature, such as thunder and lightning, and ancestral heroes who have risen to immortality. Linking these two worlds is the king, who serves as the representative in this world of those existing in *orun*. The king's head is thus sacred, and his crown, or *ade* (Fig. 11.19), rising high above his head, symbolizes his majesty and authority. Rows of beads fall over his face to shield viewers from the power of his gaze. Imagery

on the crown varies, but often refers to Ife myths of origin, similar to myths of origin found throughout the world (see Chapter 1). The first Yoruba king, Oduduwa, from whom all subsequent kings descend, is frequently represented. According to legend, Oduduwa was ordered to create a land mass out of the watery reaches of earth so that it might be populated by people. Oduduwa lowered himself down onto the waters, the legend continues, and emptied earth from a small snail shell onto the water. He then placed a chicken

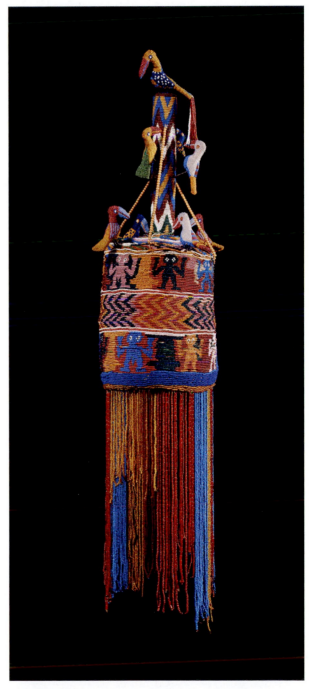

Fig. 11.19 *Ade,* **or beaded crown, Yoruba culture, Nigeria. Late 20th century.** Beadwork, height 6'1¼". © The Trustees of the British Museum. Today, approximately 50 Yoruba rulers wear beaded crowns and claim descent from King Oduduwa.

on the sand to spread it and make land. Finally he planted some palm kernels. It was at Ife that he did this, and Ife remains the most sacred of Yoruba sites.

Benin Culture

Sometime around 1170, the city-state of Benin, some 150 miles southeast of Ife, also in the Niger basin, asked the *oni* of Ife to provide a new ruler for their territory, which was, legend has it, plagued by misrule and disorder. The *oni* sent Prince Oranmiyan, who founded a new dynasty. Oranmiyan was apparently so vexed by the conditions he found that he named his new state *ibini*, "land of vexation," from which the name Benin derives. After some years, Oranmiyan returned home, but not until after he had impregnated the Benin princess. Their son Eweka would become the first king, or *oba*, as the Benin culture called their ruler, ruling from 1180 to 1246.

Already in place at the capital, Benin City, were the beginnings of a massive system of walls and moats that would become, by the fifteenth century, the world's largest human-built earthwork. According to archeologist Phillip Darling, who has studied the wall and moat system for several decades, they total some 10,000 miles in length, or some four to five times the length of the main Great Wall of China. These earthworks consist of moats, the dirt from which was piled alongside them to make walls up to 60 feet high. They were probably first dug over a thousand years ago to protect settlements and their farmlands from the nocturnal raids of the forest elephant. But as Benin grew, linear earth boundaries demarcated clan or family territories and symbolically signified the boundary between the real physical world and the spirit world. When the British arrived in the late nineteenth century, the walls were still largely intact (Fig. **11.20**), but they were soon destroyed by British forces, and what remains of them have been increasingly consumed by modern urbanization.

Like the Ife to the north, the Benin rulers also created lifelike images of their ancestor rulers. In the first half of the twentieth century, recognizing that many of the oral traditions of Benin culture were in danger of being lost, the Benin court historian, Chief Jacob Egharevba (1893–1981), recorded as many traditional tales and historical narratives as he could find and published them in his *Short History of Benin*. This is his account of the origins of brass-casting (see Chapter 2, *Materials & Techniques*, page 42) of *oba* heads in Benin culture (**Reading 11.6**):

READING 11.6

from Jacob Egharevba, *A Short History of Benin*

Oba Oguola [r. 1274–87] wished to introduce brass casting into Benin so as to produce works of art similar to those sent him from Ife. He therefore sent to the Oni of Ife for a brass-smith and Iguegha was sent to him. Iguegha was very clever and left many designs to his successors, and was in consequence deified, and is worshiped to this day by brass-smiths. The practice of making brass-castings for the preservation of the records of events was originated during the reign of Oguola.

The artists, members of the royal casters' guild, lived in their own quarters just outside the palace in Benin, where they are located to this day. Only the *oba* could order brass-work from them. These commissions were usually memorial heads, commemorating the king's royal ancestors in royal costume (Fig. **11.21**). (The head shown in Fig. 11.21 was made in the mid-sixteenth century, but heads like it were made in the earliest years of bronze production in the culture.) As in Ife culture, the *oba*'s head was the home of the spirit and the symbol of the *oba*'s capacity to organize the world and to prosper.

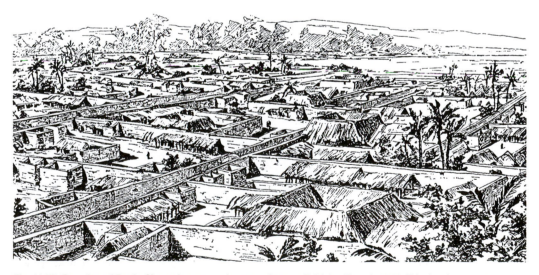

Fig. 11.20 Drawing of Benin City as it appeared to an unknown British officer in 1891. This drawing represents a small portion of the more than 2,500 square miles of walls and moats that made up Benin City in the nineteenth century.

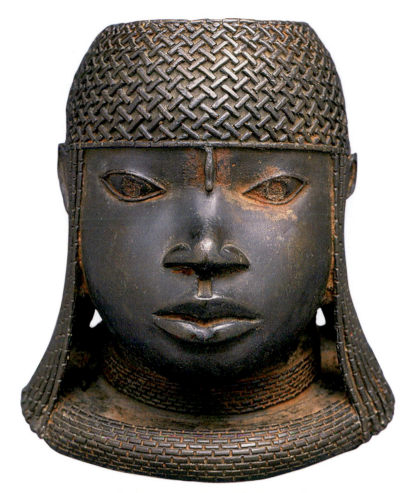

Fig. 11.21 *Head of an Oba*. **Nigeria; Edo, Court of Benin. ca. 1550**. Brass, 9¼" × 9⅝" × 9". The Metropolitan Museum of Art, New York. Such heads were usually commissioned upon the death of an *oba* by his successor, so that the deceased leader might continue to influence his community.

This power could be described and commemorated in an oral form known as a **praise poem**. Praise poems are a major part of West African culture. By praising something—a king, a god, a river—the poet was believed to gain influence over it. Almost everyone in West African culture has praise poems associated with them. These poems often use a poetic device known as **anaphora**, a repetition of words and phrases at the beginning of successive sentences that, owing to the particularities of the West African languages, is almost impossible to duplicate in translation. But the poems are intended to create a powerful and insistent rhythm that rises to a crescendo.

West African Music

The rhythm-driven crescendo of the Benin praise poem shares much with African music as a whole. In fact, the poem may have been accompanied by music. African music is part of the fabric of everyday life, accompanying work, poetry, ceremony, and dance, and often evoked by visual art. The Western idea that music can be isolated from everyday experience is almost incomprehensible to the African sensibility. Typically consisting of a single line of melody without harmony, African music is generally communal in nature, encouraging a sense of social cohesion by promoting group activity. As a result, one of the most universal musical forms throughout Africa is **call-and-response** music, in which a caller, or soloist, raises the song, and the community chorus responds to it.

Call-and-response music is by no means simple. The Yoruba language, for instance, is tone-based; any Yoruba syllable has three possible tones and this tone determines its meaning. The Yoruba reproduce their speech in the method of musical signaling known as **talking drums** (track **11.1**), performed with three types of batá drums, which imitate the three tones of the language. In ritual drumming, the drums are played for the Yoruba gods and are essentially praise poems to those gods. Characteristic of this music is its polyrhythmic structure. Here as many as five to ten different "voices" of interpenetrating rhythms and tones, often repeated over and over again in a call-and-response form, play off against one another. This method of playing against or "off" the main beat is typical of West African music and exists to this day in the "off-beat" practices of Western jazz.

Listen on **MyArtsLab**

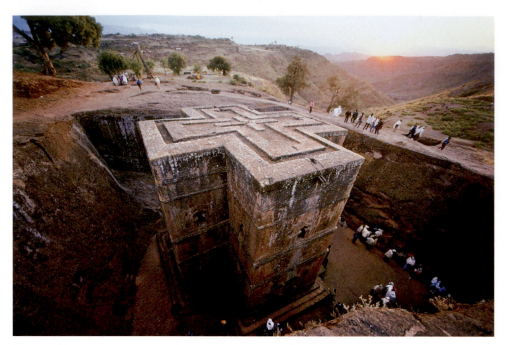

Fig. 11.22 **Beta Ghiorghis (House of Saint George), Lalibela, Ethiopia. 13th century.** Saint George Church is one of more than 1,500 stone carved churches that can still be seen in Ethiopia.

East Africa: The Zagwe Dynasty

Ironically, one of the dynasties of greatest cultural importance in medieval East Africa was also one of the shortest lived and least revered. In the region of today's Ethiopia, the Zagwe dynasty reigned for approximately 150 years, from the early twelfth century (when the declining Aksumite Empire fell), to 1270. In that year the last Zagwe ruler was deposed by a new ruling family, who claimed descent from both the Aksumite Empire that had preceded the Zagwe, and King Solomon and the Queen of Sheba. Both claims were designed to give the impression that their family had a dazzling and unbroken chain of legitimate power reaching back into biblical times. Although the new rulers embarked on a campaign to discredit the Zagwe dynasty as usurpers and their reign as a disgrace, the Zagwe rulers had already ensured their survival as a respected part of Ethiopian history by the rock churches they left behind.

The most famous of these was commissioned by the emperor Lalibela. Claiming to be instructed by God, he ordered the construction of a series of churches in the town now known by his name. Unlike most buildings, instead of being built up from the ground, the churches at Lalibela were carved downward through the soft rocks at the site. Engineers had to conceive of the completed building in advance, including decorative details, because subtractive techniques such as carving do not allow for repair of mistakes. Once the shell of the building was carved, the interior was hollowed out into rooms for use in Christian worship and study.

The last of the churches to be built, Beta Ghiorghis (Fig. **11.22**), is dedicated to the patron saint of Ethiopia, Saint George. According to legend, Lalibela had a vision in which Saint George appeared (in full armor and riding his white horse) and reproached him for not having built a church in his honor. A humbled Lalibela promised to excavate the most beautiful church of all in honor of the saint. A near-perfect cube, chiseled into the shape of a cross, the church is set some 40 feet deep into the ground, and its roof is decorated with three Greek crosses carved in relief and set inside one another.

The Swahili Coast

In the medieval era, Christian places of worship were rare in Africa. In the trading centers of the north and west, Islam was the dominant nonindigenous religion. East Africans had traded with Arab sailors since before the beginning of the common era, from trade depots along a narrow coastal strip ranging from today's Somalia through Mozambique (see Map 11.4). When these traders embraced Islam, the people the Arabs called Swahili, from the Arabic word for "shore," were quick to follow. From Mogadishu in the

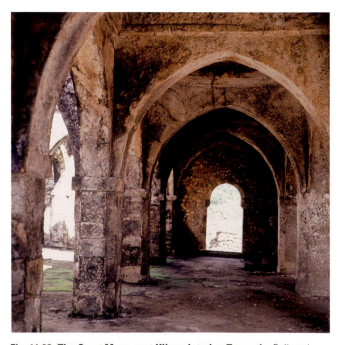

Fig. 11.23 **The Great Mosque at Kilwa, interior, Tanzania.** Built and remodeled over the centuries, it was completed with barrel vaulting and domes by the mid-fifteenth century.

north to Sofala in the south, a region known as the Swahili Coast, Arabs and Africans blended their customs to create one of the most vibrant cultures in Africa. They also created a new language—Swahili, an African language with many borrowings from Arabic.

Looking directly out onto the Indian Ocean, Swahili ports played a key role in trade with all of Asia from the medieval era onward. The great Chinese explorer Zheng He (see Chapter 18) reached the Swahili Coast, trading Chinese porcelain and other goods for African products such as spices and wild animals to take back to the Chinese emperor.

The Swahili were renowned for their architecture. Using local materials such as fossilized coral limestone, they built mosques and other buildings, carving trims and decorations directly into the stone in floral designs, arabesques, and other patterns like those used to decorate the Qur'an (see Chapter 9). So beautiful were these works that, upon visiting Kilwa, medieval explorer Ibn Battuta pronounced it "the most beautiful of cities." The Great Mosque at Kilwa (Fig. 11.23) would have been where Ibn Battuta stopped to pray. Constructed of pieces of fossilized coral bound together by cement made from sand, the pillars, arches, and walls of the mosque were coated in a glossy plaster also made from coral, into which patterns were excised.

Great Zimbabwe

In embracing Islam, the people of the Swahili Coast transformed their society, but the influence of the new faith did not spread far inland. West of Sofala, at a port at the southern end of the Swahili Coast, the Shona people built an entirely indigenous African civilization in the region of today's Zimbabwe. The Shona people, who still occupy the region today, are thought to have first come to the region by 1100 CE. At first the Shona relied on their advanced skills at mining, animal husbandry, and agriculture to sustain their communities in the rocky grasslands of the region, but as the Swahili Coast became more and more lucrative as a center of trade, the Shona positioned themselves as an inland hub of trade to which coastal traders could travel to procure goods for export. From surrounding regions, they mined or imported copper and gold, and in return received exotic goods such as porcelain and glass from Asia and the Middle East.

Between the thirteenth and fifteenth centuries, the Shona erected the massive stone buildings and walls of a city known today as Great Zimbabwe. (The word *zimbabwe* is thought to refer to "palaces of stone.") A huge city for its time, the ruins cover one square mile and are believed to have housed a population of somewhere between 10,000

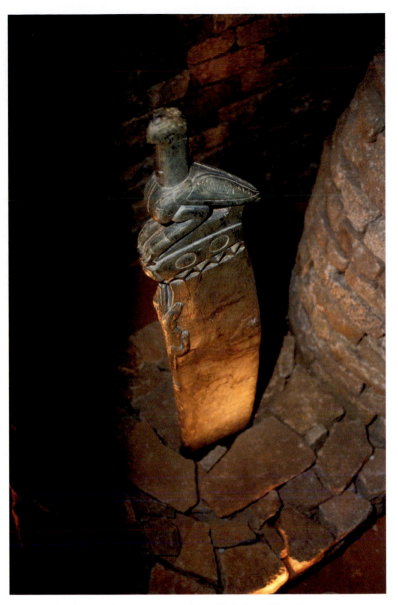

Fig. 11.24 Bird carved from soapstone, Great Zimbabwe, Zimbabwe. ca. 1200–1400 CE. Height 13½", atop a stone monolith (total height 64"). Great Zimbabwe Site Museum, Zimbabwe. One of eight such decorative monoliths at Great Zimbabwe, the bird is not a recognizable species and includes certain human features such as toes instead of talons. This has led to speculation that the figure may represent deceased Shona rulers who were believed to have the power to move between the spirit and human worlds. A crocodile, possibly another symbol of royalty, climbs up the front of the monolith.

and 20,000. Great Zimbabwe has several distinct areas. The oldest of these, a hilltop enclosure known as the Hill Ruin, probably served as a lookout, but may also have been set apart for religious ceremonies or initiation rites. Built around 1250, it has a perimeter wall of smooth stone blocks that follows the contours of the hilltop. Inside this wall are several smaller enclosures with floors of clay that were hardened and polished to a shine. The enclosures also had ceremonial platforms decorated with carved geometric patterns and tall rock monoliths topped by carved birds, possibly representing messengers from the spirit world (Fig. 11.24).

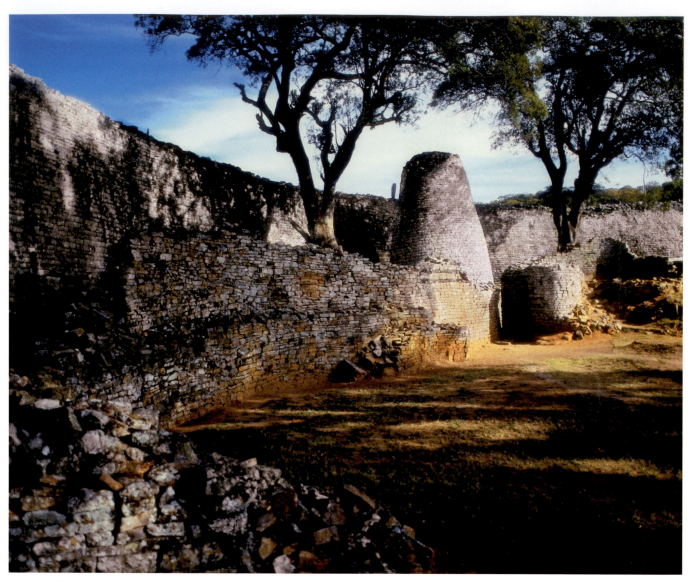

Fig. 11.25 Double perimeter wall and remains of two towers that resemble Shona granaries in the Great Enclosure, Great Zimbabwe. ca. 1200–1400 CE. The skill of the craftsmen who built these structures was extraordinary. They used no mortar, but instead fit the stones together so tightly that the walls reached 30 feet in height and were so sturdy that most of them are intact today. Only the clay smoothed over the walls, and the wooden roofs over some of the structures, have eroded away in the last eight centuries.

Below the Hill Ruin stands the Great Enclosure, a group of structures also encircled by a tall stone wall (Fig. **11.25**). This part of Great Zimbabwe was built approximately a century later, using a different style for the perimeter wall. Here, Shona craftsmen built a double wall with a space between the two walls only wide enough to allow single-file passage. They tapered the walls inward from a 17-foot-thick base for greater strength and stability, and topped the exterior wall with an alternating diagonal pattern of dark- and light-colored rocks. This decoration may have been meant to represent lightning, or perhaps the zebra, an animal frequently depicted in Shona art. These decorative stripes are echoed inside the courtyard of the enclosure, where a large platform similar to those in the Hill Ruin was constructed. One other notable feature of the Great Enclosure is two

conical structures that interrupt passage around the perimeter wall. These are likely to have been ancient granaries, for the Shona people today still use similar structures.

The remainder of Great Zimbabwe consists of clusters of smaller buildings known as the Valley Ruin. Historians and archeologists presume from this that most of the population lived in the valley and that the Great Enclosure was probably a royal residence. One intriguing mystery, however, is the reason for the massive walls of the Great Enclosure and Hill Ruin. Despite the turrets and lookout spots, the walls do not appear to have been meant for defense, and from this, scholars have surmised that the walls may have existed primarily to serve as a buffer between royalty and the common people, acting as a constant reminder of their power and status.

THE CULTURES OF MESOAMERICA AND SOUTH AMERICA IN THE CLASSIC ERA

How do the art and architecture of Mesoamerica and South America reflect the relationship of the various cultures of the region to their gods?

The cultures of pre-Columbian Mesoamerica, comprising modern-day Nicaragua, Honduras, Guatemala, Belize, and southern Mexico, possessed a great sense of their own history. They were fully aware that cultures at least as great as themselves—the Olmec in particular (see Chapter 1)—had preceded them. But during a period of about a thousand years, roughly 250 BCE to 900 CE, which archeologists

call the Classic Era, the cultures of Mesoamerica flourished. "Pre-Columbian" refers to the era before Columbus arrived in the Americas in 1492, and the title "Classic Era," borrowed from Greco-Roman culture, designates what historians consider to be the high point of pre-Columbian culture in the Americas. Three great cultures thrived in Mesoamerica during the Classic Era: the Zapotec culture in the state of Oaxaca; the somewhat mysterious but enormously influential civilization centered at Teotihuacán, just north of Tenochtitlán (present-day Mexico City); and to the south, the Maya culture in the states of Yucatan and Chiapas, and the countries of Belize and Guatemala (Map 11.5). These cultures were at once highly developed and, from a Western point of view, seemingly backward, astronomically sophisticated, with two separate but extraordinarily accurate calendars, yet lacking a domesticated beast of burden capable of

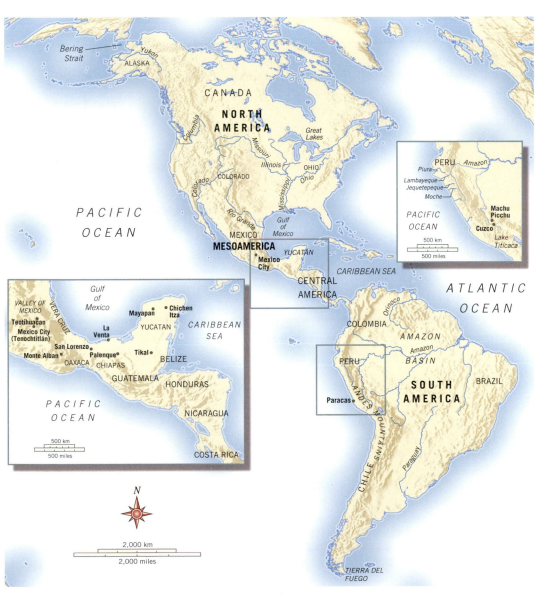

Map 11.5 The Americas. The two chief centers of cultural development in pre-Columbian times in the Americas were Mesoamerica, the semicircular land mass extending from central Mexico south and east through Guatemala and the Yucatan Peninsula, and the central Andes of South America in modern-day Peru.

carrying an adult. Even more astonishing, they lacked one of the most fundamental tools of civilization—the wheel. Although they used wheels on children's toys, they never enlarged them for use on wagons or carts. These civilizations never discovered how to process bronze or iron, yet they moved and cut stones weighing in excess of 100 tons and built enormous temples, the centerpieces of cities rivaling any in Europe or Asia. But what they lacked, they probably did not need, and what they developed was extraordinary.

Monte Albán and Zapotec Culture

Zapotec culture, which occupied the territory later controlled by the Mixtec, was centered at Monte Albán in Oaxaca. The Zapotecs had themselves been closely tied to the Olmecs (see Chapter 1), but instead of living in the alluvial lowlands of the Gulf coast, they built their capital atop a mountain overlooking the three major valleys of central Oaxaca. It seems likely that they were the first Mesoamerican people to use the 260-day calendar, and they possessed a writing system, although, with the exception of names, dates, and places, it remains largely undeciphered. Like the Olmec before them, they valued jade above all other precious stones or metal—more than gold and silver. Jade would remain the most treasured material through the entire history of the cultures of Mesoamerica, from the Olmecs to the Aztecs. The translucent green color of jade symbolized water, fertility, and vegetation—in short, the life force. Large stones were very rare, and specimen pieces were passed down from generation to generation. A particularly fine example is a bat god from Monte Albán, discovered in the grave of an early Zapotec king, and probably worn as a symbol of his power (Fig. 11.26). Its eyes, made of shell, stare fiercely out at any who would have approached him.

Teotihuacán

Teotihuacán thrived from about 50 to 750 CE. By the fourth century CE, it was a center of culture comparable to Constantinople in the Old World. In contrast to the later Mayan cities, many of which were quickly forgotten and overgrown in the jungle, Teotihuacán remained, for the Maya, the Aztecs, and other Mesoamerican civilizations, a holy site, the manifestation on earth of Tollan, the Mesoamerican mythic place of origin. Even a thousand years after it flourished, the most important Aztec rulers made pilgrimages to it.

The city is laid out in a grid system, the basic unit of which is 614 square feet, and every detail is subjected to this scheme, conveying a sense of power and mastery. A great, broad avenue, known as the Avenue of the Dead, runs through the city (Figs. 11.27 and 11.28). It links two great pyramids, the Pyramids of the Moon and the Sun, both surrounded by about 600 smaller pyramids, workshops and numerous plazas, and a giant market area. There are some 2,000 known apartment complexes—more are likely

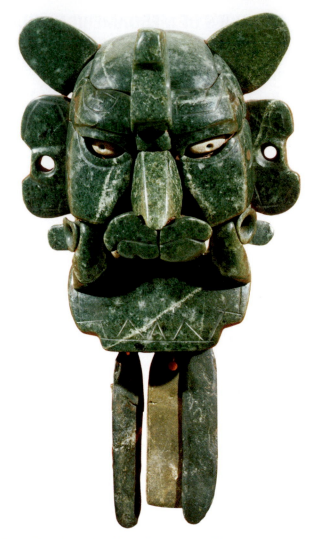

Fig. 11.26 Jade pendant, Monte Albán, State of Oaxaca, Mexico, Zapotec culture. Late pre-Classic (200 BCE–100 CE). Jade with shell inlays, 11" × 6¾". National Museum of Anthropology, Mexico City. Though found at Monte Albán, where it was discovered in a tomb, this piece may well have been passed down from the Olmecs. It represents a bat god.

to be excavated—nearly all adorned with complex murals related to ritual life. Their size, location (nearer or farther from the center), and their quality of construction is indicative of the social status of the inhabitant. The Pyramid of the Sun is oriented to mark the passage of the sun from east to west and the rising of the stellar constellation, the Pleiades, on the days of the equinox. Each of its two staircases contains 182 steps, which, when the platform at its apex is added, together total 365. The pyramid is thus an image of time. This representation of the solar calendar is echoed in another pyramid at Teotihuacán, the Temple of the Plumed (or Feathered) Serpent, which is decorated with 364 serpent fangs.

At its height, in about 500 CE, about 200,000 people lived in Teotihuacán, making it one of the largest cities in the world. Scholars believe that a female deity, associated with the moon, as well as cave and mountain rituals, played an important role in Teotihuacán culture. The placement

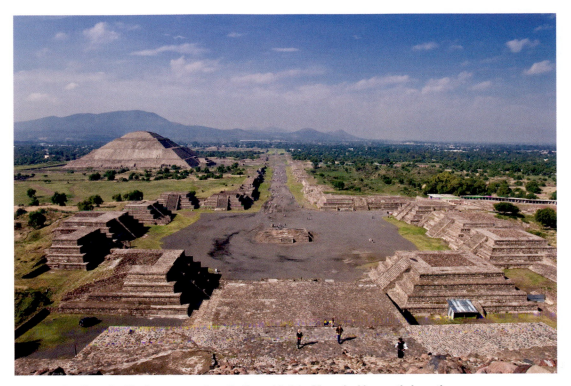

Fig. 11.27 Teotihuacán, Mexico, as seen from the Pyramid of the Moon, looking south down the Avenue of the Dead, the Pyramid of the Sun at the left. ca. 350–650 CE. One of the largest cities in the world by the middle of the first millennium, Teotihuacán covered an area of nearly 9 square miles.

👁 **Watch** an architectural simulation about Teotihuacán on **MyArtsLab**

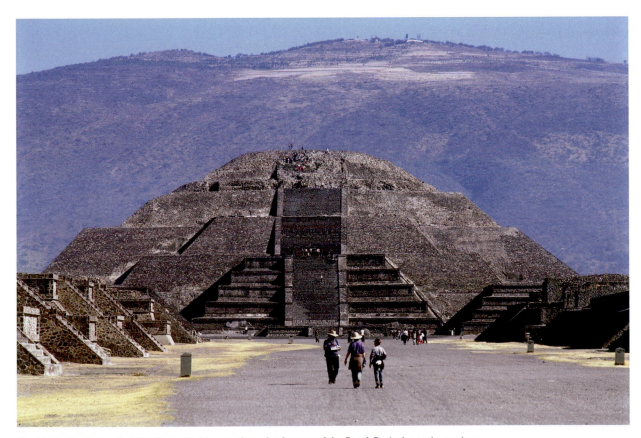

Fig. 11.28 The Pyramid of the Moon, looking north up the Avenue of the Dead. Beginning at the southern end of the city, and culminating at the Pyramid of the Moon, the Avenue of the Dead is 2½ miles long.

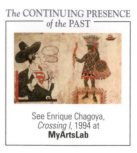

The CONTINUING PRESENCE
of the PAST

See Enrique Chagoya,
Crossing I, 1994 at
MyArtsLab

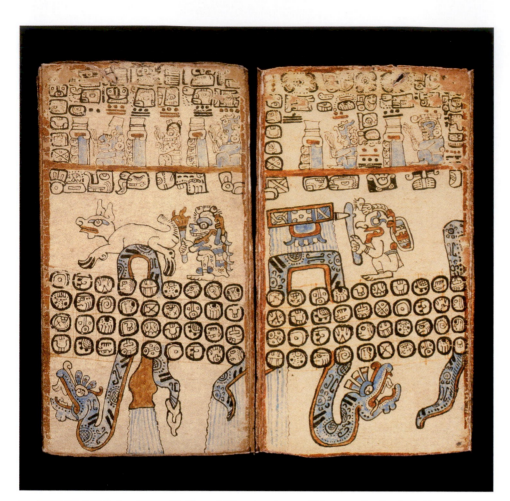

Fig. 11.29 Madrid Codex, leaves 13–16. ca. 1400 CE. Amatl paper, 56 leaves, painted on both sides and screenfolded. Museo de América, Madrid. Diviners would have used this text to predict events such as flood, drought, or an abundant harvest.

of the Pyramid of the Moon, in front of the dead volcano Cerro Gordo (see Fig. 11.28), supports this theory. It is as if the mountain, seen from a vantage point looking north up the Avenue of the Dead, embraces the pyramid in its flanks. And the pyramid, in turn, seems to channel the forces of nature—the abundant water on the mountain in particular—into the heart of the city.

Mayan Culture

To the south, another culture, that of the Maya, both predated and post-dated that of Teotihuacán. The Maya occupied several regions: the highlands of Chiapas and Guatemala; the southern lowlands of Guatemala, Honduras, El Salvador, Belize; and the northern lowlands in the states of Yucatan, Campeche, and Quintano Roo. They were never unified into a single political entity, but rather consisted of many small kingdoms that engaged in warfare with one another over land and resources.

An elaborate calendar system enabled them to keep track of their history—and, evidence suggests, predict the future. It consisted of two interlocking ways of recording time, a 260-day calendar and a 365-day calendar. The

260-day calendar probably derives from the length of human gestation, from a pregnant woman's first missed menstrual period to birth. When both calendars were synchronized, it took exactly 52 years of 365 days for a given day to repeat itself—the so-called calendar round—and the end of each cycle was widely celebrated.

The Mayan calendar was put to many uses. An example is the Madrid Codex (Fig. **11.29**), one of the four surviving Mayan codices. It consists of 56 stucco-coated bark-paper leaves, painted, with the exception of one page, on both sides. Over 250 separate "almanacs" that place events of both a sacred and secular nature within the 260-day Mesoamerican ritual calendar fill its pages. It records events concerning particularly the activities of daily life (planting, tending crops, the harvest, weaving, and hunting), rituals, astronomic events, offerings, and deities associated with them. The four horizontal rows in the lower half of each panel are composed of the glyphs of the 20 named days recycling 13 times. Sky serpents who send the rain and speak in thunder are shown weaving around the rows of glyphs. In the shorter top two leaves, standard numerology can be seen. The Mayans wrote numbers in two ways, as a system of dots and bars, seen here, and in a set of pictorial variants.

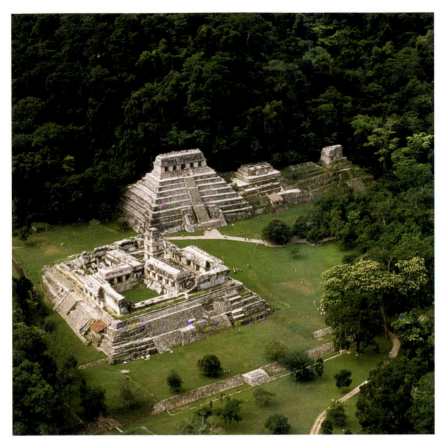

Fig. 11.30 "Palace" (foreground) and Temple of Inscriptions (tomb pyramid of Lord Pakal), Palenque, Mexico. Maya culture. 600–900 CE. These buildings formed the central complex of Palenque. Another complex to the north is composed of five temples and a ball court, and a third group of temples lies to the south. Palenque was the center of a territory that may have been populated by as many as 100,000 people.

Twenty was expressed with a glyph of the moon, and zero with a shell glyph. Zero, incidentally, was used widely in Mesoamerica many centuries before Hindu mathematicians "discovered" it in India.

The City of Palenque Among the most important Mayan cities is Palenque, one of the best-preserved of all Mayan sites. Lost in the jungle for centuries following its decline, which occurred around the year 850, Palenque was rediscovered in 1746 by a Spanish priest who had heard rumors of its existence. The Temple of Inscriptions, facing into the main courtyard of the so-called Palace, which may have been an administrative center rather than a royal residence, rises in nine steps, representing the nine levels of the Mayan Underworld (Fig. 11.30). It is inscribed with the history of the Palenque kings, who were associated with the jaguar. The first recorded king is K'uk B'alam, "Quetzal Jaguar," who, so the inscriptions say, founded the city on March 11, 431. Palenque's most powerful king was K'inich Janaab' Pakal I (Great Sun Shield), known as Pakal (603–83), who ruled for 67 years, and the Temple of Inscriptions was erected over his grave.

In 1952, Alberto Ruz, a Mexican archeologist, discovered the entrance to the tomb of Lord Pakal, under the

pyramid. It was hidden under large stone slabs in the floor of the temple at the top of the pyramid. Ruz had to clear the passage down to Pakal's tomb, at the very base of the structure, which had been back-filled with stone debris. When he reached the tomb, he found that Pakal's face was covered with a jade death mask. A small tube connected the tomb with the upper level, thus providing the dead king with an eternal source of fresh air. It also functioned as a form of communication between the living and the ancestor. Pakal was buried in a large uterus-shaped stone sarcophagus weighing over 5 tons and covered with jade and cinnabar.

The *Popol Vuh* The *Popol Vuh* is a Mayan book of creation. It was written in Quiché, a surviving Mayan dialect still spoken in the Guatemalan highlands, and produced between 1554 and 1558 by a Guatemalan Indian. Despite its late date, it probably represents Mayan belief systems that date back over a thousand years. Sometime in about 1700, a Dominican priest, Francisco Ximénez, copied the manuscript, adding a Spanish translation in a column paralleling the Quiché original. The original has since disappeared. Over a hundred years later, the Ximenez copy was found in the archives of San Carlos University in Guatemala City by Brasseur de Bourbourg, who brought it to Paris and published a version of it in 1858. It was subsequently sold to the Newberry Library in Chicago, along with other documents from the Brasseur collection, where it remained uncataloged and unknown until 1941. The *Popol Vuh* is in four parts, beginning with the deeds of Mayan gods in the darkness of a primeval sea (**Reading 11.7**):

READING 11.7

from the *Popol Vuh: The Great Mythological Book of the Ancient Maya*

Before the world was created, Calm and Silence were the great kings that ruled. Nothing existed, there was nothing. Things had not yet been drawn together, the face of the earth was unseen. There was only motionless sea, and a great emptiness of sky. There were no men anywhere, or animals, no birds or fish, no crabs. Trees, stones, caves, grass, forests, none of these existed yet. There was nothing that could roar or run, nothing that could tremble or cry in the air. Flatness and emptiness, only the sea, alone and breathless. It was night; silence stood in the dark.

In this darkness the Creators waited, the Maker, Tepeu, Gucumatz, the Forefathers. They were there in this emptiness, hidden under green and blue feathers, alone and surrounded with light. They are the same as wisdom. They are the ones who can conceive and bring forth a child from nothingness. And the time had come. The Creators were bent deep around talk in the darkness. They argued, worried, sighed over what was to be. They planned the growth of the thickets, how things would crawl and jump, the birth of man. They planned the whole creation, arguing each point until their words and thoughts crystallized and became the same thing. Heart of Heaven was there, and in the darkness the creation was planned.

Then let the emptiness fill! they said. Let the water weave its way downward so the earth can show its face! Let the light break on the ridges, let the sky fill up with the yellow light of dawn! Let our glory be a man walking on a path through the trees! "Earth!" the Creators called. They called only once, and it was there, from a mist, from a cloud of dust, the mountains appeared instantly. …

The gods try three times to create mankind, once out of animals, a second time out of mud, and a third time out of wood. Wood proves most successful, though the wooden men are killed off as well, and their descendants become monkeys. The rest of Part 1 and all of Part 2 deal with two sets of twins—the Hero Twins, Hunhapu and Xbalanque; and their half-brothers, the Monkey Twins, Hun Batz´ and Hun Chouen. Both sets of twins are ballplayers. Summoned to Xibalba (the Underworld), Hunhapu and Xbalanque undergo a series of tests, transformations, and resurrections.

The connection of the traditional Mesoamerican ball game to forces of life and death, the cycles of time, evidenced so substantially in the *Popul Vuh*, underscores its significance to the culture. Almost all major sites had ball courts (Fig. **11.31**). Players directed a heavy, solid rubber ball with their heads, thighs, or knees, padded to absorb the impact, through the opponent's ring high on the wall on each side of an I-shaped court. The game was closely associated with Mayan myths of origin and had deep religious significance. The ball represented the sun, and the duty of the players was to keep it from falling to earth as it passed through day and night (the games often lasted for several days). The sharply angled walls of the court itself were associated with the crack in the top of Creation Mountain described in the *Popul Vuh* (the Mayan word for crevice, *hom*, is also the word for "ball court"), and play was intimately tied to the gods themselves. The losing team was believed to have betrayed both the sun and the gods. Evidence suggests that the post-Classic Maya decapitated the losing team and displayed their heads on poles surrounding the ball court, and later on wooden scaffolds or stone monuments known as "skull racks."

By 900 CE, Mayan culture had collapsed as a result of a wide variety of events, including overpopulation and accompanying ecological degradation, political competition, and war. Its peoples, who survive in large numbers to this day, returned to simple farming around the ruins of their once-great cities.

The Post-Classic Era: Toltecs and Aztecs

In the north, after the decline of Teotihuacán, the Toltec culture rose to power. Centered in Tula in the modern state of Hidalgo, in terms of architecture, symbols, planning, and narrative programs, the Toltecs were a bridge between Teotihuacán and the Aztecs. When, in the twelfth century, Tula was burned and its inhabitants scattered, one of these surviving groups was the Mexica. Later known as the Aztecs, they wandered into the Valley of Mexico in about 1325 and built a village on the shores of Lake Texcoco. There they saw an eagle perching on a prickly pear cactus (*tenochtli*), a sign that their wandering was over. They dug canals and drained the shallow areas of the lake, converting them into fertile

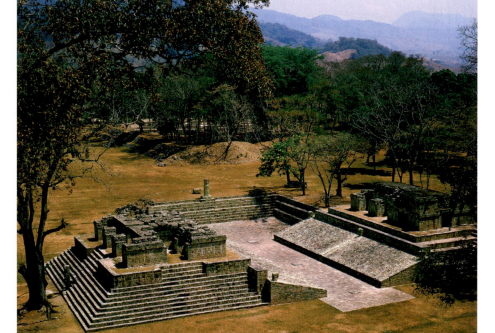

Fig. 11.31 Ball court at Copán, Honduras, Maya culture. ca. 711–36 CE. This is the second-largest ball court in Mesoamerica. The largest is at Chichen Itza.

fields, and there, as well, they built the city of Tenochtitlán on an island in the lake's center.

Blood sacrifice was central to Aztec culture, merging perfectly with the warrior traditions inherited from the Toltecs. The Aztecs believed that the sun, moon, and earth all depended upon human blood for their sustenance. Their chief activity, as a result, was war, and the chief goal of war was to capture sacrificial victims, as well as acquire territory and exact tribute to buttress the life of the elites, including quetzal feathers, copal resin for incense, and cotton for warrior uniforms. At puberty, boys were placed under jurisdiction of a local warrior house and trained for war, where they learned that success in life equaled the number of enemies captured alive for later ritual killing. Death itself, when realized in the pursuit of such honor, was the greatest honor an Aztec male could achieve.

Centered at Tenochtitlán, Aztec culture would survive until the arrival of the Spanish in 1519. In only a few years it was almost totally destroyed, its vast quantities of magnificent goldwork looted and returned to Europe to be melted down to support the warring ways of the European kings (see Chapter 18).

The Cultures of South America

As in Mesoamerica, complex cultures developed in South America during the period corresponding to the Middle Ages in Europe, particularly in the area of present-day Peru (see Map 11.5). The region is one of dramatic contrast. The snow-capped peaks and high grasslands of the Andes Mountains capture rainfall from the Pacific Ocean, creating rivers that drop quickly to the sea across one of the most arid deserts in the world.

The Moche In these river valleys, which are essentially oases in the coastal desert, Moche culture flourished for a thousand years, from about 200 BCE to 800 CE. The Moche built large mound temples made entirely of **adobe** bricks, sun-baked blocks of clay mixed with straw. The largest, located in the Moche Valley, from which the culture takes its name, is the so-called Pyramid of the Sun. It is over 1,000 feet long and 500 feet wide and rises to a height of 59 feet. In these pyramids, people buried their dead, accompanied by gold earrings, pendants, necklaces, and other ornaments, as well as elaborately decorated ceramic bowls, pots, and bottles.

The most distinctive bottles depict scenes representative of Moche culture as a whole, usually on bottles with distinctive stirrup spouts that curve elegantly away from the body of the vessel (Fig. 11.32). The list of the subjects depicted is almost endless— animals of all kinds, from seals to owls, warriors, plants, musicians, homes, children at play, women weaving, couples engaged in sex, a man washing his hair— as if the culture was intent on representing every facet of its daily life. Recent research suggests, however, that every one of these scenes has a ritual or symbolic function. This figure, for instance, may well represent the Warrior priest who presided over Moche sacrifice ceremonies, in which

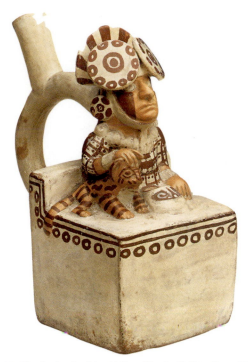

Fig. 11.32 *Moche Lord with a Feline*, Moche Valley, Peru. Moche culture. ca. **100 BCE–500 CE**. Painted ceramic, height 7½". Buckingham Fund. 1955-2281. Photograph © The Art Institute of Chicago. All rights reserved. Vessels of this kind, depicting almost every aspect of Moche life, were buried in large quantities with Moche rulers.

prisoners captured in battle were sacrificed and their blood drunk by elaborately dressed warriors.

The Inca In about 800 CE, the Moche suddenly vanished, many believe as a result of floods brought about by a series of weather events related to El Niño. This major temperature fluctuation of the waters of the Eastern Pacific Ocean results in substantial changes in rainfall levels both regionally and worldwide. The resulting political vacuum lasted for over 400 years until, around 1300, Inca culture emerged. One of many farming cultures in the southern Peruvian highlands, the Inca took advantage of the Andean camelids—llamas, alpacas, vicuñas, and guanacos, beasts of burden unknown to the cultures of Mesoamerica—to forge trading networks that eventually united the southern highlands and northern coastal lowlands under their rule. Large irrigation projects transformed both the river valleys and the desert between them into rich agricultural regions.

The Inca were, above all, masterful masons. Working with stone tools and without mortar, they crafted adjoining granite blocks that fit so snugly together that their walls have, for centuries, withstood earthquakes that have destroyed many later structures. Few of the blocks are the same size, and some have as many as 30 faces. Still, the joints are so tight that even the thinnest knife blade cannot be forced between the stones. This stonework symbolized the permanence and stability of the culture itself, and Cuzco (meaning "navel of the earth"), the capital of the Inca Empire, was laid out to resemble a giant puma, and its masonry, much of which still survives, is unmatched

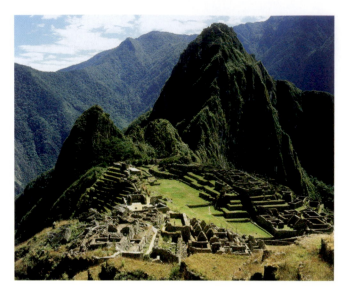

Fig. 11.33 Machu Picchu, Peru, Inca culture. ca. 1450. Machu Picchu survived destruction by the Spanish when they invaded in 1532, partly because of its remote location, high in the Andes, and partly because, compared to the Inca capital of Cuzco, it probably seemed small and comparatively insignificant. Nevertheless, by about 1537 it was abandoned as Inca civilization collapsed, victim not only of the Spanish conquistadors, but also of disease, especially smallpox.

Llamas were the source of wool for the Inca. One was sacrificed in Cuzco each morning and evening, and a white llama was kept at Cuzco as a symbol for the Inca as a whole. According to Spanish commentators, the Cuzco llama was paraded through the streets of the city during celebrations of the coming planting season each April, dressed in a red tunic and wearing gold jewelry. These processions also included life-size gold and silver images of llamas, people, and various Inca gods.

Melted for currency by the Spanish throne, none of these large objects survive. Small objects of gold and silver, which symbolized to the Inca the sun and the moon, were once scattered through the central plaza of Cuzco. The plaza—in Incan times twice as large as it is today—was excavated to a depth of between 6 and 12 inches, its sacred soil carried away to each of the four quadrants of Tahuantinsuyu, as the Inca called their homeland, "Land of the Four Quadrants." The plaza was then refilled with sand brought from the ocean, in which offerings of gold and silver llamas and human figures were distributed. The plaza thus symbolized a great body of water, at once the Pacific Ocean and Lake Titicaca, from which the Inca creator deity, Ticsivirachocha, had emerged after the great flood to repopulate the world. It was thus, for the Inca before the arrival of the Spanish, the very center of the world.

anywhere in the world. At Machu Picchu (Fig. **11.33**), stone buildings, whose thatched and gabled roofs have long since collapsed, are set on stone terraces in a setting that was designed, recent research has shown, as a royal retreat for the Inca ruler, Pachacuti Inka Yupanqui, who built the complex between 1460 and 1470 to get away from the noise and congestion of the capital. About 1,200 people lived in Machu Picchu's approximately 170 residences, most of them women, children, and priests.

The Inca also created an extraordinary network of roads, ranging from as wide as 50 feet to as narrow as 3 feet, and extending from desert to Andes peaks for some 15,000 miles. Nearly a thousand lodgings were built along the routes, and relay runners could carry news across the region in less than a week.

The Inca were especially attracted to textiles, which apparently they valued even more than gold or other minerals, at least in part because of the extremely high, and cold, elevations at which they lived. The exact meaning of the design of an Inca weaving that survives from the time of the Spanish conquest is unclear, but scholars believe it is largely symbolic (Fig. **11.34**). Most Inca tunics include only a few examples of the small square units, called *t'oqapu*, that cover this one entirely. In fact, no other known tunic incorporates such a large number and wide variety. Each of these *t'oqapu* may have held special meaning or significance, referring to specific peoples, places, or things. It seems likely that this particular tunic was worn by the ruler himself, its large number of *t'oqapu* conveying the message that he controlled an enormously diverse culture.

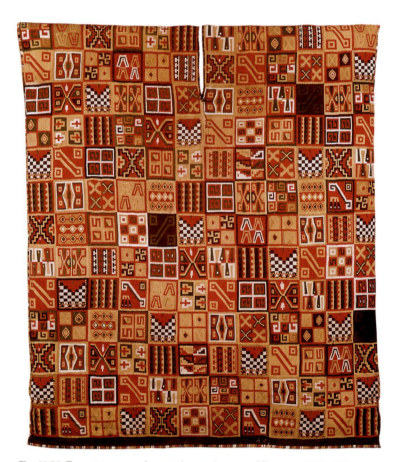

Fig. 11.34 Tapestry-weave Inca tunic, south coast of Peru. ca. 1440–1540. Camelid fiber and cotton, 35⅛" × 30". Dumbarton Oaks Research Library and Collections, Washington, D.C. Each square represents a specific group, or an individual's identity, and functions much like a heraldic device or a logo.

The Spanish and the Fate of the Inca and Aztec Capitals

One of the most elaborately decorated of all Inca sites was Cuzco's Coricancha (literally, "the corral of gold"), the Inca Temple of the Sun facing the plaza (Fig. 11.35). Dedicated to Inti, the sun god, the original temple was decorated with 700 sheets of gold studded with emeralds and turquoise and designed to reflect the sunlight admitted through its windows. Its courtyard was filled with golden statuary—"stalks of corn that were of gold—stalks, leaves and ears," the Spanish chronicler Pedro de Cieza de León reported in the mid-sixteenth century. "Aside from this," he continued, there were "more than twenty sheep [llamas] of gold with their lambs and the shepherds who guarded them, all of this metal."

After their conquest of Peru, the Spanish quickly adapted the foundations of the Inca temple to their own purposes, constructing a Dominican church and monastery on the original Inca foundations. The Inca traditionally gathered to worship at the curved, circular wall of the Coricancha, and thus the apse of Santo Domingo was purposefully constructed above it to emphasize Christian control of the native site. This story—of European control over former native sites and resources—would be all too common in the continuing history of the Western Hemisphere (see Chapter 18).

But where the Spanish in Peru incorporated Inca stone masonry into their own colonial architecture—the streets of Cuzco are lined to this day with original stone walls—in Mexico, they would obliterate the Aztec capital of

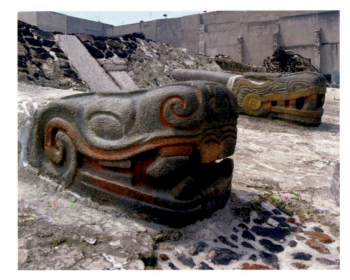

Fig. 11.36 Serpent heads in the archeological zone of the Templo Mayor, Mexico City, Mexico, Aztec culture. ca. 1469.

Tenochtitlán altogether. Even the giant temple in the heart of the city, the Templo Mayor, was brought to ruin, the Spanish building the capital of what they called New Spain atop its rubble (see Chapter 23). Not until 1978, when workers digging for an electric company excavated a huge disk over 10 feet in diameter and weighing 8.5 tons (see Fig. 18.2 in Chapter 18), did researchers determine where the temple originally stood, just to the northeast of the Zócalo, the main square of modern Mexico City. In order to accommodate excavation, 13 buildings had to be demolished, 4 dating from the nineteenth century, the others from the 1930s. The pyramid was composed of four sloped stairways, one on each side, topped by a great platform upon which stood two shrines, one dedicated to Tlaloc, the god of rain and agriculture, and one to Huitzilopochtli, god of war. Each stairway was defined by railings that flanked the stairs terminating, at the base, in menacing serpent heads (Fig. 11.36). Today the Museum of the Templo Mayor supervises continuing archeological work at the site and houses the more than 7,000 artifacts discovered there. ■

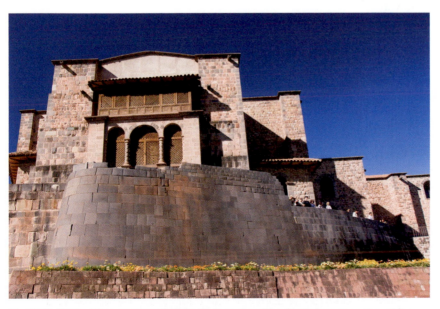

Fig. 11.35 Original Inca stone wall of the Coricancha with a Dominican monastery rising above it, Cuzco, Peru, Inca culture.

11.1 Describe how the literature, art, and architecture of the Tang and Song dynasties reflect the values of Chinese society.

Between the first and third centuries CE, Buddhism spread from India north into China, and with it came images of the Buddha. During the Tang dynasty, trade on the Silk Road flourished. As reflected in the plan of their capital Chang'an, the Tang were committed to social order. The Tang valued the arts—they were especially gifted ceramic artists—and education. Confucian, Buddhist, and Daoist philosophy informed government affairs. How did these philosophies inform the poetry of writers like Li Bai and Du Fu as well? When Marco Polo visited Hangzhou in 1274, it was still the capital city of the Southern Song dynasty. It enjoyed tremendous prosperity, controlled in no small part by a thriving merchant class whose sons had benefited from the invention of the printing press at schools that prepared them for government examinations. What did these students learn from studying the Chinese classics? Many poets and artists of the period practiced the neo-Confucian Chan Buddhism. How were these beliefs reflected in their work? In 1279, the Song fell to the Mongol leader Kublai Khan, who ruled China from Beijing as founder of the Yuan dynasty. The scholar-painters of the Chinese court, unwilling to serve under foreign domination, retreated into exile. How did their artworks reflect their resistance?

11.2 Compare and contrast the ways in which Buddhist and Hindu art and architecture embody the presence of, respectively, Buddha and the Hindu gods.

During the era known as the Middle Ages in the West, the history and art of India and Southeast Asia were dominated by the interaction of Buddhism, Islam, and Hinduism. Forced out of northern India by invading Muslims, the Buddhists retreated north into Nepal and across the Himalayas into Tibet or eastward into present-day Myanmar (formerly Burma). In Tibet, a new brand of Buddhism developed under the local religious leaders—the lamas, and the chief lama—the Dalai. How would you describe Tibetan Buddhism? Meanwhile Hinduism continued to thrive, especially in southern India and Cambodia. Distinct Hindu temple styles developed, the chief example of which is the Kandarya Mahadeva Temple at Khajuraho, which mirrored the Hindu cosmos. As Hinduism spread into Cambodia, enormous temple complexes were constructed, especially at Angkor Wat. What does the sculpture program at Angkor Wat suggest about the Hindu religion?

11.3 Describe the complex relationship between court life and spiritual practice in Heian and Kamakura Japan.

The end of the Yamato period in Japan was marked by strife between the imperial Sago clan, who were deeply attracted to Buddhism, and the Mononobe, who were in charge of the emperor's military, and the Nakatomi, in charge of Shinto ritual, both of whom opposed the introduction of Buddhism into the country. Prince Shotoku moved the capital to the Asuka Valley and introduced Confucian principles into court affairs, but his descendants were executed. Factions continued to fight even after the imperial capital was moved again to nearby Nara and then Heian-kyo (present-day Kyoto). During the more stable Heian period, conflicts continued. Nevertheless, the Heian court displayed the greatest elegance and refinement. Noble women lived in extreme seclusion, but could distinguish themselves through their correspondence and verse. Instead of writing in the official Chinese writing style, these women wrote in a new, distinctly Japanese writing system, *hiragana*. Among the most important writers at the Heian court were Sei Shonagon, author of the *Pillow Book*, and Murasaki Shikibu, whose *Diaries* are surpassed only by her monumental fictional narrative, *The Tale of Genji*. How would you describe the style of the scroll illustrations of *The Tale of Genji*? When, again, conflicts among various clans led to the downfall of the Heian dynasty, warriors known as samurai took over the country. The most powerful samurai, Minamoto Yoritomo, took the title of shogun and inaugurated the first shogunate, the Kamakura dynasty. He isolated his government from both the imperial court at Heian-kyo and the Buddhist monks at Nara. But both the court and Buddhism still thrived. What form of Buddhism became increasingly popular? Why?

11.4 Discuss the ways in which African arts serve as bridges between the temporal and supernatural worlds.

By 1100, the Yoruba civilization, centered in the West African city of Ife, was producing highly naturalistic commemorative portraits in clay and stone, probably depicting their rulers, and not long after, elegant brass sculptures as well. In Benin, a huge complex of moats and walls developed at the capital. The art of lost-wax casting was perfected there as well. What was the purpose of these sculptures? How are these same purposes reflected in praise poems? In East Africa, Ethiopia was developing monumental architecture in the form of carved rock Christian churches, while farther down the coast the Swahili culture, a hybrid of indigenous African and Arab Muslim customs and languages, fostered cosmopolitan port cities.

11.5 Understand how Mesoamerican and South American art and architecture reflect the relationship of the various cultures of the region to their gods.

Teotihuacán remained a holy site for centuries after it was abandoned, shared by the Maya, the Aztecs, and other Mesoamerican civilizations as a common place of origin. The city was designed to convey a sense of power and mastery, its Pyramid of the Sun oriented to the passage of the sun and the rise of the stellar constellation, the Pleiades, on the days of the equinox. How is it also an image of time itself?

To the south, the Mayans developed an elaborate calendar. What two cycles of time does it incorporate? How does the Temple of Inscriptions at Palenque give us another distinct sense of the passage of time and Mayan history? How does the *Popol Vuh*'s emphasis on the forces of life and death support this historical sense?

Moche culture arose in the river valleys of the coastal plains of Peru in about 200 BCE. It produced elaborate ceramic stirrup-spouted bottles that depicted every aspect of Moche life. How might we account for the disappearance of the Moche around 800 CE? Over 400 years later, the Inca emerged, with their capital at Cuzco in the high Andes, but their influence extended to the coastal plains as well. They were extraordinary masons, and they were especially attracted to textiles. The llama, from which they derived the wool to make their textile wares, was sacred to them. They decorated their temples freely with gold. What did gold represent to them? What about silver? How did all their artworks in precious metals disappear?

 Study and **review** on **MyArtsLab**

READINGS

READING 11.1

Poems by Li Bai and Du Fu

Li Bai and Du Fu are generally considered the greatest poets of the Tang dynasty. The two became close friends after Li Bai was summoned to the capital at Chang'an by the emperor Xuanzong in 742. They wrote many poems to one another, a good example of which is the second of the two poems below. The first poem below underscores Li Bai's sense of isolation and loneliness after he was expelled from court in 762. After the collapse of the Tang court in the mid-750s, Du Fu wandered down the Yangtze River, finding patrons and dreaming of his return to Chang'an, until his death in 770.

Li Bai, "Drinking Alone by Moonlight"

A pot of wine in the flower garden,
but no friends to drink with me.
So I raise my cup to the bright moon
and to my shadow, which makes us three,
but the moon won't drink
and my shadow just creeps about my heels.
Yet in your company, moon and shadow,
I have a wild time till spring dies out.
I sing and the moon shudders.
My shadow staggers when I dance. 10
We have our fun while I can stand
then drift apart when I fall asleep.
Let's share this empty journey often
and meet again in the milky river of stars.

Du Fu, "Dreaming of Li Bai"

I've swallowed sobs from the lost dead,
but this live separation is chronic grief.

From the malarial south of the river
no news comes of the exiled traveler,
but you visit my dream, old friend,
knowing I ache for you.
Are you a ghost?
No way to tell with the long road between us.
Your spirit comes through the green maple woods
slips home past darkening border fortresses. 20
You are caught in the law's net,
so how can your spirit have wings?
The sinking moon pours onto the rafters
and your face glows in my mind.
The water is deep, the waves are wide.
Don't let the dragons snatch you!

READING CRITICALLY

Both poems develop the image of moonlight. Traditionally, in China, the full moon is a symbol of good luck, harmony, and abundance. How does this symbol inform these two poems?

from Sei Shonagon, *Pillow Book*, "Hateful Things"

We know almost nothing about Sei Shonagon except what she writes about herself in the *Pillow Book*. "Hateful Things" is one of 164 such lists in Sei Shonagon's *Pillow Book*. Others include "People Who Look Pleased with Themselves," "Insects," "Things without Merit," and so on. But lists are not her only subject. She continually turns her attention to minute observations of court life, in entries such as "The Cat Who Lived in the Palace" or "The Women's Apartments along the Gallery."

One is in a hurry to leave, but one's visitor keeps chattering away. If it is someone of no importance, one can get rid of him by saying, "You must tell me all about it next time"; but, should it be the sort of visitor whose presence commands one's best behavior, the situation is hateful indeed.

One finds that a hair has got caught in the stone on which one is rubbing one's inkstick, or again that gravel is lodged in the inkstick, making a nasty, grating sound.

Someone has suddenly fallen ill and one summons the exorcist. Since he is not at home, one has to send messen- 10 gers to look for him. After one has had a long fretful wait, the exorcist finally arrives, and with a sigh of relief one asks him to start his incantations. But perhaps he has been exorcising too many evil spirits recently; for hardly has he installed himself and begun praying when his voice becomes drowsy. Oh, how hateful!

A man who has nothing in particular to recommend him discusses all sorts of subjects at random as though he knew everything.

An elderly person warms the palms of his hands over a 20 brazier and stretches out the wrinkles. No young man would dream of behaving in such a fashion; old people can really be quite shameless. I have seen some dreary old creatures actually resting their feet on the brazier and rubbing them against the edge while they speak. These are the kind of people who in visiting someone's house first use their fans to wipe away the dust from the mat and, when they finally sit on it, cannot stay still but are forever spreading out the front of their hunting costume[1] or even tucking it up under their knees. One might suppose that such behavior was restricted to people of hum- 30 ble station; but I have observed it in quite well-bred people, including a Senior Secretary of the Fifth Rank in the Ministry of Ceremonial and a former Governor of Suruga.

I hate the sight of men in their cups who shout, poke their fingers in their mouths, stroke their beards, and pass on the wine to their neighbors with great cries of "Have some more! Drink up!" They tremble, shake their heads, twist their faces, and gesticulate like children who are singing, "We're off to see the Governor." I have seen really well-bred people behave like this and I find it most distasteful. 40

To envy others and to complain about one's own lot; to speak badly about people; to be inquisitive about the most trivial matters and to resent and abuse people for not telling one, or, if one does manage to worm out some facts, to inform everyone in the most detailed fashion as if one had known all from the beginning—oh, how hateful!

One is just about to be told some interesting piece of news when a baby starts crying.

A flight of crows circle about with loud caws.

An admirer has come on a clandestine visit, but a dog 50 catches sight of him and starts barking. One feels like killing the beast.

One has been foolish enough to invite a man to spend the night in an unsuitable place—and then he starts snoring.

A gentleman has visited one secretly. Though he is wearing a tall, lacquered hat[2], he nevertheless wants no one to see him. He is so flurried, in fact, that upon leaving he bangs into something with his hat. Most hateful! It is annoying too when he lifts up the Iyo blind[3] that hangs at the entrance of the room, then lets it fall with a great rattle. If it is a head-blind, 60 things are still worse, for being more solid it makes a terrible noise when it is dropped. There is no excuse for such carelessness. Even a head-blind does not make any noise if one lifts it up gently on entering and leaving the room; the same applies to sliding-doors. If one's movements are rough, even a paper door will bend and resonate when opened; but, if one lifts the door a little while pushing it, there need be no sound.

One has gone to bed and is about to doze off when a mosquito appears, announcing himself in a reedy voice. One can actually feel the wind made by his wings and, slight though it 70 is, one finds it hateful in the extreme.

A carriage passes with a nasty, creaking noise. Annoying to think that the passengers may not even be aware of this! If I am travelling in someone's carriage and I hear it creaking, I dislike not only the noise but also the owner of the carriage.

One is in the middle of a story when someone butts in and tries to show that he is the only clever person in the room. Such a person is hateful, and so, indeed, is anyone, child or adult, who tries to push himself forward.

One is telling a story about old times when someone 80 breaks in with a little detail that he happens to know, implying that one's own version is inaccurate—disgusting behavior!

Very hateful is a mouse that scurries all over the place.

Some children have called at one's house. One makes a great fuss of them and gives them toys to play with. The children become accustomed to this treatment and start to come

[1] **hunting costume:** men's informal outdoor costume, originally worn for hunting.

[2] **tall, lacquered hat:** known as an *eboshi*, this was worn by men on the top of the head and secured by a mauve silk cord that was fastened under the chin; two long black pendants hung down from the back of the hat. The *eboshi* was a most conspicuous form of headgear and hardly suitable for a clandestine visit.

[3] **Iyo blind:** a rough type of reed blind manufactured in the province of Iyo on the Inland Sea.

regularly, forcing their way into one's inner rooms and scattering one's furnishings and possessions. Hateful!

A certain gentleman whom one does not want to see visits one at home or in the Palace, and one pretends to be asleep. But a maid comes to tell one and shakes one awake, with a look on her face that says, "What a sleepyhead!" Very hateful.

A newcomer pushes ahead of the other members in a group; with a knowing look, this person starts laying down the law and forcing advice upon everyone—most hateful.

A man with whom one is having an affair keeps singing the praises of some woman he used to know. Even if it is a thing of the past, this can be very annoying. How much more so if he is still seeing the woman! (Yet sometimes I find that it is not as unpleasant as all that.)

A good lover will behave as elegantly at dawn as at any other time. He drags himself out of bed with a look of dismay on his face. The lady urges him on: "Come, my friend, it's getting light. You don't want anyone to find you here." He gives a deep sigh, as if to say that the night has not been nearly long enough and that it is agony to leave. Once up, he does not instantly pull on his trousers. Instead he comes close to the lady and whispers whatever was left unsaid during the night.

Even when he is dressed, he still lingers, vaguely pretending to be fastening his sash.

Presently he raises the lattice, and the two lovers stand together by the side door while he tells her how he dreads the coming day, which will keep them apart; then he slips away. The lady watches him go, and this moment of parting will remain among her most charming memories.

Indeed, one's attachment to a man depends largely on the elegance of his leave-taking. When he jumps out of bed, scurries about the room, tightly fastens his trouser-sash, rolls up the sleeves of his Court cloak, over-robe, or hunting costume, stuffs his belongings into the breast of his robe and then briskly secures the outer sash—one really begins to hate him.

READING CRITICALLY

During the Heian period, the finest writers of the day were by and large aristocratic women of middle rank like Sei Shonagon. How does "Hateful Things" reflect the prominence of women in court?

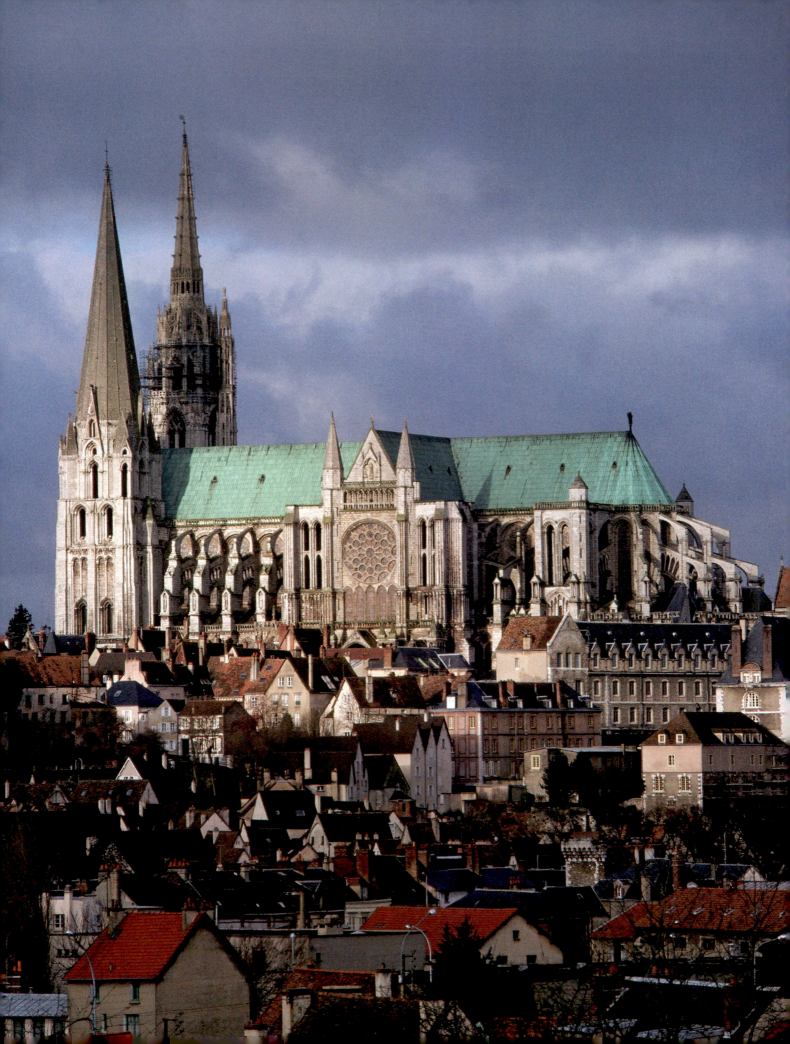

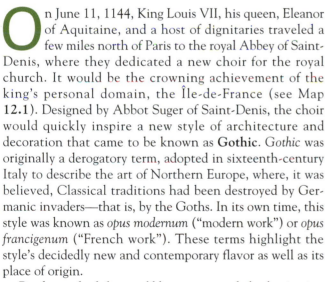

12

The Gothic Style
Faith and Knowledge in an Age of Inquiry

THINKING AHEAD

12.1 Outline the ideas, technological innovations, and stylistic developments that distinguish the Gothic style in France.

12.2 Explain why the University of Paris was preeminent among medieval institutions of higher learning.

12.3 Define the Radiant style.

12.4 Describe how the Gothic style manifested itself in Italy.

On June 11, 1144, King Louis VII, his queen, Eleanor of Aquitaine, and a host of dignitaries traveled a few miles north of Paris to the royal Abbey of Saint-Denis, where they dedicated a new choir for the royal church. It would be the crowning achievement of the king's personal domain, the Île-de-France (see Map **12.1**). Designed by Abbot Suger of Saint-Denis, the choir would quickly inspire a new style of architecture and decoration that came to be known as **Gothic**. *Gothic* was originally a derogatory term, adopted in sixteenth-century Italy to describe the art of Northern Europe, where, it was believed, Classical traditions had been destroyed by Germanic invaders—that is, by the Goths. In its own time, this style was known as *opus modernum* ("modern work") or *opus francigenum* ("French work"). These terms highlight the style's decidedly new and contemporary flavor as well as its place of origin.

By the end of the twelfth century and the beginning of the thirteenth, town after town across northern France would imitate Suger's design at Saint-Denis. At Chartres, just to the west of the Île-de-France on the Eure River (Fig.

12.1), to the north at Rouen, Amiens, and Beauvais, to the east at Laon and Reims, to the south at Bourges, and in Paris itself, Gothic cathedrals sprang up with amazing rapidity. Much of the rest of Europe would soon follow suit.

With the rise of this new Gothic style came a new standard of beauty in Western architecture and decoration. A new masonry architecture developed, eventually resulting in intricate stonework that was almost skeletal in its lightness and soaring ever higher to create lofty interior spaces. Gothic architecture matched the decorative richness of stained glass with sculptural programs that were increasingly inspired by Classical models of naturalistic representation. A new, richer liturgy developed as well, and with it, polyphonic music that by the thirteenth century was accompanied by a new instrument—the organ. The Île-de-France was the center of all these developments. It was there, as well, at the University of Paris, founded in 1200, that a young Dominican monk named Thomas Aquinas initiated the most important theological debates of the age, inaugurating a style of intellectual inquiry that we associate with higher learning to this day.

◀ **Fig. 12.1 The Cathedral of Notre-Dame, Chartres, France. ca. 1134–1220.** Chartres Cathedral rises majestically, crowning the town surrounding it. Such cathedrals were the cultural centers of their communities, the source of the community's pride and prestige.

 Listen to the chapter audio on **MyArtsLab**

SAINT-DENIS AND THE GOTHIC CATHEDRAL

What ideas, technological innovations, and stylistic developments mark the rise of the Gothic style in France?

Even as a pupil at the monastery school, Abbot Suger had dreamed of transforming the Abbey of Saint-Denis into the most beautiful church in France. The dream was partly inspired by his desire to lay claim to the larger territories surrounding the Île-de-France. Suger's design placed the royal domain at the center of French culture, defined by an architecture surpassing all others in beauty and grandeur.

After careful planning, Suger began work on the abbey in 1137, painting the walls, already almost 300 years old, with gold and precious colors. Then he added a new facade with twin towers and a triple portal. Around the back of the

ambulatory he added a circular string of chapels (Figs. **12.2** and **12.3**), all lit with large stained-glass windows (Fig. **12.4**), "by virtue of which," Suger wrote, "the whole would shine with the miraculous and uninterrupted light."

This light proclaimed the new Gothic style. In preparing his plans, Suger had read what he believed to be the writings of the original Saint Denis. (We now know that he was reading the mystical tracts of a first-century Athenian follower of Saint Paul.) According to these writings, light is the physical and material manifestation of the Divine Spirit. Suger would later survey the accomplishments of his administration and explain his religious rationale for the beautification of Saint-Denis:

> Marvel not at the gold and the expense but at the
> craftsmanship of the work.
> Bright is the noble work; but being nobly bright, the work
> Should brighten the minds, so that they may travel,
> through the true lights,
> To the True Light where Christ is the true door.

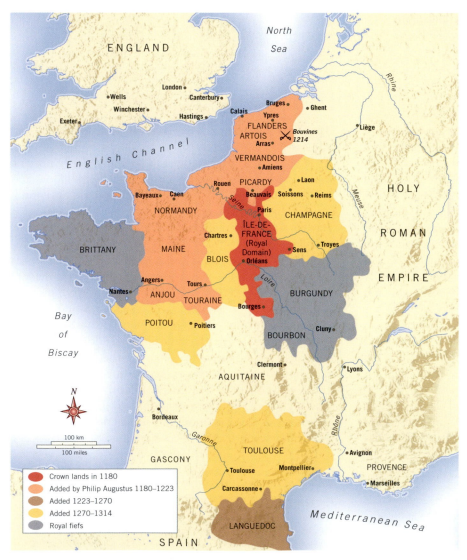

Map 12.1 The growth of the kingdom of France, 1180–1314. As France grew during the Gothic era, the Gothic style spread with it.

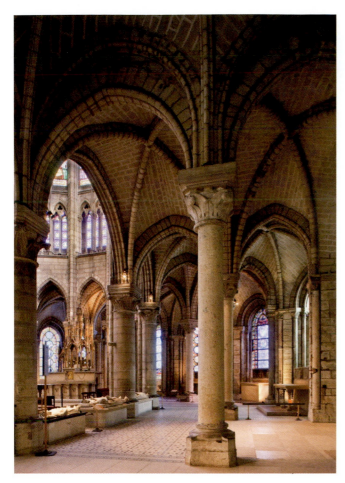

Fig. 12.2 Ambulatory choir, Abbey Church of Saint-Denis, Saint-Denis, France. 1140–44. In Abbot Suger's design, the ambulatory and radiating chapels around the apse were combined, so that the stained-glass windows—two in each chapel—fill the entire choir with light.

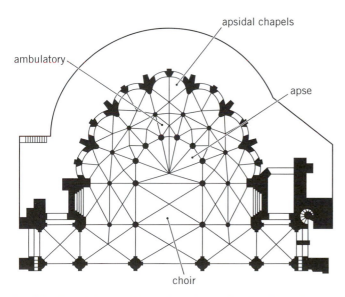
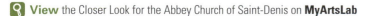

Fig. 12.3 Plan of the ambulatory choir, Abbey Church of Saint-Denis, Saint-Denis, France. 1140–44. By supporting the arches over the choir with columns instead of walls, Suger created a unified space reminiscent of the hypostyle space of the Mosque of Córdoba.

View the Closer Look for the Abbey Church of Saint-Denis on MyArtsLab

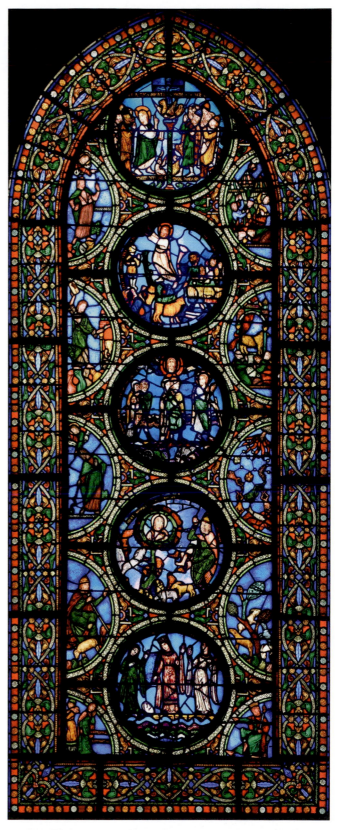

Fig. 12.4 Moses window, Abbey Church of Saint-Denis, Saint-Denis, France. 1140–44. This is the best-preserved of the original stained-glass windows at Saint-Denis. Scholars have speculated that Moses was a prominent theme at the royal Abbey of Saint-Denis because his leadership of the Israelites was the model for the French king's leadership of his people.

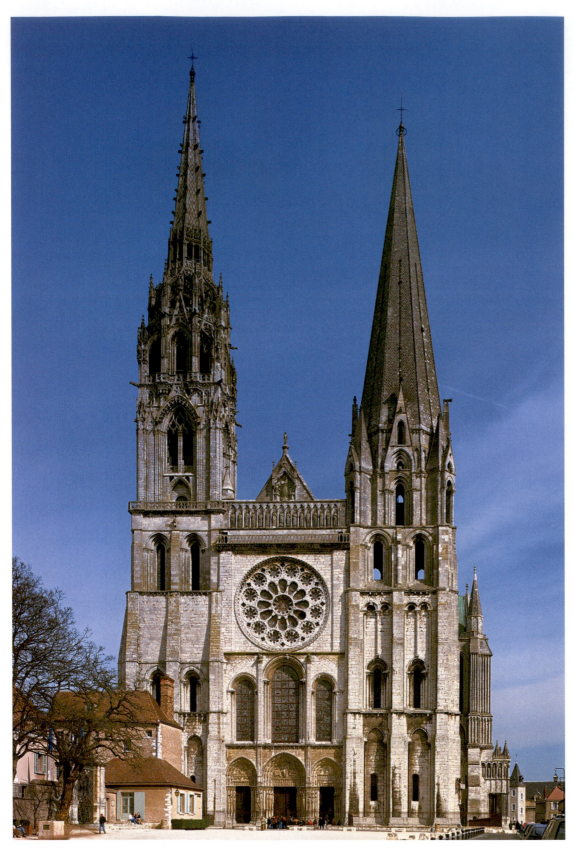

Fig. 12.5 West facade, Chartres Cathedral, France. ca. 1134–1220; south spire ca. 1160; north spire, 1507–13.
The different designs of the two towers reflect the Gothic dismissal of Romanesque absolute balance and symmetry as well as the growing refinements of the Gothic style. The later, north tower (left) was much more elaborately decorated and, in the more open framework of its stonework, more technically advanced.

✳ **Explore** the architectural panorama of Chartres Cathedral on **MyArtsLab**

The church's beauty, therefore, was designed to elevate the soul to the realm of God.

When Louis VII and Eleanor left France for the Second Crusade in 1147 (see Chapter 10), just three years after Suger's dedication of his choir, they also left the abbot without the funds necessary to finish his church. It was finally completed a century after he died in 1151. Much of its original sculptural and stained-glass decoration was destroyed in the late eighteenth century during the French Revolution. Although partially restored in the nineteenth and twentieth centuries, only five of its original stained-glass windows remain, and we must turn to other churches modeled on its design to comprehend its full effect.

Chartres Cathedral

Chief among these is the Cathedral of Notre-Dame at Chartres, which, like the other Gothic cathedrals in both the Île-de-France and its surrounding territories, drew its inspiration from Paris. The cathedral's spires can be seen for miles in every direction, lording over town and countryside as if it were the very center of its world (Fig. **12.5**, and see Fig. 12.1). Chartres was, in fact, located in the heart of France's grain belt, and its economy thrived as France exported grain throughout the Mediterranean basin. But more important, Chartres was the spiritual center of the cult of the Virgin, which throughout the twelfth and thirteenth centuries assumed an increasingly important role in the religious life of Western Europe. The popularity of this cult contributed, perhaps more than any other factor, to the ever-increasing size of the era's churches. Christians worshiped the Virgin as the Bride of Christ, Personification of the Church, Queen of Heaven, and prime Intercessor with God for the salvation of humankind. This last role was especially important, for in it the Virgin could intervene to save sinners from eternal damnation. The cult of the Virgin manifested itself especially in the French cathedrals, which are often dedicated to *Notre Dame*, "Our Lady."

Soon after the first building phase was completed at Chartres, between about 1140 and 1150, pilgrims thronged to the cathedral to pay homage to what the Church claimed was the Virgin's tunic, worn at Jesus' birth. This relic was housed in the cathedral and was believed to possess extraordinary healing powers. But in 1194, the original structure was destroyed by fire, except for the west facade, a few stained-glass windows, including one of the most beautiful, known as *Notre-Dame de la Belle Verrière* ("Our Lady of the Beautiful Window") (Fig. **12.6**), and the tunic of the Virgin. The survival of the window and the tunic was taken as a sign of divine providence, and a massive reconstruction project was begun in gratitude. Royalty and local nobility contributed their financial support, and the local guilds gave both money and work.

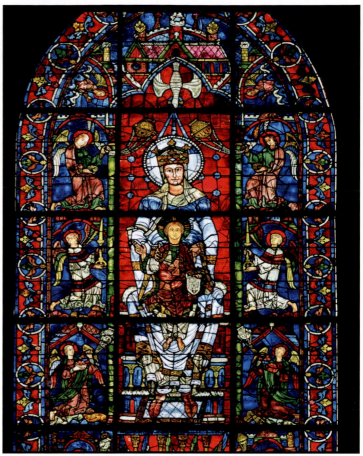

Fig. 12.6 *Notre-Dame de la Belle Verrière* ("Our Lady of the Beautiful Window") window, Chartres Cathedral. Central portion, 12th century; surrounding angels, 13th century. This window is renowned for its stunning combination of red and blue stained glass.

Behind the more or less Romanesque west facade, with its round-arch windows, rose what many consider the most magnificent of all Gothic cathedrals, its stained glass unrivaled in Europe.

Stained Glass

The stained-glass program at Chartres is immensely complex. The innovative engineering that marks Gothic architecture (to be discussed later in this chapter) freed the walls of the need to bear the weight of the structure. It also freed the walls to contain glass (see *Materials & Techniques*, page 411, and *Closer Look*, pages 412–413).

The purpose of the stained-glass programs in all Gothic cathedrals was to tell the stories of the Bible in a compelling way to an audience that was largely illiterate. The art allowed them to read the scriptural stories for themselves. At Chartres, 175 glass panels, containing more than 4,000 figures, are carefully designed, in Abbot Suger's words, "to show simple folk … what they ought to believe." Two windows are notable for their role in the cult of the Virgin.

View the Closer Look for the technique of stained glass on **MyArtsLab**

Notre-Dame de la Belle Verrière, whose central panel survived the fire of 1194, embodies the shift in style that occurred in the twelfth century as the Gothic supplanted the Romanesque. The Virgin and Child in the middle are almost Byzantine in their stiffness, their feet pointed downward, their pose fully frontal, the drapery of their clothing almost flat; compare the sixth-century mosaic of Emperor Justinian in San Vitale church, Ravenna (see Fig. 8.28 in Chapter 8). But the angels on the sides, which are thirteenth-century additions, are both less stiff and more animated. The swirls and folds of their gowns flow across their limbs, revealing the anatomy beneath them.

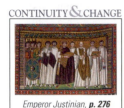

CONTINUITY & CHANGE

Emperor Justinian, **p. 276**

The second window depicts the so-called Tree of Jesse (Fig. **12.7**). Jesse trees are a common motif in twelfth- and thirteenth-century manuscripts, murals, sculpture, and stained glass, and their associated traditions are still celebrated by Christians during the season of Advent. They were thought to represent the genealogy of Christ, since they depict the Virgin Mary as descended from Jesse, the father of King David, thus fulfilling a prophecy in the Book of Isaiah (11:1): "And there shall come forth a rod out of the stem of Jesse and a Branch shall grow out of his roots." Most Jesse trees have at their base a recumbent Jesse with a tree growing from his side or navel. On higher branches of the tree are various kings and prophets of Judea. At the top are Christ and Mary. Sometimes the Virgin holds the infant Jesus, but here, as in a similar window at Saint-Denis, Mary appears in the register below Jesus. Since Jesse trees portray Mary as descending from royal lineage, they played an important role in the cult of the Virgin.

Gothic Architecture

As the Gothic style developed, important architectural innovations contributed to the goal of elevating the soul of worshipers to the spiritual realm. Key among these innovations was rib vaulting. The principles of rib vaulting were known to Romanesque architects, but Gothic architects used these techniques with increasing sophistication (see *Materials & Techniques*, page 411). Rib vaulting allowed for the massive stonework of the Romanesque style to be replaced, inside and out, by an almost lacy play of thin columns and patterns of ribs and windows, all pointing upward in a gravity-defying crescendo that carries the viewer's gaze toward the heavens. Extremely high naves—Chartres's nave is 120 feet high, Reims's nave is 125, and the highest of all, Beauvais's, is 157, the equivalent of a 15-story building—add to this emphasis on verticality, contributing a sense of elevation that is both physical and spiritual. The nave of the Cathedral of Notre-Dame at Amiens is perhaps the supreme statement of this architectural verticality (Figs. **12.8** and **12.9**). The nave is only 48 feet wide, but it soars to three times that height, 144 feet, and this narrowly proportioned space cannot help but create a sense of exaggerated height for the visitor.

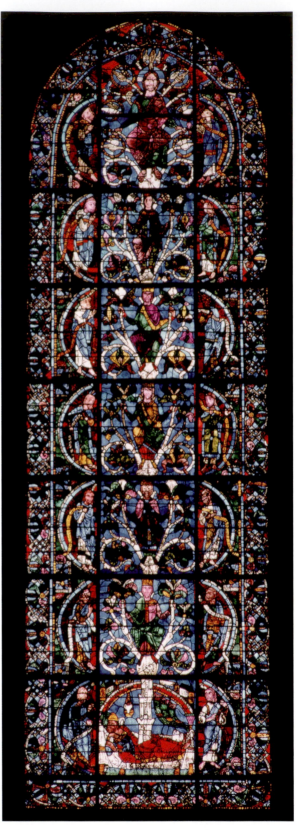

Fig. 12.7 *The Tree of Jesse* **window, Chartres Cathedral. ca. 1150–70.** Jesse was the father of King David, who, according to the Gospels, was an ancestor of Mary. At the base of the window lies the body of Jesse, a tree growing out of him. The tree branches into the four kings of Judea, one on each row. Mary is just below Christ. Seven doves, representing the seven gifts of the Holy Spirit, encircle Christ. In half-moons flanking each section of the tree stand the 14 prophets.

Materials & Techniques

Rib Vaulting

Rib vaults are a form of groin vault (see Chapter 6, *Materials & Techniques*, page 198). They are based on the pointed arch, which can reach to a greater height than a rounded arch. At the groins, structural moldings called *ribs* channel the vault's thrust outward and downward. These ribs were constructed first and supported the scaffolding upon which the masonry webbing was built. These ribs were essentially a "skeleton" filled with a lightweight masonry "skin." Throughout the late Middle Ages, more and more intricate and complex versions of this scheme were developed.

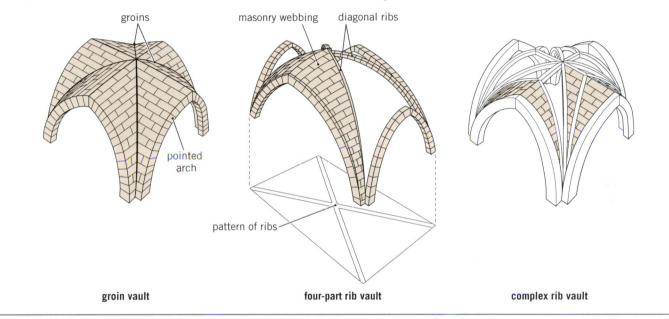

groins   masonry webbing   diagonal ribs

pointed arch

pattern of ribs

groin vault   **four-part rib vault**   **complex rib vault**

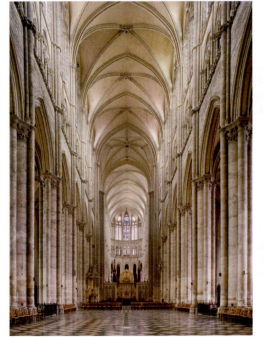

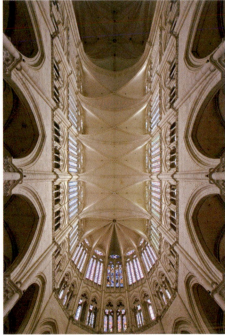

Figs. 12.8 and 12.9 Nave and vaults above the choir of the Cathedral of Notre-Dame, Amiens, France. 1220–88. Note how thin the traceries of stone between the windows at the top of the choir become, an effect that contributes further to the sense of soaring space.

👁 **Watch** an architectural simulation about the rib vault at **MyArtsLab**

The stained glass at Chartres covers more than 32,000 square feet of surface area. Although the illustration below lacks detail, we can imagine the overall effect of so many windows. The windows were donated by the royal family, by noblemen, and by merchant guilds. On an average day, the light outside the cathedral is approximately 1,000 times greater than the light inside. Thus the windows, backlit and shining in the relative darkness of the nave, seem to radiate with an ethereal and immaterial glow, suggesting a spiritual beauty beyond the here and now.

To create the windows, a variety of different colored glass was blown by artisans and rolled out into square pieces. These pieces were broken or cut into smaller fragments and assembled over a drawing marked out in chalk dust. Features of people were painted on in dark pigments, and the fragments were joined by strips of lead. The whole piece was then strengthened with an armature of iron bands, at first stretching over windows in a grid, but later shaped to follow the outlines of the design itself.

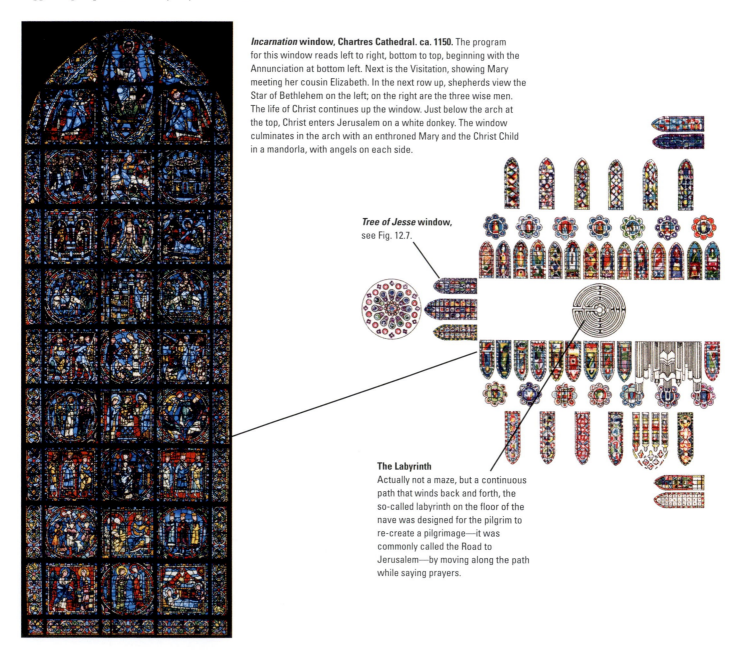

Incarnation **window, Chartres Cathedral. ca. 1150.** The program for this window reads left to right, bottom to top, beginning with the Annunciation at bottom left. Next is the Visitation, showing Mary meeting her cousin Elizabeth. In the next row up, shepherds view the Star of Bethlehem on the left; on the right are the three wise men. The life of Christ continues up the window. Just below the arch at the top, Christ enters Jerusalem on a white donkey. The window culminates in the arch with an enthroned Mary and the Christ Child in a mandorla, with angels on each side.

Tree of Jesse **window,** see Fig. 12.7.

The Labyrinth
Actually not a maze, but a continuous path that winds back and forth, the so-called labyrinth on the floor of the nave was designed for the pilgrim to re-create a pilgrimage—it was commonly called the Road to Jerusalem—by moving along the path while saying prayers.

The Stained Glass at Chartres

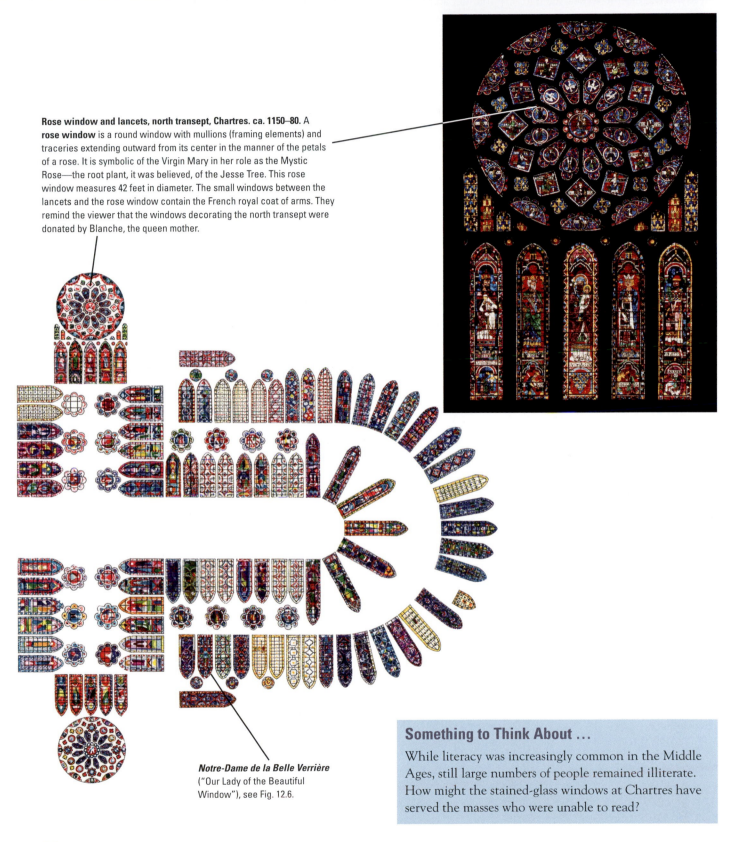

Rose window and lancets, north transept, Chartres. ca. 1150–80. A **rose window** is a round window with mullions (framing elements) and traceries extending outward from its center in the manner of the petals of a rose. It is symbolic of the Virgin Mary in her role as the Mystic Rose—the root plant, it was believed, of the Jesse Tree. This rose window measures 42 feet in diameter. The small windows between the lancets and the rose window contain the French royal coat of arms. They remind the viewer that the windows decorating the north transept were donated by Blanche, the queen mother.

Notre-Dame de la Belle Verrière ("Our Lady of the Beautiful Window"), see Fig. 12.6.

Something to Think About ...

While literacy was increasingly common in the Middle Ages, still large numbers of people remained illiterate. How might the stained-glass windows at Chartres have served the masses who were unable to read?

View the Closer Look for the stained glass at Chartres Cathedral on **MyArtsLab**

The preponderance of pointed rather than rounded arches contributes to this feeling as well. The pointed arch, in fact, possesses structural properties that contribute significantly to the Gothic style—the flatter or rounder an arch is, the greater outward thrust or pressure it puts on the supporting walls. By reducing outward thrust, the pointed arch allows for larger windows and lighter **buttresses**, pillars traditionally built against exterior walls to brace them and strengthen the vault. **Flying buttresses** (Figs. **12.10** and **12.11**, and visible as well on the exterior of Chartres Cathedral, Fig. 12.1) allow for even lighter buttressing and more windows. They extend away from the wall, employing an arch to focus the strength of the buttress's support at the top of the wall, the section most prone to collapse from the outward pressure of the vaulted ceiling. A flying buttress is basically a huge stone prop that pushes in against the walls with the same force with which the vaults push out. The thrust of the vaulted ceilings still comes down the piers and walls, but also moves down the arms of the flying buttresses, down the buttresses themselves, and into the ground. The flying buttresses help spread the weight of the vaults over more supporting stone, allowing the walls to be thinner while still supporting as much weight as earlier, thicker walls. As the magnificent flying buttresses at Notre-Dame Cathedral in Paris demonstrate, they also create a stunning visual spectacle, arching winglike from the building's side as if defying gravity.

During the thirteenth century, architects began to adorn the exteriors of their cathedrals with increasingly elaborate decoration. Stone **crockets**, leaflike forms that curve outward, their edges curling up, were added to the pinnacles, spires, and gables of the cathedrals. These were topped by **finials**, knoblike architectural forms also found on furniture. The textural richness of these forms is evident in the comparison of Chartres Cathedral (see Fig. 12.5), where they are relatively absent, and Amiens Cathedral, where they are abundant (Fig. **12.12**). The facade of Amiens is also elaborately decorated with sculpture. Most of the sculptures were made in a 20-year period by a large workshop in Amiens itself, lending the entire facade a sense of unity and coherence.

The Gothic style spread rapidly across Europe. It was especially well received in England, which, after all, was dominated by French Normans, and in Germany, where a fragmented conglomeration of independent cities, principalities,

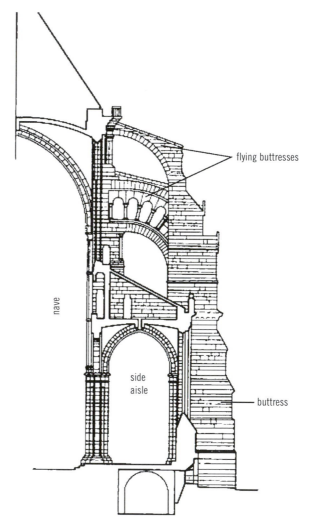

Figs. 12.10 and 12.11 Flying buttresses, Cathedral of Notre-Dame, Paris, France. 1211–90. Romanesque architects used buttressing, but concealed it under the aisle roofs. Moving the buttresses to the outside of the structure created a sense of light bridgework that contributed to the aesthetic appeal of the building as much as to its structural integrity.

✳ **Explore** the architectural panorama of the Cathedral of Notre-Dame, Paris, on **MyArtsLab**

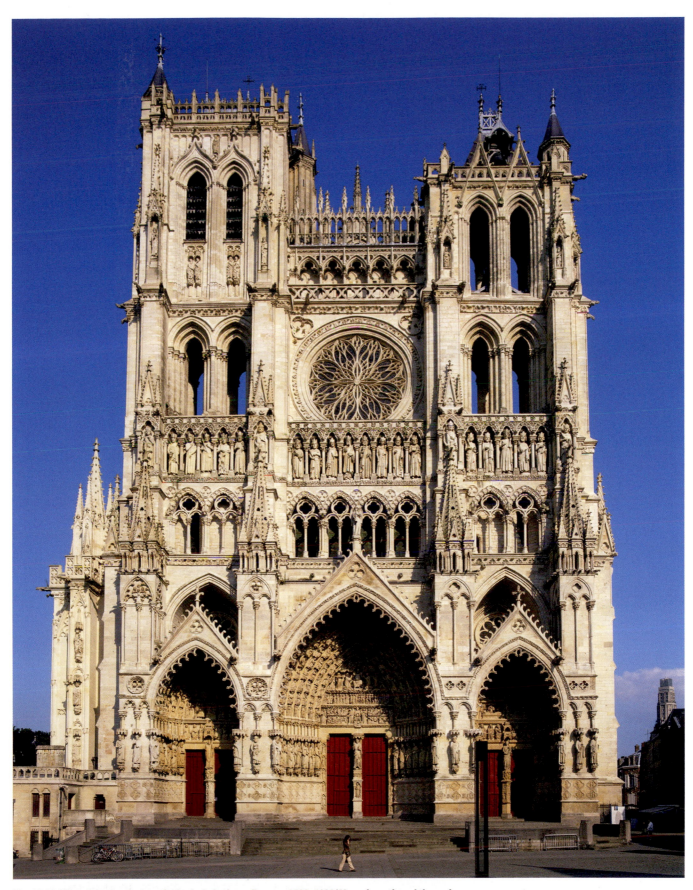

Fig. 12.12 West facade, Amiens Cathedral, Amiens, France. 1220–1236/40, and continued through the 15th century. The sculptors who decorated the facade quickly became famous and traveled across Europe, carrying their style to Spain and Italy.

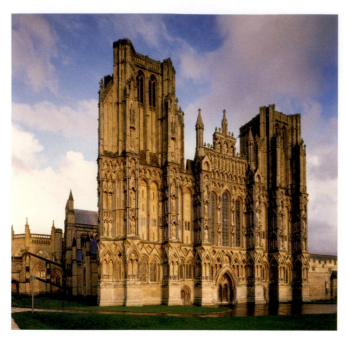

Fig. 12.13 West facade, Wells Cathedral, Wells, England. 1230–50. This cathedral exemplifies the preference for pattern and decoration in English Gothic architecture. The portal has become less important, and the rhythmic structure of the wide facade takes precedence. Life-size sculptures occupy each of the niches—originally 384 of them—representing the Last Judgment.

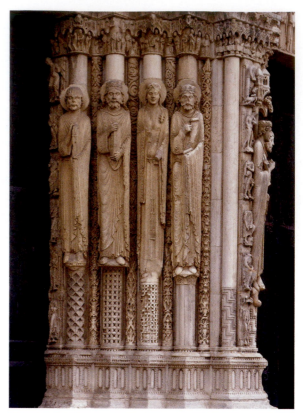

Fig. 12.14 Jamb statues, west portal, Chartres Cathedral. 1145–70. The decorative patterns at the bottom of these jamb columns are, interestingly, reminiscent of Islamic designs in Spain.

and bishoprics all sought to imitate what they conceived as the style of the French court. Wells Cathedral is one of the finest Gothic cathedrals built in England in the thirteenth century (Fig. **12.13**).

Gothic Sculpture

If we look at developments in architectural sculpture from the time of the decoration of the west portal of Chartres Cathedral (1145–70) to the time of the sculptural plan of the south transept portal (1215–20), and, finally, to the sculptures decorating the west front of Reims Cathedral (1225–55), we can see that, in a little over 100 years, Gothic sculptors had begun to reintroduce Classical principles of sculptural composition into Western art.

Although they seem almost Byzantine in their long, narrow verticality, feet pointing downward, the jamb sculptures on the west portal of Chartres mark a distinct advance in the sculptural realization of the human body (Fig. **12.14**). These, and five more sets, flank the three doorways of the cathedral's Royal Portal. The center tympanum of the portal depicts Christ Enthroned in Royal Majesty, the north tympanum the Ascension of Christ, and the south the Virgin and Child Enthroned. The jamb sculptures represent figures from the Hebrew Bible considered to be precursors of Christ. These works have little in common with Romanesque relief sculpture, typified by the *Last Judgment* tympanum on the Abbey Church of Sainte-Foy in Conques (see Fig. 10.22 in Chapter 10). While the Chartres figures remain contained by the form of the colonnade behind

them, they are fully rounded and occupy a space in front of the column itself.

When Chartres was rebuilt after the fire of 1195, a new sculptural plan was realized for the transept doors. The figures stand before a colonnade, as do the jamb figures on the west portal, but their form is hardly determined by it (Fig. **12.15**). Now they stand flat-footed. Their faces seem animated, as if they see us. The monk just to the right of the dividing column seems quite concerned for us. The portrait of the knight Saint Theodore, to the left of the column, is particularly remarkable. For the first time since antiquity, the figure is posed at ease, his hip thrusting slightly to the right, his weight falling on his right foot. He stands, in other words, in a *contrapposto* position. (Recall the Greek sculptures of the fifth century BCE, carved in that posture, such as the *Doryphoros*, Fig. 5.4 in Chapter 5). The weight of his sword belt seems to have pulled his cloak off to the right. Then, below the belt, the cloak falls back to the left. The strict verticality of the west portal is a thing of the past.

CONTINUITY & CHANGE

Doryphoros, **p. 141**

The sculptures at Reims break even further from Romanesque tradition. They are freed of their backdrop (Fig. **12.16**; see also Fig. 10.31 in Chapter 10). The Angel of the Annunciation tells Mary (the figure next to the angel on the left) that she is with child. The next

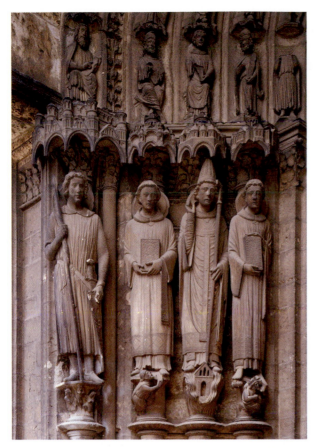

Fig. 12.15 Jamb statues, south transept portal, Chartres Cathedral. ca. 1215–20. The statue of Saint Theodore, on the left, is meant to evoke the spirit of the Crusades.

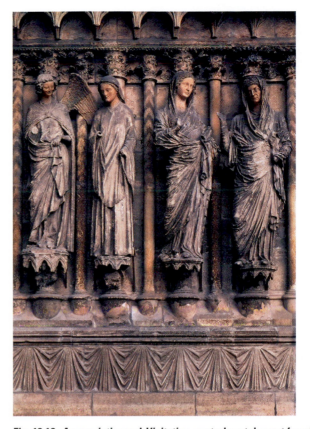

Fig. 12.16 *Annunciation* and *Visitation*, central portal, west facade, Reims Cathedral, Reims, France. *Angel of the Annunciation*, ca. 1245–55; *Virgin of the Annunciation*, 1245; *Visitation* group, ca. 1230–33. If these sculptures seem more naturalistic than any for nearly a thousand years, it is partly because they engage with one another. It is as if, looking at them, we can overhear their conversation. Note that the most naturalistic sculpture, the *Angel of the Annunciation*, dates from 15 or 20 years after the *Visitation* group, suggesting an extraordinary advance, and preference for, naturalism in a very short span of years.

two figures, to the right, represent the Visitation, when Mary tells her cousin Elizabeth that she is with child and Elizabeth in turn announces the divinity of the baby in Mary's womb. Note how the drapery adorning the pair on the left, with its simple, soft folds, differs profoundly from the drapery of the pair on the right, whose robes are Roman in their complexity. The earlier Mary bears little, if any, resemblance to the other Mary, the first probably carved by a sculptor trained in Romanesque traditions, the latter by one acquainted with Classical models.

The two pairs are as different, in fact, as the two towers of Chartres Cathedral (see Fig. 12.5), which reflect both a weakening of the Romanesque insistence on balance and symmetry as well as the fact that both were completed at different times. And yet the two pairs of sculptures share a certain emotional attitude—the good-humored smile of the angel, the stern but wise concern of Elizabeth. Even the relative ages of the persons depicted are apparent, where age would have been of no concern to a sculptor working in the Romanesque tradition. These are, in short, the most fully human, most natural sculptures since Roman times. During the Gothic period, artists developed a new visual language. The traditional narratives of biblical tradition could no longer speak through abstracted and symbolic types, but instead required believable, individual bodies to tell their stories. This new language invests the figures of Jesus, Mary,

the saints, and even the Angel of the Annunciation with personality.

Music in the Gothic Cathedral: Growing Complexity

With its vast spaces and stone walls, the Gothic cathedral could be as animated by its acoustics as by its light, or, as at Reims, the liveliness of its sculpture. Ecclesiastical leaders were quick to take advantage of this quality in constructing their liturgy. At the School of Notre-Dame, in Paris, the first collection of music in two parts, the *Magnus Liber Organi* (*The Great Book of Polyphony*), was widely distributed in manuscript by about 1160. Among its many anonymous composers was Léonin (see track **10.4**). The *Magnus Liber Organi* was arranged in song **MyArtsLab** cycles to provide music for all the feast days of the Church calendar. The *Magnus Liber* was created at a time when most polyphony was produced and transmitted only orally. What makes it so significant is that it represents the beginning of the modern sense of "composition"—that is, works attributable to a single composer.

At the end of the century, Léonin's successor, Pérotin, revised and renotated the *Magnus Liber*. One of his most famous works is *Viderunt Omnes* ("All Have Seen"), a four-part polyphonic composition based on the traditional plainchant of the same name, meant to be sung in the middle of the Christmas Mass at Notre-Dame Cathedral in Paris (track **12.1**). Throughout the piece, the choir sings a smooth, monophonic plainchant, while three soloists sing the second, third, and fourth melodic lines in **counterpoint**, that is, in opposition, to the plainchant. The clear but intertwined rhythms of the soloists build to a crescendo of sustained harmony and balance that must have inspired awe in the congregation. The music seems to soar upward, imitating the architecture of the cathedral and elevating the faithful to new heights of belief.

The words are simple, but because each syllable is sung across a range of notes and rhythms, the music takes almost 12 minutes to perform. What follows is the Latin and translation:

Viderunt omnes fines terrae salutare Dei nostri.	All the ends of the earth have seen the salvation of our God.
Jubilate Deo omnis terra.	Praise God all the earth.
Notum fecit Dominus salutare suam. Ante conspectum gentium revelavit justitiam suam.	The Lord has made known his salvation. Before the face of the people he has revealed his justice.

The complexity of such rhythmic invention mirrors the growing textural complexity of the facade of Gothic cathedrals, with their spires, gables, crockets, and finials. Developing from this polyphony was an even more complex musical form, the **motet**, consisting of three (sometimes four) voices. The tenor—from the Latin *tenere*, "to hold"—generally maintained a traditional line based on ecclesiastical chant. The tenor line might be sung or played instrumentally, perhaps by the organ, which began to replace the choir in the performance of many of these songs. In some ways, this was a practical gesture, since large choirs of the caliber needed to perform the liturgical songs were not easy to organize. The origins of the organ date back to as early as the fourth to third centuries BCE in Greece, with the invention of the hydraulis, which used water pressure to push air through the pipes. By the ninth century CE, the instrument had been modified to use air pressure, supplied by manually operated bellows, to push the air through the pipes. At any rate, the rich tones of the organ, resonating through the nave of the cathedral, gained increasing favor through the Middle Ages, and the organ became necessary to every large cathedral. In the motet, above the tenor line, two or three voices sang interweaving melodies.

By the late thirteenth century, a motet might be sung in either Latin or vernacular French, or even both simultaneously, and might consist of two, three, or four parts only loosely, if at all, related in content—sacred Latin hymns sung together with a vernacular French love song, or even a street vendor's call put to music. All these competing lines were held together like the complex elements of the Gothic facade—balanced but competing, harmonious but at odds. They reflected, in short, the great debates—between Church and State, faith and reason—that defined the age.

These debates raged at centers of higher learning, where music was part of the regular liberal-arts curriculum. It was studied as a branch of the **quadrivium** (the mathematical arts), alongside arithmetic, geometry, and astronomy, all fields dependent upon proportion and universal harmony. (The other liberal arts constituted the **trivium**, the language arts, which included grammar, rhetoric, and dialectic.) At the cathedral School of Notre-Dame in Paris, whose purpose was to train clergy, music was emphasized as an all-important liturgical tool. But by the middle of the twelfth century, cathedral schools began allowing nonclerical students to attend lectures. In 1179, a papal decree ordered the schools to provide for the teaching of the *laity* (nonclerics), the decree that would eventually give rise to the university as an institution.

THE RISE OF THE UNIVERSITY

Why did the University of Paris become preeminent among medieval institutions of higher learning?

The first university was founded in Bologna, Italy, in 1158. Two hundred years earlier, in Spain, Islamic institutions of higher learning were generally attached to mosques, since learning was considered sacred. At first, the term *university* meant simply a *union* of students and the instructors with whom they contracted to teach them. *Universitas* was an umbrella term for *collegia*, the groups of students who shared a common interest or, as at Bologna, hailed from the same geographic area. The University of Bologna quickly established itself as a center for the study of law (Fig. **12.17**), an advanced area of study for which students prepared by mastering the seven liberal arts.

Proficiency in Latin was mandatory, and students studied Latin in all courses of their first four years of study. They read the writings of the ancient Greeks—Aristotle, Ptolemy, Euclid—in Latin translation. Augustine of Hippo's *On Christian Doctrine* was required reading, as were Boethius's writings on music and arithmetic. To obtain their bachelor of arts (BA) degree, students took oral exams after three to five years of study. Further study to acquire mastery of a special field led to the master of arts (MA) degree and might qualify a student to teach theology or practice medicine or law. Four more years of study were required to acquire the title of *doctor* (from the Latin, *doctus*, "learned"), culminating in a defense of a thesis before a board of learned examiners.

The University of Paris was chartered in 1200, and soon after came Oxford and Cambridge universities in England. These northern universities emphasized the study of theology. In Paris, a house or college system was organized, at first to provide students with housing and then to help

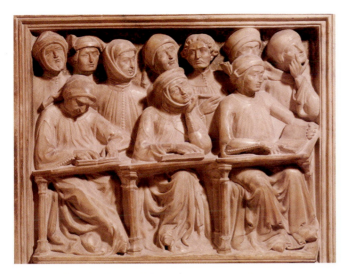

Fig. 12.17 *Law Students*, relief sculpture on tomb of a law professor at the University of Bologna. ca. 1200. Marble. Jacobello dalle Masegne and Pier Paolo dalle Masegne (fl. 1383–1409). Museo Civico, Bologna. Although women were generally excluded from the professions of medicine and law, there were exceptions. In this group of law students, the central figure in the front row appears to be a woman, Novella d'Andrea (1312–66). She lectured at the university on both philosophy and law, although it is said that she was required to speak from behind a curtain so as not to distract the male students.

them focus their education. The most famous of these was organized by Robert de Sorbon in 1257 for theology students. The Sorbonne, named after him, remains today the center of Parisian student life.

Héloïse and Abelard

The quality of its teaching most distinguished the University of Paris. Because books were available only in hand-written manuscripts, they were extremely expensive, so students relied on lectures and copious note-taking for their instruction. Peter Abelard (1079–ca. 1144), a brilliant logician and author of the treatise *Sic et Non* ("Yes and No"), was one of the most popular lecturers of his day. Crowds of students routinely gathered to hear him. He taught by the **dialectical method**—that is, by presenting different points of view and seeking to reconcile them. This method of teaching originates in the Socratic method, but whereas Socratic dialogue consisted of a wise teacher who was questioned by students, or even fools, Abelard's dialectical method presumed no such hierarchical relationships. Everything, to him, was open to question. "By doubting," he famously argued, "we come to inquire, and by inquiring we arrive at truth."

Needless to say, the Church found it difficult to deal with Abelard, who demonstrated time and again that various Church Fathers—and the Bible itself—held hopelessly opposing views on many issues. Furthermore, the dialectical method itself challenged the unquestioning faith in God and the authority of the Church. Abelard was particularly opposed by Bernard of Clairvaux, who in 1140 successfully prosecuted him for heresy. By then, Abelard's reputation as

a teacher had not faded, but his moral position had long been suspect. In 1119, he had pursued a love affair with his private student, Héloïse. Abelard not only felt that he had betrayed a trust by falling in love with her and subsequently impregnating her, but he was further humiliated by Héloïse's angry uncle, in whose home he had tutored and seduced the girl. Learning of the pregnancy, the uncle hired thugs to castrate Abelard in his bed. Abelard retreated to the monastery at Saint-Denis, accepting the protection of the powerful Abbot Suger. Héloïse joined a convent and later served as abbess of Paraclete, a chapel and oratory founded by Abelard.

The *Romance of the Rose*

The relationship of Héloïse and Abelard would be celebrated in what is undoubtedly the most extensively illuminated and popular vernacular poem of the age, the *Roman de la Rose* ("Romance of the Rose"), begun by Guillaume de Lorris (d. ca. 1235) but largely written by Jean de Meun (ca. 1240–ca. 1305). The book is the dream vision of a 25-year-old narrator who finds himself, accompanied by Dame Oyouse, or Lady Idleness, before a walled garden full of roses and pleasure seekers (Fig. **12.18**). As he selects a rose for himself, the God of Love shoots him with several arrows, leaving him forever enamored of one particular flower. His efforts to obtain the Rose meet with little success. A stolen kiss alerts the guardians of the Rose, who then enclose it behind great fortifications. At the point where Guillaume de Lorris's poem breaks off, the narrator

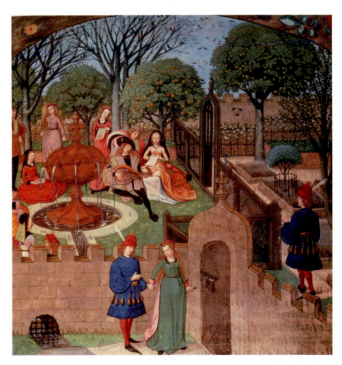

Fig. 12.18 The Master of the Prayer Books, *The Lover Being Shown the Entrance to the Garden by Lady Idleness, Roman de la Rose.* ca. 1500. British Library, London. Inside the garden, a lady, the personification of pleasure, and her companions listen to a lute player beside the fountain of Narcissus.

is left lamenting his fate. Jean de Meun concludes the narrative with a bawdy account of the plucking of the Rose, achieved through deception, which is very unlike Guillaume's idealized conception of the love quest. The book also included the first translations of the letters of Héloïse and Abelard, originally written in about 1135–36 and rendered by Meun from Latin into the vernacular. They include Héloïse's arguments to Abelard against their marriage, and her declaration of loyalty to him after she became a nun (see **Reading 12.1**, page 433).

Meun's versions of the letters are highly poeticized and bowdlerized, that is, sexual references were deleted (*bowdlerized* originates from the 1807 expurgated edition of William Shakespeare's works, *The Family Shakespeare*, edited by Thomas Bowdler to make the plays suitable for women and children). Héloïse was a woman of considerable passion. Even during the celebration of Mass, she confesses, "lewd visions" of the pleasures she shared with Abelard "take such a hold upon my unhappy soul that my thoughts are on their wantonness instead of on prayers. I should be groaning over the sins I have committed, but I can only sigh for what I have lost." Though Meun praises Héloïse for her intelligence, he especially admires her unwillingness to marry, her dedication to Abelard, and her self-sacrifice. Later medieval commentators would regard the *Roman de la Rose* as a thoroughly misogynist poem (see Chapter 13).

The Education of Women

Héloïse's story reveals much about the education of women in the Middle Ages. Intellectually brilliant, she became Abelard's private student because women were not allowed to study at the university. There were some exceptions, particularly in Italy. At Bologna, Novella d'Andrea (1312–66) lectured on philosophy and law. At Salerno, in southern Italy, the chair of medicine was held by Trotula (d. 1097), one of the most famous physicians of her time, although some scholars debate whether she was actually a woman, and convincing evidence suggests that her works are actually compendiums of works by three different authors. Concerned chiefly with alleviating the suffering of women, the major work attributed to her is *On the Diseases of Women*, commonly known throughout the Middle Ages as the *Trotula*. As the author says at the beginning of the treatise:

> Because women are by nature weaker than men and because they are most frequently afflicted in childbirth, diseases very often abound in them. … Women, from the condition of their fragility, out of shame and embarrassment do not dare reveal their anguish over their diseases (which happen in such a private place) to a physician. Therefore, their misfortune, which ought to be pitied, and especially the influence of a certain woman stirring my heart, have impelled me to give a clear explanation regarding their diseases in caring for their health.

In 63 chapters, the book addresses issues surrounding menstruation, conception, pregnancy, and childbirth, along with general ailments and diseases. The book champions good diet, warns of the dangers of emotional stress, and prescribes the use of opiates during childbirth, a practice otherwise condemned for centuries to come. It even explains how an experienced woman might pretend to be a virgin. The standard reference work in gynecology and obstetrics for midwives and physicians throughout the Middle Ages, the *Trotula* was translated from Latin into almost all vernacular languages and was widely disseminated.

Thomas Aquinas and Scholasticism

In 1245, Thomas Aquinas (1225–74), a 20-year-old Dominican monk from Italy, arrived at the University of Paris to study theology, walking into a theological debate that had been raging for nearly 100 years, ever since the conflict between Abelard and Bernard: How does the believer come to know God? With the heart? With the mind? Or with both? Do we come to know the truth intuitively or rationally? Aquinas took on these questions directly and soon became the most distinguished student and lecturer at the university.

Aquinas was accompanied to Paris by another Dominican, his teacher Albertus Magnus (ca. 1200–80), a German who taught at both Paris and Cologne and who later produced a biological classification of plants based on Aristotle. The Dominicans had been founded in 1216 by the Spanish priest Dominic (ca. 1170–1221) as an order dedicated to the study of theology. Aquinas and Magnus, and others like them, increasingly trained by Dominicans, were soon labeled *scholastics*. Their brand of theological inquiry, which was based on Abelard's dialectical method, was called **Scholasticism**.

Most theologians understood that there was a seeming conflict between faith and reason, but, they argued, since both proceeded from God, this conflict must, by definition, be a misapprehension. In the universities, rational inquiry and Aristotle's objective descriptions of physical reality were all the rage (see Chapter 5), so much so that theologians worried that students were more enthralled with logical argumentation than right outcomes. Instead of studying heavenly truths and Scriptures, they were studying pagan philosophy, dating from the fourth century BCE. Scholasticism sought to reconcile the two. One of the greatest efforts in this direction is Aquinas's *Summa Theologica*, begun in 1265 when he was 40 years old. At Albertus Magnus's request, Aquinas set out to write a theology based entirely on the work of ancient philosophers, demonstrating the compatibility of Classical philosophy and Christian religion. The *Summa Theologica* takes on virtually every theological issue of the age, from the place of women in society and the Church, to the cause of evil, the question of free choice, and whether it is lawful to sell a thing for more than it is worth. The medieval *summa* was an authoritative summary of all that was known on a traditional subject, and it was the ultimate aim of every highly educated man to produce one.

In a famous passage Aquinas takes on the largest issue of all—the *summa* of *summas*—attempting to prove the existence of God once and for all. Notice particularly the Aristotelian reliance on observation and logically drawn conclusions (**Reading 12.2**):

READING 12.2

from Thomas Aquinas, *Summa Theologica*

Is there a God?

REPLY: There are five ways in which one can prove there is a God.

The FIRST ... is based on change. Some things ... are certainly in the process of change: this we plainly see. Now anything in the process of change is being changed by something else. ... Hence one is bound to arrive at some first cause of change not itself being changed by anything, and this is what everybody understands by God.

The SECOND is based on the nature of causation. In the observable world causes are found to be ordered in series. ... Such a series must however stop somewhere. ... One is therefore forced to suppose some first cause, to which everyone gives the name "God."

The THIRD way is based on what need not be and on what must be. ... Some ... things can be, but need not be for we find them springing up and dying away. ... Now everything cannot be like this [for then we must conclude that] once upon a time there was nothing. But if that were true there would be nothing even now, because something that does not exist can only be brought into being by something already existing. ... One is forced therefore to suppose something which must be ... [and] is itself the cause that other things must be.

The FOURTH way is based on the gradation observed in things. Some things are found to be more good, more true, more noble ... and other things less [so]. But such comparative terms describe varying degrees of approximation to a superlative ... [something that is] the truest and best and most noble of things. ... There is something, therefore, which causes in all other things their being, their goodness, and whatever other perfection they have. And this we call "God."

The FIFTH way is based on the guidedness of nature. An orderedness of actions to an end is observed in all bodies obeying natural laws ...; they truly tend to a goal and do not merely hit it by accident. ... Everything in nature, therefore, is directed to its goal by someone with intelligence, and this we call "God."

Such a rational demonstration of the existence of God is, for Aquinas, what he called a "preamble of faith." What he calls the "articles of faith" necessarily follow upon and build on such rational demonstrations. So, although Christians cannot rationally know the essence of God, they can, through faith, know its divinity. Faith, in sum, begins with what Christians can know through what God has revealed to them in the Bible and through Christian tradition. Aquinas maintains, however, that some objects of faith, including the Incarnation, lie entirely beyond our capacity to understand them rationally in this life. Still, since we arrive

Read the document related to Saint Thomas Aquinas on **MyArtsLab**

at truth by means of both faith and reason—and, crucially, since all truths are equally valid—there should be no conflict between those arrived at through either faith or reason.

Although conservative Christians never quite accepted Aquinas's writings, arguing, for instance, that reason can never know God directly, his influence on Christian theology was profound and lasting. In the scope of its argument, the intellectual heights to which it soars, the *Summa Theologica* is at one with the Gothic cathedral. Like the cathedral, it is an architecture, built of logic rather than of stone, dedicated to the Christian God.

THE RADIANT STYLE AND THE COURT OF LOUIS IX

What is the Radiant style?

By the middle of the thirteenth century, the Gothic style in France had been elaborated into increasingly flamboyant patterns of repeated traceries and ornament that we have come to refer to as the *Rayonnant* or **Radiant style**. Similarly elaborate styles developed in both England and Germany. Although only 3 feet high, the *Three Towers Reliquary* (Fig. **12.19**), from Aachen Cathedral in Germany,

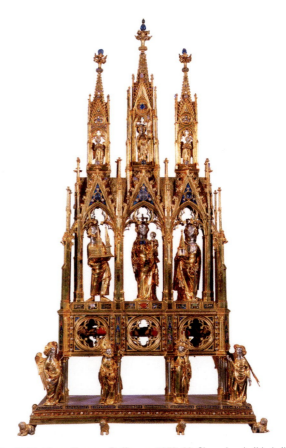

Fig. 12.19 ***Three Towers Reliquary.*** **1370–90.** Chased and gilded silver, enamel, and gems, height 36¾". Cathedral Treasury, Aachen, Germany. This reliquary, probably of Flemish origin, has transparent containers just below the top of each spire, allowing light to pass over the sacred body parts contained within.

gives a fair impression of this new, more complex style. It might as well be a model for a small church. Its pinnacles and spires soar upward. Rather than presenting us with a veil of stone—compare the facade of Amiens Cathedral (see Fig. 12.12), which, although highly decorated, is a solid mass—the reliquary seems more like a web of gossamer. It is as if the walls themselves should dissolve into air and light, as if the building—or reliquary—should float away in a halo of golden rays.

This style was associated closely with the court of Louis IX (r. 1226–70), in Paris. The Church especially valued Louis's dedication to its well-being. One of his most important contributions to the Church, and to the history of Gothic architecture, is the royal chapel of Sainte-Chapelle (Fig. **12.20**),

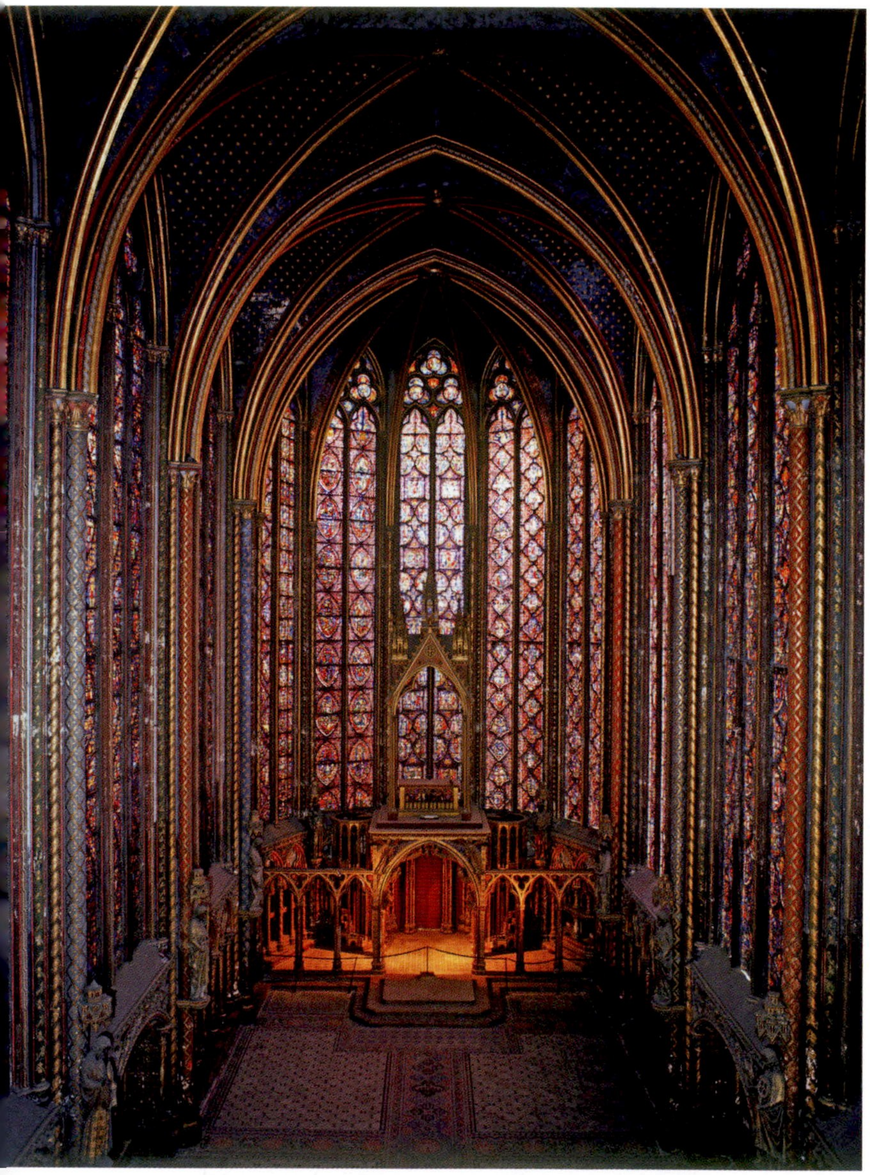

Fig. 12.20 Interior, Upper Chapel, Sainte-Chapelle, Paris. 1243–48. Although the chapel was originally surrounded by the royal castle—today it is surrounded by the Ministry of Justice—it remains more or less intact, save for a nineteenth-century repainting. Its acoustics were originally among the best in Paris and remain so today.

✳ Explore the architectural panorama of Sainte-Chapelle on **MyArtsLab**

constructed in the center of the royal palace on the Île de la Cité, not far from Notre-Dame de Paris. Louis had the chapel designed so that the royal family could enter directly from the palace, at the level of the stained glass, thus symbolizing his own eminence, while others—court officials and the like—entered through a smaller, ground-level chapel below. He created for himself, in other words, a **palatine chapel**—a palace chapel—on the model of Charlemagne's at Aachen, thus connecting himself to his great predecessor.

The chapel was nothing short of a reliquary built large. While on Crusade, Louis purchased what was believed to be the crown of thorns that Christ wore at the Crucifixion, as well as other precious objects, from the emperor of Constantinople. These precious pieces were destined to be housed in Sainte-Chapelle. No other structure in the Gothic era so completely epitomized the Radiant style even as it embodied the original vision of the Abbot Suger:

> Thus, when—out of my delight in the beauty of the house of God—the loveliness of the many-colored gems [of stained glass] has called me away from external cares, and worthy meditation has induced me to reflect, transferring that which is material to that which is immaterial, on the diversity of the sacred virtues: then it seems to me that I see myself dwelling, as it were, in some strange region of the universe which neither exists entirely in the slime of the earth nor entirely in the purity of heaven; and that, by the grace of God, I can be transported from this interior to that higher world in an analogical manner.

Bathing the viewer in the light of its stained glass—light so bright, in fact, that the viewer can hardly distinguish the details of its biblical narrative—Sainte-Chapelle is designed to relieve the faithful of any external cares and transport them into a realm of heavenly beauty. It is spiritual space, the immateriality of its light comparable, in Suger's perspective, to the immateriality of the immortal soul. The ratio of glass to stone is higher than in any other Gothic structure, the windows separated by the slenderest of columns. The lower parts of the walls, beneath the windows, are richly decorated in red, blue, and gilt, so that stone and glass seem one and the same. Golden stars shine down from the deep blue of the delicately vaulted ceiling. Louis's greatest wish was to make Paris a New Jerusalem, a city as close to paradise as could be found on earth. For many visitors, he came as close as may be humanly possible in Sainte-Chapelle.

Louis was a born reformer, as much a man of the people as any medieval king could be. Under his rule the Scholastics and Aquinas argued theology openly in the streets of Paris, just across the river from the royal palace. Louis believed in a certain freedom of thought, but even more in the rule of law. He dispatched royal commissioners into all of the provinces to check up on the Crown's representatives and ensure that they were treating the people fairly. He abolished serfdom and made private wars—which many believe to have been the ultimate motivation for the First Crusade—illegal. He reformed the tax structure and gave his subjects the right to appeal decisions in court. He was, in short, something of a saint. Indeed, the Church later beatified him as Saint Louis.

The Gothic Style in the French Ducal Courts

In the fourteenth century, the authority of the French king, though never challenged, was rivaled by the power of the ducal courts outside of the Paris region. Among these dukes were the king's relatives, the dukes of Anjou, Berry, and Burgundy, who fashioned magnificent courts in their own capitals and employed vast numbers of artists charged with decorating them in a Gothic style directly indebted to the Radiant style of the century before.

The Burgundian dukes ruled from Dijon in eastern France, but they controlled as well the region of Flanders, encompassing present-day Holland, Belgium, and Luxembourg. When, in the early fifteenth century, they moved from Dijon to Flanders, their favorite destination was Bruges, which of all the Flemish towns had been the first to build a town hall (Fig. **12.21**). Its lavish Gothic ornamentation—from the tracery patterns in the upper windows to the ornamentation of the roofs and towers—was designed to recall the palaces of the French and Burgundian nobility. Interestingly, Bruges's adaptation of this style for its civic government—a government at least theoretically independent of ducal authority—underscores not only its citizens' sense of self-worth, but also their growing independence from the very nobles they imitated.

Through the late Middle Ages, the population of Bruges ranged between 40,000 and 50,000, quite large by northern European standards. (Most cities averaged just 2,000 to 3,000 inhabitants, and across northern Europe, 70 percent of the population still lived in the countryside.) Wages in Bruges were the highest in northern Europe, especially for craftspeople, and the city took pride in providing one of the most extensive social-care networks anywhere—including 11 hospitals and hospices. The port in Bruges was one of the leading trade depots in northern Europe, where fish from the Baltic, timber, grain, and furs from Poland and Russia, and silver from the mines of central Europe were exchanged for highly prized Flemish textiles and garments, and for commodities including spices, sugar, silk, and cotton. These arrived via the Venetian fleet, which, by the early fifteenth century, was dispatching 45 merchant galleys annually to Bruges and other nearby northern ports, each carrying over 250 tons of cargo.

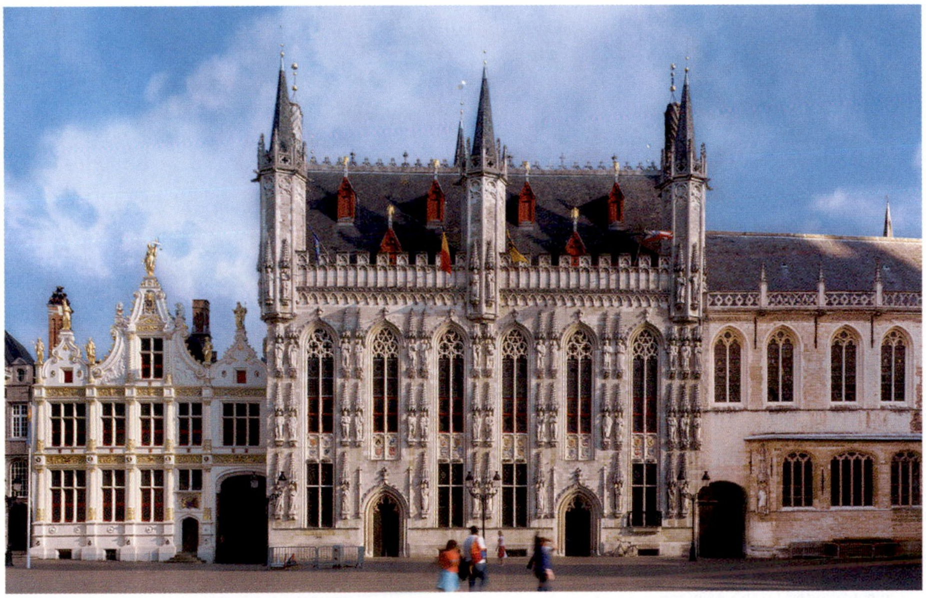

The Miniature Tradition

It is perhaps no accident that a culture so concerned with material goods and material well-being should develop, in its art, a taste for detailed renderings of material reality. The Northern European attention to detail in art derives, first of all, from the Gothic predilection for intricate traceries, the winding interplay of ornamental buds and leaves so often apparent in Gothic stone- and woodwork. As we have also seen, in the sculptural decoration of churches such as that at Reims (see Fig. 12.16), by the middle of the thirteenth century, there was a developing taste for naturalism in art. It is in the work of the medieval miniature painters of the fifteenth-century French and Burgundian courts that these two directions first merge.

A **miniature** is a very small painting associated with **illumination**, the painstakingly detailed, hand-painted decoration of manuscripts, usually in tempera on vellum. The most famous miniature painters were the Limbourg brothers (flourished 1380–1416), Paul, Jan, and Hermann, sons of a sculptor from the Netherlands. The brothers migrated to Paris in the late fourteenth century. There, they were sponsored by their uncle, the court painter to Philip the Bold, the duke of Burgundy (r. 1363– 1404). After Philip the Bold died, the Limbourgs began working for his brother Jean, Duke of Berry (r. 1360–1416). Jean was the wealthiest man in Europe at the dawn of the fifteenth century—not

Fig. 12.21 Anonymous Flemish architects, Town Hall (at right) and Greffe (at left), Bruges, Belgium. Town Hall, 1376–1402; Greffe, 1534–37. The Greffe is the office of civil clerks. The present-day sculptural decoration of the Town Hall dates from 1853. The original was destroyed during the French Revolution.

surprising, as his subjects paid the heaviest taxes in all of Europe. With those taxes, the duke funded ambitious projects designed to celebrate his status and interests. One of his most important commissions to the Limbourg brothers was the *Très Riches Heures du Duc de Berry* (*The Very Sumptuous Hours of the Duke of Berry*), an illuminated **Book of Hours** begun in 1411. The brothers died five years later, most likely of the plague, and the work remained unfinished.

A Book of Hours typically begins with a calendar illustrated with images showing daily life or special events associated with each month of the year. It continues with short prayers to be recited during the eight designated times for prayer, or the canonical hours. Among the Limbourg brothers' illustrations, many depict the Duke of Berry's residences and those of the French royal family. The *Très Riches Heures* thus provides us with a documentary record of their appearance, even though most of the buildings were destroyed long ago. Consider, for instance, their miniature painting of Mehun-sur-Yèvre (Fig. **12.22**), built near Bourges in the late fourteenth century. This Gothic structure no longer stands, but at the time, many thought it was the most beautiful private home in the world. The Limbourg brothers used

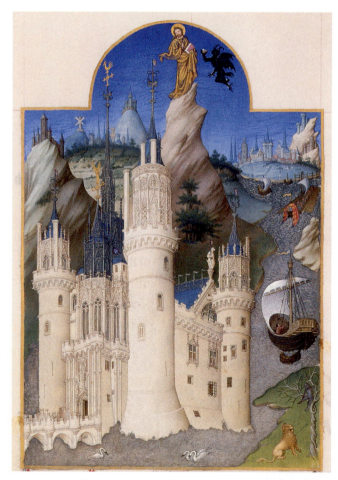

Fig. 12.22 Limbourg brothers, *The Temptation of Christ,* from *Les Très Riches Heures du Duc de Berry.* ca. 1415. Illumination on parchment, 6¾" × 4½". Musée Condé, Chantilly. Jean, Duke of Berry, was famous for the menagerie of exotic animals he kept, especially at Mehun-sur-Yèvre, including swans, bears, lions, and monkeys, as depicted in the foreground of this miniature.

it to illustrate the story of the devil's temptation of Christ. (Christ stands on the peak of a mountain at the top of the page, the devil flying beside him.) Christ refuses the riches of the world—represented by the Duke of Berry's very possessions—as if to remind the viewer, and the duke himself, of the transience of worldly things. Nevertheless, the artistry of the Limbourgs captures every detail of the home's Gothic pinnacles and points, every rib and joint across the tracery of its facade, celebrating the duke's riches even as it warns against putting too much faith in them.

The calendar section of the *Très Riches Heures* provides us with extraordinary insight into the daily lives of both nobility and peasants. The contrast between the illustration for the first calendar month, January (Fig. **12.23**), and the second, February (Fig. **12.24**), could not be more dramatic. In the first, Jean de Berry presides over a New Year's feast. At the time, New Year was known as a time for the ritual exchange of gifts, or *étrennes*. People favored, particularly, the exchange of jewelry, flasks, enameled figurines, and saltcellars. We know, for instance, that in 1411, one of Jean de Berry's sons-in-law gave him as an *étrenne* a silver saltcellar "in the fashion of an ostrich, with a belly of pearl-shell, and seated on a terrace of silver-gilt enameled with green." Art historian Brigitte Buettner has described the January scene in an article that appeared in the *Art Bulletin* in 2001:

> Clad in a *houpplande* [a loose, belted overgown with long wide sleeves] trimmed with fur and strewn with gold embroideries and diamonds, the monumental duke is differentiated from his all-male entourage of court officials and servants by redundant visual signs: the sophisticated spatial organization that at once detaches him from and binds him to his surroundings; the full profile view, glorified by the mandorla-like fire screen. … Although difficult to perceive in a reproduction, a miniature gilded bear and swan also perch on either end of the oversize *nef* at the center of the table. The *nef*, a lavish vessel used both to store trenchers or foodstuffs and as a place setting for the most honored guest, was a prized New Year's gift. … In the Limbourgs' miniature, there is an almost overwhelming sensory overload—things are carried and examined, food smelled and tasted; when looking long enough, one even starts to hear the noises made by cutting, pouring, shuffling, and rubbing, or the clinking of gilded belts and metal vessels, the crackling of the fire, the dogs barking and people shouting. The human voice is actually present in a literal way, for the chamberlain standing behind the duke … is expectorating gilded words, "Aproche, Aproche," directed to the prelate seated to Berry's right, possibly Martin Gouge. Moreover, the duke's courtiers' bodies are bedecked in costumes that are given both an optical and tactile appeal through the addition of gold embroideries, belts, and jewelry.

Behind the scene is a tapestry depicting the Trojan War, a tragic episode that could be said to have resulted from a failure to maintain the civility and hospitality of Jean de Berry's court.

This resplendent image of material well-being contrasts dramatically with the next scene, representing February.

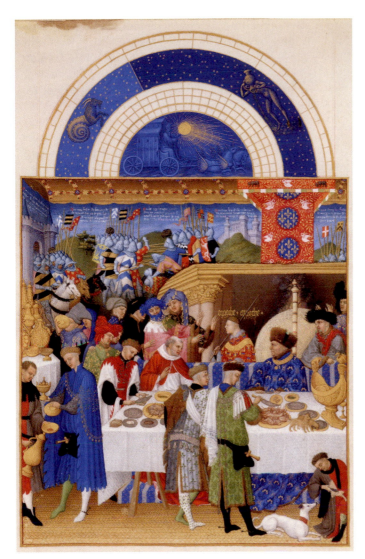

Fig. 12.23 Limbourg brothers, *January: The Feast of the Duke of Berry*, from *Les Très Riches Heures du Duc de Berry*. ca. 1415. Illumination on parchment, 6¾" × 4½". Musée Condé, Chantilly. Note that two small dogs enjoy the duke's table as much as his courtiers.

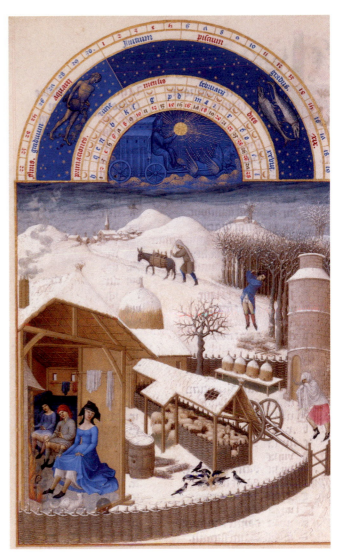

Fig. 12.24 Limbourg brothers, *February* (*Winter Scene*), from *Les Très Riches Heures du Duc de Berry*. ca. 1415. Illumination on parchment, 6¾" × 4½". Musée Condé, Chantilly. In the calendar page for July, a woman in this same blue dress and black hat is depicted shearing what may well be these same sheep.

Here we see three peasants warming themselves at a fire, one of them, probably the "lady" of the house, with her skirts raised somewhat modestly just below her knees to reveal her knickers, but the two others, clearly peasants, immodestly exposing themselves. Outside in the snowy landscape are three others: one inadequately bundled against the cold and seemingly warming her hands with her breath; a second cutting firewood, no doubt to fuel the fire the others are enjoying; and the third driving a donkey to the distant village. By contrast to the refined world of the duke himself, these peasants are boorish and vulgar. Their warmth is no better than that of the sheep huddled in their pen; their "feast" probably closer to that of the birds scratching for seed than the duke's; their shelter a far remove from even that of the bees whose hives they keep.

If the Limbourg brothers (and by extension, their patron, Jean de Berry) intended to contrast the duke's life to that of his people, there can be no doubt of the duke's superiority, but there can also be no doubt that the peasantry who owe him allegiance and work his lands are, by medieval standards, relatively well off. Their farm is tidy and, apparently, prosperous. It may be, in fact, that we are witness, in the figure of the man driving a donkey to the village perhaps to sell wood to the village dwellers, to the dawn of economic capitalism. By the fifteenth century, at any rate, feudalism was dying, a middle class (of which, perhaps, the "lady" in blue is a member) was beginning to take shape, and the power of men like Jean de Berry was beginning to wane. But these images underscore the duke's continuing prestige and his mastery of his world.

View the Closer Look for the Limbourg brothers, *February* on **MyArtsLab**

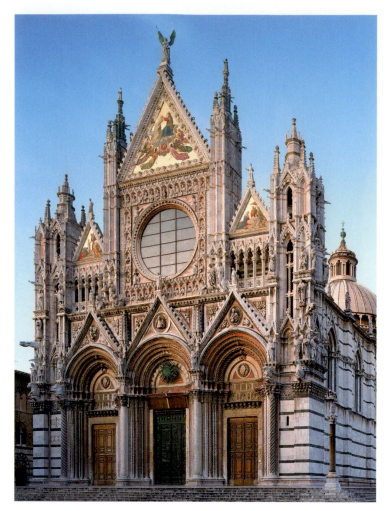

Fig. 12.25 Giovanni Pisano, lower facade, Siena Cathedral, Siena, Italy. 1284–99. Pisano designed only the lower half of the facade. Except for the rose window, the upper half of the facade dates from the fourteenth century. The mosaics in the top gables date from the nineteenth century.

THE GOTHIC IN ITALY

How did the Gothic style manifest itself in Italy?

The Gothic in Italy manifested itself in ways quite different from the rest of Europe, in no small part because Italy consisted of a number of individual city-states independent of control by a king or the Holy Roman Emperor. Even the papacy lacked real authority throughout most of the thirteenth century, since it had moved to France. Political power in these city-states—particularly in Florence and Siena—rested not with the landed aristocracy, who were often excluded from participation in civic affairs, but with the communities' leading merchant families. And these city-states competed with one another for the control of trade—and with it political influence and wealth.

This competitive atmosphere, and the civic pride associated with it, prompted civic leaders to commission new cathedrals and churches that would be, they hoped, the

envy of their neighbors. Siena took the lead, commissioning a new facade for its magnificent cathedral in 1284 (Fig. **12.25**). To the two-tone marble banding of the original Romanesque cathedral, the artist in charge, Giovanni Pisano, integrated features of the French Gothic style, such as the triple portal with its pointed gables over the tympana, the soaring finials, the rose window, and an elaborate sculpture program.

Pisano's great innovation was, in fact, this sculpture program. It incorporated freestanding sculptures of prophets and saints on the pinnacles, arches, and gables of the facade. His *Mary, Sister of Moses* (Fig. **12.26**) is an example. She leans dramatically forward, as if turning to communicate with the other figures on the facade. But her pose also is the result of Giovanni's acute sense of his public. He realized that, when seen from street level, Mary's face would be hidden behind her dress and breasts if he did not arch her neck forward. The result is a figure that stands independently of the architecture and, like the other figures on the facade, asserts its freedom in a manner comparable to the figures on the west facade portal of Reims Cathedral (see Fig. 12.16).

In 1294, Florence responded to Siena's initiative when it formed the Opera del Duomo, or Department

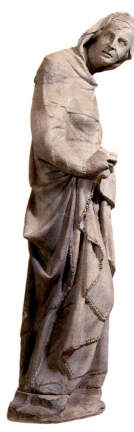

Fig. 12.26 Giovanni Pisano, *Mary, Sister of Moses*. 1284–99. Marble, height 74¾". Museo dell'Opera del Duomo, Siena. This sculpture was once on the facade of Siena Cathedral. The sculptures now in place on the facade are copies of the originals, which were removed to protect them from further deterioration.

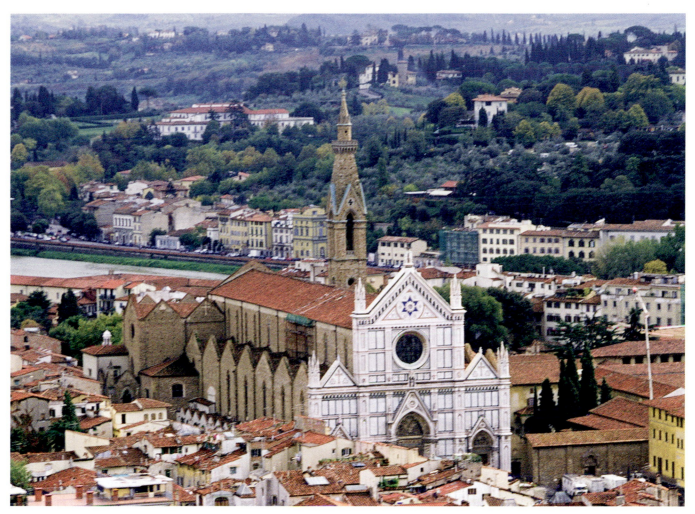

Fig. 12.27 Santa Croce, Florence, Italy. Begun 1294. Santa Croce was commissioned by the Franciscans with the support of the Florentine government and private citizens.

of Works of the Duomo (*duomo* comes from *domus dei*, or "house of God"), a committee in charge of building a new cathedral of its own. Construction began in 1296, although the building would not be completed until the first half of the fifteenth century (see Chapter 14). The city claimed that the Duomo would be "the most beautiful and honorable church in Tuscany," an assertion that everyone understood to mean it would compete with Siena's cathedral.

The New Mendicant Orders

Aside from cathedrals, civic leaders also engaged in building projects for the new urban religious orders: the Dominicans, founded by the Spanish monk Dominic de Guzman (ca. 1170–1221), whose most famous theologian was Thomas Aquinas; and the Franciscans, founded by Francis of Assisi (ca. 1181–1226). Unlike the traditional Benedictine monastic order, which functioned apart from the world, the Dominicans and the Franciscans were reformist orders, dedicated to active service in the cities, especially among the common people. Their growing popularity reflected the growing crisis facing the mainstream Church,

as isolation and apparent disregard for laypeople plagued it well into the sixteenth century.

The mainstream Church held property and engaged in business—sources, many felt, of the Church's corruption. The Dominicans and Franciscans were both **mendicant orders**—that is, they neither held property nor engaged in business, relying for their support on contributions from their communities. The Dominicans and the Franciscans were rivals, and they often established themselves on opposite sides of a city. The Dominicans' priority was preaching. The Franciscans committed themselves to a severe regimen of prayer, meditation, fasting, and mortification of the flesh, based on Francis's conviction that one could come closer to God by rejecting worldly goods. But both orders borrowed freely from one another. The Franciscans adopted the more efficient organizing principles of the Dominicans as well as their love of learning and emphasis on preaching, while the Dominicans accepted the Franciscan repudiation of worldly goods.

Franciscan and Dominican Churches In Florence, the civic government and private citizens worked with the Franciscans to build the church of Santa Croce (Fig. **12.27**).

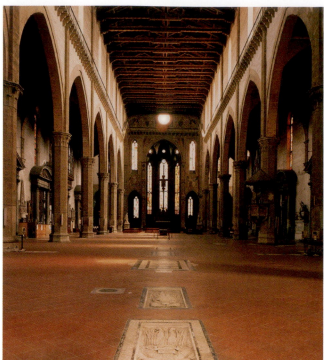

Fig. 12.28 Nave and choir, Santa Croce, Florence, Italy. Begun 1294.
The interior would come to contain the tombs of many famous Florentines, including Michelangelo, Machiavelli, Ghiberti, and Galileo (see Chapter 14).

Construction began in 1294 and continued even as the city began constructing its main cathedral. Compared to Gothic churches of the period, the mendicant churches are austere in their decoration. Nothing like the dramatic gables, finials, and sculpture program that decorate Giovanni Pisano's

Siena Cathedral distinguishes their plain facades, and their interiors are likewise unembellished. Gothic pointed arches together with vertical moldings designed to pull the eye upward decorate the nave arcade of Santa Croce (Fig. **12.28**), but instead of continuing upward into the rising vaults of the Gothic interior, the nave and choir are topped by an open, wooden-trussed ceiling. There is no structural reason that the Franciscans should have chosen to cover the nave in this manner, but perhaps they simply wanted to emphasize the simplicity of their own practice by evoking the basilica tradition of early churches such as the original Saint Paul's Outside the Walls in Rome (see Fig. 8.13 in Chapter 8).

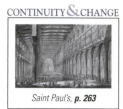

CONTINUITY & CHANGE

*Saint Paul's, **p. 263***

Santa Croce was on the eastern side of the city, and the Dominican church of Santa Maria Novella (Fig. **12.29**) was built on the western side, underscoring the rivalry between the two orders. (A Franciscan church and a Dominican church were also built in Siena.) At Santa Maria Novella, the marble striping that defines the rich surfaces of Siena's cathedral is used only on the facade, and, in fact, the facade was left unfinished above the Gothic row of niches with their Gothic portals (extended by walls both right and left) until the middle of the fifteenth century.

Families supported the construction of both Florentine mendicant churches by donating chapels, held as family property, and built on either side of the nave. Private family masses could be celebrated in these chapels, and, as opposed to the more public spaces in the churches, they were often richly decorated and their walls painted with frescoes.

Thus, a rich family expected to guarantee its salvation by contributing to the church, and the order could accept the church and its chapels as a form of alms, consistent with its vow of poverty. This emphasis on painted decoration, instead of the stained glass that marks Northern European Gothic architecture and which was also reflected in the decoration of Italian civic structures, contributed significantly to the rise of painting as an art in Italy in the thirteenth and fourteenth centuries.

The Appeal of Saint Francis Both the Dominican and Franciscan orders were sanctioned by Pope Innocent III (papacy 1198–1216). Innocent exercised papal authority as no pope had before him. He went so far as to claim that the pope was to the emperor as the sun was to the moon, a reference to

Fig. 12.29 Santa Maria Novella, Florence, Italy. Founded before 1246, nave begun after 1279. Santa Maria Novella was commissioned by the Dominicans and, like Santa Croce, its construction was supported by the Florentine government and private citizens.

the fact that the emperor received his "brilliance" (that is, his crown) from the hand of the pope. Innocent established the papacy as a self-sustaining financial and bureaucratic institution. He formalized the Church hierarchy, from pope to parish priest, and gave full sanction to the doctrine of *transubstantiation* (the belief that the bread and wine of sacrament become the true body and blood of Christ when consecrated by a priest), and also made annual confession and Easter communion mandatory for all adult Christians.

Innocent was also a remarkably gifted preacher—his sermon *On the Misery of the Human Condition* was one of the most famous of its day (see Reading 10.5 in Chapter 10)—and the power of his words, if not the fierceness of his rhetoric, served as a model for both the Dominicans and the Franciscans. But, where Innocent appealed to the fear of death and damnation, mendicant orders appealed to the promise of life and salvation. Nevertheless, Innocent clearly understood the popular appeal of preaching and the influence that preaching gave to the new mendicant orders. He especially understood the attraction offered by the example of Francis of Assisi.

The son of a rich cloth merchant, Francis became disaffected with wealth and urged his followers to lead a life of poverty. Stories detailing the deeds and miracles of Francis's life embodied the reasons that he was to be revered. In his official biography of Francis, Bonaventure of Bagnoreggio (ca. 1217–74) tells how Francis created the first crèche (**Reading 12.3**):

READING 12.3

from Bonaventure of Bagnoreggio,
Legenda Maior

He asked for and obtained the permission of the pope for the ceremony, so that he could not be accused of being an innovator, and then he had a crib prepared, with hay and an ox and an ass. The friars were all invited and the people came in crowds. The forest re-echoed with their voices and the night was lit up with a multitude of bright lights, while the beautiful music of God's praises added to the solemnity. The saint stood before the crib and his heart overflowed with tender compassion; he was bathed in tears but overcome with joy … preached to the people about the birth of the poor King, whom he called the Babe of Bethlehem. …
[T]he hay from the crib, which was kept by the people, afterwards cured sick animals and drove off various pestilences. Thus God wished to give glory to his servant Francis and prove the efficacy of his prayer by clear signs.

There were so many such stories that Pope Gregory IX (papacy 1227–41) canonized Francis two years after his death, and ordered that the Upper Church of San Francesco be built in his honor at Assisi, Francis's hometown (Fig. 12.30). Begun in 1228, it is one of the most beautiful of Italian Gothic churches. Although some of the finest stained-glass windows of the Italian thirteenth century

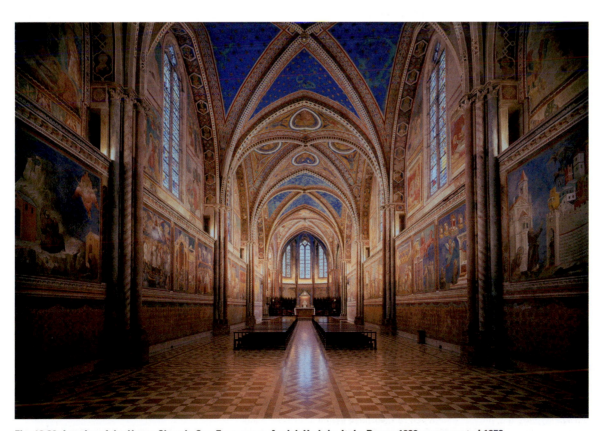

Fig. 12.30 Interior of the Upper Church, San Francesco, Assisi, Umbria, Italy. Begun 1228; consecrated 1253.
Within a few years of its completion, the church became a popular pilgrimage site.

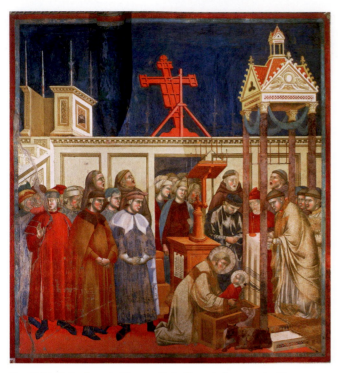

Fig. 12.31 Saint Francis Master, *Saint Francis Creates the First Christmas Crèche*, fresco in Upper Church of San Francesco, Assisi, Umbria, Italy. ca. 1295–1305. A severe earthquake gravely damaged the Assisi fresco cycle on September 26, 1997, when two sections of the church's roof collapsed.

decorate the interior, the primary decorative program consists of paintings of Old and New Testament scenes, as well as a series of 28 frescoes narrating Francis's life as told by Bonaventure. The series has often been attributed to Giotto di Bondone, the first great Italian painter of the fourteenth century (discussed in Chapter 13). The Saint Francis paintings at Assisi are stylistically different enough from Giotto's other work, however, that many art historians believe them to be the work of an unknown Roman painter, often called the Saint Francis Master.

The faces and folds of cloth in the work of the Saint Francis Master are defined with broad, lighter highlights applied over the darker background colors. Note the clothes of the two figures at the left of the scene depicting the saint creating the Christmas crèche, as narrated by Bonaventure (Fig. **12.31**). Giotto, as we will see, uses a gradual and continuous blending of dark colors to re-create the realistic appearance of shadows. Perhaps the most remarkable aspect of the painting is the artist's attempt to create an illusionistic space by means of one-point perspective (discussed more fully in Chapter 14). Here, the architectural forms recede into deep space but they do not do so in a uniform way throughout the composition.

Francis's love of the natural world was profound. In his mystical poem "Canticle of the Sun," his language suggests an intimate bond with the universe. Addressing "brother sun" and "sister moon," "brother wind" and "sister water," this poem may be the first work of literature in the vernacular, or the language spoken by the people in everyday usage, as opposed to Latin (**Reading 12.4**):

READING 12.4

Saint Francis of Assisi, "Canticle of the Sun"

Most high, all-powerful, all good, Lord!
All praise is yours, all glory, all honor
And all blessing.
To you alone, Most High, do they belong.
No mortal lips are worthy
To pronounce your name.
All praise be yours, my Lord, through all that you have made,
And first my lord Brother Sun,
Who brings the day; and light you give to us through him.
How beautiful is he, how radiant in all his splendor!
Of you, Most High, he bears the likeness.
All praise be yours, my Lord, through Sister Moon and Stars;
In the heavens you have made them, bright
And precious and fair.
All praise be yours, my Lord, through Brothers Wind and Air,
And fair and stormy, all the weather's moods,
By which you cherish all that you have made.
All praise be yours, my Lord, through Sister Water,
So useful, lowly, precious, and pure.
All praise be yours, my Lord, through Brother Fire,
Through whom you brighten up the night.
How beautiful he is; how cheerful and powerful and strong.
All praise be yours, my Lord, through Sister Earth, our mother,
Who feeds us in her sovereignty and produces
Various fruits and colored flowers and herbs.
All praise be yours, my Lord, through those who grant pardon
For love of you; through those who endure
Sickness and trial.
Happy those who endure in peace,
By you, Most High, they will be crowned.
All praise be yours, my Lord, through Sister Death,
From whose embrace no mortal can escape.
Woe to those who die in mortal sin!
Happy those She finds doing your will!
The second death can do no harm to them.
Praise and bless my Lord, and give him thanks,
And serve him with great humility.

The love of nature expressed here is fundamental to Franciscan theology. It sets out what amounts to a theology of incarnation—that is, a deep and abiding belief that God resides in the world, in his Creation, and can be understood by contemplation of that Creation.

Representing the Human

Among the surviving treasures of the Abbey Church of Saint-Denis is a sculpture of the Virgin and Child inscribed with the date 1339 and the name of Queen Jeanne d'Evreux, wife of Charles IV of France (Fig. **12.32**). Just over 2 feet high, it embodies both the cult of the Virgin and the growing preference for naturalistic representation that is so evident in the jamb sculptures at Reims (see Fig. 12.16). The Virgin holds a scepter topped by a *fleur-de-lis*, the heraldic symbol of the French monarchy, which served as a reliquary for what were said to be hairs from Mary's head. In this, she is a perfect medieval figure. But she also stands, her weight on one leg, in an exaggeration of the classical *contrapposto* pose into a pronounced S-curve, suggesting the Virgin's grace and elegance. Drapery falls around her, describing the body beneath as if it is actual flesh and bone. The softness of her face, the kindness of her expression, which the Christ Child reaches

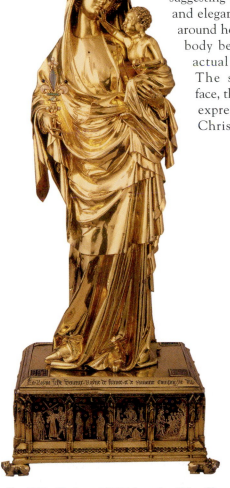

Fig. 12.32 *Virgin and Child*, **from the Abbey Church of Saint-Denis, France. ca. 1339.** Silver gilt and enamel, height 27⅛". Musée du Louvre, Paris. Inv. MR 342; MR 419.

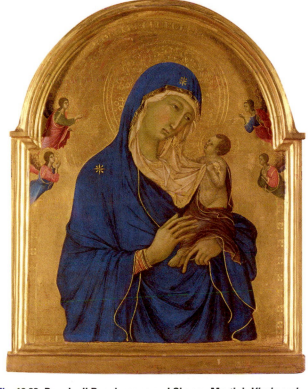

Fig. 12.33 Duccio di Buoninsegna and Simone Martini, *Virgin and Child with Saint Dominic and Saint Aurea* (detail). 1310–20. Tempera on wood, 24¼" × 34¼". National Gallery, London.

out to touch, lend her a humanity that would become a characteristic of art made in the centuries to come. It is as if she is, in this sculpture, first a mother, then the mother of Christ.

Painted at almost the same time, in Italy, is a depiction of the Virgin and Child by the Sienese master Duccio and his assistant Simone Martini (Fig. **12.33**). Here, too, the artists emphasize the human nature of the Virgin's expression, the feeling captured in the mother's facial expression—despite the obvious restraining influence of late Byzantine style on these masters. It may have been just this humanity that made the cult of the Virgin so attractive to so many. If most of the faithful found it impossible to identify with Jesus, who was, after all, a superhuman figure, they could identify with the completely human Mary. In both images, we see a hint of what would be the driving force of intellectual pursuit in the fourteenth and fifteenth centuries: the exploration not of the meaning of the Bible, but of what it means to be human. ∎

12.1 Outline the ideas, technological innovations, and stylistic developments that distinguish the Gothic style in France.

The architectural style that came to be known as Gothic originated at the Abbey Church of Saint-Denis just north of Paris, which was dedicated in 1144. It was the work of Saint-Denis's abbot, Suger, who dreamed of bringing prominence to the Île-de-France by creating an architecture surpassing all others in beauty and grandeur. How did stained glass fit into his ambitions? Chartres Cathedral, to the southwest, soon followed suit, after a fire destroyed the original structure in 1194, leaving only the west facade. The church was rebuilt into what many consider the most magnificent of all Gothic cathedrals, its stained glass unrivaled in Europe. Freed of load-bearing necessity by the innovative engineering that marks Gothic construction, the walls were thus also free to contain glass, which surrounds the entire cathedral.

As the Gothic style developed, important architectural innovations contributed to the goal of elevating the soul of worshipers to the spiritual realm. What makes the extremely high naves of Gothic cathedrals possible? During the thirteenth century, architects began to embellish the exteriors of their cathedrals with increasingly elaborate decoration, including ambitious sculptural programs. How do you account for the increasing naturalism of this sculptural decoration?

With its vast spaces and stone walls, the Gothic cathedral could easily be as animated by its acoustics as it was by its light. At the School of Notre-Dame, in Paris, the first collection of music in two parts, the *Magnus Liber Organi* (*The Great Book of Polyphony*), chiefly the work of the composers Léonin and Pérotin, was widely distributed in manuscript by about 1160. Among their most significant innovations is their emphasis on counterpoint and the complex musical form of the motet. What role did the organ play in this new music?

12.2 Explain why the University of Paris was preeminent among medieval institutions of higher learning.

In 1179, a papal decree ordered the cathedral schools to provide for the teaching of the laity (nonclerics), and the university as an institution was born. The quality of the teaching at the University of Paris distinguished it from the others. Peter Abelard, who taught by the dialectical method, was the school's most renowned lecturer. How would you describe the dialectical method? How does it differ from the Socratic method? Abelard's affair with a private female student, Héloïse, would cause them both great difficulty, and Héloïse's fate reveals much about the prospects for educated women in the Middle Ages. But probably the most important scholar at the University of Paris was Thomas Aquinas, who adopted Abelard's dialectical method to his own Scholasticism. What is Scholasticism and how does Aquinas's *Summa Theologica* reflect it?

12.3 Define the Radiant style.

By the middle of the thirteenth century, the Gothic style in France had been elaborated into increasingly flamboyant patterns of repeated traceries and ornament that we refer to as the Radiant style. How does the royal chapel of Sainte-Chapelle in Paris reflect this style?

12.4 Describe how the Gothic style manifested itself in Italy.

Siena commissioned a new facade for its cathedral from Giovanni Pisano in 1284. Florence responded to Siena's initiative by beginning construction of its own new cathedral. Aside from cathedrals, civic leaders also engaged in building churches for the new urban religious mendicant orders: the Dominicans and the Franciscans. What decorative feature of these churches distinguishes them from Gothic architecture in the north?

☑ **Study** and **review** on **MyArtsLab**

READINGS

READING 12.1

from Jean de Meun, *Romance of the Rose*

The *Romance of the Rose* is an allegorical dream vision about love, in which a young man endeavors to possess the rosebud with which he has become enamored. In Meun's hands, it becomes a satire on contemporary society. At the end of the poem, in an allegory of sexual intercourse, the lover finally penetrates the inner sanctum of the rose. The poem ends with the narrator awakening, fulfilled, at daybreak. The following represents the first publication of the letters of Héloïse and Abelard, included in the poem as part of a jealous husband's arguments against marriage.

53

… Likewise did Héloïse entreat
(The abbess of the Paraclete)
Her lover Peter Abelard,
That he would utterly discard
All thought of marriage from his mind.
This lady, noble and refined,
Of genius bright and learning great,
Loving, and loved with passionate
Strong love, implored him not to wed,
And many a well-wrought reason sped   10
To him in letters, where she showed
That hard and troublous is the code

54

Of marriage, howsoever true
Are those who bind themselves thereto;
For not alone had she in books
Studied, but all the closest nooks
Of woman's heart explored, and she
Love's throes had suffered bitterly.
Therefore she begged they might atwain,[1]
Though dying each for each, remain,   20
Bound by no bonds but those of love,
Whose gentle ties are strong above
All marriage laws, yet frank and free
Leave lovers—in sweet amity—
To follow learning, and she said,
Moreover, that long absence bred
'Twixt lovers unexpressed delight,
Most poignant when they're lost to sight.

But Peter, as himself hath writ
In burning letters, so was smit[2]   30
With passion, that nought else would serve
Till Héloïse he drew to swerve
From her sage counsel, and thence fell
On him mischance most dire to tell;
For little more their course was run
Ere she at Argenteuil as nun

Was close immured,[3] while he was reft
Of manhood by his foes, who deft
As cruel were in his despite,
Seizing him as he lay one night   40
At Paris. After this mischance
Saint Denis, patron saint of France

55

Gave shelter to him as a monk;
And when this bitter cup he'd drunk,
Down to the dregs an abbey meet
He founded, hight[4] the Paraclete,
For Héloïse, and there with good
Success she ruled the sisterhood.
Her love-lorn story hath she told
In letters which she penned with bold   50
Unshamed assurance; therein she
Declares monk Abelard to be
Her lord and master; and some say
These far-famed letters but betray
Delirious love. When first the dress
She donned of abbess, her distress
Broke forth in these wild words: If he
Who rules Rome's Empire courteously
Deigned to demand that I, as wife,
To him would dedicate my life,   60
In proud estate, I should reply
Much rather would I live and die
Thy mistress, wrapped in shame profound,
Than empress of the world be crowned.

But never since that day till now
Hath such a woman lived, I trow.[5]

READING CRITICALLY

What does Jean de Meun value most in Héloïse's rejection of marriage, and why do you think a later medieval commentary, written by one of the leading female writers of the day, would reject it as misogynist?

---

[1] **atwain:** separate.
[2] **smit:** struck.

[3] **immured:** confined.
[4] **hight:** named.
[5] **trow:** believe.

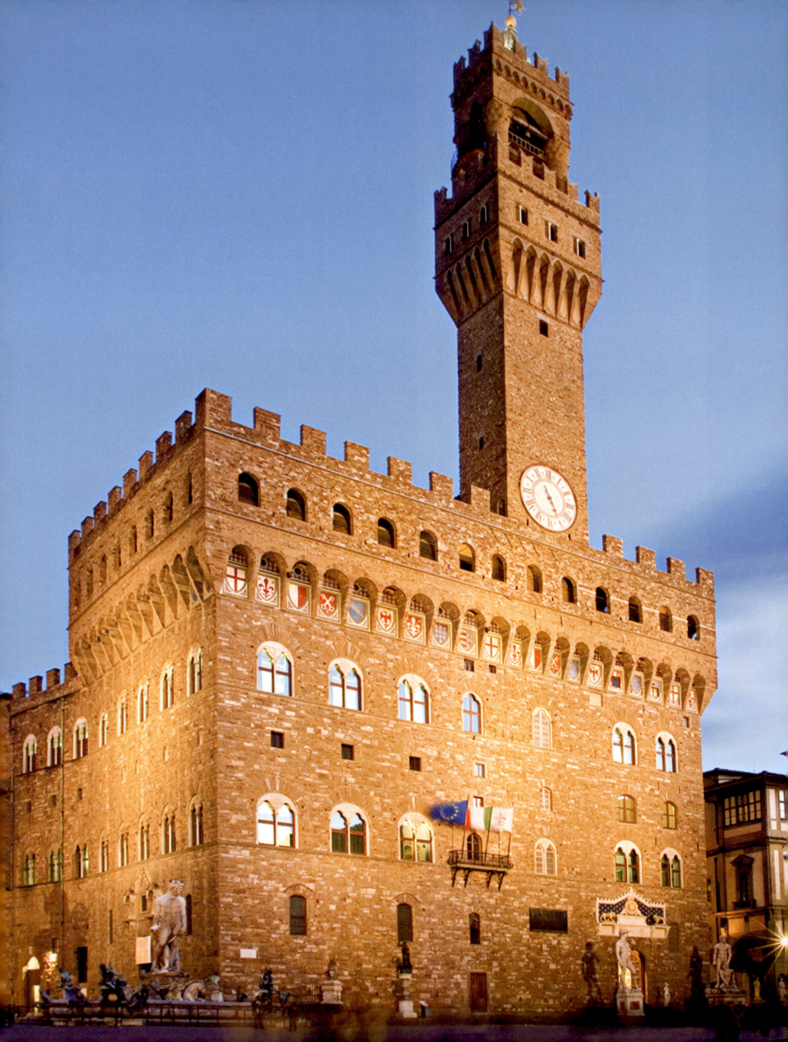

THINKING AHEAD

13.1 Compare and contrast civic life in Siena and Florence.

13.2 Outline how an increasingly naturalistic art replaced the Byzantine style in Italy.

13.3 Describe the distinguishing characteristics of Dante's *Divine Comedy*.

13.4 Examine how the vernacular style developed after the Black Death.

The city halls of Siena and Florence, begun within two years of one another (1297 and 1299 respectively), and the broad plazas that fronted them, are eloquent symbols not only of the cities' many similarities but also the intensity of their rivalry in the fourteenth century (Figs. **13.1** and **13.2**). Both buildings are more or less rectangular, decorated with crenellations meant to evoke the security and safety of the medieval fortress, and capped by tall bell towers. They dominate their urban landscapes and are reminiscent of the medieval castle's keep. Florence's Palazzo Vecchio is heavy-looking, its massive stonework reflecting the solidity of the merchant class that erected it. In contrast, the light brickwork of the facade of Siena's Palazzo Pubblico, or "public palace," is interrupted by windows composed of thin marble columns supporting Gothic arches—as if to announce the artistic refinement of the city. Siena's bell tower purposefully dwarfs that of its Florentine rival. In front of both town halls are large public squares, places for the citizenry to gather to hear government decisions.

In both Siena and Florence, the fortunes of Church and State were inextricably linked. Until the Palazzo Vecchio and the Palazzo Pubblico were built, both cities' governments met in churches. Afterward, the open squares in front of each building were used to host political events,

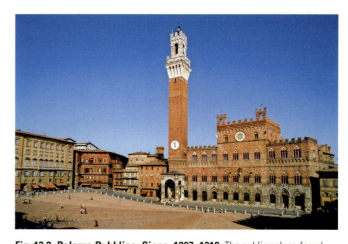

Fig. 13.2 Palazzo Pubblico, Siena. 1297–1310. The public palace faced the Campo, the large public square. Townspeople rushed back and forth, trading and bartering, and although the square was surrounded by the palaces of noble families, bankers, and merchants, the Campo was considered to be the property of all Sienese citizens. On the Campo, everyone was equal.

and public sermons supported by the government brought the Church into the government's very sphere. The local governments also invested heavily in building projects for the Church.

◄ **Fig. 13.1 Palazzo Vecchio, Florence. 1299–1310.** At the bottom right, before the main entrance, stands a replica of Michelangelo's famous sculpture of *David* (see Fig. 14.30 in Chapter 14). The original was put in place here in 1504. It was removed to protect it from damage in 1873. The replica seen here dates from 1910.

 Listen to the chapter audio on **MyArtsLab**

SIENA AND FLORENCE: CIVIC AND RELIGIOUS LIFE IN TUSCANY

How do the Sienese and Florentine republics compare?

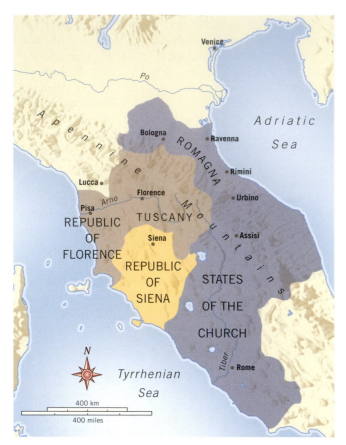

Map 13.1 Central Italy in about 1494, showing the republics of Florence and Siena and the Papal States.

The rival cities of Siena and Florence were located in Tuscany, the area of central Italy that lies between the Apennine Mountains, the central spine of the Italian peninsula, and a section of the Mediterranean known as the Tyrrhenian Sea (Map **13.1**). Siena lies in the mountainous southern region of Tuscany, at the center of a rich agricultural zone famous for its olive oil and wine. Florence is located in the Arno River valley, the region's richest agricultural district. Their rivalry dates back to the contest for supremacy between the pope and the Holy Roman Emperor during the time of Charlemagne (see Chapter 10). One faction, known as the Guelphs, sided with the pope, while another faction, the Ghibellines, sided with the emperor. Siena was generally considered a Ghibelline city, and Florence a Guelph stronghold, although factions of both parties competed for leadership within each city, especially in Florence. By the end of the thirteenth century, the pope retaliated against Siena for its Ghibelline leanings by revoking the city's papal banking privileges and conferring them instead on Florence. As a result, by the fourteenth century, Florence would become the principal economic and political power in Tuscany.

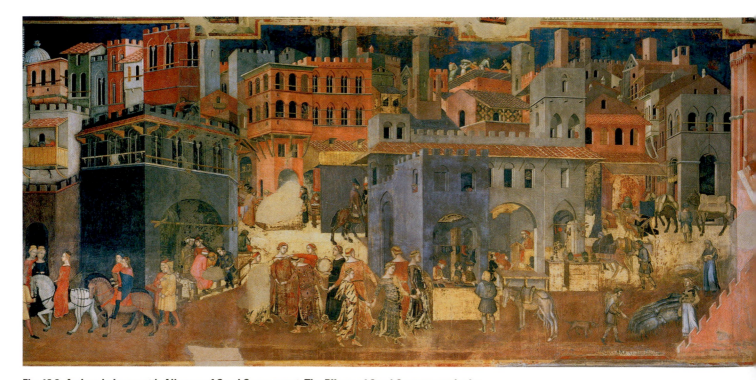

Fig. 13.3 Ambrogio Lorenzetti, *Allegory of Good Government: The Effects of Good Government in the City and Country*, fresco in the Sala della Pace, Palazzo Pubblico, Siena. 1338–39. Across from this painting, Lorenzetti also painted an *Allegory of Bad Government*, in which there is no commerce, no dancing, only man killing man, destruction and darkness all around.

Siena: A Free Commune

But in the late Middle Ages, Siena was still one of the most powerful cities in Europe. Its sense of its past lent it a feeling of historical weight. According to legend, its founders were Senius and Aschius, the sons of Remus, who with his brother, Romulus, founded Rome. Romulus had killed their father in a quarrel, and the boys, in retribution, stole Rome's she-wolf shrine and carried it back to Siena, protected by a white cloud by day and a black cloud by night. The facade of the Palazzo Pubblico celebrates their feat: Sculptures of Romulus and Remus suckled by the she-wolf decorate it, and a heraldic crest, the *balzana*, consisting of a white field atop a black one, appears under each arch.

Siena remained a small Etruscan village for 700 years, until the Roman emperor Augustus colonized it in 13 BCE. The town was dominated first by Rome and then by local nobles, Lombard and Frankish feudal counts, who arrived in successive invasions to rule in the name of their king. By the tenth century, large numbers of serfs had migrated from the surrounding countryside to three separate hilltop villages that soon merged into one. Feudal authorities were not altogether opposed to such migration. They had trained many of the serfs to manufacture the finished goods that they desired. It seemed practical to concentrate such production by chartering Siena and other towns. The charter stipulated that the townspeople would make manufactured goods, and in return, the feudal lord would protect them. Gradually, the towns gained more importance and power,

and their citizens began to pay allegiance not to feudal lords or papal authority but to the wealthiest citizens of the community, whose power base was founded on cooperation and the orderly conduct of affairs. When Siena established itself, in 1125, as a free **commune** (a collective of people gathered together for the common good), it achieved an immense advantage over its feudal neighbors. "Town air brings freedom" was a common saying in the late Middle Ages. As the prospect of such freedom attracted an increasing number of people to Siena, its prosperity was soon unrivaled.

Civic Life Crucial to the growing town's success was a new model of government, celebrated in 1338 by the painter Ambrogio Lorenzetti (active 1319–47) in a fresco called *Allegory of Good Government* (Fig. **13.3**), commissioned for the Council Chamber of Siena's Palazzo Pubblico. The fresco depicts Siena as it actually appeared. Richly dressed merchants dance in the street, one couple passing beneath the arching arms of another, followed by a chain of revelers dancing hand in hand. To the left, in an arched portico, three men play a board game. To their right is a shoe shop, behind that a schoolroom where a teacher expounds to a

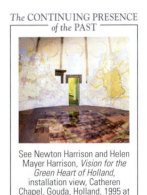

The CONTINUING PRESENCE
of the PAST

See Newton Harrison and Helen Mayer Harrison, *Vision for the Green Heart of Holland*, installation view, Catheren Chapel, Gouda, Holland, 1995 at **MyArtsLab**

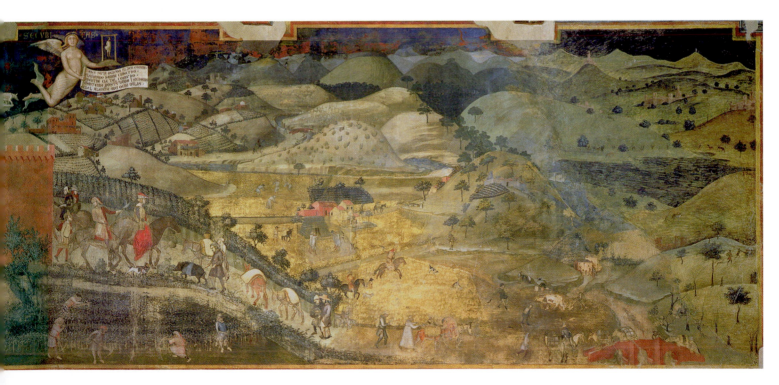

View the Closer Look for *The Effects of Good Government* on **MyArtsLab**

row of students, and beside the schoolroom, a wine shop. At the very top, masons construct a new building. Outside the city gate, to the right, the surrounding countryside is lush. Farmers bring livestock and produce to market, workers till the fields and labor in the vineyards. Above them all, floating in the sky, is the nearly nude figure of *Securitas* ("Security"), carrying a gallows in one hand and a scroll in the other, to remind citizens that peace depends upon justice. At the horizon, the sky is ominously dark, suggesting perhaps that Siena's citizens thought of themselves as living in a uniquely enlightened place.

Watching over the city's well-being was the Virgin Mary, uniting civic and religious life. The city called itself "ancient city of the Virgin," and by 1317, a *Maestà*, or *Virgin and Child in Majesty* (see Fig. 13.6), occupied the end wall of the Council Chamber of the Palazzo Pubblico. Painted by Simone Martini (active 1311–44), the *Maestà* depicts the Madonna and Christ Child surrounded by a heavenly court of saints and angels. Below, two kneeling angels offer up vessels of roses and lilies. The Virgin comments in verse, written on the platform below: "The angelic little flowers, roses and lilies, Which adorn the heavenly meadow, do not please me more than good counsel." Thus the Virgin exerts her moral influence over civic life.

The demands of daily life in Siena required divine intervention. The town had long divided itself into three distinct neighborhoods, corresponding to the three ridges of the hillside on which the city stands. With the advent of the commune, the city was ruled by three consuls, one for each neighborhood. There were other divisions as well. The wealthiest Sienese nobles, called the *grandi*, or "great ones," lorded over smaller neighborhoods, or wards, in a manner not unlike their feudal forebears. The clergy, headed by a bishop, were independent, and local churches, convents, and lay organizations devoted to deeds of charity were more or less self-governing. The common people organized themselves as military companies, which could unite to form a large Sienese army, but which also guaranteed local autonomy. And competing *arti*, or **guilds**, associations or groups of people with similar, often occupation-based interests, exercised power over their members.

The guilds became an increasingly powerful force in the commune. Leading the way was the Merchants' Guild, organized as early as 1192. The richest merchant families lent money (charging interest on their loans, despite a papal ban on the practice) and dealt in wax, pepper, and spices, as well as Flemish cloth, shoes, stockings, and belts. Other guilds, such as masons, carpenters, innkeepers,

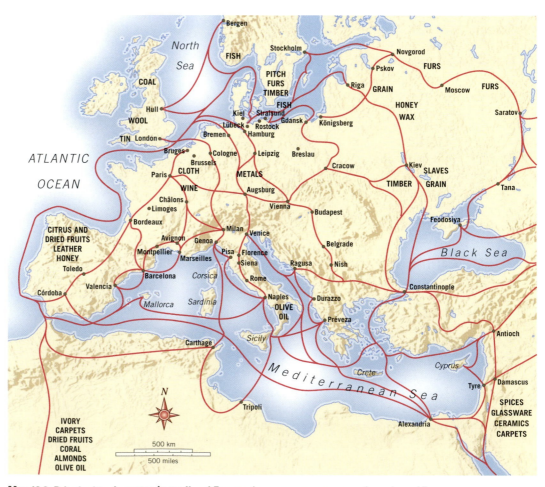

Map 13.2 Principal trade routes in medieval Europe. As commerce grew among the regions of Europe, the cities on this map grew proportionately.

barbers, butchers, and millers, quickly established themselves, but none was as powerful as the Merchants' Guild. By 1280, its members controlled city government, excluding the nobility and declaring that only "good popular merchants" should be eligible to serve on the city council.

Other guilds resented the merchants' control over the city's government, and in 1355, the people gathered in the Campo before the Palazzo Pubblico and forced their resignation. From then on, anyone belonging to a guild was technically eligible to serve on the council, except merchants and nobles. The exercise of power being what it is, however, control soon fell to the next great guilds below the merchants, the shopkeepers and notaries. By 1368, vying factions caused the disintegration of the government, as four revolutions rocked the city in as many months. The commune was a thing of the past.

Florence: Archrival of Siena

Like Siena, Florence was extremely wealthy, and that wealth was based on trade. By the twelfth century, Florence was the center of textile production in the Western world and played a central role in European trade markets (Map 13.2). The Arno River provided ample water for washing and rinsing sorted wool and finished cloth. The city's dyeing techniques were unsurpassed—to this day, the formulas for the highly prized Florentine reds remain a mystery. Dyestuffs were imported from throughout the Mediterranean and even the Orient, and each year, Florentine merchants traveled to England, Portugal, Spain, and Flanders to purchase raw wool for their manufactories.

As in Siena, it was the city's bankers and money lenders who made Florence a vital player in world trade. Florentine bankers invented checks, credit, even life insurance. Most importantly, in 1252, they introduced Europe's first single currency, the gold *florin*. By 1422, over 2 million florins were in circulation throughout Europe. This was a staggering number considering that a family could live comfortably on about 150 florins a year, and the finest palace cost about 1,000 florins. Florence was Europe's bank, and its bankers were Europe's true nobility.

The Guilds and Florentine Politics Only two other cities in all of Italy—Lucca and Venice—could boast that they were republics like Siena and Florence, and governing a republic was no easy task. As in Siena, in Florence the guilds controlled the commune. By the end of the twelfth century, there were 7 major guilds and 14 minor ones. The most prestigious was the Lawyers' Guild (the Arte dei Giudici), followed closely by the Wool Guild (the Arte della Lana) (Fig. 13.4), the Silk Guild (the Arte di Seta), and the Cloth Merchants' Guild (the Arte di Calimala). Also among the major guilds were the bankers, the doctors, and other merchant classes. Butchers, bakers, carpenters, and masons composed the bulk of the minor guilds.

As in Siena, the merchants, especially the Arte della Lana, controlled the government. They were known as the *Popolo Grasso* (literally, "the fat people"), as opposed

to *Popolo Minuto*, the ordinary workers, who comprised probably 75 percent of the population and had no voice in government. Only guild members could serve in the government. Their names were written down, the writing was placed in leather bags (*borse*) in the Church of Santa Croce (see Chapter 12), and nine names were drawn every two months in a public ceremony. (The period of service was short to reduce the chance of corruption.) Those *signori* selected were known as the *Priori*, and their government was known as the *Signoria*—hence the name of the Piazza della Signoria, the plaza in front of the Palazzo Vecchio. Of the nine Priori—six came from the major guilds, two from the minor guilds, and there was one standard-bearer.

The Florentine republic might have resembled a true democracy except for two details: First, the guilds were very close-knit so that, in general, selecting one or the other of their membership made little or no political difference; and second, the available names in the *borse* could be easily manipulated. However, conflict inevitably arose, and throughout the thirteenth century, other tensions made the problem worse, especially feuds between the Guelphs and Ghibellines. In Florence, the Guelphs were generally merchants and the Ghibellines were nobility. Thus, the

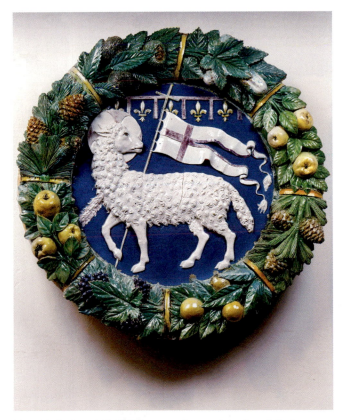

Fig. 13.4 Andrea della Robbia, coat of arms of the Arte della Lana (Wool Guild of Florence). 1487. Glazed terra cotta. Museo dell'Opera del Duomo, Florence. The guild chose for its coat of arms the Agnus Dei, the Lamb of God, carrying a banner inscribed with a red cross.

battle lines between the two were drawn in class terms, often resulting in family feuds and street violence. In fact, the tower of the Palazzo Vecchio was built on the site of a preexisting Ghibelline tower of the palace of the noble Uberti family, and the plaza in front was created by razing the remainder of the Uberti palace complex. Thus, both city hall and the public gathering place represented the triumph of Guelph over Ghibelline, the merchant class over the aristocracy.

PAINTING: A GROWING NATURALISM

What came to replace the Byzantine style of painting in Italy, and why?

Even though Saint John the Baptist was the patron saint of Florence, the city, like Siena, relied on the Virgin Mary to protect it. Her image appeared frequently in the mendicant churches and elsewhere, and these images were said to perform miracles. Pilgrims from Tuscany and beyond flocked to Florence to receive the Madonna's good graces. As in Siena, whenever the city was threatened—by war, by flood, by plague—the Madonna's image was carried through the city in ceremonial procession. The two cities put themselves under the protection of the Virgin, and it was not long before they were competing to prove who could paint her the most magnificently. In the process, they began to represent her less in the stiff, abstracted manner of the Byzantine icon and more as a real person of flesh and blood.

Duccio and Simone Martini

After the Venetian rout of Constantinople in the Fourth Crusade in 1204 (see Chapter 10), Byzantine imagery flooded Europe. One of the first artists to break from the Byzantine tradition was the Sienese native Duccio di Buoninsegna (active 1278–1318). In 1308, the commune commissioned Duccio to paint a *Maestà*, or *Virgin and Child in Majesty* (Fig. **13.5**), to be set under the dome of Siena's cathedral. The finished work was greeted with a great celebration. "On the day that it was carried to the [cathedral]," a contemporary chronicler reports

> the shops were shut, and the bishop conducted a great and devout company of priests and friars in solemn procession, accompanied by … all the officers of the commune, and all the people, and one after another the worthiest with lighted candles in their hands took places near the picture, and behind came the women and children with great devotion … making the procession around the Campo, as is the custom, all the bells ringing joyously, trumpets and bagpipes playing, out of reverence for so noble a picture as is this.

Duccio was well aware of the greatness of his achievement. Along the base of the Virgin's throne he wrote these words: "Holy Mother of God, give Siena peace and Duccio life because he painted Thee thus," announcing both the artist's piety and pride in his work and the growing prominence of artists in Italian society as a whole.

Duccio's *Maestà* begins to leave the conventions of the Byzantine icon behind and incorporates the Gothic tendency to naturalism. (Compare the Byzantine painting of

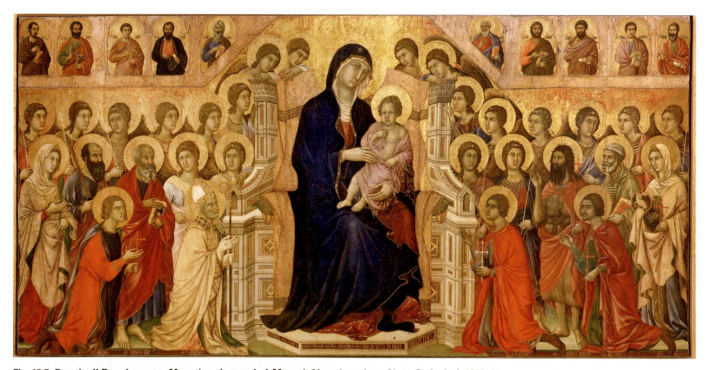

Fig. 13.5 Duccio di Buoninsegna, *Maestà*, main panel of *Maestà Altarpiece*, from Siena Cathedral. 1308–11.
Tempera and gold on wood, 7' × 13'6¼". Museo dell'Opera del Duomo, Siena. The Madonna's throne imitates the stone facade of Siena Cathedral.

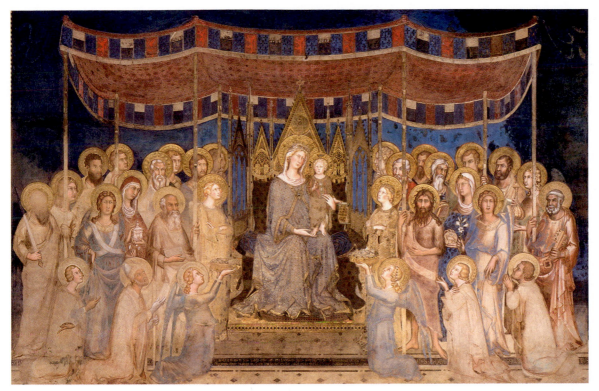

Fig. 13.6 Simone Martini, *Maestà*, Council Chamber, Palazzo Pubblico, Siena. ca. 1311–17, repaired 1321. Fresco, 25' × 31'9". Martini's fresco covers the end wall of the Council Chamber, symbolically submitting that civic body's deliberations to the Madonna's watchful gaze and care.

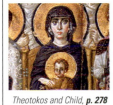

CONTINUITY & CHANGE

Theotokos and Child, p. 278

Mary from Saint Catherine's Monastery; see Fig. 8.31 in Chapter 8.) Duccio's Christ Child seems to be an actual baby, and a slightly chubby one at that. Similarly, beneath the Madonna's robes, we can sense a real body. Her knee especially asserts itself, and the drapery falling from it drops in long, gentle curves, much more natural-looking than the rigid, angular drapery of earlier, Byzantine works. Four angels peer over the top of the Madonna's throne, gazing on the child like proud relations. The saints who kneel in the front row appear to be individuals rather than types. Notice especially the aging and bearded cleric at the left. All are patron saints of the city, underscoring the fact that Duccio's painting is both an ecclesiastical and civic commission.

If Duccio's *Maestà* reflects the growing realism of Sienese art, the *Maestà* of Simone Martini, in the Hall of the Mappamondo, or Council Chamber, in Siena's Palazzo Pubblico, is even more naturalistic (Fig. **13.6**). Simone had worked on the cathedral *Maestà* as Duccio's apprentice from 1308 to 1311, and he probably modeled his own work on it. Situated in a public building, overlooking the workings of civic administration, Simone's painting announces, even more dramatically than Duccio's, the blending of the sacred and secular in Tuscan culture.

One of the great innovations of Simone's fresco is the Virgin's crown, which signifies her status as Queen of

Heaven. Surrounded by her celestial "court," she reveals the growing influence of French courtly poetry (see Chapter 10) in Italy. She becomes a model for human behavior, an emblem in the spiritual realm for the most noble types of secular love and devotion, including devotion to the right conduct of government. Highlighting the secular message, Jesus holds a parchment, adhered to the surface of the fresco, that reads, "Love Justice you who judge the earth." Like Duccio's painting, Simone's fresco carries a propagandistic message to the city fathers. As we have seen (see page 438), inscribed at the base of the throne are these words: "The angelic little flowers, roses and lilies, Which adorn the heavenly meadow, do not please me more than good counsel." The painting suggests that the Virgin is as interested in worldly affairs as divine ones. Because of the realistic way Simone has represented her, she is as human as she is divine.

Stylistic differences separate the two works as well. As in the Byzantine icon from which she derives (see Fig. 8.31 in Chapter 8), Duccio's Madonna wears no crown, her brows turn without interruption down into the length of her nose, she is draped in blue, with an orange undergarment, and her rounded hood echoes the halo behind her head. She is much larger than those attending her, conforming to the hierarchies of Byzantine art. In Simone's version of the theme, the Virgin and surrounding figures are depicted almost on the same scale. As opposed to Duccio's painting, with its stacked receding space, Simone's Virgin sits in a deep space of the canopy with its delicate Gothic arches behind the throne. Both of the Virgin's knees are visible, with the Christ Child standing firmly on one of them. Her head and neck, rather than being shrouded behind an all-embracing hood, are rounded and full beneath the crown and its softly folded train, which is itself fully rounded in shadow behind her neck. Her robe, neglecting convention, is composed of rich, transparent silks, beneath which we can see her right arm. Above all, her porcelain-white skin, tinged with pink, gives her complexion a realistic tone. Blood flows through her body, rouging her cheeks, and her flesh breathes with life. She embodies, in fact, a standard of beauty absent in Western art since Classical times—the physical beauty of the flesh as opposed to the divine beauty of the spirit. In less formal pictures, Duccio, too, used a naturalistic style.

Cimabue and Giotto

Florence, too, had its master painters of the Virgin. At about the same time that Duccio was first becoming active in Siena, a painter known as Cimabue was painting a large-scale Virgin for the altarpiece of the Church of Santa Trinità in Florence (Fig. 13.7). Cimabue's *Madonna Enthroned with Angels and Prophets* solidified his position as the leading painter in Florence. Although its Byzantine roots are clear—following closely, for instance, a Byzantine hierarchy of figures, with the Madonna larger than the figures that surround her—the painting is remarkable on several fronts. First, it is enormous. Standing over 12 feet high, it seems to have begun a tradition of large-scale altarpieces, helping to affirm the altar as the focal point of the church. But most important are Cimabue's concern for spatial volume and his treatment of human figures with naturalistic expressions. The throne is especially interesting, creating as it does a spatial setting for the scene, and the angels seem to be standing on the architectural frame; the front two clearly are. If the Virgin and Child are stock Byzantine figures, the four prophets at the base of the throne are surprisingly individualized, suggesting the increasing prominence of the individual personality in the era, an especially important characteristic, as we will see

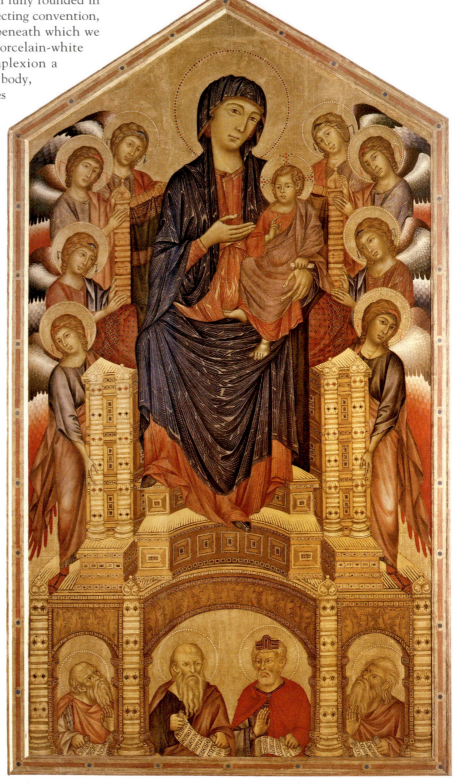

Fig. 13.7 Cimabue, *Madonna Enthroned with Angels and Prophets,* from the high altar of Santa Trinità, Florence. ca. 1285. Tempera and gold on wood, 11'7½" × 7'4". Galleria degli Uffizi, Florence. The later Renaissance historian Giorgio Vasari would claim that Cimabue had been apprenticed to a Greek painter from whom he learned the fundamentals of Byzantine icon painting.

later in the chapter, of the literature of the period. These remarkably individual likenesses also tell us that Italian artists were becoming more skillful in painting with **tempera**, which allowed them to portray the world in ever-increasing detail (see *Materials & Techniques*, page 446). Perhaps most interesting of all is the position of the Virgin's feet, the right one propped upon the throne in an almost casual position.

According to an old story, one day Cimabue discovered a talented shepherd boy by the name of Giotto di Bondone and tutored him in the art of painting. The pupil soon surpassed the teacher. The sixteenth-century historian Giorgio Vasari would later say that Giotto set "art upon the path that may be called the true one, learned to draw accurately from life and thus put an end to the crude Greek [i.e., Byzantine] manner."

Giotto's 1310 *Madonna Enthroned with Saints and Angels* (Fig. **13.8**), painted just a quarter-century after Cimabue's, is as remarkable a shift toward naturalism as Simone's *Maestà* is over Duccio's. While it retains a Byzantine hierarchy of figures—the Christ Child is almost as big as the angels and the Virgin three or four times their size—it is spatially convincing in a way that Cimabue's painting is not. Giotto apparently learned to draw accurately from life, and his figures reveal his skill. Light plays across their forms—note the folds and pleats of the angels' gowns in the foreground—and substantial bodies seem to press outward from beneath the material. Unlike the paintings in the Upper Church of San Francesco in Assisi (see Fig. 12.30 in Chapter 12), often attributed to him, Giotto's colors gradually and continuously blend from light to dark

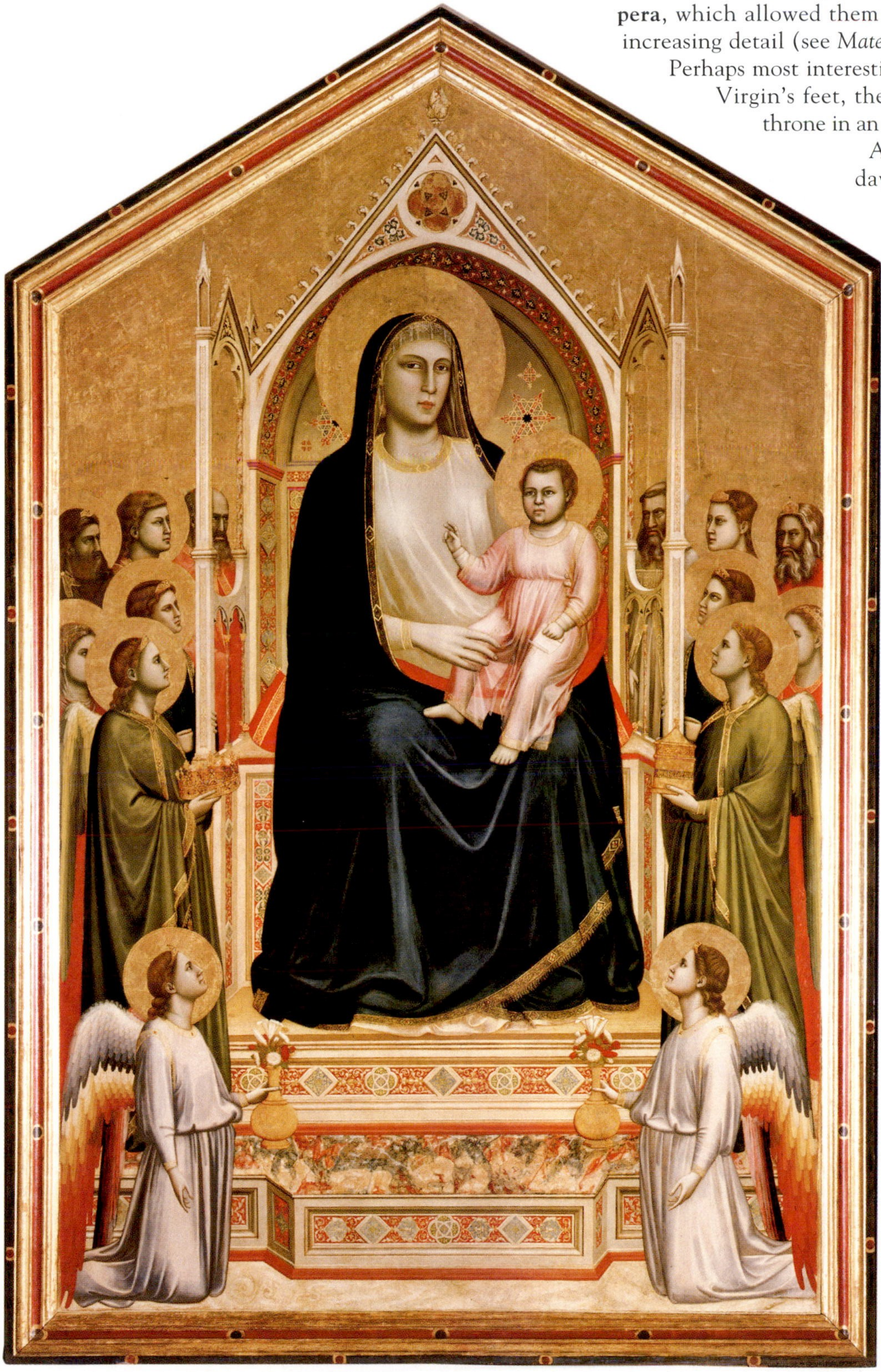

Fig. 13.8 Giotto di Bondone, *Madonna Enthroned with Saints and Angels*, from the Church of the Ognissanti, Florence. ca. 1310. Tempera and gold on wood, 10'8" × 6'8¼". Galleria degli Uffizi, Florence. Giotto's contemporary, the writer Boccaccio, discussed later in this chapter, said that he "brought back to light that art which had for many ages lain buried beneath the blunders of those who painted rather to delight the eyes of the ignorant than to satisfy the intelligence of the wise."

G iotto's greatest paintings are surely those in the Scrovegni Chapel in Padua, painted around 1305. (The chapel is also known as the Arena Chapel, after the ancient Roman arena in which it is situated.) Giotto covered virtually every space of the barrel-vaulted family chapel of the Scrovegni family with *buon fresco* (see *Materials & Techniques*, page 447), the technique of painting on wet plaster. The top of the vault is a starry blue sky, painted with lapis lazuli. Lapis lazuli does not properly combine with wet plaster, so it was applied on a dry wall. As a result, the blues of the ceiling and other blues in the frescoes have faded far more than the other colors, most of which still look fresh. On the side walls are scenes from the life of the Virgin and the life of Christ.

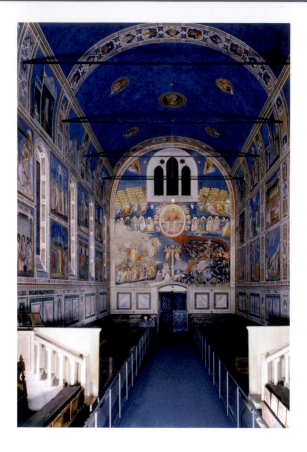

The Scrovegni Chapel, Padua. The Life of Christ and the Virgin frescoes by Giotto. 1305–06. In the bottom layer of images, closest to the floor, figures of the Virtues and Vices appear as painted, black-and-white simulations of sculpture, a technique known as *grisaille*. On the back wall above the door is a Last Judgment, figured as the final episode in the life of Christ.

Even the angels are wracked with grief.

The blue void at the center of the painting is a metaphor for the emptiness felt by the mourners.

The direction of the Virgin Mary's grief-stricken gaze continues down the diagonal line created by the barren ridge, reinforcing its emptiness.

Giotto was the first artist since antiquity to depict figures from behind, contributing to the sense that we are viewing a real drama.

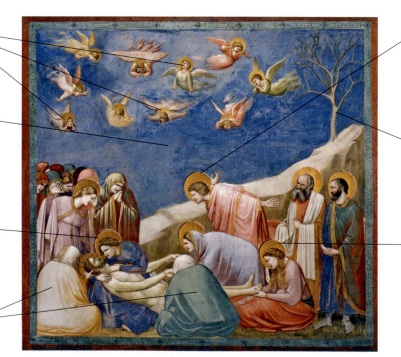

John the Evangelist flings his arms back in a gesture that echoes that of the angels, almost as if his arms were wings.

The single leafless tree is a traditional symbol of death. It sits on a barren ridge that plunges in a stark diagonal toward the dead Christ.

Mary Magdalene, recognizable by her long hair, is traditionally represented at the Crucifixion kissing Christ's feet. Here, the Crucifixion over, she holds his feet in her hands, in an act of consummate tenderness and affection.

Giotto, *The Lamentation*, Scrovegni Chapel, Padua. 1305–06. Fresco, 78½" × 73". Among the most moving scenes in the chapel is Giotto's depiction of human suffering. The painter focused on the real pain felt by Jesus' followers upon his death, rather than the promise of salvation that it symbolized.

Giotto's Scrovegni Chapel

Halley's Comet made one of its regular appearances in 1301, just a few years before this painting was made. (It was also depicted in the *Bayeux Tapestry* of 1066; see Chapter 10, *Closer Look*, page 341.) Giotto apparently modeled the star that guides the Magi on that phenomenon.

The boy looks up at the Magi's camels in astonishment. This expression of emotion is typical of Giotto's frescos. Giotto had probably never seen a camel: These have blue eyes and cows' feet.

Note Giotto's attempt to render the wooden shed in perspective. If he does not quite "get it," he is coming close.

Giotto has abandoned the Byzantine hierarchy of figures. The angels, the Magi, the Virgin, and the Child are all drawn to the same scale. (For a comparison, see Duccio's *Maestà Altarpiece*, Fig. 13.5.)

The king, Caspar, has removed his crown and placed it at the foot of the angel receiving gifts. The gesture signifies his understanding that Christ is the "King of Kings."

The blue of Mary's skirt has almost completely flaked off. Lapis lazuli, the stone used to make blue pigment, does not combine with wet plaster, so the blue had to be painted on after the plaster had dried, leaving it far more susceptible to heat and humidity, which eventually cause flaking.

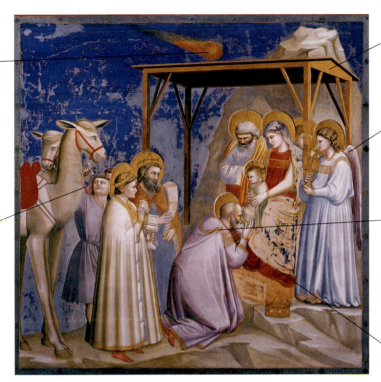

Giotto, *The Adoration of the Magi*, Scrovegni Chapel, Padua. 1305–06. Fresco, 78½" × 73". Boccaccio, author of the extraordinarily realistic story-cycle the *Decameron*, admired Giotto's painterly realism: "There is nothing in the whole creation he cannot depict," Boccaccio wrote.

Above the door is a depiction of the Last Judgment, in which the patron, Enrico Scrovegni, offers a model of the chapel to the Virgin. The purpose of the chapel seems clear: It was meant as penance on Enrico's part for his own and his father's sins—notably their flagrant usury.

The paintings depicting the life of Christ and the Virgin deliberately abandon the balance and symmetry that distinguish Byzantine painting (and, for that matter, the *Maestàs* of the period) in order to create a heightened sense of reality. In *The Lamentation*, for instance, Giotto places Christ in the lower left-hand corner of the work, at the bottom of a stark diagonal. Throughout the cycle, the action takes place on a narrow platform at the front of the painting. The architecture in the paintings is small in comparison to the figures, as in *The Adoration of the Magi*. Giotto may have been influenced by the stage sets made for the contemporary revival in Padua of Roman theater. Whatever the case, the drama of Giotto's paintings is undeniable. They possess a psychological intensity and emotional immediacy that involve the viewer directly in the scene.

Something to Think About …

If Giotto's paintings do, in fact, possess an intensity and immediacy that serve to involve the viewer directly in the scene, how might his paintings be compared to the role of music in the liturgy?

View the Closer Look for the Scrovegni (Arena) Chapel on **MyArtsLab** around the contours of his figures and their draperies, re-creating the realistic appearance of shadows.

Giotto was also a master of the human face, capable of revealing a wide range of emotion and character. The total effect is to humanize Christ, the Virgin, and the saints, to portray them as real people. This skill is particularly evident in the frescoes of the Scrovegni Chapel (see *Closer Look*, pages 444–445). The paintings in the chapel were done in **buon fresco**. In this technique, the artist applies pigments onto wet rather than dry plaster. (See *Materials & Techniques*, page 447.) Giotto's contemporaries were profoundly moved by the newfound realism of his work. In fact, the poet Dante Alighieri, whose *Divine Comedy* we will discuss in the next section of this chapter, would write in that poem: "Cimabue thought to hold the field in painting, but now Giotto has the cry, so that the other's fame, grown dim, must yield."

DANTE AND THE RISE OF VERNACULAR LITERATURE IN EUROPE

What are the distinguishing characteristics of Dante's Divine Comedy*?*

Until the early twelfth century, the language of almost all educated circles in Europe, and certainly in literature, was Latin. Gradually, however, writers began to address their works to a wider lay audience and to write in the **vernacular**, the language spoken in the streets. The French led the way, in twelfth-century works such as the *Song of Roland* (see Chapter 10) and Chrétien de Troyes's *Lancelot* (see Chapter 10), but early in the fourteenth century, vernacular works began to appear throughout Italy as well, spreading to the rest of Europe.

Dante's *Divine Comedy*

One of the greatest medieval Italian writers working in the vernacular was the poet Dante Alighieri (1265–1321). In Florence, in about 1308, he began one of the greatest works of the literary imagination, the *Divine Comedy* (Fig. **13.9**). This poem records the travels of the Christian soul from

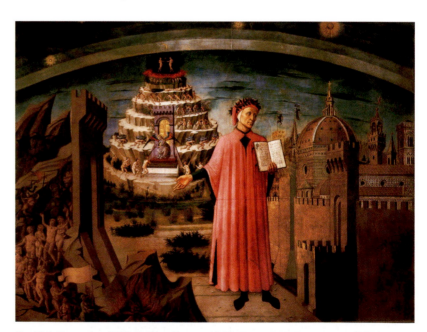

Fig. 13.9 Domenico di Michelino, *Dante and His Poem*. 1465. Fresco, 10'6" × 9'7". Florence Cathedral, Italy. To Dante's right is the Inferno, and behind him the seven-stepped hill of Purgatory. To his left is Paradise, imaged as Florence Cathedral, here topped by Brunelleschi's dome (discussed in Chapter 14). Dante himself would never live to see or even imagine the dome.

Hell to Purgatory and finally to Salvation in three books—the *Inferno*, *Purgatorio*, and *Paradiso*. It is by no means an easy journey. Dante, who is the leading character in his own poem, is led by the Roman poet Virgil, author of the *Aeneid* (see Chapter 6). (Virgil, too, visits the underworld in the sixth book of his poem.)

Virgil cannot lead Dante into Heaven in the *Paradiso*, since he is a pagan who is barred from salvation. He is thus condemned to Limbo, the first level of Hell, a place of sorrow without torment, populated by virtuous pagans, the great philosophers and authors, unbaptized children, and others unfit to enter the kingdom of heaven. Among those who inhabit the realm with Virgil are Caesar, Homer, Socrates, and Aristotle. There is no punishment here, and the atmosphere is peaceful, yet sad. Virgil is, in fact, the model of human rationality, and in the *Inferno*, he and Dante study the varieties of human sin. Many of the characters who inhabit Dante's Hell are his contemporaries—the lovers Paolo and Francesca from Ravenna and Rimini, the usurer Reginaldo Scrovegni (father of the patron of the chapel painted by Giotto; see *Closer Look*, pages 444–445), and so on. Dante also makes much of the Guelph/Ghibelline rivalries in his native Florence. He was himself a Guelph, but so divided were the Guelphs among themselves—into factions called the Blacks and the Whites, papal versus imperial bankers—that his efforts to heal their schism as one of the Priori, one of the nine leaders of the Florentine commune, resulted in a two-year exile beginning in 1302. Embittered, he never returned to Florence.

Dante's Inferno is composed of nine descending rings of sinners undergoing punishment, each more gruesome than the one before it (Fig. **13.10**). In the poem's first canto, the poet is lost in a Dark Wood of Error, where Virgil comes to his rescue, promising to lead him "forth to an eternal place" (see **Reading 13.1**, pages 460–461). In Hell, the two first encounter sinners whose passion has condemned

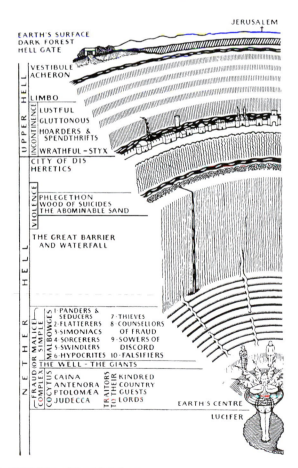

Fig. 13.10 Plan of Dante's Inferno.

them to Hell—Paolo and Francesca, whose illicit love was motivated, they tell Dante, by reading Chrétien de Troyes's *Lancelot*. The lovers are forever condemned to unreconciled love, to touch each other but never consummate their feelings. In the next ring are the gluttonous, condemned to wallow like pigs in their own excrement. Sinners, in other words, are punished not *for* their sins but *by* their sins. Dante finds intellectual dishonesty more sinful than any sin of passion, and thus flatterers, hypocrites, and liars occupy the next lower rings of Hell. The violent are farther down, immersed for eternity in boiling blood. And finally, at the very bottom of the pit, imprisoned in ice "like straws in glass," are the traitors. Among the lowest of the low are Guelphs and Ghibellines from all over Tuscany who betrayed their cities' well-being. Finally, in Canto 34, Dante once again integrates the pagan and Christian worlds as Satan himself chews on the worst of all traitors—Judas (thought to have betrayed Jesus) and Brutus and Cassius (assassins of Julius Caesar) (**Reading 13.2**):

READING 13.2

from Dante, *Inferno*, Canto 34

... With what a sense of awe I saw his head
towering above me! for it had three faces:[1]
one was in front, and it was fiery red;

the other two, as weirdly wonderful,
merged with it from the middle of each shoulder
to the point where all converged at the top of the skull;

the right was something between white and bile;
the left was about the color one observes
on those who live along the banks of the Nile.

Under each head two wings rose terribly,
their span proportioned to so gross a bird:
I never saw such sails upon the sea.

They were not feathers—their texture and their form
were like a bat's wings—and he beat them so
that three winds blew from him in one great storm:

it is these winds that freeze all Cocytus.
He wept from his six eyes, and down three chins
the tears ran mixed with bloody froth and pus.[2]

In every mouth he worked a broken sinner
between his rake-like teeth. Thus he kept three
in eternal pain at his eternal dinner.

For the one in front the biting seemed to play
no part at all compared to the ripping: at times
the whole skin of his back was flayed away.

"That soul that suffers most," explained my Guide,
"is Judas[3] Iscariot, he who kicks his legs
on the fiery chin and has his head inside.

[1] **three faces:** numerous interpretations of these three faces exist. What is essential to all explanation is that they be seen as perversions of the qualities of the Trinity.
[2] **bloody froth and pus:** the gore of the sinners he chews which is mixed with his slaver (saliva).
[3] **Judas:** note how closely his punishment is patterned on that of the Simoniacs (Canto 19).

Of the other two, who have their heads thrust forward,
the one who dangles down from the black face
is Brutus: note how he writhes without a word.

And there, with the huge and sinewy arms,[4] is the soul
of Cassius. But the night is coming on
and we must go, for we have seen the whole." ...

[4] **huge and sinewy arms:** The Cassius who betrayed Caesar was more generally described in terms of Shakespeare's "lean and hungry look." Another Cassius is described by Cicero (*Catiline III*) as huge and sinewy. Dante probably confused the two.

The rhyme scheme of the *Divine Comedy* is **terza rima**—an interlocking three-line pattern invented by Dante that goes a/b/a, b/c/b, c/d/c, and so on. (The translator here has chosen to sacrifice the melodic harmonies of Dante's original in the interest of readability and accuracy and has foregone the interlocking rhyme, rhyming only the first and third lines of each stanza.) Just as Satan has three heads, just as there are three consummate sinners in his jaws, the three-line stanza is part of a numerological pattern in the poem. Each of the three books is composed of 33 cantos, to which Dante has added an introductory canto, for a total of 100—a number signifying perfection. There are nine circles of Hell (three squared), nine circles of penitents in Purgatory, and nine spheres of Heaven.

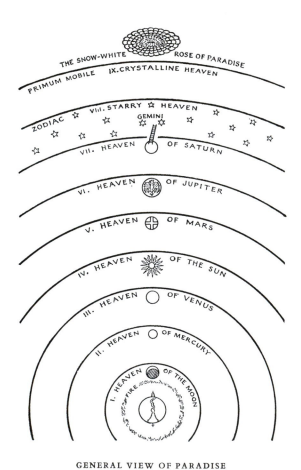

GENERAL VIEW OF PARADISE

Fig. 13.11 Plan of Dante's Paradise.

In the universe of the *Divine Comedy* (Fig. **13.11**), Virgil, as the embodiment of rationality, can take Dante no further than Hell and Purgatory, since in order to enter Paradise, faith must triumph over reason, something impossible for the pagan Roman. Dante's guide through Paradise is Beatrice, the love of his life. Beatrice was the daughter of the Florentine nobleman Folco Portinari, and Dante first saw her when she was 9 years old and he was 8. He describes meeting her in his first major work, *La Vita Nuova*: "love ruled my soul … and began to hold such sway over me … that it was necessary for me to do completely all his pleasure. He commanded me often that I should endeavor to see this youthful angel, and I saw her in such noble and praiseworthy deportment that truly of her might be said these words of the poet Homer—*She appeared to be born not of mortal man but of God.*"

Dante wrote these words in 1293. Ten years earlier, when she was 18, Beatrice had entered into a marriage, arranged when she was eight, with Simone di Bardi. It lasted only seven years, ending in her death at age 25. Dante's love for her was, then, the classic love of the courtier for his lady, marked by an unconsummated physical desire necessarily transformed into a spiritual longing, a longing he finally imagines, at the end of the *Paradiso*, as a perfect circle (**Reading 13.3**):

READING 13.3

from Dante, *Paradiso*, Canto 33

But oh how much my words miss my conception,
  which is itself so far from what I saw
  that to call it feeble would be rank deception!

O Light Eternal fixed in Itself alone,
  by Itself alone understood, which from Itself
  loves and glows, self-knowing and self-known;

that second aureole which shone forth in Thee,
  conceived as a reflection of the first—
  or which appeared so to my scrutiny—

seemed in Itself of Its own coloration
  to be painted with man's image. I fixed my eyes
  on that alone in rapturous contemplation.

Like a geometer wholly dedicated
  to squaring the circle, but who cannot find,
  think as he may, the principle indicated—

so did I study the supernal face.
  I yearned to know just how our image merges
  into that circle, and how it there finds place;

but mine were not the wings for such a flight.
  Yet, as I wished, the truth I wished for came
  cleaving my mind in a great flash of light.

Here my powers rest from their high fantasy,
  but already I could feel my being turned—
  instinct and intellect balanced equally

as in a wheel whose motion nothing jars—
  by the Love that moves the Sun and the other stars.

Dante's physical desire has been transformed into a spiritual longing that has led him to a comprehension of God's love. So ends the *Divine Comedy*, in a vision of humankind woven into the very substance and coloration of God, a vision so powerful that Dante can barely find words to express it.

THE BLACK DEATH AND ITS LITERARY AFTERMATH

How did the vernacular style continue to develop after the Black Death?

In 1316 and 1317, not long before Dante's death, crop failures across Europe resulted in the greatest famine the continent had ever known. For two summers, the sun rarely shone (no one knew that huge volcanic eruptions thousands of miles away in Indonesia had sent vast clouds of ash into the atmosphere). Furthermore, between 1000 and 1300, the continent's population had doubled to a point where it probably exceeded its ability to feed itself even in the best of times. In these dark years, which were followed by a century-long cooling period marked by too much rain to allow for good grain harvests, common people were lucky to eat, let alone eat well. Then, in December 1347, rats infested with fleas carrying bubonic plague arrived on the island of Sicily. They were carried on four Genoese ships that had set sail from Kaffa, a Genoese trading center on the Black Sea.

Since 1346, Kaffa had been under siege by Huns intent on taking control of east–west trade routes. But the Huns had fallen victim to the plague themselves, infected by traders from China, where beginning in 1334 as many as 5 million people had died. The Hun siege collapsed under the plague's scourge, but the Huns catapulted the diseased corpses of their dead into Kaffa. The four Genoese ships escaped, believing they were free of infection. Unfortunately, this was not true, and soon after the ships arrived in Sicily, the contagion spread through the port cities of Venice, Genoa, and Pisa. An already severely weakened population was almost pitifully vulnerable. Within months, the disease spread northward, through the ports of Venice, Genoa, and Pisa, across Italy, southern France, and eastern Spain.

The disease began in the lymph glands of the groin or armpits, which slowly filled with pus and turned black. The inflammations were called *buboes*—hence the name *bubonic plague*—and their black color lent the plague its other name, the *Black Death*. Since it was carried by rodents, which were commonplace even in wealthy homes, hardly anyone was spared. It was an egalitarian disease—archbishops, dukes, lords of the manor, merchants, laborers, and peasants fell equally before it. For those who survived the pandemic, life seemed little more than an ongoing burial service. In many towns, traditional funeral services were abandoned, and the dead were buried in mass graves. By 1350, all of Europe, with the exception of a few territories far from traditional trade routes, was devastated by the

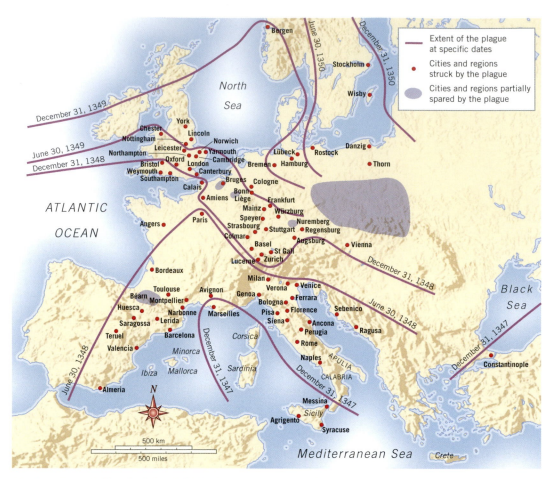

Map 13.3 **Spread of the Black Death. 1347–50.** Between 1347 and 1350, 30 to 50 percent of Europe's population—about 25 million people—died of the bubonic plague.

disease (Map **13.3**). In Tuscany, the death rate in the cities was near 60 percent. In Florence, on June 24, 1348, the feast day of the city's patron saint, John the Baptist, 1,800 people reportedly died, and another 1,800 the next day—about 4 percent of the city's population in the space of two days. Severe outbreaks of the plague erupted again in 1363, 1388–90, and 1400.

The impact of the Black Death on the popular imagination cannot be overstated. Among the most extreme reactions was that of the **flagellants**, penitents who marched from town to town beating themselves, in the belief that such behavior might atone for the human sins they were sure had caused the plague. But the social disruption that the flagellants created paled beside the outbreak of violent anti-Semitism across Europe. On October 30, 1348, officials at the village of Chatel, in the French Alps near Geneva, arrested and tortured a Jew named Agimet, forcing a false confession that he had been sent by the local rabbi to poison the drinking water of Venice, Calabria, Apulia, and Toulouse. Soon, in Spain, France, and particularly Switzerland and Germany, the citizenry began to murder their Jewish neighbors. In early January 1349, in Basel, a number of Jews were burned. A few weeks later, on Saint Valentine's Day, in Strasbourg, 900 of the town's 1,884 Jews were burned,

the rest banned from the city. In Speyer, Augsburg, Stuttgart, Regensburg, Bonn, Mainz, and town after town, the persecutions continued. In July, in Frankfurt, the Jews set their own houses on fire when they were attacked, causing much of the city to burn. The need to find a scapegoat for the plague spurred on the general population, but it seems likely that officials and city leaders, well aware that the Jews were being blamed for something they had nothing to do with, allowed these **pogroms** (massacres of Jews) to occur as a way to eliminate their own personal debts and capture Jewish wealth for themselves, much as Count Emicho of Leiningen had done during the First Crusade (see Chapter 10).

More subtle than this wave of violence were the lasting psychological effects of the epidemic, including the doubt cast upon the Church's belief in divine justice. Even more pronounced was a growing social obsession with death. A good example is a Book of Hours commissioned by Bonne of Luxembourg, wife of the dauphin of France, from her court illuminator, Jean Le Noir, at some point probably not long before her own death from the plague in 1348 (Fig. **13.12**). On the left page, three horsemen contemplate three cadavers in increasing states of decay on the right page. One horseman brings a handkerchief to his nose to fight off the stench. The cadavers address the horsemen: "What

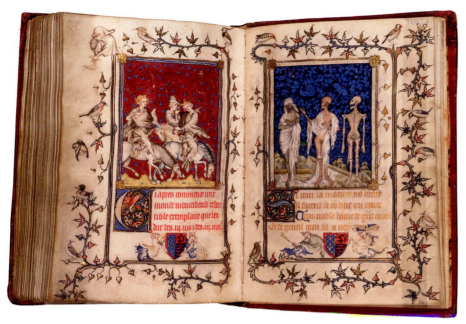

Fig. 13.12 Jean Le Noir, pages with *The Three Living* (left) and *The Three Dead* (right), from the *Psalter and Book of Hours of Bonne of Luxembourg*. Before 1349. Grisaille, color, gilt, and brown ink on vellum, 5" × 3½". The Metropolitan Museum of Art, New York. The Cloisters Collection, 1969 (69.86). Note the naturalism of the birds that decorate the margins of the manuscript.

you are we were and what we are you will be!" The artist's depiction of the human body in decay is astonishingly realistic—especially in light of the Church ban on performing autopsies. It is as if, in making us confront death, the artist is determined to bring us face to face with the ultimate truth of things.

Literature after the Black Death: Boccaccio's *Decameron*

The frank treatment of reality found in the visual arts carried over into literature, where the direct language of the vernacular proved an especially appropriate vehicle for rendering truth. The *Decameron*, or "Work of Ten Days," is a collection of framed prose tales in the manner of *The Thousand and One Nights* and Nezami's *Haft Paykar* (see Chapter 9). The Florentine writer Giovanni Boccaccio (1313–75), who lived through the plague, sets the stage for the 100 prose stories of the collection with a startlingly direct description of Florence in the ravages of the disease (**Reading 13.4**):

READING 13.4

from Boccaccio, *Decameron*

The virulence of the plague was all the greater in that it was communicated by the sick to the well by contact, not unlike fire when dry or fatty things are brought near it. But the evil was still worse. Not only did conversation and familiarity with the diseased spread the malady and even cause death,

but the mere touch of the clothes or any other object the sick had touched or used, seemed to spread the pestilence. ...

Because of such happenings and many others of a like sort, various fears and superstitions arose among the survivors, almost all of which tended toward one end—to flee from the sick and whatever had belonged to them. In this way each man thought to be safeguarding his own health. Some among them were of the opinion that by living temperately and guarding against excess of all kinds, they could do much toward avoiding the danger; and forming a band they lived away from the rest of the world. Gathering in those houses where no one had been ill and living was more comfortable, they shut themselves in. They ate moderately of the best that could be had and drank excellent wines, avoiding all luxuriousness. With music and whatever other delights they could have, they lived together in this fashion, allowing no one to speak to them and avoiding news either of death or sickness from the outer world.

Others, arriving at a contrary conclusion, held that plenty of drinking and enjoyment, singing and free living and the gratification of the appetite in every possible way, letting the devil take the hindmost, was the best preventative of such a malady; and as far as they could, they suited the action to the word. Day and night they went from one tavern to another drinking and carousing unrestrainedly. ...

Meanwhile, in the midst of the affliction and misery that had befallen the city, even the reverend authority of divine and human law had almost crumbled and fallen into decay, for its ministers and executors, like other men, had either died or sickened, or had been left so entirely without assistants that they were unable to attend to their duties. As a result everyone had leave to do as he saw fit. ...

It used to be common, as it is still, for women, friends and neighbors of a dead man, to gather in his house and mourn there with his people. ... Now, as the plague gained in violence, these customs were either modified or laid aside altogether. ... It was a rare occasion for a corpse to be followed to church by more than ten or twelve mourners— not the usual respectable citizens, but a class of vulgar grave-diggers who called themselves "sextons" and did these services for a price. ...

More wretched still were the circumstances of the common people and, for a great part, of the middle class, for, confined to their homes either by hope of safety or by poverty, and restricted to their own sections, they fell sick daily by thousands. There, devoid of help or care, they died almost without redemption. A great many breathed their last in the public streets, day and night; a large number perished in their homes, and it was only by the stench of their decaying bodies that they proclaimed their death to their neighbors. Everywhere the city was teeming with corpses. A general course was now adopted by the people, more out of fear of contagion than of any charity they felt toward the dead. Alone, or with the assistance of whatever bearers they could muster, they would drag the corpses out of their homes and pile them in front of the doors, where often, of a morning, countless bodies might be seen. Biers were sent for. When none was to be had, the dead were laid upon ordinary boards, two or three at once. It was not infrequent to see a single bier carrying husband and wife, two or three brothers, father and son, and others besides. ...

So many bodies were brought to the churches every day that the consecrated ground did not suffice to hold them, particularly according to the ancient custom of giving each corpse its individual place. Huge trenches were dug in the crowded churchyards and the new dead were piled in them, layer upon layer, like merchandise in the hold of a ship. ....

Boccaccio describes a world in virtual collapse. The social breakdown caused by the plague is especially evident in the widespread death of the ruling class and the rise of the class of men who called themselves "sextons," technically guardians of the church edifice, treasures, and vestments, but now a vile band of mercenary gravediggers. All tradition has been abandoned.

Nevertheless, a good deal of the power of Boccaccio's book is that in this atmosphere of dark matter-of-factness, he inaugurates something entirely different, suggesting that society might be ready to be reborn:

[O]n a Tuesday morning after Divine Service the venerable church of Santa Maria Novella [see Fig. 12.29 in Chapter 12] was almost deserted save for the presence of seven young ladies habited sadly[1] in keeping with the season. All were connected either by blood or at least as friends or neighbors; and fair and of good understanding were they all, as also of noble birth, gentle manners, and a modest sprightliness. In age none exceeded twenty-eight, or fell short of eighteen years. ...

One of the citizens, Pampinea, observing the dire nature of their plight, makes this suggestion:

I should deem it most wise in us, our case being what it is, if, as many others have done before us, and are still doing, we were to quit this place, and, shunning like death the evil example of others, betake ourselves to the country, and there live as honorable women on one of the estates, of which none of us has any lack, with all cheer of festal gathering and other delights, so long as in no particular we overstep the bounds of reason. There we shall hear the chant of birds, have sight of verdant hills and plains, of cornfields undulating like the sea, of trees of a thousand sorts; there also we shall have a larger view of the heavens, which, however harsh toward us, yet deny not their eternal beauty; things far fairer for eyes to rest on than the desolate walls of our city. Moreover, we shall there breathe a fresher air, find ampler store of things meet [fitting] for such as live in these times, have fewer causes of annoy[ance].

Three young men, all of whom the women know, happen to enter the church, and it is determined that they should be invited to join them, even though, as one of the young women mentions, it is well known "that they love some of us here ... [and] if we take them with us, we may thereby give occasion for scandal and censure. ..."

[1] **habited sadly:** dressed in mourning.

Thus, the entire enterprise takes place in an atmosphere of potential scandal—certainly an atmosphere outside the bounds of normal social behavior. They enter a new moral space, evidenced by the difference between the Florence they have left behind and their new surroundings:

The estate lay upon a little hill some distance from the nearest highway, and, embowered in shrubberies of divers hues, and other greenery, afforded the eye a pleasant prospect. On the summit of the hill was a palace with galleries, halls and chambers, disposed around a fair and spacious court, each very fair in itself, and the goodlier to see for the gladsome pictures with which it was adorned; the whole set amidst meads and gardens laid out with marvelous art, wells of the coolest water, and vaults of the finest wines, things more suited to dainty drinkers than to sober and honorable women.

The reader is aware that this idyllic island is surrounded by the terror of the Black Death, and that the sensual atmosphere of the setting offers—as arguably some of the best fiction always does—a refuge from the realities of everyday life.

The group determines that each day it will gather together and each will tell a story to entertain the others. As one of the young men, Dioneo, puts it, "I pray you, either address yourselves to make merry, to laugh and sing with me (so far, I mean, as may consist with your dignity), or give me leave to hie me back [return] to the stricken city." Of course, no sooner do they gather together on their first day than Dioneo challenges the ladies' dignity with a tale about a young monk from a monastery "once more saintly … than it now is" who one day spies a beautiful young woman gathering herbs in a field (see **Reading 13.5**, pages 462–463, for the tale in its entirety):

> The moment he saw her, he was passionately attacked by carnal desire. He went up to her and began a conversation. One subject led to another, and finally, they came to an understanding; he took the girl to his cell.

Dioneo's stories evoke "some qualms of shame in the minds of the ladies, as was apparent by the modest blush that tinged their faces." But the ladies are also "scarcely able to refrain their mirth." Dioneo is the embodiment of freedom, and his stories represent Boccaccio's own license to exceed the bounds of acceptable literary decorum. Not all of the other 99 tales are as ribald—that is, vulgar and indecent—as this one, but although all ten of the storytellers are aristocrats, a great many of their tales involve people of the lower, especially middle classes, and their characters, in their shrewdness and wit, ingenuity, and resourcefulness, unscrupulous behavior and bawdy desires, introduce into Western literature a kind of social realism previously unexplored. Perhaps reflecting the reality of death that surrounds them, the stories depict daily life as it is truly lived. Boccaccio's stories express the realities of life in a way that the classic tales of medieval chivalry could only intimate. His world is of flesh and blood, not knights in shining armor. If the world of the *Decameron* is a fictitious one, in its penetrating revelation of the workings of human psychology, it also represents an unprecedented brand of literary realism.

Petrarch's Sonnets

One of Boccaccio's best friends was the itinerant scholar and poet Francesco Petrarca (1304–74), known as Petrarch (Fig. **13.13**). Raised near Avignon, in France, where the papacy had established itself in 1309 and where it remained through most of Petrarch's lifetime, Petrarch studied at Montpellier and Bologna and traveled throughout northern France, Germany, and Italy. He was always in search of manuscripts that preserved the priceless literary works of antiquity—copying those he could not pry loose from monastic libraries. As he wrote to a friend in 1351, these manuscripts, in a Classical Latin and hard for monks to decipher, were in danger of being lost forever:

> It is a state of affairs that has resulted in an incredible loss to scholarship. Books that by their nature are a little hard to understand are no longer multiplied [i.e., copied and distributed], and have ceased to be generally intelligible, and so have sunk into utter neglect, and in the end have perished. This age of ours consequently has let fall, bit by

bit, some of the richest and sweetest fruits that the tree of knowledge has yielded; has thrown away the results of the vigils and labors of the most illustrious men of genius, things of more value, I am almost tempted to say, than anything else in the whole world.

It was Petrarch who rediscovered the forgotten works of the Roman orator and statesman Cicero, and his own private library consisted of over 200 Classical texts. He persuaded Boccaccio to bring the Greek scholar Leo Pilatus to Venice to teach them to read Greek. Boccaccio learned the language, but, put off by Pilatus's bad manners, Petrarch did not. Both, however, benefited from Pilatus's translation of Homer into Latin prose, as well as from his genealogy of the Greek gods.

Perhaps Petrarch's greatest work was his book of over 300 poems, the *Canzoniere* (*Songbook*), inspired by his love for a woman named Laura, whom he first met in 1327 in Avignon, where he was working for an influential cardinal. She is generally believed to have been the 19-year-old wife of Hugues de Sade. Whether Petrarch ever revealed his love to Laura, or simply poured it into his verses, remains a matter of speculation.

The majority of Petrarch's verses to Laura take the form of the **Italian sonnet**, known also as the **Petrarchan**

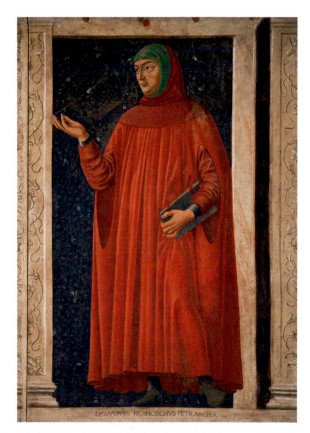

Fig. 13.13 Andrea Del Castagno, *Francesco Petrarca*. ca. 1450. Fresco transferred to wood, 97¼" × 60¼". Galleria degli Uffizi, Florence. So great was Petrarch's zeal for the classics that he would become known as the Father of Humanism, the revival of Greco-Roman culture that would come to define the Renaissance in the two centuries to follow.

sonnet because he perfected the form. Petrarch had been deeply influenced by the poetry of the troubadours, written in sonnet form (see Chapter 10). The Petrarchan sonnet is

CONTINUITY & CHANGE
Troubadour poetry, *p. 350*

composed of 14 lines divided into two parts: an *octave* of 8 lines that presents a problem, and a *sestet* of 6 lines that either attempts to solve the problem or accepts it as unsolvable. The octave is further divided into two four-line *quatrains*. The first presents the problem and the second develops the idea. Many of Petrarch's verses to Laura were composed after her death from the bubonic plague in 1348, and it seems likely that her death motivated Petrarch to circulate them. His devastation is clear in these three lines from Sonnet 338:

Earth, air, and sea should weep together,
for the human lineage, once she's gone, becomes
a meadow stripped of flowers, a gemless ring.

More influential, however, were the pure love poems. One of the most famous of these is Sonnet 134, in which Petrarch explores the complexities of his feelings—all the ambivalence, contradiction, and paradox—in the face of his love for Laura (**Reading 13.6**):

READING 13.6

Petrarch, Sonnet 134

I find no peace, and yet I am not warlike;
I fear and hope, I burn and turn to ice;
I fly beyond the sky, stretch out on earth;
my hands are empty, yet I hold the world.

One holds me prisoner, not locked up, not free;
won't keep me for her own but won't release me;
Love does not kill me, does not loose my chains,
he'd like me dead, he'd like me still ensnared.

I see without my eyes, cry with no tongue,
I want to die and yet I call for help,
hating myself but loving someone else.

I feed on pain, I laugh while shedding tears,
both death and life displease me equally;
and this state, Lady, is because of you.

Such poems would have a lasting influence, especially in the poetry of the English Elizabethan Age, because they seemed to capture all the emotional turbulence of love (see Chapter 19).

Chaucer's *Canterbury Tales*

The first Englishman to translate Petrarch was Geoffrey Chaucer (ca. 1342–1400). Well-educated, able to read both Ovid and Virgil in the original Latin, Chaucer was a middle-class civil servant and diplomat. In 1368, both he and Petrarch were guests at a wedding in Milan Cathedral, and four years later, he was in Florence, where he probably met Boccaccio. Chaucer's masterwork, *The Canterbury*

Tales, is modeled roughly on Boccaccio's *Decameron*, but it is written in verse, not prose, and is composed in **heroic couplets**. Like the *Decameron*, it is a framed collection of stories, this time told by a group of pilgrims traveling from London to the shrine of Saint Thomas à Becket, Archbishop of Canterbury. In 1170, Becket had been murdered in Canterbury Cathedral by followers of King Henry II in a dispute over the rights and privileges of the Church.

Chaucer had planned to write 120 tales. Before his death, he had completed only 22 tales and fragments of two others, but they are extraordinary in the range of characters and social types that they portray. Not only are the characters in the stories fully developed, but so are their narrators, and as a result the stories reflect perhaps the most fully developed realism of the era. Consider Chaucer's description of the Wife of Bath (Fig. **13.14**) from the Prologue to the work (**Reading 13.7**):

READING 13.7

from Chaucer, *The Canterbury Tales*, Prologue

A worthy woman there was from near the city
Of Bath, but somewhat deaf, and more's the pity.
For weaving she possessed so great a bent
She outdid the people of Ypres and Ghent.[1]
No other woman dreamed of such a thing
As to precede her at the offering.
Or if any did, she fell in such a wrath
She dried up all the charity in Bath.
She wore fine kerchiefs of old-fashioned air,
And on a Sunday morning, I could swear,
She had ten pounds of linen on her head.
Her stockings were the finest scarlet-red,
Laced tightly, and her shoes were soft and new.
Bold was her face, and fair, and red in hue.
She had been an excellent woman all of her life.
Five men in turn had taken her to wife,
Not counting other youthful company—
But let that pass for now! Over the sea
She'd traveled freely; many a distant stream
She crossed, and visited Jerusalem
Three times. She had been at Rome and at Boulogne,
At Compostella's shrine, and at Cologne.
She'd wandered by the way through many a scene.
Her teeth were set with little gaps between.[2]
Easily on her ambling horse she sat.
She was well wimpled, and she wore a hat
As wide in circuit as a shield or targe,[3]
A skirt swathed up her hips, and they were large.
Upon her feet she wore sharp-roweled spurs.
She was a good fellow; a ready tongue was hers.
All remedies of love she knew by name,
For she had all the tricks of that old game.

[1] **Ypres and Ghent:** centers of the weaving industry in Flanders.
[2] **teeth … gaps between:** for a woman to be gap-toothed was considered a sign of being highly sexed.
[3] **targe:** a type of shield.

📖 **Read** the document from *The Canterbury Tales* on **MyArtsLab**

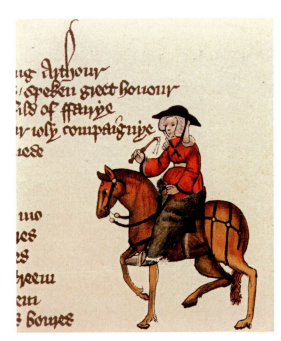

Fig. 13.14 *Wife of Bath*, from Geoffrey Chaucer's *Canterbury Tales* ("The Ellesmere Chaucer"). ca. 1400–05. Illumination on vellum. Victoria & Albert Museum, London. This image is from the earliest complete surviving text of Chaucer's work, which contains 23 portraits of the storytellers.

Chaucer accomplishes what few writers before him had—he creates character and personality through vivid detail and description. This elaborately dressed, gaptoothed, large-hipped, easy-riding survivor of five husbands comes off as a real person. The tales themselves sometimes rival Boccaccio's in their bawdy realism, but the variety of the pilgrims and the range of their moral characters create at least as profound a moral world as Boccaccio's, one whose scope even rivals that of Dante. The integrity of the Knight plays against the depravity of the Pardoner, just as the sanctity of the Parson plays against the questionable morals of the Wife of Bath. Chaucer's characters come from all three **estates**, or social ranks—the nobility, the clergy, and the common people—a fact that has led some to refer to his work as an "estates satire," a critique of social relations in his day.

Evolving English Chaucer wrote *The Canterbury Tales* in the English of his day, a language we now call Middle English. After the Norman invasion in 1066, the common people spoke one language—Anglo-Saxon (or Old English)—and the nobility another, French. The language of the learned continued to be Latin. In Chaucer's time, a new spoken vernacular, Middle English, had supplanted Anglo-Saxon among the common people. It combined elements of French, Anglo-Saxon, and the Scandinavian languages. Chaucer himself spoke French, and that he chose to write *The Canterbury Tales* in the Middle English of his day (actually a London dialect, one of about five dialects used across Britain at the time) is a significant development in the history of the English language.

Before 1385, roughly the time that Chaucer began the *Tales*, English had replaced French as the language of instruction for children. By 1362, the Chief Justice opened Parliament with a speech in English. That same year, Parliament enacted the Statute of Pleading, providing that "All pleas which shall be pleaded in his [the King's] courts whatsoever, before any of his justices whatsoever … shall be pleaded, shewed, defended, answered, debated, and judged in the English tongue." Still, the records of the pleas were kept in Latin. By mid-century, then, even the nobility, though raised speaking French, also spoke English. Chaucer's London dialect became the dominant one thanks largely to William Caxton, the London printer of Chaucer's works, who used the London dialect—the English of Britain's intellectual, political, and commercial center—in all his publications, thus making it the standard.

To provide an idea of the history of the language, here are the opening lines of the Prologue of *The Canterbury Tales* in Middle English, as Chaucer wrote them, followed by a modern rendition.

> *Whan that Aprill with his shoures soot*
>> When April with its sweet-smelling showers
> *The droghte of March hath perced to the roote,*
>> Has pierced the drought of March to the root,
> *And bathed every veyne in swich licour*
>> And bathed every vein (of the plants) in such liquid
> *Of which vertu engendred is the flour;*
>> By the power of which the flower is created;
> *Whan Zephirus eek with his sweete breeth*
>> When the West Wind also with its sweet breath,
> *Inspired hath in every holt and heeth*
>> In every wood and field has breathed life into
> *The tendre croppes, and the yonge sonne*
>> The tender new leaves, and the young sun
> *Hath in the Ram his half cours yronne,*
>> Has run half its course in Aries,
> *And smale foweles maken melodye,*
>> And small fowls make melody,
> *That slepen al the nyght with open ye*
>> Those that sleep all the night with open eyes
> *(So priketh hem Nature in hir corages),*
>> (So Nature incites them in their hearts),
> *Thanne longen folk to goon on pilgrimages. …*
>> Then folk long to go on pilgrimages. …

Chaucer understood the power of this new vernacular English to evoke the reality of fourteenth-century English life, and his keen ear for the cadences and phrasings of actual speech underscores the reality of his characters and the tales they tell.

Women in Late Medieval Society

The seven women in Boccaccio's *Decameron* and characters like Chaucer's Wife of Bath represent the increasing social prominence of women in medieval society. This is no doubt at least in part a reflection of the growing role of the Virgin in medieval religious life, and her prominence helped raise the dignity of women in general. By the thirteenth century, women were active in all trades, especially the food and clothing industries; they belonged to guilds, and increasingly had the opportunity to go to school and learn to read, at least in their vernacular languages. They were, however, still generally excluded from the learned professions of medicine and law, and they performed the same work as men for wages on the average 25 percent lower.

Women in Boccaccio and Chaucer Neither Boccaccio nor Chaucer could ever be called a feminist—in fact, both depict misogynist characters—but both do recognize these new women as real forces in contemporary social life. Chaucer's women leave prevalent and prescriptive views of women's proper roles far behind. Boccaccio's story of Filippa, told by Filostrata on the sixth day, is another case in point. It recounts how Filippa is charged by her husband with the crime of adultery, punishable by death in the town of Prato where they live, a crime to which she freely admits. But in court she argues that the law represents a double standard, one for men, quite another for women, and that, further, laws should be made by the consent of the people, and no woman ever consented to the death penalty for giving "pleasure to many more people than men ever could." If, she argues, she has always satisfied her husband's every desire,

> what was I to do with what was left over? Indeed, what am I to do with it? Throw it to the dogs? Isn't it far better to give enjoyment to some gentleman who loves me more than his life, than to let it go to waste or ruin?

The court agrees, the law is overturned, and Filippa is victorious (See **Reading 13.8**, page 463 for the tale).

Boccaccio did, in fact, write a book explicitly "for the ladies," his *De Claris Mulieribus* (*Concerning Famous Women*), a work of Latin prose published in 1362. The first collection of biographies in Western literature dedicated solely to women, it consists of 106 entries beginning with "Eve Our First Mother." It then moves on to both exemplary and notorious figures from history and mythology as well as from among Boccaccio's own contemporaries. The book was immensely popular across Europe and survives in over 100 manuscripts—an unusually high number. It was nevertheless an extremely misogynist text that assumes women's inferiority to men from the outset.

Christine de Pizan: An Early Feminist Women began to play an increasingly active role in the courts of Europe. In 1404, Philip the Bold, Duke of Burgundy, commissioned Christine de Pizan (1364–ca. 1430) to write a biography of his deceased brother, titled *The Book of the Deeds and Good Manners of the Wise King Charles V*. De Pizan had been educated at the French court, apparently against her mother's wishes, by her father, a prominent Venetian physician, who had been appointed court astrologer to King Charles V. Her husband, secretary and notary to the king, further promoted

her education. But when her father and husband died, she needed to support three children, a niece, and her mother. To do so she became the first female professional writer in European history.

As she gradually established her reputation as a writer, she worked as a copyist and illustrator, and her first successes were books of poems and ballads. In 1402, she made her reputation by attacking as misogynistic and demeaning to women the popular thirteenth-century poem the *Roman de la Rose* ("Romance of the Rose") (see Chapter 12). Two years later, in her *Book of the City of Ladies*, she again attacked male misogyny by recounting the accomplishments of women throughout the ages in an allegorical debate between herself and Lady Reason, Lady Rectitude, and Lady Justice (Fig. **13.15**). Her most immediate source was Boccaccio's *Concerning Famous Women*, but her treatment is completely different, treating only good women and freely mixing pagan and Christian examples. Her city's queen is the Virgin Mary herself, a figure whose importance confirms the centrality of women to Christianity. Thus, she opens the book by wondering why men are so inclined to demean women (**Reading 13.9**):

READING 13.9

from Christine de Pizan, *Book of the City of Ladies*

[I wondered] how it happened that so many different men—and learned men among them—have been and are so inclined to express both in speaking and in their treatises and writings so many wicked insults about women and their behavior. Not only one or two ... but, more generally, from the treatises of all philosophers and poets and from all the orators—it would take too long to mention their names—it seems that they all speak from one and the same mouth. Thinking deeply about these matters, I began to examine my character and conduct as a natural woman and, similarly, I considered other women whose company I frequently kept, princesses, great ladies, women of the middle and lower classes, who had graciously told me of their most private and intimate thoughts, hoping that I could judge impartially and in good conscience whether the testimony of so many notable men could be true. To the best of my knowledge, no matter how long I confronted or dissected the problem, I could not see or realize how their claims could be true when compared to the natural behavior and character of women.

De Pizan then turns to God for guidance and is granted a dream vision in which the three allegorical ladies encourage her to build an Ideal City, peopled with a variety of women, from Sappho to her own name-saint, all of whom help her to redefine what it means to be female.

Christine de Pizan Glorifies Joan of Arc De Pizan was writing in the context of the so-called Hundred Years' War between England and France, generally dated at 1337 to

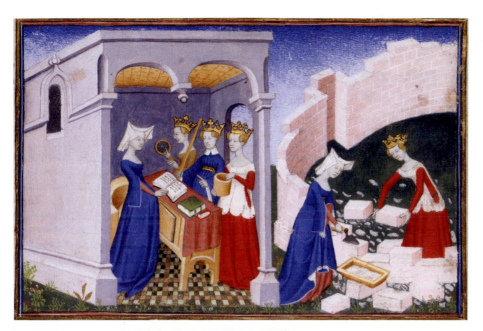

Fig. 13.15 Anonymous, _La Cité des Dames de Christine de Pizan._ ca. 1410. Illumination on parchment, page size 4¾" × 7". Bibliothèque nationale de France. On the left stands Christine de Pizan, engaged in composition while receiving the visit of Reason, Honesty, and Justice. On the right, Christine and one of the royal ladies build the Ideal City.

1429. The origins of the war went all the way back to 1216, when the English Normans (who had invaded England from France in 1066) finally lost control of all their possessions on the continent. In the early fourteenth century, the French throne was increasingly contested, and the English king proclaimed himself as the rightful heir. Thus the stage was set for war, driven largely by the English Normans' desire to recapture their homeland in Normandy. The war was fought entirely on French soil, and although the English were usually outnumbered by as much as three to one, they were generally victorious because of two technological innovations. First, the longbow's 6-foot length allowed the English infantry to pierce the chain-mail armor of the French. Second, the introduction of gunpowder and cannon made armor altogether irrelevant. Suddenly the model of heroic hand-to-hand combat, the basis of the chivalric ideal, was obsolete, and with it, the codes of loyalty, honor, and courage upon which the entire French literary tradition since the _Song of Roland_ had been based.

Even more damaging to this masculine tradition was the fact that it was a woman, Joan of Arc, who saved the French. A 17-year-old peasant girl, she approached the French king and begged him to allow her to obey the voices of the saints who ordered her to drive the English out of France. Christine de Pizan, who had retired to an abbey in 1418, after the arrival of the Burgundian troops in Paris had forced her and many others to seek protection outside the city, was overjoyed. The year before her death, de Pizan wrote a 61-stanza poem that glorified Joan's achievements (rendered in prose in **Reading 13.10**):

READING 13.10

Christine de Pizan, _Tale of Joan of Arc_

I, Christine, who have wept for eleven years in a walled abbey … begin to laugh heartily for joy …

Oh! What honour for the female sex! It is perfectly obvious that God has special regard for it when all these wretched people who destroyed the whole Kingdom—now recovered and made safe by a woman, something that 5000 men could not have done—and the traitors [have been] exterminated. Before the event they would scarcely have believed this possible.

A little girl of sixteen (isn't this something quite supernatural?) who does not even notice the weight of the arms she bears—indeed her whole upbringing seems to have prepared her for this, so strong and resolute is she! And her enemies go fleeing before her, not one of them can stand up to her. She does all this in full view of everyone, and drives her enemies out of France, recapturing castles and towns. Never did anyone see greater strength, even in hundreds or thousands of men!

For de Pizan, Joan's achievement was as much a victory for women as for France. Christine, though, would not live to see her captured by the English, betrayed, probably by Burgundian French, then tried and executed as a heretic in March 1431. Joan's mysticism, like that of Hildegard of Bingen before her (see Chapter 10), undermined the authority and (male) hierarchy of the Church. But the chief charge against her was cross-dressing! She dared challenge, in other words, the human-constructed gender roles that the Church fathers assumed to be the will of God. Still, probably no other figure better sums up the growing self-assurance of women in late medieval society and the sense of personal worth—both male and female—that would increasingly inform European society as the fifteenth century unfolded.

The Dance of Death

We do not know who, in 1424, painted a series of pictures representing a Dance of Death along the walls backing the **charnel houses**—houses where the bones of the dead were stored—that ran the length of the Cemetery of the Holy Innocents in Paris on the Rue de la Ferronnerie. These paintings were undoubtedly inspired by a clergy bent on encouraging Christian feeling and sentiment in their parishioners and on reminding them of their Christian duties in the face

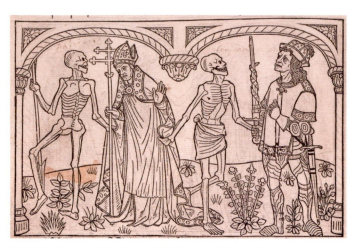

Fig. 13.16 *Dance of Death.* **ca. 1490.** Woodcut. Library of Congress, Washington, D.C. Lessing J. Rosenwald Collection. This print is one of a series copying the images that appeared on the charnel house walls of the Cemetery of the Holy Innocents.

of certain death. Every rank and order of human society was represented in this procession, the pope and emperor at its head (Fig. **13.16**), a fool and an author pulling up the rear. Verses attributed to the Chancellor of the University of Paris, Jean de Charlier de Gerson, accompany the paintings:

> By divine sentence
> No matter what your estate
> Whether good or evil, you will be
> Eaten by worms. Alas, look at us,
> Dead, stinking, and rotten.
> You will be like this, too.

The toll the Black Death wreaked on the arts was indeed devastating. In Siena, Giovanni Pisano and Ambrogio Lorenzetti were among the many victims of the Black Death. In Florence, almost all of Giotto's best students succumbed. But since the plague destroyed people and not possessions, the enormous decrease in population resulted in a corresponding increase in per capita wealth, and those who survived invested in religious art—chapels and hospitals, altarpieces and votive statues—in gratitude for being spared or in the hope of preventing future infection. Painters and sculptors turned their attention to the representation of the sufferings of Christ, the sorrows rather than the joys of the Virgin, and the miracles of the saints. The Art of Dying Well and the Triumph of Death became important themes in art and literature. The

new humanism, or belief in the value of individuals and their human potential, so evident in the realist art of Giotto and in the writings of Petrarch, Boccaccio, and Chaucer, suggests that the plague stimulated the Western imagination perhaps more than it defeated it.

Nevertheless, the specter of death, which the Black Death so thoroughly embedded in the popular imagination, haunted Western society for at least 400 years. The Cemetery of the Holy Innocents, which was the size of a large city block and occupied the area of Paris today known as Les Halles, accommodated many of the dead, but by the middle of the eighteenth century, the cemetery was almost literally exploding with corpses. Many people, who now possessed at least a rudimentary understanding of infection, argued that this cemetery was a breeding ground for disease. On December 1, 1780, a cellar wall on the Rue de la Ferronnerie burst, releasing noxious gases and fluids into the streets, and the cemetery was permanently closed. The charnel houses were demolished—along with the Dance of Death images that covered their walls. As for the dead, they were reburied in catacombs dug from ancient quarries beneath the city streets, today a tourist site.

This vast removal of the dead amounted to a banishment of the specter of death from the daily life of the city, culminating finally, in 1804, with the emperor Napoleon's Imperial Decree on Burials. Henceforth, burial was banned within the city. Each corpse would have an individual plot, permanent if space allowed, in one of four garden environments outside the city proper—among them, the bucolic Père Lachaise Cemetery, which even today attracts Parisians to its hills and paths. All were designed to aid in absorbing what the Ministry of the Interior called "cadaverous miasmata." It was envisioned that in these new Elysian Fields, children would periodically scatter flowers over the tombs. Thus, the idea of the cemetery as a kind of landscape garden, as we know it today, was born. ■

THINKING BACK

13.1 Compare and contrast civic life in Siena and Florence.

Tuscany was dominated by two competing city-states, Siena and Florence. Both were republics, and central to their success was a new form of government in which Church and State were closely aligned. Siena established itself in 1125 as a free commune. What is a commune? By the twelfth century, Florence was the center of textile production in the Western world and played a central role in European trade markets. As with Siena, it was the city's bankers and money lenders who made Florence such a vital player in world trade. Also as in Siena, in Florence, the guilds controlled the commune. How would you define a guild?

13.2 Outline how an increasingly naturalistic art replaced the Byzantine style in Italy.

In both Siena and Florence, artists began to break from the Byzantine style. One of the first was Duccio, who began to incorporate the Gothic tendency to naturalism into his *Maestà*, painted for Siena's cathedral. Even more naturalistic is Simone Martini's *Maestà*, painted for the city hall. How would you compare them? Florence, too, had its master painters of the Virgin, Cimabue and Giotto. In what did the latter exceed the others in terms of the naturalism of his art?

13.3 Describe the distinguishing characteristics of Dante's *Divine Comedy*.

In the early twelfth century, writers across Europe began to address their works to a wider lay audience and to write in the vernacular. How would you define the vernacular? What does it imply about this new literature's audience? One of the greatest medieval Italian vernacular writers was the poet Dante Alighieri, whose *Divine Comedy* records the travels of the Christian soul from Hell to Purgatory and finally to Salvation in three books—the *Inferno*, *Purgatorio*, and *Paradiso*. How does Dante's poem reflect the epic tradition? Consider its relation to, for instance, the *Odyssey* and the *Aeneid*.

13.4 Examine how the vernacular style developed after the Black Death.

In December 1347, bubonic plague arrived in Sicily. Within months, the disease spread northward, through Europe. In Tuscany, the death rate in the cities ran somewhere near 60 percent. Many blamed the Jews, who were widely persecuted. One of the most remarkable accounts of the plague opens Boccaccio's *Decameron*, a collection of stories told by young noblemen and women who have escaped Florence for the countryside. Perhaps reflecting the reality of death that surrounds them, the stories are themselves imbued with a realistic representation of life as it is truly lived. After the Black Death, the realistic treatment of life continued in vernacular literature. The sonnets of Petrarch, composed in memory of the poet's beloved Laura, inaugurate one of the most important poetic forms in Western literature. Chaucer's *Canterbury Tales*, modeled on Boccaccio's *Decameron*, approach life in the Middle Ages with a realism even more profound than Boccaccio's. Many of both Boccaccio's and Chaucer's characters are women. How do their female characters and Christine de Pizan's help to establish new roles for women?

✓ **Study** and **review** on **MyArtsLab**

READINGS

from Dante, *Inferno*, Canto 1

Dante wrote the *Divine Comedy* between 1308 and 1321, completing the *Inferno* by about 1312. The whole recounts the journey of Dante (the character, as opposed to the author) into the afterlife in three books—the *Inferno*, *Purgatorio*, and *Paradiso*—accompanied, at least as far as he can go, by the Roman poet Virgil. In the *Inferno*, Dante visits Hell. Each book is composed of 33 cantos, with the addition of one extra canto, the first, presented in full below, which serves as a prelude to the entire work. These numbers are symbolic. The number 3 is especially important. The poem is written in tercets, three-line stanzas. There are 9 (3 × 3) circles or spheres in each realm. And the number reflects, as well, the divine Trinity.

Midway in our life's journey, I went astray
   from the straight road and woke to find myself
   alone in a dark wood. How shall I say   3
what wood that was! I never saw so drear,
   so rank, so arduous a wilderness!
   Its very memory gives a shape to fear.   6
Death could scarce be more bitter than that place!
   But since it came to good, I will recount
   all that I found revealed there by God's grace.   9
How I came to it I cannot rightly say,
   so drugged and loose with sleep had I become
   when I first wandered there from the True Way.   12
But at the far end of that valley of evil
   whose maze had sapped my very heart with fear
   I found myself before a little hill   15
and lifted up my eyes. Its shoulders glowed
   already with the sweet rays of that planet
   whose virtue leads men straight on every road,   18
and the shining strengthened me against the fright
   whose agony had wracked the lake of my heart
   through all the terrors of that piteous night.   21
Just as a swimmer, who with his last breath
   flounders ashore from perilous seas, might turn
   to memorize the wide water of his death—   24
so did I turn, my soul still fugitive
   from death's surviving image, to stare down
   that pass that none had ever left alive.   27
And there I lay to rest from my heart's race
   till calm and breath returned to me. Then rose
   and pushed up that dead slope at such a pace   30
each footfall rose above the last. And lo!
   almost at the beginning of the rise
   I faced a spotted Leopard, all tremor and flow   33
and gaudy pelt. And it would not pass, but stood
   so blocking my every turn that time and again
   I was on the verge of turning back to the wood.   36
This fell at the first widening of the dawn
   as the sun was climbing Aries with those stars
   that rode with him to light the new creation.   39
Thus the holy hour and the sweet season
   of commemoration did much to arm my fear
   of that bright murderous beast with their good omen.   42
Yet not so much but what I shook with dread

at sight of a great Lion that broke upon me
   raging with hunger, its enormous head   45
held high as if to strike a mortal terror
   into the very air. And down his track,
   a She-Wolf drove upon me, a starved horror   48
ravening and wasted beyond all belief.
   She seemed a rack for avarice, gaunt and craving
   Oh many the souls she has brought to endless grief!   51
She brought such heaviness upon my spirit
   at sight of her savagery and desperation,
   I died from every hope of that high summit.   54
And like a miser—eager in acquisition
   but desperate in self-reproach when Fortune's wheel
   turns to the hour of his loss—all tears and attrition   57
I wavered back; and still the beast pursued,
   forcing herself against me bit by bit
   till I slid back into the sunless wood.   60
And as I fell to my soul's ruin, a presence
   gathered before me on the discolored air,
   the figure of one who seemed hoarse from long silence.   63
At sight of him in that friendless waste I cried:
   "Have pity on me, whatever thing you are,
   whether shade or living man." And it replied: 66
"Not man, though man I once was, and my blood
   was Lombard, both my parents Mantuan.
   I was born, though late, *sub Julio*, and bred   69
in Rome under Augustus in the noon
   of the false and lying gods. I was a poet
   and sang of old Anchises' noble son   72
who came to Rome after the burning of Troy.
   But you—why do *you* return to these distresses
   instead of climbing that shining Mount of Joy   75
which is the seat and first cause of man's bliss?"
   "And are you then that Virgil and that fountain
   of purest speech?" My voice grew tremulous: 78
"Glory and light of poets! now may that zeal
   and love's apprenticeship that I poured out
   on your heroic verses serve me well!   81
For you are my true master and first author,
   the sole maker from whom I drew the breath
   of that sweet style whose measures have brought me honor.   84
See there, immortal sage, the beast I flee.
   For my soul's salvation, I beg you, guard me from her,

for she has struck a mortal tremor through me." 87
And he replied, seeing my soul in tears:

"He must go by another way who would escape
this wilderness, for that mad beast that fleers 90
before you there, suffers no man to pass.

She tracks down all, kills all, and knows no glut,
but, feeding, she grows hungrier than she was. 93
She mates with any beast, and will mate with more
before the Greyhound comes to hunt her down.

He will not feed on lands nor loot, but honor 96
and love and wisdom will make straight his way.

He will rise between Feltro and Feltro, and in him
shall be the resurrection and new day 99
of that sad Italy for which Nisus died,
and Turnus, and Euryalus, and the maid Camilla.

He shall hunt her through every nation of sick pride 102
till she is driven back forever to Hell
whence Envy first released her on the world.

Therefore, for your own good, I think it well 105
you follow me and I will be your guide
and lead you forth through an eternal place.

There you shall see the ancient spirits tried 108
in endless pain, and hear their lamentation
as each bemoans the second death of souls.

Next you shall see upon a burning mountain 111
souls in fire and yet content in fire,
knowing that whensoever it may be
they yet will mount into the blessed choir. 114
To which, if it is still your wish to climb,
a worthier spirit shall be sent to guide you.

With her shall I leave you, for the King of Time, 117
who reigns on high, forbids me to come there
since, living, I rebelled against his law.

He rules the waters and the land and air 120
and there holds court, his city and his throne.
Oh blessed are they he chooses!" And I to him:

"Poet, by that God to you unknown, 123
lead me this way. Beyond this present ill
and worse to dread, lead me to Peter's gate
and be my guide through the sad halls of Hell." 126
And he then: "Follow." And he moved ahead
in silence, and I followed where he led.

---

1. **midway in our life's journey:** the biblical life span is three-score years and ten. The action opens in Dante's thirty-fifth year, i.e., 1300 CE.

17. **that planet:** the sun. Ptolemaic astronomers considered it a planet. It is also symbolic of God as He who lights man's way.

31. **each footfall rose above the last:** the literal rendering would be: "So that the fixed foot was ever the lower." "Fixed" has often been translated "right" and an ingenious reasoning can support that reading, but a simpler explanation offers itself and seems more competent: Dante is saying that he climbed with such zeal and haste that every footfall carried him above the last despite the steepness of the climb.

At a slow pace, on the other hand, the rear foot might be brought up only as far as the forward foot. This device of selecting a minute but exactly centered detail to convey the whole of a larger action is one of the central characteristics of Dante's style.

The Three Beasts: these three beasts undoubtedly are taken from *Jeremiah* 5:6. Many additional and incidental interpretations have been advanced for them, but the central interpretation must remain as noted. They foreshadow the three divisions of Hell (incontinence, violence, and fraud) which Virgil explains at length in Canto 11, 16–111.

38–9. **Aries ... that rode with him to light the new creation:** the medieval tradition had it that the sun was in Aries at the time of the Creation. The significance of the astronomical and religious conjunction is an important part of Dante's intended allegory. It is just before dawn of Good Friday 1300 CE when he awakens in the Dark Wood. Thus his new life begins under Aries, the sign of creation, at dawn (rebirth), and in the Easter season (resurrection). Moreover the moon is full and the sun is in the equinox, conditions that did not fall together on any Friday of 1300. Dante is obviously constructing poetically the perfect Easter as a symbol of his new awakening.

69. **sub Julio:** In the reign of Julius Caesar.

95. **The Greyhound ... Feltro and Feltro:** almost certainly refers to Can Grande della Scala (1290–1329), the great Italian leader born in Verona, which lies between the towns of Feltre and Montefeltro.

100–101. **Nisus, Turnus, Euryalus, Camilla:** all were killed in the war between the Trojans and the Latians when, according to legend, Aeneas led the survivors of Troy into Italy. Nisus and Euryalus (*Aeneid IX*) were Trojan comrades-in-arms who died together. Camilla (*Aeneid XI*) was the daughter of the Latian king and one of the warrior women. She was killed in a horse charge against the Trojans after displaying great gallantry. Turnus (*Aeneid XII*) was killed by Aeneas in a duel.

110. **the second death:** Damnation. "This is the second death, even the lake of fire." (*Revelation* 20:14)

118. **forbids me to come there since, living, etc.:** salvation is only through Christ in Dante's theology. Virgil lived and died before the establishment of Christ's teachings in Rome, and cannot therefore enter Heaven.

125. **Peter's gate:** the gate of Purgatory. (See *Purgatorio* IX, 76 ff.) The gate is guarded by an angel with a gleaming sword. The angel is Peter's vicar (Peter, the first pope, symbolized all popes: i.e., Christ's vicar on earth) and is entrusted with the two great keys.

Some commentators argue that this is the gate of Paradise, but Dante mentions no gate beyond this one in his ascent to Heaven. It should be remembered, too, that those who pass the gate of Purgatory have effectively entered Heaven.

The three great gates that figure in the entire journey are: the gate of Hell (Canto 3, 1–11), the gate of Dis (Canto 8, 79–113, and Canto 9, 86–87), and the gate of Purgatory, as above.

READING CRITICALLY

This canto serves as the prelude to the whole of the *Divine Comedy*. It introduces both Dante and his guide, Virgil. How does it also introduce Dante as the reader's guide on the same journey that he and Virgil are about to undertake?

from Boccaccio, *Decameron*, Dioneo's Tale

Boccaccio completed the *Decameron* in 1353. It is a transitional work, looking backward in many of its stories to the values and mores of medieval chivalry and mainstream Christianity even as it anticipates the individualism and ingenuity that the coming age, the Renaissance, will celebrate. A single example of its 100 tales, such as Dioneo's ribald classic below, does not do justice to the variety of subject matter and tone, the wide spectrum of human characters, and the scope of narrative structure that Boccaccio employs. But Dioneo's tale encapsulates the worldliness of the *Decameron*, a newfound frankness perhaps made possible only in the context of the Black Death, which has precipitated the book's storytellers to escape Florence and entertain one another in the countryside.

Loving ladies, if I have well understood the intention of you all, we are here to afford entertainment to one another by storytelling; wherefore, provided only nought is done that is repugnant to this end, I deem it lawful for each (and so said our queen a little while ago) to tell whatever story seems to him most likely to be amusing. … I hope to escape your censure in narrating a brief story of a monk, who by his address delivered his body from imminent peril of most severe chastisement.

In the not very remote district of Lunigiana there flourished formerly a community of monks more numerous and holy than is there to ¹⁰ be found to-day, among whom was a young brother, whose vigour and lustihood neither the fasts nor the vigils availed to subdue. One afternoon, while the rest of the confraternity slept, our young monk took a stroll around the church, which lay in a very sequestered spot, and chanced to espy a young and very beautiful girl, a daughter, perhaps, of one of the husbandmen[1] of those parts, going through the fields and gathering herbs as she went. No sooner had he seen her than he was sharply assailed by carnal concupiscence,[2] insomuch that he made up to and accosted her; and (she hearkening) little by little they came to an understanding, and unobserved by any entered his cell together. Now ²⁰ it so chanced that, while they fooled it within somewhat recklessly, he being overwrought with passion, the abbot awoke and passing slowly by the young monk's cell, heard the noise which they made within, and the better to distinguish the voices, came softly up to the door of the cell, and listening discovered that beyond all doubt there was a woman within. His first thought was to force the door open; but, changing his mind, he returned to his chamber and waited until the monk should come out.

Delightsome beyond measure though the monk found his intercourse with the girl, yet was he not altogether without anxi- ³⁰ ety. He had heard, as he thought, the sound of footsteps in the dormitory, and having applied his eye to a convenient aperture[3] had had a good view of the abbot as he stood by the door listening. He was thus fully aware that the abbot might have detected the presence of a woman in the cell. Whereat he was exceedingly distressed, knowing that he had a severe punishment to expect; but he concealed his vexation from the girl while he busily cast about in his mind for some way of escape from his embarrassment. He thus hit on a novel stratagem which was exactly suited to his purpose. With the air of one who had had enough of the girl's ⁴⁰ company he said to her: "I shall now leave you in order that I may arrange for your departure hence unobserved. Stay here quietly until I return." So out he went, locking the door of the cell, and withdrawing the key, which he carried straight to the abbot's chamber and handed to him, as was the custom when a monk was going out, saying with a composed air: "Sir, I was not able this morning to bring in all the faggots[4] which I had made ready, so with your leave I will go to the wood and bring them in." The abbot, desiring to have

better cognisance of the monk's offence, and not dreaming that the monk knew that he had been detected, was pleased with the turn ⁵⁰ matters had taken, and received the key gladly, at the same time giving the monk the desired leave. So the monk withdrew, and the abbot began to consider what course it were best for him to take, whether to assemble the brotherhood and open the door in their presence, that, being witnesses of the delinquency, they might have no cause to murmur against him when he proceeded to punish the delinquent, or whether it were not better first to learn from the girl's own lips how it had come about. And reflecting that she might be the wife or daughter of some man who would take it ill that she should be shamed by being exposed to the gaze of all the monks, he determined first of all to find ⁶⁰ out who she was, and then to make up his mind. So he went softly to the cell, opened the door, and, having entered, closed it behind him. The girl, seeing that her visitor was none other than the abbot, quite lost her presence of mind, and quaking with shame began to weep. Master abbot surveyed her from head to foot, and seeing that she was fresh and comely,[5] fell a prey, old though he was, to fleshly cravings no less poignant and sudden than those which the young monk had experienced, and began thus to commune with himself: "Alas! why take I not my pleasure when I may, seeing that I never need lack for occasions of trouble and vexation of spirit? Here is a fair wench, and no ⁷⁰ one in the world to know. If I can bring her to pleasure me, I know not why I should not do so. Who will know? No one will ever know; and sin that is hidden is half forgiven; this chance may never come again; so, methinks, it were the part of wisdom to take the boon which God bestows." So musing, with an altogether different purpose from that with which he had come, he drew near the girl, and softly bade her to be comforted, and besought her not to weep; and so little by little he came at last to show her what he would be at. The girl, being made neither of iron nor of adamant,[6] was readily induced to gratify the abbot, who after bestowing upon her ⁸⁰ many an embrace and kiss, got upon the monk's bed, where, being sensible, perhaps, of the disparity between his reverend portliness and her tender youth, and fearing to injure her by his excessive weight, he refrained from lying upon her, but laid her upon him, and in that manner disported himself with her for a long time. The monk, who had only pretended to go to the wood, and had concealed himself in the dormitory, no sooner saw the abbot enter his cell than he was overjoyed to think that his plan would succeed; and when he saw that he had locked the door, he was well assured thereof. So he stole out of his hiding-place, and set his eye to an aperture through which he saw and ⁹⁰ heard all that the abbot did and said. At length the abbot, having had enough of dalliance with the girl, locked her in the cell and returned to his chamber. Catching sight of the monk soon afterwards, and supposing him to have returned from the wood, he determined to give him a sharp reprimand and have him imprisoned, that he might thus secure the prey for himself alone. He therefore caused him to be summoned, chid him very severely and with a stern countenance, and ordered him

---

[1] **husbandmen:** farmers.
[2] **carnal concupiscence:** sexual desire.
[3] **aperture:** opening.
[4] **faggots:** firewood.

[5] **comely:** beautiful.
[6] **adamant:** diamond (i.e., a hard substance).

to be put in prison. The monk replied trippingly: "Sir, I have not been so long in the order of Saint Benedict as to have every particular of the rule by heart; nor did you teach me before to-day in what posture it behooves the monk to have intercourse with women, but limited your instruction to such matters as fasts and vigils. As, however, you have now given me my lesson, I promise you, if you also pardon my offence, that I will never repeat it, but will always follow the example which you have set me."

The abbot, who was a shrewd man, saw at once that the monk was not only more knowing than he, but had actually seen what he had done; nor, conscience-stricken himself, could he for shame mete out to the monk a measure which he himself merited. So pardon given, with an injunction to bury what had been seen in silence, they decently conveyed the young girl out of the monastery, whither, it is to be believed, they now and again caused her to return.

READING CRITICALLY

The circulation of stories such as this certainly contributed to the growing crisis of trust faced by the Church throughout the Middle Ages and into the Renaissance. How does it raise broader issues than just the question of clerical celibacy?

READING 13.8

from Boccaccio, *Decameron*, Filippa's Tale

Filippa's tale is the seventh story told on the sixth day of the *Decameron*. The story is particularly notable for its heroine's independence from received notions of proper behavior, and her astute critique of the justice system in her native Prato.

Once upon a time, in the town of Prato, there used to be a law in force—as pernicious, indeed, as it was cruel—to the effect that any woman caught by her husband in the act of adultery with a lover, was to be burned alive, like any vulgar harlot who sold herself for money.

While this statute prevailed, a beautiful lady called Filippa, a devout worshiper of Cupid, was surprised in her bedroom one night by her husband, Rinaldo de' Pugliesi, in the arms of Lazzarino de' Guazzagliotri, a high-born Adonis of a youth of that city, whom she loved as the apple of her eye.

Burning with rage at the discovery, Rinaldo could scarcely forbear running upon them, and slaying them on the spot. Were it not for the misgivings he had for his own safety, if he gave vent to his wrath, he would have followed his impulse. However, he controlled his evil intent, but could not abandon his desire to demand of the town's statute, what it was unlawful for him to bring about—in other words, the death of his wife.

As he had no lack of evidence to prove Filippa's guilt, he brought charges against her, early in the morning, at daybreak, and without further deliberation, had her summoned before the court.

Now Filippa was a high-spirited woman, as all women are who truly love, and though many of her friends and relatives advised her against going, she resolved to appear before the magistrate preferring a courageous death, by confessing the truth, to a shameful life of exile, by a cowardly flight that would have proved her unworthy of the lover in whose arms she had lain that night.

Accordingly, she presented herself before the provost, with a large following of men and women who urged her to deny the charges. She asked him firmly and without moving a muscle what he desired of her. The provost, seeing her so beautiful, courteous and so brave—as her words demonstrated—felt a certain pity stirring in his heart at the thought that she might confess a crime for which he would be obliged to sentence her to death to save his honor. But then, seeing he could not avoid cross-questioning her on the charge proffered against her, he said:

"Madame, here as you see, is Rinaldo, your husband, who is suing you on the grounds of finding you in the act of adultery with another man, and who therefore demands that I sentence you to death for it, as the law, which is in force, requires. I cannot pass sentence if you do not confess your guilt with your own lips. Be careful of our answers, then, and tell me if what your husband charges you with is true."

Filippa, not at all daunted, replied in a very agreeable voice: "Your honor, it is true that Rinaldo is my husband, and that last night he found me in the arms of Lazzarino, where I had lain many another time, out of the great and true love I bear him. Far be it from me ever to deny it.

"As you are doubtless aware, laws should be equal for all, and should be made with the consent of those whom they may affect. Such is not the case with this particular statute, which is stringent only with us poor women, who, after all, have it in our power to give pleasure to many more people than men ever could. Moreover, when this law was drawn up, not a single woman gave her consent or was so much as invited to give it. For all these reasons, it surely deserves to be considered reprehensible. If you insist upon enforcing it, not at the risk of my body, but of your immortal soul, you are at liberty to do so; but before you proceed to pass judgment, I beg you to grant me a small request. Simply ask my husband whether I have ever failed to yield myself to him entirely, whenever he chose, and as often as he pleased."

Without waiting for the magistrate to question him, Rinaldo immediately answered that there was no doubt Filippa had always granted him the joy of her body, at each and every request of his.

"That being the case, your honor," she went on directly, "I'd like to ask him, since he has always had all he wanted of me and to his heart's content, what was I to do with all that was left over? Indeed, what am I to do with it? Throw it to the dogs? Isn't it far better to let it give enjoyment to some gentleman who loves me more than his life, than to let it go to waste or ruin?"

As it happened the whole town had turned out to attend the sensational trial that involved a lady of such beauty and fame, and when the people heard her roguish question, they burst into a roar of laughter, shouting to a man that she was right and had spoken well.

That day before court was adjourned, that harsh statute was modified at the magistrate's suggestion to hold only such women as made cuckolds of their husbands for love of money.

As for Rinaldo, he went away crest-fallen at his mad venture, while Filippa returned home victorious, feeling in her joy that she had, in a sense, been delivered from the flames.

READING CRITICALLY

When Filippa declares that "laws should be equal for all, and should be made with the consent of those whom they may affect," she anticipates arguments that will be used to justify, for instance, the American Revolution in 1776. What is surprising about finding such arguments in a story written in 1351?

The Renaissance and the Age of Encounter

1400–1600

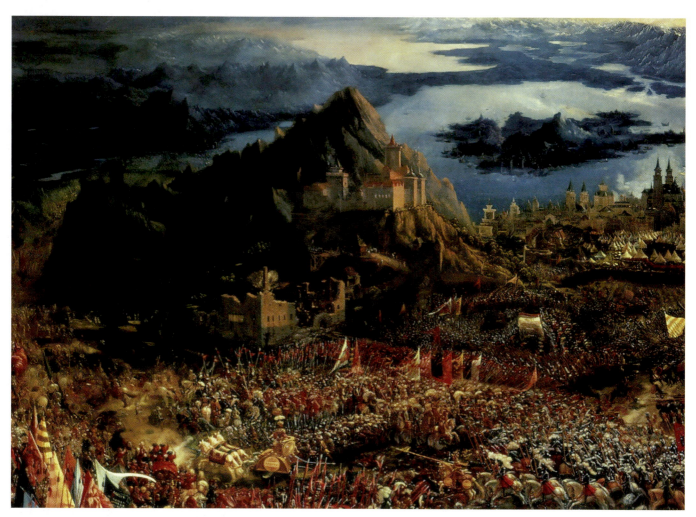

Albrecht Altdorfer, *The Battle of Issus* (detail). 1529 (see Fig. 17.1 in Chapter 17).

During the period extending from about 1400 to 1600, Western European culture experienced a rebirth of Classical learning and values. For this reason we call the period the Renaissance, which means "rebirth" in French. By the middle of the fourteenth century, Dante Alighieri had picked the ancient Roman poet Virgil as his guide through his fictional Inferno and Purgatory, Petrarch was busy amassing his own Classical library, and Boccaccio, who like Dante wrote in the vernacular Italian instead of Latin, was also learning Greek.

At the dawn of the Renaissance, then, the values of the Classical past—simplicity, balance, and restraint in design, proportionality of parts, and purity of form—had already firmly established their place in Western culture. These values stimulated the emergence of humanism—the recovery, study, and spread of the art and literature of Greece and Rome, and the application of their principles to education, politics, social life, and the arts in general. In turn, humanism stimulated a new sense of the value of the individual. Each person had the capacity for self-determination in the search for truth and morality. Faith, sacred texts, or religious tradition were no longer the only guides.

After the Black Death, it seemed possible, even necessary, to begin again. In politics, feudal rule gave way to centralized forms of government. City-states flourished, strengthened by the influx of workers migrating from the countryside, as manufacture and trade supplanted agriculture as the basis of the European economy. The Church, which in medieval times had been the very foundation of Western culture, found itself challenged on all fronts. Politically, European monarchs questioned its authority. Philosophically, a growing class of intellectuals challenged its long-held doctrines. Morally, many of these same intellectuals denounced the behavior of its clergy and called for reform.

It was a time of invention and encounter. The printing press in Germany became a major instrument of change by making available to an ever-growing middle class works of literature, political tracts, and philosophical arguments that literally transformed their way of thinking. Even as the telescope revised human understanding of the cosmos and the world's place in it, previously unknown civilizations in the Americas, Africa, and the Far East changed the Western understanding of its world. The Age of Encounter, which began in the fifteenth century and ended in the seventeenth, resulted in the colonization of most of the non-Western world. The effect of Western colonization was the displacement, enslavement, and large-scale death of native peoples. Those cultures that the West did not come to dominate—China and Japan especially—were deeply affected by their encounters with the West.

By the start of the sixteenth century, the humanistic spirit had begun to generate new forms of art and literature. The use of the rules of scientific perspective allowed for the convincing representation of three-dimensional space on the two-dimensional surface of a panel or canvas. The introduction of oil painting as a medium contributed to this naturalism by enabling artists to render the natural world in more precise detail than did tempera and to imitate effects of light and shadow both in the atmosphere and on the surface of objects. In architecture, structural innovations permitted the construction of the largest spaces since antiquity. New literary forms—the English sonnet, the personal essay, and popular theater—responded to a growing secular taste. And in music, where the courts maintained their own rosters of musicians, vernacular song and dance became popular even as the Church sanctioned innovative forms of polyphonic music for its liturgy. In this atmosphere, individual composers began to be recognized across Europe, and their works were published and widely circulated. Following the lead of the early fifteenth-century writer Christine de Pizan, women increasingly insisted on their own worth and dignity, assuming important roles as patrons, as artists in their own right, and, in England, as heads of state. All of these developments combined to bring Western culture to the threshold of modern life.

1404–35
Chinese emperor Zhu Di sponsors naval expeditions to Indian Ocean and African coast

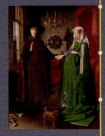

1420–36
Filippo Brunelleschi, dome of Duomo at Florence

ca. 1434
Jan van Eyck, *Giovanni Arnolfini and His wife Giovanna Cenami*

1435
Architect Leon Battista Alberti codifies optical perspective in *On Painting*

1455–56
Johannes Gutenberg, *Gutenberg Bible*

1480–1550
Portuguese extend African slave trade to Europe, Brazil

ca. 1482
Sandro Botticelli, *Primavera*

1486
Pico della Mirandola writes *Oration on the Dignity of Man*, philosophical treatise

1492
Spanish King Ferdinand II and Queen Isabella finance Columbus's voyage to the New World

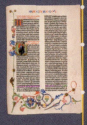

1508
Michelangelo begins Sistine Chapel ceiling

1513
Machiavelli writes *The Prince*

1517
Martin Luther posts *Ninety-Five Theses* on church door at Wittenberg

ca. 1488–1576
Lifetime of Titian, *Venus of Urbino* (ca. 1538)

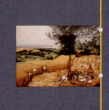

1519–21
Hernán Cortés conquers Aztec Empire of Mexico

ca. 1525–69
Lifetime of Pieter Bruegel the Elder, *Harvesters* (1565)

1542–63
Council of Trent convened to plan Catholic Church reform; Pope Paul III initiates Inquisition

1564–1616
Lifetime of William Shakespeare, poet and playwright

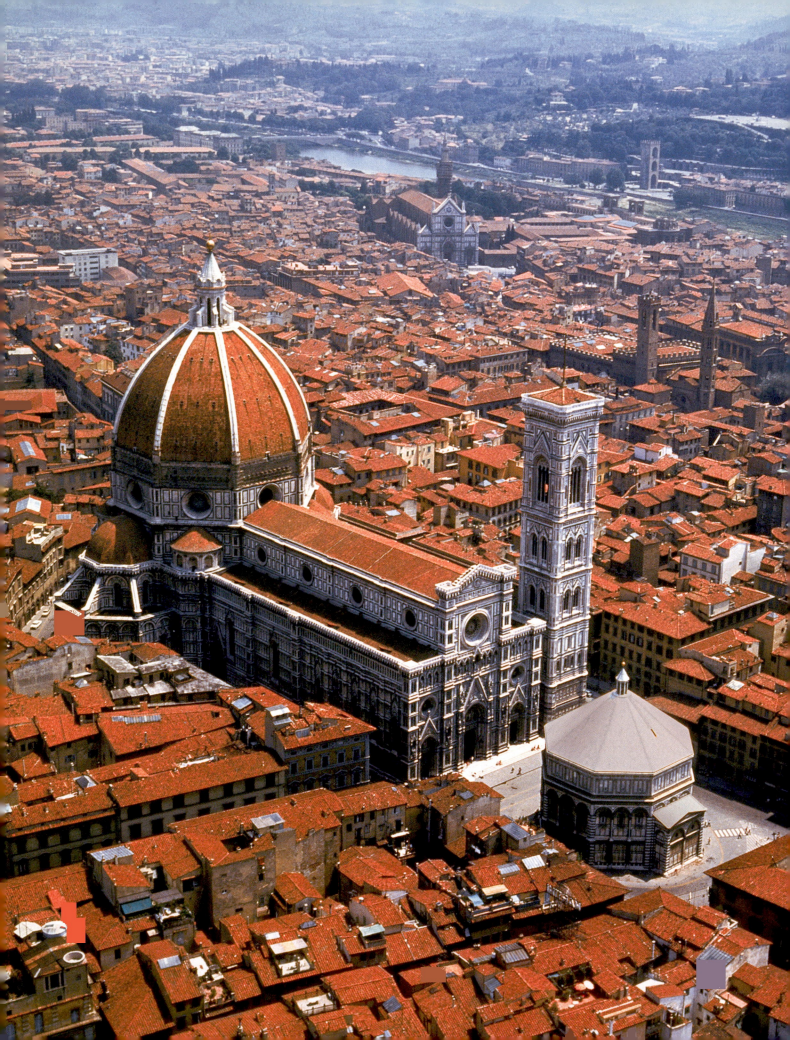

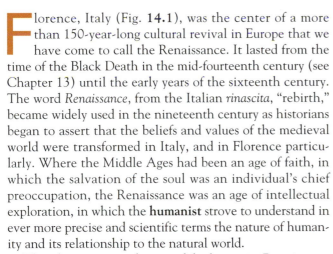

14

Florence and the Early Renaissance

Humanism in Italy

THINKING AHEAD

14.1 Examine how sculpture and the use of scientific perspective were instrumental in the early development of the Italian Renaissance.

14.2 Discuss the influence of the Medici family on Florentine art and the development of humanist thought.

14.3 Describe how other Italian courts followed the lead of the humanist court in Florence.

14.4 Explain the symbolic significance of Michelangelo's *David*.

lorence, Italy (Fig. **14.1**), was the center of a more than 150-year-long cultural revival in Europe that we have come to call the Renaissance. It lasted from the time of the Black Death in the mid-fourteenth century (see Chapter 13) until the early years of the sixteenth century. The word *Renaissance*, from the Italian *rinascita*, "rebirth," became widely used in the nineteenth century as historians began to assert that the beliefs and values of the medieval world were transformed in Italy, and in Florence particularly. Where the Middle Ages had been an age of faith, in which the salvation of the soul was an individual's chief preoccupation, the Renaissance was an age of intellectual exploration, in which the **humanist** strove to understand in ever more precise and scientific terms the nature of humanity and its relationship to the natural world.

This chapter traces the rise of the humanist Renaissance city-state as a center of culture in Italy in the fifteenth century, concentrating first on the republic of Florence, where the Medici family, whose wealth derived from their considerable banking interests, did much to position the city as a model that others felt compelled to imitate. Among these others were a number of smaller city-states ruled by Italian nobility—the Montefeltro court in Urbino, the Gonzaga court in Mantua, and the Sforza court in Milan. In each place, Church and State worked side by side for the good of the whole, championed by leaders who prepared the citizenry for lives of virtuous action. This brand of civic humanism reached its apex in Florence where, in response to the aggressive expansionism of Milan, a patriotic exaltation of liberty and a republican form of government developed through the citizenry's understanding that each citizen was responsible for every other citizen and participated in public life for the common good.

In this environment of enlightened leadership, the arts flourished. Across the Italian city-states, naturalism supplanted the formulaic pictorial traditions of the Middle Ages as artists came to understand the physical universe as a manifestation of the divine and thus worth copying in the greatest detail. In each place, humanist values helped to redefine the relation of the individual to the state, and philosophers insisted on the dignity of the individual.

◀ **Fig. 14.1 Florence, Italy.** The Duomo, Florence's magnificent cathedral, rises over the city. Its octagonal baptistery sits in the square before it. Just above and to the right of its bell tower, or *campanile*, designed by Giotto and built between 1334 and 1359, is the tower of the Palazzo Vecchio (see Fig. 13.1 in Chapter 13), and farther back toward the River Arno is Santa Croce (see Fig. 12.27 in Chapter 12).

((**Listen** to the chapter audio on **MyArtsLab**

THE STATE AS A WORK OF ART: THE BAPTISTERY DOORS, FLORENCE CATHEDRAL, AND A NEW PERSPECTIVE

How did sculpture and the use of scientific perspective contribute to the "rebirth" that is the Italian Renaissance?

Florence was, in fact, so thoughtfully and carefully constructed over the course of the fifteenth century that later scholars would come to view it as a work of art in its own right. No event better exemplifies its character—and the character of the Italian Renaissance in general—than a competition held at the very beginning of the century, in 1401, to choose a designer for a pair of bronze doors for the north entrance to the city's **baptistery** (Map **14.1**; and see Fig. 14.1). The bapistery is a building standing in front of a cathedral and used for the Christian rite of baptism.

By the thirteenth century, a legend had developed that the Baptistery stood on the site of a Roman temple to Mars, subsequently rededicated to Saint John the Baptist. The octagonal building was thus the principal civic monument connecting Florence to its Roman roots, and it stood at the very heart of the city, in front of the cathedral, which was still under construction in 1401. The original doors, at the south entrance, had been designed by Andrea Pisano in 1336, before the advent of the Black Death, and the Wool Guild, or Arte della Lana (see Chapter 13), which was in charge of the Opera del Duomo—literally, the "Works of the Cathedral"—was determined to create a new comparable set of doors for the north entrance.

In many ways, it is remarkable that the competition to find the best design for the Baptistery doors could even take place. As much as four-fifths of the city-state's population had died in the Black Death of 1348, and the plague had returned, though less severely, in 1363, 1374, 1383, and 1390. Finally, in the summer of 1400, it came again, this time killing 12,000 Florentines, about one-fifth of the population. Perhaps the guild hoped that a facelift for the Baptistery might appease an evidently wrathful God. Furthermore, civic pride and patriotism were also at stake. Milan, the powerful city-state to the north, had laid siege to Florence, blocking trade to and from the seaport at Pisa and

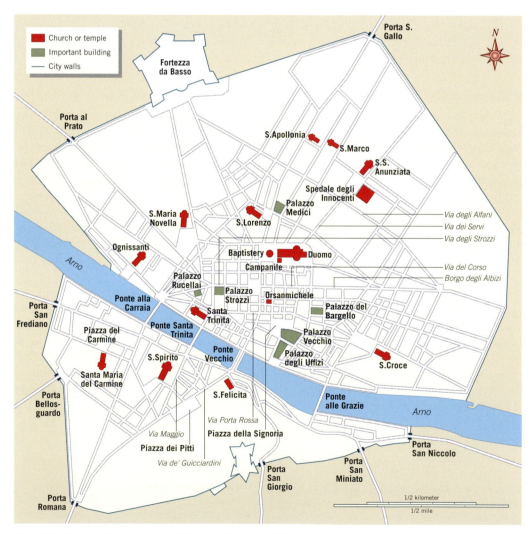

Map 14.1 Streets and monuments of Florence, Italy. ca. 1500.

creating the prospect of famine. The fate of the Florentine republic seemed to be in the balance.

So the competition was not merely about artistic talent. The general feeling was that if God looked with favor on the enterprise, the winner's work might well be the city's salvation. In fact, during the summer of 1402, as the competition was concluding, the duke of Milan died in his encampment outside the walls of Florence. The siege was over, and Florence was spared. If the Wool Guild could not take credit for these events, at least no one could deny the coincidence.

Thirty-four judges—artists, sculptors, and prominent citizens, including a Medici—chose the winner from among the seven entrants. Each artist was asked to create a bronze relief panel depicting the Hebrew Bible's story of the Sacrifice of Isaac (Genesis 22) in a 21 by 17½-inch *quatrefoil* (a four-leaf-clover shape set on a diamond). All but two designs were eliminated, both by little-known 24-year-old goldsmiths: Filippo Brunelleschi (1377–1446) and Lorenzo Ghiberti (1378–1455).

The Sacrifice of Isaac is the story of how God tested the faith of the patriarch Abraham by commanding him to sacrifice Isaac, his only son. Abraham took Isaac into the wilderness to perform the deed, but at the last moment, an angel stopped him, implying that God was convinced of Abraham's faith and would be satisfied with the sacrifice of a ram instead. Brunelleschi and Ghiberti both depicted the same aspect of the story, the moment when the angel intervenes.

Brunelleschi placed Isaac in the center of the panel and the other figures, whose number and type were probably prescribed by the judges, all around (Fig. 14.2). The opposition between Abraham and the angel, as the angel grabs Abraham's arm to stop him from plunging his knife into his son's breast, is highly dramatic and realistic, an effect achieved by the figures' jagged movements. Ghiberti, in contrast, set the sacrifice to one side of the panel (Fig. 14.3). He replaced a sense of physical strain with graceful rhythms, so that Isaac and Abraham are unified by the bowed curves of their bodies, Isaac's nude body turning on its axis to face Abraham. The angel in the upper right corner is represented in a more dynamic manner than in Brunelleschi's panel. This heavenly visitor seems to have rushed in from deep space. The effect is achieved by **foreshortening**, a technique used to suggest that forms are sharply receding. In addition, the strong diagonal of the landscape, which extends from beneath the sacrificial altar and rises up into a large rocky outcrop behind the other figures, creates a more vivid sense of real space than Brunelleschi's scene.

Despite the artistic differences in the two works, the contest might have been decided by economics. Brunelleschi cast each of his figures separately and then assembled them on the background. Ghiberti cast separately just the body of Isaac, which required only two-thirds of the bronze used by his rival. The process also resulted in a more unified panel, and this may have given Ghiberti the

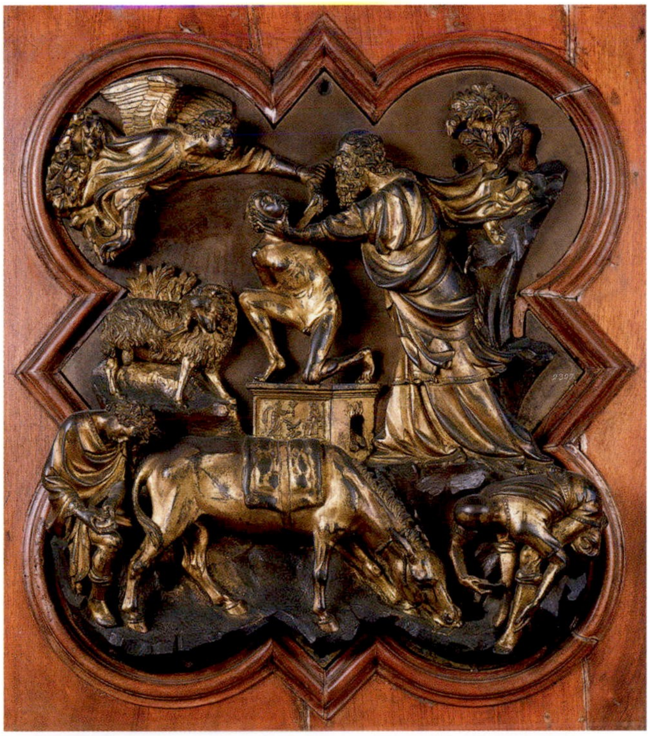

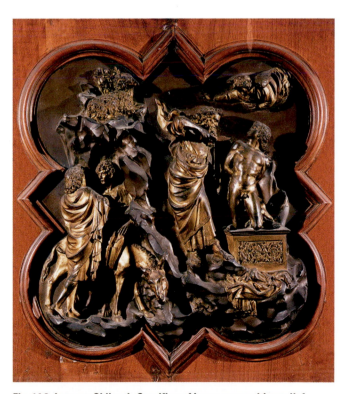

Fig. 14.2 Filippo Brunelleschi, *Sacrifice of Isaac*, competition relief commissioned for the doors of the Baptistery. 1401–02. Parcel-gilt bronze, 21″ × 17½″. Museo Nazionale del Bargello, Florence. Brunelleschi's background seems to be little more than a flat surface against which his forms are set.

Fig. 14.3 Lorenzo Ghiberti, *Sacrifice of Isaac*, competition relief commissioned for the doors of the Baptistery. 1401–02. Parcel-gilt bronze, 21″ × 17½″. Museo Nazionale del Bargello, Florence. As opposed to Brunelleschi's, Ghiberti's background seems to be real, deep space.

edge. Disappointed, Brunelleschi left Florence for Rome and gave up sculpture forever. Their competition highlights the growing emphasis on individual achievement in the young Italian Renaissance: The work of the individual craftsperson was replacing the collective efforts of the guild or workshop in decorating public space. The judges valued the originality of Brunelleschi's and Ghiberti's conceptions. Rather than placing their figures on a shallow platform, as one might expect in the shallow space available in a relief sculpture, both sought to create a sense of a deep, receding space, enhancing the appearance of reality.

As humanists, Ghiberti and Brunelleschi valued the artistic models of antiquity and looked to Classical sculpture for inspiration. Notice the twisting torso of Ghiberti's nude Isaac and Brunelleschi's servant at the lower left of the relief, a direct quotation of an ancient Roman bronze known as the *Thorn-Puller* (see Fig. 6.10 in Chapter 6). Finally, the artworks they created captured human beings in the midst of a crisis of faith with which every viewer might identify. In all this, their competition looked forward to the art that defines the Italian Renaissance itself.

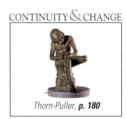

CONTINUITY & CHANGE

Thorn-Puller, **p. 180**

The *Gates of Paradise*

Ghiberti worked on the north-side doors for the next 22 years, designing 28 panels in four vertical rows illustrating the New Testament (originally the subject had been the Hebrew Bible, but the Wool Guild changed the program). Immediately upon their completion in 1424, the guild commissioned a second set of doors from Ghiberti for the east side of the Baptistery. These would take him another 27 years. Known as the *Gates of Paradise* because they open onto the *paradiso*, Italian for the area between a baptistery and the entrance to its cathedral, these doors depict scenes from the Hebrew Bible in ten square panels (Fig. **14.4**). The borders surrounding them contain other biblical figures, as well as a self-portrait (Fig. **14.5**). The artist's head is slightly bowed, perhaps in humility, but perhaps, situated as it is just above the average viewer's head, so that he might look out upon his audience. The proud image functions as both a signature and a bold assertion of Ghiberti's own worth as an artist and individual.

Each of the panels in the east doors depicts one or more events from the same story. For instance, the first panel, at the upper left of the doors (Fig. **14.6**), contains four episodes from the Book of Genesis: the Creation of Adam, at the bottom left; the Creation of Eve, in the center; the Temptation, in the distance behind the Creation of Adam; and the Expulsion, at the bottom right. This portrayal of sequential events in the same frame harkens back to medieval art. But if the content of the space is episodic, the landscape is coherent and realistic, stretching in a single continuity from the foreground into the far distance. The figures themselves hark back to Classical Greek and

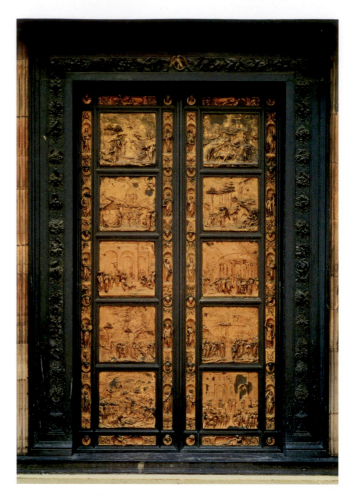

Fig. 14.4 Lorenzo Ghiberti, *Gates of Paradise*, east doors of the Baptistery, Florence. ca. 1425–52. Gilt bronze, height 15′. Ghiberti wrote of the doors in his *Commentaries* (ca. 1450–55): "I strove to imitate nature as clearly as I could, and with all the perspective I could produce, to have excellent compositions with many figures."

Roman sculpture. Adam, in the lower left-hand corner, resembles the recumbent god from the east pediment of the Parthenon (see Fig. 5.10 in Chapter 5), and Eve, in the right-hand corner, is a Venus of recognizably Hellenistic origin; compare Praxiteles' fourth-century BCE *Aphrodite of Knidos* (see Fig. 5.20 in Chapter 5).

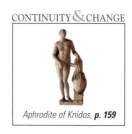

CONTINUITY & CHANGE

Aphrodite of Knidos, **p. 159**

Ghiberti meant to follow the lead of the ancients in creating realistic figures in realistic space. As he wrote in his memoirs: "I strove to observe with all the scale and proportion, and to endeavor to imitate Nature ... on the planes one sees the figures which are near appear larger, and those that are far off smaller, as reality shows." Not only do the figures farther off appear smaller, they also decrease in their projection from the panel, so that the most remote ones are in very shallow relief, hardly raised above the gilded bronze surface.

Whereas medieval artists regarded the natural world as an imperfect reflection of the divine, and hardly worth

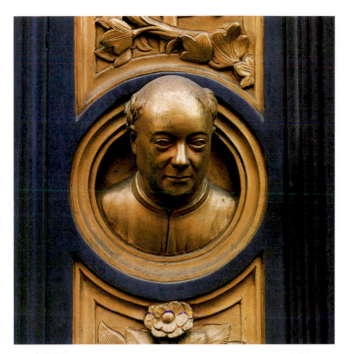

Fig. 14.5 Lorenzo Ghiberti, self-portrait from the *Gates of Paradise*, east doors of the Baptistery, Florence. ca. 1425–52. Gilt bronze. Ghiberti included his self-portrait among the prophets and other biblical figures framing the panels, as he had earlier on the north doors. The extreme naturalism of this self-portrait underscores the spirit of individualism that characterizes the Renaissance.

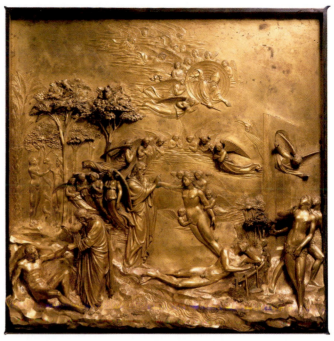

Fig. 14.6 Lorenzo Ghiberti, *The Story of Adam and Eve*, from the *Gates of Paradise*, east doors of the Baptistery, Florence. ca. 1425–52. Gilt bronze, 31¼" × 31¼". The influence of Classical antiquity is clear in the portrayal of Eve, whose pose, at the center, derives from Birth of Venus sculptures, and, on the right, from images of the Venus Pudica, or "modest" Venus.

attention (see Chapter 10), Renaissance artists understood the physical universe as an expression of the divine and thus worth copying in the greatest detail. To understand nature was, in some sense, to understand God. Ghiberti's panel embodies this growing desire in the Renaissance to reflect nature as accurately as possible. This provided a major motivation for the development of perspective in painting and drawing.

The work had political significance as well. The only panel to represent a single event in its space is the *Meeting of Solomon and Sheba* (Fig. **14.7**). Here, the carefully realized symmetry of the architecture, with Solomon and Sheba framed in the middle of its space, was probably designed to represent the much-hoped-for reunification of the Eastern Orthodox and Western Catholic branches of the Church. Solomon was traditionally associated with the Western Church, while the figure of Sheba, queen of the Arabian state of Sheba, was meant to symbolize the Eastern. Cosimo de' Medici would finance a Council of Churches that convened in Florence in 1438, and as Ghiberti finished the doors a year earlier, it seemed possible, even likely, that reunification might become a reality. This would have restored symmetry and balance to a divided Church just as Ghiberti had achieved balance and symmetry in his art. But above all, especially in the context of the other nine panels, all of which possess multiple events with multiple focal points, this composition's focus on a single event reflects the very image of the unity sought by the Church.

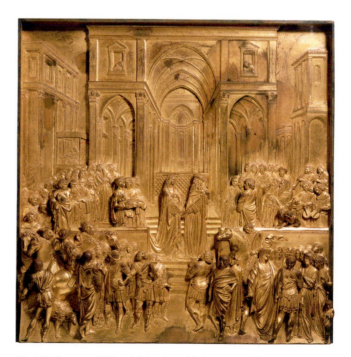

Fig. 14.7 Lorenzo Ghiberti, *Meeting of Solomon and Sheba*, from the *Gates of Paradise*, east doors of the Baptistery, Florence. ca. 1425–52. Gilt bronze, 31¼" × 31¼". The reunification of the Eastern and Western churches, symbolically represented here, was announced on the steps of Florence Cathedral on July 9, 1439, with the emperor of Byzantium present. The agreement was short-lived, and by 1472, the Eastern Church had formally rejected the Florence accords.

Florence Cathedral

Construction of the Duomo (see Fig. 14.1), as Florence Cathedral is known, began in 1296 (see Chapter 12) under the auspices of the Opera del Duomo, which was controlled by the Wool Guild. The cathedral was planned as the most beautiful and grandest in all of Tuscany. It was not consecrated until 140 years later, and even then, was hardly finished. Over the years, its design and construction became a group activity as an ever-changing panel of architects prepared model after model of the church and its details were submitted to the Opera and either accepted or rejected.

Competing Plans and Brunelleschi's Dome The first architect involved in the Duomo's planning was Arnolfo di Cambio (ca. 1245–ca. 1302), a student of Nicola Pisano who was charged with replacing the medieval church, Santa Reparata, which stood on the site of the new cathedral. His plan dwarfed the earlier church, but only the first two bays had been completed when the guild appointed Giotto di Bondone *capomaestro* of the structure in 1334. The campanile, the cathedral's freestanding bell tower, was completed in the 1350s, well after Bondone's death in 1337. Exactly what he planned for the cathedral itself is not known, but the present building follows plans for the choir end of the building first developed by Francesco Talenti (active 1300s) in 1355 and then refined several times by others.

Ultimately, the octagonal plan of the crossing, mirroring the octagonal structure of the Baptistery, was agreed upon. Throughout this period of revision (from the late 1350s to the late 1360s), the Opera del Duomo periodically submitted competing plans to the people for a vote, suggesting the civic investment in the structure. In August 1418, the Opera del Duomo announced a competition to crown Florence Cathedral with a dome. Brunelleschi was one of the entrants.

During visits to Rome, Brunelleschi had carefully measured the proportions of ancient buildings, including the Colosseum, the Pantheon, the remains of the Baths of Caracalla, and the Domus Aurea ("Golden Palace") of Nero. Using these studies, Brunelleschi produced the winning design for the dome of Florence Cathedral. The design guaranteed his reputation as one of the geniuses of Renaissance Florence, even in his own day. (See *Closer Look*, pages 474–475.)

Brunelleschi completed the dome in 1436. In yet another competition, he then designed a **lantern** (a windowed turret at the top of a dome and visible in Fig. 14.1) to cover the **oculus** (hole) and thus put the finishing touch on the dome. It was made of over 20 tons of stone. Brunelleschi designed a special hoist to raise the stone to the top of the dome, but construction had barely begun when he died in 1446.

"Songs of Angels": Music for Church and State For the consecration of Florence Cathedral, rededicated as Santa Maria del Fiore (Saint Mary of the Flower) on March 25, 1436, Brunelleschi constructed a 1,000-foot walkway, 6 feet high and decorated with flowers and herbs, on which

to guide celebrated guests into the cathedral proper. These included Pope Eugenius IV and his entourage of 7 cardinals, 37 bishops, and 9 Florentine officials (including Cosimo de' Medici), all of whom were observed by the gathered throng. Once inside, the guests heard a new musical work, picking up the floral theme of the day, called *Nuper rosarum flores* ("The Rose Blossoms") (track **14.1**). It was composed especially for the consecration by French composer Guillaume Dufay (ca. 1400–74), who worked in both France and Italy. The piece is a **motet**, a form of polyphonic vocal work that had gained increasing popularity since the mid-thirteenth century (see Chapter 12). Dufay's motet introduced a richer and fuller sonority to the form, combining both voices and instruments. (The issue of using instruments, other than the organ, in church performance would remain a matter of controversy for many centuries in the Catholic Church.) The *cantus firmus*—or "fixed melody"—on which the composition is based is stated in not one but two voices, both moving at different speeds.

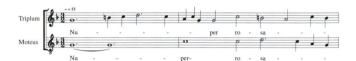

Cantus firmus* melody from Dufay's *Nuper rosarum flores

The melody derives from a chant traditionally used for the dedication of new churches, *Terribilis est locus iste* ("Awesome Is This Place").

Dufay's motet also reflects the ideal proportions of the Temple of Solomon in Jerusalem (see Chapter 2), which, according to I Kings, was laid out in the proportions 6:4:2:3, with 6 being the length of the building, 4 the length of the nave, 2 the width, and 3 the height. Florence Cathedral followed these same proportions, and Dufay mirrors them in his composition by repeating the *cantus firmus* four times, successively based on 6, 4, 2, and 3 units per *breve* (equivalent to two whole notes in modern notation). Hearing the entire work, one witness wrote, "it seemed as though the symphonies and songs of the angels and divine paradise had been sent forth from Heaven to whisper in our ears an unbelievable celestial sweetness." It is not surprising, given this reaction, that Dufay was regarded as the greatest composer of the fifteenth century. It is even less surprising that the Florentines selected him to celebrate the consecration of their new cathedral and its dome by creating an original work. In performing this service he announced the preeminence of both the cathedral and the city that had built it.

Scientific Perspective and Naturalistic Representation

No aspect of the Renaissance better embodies the spirit of invention evidenced by both Brunelleschi's dome and Dufay's music than **scientific**, or **linear perspective**, which allowed artists to translate three-dimensional space onto a two-dimensional surface, thereby satisfying the age's increasing taste for naturalistic representations of the physical world. It was the basis of what would later come to be called *buon disegno*, literally "good design" or "drawing," but the term refers more to the intellectual conception of the work than to literal drawing. Giorgio Vasari (1511–74), whose *Lives of the Most Excellent Painters, Architects, and Sculptors* is one of our most important sources of information about Italian Renaissance art in the fourteenth, fifteenth, and sixteenth centuries, defined it as follows: "Design (*disegno*) is the imitation of the most beautiful things of nature in all figures whether painted or chiseled, and this requires a hand and genius to transfer everything which the eye sees, exactly and correctly, whether it be in drawings, on paper panel, or other surface, both in relief and sculpture." It distinguished, in his mind, the art of Florence above all others.

Brunelleschi, Alberti, and the Invention of Scientific Perspective It was Brunelleschi who first mastered the art of scientific perspective sometime in the first decade of the fifteenth century. The ancient Greeks and Romans had at least partially understood its principles, but their methods had been lost. Brunelleschi almost certainly turned to them for the authority, at least, to "reinvent" it. His investigation of optics in Arab science also contributed to his understanding, particularly Alhazen's *Perspectiva* (ca. 1000 CE), which integrated the Classical works of Euclid, Ptolemy, and Galen. Their understanding of the principles of geometry, and the sense of balance and proportion that geometry inspired, affected every aspect of Brunelleschi's architectural work.

But it was geometry's revelation of the rules of perspective that most fascinated Brunelleschi. As he surveyed the Roman ruins, plotting three-dimensional architectural forms on flat paper, he mastered its finer points. Back in Florence, he would demonstrate the principles of perspective in his own architectural work. In the 1420s, while the cathedral dome was under construction, the Medici commissioned Brunelleschi to redesign the family parish church of San Lorenzo (Fig. **14.8**). The design owes much to the basilica churches of fourth- and fifth-century Christian Rome. Compare San Lorenzo, for example, with the interior of Saint Paul's Outside the Walls (see Fig. 8.13 in Chapter 8). Brunelleschi's design emphasizes the balance, symmetry, and proportion of its Classical precedents. He has composed the space in regular square

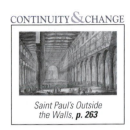

CONTINUITY & CHANGE

*Saint Paul's Outside the Walls, **p. 263***

blocks, with each bay nave twice as wide as the side aisles and the side aisles twice the size of each side chapel. The crossing is four times the size of each aisle. The space thus created, the wide arches revealing the whole of the architecture, is much more open than the Classical basilicas that inspired him, in which more tightly spaced columns tended to hide the side aisles and chapels from view. This clarity and order is the very basis of scientific perspective. Visitors standing at the entrance to San Lorenzo and looking down the nave feel as if they have just walked into a perspective drawing come to life, with all of the church's lines converging on the altar and choir at the far end of the nave.

Brunelleschi's findings were codified in 1435 by the architect Leon Battista Alberti (1404–74) in his treatise *On Painting*. Painting, Alberti says, is an intellectual pursuit, dedicated to replicating nature as accurately as possible. A painting's composition should be based on the orderly arrangement of parts, which relies on rendering

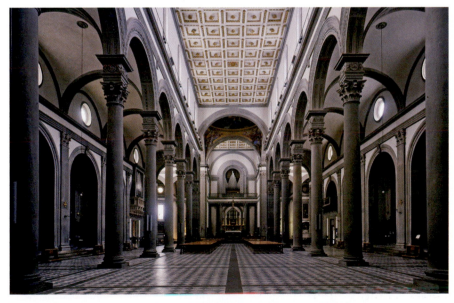

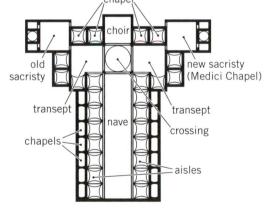

Fig. 14.8 Brunelleschi, nave and plan of San Lorenzo, Florence. ca. 1421–69. San Lorenzo was not completed until 23 years after Brunelleschi's death, and its exterior remains unfinished to this day, but it remains true to Brunelleschi's Classical vision.

✳ **Explore** the architectural panorama of the Church of San Lorenzo on **MyArtsLab**

I n the fourteenth century, with the nave of Florence Cathedral completed and vaulted, master mason Neri di Fioravanti had created a plan for a dome unlike anything ever built. Its diameter of 143 feet 6 inches was wider than the Roman Pantheon, and vaulting would not even begin until the building was 170 feet high—13 feet higher than the top of the highest Gothic cathedral, the one at Beauvais in France (and it had partially collapsed). This plan was a technical challenge that would not be met until the fifteenth century, when Filippo Brunelleschi won the competition sponsored by the Opera del Duomo to create a workable design.

Brunelleschi's design for the dome of Florence Cathedral was the triumph of his career. It solved a number of technical problems. For one thing, it eliminated the need for the temporary wooden scaffolding normally used to support the dome vaulting as it was raised. Though critics disagreed, Brunelleschi argued that a skeleton of eight large ribs, visible on the outside of the dome, alternating with eight pairs of thinner ribs beneath the roof, all tied together by only nine sets of horizontal ties, would be able to support themselves as the dome took form. The thinner ribs would lie between two shells—the outer roof and the interior ceiling—again creating a dome much lighter in weight than a solid structure. Scaffolding would be cantilevered out from the base of the drum and moved up, horizontal band by horizontal band, as the dome rose up. Additional support could be achieved through the use of lightweight bricks set in an interlocking herringbone pattern.

Something to Think About …

Many later Italians came to think of Brunelleschi's dome as a supreme example of *sprezzatura* (see page 488, later in this chapter). Can you explain?

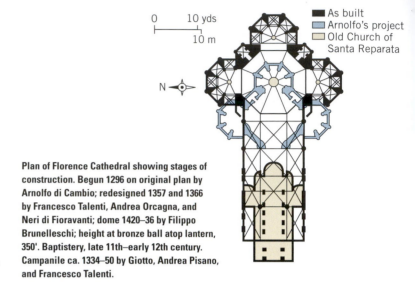

Plan of Florence Cathedral showing stages of construction. Begun 1296 on original plan by Arnolfo di Cambio; redesigned 1357 and 1366 by Francesco Talenti, Andrea Orcagna, and Neri di Fioravanti; dome 1420–36 by Filippo Brunelleschi; height at bronze ball atop lantern, 350'. Baptistery, late 11th–early 12th century. Campanile ca. 1334–50 by Giotto, Andrea Pisano, and Francesco Talenti.

- ■ As built
- ■ Arnolfo's project
- ☐ Old Church of Santa Reparata

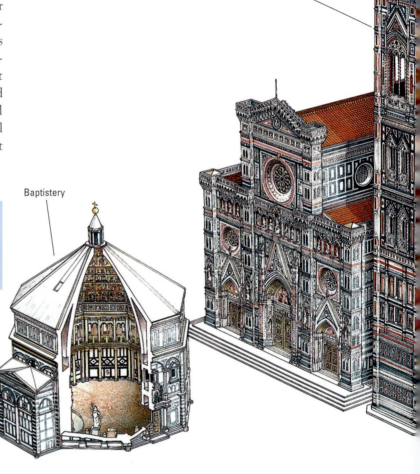

The campanile, or bell tower, was designed by Giotto and built between 1334 and 1359.

Baptistery

✳ **Explore** the architectural panorama of Florence Baptistery on **MyArtsLab**

Brunelleschi's Dome

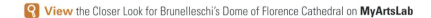 **View** the Closer Look for Brunelleschi's Dome of Florence Cathedral on **MyArtsLab**

The gilt bronze ball at the top of the dome was created by Andrea del Verrocchio between 1468 and 1471. It was raised into position by a machine built with the help of Leonardo da Vinci. The ball fell off after being struck by lightning on July 17, 1600, and was replaced two years later by a larger one.

The lantern, designed to cover the oculus, reveals Brunelleschi's Classical borrowing, for it adopts, perfectly, the Corinthian order.

Ribs and horizontal bands within the dome. The eight visible ribs are each 13 feet deep. Sixteen other concealed ribs radiate beneath the brickwork from the center. All meet at the oculus, over which Brunelleschi constructed his lantern. The horizontal ribs absorb the pressure caused by the thrust of the ribs against the wall of the dome.

Stone blocks at the base of the dome tie the inner and outer domes together. The projecting nibs supported platforms that were used by the masons for constructing the brickwork shell.

Cross-section of Brunelleschi's dome. This gives some idea of the enormous space beneath the dome. A drum (the wall designed to support the dome) was added to the octagonal crossing, extending the height of the crossing to 170' at the dome's base. The dome itself is another 100' high, and the lantern another 47½', making the whole well over 300' high.

Diagram of Dante's circles of Hell. Brunelleschi was an avid reader of Dante's *Divine Comedy* (see Chapter 13), and actually calculated the precise dimensions of Paradise. Scholars have noted that the nine circles of Brunelleschi's dome invert the nine circles of Dante's Inferno, suggesting that the dome was conceived as a model of Paradise.

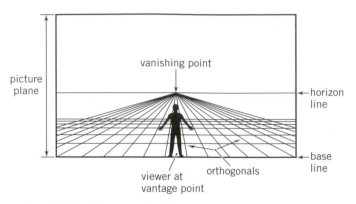

Fig. 14.9 Alberti's perspective diagram.

appear to converge at a single **vanishing point** on the horizon (think of train tracks merging in the distance); (2) These parallel lines are realized on the **picture plane**—the two-dimensional surface of the panel or canvas, conceived as a window through which the viewer perceives the three-dimensional world—as diagonal lines called **orthogonals**; (3) Forms diminish in scale as they approach the vanishing point along these orthogonals; and (4) The vanishing point is directly opposite the eye of the beholder, who stands at the **vantage point**, thus, metaphorically at least, placing the individual (both painter and viewer) at the center of the visual field.

Perspective and Naturalism in Painting: Masaccio

Although Alberti dedicated *On Painting* first and foremost to Brunelleschi, he also singled out several other Florentine

space in **one-point perspective**. He provides step-by-step instructions for the creation of such space, and provides diagrams as well (Fig. **14.9**). The basic principles of the system are these: (1) All parallel lines in a visual field

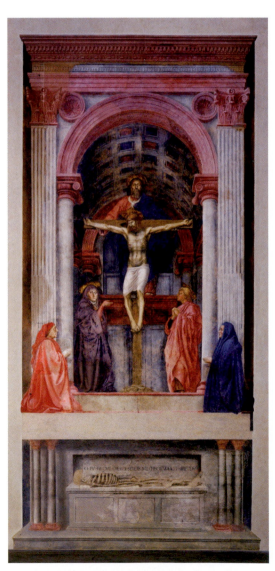

Fig. 14.10 Masaccio, *Trinity with the Virgin, Saint John the Evangelist, and Donors*, Santa Maria Novella, Florence. ca. 1425. Fresco, 21' × 10'5". The Trinity consists of Christ, God the Father behind him, and the Holy Spirit, represented as a dove flying between the two.

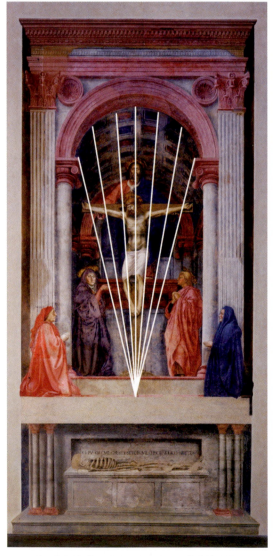

Fig. 14.11 Diagram of Masaccio's *Trinity with the Virgin, Saint John the Evangelist, and Donors*, showing the orthogonal lines that produce one-point scientific perspective.

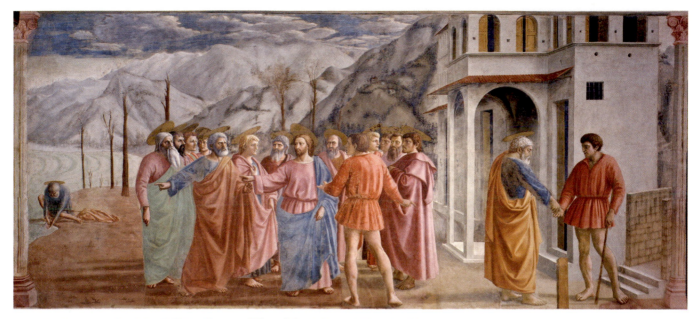

Fig. 14.12 Masaccio, *The Tribute Money*, Brancacci Chapel, Santa Maria del Carmine, Florence.
1420s. Fresco, 8¼' × 19'7". When this fresco was restored between 1981 and 1991, cleaning revealed that every character in this scene originally had a gold-leaf halo, except the tax collector, probably not a Christian. Masaccio drew these halos according to the laws of scientific perspective.

View the Closer Look for *The Tribute Money* on **MyArtsLab**

artists. One of these was Masaccio, whose *Trinity* (Fig. **14.10**) was probably painted in 1425. This fresco is painted directly on the wall of the Church of Santa Maria Novella in Florence and represents a chapel off the nave of that building. All of its architectural features are painted according to the laws of perspective, and the man and woman who kneel on what looks like a narrow ledge on either side of this chapel are so realistically positioned and naturalistically rendered that they seem to exist within our own space. (They are actually images of the donors who commissioned the work.)

In the carefully contrived perspectival scheme of this fresco, the horizon line is just above the base of the cross (Fig. **14.11**). Here, the central mystery of Christian faith—God as Father, Son, and Holy Spirit—is contained within the rational scheme of scientific perspective. This contrast between faith and naturalism is highlighted by the sarcophagus depicted at the bottom of the painting. A skeleton lies beneath its opened lid, and an inscription above it reads: "I was once that which you are, and what I am you also will be."

Masaccio's masterpiece of naturalistic representation is actually a somewhat earlier work, *The Tribute Money* (Fig. **14.12**). Commissioned by a member of the Brancacci family in the 1420s as part of a program to decorate the family's chapel in the Church of Santa Maria del Carmine in Florence, it illustrates an event in the Gospel of Matthew (17:24–27). Christ responds to the demand of a Roman tax collector for money by telling Saint Peter to catch a fish in the Sea of Galilee, where he will find, in its mouth, the required amount. This moment occurs in the center of the painting. Behind the central group, to the left, Saint Peter finds the money, and to the right, he pays the tax. The vanishing point of the painting is behind the head of Christ, where the orthogonals of the architecture on the right converge. In fact, the function of the architecture appears to be to lead the viewer's eyes to Christ, identifying him as the most important figure in the work.

Another device, known as **atmospheric perspective**, also gives the painting the feeling of naturalism. This system depends on the observation that the haze in the atmosphere makes distant elements appear less distinct and bluish in color, even as the sky becomes paler as it approaches the horizon. As a result, the house and trees on the distant hills in this fresco are loosely sketched, as if we see them through a hazy filter of air. The diminishing size of the barren trees at the left also underscores the fact that, in a perspectival rendering of space, far-off figures seem smaller (as does the diminished size of Saint Peter at the edge of the sea).

Perhaps the greatest source of naturalism in the scene comes from the figures themselves, who provide a good imitation of life through their dynamic gestures and poses, their individuality, and their emotional engagement in the events. Here the human figure is fully alive and active. This is especially evident in the *contrapposto* pose of the Roman tax collector, whom we see both with his back to us in the central group of figures and at the far right, where Saint Peter is paying him. Christ, too, throws all of his weight to his right foot. This is a naturalistic device that Masaccio borrowed from antiquity. Indeed, the blond head of Saint John is almost surely a copy of a Roman bust.

The Classical Tradition in Freestanding Sculpture: Donatello

Masaccio probably learned about the Classical disposition of the body's weight from Donatello, who had accompanied Brunelleschi to Rome years before. Many of Donatello's own works seem to have been inspired by antique Roman sculpture.

This Classical inspiration is visible in one of his earliest commissions, a statue of Saint Mark created for one of Florence's lesser guilds, the linen weavers and peddlers (Fig. **14.13**). It was one of a number of commissions by the city's guilds to decorate niches on the outer walls of Orsanmichele, a building originally constructed in 1336 as a market and grain store (in case of famine or siege). As early as 1339, it was decided that each of the city's guilds should provide a statue of their respective patron saints to decorate each of the niches on the Orsanmichele's outer walls, but by 1400, only three of the guilds had complied. As civic pressure was brought to bear on the guilds to fulfill their obligations in the first years of the fifteenth century, the city was treated to a virtual exposition of the new Classical direction in sculpture, a direction matched only by Ghiberti's work on his two sets of doors for the Baptistery, the other great commissions of the era.

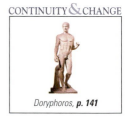

CONTINUITY & CHANGE

Doryphoros, **p. 141**

Donatello's *Saint Mark* stands in a fully Classical *contrapposto* pose reminiscent of Greek sculpture such as Polyclitus' *Doryphoros* (see Fig. 5.4 in Chapter 5). The folds of the drapery covering his body reveal the form of his body beneath, particularly his left knee as it projects forward, relieved of the necessity of bearing weight, and the drapery falls naturally across his upper body to gather at his waist. His beard and hair appear natural, his look remarkably intent. He is, in other words, a fully realized *human* form.

Dating from nearly 30 years later, Donatello's *David* (Fig. **14.14**), which celebrates this Hebrew Bible hero's victory over the giant Goliath, indicates how completely the sculptor had absorbed Classical tradition. The first life-size freestanding nude sculpted since antiquity (see again Polyclitus' *Doryphoros*, Fig. 5.4 in Chapter 5), it is revolutionary in other ways as well. The *contrapposto* pose is almost exaggerated, especially the positioning of the back of the hand against the hip. The young adolescent's youthful gaze stands in marked contrast to the bearded head of Goliath at his feet. Donatello seems to celebrate not just the human body, but its youthful vitality, a vitality his figure shared with the Florentine state itself.

It is difficult, in other words, to imagine that such a slight, adolescent figure could have slain a giant. It is as if Donatello portrayed David as an unconvincing hero in order to underscore the ability of virtue, in whatever form, to overcome tyranny. And so this young man might represent the vigor and virtue of the Florentine republic as a whole and the city's persistent resistance to domination.

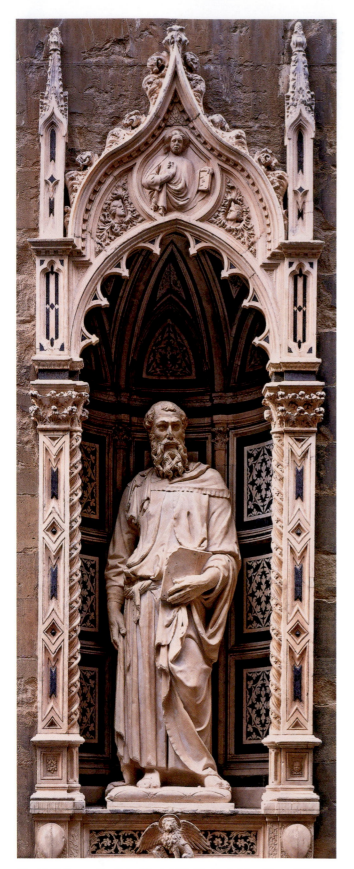

Fig. 14.13 Donatello, *Saint Mark.* **1411.** Marble, height of figure 93". Museo di Orsanmichele, Florence. The sculpture seen *in situ* here is a copy of the original, which has been removed to protect it from the elements and is now in the Museo di Orsanmichele.

In fact, when in 1469 the statue stood in the courtyard of the Medici palace, it bore the following inscription: "The victor is whoever defends the fatherland. All-powerful God crushes the angry enemy. Behold a boy overcame the great tyrant. Conquer, O citizens." The Medici thus secularized the religious image even as they implicitly affirmed their right to rule as granted by an all-powerful God whose might they shared.

THE MEDICI FAMILY AND HUMANISM

How did the Medici family help shape humanist Florence?

The Medici were the most powerful family in Florentine affairs for 76 years, from 1418, when they became banker to the papacy, until 1494, when irate citizens removed them from power. (They were briefly exiled earlier, for one year, in 1433.) A family of bankers with offices in Pisa, Rome, Bologna, Naples, Venice, Avignon, Lyon, Geneva, Basel, Cologne, Antwerp, Bruges, and London during the fifteenth century, the Medici never ruled Florence outright, but they managed its affairs from behind the scenes.

Over the course of those 76 years, they molded and manipulated, controlled and cajoled, persuaded and provoked the citizens of Florence into becoming a citizenry befitting the city they envisioned, a city that in some sense they sculpted, painted, and built. For them, the city was their own personal work of art. But the Medici trained the citizenry so well, especially imbuing it with a fierce independence of spirit, that the people eventually chafed at the control that the family exercised, and rebelled.

Cosimo de' Medici

The family's power was fully cemented by Cosimo de' Medici (1389–1464), who, as banker to the papacy, secured Florence's domination over rival Siena (see Chapter 13), putting the city at the very center of Italian politics. He had inherited great wealth from his father and secured the family's hold on the political fortunes of the city. Without upsetting the appearance of republican government, he mastered the art of behind-the-scenes power by controlling appointments to chief offices. But he also exerted considerable influence through his patronage of the arts. His father had headed the drive to rebuild the Church of San Lorenzo (see Fig. 14.8), which stood over the site of an early Christian basilica dedicated in 393. San Lorenzo thus represented the entire Christian history of Florence, and after his father's death, Cosimo himself paid to complete its construction and decorate it. In return, it was agreed that no family crest other than the Medici's would appear in the church. Cosimo also rebuilt the old monastery of San Marco for the Dominican Order, adding a library, cloister, chapter room, bell tower, and altarpiece. In effect,

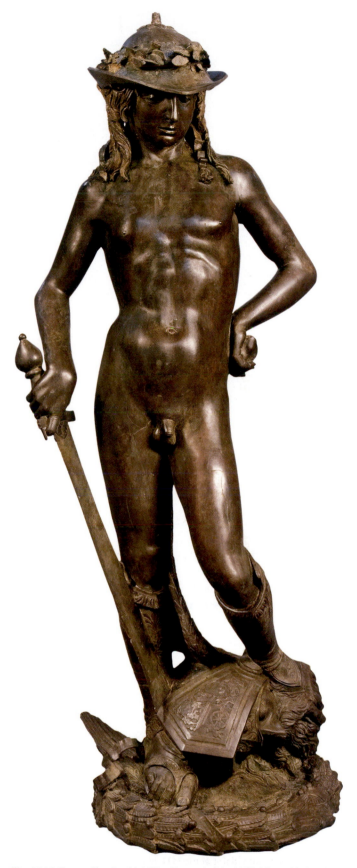

Fig. 14.14 Donatello, *David*. 1440s. Bronze, height 62¼". Museo Nazionale del Bargello, Florence. By 1469, this sculpture stood in the courtyard of the Medici palace as a symbol of the Florentine state.

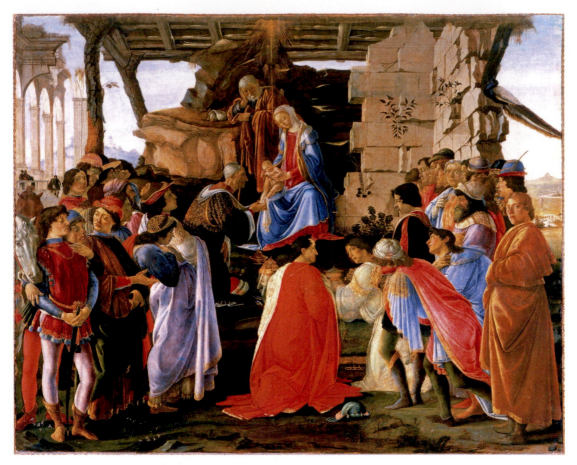

Fig. 14.15 Sandro Botticelli, *Adoration of the Magi*. 1470s. Tempera on panel, 43¾" × 52¾". Galleria degli Uffizi, Florence. On the right, the standing figure in the yellow robe staring out at the viewer is the artist himself, Botticelli.

Cosimo had made the entire religious history of Florence the family's own.

They even found themselves painted into that history. In an *Adoration of the Magi* (Fig. **14.15**) commissioned by Gaspare del Lama, a banker in the House of Medici, from painter Sandro Botticelli (1445–1510) sometime in the 1470s, Cosimo is dressed as the eldest Magus and kneels before the Christ Child. Looking on from the right side, in a black robe with a red stripe, is Lorenzo the Magnificent, Cosimo's grandson, who later guided the family's fortunes. Here art mimics life, for each year the Medici men participated in a procession that moved through the city on January 6, the feast day of the Magi, from the monastery church of San Marco, to the Baptistery beside Florence Cathedral (see Map 14.1). In both the procession and the painting, the Medici embodied not only the wisdom of the Magi but their kingship as well; through both, they affirmed their political power despite the ostensibly republican government of the city.

The procession of the Magi was staged each year by the Confraternity of the Magi, to which all the Medici belonged. The **confraternity** was the most characteristic form of organization in the Catholic Church in Renaissance Italy. As opposed to guilds, which were organized by trade, confraternities were religious brotherhoods for laypeople

and were designed to promote their common religious life. The Confraternity of the Magi was the most powerful confraternity in Florence and provided the Medici with a ready-made vehicle for public charity and self-promotion. Seven years after Cosimo's death, his grandson Lorenzo claimed that the Medici had spent over 600,000 florins for public purposes since 1434, much of it distributed through the Confraternity of the Magi. (Though the value of the florin varied considerably, a florin in Cosimo's time was worth perhaps $200 in today's currency, making Cosimo's expenditures roughly $40 million.) This was about twice as much as Cosimo had left his heirs, a generosity hardly lost on fellow Florentines and one, Lorenzo said, that "casts a brilliant light upon our condition in the city."

Marsilio Ficino and Neoplatonism Cosimo surrounded himself with humanists. He collected ancient Greek and Roman art, bringing to Florence the finest examples of sculpture he could find. He also sought the humanists' guidance about what books and manuscripts of the ancients he ought to collect, and commissioned translations of Greek philosophy and literature, since he himself could not master the language. Especially after the fall of Constantinople in 1453, Greek texts and Greek scholars arrived in large numbers from the East. Cosimo was particularly impressed by one scholar, the young priest Marsilio Ficino (1433–99).

Beginning in about 1453, Cosimo supported Ficino in his translations and interpretations of the works of Plato and later philosophers of Platonic thought. (The translations were from the Greek to Latin, which all educated people knew and read.) Platonic thought distinguished between a sphere of being that is eternal and unchanging and the world in which we actually live, in which nothing is fixed forever. Following Plato's lead, Ficino argued that human reason belonged to the eternal dimension, as human achievement in mathematics and moral philosophy demonstrated, and that through human reason we can commune with the eternal sphere of being.

Inspired by Ficino, who conceived it his duty to harmonize Christian and pagan traditions, Cosimo founded the Platonic Academy in Florence. Often gathering at a suburban villa, with Cosimo in attendance, the academy discussed Plato under Ficino's guidance. Inspired especially by Plato's *Symposium* (see Reading 5.6 in Chapter 5), Ficino coined the term **Platonic love** to describe the ideal spiritual (never physical) relationship between two people, based on Plato's insistence on striving for and seeking out the good, the true, and the beautiful. The source of Ficino's thought is his study of the writings of Plotinus (ca. 205–70 CE), a Greek scholar of Platonic thought who had studied Indian philosophy (both Hinduism and Buddhism) and who believed in the existence of an ineffable and transcendent One, from which emanated the rest of the universe as a series of lesser beings. For Plotinus, human perfection (and, therefore, absolute happiness) was attainable in this world through philosophical meditation. This **Neoplatonist** philosophy (a modern usage) recast Platonic thought in contemporary terms. It appealed immensely to Cosimo. He could see everywhere in the great art and literature of antiquity the good, the true, and the beautiful he sought, and so he surrounded himself with art and literature, both contemporary and Classical, and lavished them upon his city.

Humanist scholarship, in fact, encouraged Cosimo's politics as well. Aristotle had defined human beings as "political animals" (see Chapter 5, page 137) and the Roman orator Cicero had insisted that civic responsibility was the chief duty of citizens (see *On Duty*, Reading 6.2 in Chapter 6). Cosimo saw his patronage—especially insofar as Church and State were inextricably linked in Renaissance Florence—as activity for the good of God that would in turn benefit the city.

Domestic Architecture for Merchant Princes, In 1444, Cosimo commissioned for the family a new **palazzo** ("palace") that would redefine domestic architecture in

CONTINUITY & CHANGE
Plato's *Symposium*, **p. 171**

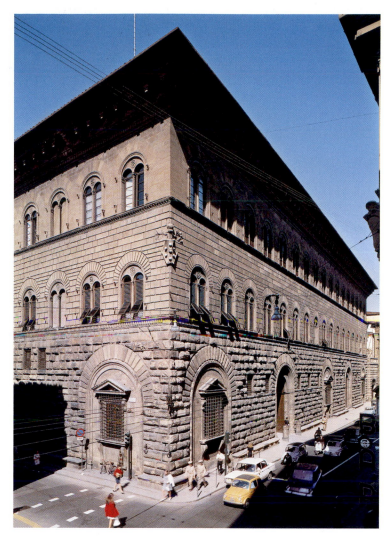

Fig. 14.16 Michelozzo di Bartolommeo. Palazzo Medici-Riccardi, Florence. Begun 1444. If it seems odd to think of such a structure as a palace, it is worth remembering that the Italian word *palazzo* refers to any reasonably large urban house.

the Renaissance. He first rejected a plan by Brunelleschi, considering it too grand, and built instead a palace designed by Michelozzo di Bartolommeo (1396–1472), now known as the Palazzo Medici-Riccardi (Fig. **14.16**). Cosimo filled it with the art of the day (including Donatello's *David*, Fig. 14.14). The bottom story is 20 feet high and made of rough-cut stone meant to imitate the walls of ancient Roman ruins and designed to suggest the Medici's adherence to tradition. The outside of the second story, which housed the living quarters, is cut into smooth stones, with visible joints between them. The outside of the third story, reserved for servants, is entirely smooth, thus giving the facade the appearance of decreasing mass and even airiness.

The Palazzo Medici became the standard for townhouses of wealthy Florentine merchants. Two years later, Leon Battista Alberti, author of *On Painting* and a close friend and adviser to Cosimo, designed a home for the Florentine patrician Giovanni Rucellai that brought the more or less subtle Classical references of Michelozzo's design

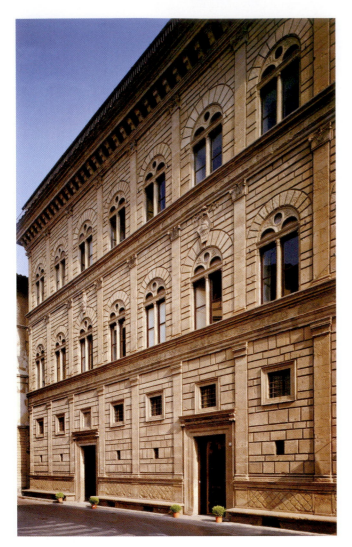

Fig. 14.17 Leon Battista Alberti, Palazzo Rucellai, Florence. 1446–51. In Alberti's time, the house extended to the right by four more bays and one more doorway, or portal.

for Cosimo to full light. The Palazzo Rucellai (Fig. **14.17**) reflects on a domestic level many of the ideas that Alberti would publish in about 1450 in his *On the Art of Building*.

For Alberti, architecture is the highest art and all buildings need to reflect properly their social "place." Thus the Duomo, which Alberti believed to be the most important building in Florence, is at the heart of the city and rises high above it, the very center of Florentine culture. It follows that leading families should live in houses that reflect those families' stability and strength.

The Palazzo Rucellai does that and more. In direct imitation of the Roman Colosseum (see Fig. 6.20 in Chapter 6), Alberti uses three Classical orders, one for each of the three stories: the Tuscan (substituting for the Doric) at the bottom, the Ionic at the second story, and the Corinthian at the top. As at the Colosseum, the columns

CONTINUITY & CHANGE

The Colosseum, **p. 195**

are decorative rather than functional, and an arch is set between them. Many people thought Alberti's plan was too grand because, in its reference to the Colosseum, it embodied not Republican but Imperial Rome. However, Alberti's design reflected the real state of affairs in Florence at that time. For the city was ruled by what was in fact a hereditary monarchy—the Medici—supported by a wealthy, albeit mercantile, "nobility," consisting of families such as the Rucellai.

Lorenzo the Magnificent: "... I find a relaxation in learning."

After Cosimo's death in 1464, his son Piero (1416–69) followed in his father's footsteps, championing the arts, supporting the Platonic Academy, and otherwise working to make Florence the cultural center of Europe. But when Piero died only five years after his father, his 20-year-old son Lorenzo (1449–92) assumed responsibility for leading the family and the city. So great and varied were his accomplishments that in his own time he was known as *il Magnifico*— "the Magnificent."

Lorenzo did not have his grandfather's wealth, so it was impossible for him to commission many works himself. But he saw to it that the artists and architects he attracted to the city received ample commissions from other patrons. He himself was an accomplished musician and poet, imitated by many, and he also started the collection of books that became the Medici Library, his agents retrieving large numbers of previously unknown Classical works from Greece, Egypt, and the Middle East. A large workshop of copyists employed by Lorenzo guaranteed that these works were diffused across the European continent. By the time of his death, he had created a model humanist city, the envy of all Italy. In Urbino, Mantua, and Milan, local rulers imitated Lorenzo's court and the traditions of artistic and philosophic achievement that had marked Florentine culture since the very beginning of the fifteenth century.

As a young man, Lorenzo had been tutored by Ficino, and among his favorite pastimes was spending the evening talking with Ficino and other friends. "When my mind is disturbed with the tumults of public business," he wrote Ficino in 1480, "and my ears are stunned with the clamors of turbulent citizens, how would it be possible for me to support such contentions unless I found a relaxation in learning?" In support of learning, Lorenzo rebuilt the University of Pisa and continued to support the study of Greek philosophy and literature in Florence at the Platonic Academy.

Lorenzo's own circle of acquaintances included many of the greatest minds of the day. Delighted by a copy of an ancient Greek or Roman faun's head made by an unknown adolescent named Michelangelo Buonarroti, Lorenzo invited the sculptor to live in the Medici palace, and the young man was soon a regular in the philosophical discussions that occupied Lorenzo for so many evenings. Besides Ficino, other frequent guests included the composer

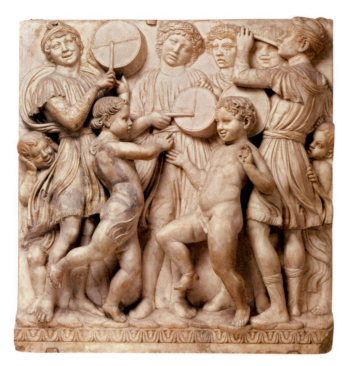

Fig. 14.18 Luca della Robbia, *Drummers* (detail of the *Cantoria*). 1433–40. Marble, 42⅛" × 41". Museo dell'Opera del Duomo, Florence. The 17-foot length of the space containing the *Cantoria*, or singer's gallery, would have accommodated small choirs and portable organs.

complex polyphony and counterpoint of church music (see the discussions of music in Chapters 10 and 12) in favor of simple harmonies and dancelike rhythms. Most *frottole* consist of three musical parts, with the melody in the highest register. The melodic line is generally taken by a soprano voice, accompanied in the two lower parts by either a lute and viol, two viols, other instruments, or two other voices. A typical *frottola* rhythm, such as from *Un di Lieto* ("One of Good Cheer"), might go something like this:

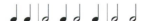

Typical *frottola* rhythm

From Lorenzo's point of view, such songs, sung in his native Italian, not Greek or Latin, demonstrated once and for all that Italian was the most harmonious and beautiful of languages when set to music. This sentiment would go on to have a lasting impact, especially on the development of the musical genre known as *opera* in the sixteenth and seventeenth centuries.

Poliziano: Humanist Poet Poliziano (1454–94) was a humanist as well as a poet and one of the foremost scholars of his day. He had translated Homer's *Iliad* into Latin and dedicated the work to Lorenzo, who soon made the young man his secretary and tutor to his sons. Poliziano wrote sonnets, dance songs, and carnival songs for a singer and instruments. His greatest work is undoubtedly *Stanzas for the Joust of Giuliano de' Medici*, a long poem written in vernacular Latin around 1475–78, the years immediately after Giuliano, Lorenzo's younger brother, had won a jousting tournament. It celebrates not only Giuliano's victory, but also his love for the beautiful Simonetta Vespucci, a married woman who was his mistress and tragically died in 1476.

In Book 1, verse 43 of Poliziano's poem, Giuliano sees a nymph while wandering in the woods, and Cupid immediately strikes him with Love's arrow. The nymph turns out to be Simonetta, whom Poliziano describes as follows (**Reading 14.1**):

Heinrich Isaac, the poet Poliziano, the painter Botticelli, and the philosopher Pico della Mirandola.

Heinrich Isaac: Humanist Composer Lorenzo's love of music was equaled only by his love of painting and poetry, and music was an important part of Florentine life, so much so that in 1433, the Opera del Duomo commissioned a series of eight reliefs from Luca della Robbia celebrating music. The reliefs were to be displayed in a gallery above the north door of the sacristy (Fig. **14.18**). They were conceived to illustrate Psalm 150, which calls for worshipers to praise God "with sound of the trumpet … with psaltry and harp … with timbrels and dance … with stringed instruments and organs … upon the high-sounding cymbals." Luca's youthful figures are the very embodiment of the joy and harmony that made music such an ideal manifestation of the humanist spirit.

Lorenzo's household employed its own private music master, and in 1475, Lorenzo appointed the Flemish composer Heinrich Isaac (1450–1517) to the position. Isaac oversaw the Medici's five household organs, taught music to Lorenzo's sons, served as organist and choirmaster at Florence Cathedral, and, before he knew it, found himself collaborating with Lorenzo writing songs for popular festivals.

The scores for many of the songs produced by this collaboration survive. They are examples of a musical genre known as the *frottola*, from the Italian for "nonsense" or "fib," and are extremely lighthearted. These *frottole* offer evidence of a strongly Italian movement away from the

> ## READING 14.1
>
> **from Poliziano, *Stanzas for the Joust of Giuliano de' Medici* (1475–78)**
>
> She is fair-skinned, unblemished white, and white is her garment, though ornamented with roses, flowers, and grass; the ringlets of her golden hair descend on a forehead humbly proud. The whole forest smiles about her, and, as it may, lightens her cares; in her movement she is regally mild, her glance alone could quiet a tempest.

Poliziano stopped writing in the middle of the second book, probably because Giuliano was assassinated in 1478. Poliziano was present when, on April 26, the rival Pazzi

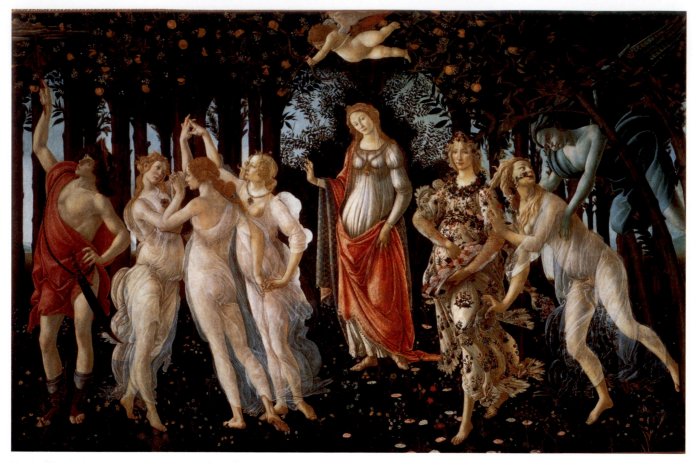

Fig. 14.19 Sandro Botticelli, *Primavera*. Early 1480s. Tempera on panel, 6'8" × 10'4". Galleria degli Uffizi, Florence. *Primavera* means both "spring" and "first truth" in Italian. Though the title is strongly allegorical, its exact meaning is still debated.

View the Closer Look for *Primavera* on **MyArtsLab**

family attacked Lorenzo and Giuliano during High Mass in the cathedral. Lorenzo was wounded in the shoulder, saved by Poliziano, but Giuliano died at the scene. The Pazzi were severely punished—though Lorenzo saved innocent family members from raging Florentine mobs—but Poliziano could never bring himself to finish the poem.

Sandro Botticelli: Humanist Painter It seems very likely that Poliziano's poem, or at least the sentiments surrounding it, inspired Sandro Botticelli to paint his *Primavera* ("Spring"), perhaps on commission from Lorenzo di Pierfrancesco de' Medici, Lorenzo the Magnificent's cousin and a student of both Ficino and Poliziano (Fig. **14.19**). In Botticelli's *Primavera*, the nymph stands in the center, depicted as Venus, goddess of love, surrounded by other mythological characters, who appear to move through the garden setting from right to left. To the humanists in Lorenzo's court, Venus was an allegorical figure who represented the highest moral qualities. According to Ficino, she was the very embodiment of "Humanitas … her Soul and mind are Love and Charity, her eyes Dignity and Magnanimity, the hands Liberality and Magnificence, the feet Comeliness and Modesty. The whole, then, is Temperance and Honesty, Charm and Splendor." On the far right of the embodiment of the humanities, Zephyrus, god of the west wind, attempts to capture Chloris, the nymph of spring, in his cold, blue grasp. But Flora, goddess of flowers, who stands beside the nymph, ignores the west wind's threat, and distributes blossoms across the path. To the left of Venus, the three Graces, daughters of Zeus and personifications of beauty, engage in a dance that recalls a specific one created for three people by Lorenzo in the 1460s. Lorenzo called the dance "Venus" and described it as based on the movement of two figures around a third one:

> First they do a slow side-step, and then together they move with two pairs of forward steps, beginning with the left foot; then the middle dancer turns round and across with two reprises, one on the foot sideways and the other on the right foot, also across; and during the time that the middle dancer is carrying out these reprises the other two go forward with two triplet steps and then give half a turn on the right foot in such a way as to face each other.

Finally, to the left, Mercury, messenger of the gods, holds up his staff as if to brush away the remnants of a straying cloud. Over the whole scene and positioned just above the head of Venus, Cupid reigns.

Primavera captures the spirit of the Medici. It celebrates love, not only in a Neoplatonic sense, as a spiritual, humanist endeavor, but also in a more direct, physical way. For Lorenzo hardly shied from physical pleasure. A prolific poet himself, his most famous poem, the 1490 "Song of Bacchus," deliberately invites the kind of carefree behavior we associate with carnivals, lavish festivities that Lorenzo regularly sponsored, complete with floats, processions through mythological settings, dance, and song (**Reading 14.2**):

READING 14.2

"Song of Bacchus," or "Triumph of Bacchus and Ariadne" from *Lorenzo de' Medici: Selected Poems and Prose*

How lovely is youth in its allure,
Which ever swiftly flies away!
Let all who want to, now be gay:
About tomorrow no one's sure.

Here are Bacchus, Ariadne,
For one another all afire:
Because time flies and plays us false,
They always yield to their desire.
These nymphs of theirs and other folk
Are merry every single day.
Let all who want to, now be gay:
About tomorrow no one's sure.

Those who love these pretty nymphs
Are little satyrs, free of cares,
Who in the grottoes and the glades
Have laid for them a hundred snares.
By Bacchus warmed and now aroused
They skip and dance the time away.

Let all who want to, now be gay:
About tomorrow no one's sure.

In fact, it seems likely that Botticelli's painting decorated Lorenzo di Pierfrancesco's wedding chamber. Clearly, a lighthearted spirit of play tempered all of Lorenzo the Magnificent's followers. As Machiavelli would later say of him: "If one examines the light and serious side of his life, one sees in him two different persons joined in an almost impossible conjunction."

Pico della Mirandola: Humanity "at the ... center of the world. ..." Cultural life in Lorenzo's court was grounded on moral philosophy. The young humanist philosopher, Pico della Mirandola (1463–94), shared Lorenzo's deep interest in the search for divine truth. By age 23, in 1486, Pico had compiled a volume of some 900 theological and philosophical theses, 13 of which Pope Innocent VIII (papacy

1484–92) considered heretical. When Pico refused to recant the 13 theses, Innocent condemned all 900.

Pico's thinking was based on wide reading in Hebrew, Arabic, Latin, and Greek, and he believed that all intellectual endeavors shared the same purpose—to reveal divine truth. Pico proposed defending his work, in public debate in Rome, against any scholar who might dare to confront him, but the pope banned the debate and even imprisoned him for a brief time in France, where he had fled. Lorenzo offered Pico protection in Florence, defying the pontiff in a daring assertion of secular versus papal authority. As a result, Pico became an important contributor to Lorenzo's humanist court.

In his 1486 *Oration on the Dignity of Man*—the introduction to his proposed debate and one of the great manifestos of humanism—Pico argued that humanity was part of the "great chain of being" that stretches from God to angels, humans, animals, plants, minerals, and the most primal matter. This idea can be traced to the Idea of the Good developed by Plato in Book 7 of the *Republic*, an idea of perfection to which all creation tends. Plotinus' brand of Neoplatonic thought took it a step further in proposing that the material world, including humanity, is but the shadowy reflection of the celestial, a condition that the pursuit of knowledge allows humanity, if it chooses, at least to begin to overcome. According to Pico, humanity finds itself in a middle position in the great chain of being—not by natural law but by the exercise of its own free will. Humans, then, are not fixed in the middle position. They are, in fact, pure potential, able to make of themselves what they wish. Humanity, it follows, is God's greatest miracle: "There is nothing to be seen more wonderful than man," Pico wrote. In his *Oration*, he has God explain to Adam that he has placed him "at the very center of the world" and given him the gift of pure potential to shape himself (**Reading 14.3**):

READING 14.3

from Pico della Mirandola, *Oration on the Dignity of Man* (1486)

We have given you, Oh Adam, no visage proper to yourself, nor any endowment properly your own, in order that whatever place, whatever form, whatever gifts you may, with premeditation, select, these same you may have and possess through your own judgment and decision. The nature of all other creatures is defined and restricted within laws which We have laid down; you, by contrast, impeded by no such restrictions, may, by your own free will, to whose custody We have assigned you, trace for yourself the lineaments of your own nature. I have placed you at the very center of the world, so that from that vantage point you may with greater ease glance round about you on all that the world contains. ... You may, as the free and proud shaper of your own being, fashion yourself in the form you prefer. It will be in your power to descend to the lower, brutish forms of life; [or] you will be able, through your own decision, to rise again to the superior orders whose life is divine.

For Pico, the role of the philosopher in this anthropocentric ("human-centered") world is as "a creature of heaven and not of earth." This is because "unmindful of the body, withdrawn into the inner chambers of mind," the philosopher is part of "some higher divinity, clothed with human flesh." It is imperative, therefore, in Pico's view, for individuals to seek out virtue and knowledge, even while knowing their capability of choosing a path of vice and ignorance. Taking the idea of "freedom of judgment" to a new level, Pico argues that humanity is completely free to exercise its free will. And this gift of free will makes humans "the most fortunate of living things."

Such thinking reflects what may be the most important transformation wrought by Renaissance thinkers on medieval ideas. Art, literature, and philosophy, as the free expression of the individual's creative power, can, if they aim high enough, express not only the whole of earthly creation but the whole of the divine. The human being is a *parvus mundus*, a "small universe."

BEYOND FLORENCE: THE DUCAL COURTS AND THE ARTS

How did the art and literature created in the ducal courts of Italy reflect Florentine humanist values?

Pico's message of individual free will and of humanity's ability to choose a path of virtue and knowledge inspired Lorenzo's circle and the courts of other Italian city-states as well. These leaders were almost all nobility, not merchants like the Medici (who, it must be said, had transformed themselves into nobility in all but name), and each court reflected the values of its respective duke—and, very often, his wife. But if they were not about to adopt the republican form of government of Florence, they nevertheless all shared the humanistic values that were so thoroughly developed there.

The Montefeltro Court in Urbino

One of the most prominent of these city-states was Urbino, some 70 miles east of Florence across the Apennine Mountains, where the military strategist and learned Duke Federigo da Montefeltro (1422–82) ruled. Federigo surrounded himself with humanists, scholars, poets, and artists, from whom he learned and from whom he commissioned works to embellish Urbino. He financed these expenditures through his talents as a *condottiero*, a mercenary soldier who was a valuable and highly paid ally to whomever could afford both him and his army. His court was also a magnet for young men who wanted to learn the principles of noble behavior.

Piero and Painting in Urbino Federigo's interest in scientific perspective was shared by the painter Piero della Francesca (ca. 1420–92), who first visited the Urbino court in 1469 and developed strong ties with it.

The political ideal of Federigo's court was projected by Piero in a state portrait of Federigo and his wife Battista Sforza (Fig. 14.20). In it, husband and wife gaze toward each other in profile situated in front of a landscape that most probably symbolizes the territory they ruled together. Their collars are aligned with the horizon, linking

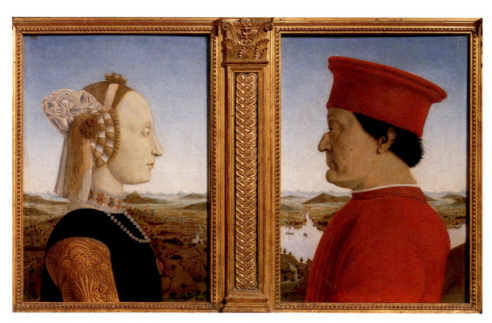

Fig. 14.20 Piero della Francesca, *Battista Sforza and Federigo da Montefeltro*. ca. 1472. Oil and tempera on panel, each 18½" × 13". Galleria degli Uffizi, Florence. Despite the idealism of Federigo's portrait—the profile view hides the disfigurement of the other side of his face—viewers sense they are looking at a realistic portrait because of such details as the moles on his cheek.

them together across the division of the canvas, but while the landscape behind Federigo is expansive and open to the sea, the landscape behind Battista is enclosed and fortified. Although Battista was Federigo's closest confidant, ruling Urbino during her husband's absences, her possibilities, the painting suggests, are limited, while Federigo's are not. And the shadow behind her suggests something else. A few years before Piero painted this work, Battista died, at the age of 26, six months after the birth of their ninth child, their son and heir, Guidobaldo. Federigo never remarried, and this portrait in some measure marks his devotion to her. These are idealized portraits, painted in profile no doubt because Federigo had lost his right eye and part of his nose in a sword fight, but also, in following tradition, by replicating ancient coin prototypes. Battista is portrayed as the ideal Renaissance beauty, her hairline plucked in order to achieve the rounded geometry of what was considered the ideal female face. But the painting is symbolically idealized as well. On the back of the double portrait are two facing images of the couple riding in chariots, his drawn by white horses, symbols of his political virtue, hers by unicorns, symbols of chastity (Fig. **14.21**). Battista is represented as Venus, goddess of love, but also, as in Botticelli's *Primavera*, the very embodiment of *humanitas*, and Federigo as Mars, god of war and the embodiment of male leadership. In Greek mythology, the product of their relationship is the goddess Harmonia, "Harmony," in this case the city-state of Urbino itself. But for Piero—and humanists in general—*harmonia* also suggested the mathematical harmonies of the universe, the perfection embodied in scientific perspective and its measured realization of space.

Baldassare Castiglione and *"L'Uomo Universale"* One of the most important books of the age, written between 1513 and 1518, recalled conversations, probably imaginary, that took place in 1507 among a group of aristocrats at the Urbino court of Guidobaldo da Montefeltro (1472–1508), the son of Federigo. *The Book of the Courtier* by Baldassare Castiglione (1478–1529) takes the form of a dialogue in which the eloquent courtiers at Urbino compete with each other to describe the perfect courtier—the man (or woman) whose education and deportment is best fashioned to serve the prince. It was not published until 1528, but by 1600, the book had been translated into five languages and reprinted in 57 editions.

The Book of the Courtier is, in essence, a nostalgic re-creation of Castiglione's nine years (1504–12) in the Urbino court, which he labeled "the very abode of joyfulness." It takes place on four successive evenings in the spring of 1507. The dialogue is in the form of a dialectic, as the viewpoints of some speakers are challenged and ridiculed by others. The first two books debate the qualities of an ideal gentleman (see **Reading 14.4**, pages 497–498). The goal is to be a completely well-rounded person, *l'uomo universale*. Above all, a courtier must be an accomplished soldier (like Federigo), not only mastering the martial arts but demonstrating absolute bravery and total loyalty in war. His liberal education must include Latin and Greek, other modern languages such as French and Spanish (necessary for diplomacy), and study of the great Italian poets and writers, such as Petrarch, Boccaccio, and Poliziano, so that he might imitate their skill in his own verse and prose, both in Latin and in the vernacular. The courtier must also be able to draw, appreciate the arts, and excel in dance and

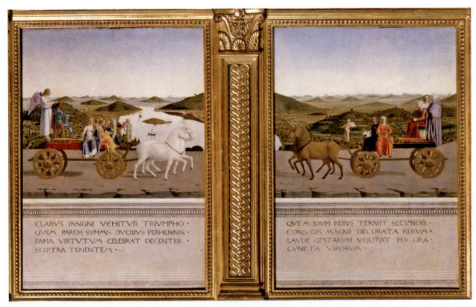

Fig. 14.21 Piero della Francesca, *Triumph of Federigo and Battista da Montefeltro*. ca. 1472. Reverse of Fig. 14.20. Galleria degli Uffizi, Florence. Federico's inscription reads: "He that the perennial fame of virtues right celebrates holding the scepter, equal to the highest dukes, the illustrious, is borne in outstanding triumph." Battista's reads: "She that kept her modesty in favorable circumstances, flies on the mouths of all men, adorned with the praise of the acts of her great husband."

music (though one must avoid the wind instruments since they deform the face). Above all, the courtier must demonstrate a certain *grazia* ("gracefulness") tempered by *gravitas* ("dignity") in all things. This balanced character trait is obtained, Castiglione explains in *The Book of the Courtier*, by means of "one universal rule":

> Flee as much as possible … affectation; and, perhaps to coin a word … make use in all things of a certain sprezzatura, which conceals art and presents everything said and done as something brought about without laboriousness and almost without giving it any thought.

Sprezzatura means, literally, "undervaluing" or "setting a small price" on something. For the courtier, it means simply doing difficult things as if effortlessly and with an attitude of nonchalance. The ideal gentleman, in other words, is a construction of absolute artifice, a work of art in his own right who cuts *una bella figura*, "a fine figure," that all will seek to emulate. Ultimately, Castiglione suggests, a state led by such perfect gentlemen would itself reflect their perfection, and thus the state does not create great individuals so much as great individuals create the perfect state, in the kind of exercise of free will that Pico discussed.

The Gonzaga Court in Mantua

The marquis Ludovico Gonzaga (1414–78) brought his northern Italian city-state of Mantua, located on a marsh-surrounded plain between Milan and Venice, into prominence among the Italian courts in the middle of the fifteenth century. Like Federigo da Montefeltro in Urbino, the Gonzagas hired themselves out as mercenaries to other city-states, accumulating enormous wealth in this manner. At the same time, they encouraged literary studies and commissioned works of architecture and the other visual arts. The Gonzaga court exhibited the same mixture of humanist and chivalric values found at other Renaissance courts and likewise reflected the values of its ruler.

Ludovico had a taste for Classical antiquity. It was stimulated, in part, by the work of Andrea Mantegna (ca. 1431–1506), who in 1460 accepted Ludovico's invitation to serve as court painter. Mantegna held this position for over 40 years. It was the painting of Mantegna that helped to bring the marquis's court to prominence.

In 1465, Mantegna began his most famous work, the *Camera Picta*, or "painted chamber," an elaborate fresco for the square room that served as both Ludovico's bridal

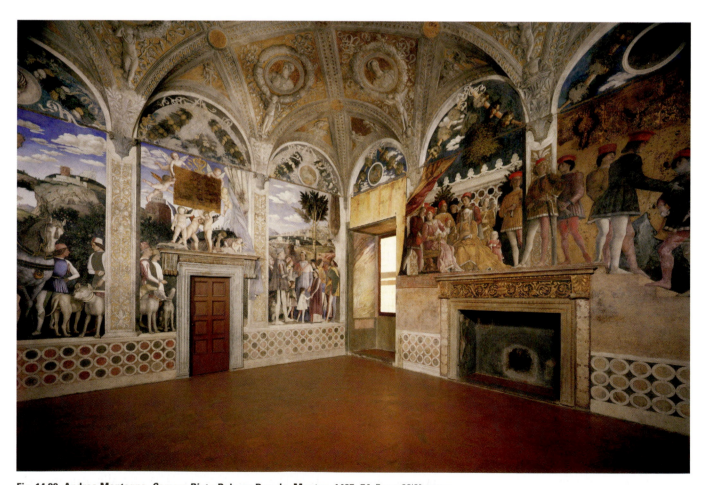

Fig. 14.22 Andrea Mantegna, ***Camera Picta*,** **Palazzo Ducale, Mantua. 1465–74.** Room 62'6" square.
To the right of the doorway, the family greets Cardinal Francesco, head of the Church of Sant'Andrea in Mantua and Ludovico's son.

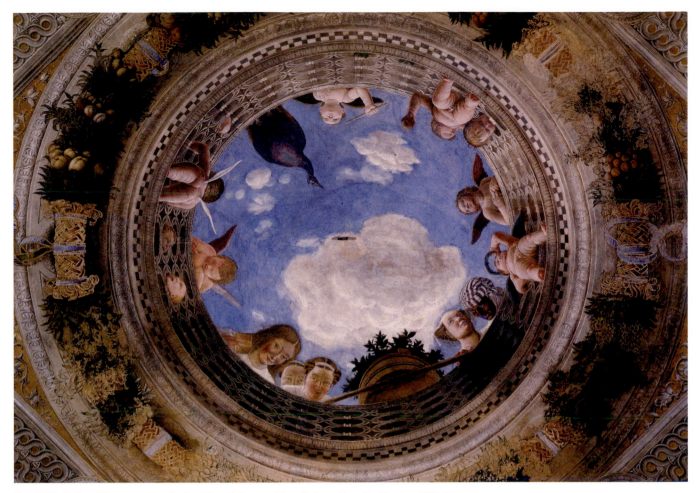

Fig. 14.23 Andrea Mantegna, detail of ceiling of *Camera Picta*, Palazzo Ducale, Mantua. 1465–74.
Fresco, diameter of balcony 5'. Mantegna plays on the idea of voyeurism, of women of the court peering into the room that served both as official reception chamber and bridal chamber. The implicit lesson is that the prince is always observed in all of his affairs.

chamber and the chamber in which he received visiting dignitaries. It took Mantegna nearly nine years to complete his work. On the walls are paintings of the Gonzaga family done partly *a secco* on dry plaster with an oil varnish (Fig. **14.22**). They depict the Gonzagas hunting in one fresco, participating in political life in another. Over the fireplace, Ludovico and Barbara of Brandenburg gather with their entire family as courtiers arrive to visit.

The ceiling of the *Camera Picta* is a tour de force. Mantegna painted a highly decorative dome over the room with a large illusionistic oculus (round opening) at its center that provides a view into a blue sky (Fig. **14.23**). It demonstrates his mastery of the *di sotto in sù* technique, the depiction of objects as seen from below, especially foreshortened figures such as the naked *putti*, or baby angels, perched inside the railing. Two groups of women peer over the edge of the oculus balustrade, including one who may be a visitor or servant from Muslim Africa. A peacock looks across at them, and a heavy potted plant rests precariously on a wooden pole. Of the eight pudgy *putti* who play along the railing, three appear to have gotten their heads stuck in

the balustrade, and one is about to drop an apple. This is perhaps a lighthearted play upon words in which *gravitas*—literally the dignity embodied in the ideal ruler—is transformed into *gravity*.

The *Camera Picta* instantly became famous, drawing attention to Ludovico's court. Mantegna's extremely accomplished realization of illusionistic space, brought off with panache and wit, makes the room's decorations the very model of *sprezzatura* in painting. That Ludovico had been able to attract such a skilled artist as Mantegna to his employ simply added to the Gonzaga prestige.

The Sforza Court in Milan and Leonardo da Vinci

The Sforza family's control over the court of Milan was somewhat less legitimate than most other ducal city-states in Italy. Francesco Sforza (1401–66) became ruler of Milan by marrying the illegitimate daughter, but sole heir, of the duke of Milan. His own illegitimate son, Ludovico (1451–1508), called *il Moro*, "the Moor," because of his dark complexion, wrested control of the city from the family of Francesco's legitimate brother and proclaimed himself Duke of Milan in 1494. Both Francesco and Ludovico understood the tenuousness of their claims to rule, and they actively sought to win the support of the people through the arts. They welcomed artists from throughout central Italy to their city and embraced humanism.

The most important of these artists was Leonardo da Vinci (1452–1519), who first arrived in Milan in 1482 as the emissary of Lorenzo de' Medici to present a silver lyre, perhaps made by Leonardo himself, to Ludovico Sforza. Ludovico was embroiled in military matters, and Leonardo pronounced himself a military engineer, capable of constructing great "machines of war," including designs for a catapult and covered vehicles that resemble modern-day armored cars.

Leonardo's restless imagination, in fact, led him to the study of almost everything: natural phenomena like wind, storms, and the movement of water; anatomy and physiology; physics and mechanics; music; mathematics; plants and animals; geology; and astronomy, to say nothing of painting and drawing. Leonardo was a humanist, and as such was deeply swayed by Neoplatonic thought. He saw connections among all spheres of existence and wrote of them:

If man has in himself bones, the supports and armature for the flesh, the world has the rocks, the supports of the earth; if man has in himself the lake of blood, in which the lungs increase and decrease in breathing, the body of the earth has its oceanic sea, which likewise increases and decreases every six hours with the breathing of the world; if from the said lake veins arise, which proceed to ramify throughout the human body, the oceanic sea fills the body of the earth with infinite veins of water.

Thus, the miracle of the fetus in the womb, which Leonardo depicts in a famous anatomical study from his notebooks (Fig. **14.24**), is analogous in his mind to the mysteries that lie deep within the body of the earth. "I came to the entrance of a great cavern," he writes in one note. "There immediately arose in me two feelings—fear and desire—fear of the menacing, dark cavity, and desire to see if there was anything miraculous within." Leonardo's fascination with the human body—an image, for him, of both attraction and repulsion—led him to produce this and his other precisely drawn dissections of the human body in 1510 to 1512, probably working under the direction of a young professor of anatomy.

In his *Lives of the Most Excellent Painters, Architects, and Sculptors*, which first appeared in 1550 and

was subsequently revised and greatly expanded in 1568, Giorgio Vasari underscores the inquisitiveness that Leonardo's dissections reveal. Born in 1511, Vasari could never have known Leonardo personally, but as a painter and architect, as well as a historian, he did know many other Renaissance artists, including Michelangelo, and his *Lives* remains one of our primary sources on Renaissance art.

Vasari focuses on demonstrating the individual creative genius of each artist he discusses. Vasari's treatment of Leonardo is typical of the other biographies in *Lives*. From the very opening lines of the "Life of Leonardo," Vasari presents him as a prototypical Renaissance man, endowing him with "beauty of body, infinite grace in all his actions" and of such genius "that to whatever difficulties he turned his mind, he solved them with ease" (see **Reading 14.5**, pages 498–499).

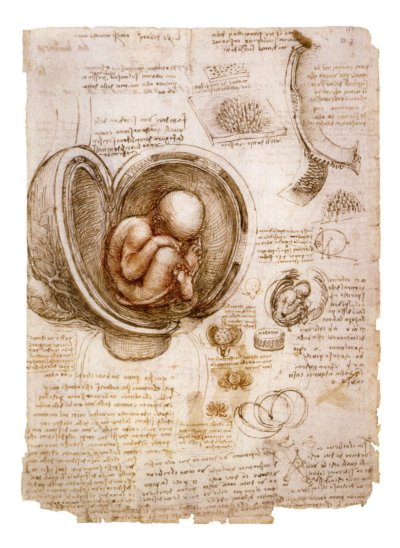

Fig. 14.24 Leonardo da Vinci, *Embryo in the Womb*. ca. 1510. Pen and brown ink, 11¾" × 8½". The Royal Collection © 2011 Her Majesty Queen Elizabeth II. Leonardo's notes on this page from one of his notebooks relate not only to standard questions of anatomy and physiology, including the nourishment of the fetus, but also to the relationship of the fetus's soul to that of its mother.

📖 **Read** the document from Vasari's *Lives* on **MyArtsLab**

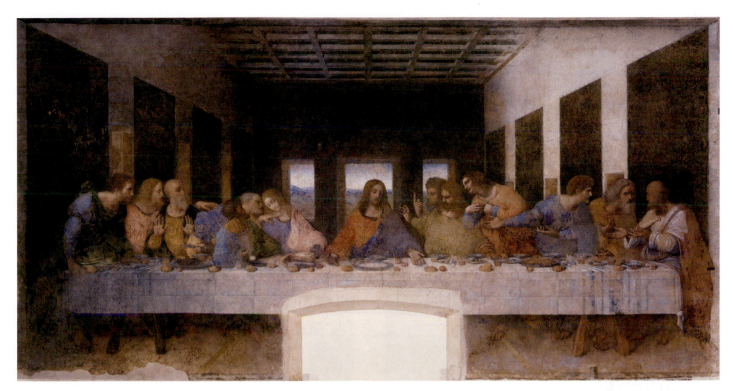

Fig. 14.25 Leonardo da Vinci, *Last Supper,* **wall painting in refectory, Monastery of Santa Maria delle Grazie, Milan. ca. 1495–98.** Fresco, oil, and tempera on plaster, 15'1⅛" × 28'10½". Today, even after "restoration," Leonardo's original painting remains in very bad shape. The fault is almost entirely Leonardo's—or maybe Ludovico Sforza's, who rushed him to complete it. Instead of using the established fresco technique of painting tempera on wet plaster, Leonardo applied tempera to dry plaster. As early as 1517, the paint began to flake off, unable to adhere to the wall.

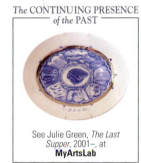

The CONTINUING PRESENCE of the PAST

See Julie Green, *The Last Supper,* 2001–, at **MyArtsLab**

In 1495, Ludovico commissioned Leonardo to paint a monumental fresco of the Last Supper for the north wall of the refectory of the Dominican monastery of Santa Maria delle Grazie (Fig. **14.25**). The intent was that at every meal the monks would contemplate Christ's last meal in a wall-sized painting. Like Masaccio's illusionistic chapel extending off the nave of Santa Maria Novella in Florence (see Fig. 14.10), the *Last Supper* illusionistically extends the refectory walls in a modified one-point perspective (the tabletop is tipped toward the viewer), carrying the present of architectural space into the past of the painting's space (Fig. **14.26**).

The moment Leonardo chose to depict is just after Christ has announced to the apostles that one of them will betray him. Each apostle reacts in his characteristic way. Saint Peter grabs a knife in anger, while Judas turns away and Saint John appears to faint. The vanishing point of the painting is directly behind Christ's head, focusing the viewer's attention and establishing Christ as the most important figure in the work. He extends his arms, forming a perfect equilateral triangle at the center of the painting, an image of balance and a symbolic reference to the Trinity. What is unique about this painting of an otherwise completely traditional subject for a refectory is the psychological realism that Leonardo lends to it. We see this in the sense of agitated doubt and confusion among the apostles, their intertwined bodies twisting and turning as if drawn toward

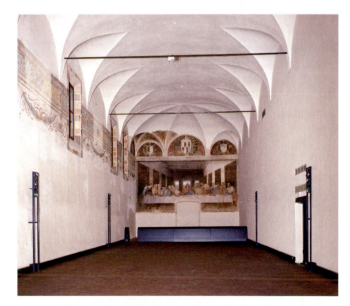

Fig. 14.26 The refectory, Monastery of Santa Maria delle Grazie, Milan, with Leonardo da Vinci's *Last Supper* **at far end.** The monks at the monastery would have consumed their own meals beneath this depiction of Christ's Last Supper.

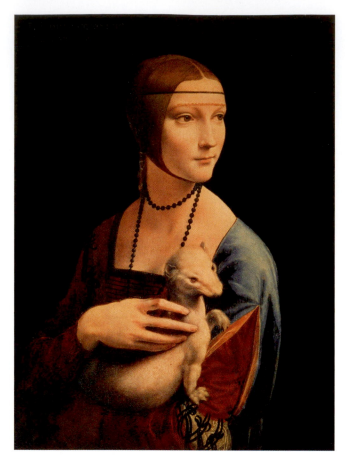

Fig. 14.27 Leonardo da Vinci, *Cecelia Gallerani* (*Lady with an Ermine*). 1483–85. Oil on panel, 21" × 15½". Czartoryski Museum, Cracow. Leonardo's ability to evoke his sitter's personality is clearly evident.

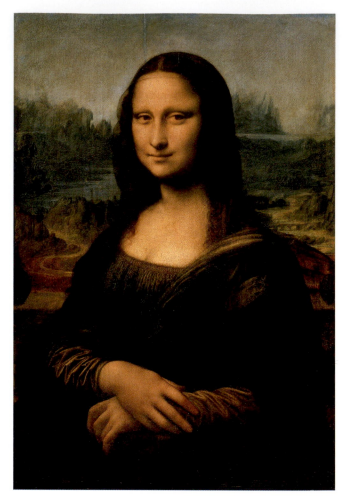

Fig. 14.28 Leonardo da Vinci, *Mona Lisa*. 1503–15. Oil on wood, 30¼" × 21". Musée du Louvre, Paris. Recent research tends to suggest that the woman in this picture is the wife of the Florentine patrician Francesco del Giocondo. She is seated on a balcony, originally between two columns that have been cut off (the base of the left column is just visible).

View the Closer Look for the *Mona Lisa* on **MyArtsLab**

the self-contained and peaceful image of Christ. The apostles, even Judas, are revealed in all their humanity, while Christ is composed in his compassion for them.

Because Leonardo was already known for his skill as a portrait painter when he arrived in Milan, Sforza commissioned him to paint his 16-year-old mistress, Cecelia Gallerani. The painting, sometimes known as *Lady with an Ermine*, represents something of a new direction in portraiture (Fig. **14.27**). The three-quarter view, head turned sharply to the right, is a new pose, but the truly unique aspect of the painting is the psychological reality of her gaze. It is as if we can see, in the blackness of the space behind her, something of the sitter's inner character. The long, sleek face of the white-furred ermine that she holds in her arms—an aristocratic and highly prized pet in the Renaissance as well as a symbol of purity and chastity—mirrors the features of its mistress, in whose family name, Gallerani, is embedded the Greek word for ermine, *galé*.

Leonardo's fascination with revealing the human personality in portraiture is nowhere more evident than in his *Mona Lisa* (Fig. **14.28**); Leonardo fuses his subject with the landscape behind her by means of light. This technique is called *sfumato* ("smokiness"). Its hazy effects, which create a half-waking, dreamlike quality reminiscent of dusk, could only be achieved by building up color with many layers of

transparent oil paint—a process called **glazing**. But it is the mysterious personality of Leonardo's sitter that most occupies the viewer's imagination. For generations, viewers have asked, Who is this woman? What is she thinking about? What is her relation to the artist? Leonardo presents us with a particular personality, whose half-smile suggests that he has captured her in a particular, if enigmatic, mood. And the painting's hazy light reinforces the mystery of her personality. Apparently, whatever he captured in her look he could not give up. The *Mona Lisa* occupied Leonardo for years, and it followed him to Rome and then to France in 1513, where King Louis XII offered him the Château of Cloux near Amboise as a residence. Leonardo died there on May 2, 1519.

In 1499, the French, under Charles VIII, deposed Ludovico and imprisoned him in France, where he died in 1508. Leonardo abandoned Milan, eventually returning to Florence in about 1503. Both of Ludovico's sons would briefly rule as Duke of Milan in the early sixteenth century, but both were soon deposed, and the male line of the Sforza family died out.

FLORENCE AFTER THE MEDICI: THE NEW REPUBLIC

How did Michelangelo's David *symbolize the new Florentine republic?*

In November 1494, the domination of Florence by the Medici family came to an end. Lorenzo had died two years earlier, and his successor, Piero the Unfortunate, faced with the threat of the same French invasion that ousted Ludovico Sforza in Milan, had blundered through a series of political moves and alliances until finally agreeing to cooperate with the French king, Charles VIII (1470–98). The Florentines would have none of it, and a mob drove Piero from the city. Into this power vacuum stepped a Dominican friar, Girolamo Savonarola (1452–98), abbot of the monastery of San Marco. Although, as a priest, he could not hold office, and although the city, freed of the Medici, was ostensibly a republic once again, Savonarola wielded tremendous political control. He appealed, first and foremost, to a moralistic faction of the populace that saw, in the behavior of the city's upper classes, and in their humanistic attraction to Classical Greek and Roman culture, clear evidence of moral decadence. He appealed as well to the Florentine populace's desire to reestablish its identity as a republic, which by 1490 everyone recognized had been lost, so dominant had the Medici family become. As early as 1491, Savonarola had preached that Florence was little more than a den of thieves. The arrival of Charles VIII was the scourge of the Lord, he said, ridding the city of the decadent and tyrannical Medici.

Savonarola railed against the Florentine nobility, going so far as to organize troops of children to collect the city's "vanities"—everything from cosmetics to books and paintings—and burn them in giant bonfires. Finally, in June 1497, an angry Pope Alexander VI excommunicated him for his antipapal preachings and for disobeying his directives for the administration of the monastery of San Marco. Savonarola was commanded not to preach, an order he chose to ignore. On May 28, 1498, he was forcibly removed from San Marco, tortured as a heretic along with two fellow friars, hanged until nearly dead, and then burned at the stake (Fig. **14.29**). His ashes were subsequently thrown into the Arno River. Once again, Florence felt itself freed from tyranny.

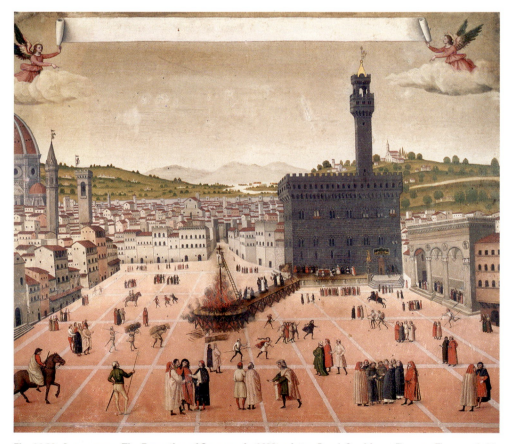

Fig. 14.29 Anonymous, *The Execution of Savonarola*. **1498 or later.** Panel. San Marco, Florence. The remarkable thing about this painting, which depicts an event taking place in the Piazza della Signoria, is that many passersby appear to be totally oblivious to the burning of Savonarola at the stake. In fact, we know from other documents that the piazza was packed with people intent on seeing the execution.

With the fall of Savonarola, the Signoria, Florence's governing body, quickly moved to assert the republic's survival in visual terms. It moved Donatello's *David* (see Fig. 14.14) from the Medici palace to the Palazzo della Signoria, where the governing body met to conduct business. It also asked Michelangelo, who had left for Rome in 1496, to return to Florence in 1501 to work on an old, weathered, and partially cut block of marble that all other sculptors had abandoned in dismay. It was to be another freestanding statue of the biblical hero David, but colossal in scale. Michelangelo rose to the challenge.

The completed figure (Fig. **14.30**), over 17 feet high—even higher on its pedestal—intentionally references Donatello's boyish predecessor but then challenges it. Michelangelo represents David before, not after, his triumph, sublimely confident, ready to take on whatever challenge faces him, just as the republic itself felt ready to take on all comers. The nudity of the figure and the *contrapposto* stance are directly indebted to the Medici celebration of all things ancient Greek. Its sense of self-contained, even heroic individualism captures perfectly the humanist spirit. Michelangelo's triumph over the complexity of the stone transformed it into an artwork that his contemporaries lauded for its almost unparalleled beauty. It was an achievement that Michelangelo would soon equal, in another medium, in his work on the Sistine Chapel ceiling at the Vatican, in Rome.

Michelangelo's *David* can be thought of as truly inaugurating the High Renaissance, the short-lived period from the late fifteenth century until about 1520 that is traditionally associated with the mature work of Leonardo, Michelangelo, Raphael, and the Venetian artists Giorgione and Titian. By 1520, Leonardo, Raphael, and Giorgione were dead. Seven years later, Rome was sacked by Charles V of France, and the teachings of the German monk Martin Luther were gaining an increasingly large following in the north, undermining the authority of Rome. Luther's Protestant Reformation decried the corruption and excess of the Catholic Church and inspired a period of moral piety that affected Protestants and Catholics alike.

The fate of the *David* underscores the political and moral turbulence of the times. Each night, as workers slowly moved the statue from Michelangelo's workshop to the Piazza della Signoria, supporters of the exiled Medici hurled stones at it, understanding, correctly, that the statue was a symbol of the city's will to stand up to any and all tyrannical rule, including that of the Medici themselves. Another group of citizens soon objected to the statue's nudity, and before it was even installed in place, a skirt of copper leaves was prepared to spare the general public any possible offense. The skirt is long gone, but it symbolizes the conflicts of the coming age, even as the sculpture itself embodies the grandeur and ambition of the High Renaissance as a whole.

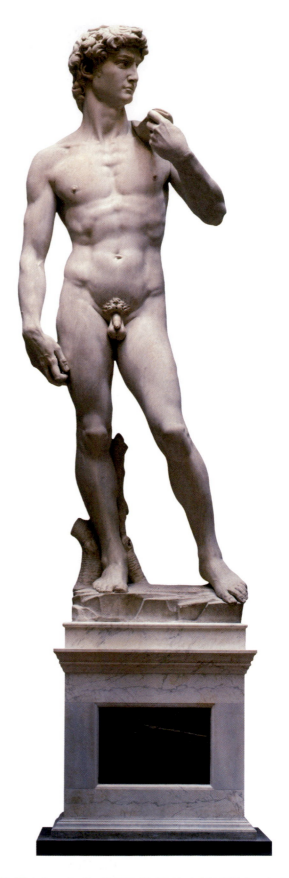

Fig. 14.30 Michelangelo, *David*. 1501–04. Marble, height 17'3". Accademia, Florence. The *David* was originally conceived to be placed high on the facade of Florence Cathedral. It was probably situated in the Piazza della Signoria because it could not be lifted into place.

Michelangelo in Rome

Even as Florence sought to exert its preeminence as a republic, Rome became the focal point of Italian Renaissance art as the popes sought to make the city the very center of Christian culture by commissioning many new works of art and architecture. Soon after finishing the *David* in 1504, Michelangelo was called to Rome to create a monumental tomb for Pope Julius II. (The pope was alive and well—he was simply planning ahead, fully intending to celebrate his glory and grandeur in perpetuity after his death.) The initial plan called for a three-story stepped-pyramidal structure, each level decorated by sculptures and topped by Julius's sarcophagus. But work on the tomb was soon interrupted. First, the pope awarded the commission to enlarge Saint Peter's Basilica to Donato Bramante, so angering the jealous Michelangelo that he left Rome for two years. When he returned, essentially coerced by the pope, Julius decided that the tomb could wait and ordered him to paint the ceiling of the Sistine Chapel. That project took Michelangelo, whose first love was sculpture and who wanted most of all to work on the sculptures for the tomb, four years to complete, from 1508 to 1512. Then, even as he got back to work on the tomb, Julius died, and his successor, Leo X (son of Lorenzo de' Medici), sent Michelangelo back to Florence to work on projects for the Medici family, who had returned to power. The tomb project lagged. Not until 1545 was a much-reduced version installed in the Church of San Pietro in Vincoli (Saint Peter in Chains) in Rome, thus concluding what Michelangelo referred to as "the tragedy of the tomb."

However, one of Michelangelo's very greatest sculptures, the *Moses* (Fig. **14.31**), stands at eye level in the center of the final installation. Originally designed to be placed on the second level of the tomb, and thus to be seen from below, it possesses what Vasari would call *terribilità*—a terrifying and awesome force. In the sculpture, Moses has just received the Ten Commandments. Two horns top his head, a traditional attribute based on a mistranslation of the Hebrew word for *light* in the Latin Bible. They signify the divine favor bestowed upon Moses by God. But Michelangelo has captured Moses in a particularly conflicted moment, for even as he has received God's favor, he has come down from Mount Sinai to witness the Hebrews worshiping a golden calf. The sculpture seems to capture both Moses' anger and his ability to control that rage, an emotional complexity that typifies the art of the High Renaissance and that would intrigue admirers of the statue for centuries, including the father of psychiatry, Sigmund Freud, who in the early twentieth century would write an essay on the psychological complexity of the work. ■

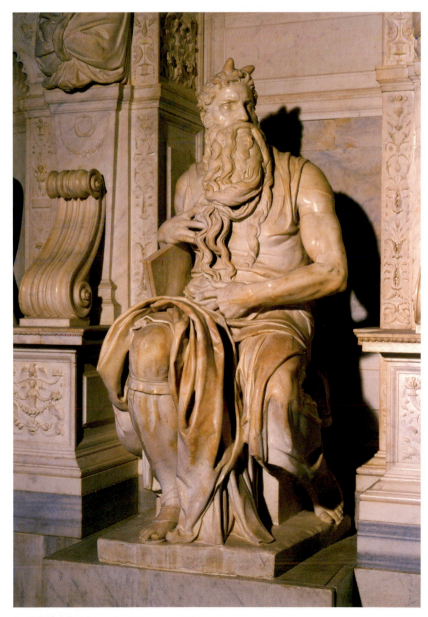

Fig. 14.31 Michelangelo, *Moses*. ca. 1513–15. Marble, height 7'8½". San Pietro in Vincoli, Rome.

14.1 Examine how sculpture and the use of scientific perspective were instrumental in the early development of the Italian Renaissance.

Florence was the center of the cultural revival that we have come to call the Renaissance, a "rebirth" that amounted to a revolution in human consciousness. How does the Baptistery doors competition of 1401 exemplify this new consciousness? How does Lorenzo Ghiberti's new set of doors, the *Gates of Paradise*, articulate Renaissance values even more?

By 1418, Florence Cathedral still lacked a dome above its octagonal crossing. Brunelleschi won the competition for the dome's design, a feat of architectural engineering unsurpassed in his day. For the cathedral's consecration on March 25, 1436, French composer Guillaume Dufay created a new musical work, a motet called *Nuper rosarum flores* ("The Rose Blossoms"). How does Dufay's composition reflect Brunelleschi's feat?

Brunelleschi was also the first Renaissance artist to master the art of scientific perspective, probably as a result of his humanistic study of optics in Arab science and his own surveying of Roman ruins. What values does his interest in scientific perspective reflect? How does the work of sculptor Donatello also reflect these values?

14.2 Discuss the influence of the Medici family on Florentine art and the development of humanist thought.

Medici control of Florentine politics was secured by Cosimo de' Medici, who surrounded himself with humanists. He sought their guidance about which books and manuscripts of the ancients to collect, and he commissioned translations of Greek philosophy and literature, championing especially the translations and interpretations of the works of Plato by Marsilio Ficino. How would you describe Ficino's Neoplatonist philosophy? How does

it recast Platonic thought? Cosimo's grandson, Lorenzo, "the Magnificent," continued the Medici tradition. His own circle of acquaintances included many of the greatest minds of the day, including the composer Heinrich Isaac, the poet Poliziano, the painter Botticelli, and the philosopher Pico della Mirandola. Can you describe how the work of each reflects humanistic principles?

14.3 Describe how other Italian courts followed the lead of the humanist court in Florence.

Lorenzo's court inspired the courts of the leaders of other Italian city-states, the leaders of which were almost all nobility. In Urbino, Duke Federigo da Montefeltro championed the use of scientific perspective in the painting of Piero della Francesca. Also at Urbino, Baldassare Castiglione wrote *The Book of the Courtier*. How does this treatise define *l'uomo universale*? In Mantua, Ludovico Gonzaga commissioned the painter Andrea Mantegna to decorate his palazzo with highly illusionistic frescoes. And in Milan, Ludovico Sforza commissioned Leonardo da Vinci to paint the *Last Supper* for the Dominican monastery of Santa Maria delle Grazie. What would you say is Leonardo's greatest strength as a painter? How does his portraiture reflect humanistic values?

14.4 Explain the symbolic significance of Michelangelo's *David*.

In 1494, a Florentine mob drove the last of the Medici rulers from the city. Yet, into the breach stepped the Dominican friar Girolamo Savonarola, who preached a moralistic brand of fire and brimstone, condemning humanist values. At first wielding great political power, Savonarola was finally tried as a heretic in 1498, and burned at the stake. Afterward, a relieved city council sought to reassert republican values in visual terms, and commissioned the giant nude sculpture. Why did the story of David seem so appropriate a subject?

✔ **Study** and **review** on **MyArtsLab**

READINGS

READING 14.4

from Baldassare Castiglione, *The Book of the Courtier*, Book 1 (1513–18; published 1528)

Castiglione spent his life in the service of princes, first in the courts of Mantua and Urbino, and then in Rome, where he served the papacy. His *Book of the Courtier* was translated into most European languages and remained popular for two centuries. It takes the form of a series of fictional conversations between the courtiers of the duke of Urbino in 1507, and includes the duchess. In the excerpt below, the separate speakers have not been identified to facilitate ease of reading. The work is a celebration of the ideal character of the Renaissance humanist and the ethical behavior associated with that ideal.

[The Perfect Courtier]

Within myself I have long doubted, dearest messer Alfonso, which of two things were the harder for me: to deny you what you have often begged of me so urgently, or to do it. For while it seemed to me very hard to deny anything (and especially a thing in the highest degree laudable) to one whom I love most dearly and by whom I feel myself to be most dearly loved, yet to set about an enterprise that I am not sure of being able to finish, seemed to me ill befitting a man who esteems just censure as it ought to be esteemed. …

You ask me then to write what is to my thinking the form of Courtiership most befitting a gentleman who lives at the court of princes, by which he may have the ability and knowledge perfectly to serve them in every reasonable thing, winning from them favor, and praise from other men; in short, what manner of man he ought to be who may deserve to be called a perfect Courtier without flaw. …

So now let us make a beginning of our subject, and if possible let us form such a Courtier that any prince worthy to be served by him, although of but small estate, might still be called a very great lord.

I wish then, that this Courtier of ours should be nobly born and of gentle race; … for noble birth is like a bright lamp that manifests and makes visible good and evil deeds, and kindles and stimulates to virtue both by fear of shame and by hope of praise. … And thus it nearly always happens that both in the profession of arms and in other worthy pursuits the most famous men have been of noble birth, because nature has implanted in everything that hidden seed which gives a certain force and quality of its own essence to all things that are derived from it, and makes them like itself: as we see not only in the breeds of horses and of other animals, but also in trees, the shoots of which nearly always resemble the trunk; and if they sometimes degenerate, it arises from poor cultivation. And so it is with men, who if rightly trained are nearly always like those from whom they spring, and often better; but if there be no one to give them proper care, they become like savages and never reach perfection.

It is true that, by favor of the stars or of nature, some men are endowed at birth with such graces that they seem not to have been born, but rather as if some god had formed them with his very hands and adorned them with every excellence of mind and body. So too there are many men so foolish and rude that one cannot but think that nature brought them into the world out of contempt or mockery. Just as these can usually accomplish little even with constant diligence and good training, so with slight pains those others reach the highest summit of excellence. …

Besides this noble birth, then, I would have the Courtier favored in this regard also, and endowed by nature not only with talent and beauty of person and feature, but with a certain grace and (as we say) air that shall make him at first sight pleasing and agreeable to all who see him; and I would have this an ornament that should dispose and unite all his actions, and in his outward aspect give promise of whatever is worthy the society and favor of every great lord.

But to come to some details, I am of opinion that the principal and true profession of the Courtier ought to be that of arms; which I would have him follow actively above all else, and be known among others as bold and strong, and loyal to whomsoever he serves. And he will win a reputation for these good qualities by exercising them at all times and in all places, since one may never fail in this without severest censure. And just as among women, their fair fame once sullied never recovers its first lustre, so the reputation of a gentleman who bears arms, if once it be in the least tarnished with cowardice or other disgrace, remains forever infamous before the world and full of ignominy. Therefore the more our Courtier excels in this art, the more he will be worthy of praise …

… And of such sort I would have our Courtier's aspect; not so soft and effeminate as is sought by many, who not only curl their hair and pluck their brows, but gloss their faces with all those arts employed by the most wanton and unchaste women in the world; and in their walk, posture and every act, they seem so limp and languid that their limbs are like to fall apart; and they pronounce their words so mournfully that they appear about to expire upon the spot: and the more they find themselves with men of rank, the more they affect such tricks. Since nature has not made them women, as they seem to wish to appear and be, they should be treated not as good women but as public harlots, and driven not merely from the courts of great lords but from the society of honest men.

Then coming to the bodily frame, I say it is enough if this be neither extremely short not tall, for both of these conditions excite a certain contemptuous surprise, and men of either sort are gazed upon in much the same way that we gaze on monsters. Yet if we must offend in one of the two extremes, it is preferable to fall a little short of the just measure of height than to exceed it, for besides often being dull of intellect, men thus huge of body are also unfit for every exercise of agility, which thing I should much wish in the Courtier. And so

I would have him well built and shapely of limb, and would have him show strength and lightness and suppleness, and know all bodily exercises that befit a man of war; whereof I think the first should be to handle every sort of weapon well on foot and on horse, to understand the advantages of each, and especially to be familiar with those weapons that are ordinarily used among gentlemen; for besides the use of them in war, where such subtlety in contrivance is perhaps not needful, there frequently arise differences between one gentleman and another, which afterwards result in duels often fought with 100 such weapons as happen at the moment to be within reach: thus knowledge of this kind is a very safe thing. …

Moreover I deem it very important to know how to wrestle, for it is a great help in the use of all kinds of weapons on foot. Then, both for his own sake and for that of his friends, he must understand the quarrels and differences that may arise, and must be quick to seize an advantage, always showing courage and prudence in all things. Nor should he be too ready to fight except when honor demands it; for besides the great danger that the uncertainty of fate entails, he who rushes into such 110 affairs recklessly and without urgent cause, merits the severest censure even though he be successful. But when he finds himself so far engaged that he cannot withdraw without reproach, he ought to be most deliberate, both in the preliminaries to the duel and in the duel itself, and always show readiness and daring. Nor must he act like some, who fritter the affair away in disputes and controversies, and who, having the choice of weapons, select those that neither cut nor pierce, and arm themselves as if they were expecting a cannonade; and thinking it enough not to be defeated, stand ever on the defensive 120 and retreat—showing therein their utter cowardice. …

READING CRITICALLY

Why do you suppose Castiglione places so much emphasis in this excerpt on physical characteristics and prowess?

READING 14.5

from Giorgio Vasari, "Life of Leonardo: Painter and Sculptor of Florence," in *Lives of the Most Excellent Painters, Architects, and Sculptors* (1550, 1568)

First published in 1550 and then revised and greatly expanded in 1568, Vasari's *Lives of the Most Excellent Painters, Architects, and Sculptors*, from which this "Life of Leonardo" is taken, is the first full account of Renaissance artists ever written. It is based on interviews that Vasari conducted throughout Italy. Born in 1511, Vasari could never have known Leonardo personally, but he did know many other Renaissance artists, including Michelangelo, whom he idolized. Art historians today discredit many of his narrative's details, but his book remains the starting point for the study of Renaissance art.

The greatest gifts are often seen, in the course of nature, rained by celestial influences on human creatures; and sometimes, in supernatural fashion, beauty, grace, and talent are united beyond measure in one single person, in a manner that to whatever such an one turns his attention, his every action is so divine, that, surpassing all other men, it makes itself clearly known as a thing bestowed by God (as it is), and not acquired by human art. This was seen by all mankind in Leonardo da Vinci, in whom, besides a beauty of body never sufficiently extolled, there was an infinite grace in all his actions; and so 10 great was his genius, and such its growth, that to whatever difficulties he turned his mind, he solved them with ease. In him was great bodily strength, joined to dexterity, with a spirit and courage ever royal and magnanimous; and the fame of his name so increased, that not only in his lifetime was he held in esteem, but his reputation became even greater among posterity after his death.

Truly marvellous and celestial was Leonardo, the son of Ser Piero da Vinci; and in learning and in the rudiments of letters he would have made great proficience, if he had not 20 been so variable and unstable, for he set himself to learn many things, and then, after having begun them, abandoned them. Thus, in arithmetic, during the few months that he studied it, he made so much progress, that, by continually suggesting doubts and difficulties to the master who was teaching him, he would very often bewilder him. He gave some little attention to music, and quickly resolved to learn to play the lyre, as one who had by nature as spirit most lofty and full of refinement: wherefore he sang divinely to that instrument, improvising upon it. Nevertheless, although he occupied 30 himself with such a variety of things, he never ceased drawing and working in relief, pursuits which suited his fancy more than any other. Ser Piero, having observed this, and having considered the loftiness of his intellect, one day took some of his drawings and carried them to Andrea del Verrocchio, who was much his friend, and besought him straitly [*sic*] to tell him whether Leonardo, by devoting himself to drawing, would make any proficience. Andrea was astonished to see the extraordinary beginnings of Leonardo, and urged Ser Piero that he should make him study it; wherefore he arranged with 40 Leonardo that he should enter the workshop of Andrea, which Leonardo did with the greatest willingness in the world. And he practiced not one branch of art only, but all those in which drawing played a part; and having an intellect so divine and marvellous that he was also an excellent geometrician, he not only worked in sculpture, making in his youth, in clay, some heads of women that are smiling, of which plaster casts are still taken, and likewise some heads of boys which appeared to have issued from the hand of a master; but in architecture, also, he made many drawings both of ground-plans and of other 50 designs of buildings; and he was the first, although but a youth, who suggested the plan of reducing the river Arno to a navigable canal from Pisa to Florence. He made designs of flour-mills, fullingmills, and engines, which might be driven by the force of water; and since he wished that his profession should be painting, he studied much in drawing after nature, and sometimes in making models of figures in clay, over which he would lay soft pieces of cloth dipped in clay, and then set himself patiently to draw them on a certain kind of very fine Rheims cloth, or prepared linen; and he executed them in black 60 and white with the point of his brush, so that it was a marvel, as some of them by his hand, which I have in our book of drawings, still bear witness; besides which, he drew on paper with such diligence and so well, that there is no one who has ever equalled him in perfection of finish; and I have one, a head drawn with the style in chiaroscuro, which is divine.

And there was infused in that brain such grace from God, and a power of expression in such sublime accord with the intellect and memory that served it, and he knew so well how to express his conceptions by draughtmanship, that he vanquished with his 70 discourse, and confuted with his reasoning, every valiant wit. And he was continually making models and designs to show men how to remove mountains with ease, and how to bore them in order to pass from one level to another; and by means of levers, windlasses, and screws, he showed the way to raise and draw great weights, together with methods for emptying harbours, and pumps for removing water from low places, things which his brain never ceased from devising. …

READING CRITICALLY

Vasari focuses on demonstrating the individual creative genius of Leonardo and many of the other artists he discusses. Why, as a humanist, does "genius" matter so much to him?

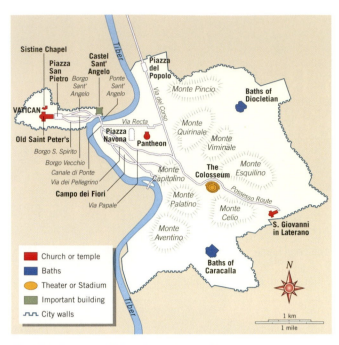

Map 15.1 Rome, ca. 1400, at the birth of the Renaissance.

Legend:
- Church or temple
- Baths
- Theater or Stadium
- Important building
- City walls

for Rome in 1505 and commissioned major paintings and monuments from the then 30-year-old artist. In 1508, Michelangelo was followed by Raphael (Raffaello Santi or Sanzio, 1483–1520), a young painter from Urbino who had arrived in Florence in 1505. Julius set him the task of decorating the papal apartments. Rome must have seemed something of a Florentine place. In fact, when the Medici returned to power in Florence in 1512, they did so under the sway of two great Medici popes: Leo X (papacy 1513–21), who was Lorenzo the Magnificent's son, Giovanni de' Medici; and Clement VII (papacy 1523–34), who was Lorenzo's nephew, Giulio de' Medici. Whether in the church or the republic, Rome or Florence, the men of this patrician family were a dominant force.

That said, the Medici exerted little influence over Venice to the north. Fifteenth-century Venice defined itself as both the most cosmopolitan and the most democratic city in the world. Since the seventh century, the citizens of this watery city had elected the Venetian Republic's ruler, the *doge*, for life. Admittedly, not everyone could govern. Election to the city's Grand Council was limited to a small, elite group, but everyone did participate equally in the city's daily affairs. It owed its cosmopolitan atmosphere to the fact that, throughout the Middle Ages, it had dominated trade in the eastern Mediterranean and the Middle East. Its navy was unrivaled, and through it, goods from northern Europe flowed into the Mediterranean, and goods from the Mediterranean and points east flowed into Europe. After Constantinople fell to the Ottoman Empire in 1453, large numbers of artists and scholars arrived from the east, adding to the city's already considerable cosmopolitan atmosphere. Trade with the north brought Venetian artists into contact with the technique of painting in oils, and they responded

with enthusiasm to the effects they could achieve with the new medium. With oil paint, artists could render the world with a greater luminosity and realism than was possible with tempera or fresco (favored in Florence and Rome).

From our modern perspective, we tend to view Venice as engaged in some sort of competition with Florence and Rome for preeminence among Italian cities. But from the Venetian point of view, there was never any question that Venice was the very center of culture. Nevertheless, among the three cities they articulated the values that we have come to associate with the High Renaissance—a self-confident humanism, a shared admiration for Classical tradition, and a keen sensitivity to balance, order, and a harmony among parts. These values were, in short, the standards of Classical beauty, and so successful were some artists at meeting them—Michelangelo in Florence and Rome, Raphael in Rome, Giorgione and Titian in Venice—that together with Leonardo's their work came to be considered the product of divinely inspired creative genius. Invention and originality became the hallmarks of success in all the arts.

THE ART OF THE PAPAL COURT IN ROME

How did papal patronage impact the arts in Rome?

Of all the fifteenth-century popes, Sixtus IV was the most successful in fulfilling the Church's mission to rebuild Rome. He rebuilt the city's port, repaved its streets, and built a new, functional bridge across the Tiber. He restored and refreshed the city's water supply, once the pride of the Roman emperors. All around the city, he rebuilt old churches and constructed new ones. He founded the Vatican Library, where a fresco showed Sixtus, his nephews, and the humanist scholar Platina (Fig. **15.2**). At the bottom, an inscription commends Sixtus for these accomplishments: "Rome, once full of squalor, owes to you, Sixtus, its temples, foundling hospital, street squares, walks, bridges, the restoration of the Acqua Vergine at the Trevi fountain, the port for sailors, the fortifications on the Vatican Hill, and now this celebrated library."

Over the next 100 years, the popes and their cardinals would continue to widen and redesign Rome's streets and plazas. The new monuments and palaces they commissioned would enhance the image of the Church as well as Rome itself. As the humanist scholar and literary historian Paolo Cortesi argued, "attractively designed and sumptuously executed" palaces served to bring "the ignorant mob" into submission to the Church's authority and might. The fresco of Sixtus IV illustrates these aspirations. The room in which he and his retinue gather is richly appointed. Column capitals are trimmed in gold, the ceiling is coffered, marble covers almost every surface, and an elaborate Corinthian capital supporting a large, arched space in the background sits at the vanishing point of the painting's carefully

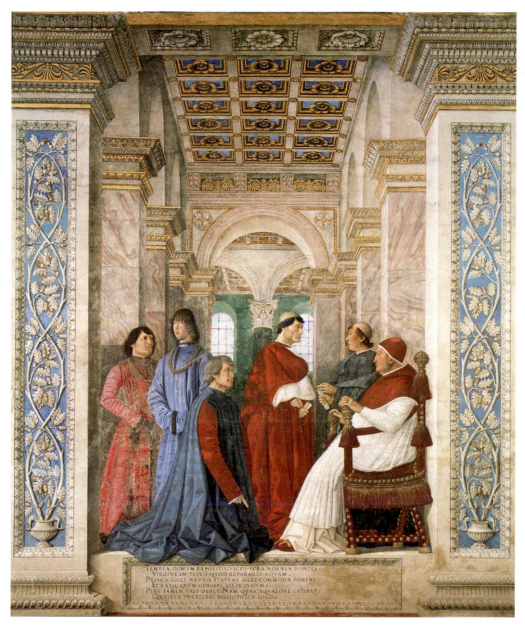

Fig. 15.2 Melozzo da Forli, *Sixtus IV, His Nephews, and Platina.* **1480–81.** Detached fresco, 12'2¼" × 10'2½". Vatican, Rome. The Vatican librarian and humanist scholar Platina kneels before the pope, pointing to an inscription that praises Sixtus's rebuilding of Rome.

conceived perspective. The splendor that was Rome, the architecturally rendered space suggests, is reborn.

But the painting also makes clear that there is more at stake than architectural restoration. Surrounding Sixtus are his "nephews"—a word that in Renaissance Italy means any male family member—and the humanist scholar Platina (1421–81) who kneels before him. If both Platina's presence and the Classical construction of the scene symbolize the humanist ideals of the papal court, the presence of four cardinals in the pope's family, all members of the Riario/Rovere clan, suggests the political reality of the cardinal-as-courtier. As the Medici ruled Florence, so the Riario/Rovere clan controlled not just Rome but Christendom.

The Patronage of the Cardinals

The papal court of Sixtus IV—especially its cardinals—commissioned as many or more works than the pope himself. Sixtus VI's nephew, Cardinal Raffaele Riario, built a huge palace for himself and also managed to lure the youthful Michelangelo to Rome, commissioning him to sculpt a nearly 7-foot-tall *Bacchus*. This staggering, drunken depiction of the god of wine eventually ended up in the collection of Michelangelo's friend, the Roman banker Jacopo Galli, perhaps because it seemed unsuitable for the collection of a cardinal. Galli, in turn, seems to have arranged for Michelangelo's second commission in Rome, a contract with another cardinal that boldly promised to

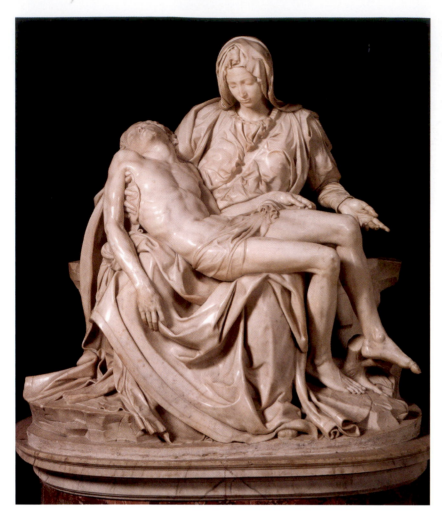

Fig. 15.3 Michelangelo, *Pietà*. 1497–1500. Marble, 5'8" × 6'5" × 27". Cappella della Pietà, Saint Peter's, Vatican, Rome. This is the only work Michelangelo ever signed. The Latin inscription reads *Michael Angelus Bonarotus Florentinus Faciebat,* "Michelangelo Buonarroti the Florentine Made This."

View the Closer Look for Michelangelo's *Pietà* on **MyArtsLab**

Bramante and the New Saint Peter's Basilica

Shortly after he was elected pope in 1503, Julius II made what may have been the most important commission of the day. He asked the architect Donato Bramante (1444–1514) to renovate the Vatican Palace and serve as chief architect of a plan to replace Saint Peter's Basilica with a new church. The pope took the name Julius to emphasize his own imperial authority. He grew a beard, emulating Julius Caesar, who in 54 BCE had let his beard grow after the Gauls had slaughtered his troops. (Caesar swore to let his beard and hair go uncut until he had taken his vengeance.) Like Caesar, Julius II was intent on defeating the hated French and driving them out of northern Italy, a triumph the papal forces accomplished in 1512 with the help of a Spanish army. His decision to demolish the Old Saint Peter's Basilica, which had been built by the emperor Constantine in about 330, and erect a magnificent new one in its place, was the ultimate expression of his majesty and power.

The pope's chosen architect, Bramante, had worked with Leonardo da Vinci in Milan, and Julius was deeply impressed by Leonardo's understanding of the writings of the ancient Roman architectural historian Vitruvius, specifically the ten books constituting *De architectura* (*Concerning Architecture*). For Vitruvius, whose acquaintance with Polyclitus' *Canon* of proportion is our only firsthand account of the now-lost original (see Chapter 5), the circle and square were the ideal shapes. Polyclitus' theory of proportion was the geometrical equivalent of Pythagoras' **music of the spheres**—which Vitruvius discusses in Book 5 of *De architectura*—the theory that each planet produced a musical sound, fixed mathematically by its velocity and distance from Earth, which harmonized with those produced by other planets and was audible but not recognized on Earth. Thus, according to Vitruvius, the human head "from the chin to the crown is an eighth" of the whole height, and the human body itself fits into the ideal musical interval of the **octave**, the interval that gives the impression of duplicating the original note at a higher or lower pitch. For Vitruvius, symmetry, proportion, and ratio derive from the perfection of the human figure in all its parts, and the perfectly symmetrical shapes of the circle and square find their source in the figure and are generated by the figure geometrically. Thus these shapes are profoundly humanist in character. Leonardo had captured this notion in his *Vitruvian Man*, a drawing in which he placed the human figure at the center of a perfect circle inscribed over a square (Fig. **15.4**).

provide the cardinal with the most beautiful statue in the city. Michelangelo was not yet 25, yet he succeeded in creating a sculpture of enormous emotional intensity, the *Pietà*, a word meaning both "pity" and "piety" in Italian, and generally used to describe Mary grieving over her dead son lying in her arms (Fig. **15.3**). In this *Pietà*, Michelangelo has enlarged Mary's body, though not her face, and thus diminished Christ in relation to her. As a result, Christ's supple body, unaffected by rigor mortis, veins bulging as if blood still coursed through them, fits neatly into the soft folds of his mother's dress and draperies, the carving of which demonstrated the sculptor's mastery of his material. Christ seems almost alive—at least more asleep than dead—probably a metaphor of his spiritual rebirth. Likewise, though Mary would have been middle-aged at Christ's death, Michelangelo portrays her as still young and beautiful because she is more a timeless image of purity and chastity than a real person. Nevertheless, though the scene is idealized, the emotions it evokes in the viewer are very real indeed.

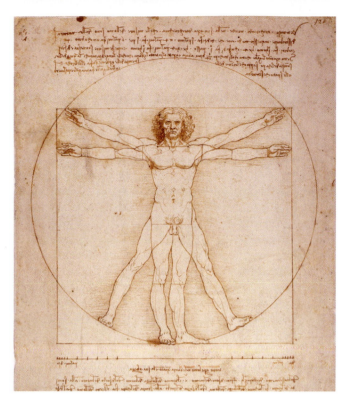

Fig. 15.4 Leonardo da Vinci. *Vitruvian Man.* ca. 1485–90. Pen and ink, 13½" × 9⅝". Gallerie dell'Accademia, Venice. Vitruvius specifically related the harmonious physical proportions of man, which reflect those of his divine creator, to the proportions of architecture.

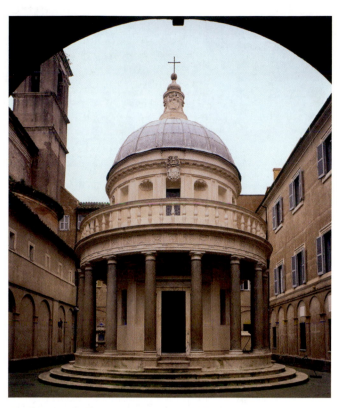

Fig. 15.5 Donato Bramante, Tempietto. 1502. San Pietro in Montorio, Rome. This chapel was certainly modeled after a Classical temple. It was commissioned by King Ferdinand and Queen Isabella of Spain, financiers of Christopher Columbus's voyages to America. It was undertaken in support of Pope Alexander VI, who was himself Spanish.

The CONTINUING PRESENCE
of the PAST

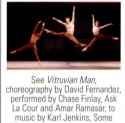

See *Vitruvian Man*, choreography by David Fernandez, performed by Chase Finlay, Ask La Cour and Amar Ramasar, to music by Karl Jenkins, Some Dance Company, New York City, February 2012 on **MyArtsLab**

In Rome, Bramante quickly applied this emphasis on geometrical figures to one of his earliest commissions, a small freestanding circular chapel in the courtyard of a Spanish church in Rome, San Pietro in Montorio, directly over what was revered as the site of Saint Peter's martyrdom. Because of its small size and the fact that it was modeled on a Classical temple that was excavated in Rome during the reign of Sixtus IV, this structure is known as the Tempietto ("Little Temple") (Fig. **15.5**). The 16 exterior columns are Doric—in fact, their shafts are original ancient Roman granite columns—and the frieze above them is decorated with objects of the Christian liturgy in sculptural relief. The diameter of the shafts defines the entire plan. Each shaft is spaced four diameters from the next, and the colonnade they form is two diameters from the circular walls. In its Classical reference, its incorporation of original Classical Roman columns into its architectural scheme, and, above all, the mathematical orderliness of its parts, the Tempietto is the very embodiment of Italian humanist architecture in the High Renaissance.

The task of replacing Old Saint Peter's was a much larger project and Bramante's most important one. Old Saint Peter's was a **basilica**, a type of ancient Roman

building with a long central nave, double side aisles set off by colonnades (see Fig. 6.35 in Chapter 6), an apse in the wall opposite the main door, and a transept near the apse so that large numbers of visitors could approach the shrine to Saint Peter. In his plan for a new Saint Peter's (Fig. **15.6a**),

CONTINUITY & CHANGE

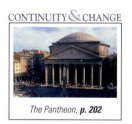

The Pantheon, **p. 202**

Bramante adopted the Vitruvian square, as illustrated in Leonardo's drawing, placing inside it a **Greek cross** (a cross in which the upright and transverse shafts are of equal length and intersect at their middles) topped by a central dome purposely reminiscent of the giant dome of the Pantheon (see Fig. 6.26 in Chapter 6). The resultant central plan is essentially a circle inscribed within a square. In Renaissance thinking, the central plan and dome symbolized the perfection of God. Construction began in 1506.

Julius II financed the project through the sale of **indulgences**, a remission of penalties to be suffered in the afterlife, especially release from purgatory. This was the place where, in Catholic belief, individuals temporarily reside after death as punishment for their sins. Those wanting to enter heaven more rapidly than they otherwise might could shorten their stay in purgatory by purchasing an indulgence. The Church had been selling these documents since

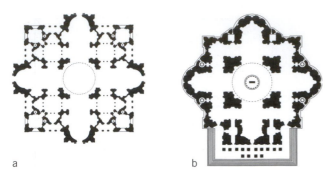

a   b

Fig. 15.6 Plans for Saint Peter's, Rome, by (a) Donato Bramante and (b) Michelangelo. Bramante's original plan (a), in the form of a Greek cross, was sporadically worked on after Julius II's death in 1513. The project came to a complete halt for a decade after the Sack of Rome by the troops of the Hapsburg emperor Charles V in 1527. In 1547, Pope Paul III appointed Michelangelo as architect, and he revived Bramante's original plan but added more support for the dome and thickened the walls. He also added a portico consisting of ten columns in the second row and four in the front, which created the feeling of a Latin cross, especially when extended by his other addition to Bramante's scheme, the massive flight of steps rising to the main portal (b).

👁 **Watch** an architectural simulation of Saint Peter's Basilica on **MyArtsLab**

the twelfth century, and Julius's building campaign intensified the practice. (In protest against the sale of indulgences, Martin Luther would launch the Protestant Reformation in Germany in 1517; see Chapter 17.) The New Saint Peter's would be a very expensive project, but there were also very many sinners willing to help pay for it. With the deaths of both pope and architect, in 1513 and 1514 respectively, the project came to a temporary halt. Its final plan would be developed in 1546 by Michelangelo (Fig. **15.6b**).

The Sistine Chapel

Just as the construction of the New Saint Peter's was about to get under way, Julius II commissioned Michelangelo to design his tomb. It would be a three-storied monument, over 23 feet wide and 35 feet high, and it represents Michelangelo's first foray into architecture. For the next 40 years, Michelangelo would work sporadically on the tomb, but from the beginning, he was continually interrupted, most notably in 1506 when Julius himself commanded the artist to paint the 45 by 128-foot ceiling of the Sistine Chapel, named after Sixtus IV, Julius's uncle, who had commissioned its construction in 1473. Ever since its completion, the chapel has served as the meeting place of the conclave of cardinals during the election of new popes. Michelangelo at first refused Julius's commission, but by 1508, he reconsidered, signed the contract, and began the task.

The chapel, built in the space between Old Saint Peter's and the papal palace, used the same proportions described in the Hebrew Bible for the Temple of Solomon. It was already impressively decorated with frescoes commissioned by Sixtus IV when Julius II asked Michelangelo to paint the ceiling (Fig. **15.7**). Whatever he did had to harmonize at some level with the extraordinary painting cycles in the

lower levels of the chapel and yet fulfill the program planned by the pope. Julius first proposed filling the spandrels between the windows with paintings of the 12 apostles and then decorating the ceiling proper with ornamental designs. But when Michelangelo objected to the limitations of this plan, the pope freed him to paint whatever he liked, and Michelangelo undertook for himself a far more ambitious task—nine scenes from Genesis, the first book of the Hebrew Bible, on the ceiling proper surrounded by prophets, sibyls, the ancestors of Christ, and other scenes (Figs. **15.8** and **15.9**). Thus, the ceiling would narrate events before the coming of the law of Moses, and would complement the narrative cycles on the walls below.

Throughout the ceiling, Michelangelo includes the della Rovere heraldic symbols of oak (*rovere*) and acorn to symbolize the pope's patronage, usually in the hands of ***ignudi***, nude youths who sit at the four corners of alternate central panels. These same panels are framed by bronze shields that underscore the patron's military prowess. The whole is contained in an entirely illusionistic architecture that appears to open at each end to the sky outside. Only the spandrels over the windows and the **pendentives** (concave triangular sections that form a transition between a rectilinear and a dome shape) at each corner are real.

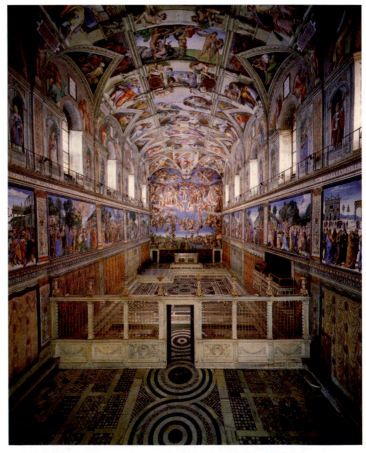

Fig. 15.7 Interior, Sistine Chapel, Vatican, Rome. Built 1475–81; side wall frescoes painted 1482–83; ceiling painted 1508–12; end wall 1536–41. On the end wall is Michelangelo's *Last Judgment* (see Fig. 20.4 in Chapter 20).

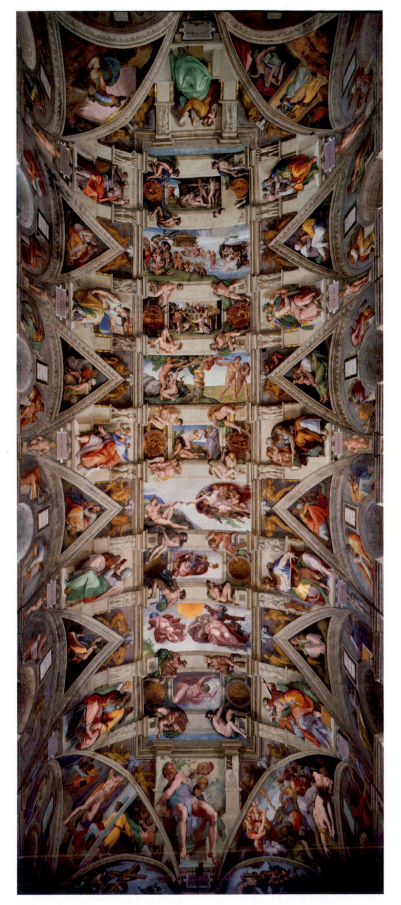

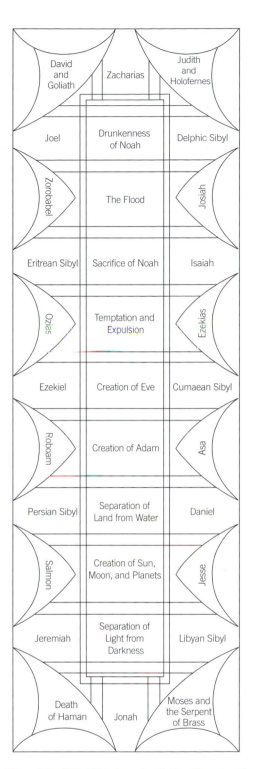

David and Goliath	Zacharias	Judith and Holofernes
Joel	Drunkenness of Noah	Delphic Sibyl
Zorobabel	The Flood	Josiah
Eritrean Sibyl	Sacrifice of Noah	Isaiah
Ozias	Temptation and Expulsion	Ezekias
Ezekiel	Creation of Eve	Cumaean Sibyl
Roboam	Creation of Adam	Asa
Persian Sibyl	Separation of Land from Water	Daniel
Salmon	Creation of Sun, Moon, and Planets	Jesse
Jeremiah	Separation of Light from Darkness	Libyan Sibyl
Death of Haman	Jonah	Moses and the Serpent of Brass

Fig. 15.8 and Fig. 15.9 Michelangelo, Sistine Chapel ceiling and plan of its narrative program, Vatican, Rome. 1508–12. Fresco, 45' × 128'. The intense and vibrant colors of the ceiling were revealed after a thorough cleaning, completed in 1990. Centuries of smoke and grime were removed by a process that involved the application of a solvent, containing both a fungicide and an antibacterial agent, mixed with a cellulose gel that would not drip from the ceiling. This mixture was applied in small sections with a bristle brush, allowed to dry for three minutes, and then removed with sponge and water. Until the cleaning, no one for centuries had fully appreciated Michelangelo's daring, even sensual, sense of color.

✳ **Explore** the architectural panorama of the Sistine Chapel ceiling on **MyArtsLab**

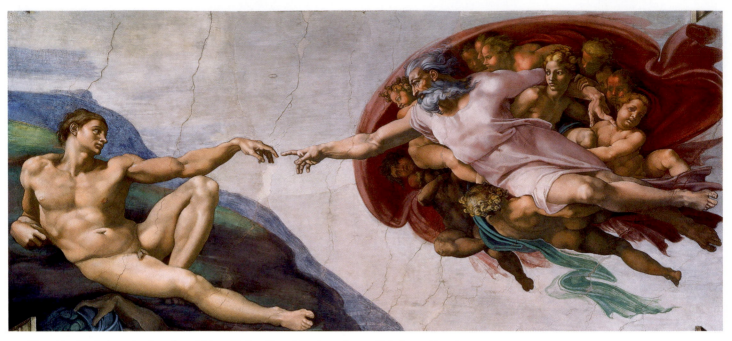

Fig. 15.10 Michelangelo, *Creation of Adam*, Sistine Chapel, Vatican, Rome. 1510. Fresco. Note the analogy Michelangelo creates between Adam and God, between the father of humankind and God the Father. Although they face one another, Adam and God are posed along parallel diagonals, and their right legs are in nearly identical positions. The connection is further highlighted by the fluttering green ribbon in God's space that echoes the colors of the earth upon which Adam lies.

The nine central panels tell the story, in three panels each, of Creation, Adam and Eve, and Noah. The series begins over the chapel altar with the *Separation of Light from Darkness*, a moment associated with the eternal struggle between good and evil, truth and falsehood. In fact, this pairing of opposites characterizes the entire program. At the center of the ceiling is the *Creation of Eve*. Life and death, good and evil, the heavenly and the earthly, the spiritual and the material, pivot around this central scene. Everything between here and the altar represents Creation before the knowledge of good and evil was introduced to the world by the temptation of Eve in the Garden of Eden, a scene represented, together with the Expulsion, in the panel just to the right. From here to the panel over the door to the chapel, we witness the early history of fallen humankind, for viewers entering the chapel look up to see directly above them the *Drunkenness of Noah*, an image symbolic of their own frailty. They see the goodness and truth of God's creation only at the greatest remove from them, far away at the chapel's other end.

The tension between the spiritual and the material worlds is nowhere better represented on the ceiling than in the *Creation of Adam* (Fig. **15.10**). Adam is earthbound. He seems lethargic, passive, barely interested, while a much more animated God flies through the skies carrying behind him a bulging red drapery that suggests both the womb and the brain, creativity and reason. Under his arm is a young woman, who may be Eve, who prefigures the Virgin, while God's left hand touches the shoulder of an infant, who may symbolize the future Christ. The implication of the scene

is that in just one moment, God's finger will touch Adam's and infuse him with not just energy but soul, not just life but the future of humankind.

As the work progressed, it appears that Michelangelo grew more comfortable, for his style became increasingly energetic and bold. This is especially apparent in his depiction of the *ignudi*, sibyls, and prophets, which he presented with increasing skill in more poses exhibiting greater physical movement as he progressed down the ceiling from entrance to altar. His accomplishment becomes even clearer when we compare the final painting to the preparatory studies. In a drawing of one of the later figures painted, the *Libyan Sibyl* (Fig. **15.11**), the figure's hands are balanced evenly, at the same level, but by the time he painted her (Fig. **15.12**), the left hand had dropped below the right to emphasize her downward turn, emphasizing the fact that she is bringing knowledge down to the viewer. The artist has paid special attention to the left foot, seeing the need to splay the four smaller toes backward. And finally, his model in the drawing was apparently male. In his reworking of the face at the lower left of the drawing, he softens the figure's cheekbones and fills out her lips. In the final painting, he reduces the model's prominent brow, hides the musculature of the model's back, and exaggerates the buttocks and hips, feminizing the original masculine sketch. As graceful as it is powerful and majestic, the *Libyan Sibyl* is a virtuoso display of technical mastery.

Michelangelo worked on the ceiling from May 1508 until 1512. To paint the ceiling, Michelangelo had to construct a scaffold that moved down the chapel from the

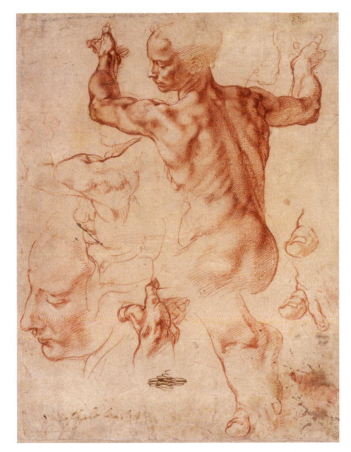

Fig. 15.11 Michelangelo, *Studies for the Libyan Sibyl.* **ca. 1510.** Red chalk, 11⅜" × 8⁷⁄₁₆". The Metropolitan Museum of Art, New York, Joseph Pulitzer Bequest, 1924 (24.197.2). Very few of Michelangelo's drawings for the Sistine Chapel survive, even though he prepared hundreds as he planned the ceiling.

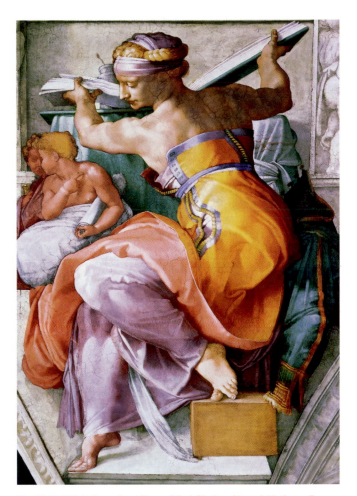

Fig. 15.12 Michelangelo, *Libyan Sibyl,* **Sistine Chapel, Vatican, Rome. 1512.** Fresco. In Michelangelo's program for the ceiling, the Sibyls alternate with Hebrew Bible prophets around the room. One of the most striking characteristics of these figures is the way they seem to project in front of the decoration and enter into the real space of the chapel, creating a stunning illusionistic effect.

entrance to the altar. Thus, the first frescoes painted were the Noah group, and the last, the Creation. In a sonnet he wrote in about 1510, Michelangelo describes the difficulties he faced (**Reading 15.1**):

READING 15.1

Sonnet to John of Pistoia on the Sistine Ceiling (ca. 1510)

I've got myself a goiter from this strain,
As water gives the cats in Lombardy
Or maybe it is in some other country;
My belly's pushed by force beneath my chin.

My beard toward Heaven, I feel the back of my brain
Upon my neck, I grow the breast of a Harpy;
My brush, above my face continually,
Makes it a splendid floor by dripping down.

My loins have penetrated to my paunch,
My rump's a crupper, as a counterweight,
And pointless the unseeing steps I go.

In front of me my skin is being stretched
While it folds up behind and forms a knot,
And I am bending like a Syrian bow.

And judgment, hence, must grow,
Borne in the mind, peculiar and untrue;
You cannot shoot well when the gun's askew.

John, come to the rescue
Of my dead painting now, and of my honor;
I'm not in a good place, and I'm no painter.

These lines affirm that Michelangelo painted the ceiling standing, not lying down, his eyes focused on the work above him. They also affirm the considerable difficulty of the project, and, somewhat surprisingly, given the genius of his achievement, his general distaste for painting. He was, he believed, a sculptor above all else.

Raphael and the Stanza della Segnatura

Meanwhile, in about 1505, a young painter named Raphael (Raffaello Santi or Sanzio) arrived in Florence from Urbino and began to receive a great deal of attention as a painter of portraits of wealthy Florentine citizens. He also produced a series of small, beautifully executed paintings of the Virgin and Child. The latter, of course, embraced a theme that stretched back to the Byzantine icon, down through the work of the Sienese painters, Duccio and Martini, and the Florentines, Cimabue and Giotto (see Chapter 13). However, the naturalism that these earlier painters had striven to achieve reached new heights in Raphael's work. His paintings were immediately approachable—linearly precise, coloristically rich, and compositionally simple.

The *Small Cowper Madonna* (Fig. 15.13) is an example. Both the Virgin and Child are imbued with an almost celestial serenity—owing in no small part to the fact that their heads are framed by the radiant light of Raphael's

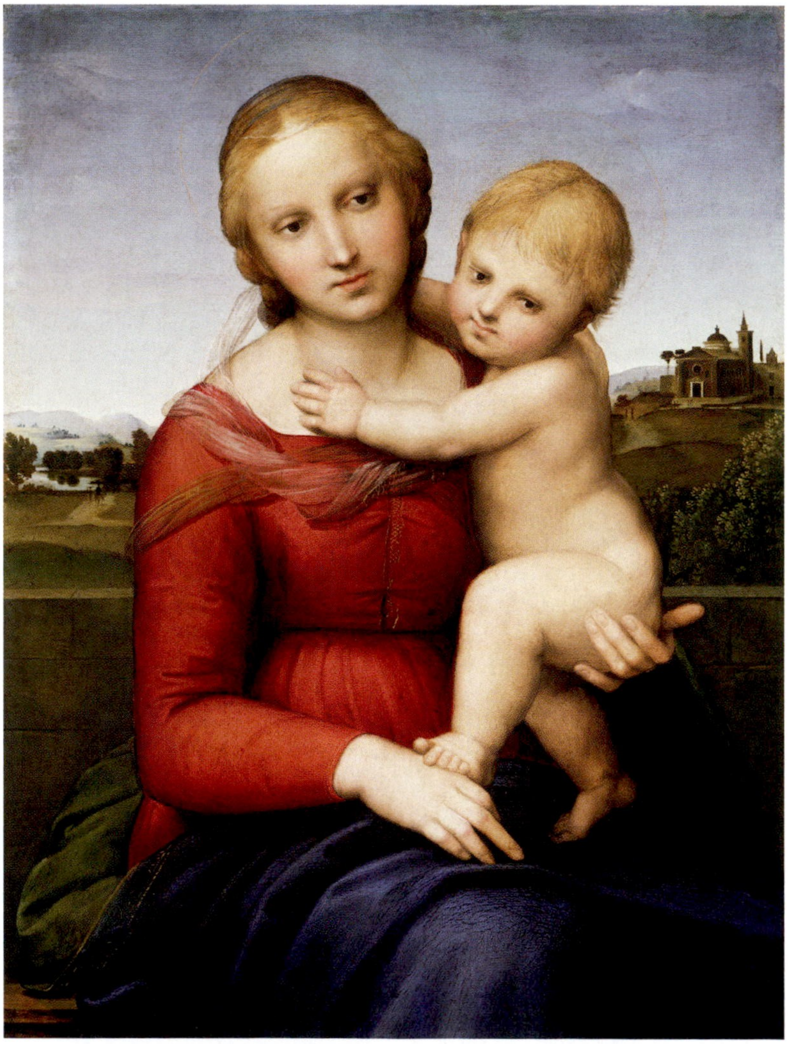

Fig. 15.13 Raphael, *Small Cowper Madonna*. ca. 1505. Oil on panel, 23⁷⁄₁₆" × 17⁵⁄₁₆". National Gallery of Art, Washington, D.C., Widener Collection (1942.9.57). Photograph © Board of Trustees, National Gallery of Art. The painting takes its name from its owner, George Nassau Clavering, the third Earl Cowper (1738–89), who visited Italy in 1760 and remained there for the rest of his life, amassing an extraordinary collection of Italian Renaissance paintings.

sky. But what strikes us most is their very humanity—the fact that they seem absolutely alive with a sense of touch, the Child's toes resting on her right hand, her left supporting his naked buttocks. Lending the scene a sense of reality is the landscape itself, which is a real one, featuring the Church of Bernadino, 2 miles outside of Raphael's native Urbino and the burial place of Federigo da Montefeltro and Battista Sforza (see Fig. 14.20 in Chapter 14). But perhaps more than anything else, the self-reflective gaze of the Virgin captures the viewer's imagination, as if we have caught her literally in the moment, thinking who knows what, but deep in thought nonetheless. Divinity and humanity are here perfectly balanced.

In 1508, the young Raphael left Florence to arrive in Rome as Michelangelo was beginning work on the Sistine Chapel ceiling. He quickly secured a commission from Julius II to paint the pope's private rooms in the Vatican Palace. The first of these rooms was the so-called Stanza della Segnatura ("Room of the Signature"), where subsequent popes signed official documents, but which Julius used as a library. Julius had determined the subjects. On each of the four walls, Raphael was to paint one of the four major areas of humanist learning: Law and Justice, to be represented by the *Cardinal Virtues*; the Arts, to be represented by *Mount Parnassus*; Theology, to be represented by the *Disputà*, or *Dispute over the Sacrament*; and Philosophy, to be represented by the *School of Athens* (see *Closer Look*, pages 512–513). In an apparent attempt to balance Classical paganism and Christian faith, a gesture completely in keeping with Julius's humanist philosophy, two of these scenes—*Mount Parnassus* and the *School of Athens*—had Classical themes, the other two Christian. The *Disputà* (Fig. 15.14) is the fullest account in Christian art of the sacrament of the Eucharist, the central ritual of Christian faith. At the center of the painting, at the vanishing point placed on an altar, is a monstrance, a container for displaying the consecrated Host (bread) of the Holy Eucharist. According to the Catholic doctrine of Transubstantiation, in the celebration of the mass at the moment of consecration, the bread and wine literally become the body and blood of Christ. To the left of the altar is a figure who raises his arm in a horizontal gesture to suggest the earthly reality of the wine and bread. On the other side of the altar, another figure points heavenward to suggest the transubstantiation of the wine and bread into the blood and body of Christ. A dove, enclosed in a circle of gold and symbolizing the Holy Spirit, is depicted directly above the monstrance. In the heavenly realm, directly above the dove, Christ sits in majesty, flanked by the Virgin and John the Baptist, and above him, God the Father.

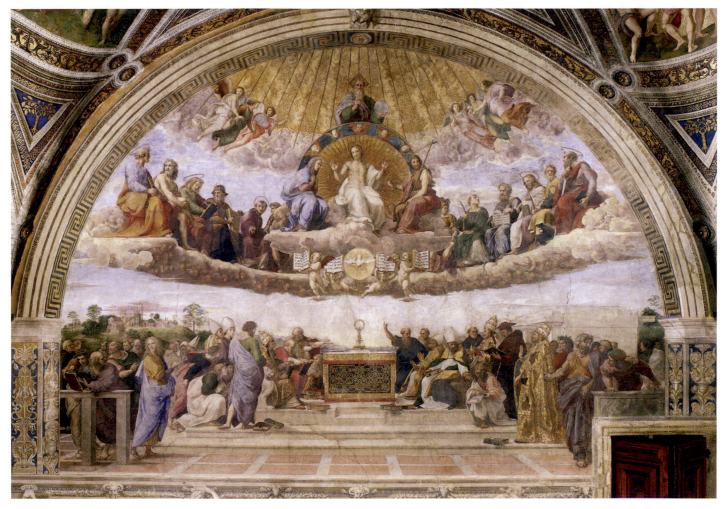

Fig. 15.14 Raphael, *Disputà*. 1508–11. Fresco, 19' × 27'. Stanza della Segnatura, Vatican Palace, Rome. In the earthly realm, to the right, Dante can be seen wearing a laurel wreath. Directly in front of him is Pope Sixtus IV, wearing a gold robe and papal tiara.

Directly across from the *Disputà* is the *School of Athens*, with Plato and Aristotle, the cornerstones of Classical philosophy, at a vanishing point of the horizon line. Both scenes are framed in *trompe l'oeil* (illusionistic) arched vaults, the one framing the heavens, the other an immense barrel-vaulted interior perhaps inspired by Bramante's new design for Saint Peter's. (Bramante, in fact, is pictured in the *Disputà*, leaning on the railing at the lower left, looking at what may be his plans for the church.) The same duality between the heavenly and the earthly, the spiritual and the material, that animates the Sistine ceiling, which Michelangelo was in the midst of painting just across an intervening courtyard, informs Raphael's work. (This suggests that Julius II had his say in both projects.) And it informs the individual frescoes as well. In the *School of Athens*, as in the *Disputà*, gestures of central figures indicated heavenly and earthly duality. Plato points toward the heavens, the realm of ideal forms that so informs his work, while Aristotle stretches out his hand palm down toward the earth, from where, in his view, all knowledge originates in empirical observation. Other philosophers are spread out across the room, those ranked on Plato's side beneath a niche containing a statue of Apollo, the god of sunlight, rationality, poetry, music, and the fine arts; those on Aristotle's side beneath a statue of Minerva, goddess of wisdom and the mechanical arts. But for Raphael and many other humanists, Plato and Aristotle were more alike than dissimilar. They believed that the greatest difference between the two was more a matter of style than substance. Plato's poetic images and Aristotle's rational analysis were actually arguing for the same things but from different directions. The painting is, after all, entitled *School of Athens*, not *Schools of Athens*. This unified humanist philosophical tradition is mirrored, then, in the balanced clarity of the painting's composition.

The Medici Popes

Pope Julius II died in 1513, not long after Michelangelo had completed the Sistine Chapel ceiling and Raphael the Stanza della Segnatura. He was succeeded by Leo X, born Giovanni de' Medici, son of Lorenzo the Magnificent.

The *School of Athens*, also known as *Philosophy*, is generally acknowledged as the most important of Raphael's four paintings for the Stanza della Segnatura of the Vatican Palace in Rome. Its Classicism is clearly indicated in several ways: by its illusionistic architectural setting, based on ancient Roman baths; by its emphatic one-point perspective, which directs viewer attention to the two central figures, Plato and Aristotle, fathers of philosophy; and by its subject matter, the philosophical foundation of the Renaissance humanistic enterprise. All of the figures here—the Platonists on the left, the Aristotelians on the right, though not all have been identified—were regarded by Renaissance humanists as embodying the ideal of continual pursuit of learning and truth. The clarity, balance, and symmetry that distinguish this Raphael composition became a touchstone for painters in centuries to come.

Plato (ca. 428–348 BCE) resembles a self-portrait of Leonardo da Vinci. He points upward to the realm of ideas. (Note the resemblance of this gesture to that of Doubting Thomas in Leonardo's *Last Supper*, see Fig. 14.25 in Chapter 14). He carries the *Timaeus*, the dialogue on the origin of the universe, in which he argued that the circle is the image of cosmic perfection.

Apollo, holding a lyre, is god of reason, patron of music, and symbol of philosophical enlightenment.

Epicurus (341–270 BCE) reads a text and wears a crown of grape leaves, symbolic of his philosophy that happiness could be attained through the pursuit of pleasures of the mind and body.

Pythagoras (ca. 570–490 BCE), the Greek mathematician, illustrates the theory of proportions to interested students—among them, wearing a turban, the Arabic scholar **Averroës** (1126–98).

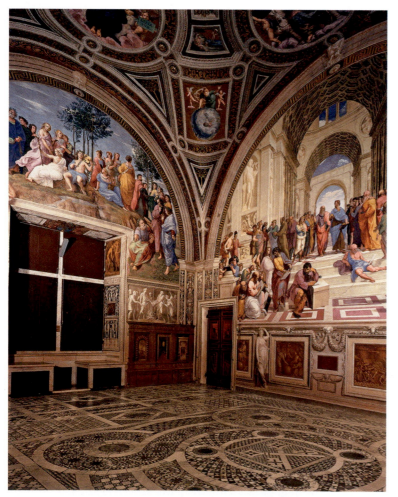

Something to Think About ...

Why do you suppose that Raphael chose to use the likenesses of so many of his contempories as models for the figures from Classical antiquity depicted in the painting?

Stanza della Segnatura, Vatican, Rome.
Fresco on the left lunette, *Parnassus*; on the right lunette, *School of Athens*.

 View the Closer Look for the *School of Athens* on **MyArtsLab**

Aristotle (384–322 BCE) carries his *Nicomachean Ethics* and gestures outward toward the earthly world of the viewer, emphasizing his belief in empiricism—that we can only understand the universe through the careful study and examination of the natural world.

Minerva, the goddess of wisdom, is the traditional patron of those devoted to the pursuit of truth and artistic beauty.

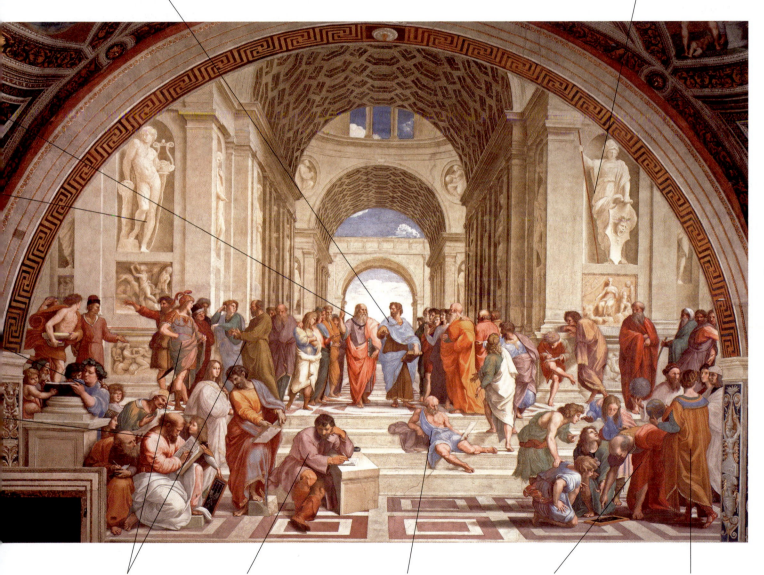

Alexander the Great (356–323 BCE) debates with **Socrates** (ca. 469–399 BCE), who makes his points by enumerating them on his fingers.

Heraclitus (ca. 535–475 BCE), the brooding Greek philosopher who despaired at human folly, wears stonecutter's boots and is actually a portrait of **Michelangelo**.

Diogenes the Cynic (ca. 412–323 BCE), who roamed the streets of Athens looking for an honest man, hated worldly possessions, and lived in a barrel.

Euclid (third century BCE), whose *Elements* remained the standard geometry text down to modern times, is actually a portrait of **Bramante**.

Ptolemy, the second-century astronomer and philosopher, holds a terrestrial globe, while **Zoroaster** (ca. 628–551 BCE) faces him holding a celestial globe. Both turn toward a young man who looks directly out at us. This is a self-portrait of **Raphael**.

Raphael, *School of Athens*. **1510–11.** Fresco, 19′ × 27′. Stanza della Segnatura, Vatican, Rome.

Leo's papacy began a nearly 21-year period of dominance from Rome by the Medici popes (interrupted only by the 21-month rule of a Dutch cardinal, Adrian VI, who deplored the artistic patronage of the Medici popes as both extravagant and inappropriate) that ended with the ten-year reign of Giulio de' Medici as Clement VII. The patronage and politics of these Medici popes had a significant effect on both art and literature.

Leo X and Raphael After his work in the Stanza, Leo was quick to hire Raphael for other commissions. When Bramante died in 1514, Leo appointed the young painter as papal architect, though Raphael had never worked on any substantial building project. It was not long before Leo asked Raphael to paint his portrait.

Raphael's *Portrait of Pope Leo X with Cardinals Giulio de' Medici and Luigi de' Rossi* (Fig. **15.15**), painted in 1517, suggests a new direction in Raphael's art. The lighting is more somber than in the vibrantly lit paintings of the Stanza della Segnatura. Architectural detail is barely visible as the figures are silhouetted, seated against an intensely black ground. Although posed as a group, the three figures look in different directions, each preoccupied with his own concerns. It is as if they have just heard something familiar but ominous in the distance, something that has given them all pause. There is, furthermore, a much greater emphasis on the material reality of the scene. One can almost feel the slight stubble of Leo's beard, and the beards of the two cardinals are similarly palpable. The velvet of Leo's ermine-trimmed robe contrasts dramatically with the silk of the cardinals' cloaks. And the brass knob on the pope's chair reflects the rest of the room like a mirror, including a brightly lit window that stands in total opposition to the darkness of the rest of the scene. All in all, the painting creates a sense of drama, as if we are witness to an important historical moment.

In fact, in 1517, the papacy faced some very real problems. To the north, in Germany, Martin Luther had published his *Ninety-Five Theses*, attacking the practice of papal indulgences and calling into question the authority of the pope (see Chapter 17). Back in Florence, where the Medici had resumed power in 1512, the family maintained control largely through its connections to Rome, and its control was constantly threatened. Despite these difficulties, as Leo tried to rule the Church in Rome and Florence from the *stanze* of the Vatican, he continued his patronage of the arts unabated. He commissioned Raphael to decorate more rooms in the papal apartments and to develop a series of ten **cartoons** (full-scale drawings used to transfer a design onto another surface) for tapestries depicting the lives of Saints Peter and Paul, to cover the lower walls of the Sistine Chapel.

The enormous *Saint Paul Preaching at Athens* (Fig. **15.16**) is one such cartoon. Paul is preaching at the Areopagus (the seat of the Athenian judicial council). Behind Paul are Raphael's contemporaries, his patron, Leo X, in the red hat, and Janus Lascaris, a Greek whom Leo had recently

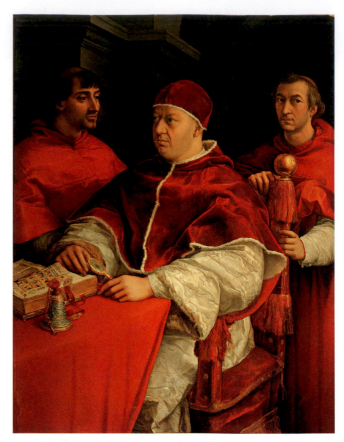

Fig. 15.15 Raphael, *Pope Leo X with Cardinals Giulio de' Medici and Luigi de' Rossi*. 1517. Panel, 60½" × 47". Galleria degli Uffizi, Florence. The illuminated manuscript on the table in front of the pope is from his private collection. It contributes significantly to the highly naturalistic feeling of the scene, even as it symbolizes his humanism.

appointed director of the new Greek academy in Rome. One of Leo's pet peeves was poor preaching, and he and Janus Lascaris listen intently to the master of all preachers in one of his greatest moments. The cartoon was first drawn in charcoal on paper (as many as 160 to 170 separate sheets were glued together to form the larger than life-size image) and then overpainted with color. It was then shipped with the other cartoons to Brussels, where the tapestries were woven in the workshop of Pieter van Aelst. The final tapestry (Fig. **15.17**) is reversed from the drawing, since the weavers worked from behind the cartoon. The borders of the final tapestry are, incidentally, also Raphael's design.

Leo X and Michelangelo In addition to Raphael's tapestries, Leo also celebrated his papacy with a series of commissions at San Lorenzo, the neighborhood church in Florence that had served as the Medici family mausoleum for nearly 100 years. Perhaps inspired by Michelangelo's project for the tomb of Julius II in Rome (see Fig. 14.31 in Chapter 14), he hired Michelangelo to design a new funerary chapel there, the so-called New Sacristy, for recently deceased members of the family.

The plan was that the tombs of four of the Medici would be placed in this New Sacristy, those of Leo X's father,

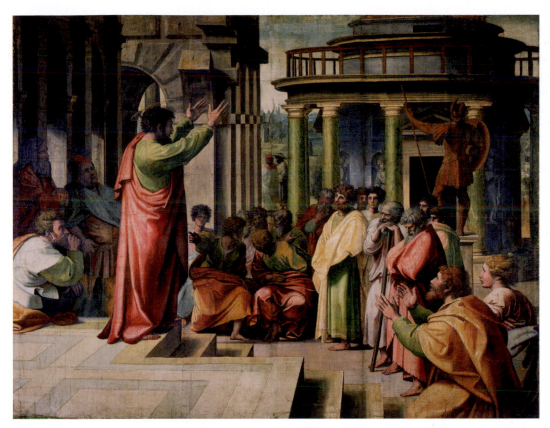

Fig. 15.16 Raphael, *Saint Paul Preaching at Athens*. 1515–16. Bodycolor on paper mounted onto canvas (tapestry cartoon), 11'1¾" × 14'5¼". Victoria and Albert Museum, London. To the right, with its back turned to the Apostle, is a statue of Mars. The moment is that described in Acts 17:22: "Then Paul stood in the middle of Mars' hill, and said, You men of Athens, I perceive that in all things you are too superstitious."

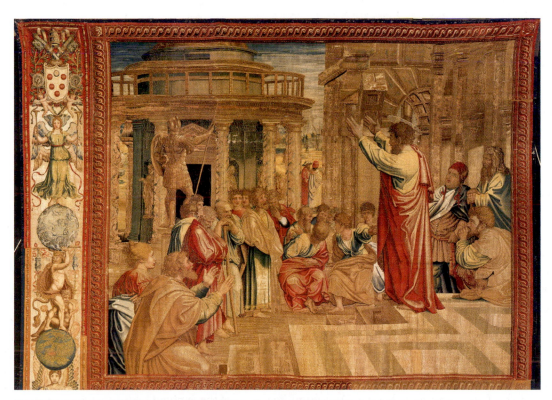

Fig. 15.17 Raphael, *Saint Paul Preaching at Athens*. Completed 1519–21. Tapestry. Pinacoteca, Vatican Museums, Vatican State. This was not among the first seven tapestries mounted in the Sistine Chapel in time for a mass celebrated by the Pope on December 26, 1519, but it was hanging in the Sistine Chapel by 1521.

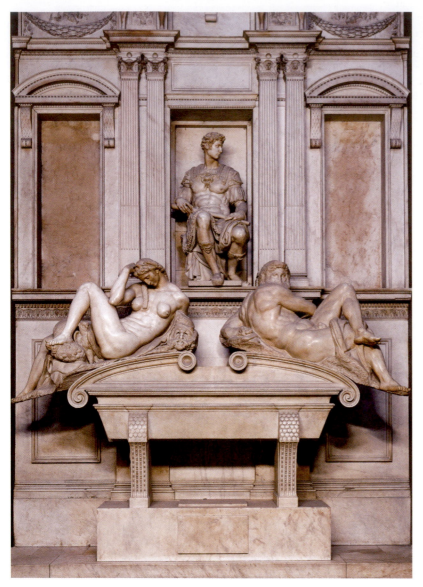

Fig. 15.18 Michelangelo, *Tomb of Giuliano de' Medici*. 1519–34. Height of central figure, 71". New Sacristy, San Lorenzo, Florence. The positions of the two nudes would have seemed less precarious if Michelangelo had ever finished the two river gods he meant to install below them.

reportedly explained: "A thousand years from now, nobody will know what he looked like."

Niccolò Machiavelli, Papal Politics, and the Perfect Prince If Michelangelo's design for the New Sacristy at San Lorenzo idealized the prince, the politics of the era led the political philosopher Niccolò Machiavelli (1469–1527) to approach the question of princely leadership in far more practical terms. Machiavelli's treatise *The Prince* (1513) is part of a long tradition of literature giving advice to rulers that stretches back to the Middle Ages. Although its division into chapters (there are 26) and even some of its headings follow the conventional form, Machiavelli's revolutionary political pragmatism sets the work apart. Humanist education had been founded on the principle that it alone prepared people for a life of virtuous action. Machiavelli's *Prince* challenged that assumption.

Machiavelli had served the Florentine city-state for many years when, on June 19, 1498, three weeks after the death of Savonarola, he assumed the post of second chancellor to the Florentine Republic. In that role, he served on the various Florentine military committees and worked as a diplomat. He engaged in the tough negotiations between Florence and its many enemies, particularly the Borgia papacy of Alexander VI (papacy 1492–1503). The moral laxness of Alexander's court had brought on the wrath of Savonarola in the first place (see Chapter 14). A humanist scholar, Machiavelli had studied the behavior of ancient Roman rulers and citizens at great length, and he admired particularly their willingness to act in defense of their country. On the other hand, he disdained the squabbling and feuding that marked Italian internal relations in his own day.

In his *Discourses on the First Ten Books of Titus Livy*, completed in about 1519, he argues that the ancient Romans were exemplary in leading lives of manly action, courage, and assertiveness, in contrast to Christians, whom he sees as passive, submissive, and ineffectual. He even praises Romulus, the legendary founder of Rome, for murdering his brother Remus, arguing that the end justified the means: "Reprehensible actions may be justified by their effects," he wrote, "and when the effect is good, as it was in the case of Romulus, it always justifies the action." Assessing the situation in the Italian politics of his day, he concluded that only the strongest, most ruthless leader could impose order on the Italian people.

Even though the Borgias threatened the well-being of Florence, Machiavelli admired them for their ruthless determination. Alexander VI might have bribed his way

Lorenzo the Magnificent, Lorenzo's brother Giuliano, and two younger members of the family, also named Lorenzo and Giuliano. Working on the project from 1519 to 1534, Michelangelo would complete only the tombs of the two younger Medici. Nearly mirror images of each other, each consists of a sarcophagus topped by two reclining nudes that form the base of a triangle topped by a seated armored figure representing the deceased (Fig. **15.18**). The two reclining nudes are allegorical figures representing Day, on the right, and Night, on the left. A note on one of Michelangelo's sketches for the ensemble reads: "Day and Night speak, and say: We with our swift course have brought Duke Giuliano to death. ..." The portrait of the Prince above, turned to face what would have been the tomb of Lorenzo the Magnificent, is that of an idealized Roman warrior. Notably, it bore no resemblance to Giuliano. As Michelangelo himself into the papacy, lived openly with his mistress in the Vatican, and indulged in the most blatant forms of nepotism, deeding vast papal properties to his family, but he had not shied from asserting his power. After all, he had quickly disposed of Savonarola's threat. And Machiavelli saw in Cesare Borgia (1475–1507), Alexander's son by his mistress, a role model for the perfect prince.

From Machiavelli's point of view, Cesare Borgia's chief virtue was his ethical pragmatism. For the statesman's first duty, he believed, was to preserve his country and its institutions, regardless of the means he used. Thus, a prince's chief preoccupation, and his primary duty, says Machiavelli in Chapter 14, is to wage war (**Reading 15.2a**):

READING 15.2a

from Niccolò Machiavelli, *The Prince*, Chapter 14 (1513)

A Prince ... should have no care or thought but for war, and for the regulations and training it requires, and should apply himself exclusively to this as his peculiar province; for war is the sole art looked for in one who rules and is of such efficacy that it not merely maintains those who are born Princes, but often enables men to rise to that eminence from a private station; while, on the other hand, we often see that when Princes devote themselves rather to pleasure than to arms, they lose their dominions.

His attention turned to war, the prince must be willing to sacrifice moral right for practical gain, for "the manner in which we live, and that in which we ought to live, are things so wide asunder, that he who quits the one to betake himself to the other is more likely to destroy than to save himself." Therefore, "it is essential ... for a Prince who desires to maintain his position, to have learned how to be other than good." Goodness, from Machiavelli's point of view, is a relative quality anyway. A prince, he says, "need never hesitate ... to incur the reproach of those vices without which his authority can hardly be preserved; for if he well consider the whole matter, he will find that there may be a line of conduct having the appearance of virtue, to follow which would be his ruin, and that there may be another course having the appearance of vice, by following which his safety and well-being are secured." The well-being of the prince, in other words, is of the utmost importance because upon it rests the well-being of the state. (See **Reading 15.2** on pages 538–539 for a longer selection from the text of Chapters 15–18 of *The Prince*.)

Machiavelli further argues that the prince, once engaged in war, has three alternatives for controlling a state once he has conquered it: He can devastate it, live in it, or allow it to keep its own laws. Machiavelli recommends the first of these choices, especially if the prince defeats a republic (**Reading 15.2b**):

READING 15.2b

from Niccolò Machiavelli, *The Prince*, Chapter 5 (1513)

In republics there is a stronger vitality, a fiercer hatred, a keener thirst for revenge. The memory of their former freedom will not let them rest; so that the safest course is either to destroy them, or to go and live in them.

This is probably a warning directed at the absentee Medici popes, far away in Rome and not tending to business in Florence, for Machiavelli originally planned to dedicate the book to Giuliano de' Medici, by then Pope Leo X. (He eventually dedicated it to Lorenzo de' Medici, then Duke of Florence, hoping to secure political favor.) Its lessons, drawn from Roman history, were intended as a guide to aid Italy in rebuffing the French invasions.

Finally, according to Machiavelli in Chapter 17 of *The Prince*, the prince should be feared, not loved, for "Men are less careful how they offend him who makes himself loved than him who makes himself feared." This is because "love is held by the tie of obligation, which, because men are a sorry breed, is broken on every whisper of private interest; but fear is bound by the apprehension of punishment which never relaxes."

From Machiavelli's point of view, humans are "fickle," "dishonest," "simple," and, as he says here, all in all a "sorry breed." The state must be governed, therefore, by a morality different than that governing the individual. Such moral and ethical pragmatism was wholly at odds with the teachings of the Church. In 1512, Pope Julius II's troops overran the Florentine republic, restored the Medici to power in Florence, and dismissed Machiavelli from his post as second chancellor. Machiavelli was then (wrongfully) accused of involvement in a plot to overthrow the new heads of state, imprisoned, tortured, and finally exiled permanently to a country home in the hills above Florence. It is here, beginning in 1513, that he wrote *The Prince*.

Although widely circulated, *The Prince* was too much at odds with the norms of Christian morality to be well received in the sixteenth century. Throughout the seventeenth and eighteenth centuries, it was more often condemned than praised, particularly because it appeared to be a defense of absolute monarchy. Today we value *The Prince* as a pioneering text in political science. As an essay on political power, it provides a rationalization for political expediency and duplicity that society has all too often witnessed in modern political history.

Clement VII and the Laurentian Library When Leo X died in 1521, he was briefly succeeded by Adrian VI, a non-Medici who died only 21 months into his reign, and when Giulio de' Medici succeeded him as Clement VII (papacy 1523–34), artists and humanists reacted enthusiastically. As cardinal, he had commissioned major works from Raphael and others, and he had worked closely with Leo on Michelangelo's New Sacristy at San Lorenzo in Florence. But Clement was never able to sustain the scale of patronage in Rome that his uncle had managed. This failure resulted in part from the Sack of Rome by the German mercenary troops of Holy Roman Emperor Charles V in 1527. During this crisis, many of the artists' workshops in the city were destroyed, and many artists abandoned the city altogether.

In Florence, Clement was more successful in his patronage efforts, especially at San Lorenzo. In 1523, he commissioned Michelangelo to build a library complex over the preexisting cloister, even as he was at work on the New Sacristy. The Laurentian Library was designed to house the enormous book collection of the Medici family and serve as a place of quiet refuge and study. Michelangelo's most original contribution to the library is the large triple stairway leading from the vestibule to the library reading room a story above (Fig. **15.19**). The central flight is composed of three oval steps at the bottom and one at the top, with segments of ovals ending in scrolls in between. Two rectangular flights flank the central staircase and are separated from it by wide banisters. These side flights have no outside banister and end at a square that turns into the central stairs about two-thirds of the way up, a turning emphasized by broad scrolls that rise up to the central banisters. The trapezoidal form of the staircase creates a perspective rise to the doorway into the library, which is flanked by pairs of heavy Tuscan columns. These columns continue around the room, placed in niches as if they were sculptures in their own right.

The overall effect is more sculptural than architectural, and in its combination of Classical and nonclassical forms—for instance, Tuscan columns juxtaposed with oval stairs, and rigid horizontals and verticals juxtaposed with sensuous scrolls—it announces a new architectural freedom undoubtedly related to the freedom of movement in paintings such as the *Libyan Sibyl* (see Fig. 15.12) in the Sistine Chapel. Michelangelo once described this

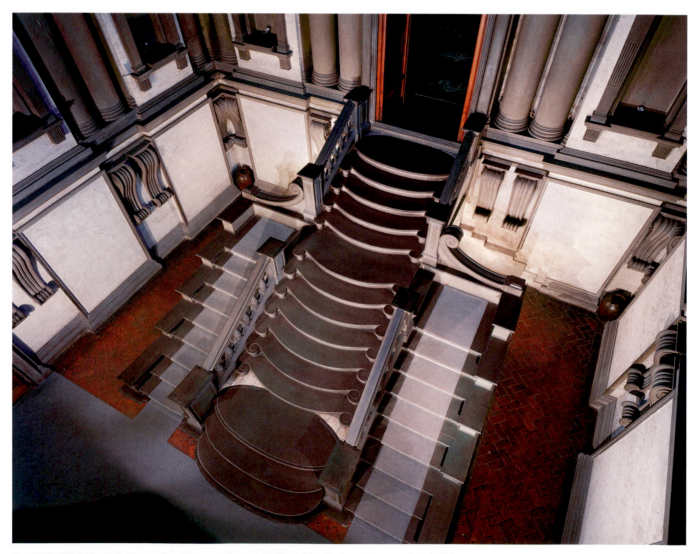

Fig. 15.19 Michelangelo, Laurentian Library staircase. Designed beginning 1524, completed 1559.
San Lorenzo, Florence. In *On Architecture*, Alberti advised that interior staircases occupy as little room as possible. Michelangelo ignored his recommendation, asserting his independence from the strictures of tradition.

project as "a certain stair that comes back to my mind as in a dream," and its cascading waterfall effect, filling the space of the vestibule as no other stair had done before, certainly suggests that Michelangelo was becoming increasingly interested in exploring realms of the imagination beyond the humanist vision of a rational world governed by structural logic.

The Sistine Chapel Choir

The inventiveness that marks the patronage of the Medici popes and cardinals as well as the work of Raphael, Leonardo, and Michelangelo was a quality shared by Renaissance musicians, especially in the virtuosity of their performances. Such originality was the hallmark of the Sistine Chapel Choir, founded in 1473 by Sixtus IV. It performed only on occasions when the pope was present and typically consisted of between 16 and 24 male singers. The choir's repertory was limited to the polyphonic forms common to the liturgy: motets, masses, and psalm settings. These were arranged in four parts (voices), for boy sopranos, male altos, tenors, and basses. The choir usually sang without instrumental accompaniment, a cappella, "in the manner of the chapel," an unusual practice at the time, since most chapel choirs relied on at least organ accompaniment.

Josquin des Prez

Composers from all over Europe were attracted to the Sistine Chapel Choir. Between 1489 and 1495, one of the principal members of the choir was the Franco-Flemish composer Josquin des Prez (ca. 1450–1521). Afterward, beginning in about 1503, he served as musical director of the chapel at the court of Ferrara. During his lifetime, he wrote some 18 masses, almost 100 motets (see Chapter 12 and the discussion of Guillaume Dufay in Chapter 14), and some 70 songs, including three Italian *frottole*.

Josquin's last mass, the *Pange lingua* ("Sing, My Tongue"), written some time after 1513, is structured by means of **paraphrase**. In paraphrase structure, all voices elaborate on an existing melody. One voice introduces a musical idea that is subsequently repeated with some variation in sequence by each of the other voices throughout the entire work or section of a work, so that all the parts are rhythmically and melodically balanced. This creates the richly polyphonic texture of the whole. This contrasts with *cantus firmus*, which is the plainchant (monophonic) "fixed melody" on which the composition is based (see Chapter 14). The source of Josquin's melody in *Pange lingua* is a very well-known plainchant hymn written in the sixth century by Venantius Fortunatus (ca. 530–609), one of the earliest medieval poets and composers. Josquin transforms the original hymn into a completely new composition, even as he leaves the melody entirely recognizable.

The opening *Kyrie* (Fig. **15.20**) (track **15.1**) is based on the opening of the Fortunatus plainchant. In a technique known as **point of imitation**, this musical theme is taken up by all the voices of Josquin's polyphonic composition in succession so that all four voices weave round one another in imitation. This kind of innovative play upon a more or less standard theme is testimony to Josquin's ingenuity and humanist individualism. And it brings a level of expressiveness to the liturgy that far exceeds the more or less unemotional character of the plainchant. Largely because of this expressiveness, his compositions were among the first polyphonic works to be widely performed long after the death of their composer.

Listen on MyArtsLab

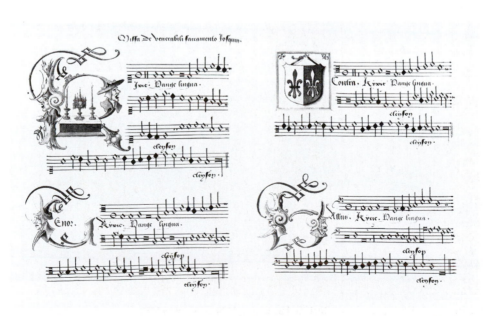

Fig. 15.20 Score for the opening bars of Josquin des Prez's *Pange lingua* mass. 16th century. The four voices of the mass are represented here, each one indicated by the decorative capital at the beginning of the line.

THE HIGH RENAISSANCE IN VENICE

What distinguishes Venetian culture from that of Florence and Rome?

In a mid-fifteenth-century painting by Vittore Carpaccio (1450–1525) of Saint Mark's lion (Fig. **15.21**), symbol of the Venetian republic, the lion stands with its front paws on land and its rear paws on the sea, symbolizing the importance of both elements to the city. In the sixth or seventh century, invading Lombards from the north had forced the local populations of the Po River delta to flee to the swampy lagoon islands that would later become the city of Venice. Ever since, trade had been the lifeblood of Venice.

Not only did the city possess the natural fortification of being surrounded on all sides by water (Map **15.2**), but, as a larger city-state, it also controlled the entire flood-plain north of the Po River, including the cities of Padua and Verona and extending eastward nearly to Milan (Map **15.3**). This larger territory was called Terraferma (from the Latin *terra firma*, "firm ground"), to distinguish it from the watery canals and islands of the city proper. From Terraferma, the Venetians established trade routes across the Alps to the north, and eastward across Asia Minor, Persia, and the Caucasus. As one Venetian historian put it in a thirteenth-century history of the city: "Merchandise passes through this noble city as water flows through fountains." By the fifteenth century, the city had become a center of fashion. In 1423, the doge observed, "Now we have invested in our silk industry a capital of 10 million ducats [roughly $39 million today] and we make 2 million [roughly $7.8 million] annually in export trade; 16,000 weavers live in our city." These weavers produced satins, velvets, and brocades that were in demand across the continent. On

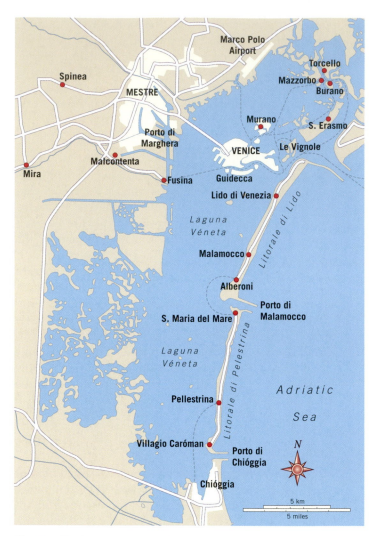

Map 15.2 The islands of Venice, the lagoon, and (at the left), the Italian mainland.

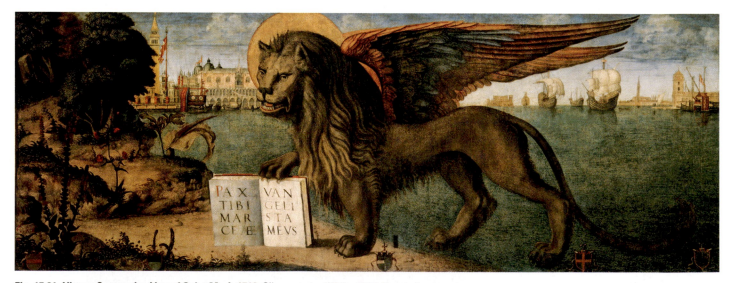

Fig. 15.21 Vittore Carpaccio, *Lion of Saint Mark*. 1516. Oil on canvas, 4'6¾" × 12'1". Doge's Apartments, Doge's Palace, Venice. Venetians believed that an angel visited Saint Mark and prophesied that he would be buried in Venice, on the very spot where Saint Mark's Cathedral stands. So they felt justified in removing his relics from Egypt and bringing them to Venice.

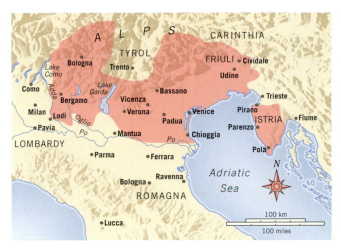

Map 15.3 Venice and the Venetian Terraferma, the Venetian-controlled mainland, at the end of the 15th century. Venice controlled all the land inside the dotted line. Its territories extended almost to Milan in the west, northward into the Alps, and almost as far as Ferrara and Mantua to the south. A causeway connecting Venice to the mainland was constructed in the middle of the nineteenth century. Until then, the city was approachable only by water.

this tide of merchandise flowed even greater wealth. As a result, the city became a great naval power and a preeminent center of shipbuilding, able to protect and contribute to its maritime resources as no other European city (except possibly Genoa) could even imagine.

Venice considered itself blessed by Saint Mark, whose relics resided in the Cathedral of Saint Mark's. Protected by its patron saint, the city could prosper in peace. "Peace unto you, Mark my evangelist," reads the Latin inscription in the book the lion holds with its right paw in Carpaccio's painting. Behind the lion, visible across the lagoon, is the Piazza San Marco (Saint Mark's Square), with its tall campanile, or bell tower, the domes of Saint Mark's, and the Palace of the Doge, the Venetian Republic's leader, whom they elected for life. In almost every other Italian city, Church and State were physically separated, but in Venice, the political and religious centers of the city stood side by side. Peace, prosperity, and unity of purpose were the city's greatest assets—and the citizens of Venice believed, above all, in those principles.

Venetian Architecture

During the Renaissance, an elaborate, sensuous style of architecture would develop in Venice, influenced by the elaborate Gothic style of facades of buildings such as the Doge's Palace, which was begun in 1340 (Fig. 15.22). There is no hint in this building of any need to create a defensible space to protect the state. Two stories of open arcades, rising in pointed arches and topped by open quatrefoils, provide covered walkways around the outside, as if to invite the citizenry into its halls. The diamond pattern of the stonework in the upper stories creates a sense of lightness to what might otherwise seem a massive facade. And the color of the ornament and stone—white and pink—seem calculated to reflect light itself, so that the building might shine like a gemstone set in the public square,

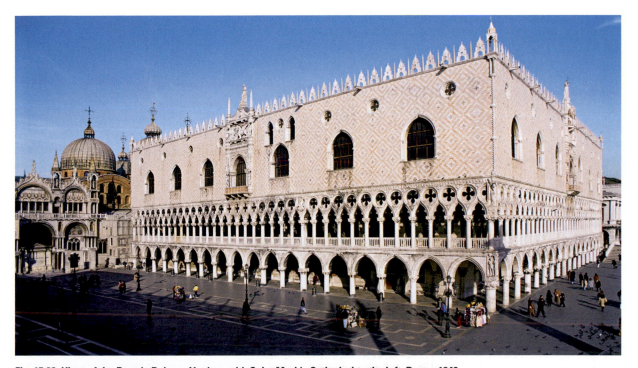

Fig. 15.22 View of the Doge's Palace, Venice, with Saint Mark's Cathedral to the left. Begun 1340.
During the Renaissance, an elaborate, more sensuous style of art would develop in Venice, influenced by the elaborate Gothic style of facades such as this one.

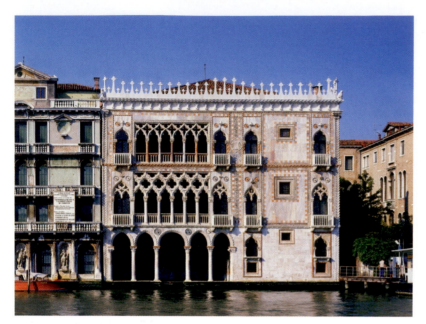

Fig. 15.23 Giovanni and Bartolomeo Bon, Ca' d'Oro ("House of Gold"), Contarini Palace, Venice. 1421–37. The Ca' d'Oro, built for one of Venice's most prominent families, is still spectacular today. We can only imagine how it must have looked with its original gilded ornamental detail. The attic, where servants lived, is not visible in this view.

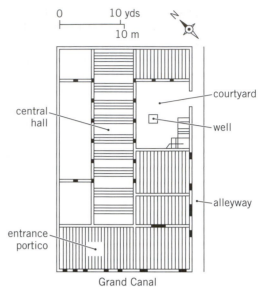

Fig. 15.24 Floor plan of ground level, Ca' d'Oro, Venice.

literally a reflection of the city's wealth and well-being. The building's emphasis on texture and the play of light and shadow across richly elaborated surfaces would become one of the hallmarks of Venetian art and architecture.

The wealth and general well-being of Venice were evident along the city's main, curving thoroughfare, the Grand Canal, where its most important families built their homes. One of the most magnificent of these is the Ca' d'Oro (Fig. **15.23**), built by the head of the Contarini family. (*Ca'* is a Venetian abbreviation of *casa*, "house," and *Ca' d'Oro* means "House of Gold.") Although built in the Renaissance, the house, like the Doge's Palace (see Fig. 15.22), is distinctly Gothic in character. Venetian palazzi and civic architecture retained Gothic elements for so long probably because the citizens regarded their continued use as a sign of the stability of the city's culture.

The asymmetry of the Ca' d'Oro facade, with its three distinct loggias, or arcades, is characteristic of the design of other moderate-sized Venetian palazzi. Originally, Contarini ordered that the stone carved for the tracery work be painted with white lead and oil to make it shine like marble. The red Verona marble used in the detailing was oiled and varnished to bring out its deepest and richest hues. The balls atop the facade's parapet, the rosettes at the bottom of the arches, the leaves on the capitals at the corners, the architectural moldings, window finials, and the roundels over the windows and the portico arches were all gilded—giving the house its name. Finally, the backgrounds of the capitals, and other details, were painted with very expensive ultramarine blue, made of ground lapis lazuli, an imported semiprecious stone.

Despite the lavishness of the facade, the plan of the Ca' d'Oro (Fig. **15.24**) is typical of Venetian architecture. The entrance portico, at canal level, opens to a long open hall with storerooms along its length. Toward the back of the house is an open courtyard and garden, from which a staircase rises to the second story. There, the Contarini received guests and entertained in the main reception room. The family's private rooms were on the third story, and servants' quarters in the attic.

The Contarini finished the Ca' d'Oro just seven years before Cosimo de' Medici began the Medici palace in Florence (see Fig. 14.16 in Chapter 14), but nothing could be more distant in feeling and taste. Contarini's palace, with its airy traceries and ornamentation, is light and refined; Cosimo's palace, with its monumental facade, is massive—a wall of stone. One opens to the canal; the other turns inward away from the street. The Ca' d'Oro is an ostentatious celebration of personal wealth and social status; the Medici palace projects state authority and power. The pomp and extravagance we sense in Venetian homes such as this one, the sensitivity to light and air, the luxury of detail and design, and the opulent variety of pattern and texture all define the Venetian visual world, and all came to define Venetian art and architecture in the Renaissance.

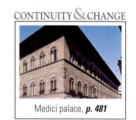

CONTINUITY & CHANGE

Medici palace, *p. 481*

The *Scuole*, Painting, and the Venetian Style

At the end of the thirteenth century, Venice's Grand Council divided the city's population into three social classes. The nobility were the patrician families, from whose members the doge was elected. Beneath this small, upper-echelon group were male citizens, essentially a bourgeois mercantile class of people who rotated through the elective offices of the government. To enter their ranks, one had to prove that no one in the family had ever performed manual labor. The rest of the population made up roughly 90 percent of the city's inhabitants. They were artisans, craftspeople, shipbuilders, shopkeepers, and all foreigners, no matter how wealthy.

Cutting across these distinct political groups were the *scuole* ("schools"), religious confraternities like those in Florence (see Chapter 14) that engaged in charity, sponsored social functions, and marched in sometimes elaborate processions associated with civic and religious festivals. Each *scuola* had a patron saint, after whom it took its name. All political groups came together in the *scuole*; rich and poor, patrician and commoner worked together for the common good, and nobles were specifically prohibited from holding office in order to underscore the sense of equality and brotherhood that these organizations fostered. Despite internal equality, each *scuola* competed with other *scuole* for civic prestige and to enhance their city's fame. The *scuole*, therefore, commissioned architects to produce ever grander headquarters and artists to paint ever larger and more magnificent works to decorate them.

One of the largest *scuole* in Venice was that of Saint John the Evangelist. Its prestige and a great deal of its income derived from a relic, a gift from the grand chancellor of Cyprus. The relic was purported to be from the True Cross (the cross on which Christ was crucified). This relic was the subject of much of the art that decorated the confraternity's meetinghouse. Two of the most important Venetian painters of the late fourteenth and early fifteenth centuries, Gentile Bellini (ca. 1429–1507) and Vittore Carpaccio, were involved in its adornment. The Scuola di San Giovanni Evangelista (Saint John the Evangelist) commissioned both men to paint images for them, Carpaccio paintings of various miracles and Bellini the annual procession of all the *scuole* through the streets of Venice, culminating in the Piazza San Marco.

The procession occurred on the feast day of Saint Mark, and the Scuola di San Giovanni Evangelista carried its relic of the True Cross through the streets of the city. Gentile Bellini's painting of the procession (Fig. 15.25) celebrates a famous occasion in 1444, when it was claimed that a terminally ill child had been miraculously healed by the presence of the relic. The child's father, wearing a red robe, kneels in thanks, to the right of the break in the procession behind the reliquary. Members of the Scuola di San Giovanni Evangelista, identified by their white robes, march across the foreground. The coats of arms of all the *scuole* in the city decorate the canopy covering the reliquary, and it seems as if the entire population has come out to the piazza to celebrate the occasion. The realism of the scene—with each individual rendered in a portrait likeness—seems to affirm the truth of the miracle.

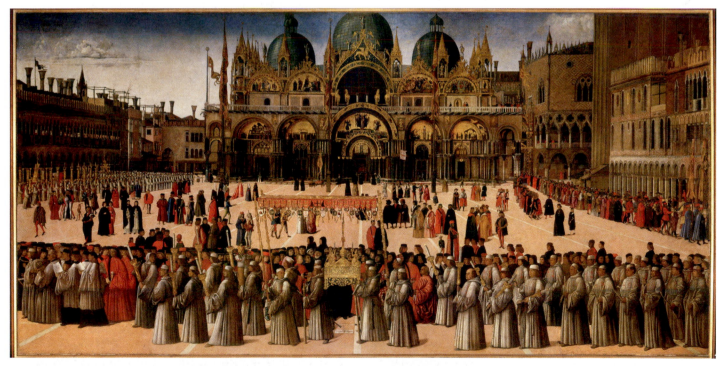

Fig. 15.25 Gentile Bellini, *Procession of the Reliquary of the True Cross in Piazza San Marco.* **1496.** Oil on canvas, 12'½" × 24'5¼". Gallerie dell'Accademia, Venice. Venetian painting was deeply influenced by technical advances in Flanders (see Chapter 16), specifically the use of oil-based paints on canvas and board. The method allows for much greater detail than does tempera. Using it, artists could create intensely realistic scenes such as this one.

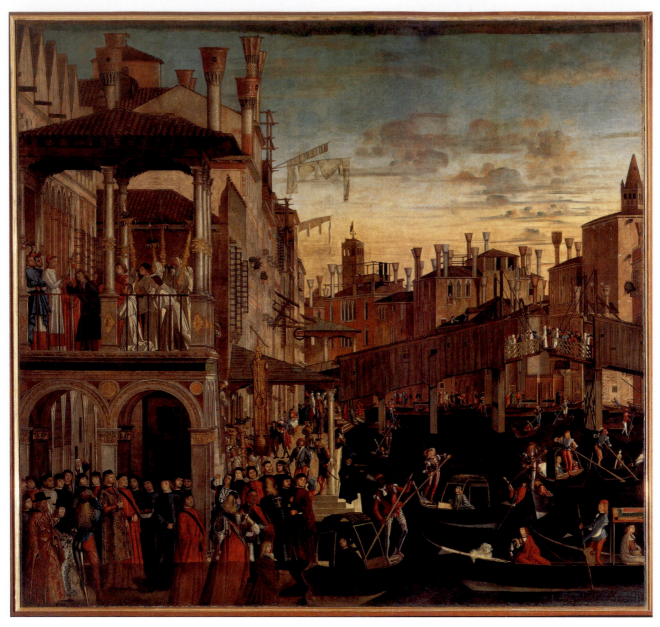

Fig. 15.26 Vittore Carpaccio, *Miracle at the Rialto* (*Healing of the Possessed Man*). ca. 1494. Oil on canvas, 11'11¾" × 12'9¼". Gallerie dell'Accademia, Venice. At the far end of the walkway stand two turbaned and white-bearded Muslims and a black African. A worker carries a barrel halfway down the walkway. All details symbolize Venice's civic harmony.

In the same vein, Vittore Carpaccio's *Miracle at the Rialto* (Fig. **15.26**) almost casually asserts the truth of its subject through the realism of its style. On the balcony at the left, a possessed man with rolling eyes and contorted expression surrounded by members of the confraternity is healed by the relic of the cross. But the painting hardly seems to be about this miracle. Its subject is the urban life of Venice itself. The scene is the canal in front of the Rialto Bridge, a wooden drawbridge over the Grand Canal that was not replaced by the present stone structure until the late sixteenth century. All of the city's diverse population are represented here, including elaborately costumed gondoliers. Note that the gondolier closest to the

left bank is of African origin, a reminder of Venice's vast trading connections. The dog in the gondola to his right is a terrier, an import from England. Laundry hangs on poles extended from the rooftops, and the richly decorated and distinctive Venetian chimney pots dominate the horizon.

In a Florentine painting, the miracle would have been the focus of the composition. But here and in Bellini's painting as well, the religious subject—the miracle—is moved to the periphery of the composition, and the artist concentrates instead on detailing the familiar sights and features of Venice itself. This approach probably owes a debt to Northern European painting, which habitually portrays sacred events in highly localized landscapes and settings. But it is this emphasis on the realistic details of everyday life that sets Venetian painting apart from both its medieval predecessors and other Renaissance painting in Italy.

This level of detail was made possible by the new technique of **oil painting** developed by Netherlandish painters in the first half of the fifteenth century (see Chapter 16). The pigments used in oil painting are the same as those used in tempera (see Chapter 13), but oil is a translucent medium in which the pigment is suspended. When oil is applied in many thin layers, light penetrates the layers and is reflected, creating a kind of luminosity, the sensation that the painting is itself generating light. Scholars have recently discovered that Venetian artists often mixed pulverized glass, which reflects light prismatically, into their oil paints, thus heightening the luminous effects. Furthermore, oil dries very slowly, allowing the artist to blend colors and create very subtle modulations of tone and detail, whereas tempera is difficult to blend and appears flat and opaque. In Carpaccio's painting, the medium creates an almost palpable sense of atmosphere as the afternoon light seems to warm the buildings and figures against the dark water of the canal.

Masters of the Venetian High Renaissance: Giorgione and Titian

The two great masters of painting in the Venetian High Renaissance were Giorgione da Castelfranco, known simply as Giorgione (ca. 1478–1510), and Titian (ca. 1488–1576). Both painters were students of Giovanni Bellini, and Giorgione had been especially inspired by Leonardo's visit in 1500. In the first decade of the sixteenth century, they worked sometimes side by side with Bellini, gaining increased control of their surfaces, building up color by means of glazing, as Leonardo did in his soft, luminous landscapes. Their paintings, like the great palaces of Venice whose reflections shimmered on the Grand Canal, demonstrate an exquisite sensitivity to the play of light and shadow, to the luxurious display of detail and design, and to an opulent variety of pattern and texture.

Giorgione The mysterious qualities of Leonardo's highly charged atmospheric paintings like the *Mona Lisa* (Fig. 14.28 in Chapter 14) are fully realized in Giorgione's *Tempest* (Fig. **15.27**). The first known mention of the painting dates from 1530, when the painting surfaced in the collection of a Venetian patrician. We know almost nothing else about it, which contributes to its mystery. At the right, an almost nude young woman nurses her child. At the left, a somewhat disheveled young man, wearing the costume of a German mercenary soldier, gazes at the woman and child with evident pride. Between them, in the foreground, stands a pediment topped by two broken columns. A creaky wooden bridge crosses the estuary in the middle ground, and lightning flashes in the distance, illuminating a densely built cityscape. What, we must ask, is the relationship between the two figures? Are they husband and wife? Or are they lovers, whose own

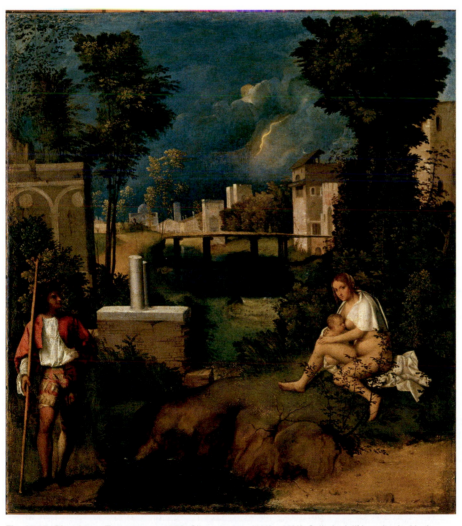

Fig. 15.27 Giorgione, *Tempest.* **ca. 1509.** Oil on canvas, 31¼" × 28¾". Gallerie dell'Accademia, Venice. There is nothing about this painting that could be called controlled. The landscape is overgrown and weedy—just as the man and woman are disheveled and disrobed. It is as if, for a moment, the lightning has revealed to the viewer a scene not meant to be witnessed.

View the Closer Look for *Tempest* on **MyArtsLab**

tempestuous affair has resulted in the birth of a child? These are questions that remain unanswered.

Giorgione evidently began work on his paintings without preliminary drawings, and X-ray examination of this one reveals that in the young man's place there originally stood a second young woman stepping into the pool between the two figures. At the time that the work surfaced in the wealthy Venetian's collection in 1530, it was described simply as a small landscape with a soldier and a gypsy. It seems to have satisfied the Venetian taste for depictions of the affairs of everyday life, and even though its subject remains obscure, the painting continues to fascinate us.

The fact that Giorgione did not make preliminary drawings for his paintings led Vasari, in his *Lives of the Most Excellent Painters, Architects, and Sculptors*, to charge that he was simply hiding his inability to draw well beneath a virtuoso display of surface color and light. The shortcoming of all Venetian artists, Vasari claimed, was their sensuous painterly technique, as opposed to the intellectual *buon disegno* ("good design') of the Florentines (see Chapter 14), epitomized by their careful use of scientific perspective and linear clarity.

Titian In a certain sense, Vasari was right. Sensuality, even outright sexuality, would become a primary subject of Venetian art, as many of Titian's paintings make clear. When Giorgione died of the plague in 1510, at only 32 years of age, it seems likely that his friend Titian, 10 years younger, finished several of his paintings. While lacking the sense of intrigue that his elder mentor captured in the *Tempest*, Titian's *Sacred and Profane Love* (Fig. **15.28**) is similarly addressed to the relations between the sexes, only a little more indirectly. The nude figure at the right holds a lamp, perhaps symbolizing divine light and connecting her to the Neoplatonic ideal of the celestial Venus and thus sacred love. The luxuriously clothed, fully dressed figure on the left, whom we might think of as the "*earthly* lady," or profane love, holds a bouquet of flowers, a symbol of her fecundity. Between the two, Cupid reaches into the fountain.

The painting was a commission from Niccolò Aurelio on the occasion of his marriage to Laura Bagarotto in 1514. Behind the clothed figure on the left, two rabbits cavort in the grass, underscoring the conjugal theme of the image. It seems probable that the two female figures represent two aspects of the same woman, and thus embody the range of roles that the Renaissance woman filled for her humanist husband, combining Classical learning and intelligence with a candid celebration of sexual love in marriage.

Titian's *Venus of Urbino* (Fig. **15.29**), painted for Duke Guidobaldo della Rovere of Urbino in 1538, more fully acknowledges the sexual obligations of most Renaissance women. This "Venus"—more a real woman than an ethereal goddess, and referred to by Guidobaldo as merely a "nude woman"—is frankly available. She stares out at the viewer, Guidobaldo himself, with matter-of-factness, suggesting she is totally comfortable with her nudity. (Apparently the lady-in-waiting and maid at the rear of the palatial rooms are searching for suitably fine clothing in which to dress her.) Her hand both covers and draws attention to her genitals. Her dog, a traditional symbol of both fidelity and lust, sleeps lazily on the white sheets at her feet. She may be, ambiguously, either a courtesan or a bride. (The chest from which the servant is removing clothes is a traditional reference to marriage.) In either case she is, primarily, an object of desire.

As Titian's work continued to develop through the 1550s, 1560s, and 1570s, his brushwork became increasingly loose and gestural (see Chapter 20). The frank sensuality conveyed by crisp contours in *Sacred and Profane Love* and the *Venus of Urbino* found expression, instead, in the artist's handling of paint itself. Indeed, the viewer can feel Titian's very hand in these later works, for he would

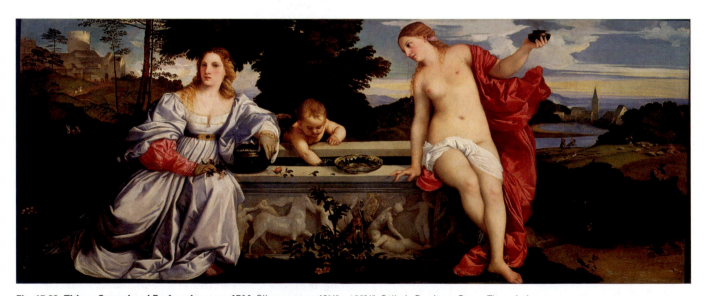

Fig. 15.28 Titian, *Sacred and Profane Love*. ca. 1514. Oil on canvas, 46½" × 109⅞". Galleria Borghese, Rome. The painting was commissioned by Niccolò Aurelio, a Venetian, to celebrate his marriage to Laura Bagarotto and was probably intended for the couple's sleeping chamber. The husband's coat of arms is carved on the fountain; the wife's is inside the silver bowl on the fountain's ledge.

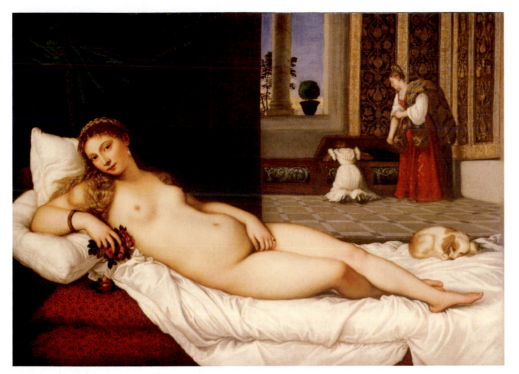

Fig. 15.29 Titian, *Reclining Nude* (*Venus of Urbino*). ca. 1538. Oil on canvas, 47" × 65". Galleria degli Uffizi, Florence. Titian's technique contributes significantly to the power of the painting. Although not visible in reproduction, the nude's skin is built up of layers of semitransparent yellow-whites and pinks that contrast with the cooler bluish whites of the bed sheets. Behind her, the almost black panel and curtain further contrast with the luminous light on her body.

actually paint with his fingers and the stick end of his brush too. But Titian's mastery of color—the rich varieties of warm reds, the luminosity of his glazes—so evident in these paintings, never altered. In fact, his color came to define the art of Venice itself. When people speak of "Venetian" color, they have Titian in mind.

WOMEN IN ITALIAN HUMANIST SOCIETY

How did women fare in the Italian Renaissance?

The paintings of both Giorgione and Titian raise the issue of the place of women in Italian humanist society. It remained commonplace, especially in Venice, to paint portraits of women whose identity was unknown but who represented ideal beauty. Titian's *La Bella* (Fig. **15.30**) seems to be the same person depicted in the *Venus of Urbino* (and she appears in at least two other Titian portraits), but her identity is a mystery, if in fact she was ever a "real" woman and not simply the embodiment of Titian's idea of "true" beauty. Something of a canon of female beauty had been codified by Petrarch, in his sonnets, and Poliziano in his poems (see Reading 14.1 in Chapter 14). In her book *Women in Italian Renaissance Art: Gender, Representation, Identity*, Paola Tinagli sums up the canon: "Writers praised

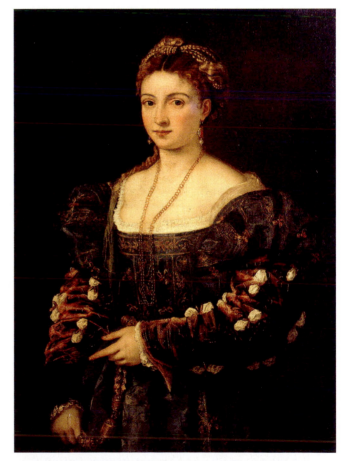

Fig. 15.30 Titian, *La Bella* (*Woman in a Blue Dress*). ca. 1538. Oil on canvas, 39⅜" × 30". Palazzo Pitti, Florence. The sumptuousness of the dress adds considerably to the sense of beauty Titian seeks to convey. It was painted with extremely expensive lapis lazuli pigments.

[painters for] the attractions of wavy hair gleaming like gold; of white skin similar to snow, to marble, to alabaster or to milk; they admired cheeks which looked like lilies and roses, and eyes that shone like the sun or the stars. Lips are compared to rubies, teeth to pearls, breasts to snow or apples." Portraits of Venetian women who embodied such traits are emblems of the beautiful more than representations of real beings.

But as humanist values helped redefine the relation of the individual to the state throughout the Italian city-states and gave male citizens a greater degree of freedom, women began to benefit as well. While at all levels of culture their role might still be relegated to the domestic side of life, they were increasingly better educated and therefore better able to assert themselves. This is particularly true of middle- and upper-class women. And occasionally these women, through their accomplishments, achieved a remarkable level of stature.

The Humanist Education of Women

In the Italian humanist courts, the wives of rulers and their daughters—who were, after all, prospective wives of other rulers—received a humanist education. Like the medieval author of the *Book of the City of Ladies*, Christine de Pizan (see Chapter 13), they possessed knowledge of French and Latin, the ability to write in their native language with grace and ease, a close acquaintance with both Classical and vernacular Italian literature, and at least a passing knowledge of mathematics and rhetoric. They were expected to be good musicians and dancers. In addition, the rise of the merchant class to a position of wealth and social responsibility necessitated at least some degree of education for the women whose husbands were members of the guilds and confraternities of the city.

The Florentine mercantile system required of every man a working knowledge of mathematics and accounting, and the ability to read. As we have seen, the guilds, where these skills were practiced daily, were also the chief sponsors of public works, from cathedrals and churches to the sculptures and paintings that adorned them. In general, the wives of these merchant guildsmen were not only conversant with their husbands' affairs, but with the greater affairs of the city as well. Many took a more active role in both. Indeed, since women customarily married between the ages of 13 and 17 and to men generally much older than themselves, they often inherited the family businesses. In order to maintain their financial and personal independence, many chose not to remarry.

The most influential women in Rome, for instance, were connected to the Church hierarchy either by blood or marriage. Their brothers and brothers-in-law, uncles and nephews, were the cardinals and popes who lavished the city with their wealth and largesse. As executors of their husbands' estates and as widows, many of these women became important patrons of convents, where they were able to escape the social strictures of widowhood.

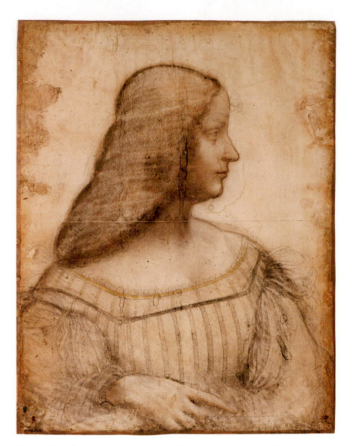

Fig. 15.31 Leonardo da Vinci, *Isabella d'Este.* **1499–1500.** Pastel, 18½" × 14½". Musée du Louvre, Paris. Isabella had several copies made of this drawing, and, as a result, we know that originally Leonardo depicted her with a book at her fingertips, a symbol of her humanist learning. This original drawing has been cut down on all sides.

Of all Renaissance woman patrons, none matches Isabella d'Este (1474–1539), Duchess of Mantua and wife to Francesco Gonzaga, grandson of Ludovico (see Chapter 14). Leonardo's pastel portrait of her (Fig. **15.31**), in profile, but with her torso turned toward the viewer, subtly reveals her authority and power, equating her, as it does, to male rulers such as those found on Roman coins. Isabella was a gifted musician, and her accomplishments in music and dance were widely admired by her contemporaries. She mastered the lute and the *lira da braccio*, a bowed string instrument that is the precursor of the modern violin. Although only one musical manuscript—a book of songs—can be associated with her patronage, she supported a large band of court musicians for secular music-making (her husband Francesco hired the musicians and singers for his prestigious chapel choir), and like Lorenzo de' Medici (see Chapter 14) she delighted in *frottole*, lighthearted vernacular poetry set to music.

Isabella was an avid collector of art and antiques, for which, she admitted, she was "hungry" and "insatiable." She regularly bought works by Italian artists, not for their subject matter, but because she wanted their work represented in her collection. And although her ambitions as a patron were restricted by her lack of personal funds, she surrounded herself with experts in the arts and humanities. She sought their advice whenever she could manage to commission work from the leading artists of the day, including Mantegna, Perugino, and Leonardo.

Women and Family Life

Still, for most women the husband's role was one of active, public life, and the wife's was to manage domestic affairs. In *On the Family*, a book published in 1443 by the same Leon Battista Alberti whose *On Painting* had outlined the principles of perspective, the author approvingly quotes a young groom introducing his bride to his household:

> After my wife had been settled in my house a few days, and after her first pangs of longing for her mother and family had begun to fade, I took her by the hand and showed her around the whole house. ... At the end there were no household goods of which my wife had not learned both the place and purpose. Then we returned to my room and having locked the door, I showed her my treasures, silver, tapestry, garments, jewels, and where each thing had its place.

For Alberti, clearly, the family is an orderly system. Each thing in the household has its proper place, just as, not coincidentally, each object in a perspectival drawing has its right and proper place. And the woman's proper place was in the service of her husband.

Much of what we know about what was accepted as the proper behavior of ladies of the court derives from Castiglione's *Book of the Courtier* since, as part of its concern with the conduct of the aristocratic gentleman, it details the gentleman's expectations of his lady (see Chapter 14). It was generally agreed, for instance, by the conversationalists at the Urbino court that a courtier's lady should profit from most of the rules that serve the courtier. Thus, her accomplishments should demonstrate the casual effortlessness of *sprezzatura*. In one of the book's conversations, for instance, Giuliano de' Medici addresses a gathering of ladies and gentlemen, intent on pointing out what the lady needs *beyond* the accomplishments of her husband (**Reading 15.3**):

READING 15.3

from Baldassare Castiglione, *The Courtier*, Book 3 (1513–18; published 1528)

[The court lady] must have not only the good sense to discern the quality of him with whom she is speaking, but knowledge of many things, in order to entertain him graciously; and in her talk she should know how to choose those things that are adapted to the quality of him with whom she is speaking, and should be cautious lest occasionally, without intending it, she utter words that may offend him. ... Let her not stupidly pretend to know that which she does not know, but modestly seek to do herself credit in that which she does know. ... I wish this Lady to have knowledge of letters, music, painting, and to know how to dance and make merry; accompanying the other precepts that have been taught the Courtier with discreet modesty and with the giving of a good impression of herself. And thus, in her talk, her laughter, her play, her jesting, in short, in everything, she will be very graceful, and will entertain appropriately, and with witticisms and pleasantries befitting her, everyone who shall come before her. ...

Whereas, for Castiglione, the courtier must strive to exemplify the perfectly well-rounded *l'uomo universale*, the court lady must use her breeding and education to further the perfection of the home.

Laura Cereta and Lucretia Marinella: Renaissance Feminists

Many fifteenth-century women strove for a level of education beyond the mere "knowledge of letters, music, painting" called for by Castiglione. One of the most interesting is Laura Cereta (1469–99). She was the eldest child of a prominent family from the city of Brescia in the Venetian Terraferma. Until she was 11, she was educated by nuns at a convent school. There, she studied reading, writing, embroidery, and Latin until her father called her home to help raise her siblings. But he encouraged her to continue her studies, and in his library, she read deeply in Latin, Greek, and mathematics. At 15, however, Cereta chose motherhood over the pursuit of her studies and married a local merchant. When he died, two years later, she returned to her studies. In 1488, at just 19 years of age, she published *Family Letters*, a Latin manuscript containing 82 letters addressed to friends and family, an unusually large number of them women, as well as a mock funeral oration in the Classical style.

Cereta's letter, known as the *Defense of Liberal Instruction for Women*, is one of the most remarkable fifteenth-century Italian documents. It is a response to a critic who had praised her as a prodigy, implying that true women humanist scholars were rare and that, perhaps, her father had authored her letters. In the *Defense*, Cereta explains why so few women were scholars and then defends her own learning (**Reading 15.4**):

READING 15.4

from Laura Cereta, *Defense of Liberal Instruction for Women* (1488)

Only the question of the rarity of outstanding women remains to be addressed. The explanation is clear: women have been able by nature to be exceptional, but have chosen lesser goals. For some women are concerned with parting their hair correctly, adorning themselves with lovely dresses, or decorating their fingers with pearls and other gems. Others delight in mouthing carefully composed phrases, indulging in dancing, or managing spoiled puppies. Still others wish to gaze at lavish banquet tables, to rest in sleep, or, standing at mirrors, to smear their lovely faces. But those in whom a deeper integrity yearns for virtue, restrain from the start their youthful souls, reflect on higher things, harden the body with sobriety and trials, and curb their tongues, open their ears, compose their thoughts in wakeful hours, their minds in contemplation, to letters bonded to righteousness. For knowledge is not given as a gift, but [is gained] with diligence. The free mind, not shirking effort, always soars zealously toward the good, and the desire to know grows ever more wide and deep. It is because of no special holiness, therefore, that we [women] are rewarded by God the Giver with the gift of exceptional talent. Nature has generously lavished its gifts upon all people, opening to all the doors of choice through which reason sends envoys to the will, from which they learn and convey its desires. The will must choose to exercise the gift of reason.

Cereta's argument parallels Pico della Mirandola's in the *Oration on the Dignity of Man* (see Chapter 14). Women, like men, can choose to exercise their free will in the pursuit of learning. If Adam could choose to fashion himself in whatever form he might prefer, so could Eve.

One hundred years later, in Venice, things had hardly changed, as is evident in Lucretia Marinella's (1571–1653) *The Nobility and Excellence of Women and the Defects and Vices of Men*, published in Venice around 1600 and widely circulated. (See **Reading 15.5a**.) Marinella was one of the most prolific writers of her day. She published many works, including a pastoral drama, musical compositions, religious verse, and an epic poem celebrating Venice's role in the Fourth Crusade, but her sometimes vitriolic polemic against men is unique in the literature of the time. *The Nobility and Excellence of Women* is a response to a contemporary diatribe, *The Defects of Women*, written by her Venetian contemporary, Giuseppe Passi.

It is clear enough to Marinella, who had received a humanistic education, that any man who denigrates women is motivated by such reasons as anger and envy (see **Reading 15.5**, pages 540–541, for an extended excerpt).

READING 15.5a

from Lucretia Marinella, *The Nobility and Excellence of Women* (1600)

When a man wishes to fulfill his unbridled desires and is unable to because of the temperance and continence of a woman, he immediately becomes angry and disdainful, and in his rage says every bad thing he can think of, as if the woman were something evil and hateful. … When a man sees that a woman is superior to him, both in virtue and in beauty, and that she is justly honored and loved even by him, he tortures himself and is consumed with envy. Not being able to give vent to his emotions in any other way, he resorts with sharp and biting tongue to false and specious vituperation and reproof. … But if with a subtle intelligence, men should consider their own imperfections, oh how humble and low they would become! Perhaps one day, God willing, they will perceive it.

From Marinella's point of view, Renaissance women possess the fullest measure of Castiglione's moral virtue and humanist individualism, not the courtiers themselves. The second part of the book, on the defects and vices of *men*, is a stunning and sometimes amusing reversal of Passi's arguments, crediting men with all the vices he attributes to women. But perhaps Marinella's most important distinction is her insistence that women are autonomous beings, who should not be defined only in relation to men.

Veronica Franco: Literary Courtesan

Among Venice's most educated citizens were its so-called "honest courtesans" who, unlike common prostitutes, who sold only their sexual favors, were highly sophisticated intellectuals who gained access to the city's aristocratic circles. "Thou wilt find the Venetian Courtezan a good Rhetorician and an elegant discourser," wrote one early seventeenth-century visitor to the city. Although subject to the usual public ridicule—and often blamed, together with the city's Jews, for any troubles that might befall the republic—they were understood by writers such as Lucretia Marinella to be more products of men's own shortcomings and desires than willful sinners in their own right. This group of courtesans, in fact, dominated the Venetian literary scene. Many of their poems transform the clichés of courtly love poetry into frankly erotic metaphors, undermining the superior position of men in Italian society in ways comparable to the proto-feminist writings of the likes of Cereta and Marinella.

Among the most remarkable Venetian courtesans was Veronica Franco (1546–91), who published two volumes of poetry: *Terze rime* (1575), named after the plural of the Italian poetic form first introduced by Dante in his *Divine Comedy* (see Chapter 13), and *Homely Letters to Diverse People* (1580). She also collected the works of other leading writers in respected anthologies, and founded and funded a charity for courtesans and their children.

Franco first gained notoriety in the 1570s at a renowned Venetian literary salon where male and female poets read and exchanged their works. Her poetry celebrates her sexual expertise as a courtesan and, in the slightly veiled imagery of the courtly tradition, promises to satisfy her interlocutor's desires. Consider *Capitolo* 13, in which she playfully challenges a lover to a "duel" (**Reading 15.6**):

READING 15.6

from Veronica Franco, *Terze rime*, *Capitolo* 13

No more words! To deeds, to the battlefield, to arms!
For, resolved to die, I want to free myself
from such merciless mistreatment.
Should I call this a challenge? I do not know,
since I am responding to a provocation;
but why should we duel over words?
If you like, I will say that you challenged me;
if not, I challenge you; I'll take any route,

---

and any opportunity suits me equally well.
Yours be the choice of place or of arms,
and I will make whatever choice remains;
rather, let both be your decision. ...

Come here, and, full of most wicked desire,
braced stiff for your sinister task,
bring with daring hand a piercing blade.
Whatever weapon you hand over to me,
I will gladly take, especially if it is sharp
and sturdy and also quick to wound.
Let all armor be stripped from your naked breast,
so that, unshielded and exposed to blows,
it may reveal the valor it harbors within.
Let no one else intervene in this match,
let it be limited to the two of us alone,
behind closed doors, with all seconds sent away. ...

To take revenge for your unfair attack,
I'd fall upon you, and in daring combat,
as you too caught fire defending yourself,
I would die with you, felled by the same blow.
O empty hopes, over which cruel fate
forces me to weep forever!
But hold firm, my strong, undaunted heart,
and with that felon's final destruction,
avenge your thousand deaths with his one.
Then end your agony with the same blade. ...

Here Franco transforms the language of chivalric knighthood into the banter of the bedroom in a masterful use of **double-entendre**, a figure of speech in which a phrase can be understood in either of two ways. This duality, the simultaneous expression of intellectual wit and erotic sensuality, is fundamental to the Venetian style.

NEW TRENDS IN VENETIAN LITERATURE, MUSIC, AND ARCHITECTURE

What new literary attitudes, musical forms, and architectural innovations distinguish the Venetian High Renaissance?

As the remarkable intellectual inventiveness of its women citizens suggests, Venice prided itself on its spirit of innovation. Ludovico Ariosto's epic poem, *Orlando Furioso*, so enthralled audiences with its combination of parodic wit and wildly exciting narrative that it quickly became one of the very first examples of a truly popular literature. In music, the city hosted two of the most important composers of a new secular musical form, the madrigal. And the country homes of Andrea Palladio on the Venetian mainland would establish a new Classical standard in domestic architecture.

Ludovico Ariosto's *Orlando Furioso*

The satiric approach to chivalry and courtly love also appears in the romantic epic *Orlando Furioso* ("The Madness of Orlando") by Ludovico Ariosto (1474–1533), a writer working in the nearby Ferrara court. Published in Venice in 1515 under the authority of the doge, *Orlando Furioso* would become the most popular book of the day, constantly revised and expanded to reflect events in contemporary Italian history artfully disguised in the conventions of medieval romance. The heroism and intellectual superiority of its many female characters served to inspire Lucretia Marinella. It also inspired artists to depict scenes from its narrative, such as the **maiolica** plate illustrated here (Fig. **15.32**), made by a native of the town of Rovigo in the Venetian Terraferma, Francesco Xanto Avelli, known as Xanto. Maiolica is made with a tin-glazing technique first used by the Babylonians in the ancient Middle East. Tin glaze creates a brilliant white, opaque surface, which is then painted over with underglazes that absorb the pigment like fresco, resulting in brilliant colors.

The plot of Ariosto's epic is a conscious nod in the direction of the medieval French *chanson de geste* ("songs of heroic deeds") known as the *Song of Roland* (see Chapter

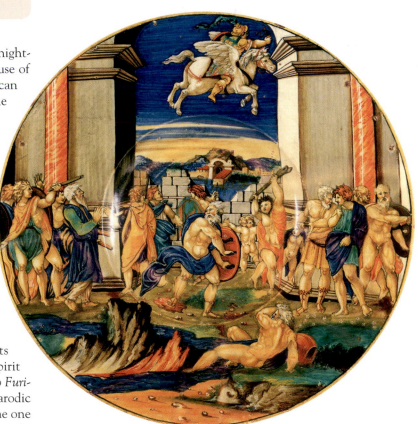

Fig. 15.32 Francesco Xanto Avelli da Rovigo, dish with a scene from *Orlando Furioso* showing Ruggiero escaping the castle of Atlante on Atlante's hippogriff, a winged horse. 1531. Tin-glazed earthenware, diameter 17¾". Los Angeles County Museum of Art. William Randolph Hearst Collection, 49.26.3. Pieces like this one were often displayed on a sideboard or buffet—much as they are today.

10). It takes place within the context of the largely mythologized history of Charlemagne's wars against the encroaching forces of Islam, heading north from Africa through Spain. The poem's hero, Orlando (the Roland of the French poem), goes mad (that is, *furioso*) halfway through the epic poem, when he cannot come to terms with his unrequited love for the beautiful Angelica. The poem opens with the lines "Of wives and ladies, knights and arms, I sing, / of courtesies and many a daring feat," a purposefully unheroic echo of the opening of Virgil's *Aeneid*, "Of arms and the man I sing." These lines set in motion a fantastic set of adventures. Angelica, the beloved of Orlando, is being pursued by a knight traveling on foot, in other words a horseless horseman, and this irregularity sets up the sense of parody and irony that dominates the poem. The ill-mannered knight, Rinaldo, not even remotely a true gentleman, as his horselessness implies, chases Angelica into the woods in a scene meant to parody Dante's descent into the "dark forest" in the first Canto of the *Inferno* (see Chapter 13 and **Reading 15.7a**):

The poem leaps from scene to scene, dropping one plot line and picking up another every time the action seems to heat up. Each "new affright" of its structure seemingly imitates the "strange and crooked paths" followed by Angelica. Knights fly around on winged horses and wander through a magic castle. A valiant female knight, Bradamante, visits Merlin, the magician of Arthurian legend, deep in a cavernous tomb, and he instructs her on how to rescue her love, Ruggiero. An English aristocrat named Astolfo flies to the moon to rescue Orlando's wits, which Orlando does not even realize he has lost. Ladies are constantly imperiled (sometimes as much by their rescuers, who seem universally to expect sexual favors in return for their heroic deeds), as action follows fast upon action throughout the poem.

The poem, in short, demonstrates that traditional chivalric virtues—those that Castiglione was outlining in *The Book of the Courtier* (see Chapter 14) even as Ariosto was writing his poem—had little or no relevance to the modern Italian court, just as armor, swords, and lances had been made irrelevant by the invention of gunpowder. On the subject of gunpowder, the poem makes the following lament (**Reading 15.7b**):

Love is never ennobling in the poem—and rarely chivalric—but leads only to insult, rejection, madness, and death. The only way to save oneself is not to love at all. But however unsympathetic the poem is to the chivalric code, Ariosto's ability to create an exciting narrative of nonstop action that moves across the globe in large part accounts for his poem's extraordinary success. Throughout the sixteenth century, new readers discovered the poem as the printing press (see Chapter 16) made it more widely available, especially to a popular audience that had little use for the conventions of chivalry.

Music of the Venetian High Renaissance

Almost without exception, women of literary accomplishment in the Renaissance were musically accomplished as well. As we have seen, Isabella d'Este played both the lute and the *lira da braccio*, the precursor to the modern violin. Through her patronage, she and her sister-in-law Lucrezia Borgia, Duchess of Ferrara, competed for musicians and encouraged the cultivation of the *frottola*. Courtesans such as Veronica Franco could both sing and play. And both Isabella and Elisabetta Gonzaga, Duchess of Urbino, were well known for their ability to improvise songs. By the last decades of the sixteenth century, we know that women were composing music as well. The most famous of these was the Venetian Madalena Casulana.

Madalena Casulana's Madrigals Madalena Casulana was the first professional woman composer to see her own compositions in print. In 1566, her anthology entitled *The Desire* was published in Venice. Two years later, she dedicated her first book of songs to Isabella de' Medici Orsina with these words: "I would like … to show the world … the vain error of men, who so much believe themselves to be the masters of the highest gifts of the intellect, that they think those gifts cannot be shared equally by a woman."

Casulana's known work consists almost entirely of madrigals. The **madrigal** is a secular vocal composition for three or more voices. It became popular throughout Italy in the sixteenth century, where it dominated secular music. Whereas the *frottola* uses the same music for each successive stanza (see Chapter 14), the madrigal is through-composed—that is, each line of text is set to new music (allowing for the repetition of various earlier themes or motives). This allows for **word painting**, where the musical elements imitate the meaning of the text in mood or action. Anguish, for example, is conveyed with an unusually low pitch, as in Casulana's *Morir non può il mio cuore* ("My Heart Cannot Die") (track **15.2**). The song laments a relationship gone bad, and the narrator contemplates driving a stake through her heart because it is in so much pain. When she says that her suicide might kill her beloved—*so che morreste voi* ("I know that you would die")—the word painting by rising progression of the melody suggests that, for her, his death might not be such a bad thing.

The ladies of the courts of Mantua and Ferrara were especially well known for their vocal accomplishments. At Ferrara, the "Ensemble of Ladies" attracted many of the most prominent madrigal composers of the day. But even when such ensembles were not available, madrigals and other songs could be performed by a single voice, accompanied by, perhaps, a flute and a lute. The words themselves were of paramount importance, however the music was performed.

Adrian Willaert's Innovations for Polyphonic Form Without question, the figure most responsible for the popularity of the genre of the madrigal in sixteenth-century Venice was Adrian Willaert (1490–1562), a Netherlander who was appointed to the highest musical position in Venice in 1527, choirmaster of Saint Mark's. By the time he accepted the position, he had already been a leading figure at the court of Ferrara for over a decade. He brought to his new position a deeply felt humanist spirit, one dedicated to innovation and originality even as it acknowledged the great achievements of the past. Willaert's chief interest was polyphonic music such as the motet and the madrigal. To both of these genres he brought radical new ideas as exemplified in the corpus of 27 motets and 25 madrigals for between four and seven voices called *New Music*, published in 1559, but probably written for the most part between the late 1530s and mid-1540s.

The madrigals of the *New Music* departed from all previous ones by consistently setting complete sonnets—all but one of them by the fourteenth-century Italian poet Petrarch (see Chapter 13)—in the form of the motet and by adapting a dense counterpoint formerly reserved for sacred music. Willaert's chief aim was to present Petrarch's words with as much clarity and restraint as possible. His choice of the Petrarchan sonnet, with its sense of *gravitas*, as the source of his lyrics was most likely driven by a desire to raise secular song to the level of the religious motet. Both were, at least musically, of equal weight and importance. And although Petrarch's sonnets spoke of worldly love, they most often did so as metaphor for spiritual love.

Willaert's love of polyphonic forms led to other innovations as well. At Saint Mark's, he regularly used two choirs—sometimes more—to create a **polychoral style** in which choirs on either side of the church sang to and against each other in increasingly complicated forms that anticipated by over four centuries the effects of stereophonic music. This arrangement drew notice after the publication in 1550 of his *Salmi spezzati* (literally "broken psalms," but a reference to alternating choirs). He also added new instrumental forms to the liturgy, including an organ *intonazione* (short prelude) and a virtuoso prelude, also for organ, called the **toccata** (from the Italian *toccare*, "to touch"), designed to feature both the range of the instrument and the manual dexterity of the performer. Both were soon widely emulated across Europe. The richness of musical experience in Willaert's Venice, then, was not unlike the richness of its painting—full of light and emotion, as words found their emotional equivalent in sound.

Andrea Palladio and the New Rural Architecture

The setting of Titian's *Sacred and Profane Love* (see Fig. 15.28) represents an escapist tendency that we first saw in Boccaccio's *Decameron* (Chapter 13). In Boccaccio's stories, a group of young men and women flee the onset of the plague in Florence, escape to the country, and for ten days entertain each other with a series of tales, many of which are alternately ribald and erotic, moral and exemplary. Renaissance humanists considered retreats to the country to be an honored ancient Roman tradition, the pleasures of which were richly documented by such Roman poets as Horace in his *Odes* (Chapter 6):

> How in the country do I pass the time?
> The answer to the question's brief:
> I lunch and drink, I sing and play,
> I wash and dine, I rest.

By the High Renaissance, wealthy Venetian families, following strong Classical precedent, routinely escaped the heat and humidity of the city to private villas in the countryside. The architecture of Andrea Palladio set the standard for the country villa.

Palladio was a careful student of Vitruvius, as was Leonardo. On a visit to Rome, in the summer of 1541, he became fascinated by ancient monuments (**Reading 15.8a**):

READING 15.8a

from Andrea Palladio, *Four Books on Architecture* (1570)

I set myself the task of investigating the remains of the ancient buildings that have survived despite the ravages of time and the cruelty of the barbarians, and finding them much worthier of study than I had at first thought, I began to measure all their parts minutely and with the greatest care. ... It will be obvious to anyone not absolutely devoid of common sense that the methods by which the ancients built were excellent because the ruins

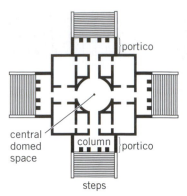

central domed space — column — portico — portico — steps

Fig. 15.33 Andrea Palladio, Villa La Rotonda and plan of main floor (*piano nobile*). Begun 1560s. The building's Ionic columns, Classical plinths, porticos, and other details, as well as its use of elemental geometric forms—circle, cube, and sphere—make it one of the closest realizations of Classical ideals in all of architecture.

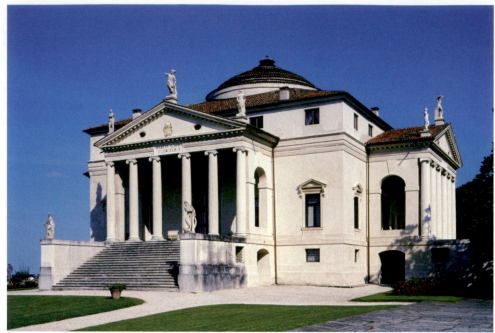

👁 **Watch** a Students on Site video about the Villa La Rotonda on **MyArtsLab**

of so many magnificent buildings survive in and outside Italy after such a vast amount of time and so many changes and falls of empires; because of this we have absolute proof of the extraordinary virtue of the Romans which otherwise, perhaps, nobody would believe in.

It is no accident, then, that the centralized plan of the house that many think of as his masterpiece, the Villa La

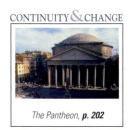

CONTINUITY & CHANGE

The Pantheon, p. 202

Rotonda, located just outside the city of Vicenza, and built in the 1560s for a humanist churchman, recalls Leonardo's *Vitruvian Man* (see Fig. 15.4) and that its central dome is modeled after the Pantheon (see Fig. 6.26 in Chapter 6), which was itself known in the sixteenth century as La Rotonda, as was any large, domed circular room (Fig. 15.33). Although lacking the Pantheon's coffered ceiling and size, Palladio's villa was originally distinguished by a 7-foot-diameter oculus, open to the sky, but today covered by a small cupola. Directly below the oculus, a stone drain in the shape of a faun's face allowed rainwater to fall into the basement. As in the Vitruvian ideal, the main floor, with its central rotunda surrounded by reception rooms, is perfectly symmetrical. Although Venice depended on the agricultural economy of the Terraferma, the Villa La Rotonda was not designed to be a working farm. The house was designed for family life and entertaining.

As in so much Venetian architecture, the house looks outward, toward the light of the countryside, rather than inward to the shadow of a courtyard. It is situated on the crest of a hill. On each of its four sides, Palladio has placed

a pedimented loggia, approached by a broad staircase, designed to take advantage of the view. In his *Four Books on Architecture*, published near the end of his life, Palladio described the building's site and vistas (**Reading 15.8b**):

READING 15.8b

from Andrea Palladio, *Four Books on Architecture* (1570)

The site is one of the most pleasing and delightful that one could find because it is on top of a small hill which is easy to ascend; on one side it is bathed by the Bacchiglione, a navigable river, and on the other is surrounded by other pleasant hills which resemble a vast theater and are completely cultivated and abound with wonderful fruit and excellent vines; so, because it enjoys the most beautiful vistas on every side, some of which are restricted, others more extensive, and yet others which end at the horizon, loggias have been built on all four sides; under the floor of these loggias and the hall are the rooms for the convenience and use of the family.

According to architectural historian Witold Rybczynski, Palladio's greatness lies in "his equilibrium, his sweet sense of harmony. He pleases the mind as well as the eye. His sturdy houses, rooted in their sites, radiate order and balance, which makes them both of this world and otherworldly." Palladio built many villas in the vicinity of Venice. Each of them is interesting in a different way, and they constitute an important body of High Renaissance architecture that influenced architects in many countries and later centuries down to our own day.

The Self-Portrait

When Titian died in 1576, he was almost 90 years old, and his active career had spanned two-thirds of the sixteenth century. He was, without question, the most sought-after painter in Europe, the intimate of popes, kings, and the nobility of Germany, Italy, and Spain. This was partly due to his ability as a portrait painter to reveal nuances of character and personality. He was appreciated as well as a painter of erotic and sexually charged imagery, a talent suited to the painterly and sensuous technique of the Venetian style. His brushwork was loose and gestural, laden with emotion, and charged by a deep understanding of the effects of dramatic contrasts of light and dark.

In the years after his death, no aspiring painter could ignore Titian's place in the history of art. If we compare Titian's self-portrait of about 1570 (Fig. **15.34**) to that of the Dutch painter Rembrandt van Rijn of 1659 (Fig. **15.35**), his influence is evident, despite the fact that Rembrandt was working nearly 100 years later and in a different country. Both men sit in a rich, luminous light, their faces infused with a spirituality previously reserved for Christian saints and martyrs. Their hands, the symbols of their craft—Titian even holds a brush in his—emerge out of the darkness. These are humanist images: images of men of originality and talent who have worked, learned, mastered their world and its history. Above all, they are *self*-portraits, signature images in which both painters declare their own authority and importance, a genre that Rembrandt would exploit in the period of the Baroque (see Chapter 22) as no other artist before him. ■

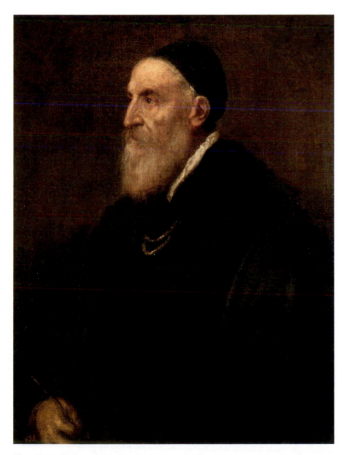

Fig. 15.34 Titian, *Self-Portrait*. ca. 1570. Oil on canvas, 34" × 27¼". Museo del Prado, Madrid.

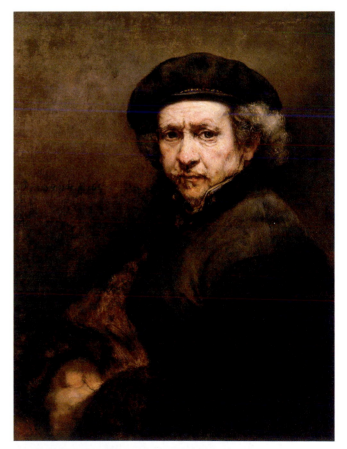

Fig. 15.35 Rembrandt van Rijn, *Self-Portrait*. 1659. Oil on canvas, 33¼" × 26". National Gallery of Art, Washington, D.C. Andrew W. Mellon Collection. Photograph © Board of Trustees, National Gallery of Art.

15.1 Describe the impact of papal patronage on the art of the High Renaissance in Rome.

In the fifteenth century, the grandeur that had once distinguished the city of Rome had almost entirely vanished. But beginning with the ascension of Sixtus IV to the papacy in 1471, and lasting until 1527, when German mercenaries in the employ of the Holy Roman Emperor Charles V sacked the city, the patronage of the popes and their cardinals transformed Rome. This period is known as the High Renaissance. Many of the greatest works of the period, including Michelangelo's frescoes for the Sistine Chapel ceiling, Bramante's Tempietto and his new basilica for Saint Peter's, and Raphael's frescoes for the Stanza della Segnatura, were commissioned by Pope Julius II. How would you describe Julius II's personality?

Julius II was followed in 1513 by Leo X, born Giovanni de' Medici. Leo particularly favored Raphael as an artist. In 1523, Giulio de' Medici became pope as Clement VII. The Sack of Rome in 1527 caused many artists to leave the city and substantially diminished Clement's ability to sustain the same scale of patronage as his predecessors. Niccolò Machiavelli's treatise *The Prince* reflects the turmoil surrounding papal politics in this era. What does he suggest is the prince's primary duty? Do you think Machiavelli's outlook is applicable today?

Renaissance musicians shared with other artists of the age its spirit of inventiveness. The Sistine Chapel Choir, founded in 1473 by Sixtus IV, usually sang a cappella (without instrumental accompaniment). Between 1489 and 1495, one of the principal members of the Sistine Chapel Choir was the Franco-Flemish composer Josquin des Prez. His compositions include 18 masses. What is a mass?

15.2 Compare the social fabric and artistic style of Renaissance Venice to that of both Florence and Rome.

Fifteenth-century Venice defined itself as both the most cosmopolitan and the most democratic city in the world. Its religious and political centers—Saint Mark's Cathedral and the Doge's Palace—stood side by side, symbolizing peace, prosperity, and, above all, unity of purpose. How does this compare to cities like Florence and Siena? How does it compare to Rome?

The city's *scuole* ("schools"), religious confraternities which engaged in charity, sponsored social functions, and marched in sometimes elaborate processions associated with civic and religious festivals, reflected its democratic values. The wealth and general well-being of Venice was displayed along the Grand Canal, where its most important families built their homes. These magnificent homes were Gothic in character. How can we account for the city's taste for this medieval style? Two of the most important Venetian painters of the late fourteenth and early fifteenth centuries, Gentile Bellini and Vittore Carpaccio, received commissions from the Scuola di San Giovanni Evangelista (Saint John the Evangelist). Why were Venetian painters like Giorgione and Titian attracted to oil painting as a medium? In what ways does their painting style differ from other High Renaissance painters such as Michelangelo and Raphael?

15.3 Outline the place of women in Renaissance Italy.

In many ways the paintings of both Giorgione and Titian reflect Venetian attitudes toward women. What does Titian's *La Bella* reveal about these attitudes? In the Italian humanist courts, the wives of rulers and their daughters received a humanist education. Much of what we know about customary behavior of ladies at court derives from Castiglione's *Book of the Courtier*. Several notable women strove for a level of education beyond the mere "knowledge of letters, music, painting" called for by Castiglione. Among these were Isabella d'Este, the duchess of Mantua and wife to Francesco Gonzaga, who owned an important collection of art and antiques, and two women who frankly rebelled against male attitudes toward them, Laura Cereta and Lucretia Marinella. What is the relation between Cereta's *Defense of Liberal Instruction for Women* and Pico della Mirandola's *Oration on the Dignity of Man*? How would you describe Marinella's sense of women's place?

The Venetian literary scene was dominated by a group of so-called "honest courtesans" whose reputations were built upon the ability to combine sexual and intellectual pursuits. The poetry of one of these courtesans, Veronica Franco, exemplifies their literary production.

15.4 Discuss the new literary attitudes, musical forms, and architectural innovations of the Venetian High Renaissance.

Ludovico Ariosto's romantic epic *Orlando Furioso* is a landmark in Venetian literature. What aspects of its style and subject matter helped to make it so popular?

By the last decades of the sixteenth century, women began to compose music as well. The most famous of these was the Venetian Madalena Casulana, the first professional woman composer to see her own compositions in print. How do her madrigals compare to the *frottola*, the genre of musical song so popular in Florence? Without question, the figure most responsible for the popularity of the madrigal form in sixteenth-century Venice was Adrian Willaert, choirmaster of Saint Mark's. His chief interest was polyphonic music such as the motet and the madrigal. What radical new ideas did Willaert bring to his music?

By the High Renaissance, wealthy Venetian families, following Classical precedent, routinely escaped the heat and humidity of the city to private villas in the countryside. Architect Andrea Palladio's Villa La Rotonda set the standard for the country villa. How does it reflect Classical architectural values?

☑ **Study** and **review** on **MyArtsLab**

READINGS

from Niccolò Machiavelli, *The Prince*,[1] Chapters 15–18 (1513)

The Prince is a reflection of Machiavelli's experiences in the world of power politics. He served as defense secretary of the Florentine republic until imprisoned, tortured, and exiled by the Medici family upon their return to power in 1512. *The Prince* was written in order to regain his status in the Florentine government and for presentation to Giuliano de' Medici, although the dedication was changed upon Giuliano's death to Lorenzo de' Medici, who almost certainly did not read it. By and large, Machiavelli's contemporaries were shocked by the ruthless and amoral political policy that he appears to advocate, but he no doubt saw his work as a realistic account of political circumstance in his time and place.

CHAPTER 15

Of the Qualities in Respect of Which Men and Most of All Princes, Are Praised or Blamed

It now remains for us to consider what ought to be the conduct and bearing of a Prince in relation to his subjects and friends. And since I know that many have written on this subject, I fear it may be thought presumptuous in me to write of it also; the more so, because in my treatment of it I depart from the views that others have taken.

But since it is my object to write what shall be useful to whosoever understands it, it seems to me better to follow the real truth of things than an imaginary view of them. For many Republics and Princedoms have been imagined that were 10 never seen or known to exist in reality. ...[2]

Laying aside, therefore, all fanciful notions concerning a Prince, and considering those only that are true, I say that all men when they are spoken of, and Princes more than others from their being set so high, are characterized by some one of those qualities which attach either praise or blame. Thus one is accounted liberal,[3] another miserly (which word I use, rather than *avaricious*, to denote the man who is too sparing of what is his own, *avarice* being the disposition to take wrongfully what is another's); one is generous, another greedy; one cruel, 20 another tender-hearted; one is faithless, another true to his word; one effeminate and cowardly, another high-spirited and courageous; one is courteous, another haughty; one impure, another chaste; one simple, another crafty; one firm, another facile; one grave, another frivolous; one devout, another unbelieving; and the like. Every one, I know, will admit that it would be most laudable for a Prince to be endowed with all of the above qualities that are reckoned good; but since it is impossible for him to possess or constantly practice them all, the conditions of human nature not allowing it, he must be dis- 30 creet enough to know how to avoid the infamy of those vices that would deprive him of his government, and, if possible, be on his guard also against those which might not deprive him of it; though if he cannot wholly restrain himself, he may with less scruple indulge in the latter. ...

CHAPTER 16

Of Liberality and Miserliness

Beginning, then with the first of the qualities above noticed, I say that it may be a good thing to be reputed liberal, ... [In] time he will come to be regarded as more and more liberal, when it is seen that through his parsimony his revenues are sufficient; that he is able to defend himself against any who 40 make war on him; that he can engage in enterprises against others without burdening his subjects; and thus exercise liberality towards all from whom he does not take, whose number is infinite, while he is miserly in respect of those only to whom he does not give, whose number is few.

In our own days we have seen no Princes accomplish great result save those who have been accounted miserly. All others have been ruined. Pope Julius II, after availing himself of his reputation for liberality to arrive at the Papacy, made no effort to preserve that reputation when making war on the King of 50 France, but carried on all his numerous campaigns without levying from his subjects a single extraordinary tax, providing for the increased expenditure out of his long-continued savings. ...

A Prince, therefore, if he is enabled thereby to forbear from plundering his subjects, to defend himself, to escape poverty and contempt, and the necessity of becoming rapacious, ought to care little though he incur the reproach of miserliness, for this is one of those vices which enable him to reign. ...

CHAPTER 17

Of Cruelty and Clemency and Whether It Is Better to Be Loved or Feared

Passing to the other qualities above referred to, I say that every 60 Prince should desire to be accounted merciful and not cruel. Nevertheless, he should be on his guard against the abuse of this quality of mercy. Cesare Borgia was reputed cruel, yet his cruelty restored Romagna, united it, and brought it to order

---

[1] Translated by N. Hill Thomson. Machiavelli knew the world of power politics first-hand. As defense secretary of the Florence republic, he traveled widely and met many European princes, including Cesare Borgia. When the Medici family returned to power in Florence, Machiavelli was dismissed from office, imprisoned, and tortured. Upon his release, he retired in his mid-forties to his country estates and spent the rest of his life writing works about politics, as well as poems and plays. His contemporaries professed to be shocked by "Machiavellianism," the ruthless, amoral policy described in *The Prince*; modern readers are more likely to see it as a realistic description of how politics works, behind idealistic rationalizations.

[2] For example, in Plato's *Republic*.

[3] Free-giving; generous.

and obedience; so that if we look at things in their true light, it will be seen that he was in reality far more merciful than the people of Florence, who, to avoid the imputation of cruelty, suffered Pistoia to be torn to pieces by factions.[4]

A Prince should therefore disregard the reproach of being thought cruel where it enables him to keep his subjects united 70 and obedient. For he who quells disorder by a very few signal examples will in the end be more merciful than he who from too great leniency permits things to take their course and so to result in rapine and bloodshed; for these hurt the whole State whereas the severities of the Prince injure individuals only. ...

And here comes in the question whether it is better to be loved rather than feared, or feared rather than loved. It might perhaps be answered that we should wish to be both; but since love and fear can hardly exist together, if we must choose between them, it is far safer to be feared than loved. 80 For of men it may generally be affirmed that they are thankless, fickle, false, studious to avoid danger, greedy of gain, devoted to you while you are able to confer benefits upon them, and ready, as I said before, while danger is distant, to shed their blood, and sacrifice their property, their lives, and their children for you; but in the hour of need they turn against you. The Prince, therefore, who without otherwise securing himself builds wholly on their professions is undone. For the friendships which we buy with a price, and do not gain by greatness and nobility of character, though they be fairly earned are not 90 made good, but fail us when we have occasion to use them.

Moreover, men are less careful how they offend him who makes himself loved than him who makes himself feared. For love is held by the tie of obligation, which, because men are a sorry breed, is broken on every whisper of private interest; but fear is bound by the apprehension of punishment which never relaxes its grasp.

Nevertheless a Prince should inspire fear in such a fashion that if he do not win love he may escape hate. For a man may very well be feared and yet not hated, and this will be the 100 case so long as he does not meddle with the property or with the women of his citizens and subjects. And if constrained to put any to death, he should do so only when there is manifest cause or reasonable justification. But, above all, he must abstain from the property of others. For men will sooner forget the death of their father than the loss of their patrimony. Moreover, pretexts for confiscation are never to seek, and he who has once begun to live by rapine always finds reasons for taking what is not his; whereas reasons for shedding blood are fewer, and sooner exhausted. ... 110

CHAPTER 18

How Princes Should Keep Faith

Every one understands how praiseworthy it is in a Prince to keep faith, and to live uprightly and not craftily. Nevertheless, we see from what has taken place in our own days that Princes who have set little store by their word, but have known how to overreach men by their cunning, have accomplished great things, and in the end got the better of those who trusted to honest dealing.

Be it known, then, that there are two ways of contending, one in accordance with the laws, the other by force; the first of which is proper to men, the second to beasts. But since 120 the first method is often ineffectual, it becomes necessary to resort to the second. A Prince should, therefore, understand how to use well both the man and the beast. ...

But since a Prince should know how to use the beast's nature wisely, he ought of beasts to choose both the lion and the fox; for the lion cannot guard himself from the toils, nor the fox from wolves. He must therefore be a fox to discern toils, and a lion to drive off wolves. ...

It is not essential, then, that a Prince should have all the good qualities which I have enumerated above, but it is most 130 essential that he should seem to have them; I will even venture to affirm that if he has and invariably practices them all, they are hurtful, whereas the appearance of having them is useful. Thus, it is well to seem merciful, faithful, humane, religious, and upright, and also to be so; but the mind should remain so balanced that were it needful not to be so, you should be able and know how to change to the contrary. ...

A Prince should therefore be very careful that nothing ever escapes his lips which is not replete with the five qualities above named, so that to see and hear him, one would think 140 him the embodiment of mercy, good faith, integrity, humanity, and religion. And there is no virtue which it is more necessary for him to seem to possess than this last; because men in general judge rather by the eye than by the hand, for every one can see but few can touch. Every one sees what you seem, but few know what you are, and these few dare not oppose themselves to the opinion of the many who have the majesty of the State to back them up. ...

A certain Prince of our own days, whose name it is as well not to mention,[5] is always preaching peace and good faith, 150 although the mortal enemy of both; and both, had he practiced them as he preaches them, would oftener than once, have lost him his kingdom and authority.

READING CRITICALLY

The term *Machiavellianism* is often employed as a synonym for evil, invoked, for instance, by some psychologists to describe a person's tendency to deceive and manipulate others for gain. What in the reading suggests that Machiavelli understood politics far more subtly and complexly than this term suggests?

---

[4] Pistoia was a city near Florence, under its control. Florence failed to assert its power and allowed a bloody war to continue.

[5] King Ferdinand of Spain.

from Lucretia Marinella, *The Nobility and Excellence of Women and the Defects and Vices of Men* (ca. 1600)

Not much is known about Marinella other than that she was a prolific writer and composer, publishing religious verse, a pastoral drama, a life of the Virgin, an epic poem celebrating Venice's role in the Fourth Crusade, and a variety of madrigals. *The Nobility and Excellence of Women and the Defects and Vices of Men*, published around 1600, is her reply to a thoroughly misogynistic attack on women written by her Venetian contemporary Giuseppe Passi in 1599. In it she contends that women surpass men on almost all counts. Her argument is based on the Neoplatonic assertion that beauty is a reflection of goodness and that woman's beauty is the driving force behind the development of virtue in men.

A reply to the flippant and vain reasoning adopted by men in their own favor

It seems to me that I have clearly shown that women are far nobler and more excellent than men. Now it remains for me to reply to the false objections of our slanderers. …

I do not, however, wish to wrong famous men in denying their conclusions, since certain obstinate people would regard this as being unjust. I say, therefore, that various reasons drove certain wise and learned men to reprove and vituperate women. They included anger, self-love, envy, and insufficient intelligence. It can be stated therefore that when Aristotle or some other man reproved women, the reason for it was either 10 anger, envy, or too much self-love.

It is clear to everyone that anger is the origin of indecent accusations against women. When a man wishes to fulfil his unbridled desires and is unable to because of the temperance and continence of a woman, he immediately becomes angry and disdainful and in his rage says every bad thing he can think of, as if the woman were something evil and hateful. The same can be said of the envious man, who when he sees someone worthy of praise can only look at them with a distorted view. And thus when a man sees that a woman is superior to him, 20 both in virtue and in beauty, and that she is justly honored and loved even by him, he tortures himself and is consumed with envy. Not being able to give vent to his emotions in any other way, he resorts with sharp and biting tongue to false and specious vituperation and reproof. The same occurs as a result of the too great love that men bear for themselves, which causes them to believe that they are more outstanding in wit and intelligence and by nature superior to women—an exaggerated arrogance and over-inflated and haughty pride. But if with a subtle intelligence they should consider their own imperfec- 30 tions, oh how humble and low they would become! Perhaps one day, God willing, they will perceive it. …

Of men who are ornate, polished, painted, and bleached

For men born to politics and civil life it is becoming, to a certain extent, to be elegant and polished. Everyone knows this, and it has been verified by Della Casa, Guazzo, Sabba, and *The Book of the Courtier*.[1] If, according to these authors' reason-

ing, this is right for men, we must believe that it is even more right for women, since beauty shines brighter among the rich and elegantly dressed than among the poor and rude. Tasso[2] demonstrates this in *Torrismondo*, by means of the Queen's 40 speech to Rosmonda:

Why do you not adorn your pleasing limbs and with pleasing clothes augment that beauty which heaven has given you courteously and generously? Unadorned beauty in humble guise is like a rough, badly polished gem, which in a humble setting shines dully.

Since beauty is woman's special gift from the Supreme Hand, should she not seek to guard it with all diligence? And when she is endowed with but a small amount of that excellent quality, should she not seek to embellish it by every 50 means possible, provided it is not ignoble? I certainly believe that it is so. When man has some special gift such as physical strength, which enables him to perform as a gladiator or swagger around, as is the common usage, does he not seek to conserve it? If he were born courageous, would he not seek to augment his natural courage with the art of defense? But if he were born with little courage would he not practice the martial arts and cover himself with plate and mail and constantly seek out duels and fights in order to demonstrate his courage rather than reveal his true timidity and cowardice? 60

I have used this example because of the impossibility of finding a man who does not swagger and play the daredevil. If there is such a one people call him effeminate, which is why we always see men dressed up like soldiers with weapons at their belts, bearded and menacing, and walking in a way that they think will frighten everyone. Often they wear gloves of mail and contrive for their weapons to clink under their clothing so people realize they are armed and ready for combat and feel intimidated by them.

What are all these things but artifice and tinsel? Under these trappings of courage and valor hide the cowardly souls 70 of rabbits or hunted hares, and it is the same with all their other artifices. Since men behave in this way, why should not those women who are born less beautiful than the rest hide their less fortunate attributes and seek to augment the little beauty they possess through artifice, provided it is not offensive?

Why should it be a sin if a woman born with considerable beauty washes her delicate face with lemon juice and the

---

[1] A reference to four famous sixteenth-century handbooks on manners.

[2] The Italian poet Torquato Tasso (1495–1544), whose tragedy *Torrismondo* was published in 1586.

water of beanflowers and privets[3] in order to remove her freckles and keep her skin soft and clean? Or if with columbine, white bread, lemon juice, and pearls she creates some other potion to keep her face clean and soft? I believe it to be merely a small one. If roses do not flame within the lily pallor of her face, could she not, with some art, create a similar effect? Certainly she could, without fear of being reproved, because those who possess beauty must conserve it and those who lack it must make themselves as perfect as possible, removing every obstacle that obscures its splendor and grace. And if writers and poets, both ancient and modern, say that her golden hair enhances her beauty, why should she not color it blonde and make ringlets and curls in it so as to embellish it still further? ...

But what should we say of men who are not born beautiful and who yet make great efforts to appear handsome and appealing, not only by putting on clothes made of silk and cloth of gold as many do, spending all their money on an item of clothing, but by wearing intricately worked neckbands? What should we say of the medallions they wear in their caps, the gold buttons, the pearls, the pennants and plumes and the great number of liveries[4] that bring ruin on their houses? They go around with their hair waved, greased, and perfumed so that many of them smell like walking perfumeries. How many are there who go to the barbers every four days in order to appear close-shaven, rosy-cheeked, and like young men even when they are old? How many dye their beards when the dread arrival of old age causes them to turn white? How many use lead combs to tint their white hairs? How many pluck out their white hairs in order to make it appear that they are in the flower of youth? I pass over the earrings that Frenchmen and other foreigners wear and the necklaces, of Gallic invention, which we read of in Livy.

How many spend three or four hours each day combing their hair and washing themselves with those balls of soap sold by mountebanks in the *piazza*![5] Let us not even mention the time they spend perfuming themselves and putting on their shoes and blaspheming against the saints because their shoes are small and their feet are big, and they want their big feet to get into their small shoes. How ridiculous! ...

READING CRITICALLY

In what ways might Marinella's defense of women have found inspiration in Castiglione's *Book of the Courtier* (see Chapter 14)?

[3]Flowering shrub.
[4]Servants.

[5]A broad, open public space.

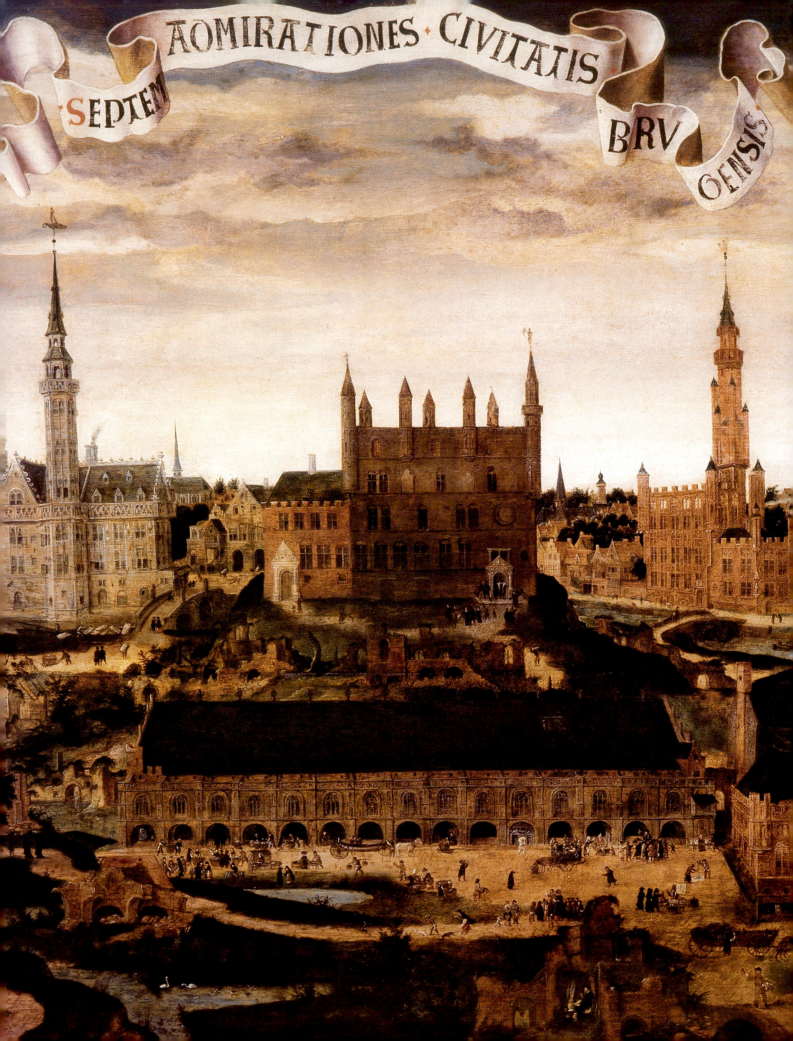

16 The Renaissance in the North
Between Wealth and Want

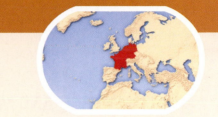

THINKING AHEAD

16.1 Explain the effect of commerce and mercantile wealth on the development of both religious and secular painting in Northern Europe.

16.2 Describe the tension between financial wealth and ethical behavior as reflected in literature, music, and dance.

16.3 Compare and contrast the mysticism of Germans such as Grünewald and the new style of art introduced by Dürer.

Fifteenth- and sixteenth-century Italy did not hold a monopoly on the arts in Europe. To the north, the Flemish city of Bruges was a major center of culture, rivaling the Italian city-states in both art and commerce. The financial capital of the North, the city was home to the Medici banking interests in the region and had a strong merchant class of its own. Although inland, its link to the North Sea gave Bruges access to other mercantile centers by a waterway, closed off at the mouth of the sea by a lock, where, in the words of one sixteenth-century report, "it is a pleasure and a marvel to behold the wild sea let in and out, as it were, through a wooden door, with artfulness and human ingenuity." The waterway terminated in the heart of the city at the Water Hall, a long warehouse where ships could load and unload goods (Fig. **16.1**).

The city's prosperous merchant class, like the nobility, actively supported the arts. Their court was obsessed with chivalry, poetry, music, and art, and since Bruges was home to a thriving community of painters, the dukes were particularly attracted to it. There they commissioned paintings, sculptures, manuscripts, and gold work from throughout the region, often competing with the merchant class. Thus, both the nobility and the merchant class contributed

to the city's position at the center of the arts in Northern Europe. But there was a darker side to the North's growing prosperity. In his classic text on the rise of the Renaissance in the north, *The Autumn of the Middle Ages*, Johan Huizinga describes the tensions that informed life in the region:

> There was less relief available for misfortune and for sickness; they came in a more fearful and more painful way. Sickness contrasted more strongly with health. The cutting cold and the dreaded darkness of winter were more concrete evils. Honor and wealth were enjoyed more fervently and greedily because they contrasted still more than now with lamentable poverty. A fur-lined robe of office, a bright fire in the oven, drink and jest, and a soft bed still possessed … high value for enjoyment. …
>
> So intense and colorful was life that it could stand the mingling of the smell of blood and roses. Between hellish fears and the more childish jokes, between cruel harshness and sentimental sympathy the people stagger—like the giant with the head of a child, hither and thither. Between the absolute denial of all worldly joys and a frantic yearning for wealth and pleasure, between dark hatred and merry conviviality, they live in extremes.

◀ **Fig. 16.1 Pieter I Claeissens (?),** ***The Seven Wonders of Bruges*** **(detail). ca. 1550–60.** Panel, 34⅝″ × 48⅜″. Private collection. LUKAS, Art in Flanders, Belgium. This view gathers widely separated buildings into a single scene. The long building in the center foreground is the Water Hall, a warehouse and market complex near the center of the city. Behind the Water Hall is the town hall, symbol of the prosperity the city enjoyed throughout the northern regions of Europe as a result of trade and unprecedented mercantile activity.

((⸱ **Listen** to the chapter audio on **MyArtsLab**

The Church itself offered little solace, since it seemed to many the very center of sin and corruption. In the magnificence of the art it commissioned to glorify God, a Northerner would likely be reminded of the poverty and darkness that surrounded him. The Northern imagination was, in fact, pervaded by a sense of pessimism. From a pessimist's point of view, Christ's Crucifixion represented the inevitability of pain and suffering, not the promise of the glory of the afterlife. In art, this pessimism was reflected in the painstakingly rendered depictions of suffering, realized particularly in Germany. At the same time, humanist ideals imported from Italy began to assert themselves as well.

ART, COMMERCE, AND MERCHANT PATRONAGE

How did commerce and mercantile wealth influence the development of both religious and secular painting in Northern Europe?

In Bruges, painting was a major commodity, second only to cloth. The Corporation of Imagemakers produced for sale many small devotional panels, private prayer books, portraits, and town views. Each May, the city of Bruges sponsored a great fair, where painters, goldsmiths, booksellers, and jewelers displayed their wares in over 180 rented stalls on the grounds of a Franciscan cloister. Especially popular, because they were relatively inexpensive, were oil paintings. The medium of oil painting had been known for several centuries, and medieval painters had used oils to decorate stone, metal, and occasionally plaster walls. As we will see, oil painting enabled artists such as Jan van Eyck to add the kind of detail and subtle color and value gradations to their paintings that resulted in a remarkable realism. For many art historians, this detailed naturalism is the most distinctive feature of Northern European art. By the sixteenth century, at any rate, Bruges printmaker Johannes Stradanus popularized the idea of van Eyck's mastery of the medium with the publication of his print, *Jan van Eyck's Studio* (Fig. 16.2). This print shows van Eyck's Bruges studio as a factory where paintings are made as goods for consumption by a rising middle class.

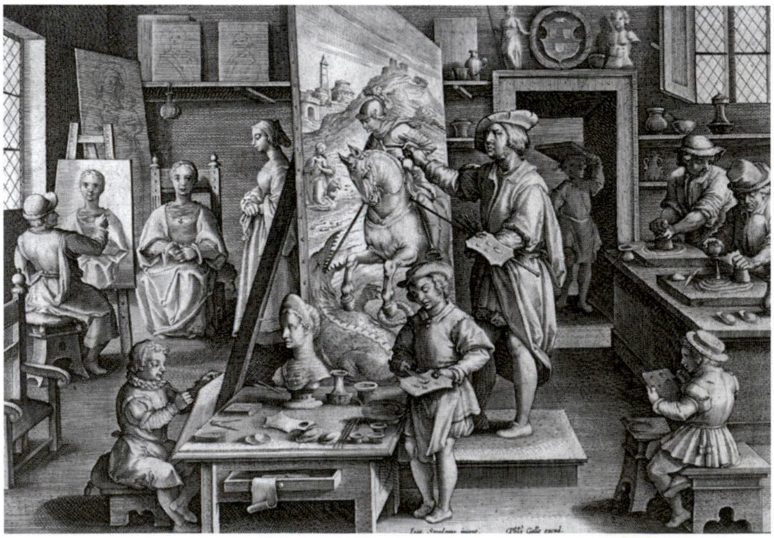

By the middle of the fifteenth century, the Flanders city of Antwerp, on the River Scheldt, had supplanted Bruges in importance. In a quirky instance of geography influencing history, silt built up in Bruges's canal system, making its harbor inaccessible to large vessels. Antwerp did not hesitate to take advantage. All artwork in Antwerp was sold at its fair. By the middle of the sixteenth century, huge quantities of art were bought and sold at the building where the fair was held, and nearly 300 painters lived nearby. In 1553 alone, Spanish and Portuguese ships left the Antwerp docks with more than 4 tons of paintings and 70,000 yards of tapestries—all purchased at the fair. And the trade in art went both ways. While Antwerp was the chief distribution center for the arts in northern Europe, it also received goods from centers of culture across the region (Map 16.1). From the printing presses of Nuremberg, in Germany, an ever-increasing trade in fine art prints was initiated (discussed in Chapter 17). From Cologne, home to a community of painters rivaling that of Bruges, came paintings; from Paris, illuminated manuscripts; and from Arras, Brussels, and Tournai, tapestries. Art and commerce were now inextricably linked.

One of the greatest differences between the Renaissance cultures of the North and South is the nature of patronage that developed in each. In the south of Europe, the most important patrons were the politically powerful families. The Medici, the Gonzagas, and the Montefeltros—and the papacy (often members of these same families)—all used their patronage to further their political prestige. In the North, trade had created a wealthy and relatively large class of merchants, who soon rivaled the French and Burgundian courts as the most important patrons of the day. Wealthy nobles, like Philip the Good of Burgundy, certainly influenced artistic developments, but gradually, the taste of the new business class came to dominate the production and distribution of works of art. This new business class represented a new audience for artists, in both the North and South. Motivated by the marketplace, artists sought to please this new class. In turn, members of the business class fostered the careers of several artists who were highly skilled in the use of oil paint. These artists, Robert Campin, Jan van Eyck, Rogier van der Weyden, and Hieronymus Bosch, are associated with particular northern centers of culture.

Fig. 16.2 Johannes Stradanus, *Oil Painting*, or *Jan van Eyck's Studio*. Late 16th century. 8″ × 10½″. Stedelijke Museum, Bruges. LUKAS, Art in Flanders, Belgium. In his *Lives of the Painters*, Giorgio Vasari wrote that van Eyck had discovered oil painting. Vasari had met Stradanus, from whom he learned of van Eyck's work.

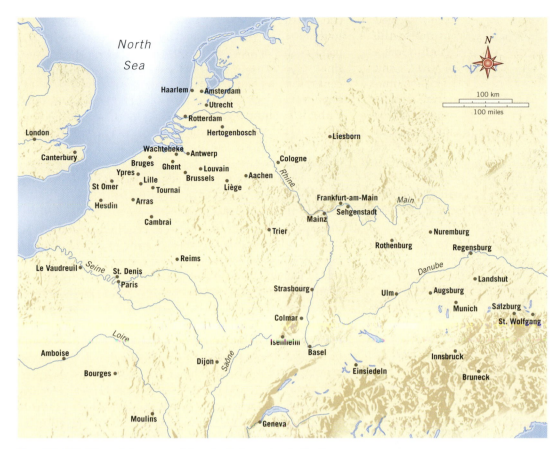

Map 16.1 **Chief financial, commercial, and artistic centers in Northern Europe in the 15th and 16th centuries.**

Robert Campin in Tournai

The growing influence of the merchant class pervades the *Mérode Altarpiece* (Fig. **16.3**), painted by the so-called Master of Flémalle. His real name, say many scholars, was Robert Campin (ca. 1375–1444). Campin was a member of the painters' guild and the city council in Tournai. Since the Middle Ages, this city near the southern border of Flanders was known for metalwork, jewelry, and architectural sculpture. We know little about Campin's life, but we do know that the Tournai city fathers condemned him for

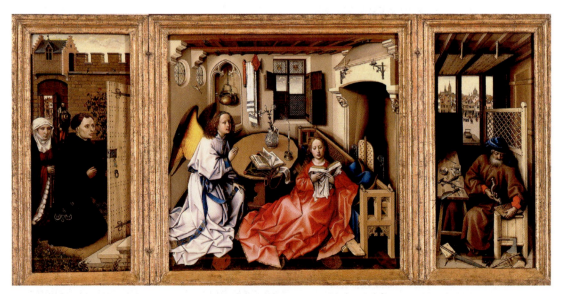

Fig. 16.3 **Robert Campin (Master of Flémalle),** *Mérode Altarpiece.* **ca. 1426.** Oil on panel, center 25⁵⁄₁₆″ × 24⅛″, each wing 25⅜″ × 10⅞″. The Metropolitan Museum of Art, New York. The Cloisters Collection, 1956 (56.70). The two donors kneel at the left, Mary and the archangel Gabriel are in the center, and Joseph works in his carpenter's shop at the right.

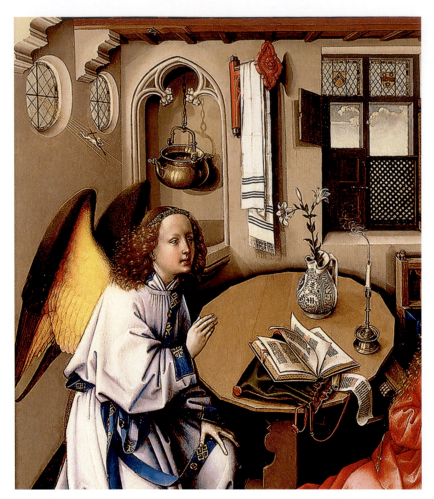

Fig. 16.4 Robert Campin (Master of Flémalle), *Mérode Altarpiece* (detail). ca. 1426. The Metropolitan Museum of Art, New York. The Cloisters Collection, 1956 (56.70). The extraordinarily fine detail of Campin's painting was made possible by his use of oil paint.

carrying the cross flies into the room (Fig. **16.4**). Campin is telling the viewers that the entire life of Christ, including the Passion itself, enters Mary's body at the moment of conception. The candle on the table beside her, symbolic of the "old faith" (that is, Judaism), is extinguished by the "true light" of Christ entering the room. This potent theological proposition kindled the anti-Jewish sentiment that erupted in medieval Spain and during the Crusades (see Chapter 10). It would also underlie anti-Semitic feelings from the later Renaissance Inquisitions, in which Jews were required to convert to Christianity or face exile or death, down to the Holocaust in the twentieth century. The lilies in the vase on the table are a traditional symbol of Mary's purity, although, since there are three of them, they may also represent the Trinity.

In the next room, behind the fireplace and settee next to which Mary reads and in the right-hand panel, Joseph works as a carpenter. On the table in front of him is a recently completed mousetrap, probably a reference to a metaphor created by Saint Augustine to the effect that the Passion of Christ is a trap baited by Christ's own blood to catch Satan. Another mousetrap sits outside on the window ledge, apparently for sale. Joseph is in the act of boring holes in a piece of wood, perhaps a grape press and thus another reference to the blood of Christ—Christ's declaration of wine as his own blood in the Eucharist. Through the window, its shutters latched to the ceiling above, we can see the main square of a typical Flemish town, perhaps Tournai itself.

This Annunciation is clearly an entirely local and bourgeois affair. Mary is a Flemish housewife, Joseph, a Flemish carpenter and owner of the house, even though the two were not yet married at the time of Annunciation. Time has collapsed—the New Testament becomes a current event. Every element seems a necessary and real part of everyday Flemish life. Each common object in this middle-class home serves a real, material purpose as well as a religiously symbolic one.

Another noteworthy aspect of Campin's triptych is its astonishingly small size for an altarpiece. If its two side panels were closed over the central panel, as they are designed to work, the altarpiece is just over 2 feet square—making it easily portable. This little altarpiece is itself a material object, so intimate and detailed that it functions more like the book that lies open on the table within its frame than a painting. It is very different from the altarpieces being made in Italy during the first half of the fifteenth century. Most were monumental in scale and painted in fresco, permanently embedded in the wall, and therefore not portable.

leading a dissolute life with his mistress. His punishment was reduced, but the story shows the moral seriousness of Northern European culture in the fifteenth century, a seriousness that would grow even greater during the later Protestant Reformation.

The *Mérode Altarpiece* is a three-part work, or **triptych** (see *Context*, page 553). The left-hand panel depicts the altarpiece's patrons, Ingelbrecht of Mechlin and his wife, kneeling. They are ordinary people, though a little wealthier than most, and their family coats of arms decorate the top windows in the center panel. Here, in the living room of a middle-class Flemish home, the magic of the Annunciation takes place. Mary sits on the footrest of a wooden settee before the fireplace, intently reading a book. Another book, richly illustrated, lies on the table beside her. **Finials**, or ornamental tops, at each corner of the settee depict dogs, symbols of fidelity and domesticity, and lions, symbols of Jesus and his Resurrection. The archangel Gabriel approaches Mary from the left, almost blocking the view of the two patrons, who peer in through the doorway. Seven rays of sunlight, directed toward Mary's abdomen, illuminate the room. On one of the rays, a miniature Christ

Oil Painting

None of the materials used in oil painting were new when painters in Flanders began working with the medium. The support, a wooden panel with a layer of white plaster, or **gesso**, sometimes incorporating a layer of linen or canvas between the wood and the plaster, had been used in tempera painting. And the pigments were the same as those used by tempera artists. Sometimes, artists working in tempera would use oil to create a luminous finish on the surface of the painting.

What the Flemish panel painters brought to this mix was the understanding that by using oil as the *primary* vehicle for the paint, they could create layers of paint with greater or lesser translucency, depending on the density of the pigment suspended in the oil. As light penetrates the paint layers, it is reflected back at the viewer, creating a gemlike brilliance of color. This sense of seeing colored light in the painting is the distinguishing characteristic of Flemish oil painting.

Oil offers other advantages as a painting medium. It dries much more slowly than tempera, and the drying process can be further slowed by adding extra oil. Slow-drying paint allows artists to blend the colors in minute amounts, creating subtle modulations of tone that suggest a sense of light falling across an object. Furthermore, using oil paint, the artist can work with extremely soft, fine brushes, eliminating any hint of brushstrokes. The smooth

Diagram of a section of a 15th-century Flemish painting, demonstrating the luminosity of the oil medium. The large arrow suggests how light penetrates the translucent glazes of the medium and is reflected back to the viewer.

finish that results heightens the illusion that the viewer is looking at the object itself. Implicit in the Flemish artist's sensitivity to the light-enhancing qualities of the oil medium is the understanding that light suggests spiritual truth. So, as light falls across an object and is literally reflected back at the viewer, the object assumes, at least potentially, a deeper symbolic resonance or meaning. From this point of view, the world and its objects become "alight" with the Creator, and painters can find in their task a profound spiritual importance.

Campin's altarpiece is made to be held up close, in the hands, not surveyed from afar, suggesting its function as a private, rather than public, devotional object.

As an exploration of the private nature of religious experience, the painting's subtext is *touch*. Working with oil paint, Campin and other contemporary Northern painters were able to blend, shade, and bleed colors so skillfully that textures—Gabriel's exquisitely curly hair, Mary's soft skin and velvet dress, Joseph's wool robe, the brass pot hanging in the back alcove, even the transparent smoke rising from the candle—become nearly palpable (see *Materials & Techniques*, above). Light seems to emanate from within the painting itself. Gabriel's wings glow, an effect created by layering very thin, almost transparent coats of oil paint on the surface of the painting—a process known as **glazing**.

The wings literally contain light, lending the archangel a physical presence and material reality. The spiritual is made real. In fact, the archangel appears no less (and no more) "real" than the brass pot above his head.

Because of its intimacy and portability, its realism and emphasis on physical things, the *Mérode Altarpiece* and other Northern Renaissance paintings like it introduced a new set of possibilities for painting. Patrons in the south gained personal satisfaction and even honor from their patronage—compare the Medici family portraits in Botticelli's *Adoration of the Magi* (see Fig. 14.15 in Chapter 14) or the donors in Masaccio's *Trinity* (see Fig. 14.10 in Chapter 14)—but such acts were intended to enhance the glory of the city-state, the guild, the *scuole*, or the Church. But here, the motive of Ingelbrecht of Mechlin and his wife seems wholly personal.

👁 **Watch** a video about the technique of making oil paint and oil painting on **MyArtsLab**

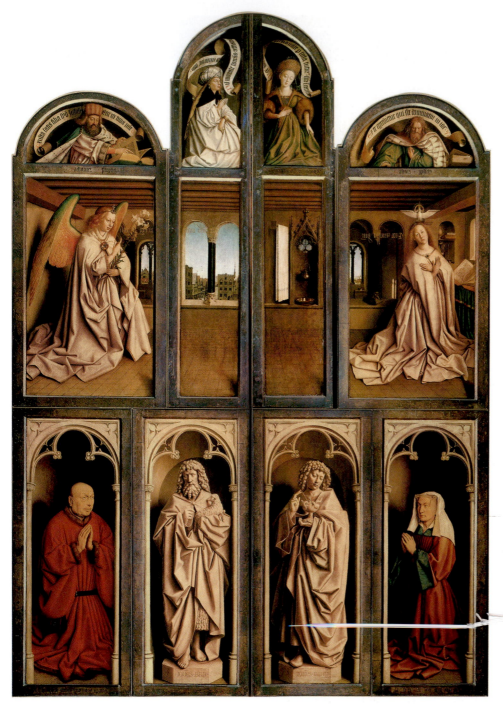

Fig. 16.5 Jan and Hubert van Eyck, *Ghent Altarpiece*. ca. 1425–32. Oil on panel, closed 11'5¾" × 7'6¾". Saint Bavo Cathedral, Ghent. This monumental work has had a dramatic history. In 1566, the parishioners of Saint Bavo, frightened that anti-Catholic Protestants might destroy the altarpiece, dismantled it and hid it away. In 1894, when it was part of the royal collection in Berlin, it was disassembled so that both sides of the panels could be viewed simultaneously. After the German defeat in World War I, the altarpiece was returned to Ghent, disassembled again for safekeeping during World War II, and finally, in 1950 to 1951, permanently reassembled at Saint Bavo Cathedral.

One of the most distinctive features of Campin's painting is the everyday appearance of the scene. This ordinariness lends the image of Christian miracle a reality never before seen in European painting. The reality was heightened by the depiction of objects through the medium of oil paint.

Jan van Eyck in Ghent and Bruges

Even a painting so monumental in size and so important to an entire community as the *Ghent Altarpiece*, by Hubert and Jan van Eyck (ca. 1395–1441), originated in its merchant-class patrons' hope for personal salvation. The city of Ghent was a major port and flourishing center of the cloth industry. There, a prosperous couple, Jodocus Vijd and his wife, Isabel Borluut, sponsored a private chapel for the Cathedral of Saint Bavo, and commissioned this altarpiece for its interior. The artist depicted both patrons life-size, at the bottom of the closed doors of the altarpiece flanking painted sculptures of John the Baptist and John the Evangelist (Fig. **16.5**). An inscription below them reads: "Hubert van Eyck, the most famous painter ever known, started this work of art at the request of Jodocus Vijd; his brother Jan, who was the second in art, finished the monumental commission. With this verse the donor consigns the work to your charge on May 6, 1432." Very little is known about Hubert, who died before September 18, 1426, not long after he started the painting. He probably painted some of the panels, though his younger brother Jan probably finished most or all of them. It is not really possible to distinguish their work since other artists in Jan's workshop also had a hand in painting the altarpiece. Most recent scholarship attributes the design and execution to Jan and his workshop.

The doors to the polyptych (an altarpiece constructed from multiple panels) remained closed except each year at

Under the patronage of the merchant class of the north, painting begins to function something like the mousetrap Joseph has set outside his window for sale; that is, as a commodity. And in fact, the patrons of the *Mérode Altarpiece* have conceived of it as a kind of object of barter. Its commission is a form of indulgence, or payment, which spares them from purgatory and paves their way into heaven.

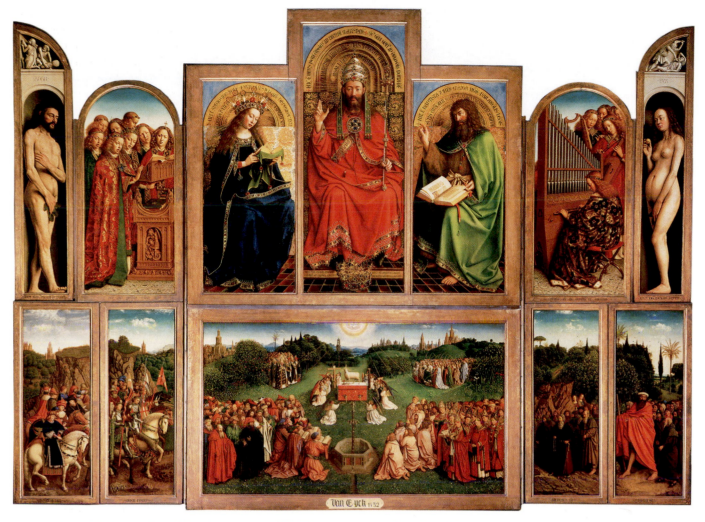

Fig. 16.6 Jan and Hubert van Eyck, *Ghent Altarpiece*. ca. 1425–32. Oil on panel, open 11'5¾" × 15'½". Saint Bavo Cathedral, Ghent. Unlike the altarpiece's flat depiction in this photograph, the wings were opened at a slight angle to the central panels, thus allowing Adam and Eve to gaze more directly at their God.

🔎 **View** the Closer Look for the *Ghent Altarpiece* (open) on **MyArtsLab**

Easter. For most of the year, therefore, the patrons actually worshiped below *The Annunciation*, a painting rendered across four panels that gave the impression of a single room. At the left, Gabriel arrives with a bouquet of lilies in his hands. In gold letters that extend across the panels toward Mary, he speaks the Latin words "*Ave gracia plena d[omi]n[u]s tecu[m]*" ("Hail to thee who art full of grace; the Lord is with you"). She responds, "*Ecce ancilla d[omi]ni*" ("Behold the handmaiden of the Lord"). With this gold lettering, van Eyck illustrates the traditional story of Mary's impregnation—through her ear by the Word of God.

On the inner panels, van Eyck illustrates *The Adoration of the Lamb by All Saints* (Fig. **16.6**). The bottom five panels form a single coherent scene from the Book of Revelation in which the Lamb, the embodiment of Christ himself, stands on an altar while its blood drips into a golden chalice. In front of the altar is the Fountain of Life, from which water flows, washing away the sins of those who worship there. Above the altar is the Holy Spirit, a semicircular

orb of light, from which rays of light descend on the crowd below, including the 12 apostles on the right, and Hebrew Bible figures on the left. In each of the side panels, pilgrims representing the range of society, from knights to hermits, arrive to worship at the altar. In the background, rising above the meadow, is the skyline of Ghent, including Saint Bavo Cathedral.

Unlike the bottom panels, the seven panels across the top of the altarpiece do not create a single space. But in their symmetry, with God the Father in the center, bracketed on the outside by Adam and Eve, they form a unified space. To God's left and right are the Virgin, crowned as the Queen of Heaven, and John the Baptist. Separating them from Adam and Eve are groups of angels playing musical instruments.

In the depiction of Adam and Eve, the largest painted nudes since antiquity, Jan van Eyck clearly demonstrated his extraordinary skill. Eve holds the shriveled forbidden fruit. Her belly protrudes in a manner that was the

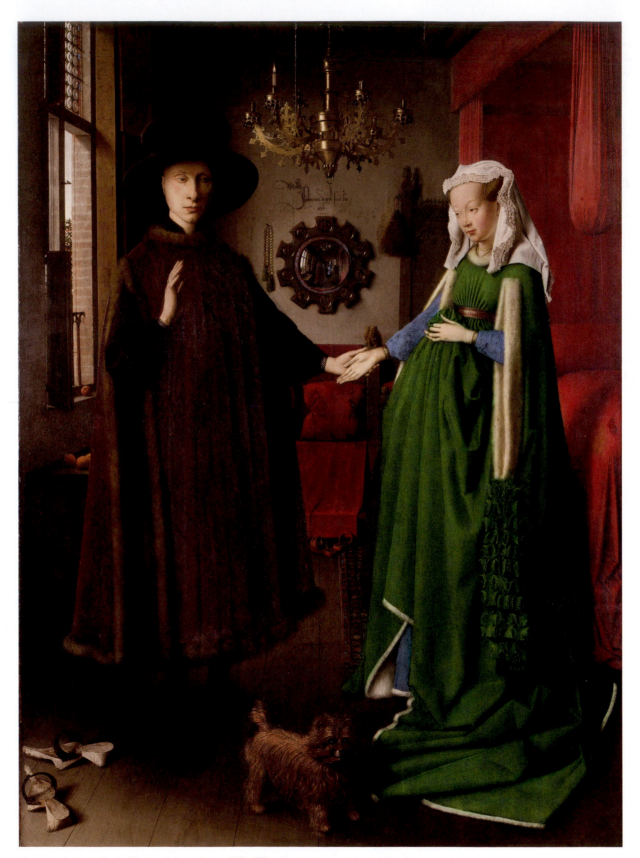

Fig. 16.7 Jan van Eyck, *Giovanni Arnolfini and His Wife Giovanna Cenami*. ca. 1434. Oil on panel, 32¼" × 23½". National Gallery, London. Giovanna may look pregnant, but she is probably not. However, she has pulled her robe up before her abdomen and dressed in green to suggest her fertility. Note the comparable body type exhibited by Eve in the *Ghent Altarpiece* (see Fig. 16.6).

View the Closer Look for *Giovanni Arnolfini and His Wife Giovanna Cenami* on **MyArtsLab** preferred female body-type of the age; the posture suggests that though she is not pregnant, she is fertile. The clarity and realism of detail is astonishing. We can see almost every strand of her hair as it flows over her shoulder, while the nudity of the pair seems pure flesh. As opposed to God the Father, the Virgin, and Saint John, all of whom are presented in perspective as if the viewer were standing at eye level, Adam and Eve are presented as if viewed from below. Note how Adam's toes seem to extend out of the picture plane above our heads, affirming our own position, on the ground below them, looking up. This presentation underscores our own lowly human condition in relation to this scene of miracles and hope. And in it, Adam and Eve are no longer types, but individuals of real flesh and bone, in whom we can see ourselves.

This celebration of individual identity marks Renaissance art in both the North and South. It is especially apparent in van Eyck's double portrait of Giovanni Arnolfini, an Italian merchant representing Medici interests in Bruges, and his wife, Giovanna Cenami (Fig. **16.7**). Scholars continue to debate the meaning and purpose of the work, but most have agreed that the couple are exchanging marriage

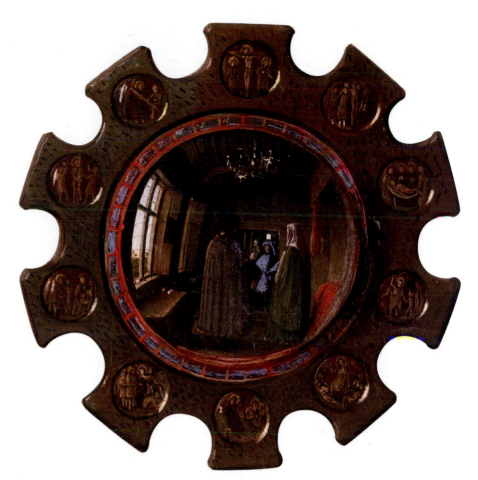

Fig. 16.8 Jan van Eyck, *Giovanni Arnolfini and His Wife Giovanna Cenami* **(detail). ca. 1434.** Each of the ten small circles around the mirror contains a scene of Christ's Passion.

vows in a bedroom before two witnesses. One of them is van Eyck himself, who is reflected in the mirror at the back of the room (Fig. **16.8**). (Above the mirror he inscribed in Latin "*Johannes de Eyck fuit hic. 1434*" ["Jan van Eyck was here, 1434"]). Recently a persuasive argument has been made that this scene represents an engagement rather than a marriage—a touching of the hands was the traditional sign of an agreement to wed—and that the scene takes place in the front parlor of a Dutch home, a room that was commonly decorated with a canopied bed as a symbol of hospitality.

The painting abounds with other symbolic elements, transforming what is at first glance a wholly secular image into one filled with religious significance, a characteristic feature of Northern art. Many scholars speculate that the little dog at the feet of the couple represents fidelity, and the two pair of shoes, at the left front of the painting and at the back of the room, suggest that the couple stand on ground hallowed by the sacred character of the ceremony that engages them. The chandelier, with its single burning candle, is traditionally thought to represent the presence of Christ. The fruits on the window ledge and table behind Arnolfini suggest abundance. Atop the high chairback at the back of the room is a sculptural finial representing either Saint Margaret, the patron saint of childbirth, or

Saint Martha, the patron saint of housewives. The dusting brush beside it probably symbolizes the wife's household duties. Above all, the painting seems to celebrate the couple's spiritual and material well-being. Its many textures, from Arnolfini's fur robe to the rich red velvet of the bed, symbolize what we might call "the good life," a phrase with a long Classical history.

In his paintings, van Eyck expresses his love of detail through his ability to render in oil paint the texture of things and the way light plays across their surfaces. This skill is apparent in the glittering jewels of God's crown in the *Ghent Altarpiece*, for instance, and in the green wool of Giovanna Cenami's dress or the ermine of Giovanni Arnolfini's robe. This love of detail, presented through a smooth surface that does not show brushstrokes, is the hallmark of Northern Renaissance painting, the characteristic that distinguishes it most from painting in the South.

Rogier van der Weyden of Brussels

The tension between material well-being and spiritual narrative that we see in the Arnolfini portrait appears in all Northern painting. The religious narratives painted by Rogier van der Weyden (ca. 1399–1464), who studied with Robert Campin in Tournai, are a good example.

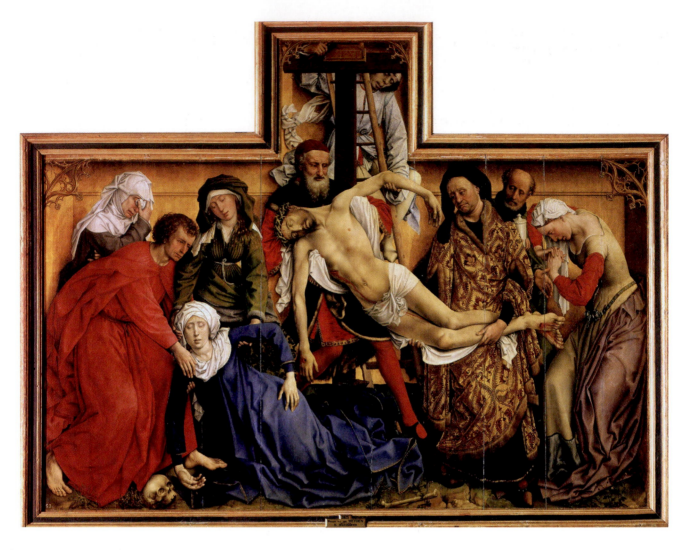

Fig. 16.9 Rogier van der Weyden, *Descent from the Cross*. ca. 1435. Oil on panel, 7'2⅝" × 8'7⅛".
Museo del Prado, Madrid. The subject matter is human suffering, with no hint of the miracle of the Resurrection
to follow. This focus on emotional seriousness is a particularly Northern characteristic.

View the Closer Look for *Descent from the Cross* on **MyArtsLab**

In his *Descent from the Cross* (Fig. **16.9**), notice the contrast between the extraordinary expression of individual emotion and the gorgeous colors and complex textures of the clothing worn by the figures. Nothing better defines the North's contribution to Renaissance art than this portrayal of Christ's followers. Their startlingly realistic expressions, underscoring their individual identities and feelings, are combined with a painstaking attention to detail. In fact, spiritual truth and material richness combine in van der Weyden's painting to constitute a coherent whole.

In his monumental *Descent from the Cross*, commissioned by the Louvain Crossbowmen's Guild about 1435, van der Weyden contained the Deposition in a shallow golden sepulcher, as if purposefully avoiding the detailed landscapes that dominate the backgrounds of Campin's and van Eyck's work. He draws the viewer's attention to the drama of human feeling. In this closed, shallow space, the protagonists press forward toward the picture plane. Every wrinkle on every brow,

every tear on every face (six of the ten figures are crying), every quivering lip seems to come alive. These are physical presences, emotionally caught up in the tragedy before them.

The composition of the painting supports the emotional pitch. In keeping with the painting's theme, the compositional weight of the painting falls with Christ to the ground, to death. Christ's body hangs in the hands of Joseph of Arimathea, who offered his newly built tomb for Christ's burial, and the figure on the ladder supports his arm. The swooning body of the Virgin echoes the curve of Christ's own, her right arm similarly falling straight downward toward a skull (perhaps the skull of Adam), while another Mary supports her left arm. John the Baptist, wearing a red robe and holding the Virgin up, forms a sort of visual parenthesis with the almost grotesquely contorted Mary Magdalene on the far right. As a group, the figures seem to fall physically under the weight of Christ's body even as they collapse emotionally under the weight of the moment.

Altars and Altarpieces

The **altar** in a Christian church is deeply symbolic, representing both the table of Jesus' Last Supper and the tombs of Christ and the saints. Its top is called the **mensa** (from Latin for "table"), and its side supports are called **stipes** (from Latin for "post"). The front, often decorated, is called the **antependium**.

An **altarpiece** is a painted and/or carved construction placed behind the altar so as to appear visually joined to it. Originally a single panel, the altarpiece had evolved by the fifteenth century into an elaborate architectural construction. Before the Renaissance, altarpieces were generally fixed in place (and were often painted in fresco). Painting on panel freed artists to create these more elaborate constructions. The altarpiece's base, or **predella**, is usually decorated with images. Above this might appear a **diptych** or triptych, two- or three-paneled, hinged paintings, designed to fold around and seemingly embrace the altar. The triptych soon evolved into a winged triptych, in which two panels, often painted on both sides, fold over the central section, and then into a **polyptych**, a multipaneled construction also painted on both sides, which could be opened and closed to form different arrangements according to the specific liturgical needs of the church year.

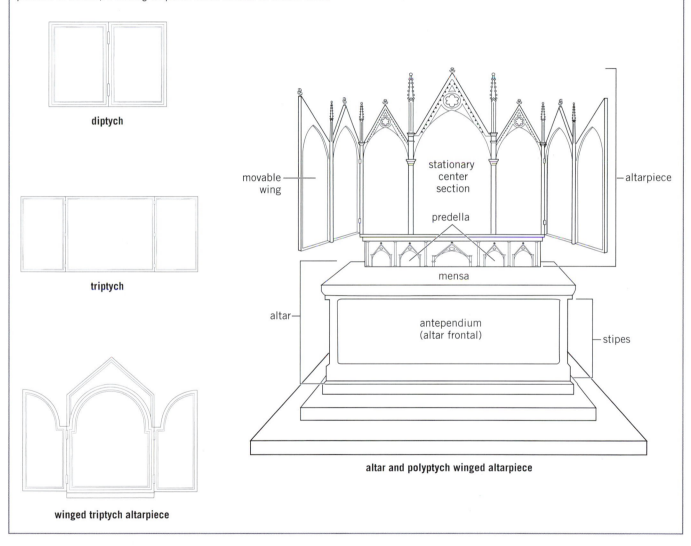

diptych

triptych

winged triptych altarpiece

movable wing

stationary center section

predella

altarpiece

mensa

altar

antependium (altar frontal)

stipes

altar and polyptych winged altarpiece

As the official painter to the city of Brussels, van der Weyden maintained a large workshop with many assistants. He received commissions not only from Philip the Good and his court, but also from foreign princes, the Church, and merchant guilds.

Hieronymus Bosch in 's-Hertogenbosch

Hieronymus Bosch (1450–1516) was born, lived, and worked in the town of 's-Hertogenbosch (now in southern Holland). The town owed its prosperity to wool and cloth. Bosch was a contemporary of the painters in southern Europe who worked in the so-called High Renaissance. Such a distinction seems inappropriate in the North, where there was greater continuity between fifteenth- and sixteenth-century art. (Only Albrecht Dürer, a German, discussed later in the chapter, fits comfortably into the High Renaissance cult of the individual creative genius.) Bosch's paintings are at once minutely detailed and brutally imaginative, casting a dark, satiric shadow over the materialistic concerns of his Northern predecessors. In *Carrying of the Cross* (Fig. **16.10**), Bosch presents Christ in the middle of the painting, the crown of thorns on his head, bent under the weight of the cross, his eyes closed, and several days' growth of beard on his face. It is difficult to say whether he closes his eyes from exhaustion or from sorrow and pity for the grotesque menagerie of humanity that surrounds him. From their faces, these participants in Christ's pain and

Fig. 16.10 Hieronymus Bosch. *Carrying of the Cross*. ca. 1490. Oil on panel, 30⅛″ × 32⅞″. Museum voor Schone Kunsten, Ghent. It seems likely that Bosch knew of Leonardo da Vinci's studies in the 1490s of grotesque human visages, studies that Leonardo believed revealed the character and personalities of those depicted.

humiliation seem morally bankrupt, hideously evil, almost sublimely stupid, if not criminally insane.

Such pessimism derives at least partly from a sense of doom that was characteristic of the North. It continues from the medieval sermon tradition stressing the wretchedness and worthlessness of human existence, exemplified by Pope Innocent III's *On the Misery of the Human Condition* (see Reading 10.5 in Chapter 10) through the devastation of the bubonic plague. From the 1340s well into the sixteenth century, the plague periodically ravaged northern cities due to the colder climate and harsher conditions that defined day-to-day life in the North.

Northern pessimism manifests itself most dramatically in Bosch's most ambitious painting, a triptych with closing doors known as the *Garden of Earthly Delights*, painted around 1505 to 1510 (see *Closer Look*, pages 556–557). Although the painting takes the form of a triptych winged altarpiece, it was never intended for a religious setting. The *Garden of Earthly Delights* hung in a palace in Brussels, where invading Spanish troops seized it in 1568 and took it to Madrid, where it remains.

The painting is really a **conversation piece**, a work designed to invite discussion of its meaning. Bosch has given us an enigmatic essay on what the world might be like if the fall of Adam and Eve had never happened. It presents, in other words, a world technically without sin, yet rampant with behavior that its viewers, the fallen sons and daughters of Adam and Eve, could only identify as sinful.

Other parts of the painting, the right panel in particular, seem to suggest life after the fall, life in which Adam and Eve's sin has made humankind aware of good and evil. These are the painting's paradoxes and its source of endless fascination. Equally intriguing is its meticulous detail, which gives the most grotesquely imaginative landscapes a sense of reality.

LITERATURE, TAPESTRY, DANCE, AND MUSIC IN NORTHERN EUROPE

What tensions existed between the financial wealth of the North and its ethical and moral climate?

The pessimism and moral ambiguity of Bosch's paintings ran through the Northern intellectual climate as a whole: The human body was widely regarded as the vehicle and instrument of sin. This is in stark contrast to the Southern humanist approach to the body as an object of beauty that reflects the beauty of God. (See, for example, Donatello's *David*, Fig. 14.14 in Chapter 14.) And, rather than offering hope, the Church seemed to many to be morally bankrupt

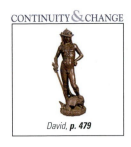
CONTINUITY & CHANGE

David, p. 479

and intent on bankrupting the faithful as it rebuilt Rome. Toward the end of the fifteenth century, the French poet Jean Meschinot (1420–91) summed up the sense of physical and spiritual melancholy that pervaded the North with these words: "O miserable and very sad life! … We suffer from warfare, death and famine; Cold and heat, day and night, sap our strength; Fleas, scabmites and so much other vermine make war upon us. In short, have mercy, Lord, upon our wicked persons, whose life is very short." As Johan Huizinga noted in the passage from his *Autumn of the Middle Ages* quoted on page 543, in the North: "Sickness contrasted more strongly with health. The cutting cold and the dreaded darkness of winter were more concrete evils. Honor and wealth were enjoyed more fervently and greedily because they contrasted still more than now with lamentable poverty." Thus, in a painting like van Eyck's Arnolfini portrait, Giovanna's robe, in all its bright color and fur-lined warmth, would also have evoked in the Northern imagination its opposite—dismal darkness, poverty, and cold.

The Literature of Ambiguity

By the first half of the sixteenth century, pessimism and doubt still pervaded Northern thought. Skepticism, about the Church in particular, reached even the highest ranks of the Northern European aristocracy. They regarded it with ambiguous feelings worthy of Bosch. This skepticism was poignantly expressed in the writings of Marguerite de Navarre (1492–1549), sister of the French king Francis I (1494–1547). She governed France herself when her brother was imprisoned in 1524 by the Holy Roman Emperor Charles V. She invested large sums of money and energy in order to reform monasteries and convents and establish hospitals across France. As a writer, Marguerite expressed the nuances of human relationships with a subtlety rare in her own day. Clearly a person of high moral and ethical character, she could nevertheless sympathize with sensibilities far less refined than her own, as the 72 stories that make up the *Heptameron* indicate time and again.

Modeled on Boccaccio's *Decameron* (see Chapter 13), the stories are told by ten persons of aristocratic birth, who through a variety of misadventures find themselves thrown together at the abbey of Our Lady of Sarrance in the Pyrenees Mountains. Informed that the French royal family wishes a French equivalent of the *Decameron*, they undertake the task, each telling a tale a day, although they complete only the first seven days. (Marguerite's own death may have terminated the cycle.) Story 55 (see **Reading 16.1**, pages 566–567) is short, but shows Marguerite's skill to the fullest. It is about a Spanish widow's strategy to circumvent her dying husband's wish to sell his valuable horse in order

Read the document from *The Tales of the Heptameron* on **MyArtsLab**

to purchase an indulgence for himself. Her scheme is clever, but the real interest of the work lies elsewhere. Marguerite's tales are, like Bosch's *Garden of Earthly Delights*, conversation pieces, designed to provoke dialogue and debate among their listeners. In this case, the conversation turns to the subject of Franciscan friars, who stand for the greed of the Church and, as other tales in the *Heptameron* make clear, the hostility toward women of the entire monastic system. In this tale, the wife's clever scheme to avoid paying alms to the Church, while technically immoral and sacrilegious, is honored by at least some of the group as wise and even noble.

Marguerite's tale is characteristically Northern in its emphasis on money. The social fabric of the North was deeply divided between those with wealth and those without it. In the calendar pages of the Limbourg brothers' 1416 *Très Riches Heures du Duc de Berry*, for example, the daily lives of nobility and peasants are contrasted (see Figs. 12.23 and 12.24 in Chapter 12). The very large peasant class regarded the aristocracy, the Church, and the mercantile middle class with equal suspicion. In fact, in France, the peasants rebelled in 1358 against the heavy tax burden imposed upon them by the Hundred Years' War. They revolted also in England, in 1381, and in Germany, culminating in the so-called Peasant War (see Chapter 17) of 1524 to 1526. As a result, the aristocracy, the clergy, and the middle class viewed peasants with deep suspicion too. In fact, since before the fall of Rome in the fifth century CE, the Latin word for "peasant," *paganus*, had been synonymous with "pagan." Peasants were assumed to be ungodly.

Tapestry

In this atmosphere, the great fairs of both Bruges and Antwerp still overflowed with luxury goods. Goldsmiths and jewelers rented stalls, featuring elaborately decorated ornaments, wine canisters, goblets, punch bowls, and drinking cups. Picture frames were a specialty, and the joiners (specialized carpenters) who crafted these also sold pulpits, church benches, altars, organ cases, and furniture. The textile merchants conducted a brisk trade in very costly luxury broadcloth, usually woven from British wool. The most luxurious of these rivaled Italian silks in their fine, soft, and close weaves. The stalls of the tapestry merchants were among the busiest. These luxury goods supplemented the fine art market, and along with the popular art forms in dance and music, constituted a rich cultural heritage.

The stone walls of the palaces and private residences of French and Burgundian royalty were covered with **tapestries** from Arras, Brussels, and Tournai (see *Materials & Techniques*, page 558). These heavy, handwoven textiles with decorative designs usually depicting historical or current scenes hung from metal hooks on the wall and were used to help warm the rooms in the cold winter months. They were highly transportable and moved with their itinerant courts. It is possible that the transportability of tapestries may have inspired painters to create their own imagery on highly transportable panels.

CLOSER LOOK

Hieronymus Bosch's *Garden of Earthly Delights* is full of strange hybrid organisms, part animal or bird, part human, part plant, sometimes part mechanical contraption. In the left panel of the triptych, we see the Garden of Eden, populated with such strange creatures as albino giraffes and elephants, unicorns, and flying fish. In the right panel, we see Bosch's deeply disturbing vision of hell, in which fire spits from the skyline and tortured souls are impaled on musical instruments or eaten alive by monsters. The central panel presents an image of life on earth, with hundreds of naked young men and women frolicking in a garden full of giant berries and other fruits. Lovers are variously contained in transparent columns or globes of glass—a reference to the proverb "Happiness and glass, how soon they pass." This landscape is like a parody of the central meadow in van Eyck's depiction of the Adoration of the Lamb in the *Ghent Altarpiece* (see Fig. 16.6). The world here has gone awry. Illicit lust replaces love of God, wanton seduction replaces beauty, and Bosch's own wild imagination replaces reason.

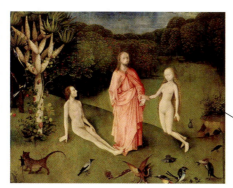

Even as God commands Adam and Eve to "be fruitful and multiply and fill the earth and subdue it," (Gen. 1:26) death is imminent: A cat walks off to the left with a mouse in its teeth, and ravens perch above on the Fountain of Life.

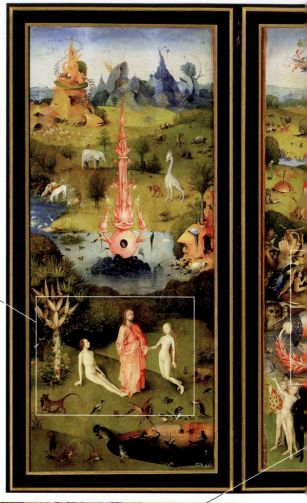

Something to Think About ...

Look at the painting of a *Meat Stall* by Peter Aertsen (see Fig. 17.15 in Chapter 17) painted some 40 years after Bosch's *Garden of Earthly Delights*. What do the two paintings have in common?

Hieronymus Bosch, *Garden of Earthly Delights*, closed. ca. 1505–10. Oil on panel, each wing 7'2½" × 38". Museo del Prado, Madrid. When closed, the triptych reveals the world at the moment of Creation. At the top left-hand corner, God floats on a cloud and looks down at the earthly orb. The landscape has no people. Inscribed across the top are these words from Psalms 33:9: "*Ipse dixit et facta su[nt]. Ipse ma[n]davit et creata su[n]t*"—"He himself spoke, and they were made; he himself commanded, and they were created." The irony of what is hidden inside these exterior panels could not be greater.

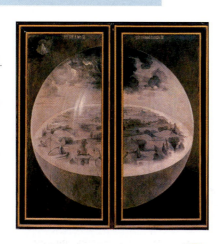

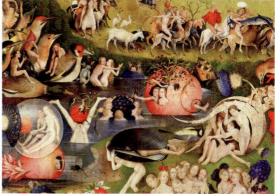

Here are the results of God's command to Adam and Eve to "be fruitful and multiply." Recall that it was eating the forbidden fruit of the Garden of Eden that was the Original Sin. Swimmers suck at the blackberry in the middle of the pool or float upside down, with fruit atop their genitals, or peek out of a floating orange, an image of gluttony. In fact, all of the Seven Deadly Sins are here—Pride, Envy, Greed, Gluttony, Anger, Sloth, and, above all, Lust.

View the Closer Look for *Garden of Earthly Delights* on **MyArtsLab**

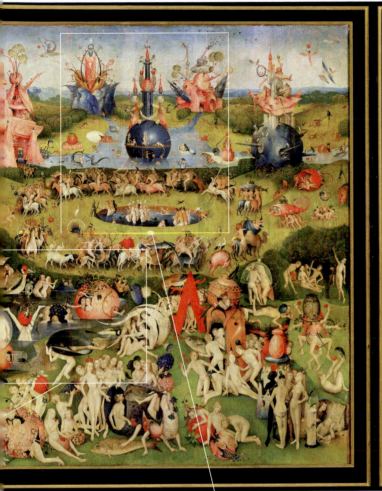

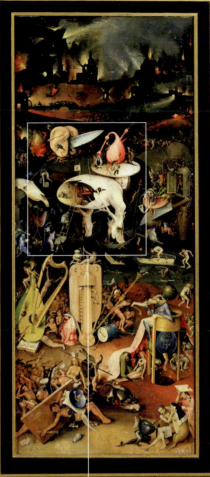

Hieronymus Bosch, *Garden of Earthly Delights*, open. ca. 1505–10. Oil on panel, center 7′2½″ × 6′4¾″; each wing 7′2½″ × 38″.

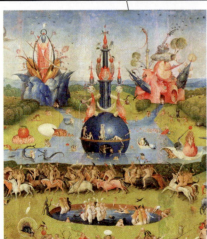

The focus of the central panel is this pool surrounded by the four so-called Castles of Vanity (this detail shows two of them). Horns, a symbol of cuckoldry, decorate the central fountain, known as the Tower of Adulteresses. Circling around the lower pool of bathing women, called the Bath of Venus, young men ride pigs, horses, goats, griffins, and other animals, apparently intent on "riding" the young women as well.

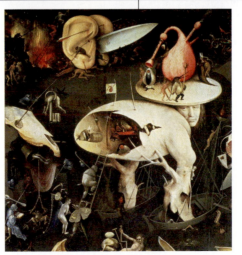

This strange creature presides over hell. Its legs are supported by tree trunks, each standing in a boat; its eggshell stomach is cracked open; and its head, with an astonishingly realistic face, is topped by a disk with bagpipe (a traditional symbol of lust). Behind it, two ears, pierced by arrows, flank a knife blade, like some monstrous cannon or hellish phallus.

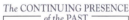

The CONTINUING PRESENCE
of the PAST

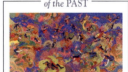

See Raqib Shaw, *Garden of Earthly Delights X*, 2004 at **MyArtsLab**

Materials & Techniques

Tapestry

Tapestries are heavy textiles handwoven on looms. The looms range in size from small, handheld models to large, freestanding structures. They serve as frames, holding in tension supporting threads, called the **warp**, so that striking threads, called the **weft**, can be interwoven between them. Warp threads are made of strong fibers, usually wool or linen, while weft threads are brightly colored strands of silk, wool, or spun gold or spun silver threads. Once the warp threads are stretched on the loom, the weaver places a **cartoon**, or full-scale drawing, below or behind the loom. The weaver then works on the back side of the tapestry, pushing the weft threads under and over the warp threads, knotting alternating colors together in a single strand, to match the cartoon's design so that the front side of the tapestry reproduces the design in reverse. The design can approach painting in its compositional complexity, refinement, and the three-dimensional rendering of forms.

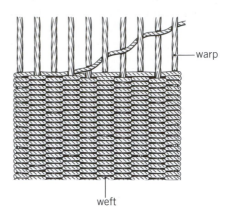

The vertical warp threads of a tapestry are interwoven with horizontal weft threads

Few tapestries from the period survive, but they could be over 30 feet wide and nearly as tall. The figures in them were often at least life-size—sometimes larger—so they were legible even in the largest room or church. Most tapestries were woven with dyed wool and silk, and their original coloration was often brilliant, even intense. Their color could be enhanced with silver- and gold-wrapped threads. This ultimately led to their destruction, especially during the French Revolution in the late eighteenth century, when they were burned to retrieve the precious metals.

Tapestries in churches often served the same iconographic and liturgical functions as frescoes in Southern Europe. A fifteenth-century tapestry showing the *Adoration of the Magi* (Fig. 16.11), commissioned by a French cardinal, the Archbishop of Lyon, in 1476, is a rare surviving example. It was designed to hang across the front of the altar of the earliest of the great French Gothic cathedrals, Saint-Étienne in Sens, halfway between Paris and Lyon. The cardinal's own coat of arms, with the motto, *N'espoir ne peur* ("No hope, no fear"), lines the

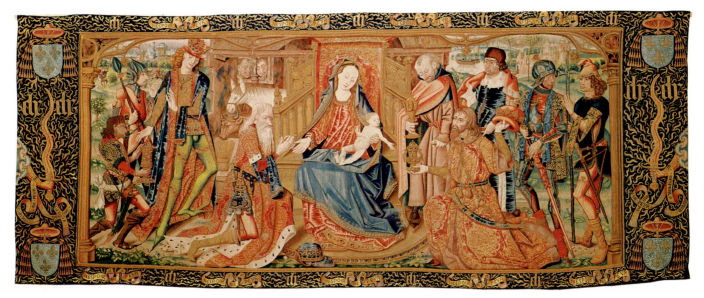

Fig. 16.11 Anonymous Brussels weaver (perhaps after a design by the Master of the View of Saint Gudule), *Adoration of the Magi*. **ca. 1476–88.** Wool, silk, silver, and gilt-metal-wrapped thread, 4′6½″ × 10′10½″. Cathedral Treasury, Sens, France. The unknown Master of the View of Saint Gudule takes his name from a surviving painting by his distinctive hand that includes a view of the cathedral of Saint Gudule in Brussels.

View the Closer Look for the technique of tapestry on **MyArtsLab** border top and bottom, and his red cardinal's hat decorates each corner. It would have been just one of many such tapestries decorating the interior of the cathedral. Another companion tapestry, an *Assumption of the Virgin*, served as the cathedral's altarpiece. From the landscape in the background of the *Adoration of the Magi* to the realistic faces of the figures and the luminous surfaces of lighted objects (an effect achieved here by means of silver and gold threads instead of oil paint), the influence of Flemish painting on this design is clear.

Dance and Music

Elaborate decorative programs were not limited to palaces and churches. Many town halls across Northern Europe were richly decorated as well, and the great halls in these buildings often played host to important civic social gatherings, including dances. In 1477, the Munich town council commissioned for the city's new feast room sculptures of 16 Morris dancers by Erasmus Grasser (ca. 1445/50–1518) (Fig. 16.12). Over 2 feet tall, each of the sculptures depicts a dancer leaping or twisting around to what, in real life, would be flute and drum music. Morris dancing is thought to have originated in Moorish Spain, *Morris* being a corruption of *Moorish*. The dances were popular not only among the common people—Morris dance troupes often wandered from town to town performing at carnivals and festivals—but as interludes at more formal dance occasions.

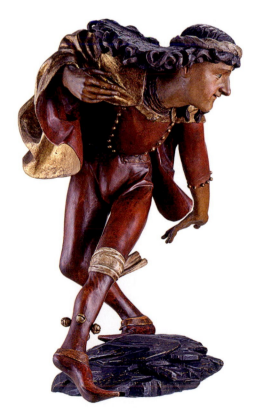

Fig. 16.12 Erasmus Grasser, *Morris Dancer* (*Bridegroom*). 1480.
Limewood with modern polychrome, height 24¼". Stadtmuseum, Munich. This figure's nickname—the "Bridegroom"—suggests the erotic nature of Morris dancing as a genre.

The garments of most of the Morris dancers were adorned with bells, which made an agreeable tinkle as the dancers moved. The dances were often frankly slapstick, a source of great amusement to their audience.

Popular dances such as the Morris dance found their musical equivalent in the madrigal, the genre of song inspired in Southern Europe by setting the sonnets of the Italian poet Petrarch to music (see Chapter 13). In the North, they were often more lighthearted and frivolous, a subgenre of madrigal referred to as **villanella**, a word meaning "country girl." (The root of villanella is *villa*, a country house, and is thus associated with pagan or peasant—that is, ungodly—behavior.) Such songs were extremely popular and widely published. Among the most famous is *Matona, mia cara* ("My Lady, My Beloved"), written by the Flemish composer Roland De Lassus (1532–94), a frequent guest in princely courts across Europe and known throughout Southern Europe as Orlando di Lasso (track **16.1**). Of his more than 2,000 compositions, nearly 200 were madrigals, and this one was written when he was only 18 years of age.

Based on a German soldier's song, it pokes fun at the heavy accent of a German mercenary trying to seduce a young woman in broken Italian. Translated into English, a rough equivalent of its opening line might read something like, "My leddy, my b'loved, I vant make song under vindow." Each verse ends in a group of nonsense syllables—"Dong, dong, dong, derry, derry, dong, dong, dong, dong"—which, depending on one's inclination and their context, might also be understood as sexually suggestive: "Lancer makes good companion, Dong, dong, dong. ..." When finally the German lancer pleads that he "knows no Petrarch," we understand that, in many ways, this madrigal is something of a spoof on the madrigal genre as a whole.

THE GERMAN TRADITION

How does Albrecht Dürer's work compare to that of Matthias Grünewald?

By 1500, cities in the German-speaking regions to the southeast of Flanders and in the Netherlands to the northeast had begun to grow rapidly. Many of the larger cities had doubled in size in the century after 1400. The population of Cologne, the largest city in Germany, was about 40,000, and Nuremberg, Strasbourg, Vienna, Prague, and Lübeck could all claim between 20,000 and 30,000 residents, which made them substantial centers of culture, though smaller than Florence, Paris, and London at about 100,000 inhabitants. In all these cities, an increasingly wealthy, self-made mercantile class supported the production of art. Caught between North and South, between the richly detailed and luminous oil painting of a van Eyck and the more linear, scientific, and Classically idealized style of a Raphael, German painters at the dawn of the sixteenth century exhibited instances of each.

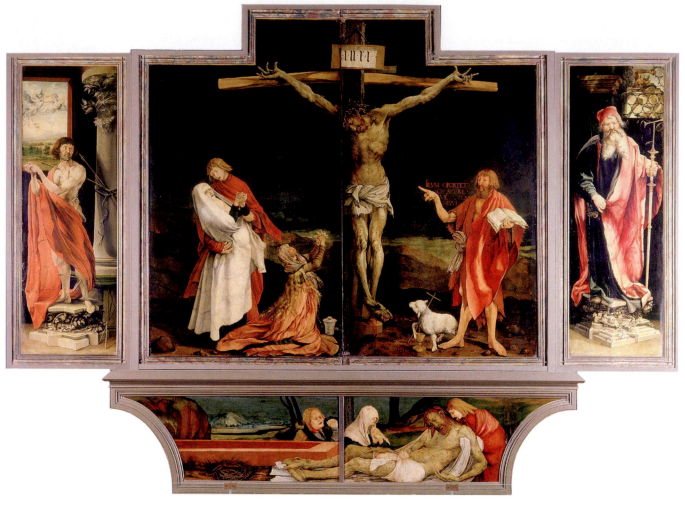

Fig. 16.13 **Matthias Grünewald,** *Isenheim Altarpiece,* **closed. ca. 1510–15. Main body,** *Crucifixion;* **base,** *Lamentation;* **side panels,** *Saint Sebastian* **(left) and** *Saint Anthony* **(right).** Oil on wood, center: 9′9½″ × 10′9″; each wing: 8′2½″ × 3½′; base: 2′5½″ × 11′2″. Musée d'Unterlinden, Colmar, France. Saint Sebastian appears in his role as protector from the plague. Saint Anthony, patron saint of the Isenheim hospital, stands before a window through which a demon, representing the plague, blows its evil breath. The altarpiece was designed to complement Saint Anthony's shrine.

Emotion and Christian Miracle:
The Art of Matthias Grünewald

The intensity of feeling and seriousness that we saw in the painting of van der Weyden and Bosch also appear in the work of Matthias Grünewald (ca. 1470–1528). Multitalented Grünewald served as architect, engineer, and painter to the court of the archbishops of Mainz. His most famous work is the so-called *Isenheim Altarpiece,* a monumentally large polyptych painted around 1510 to 1515 for the hospital of the Abbey of Saint Anthony, a facility in Isenheim, near Strasbourg, dedicated to the treatment of people with skin diseases. These included syphilis, leprosy, and ergotism, a gangrenous condition caused by eating grain contaminated with the ergot fungus. Physical illness was viewed as a function of spiritual illness, and so Grünewald's altarpiece, like Pope Innocent III's sermon *On the Misery of the Human Condition* of nearly 300 years earlier, was designed to move these sinners to repentance.

But it also reminded the patients at the Abbey that they were not alone in their suffering, that Christ had suffered like them.

The Crucifixion in the *Isenheim Altarpiece* is among the grimmest ever painted (Fig. **16.13**), Christ's flesh ripped and torn by thorns, more startlingly realistic in its detail than any Crucifixion ever painted in the South. His body seems emaciated, his ashen skin drawn tightly across his abdomen and rib cage. He hangs limply from the cross, which seems to bend under his weight, his hands splayed open, contorted by pain. His lips are blue, and, as if to emphasize Christ's morbidity, Grünewald's palette of purple-green and yellow-brown almost reeks of rotten flesh. All is darkness, echoing the account of the Crucifixion in the Gospel of Mark (15:33): "And when the sixth hour was come, there was darkness over the whole land until the ninth hour." Below, in the predella, or supporting base, of the altarpiece, a Lamentation shows Christ's body, stiff in rigor mortis, as it is settled into the tomb.

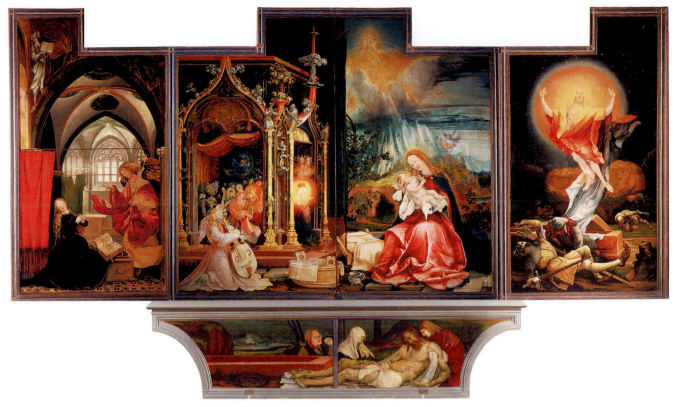

Fig. 16.14 Matthias Grünewald, *Isenheim Altarpiece*, first opening. ca. 1510–15. Left, *Annunciation*; middle, *Virgin and Child with Angels*; right, *Resurrection*. Oil on panel, center: 9′9½″ × 10′9″; each wing: 9′9½″ × 5′4½″. Musée d'Unterlinden, Colmar, France. In the left-hand panel, the gesture of the angel of the Annunciation as he points to Mary echoes the gesture of Saint John pointing to the crucified Christ in the closed altarpiece, underscoring the transformation of spirit between the closed and the open doors.

The altarpiece is composed of one set of fixed wings, two movable sets, and one set of sliding panels to cover the predella so that the altarpiece could be exhibited in different configurations. Hospital patients saw the horrifying realism of Grünewald's *Crucifixion* and *Lamentation* on the closed wings throughout the week, but on holy days and possibly Sundays, the altarpiece was opened to reveal, inside, brightly lit scenes of the *Annunciation*, the *Virgin and Child with Angels*, and the *Resurrection* (Fig. 16.14). In the *Annunciation* panel, the angel appears to Mary in a Gothic church. The Bible on her lap is open to Isaiah 11:1: "And there shall come forth a rod out of the stem of Jesse, and a Branch shall grow out of his roots." Above her, the dove of the Holy Spirit hovers on suspended wings and is bathed in a luminous light. In the central panel, Mary cares for the Christ Child in an array of detail that a patient at the hospital of the Abbey of Saint Anthony would recognize—torn linen rags for cleansing the skin, a bed, a tub, a towel, and even a chamber pot. In the *Resurrection* panel on the right, Christ soars up in an aureole of translucent light, the Roman soldiers blown to the ground as he explodes from the tomb. Christ's skin is now white and pure in contrast to the gangrenous green of the closed panel. So the promise of salvation—the Christian miracle—was always at least latent in the patient's mind, the glory and joy of the hereafter always imaginable behind the pain and suffering of the moment.

Grünewald's altarpiece underscores the Northern European preoccupation with death. In the face of recurring plagues ever since the Black Death of 1348, the fragility of life and the ultimate horror of death were constant thematic concerns. It is hardly surprising that among the most popular texts in Northern Europe was the *Art of Dying Well*. Although its origins are unclear, over 100 different versions appeared in several different languages between the 1460s and 1500. Grünewald's altarpiece is typical of Northern European art in its unswerving attention to the reality of death, represented in the minutest detail, but it is also uniquely German in its intense emotionalism and almost mystical sense of transcendence.

Women and Witchcraft

Grünewald's altarpiece captures the miracle of the Christian story as powerfully as any work of its age. Yet since the Middle Ages, other apparent miracles had occurred more routinely in secular society, and the Church could not tolerate them. Local legends had it that practicing miracle workers caused impotence, droughts, multiple births,

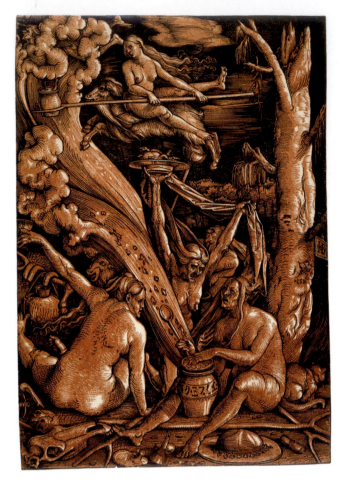

Fig. 16.15 Hans Baldung Grien, *Witches' Sabbath*. 1510. Chiaroscuro woodblock with orange tone block, 14¹⁵⁄₁₆″ × 10¼″. © The Trustees of the British Museum. Baldung's nickname, "Grien," or "Green," refers to his habit of wearing green when he worked as an apprentice to Dürer from 1503 to 1509.

most influential documents of the age was a guide on how to bring these laypeople to justice. The *Malleus Maleficarum* (*The Hammer of Witches*) was written chiefly by Heinrich Krämer, a German theologian driven to the task apparently by his extreme misogyny. In its own time, the *Malleus Maleficarum* was little respected. Nevertheless, the *Malleus* remained one of the few documents of its kind in print, and as witch trials erupted across Europe in the sixteenth century, it provided an important reference point for the civil courts charged with conducting the trials.

Hans Baldung's woodblock print *Witches' Sabbath* (Fig. **16.15**) of 1510 captures the essence of what the Church most feared. Here, beneath a dead tree hung with moss, the witches perform a black mass. One witch raises a lizard above her head in a mockery of the consecration of the Host, the moment in the celebration of the Catholic Mass when bread and wine are reputedly changed into the body and blood of Christ. Another witch rides backward on a goat (symbol of the devil) across the top of the print. The nudity of the figures suggests the sexual perversion of their activities. The print confirms the misogynistic thinking of Krämer's *Malleus*, where he answers the question, "Why is Superstition chiefly found in Women?" (see **Reading 16.2**):

READING 16.2

from Heinrich Krämer, *Malleus Maleficarum* (1486)

Now the wickedness of women is spoken of in Ecclesiastes xxv: There is no head above the head of a serpent: and there is no wrath above the wrath of a woman. I had rather dwell with a lion and a dragon than to keep house with a wicked woman. And among much which in that place precedes and follows about a wicked woman, he concludes: All wickedness is but little to the wickedness of a woman. Wherefore S. John Chrysostom says on the text, It is not good to marry (S. Matthew xix): What else is woman but a foe to friendship, an inescapable punishment, a necessary evil, a natural temptation, a desirable calamity, a domestic danger, a delectable detriment, an evil of nature, painted with fair colors! ... We may add to what has already been said the following: that since they are feebler both in mind and body, it is not surprising that women should come more under the spell of witchcraft. ... But the natural reason [why superstition is chiefly found in woman] is that she is more carnal than a man, as is clear from her many carnal abominations. And it should be noted that there was a defect in the formation of the first woman, since she was formed from a bent rib, that is, a rib of the breast, which is bent as it were in a contrary direction to a man. And since through this defect she is an imperfect animal, she always deceives.

and miraculous recovery from disease—anything that seemed unnatural. From 1400 to 1700, across Europe and especially in Germany, the threat of witchcraft seemed very real. In this time period, somewhere between 70,000 and 100,000 people were sentenced to death for the practice of "harmful magic," and 80 percent of the witchcraft trials over the three centuries were conducted against women. In village culture, people with apparently special gifts—the "cunning folk"—had traditionally been called upon during times of crisis: plague, drought, or personal problems, such as disability and the inability to conceive. These "cunning folk" were often single women and widows who also functioned as midwives and were almost totally estranged from the community financially. Through the practice of their putative magical powers, they achieved, on the other hand, a certain real status in the community.

Although the Church also believed its clergy to possess magical powers—the exorcism of demons, for instance—it attacked the practice of magic by laypeople based on what it considered to be a legitimate fear of the devil. One of the

In its extreme misogyny, the *Malleus* does not accurately represent the feelings of the age. But it does reveal a side of European thought, and a tradition in the Church, which had subjected women to secondary status for centuries. The rhetoric of the *Malleus* demonstrates the most virulent strain of the thinking that would cause Lucretia Marinella, for instance, to write her *Nobility and Excellence of Women and the Defects and Vices of Men* (see Reading 15.5 in Chapter 15).

Northern Detail Meets Southern Humanism: The Art of Albrecht Dürer

Born in 1471 in the city of Nuremberg, Albrecht Dürer represents a trend in German culture distinct from the emotionalism and mysticism of Grünewald or the superstition and misogyny of Krämer, one based on humanism. By his death in 1528, he had become one of the leading painters of the Renaissance, successfully wedding his German-Netherlandish Gothic heritage with the Renaissance interest in perspective, empirical observation, and rules of ideal beauty for representing the human figure.

Dürer's landscape studies, such as *The Large Turf* (Fig. **16.16**), display his Northern interest in the minutest details of nature but also his scientific mind, and his humanist interest in the phenomena of the natural world. This he shared with Leonardo da Vinci. In fact, after visiting Italy in 1505 to 1506 to learn the laws of scientific perspective from the Italian masters, Dürer was determined to introduce a more scientific approach to painting to Germany. To do so, he published theoretical treatises on drawing, perspective, proportion, measurement, and the techniques of painting.

The *Draftsman Drawing a Reclining Nude* (Fig. **16.17**), from one of these treatises, is an example of Dürer's attempt to marry the detailed textural

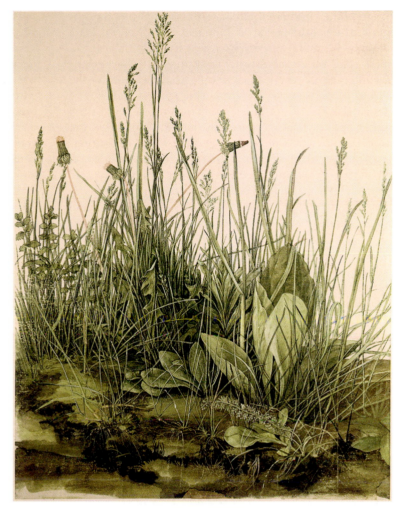

Fig. 16.16 Albrecht Dürer, *The Large Turf*. 1503. Watercolor, 16¼″ × 12⅛″. Albertina, Vienna. Dürer's interest in nature reached a scientific dimension, demonstrated here.

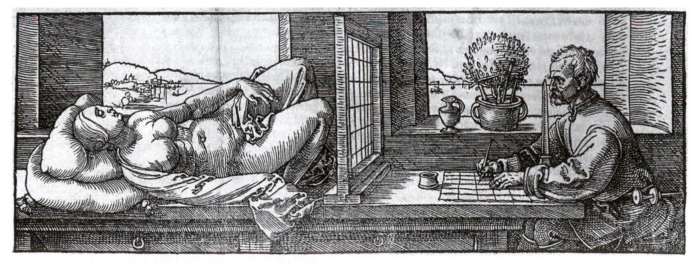

Fig. 16.17 Albrecht Dürer, *Draftsman Drawing a Reclining Nude*. ca. 1525. Woodcut, second edition, 3″ × 8½″. One of 138 woodcuts and diagrams in *Teaching of Measurement with Compass and Ruler*. The artist looks at his foreshortened model through a grid from a fixed point and then transfers what he sees to a similarly gridded paper. This gives him an accurate representation of the figure in foreshortened perspective.

vision of the Northern tradition with the scientific human-ism of the South. The artist's model here is frankly, even shockingly, nude—especially given the artist's point of view—and yet he subjects her to an intensely mathematical and rational regime. Functioning as a metaphor for the ability of the artist to subject nature to the discipline of his gaze is a series of tensions: between the grid of the screen and the paper; between the curvilinear folds of the model's body and the drapery; and between "measuring" the world and submitting to the feelings that the world might provoke. Dürer presents the artist as a disinterested observer. His imagination is moved by the objective recording of reality, not by the subjective feelings the model might inspire in him. And, like Johannes Stradanus's vision of *Jan van Eyck's Studio* (see Fig. 16.2), this print is a look into the artist's private world, a revelation of his technical means. These feelings—his love for his craft and his passion for his art—may actually be the real subject of the illustration.

Like other Northern artists, Dürer was a master of oil painting. *Self-Portrait* of 1500 (Fig. **16.18**) takes full advantage of its oil medium to create a highly textured surface that glows with a light that seems to emanate from within the artist himself. Acknowledging his own skill with oil colors, Dürer inscribed the painting as follows: "Thus I, Albrecht Dürer from Nuremburg, painted myself with undying colors at the age of 28 years." The intimation of artistic immortality embodied in the word "undying" is underscored in the way that Dürer self-consciously paints himself as a sort of icon. His frontal pose, bearded face, and intense gaze recall traditional images of Christ. At the very least, he means for us to see in his face evidence of divine inspiration. "Art," he would write, "derives from God; it is God who has created all art; it is not easy to paint artistically. Therefore, those without aptitude should not attempt it, for it is an inspiration from above." For Dürer, creating art was a sacred act; it made manifest God's work, from the Creation to Christ's Passion.

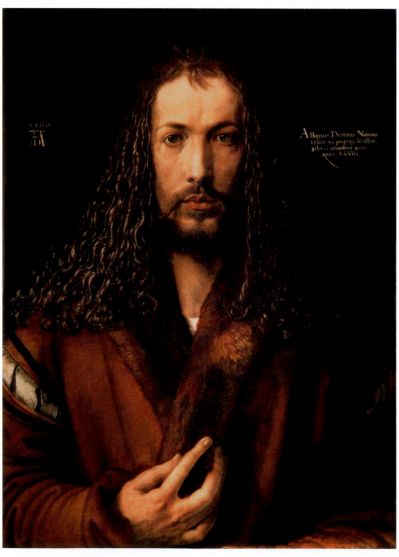

Fig. 16.18 Albrecht Dürer, *Self-Portrait*. 1500. Oil on panel, 26¼″ × 19¼″. Alte Pinakothek, Munich. Dürer's skill as a portraitist is embodied in the story that his dog once barked and wagged its tail at one of his self-portraits. We cannot vouch for the accuracy of the story.

The Modern Devotion and a New Austerity in Art

In 1517, the events of history would overtake Dürer and his art. In fact, they would overtake all artistic and cultural production in Europe, changing the course of the arts forever. The person responsible for this extraordinary change was Martin Luther, a German monk and humanist scholar bent on religious reform. The technology responsible was the printing press, which gave Luther the means to transmit his radical ideas across Europe.

Luther's Protestant Reformation (see Chapter 17), as it came to be called, was the result of a century-long reexamination of the role of the Church in daily life. Throughout the fifteenth century in Northern Europe, a new religious movement, known as the "modern devotion," had taken hold in city after city. Lay citizens gathered in houses organized to promote a lifestyle similar to that of monks and nuns, though they stopped short of taking monastic vows. These Brothers and Sisters of the Common Life, as they came to be known, tried to bring the message of Jesus into daily practice. But the life of austerity and simplicity that such popular religious movements promoted clashed sharply with the prosperity and material pleasures of the Northern mercantile class.

The values of the modern devotion clashed even more dramatically with the extravagance and corruption of the Church in Rome. One of the most vigorous opponents of Church excesses was Desiderius Erasmus (ca. 1466–1536). Like Luther, Erasmus was a monk and humanist scholar, but he had been raised in Rotterdam among the Brothers of the Common Life. By his mid-thirties, he had become one of Europe's most sought-after educators (see Chapter 17). He was also the first humanist to take advantage of the printing press, as the books that dominate the foreground of Dürer's engraved portrait of him (Fig. **16.19**) suggest.

Although a strident critic of the papacy, Erasmus remained committed to the Church throughout his life. He also remained committed to beauty, as the flowers in the vase on his desk in the Dürer portrait affirm. In fact, Erasmus greatly admired Dürer's art, especially his printmaking ability. According to Erasmus, Dürer could accomplish with line alone what the Greek painter Apelles could manage only with the addition of color. But in the sixteenth century, in the North, Erasmus's tolerance,

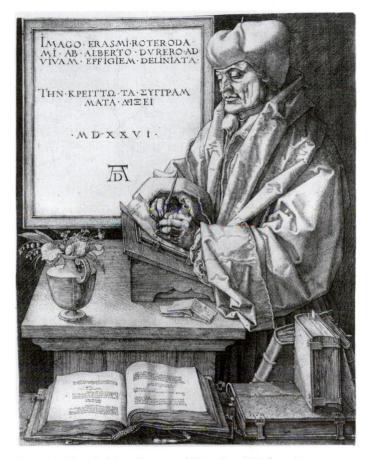

Fig. 16.19 Albrecht Dürer, *Erasmus of Rotterdam*. 1526. Engraving, 9¾" × 7½". © The Trustees of the British Museum. The Latin inscription on the wall behind Erasmus reads: "This image of Erasmus of Rotterdam was drawn from life by Albrecht Dürer." The Greek inscription below reads: "The better image will reveal his writings," suggesting that Dürer understands that his art can never reflect the intellectual scope of Erasmus's writings. The combination of both Latin and Greek inscriptions is symbolic of Erasmus's— and Dürer's—humanism.

even love, of art and beauty would be challenged by a new iconoclasm, inspired by the Protestant Reformation. This movement would see, in the lavish decoration of the Vatican, the very image of corruption in the Church as a whole. ∎

16.1 Explain the effect of commerce and mercantile wealth on the development of both religious and secular painting in Northern Europe.

The center of commercial activity in Flanders by the beginning of the fifteenth century was Bruges. Each year, it sponsored a great fair where luxury art goods, especially tapestries and paintings, were sold to a rising merchant class, for both local consumption and export. Flemish painters took oil painting to new heights. Often, the objects depicted in these paintings seem so real that the viewer might actually touch them. What effects does oil painting make possible in altarpieces? How do these effects contribute to the presentation of the Christian story, and in more secular works, such as van Eyck's portrait of Giovanni Arnolfini and his wife, to the symbolic complexity of the work? How do these effects contribute, less optimistically, to Bosch's work, especially the conversation piece, the *Garden of Earthly Delights*?

16.2 Describe the tension between financial wealth and ethical behavior, as reflected in literature, music, and dance.

The sister of the French king, Marguerite de Navarre, governed France while her brother was a prisoner of the Holy Roman Emperor. A woman of refined sensibilities, she also wrote a collection of insightful stories modeled after Boccaccio's *Decameron*. What does Marguerite de Navarre's *Heptameron* share with the paintings of Hieronymus Bosch? What does the work reveal about the moral and ethical climate of the period?

Tapestries were an especially important Flemish art form that often imitated the realism of Flemish painting. What accounts for the popularity of tapestries? Also extremely popular were Morris dances, which were performed to flute and drum music at carnivals and festivals and as interludes at more formal affairs. How are the Morris dance's sensibilities reflected in Northern European madrigals, especially in the subgenre of the villanella?

16.3 Compare and contrast the mysticism of Germans such as Grünewald and the new style of art introduced by Dürer.

Matthias Grünewald's *Isenheim Altarpiece* is grimly realistic in its portrayal of death, and yet transcendently emotional. How does his work compare to that of the Flemish painters? How does mysticism inform German art and literature? Perhaps the most interesting development in Germany is Nuremburg artist Albrecht Dürer's attempt to synthesize the Northern interest in detailed representation with the traditions of Italian humanism he had assimilated on his visit there in 1505 to 1506. How does this synthesis manifest itself in his art?

✔ **Study** and **review** on **MyArtsLab**

READINGS

READING 16.1

from Marguerite de Navarre, *Heptameron*, Story 55 (1558)

The *Heptameron* is a prose fiction work published after Marguerite de Navarre's death and modeled on Boccaccio's *Decameron* (see Chapter 13). It consists of 72 tales, many of which convey the hostility and dismay of their narrators about the state of the Catholic Church, most specifically the decadent behavior of priests and monks, whose actions are described in the most vivid terms, and unfortunate Christians who believe in the efficacy of good works. The fifty-fifth tale, which follows, is one of these.

Story 55

In the town of Saragossa there was a rich merchant. Seeing that his death was near, and that he could not take his wealth with him—wealth which perhaps he had not acquired altogether honestly—he thought that he might make some amends for his sins by making some little donation or other to God. As if God grants his grace in return for money! Anyway, he made arrangements regarding his house, and gave instructions that a fine Spanish horse of his should be sold, and the proceeds distributed to the poor mendicants. It was his wife whom he requested to carry out these instructions as soon as possible after his death. No sooner was the burial over and the first few tears shed, than the wife, who to say the least was no more stupid than Spanish women in general, approached her servant, who had also heard her husband's wishes.

"I think I've lost enough," said she, "in losing my husband whom I loved so dearly, without losing his property as well. Not that I want to disobey his instructions. In fact, I want to carry out his wishes even better than he intended. You see, the poor man was so taken in by those greedy priests. He thought he would make a sacrifice to God after his death by giving away a sum of money, not a single écu of which he would have given away during his lifetime, however great the need, as you know. So I've made up my mind that we shall do what he instructed us to do after his death—indeed we shall do better, and do what he *would* have done himself, had he lived a fortnight longer. Only not a soul must hear of it!"

The servant gave his word, and she went on: "You will go and sell his horse, and when they ask you how much you want, you will say one ducat. But I also have an excellent cat that I want to sell, and you will sell it at the same time, for ninety-nine ducats. Together the horse and the cat will fetch a hundred ducats, which is what my husband wanted for the horse alone."

So the servant promptly went off to do as his mistress requested. As he was leading the horse across the square, carrying the cat in his arms, he was approached by a certain nobleman who had seen the horse before and was interested in acquiring it. Having asked the price, the nobleman received the answer: "One ducat!"

"I should be obliged if you would be serious," said the man.

"I assure you, Monsieur, that the price is one ducat. ... I can't let the cat go for less than ninety-nine ducats!"

The nobleman thought this was a fair enough bargain. On the spot he paid one ducat for the horse, and ninety-nine for the cat, as requested, and led his purchases away. The servant took the money back to his mistress, who was extremely pleased, and lost no time in giving away the proceeds from the sale of the horse to the poor mendicants. As for the rest, that went to provide for the wants of herself and her children.

"Well, what do you think of her? Wasn't she wiser than her husband, and wasn't she just as much concerned about his conscience as she was about doing well for her family?"

"I think she loved her husband," said Parlamente, "but realized that most men's minds wander when they're on their deathbeds, and knowing what his real intention was, she wanted to interpret his wishes for the benefit of their children, and I think it was very wise of her to do so."

"What!" exclaimed Geburon. "Do you not think it a grave error to fail to execute the last will and testament of deceased friends?"

"Indeed I do!" replied Parlamente. "Provided the testator is sound of mind and not deranged."

"Do you call it deranged," replied Geburon, "to give away one's goods to the Church and to the poor mendicants?"

"I do not call it deranged," she replied, "if a man distributes to the poor that which God has placed within his power. But to give away as alms what belongs to other people—I do not think that shows great wisdom. It's all too common to see the world's greatest usurers putting up ornate and impressive chapels, in the hope of appeasing God for hundreds of thousands of ducats' worth of sheer robbery by spending ten thousand ducats on a building! As if God didn't know how to count!"

"Indeed, I am frequently astonished," said Oisille, "that they presume to be able to appease God by means of the very things, which, when He came to earth, He condemned—things such as fine buildings, gilded ornaments, decorations and paintings. But, if they had rightly understood what God has said of human offerings in a certain passage—that 'the sacrifice of God is a troubled spirit: a broken and contrite heart, O God, shalt thou not despise'—and again, in another passage, what Saint Paul has said—that 'ye are the temple of the living God, in which He will dwell'—if they had rightly heard these words, I say, they would have taken pains to adorn their conscience while they were yet alive. They would not have waited till a time when man can do neither good nor evil. Nor would they have done what is even worse and placed upon those who remain the burden of dispensing their alms to those upon whom, during their lifetime, they did not even deign to look. But He who reads men's hearts will not be deceived, and He will judge them not only according to their works, but according to the faith and charity that they have shown towards Him."

"Why is it, then," said Geburon, "that the Franciscans and Mendicants talk of nothing else when a man's dying but of how we ought to make bequests to their monasteries, with the assurance that they will send us to Paradise whether we want or not?"

"What, Geburon!" broke in Hircan. "Have you forgotten your story about the Franciscans, that you're asking how men like that can possibly lie? I'll tell you, as far as I'm concerned, there's no one on this earth tells lies like they do. It may be that those who speak for the good of their community as a whole aren't to be criticized; but there are some who forget their vow of poverty in order to satisfy their own greed."

READING CRITICALLY

How might the reader understand, even justify in humanist terms, the Spanish wife's actions?

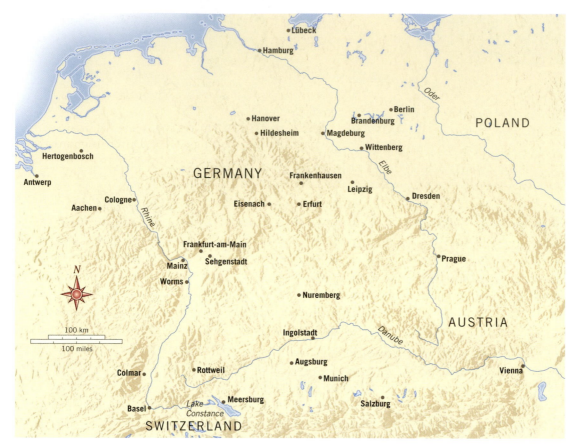

Map 17.1 Germany during the Reformation. ca. 1517.

They jailed Pope Clement VII (Giulio de' Medici) and forced him to pay a large ransom for his release. And if the Christian world had been torn asunder by those events, it was even more threatened by the challenge of Martin Luther (1483–1546), a rogue priest from Wittenberg, Germany, far to the north on the Elbe River (Map 17.1), who on October 31, 1517, had posted *Ninety-Five Theses* on the door of the town's All Saints Church. The door served as a sort of kiosk for university-related announcements, and since Luther was a professor of theology at the university, it seemed the proper forum to announce the terms of his protest against the practices of the Catholic Church. His aim was to reform the Church, and by 1529, his movement had become known as the Protestant Reformation. As Altdorfer worked on his painting, the Church seemed to be threatened from both within and without. From Luther's point of view, the Sack of Rome signaled the bankruptcy of the Church and God's displeasure with it. From the Catholic point of view, Luther's challenge to papal authority signaled the disintegration of belief that presaged the Second Coming and the Day of Judgment (when, they were sure, the likes of Luther would be sent directly to hell). But equally, for both, the Apocalypse seemed at hand.

Apocalyptic fervor had swept Europe since the late fifteenth century. Seizing on this widespread fear, in 1498, Albrecht Dürer executed a series of prints illustrating the Apocalypse and, in *The Four Horsemen of the Apocalypse*, its chief signs—pestilence, war, famine, and death (Fig. 17.2). The prints were reproduced by the thousands and distributed across Germany and the rest of Europe, effectively securing Dürer's income for life. By the mid-1520s, as the Turks pressed on Vienna, even Martin Luther saw their invasion as a sign that the Apocalypse was at hand. In a treatise entitled *On the War Against the Turks*, he wrote that they were "the rod of God's wrath" by which "God is punishing the world." Their war, he said, "is nothing but murder and bloodshed ... a tool of the devil himself." From his point of view, the only thing a Christian could do was repent and prepare for the end.

This chapter outlines the causes of Luther's Reformation and its impact on political, social, and cultural life in sixteenth-century Germany and France. As if Luther's theses were a giant stone of questioning dropped into the pool of European faith, his message quickly spread in waves from its center in Wittenberg to other countries across Northern Europe. Luther's message had broad appeal, largely because he understood the need to address ordinary people. By successfully communicating with this wider audience, he could be said to have changed the humanist enterprise forever. Although late medieval writers like Boccaccio, Dante, and Chaucer had created a vernacular literature (see Chapter 13), Luther permanently transformed the nature of learning by translating the Latin Bible into vernacular German

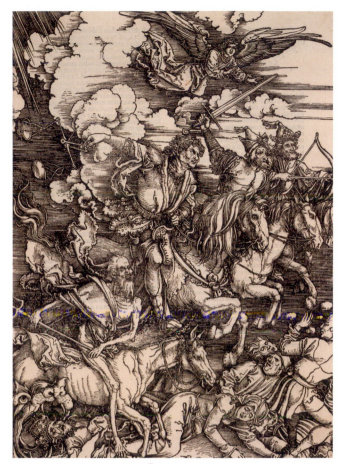

Fig. 17.2 Albrecht Dürer, *The Four Horsemen of the Apocalypse*. 1498. Woodcut, 15½" × 11⅛". Yale University Art Gallery. Library Transfer, Gift of Paul Mellon, B.A. 1929, L.H.D.H. 1967. 1956.16.3e. Dürer represents eight verses of Saint John's vision in the Book of Revelation (6:1–8). The rider with a bow represents pestilence. Next to him, raising his sword, is war. The third rider, with the empty scales, is famine. In the foreground rides Death, sweeping a king and his people backward into the jaws of Hades (at the bottom left).

and writing hymns that could be sung by the entire congregation. He also arranged for his community to provide for those in need. These accomplishments undermined the traditional authority of the Church, just as they undermined the authority of the Catholic nobility. Other Church leaders soon took up the reformist cause, often resulting in strife.

What probably contributed most to the spread of Luther's ideas was the printing press. Far faster and cheaper than hand-lettering, printing books could put written ideas into the hands of many more people. Ordinary citizens now could own their own Bibles, which previously had been available only in churches and monasteries, and they could interpret scripture for themselves. New humanist writers, often sympathetic to reformist goals, could publish and rapidly distribute their own ideas. Printmaking also made imagery, another transmitter of reformist ideals, widely available. And artists, responding to the distaste of many Protestant reformers for religious imagery, increasingly turned their attention to nonreligious subject matter.

ERASMUS, LUTHER, AND THE REFORMATION

How did Erasmus and Luther seek to reform the Roman Catholic Church?

Luther's own antipapal feelings were inspired, at least in part, by his reading of the Dutch humanist and scholar Desiderius Erasmus, whose 1516 translation of the Greek New Testament into Latin especially impressed the young Augustinian monk (see Chapter 16, *Continuity & Change*, page 565). Luther's early teachers, like those of Erasmus, were all Augustinians, so he was predisposed to be impressed by Erasmus's attack on the corruption of the clergy.

The Satires of Erasmus

Erasmus's chief tool was satire. **Satire** is a literary genre designed to convey the contradictions between real and ideal situations. It had lain dormant in Western culture since Greek and Roman times when such writers as Aristophanes, in his comedies, and Horace and Juvenal, in their poems and essays, used it to critique the cultures of their own day. Humanist scholars like Erasmus and More, thoroughly acquainted with these Classical sources, reinvigorated the genre.

Luther was also impressed by Erasmus's anonymously published attack on Pope Julius II in *Julius Excluded from Heaven* (1513). In this satiric dialogue, Saint Peter and the pope encounter each other at the doors to paradise (**Reading 17.1**):

READING 17.1

from Desiderius Erasmus, *Julius Excluded from Heaven* (1513)

PETER: Immortal God, what a sewer I smell here! Who are you?

JULIUS: ... so you'll know what sort of prince you insult, listen up. ... Even though I supported such a great army, celebrated so many splendid triumphs, erected buildings in so many places, still, when I died I left five million ducats. ...

PETER: Madman! ... all I hear about is a leader not of the church but of this world. ...

JULIUS: Perhaps you are still dreaming of that old church. ... What if you could see today so many sacred buildings erected by kingly wealth, so many thousands of priests everywhere (many of them very rich), so many bishops equal to the greatest kings in military power and in wealth, so many splendid palaces belonging to priests. ... What would you say?

PETER: That I was looking at a tyrant worse than worldly, an enemy of Christ, the bane of the church.

Julius believes that his "good works"—his military victories, his public projects, even the wealth he has brought to the Church—are going to get him admitted to paradise. Saint Peter—and, of course, Erasmus and Luther—believed otherwise. (Although extremely critical of the Church, Erasmus would remain a Catholic to the end of his life.)

Erasmus wrote his most famous satire, *In Praise of Folly*, while living in the home of his friend the English humanist, philosopher and statesman Thomas More (1478–1535) in London (the work's Latin title, *Encomium Moriae*, is a pun that can also be translated "In Praise of More"). Like the later tract, *Julius Excluded from Heaven*, the work, an attack upon the vices and follies of contemporary society, went through more than two dozen editions in Erasmus's lifetime.

In Praise of Folly helped to secure Erasmus's reputation as the preeminent humanist in Europe and was his most influential work. It is written in the voice, or persona, of an allegorical figure named Folly (*Moria*). She is a fool, and plays the fool. Thus, in the work's opening pages, she addresses her readers as follows, pleading for her reputation by noting how pervasive in human behavior is her rule (**Reading 17.2a**):

READING 17.2a

from Desiderius Erasmus, *In Praise of Folly* (1509)

[T]ell me whether fools … are not infinitely more free and happy than yourselves? Add to this, that fools do not barely laugh, and sing, and play the good-fellow alone to themselves: but … impart their mirth to others, by making sport for the whole company they are at any time engaged in, as if providence purposely designed them for an antidote to melancholy: whereby they make all persons so fond of their society, that they are welcomed to all places, hugged, caressed, and defended, a liberty given them of saying or doing anything; so well beloved, that none dares to offer them the least injury; nay, the most ravenous beasts of prey will pass them by untouched, as if by instinct they were warned that such innocence ought to receive no hurt.

Through the device of Folly, therefore, Erasmus is free to say anything he pleases, and, as Folly reminds us, "It is one further very commendable property of fools, that they always speak the truth." Erasmus spares virtually no one among Folly's "regiment of fools," least of all theologians and Church officials. He attacks, especially, those who "maintain the cheat of pardons and indulgences"—a sentiment that would deeply influence Martin Luther (**Reading 17.2b**):

📖 **Read** the document related to Martin Luther on **MyArtsLab**

READING 17.2b

from Desiderius Erasmus, *In Praise of Folly* (1509)

By this easy way of purchasing pardons, any notorious highwayman, any plundering soldier, or any bribe-taking judge, shall disburse some part of their unjust gains, and so think all their grossest impieties sufficiently atoned for; so many perjuries, lusts, drunkenness, quarrels, blood-sheds, cheats, treacheries, and all sorts of debaucheries, shall all be, as it were, struck a bargain for, and such a contract made, as if they had paid off all arrears, and might now begin upon a new score.

The rhetorical power of such verbal abuse accounts for much of the appeal of Erasmus's prose. So too does his sense of **irony**, his ability to say one thing explicitly but implicitly mean another—to speak with "tongue in cheek." Irony

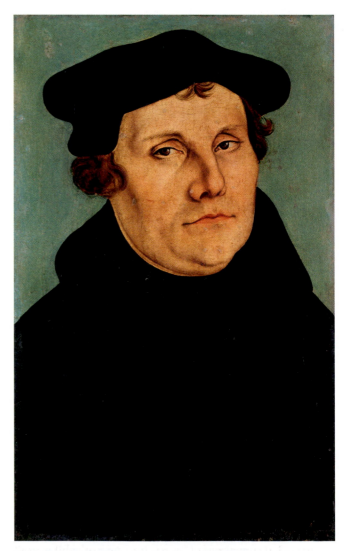

Fig. 17.3 Lucas Cranach, *Martin Luther*. ca. 1526. Oil on panel, 15" × 9". Galleria degli Uffizi, Florence. A remarkable aspect of this painting is Luther's sideways glance, which suggests a personality capable of concentrating on more than one thing at once.

is, in fact, one of the chief tools of satire, and is embodied in the very title of Erasmus's work. *In Praise of Folly* is, of course, a *condemnation* of human folly.

Martin Luther's Reformation

The satire of Erasmus was rather too lighthearted for Luther himself. If he and Erasmus recognized the same problems with the Church, they were too serious, from Luther's point of view, to be dismissed as mere "folly." Even a cursory comparison of Luther's demeanor in Lucas Cranach's portrait of the Wittenberg professor (Fig. **17.3**) and the expression of Erasmus in Dürer's portrait of the Dutch humanist (see Fig. 16.19 in Chapter 16), executed at approximately the same time, reveals their difference in temperament.

Luther's own early years in the Church underscore how seriously he took his calling. He had entered the Order of the Hermits of Saint Augustine in Erfurt, in 1505, at the age of 22. This decision was apparently motivated by an oath he had taken when, in a severe lightning storm, he had promised to become a monk if he survived the storm. By 1511, he had moved to the Augustinian monastery in Wittenberg, earning a doctorate in theology in 1512. In the winter semester of 1513 to 1514, he began lecturing at the university there. His primary subject was the Bible.

In the preface to the complete edition of his writings, published just a year before his death, Luther recalled the crisis in belief that preoccupied him between 1513 and 1517 (**Reading 17.3**):

This was the source of Luther's frustration, even anger. God, Luther was certain, accepts all believers *in spite of*, not because of, what they do. The Bible, he argued, rejects "the wicked idea of the entire kingdom of the pope, the teaching that a Christian man must be uncertain of the grace of God toward him. If this opinion stands, then Christ is completely useless. … Therefore the papacy is a veritable torture chamber of consciences and the very kingdom of the devil." From Luther's point of view, Christ had already atoned for humankind's sins—what was the point of his sacrifice?—and he provided the faithful with the certainty of their salvation. So Luther began to preach the doctrine of salvation by faith rather than by works.

Like both Dante and Chaucer before him, Luther was particularly bothered by the concept of **indulgences**, remissions of penalties to be suffered in purgatory. Theoretically, indulgences pave the way to heaven for any sinner, and given the apocalyptic fervor of the day, they were especially popular. Luther's specific target was Johannes Tetzel, a Dominican monk notorious as a traveling seller of indulgences (Fig. **17.4**). Tetzel had been jointly hired by Archbishop Albrecht of Mainz and Pope Leo X to raise money to cover the archbishop's debts and to fund Leo's rebuilding of Saint Peter's in Rome. The sale of indulgences supported these projects.

In general terms, Luther detested both the secular or materialist spirit evident in Church patronage of lavish decorative programs and the moral laxity of its cardinals in Rome. He longed for the Church to return to the spiritual

---

READING 17.3

from Martin Luther, Preface to *Works* (1545)

Though I lived as a monk without reproach, I felt that I was a sinner before God with an extremely disturbed conscience. … I was angry with God, and said, "As if, indeed, it is not enough, that miserable sinners, eternally lost through original sin, are crushed by every kind of calamity … without having God by the gospel threatening us with his righteousness and wrath!" Thus I raged with a fierce and troubled conscience. …

At last, by the mercy of God, meditating day and night, I gave heed to the context of the words, namely, "In it the righteousness of God is revealed, as it is written, 'He who through faith is righteous shall live'" [Romans 1:17]. There I began to understand that the righteousness of God is that by which the righteous [person] lives by a gift of God, namely by faith. … Here I felt that I was altogether born again and had entered paradise itself through open gates.

Luther's thinking amounts to an almost total rejection of traditional Church doctrine. He argued that the moral virtue that God commands of humanity does not exhibit itself in good deeds or works—in commissioning an altarpiece, for instance—for if this were true, people could never know if they had done enough good works to merit salvation.

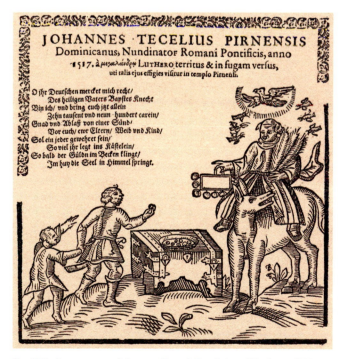

Fig. 17.4 Anonymous, *Johannes Tetzel, Dominican Monk*. ca. 1517. The last lines of the poem at the top of this contemporary caricature read: "As soon as the coin in the basin rings, Hurray the soul into heaven springs."

ways of the early Church and to back away from the power and wealth that were corrupting it. In particular, Luther found the practice of selling indulgences to be contradictory to scripture. In the *Ninety-Five Theses*, which he nailed to the church door at Wittenberg on October 31, 1517, he wrote: "Those who believe that, through letters of pardon, they are made sure of their own salvation will be eternally damned along with their teachers" (thirty-second thesis). More to the point, he wrote in the eighty-sixth thesis: "Why does not the Pope, whose riches are at this day more ample than those of the wealthiest of the wealthy, build the single Basilica of Saint Peter with his own money rather that with that of poor believers?" (See **Reading 17.4**, page 593, for more selections from the *Ninety-Five Theses*.)

At the heart of his opposition, in fact, was class division. Only the rich could afford to pay for the remission of their sins and those of their families. If the poor did buy them, they did so at great sacrifice to the well-being of their families. Then they had to watch the proceeds from the practice build the most extravagant, even profligate of projects in Rome. Such injustice and inequity fueled Luther's rage.

Church Reaction to the *Ninety-Five Theses*

The Church initially reacted to Luther's *Theses* by turning the case over to a Dominican theologian named Prierias (1456–1527), who responded in 1518 with a *Dialogue Against the Arrogant Theses of Martin Luther Concerning the Power of the Pope*. Luther considered his *Theses* more the exercise of an academic freedom—the right of a member of the university faculty to offer theses for acceptance or refutation. And if he was impressed by the ferocity of Prierias's response, he was not by its intelligence: "I thought, 'Good God, has it come to this that the matter will go before the pope?' However, our Lord God was gracious to me, and the stupid dolt wrote such wretched stuff that I had to laugh. Since then I've never been frightened."

On August 7, 1518, Luther was summoned to appear in Rome within 60 days to answer a charge of heresy. Frederick the Wise, the founder and patron of the University of Wittenberg, intervened. He had conferred with Erasmus about the publication of the *Theses*, and Erasmus had admiringly replied: "He has committed a great sin—he has hit the monks in their belly and the Pope in his crown!" Frederick understood the importance of the reforms Luther was advocating, and he arranged for Luther to face charges on neutral ground in what is now the Bavarian city of Augsburg. But Luther infuriated his inquisitor, refused to recant, and barely escaped being seized and sent to Rome in chains.

This experience did not cow Luther. In June 1519, in Leipzig, he entered into a debate with Professor Johann Eck of the University of Ingolstadt. In the course of the disputations, which were attended by armed students from both universities, Luther not only challenged the authority of the pope, arguing that both the pope and his councils could and did err, but also claimed, for the first time, that scripture, and scripture alone, held sole authority in all matters

of faith. Within a few months, he had published three pamphlets that sealed his fate. In the first, *The Address to the Christian Nobility of the German Nation*, he urged the German princes to reform the Roman Church and curtail its political and economic activities in Germany. In the second, *The Babylonian Captivity of the Church*, he argued that only two of the seven sacraments—Baptism and the Eucharist—were proper. And in the third, *The Freedom of a Christian*, he argued for salvation by force of faith alone.

Luther's friend, the artist Lucas Cranach the Elder (1472–1553), illustrated this last principle in a woodcut executed around 1530 (Fig. **17.5**). Through the device of a half-living, half-dead tree, Cranach shows the difference between Catholic dependency on good works and Protestant reliance on grace or faith. On the dead side of the tree, a poor sinner is condemned to hell quite simply because, as a descendent of Adam and Eve (at the back), he will inevitably fail to conform to God's Law, as represented by the tablets of Moses, held up to him by the figure just to the left of the tree. On the live side of the tree, Christ freely sacrifices himself and rises anew from the tomb, stepping on Death and the Devil as he does so. In the background, angels announce Christ's birth to the shepherds, while a sinner, bathed in the freely shed blood of Christ, is saved not by what he has done on earth, but by his very belief.

On January 3, 1521, the Church excommunicated Luther for the beliefs he had set forth in his writings. In April, at the Diet of Worms (a city on the Rhine in southwest Germany), the newly elected emperor Charles V ordered Luther to recant. (A *Diet* is a formal assembly called to discuss state affairs.) But Luther, who on his way to Worms had been greeted by cheering mobs in town after town, unhesitatingly refused, indicating that to do otherwise would violate scripture, reason, and his own conscience. Finally, on May 26, 1521, Luther and all his followers, known as Lutherans, were outlawed. All his writings were declared heretical and ordered burned. By 1526, menaced by threats from France and Turkey, and in order to keep peace at home, the emperor granted each German territory and city discretion in choosing whether to follow Luther's example. However, three years later, he rescinded the order, resulting in 18 German states signing a *protestatio*, the act of protest that actually gave rise to the term *Protestant*.

Luther's Popular Appeal: The Vernacular Bible

Excommunicated, his life in danger, Luther took refuge in Frederick's Wartburg Castle, in central Germany, where he spent the next year disguised as a knight. The desperate nature of his situation was mitigated by the broad base of his growing popular support.

At Wartburg, Luther occupied himself with translating Erasmus's New Testament Bible from Latin into vernacular German, "not word for word but sense for sense," as he put it. His object was to make the Bible available to ordinary people, in the language they spoke on the street, so that

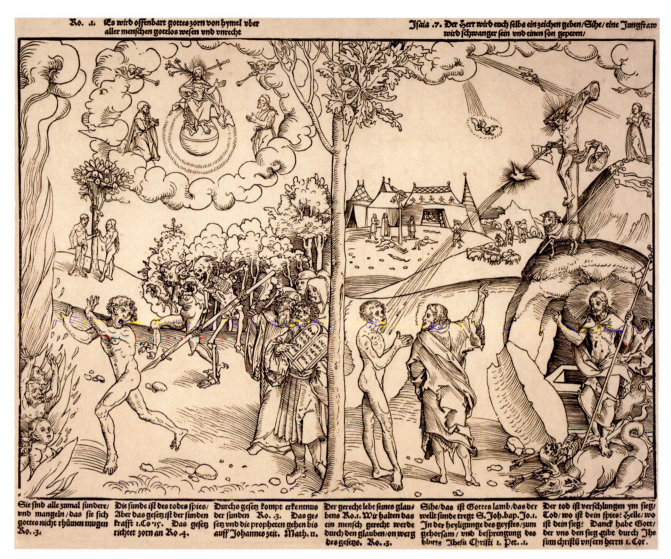

they could meditate for themselves on its meanings without the intervention of a priest. No longer would the Catholic Church be the sole authority of biblical interpretation.

Soon after his return to Wittenberg in September 1522, his popularity helping to assure his safety, Luther's vernacular New Testament was published. The entire printing of 3,000 copies sold out within three months, and a second printing quickly followed. Considering that the entire population of Wittenberg was only 2,500, the sellout of the first printing was astonishing.

Reformation Music: The Chorale

Luther also sought to reform Church liturgy, especially the use of music in the church service. He was a trained musician and understood the power of a hymn sung in the vernacular by the entire congregation, a form known as the **chorale**, rather than in Latin by a chorus of monks separated from the worshipers. While he did not invent

the chorale form, between 1524 and 1545, he composed and compiled nine hymnals, consisting of Latin hymns, popular religious songs, and secular tunes recast with religious lyrics. The most famous of Luther's chorales is *Ein feste Burg ist unser Gott* ("A Mighty Fortress Is Our God") (track **17.1**), still widely sung today. Luther probably wrote the melody, and he adopted the text from Psalm 46 ("God is our refuge and our strength …"). When sung in unison by all the voices in the congregation, it embodies Luther's sense that "next to the Word of God, music deserves the highest praise."

Although many later Protestants insisted on unison—that is, monophonic—chorales, and some even banned music altogether on the grounds that it was a needless sensual adornment to God's word, Luther consistently praised music and even embraced polyphonic musical settings. In 1551, Johann Walter would in fact write a polyphonic setting for Luther's *Ein feste Burg ist unser Gott* that would become widely popular.

Attack on Celibacy and Support of Charity

Luther appealed to the wider populace in other ways as well. He attacked what many considered the absurdity of monasticism and clerical celibacy by marrying a former nun and fathering six children. The Catholic Church had argued that only those who practiced the three "counsels"—poverty, celibacy, and obedience—could have a religious vocation. But for Luther, faith equalized everyone, and monastic vows conflicted with faith because they embrace the notion of good works instead.

Luther's position on faith did not mean that his parishioners were freed from performing good works. No one should have to beg in Wittenberg, he argued, and so in late 1520, he established the "community chest" to support the needy. When his parishioners failed to contribute to it, he declared his unwillingness to be "the shepherd of such pigs" and actually quit preaching until the coffers were filled. "Christ and all saints are one spiritual body," he preached, "just as the inhabitants of a city are one community and a body, each citizen being a member of the other and of the entire city." While Luther hoped that other churches outside Wittenberg would adopt his reforms, the evidence suggests that other parishes encountered similar difficulties in actually implementing his ideas.

THE SPREAD OF THE REFORMATION

How did the Reformation change as it spread to Geneva and Zurich in particular?

Even as Luther led the Reformation in Germany, other reformists initiated similar movements in France and Switzerland (Map **17.2**), and still others radicalized his thinking. The appeal of Luther's Reformation was as much due to its political as its religious implications. His defense of the individual conscience against the authority of the pope was understood to free the German princes of the same papal tyranny that plagued him. And to many townspeople and peasants, freedom from the pope's authority seemed to justify their own independence from authoritarian rule, whether of a peasant from his feudal lord, a guild from local government, or a city from its prince.

Thomas Müntzer and the Peasant War

By 1524, peasant leaders across Germany, many of whom were Lutherans, were openly requesting Luther's support in their struggle for political and economic freedom, especially release from serfdom. Luther was hesitant to endorse the

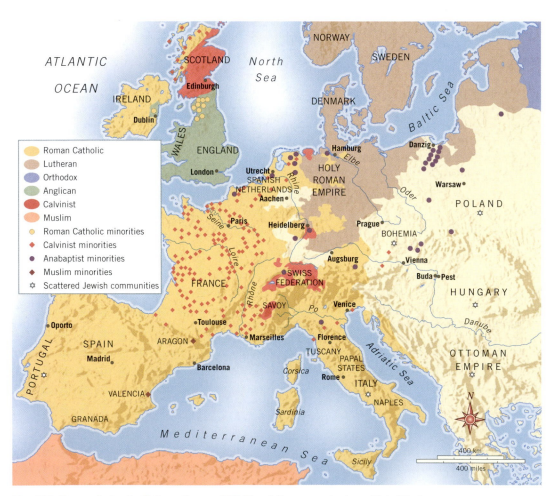

Map 17.2 Europe during the Reformation. ca. 1560. Though Europe remained—and is to this day—predominantly Roman Catholic, the Protestant Reformation had a major impact in the North.

aims of the peasants, but Thomas Müntzer (ca. 1489–1525), a German cleric who had studied at Wittenberg, was not. Müntzer thoroughly believed that reform of the Church required the absolute abolition of the vestiges of feudalism, the rule of what he called the "Godless princes" and the self-serving scholars and priests who worked for them. He numbered Luther among these.

Müntzer differed from Luther theologically in that he saw Luther's "faith" as based on scripture whereas he, Müntzer, believed that God spoke spiritually to every individual with faith, and that God's word came in visions and dreams as well as from scripture. Politically, their differences were even more extreme. Müntzer's revelations—his spiritual conversations with his God—led him to believe that a revolutionary transformation of society was required. When Luther objected, Müntzer replied in an invective-ridden tract, *A Highly Provoked Vindication and a Refutation of the Unspiritual Soft-Living Flesh in Wittenberg Whose Robbery and Distortion of Scripture Has So Grievously Polluted Our Wretched Christian Church,* published in 1524. "The great do whatever they please," Müntzer wrote, "and Doctor Liar [Luther] responds, Amen. It is the lords themselves who make the poor man their enemy. If they refuse to do away with the causes of insurrection, how can trouble be avoided? If saying that makes me an inciter to insurrection, so be it!"

Luther was actually sympathetic to the peasants' plight, but he lacked the militancy of Müntzer, who soon raised an army and joined forces with the rebels in Frankenhausen. Within days, the troops of the princes encircled the town, and Müntzer, certain that God was on his side, led the peasants against the princes in the so-called Peasant War. In the ensuing battle, the princes lost six men, Müntzer 6,000. Ten days later, Müntzer was executed.

Luther condemned the Peasant War of 1524 to 1526 in the strongest terms, calling on the German princes to put down the rebellion. He had first urged the German rulers to "try kindness" and negotiate with the peasants, and as the rebellion proceeded, he advocated mercy. But finally, in a tract called *Against the Robbing and Murdering Hordes of Peasants,* he called upon the rulers to put the rebellion down (**Reading 17.5**):

READING 17.5

from Martin Luther, *Against the Robbing and Murdering Hordes of Peasants* (1525)

For rebellion is not just simple murder; it is like a great fire, which attacks and devastates a whole land. Thus rebellion brings with it a land filled with murder and bloodshed; it makes widows and orphans, and turns everything upside down, like the worst disaster. Therefore let everyone who can, smite, slay, and stab, secretly or openly, remembering that nothing can be more poisonous, hurtful, or devilish than a rebel. It is just as when one must kill a mad dog; if you do not strike him, he will strike you, and a whole land with you.

Nearly 100,000 peasants were killed across Germany in the two years of the conflict, and the peasants themselves felt Luther had completely betrayed them.

The Peasant War was not an isolated incident. The feelings that erupted so violently in Germany were the result of long-standing socioeconomic discontent across Europe. As rising expectations for increased economic prosperity and a moderate degree of social freedom energized the general population—especially the rural peasants—the thought that anyone might thwart those expectations met increasing opposition.

Ulrich Zwingli in Zurich

In 1519, Ulrich Zwingli (1484–1531), strongly influenced by Erasmus, entered the contest to be chosen as people's priest of the Great Minster Church in Zurich, Switzerland. The town council had been granted authority by the Church to select its own clergy. Zwingli's candidacy was compromised by the fact that he lived openly with a woman with whom he had fathered six children. The open rejection of celibacy galvanized the electorate, who believed celibacy to be an entirely unfair demand on the clergy. Zwingli was elected, and from that position of power, he soon challenged not only the practice of clerical celibacy, but also such practices as fasting, the veneration of saints, the value of pilgrimages, and the ideas of purgatory and transubstantiation. On this last point, he was especially at odds with Luther. From Zwingli's point of view, communion was symbolic, while Luther held that consubstantiation, the coexistence of the bread and wine with the blood and body of Christ, did indeed occur when the bread and wine of the Eucharist were blessed. Had the two been able to agree on this point, a single, unified Protestant church might have transpired.

Zwingli quickly instituted a program of iconoclasm in Zurich. Churches were purged of all imagery on the grounds that images provoked at least the potential for idolatry. Such works were seen, as well, as the embodiment of the Catholic taste for material, rather than spiritual, well-being. Outraged at the pomp, expense, and seeming excess with which the Vatican was decorating Rome, Zwingli used the authority of the prohibition against worship of false idols in the Ten Commandments to argue that art's appeal to the senses rather than the intellect was contrary to proper religious practice and unbecoming to the dignity of any place of worship. In Zurich, the churches were closed for 13 days in August 1523, while all offending objects were removed—metal items were melted for reuse and the rest destroyed—and the walls were whitewashed. Zwingli was ecstatic: "In Zurich we have churches which are positively luminous; the walls are beautiful white!"

By the late 1520s, civil war between Protestant and Catholic cantons, or states, broke out in Switzerland. The Protestants won the first major battle, but during the second battle, Zwingli was wounded by his Catholic adversaries, then summarily executed, and his remains were scattered so that no relics would survive his death. The compromise that resulted was that each Swiss canton was now free to choose its own religion.

John Calvin in Geneva

The iconoclasm that marked Zwingli's Zurich erupted in the canton of Geneva in the mid-1530s, as the residents successfully revolted against their local prince (who also happened to be the bishop), and bestowed power on a city council. In May 1536, the city voted to adopt the Reformation and "to live according to the Gospel and Word of God … [without] any more masses, statues, idols, or other papal abuses." Two months later, with the city essentially purged by iconoclasts, John Calvin (1509–64) arrived.

Calvin was a French religious reformer who had undergone a religious conversion of extreme intensity. Calvin was convinced that the city could become a model of moral rectitude and Christian piety. For four years, he fought to have the city adopt strict moral codes, locking horns with the city's large population of Catholics. In 1538, his insistence that church worship and discipline belonged in the hands of the clergy, not politicians, led to his banishment from the city. But in 1541, the city recalled him, and he began to institute the reforms that he thought were necessary.

Calvin believed in a doctrine of **predestination**, the idea that people are "elected" by God to salvation prior to coming into the world, and that anyone so elected self-evidently lives in a way that pleases God. In fact, later Calvinists would come to believe that living a pure and pious life—often coupled with business success—made one's election manifest to one's neighbors. As Calvin explained election in his *Institutes of the Christian Religion* (1536): "God divinely predestines some to eternal salvation—the Elect—and others to eternal perdition—the Damned; and since no one knows with absolute certainty whether he or she is one of the Elect, all must live as if they were obeying God's commands." In effect, one could only intuit one's election, but never know it with certainty.

To this end, Calvinist Geneva—a city where all lived by God's commands—prohibited dancing and singing ("If any one sing immoral, dissolute, or outrageous songs, or dance the virollet or other dance, he shall be put in prison for three days. …"), drunkenness ("If any one be found intoxicated he shall pay for the first offense 3 sous … for the second offense he shall be held to pay the sum of 6 sous, and for the third 10 sous and be put in prison"), and blasphemy. Women were prohibited from wearing rouge, lace, and jewelry; men from gambling and playing cards. Men who beat their wives were severely punished, quickly giving the city a reputation as "a paradise for women." So vigilant—and intolerant—was Calvin's Consistory, the ecclesiastical court that supervised the morals of the city and that was made up of 12 city elders and the pastors of its churches, that in some ways Geneva came to resemble a religious police state. When theologian and scientist Michael Servetus (1511–53), discoverer of the pulmonary circulation of blood, arrived in Geneva in 1553, Calvin had already condemned his theological writings as the most "impious ravings of all the ages." Servetus argued that infant baptism was diabolical, that there was no such thing as original sin, and that the Trinity was a "three-headed Cerberus," the mythological dog guarding the gates to Hades. He was promptly arrested—Calvin serving as the chief witness against him—and condemned to death at the stake over a slow-burning green wood fire.

Nevertheless, by the time he was done instituting these reforms, Calvin was extremely popular. Before his death in 1564, nearly 7,000 religious refugees had arrived in Geneva seeking protection for their own religious practice. Many of these carried his teachings back to their homelands—to France, the Netherlands, England, Scotland, Poland, and even the fledgling Americas. So austere was the life they had learned in Geneva that, in England, they soon became known by the name of "Puritans." The intolerance of Calvin's Geneva migrated with them, especially to the Puritan colonies in North America.

Calvinist iconoclasm spread across Europe in the process, reaching a peak in the summer of 1566 (Fig. **17.6**). The extent of the devastation varied from town to town. In Nuremberg, a great sculpture of Mary and Gabriel hanging over the high altar of the Church of Saint Lorenz

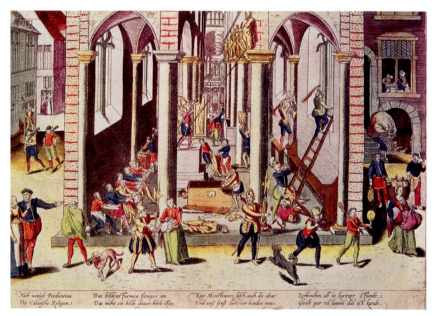

Fig. 17.6 Franz Hogenbergh, *Netherlandish Iconoclasm.* ca. 1566. Etching, 16½″ × 22″. Hamburger Kunsthalle, Hamburg. To the right, the iconoclasts have begun plundering local shops, suggesting that, from Hogenbergh's point of view, the iconoclasm was informed by a certain hooligan element.

believed to be a race rejected by God for denying Jesus and crucifying him. Both Calvin and Luther were deeply disappointed that Jews did not willingly convert to Christianity in great numbers upon seeing the reforms that the Protestants had put in place. As Calvin put it, "the rotten and unbending stiffneckedness [of Jews] deserves that they be oppressed unendingly and without measure or end and that they die in their misery without the pity of anyone."

Luther was even more agitated, publishing in 1543, three years before his death, a book entitled *On the Jews and Their Lies*. Earlier in his career, in a 1523 tract entitled *That Jesus Christ Was Born a Jew*, he had preached tolerance: "You will find plenty of Christians—and indeed the greater part of them—who are worse in their secret belief than any Jew, heathen Turk, or heretic. A heathen is just as much a man or a woman—God's good creation—as Saint Paul, Saint Peter, and Saint Lucy, not to speak of a slack and spurious Christian." But by the 1540s, he had evidently changed his mind. *On the Jews and Their Lies* would blacken his reputation forever after it was taken up in the twentieth century by Adolf Hitler's Nazi regime and quoted endlessly to support the Holocaust.

Luther calls Jews devils and blasphemers, a "miserable, blind and senseless" people. They are, he says, "nothing but thieves and robbers who daily eat no morsel and wear no thread of clothing which they have not stolen and pilfered from us by means of their accursed usury." Furthermore, he calls for these "poisonous, envenomed worms" to be ejected from Germany, even as their houses, synagogues, schools, and writings should be burned, their money, gold, and silver confiscated, and safe conduct on the highways denied them. Nothing could be more alien to the humanist tolerance that Luther had preached earlier in his life.

THE PRINTING PRESS: A FORCE FOR IDEAS AND ART

How did the printing press impact both the Reformation and the art and literature of the era?

It is debatable whether the Reformation would have occurred without the invention, a half-century earlier, of the printing press. Sometime between 1435 and 1455, in the German city of Mainz, Johannes Gutenberg (ca. 1390–1468) discovered a process for casting individual letterforms by using an alloy of lead and antimony. The letterforms could be composed into pages of type and then printed on a wooden standing press using ink made of lamp-black and oil varnish. Although the Chinese alchemist Pi Sheng had invented **movable type** in 1045 CE, now, for the first time the technology was available in the West, and identical copies of written works could be reproduced over and over again.

In 1455, Gutenberg published his first major work, the *Gutenberg Bible* (Fig. **17.7**)—also known as the

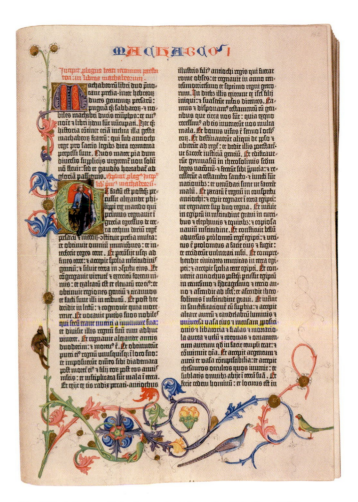

Fig. 17.7 Johannes Gutenberg, page from the Gutenberg Bible, text printed with movable letters and hand-painted initials and marginalia: page 162 recto with initials "M" and "E" and depiction of Alexander the Great; Mainz. 1455–56. Staatsbibliothek, Berlin. An artist added the colors of the still-Gothic decorative designs by hand after the page was printed to lend the book the feeling of a medieval manuscript. The appearance of Alexander the Great in the design further contributes to the effect.

was spared destruction, but by decree of the town council it was covered over by a cloth, not to be permanently uncovered until the nineteenth century. In Antwerp, iconoclasts destroyed all the sculpture and painting that decorated the city's 30 churches, including most of the cathedral's 70 altars. In Ghent, at Saint Bavo Cathedral, Van Eyck's *Ghent Altarpiece* (see Figs. 16.5 and 16.6 in Chapter 16) was dismantled and hidden in the tower by local authorities just three days before the city's churches were sacked.

Protestant Anti-Semitism

Given the intolerance of Calvin's Consistory, it is not surprising that Jews were not welcome in Geneva. In fact, they were expelled from the city at the end of the fifteenth century and not allowed to return until the beginning of the nineteenth. They had been blamed for the plague in the fourteenth century (see Chapter 13), and they were also

Forty-Two-Line Bible because each column of type contains 42 lines—the first substantial book to be published from movable type in Europe. The text is Saint Jerome's translation into Latin of the original Hebrew and Greek. The book's typeface is heavily influenced by the Gothic manuscript tradition, probably because the printer wanted it to look as if it were hand-copied. The publication of another Bible, the so-called *Thirty-Six-Line Bible*, quickly followed in 1458 to 1461. By the end of the century, printing presses were churning out a wide variety of books in at least 60 German cities and in 200 others throughout Europe. Publishers were quick to print the great humanist texts. Gutenberg's press published the writings of Augustine of Hippo in the early 1460s, the writings of Cicero in 1465, and Dante's *Divine Comedy* in 1472. Even an Arabic edition of the Qur'an was printed in Italy in 1500.

More popular than the humanist texts, however, was the Bible, which was the Continent's best seller. Up to this time, the Bible had been an item of some rarity, available only in churches and monasteries. A vellum edition required 170 calfskins or 300 sheepskins, and therefore was prohibitively expensive. Now the less costly, printed Bible found its way into the homes of individual citizens. By the time of Luther's death in 1546, 3,830 separate editions of the Bible—all together about 1 million copies—had been published, many in vernacular German. Although there were still a large number of variant texts, there were many fewer than before, and something close to the standardization of scripture was beginning to take place. In England, William Tyndale (ca. 1494–1536) translated the Bible into English, and the works of Luther as well. The bishop of London, Cuthbert Tunstall (1474–1559), was mortified at the prospect of the people being able to interpret the Bible for themselves. "We must root out printing," he warned,

"or printing will root out us." In Antwerp in 1535, imperial authorities arrested the "dangerous" Tyndale, strangled him, and then burned him at the stake. Ironically, when King James I of England instructed translators to create what has come to be known as the King James Version of the Bible in 1604, it was a lightly edited version of Tyndale's translation that provided the basis for the work; as much as 80 percent of the text is Tyndale's. The King James Version would have a profound impact on all subsequent Bible translations and on English literature as a whole.

Luther's fame protected him from such hostile acts. He was the Continent's best-selling author. It is estimated that between 1518 and 1525, one-third of all texts published in Germany were by him—roughly 300,000 a year. His *Address to the Christian Nobility of the German Nation* sold 4,000 copies in three weeks in Wittenberg alone. In the next two years, it went through 13 editions. For Luther, the printing press was a true gift from God, and he understood how to use it. Not only did the literate few, about 30 percent of the urban population, heed his words, but so did those to whom Luther's texts were read aloud. "Faith," Luther wrote, "comes by hearing." His writings, he knew, were well heard.

Printmaking: Book Illustration and Fine Art

The art of printmaking was reasonably well known before the advent of the printing press in the West. As early as the sixth century, Europeans decorated textiles with printed images, and produced **woodcut** playing cards in Germany by the beginning of the fifteenth century (see *Materials & Techniques*, page 581). The Japanese made woodblock rubbings of Buddhist images in the mid-eighth century. But with the printing press, printmaking came into its own as

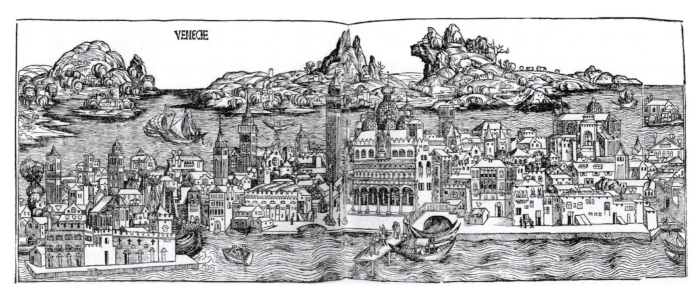

Fig. 17.8 *Venice*, **from Hartmann Schedel's** *The Nuremberg Chronicle*. **1493.** Woodcut, illustration size approx. 10″ × 20″. The Metropolitan Museum of Art, New York. Rogers Fund, 1921 (21.36.145). This is one of the more accurate woodcuts in the book, since most people knew something of Venice. The Doge's Palace, the Campanile, and Saint Mark's are recognizable in the center of the panorama, but the image is still largely a work of the imagination.

Printmaking

A **print** is a single impression of a multiple **edition** of impressions, made on paper from the same master image carved, etched, engraved, or otherwise drawn on a block or plate. There are two basic types of printmaking, *relief* and *intaglio*. Both processes are illustrated here.

In **relief** processes, the image to be printed is *raised above* the background in reverse. Common rubber stamps are examples of relief printing, and Gutenberg's metal type is a form of the same process. The **woodcut** was a popular form of relief printing from the early fifteenth century on. In the woodcut process, the artist draws the design on the surface of a woodblock and cuts away the parts that are to appear white with a sharp tool called a gouge, leaving elevated the areas to be printed. To create a dark line, for instance, the artist or carver cuts away the block on each side of it. Next, the printer rolls the elevated surface with ink, thick and sticky enough not to flow into the hollows, and then a piece of paper is pressed directly against this raised, inked surface, resulting in the finished print. All the illustrations in *The Nuremberg Chronicle* are woodcuts (see Fig. 17.8).

In **intaglio** processes, the area to be printed is *below* the surface of the plate in reverse. *Intaglio*, which means "engraving" in Italian, derives from **engraving** techniques used by armorers to ornament armor. Nuremberg was a center for manufacturing arms and armor, and artists there, like Albrecht Dürer (see Fig. 17.9), perfected this intaglio technique in the late fifteenth and early sixteenth centuries. In an engraving, the artist or carver incises lines into a metal plate with a sharp tool called a burin. The printer then fills the incised lines with ink, wipes clean the surface of the plate, and presses a sheet of dampened paper into the plate with a very powerful roller. The paper essentially fills the incised grooves, resulting in a final print with slightly raised lines.

Relief Printing

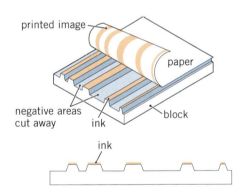

Intaglio Printing

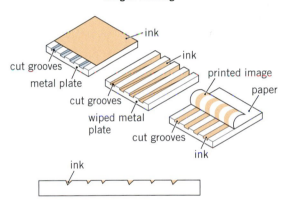

a method of illustrating printed books. In addition, artists produced single-sheet prints in multiple copies as a form of art, not illustration.

Illustrated Books One of the most ambitious of the early illustrated books was a history of the world from Creation to date known as *The Nuremberg Chronicle* (Fig. **17.8**). Published in 1493 in two editions, one in black and white and another with hand-colored illustrations, it is the first book about which we know almost every detail of its making. The author of *The Nuremberg Chronicle* was Hartmann Schedel (1440–1514) who sometime around 1490 convinced two wealthy Nurembergers to finance the work and make it available "for the common delight." The 600-page book included over 1,800 illustrations, an average of 3 per page. To create the 1,800 images, the artists made only 654 different blocks, so the same blocks were used over again

to depict different cities. Few readers would have noticed. Most had not traveled widely enough to tell the difference between, say, Padua and Siena. Forty-four images of men and women were repeated 226 times to represent different historical personages.

Albrecht Dürer served as an apprentice in the studio where many of the illustrations in *The Nuremberg Chronicle* were produced. Dürer also happened to be the godson of the book's publisher, and it seems likely that he worked on at least some of the *Chronicle*'s blocks. By the end of the century, at any rate, Dürer was not only recognized as a great painter, as we saw in the previous chapter, but was widely held to be the greatest printmaker of the day, a master at both woodcut and engraving.

Single-Sheet Prints Dürer treated prints as an art form and produced many single-sheet engravings, images not

Watch a video about the technique of intaglio printmaking on **MyArtsLab**

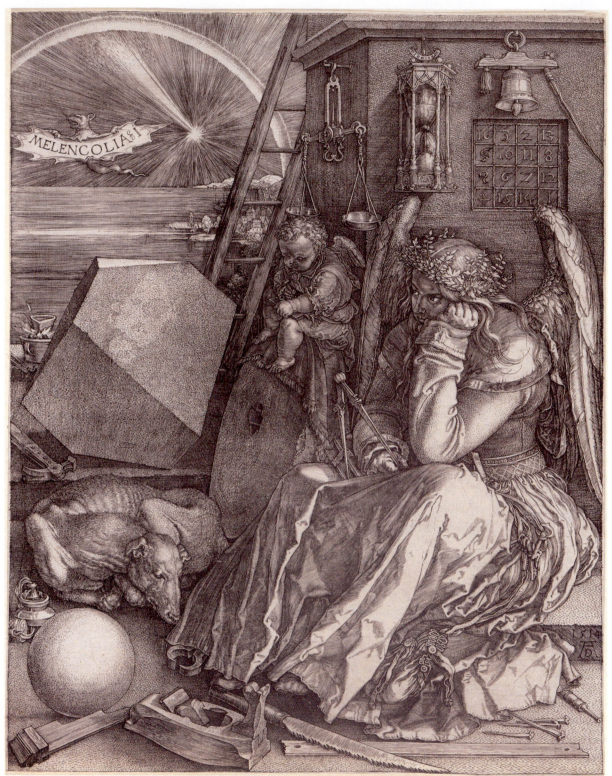

Fig. 17.9 Albrecht Dürer, *Melancholia I.* **1514.** Engraving, 9⅞" × 7⅜". Yale University Art Gallery. Fritz Achelis Memorial Collection, Gift of Frederic George Achelis, B.A. 1907. In the background, a bat carries a sign bearing the print's title. A creature of the night, the bat symbolizes darkness, as behind it the sun (the light of inspiration) descends towards the western horizon.

🔎 **View** the Closer Look for *Melancholia I* on **MyArtsLab**

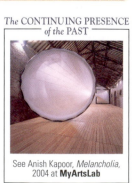

The CONTINUING PRESENCE
of the PAST

See Anish Kapoor, *Melancholia,*
2004 at **MyArtsLab**

intended as book illustrations. Among Dürer's many great engravings is *Melancholia I* (Fig. **17.9**) of 1514. It is a fully humanist image, a complex depiction of failed inspiration and genius, informed by a wealth of Classical allusion. Dürer himself suffered from melancholy, or depression, and this can be understood as an image of his own muse. She is at once divinely inspired (note her wings) and incapable of action. Note the way she carelessly holds the compass. With head resting on hand, she strikes the traditional pose of a melancholic personality. Raphael had portrayed Michelangelo as Heraclitus in a similar position just a few years earlier in his *School of Athens* (see Chapter 15, *Closer Look*, pages 512–513.) Tools lie idly beneath her feet. Time passes (indicated by the hourglass on the wall behind her). Even a pudgy cupid, almost always busy at work, sits dejected and uninspired beside her.

In *Melancholia I*, Dürer's extraordinary skill as an engraver is evident. As in drawing, he models and shades his subject by hatching, but he also uses **stippling**, in which dots of greater density create a deeper and darker shadow. Dürer employs this contrast between dark and light as a metaphor for the contrast between melancholy and inspiration, the subject of his earlier engraving *Adam and Eve* (see *Closer Look*, pages 584–585).

Writing for Print: The New Humanists

The sudden availability of books in large numbers transformed not only the spread of knowledge but its production as well. Suddenly, scholars could work in their own personal libraries and write knowing that their thinking could quickly find its way into print. Similarly, composers could see their music in print and expect it to be performed across the Continent. In short, the printing press created a new economy that transformed the speed at which information traveled.

François Rabelais No one better expressed his wonder at print and how it was transforming society than the French writer François Rabelais (ca. 1494–ca. 1553). A former Franciscan and Benedictine monk, Rabelais left the monastery to study at the Universities of Poitiers and Montpellier before moving to Lyon, one of the intellectual centers of France, to practice medicine. In his spare time, he wrote and published humorous pamphlets critical of established authority and stressing individual liberty. Written in a satirical voice, Rabelais's pamphlets contain keen observations of the social and political events in the first half of the sixteenth century.

Gargantua and Pantagruel, his first book, is a connected series of five novels published over 32 years. It tells the story of two giants, Gargantua and his son Pantagruel, in a highly amusing and witty mock-epic style because, Rabelais says in his introduction, "to laugh is proper to the man." There is much scatological humor and violence. In one of the story's more serious moments, Gargantua writes a letter to Pantagruel extolling the virtues of a humanist education (**Reading 17.6**):

READING 17.6

from François Rabelais, *Gargantua and Pantagruel*, Book 2, Chapter 7 (1532)

Even though my late father Grandgousier, of blessed memory, strove with all his ability that I should profit from and learn political knowledge, and even though my labors and studies matched or even surpassed his desires, nevertheless, as you can well understand, the times were not fit or favorable for learning as is the present; and I did not have the abundance of such instructors as you have had. The times were still dark, and reflected the misery and calamity caused by the Goths, who had destroyed all good scholarship. But, through divine grace, during my life light and dignity have been restored to learning; and we witness in them so much improvement that now I would have trouble being accepted into a children's beginning class, I who in my maturity was reputed (and not wrongly) the most learned man of the time. I do not say this out of vain boasting—even though I could properly do so in writing to you as you may understand by the authority of Marcus Tullius Cicero in his book Old Age, and the teachings of Plutarch in his book titled How to Praise Oneself Honorably—but to inspire in you the desire to strive for the highest achievements.

Now all the disciplines have been restored, languages revived: Greek, without which it is shameful for a person to call himself learned: Hebrew, Chaldean, and Latin. Elegant and correct printed editions are available, the result of a divinely inspired invention of my time, as are in contrast guns—the product of diabolical suggestion. The world is full of learned men, fine teachers, ample libraries; and it is my opinion that neither in the time of Plato, nor of Cicero … were there such opportunities for study as we see today; and no one should now go out in public who has not been well polished in Minerva's workshop. I see the robbers, hangmen, freebooters and grooms of today more learned than the theologians and preachers of my day. What can I say? Even women and girls aspire to the honor and celestial manna of good learning. Things have changed so much that at my advanced age I have had to learn Greek, which I had not rejected like Cato, but which I had not had the leisure to learn in my youth; and I delight in reading the Morals of Plutarch, the beautiful Dialogues of Plato … as I await the hour at which it may please God, my Creator, to summon and order me to leave this world.

The objects of Rabelais's attack on the "dark" Middle Ages are the fundamental dogmas and sacraments of medieval theology, for which his novel was condemned by the Roman Catholic Church. He was more than sympathetic to the reforms proposed by Martin Luther, and he conceived of his own humor as a liberating force in the fight against traditional religious practice and the corruption that accompanied it. Rabelais was also deeply troubled by the religious conflicts of the day, especially when they erupted into violence. This sentiment informs Gargantua's remark contrasting the "divinely inspired" printing press to the "diabolical" character of guns.

CLOSER LOOK

n his engraving of 1504, *Adam and Eve*, Dürer depicts the biblical couple before the Fall as two ideal nudes constructed according to what he believed were perfect proportions as derived from Classical theories of beauty. The play of light on the bodies of the couple emphasizes their physical beauty and is a metaphor for inspiration—both God's and Dürer's own. This early example of Dürer's interest in ancient Greek and Roman models of ideal physical proportion is filled with symbolic content. It also demonstrates the artist's skillful use of engraving techniques. The print was an immediate sensation, widely distributed across the Continent. It became a model for many other artists.

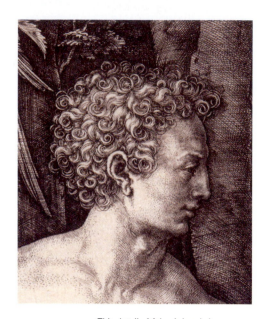

This detail of Adam's head shows how Dürer modeled rounded forms by means of **hatching** (closely spaced parallel lines) and **cross-hatching** (two or more sets of parallel lines set at an angle to one another). The denser the lines, the deeper the shadow.

Something to Think About …

Creating art was, for Dürer, a sacred act, as a consideration of his *Self-Portrait* of 1500 makes clear (see Fig. 16.18 in Chapter 16). How does this print reflect that attitude?

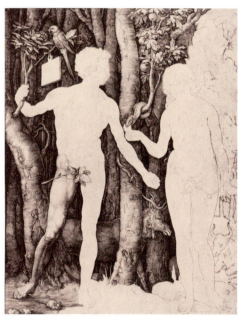

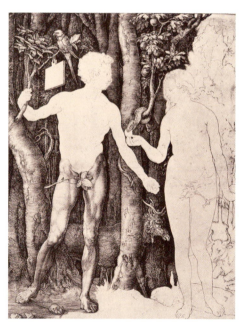

Albrecht Dürer, *Adam and Eve*, **first state (left) and second state (right). 1504.** Engravings, each 9⅞" × 7⅜". Albertina, Vienna. These two trial **proofs** provide insight into the artist's process. Dürer pulled each proof to consider how well the incised lines would hold and transfer ink to paper. He also wanted to see the actual image itself, since on the plate it is in reverse. In each of these states, or stages, in the process, Dürer lightly outlined his entire composition. In the first state, he incised all of the background except for the area over Eve's shoulder. In the second, he completed Adam's entire lower body.

Dürer's *Adam and Eve*

The **parrot** is the embodiment of wisdom and language. It is associated with Adam, as opposed to Eve, who feeds the snake.

A **placard** inscribed with the words "Albrecht Dürer of Nuremberg made [this in] 1504" hangs from the Tree of Life, a witty allusion by Dürer to the immortality of his own art.

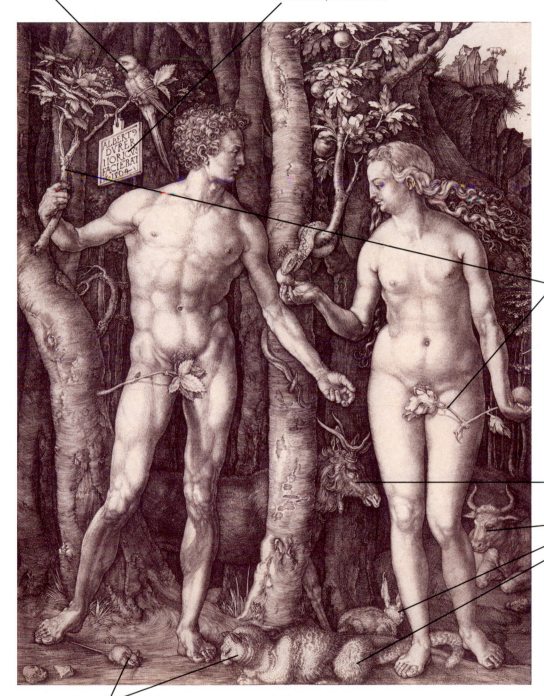

Albrecht Dürer. *Adam and Eve.* **1504.** Engraving, 9⅞" × 7⅜". Yale University Art Gallery, Fritz Achelis Memorial Collection, Gift of Frederic George Achelis, B.A. 1907; reacquired in 1972 with the Henry J. Heinz II, B.A. 1931.

Adam holds a **branch** of mountain ash, the Tree of Life, while Eve holds a **branch** of a fig tree, the forbidden Tree of Knowledge.

Fluids in the body, known as the **four humors**, were thought to influence health and personality. Medieval philosophers believed that before the Fall, the humors were in perfect balance. The elk represents **melancholy** (black bile); the ox, sluggishness or **laziness** (phlegm); the rabbit, **sensuality** (blood); and the cat, **anger** and **cruelty** (yellow bile).

The **cat** at Eve's feet is preparing to jump on the mouse at Adam's feet, suggesting the introduction of death into the world at the moment of the Fall.

View the Closer Look for *Adam and Eve* on **MyArtsLab**

Michel de Montaigne A generation younger than Rabelais, Michel de Montaigne (1533–92) was nevertheless equally affected by the conflicts between Catholics and Protestants in the mid-sixteenth century. He was the son of a wealthy merchant and mayor of Bordeaux, who sent him away at birth to be nursed by a peasant woman so that he might develop a love and respect for the common folk. A resident German tutor taught him Latin as he learned to speak, so that, in fact, Latin was his native tongue. By the age of 6, he was enrolled in the prestigious Collège de Guienne, in Bordeaux, and by the age of 21, he had finished law school. At 24, he became one of 60 magistrates charged with enforcing the king's law in Bordeaux. In that capacity, watching the sometimes vicious persecution of the Huguenot "heretics," he developed a lifelong distaste for brutality and cruelty.

In 1570, after 13 years of service as a magistrate, Montaigne retired from public life to the Montaigne estate and the sanctuary of his library: "It is on the third story of a tower," he later wrote. "The first contains my chapel; the second a bed-chamber with a dressing-room. … My library is round in shape, squared off only for the needs of my table and chair and, as it curves around, it offers me a single glance at all my books." Before the printing press, such private libraries were virtually nonexistent, but in the privileged surroundings of his books, Montaigne invented a new style of writing, the **personal essay**. *Essai*, in French, means "try out," or "attempt," and the form is a vehicle for trying out ideas, testing them even as they are written. In his essays, Montaigne revealed his own mind at work, often contradicting himself, openly challenging his own assumptions, and, in short, approaching the workings of his own mind with a significant measure of skepticism. Like Rabelais, Montaigne in his essays often posed more questions than he answered, and any answer was, almost by definition, tentative. Among his most famous essays is "Of Cannibals," a work that reflects his fascination with reports from the New World (see Chapter 18). The essay delights in the captivating details of cannibal life, but it also, tellingly, draws analogy to the writer's own world and the religious conflicts that were, in his view, tearing French society apart. "So we may call these people barbarians," he writes, "in respect to the rules of reason, but not in respect to ourselves, who surpass them in every type of barbarity." (See **Reading 17.7**, pages 594–595, for the complete essay.)

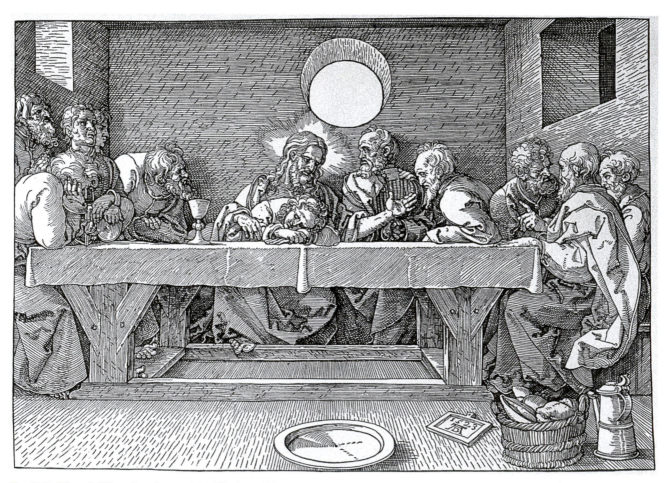

Fig. 17.10 Albrecht Dürer, *Last Supper*. 1523. Woodcut, 8¾" × 11¹³⁄₁₆". Private collection. The table, with its heavy wooden carpentry, is of a kind ordinary Germans might have had in their homes. It suggests, as a result, the close connection between Christ, his disciples, and the common people.

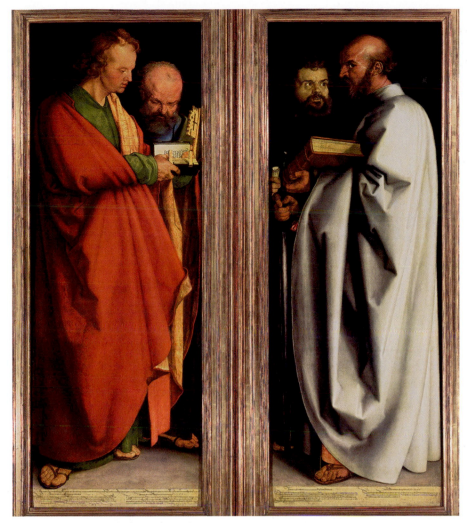

Fig. 17.11 Albrecht Dürer, *Four Apostles*. 1526. Oil on panel, each panel 7'1½" × 2'6". Alte Pinakothek, Munich. John and Mark assume primary status here, probably because John was Luther's favorite apostle and Mark the favorite of Protestants generally.

FROM RELIGIOUS TO SECULAR ART

How did the Reformation transform art in the North?

In the fever of iconoclasm that swept Europe, most artists working in the North saw at least some of their work destroyed, and those who depended on religious commissions lost their livelihood. Some artists, such as Dürer, discovered ways of working that seemed compatible with the developing Protestant aesthetic of restraint and propriety. Others made the best of things, turning to the creation of more secular imagery—landscape and portraiture, for instance.

Dürer's Protestant Imagery

Dürer's *Melancholia I* is an elaborate and complex humanist image, and it contrasts dramatically with his *Last Supper* (Fig. 17.10). The latter is a woodcut dating from 1523—that is, after Dürer had come under the influence of

Martin Luther. The image is simple, straightforward, and clear. Gone is the elaborate composition that defined his earlier work. Dürer's task is now to portray, as unambiguously as possible, Lutheran doctrine, in this case a point that Luther had just made concerning Holy Communion. Luther had reaffirmed the sacrament of Communion, not as transubstantiation, in which the bread and wine literally disappear and are transformed into the body and blood of Christ, but as consubstantiation, in which Christ's body and blood are present "in, with, and under" the bread and wine. Thus the chalice on the table and the empty plate on the floor wait to be filled by the basket of bread and pitcher of wine at the bottom right.

Dürer's most direct assertion of his Lutheran faith is the 1526 oil painting *The Four Apostles* (Fig. 17.11). Donated to the city of Nuremberg, it may have been intended to show the citizens an example of what a new, Protestant art might look like. As he wrote, in defense of his own practice: "A Christian would no more be led to superstition by a picture or effigy than an honest man to commit murder

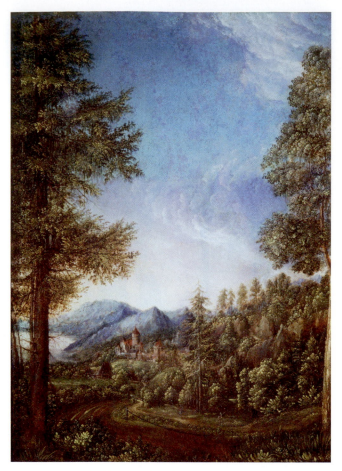

because he carries a sword by his side. He must indeed be an unthinking man who would worship picture, wood, or stone. A picture therefore brings more good than harm, when it is honestly, artistically, and well made." So Dürer's *Four Apostles*, with John standing in front of Peter at the left, and Mark the Evangelist in front of Matthew at the right, carries an admonition to all viewers across the bottom. It says, do not worship "false prophets," and pay particular heed to the words of the New Testament. This warning accompanies excerpts from Luther's new German translation of the gospels.

Landscapes, Cycles, and Still Lifes

Other artists were not so confident in their practice, and at a time when the worth of religious imagery was being questioned, the market for it was diminishing as well. The growing middle class, which was increasingly interested in decorating their homes with art and regularly purchased it, began to exhibit a taste for secular as opposed to religious imagery. Many conservative Protestant sects deemed religious art a sin. Zwingli not only "cleansed" Zurich's churches of imagery, but also went so far as to nail closed the church organs. Religious commissions that had served artists like Campin and van Eyck a century earlier were essentially nonexistent, at least in the Protestant North. Portraiture would increasingly become a staple of the painter's livelihood (see Chapters 19 and 22).

Landscape, often completely without human figures, also began to establish itself. In this genre, *Danube Landscape*

Fig. 17.12 Albrecht Altdorfer, *Danube Landscape*. ca. 1525. Oil on panel, 12″ × 8¾″. Alte Pinakothek, Munich. Although this scene may seem a little fanciful, it may be more realistic than not in capturing the feel of Altdorfer's native Bavaria.

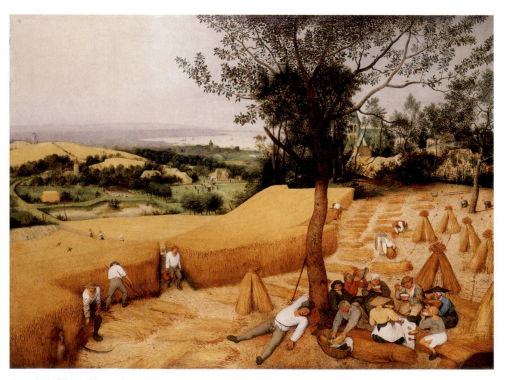

Fig. 17.13 Pieter Bruegel the Elder, *Harvesters*. 1565. Oil on panel, 43¾″ × 52¾″. The Metropolitan Museum of Art, New York. Five of the six paintings in this cycle survive. The other four are *The Gloomy Day, Hunters in the Snow, The Return of the Herd* (all in the Kunsthistorisches Museum, Vienna), and *Haymaking* (in the Roudnice Lobkowicz collection, Nelahozeves, Czech Republic).

by Albrecht Altdorfer, whose *Battle of Issus* opened this chapter, marks an important shift in Western consciousness (Fig. **17.12**). Painted about 1525, some four years before *The Battle of Issus*, this is no pastoral or garden scene, no pleasantly cultivated landscape in which humans and nature appear in harmony. Rather, its trees and sky, gathering clouds, and approaching storm, create something of the same ominous feeling that informs the landscape elements of *The Battle of Issus*. Despite the red-roofed castle at the end of a winding road, which implies human habitation, the painting celebrates the grandeur and awesome immensity of nature. It is as if the dramatic background of a painting like Leonardo's *Mona Lisa* (see Fig. 14.28 in Chapter 14) has elevated itself to the foreground.

Another popular type of painting for Northern homes was the cycle, a series of paintings on a secular theme such as the Five Senses, the Months of the Year, or the Four Seasons. These often took the form of landscape as well. *Harvesters* (Fig. **17.13**) by Pieter Bruegel the Elder (ca. 1525–69) is one of a cycle of six paintings that each represent two months of the year—in this case August and September—commissioned by a wealthy Antwerp merchant for

his suburban home. Bruegel's theme is the harmonious relation between the natural world and the people who inhabit it. *Harvesters* depicts a peasantry blessed with a bountiful harvest, unencumbered by authority, and enjoying the good life. Some viewers detect in Bruegel's depictions of Flemish peasants a moralizing attitude—seeing, for instance, the man who is sleeping under the tree as an image of sloth. But if Bruegel is moralizing here, then he does it with a sense of good humor, and he tempers that judgment by portraying the industry of the other peasants still working in the fields even as the larger group relaxes under the pear tree, a traditional symbol of the life force.

In this sense, *Harvesters* could be said to depict the human condition in benign if not idealized terms. This no doubt reflects in some manner the attitude of Bruegel's patron as well as middle-class nostalgia for the simplicities of rural life. These are people who know their place, and are content with it.

So the painting can be read as something of a moral lesson. Certainly, other paintings by Bruegel have moral overtones and some even contrast starkly with the theme of this painting. *The Triumph of Death* (Fig. **17.14**), which

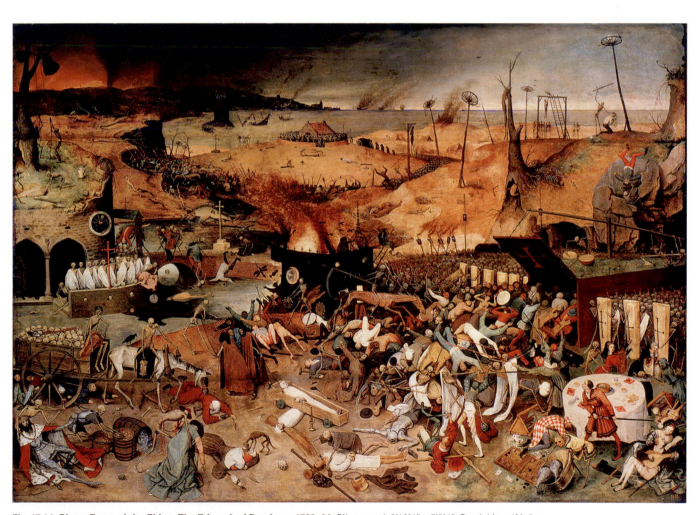

Fig. 17.14 Pieter Bruegel the Elder, *The Triumph of Death***. ca. 1562–64.** Oil on panel, 3'10¾" × 5'3¾". Death himself is in the center of the painting, wielding a scythe and leaping over the crowd on his scrawny horse, reminiscent of the one ridden by Death in Dürer's *Four Horsemen of the Apocalypse* (see Fig. 17.2), a print that Bruegel undoubtedly knew.

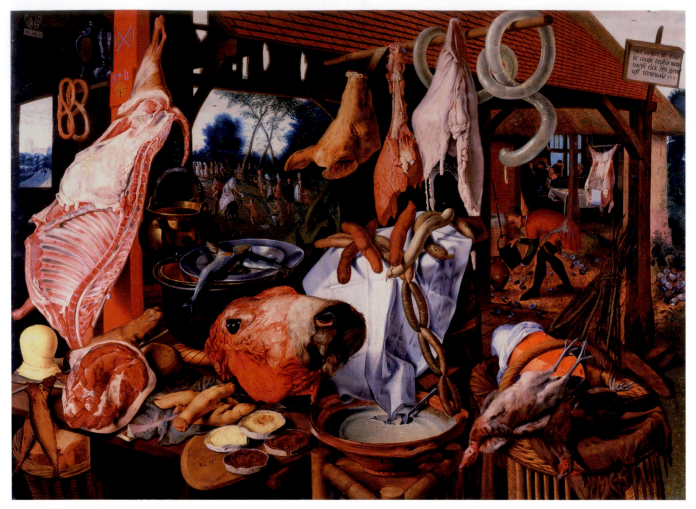

Fig. 17.15 Peter Aertsen, *The Meat Stall*. 1551. Oil on panel, 4'⅜" × 6'5¾". Private collection. The bowl in front is filled with lard for cooking. The boy in the background appears to have been shucking oysters, a symbol of gluttony and sensual pleasure.

Bruegel painted just a couple of years before this cycle, is an example. It was painted 40 years after the Peasant War and in the manner of Hieronymus Bosch (see Chapter 16, *Closer Look*, pages 556–557), who was a generation older than Bruegel. This pointedly political work depicts a massive army of skeletons laying waste to all living things. Men are hanged from scaffolds, beheaded by swords, and crushed beneath the wheels of a death cart. The natural world is transformed into a desert. But most pertinent to the political climate are the figures in the lower corners. On the right, the aristocracy is overcome as a gentleman plays the lute and sings a love song to his lady, both of them damningly indifferent to the destruction going on behind them. At the lower left, an emperor or king succumbs as skeletons help themselves to his gold and jewels, an image suggesting that wealth is incapable of saving even the monarchy. The painting underscores the division between the aristocracy and the common people, even as it argues for the equality of everyone in the face of death.

The Dutch and Flemish were generally predisposed to finding moral implications in otherwise decorative works of art, if for no other reason than to justify owning them. Such moralizing is consistent with the religious piety of the Protestant North. *The Meat Stall*, painted in 1551 by Dutchman Peter Aertsen (1508–75), is more directly religious (Fig. **17.15**). Yet its religious sentiments are not immediately visible through its facade of sausages, cow's head, ham hocks, fowl, fish, and various meats hanging in a shed. It seems, at first, a celebration of abundance and prosperity. And yet, through the shed opening in the left rear, we see the Holy Family giving alms to some beggars. This act of charity contrasts dramatically with the storehouse of food that dominates the foreground and with the private feast about to take place inside the house at the back right. The still life's meat reminds us of our mortality, while the scene as a whole chides us for attending to our material rather than spiritual well-being. In the art of still life and landscape, the religious sentiments of the Reformation have found a new voice.

The Church Strikes Back

No movement as radical as the Reformation could take place without a strong reaction from the Roman Catholic Church. The challenge of Protestantism to the moral authority of the pope threatened the Church with downfall, and Rome soon recognized this. Yet the Roman Catholic Church had come to some of the same conclusions about its shortcomings as its Northern critics. In self-defense, therefore, it launched a Counter-Reformation, both to strike back against the fundamental ideas defended by reformists like Luther and to implement reforms of its own.

The Counter-Reformation (see Chapter 20) had the support of clergy and laypeople through newly organized groups such as the Modern Devotion and the Oratory of Divine Love. These groups encouraged a return to the principles of simplicity, ethical living, and piety that Erasmus had championed. The Society of Jesus, known more familiarly as the Jesuits, took a tougher approach. Founded by Ignatius of Loyola in the 1530s, it advocated a return to strict and uncompromising obedience to the authority of the Church and its ecclesiastical hierarchy. The society's Rule 13 sums up its notion of obedience: "I will believe that the white that I see is black if the hierarchical Church so defines it." Then, in 1545, Pope Paul III convened the Council of Trent in order to define Church doctrine and recommend far-reaching reforms in the abuses practiced by the Church, particularly the selling of indulgences.

The Council of Trent, which convened in two more sessions between 1545 and 1563, also decided to counter the Protestant threat "by means of the stories of the mysteries of our Redemption portrayed by paintings or other representations, [so that] the people be instructed and confirmed in the habit of remembering and continually revolving in mind the articles of faith." The arts should be directed, the Council said, toward clarity and realism, in order to increase understanding, and toward emotion, in order to arouse piety and religious fervor. While the Council of Trent generally preached restraint in design, its desire to appeal to the emotions of its audience resulted in increasingly elaborate church architecture, so that the severe simplicity of the Calvinist church (Fig. 17.16), devoid of any art, would seem emotionally empty beside the grand expanse of the Catholic interior (Fig. 17.17). Yet the basic configuration would remain the same. For the next two centuries, both churches would vie for the souls of Christians in Europe and the Americas. ■

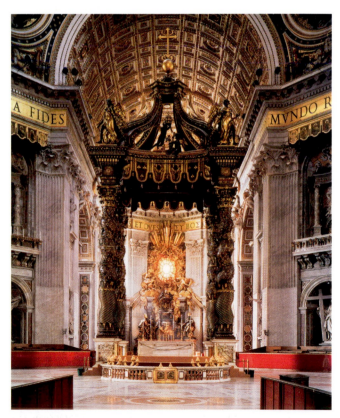

Fig. 17.17 **Gianlorenzo Bernini, Baldachino, Saint Peter's Basilica, Vatican, Rome. 1624–33.** Gilt bronze, marble, stucco, and glass, height approx. 100′.

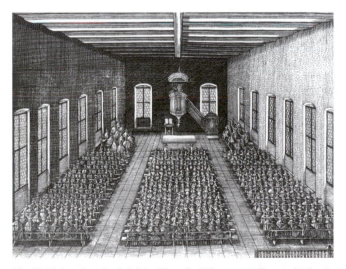

Fig. 17.16 **Interior of a Calvinist Church. 17th century.** German National Museum, Nuremberg.

THINKING BACK

17.1 Describe both Erasmus's and Luther's calls for reform of the Roman Catholic Church.

On October 31, 1517, the German priest and professor Martin Luther posted his *Ninety-Five Theses* on the door of Wittenberg's All Saints Church. His feelings about the Church were in many ways inspired by the writings of the Dutch humanist scholar Desiderius Erasmus, who is most noted for his satirical attack on the corruption of the Roman Catholic Church entitled *In Praise of Folly*. In what terms does Erasmus "praise" human folly? What are the characteristics of satire, and how does irony contribute to it?

Luther's calling for the reform of the Roman Catholic Church unleashed three centuries of social and political conflict. Luther deplored the concept of indulgences and he detested the secular spirit apparent in both Church patronage of lavish decorative programs and the moral laxity of the cardinals in Rome. What are indulgences? The Church charged Luther with heresy, but he continued to publish tracts challenging the authority of the pope. The Church excommunicated him, declared all of his writings heretical, and ordered them burned. In hiding, Luther translated Erasmus's New Testament Bible from Latin into vernacular German. How did Luther transform the liturgy? How did he address the issue of clerical celibacy?

17.2 Discuss the spread of the Reformation and its different manifestations in Zurich and Geneva.

In Germany, Luther's defense of individual conscience against the authority of the pope seemed to peasants a justification for their own independence from their feudal lords. What resulted from this newfound sense of freedom? Ulrich Zwingli, in Zurich, and John Calvin, in Geneva, followed Luther's lead, both convinced that their respective cities could become models of moral rectitude and Christian piety. How did their approach to Church doctrine differ from Luther's? What effect did their iconoclasm have?

17.3 Assess the impact of the printing press on both the Reformation and the art and literature of the era.

One of the most important contributors to the Reformation was Johannes Gutenberg's printing press. It made the Bible a best seller. How did the widespread distribution of his texts fuel reformist movements? Printmaking came into its own as a way to illustrate printed books. How did Albrecht Dürer take advantage of the medium? Humanist thinkers quickly took advantage of print to distribute their works—François Rabelais and Michel de Montaigne, in particular. What new form of writing did the latter invent?

17.4 Recognize how the Reformation transformed art throughout Northern Europe.

The Reformation had a profound effect on the arts throughout Northern Europe. Most artists working in Northern Europe saw at least some of their work destroyed by iconoclasts, and artists who depended on religious commissions lost their livelihood. Dürer attempted to create a new, simpler imagery compatible with the developing Protestant sense of restraint. How would you describe his new style? Other artists turned away from religious themes to take up more secular subject matter. What were some of these new subjects?

✓ **Study** and **review** on **MyArtsLab**

READINGS

from Martin Luther, *Ninety-Five Theses* (1517)

Luther's *Ninety-Five Theses* represent the first protest of the Protestant Reformation. Nailed to the church door at Wittenberg on October 31, 1517, their prime target was the sale of indulgences, particularly by the cleric Johannes Tetzel, whose visit to Wittenberg raised Luther's ire. The following 24 theses (theses 27–50) represent the key points in Luther's attack on the practice.

27 There is no divine authority for preaching that the soul flies out of purgatory immediately the money clinks in the bottom of the chest.

28 It is certainly possible that when the money clinks in the bottom of the chest avarice and greed increase; but when the Church offers intercession, all depends on the will of God.

29 Who knows whether all souls in purgatory wish to be redeemed in view of what is said of St. Severinus and St. Paschal.[1]

30 No one is sure of the reality of his own contrition, much less of receiving plenary forgiveness.[2]

31 One who *bona fide* buys indulgences is as rare as a *bona fide* penitent man, i.e., very rare indeed.

32 All those who believe themselves certain of their own salvation by means of letters of indulgence, will be eternally damned, together with their teachers.

33 We should be most carefully on our guard against those who say that the papal indulgences are an inestimable divine gift, and that a man is reconciled to God by them.

34 For the grace conveyed by these indulgences relates simply to the penalties of the sacramental "satisfactions" decreed merely by man.

35 It is not in accordance with Christian doctrine to preach and teach that those who buy off souls, or purchase confessional licenses, have no need to repent of their own sins.

36 Any Christian whatsoever, who is truly repentant, enjoys plenary remission from penalty and guilt, and this is given him without letters of indulgence.

37 Any true Christian whatsoever, living or dead, participates in all the benefits of Christ and the Church; and this participation is granted to him by God without letters of indulgence.

38 Yet the pope's remission and dispensation are in no way to be despised, for, as already said, they proclaim the divine remission.

39 It is very difficult, even for the most learned theologians, to extol to the people the great bounty contained in the indulgences, while, at the same time, praising contrition as a virtue.

40 A truly contrite sinner seeks out, and loves to pay, the penalties of his sins; whereas the very multitude of indulgences dulls men's consciences, and tends to make them hate the penalties.

41 Papal indulgences should only be preached with caution, lest people gain a wrong understanding, and think that they are preferable to other good works: those of love.

42 Christians should be taught that the pope does not at all intend that the purchase of indulgences should be understood as at all comparable with works of mercy.

43 Christians should be taught that one who gives to the poor, or lends to the needy, does a better action than if he purchases indulgences.

44 Because, by works of love, love grows and a man becomes a better man; whereas, by indulgences, he does not become a better man, but only escapes certain penalties.

45 Christians should be taught that he who sees a needy person, but passes him by although he gives money for indulgences, gains no benefit from the pope's pardon, but only incurs the wrath of God.

46 Christians should be taught that, unless they have more than they need, they are bound to retain what is necessary for the upkeep of their home, and should in no way squander it on indulgences.

47 Christians should be taught that they purchase indulgences voluntarily, and are not under obligation to do so.

48 Christians should be taught that, in granting indulgences, the pope has more need, and more desire, for devout prayer on his own behalf than for ready money.

49 Christians should be taught that the pope's indulgences are useful only if one does not rely on them, but most harmful if one loses the fear of God through them.

50 Christians should be taught that, if the pope knew the exactions of the indulgence-preachers, he would rather the church of Saint Peter were reduced to ashes than be built with the skin, flesh, and bones of his sheep.

READING CRITICALLY

How would you summarize Luther's protestation against the selling of indulgences?

---

[1] Both saints are said to have refused to have their periods of penance in Purgatory shortened.

[2] Complete forgiveness.

from Michel de Montaigne, "Of Cannibals" (1580)

Montaigne's essay "Of Cannibals" reflects his fascination with reports of native civilizations in the New World. It is not the exotic details of cannibal life that lie at the center of the essay, however, but rather Montaigne's own love of simplicity and "naturalness." In fact, like the *Essays* as a whole, the piece is more about Montaigne himself than anything else. Montaigne is as interested in how his own life compares with that of the "noble savages" as he is in the savages themselves. Such personal reflections represent a new genre in Western literature—the informal meditation that tracks the meanderings of a charming, witty, and deeply intelligent mind.

… I had with me for a long time a man who had lived for ten or twelve years in that other world which has been discovered in our century, in the place where Villegaignon landed, and which he called Antarctic France. This discovery of a boundless country seems worthy of consideration. I don't know if I can guarantee that some other such discovery will not be made in the future, so many personages greater than ourselves having been mistaken about this one. I am afraid we have eyes bigger than our stomachs, and more curiosity than capacity. We embrace everything, but we clasp only wind. … [10]

This man I had was a simple, crude fellow—a character fit to bear true witness; for clever people observe more things and more curiously, but they interpret them; and to lend weight and conviction to their interpretation, they cannot help altering history a little. They never show you things as they are, but bend and disguise them according to the way they have seen them; and to give credence to their judgment and attract you to it, they are prone to add something to their matter, to stretch it out and amplify it. We need a man either very honest, or so simple that he has not the stuff to build up false inventions and give [20] them plausibility; and wedded to no theory. Such was my man; and besides this, he at various times brought sailors and merchants, whom he had known on that trip, to see me. So I content myself with his information, without inquiring what the cosmographers say about it.

We ought to have topographers who would give us an exact account of the places where they have been. But because they have over us the advantage of having seen Palestine, they want to enjoy the privilege of telling us news about all the rest of the world. I would like everyone to write what he knows, and as [30] much as he knows, not only in this, but in all other subjects; for a man may have some special knowledge and experience of the nature of a river or a fountain, who in other matters knows only what everybody knows. However, to circulate this little scrap of knowledge, he will undertake to write the whole of physics. From this vice spring many great abuses.

Now, to return to my subject, I think there is nothing barbarous and savage in that nation, from what I have been told, except that each man calls barbarism whatever is not his own practice; for indeed it seems we have no other test of truth and [40] reason than the example and pattern of the opinions and customs of the country we live in. There is always the perfect religion, the perfect government, the perfect and accomplished manners in all things. Those people are wild, just as we call wild the fruits that Nature has produced by herself and in her normal course; whereas really it is those that we have changed artificially and led astray from the common order, that we should rather call wild. The former retain alive and vigorous their genuine, their most useful and natural, virtues and properties, which we have debased in the latter in adapting them to gratify [50] our corrupted taste. And yet for all that, the savor and delicacy of some uncultivated fruits of those countries is quite as excellent, even to our taste, as that of our own. It is not reasonable that art should win the place of honor over our great and powerful mother Nature. We have so overloaded the beauty and richness of her works by our inventions that we have quite smothered her. Yet wherever her purity shines forth, she wonderfully puts to shame our vain and frivolous attempts:

Ivy comes readier without our care;
In lonely caves the arbutus grows more fair; [60]
No art with artless bird song can compare.
PROPERTIUS

All our efforts cannot even succeed in reproducing the nest of the tiniest little bird, its contexture, its beauty and convenience; or even the web of the puny spider. All things, says Plato, are produced by nature, by fortune, or by art; the greatest and most beautiful by one or the other of the first two, the least and most imperfect by the last.

These nations, then, seem to me barbarous in this sense, that they have been fashioned very little by the human mind, and are [70] still very close to their original naturalness. The laws of nature still rule them, very little corrupted by ours; and they are in such a state of purity that I am sometimes vexed that they were unknown earlier, in the days when there were men able to judge them better than we. I am sorry that Lycurgus and Plato did not know of them; for it seems to me that what we actually see in these nations surpasses not only all the pictures in which poets have idealized the golden age and all their inventions in imagining a happy state of man, but also the conceptions and the very desire of philosophy. They could not imagine a naturalness so pure [80] and simple as we see by experience; nor could they believe that our society could be maintained with so little artifice and human solder. This is a nation, I should say to Plato, in which there is no sort of traffic, no knowledge of letters, no science of numbers, no name for a magistrate or for political superiority, no custom of servitude, no riches or poverty, no contracts, no successions, no partitions, no occupations but leisure ones, no care for any but common kinship, no clothes, no agriculture, no metal, no use of wine or wheat. The very words that signify lying, treachery, dissimulation, avarice, envy, belittling, pardon—unheard of. How far [90] from this perfection would he find the republic that he imagined: *Men fresh sprung from the gods* [Seneca].

For the rest, they live in a country with a very pleasant and temperate climate, so that according to my witnesses it is rare to see a sick man there; and they have assured me that they never saw one palsied, bleary-eyed, toothless, or bent with age. They are settled along the sea and shut in on the land side by great high mountains, with a stretch about a hundred leagues wide in between. They have a great abundance of fish and flesh which bear no resemblance to ours, and they eat them with no other artifice than cooking. The first man who rode a horse there, though he had had dealings with them on several other trips, so horrified them in this posture that they shot him dead with arrows before they could recognize him. ... 100

They have their wars with the nations beyond the mountains, further inland, to which they go quite naked, with no other arms than bows or wooden swords ending in a sharp point, in the manner of the tongues of our boar spears. It is astonishing what firmness they show in their combats, which never end but in slaughter and bloodshed; for as to routs and terror, they know nothing of either. 110

Each man brings back as his trophy the head of the enemy he has killed, and sets it up at the entrance to his dwelling. After they have treated their prisoners well for a long time with all the hospitality they can think of, each man who has a prisoner calls a great assembly of his acquaintances. He ties a rope to one of the prisoner's arms, by the end of which he holds him, a few steps away, for fear of being hurt, and gives his dearest friend the other arm to hold in the same way; and these two, in the presence of the whole assembly, kill him with their swords. This done, they roast him and eat him in common and send some pieces to their absent friends. This is not, as people think, for nourishment, as of old the Scythians used to do; it is to betoken an extreme revenge. And the proof of this came when they saw the Portuguese, who had joined forces with their adversaries, inflict a different kind of death on them when they took them prisoner, which was to bury them up to the waist, shoot the rest of their body full of arrows, and afterward hang them. They thought that these people from the other world, being men who had sown the knowledge of many vices among their neighbors and 130

were much greater masters than themselves in every sort of wickedness, did not adopt this sort of vengeance without some reason, and that it must be more painful than their own; so they began to give up their old method and to follow this one.

I am not sorry that we notice the barbarous horror of such acts, but I am heartily sorry that, judging their faults rightly, we should be so blind to our own. I think there is more barbarity in eating a man alive than in eating him dead; and in tearing by tortures and the rack a body still full of feeling, in roasting a man bit by bit, in having him bitten and mangled by dogs and swine 140 (as we have not only read but seen within fresh memory, not among ancient enemies, but among neighbors and fellow citizens, and what is worse, on the pretext of piety and religion), than in roasting and eating him after he is dead. ...

So we may well call these people barbarians, in respect to the rules of reason, but not in respect to ourselves, who surpass them in every kind of barbarity.

Their warfare is wholly noble and generous, and as excusable and beautiful as this human disease can be; its only basis among them is their rivalry in valor. They are not fighting for the 150 conquest of new lands, for they still enjoy that natural abundance that provides them without toil and trouble with all necessary things in such profusion that they have no wish to enlarge their boundaries. They are still in that happy state of desiring only as much as their natural needs demand; anything beyond that is superfluous to them. ...

READING CRITICALLY

What is Montaigne's point of view on the relationship between nature and culture, and how does that point of view inform his understanding of cultural difference?

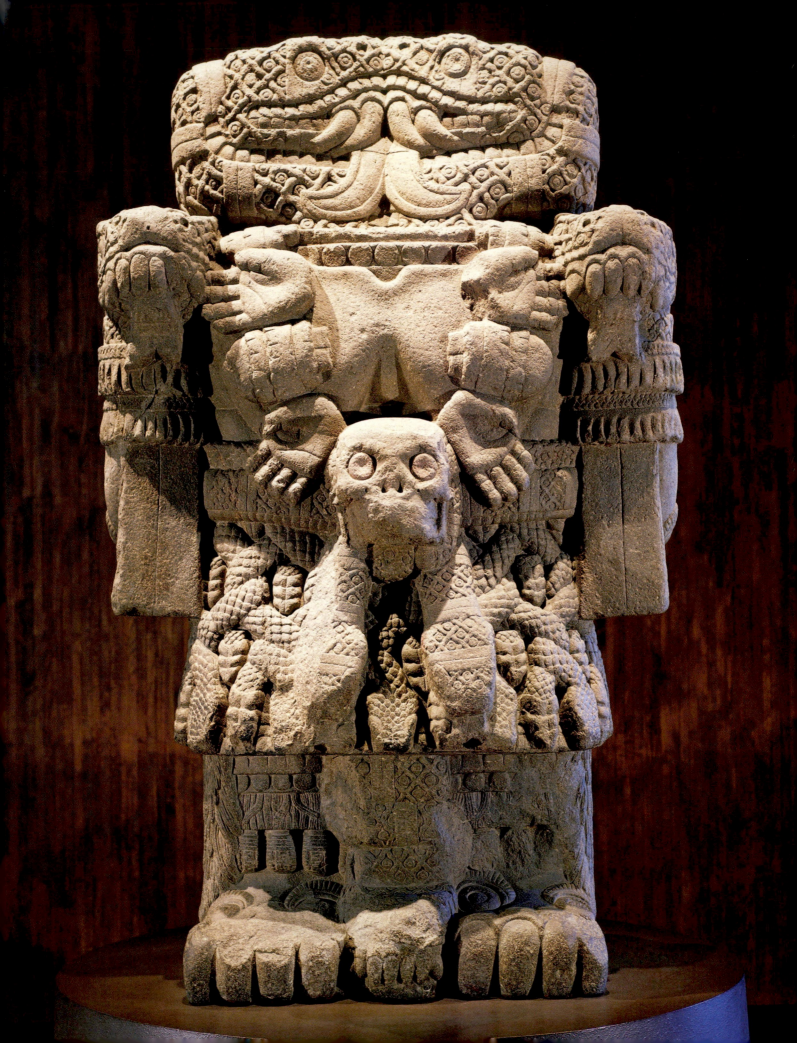

18 Encounter and Confrontation

The Impact of Increasing Global Interaction

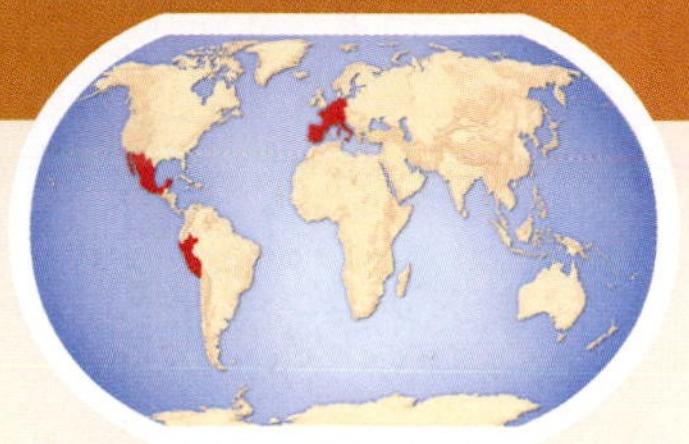

In 1519 to 1521, the Aztec Empire of Mexico was conquered by the Spanish *conquistador* ("conqueror") Hernán Cortés (1485–1547) and his army of 600 men through a combination of military technology (gunpowder, cannon, and muskets), disease inadvertently introduced by his troops, and a series of lies and violations of trust. The Aztecs possessed neither guns nor horses, nor much in the way of clothing or armor, all of which made them appear if not uncivilized, then completely vulnerable. They were also vulnerable because other native populations in Mexico deeply resented the fact that the Aztecs regularly raided their villages to obtain victims for blood sacrifice. According to Aztec legend, at the time of their exile from Tula, the supreme spiritual leadership of the culture was assumed by the bloodthirsty Huitzilopochtli, the god of war, who had emerged fully grown from the womb of his mother Coatlicue, the earth goddess, wielding his weapon, the Fire Serpent, Xiuhcoatl. A sculpture depicting Coatlicue may have originally stood in the temple to Huitzilopochtli at Tenochtitlán atop the Templo Mayor (Fig. **18.1**; and see Fig. 11.36 in

Chapter 11). Her head is composed of two fanged serpents, symbolizing two rivers of blood flowing from her decapitated head. She wears a necklace of human ears, severed hands, and, at the bottom, a human skull. The connection of blood to fertility is made clear in the snake that descends between her legs, which suggests both menstruation and the phallus.

Huitzilopochtli was born full-grown out of Coatlicue of necessity. Coatlicue was also mother of Coyolxauhqui, the Moon, and one day, while she was sweeping her temple on top of Coatepec hill, symbolically represented in Tenochtitlán by the Templo Mayor, she had been miraculously impregnated with Huitzilopochtli by a ball of feathers that floated down from the sky. Coyolxauhqui viewed the pregnancy of her mother as an affront, and she conspired to kill her mother. At that moment, Huitzilopochtli was born. He decapitated his treacherous sister, and cast her down from the top of Coatepec hill. At each tumble of her fall, she was further dismembered. This is the Aztec explanation for the phases of the moon. As the moon wanes each month, more and more of it disappears.

◀ **Fig. 18.1 *Coatlicue*, Aztec. 15th century.** Basalt, height 8'3". National Museum of Anthropology, Mexico City. Coatlicue is represented as headless because, as legend has it, she was decapitated at the beginning of the present creation.

((**Listen** to the chapter audio on **MyArtsLab**

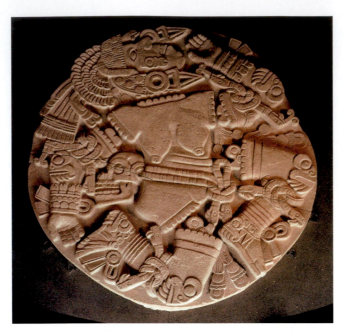

Fig. 18.2 *The Moon Goddess Coyolxauhqui,* **Aztec, from the Sacred Precinct, Templo Mayor, Tenochtitlán. ca. 1469.** Stone, diameter 10'11". Museo Templo Mayor, Mexico City. The sculpture was found lying at the base of the Templo Mayor, as if cast down by Huitzilopochtli.

A giant disk, over 10 feet across, found at the base of the Templo Mayor, depicts the goddess (Fig. 18.2), decapitated, arms and legs dismembered. She is adorned with a two-headed serpent belt bearing a skull, like the necklace of her mother Coatlicue in Fig. 18.1. Her torso, with flaccid breasts, is shown frontally. Issuing from her mouth is what appears to be her last breath. Thus victorious over the moon, Huitzilopochtli ordered the Aztec priests to search for a cactus with a great eagle perched upon it and there establish a city in his name. They soon found the place on the shores of Lake Texcoco. The cactus bore red fruit in the shape of the hearts that Huitzilopochtli devoured, and the eagle was the symbol of the god himself. The Aztecs proceeded to build their great city, Tenochtitlán, "the place of the prickly pear cactus."

Anthropological evidence suggests that just before Cortés's arrival, in about 1450, the Aztecs, in their thirst for blood sacrifice, had wiped out the entire population of Casas Grandes, near present-day Chihuahua in northern Mexico, a trading center containing over 2,000 pueblo apartments. Given such Aztec behavior, other tribes were willing to cooperate with Cortés. Cortés also had the advantage of superior weaponry, and he quickly realized that he could exploit the Aztecs' many vulnerabilities. One of the most important documents of the Spanish conquest, the 1581 *History of the Indies of New Spain*, by Diego de Durán, depicts Cortés's technological superiority (Fig. 18.3). Durán was a Dominican priest fluent in Nahuatl, the Aztec language. His *History* is the product of extensive interviews and conversations with the Aztecs themselves. It represents a concerted effort to preserve Aztec culture, recounting Aztec history from its creation story through the Spanish conquest. In this illustration,

a well-armed army led by Pedro de Alvarado, one of Cortés's generals, confronts the Aztec military orders of the Eagle and the Jaguar. The Spanish wear armor and fight with crossbows and firearms, while the Aztecs have only spears.

Despite their technological superiority, Alvarado's men were in some jeopardy. Alvarado was besieged by Aztecs angry at the slaughter of hundreds of Aztecs during the Fiesta of Toxcatl, staged to impress their Spanish visitors. The massacre by the Spaniards is illustrated in Durán's *History* (Fig. 18.4). The infamy of the Spaniards' attack and the Aztec retaliation are also described by a Franciscan missionary, Bernardino de Sahagún. Like Durán, Sahagún was fluent in Nahuatl, and he based his *History of the Things of New Spain* on interviews with surviving Aztecs (see **Reading 18.1**, page 631, for his full account).

Throughout these events, the Aztec king Motecuhzoma (formerly spelled Montezuma) had remained a prisoner of the Spanish forces. Cortés had pledged his friendship, but once he had been admitted into Tenochtitlán itself, he imprisoned Motecuhzoma. The Spanish conquistador had learned of an Aztec myth concerning Quetzalcóatl, the Feathered Serpent, who was widely worshiped throughout Mexico. In this myth, Quetzalcóatl was dethroned by his evil brother, Tezcatlipoca, god of war, and fled to the Gulf of Mexico, where he burst into flames and ascended to the heavens, becoming the Morning Star, Venus. In yet another version, he sailed away across the sea on a raft of

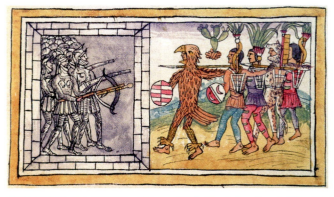

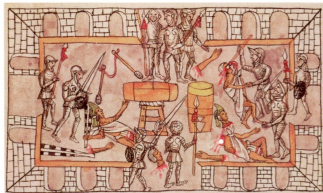

Figs. 18.3 and 18.4 (top) Aztecs confront the Spaniards; and (bottom) the Spanish massacre Aztec nobles in the temple courtyard. Both from Diego de Durán's *History of the Indies of New Spain*, 1581. Biblioteca Nacional, Madrid. Durán's work was roundly criticized during his lifetime for helping the "heathen" Aztecs maintain their culture.

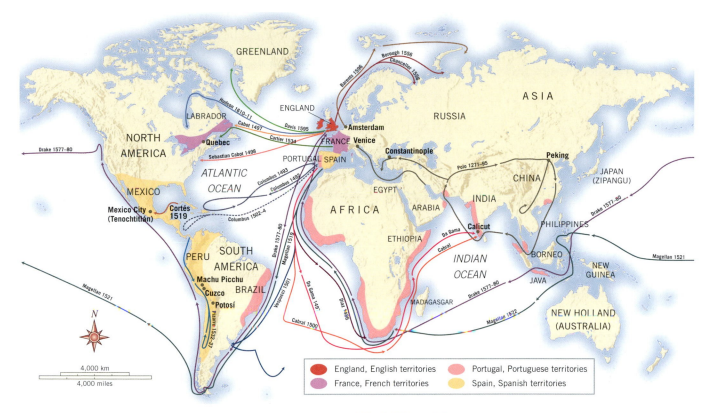

Map 18.1 **World exploration. 1486–1611.** Note Marco Polo's overland route to China in 1271 to 1295, which anticipated the great sea explorations by 200 years.

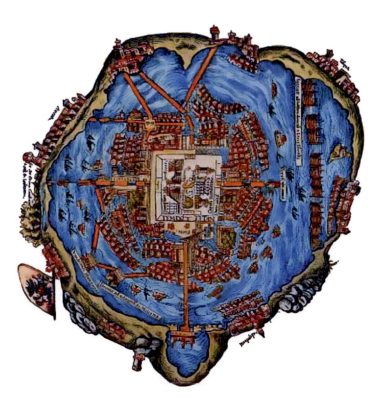

Fig. 18.5 Plan of Tenochtitlán, from Cortés's first letter to the king of Spain. 1521. Bernal Díaz, one of Cortés's conquistadors, compared the plan of Tenochtitlán to Venice. Set in the middle of Lake Texcoco, it was crisscrossed by canals. In the center of the island is the Templo Mayor.

serpents, promising one day to return. It was reputed that Quetzalcóatl was fair-skinned and bearded. Evidently, Motecuhzoma believed that Cortés was the returning Quetzalcóatl and welcomed him without resistance. Within two years, Cortés's army had crushed Motecuhzoma's people in the name of Spain. Of the 20 to 25 million inhabitants of Mexico at that time, only about 2 million survived—the remainder were wiped out by war and disease. Their beautiful capital, Tenochtitlán, surrounded by the waters of Lake Texcoco (Fig. **18.5**), would be quickly transformed into the capital of New Spain, its Templo Mayor reduced to rubble (see Fig. 11.36 in Chapter 11).

The imperial adventuring of Cortés in the Americas was mirrored around the globe, as Europeans sought to establish their power not only in the Americas, but in Africa, India, China, and Japan as well. This chapter considers the cultures of the Americas, Africa, India, China, and Japan in this period, and considers how Europe transformed these cultures as it explored the world (see Map **18.1**) and was itself transformed by contact with them. But European contact was not the only interaction these cultures experienced in the era. They also impacted one another. From a Western perspective, these cultures represented a wider world with Europe at its center. But from the point of view of these cultures, Europe represented the periphery, a cultural force invading their own centers of culture from the outside.

THE SPANISH IN THE AMERICAS

How did the Spanish impact the indigenous cultures of the Americas?

When Cortés entered the Aztec island capital of Tenoch-titlán, more than 200,000 people lived there. Gold-laden temples towered above the city. Gardens rich in flowers and fruit, and markets with every available commodity, dominated the city itself as Bernal Díaz (1492–1584), one of Cortés's conquistadores, would later recall the sight (**Reading 18.2**):

READING 18.2

from Bernal Díaz, *True History of the Conquest of New Spain* (ca. 1568; published 1632)

We were astounded. ... These buildings rising from the water, all made of stone, seemed like an enchanted vision. ... Indeed some of our soldiers asked whether it was not all a dream. ... It was all so wonderful that I do not know how to describe this first glimpse of things never heard of, seen, or dreamed of before. ...

Let us begin with the dealers in gold, silver, and precious stones, feathers, cloaks, and embroidered goods, and male and female slaves who are also sold there. ... Next there were those who sold coarser cloth, and cotton goods and fabrics made of twisted threads, and there were chocolate merchants with their chocolate. In this way you could see every kind of merchandise to be found anywhere in New Spain. ... We were astounded at the great number of people and the quantities of merchandise, and at the orderliness and good arrangements that prevailed.

What most astonished Cortés himself, as it had Díaz, was that Aztec civilization was as sophisticated as his own and unlike the civilization Columbus had encountered, with its naked, seemingly innocent natives. "So as not to tire Your Highness with the description of things of this city," Cortés wrote Queen Isabella of Spain, "I will say only that these people live almost like those in Spain, and in as much harmony and order as there, and considering that they are barbarous and so far from the knowledge of God and cut off from all civilized nations, it is truly remarkable to see what they have achieved in all things." This inclination to see a thriving civilization as uncivilized because it is unlike one's own is typical of the attitude of Westerners toward the peoples with whom they came into contact during the Age of Encounter. Other peoples were exactly that—the "Other"—a separate category of being that freed Western colonizers from any obligation to identify these peoples as equal, or even similar, to themselves (see *Context*, page 604).

It seemed paramount to the Spanish crown to begin to raise the native population from its "barbarous" condition by bringing it, as Columbus had put it from the beginning, to "the knowledge of God." The Spanish essentially obliterated the traditions of the Native American cultures they encountered, burning all their books, destroying almost every record of their history that they could lay their hands on, and crippling for all time our ability to adequately piece together a full picture of their culture. Churches were quickly built in Mexico City. And as the Church sought to convert native populations to the Catholic faith, the musical liturgy became a powerful tool. As early as 1523, Spanish monks created a school for Native Americans in Texcoco, Mexico (just east of Mexico City), and began teaching music, including Gregorian chant, the principles of polyphony, and composition, on an imported organ. Throughout the sixteenth century, missionaries used music, dance, and religious dramas to attract and convert the indigenous population to Christianity. A syncretic culture quickly developed, in which European styles were Indianized, and Indian culture was Christianized. An interesting example can be seen in the paintings depicting festival days in the seventeenth century, where Christian sacraments—in this case, marriage—occur side by side with traditional Aztec and Mayan rituals (see *Closer Look*, pages 602–603).

Pizarro in Peru

Spain conquered Peru in 1533 through the exploits of Francisco Pizarro (1474–1541) with an army of only 180 men. The Inca Empire Pizarro found in Peru was one of the largest empires in the world and included, in addition to Peru itself, most of what is now Ecuador, Bolivia, northern Chile, and part of Argentina (see Chapter 11). Pizarro's military strategy was aided by simple deceit. He captured the Inca emperor, Atahuallpa, who offered Pizarro a ransom of 13,420 pounds of gold and 26,000 pounds of silver. Pizarro accepted the ransom and then executed the unsuspecting emperor. He next proceeded to plunder Peru of the gold and silver artifacts that were part of its religious worship of the sun (gold) and moon (silver).

No work better may exemplify the impact of Spanish colonization on the native Inca of Peru than a portrait of Atahuallpa painted in Cuzco, the traditional capital of the Inca Empire, in the mid-eighteenth century (Fig. **18.6**). It is one of a series of 14 portraits of the Inca kings, most of which are based on an engraving by Antonio de Herrera in *General History of the Deeds of the Castilians*, first published in 1615, some 80 years after Pizarro's betrayal of Atahuallpa. Representations of the Inca kings were very popular in Peru in the seventeenth and eighteenth centuries, especially in the Cuzco households of the Peruvian *caciques*—Indian nobility who proudly traced their heritage back to the royal Inca families. Although painted by Cuzco Indians, the framing device and the portrait conventions are entirely European. Even more remarkable is the text around the frame identifying Atahuallpa. It labels him the "Bastard Tyrant," suggesting that this particular series of portraits may have been destined for a Spanish

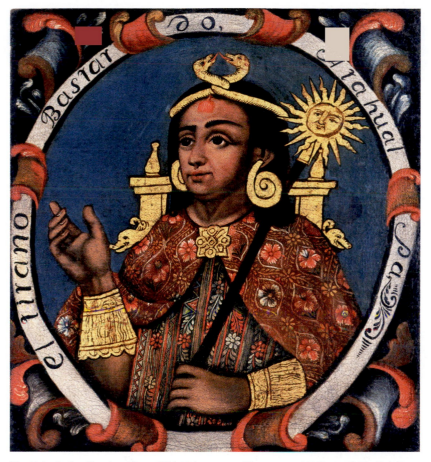

Fig. 18.6 *Atahuallpa*, from Peru. Mid-18th century. Oil on canvas, 23¾" × 21⅝". The Brooklyn Museum. 45.128.189. Note Atahuallpa's scepter, with its golden sun. Gold, for the Inca, was the "sweat of the sun." Each year, as the winter solstice approached and the sun seemed to disappear more each day, a priest would hold a ceremony at a large stone column called the *intihuatana*, meaning "for tying the sun," in order to prevent the sun from disappearing altogether. The Spanish destroyed the *intihuatanas*, but one survives at Machu Picchu.

and missiles; very odd clothing, bedding, and all sorts of strange articles for human use, all of which is fairer to see than marvels. These things were all so precious that they were valued at a hundred thousand guilders. But I have never seen in all my days that which so rejoiced my heart, as these things. For I saw among them amazing artistic objects, and I marveled over the subtle ingenuity of the men in these distant lands. Indeed I cannot say enough about the things which were there before me.

Accounts like this helped give rise to the belief in an entire city of gold, El Dorado, which continued to elude the grasp of the conquistadors under royal order who followed in Pizarro's footsteps in Peru, often with unhappy results. The treasures of gold and silver that were brought back would be melted down for currency, far more important than their artistic value to the warring Spanish monarchy. In fact, almost no gold or silver objects survive from the conquest.

Throughout the first half of the sixteenth century, the Spanish purchased thousands of slaves from the Portuguese and set them to work panning gold in the mountains of the Americas. But in 1555, the process for isolating silver from waste by combining it with mercury was developed, and silver began to be mined at an extraordinary rate. The largest silver mine in the Americas was at Potosí, Bolivia, 13,000 feet high in the Andes. From 1580 to 1650, the mines at Potosí never produced less than 7.6 million pesos annually, minted into coins near the mines. The city's population in 1547 was about 14,000. By 1650, Potosí had become the largest city in the Americas, with a population of nearly 160,000.

The Spanish conscripted Indians from their traditional agricultural chores to work the mines at Potosí. (African slaves worked almost all other mines in the Americas, but they were unable to adjust to the extremely high elevation of Potosí.) Spain instituted the *repartimiento*—called the *mita* by the Indians—requiring adult male Indians to devote a certain number of days each year to working for Spanish economic interests. At Potosí, 13,300 Indians were conscripted annually under the *mita*, one-third of them working at any one time. Literally thousands upon thousands of Indians rotated through the mine in the 70 years of its maximum output, and many thousands of them died in its inferno-like conditions. Under the *mita*, the Indians received minimum wages and had to buy supplies from the mine owners. This created a system of *debt patronage* that lasted into the early twentieth century across South America and Mesoamerica.

colonial household. After a series of rebellions throughout Peru in the late eighteenth century, however, Spanish rulers banned portraits of the Inca kings and destroyed many of them. At the same time, they banned native costumes, especially the elaborate costumes of the nobility that adorn Atahuallpa in this work.

Gold and Silver: The Monetary Motive

The acquisition of gold, silver, and other treasure was a strong motivation for European colonization of the Americas. Great masses of treasure were sent home from the New World. When the first Royal Fifth (that is, one-fifth of the treasures collected by Cortés and earmarked by contract for the king) arrived in Brussels, the German artist Albrecht Dürer was present:

I saw the things which were brought to the King from the New Golden Land: a sun entirely of gold, a whole fathom [six feet] broad; likewise, a moon, entirely of silver, just as big; likewise, sundry curiosities from their weapons, armor,

CLOSER LOOK

This monumental *biombo* (folding screen) is a work exceptional for its depiction of the syncretism of Christian and native traditions in seventeenth-century Mexico. The Spanish and Portuguese word *biombo* was derived from the Japanese word for folding screen, *byobu* (literally, "protection from the wind"). *Biombos* were first introduced to New Spain (Mexico) from Japan through the legendary Manila galleons that traded across the Pacific at the end of the sixteenth century. By the seventeenth century, they had become a standard and fashionable decoration in elite households. This *biombo* depicts festivities taking place in a village situated near canals—probably Santa Anita Ixtacalco, a famous site in the environs of Mexico City.

Something to Think About ...

What does this *biombo* have in common with the casta painting tradition (see Fig. 18.17)?

Here an Indian lies on the ground and juggles a log with his feet; the surrounding crowd includes Spaniards, recognizable by their seventeenth-century capes and collars.

The foreground is filled with Indians, many of them in native costume.

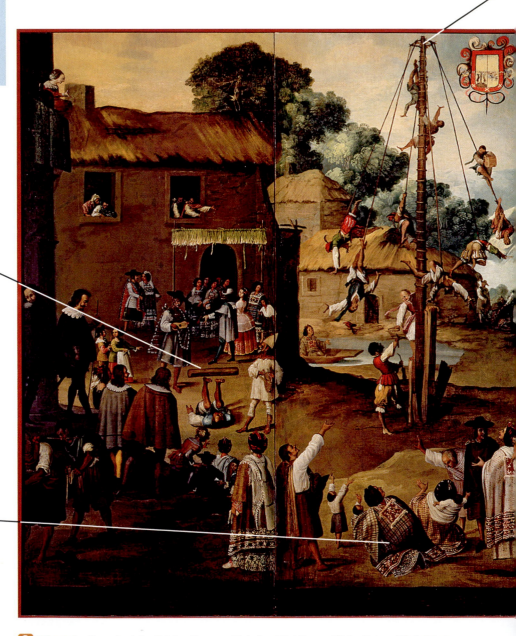

View the Closer Look for *Folding Screen with Indian Wedding and Flying Pole* on **MyArtsLab**

A *palo volador*, or flying pole, from which men called *voladores* swing to the ground on ropes. It represents a long-standing tradition preserved from pre-Hispanic times. Archeologist Demetrio Sodi has described *El Volador*, the original dance as performed by the Maya: "Five men are chosen to perform the dance. In the past, the dancers dressed as eagles or other birds. [Here all pretence of costume has been forsaken, suggesting that its purpose is more entertainment than ritual.] One is the captain and four take the roles of birdmen. A tall, strong, straight tree is stripped of its branches and bark and set upright in the main square of the town. A wooden cylinder is attached to the top of the trunk, with a frame from which hang the four ropes to which the birdmen are tied. The captain stands on top of the cylinder, playing a drum and flute, and dances, turning to the four corners of the universe. [This figure is likewise missing in the painting.] Then the four birdmen, tied by their ankles and hanging head down, slowly descend. The number of circles they turn before touching the earth varies, but in pre-Hispanic times, and even now on certain occasions, they circled thirteen times. The number of turns multiplied by the four birdmen equals the number of years of the pre-Hispanic calendar: fifty two, divided by four, thirteen year periods. *El Volador* undoubtedly has an intimate relation to worship of the sun. The captain who turns toward the cardinal points and the birdmen dressed as eagles (birds of the sun), make this clear."

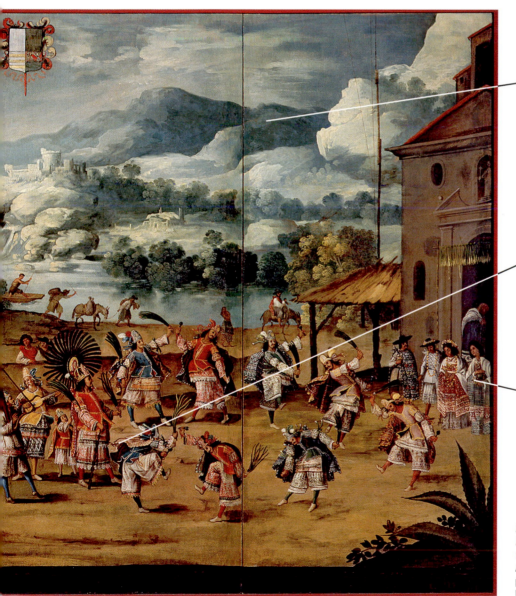

The landscape is completely imaginary, based on the Flemish landscape tradition or the Italian landscapes of Annibale Carracci.

Here nine Indians perform a *tecontin*, or Dance of Motecuhzoma. At the left, a sumptuously dressed figure plays the part of Motecuhzoma. An attendant holds a *mosqueador*, a large feather fan, over his head. The eight other dancers imitate the dance performed by the Aztec king, accompanied by a harpist and guitarist.

Indian newlyweds leave the church. Contemporary accounts tell us that at the dance's conclusion, the Motecuhzoma figure would lead all present in celebrating the Christian sacrament of marriage.

Folding Screen with Indian Wedding and Flying Pole (Biombo con desposorio indígena y palo volador). ca. 1690. Oil on canvas, 66" × 120". Los Angeles County Museum of Art. Purchased with funds provided by the Bernard and Edith Lewin Collection of Mexican Art Deaccession Fund. M.2005.54.

The "Other" in Western Consciousness

Any history of Western civilization must account for the relation of Western cultures to the other cultures with which they came into contact. The Age of Encounter, which began in the fifteenth century and ended in the seventeenth, resulted in the colonization of most of the non-Western world. Only the vast interior of Asia escaped Western domination. The effect of Western colonization was the displacement, enslavement, and large-scale death of native peoples. This last effect was at least partly unintentional, as Europeans introduced into the uncharted territories of their conquest common European diseases that the immune systems of native populations could not successfully fight. From the Western perspective, it hardly mattered. Europeans thought of these peoples as being in a state of cultural childhood, and because childhood mortality was extremely high in the Renaissance and something Europeans accepted as natural, they could absorb the deaths of these New World "children" with composure. Above all, these "innocents" were "primitive"—that is, they knew nothing of the Christian God and Western culture. At the very least, they required "civilizing."

Homi Bhaba, a great student of contemporary global culture, has reminded us of the "artifactual" consequences of Western colonization in an essay exploring the connection between contemporary culture and its colonial heritage. "The great remains of the Inca or Aztec world are the debris ... of the Culture of Discovery," he writes. "Their presence in the museum should reflect the devastation that has turned them from being signs in a powerful cultural system to becoming the symbols of a destroyed culture." The headdress of Motecuhzoma, presented to the Holy Roman Emperor Charles V by Cortés and now in the Museum of Ethnology in Vienna, is a case in point. Consisting of 450 green tail feathers of the quetzal bird, blue feathers from the cotinga bird, beads, and gold, it is a treasure of extraordinary beauty and can be appreciated in purely aesthetic terms, as the museum presents it. Yet as Homi Bhaba points out, "It seems appropriate ... [to make] present in the display of art what is so often rendered unrepresentable or left unrepresented—violence, trauma, dispossession." In other words, Bhaba believes that the headdress's history, the tale of Cortés and his betrayal of Motecuhzoma, should enter into the museum display.

Bhaba is critiquing museum practice, but his admonition applies as well to this text. Many of the images in this chapter are symbols of destroyed cultures. They were once signs of power. They were quickly consigned, in Western consciousness, to the category of the "Other." Those classified as "Other" were thought to be incapable of utilizing their own natural resources for themselves. The West considered those whom they colonized to be weak (because unsophisticated in the uses of Western technology), uneducated (though highly trained in their own traditions), and morally bankrupt (because "bloodthirsty," "naked," and "uninhibited"). Remember, the Greeks called all peoples who did not speak Greek "barbarians" (see Chapter 5). And just as the Romans tried to "Romanize" their provincial holdings, so too did Western colonizers from the era of the great explorers try to "civilize" the peoples they encountered.

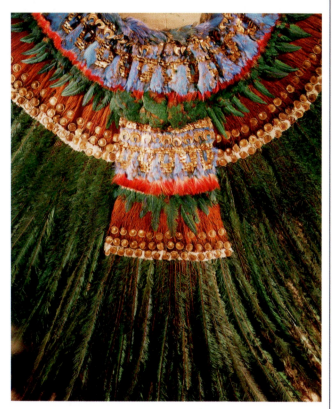

Quetzal feather headdress, Aztec. ca. 1520. Museum für Völkerkunde, Vienna. There is speculation but no proof that this headdress was worn by the Aztec emperor Motecuhzoma.

The wealth generated by the Potosí mine was arguably responsible for the ascendancy of Spain as an empire during the sixteenth century. But the exploitation of the people and natural resources of the Americas that the Potosí mine represents thrusts the dark side of the Age of Encounter into astonishing relief. The Dominican monk Francisco de la Cruz was one Spaniard who recognized this: "One of the reasons God will punish Spain is because it has not given due succour and salvation to the Indians. ... The time will come when Peru will be ruled independent of Spain." The Inquisition burned de la Cruz at the stake in Lima on April 13, 1578, for such progressive thinking.

WEST AFRICAN CULTURE AND THE PORTUGUESE

What impact did the Portuguese have on African culture and what kinds of traditions did these cultures maintain after contact?

Portugal was as active as Spain in seeking trading opportunities through navigation, but focused on Africa and the East instead of the Americas. In 1488, Bartholomeu Dias (ca. 1450–1500), investigating the coast of West Africa (Map **18.2**), was blown far south by a sudden storm, and turning northeast, found that he had rounded what would later be called the Cape of Good Hope and entered the Indian Ocean. Following Dias, Vasco da Gama (ca. 1460–1524) sailed around the cape with four ships in 1497 and reached Calicut, India, 10 months and 14 days after leaving Lisbon. Then, in 1500, Pedro Cabral (ca. 1467–ca. 1520), seeking to repeat da Gama's voyage to India, set out from the bulge of Africa. Sailing too far westward, he landed in what is now Brazil, where he claimed the territory for Portugal.

After Bartholomeu Dias's exploration of the west coast of Africa, it did not take long for European and African traders to extend existing practices of human exploitation that were common on both continents. This trade in human labor would eventually take on a scope and dimension not previously seen. The Portuguese exploitation of African labor was

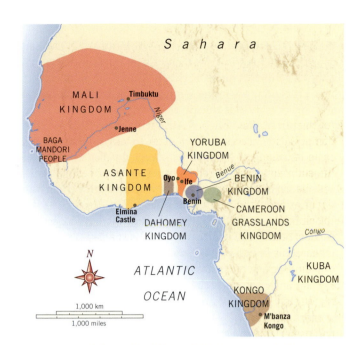

Map 18.2 Sub-Saharan West Africa. 1200–1700. While Muslim traders had extensive knowledge of North Africa, little was known of sub-Saharan Africa before the Portuguese explorations of the fifteenth and sixteenth centuries.

financed principally by a Florentine banker together with a group of other financiers from Genoa. Over the course of four centuries, the Portuguese transported millions of Africans across the Atlantic (Map **18.3**) on the **Middle Passage**, so named because it formed the base of a triangular trade system: Europe to Africa, Africa to the Americas (the

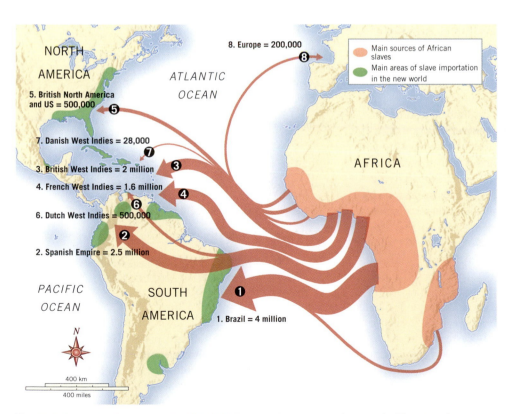

Map 18.3 Transatlantic slave trade. 1450–1870. These numbers are approximate, and subject to much scholarly debate.

Middle Passage), and the Americas to Europe. No one can say with certainty just how many slaves made the crossing, although estimates range between 15 and 20 million. Part of the problem is the unknown numbers who died of disease and harsh conditions during the voyage. For instance, in 1717, a ship reached Buenos Aires with only 98 survivors of an original 594 slaves. Such figures, though, were probably not unusual.

For a while, at least, the Portuguese enjoyed a certain status as divine visitors from the watery world, the realm of Olokun, god of the sea. They were considered to be the equivalent of the mudfish, because they could both "swim" (in their boats) and walk on land. The mudfish was sacred to the people of Benin, who saw it as a symbol of both transformation and power. (It lies dormant all summer on dry mudflats until fall when the rains come and it is "reborn.") The fish is a symbol of power because it can deliver strong electric shocks and possesses fatal spines. Likewise, the Portuguese seemed to be born of the sea and possessed fatal "spines" of their own—rifles and musketry.

An example of this association of the mudfish with the Portuguese is a decorative design that forms the tiara of an ivory mask worn as a hip pendant by the *oba* Esigie (r. 1504–50) (Figs. **18.7** and **18.8**). (An *oba* is the supreme traditional head of a Yoruba town.) The pendant probably depicts the queen mother (that is, the *oba*'s mother), or *iyoba*. Esigie's mother was named Idia, and she was the first woman to hold officially the position of *iyoba*. Apparently, when the neighboring Igala people of lower Niger threatened to conquer the Benin, Idia raised an army and by using magical powers helped Esigie defeat the Igala army. Part of her magic may have been the enlistment of Portuguese help. In acknowledgment of the Portuguese aid, the *iyoba*'s collar bears decorative images of bearded Portuguese sailors and alternating sailors and mudfish at the top of her tiara.

The impact of the Portuguese merchants, and of the Catholic missionaries who followed them, was not transforming, though it was undeniable and at times devastating. The Benin culture has remained more or less intact since the time of encounter. Today, for instance, during rituals and ceremonies, the *oba* wears at his waist five or six replicas of masks such as the *iyoba*'s, as well as the traditional coral-bead headdress. Oral traditions, like the praise poem (see Chapter 11), remain in place, despite attempts by Western priests to suppress them. If anything, it has been the last 50 years that have most dramatically transformed the cultures of Africa. But it was the institution of slavery, long practiced in Africa and the Middle East and by the Yoruba of Ife (their founding city) and the Benin peoples, that most dramatically impacted Portuguese and Western culture.

At first Benin had traded gold, ivory, rubber, and other forest products for beads and, particularly, brass. The standard medium of exchange was a horseshoe-shaped copper or brass object called a *manilla*, five of which appear in an early sixteenth-century Benin plaque portraying a Portuguese warrior (Fig. **18.9**). Such metal plaques decorated

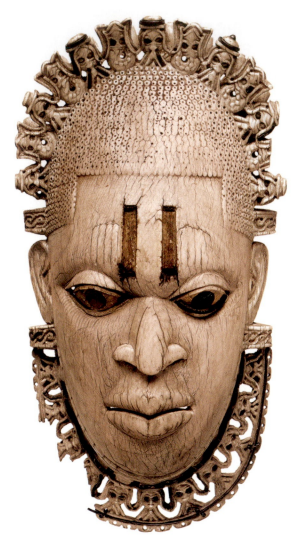

Fig. 18.7 Mask of an *iyoba* (queen mother), probably Idia, Court of Benin, Nigeria. ca. 1550. Ivory, iron, and copper, height 9⅜". The Metropolitan Museum of Art, New York. The Michael C. Rockefeller Memorial Collection, Gift of Nelson A. Rockefeller, 1972 (1978.412.323). The scarification lines on the forehead were originally inlaid with iron, and so were its pupils, both symbols of strength.

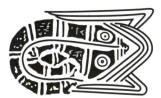

Fig. 18.8 Symbol of a coiled mudfish. Found throughout the art of Benin and in the tiara worn by the *iyoba* in Fig. 18.7.

the palace and royal altar area particularly, and here the soldier brings with him the very material out of which the plaque is made. If his weapons—trident and sword—suggest his power, it is a power in the service of the Benin king, at least from the Benin point of view.

The Portuguese also picked up thousands of small objects—amulets, trinkets, and so on—that they termed practice. At the start of the era, around 1492, there were an estimated 140,000 to 170,000 African slaves in Europe and they were represented in the art of the West (see Fig. 14.23 in Chapter 14 and Fig. 15.26 in Chapter 15). But in about 1551, the Portuguese began shipping thousands more slaves to Brazil to work in the sugar plantations there. War captives proved an insufficient source of bodies, and the Portuguese took whomever they could get their hands on. Furthermore, they treated these slaves much more harshly than the Muslims had. They chained them, branded them, and often literally worked them to death. In short, the Portuguese inaugurated a practice of **cultural hegemony** (cultural domination) that set the stage for the racist exploitation that has haunted the Western world ever since.

Kingdom of the Kongo

A thousand miles south of Benin, in the basin of the Congo River, comprising parts of present-day Angola, Gabon, the Democratic Republic of Congo, and the Republic of Congo, the kingdom of the Kongo rose to prominence sometime around 1400. Like many of the West African cultures to the north, its resources derived from the equatorial forest. Its capital city, Mbanza Kongo, was home to from 2 to 3 million people. *Mbanza* means "residence of the king," and its king lived in a royal residence on the top of a hill overlooking the Lulunda River.

One of the king's titles was *Matombola*, "the one who summons spirits from the land of the dead." This land, the Kongolese believed, lay across the sea, beneath the waters of the earth. Thus, when the Portuguese arrived by sea, they were believed to be visitors from that other world, and it was assumed that their king was the Kongo ruler's counterpart among the dead. As a result, one of the first gifts that the Kongolese king sent to the king of Portugal was an ivory horn carved from an elephant tusk (Fig. **18.10**), associated in the Kongolese mind with all royalty. The gift served to establish, at least from the point of view of the Kongolese king, the equality of the two rulers. An account of a visit to Mbanza Kongo by Portuguese missionaries in 1491 describes how horn players painted in white in memory of their ancestors met them. They played their song 12 times, a deep resonating melody that the missionaries found

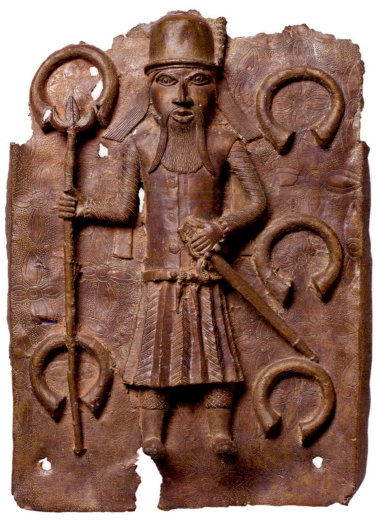

Fig. 18.9 *Portuguese Warrior Surrounded by Manillas,* **Court of Benin, Nigeria. 16th century.** Bronze, 18" × 13" × 3". Kunsthistorisches Museum, Vienna. Notice the background of the bronze, which is incised with jungle floral images.

fetisso, a sixteenth-century Afro-Portuguese pidgin word from which derives our word **fetish,** an object believed to have magical powers similar to those of Western objects such as rosaries or reliquaries. But eventually the trade turned to slaves. Africans had long been selling slaves, the victims of war with neighboring territories, to Muslim traders. But the Portuguese dramatically expanded the

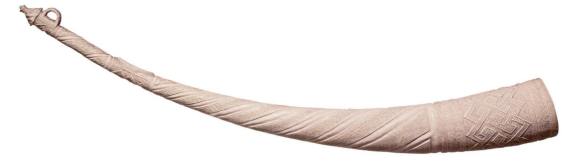

Fig. 18.10 *Mpungi,* **an ivory horn, from Kongo. Collected before 1553.** Length 32½". Museo degli Argenti, Florence. Ivory horns are found throughout equatorial Africa, almost always associated with the royal court. They are used today to announce the arrival of a king, among other things.

wholly melancholy. In fact, the Kongolese believed that the dead understood these notes, and that at their sound the ancestors of the royal line rose up to aid the ruler in governing his people.

The Kongolese were attracted to Christianity. As early as 1491, the Kongo king Nzinga aNkuwa converted and was baptized as Joao I. Not long after, his son and heir ordered that Christianity become the state religion. The interest shown by the African peoples in the message of the Christian missionaries (as well as earlier, in the sub-Sahara, to Islamic missionaries) can be explained by the fact that they, too, traditionally accepted the duality of the universe and the existence of an afterlife. And yet the Africans showed an amazing capacity to adapt the outward forms of Christianity to their own cultural practices. For instance, across almost all of West Africa, the cross traditionally stood for the order of the cosmos, and was a talisman of extraordinary power usually associated with royal authority. Furthermore, in the Kongo in particular, the cross shape echoed the shape of the iron swords that served as the symbol of Kongo political authority. It is hardly surprising, then, that Christian crosses were soon adapted to the traditional ritual practices of the Kongo royal court. They could help the ruler in his role as healer, judge, or even rainmaker—any time it might be necessary to make contact with ancestral spirits.

Such Africanization of the postmedieval Christian practice is especially apparent in an ivory Crucifixion plaque from the Vili culture (a subset of the Kongo kingdom) on the Atlantic coast north of the Congo River (Fig. 18.11). The Vili artist depicted Christ with African facial features, as well as the beard (symbol of wisdom) and hairstyle of the Kongo nobility. Attendants kneel beside Christ in the traditional posture of respect, touching his loincloth, which he wears in the Vili royal manner, in admiration for the material itself. It is not so clear, in other words, whether the Vili artist who made this plaque was representing Christian doctrine or adapting it to African tradition by equating Christ with Kongolese royalty—in much the same way that Europeans rulers, especially the pope, identified themselves and their governments with the Church. What this and other images like it demonstrate is the complex exchange between cultures that the Age of Encounter inaugurated. We must read these images, simultaneously, as emblems of the forcible transformation of other cultures into the likeness of the West and as adaptive strategies for cultural survival.

Strategies of Cultural Survival: The Dance

Almost all African cultures emphasized the well-being of the group over the individual, a conviction invoked, guaranteed, and celebrated by the masked dance. In the face of European challenges to the integrity of African cultures, dance became an especially important vehicle in maintaining cultural continuity. The masked dance is, in fact, a ritual activity so universally practiced from one culture

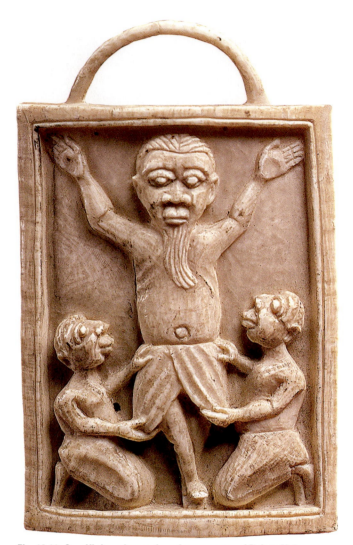

Fig. 18.11 Crucifixion plaque, from Loango area of Pointe Noire (Democratic Republic of the Congo), Vili culture. Collected in 1874. Ivory, 3¼" × 2¼". Museum für Völkerkunde, Berlin. The Portuguese claimed to have converted the kingdom of the Kongo to Christianity as early as the 1490s.

to the next across West Africa that it could be called the focal point of the region's cultures. It unites the creative efforts of sculptors, dancers, musicians, and others. Originally performed as part of larger rituals connected with stages in human development, the passing of the seasons, or stages of the agricultural year, the masked dance in recent years has become increasingly commercial—a form of entertainment disconnected from its original social context. A modern photograph of the *banda* mask being used by the Baga Mandori people who live on the Atlantic coastline of Guinea is unique, however, in capturing an actual *banda* dance (Fig. 18.12). The *banda* mask dance is always performed at night, with only torches for illumination, but in 1987 villagers agreed, for the sake of photography, to begin the performance at dusk. The photographs taken that evening by Fred Lamp, Curator of African Art at the Yale University Art Gallery, are the only extant photographs of an actual *banda* performance.

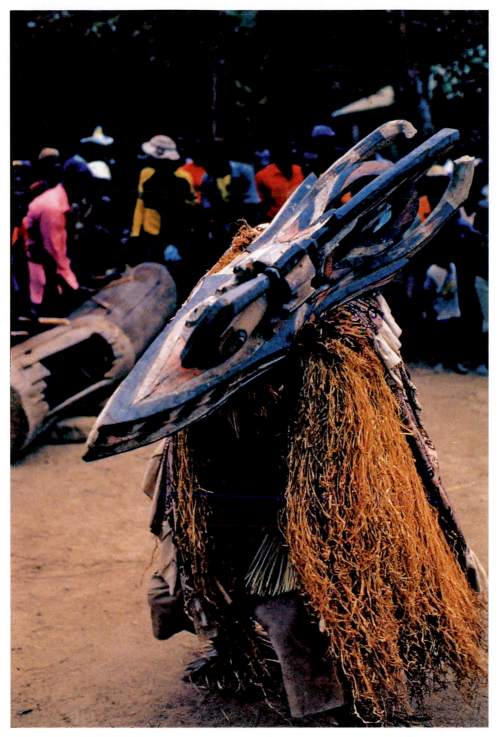

Fig. 18.12 Dance of *banda*, Baga Mandori, Guinea, 1987. The choreography of the dance involves the dancer spinning madly while holding the headdress aloft, then twirling the mask in a series of figure 8s, finally dashing it down to the ground before returning it to his head, all in one seamless burst of movement.

The *banda* mask is a sort of amalgam of different creatures, combining the jaws of a crocodile, the face of a human, the elaborate hairstyle of a woman, the body of a serpent, the horns of an antelope, the alert ears of a deer, and, rising between the horns, the tail of a chameleon. The *banda* mask dance is generally performed at initiations, harvest ceremonies, and funerals, and is renowned for

its spectacular acrobatics, with the wearer spinning high in the air and low to the ground, as if in defiance of the enormous weight of the mask itself. Like Native American kachina dolls (see Fig. 1.19 in Chapter 1), the *banda* mask is believed to possess *agency*. That is, it helps to effect change—the transformation (as symbolized by the chameleon's tail) from adolescence to adulthood, from fall to

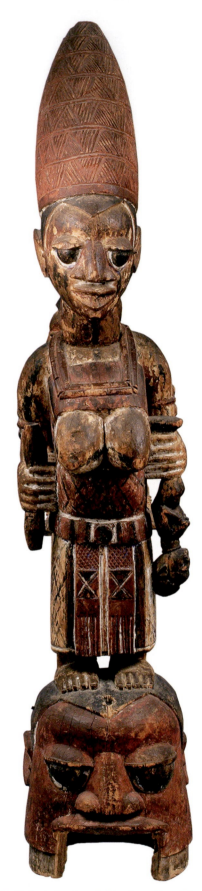

Fig. 18.13 *Elefon* **helmet mask, Yoruba culture, Nigeria. After 1900.** Wood, height 51½". The University of Iowa Museum of Art, Stanley Collection. When not in use in a ritual dance, such masks were kept in the shrine of the family patriarch, where they were worshiped.

winter, from life to death. And it embodies the collective consciousness of the group by incorporating into its single visage the diversity of the natural world.

Interestingly, African cultures do not have a word for "mask." Rather, each mask has a particular name that is generally the word for the ancestor or supernatural being that the mask helps to make manifest. The mask, then, is not so much an object in its own right as it is a thing to be danced. Thus the *elefon* helmet mask (Fig. **18.13**), from the Yoruba culture at the eastern end of the West African forests, near the Niger River, evokes the spirit of the ancestral emperors of the Yoruba city of Oyo, who were called *Elefon*. Like most African masks, this one was worn by a male, and the mask proper—its bottom quarter—is male. But the top three-quarters consist of a representation of a female. She carries a fly whisk in one hand and wears a tall conical crown and a necklace of large coral beads—all symbols of a Yoruba chief. And indeed, though rare, there are instances of Yoruba women serving as chief. The highest-ranking woman was called *Iyalode*, or "mother of all." The female figure on the *elefon* mask holds the upside-down figure of another woman in her left hand. This gesture represents the power of the *Iyalode* to exercise discipline over women who have erred. The *Iyalode* also represented the collective interests of women before the king.

Strategies of Cultural Survival: Communicating with the Spirit World

Throughout Africa, from the moment of European contact onward, traditional systems of belief, ritual practices, and local customs have continued to exhibit a strong presence despite the ongoing influence of Western and Islamic cultures. It is almost certain that many, if not most, of these beliefs, rituals, and customs date back centuries and help to establish a very real sense of cultural continuity.

The ritualistic use of objects connected with birth, death, and ancestral connections to the spirit world figure prominently in maintaining this sense of continuity. A fascinating example in Yoruba culture is the carving of *ere ijebi*, or "twin figures" (Fig. **18.14**) when a twin dies. Since the Yoruba have one of the highest rates of twin births in the world (45 for every 1,000 births), and since twins are generally smaller and weaker than single-born infants, twin deaths are comparatively common. While the *ere ijebi* are being carved, the mother of the deceased child lavishes gifts of food on the carver, and when the sculpture is finished, she carries it home on her back, wrapped as if it were living, while the women of the village sing songs to accompany her. The mother then performs various tasks to honor the figure, washing it as if it were alive, rubbing its body with powder and oil, offering it what are believed to be the favorite foods of twins—beans and palm oil—and dressing it in rich garments and beads. Honored in this way, the spirit of the deceased twin will, it is believed, bring to its parents both wealth and good fortune.

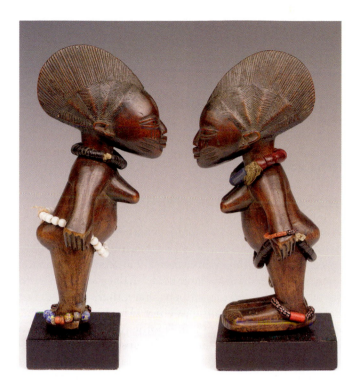

Fig. 18.14 Twin Figures (*ere ibeji*), Yoruba culture, Nigeria. 20th century. Wood, height 7⅞". The University of Iowa Museum of Art, Stanley Collection. This pair of *ere ibeji* appear to have been carved at the same time, by the same artist in the Yoruba city of Abeokuta. A strong case has been made that they are the work of Akiode, who died in 1936.

The Baule people of the Côte d'Ivoire lavish this same sort of attention upon what are known as "spirit spouses" (Fig. 18.15). The Baule believe that a spirit world exists as a sort of parallel universe to their own. We all lived, they believe, in this spirit world before we were born, and we lived there very much as we do in this world, in families and communities, as husband and wife. Sometimes our attachment to our spirit spouse is so strong that in this world we continue to dream of him or her. As a result, we cannot function in this world in the manner that might be expected. A woman still attached to her spirit spouse might not be able to bear children. A man might not achieve the level of status that his parents expect, or he might not marry. Sometimes a spirit spouse gets jealous of his or her earthly counterpart and causes discord in the marriage. In order to appease the spirit spouse or right the balance between the spirit world and the earthly realm, so that life on earth will move on smoothly, a village diviner will order that a carving be made representing the otherworld wife (*blolo bla*) or the otherworld husband (*blolo bian*). Just as the Yoruba women care for their twin figures, the Baule dress their spirit spouses in beautiful textiles and jewelry, wash and oil them, and generally appease them with caresses until they take on a highly glossed sheen that demonstrates how much attention has been lavished upon them. The resulting beauty of the figure announces its

owner's success in appeasing and communicating with the spirit world.

In the Kongo kingdom in the late nineteenth century, figures were carved that embodied the Kongolese resistance to the imposition of foreign ideas as European states colonized the continent. Throughout Central Africa, all significant human powers are believed to result from communication with the dead. Certain individuals can communicate with the spirits in their roles as healers, diviners, and defenders of the living. They are believed to harness the powers of the spirit world through magical figures called *minkisi* (singular *nkisi*). Among the most formidable

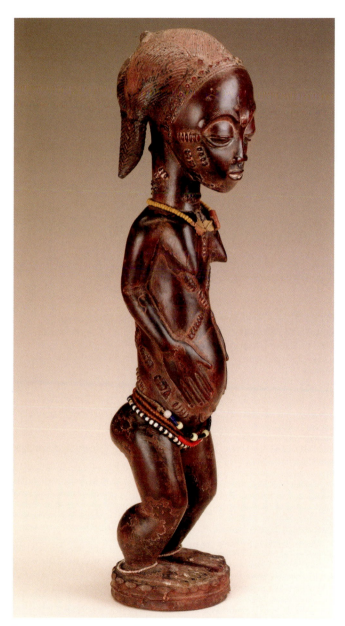

Fig. 18.15 Spirit Spouse (*blolo bla*), Baule culture, Côte d'Ivoire. Early to mid-20th century. Wood, glass beads, gold hollow beads, plant fiber, white pigment encrustation, height 19¼". National Museum of African Art, Smithsonian Institution, Washington, D.C. (85-15-2). Such figures were placed in private shrines, usually in the bedroom.

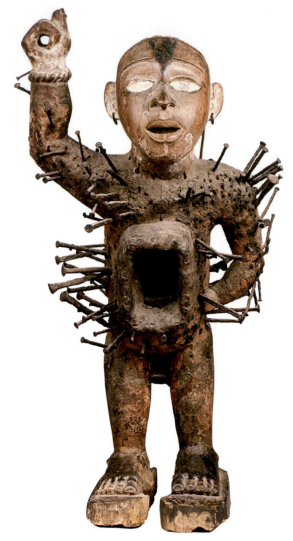

Fig. 18.16 Magical figure (*nkisi nkonde*), Kongo (Muserongo), Zaire. Late 19th century. Wood, iron nails, glass, and resin, height 20". The University of Iowa Museum of Art, Stanley Collection. The *bilongo* ("medicine") is placed in the figure's *mooyo*, a term that means both "belly" and "life."

View the Closer Look for a *nkisi nkonde* figure on **MyArtsLab**

of *minkisi* is the type known as *minkonde* (singular *nkonde*). These are said to pursue witches, thieves, adulterers, and wrongdoers by night (Fig. **18.16**). The communicator activates a *nkonde* by driving nails, blades, and other pieces of iron into it so that it will deliver similar injuries to those worthy of punishment.

Minkonde figures stand upright, as if ready to spring forward. In many figures, one arm is raised and holds a knife or spear (often missing, as here), suggesting that it is ready to attack. Other *minkonde* stand upright in a stance of alertness, like a wrestler challenging an opponent. The hole in the stomach of the figure illustrated here contained magical "medicines," known as *bilongo*, sometimes blood or plants, but often kaolin, a white clay believed to be closely linked to the world of the dead, and red ocher, linked symbolically to blood. Such horrific figures—designed

to evoke awe in the spectator—were seen by European military commanders as evidence of an aggressive native opposition to colonial control and by European missionaries as direct evidence of African idolatry and witchcraft, and so many of them were destroyed. More accurately, the *minkonde*, like the Baule spirit spouses and Yoruba twins, represented a form of *animism*, a belief in the existence of souls and a conviction that nonhuman things can also be endowed with a soul. Animism is the foundation of many world religions.

The Slave Trade: Africans in the Americas

Adaptive strategies were especially important to those Africans transported across the Atlantic in the Portuguese slave trade. Torn from their native cultures, and often re-situated with other Africans from cultures utterly unfamiliar to them, their cultural identity was severely challenged. But before long, across South America and Mexico, Africans outnumbered white Spaniards roughly two to one. Because of the almost total absence of European women in the Americas during the sixteenth century, the Spanish turned to other women for sexual partners. Very soon there were large numbers of people of variously mixed race, called *castas* or *castes*. The most common castas were *mestizo* (Spanish-Indian), *mulatto* (Spanish-black), *zambo* (black-Indian), and then later, in the seventeenth century, *castizo* (a light-skinned mestizo) and *morisco* (a light-skinned mulatto). By the eighteenth century, as growing numbers of Philippinos and other Asian populations arrived in Mexico (generally as slaves), and as the various castes themselves intermingled, a new term came into the language to indicate racial indeterminacy, *tente en el aire*, "hold yourself in the air." By the end of the century, fully one-quarter of the population was of mixed race.

Indeed, by the early years of the eighteenth century, a distinct genre of painting even developed, so-called **casta painting** (Fig. **18.17**). By and large, casta paintings exist in sets of 16, recording the process of race-mixing in the Americas. Each portrays a man and a woman of different races with one or two of their children, and each is titled with a sort of equation, as in the image illustrated here, a Spaniard plus a black equals a mulatto. These casta paintings are generally arranged hierarchically, with pure-blooded Spanish or *criollo* (descendants of pure-blooded Spanish born in Mexico) parents producing equally pure-blooded offspring in the first position. The offspring of black parents were at the bottom, and Indians variously in the middle. The painting reproduced here is positioned, as inscribed at the top left, in sixth place in the hierarchical scale (so high, despite the black mother, because of the Spanish father). The Spaniard's African wife is making hot chocolate at the stove, while his mulatto son brings him a brazier to light his cigarette. The social difference between father and son is highlighted by the distinct difference in the richness of their clothing.

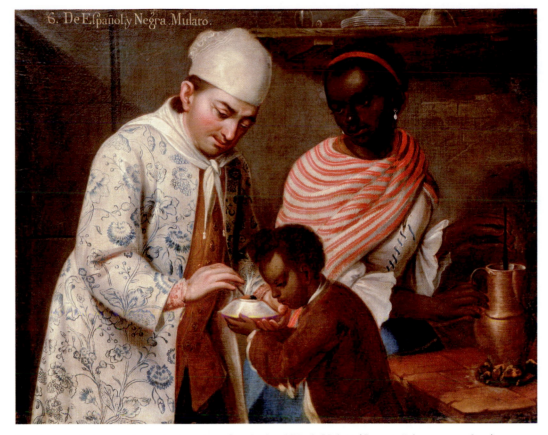

Fig. 18.17 Attributed to José de Alcíbar, *From Spaniard and Black, Mulatto* (*De español y negra, mulatto*). ca. 1760. Oil on canvas, 31" × 38¼". Denver Art Museum, Collection of Jan and Frederick R. Mayer. The man's coat underscores the cultural complexity of the scene. It is chintz, imported from India.

While it is clear that the casta paintings are indicative of the Spanish obsession with racial genealogy and a genuine interest in dynamics of racial intermixing—never before so readily apparent—that obsession was at least partly based on the Spanish nobility's insistence on affirming its own position at the top of the ladder. That said, the Franciscan priest Fray Juan de Torquemada, one of the first great historians of New Spain, could see in the great diversity of skin color that abounded in Mexico, the manifestation of divine purpose (**Reading 18.3**):

READING 18.3

from Fray Juan de Torquemada, *Indian Monarchies* (1615)

There is no other reason for this [variation in human complexion] than God's wish to display his marvels through the variety of colors. Like the colors of the flowers in a field, he wished for them to preserve that given to them by Nature. In this way, just as God is praised in the many shades of the flowers, so too is the Almighty blessed and praised in the different and varied colors of mankind. It is through his artifices and paintings that he chose to show the boundlessness of his wisdom.

The full title of Torquemada's book is *The Twenty-One Ritual Books and Indian Monarchy with the Origin and Wars of the West Indians, of Their Populations, Discoveries, Conquest, Conversion and Other Marvelous Things of the Same Land*, and this passage is taken from Ilona Katzew's groundbreaking study of 2004, *Casta Painting*, easily the most extensive survey of the genre ever compiled. Katzew argues that in the sense of heterogeneity established both in the writings of Torquemada and others and in casta paintings themselves, New Spain established an identity distinct from the Old World—and, it is worth pointing out, distinct from that of its neighbors to the north as well.

The cultures of New Spain and Peru comprised a diverse and pluralistic society like none before it in the world. Black Africans from widely divergent cultures in the Gulf of Guinea, the Congo River basin, and what is now Angola, introduced new words into the Spanish-Mexican language and new musical instruments (notably the marimba) and rhythms into popular music. As we saw, the religions of their native Africa had accepted a division of existence into a dual system roughly approximating the Christian division of body and soul, and they accepted the idea of an afterlife. So black Africans in the Americas readily accepted Christianity, to which they brought their own African practices, many of which have survived.

INDIA AND EUROPE: CROSS-CULTURAL CONNECTIONS

How did European contact affect Mogul India?

The synthesis of cultures so evident in the pluralistic society that developed in New Spain is also apparent in the art of India during roughly the same period. But in India, the synthesis was far less fraught with tension. The reason has much to do with the tolerance shown by India's leaders in the seventeenth and eighteenth centuries toward forces from the outside, which, in fact, they welcomed.

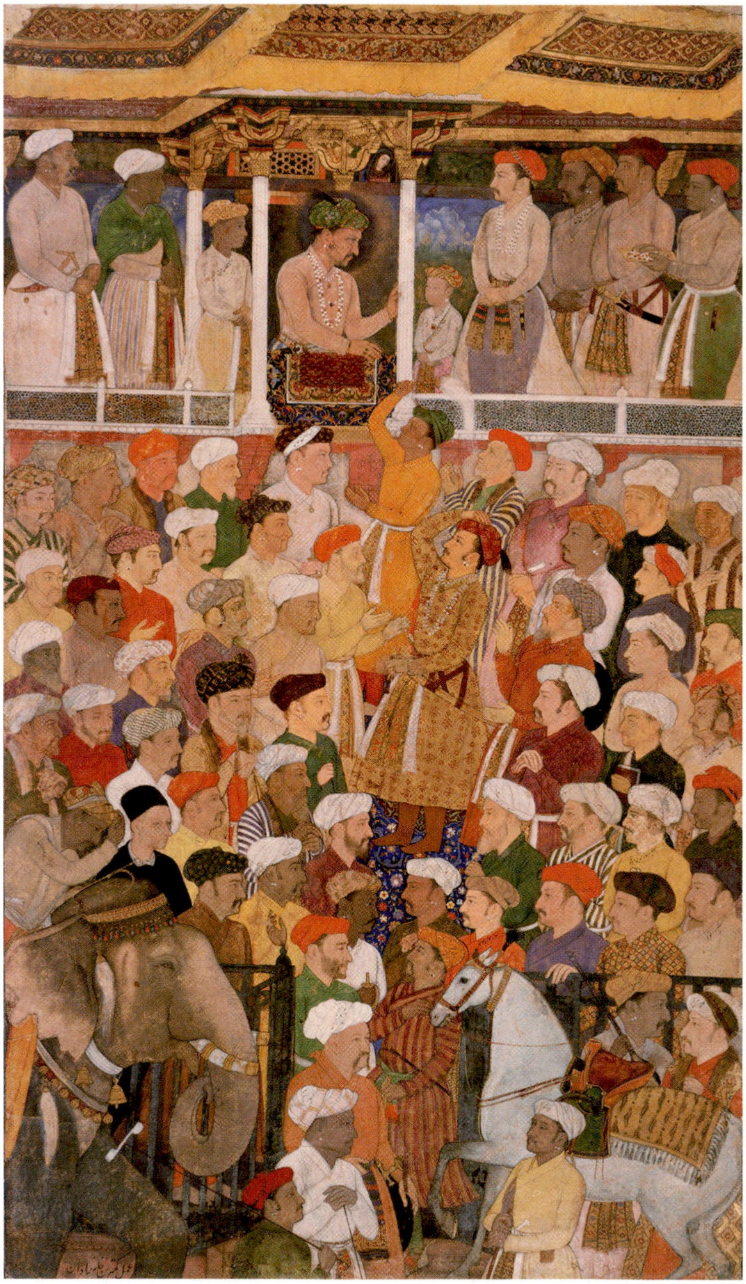

Islamic India: The Taste for Western Art

India's leaders in the seventeenth and eighteenth centuries were Muslim. Islamic groups had moved into India through the northern passes of the Hindu Kush by 1000 and had established a foothold for themselves in Delhi by 1200. In the early sixteenth century, a group of Turko-Mongol Sunni Muslims known as *Moguls* (a variation on the word *Mongol*) established a strong empire in northern India, with capitals at Agra and Delhi, although the Hindus temporarily expelled them from India between 1540 and 1555.

Their exile, in Tabriz, Persia, proved critical. Shah Tamasp Safavi (r. 1524–76), a great patron of the arts who especially supported miniature painting, received them into his court. The Moguls reconquered India with the aid of the shah in 1556. The young new Mogul ruler, Akbar (r. 1556–1605), was just 14 years of age when he took the throne, but he had been raised in Tabriz and he valued its arts. He soon established a school of painting in India, open to both Hindu and Islamic artists, taught by Persian masters brought from Tabriz. He also urged his artists to study the Western paintings and prints that Portuguese traders began to bring into the country in the 1570s. By the end of Akbar's reign, a state studio of more than 1,000 artists had created a library of over 24,000 illuminated manuscripts.

Akbar ruled over a court of thousands of bureaucrats, courtiers, servants, wives, and concubines. Fully aware that the population was largely Hindu, Akbar practiced an official policy of religious toleration. He believed that a synthesis of the world's faiths would surpass the teachings of any one of them. Thus he invited Christians, Jews, Hindus, Buddhists, and others to his court to debate with Muslim scholars. Despite taxing the peasantry heavily to support the luxurious lifestyle that he enjoyed, he also instituted a number of reforms, particularly banning the practice of immolating surviving wives on the funeral pyres of their husbands.

Under the rule of Akbar's son, Jahangir (r. 1605–27), the English taste for portraiture (see Chapter 19) found favor in India. The painting *Jahangir in Darbar* is a good example (Fig. **18.18**). It shows Jahangir, whose name means "World Seizer," seated between the two pillars at the top of the painting, holding an audience, or *darbar*, at court. His son, the future emperor Shah Jahan, stands just behind him. The figures in the street are a medley of portraits, composed in all likelihood from albums of portraits kept by court artists. Among them is a Jesuit priest

Fig. 18.18 Attributed to Manohar, *Jahangir in Darbar*. Northern India. Mogul period, about 1620. Opaque watercolor and gold on paper, 13¾″ × 7⅛″. Museum of Fine Arts, Boston. Francis Bartlett Donation of 1912 and Picture Fund 14.654. Photograph © 2013 Museum of Fine Arts, Boston. Nothing underscores the Mogul lack of interest in Western perspective more than the way in which the figure in the middle of the street seems to stand on the head of the figure below him.

from Europe dressed in his black robes (although nothing in the painting shows a familiarity with Western scientific perspective). The stiff formality of the figures, depicted in profile facing left and right toward a central axis, makes a sharp contrast to the variety of faces with different racial and ethnic features that fills the scene.

The force behind this growing interest in portraiture was the British East India Company, founded by a group of enterprising and influential London businessmen in 1599. King James I awarded the Company exclusive trading rights in the East Indies. A few years later, James sent a representative to Jahangir to arrange a commercial treaty that would give the East India Company exclusive rights to reside and build factories in India. In return, the Company offered to provide the emperor with goods and rarities for his palace from the European market.

Jahangir's interest in all things English is visible in a miniature, *Jahangir Seated on an Allegorical Throne*, by an artist named Bichitr (Fig. **18.19**). The miniaturist depicts Jahangir on an hourglass throne, a reference to the brevity of life. The shah hands a book to a Sufi teacher, evidently preferring the mystic's company to that of the two kings who stand below, an Ottoman Turkish ruler who had been conquered by Jahangir's ancient ancestor Tamerlane and, interestingly, King James I of England. The English monarch's pose is a three-quarter view, typical of Western portraiture but in clear contrast to the preferred profile pose of the Mogul court, which Jahangir assumes. The figure holding a picture at the bottom left-

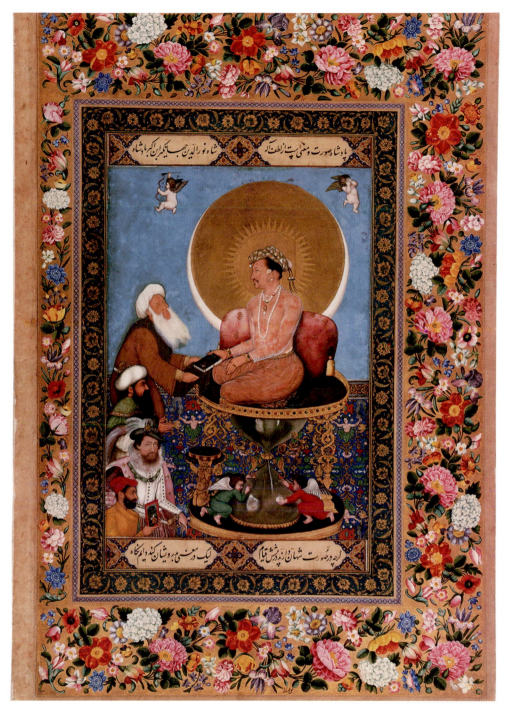

Fig. 18.19 Bichitr, *Jahangir Seated on an Allegorical Throne,* **from the** *Leningrad Album of Bichitr.* **ca. 1625.** Opaque watercolor, gold, and ink on paper, 10" × 7⅛". Freer Gallery of Art, Smithsonian Institution, Washington, D.C. (42.15V). Behind the shah is a giant halo or nimbus consisting of the sun and a crescent moon. It recalls those behind earlier images of Buddha.

hand corner of the composition may be the artist Bichitr himself. Two Western-style *putti* (cherubs) fly across the top of the composition: The one at the left is a Cupid figure, about to shoot an arrow, suggesting the importance of worldly love. The one at the right apparently laments the impermanence of worldly power (as the inscription above reads). At the bottom of the hourglass, two Western-style angels inscribe the base of the throne with the prayer, "Oh Shah, may the span of your life be a thousand years." The throne itself is depicted in terms of scientific perspective, but the carpet it rests upon is not. Framing the entire image is a border of Western-style flowers, which stand in marked contrast to the Turkish design of the interior frame. All told, the image is a remarkable blend of stylistic and cultural traditions, bridging the gap between East and West on a single page.

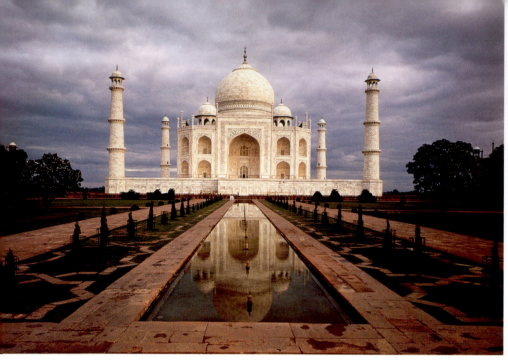

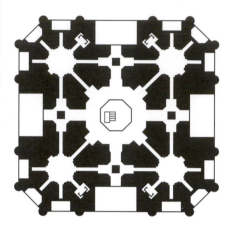

Fig. 18.20 Taj Mahal, Agra, India. Mogul period, ca. 1632–48. Originally Shah Jahan planned to build his own tomb across the river, a matching structure in black marble, connected to the Taj Mahal by a bridge. The shah's tomb was never built, and he is buried, with his beloved wife, in a crypt in the mausoleum's central chamber.

Fig. 18.21 Plan of the Taj Mahal, Agra. ca. 1632–48.

🔍 **View** the Closer Look for the Taj Mahal on **MyArtsLab**

Mogul Architecture: The Taj Mahal

Addicted to wine laced with opium, Shah Jahangir died in 1628, not long after the completion of the miniature wishing him a life of a thousand years. While his son Shah Jahan (r. 1628–58) did not encourage painting to the degree his father and grandfather had, he was a great patron of architecture. His most important contribution to Indian architecture—and arguably one of the most beautiful buildings in the world—is the Taj Mahal ("Crown of the Palace"), constructed as a mausoleum for Jahan's favorite wife, Mumtaz-i-Mahal (the name means "Light of the Palace"), who died giving birth to the couple's fourteenth child (Fig. **18.20**).

Sited on the banks of the Jumna River at Agra in northern India, the Taj Mahal is surrounded by gardens meant to evoke a vision of paradise as imagined in the Qu'ran. It is interesting to compare the wall mosaic of a landscape in the Great Mosque (see Fig. 9.9 in Chapter 9). Measuring 1,000 by 1,900 feet, the garden is interspersed with broad pathways, reflecting pools, and fountains that were originally lined by fruit trees and cypresses, symbols, respectively, of life and death. To the west of the building, in the corner of the property, is a red sandstone mosque, used for worship. Rising above the garden, and reflected in its pools, is the delicate yet monumental mausoleum of Taj Mahal itself.

The white marble tomb is set on a broad marble platform with minarets at each corner, their three main sections corresponding to the three levels of the mausoleum proper, thus uniting them with the main structure. At the top of these minarets are **chattri**, or small pavilions that are traditional embellishments of Indian palaces, from which muezzins can call the faithful to worship at the property's mosque. The main structure, the Taj Mahal proper, is basically square, although each corner is sliced off in order to create a subtle octagon. Each facade is identical: a central **iwan** (a traditional Islamic architectural feature consisting of a vaulted opening with an arched portal), flanked by two stories of smaller **iwans**. These voids in the facade contribute to the sense of weightlessness the building seems to possess. Four octagonal **chattris** positioned at each corner of the roof provide a transition to the central onion dome, which rises on its drum in a graceful swelling curve. The facades are inlaid with inscriptions and arabesques of semiprecious stones—carnelian, agate, coral, turquoise, garnet, lapis, and jasper—but these are so delicate and lacelike that they emphasize the whiteness of the whole rather than call attention to themselves.

Inside the Taj Mahal, the sequence of rooms is set out according to the favorite pattern of the Mogul period: an interpenetrating square and cross. There are eight small rooms on each of the two stories: one in each corner and one behind each **iwan**. The largest chamber is the octagonal central area, which rises two stories to a domed ceiling beneath the outer dome (Fig. **18.21**). An intricately carved openwork marble screen surrounds this central area.

With the Taj Mahal, Shah Jahan brought the Mogul style of architecture to its peak of beauty and splendor. Yet, in its placement among expanses of water and gardens, the Taj Mahal is similar to other buildings of the time, such as the Red Fort, the nickname for the palace which was

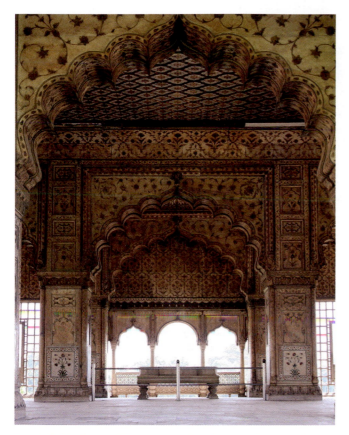

Fig. 18.22 The Peacock Throne Room, Red Fort (Shahjahanabad), Delhi. Mogul period, after 1638. The design of the Peacock Throne itself has been attributed to one Austin de Bordeaux, whom the French physician François Bernier (1625–88) described, in his *Travels in the Mogul Empire* (1670), as "a Frenchman by birth, who after defrauding several of the Princes of Europe, by means of false gems, which he fabricated with peculiar skill, sought refuge in the great Mogul's court, where he made his fortune."

constructed by Shah Jahan across the Jumna River from the Taj Mahal in Delhi. He fully intended it to be the most magnificent palace on the face of the earth. At its center, surrounded by gardens, pavilions, and baths, was the Peacock Throne Room (Fig. **18.22**). There, the shah sat upon an enormous solid gold throne (subsequently destroyed and looted by Persian warriors in 1732), set upon a 6 by 4-foot platform. The platform throne itself supported 12 pillars covered with emeralds, over which was an enameled canopy inlaid with diamonds, emeralds, rubies, and garnets. It was flanked on each side by jeweled peacocks. The marble walls of the room were themselves inlaid with precious and semiprecious stones in a mosaic technique the Moguls had learned from the Italians, called *pietra dura* (Italian for "hard stone"), also employed at the Taj Mahal. Around the ceiling of the room, the shah had these words inscribed: "If there is a paradise on the face of the earth, It is this, oh! it is this, oh! it is this." Such architectural splendor served one purpose—to glorify the worldly power of the ruler.

In 1658, Shah Jahan became very ill, and his four sons battled each other for power. The conservative, Aurangzeb (r. 1658–1707), eventually triumphed and confined his father to the Red Fort. Aurangzeb reinstituted traditional forms of Islamic law and worship, ending the pluralism that had defined the Mogul court under his father and grandfather even as he began to reinstate traditional Muslim prohibitions against figural art. But from his rooms in the Red Fort, Shah Jahan could look out over the Jumna River to the Taj Mahal and re-create in poetry the paradise where he believed he would come to rest with his wife (**Reading 18.4**):

READING 18.4

Shah Jahan, inscription on the Taj Mahal (ca. 1658)

Like a garden of heaven a brilliant spot,
Full of fragrance like paradise fraught with ambergris.
In the breadth of its court perfumes from the nose-gay of
    sweetheart rise,
The nymphs of paradise use their eye-lids for cleaning its
    threshold.

Shah Jahan's tomb is, in fact, next to his wife's in the crypt below the central chamber of the Taj Mahal. Above both tombs are their marble cenotaphs, beautifully inlaid in *pietra dura* by the artisans of northern India.

CHINA: THE MING DYNASTY (1368–1644)

How did China resist foreign influence even as trade with the wider world flourished?

The **cultural syncretism**, or intermingling of cultural traditions, that marks the Americas, was largely resisted by Chinese populations when Europeans arrived on their shores. The reasons are many, but of great importance was the inherent belief of these cultures in their own superiority. For centuries, the Chinese had resisted Mongolian influence, for instance, and at the same time had come to prefer isolation from foreign influence.

This is not to say that the Chinese totally removed themselves from the world stage. Some 92 years before the Portuguese explorer Vasco da Gama landed in Calicut, India, inaugurating Portuguese sea trade in the eastern oceans, a massive Chinese fleet had sailed into that port to inaugurate a sea trade of its own. It was the brainchild of the emperor Zhu Di (r. 1402–24). His father Zhu Yuanzhang (r. 1368–98), had driven the Mongols out of China in 1368, restored Chinese rule in the land, and established the dynasty called Ming ("bright" or "brilliant") at Nanjing. Confucian scholars, who under the Mongolian rule of the Yuan dynasty had found themselves utterly neglected (see Chapter 11), were once again welcomed at court.

The Ming emperors were consumed by fear of Mongol reinvasion and in defense created what was arguably the most despotic government in Chinese history. Zhu Yuanzhang enlisted thousands of workers to reinforce the Great Wall of China (see Fig. 7.1 in Chapter 7) against invasion

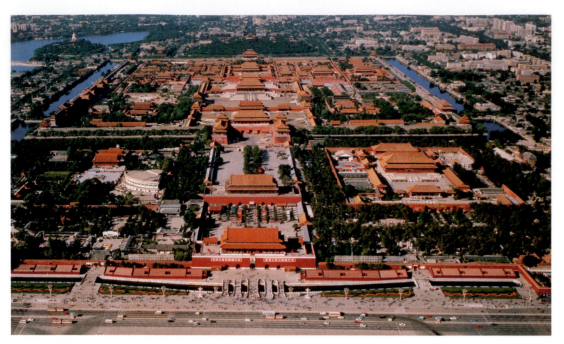

Fig. 18.23 The Forbidden City, now the Palace Museum, Beijing. Mostly Ming dynasty (1368–1644).
View from the south.

👁 **Watch** an architectural simulation of the Forbidden City on **MyArtsLab**

from the north, and untold numbers of them perished in the process. He equipped huge armies and assembled a navy to defend against invasion from the sea. Artists whose freedoms had been severely restricted under the Mongols (see Chapter 11) were even less free under the Ming. But in a bow to scholarship and the arts, Zhu Di commissioned the compilation of an authoritative 11,095-volume encyclopedia of Chinese learning. He also undertook the construction of an Imperial Palace compound in Beijing on the site of Kublai Khan's ruined capital (Figs. **18.23** and **18.24**). The palace complex, known as the Forbidden City, was, among other things, the architectural symbol of his rule.

The name refers to the fact that only those on official imperial business could enter its gates. Although it was largely rebuilt in the eighteenth century during the Qing dynasty (1644–1900), the general plan is Ming but based on Mongol precedents. In fact, the Mongols had reserved the entire northern side of Beijing for themselves, and the resident Chinese had lived only in the southern third of the city. Ming emperors preserved this division, allowing ministers and officials to live in the northern or Inner City and commoners in the southern or Outer City.

The Forbidden City itself was in the middle of the Inner City. Like the Tang capital of Chang'an (see Chapter 11), Beijing is laid out on a grid, and the Forbidden City is laid out on a grid within the grid along a north–south axis according to the principles of *feng shui* ("wind and water"). In Daoist belief, certain "dragon lines" of energy, or *qi*, flow through the earth, along mountains and ridges, down streams and rivers, influencing the lives of people near them. Evil forces were believed to come from the

north and so the city opened to the south. Since emperors were considered divine and closely connected to the forces of the cosmos, the practice of *feng shui* was especially crucial in constructing royal compounds.

Following traditional practice, the Forbidden City covers about 240 acres and is walled by 15 miles of fortifications. It is composed of 9,999 buildings and rooms, each constructed with nails, nine nails per row. The number 9 in Chinese sounds like the word for "everlasting," and because 9 was believed to be the extreme of positive numbers, the maximum of the singular, it was thus reserved for use only by the emperor. The buildings in the complex follow traditional patterns of post-and-lintel construction that date back to the Shang and Zhou periods.

The emperors and their families rarely left the Forbidden City's confines. Visitors entered through a monumental U-shaped Meridian Gate and then crossed the Golden Water River, spanned by five arched marble bridges. Across the courtyard stands the Gate of Supreme Harmony, on the other side of which is another giant courtyard leading to the Hall of Supreme Harmony. Here, on the most important state occasions, the emperor sat on his throne, facing south, his back to the evil forces of the north. Behind the Hall of Supreme Harmony were increasingly private spaces, devoted to day-to-day routine and living quarters. The balance and symmetry of the compound were believed to mirror the harmony of the universe. Situated, as it was believed, in the middle of the world, the Forbidden City was the architectural symbol of the emperor's rule and of his duty as the Son of Heaven to maintain order, balance, and harmony in his land.

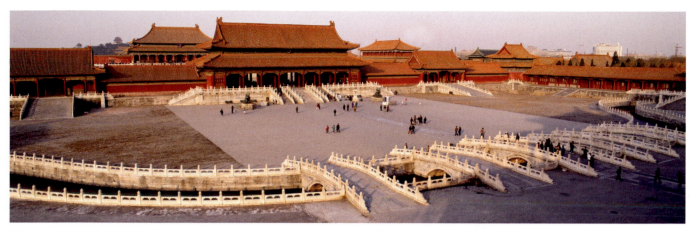

Fig. 18.24 The Hall of Supreme Harmony. As seen from across the square beyond the Gate of Supreme Harmony. Height 115'. Elevated on three tiers of marble platforms, the hall is the largest building in the complex. No other building, anywhere in the empire, was allowed to be higher. It houses the main throne of the emperor, from which he presided over ceremonies celebrating the winter solstice, the new year, and his own birthday. Along the stairs rising to the hall are 18 *dings*—bronze food vessels (see Chapter 7)— that represent the 18 provinces of Ming China. On the terrace stand a bronze crane and a bronze tortoise, symbols of everlasting rule and longevity. Red and gold lacquered brackets resting on the lintels support flaring upswept eaves, which disguise the enormous weight of the tiled roof. These brackets are carved in a variety of calligraphic designs, many of which also appear on Shang and Zhou bronzes. The red walls contrast dramatically with the roof tiles lacquered in a glowing yellow, a color reserved for imperial structures.

The Treasure Fleet: Extending China's Influence

Zhu Di called himself the Yongle emperor, meaning "lasting joy," a propagandistic name designed to deflect attention from the tyranny of his court. His massive construction projects served to establish the grandeur of his authority. Among the largest of these was his "treasure fleet" of 317 ships, crewed by 27,000 men and headed by a ship that was 440 feet long, one of the largest wooden ships ever built. Unlike the European ocean expeditions undertaken a century later, these voyages were not primarily motivated by trade and exploration, but rather by the desire of the Yongle emperor to extract tribute from states throughout the Indian Ocean and the Southeast Asia. Still, trade was the result. Under the command of Zheng He (1371–1435), a Muslim eunuch who had served Zhu Di since childhood, the fleet sailed in seven expeditions between 1404 and 1435 throughout the oceans of Southeast Asia to India, Saudi Arabia, and down the African coast (see Map **18.4**).

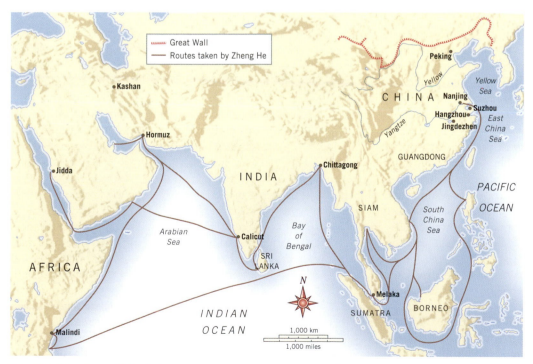

Map 18.4 Ming China, 1368–1644. This map also shows the routes taken by Zheng He and the Chinese "treasure fleet." In 30 years, Zheng He traveled more than 186,000 miles, the equivalent of 7½ circumnavigations of the world.

China, like many cultures, saw itself through ethnocentric eyes. It viewed itself as the great Middle Kingdom, believed to be at the center of the four seas and at the heart of the four cardinal directions. Zhu Di conceived of the treasure fleet as his chief means to extend Chinese influence throughout the "four corners" of the world. To that end, all the provinces of China had to provide goods for the fleet to trade—from Suzhou and Hangzhou, fine silks and brocades; from the imperial porcelain works at Jingdezhen, fine white porcelain; from Jiaxing, lacquerware; and from Guangdong, iron, required not only for trade but for construction of the fleet itself.

Zheng He's first voyage was to Calicut, the center of the spice trade. Here he obtained cardamom, cinnamon, ginger, turmeric, and, above all, pepper, literally worth its weight in gold. (The small cargo of pepper that Vasco da Gama eventually brought back from Calicut paid for his voyage several times over.) Calicut became a regular port of call for the fleet, as did Malacca, on the Malay peninsula, where cloves, nutmeg, sambal oelek (a red hot pepper), and other Indonesian spices were available. He also acquired precious tree resins, such as camphor and frankincense, used for making incense. In Siam (now Thailand), he discovered mahogany, a hard wood, excellent for making ship rudders, and he paid the Siamese in gold for the trees. But the Middle East and Africa yielded some of the most precious treasures. Hormuz, on the Persian Gulf, was famous for its pearls from the banks off what is now Bahrain, but it was also a center of trade in precious stones. In return for porcelains and silks, Zheng He acquired sapphires, rubies, topaz, and amber, as well as Middle Eastern woolens and carpets.

Luxury Arts

The lavish lifestyle of the Ming court ensured the production of vast quantities of decorative luxury goods. In addition, as trade flourished, many Chinese merchants became increasingly wealthy and began to collect paintings, antiques, finely made furniture, and other quality objects for themselves. **Lacquerware** was extremely popular. Made from the sap of the Chinese *Rhus vernicifera* tree (a variety of sumac), lacquer is a clear, natural varnish that, when applied to wood, textiles, or other perishable materials, makes them airtight, waterproof, and resistant to both heat and acid. A surface coated with many thin layers of lacquer can be carved through into all manner of designs. Lacquerware furniture, bowls, dishes, and other small articles were very desirable.

One of the commodities most prized by the Chinese themselves and by those who traded with China was **porcelain** ceramic ware (see *Materials & Techniques*, page 621). The Chinese had invented the process for making porcelain around 1004 CE at Jingdezhen, which by the beginning of the Ming dynasty boasted 20 kilns. At Zhu Di's death in 1424, it had almost tripled in size to 58 kilns.

Ming painters decorated the unfired surfaces of their porcelain ware with blue cobalt glazes, covered everything with a layer of white glaze, and then fired their works. During the reign of Zhu Di, the look of Chinese porcelain improved dramatically. This was due largely to the fact that Zheng He had traded Chinese produce for a cobalt ore, probably from Kashan, Persia, high in iron and low in manganese (just the opposite of Chinese ore), which allowed for a new richness of color. Among the Ming artists' favorite motifs were fish, waves, and sea monsters, but particularly dragons, because they symbolized the emperor. His veins were said to flow with the dragon's blood (Fig. **18.25**). The dragon was everywhere on Ming art, from textiles to lacquerware and jade carvings. Note that the two vases in Fig. 18.25 are mirror images, the finely outlined forms of the dragons seemingly mimicking each other's flight. Their gestures, in fact, suggest the graceful movements of **T'ai Chi Ch'uan**, the Chinese martial art that includes solo forms, or routines, and two-person forms, known as "pushing hands." These two dragons, their bony claws reaching toward one another, particularly evoke the "pushing hands" form. The two vases create a sense of balance, like the balance of *yin* and *yang* (see Fig. 7.5 in Chapter 7), the symbol for which is, in fact, the symbol for t'ai chi itself.

Painting and Poetry: Competing Schools

The imperial court and the newly rich merchant class also acquired paintings, considered luxury goods in their own right. As in the Tang dynasty (see Chapter 11), a class of

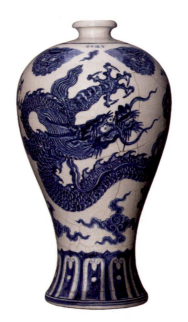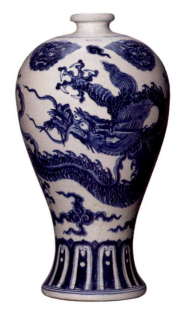

Fig. 18.25 Pair of porcelain vases with cobalt blue underglaze. Ming dynasty, Xuande period (1426–35). Height 21¾". The Nelson-Atkins Museum of Art, Kansas City, Missouri. As early as the Bronze Age, the Chinese associated the dragon with sudden manifestations of nature, such as wind, rain, and lightning. By the Song and Tang dynasties (fifth–tenth centuries), painting pictures of dragons was a method of praying for rain. For Chan Buddhists (see Chapter 11), the dragon symbolized sudden enlightenment.

Porcelain

Porcelain is a ceramic ware that is made by combining clays rich in kaolin, a highly refined mineral found in abundance near Jingdezhen, with the mineral feldspar and sometimes quartz. Porcelain requires extremely high firing temperatures, and it seems likely that the Chinese developed the techniques for firing porcelain while casting bronze vessels. When fired at 1800°F to 2400°F (1000°C to 1300°C), the minerals in the kaolin clay fuse into a translucent, glasslike, and extremely strong ceramic ware. In fact, the ceramic contains a high percentage of actual body glass. As a result, porcelains tend to transmit light and make a clear, ringing sound when struck. Imperial porcelain was traditionally thought to be "as white as jade, as bright as a mirror, as thin as paper, with a sound as clear as a bell." Europeans tried desperately to match Chinese quality but did not succeed until kaolin was discovered in Saxony in the early 1700s, leading to the creation of the great Meissen porcelain factory in Germany.

highly educated **literati**, or literary intelligentsia—artists equally expert in poetry, calligraphy, and painting—executed the works. Many paintings combine image and poem, the latter written in a calligraphy distinctly the artist's own.

Late in the Ming dynasty, an artist, calligrapher, theorist, and high official in the government bureaucracy named Dong Qichang (1555–1636) wrote an essay that has affected the way we have looked at the history of Chinese painting ever since, although many scholars, even in Dong Qichang's time, viewed it as oversimplified. He divided the history of Chinese painting into two schools, Northern and Southern, although geography had little to do with it. It was not place but the spirit in which the artist approached the painting that determined its school. A painter was Southern if unorthodox, radical, and inventive, like the Southern brand of Chan (Zen) Buddhism; a painter was Northern if conservative and traditional in approach, like the Northern brand of Chan Buddhism.

Northern School *Hundreds of Birds Admiring the Peacocks* by Yin Hong, a court artist active in the late fifteenth and early sixteenth centuries, is an example of the Northern style (Fig. **18.26**). It has a highly refined decorative style, which emphasizes the technical skill of the painter. It also has a rich use of color and reliance on traditional Chinese painting, in this case the birds-and-flowers genre that had been extremely popular in the Song dynasty, which flourished contemporaneously with the Early Middle Ages in the West. Like Guo Xi's Song dynasty painting *Early Spring* (see Chapter 11, *Closer Look*, pages 370–371), the Yin Hong painting also has a symbolic meaning that refers directly to the emperor. Just as the central peak in *Early Spring* symbolizes the emperor himself, with the lower peaks and trees subservient to him, here a peacock symbolizes the emperor, and around it "hundreds of birds"—that is, the court officials—gather in respect and submission.

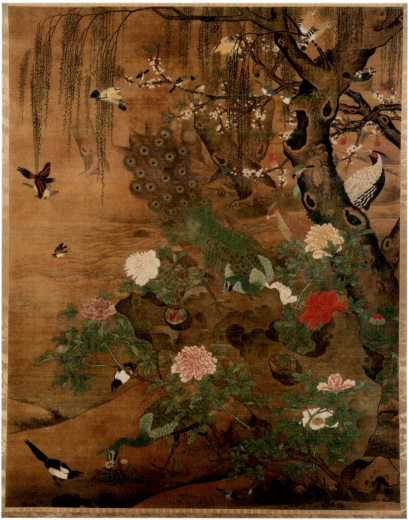

Fig. 18.26 Yin Hong, *Hundred Birds Admiring the Peacocks*. Ming dynasty, late 1400s–early 1500s. Hanging scroll, ink and color on silk, 94⁷⁄₁₆″ × 76¹⁵⁄₁₆″. The Cleveland Museum of Art, purchase from the J.H. Wade Fund, 1974.31. The Chinese traded in the Middle East for peacocks, considered the most supreme of all ornamental birds, in exchange for silk.

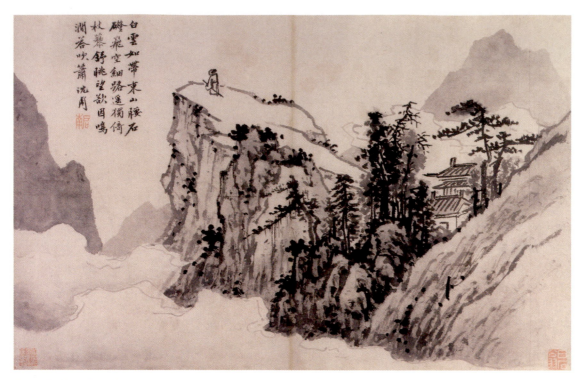

Fig. 18.27 Shen Zhou, *Poet on a Mountaintop*, leaf from an album of landscapes; painting mounted as part of a handscroll. Ming dynasty, ca. 1500. Ink and color on paper, 15¼" × 23¾". The Nelson-Atkins Museum of Art, Kansas City, Missouri. Shen Zhou places himself at the center of this composition in a relaxed and casual manner that reflects Chan Buddhism, which is more intuitive than intellectual. Note the informal simplicity of his brushwork and calligraphy.

📖 **Read** the document related to Shen Zhou on **MyArtsLab**

Southern School The Southern style is much more understated than the Northern School, preferring ink to color and free brushwork (emphasizing the abstract nature of painting) to meticulously detailed linear representation. For the Southern artist, reality rested in the mind, not the physical world, and so self-expression is the ultimate aim. Furthermore, in the Southern School, the work of art more systematically synthesized the three areas of endeavor that any member of the literati should have mastered: poetry, calligraphy, and painting.

So, a Southern-School painting like *Poet on a Mountaintop* by Shen Zhou (1427–1509) radicalizes traditional Chinese landscape (Fig. **18.27**). In the earlier Song dynasty landscapes, the unifying embrace of the natural world dwarfs human figures (see Chapter 11, *Closer Look*, pages 370–371). But in Shen Zhou's Ming dynasty painting, the poet is the central figure. He faces out over an airy void in which hangs the very image of his mind, the following poem:

> White clouds like a belt encircle the mountain's waist
> A stone ledge flying in space and the far thin road.
> I lean alone on my bramble staff and gazing contented into space
> Wish the sounding torrent would answer to your flute.

An artist capable of putting himself at the center of both painting and poem would have had no desire to enter the government bureaucracy. Shen Zhou lived out his life in the district of Suzhou, far from court. But, interestingly, it was Shen Zhou's style of work, and the style of other literati painters in the Southern School, that the Ming theorist Dong Qichang most preferred and that would become the dominant, orthodox style of painting in the Qing dynasty to follow.

JAPAN: COURT PATRONAGE AND SPIRITUAL PRACTICE

What new developments in the arts were championed by the Ashikaga shoguns, and how did contact with the West impact Japan in the Azuchi-Momoyama period?

Long before Ming rulers finally overthrew the Mongol Yuan dynasty in China in 1368, the Japanese rulers of the Kamakura period (see Chapter 11) had repelled the Mongol Kublai Khan's attempts to conquer their island country in both 1274 and 1281. The cost was high, and the islands were left impoverished. Conflict between competing lines of succession to the imperial throne destabilized the court. Gradually, in the provinces, localized village-level military leaders gained more and more authority until they controlled, after several generations, large regional areas of land. These lords, who would come to be known as *daimyo*, or "great names," gained increasing strength, competing with the shogunate for power even as they began to war among themselves, seeking control of the entire nation. The power of the emperor was, however, rarely challenged, and the *daimyo* were important patrons of the imperial court, as well as major consumers of court-based arts and crafts. The principles and ethics of Zen Buddhism, the Japanese version of Chinese Chan Buddhism (see Chapter 11), also appealed to them. Throughout the twelfth and thirteenth centuries, Chan teachings gained an increasing foothold in Japan. The carefully ordered monastic lifestyle of Chan monks contrasted dramatically with the sometimes extravagant lifestyles of the Buddhist monasteries of the Heian period. And the Chan advocacy of the possibility of immediate enlightenment through meditation and self-denial presented, like Pure Land Buddhism (see Chapter 11), with which it competed for followers, an especially attractive spiritual practice.

The Muromachi Period (1392–1573): Cultural Patronage

By 1392, one shogun family, the Ashikaga, had begun to exercise increased authority over Japanese society. They had their headquarters in the Muromachi district of Kyoto (hence the alternative names for the period in which they ruled.) It was a period of often brutal civil war as the *daimyo* vied for power. Although Kyoto remained in a state of near-total devastation—starvation was not uncommon—the Ashikaga shoguns built elaborate palaces around Kyoto as refuges from the chaos outside their walls. One of the most elaborate of these, now known as Kinkakuji, the Golden Pavilion (Fig. 18.28), was built as a setting for the retirement of the Ashikaga shogun Yoshimitsu (1358–1408). Begun in 1399, its central pavilion is modeled on Chinese precedents. Its first floor was intended for relaxation and contemplation of the lake and gardens. A wide veranda for viewing the moon, a popular pastime, fronted its second floor. And the top floor was designed as a small Pure Land Buddhist temple, containing a sculpture of Amida Buddha, the Buddha of Infinite Light and Life who dwells in the paradise of the Western Pure Land, along with 25 bodhisattvas. The gardens surrounding the pavilions at Kinkakuji provided the casual stroller with an ever-changing variety of views, thus creating a tension between the multiplicity of scenes and the unity of the whole. As a matter of policy, Yoshimitsu associated himself with the arts in order to lend his shogunate authority and legitimacy. Therefore, he and later Ashikaga shoguns encouraged some of the most important artistic developments of the era in painting and garden design. They also championed important new forms of expression, including the tea ceremony and Noh drama.

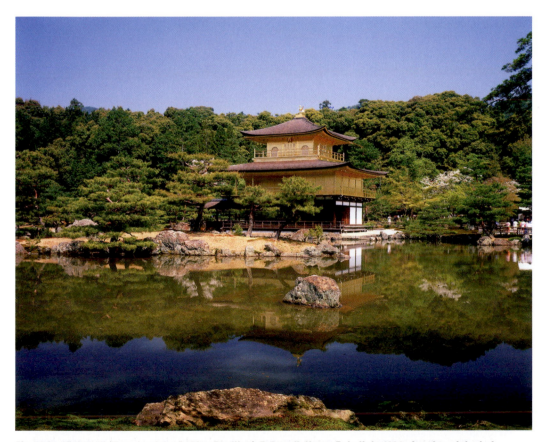

Fig. 18.28 Kinkakuji (Temple of the Golden Pavilion), Rokuonji, Kyoto. Rebuilt in 1964 after the original of the 1390s. The original Kinkakuji was set ablaze and completely destroyed in 1950 by a young monk protesting the commercialization of Buddhism after World War II. The restoration closely approximates its original appearance.

Painting in the New Zen Manner The question of the extent of the influence of Zen on Japanese art is a problematic one. As has often been pointed out, the features normally associated with Zen (Chan) Buddhism in the arts—simplicity of design, suggestion rather than description, and controlling balance through irregularity and asymmetry—are also characteristic of indigenous Japanese taste. Still, a number of Japanese artists, usually Zen monks themselves, turned to China and its Chan traditions for inspiration. In order to acquaint himself more fully with Chinese traditions, for instance, Sesshu Toyo (1420–1506), a Zen priest-painter, traveled to China in 1468–69, copying the Song dynasty masters and becoming adept at the more abstract forms of representation practiced by the Chan Buddhist literati. Like other painters of his era inspired by the Chinese, Sesshu worked in multiple pictorial modes—depictions of Buddhist scenes, portraits, flower and bird painting, and, most famously, landscapes. *Haboku Landscape* is an example of the latter, painted in the new Zen Buddhist manner known as *haboku* (Fig. **18.29**). *Haboku* means "broken or splashed ink," the application of one layer of ink over another, "breaking" the initial surface or description. No mark on this painting could actually be thought of as representational. Rather, the denser ink suggests trees and rocks, while the softer washes evoke tall mountains in the distance, water, and mist. And instead of the panoramic landscapes of the Chinese Song dynasty that Sesshu studied in China, with its deep space, symmetrical balance, and vast array of richly detailed elements (compare Guo Xi's *Early Spring*; Chapter 11, *Closer Look*, pages 370–371), Sesshu's landscape is startlingly simple, almost impressionistic in its mistiness, and asymmetrical in its composition.

Zen Gardens Perhaps inspired by the gardens surrounding shogun palaces such as Kinkakuji, designers made gardens a regular feature of Muromachi Zen temples, especially the *karesansui*, or "withered or **dry landscape**" garden. Japanese gardeners had long featured water as an important, even primary element, but around Kyoto, with its limited number of springs and mountain streams, gardeners turned their attention away from the streams and ponds that characterize the Golden Pavilion at Kinkakuji and increasingly focused their attention on rocks and a few carefully groomed plantings as the primary feature of garden design.

An especially remarkable example is a garden in the precinct of Daisen-in, a subtemple of the Daitokuji compound founded in 1509 in Kyoto by Kogaku Soko (1465–1548). Its design is usually attributed to the painter Soami (d. 1525). The garden of the Daisen-in is actually a series of separate gardens arranged around Soko's residence, itself decorated with a variety of Soami's paintings. The garden that flanks two sides of the residence is a miniature landscape, the vertical rocks of which represent a mountain (Fig. **18.30**). A waterfall, suggested by a vein of white quartz, cascades down one rock, forming a river of white gravel across which a slab of stone has fallen like a natural bridge, connecting islands in the stream. Farther down, a boat-shaped rock sails in the

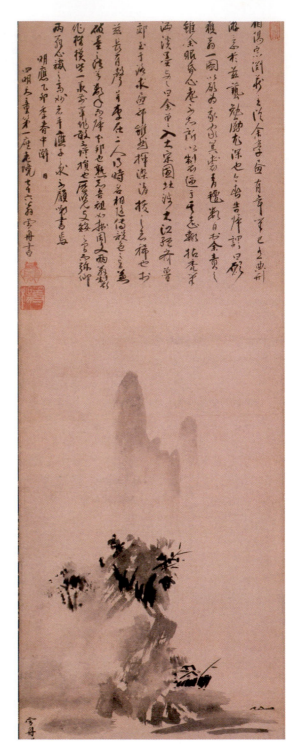

Fig. 18.29 Sesshu Toyo, *Haboku Landscape*. 1400s–early 1500s. Hanging scroll, ink on paper, 28¼" × 10½". The Cleveland Museum of Art, Gift of the Norweb Foundation, 1955.43. This painting is mounted on a scroll some 5 feet in length.

wider expanse of the river. On the other side of the residence, the gravel stream flows into an expanse of carefully raked white gravel punctuated by two cones constructed of the same material. This wide expanse is meant to suggest the ocean, its raked lines waves rising to meet what may be two volcanic islands. (This last attribution remains a matter of speculation.) Taken as a whole, the flow of the pebble

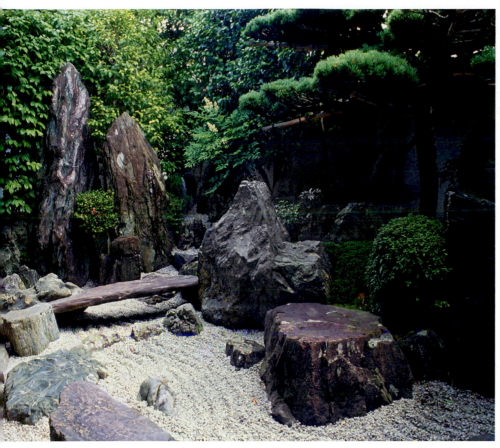

Fig. 18.30 Attributed to Soami, Garden of the Daisen-in of Daitokuji, Kyoto. Muromachi period, ca. 1510–25. Note the similarity between the two tallest rocks in this garden and the two mist-covered mountains in the distance of Sesshu Toyo's *Haboku Landscape* (see Fig. 18.29). Both, it would seem, are realizations of the same aesthetic in different mediums, though it seems unlikely that either directly influenced the other.

stream, from mountaintop to ocean, might best be viewed as a narrative, perhaps a metaphor for the passage of time, or even the passage of a Zen Buddhist philosopher from the relative complexity and confusion of early life to the expansive simplicity and enlightenment of maturity.

The Tea Ceremony *Matcha*, literally "finely powdered tea," was introduced into Japan from China during the early Kamakura period. By the end of the Kamakura period, tea contests to discern different teas and the regions in which they were grown had become popular. By the early Muromachi period, rules for the ways in which tea was to be drunk began to be codified, especially in Zen temples. By the sixteenth century, these rules would come to be known as the **Way of Tea**, *chanoyu*. In small rooms specifically designed for the purpose and often decorated with calligraphy on hanging scrolls or screens, the guest was to leave the concerns of the daily world behind and enter a timeless world of ease, harmony, and mutual respect. The master of the ceremony would assemble a few examples of painting and calligraphy, usually *karamono*, treasures imported from China, of which the Ashikaga shogun Yoshimasa (1430–90), grandson of Yoshimitsu, had the finest collection.

Late in the fifteenth century, in a transformation traditionally attributed to Murata Shuko, a former Zen priest, the taste for displaying *karamono* in the tea ceremony was replaced by a taste for things possessing the quality of **wabi**—that is, things evidencing qualities of austerity and simplicity and showing the effects of time. These objects were thought to reflect a taste more Japanese than Chinese, a taste reflected in a comment attributed to Shuko: "The moon is not pleasing unless partially obscured by a cloud." The master of the ceremony would assemble a few examples of painting and calligraphy together with a variety of different objects and utensils for making tea—the kettle, the water pot, the whisk, the tea caddy, and above all the tea bowl, each prized for its aesthetic shape and texture. In a quiet, muted light, and on a floor covered with *tatami*, woven straw mats, the master and his guest would contemplate the tea, its preparation, and the objects accompanying the ensemble, which, it was understood, expressed the master's artistic sensibility. Together, guest and master would collaborate in a ritual of meditation to transform the drinking of tea into a work of highly refined art, known as the *wabicha*.

Interestingly, it was not at court where the *wabicha* developed into the classic tea ceremony, but among the rich merchant classes. Two merchants from Sakai, Takeno Joo (1502–55) and Sen no Rikyu (1522–91), are traditionally credited with inventing the ceremony proper. As Rikyu defined the ceremony:

Chanoyu performed in a plain hut is above all an ascetic discipline, based on the Buddhist law, that is aimed at achieving spiritual deliverance. To be concerned about the quality of the dwelling in which you serve tea or the flavor of the food served with it is to emphasize the mundane. It is enough if the dwelling one uses does not leak water and the food served suffices to stave off hunger. This is in accordance with the teachings of Buddha and is the essence of the *chanoyu*. First, we fetch water and gather firewood. Then we boil the water and prepare tea. After offering some to the Buddha, we serve our guests. Finally, we serve ourselves.

The prominence of Rikyu and Joo in the development of the *chanoyu* presages a dramatic shift in Japanese culture, as the military class that had dominated Japanese society for centuries was beginning to give way to the interests of commerce and trade.

Noh Drama The Ashikaga shoguns, including Yoshimitsu and Yoshimasa, also enthusiastically supported the development of the important literary genre of Noh drama. The Noh drama was primarily the result of the efforts of Kan'ami Kiyotsugu (1333–84) and his son Zeami Motokiyo (1363–1443). They conceived of a theater incorporating music, chanting, dance, poetry, prose, mime, and masks to create a world of sublime beauty based on the ideal of *yugen*, which almost defies translation but refers to the suggestion of vague, spiritual profundity lying just below the surface of the Noh play's action (or, rather, the stillness of its inaction).

The word *noh* means "accomplishment," and it refers to the virtuoso performance of the drama's main character, whose inner conflicts must be resolved before his or her soul can find peace. There were five kinds of Noh plays, including "warrior plays" and "woman plays." The main characters of the warrior plays, which did not exist before Zeami, were historical personages of the samurai class derived from the same accounts as the Taira and Minamoto conflicts upon which the scroll painting *Night Attack on the Sanjo Palace* is based (see Fig. 11.17 in Chapter 11).

The Noh play *Semimaru*, written by Zeami in the early fifteenth century, belongs to the fourth, "miscellaneous" category of Noh plays, plays that treat, among other things, madness and vengeful ghosts. It re-creates the medieval Japanese legend of Semimaru, a blind prince who lived as a beggar in a bamboo hut on Mount Osaka (see **Reading 18.5**, pages 632–633, for the first half of the play). His blindness was attributed to laxity in the performance of his religious duties in a former life, for which his emperor father exiled him from court, as Semimaru explains to his attendant, Kiyotsura, so that his ascetic lifestyle might "purge in this world my burden from the past, / And spare me suffering in the world to come." In the play, Semimaru meets up with his deranged sister, who was apparently similarly lacking in her performance of religious duties and is thus condemned to wander the countryside. She hears him playing the *biwa*, a short-necked lute. In fact, traditionally Semimaru was considered the greatest master of the *biwa* and flute, the music of which apparently brought his soul to a state of peace.

Noh is very different from Western drama. Semimaru wears a beautifully crafted mask with shut eyes that signify his blindness. He is accompanied by a chorus, which narrates events to the sound of wind instruments and drums, and by secondary characters, who help him accomplish his goals. The plot, which the audience would know quite well, is almost irrelevant—certainly it does not drive the action of the drama forward. The characters speak their lines in a stylized manner, and make no attempt at realistic tonal inflections. Three drums and a flute accompany their lines, their movements turn into dance, and the performance lasts for a much longer time than it takes simply to read it. In fact, although Noh plays often read well on the page, the total effect is lost without the nonverbal elements. Zeami's own explanation of the power of silence in Noh drama, from his essay "The One Mind Linking All Powers," gives a hint at what one would miss in reading (**Reading 18.6**):

READING 18.6

from Zeami Motokiyo, "The One Mind Linking All Powers" (early 15th century)

Sometimes spectators of the Noh say that the moments of "no action" are the most enjoyable. This is one of the actor's secret arts. Dancing and singing, movements on the stage, and the different types of miming are all acts performed by the body. Moments of "no action" occur in between. When we examine why such moments without action are enjoyable, we find that it is due to the underlying spiritual strength of the actor, which unremittingly holds the attention.

The audience, in other words, is invited to see beyond everyday reality into the farther reaches of existence, into the aesthetic realm of the *yugen*.

The Azuchi-Momoyama Period (1573–1615): Foreign Influences

Even as Japanese culture flourished under the patronage of the Ashikaga shoguns, the country simultaneously endured many years of sometimes debilitating civil war. By the middle of the sixteenth century, the Ashikaga family had lost all semblance of power, and various *daimyo* controlled the provinces once again. Finally, one of their number, Oda Nobunaga (1534–82), son of a minor vassal, forged enough alliances to unify the country under a single administration. By 1573, Nobunaga had driven what remained of the Ashikaga out of Kyoto, inaugurating a period now known as the Azuchi-Momoyama, named for the location of Nobunaga's castle at Azuchi on Lake Biwa and that of his successor, Hideyoshi (1537–98), at Momoyama, literally "Peach Hill," after an orchard of peach trees later planted on the ruins of the castle, south of Kyoto.

Nobunaga's victory was aided by the gunpowder and firearms introduced to Japan by Portuguese traders after they arrived in 1543. During the reign of Nobunaga, the West greatly expanded trade throughout Japan. In 1543, Portuguese traders first entered Japanese waters, and, from the Portuguese, the Japanese *daimyo* soon learned about Western firearms. Within 30 years, the civil conflict that Hideyoshi would bring to an end in 1590 was being fought with guns and cannon. Almost at the same time, in 1549, the priest Francis Xavier (1506–52), one of the founders of the Jesuits, landed at Kagoshima dedicated to bringing Christianity to Japan. By the 1580s, the Church had converted as many as 150,000 Japanese to Catholicism.

The Momoyama Castle Although the arrival of gunpowder surely encouraged the Azuchi-Momoyama rulers to build much larger, more defensible castles than those of the

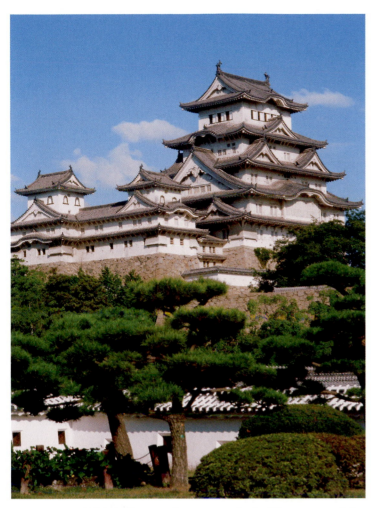

earlier shoguns, the primary purpose of the castles was more to impress upon the world the power and majesty of the *daimyo*. The Himeji Castle near Osaka (Fig. **18.31**) is an example. Like most other castles of the era—roughly 40 were constructed across the country—it was built at the crest of a hill topped by a ***tenshu***, a defensible refuge of last resort much like the keep of an English castle (see Chapter 10). Lower down the hill's slope was a massive wall of stone.

The original *tenshu* was three stories high, but three more *tenshu* were added later. Two are three stories and one rises five stories above the hilltop. The resulting fortress is at once virtually impregnable and almost delicate in appearance, with its winglike white plaster rooflines and sharply pointed triangular tiled gables. In fact, because of the graceful, ascending rhythms of its forms, it has come to be known as White Heron Castle.

Namban* and Kano-School Screen Painting** The presence of foreign traders in Japan, principally Portuguese and Dutch, soon found its way into Japanese painting, particularly in a new genre of screen painting known as ***namban. *Namban* literally means "southern barbarian," referring to the "barbarian" Westerners who arrived from the south by ship. In the most popular theme of this genre, a foreign galleon arrives in Kyoto harbor (Fig. **18.32**). The ship's crew unloads goods, and the captain and his men proceed through the streets of the city to Nambanji, the Jesuit church in Kyoto. The priests themselves are Japanese converts to Christianity.

The uniqueness of these paintings is that they present a convergence of cultures, encouraged by the prospect of trade, not only with Europeans but with the peoples of other Asian countries, unparalleled in world history. The Portuguese, with the help of slave labor

Fig. 18.31 Himeji Castle, Hyogo prefecture, near Osaka. Momoyama period, 1581; enlarged 1601–09. The Tokugawa shoguns destroyed most of the Momoyama castles in the early seventeenth century because they believed the castles encouraged other *daimyo* to challenge their power.

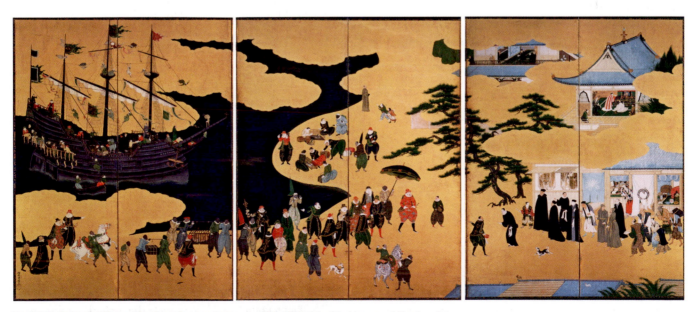

Fig. 18.32 School of Kano, *Namban* six-panel screen. 1593–1600. Kobe City Museum of Namban Art, Japan. Across the bottom left of the screen, African slaves, dressed in Portuguese costume, carry goods. In the center panel, another holds an umbrella over the head of a figure dressed in red.

from Africa, had established a base in Macao, which they had been ceded by the Chinese in return for suppressing piracy on the Chinese coast, and they served as the conduit between China and Japan, exchanging Japanese silver for Chinese raw silk, which the Japanese processed into textiles, particularly kimonos, of remarkable quality. Only the cultural syncretism of New Spain even begins to compare.

The *namban* screens are only one example of the many types of screens commissioned by the Azuchi-Momoyama *daimyo* to decorate their palaces and castles. Traditional Japanese interiors consisted of mostly open rooms with little or no furniture. These angular spaces could be softened and subdivided by the placement of screens. They were often used as a backdrop behind an important person, or to create an eating area, a reception area, or a sleeping area. Themes depicted on the screens include cityscapes, mythological scenes, depictions of great battles, and images of dramatic performances, daily life in the court, and the common people working in the countryside. Perhaps the most famous screens of the Momoyama period are those produced by the Kano School. The many talented members of the Kano family first attracted the attention of the Ashikaga court in the late fifteenth century, but they reached their ascendancy in the Azuchi-Momoyama period in the work of Kano Eitoku (1543–90), great-grandson of the school's founder.

The most important screens and door-panel paintings by Eitoku were destroyed when Nobunaga's castle at Azuchi was destroyed in 1582 after Nobunaga's assassination, but one door-panel painting attributed to him does survive, *Cypress Trees*, originally a set of panels for a paper-covered sliding door, over 5½ feet high (Fig. **18.33**). The twisted branch of a cypress extends from the right across the foreground of the composition. Behind it is a broad landscape of shoreline and cliffs, half-covered in gold-leafed clouds. The panoramic sweep of such paintings is in keeping with the grandeur of the castles they most often decorated, and served to confirm the preeminent position of the Azuchi-Momoyama rulers and aristocracy who commissioned them.

The Closing of Japan

Nobunaga's successor, Hideyoshi, was deeply suspicious of Christianity. By 1587, he had prohibited the Japanese from practicing it and, in 1597, went so far as to execute 26 Spanish and Japanese Jesuits and Franciscans in Nagasaki. Succeeding rulers pursued an increasingly isolationist foreign policy. In 1603, Hideyoshi's successor, Tokugawa Ieyasu (1542–1616) instituted a shogunate based at his castle in Edo (present-day Tokyo) that was to last, in peace, for 250 years. Christianity, even as practiced by foreigners, was banned altogether in 1614. The new Tokugawa shoguns espoused a Confucianist philosophy based on the belief that every individual should be happy in their place if they understood and appreciated their role in a firmly structured society. While the emperor and his court were at the top of this structure, the Tokugawa shoguns were its effective leaders, with 250 or so regional *daimyo* under the shogun exercising regional authority. The Tokugawa shogunate forbade the Japanese to travel abroad in 1635, and limited foreign trade in 1641 to the Dutch, whom they confined to a small area in Nagasaki harbor, and the Chinese, whom they confined to a quarter within the city of Nagasaki itself.

Japan would remain sealed from foreign influence until 1853, when the American commodore Matthew Perry sailed into Edo Bay with four warships and a letter from the president of the United States urging the Japanese to receive the American sailors. The following year, Japan formally reopened its ports to the world.

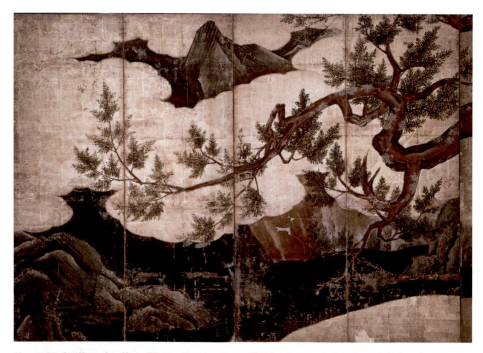

Fig. 18.33 Attributed to Kano Eitoku, *Cypress Trees*. Momoyama period, 16th century.
Eight-fold screen (four shown), gold leaf, color, and ink on paper, height 67". Tokyo National Museum, Japan. The cypress is a traditional Japanese symbol of endurance.

The Influence of Zen Buddhism

Once Japan reopened its doors to world trade in 1853, the culture that it had developed over the 11 preceding centuries had an almost immediate impact on the West. Western artists of the nineteenth century, including Claude Monet, Vincent van Gogh, and Mary Cassatt, were fascinated by Japanese prints, which flooded European and New York markets in what amounted to an avalanche of images. Noh theater generated considerable excitement among Western writers. German playwright Bertolt Brecht and Irish poet William Butler Yeats would each write Noh plays of their own, and the American poet Ezra Pound freely adapted a number of traditional Noh plays. Especially appealing to Western sensibilities was Zen Buddhist philosophy, especially in forms more or less intentionally constructed to appeal to the modern Western mind.

The most influential disseminator of a specifically modern version of Zen Buddhist philosophy in the West was the Japanese scholar D.T. Suzuki (1870–1966). In 1921, he and his wife began publishing *The Eastern Buddhist*, an English-language quarterly intended mostly for Westerners. His *Essays in Zen Buddhism*, published in London in 1927 and expanded upon in both 1933 and 1934, firmly established Suzuki's reputation. When, in April 1936, Suzuki was invited to London to speak at the World Congress of Faiths, he met the 20-year-old Alan Watts, who later the same year would publish his own very influential book, *The Spirit of Zen*.

After spending World War II in seclusion at Enkakuji, an important Zen temple in Kamakura, Suzuki moved to California in 1949, then to New York City, where from 1952 to 1957 he taught seminars on Zen at Columbia University. Composer John Cage attended these seminars for two years, and they deeply influenced his musical direction. A number of other twentieth-century Western intellectuals absorbed Suzuki's teachings as well, including psychoanalyst Carl Jung; poets Thomas Merton, Gary Snyder, and Allen Ginsberg; novelist Jack Kerouac; and potter Bernard Leach.

The many Asian members of the international Fluxus movement of artists, composers, and designers in the 1960s and 1970s, including Yoko Ono, popularized the Zen philosophical practice of posing riddles as a way to lead students to enlightenment. Ono's Fluxus compatriot, the Korean-born

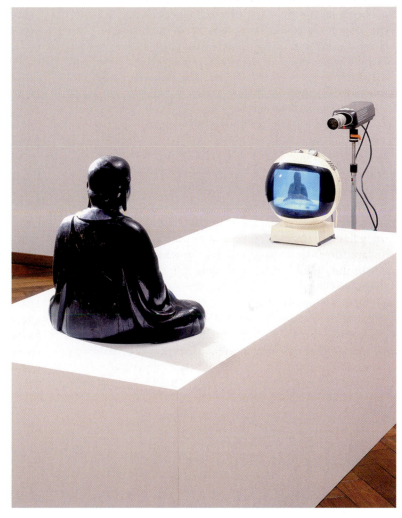

Fig. 18.34 **Nam June Paik,** *TV Buddha*. **1974.** Video installation with statue. Collection Stedelijk Museum, Amsterdam. Paik was deeply influenced by D.T. Suzuki through his close friendship with composer John Cage.

Nam June Paik (1932–2006), one of the great innovators of video art, poses just such a riddle in his *TV Buddha* of 1974 (Fig. **18.34**). How, if he were alive today, would Buddha withdraw from the culture around him in order to meditate in pursuit of enlightenment? How, in meditating upon his own image reflected back to him on a TV screen, would he escape the charge of self-indulgent narcissism? Or would he escape it at all? What does it really mean to reflect upon oneself? These are the kind of questions that a Zen master might ask of Paik's work, just as they are the kind of questions a contemporary viewer might ask as well, which begins to suggest just how much Eastern philosophy has come to influence Western thought. ∎

THINKING BACK

18.1 Discuss the impact of the Spanish on the indigenous cultures of the Americas.

The arrival of Christopher Columbus in the Americas in 1492 inaugurated 125 years of nautical exploration of the globe by Europeans. Spain concentrated on the Americas. The Spanish did not come in family groups to settle a New World. Instead, Spanish men came in hopes of plundering America's legendary wealth of precious metals. The absence of Spanish women accelerated the intermingling of races in New Spain. How do you account for the inhuman treatment of native cultures by European explorers and colonial administrators?

18.2 Describe the impact of the Portuguese on African life and the kinds of ritual traditions that have contributed to the cultural survival of African communities after contact.

The Portuguese slave trade transported many millions of Africans across the Atlantic on the Middle Passage, and the presence of the Portuguese is evident in much of the art produced in West Africa in the sixteenth century. How were the Portuguese first received in Africa? How is their presence reflected in West African art? How did the slave trade affect the population of New Spain?

Nevertheless, African cultures managed to maintain their cultural identity by continuing to engage in ritual practices and traditions. How did dance serve this purpose? What powers did their sculpture contain?

18.3 Outline the ways in which contact with Europe affected Mogul India.

Mogul leaders in India, particularly Akbar and Jahangir, not only introduced conventions of Islamic art to India but opened the doors of the country to English traders. The style of representation that resulted from this contact is a blend of stylistic and cultural traditions, East and West. The Taj Mahal, on the other hand, is a distinctly Mogul achievement. What aesthetic taste does it reflect?

18.4 Assess the impact of contact with the wider world on Ming China and its cultural traditions.

Nearly 100 years before the Portuguese sailed into the Indian Ocean, the Chinese emperor Zhu Di's treasure fleet, commanded by Zheng He, conducted trade expeditions throughout the area. What was the Chinese attitude toward the populations they encountered? One of the most important undertakings of Zhu Di's reign was the construction of the royal compound in Beijing, known as the Forbidden City. From what various cultural traditions does its design draw? In the Ming court, Dong Qichang wrote an essay dividing the history of Chinese painting into two schools, Northern and Southern. What are the characteristics of each?

18.5 Explain the cultural patronage of the Ashikaga shoguns and the impact of the West on Japan in the Azuchi-Momoyama period.

In Japan, political turmoil caused by war with the Mongols, instability at the imperial court, and, in the provinces, the increasing power of local military rulers, who would come to be known as *daimyo*, was finally mitigated by the ascendancy of Ashikaga shoguns in the Muromachi period (1392–1573). In the midst of what often amounted to civil war, the Ashikaga shoguns were great cultural patrons. Why did they associate themselves with the arts? What was their attitude toward China and Chan (Zen) in particular? What elements of Japanese taste began to assert themselves in painting? In garden design? In the tea ceremony? What aesthetic feeling manifests itself particularly in Noh drama? How did trade with the Portuguese in the Azuchi-Momoyama period (1573–1615) influence Japanese culture? Screen painting became especially popular and depicted a wide variety of subjects. How does *namban* painting reflect Japan's increasing cultural syncretism? What aesthetic principles inform the large-scale landscapes of the Kano School?

✔ **Study** and **review** on **MyArtsLab**

READINGS

from Bernadino de Sahagún, *History of the Things of New Spain* (ca. 1585)

The *History of the Things of New Spain* was written in the Nahuatl language under the supervision of the Benedictine monk Bernadino de Sahagún. First completed in about 1555, it relies on the memories of aging native Aztecs who had actually been alive during the conquest. The 1555 version has been lost. But in about 1585, Bernadino prepared a second version in Nahuatl. The description of Pedro de Alvarado's massacre of the Aztecs at the Fiesta of Toxcatl, which follows, is from that later version and is particularly chilling.

The Beginning of the Fiesta

… All the young warriors were eager for the fiesta to begin. They had sworn to dance and sing with all their hearts, so that the Spaniards would marvel at the beauty of the rituals.

The procession began, and the celebrants filed into the temple patio to dance the Dance of the Serpent. When they were all together in the patio, the songs and the dance began. Those who had fasted for twenty days and those who had fasted for a year were in command of the others; they kept the dancers in file with their pine wands. (If anyone wished to urinate, he did not stop dancing, but simply opened his clothing at the hips and separated his clusters of heron feathers.) 10

If anyone disobeyed the leaders or was not in his proper place they struck him on the hips and shoulders. Then they drove him out of the patio, beating him and shoving him from behind. They pushed him so hard that he sprawled to the ground, and they dragged him outside by the ears. No one dared to say a word about this punishment, for those who had fasted during the year were feared and venerated …

The great captains, the bravest warriors, danced at the head of the files to guide the others. The youths followed at a slight 20 distance. Some of the youths wore their hair gathered into large locks, a sign that they had never taken any captives. Others carried their headdresses on their shoulders; they had taken captives, but only with help.

Then came the recruits, who were called "the young warriors." They had each captured an enemy or two. The others called to them: "Come, comrades, show us how brave you are! Dance with all your hearts!"

The Spaniards Attack the Celebrants

At this moment in the fiesta, when the dance was loveliest and when song was linked to song, the Spaniards were seized with 30 an urge to kill the celebrants. They all ran forward, armed as if for battle. They closed the entrances and passageways, all the gates of the patio: the Eagle Gate in the lesser palace, the Gate of the Canestalk and the Gate of the Serpent of Mirrors. They posted guards so that no one could escape, and then rushed into the Sacred Patio to slaughter the celebrants. They came on foot, carrying their swords and their wooden or metal shields.

They ran in among the dancers, forcing their way to the place where the drums were played. They attacked the man who was drumming and cut off his arms. Then they cut off his 40 head, and it rolled across the floor.

They attacked all the celebrants, stabbing them, spearing them, striking them with their swords. They attacked some of them from behind, and these fell instantly to the ground with their entrails hanging out. Others they beheaded: they cut off their heads, or split their heads to pieces.

They struck others in the shoulders, and their arms were torn from their bodies. They wounded some in the thigh and some in the calf. They slashed others in the abdomen, and their entrails all spilled to the ground. Some attempted to run away, 50 but their intestines dragged as they ran; they seemed to tangle their feet in their own entrails. No matter how they tried to save themselves, they could find no escape.

Some attempted to force their way out, but the Spaniards murdered them at the gates. Others climbed the walls, but they could not save themselves. Those who ran into the communal houses were safe there for a while; so were those who lay down among the victims and pretended to be dead. But if they stood up again, the Spaniards saw them and killed them. 60

The blood of the warriors flowed like water and gathered into pools. The pools widened, and the stench of blood and entrails filled the air. The Spaniards ran into the communal houses to kill those who were hiding. They ran everywhere and searched everywhere; they invaded every room, hunting and killing.

The Aztecs Retaliate

When the news of this massacre was heard outside the Sacred Patio, a great cry went up: "Mexicanos, come running! Bring your spears and shields! The strangers have murdered our warriors!"

This cry was answered with a roar of grief and anger: the 70 people shouted and wailed and beat their palms against their mouths. The captains assembled at once, as if the hour had been determined in advance. They all carried their spears and shields.

Then the battle began. The Aztecs attacked with javelins and arrows, even with the light spears that are used for hunting birds. They hurled their javelins with all their strength, and the cloud of missiles spread out over the Spaniards like a yellow cloak.

The Spaniards immediately took refuge in the palace. They began to shoot at the Mexicans with their iron arrows and to fire their cannons and arquebuses. And they shackled 80 Motecuhzoma in chains.

READING CRITICALLY

When Cortés rescued Alvarado, the latter claimed that informants had told him the Aztecs planned to attack when the Fiesta of Toxcatl was over in order to free Motecuhzoma. Does this claim alter your reaction to this Nahuatl version of events?

from Zeami Motokiyo, *Semimaru* (early 15th century)

Noh theater is very different from Western theater. It incorporates music, chanting, dance, poetry, prose, mime, and elaborate masks and costumes to create a total theatrical experience. It is perhaps closest to our musical form opera. But even opera cannot match the slow, ritualistic pace of Noh plays, which seek to create in their audience an ethereal sense of a transcendent, Zen Buddhist world. The following text, representing approximately the first half of the play, was written by one of the founders of the Noh tradition.

Persons

Prince Semimaru (*tsure*)
Kiyotsura, An Imperial Envoy (*waki*)
Two Palanquin Bearers (*wakizure*)
Hakuga No Sammi (*Kyōgen*)
Princess Sakagami, Semimaru's Sister (*shite*)[1]

Place

Mt. Ōsaka in Ōmi Province

Time

The Reign of Emperor Daigo: The Eighth Month

[*The stage assistant places a representation of a hut at the* waki-*position. Semimaru enters, wearing the* semimaru *mask. He is flanked by two Palanquin Bearers who hold a canopy over him. Kiyotsura follows them.*]

KIYOTSURA: The world is so unsure, unknowable;
  Who knows—our griefs may hold our greatest hopes,
  This nobleman is the Prince Semimaru   10
  Fourth child of the Emperor Daigo.

KIYOTSURA AND ATTENDANTS: Truly in this uncertain world
  All that befalls us comes our way
  As recompense for what we've done before.
  In his previous existence
  He observed intently the laws of Buddha
  And in this life was born a prince,
  Yet why was it—ever since he lay,
  An infant wrapped in swaddling clothes
  His eyes have both been blind. For him   20
  The sun and moon in heaven have no light;
  In the black of night his lamp is dark;
  The rain before the dawn never ends.

KIYOTSURA: His nights and days have been spent this way,
  But now what plan has the Emperor conceived?
  He ordered us to escort the Prince in secret,
  To abandon him on Mount Ōsaka
  And to shave his head in priestly tonsure.
  The Emperor's words, once spoken
  Are final—what immense pity I feel!   30
  Yet, such being the command, I am powerless.

KIYOTSURA AND ATTENDANTS: Like lame-wheeled carriages
  We creep forth reluctantly
  On the journey from the Capital;
  How hard it is to say farewell
  As dawn clouds streak the east!
  Today he first departs the Capital
  When again to return? His chances are as fragile
  As unraveled threads too thin to intertwine,
  Friendless, his destination is unknown.   40
  Even without an affliction
  Good fortune is elusive in this world,
  Like the floating log the turtle gropes for
  Once a century: The path is in darkness
  And he, a blind turtle, must follow it.[2]
  Now as the clouds of delusion rise
  We have reached Mount Ōsaka
  We have reached Mount Ōsaka.

[*Semimaru sits on a stool before the Chorus. Kiyotsura kneels at the shite-pillar. The Bearers exit through the slit door.*]   50

SEMIMARU: Kiyotsura!

KIYOTSURA: I am before you.

[*From his kneeling position, he bows deeply.*]

SEMIMARU: Are you to leave me on this mountain?

KIYOTSURA: Yes, your highness, So the Emperor has
  commanded, and I have brought you this far,
  But I wonder just where
  I should leave you,
  Since the days of the ancient sage kings
  Our Emperors have ruled the country wisely,   60
  Looking after its people with compassion—
  But what can his Majesty have had in mind?
  Nothing could have caught me so unprepared.

SEMIMARU: What a foolish thing to say, Kiyotsura, I was born
  blind because I was lax in my religious duties in a former life,
  That is why the Emperor, my father,
  Ordered you to leave me in the wilderness,
  Heartless this would seem, but it's his plan
  To purge in this world my burden from the past,

---

[1] The parenthetical terms designate each character's role: *tsure*, accompanying the main actor; *waki*, a secondary actor; *wakizura*, accompanying the *waki*; *Kyōgen*, an interlude actor; and *shite*, the main actor.

[2] In certain Buddhist texts, the rarity of meeting a Buddha is compared to the difficulty of a blind sea turtle's chances of bumping into a log to float on. The turtle emerges to the surface only once a century and tries to clutch the log, but it has a hole and eludes his grasp; this was a simile for the difficulty of obtaining good fortune.

And spare me suffering in the world to come,
This is a father's true kindness,
You should not bewail his decree.

KIYOTSURA: Now I shall shave your head,
His Majesty has so commanded.

SEMIMARU: What does this act signify?

KIYOTSURA: It means you have become a priest,
A most joyous event.

[Semimaru rises. The stage assistant removes his nobleman's outer robe and places a priest's hat on his head.]

SEMIMARU: Surely Seishi's poem described such a scene: 80
"I have cut my fragrant scented hair
My head is pillowed half on sandalwood."[3]

KIYOTSURA: Such splendid clothes will summon thieves, I fear.
Allow me to take your robe and give you instead
This cloak of straw they call a *mino*.

[Semimaru mimes receiving the *mino*.]

SEMIMARU: Is this the mino mentioned in the lines,
"I went to Tamino Island when it rained"?[4]

KIYOTSURA: And I give you this *kasa* rainhat
To protect you also from the rain and dew. 90

[He takes a kasa *from the stage assistant and hands it to* Semimaru.]

SEMIMARU: Then this must be the *kasa* of the poem
"Samurai—take a *kasa* for your lord."[5]

[Semimaru puts down the kasa.]

KIYOTSURA: And this staff will guide you on your way,
Please take it in your hands.

[He takes a staff from the stage assistant and hands it to Semimaru.]

SEMIMARU: Is this the staff about which Henjō wrote: 100
"Since my staff was fashioned by the gods
I can cross the mountain of a thousand years"?[6]

[Kiyotsura kneels at the shite-pillar.]

KIYOTSURA: His staff brought a thousand prosperous years,[7]

SEMIMARU: But here the place is Mount Ōsaka,

KIYOTSURA: A straw-thatched hut by the barrier;

SEMIMARU: Bamboo pillars and staff, my sole support,

KIYOTSURA: By your father, the Emperor,

SEMIMARU: Abandoned,

CHORUS: I meet my unsure fate at Mount Ōsaka. 110
You who know me, you who know me not[8]
Behold—this is how a prince, Daigo's son,
Has reached the last extremity of grief,

[He lowers his head to give a sad expression to his mask.]

Travelers and men on horses
Riding to and from the Capital,
Many people, dressed for their journeys,
Will drench their sleeves in sudden showers;
How hard it is to abandon him,
To leave him all alone; 120
How hard it is to abandon him,
To tear ourselves away.

[Kiyotsura bows to Semimaru.]

But even farewells must have an end;
By the light of the daybreak moon
Stifling tears that have no end, they depart.

[Weeping, Kiyotsura goes to the bridgeway.]

Semimaru, the Prince, left behind alone,
Takes in his arms his lute, his one possession,
Clutches his staff and falls down weeping. 130

[Semimaru picks up the staff and kasa, comes forward, and turns toward the departing Kiyotsura. Kiyotsura stops at the second pine and looks back at him, then exits. Semimaru retreats, kneels, drops his kasa and staff, and weeps. Hakuga no Sammi enters and stands at the naming-place.] ...

READING CRITICALLY

One of the aims of Noh theater is to reveal the inner strength of a character even in the most tragic circumstances. How does this selection reflect Semimaru's inner strength?

[3] The poem referred to is by Li Ho and is actually a description of Hsi-shih (Seishi) rather than a poem by her. The meaning of the original verses was that Seishi's fragrant locks rivaled the perfume of cloves or sandalwood; however, the dramatist here misunderstood the Chinese and interpreted it as meaning she had cut her locks and now would have to rest her head on a hard pillow of sandalwood.
[4] From the poem by Ki no Tsurayuki, no. 918 in the *Kosinshu*. [The *Kosinshu* is an early anthology of *waka* poems dating from the Heian period; see the discussion of *waka* poetry in Chapter 11.]
[5] From the anonymous poem, no. 1091 in the *Kosinshu*.
[6] From the poem by the priest Henjō, no. 348 in the *Kosinshu*.

[7] There is a pivot-word embedded here: *chitase no saka*, the slope of a thousand years; and *saka yuku tsue*, the staff that brings steady prosperity. [Pivot-words are a device used in *waka* poetry in which the literal meaning of a word suggests, when pronounced, a different, fuller meaning, in the way, for instance, that an English-speaking poet might write "see" but suggest "sea."]
[8] An allusion to the poem, attributed to Semimaru himself, no. 1091 in the *Gasenshū* [a collection of Zen Buddhist texts]. The poem, about the Barrier of Osaka, originally had a meaning something like: "This is the Barrier where people come and go exchanging farewells; for friends and strangers alike this is Meeting Barrier."

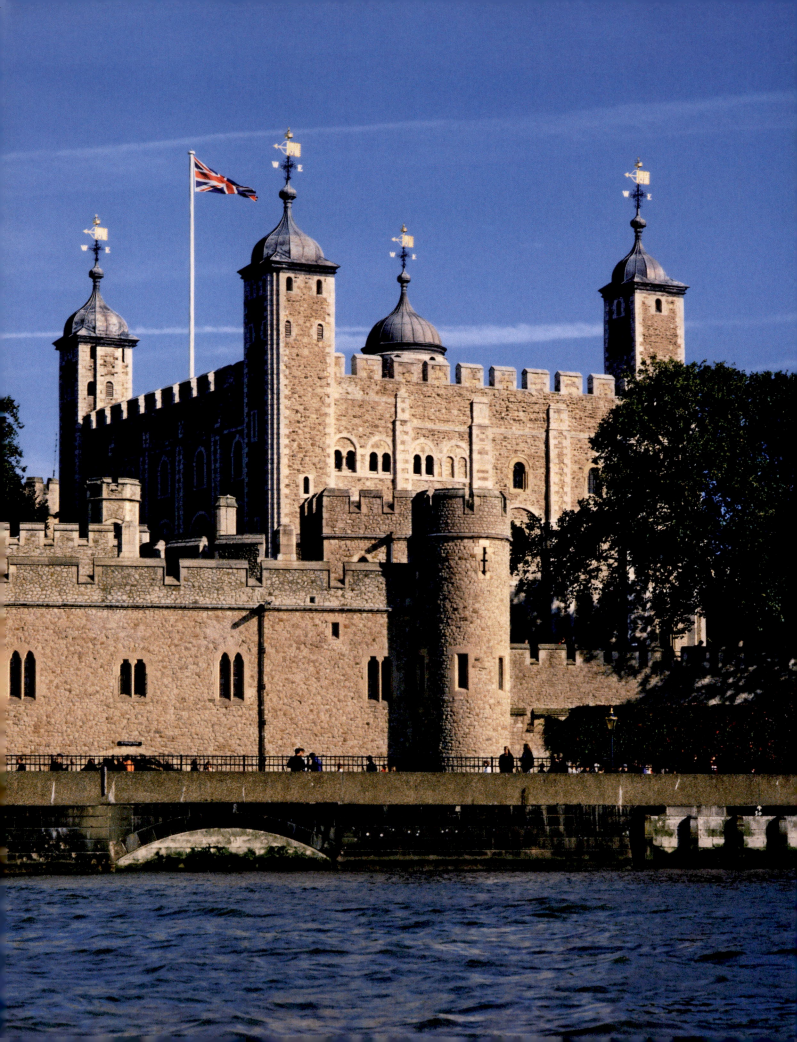

19

England in the Tudor Age
"This Other Eden"

THINKING AHEAD

19.1 Explain how Henry VIII transformed England.

19.2 Outline the flourishing of the arts under the rule of Queen Elizabeth I.

19.3 Characterize the Elizabethan stage and the contributions to it of both Marlowe and Shakespeare.

19.4 Describe the unique features of the English colonization of the Americas.

The city of London was crowded with spectators on February 20, 1547, as the coronation procession of Edward VI (r. 1547–53) passed through the streets. The route originated at the Tower of London (Fig. **19.1**), the political center of the city and principal London residence of the English kings. It proceeded to Westminster Abbey, where the coronation ceremony would take place (Fig. **19.2**). Edward was just 10 years old, the sole surviving male in the Tudor dynasty inaugurated by his grandfather, Henry VII (r. 1485–1509). Edward's father, Henry VIII (r. 1509–47), had died just a month before, his mother, Jane Seymour, many years earlier. His uncle, Edward Seymour, Duke of Somerset, had been named his protector and regent, to rule on his behalf during his minority.

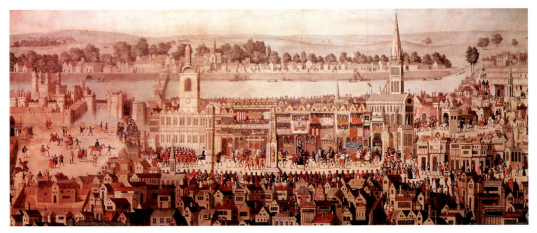

Fig. 19.2 *The Coronation Procession of King Edward VI.* **1547.** Society of Antiquaries, London. The major features of the London landscape in the mid-sixteenth century are all visible here. At the left, the procession leaves the Tower of London. Just to the right is London Bridge, still covered with shops and houses. The procession passes by the medieval church of Saint Mary-le-Bow and Saint Paul's Cathedral, and proceeds out through Ludgate to Westminster in the distance.

◄ **Fig. 19.1 The Tower of London as seen from the Thames.** The Tower of London served as the London palace of English kings beginning with William the Conqueror, who first built the nine-story inner White Tower on the site of a Roman fortress. Henry VIII remodeled it to house his new queen, Anne Boleyn.

((**Listen** to the chapter audio on **MyArtsLab**

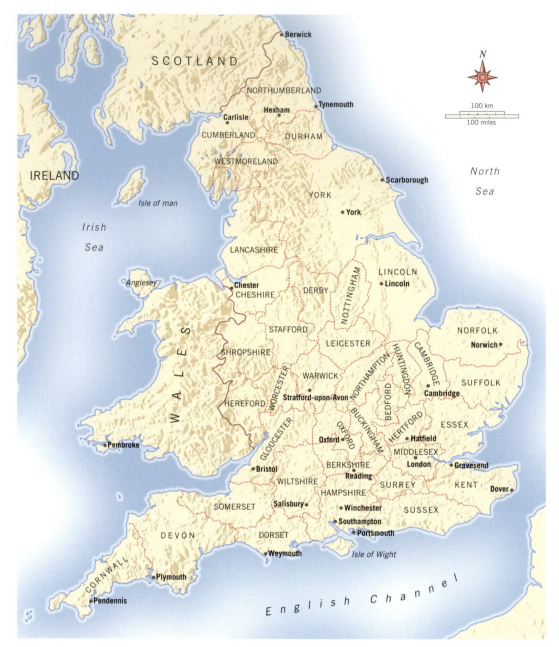

Map 19.1 Tudor England in the 16th century.

Renaissance London in 1547 was a port city on the banks of the River Thames in the southeast corner of the British Isles (Map **19.1**). Its 80,000 or so inhabitants constituted only about 4 percent of the entire English population, but this was about to change. By 1700, London would house almost half a million people—10 percent of the country's total population—even though the plague wracked the city throughout the sixteenth century.

As the densely packed foreground in Fig. 19.2 indicates, London in 1547 was just beginning a construction boom almost unprecedented in the Western world. Precipitating the boom was the Dissolution Act of 1536 dissolving the monasteries and selling off Church holdings. Henry VIII's high-handed decree was motivated primarily by a need for money, though Henry's quarrel with the Roman

Church and his desire to assert authority as head of the Church in England may have played a part. Considerable wealth was required to support his numerous estates and the palaces he was in the habit of building—as well as the enormous court that followed him everywhere. One day in 1532, for instance, as the king and his traveling household were headed to Calais, they reportedly consumed 6 oxen, 8 calves, 40 sheep, 12 pigs, 132 capons, 7 swans, 20 storks, 34 pheasant, 192 partridges, 192 cocks, 56 herons, 84 young hens, 720 larks, 240 pigeons, 24 peacocks, and 192 plovers and teals. Feeding the court alone cost Henry the equivalent of approximately $9 million per year.

Even though the vast revenues of the monasteries flowed directly into the king's coffers after the Dissolution, it was the sale of the monastic lands that contributed most to his

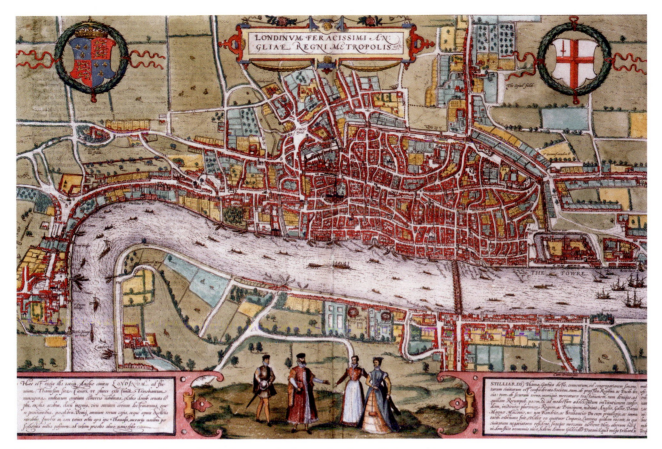

Map 19.2 London in the time of Queen Elizabeth, taken chiefly from the plan by R. Aggnes. 1560.
Westminster is at the bottom left and the Tower of London at the center right, just to the right of London Bridge. Saint Paul's Cathedral stands squarely in the center top. The two circular structures on the south bank of the river, across from Saint Paul's, are bear-baiting arenas, where dogs were set upon a captive bear as a form of entertainment.

wealth, transforming London in the process. Before the Dissolution, as much as 60 percent of the property in some parts of the city was in ecclesiastical hands, and the Church had vast holdings outside the city as well. Henry sold these properties to wealthy gentry, who used the rural parcels for country estates, the urban ones for townhouses. In Tudor times, the vast majority of London's population lived inside the gates of the city walls (see Map **19.2**). There the gentry in their magnificent townhouses butted up against butchers and bakers, brewers and millers, glassmakers and haberdashers, with their stalls and stores, stables and furnaces. As people flocked to the city from the countryside—especially young men intent on making their fortunes—adequate lodging became a growing problem. Makeshift hovels filled the alleyways just off the main thoroughfares, poor families lived in cellars, and upper-story rooms were subdivided. Financially, the city was the direct beneficiary of the collapse of Antwerp as a center of trade in 1585, following the Dutch rebellion against Spanish rule. Also, as maritime activity increased, including the circumnavigation of the globe by Sir Francis Drake (ca. 1540–96) and early seventeenth-century exploration founded the first British settlement to survive in North America at Jamestown, Virginia, the community of merchants increased proportionally. In 1592, the Levant Company was founded to trade with the eastern Mediterranean, and seven years later, in 1599, the East India Company was formed to trade around the Cape of Good Hope with southern Asia.

The dissolution of the monasteries affected not only the growth of London and the wealth of the Crown but also Henry's political power. This is because those who received properties from him tended to support his split with Rome, and because Parliament was able to raise money without raising taxes. Politically, the city was unique in Renaissance Europe, both self-governing and under royal rule. Its lord mayor was the city's voice in dealing with the king as well as the king's agent in the city. A group of aldermen served as justices of the peace and presided over the city's courts and jails. They controlled the city's charities, assisted in levying its taxes, and often served as members of Parliament. Thus, in the city, they exercised something like democratic rule within the overarching rule of the monarch. Henry VIII and his successors, particularly Queen Elizabeth I (r. 1558–1603), rarely meddled in city politics, and in return the city bestowed upon its monarch almost undivided loyalty. By 1603, when James I (r. 1603–25), the first of the Stuart monarchs, succeeded Elizabeth on the throne, the size of the city was close to 200,000 people. The new monarch, considering this fact, drolly remarked, "Soon London will be all England."

This chapter outlines the rise of London as a great center of culture in the sixteenth century, a time of extraordinarily complex political maneuvering on the part of Henry VIII. Although a Catholic at heart, Henry felt obliged to split with the Church and align himself with Protestant reformers. England's messy political climate discouraged the production of religious art. In fact, Henry's reign is noted most of all for the destruction of religious art, brought on largely by his suppression of the monasteries. But Henry was a man of deep and profound learning, a poet, musician, and lyricist of considerable accomplishment, and he surrounded himself with artists and intellectuals. Portrait painting became the chief occupation of court artists. Humanist scholars served as his personal advisers. He loved music and encouraged theatrical productions at court. And while political turmoil continued under the rule of his three heirs, the secular arts continued to thrive. This was particularly so during the reign of his daughter, Elizabeth I, when writing poetry became common court practice, with the sonnet as the preferred form. But the art that most distinguished Elizabeth's London was the theater, its most popular form of entertainment. Audiences flocked to the south bank of the River Thames to see the plays performed in such theaters such as the Globe, where William Shakespeare of Stratford-upon-Avon rose to preeminence as the greatest playwright of the day.

THE REIGN OF HENRY VIII

How did Henry VIII transform England?

However controversial he may have been, Henry VIII brought England to a position of international prominence. By the end of his daughter Elizabeth's reign in 1603, London could, with some justification, claim to be the very center of Western culture. It was Henry who first insisted the monarch be addressed as "Your Majesty," rather than "Your Grace" or "Your Highness," in accord with the air of magnificence that he cultivated in all things associated with his court.

Henry VIII was, in almost every way, extraordinary. In his youth, he was a great athlete and intensely competitive. Even after his coronation and despite the protests of his advisers, he regularly participated in royal jousts and games, which he won routinely (very often in disguise, so as to discourage sycophants from allowing him to win). As he grew older, he grew larger, so that by the time German artist Hans Holbein the Younger (ca. 1497–1543) painted his portrait in 1540 (Fig. **19.3**), at the age of 49, his 6-foot-2-inch frame (quite tall for the age) was supporting an imposing 54-inch waistline. This girth did not impede his sexual appetite, for the monarch married repeatedly—he had six wives, and ordered the beheading of two. These marriages produced three children (see *Context*, page 641). The right to divorce and remarry, in fact, was another reason behind his split with the Church. Henry's mind was

arguably the best of any European ruler of the age. When he was 8 years old, the great Dutch humanist Desiderius Erasmus (see Chapter 17) visited him, and subsequently the two began an extensive correspondence in Latin, the international language of the day. Erasmus called him "a universal genius," and throughout his reign, Henry surrounded himself with humanist scholars. These men of the mind tested his formidable intellect and brought prestige to his court. Henry was a passionate musician who also composed popular tunes, including the traditional Christmas song "Green Groweth the Holly." He practiced daily and played almost every instrument, including the lute, the virginal (a keyboard instrument similar to a harpsichord), the recorder, cornet, regal (a kind of portable organ), and perhaps even the harp. He loved both astronomy and mapmaking, and his passion for them is probably reflected in the objects that decorate Hans Holbein's famous painting *The Ambassadors* (see *Closer Look*, pages 644–645). His learning was so great that on the day of Henry's coronation, June 24, 1509, the humanist philosopher, author, and statesman Thomas More (1478–1535), wrote: "This day consecrates a young man who is the everlasting glory of our age."

Humanism in Tudor England: Desiderius Erasmus and Thomas More

The same year Henry assumed the throne, in 1509, Desiderius Erasmus wrote *In Praise of Folly* (see Chapter 17), the work that so influenced Martin Luther. Erasmus had an incalculable influence on Henry VIII's thinking about kingship. For one thing, his attack on monastic life in *In Praise of Folly* certainly helped Henry justify the dissolution of the monasteries. In his *Adages*, written off and on from 1500 to 1533, Erasmus opened with a piece about the lessons of Homer's *Iliad* (see Chapter 4) that Henry could only have understood as an admonition about his own behavior, particularly his predilection for changing wives at a whim, and the lavishness of his court (**Reading 19.1**):

READING 19.1

from Desiderius Erasmus, *The Adages of Erasmus* (1500–33)

What could be more idiotic than to be up in arms so childishly for the sake of a chit from a barbarous land, and then when he couldn't keep his sweetheart, to snatch the girl belonging to Achilles, and put the whole army in danger? And then there is Achilles himself—how foolishly he rages when bereft of his lady-love and how childishly he goes crying to his mother! And yet he is the one whom the poet sets before us as the perfect example of an excellent prince.

Indeed Hesiod (whom some think older than Homer) calls princes "gift-greedy" and "childish"—I suppose on account of their small wisdom in government, and the way they strained after the accumulation of riches by fair means and foul, rather than after the public good.

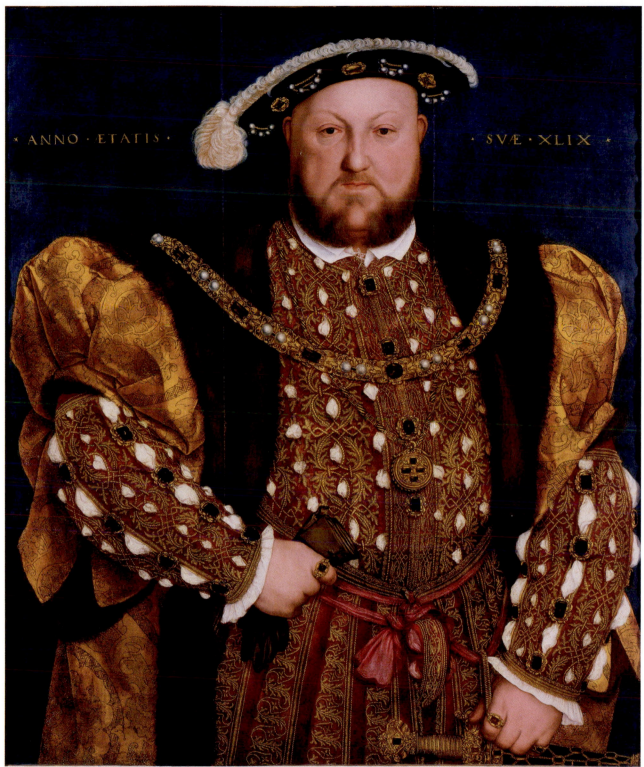

Fig. 19.3 Hans Holbein the Younger, *Henry VIII in Wedding Dress*. 1540. Oil on panel, 32½″ × 29″.
Galleria Barberini, Rome. Henry is in the clothes that he wore when he married the 25-year-old Anne of Cleves
in 1540. He was 49.

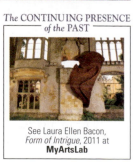

The CONTINUING PRESENCE
of the PAST

See Laura Ellen Bacon,
Form of Intrigue, 2011 at
MyArtsLab

For it was not ill-advisedly that the divine Plato wrote that the only way for a state to attain happiness was for the supreme command to be given to philosophers, or else, inversely, that those who govern should themselves follow philosophy. And to follow philosophy is not just to wear a mantle and to carry a bag round, or let your beard grow. What is it then? It is to despise those things which the common herd goggles at, and to think quite differently from the opinions of the majority. ...

To Henry's credit, he allowed, even encouraged this kind of critique. When Thomas More published his *Utopia* in 1516, it was widely understood to be more than just a description of an unrealized, ideal state—in Greek, *eu* means "good" and *topos* "place," hence "Good place," but also, the root might be, *ou* meaning "not," hence "No place"—and thus a profound critique of the English political system. At the heart of the critique is More's implicit comparison between his own corrupt Christian society and the ideal society he imagines. This ideal society was inspired, at least in part, by the accounts of explorers returning from the Americas. Its fictional narrator is himself an explorer who has discovered an island culture in which people share goods and property, where war is held in contempt, personal vanity despised, education available to all (except, notably, slaves—a blind spot in More's cultural critique), and freedom of religion a given. Each individual works (six hours a day) for the common good, assuming personal responsibility for social justice rather than entrusting it to some higher authority. Equality, kindness, and charity are the virtues most esteemed by all. In short, Utopia seemed the very antithesis of More's England (see **Reading 19.2**, page 661, for a description of some of the virtues of his Utopia).

By the time *Utopia* was published, More was the king's unofficial secretary. As if to endorse More's point of view, Henry promoted him within the year to a position on his advisory council. This was the first of many advancements, culminating in More's appointment as Lord Chancellor, the presiding officer of the House of Lords, in 1529. In *Utopia*, More dedicated considerable discussion to matters of religion, in many ways anticipating the Reformation politics that would begin in the following year. Utopus, king of Utopia, enforces a practice of religion (**Reading 19.2a**):

READING 19.2a

from Thomas More, *Utopia*, Book 2 (1516)

By those among them [the Utopians] that have not received our religion [Christianity], do not fright any from it, and use none ill that goes over to it; so that all the while I was there, one man was only punished on this occasion. He being newly baptized, did, notwithstanding all that we could say to the contrary, dispute publicly concerning the Christian religion with more zeal than discretion; and with so much heat, that he not only preferred our worship

to theirs, but condemned all their rites as profane; and cried out against all that adhered to them, as impious and sacrilegious persons, that were to be damned to everlasting burnings. Upon his having frequently preached in this manner, he was seized, and after trial he was condemned to banishment, not for having disparaged their religion, but for his inflaming the people to sedition: for this is one of their most ancient laws, that no man ought to be punished for his religion. At the first constitution of their government, Utopus having understood that before his coming among them the old inhabitants had been engaged in great quarrels concerning religion ... he made a law that every man might be of what religion he pleased, and might endeavor to draw others to it by force of argument, and ... that he ought to use no other force but that of persuasion, and was neither to mix with it reproaches nor violence. ... This law was made by Utopus, not only for preserving the public peace, which he saw suffered much by daily contentions and irreconcilable heats, but because he thought the interest of religion itself required it.

If such moderation was the ideal that More presented to Henry VIII, his king found it somewhat difficult to live up to the example of the fictional Utopus.

Martin Luther presented the first test of Henry's ability to live up to More's ideal. As a devout Catholic and leader, Henry felt obliged to rebuke the upstart German cleric, for he was wary of precisely the kind of religious division More had warned about in *Utopia* working its way into England. An added benefit of taking Luther on, Henry reasoned, would be the pope's probable conferral of a title like "the most Catholic King" or "Protector of the Holy See." Such a title had already been bestowed upon Charles V of Germany and Francis I of France, and Henry coveted one for himself. In 1521, Henry published a short but pointed Latin tract, translated as *A Defense of the Seven Sacraments against Martin Luther*. In it, referring to himself in the third person, he said he intended "to defend the Church, not only with his armies but the resources of his mind." After reading it, More urged the king to tone down his attack, but Henry would not comply. "What serpent so venomously crept in as he who called the Most Holy See of Rome 'Babylon' and the Pope's authority 'Tyranny,' and turns the name of the Most Holy Bishop of Rome into 'Anti-Christ'?" Henry exclaimed about Luther. The publication of Henry's tract was followed by a public burning of Luther's works in London and the presentation of a gold-bound edition of Henry's essay to Leo X in Rome. The pope expressed his gratitude by conferring on Henry the title he desired, "Defender of the Faith." Ironically, Henry later used this title to legitimize the founding of the Anglican Church in England.

Henry would quickly find it difficult to live up to his newly won title, just as More would soon find it difficult to live up to the expectations of his king. But in the meanwhile, Henry's favorite painter, Hans Holbein, would celebrate

Read the document related to Thomas More on **MyArtsLab**

The Tudor Genealogy

The House of Tudor was founded in the fifteenth century by Owen Tudor (ca. 1400–1461), but the dynasty occupying the throne of England did not begin until 1485, when Henry VII took the throne. His son, Henry VIII, had three direct heirs—Mary, Elizabeth, and Edward—but none of them had any children. This enabled James VI of Scotland to assume the English throne as James I, the first Stuart king.

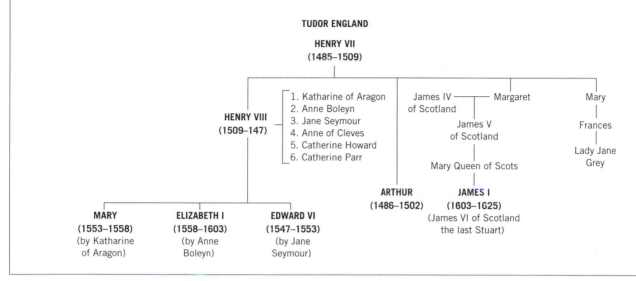

TUDOR ENGLAND

HENRY VII
(1485–1509)

HENRY VIII
(1509–147)
1. Katharine of Aragon
2. Anne Boleyn
3. Jane Seymour
4. Anne of Cleves
5. Catherine Howard
6. Catherine Parr

James IV ——— Margaret   Mary
of Scotland

James V   Frances
of Scotland

Mary Queen of Scots   Lady Jane
Grey

ARTHUR   **JAMES I**
(1486–1502)   **(1603–1625)**
(James VI of Scotland
the last Stuart)

MARY   **ELIZABETH I**   **EDWARD VI**
(1553–1558)   **(1558–1603)**   **(1547–1553)**
(by Katharine   (by Anne   (by Jane
of Aragon)   Boleyn)   Seymour)

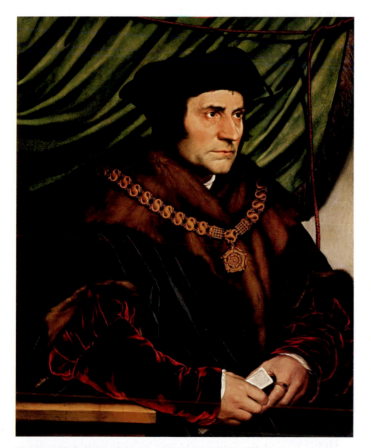

Fig. 19.4 Hans Holbein the Younger, *Thomas More*. 1527. Tempera on oak, 27½″ × 23½″. Frick Collection, New York. Holbein's portrait captures the power of More's intellect and celebrates his service to the king.

More in a portrait painted soon after his appointment as Lord Chancellor in 1529 (Fig. **19.4**). In fact, Henry promoted portrait painting over other art genres, as did the English people generally throughout the sixteenth century.

Hans Holbein and Portrait Painting

Hans Holbein was one of the most important portraitists of wealthy society in Europe, and he painted hundreds of works during his two extended visits to England (1526–28, 1532–43), including many of Henry (see Fig. 19.3), four of his six wives, scores of portraits of English courtiers and humanists, and just as many of the London German merchant community. Each portrait conveyed the sitter's status and captured something of the sitter's identity. The English taste for this genre of painting can be understood as an expression of the culture's general humanist emphasis on individualism.

As in Northern Renaissance painting as a whole, Holbein's portrait of More is richly detailed. Over a white shirt, which shows at his neck and wrists, More wears a black velvet cloak with brown fur lining and collar, and a doublet with red velvet sleeves. Around his neck is a double-S gold chain and medallion symbolizing his work in the service of the king: It stands for the French expression *souvent me souviens*, "think of me often." The chain is painted in gold leaf (as is the ring on his left index finger), and it frames his face even as it echoes the curve of his forearms, themselves a highly realistic rendering of red velvet. The true subject of the painting is the quality of More's mind.

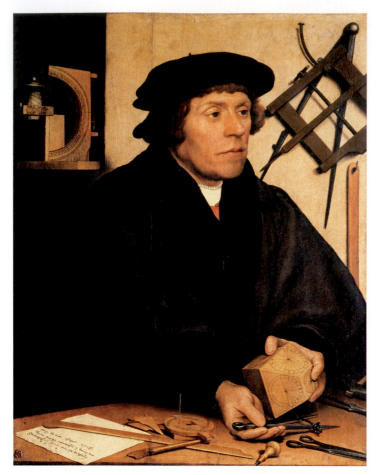

Fig. 19.5 Hans Holbein the Younger, *Nicolaus Kratzer*. 1528. Tempera on panel, 32⅔" × 25⅓". Musée du Louvre, Paris. Although Kratzer, a native of Germany, served as Henry's court astronomer from about 1517 to 1547, he never mastered the English language, complaining to Henry that 30 years was insufficient time in which to learn such a difficult tongue.

holds dividers (a pair of compasses used to divide lines), and other parts of the incomplete instrument lie alongside a ruler and a woodcutting knife on the left on the table. Other tools include an auger, scissors, a divider, and a hammer. Like More, Kratzer wears the black cap of a scholar and stares off into space, as if deep in thought. But the brilliant contrast of red and green in the More portrait is replaced by a subtle range of cream, brown, and black. Despite Kratzer's position, Holbein's portrait is not concerned with the trappings of the king's court—fine clothes and gold chains—but with the pure pursuit of humanist learning. It celebrates a man of science.

Henry's Marriages and His Defiance of Rome

One of Holbein's most challenging tasks was painting the portraits of Henry's succession of wives. These portraits were politically sensitive, as Henry's marriages posed a serious threat to his position as "Defender of the Faith." His marriage to Katharine of Aragon forced the issue. By 1527, Katharine had endured many miscarriages and stillbirths, and had successfully delivered only two children, one of whom survived, Mary, born February 18, 1516. Henry, who desperately wanted a male heir, had also fallen in love with one of Katharine's ladies-in-waiting, Anne Boleyn. He could not marry Anne unless the pope agreed to annul his marriage to Katharine, and the pope might not see Henry's side of the argument. Not only had Katharine borne two children during their 18-year marriage, but she was also the aunt of Charles V, who happened to be holding Pope Clement VII hostage in 1527 after the Sack of Rome. Furthermore, Henry's marriage to Katharine had required a special papal dispensation in the first place (since Katharine had first been married to Henry's now-deceased brother Arthur). When Henry's annulment was denied, he convened what became known as the Protestant Parliament, which quickly recognized Henry, not the pope, as head of the Church of England. England was now in open defiance of the papacy, and Henry no longer its "Defender of the Faith," although he continued to claim the title for the English crown. In January 1533, he married the pregnant Anne Boleyn.

What might be called the *de facto* Protestantization of the Catholic Church quickly followed. In order to assert his kingship, Henry was forced to defy Rome, and in doing so he legitimized English Protestantism. Yet he remained, at least temperamentally, Catholic. He was capable, furthermore, of wielding power as an extreme despot. He executed his friend Thomas More for suggesting that Katharine's daughter Mary was the legitimate heir to the throne, not Anne Boleyn's child. Boleyn was herself soon executed for treason, and Henry proceeded through a string of four more wives: Jane Seymour, who died in 1537 shortly after giving birth to the future Edward VI; Anne of Cleves, whom he married sight-unseen in order to create an alliance with the

Posed in three-quarters profile, More looks past the viewer as if deep in thought. His face is distinguished by a two-days' growth of beard—as if he has been too busy to bother shaving—by tiny wrinkles that radiate from his right eye and suggest wisdom, and by the weary sagging of skin below his right eye. The whole, in short, is an emblem of More's tireless service to the king and a lasting symbol of the power of this great humanist scholar's mind.

Holbein's portrait of Nicolaus Kratzer (1487–ca. 1550), painted in 1528 (Fig. **19.5**), is more subdued. Kratzer was a close friend of More, tutor of his daughters, and lived in More's household. He also served as the royal court astronomer to Henry VIII, and most of the instruments in this portrait of him reoccur in one of Holbein's most interesting works, *The Ambassadors* (see *Closer Look*, pages 644–645). Behind Kratzer, on the shelf, is a conventional sundial, a symbol of measuring time but largely supplanted by the clock in the fourteenth through sixteenth centuries. In his hands, he holds what is known as a *polyhedral sundial*—a pair of identically truncated square pyramids placed base to base, less accurate than the instrument behind him—which he is in the process of constructing. In his right hand, he

European Protestants, but finding her to bear a remarkable resemblance to a horse, had Parliament annul the union; Catherine Howard, whom he had beheaded for adultery in 1542; and, finally, his last wife, Catherine Parr, a humanist and reformer, who survived his death in 1547.

Edward, Mary, and Elizabeth: The Continuing Religious Conflict

Edward VI was only 10 years of age when he became king in 1547. A Protestant himself, and influenced by his Protestant regents, Edward ordered the removal of images and altars from churches, decreed salvation by faith alone and the supremacy of the Bible, and overturned Catholic doctrines that his father had upheld even as he had revolted from the Church itself.

The changes were short-lived, for when Edward died at age 16 in 1553, his half-sister Mary I (Fig. **19.6**), a devout Catholic, assumed the throne. She quickly restored Catholic doctrine and practice. She also made a political marriage with the militant Prince Philip of Spain in

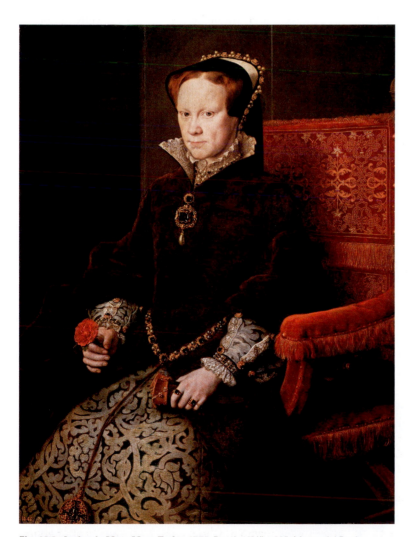

Fig. 19.6 Anthonis Mor, *Mary Tudor*. 1554. Panel, 42⅞″ × 33″. Museo del Prado, Madrid. Mary holds a rose, emblem of the Tudor family, and here a symbol of the legitimacy of her rightful claim to the English throne.

1554—making the Catholic Philip king of England (he would become King Philip II of Spain in 1556—see Chapter 22). Mary executed 282 Protestants by burning them at the stake, and forced hundreds of others into exile in Germany and Switzerland. Mary died only five years into her reign, and Elizabeth I took the throne in 1558. Like Edward, she had been raised a Protestant, but Elizabeth strove to find a middle ground by merging, in her new Anglican Church—more formally known as the Church of England—traditional Catholic ritual and a broadly defined Protestant doctrine.

Still, extremists would have none of it. On the one hand, many English Protestants sought religious autonomy. Known as nonconformists, or Puritans, they wanted to purify the Anglican Church of all vestiges of what they believed were papist ritual and doctrine. One group of Puritans, the Presbyterians, wanted to replace the bishop with councils of elders, or *presbyters*, while another group, the Congregationalists, wanted to make each congregation a wholly independent body. Elizabeth allowed these groups to work in Parliament for the reforms they wanted, but gave up nothing that challenged the hierarchy of the Anglican Church and her control over it. Finally, in 1593, she acted against the Congregationalists: They could either conform or face exile or death.

The Catholic threat was somewhat different. Catholic extremists within the country wanted to replace Elizabeth with Mary Stuart, queen of the Scots and a Catholic. When, in 1586, a plot against Elizabeth was conceived with Mary's complicity, Elizabeth felt she had no choice but to execute Mary. Most Catholics viewed the execution as the equivalent of an act of war, for in their eyes, Mary was the rightful heir to the throne, not Elizabeth. Philip II of Spain, following in the footsteps of his father, Charles V, was determined to avenge Mary. To that end, he gathered an enormous fleet of 130 ships bearing 25,000 soldiers—the Spanish Armada—to invade England and defend Catholicism. It set sail on July 22, 1588, for the Netherlands, where it meant to pick up an additional force of 17,000 men from the army of Flanders. On the night of August 7, in the waters of the English Channel off Calais, the English sent six small ships packed with explosives into the midst of the Spanish fleet, many of which hoisted anchor and fled. At dawn, the remaining ships found themselves facing the entire English fleet, which had arrived during the night. After a nine-hour battle, about 18 Spanish ships were lost, and casualties were high. The Armada fled into the North Sea and most of the ships subsequently perished in Atlantic storms. Only 60 of the 130 galleons that originally had set sail returned to Spain, and some 15,000 men perished. Henceforth, Elizabeth could rightly claim the supremacy of England in world affairs.

Hans Holbein's *The Ambassadors* depicts two French ambassadors to the court of Henry VIII. Jean de Dinteville, on the left, commissioned the painting, and Georges de Selve, on the right, was the bishop-elect of Lauvau. Both represent the interests of Francis I, and, therefore, of the Catholic Church (see Chapter 20). It seems clear that both were present at court to negotiate with Henry about his insistence on annulling his marriage to Katharine of Aragon and marrying Anne Boleyn (see page 638) and the subsequent separation of the Church of England from the Catholic Church. In fact, Henry had married Anne just three months before this work was painted, in January 1533. A cylindrical dial on the table between the two ambassadors tells us that it is April 11, 1533. The other objects on the two-tiered table between the ambassadors—the Lutheran hymnal, the terrestrial globe, the celestial globe, and the astronomical instruments—all indicate the men's willingness to strike a balance between Catholic and Protestant interests. The skull, placed between the viewer and the ambassadors, in what is known as an *anamorphic projection*, suggests that the two men understand the fate that awaits us all.

🔎 **View** the Closer Look for *The Ambassadors* on **MyArtsLab**

Something to Think About ...

The painting was commissioned as a portrait, but its allegorical content renders it far more complex than most portraiture. How does this complexity underscore its humanist principles, and why would the two ambassadors want to present themselves in humanist terms?

The lute is in perfect linear perspective, in contrast to the distorted perspective of the skull. One of the 11 strings is broken, probably symbolizing the lack of harmony between Catholic and Protestant interests.

The tiled floor is a direct copy of the floor of the sacred area in front of the high altar of Westminster Abbey. The tiles are colored glass and stone, from Rome, Egypt, and the Middle East. By using this design, Holbein suggests that his ambassadors stand on holy ground and are engaged in some holy purpose.

This Lutheran hymnal is Johannes Walther's 1525 *The Little Hymn-Book*. The hymn on the left is "Come, Holy Ghost, our souls inspire," one of Martin Luther's best-known compositions. The hymn on the right is also by Luther: "Man, if thou wouldst live a good life and remain with God eternally."

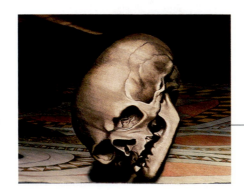

Holbein's highly distorted skull, as seen if viewed from a low position to the right of the painting. Painted in this way, it suggests that one's point of view determines what one is capable of seeing—perhaps the principal lesson of diplomacy. But perhaps more important, the skull symbolizes the vanity of life, the transience of material possessions, and possibly, the ultimate meaninglessness of petty politics.

The Ottoman rug covering the table reminds the viewer of another division threatening Europe, that of Suleiman the Magnificent and the Turkish Empire, which had admittedly failed in its siege of Vienna in 1529, but which remained a potent force in Eastern Europe and the Mediterranean.

The handled globe shows all of Europe, in brown and upside down, and most of Africa. To the right side is the coast of the Americas. The globe is positioned so that Rome lies at the center, balancing the Lutheran hymnal on the same shelf. Below the globe, held open by a triangle used for drawing, is a book of arithmetic. The two examples of long division may be an allegorical reference to the division or disharmony between Protestants and Catholics.

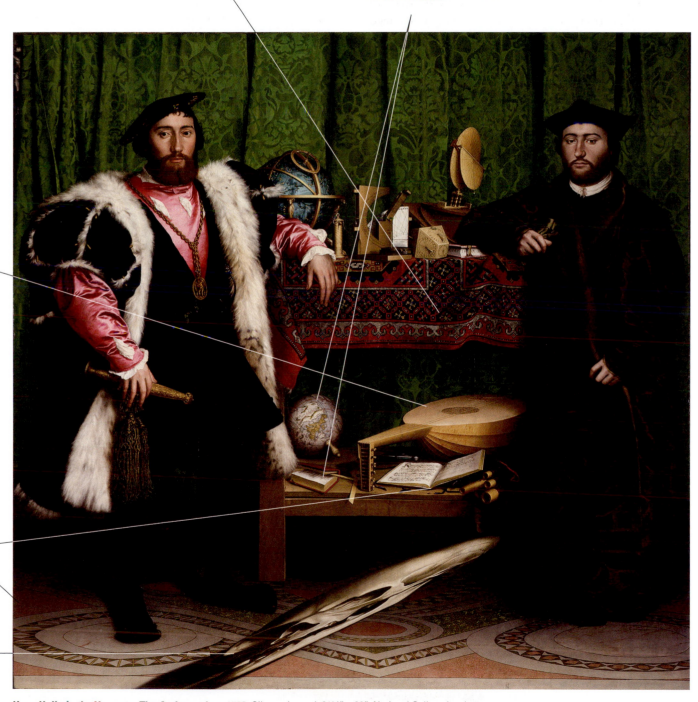

Hans Holbein the Younger, *The Ambassadors*. **1533.** Oil on oak panel, 81½″ × 82″. National Gallery, London.

ELIZABETHAN ENGLAND

How did the arts flourish under Queen Elizabeth I?

England flourished under Elizabeth I, even though it remained religiously divided, sometimes beset by rebellion, mired in personal and political intrigue, and threatened by Catholic Europe. What held English society together was a common sense of destiny and purpose, a shared belief in the greatness of England itself, and a booming national economy. Some in England soon came to see it as the center of culture, or even of the world, with London as its shining light. We find these feelings of national pride articulated by the princely character John of Gaunt, Duke of Lancaster, in the historical play *Richard II*, written by William Shakespeare (1564–1616) a mere six years after the defeat of the Spanish Armada by the English navy (**Reading 19.3**):

READING 19.3

from William Shakespeare, *Richard II*, Act 2, Scene 1 (1594)

This royal throne of kings, this sceptred isle,
This earth of majesty, this seat of Mars,
This other Eden, demi-paradise,[1]
This fortress built by Nature for herself
Against infection[2] and the hand of war,   5
This happy breed of men, this little world,
This precious stone set in the silver sea,
Which serves it in the office[3] of a wall,
Or as [a] moat defensive to a house,
Against the envy of less happier lands;   10
This blessed plot, this earth, this realm, this England . . .

[1] **demi-paradise:** little paradise.
[2] **infection:** (1) pestilence; (2) moral contamination.
[3] **office:** function.

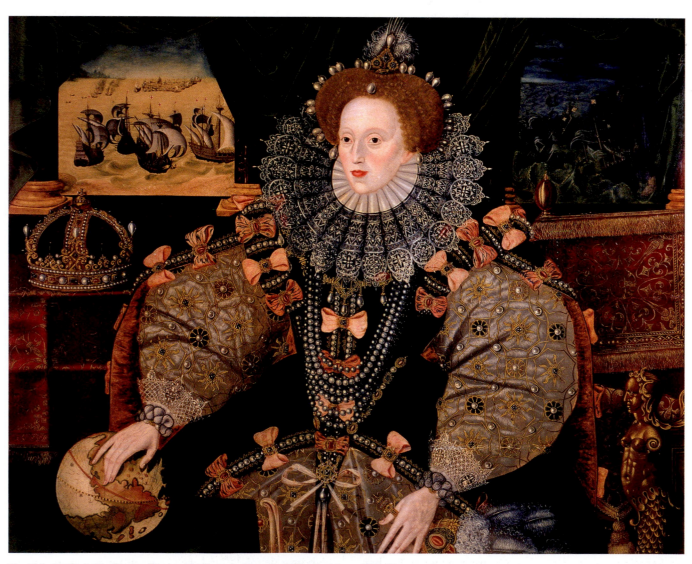

Fig. 19.7 Attributed to George Gower, *The Armada Portrait of Elizabeth I*. ca. 1588. Oil on panel, 38½" × 28½". Private collection. The victorious English fleet sails in bright sunshine behind the queen on the left, while the Spanish Armada sinks in Atlantic storms through the window at the right.

For Gaunt, England is not merely an earthly paradise protected from the turmoil of the world by the sea that surrounds it, but something grander. These last lines crescendo from the small and near ("this blessed plot"), to the broad expanse ("this earth"), to the kingdom as a whole ("this realm"), to finally "this England," something larger yet—empire. Notice that in the so-called *Armada Portrait of Elizabeth I* (Fig. **19.7**), the queen's hand rests firmly on the globe, which Sir Francis Drake had circumnavigated at Elizabeth's behest in 1577 to 1580.

The booming English economy owed much to the extraordinary growth in national wealth that followed the sale of monastic lands initiated by Henry VIII. London benefited most directly. However, the sale of ecclesiastical properties in the countryside to middle- and upper-class citizens had also created a new population of landed gentry. The playwright William Shakespeare is a prime example. Shakespeare's father was a common merchant in the Midlands market town of Stratford-upon-Avon who took advantage of the newfound wealth in the countryside to rise to a position of considerable prominence, serving as both mayor and alderman. The town of Stratford announced its chief interests in its street names—Sheep Street, Bull Lane, Swine Street, and, of course, Church Lane. But after his success in the London theater, William Shakespeare owned the largest house in town, possessed a coat of arms (actually awarded to his father), and referred to himself as "William Shakespeare of Stratford-upon-Avon, gentleman."

There was, in short, a breakdown in traditional class distinctions accompanied by a social mobility unprecedented in European history. Wages were as much as 50 percent higher in London than in the provinces, causing an increasing number of people to move to the city. There they helped to create a new culture of achievement, in which the individual's ability to realize desires for wealth and fame, property and respect, overthrew the traditional hierarchies of medieval society once and for all. London was in some ways the first modern culture: extremely competitive, even cutthroat. But no longer was a person's place in society determined at birth. Even actors or playwrights could get rich—if audiences liked them.

Elizabeth I and the Arts: Painting and Poetic Forms

Shakespeare was the direct beneficiary of a monarchy that championed the arts, especially the literary arts. Elizabeth I could speak Latin, French, and Italian, and was reasonably

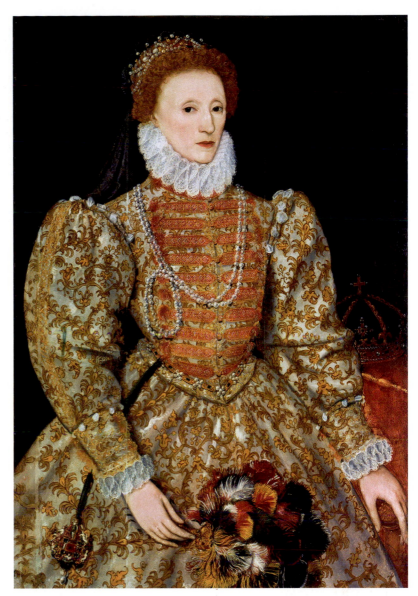

Fig. 19.8 Attributed to Federigo Zuccaro, *The Darnley Portrait of Elizabeth I.* ca. 1575. Oil on panel, 44½″ × 31″. National Portrait Gallery, London. No other portrait of Elizabeth better conveys her steadfast determination, even toughness, while still capturing something of her beauty. By all accounts, she could alternately swear like a common prostitute and charm like the most refined diplomat.

competent in Greek. In painting, she favored portraiture, like her father, and was herself the subject of many portraits. Her *Armada Portrait* (see Fig. 19.7) is typical of post-Holbein portraiture in the Elizabethan court. Few English painters could match Holbein's skill in depicting volume, texture, and light. Most tended to concentrate on elaborate decorative effects. Set behind the flat patterning of her lace collar, pearl necklaces, and jewel-encrusted dress, Elizabeth appears almost bodiless—the exact opposite of Holbein's emphatically embodied portrait of Henry VIII (see Fig. 19.3). This sense of two-dimensionality appears, too, in the elaborate detail of Elizabeth's gown in the so-called *Darnley Portrait of Elizabeth I* (Fig. **19.8**), with its repetitive interlace of intricate pattern and rich texture.

The Sonnet

The **sonnet** is a lyric poem of 14 lines, following one or another of several set rhyme schemes. There are two primary types of sonnet: the Italian (Petrarchan) and the English (Shakespearean). The Italian sonnet is characterized by an eight-line **octave** rhyming abbaabba, and a six-line **sestet** rhyming cdecde, cdccdc, cddcdd, or cdedec. Usually, the octave expresses some problem, doubt, or passion that the sestet then resolves or explains.

The English sonnet consists of three **quatrains,** four-line stanzas, each with its own rhyme scheme, followed by a rhymed **couplet,** two lines of verse with similar end rhymes. The complete rhyme scheme looks like this: abab cdcd efef gg.

Both sonnet forms play much variation on a standard rhythm, or meter, called **iambic pentameter**, consisting of ten syllables with five stressed beats, short/long, short/long, short/long, short/long, short/long. A line from Shakespeare's Sonnet 130 scans as follows:

If snow be white, why then her breasts are dun

This is also the **basic meter** that Shakespeare employs in the unrhyming **blank verse** of his plays, as in this line from *Romeo and Juliet*:

But soft! What light through yonder window breaks?

Paintings such as these, which emphasized decorative patterning over physical form, reflected the English taste for intricate, elaborately designed poetic forms. Elizabeth encouraged the literary life as an admirable and worthy pursuit. Poets brought their work to court, where they shared it with one another, seeking the praise and patronage of the queen and aristocracy. Many poems were, in fact, dedicated to the queen, most notably Edmund Spenser's long allegorical epic, *The Faerie Queene*, which celebrates the Tudor monarchy, which culminated in Elizabeth's reign. Elizabeth herself was an accomplished poet; "On Monsieur's Departure" of 1582 gives a fair idea of her skill (**Reading 19.4**):

READING 19.4

Elizabeth I, "On Monsieur's Departure" (1582)

I grieve and dare not show my discontent,
I love and yet am forced to seem to hate,
I do, yet dare not say I ever meant,
I seem stark mute but inwardly do prate.
   I am and not, I freeze and yet am burned,   5
   Since from myself another self I turned.
My care is like my shadow in the sun,
Follows me flying, flies when I pursue it,
Stands and lies by me, doth what I have done.
His too familiar care doth make me rue it.   10
   No means I find to rid him from my breast,
   Till by the end of things it be supprest.
Some gentler passion slide into my mind,
For I am soft and made of melting snow;
Or be more cruel, love, and so be kind.   15
Let me or float or sink[1], be high or low.
   Or let me live with some more sweet content,
   Or die and so forget what love ere meant.

[1] **or float or sink:** either float or sink.

The poem is a remarkably candid statement of the tension between Elizabeth's personal and political lives. Her position as queen forces her to hide her true feelings for her lover, but these find full expression in the poem. Elizabeth used several elaborate and witty images, or conceits, that would become characteristic of the poetry of the Elizabethan age. Here, the poet's "care," first referred to in line 7, is both the emotional side of her personality—the feelings that she says, in line 1, she "dare not show"—and also her lover. When she says, in line 15, "Or be more cruel, love, and so be kind," she invites her lover to spurn her and thus relieve her of her feelings. This witty reversal of expectation is a standard Elizabethan poetic practice. And in the final couplet, the word "die" is standard wordplay as well, referring not only to literal death but also to sexual orgasm.

In the sixteenth century, such elaborate conceits were normally employed in **sonnets**, or "little songs," tightly woven lyric verses of 14 lines with strict schemes of rhyme and rhythm. Elizabeth's poem, while not technically a sonnet—it is 18 lines long—is indicative of the attraction to complex forms that the sonnet embodies. English writers generally employed one of two sonnet forms, the Italian (Petrarchan) or the English (Shakespearean). (See *Context*, above.) The Italian form was brought to England by Sir Thomas Wyatt (1503–42) through his translations of the Italian poet Petrarch (see Chapter 13). Rumors had linked Wyatt romantically to Anne Boleyn, Henry VIII's second wife. Suspicious, Henry imprisoned Wyatt in the Tower of London, but released him after Anne's execution and appointed him ambassador to the court of Charles V in 1537. Wyatt was back in the Tower in 1541, following accusations of misconduct as ambassador, but Henry pardoned him once more. One of Wyatt's most famous sonnets, based on Petrarch, is "List to Hunt" (**Reading 19.5**):

Thomas Wyatt, "List to Hunt"
(first published 1557)

Whoso list to hunt, I know where is an hind,[1]
But as for me, hélas, I may no more.
The vain travail hath wearied me so sore,
I am of them that farthest cometh behind.
Yet may I by no means my wearied mind   5
Draw from the deer, but as she fleeth afore
Fainting I follow. I leave off therefore,
Sithens[2] in a net I seek to hold the wind.
Who list her hunt, I put him out of doubt,
As well as I may spend his time in vain.   10
And graven with diamonds in letters plain
There is written, her fair neck round about:
Noli me tangere, for Caesar's I am,
And wild for to hold, though I seem tame.

[1] **Whoso … hind:** Whoever wishes to hunt, I know where there is a female
red deer (Anne Boleyn's hair was red).
[2] **Sithens:** since.

Here, the first eight lines, the octave, announce the poet's withdrawal from the pursuit of his love, since trying to catch her is like trying to hold the wind in a net. The last six lines, the sestet, warn others who might choose to pursue her that she is untouchable. The message worn round her neck is an especially interesting conceit. The Latin words *Noli me tangere* ("Do not touch me") are the words Christ is said to have spoken to Mary Magdalene when he appeared to her after the Crucifixion and she tried to embrace him. He explained to her that he now existed in a new form somewhere between the physical and the spiritual. The implication is that the poet's lady exists in a comparable dimension. Since Wyatt was rumored to be the lover of Anne Boleyn, the reference to Caesar probably means the king, and for the poet to woo the king's wife would have been a very wild pursuit indeed.

Individual sonnets were often gathered into a collection or **sonnet sequence** dedicated to a particular love affair. The most notable of the many sonnet sequences are *Astrophel and Stella* by Sir Philip Sidney (1554–86), the *Amoretti* by Edmund Spenser, and the sequence of 154 sonnets by William Shakespeare. Shakespeare used the English form so successfully that it has been given his name—Shakespearean. The poems in his sequence often poke fun at the conventions of the Petrarchan love sonnet. Sonnet 130 is an example (**Reading 19.6**):

William Shakespeare, Sonnet 130 (1609)

My mistress' eyes are nothing like the sun;
Coral is far more red than her lips' red:
If snow be white, why then her breasts are dun;[1]

If hairs be wires, black wire grows on her head.
I have seen roses damasked,[2] red and white,   5
But no such roses see I in her cheeks;
And in some perfumes is there more delight
Than in the breath that from my mistress reeks.
I love to hear her speak, yet well I know
That music hath a far more pleasing sound: 10
I grant I never saw a goddess go;
My mistress, when she walks, treads on the ground:
    And yet, by heaven, I think my love as rare
    As any she belied with false compare.

[1] **dun:** grayish brown.
[2] **damasked:** pink.

Shakespeare's ironic strategy here is to knock the courtly conventions of love off their pedestal, as it were, and bring them down to the "ground." The poem speaks to an audience much larger than the court, an audience of everyday people, the same audience that his plays would so directly address. But Shakespeare's more commonplace love is no less real than a courtier's. Notably, the English sonnet does not generally resolve or explain itself until the last couplet, and here the couplet overturns the rest of the poem by announcing the depth and reality of the poet's love.

However, in many of his sonnets, Shakespeare openly celebrates Petrarchan themes such as unquestioning devotion to his beloved and the enduring nature of love itself. Sonnet 18, for instance, compares his love to an "eternal summer's day" (**Reading 19.7**):

William Shakespeare, Sonnet 18 (1609)

Shall I compare thee to a summer's day?
Thou art more lovely and more temperate,
Rough winds do shake the darling buds of May,
And summer's lease[1] hath all too short a date.
Sometime too hot the eye[2] of heaven shines,   5
And often is his gold complexion dimm'd;
And every fair from fair sometimes declines,[3]
By chance or nature's changing course untrimm'd,[4]
But thy eternal summer shall not fade
Nor lose possession of that fair thou ow'st,   10
Nor shall Death brag thou wand'rest in his shade,
When in eternal lines to time thou grow'st,[5]
    So long as men can breathe or eyes can see
    So long lives this[6] and this gives life to thee.

[1] **lease:** allotted time.
[2] **eye:** the sun.
[3] **every fair from fair … declines:** beauty eventually leaves all things once
beautiful—that is, beauty eventually fades.
[4] **untrimm'd:** deprived of adornment.
[5] **When in … thou grow'st:** when in this verse your fame will grow as
time elapses.
[6] **this:** this sonnet itself.

Read the document related to Edmund Spenser at **MyArtsLab**

The sonnet underscores Shakespeare's understanding of the importance of the written word. The poem survives, lending its subject and author a kind of immortality. The theme of immortality conferred by literature is commonplace in English poetry of the era. In the *Amoretti* sonnet sequence, Edmund Spenser addresses it in an intriguing way (**Reading 19.8**):

READING 19.8

Edmund Spenser, Sonnet 75, from the *Amoretti* (1595)

One day I wrote her name upon the strand,
But came the waves and washed it away:
Again I write it with a second hand,
But came the tide, and made my pains his prey.
Vain man, said she, that doest in vain assay,[1]   5
  A mortal thing so to immortalize,
  For I myself shall like to this decay,
  And eek[2] my name be wiped out likewise.
Not so, (quod[3] I) let baser things devise
  To die in dust, but you shall live by fame:
  My verse, your virtues rare shall eternize,
  And in the heavens write your glorious name.
Where whenas death shall all the world subdue,
Our love shall live, and later life renew.

[1] **assay:** try.
[2] **eek:** also.
[3] **quod:** said.

The play here is between the ephemeral nature of the word written on the beach, where it is continually erased by the incoming tide, and the immortality of Spenser's verse. But it is not just the immortality of Spenser's verse that the poem celebrates—it is also the prospect of Christian resurrection and reunion with God (and his lady) after the Last Judgment, when "death shall all the world subdue." When read aloud, the reader can experience the wavelike rhythms of Spenser's poem. Its lines are bound together by a series of **alliterations**, words beginning with the same sound (for instance, *waves/washed* in line 2), that lend the poem a feeling of rocking back and forth.

Music in the Elizabethan Age

Elizabeth was an accomplished musician and an avid fan of the madrigal. Her enthusiasm for this musical form probably accounts for its popularity in England during the late sixteenth and early seventeenth centuries. A madrigal is a complex polyphonic unaccompanied song based on a secular text (see Chapter 15). In 1588, *Music from across the Alps*, an anthology of 57 Italian madrigals translated into English, was published in London. Two years later, *Italian Madrigals Englished* appeared. But English composers were not to be outdone. Thomas Morley, the organist at Saint Paul's Cathedral, complained about the English public's

penchant for liking "whatever cometh from beyond the seas (and specially from Italy) be it ever so simple, [while] condemning that which is done at home though it be never so excellent." Morley was owner of the monopoly on publishing music in England, so his sentiments were obviously self-serving. Nevertheless, he wrote and published more madrigals than any other English composer, many of them inspired by Italian sources. In 1601, he also published an anthology of madrigals honoring Elizabeth, *The Triumphs of Oriana*, named for a mythological shepherd queen, Oriana, who personified Elizabeth.

Morley's compositions sometimes employ very short texts and, as a result, repeat each phrase many times. The text of "Fyre and Lightning", a madrigal for two tenor voices, reads:

> Fyre and lightning from heaven fall
> And sweetly enflame that hart with love arightfull,
> O Flora my delightfull,
> So faire but yet so spightfull.

The musical setting is based on imitation, the two voices copying each other in turn (track **19.1**). At times, the imitation is very close, the second voice following so closely on the heels of the first that a feeling of emotional intensity or agitation develops. The song ends with both voices singing in **homophonic harmony**, a unison movement of the voices in chords that employs a dissonant chord to underscore in word painting the last stinging word, "spitefull." Listen on **MyArtsLab**

Sacred music during the Elizabethan age was directly inspired by the publication, in 1549, of *The First Book of Common Prayer*. Despite Henry VIII's break with the papacy, the Church of England had continued to use its Latin liturgies. But when Edward VI assumed the throne, the English bishops agreed to translate the Latin liturgy into English. The project was led by Thomas Cranmer (1487–1556), whom Henry had appointed Archbishop of Canterbury in 1533. Cranmer created a text whose rhythms and diction would influence writing in English perhaps even more profoundly than the King James Bible. Additionally, he revised the order of the Mass to exclude the doctrine of transubstantiation. (This last accomplishment was considered the greatest of the "heresies" that provoked Queen Mary to have him burned at the stake in 1556.)

Since the liturgy, now known as the Communion Service, still contained music, musicians were able to maintain their existing repertory by converting the existing mass settings and motets into English. Soon composers started to write original motets in English as well. These works came to be known as **anthems**, and they took two forms: the **full anthem** sung by a chorus throughout, and the **verse anthem**, in which choral passages alternate with solo voice and instrumental accompaniment. An example is "Verily, Verily I Say Unto You," by Thomas Tallis (1505–85) (track **19.2**). It Listen on **MyArtsLab** typifies the early English full anthem. It is almost entirely chordal, and reflects the post-Reformation taste for simplicity of style.

Perhaps the greatest composer of the day was William Byrd (ca. 1540–1623). Byrd composed in all genres except for the stage. A Catholic in an Anglican country, he had to be extremely cautious in his dealings with the royal court. He practiced his faith in secret, and he wrote a great deal of music for the Catholic liturgy, including Latin masses. But he also wrote in English for the Anglican liturgy, as well as madrigals and other songs. He published a group of these in 1588 in a collection entitled *Psalms, Sonnets, & Songs*, in the preface to which he outlined eight reasons why all people should learn to sing (**Reading 19.9**):

READING 19.9

from William Byrd, *Psalms, Sonnets, & Songs* (1588)

Reasons briefly set down by the author to persuade everyone to learn to sing.

1. First it is a Knowledge easily taught, and quickly learned where there is a good Master, and an apt Scholar.
2. The exercise of singing is delightful to Nature & good to preserve the health of Man.
3. It doth strengthen the parts of the breast, & and doth open the pipes.
4. It is a singularly good remedy for a stuttering & stammering in the speech.
5. It is the best means to procure a perfect pronunciation & to make a good Orator.
6. It is the only way to know where Nature hath bestowed the benefit of a good voice: which gift is so rare, as there is not one among a thousand, that hath it; and in many, that excellent gift is lost, because they want Art to express Nature.
7. There is not any Music of Instruments whatsoever, comparable to that which is made of the voices of Men, where the voices are good, and same well sorted and ordered.
8. The better the voice is, the better it is to honor and serve God therewith: and the voice of man is chiefly to be employed to that end.

Onmis spiritus laudet Dominum ["Let every spirit praise the Lord"]

Since singing is so good a thing,
I wish all men would learn to sing.

Byrd was also one of the greatest keyboard composers of his day, serving as organist at the Chapel Royal in London. His compositions were represented in the first collection of keyboard music ever published in England, the *Parthenia* of 1611, and in two important manuscript collections, the *Fitzwilliam Virginal Book*, which includes 69 of his keyboard works, and a group of 42 compositions preserved in a manuscript transcribed in 1591 and presumably written for a pupil or patron, entitled *My Ladye Nevells Booke*.

THE ELIZABETHAN STAGE

What are the characteristics of the Elizabethan stage and what were Marlowe's and Shakespeare's contributions to it?

The most remarkable cultural characteristic of Elizabethan England was the rise of drama as a popular art form. The rise of theater coincided with the growth of the middle and upper classes, who now had the leisure time to enjoy an occasional play or two. For centuries, the English had adored theatrical pageantry—minstrels and acrobats passing through town, guild pageants traveling through city streets (*pageant* literally means "movable stage" in Middle English), and especially religious plays. Chief among the last of these are the so-called miracle and morality plays.

In a strict sense, **miracle plays** are nonscriptural dramas based upon the legend of some saint or of a miracle performed by some saint or sacred object. In a broader sense, they include scriptural dramas. Miracle plays became very popular in the early fourteenth century. Easter and Christmas plays were joined into cycles representing the whole course of sacred history from the Creation to the Last Judgment. They were performed at a number of locations around the city in a single day, generally by townspeople. Four such cycles survive—the Towneley, Chester, York, and Coventry plays. The **morality plays** developed out of the miracle plays in the fifteenth century. In these dramatized allegories, abstract virtues and vices or other human qualities appear in human form (a device known as **personification**) and either struggle for the human soul or act out some moral truth or lesson.

Early in Elizabeth's reign, government authorities banned performances of most of these religious plays, fearing that the Catholic origins and sentiments of these dramas might stir up religious tensions. But the court itself was extremely supportive of theater in general. Henry VIII had loved what were called **revels**, large-scale entertainments that depicted mythological or chivalric themes in an allegorical manner organized by the king's Master of the Revels. Henry often participated in them himself. He also employed traveling bands of players to perform **interludes** during breaks in the larger entertainments. Often written in doggerel verse, interludes were generally comical or allegorical. "Pyramus and Thisbe," the play-within-a-play in Shakespeare's *A Midsummer's Night Dream*, is just such an interlude.

Until 1576, no permanent theater existed in England. Amphitheaters in Southwark, on the south bank of the Thames (see Map 19.2), were used for bear-baiting, and many inns made for natural playhouses, as they were designed around inner courtyards with upstairs rooms looking in. Companies of actors were officially adopted by noblemen, wore their patron's feudal livery, and were officially his servants. James Burbage belonged to a troupe adopted by the earl of Leicester, known as Leicester's

Men. In the spring of 1576, Burbage opened the Theater of Shoreditch, just outside the walls of London, and the relationship between actors and patrons changed. Troupes of actors no longer depended completely on their masters; now they could also rely on the popularity of their plays to bring in profits and support themselves.

The basic price of admission to Burbage's Theater was one penny, which in 1600 could buy one chicken or two tankards of ale. A laborer's wage was three or four pence, or pennies, a day. Burbage's Theater was thus affordable, which partly accounts for its success; one penny soon became the standard base price of admission for all London theaters. Although public playhouses varied, in general they were open-air structures consisting of three tiers of covered galleries (in which seats cost between three and six pence). In front of the stage, an open courtyard area held the **groundlings**. These theatergoers paid the one-penny base price of admission, stood throughout the performance, and wandered in and out at will, eating and drinking as they enjoyed the play. A rectangular stage, about 40 feet wide, projected into the courtyard. Behind it were exits to

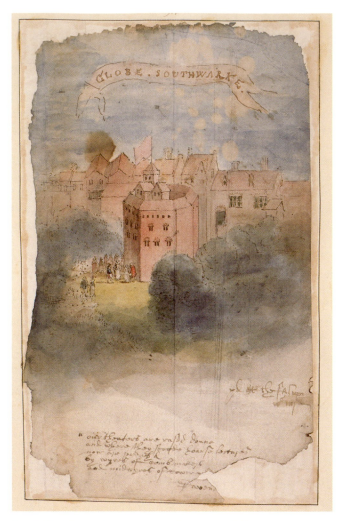

Fig. 19.10 J.C. Visscher, *The Globe Theater*. ca. 1599.
© The Trustees of the British Museum. The Globe opened its doors in 1599 with a performance of Shakespeare's *Henry V*. It burned down 14 years later during a performance of *Henry VIII*.

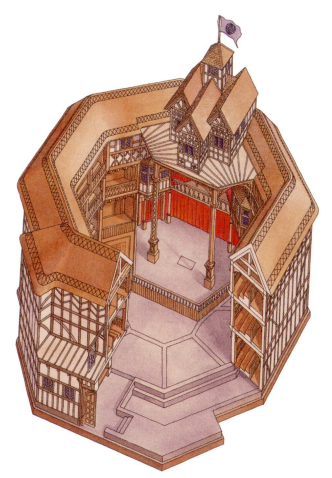

Fig. 19.9 Reconstruction and cross-section of the Globe Theater. 1599–1613. The stage was surrounded on three sides by three stories of tiered seating. Groundlings, those who paid one penny for admission, stood in the open area in front of the stage. Admission to the lower gallery was another penny, to the middle galleries yet another.

dressing rooms and balconies where players might look out on the action beneath them on the stage proper. Out of a trap door, in center stage, a ghost might rise.

In 1598, Burbage's company, now headed by James's son Richard, tore down the Shoreditch theater, in a dispute over the lease, and rebuilt it across the river in Southwark at Bankside, in the neighborhood previously associated with bear-baiting. He re-named it "The Globe" (Figs. **19.9** and **19.10**). It could seat 3,000 people. The Swan and the Rose, large theaters that were already established at Bankside, could seat about the same. Watermen who transported London audiences across the river to the theaters claimed to carry 3,000 to 4,000 theatergoers to Bankside every afternoon. Including those arriving by foot across London Bridge, as many as 9,000 Londoners descended on the playhouses each day.

Women were prohibited from appearing on stage, and so males—generally boys—played all female roles, which, in turn, required elaborate costuming. Stage props were sometimes minimal, consisting of no more than a chair or two, a chest, or the like, but some companies possessed elaborate sets. Lighting was nonexistent. Thus, under the light of an afternoon sky, the playwright might evoke night or storm by having one of the lesser actors carry a torch or lantern, and the audience would have to suspend its disbelief and imagine the scene (just as they had to accept boys as women). As a result, Elizabethan drama often focuses on the relation between illusion and reality, questioning what is "real" and what is not.

Christopher Marlowe: The Legend of Faustus

The relationship between illusion and reality, and our inability to distinguish between the two, is, in fact, the focus of one of the most important pre-Shakespearean plays performed in London, *The Tragical History of Dr. Faustus* by Christopher Marlowe (1564–93). It was first performed in 1588, with great success. We know very little about Marlowe's life, although it is clear that he served the throne in some capacity. At the time of his death, rumors surfaced that he was a spy. We do know, from a coroner's report discovered in 1923, that he was stabbed in the eye in a brawl over a bar tab on June 1, 1593.

Dr. Faustus owes a great debt to the morality plays of the previous century. Faustus is a German professor at Luther's Wittenberg, dissatisfied with what traditional scholarship can teach him. He turns to black magic when Mephistopheles, Lucifer's assistant, reveals its power to him in a vision. In a scene deeply indebted to the morality play, a Good Angel and a Bad Angel argue for control of Faustus's conscience. He signs over his soul to Lucifer for what he believes will be 24 years of pleasure and intellectual power. Although Faustus is tempted to repent, Mephistopheles wins him for good with a mimed show of the Seven Deadly Sins, a scene that also derives directly from the example of the morality plays. In a series of interludes that the audience is to understand as taking place over the passage of a great deal of time, Faustus plays a practical joke on the papal court, presents the emperor Charles V with a vision of Alexander the Great and his lover, and makes the spirit of Helen of Troy appear in a debate with his students over the question "Who is the most beautiful woman in the world?" At his death he finally realizes his mistake, expressing his thoughts in a **soliloquy**, or **interior monologue** (**Reading 19.10**). (A soliloquy expresses a character's innermost thoughts. On the stage, the character appears to be talking to him- or herself, oblivious to anyone present.)

READING 19.10

from Christopher Marlowe, *The Tragical History of Dr. Faustus*, Scene 14 (1604)

Ah, Faustus,
Now hast thou but one bare hour to live,
And then thou must be damn'd perpetually!

Stand still, you ever-moving spheres of Heaven,
That time may cease, and midnight never come;
Fair Nature's eye, rise, rise again and make
Perpetual day; or let this hour be but
A year, a month, a week, a natural day,
That Faustus may repent and save his soul! …
O God!
If thou wilt not have mercy on my soul,
Yet for Christ's sake whose blood hath ransom'd me,
Impose some end to my incessant pain;
Let Faustus live in hell a thousand years—
A hundred thousand, and—at last—be sav'd!
O, no end is limited to damned souls!

With this last thought, knowing that he is forever condemned to hell, Faustus dies and falls into "ugly hell."

The play originally consisted of 14 scenes, alternating between Faustus's serious scenes and comic interludes involving an array of "low" or common characters that serve to undercut the overreaching ambitions of Faustus himself. This blending of tragic and comic modes would become a standard feature of the Elizabethan stage. But it is Faustus's unquenchable thirst for the unattainable that defines Marlowe's tragic hero and that constitutes the type of hero that is his most important gift to the theater.

William Shakespeare: "The play's the thing!"

The Rose Theatre hosted the first of Shakespeare's plays known to have been staged in London: *Henry VI, Part I*, and *Titus Andronicus*, both performed in 1592. We actually know almost nothing about Shakespeare's preparation to be a playwright. When he was in his twenties, during the 1580s, he lived in almost total obscurity. But beginning in about 1590, two years before his first two plays were staged, he was active in the London theater. Shakespeare's company was Burbage's newly renamed Lord Chamberlain's Players at the Globe, and he earned 10 percent of its profits. He wrote his plays with specific actors in the company in mind and played only minor roles himself. Richard Burbage was the leading man, playing the title role in Shakespeare's major tragedies *Richard II*, *Romeo and Juliet*, *Hamlet*, *Othello*, and *King Lear*. Though many of Shakespeare's characters sing—and music plays an important role in the plays— none of the characters played by Burbage ever sing a note, because Burbage himself was tone-deaf.

While there were other great playwrights in the Elizabethan era—Christopher Marlowe, as we have already noted, and Thomas Kyd (1558–94) chief among them— Shakespeare even in his own time was the acknowledged master of the medium. He wrote 37 plays: great cycles narrating English history; romantic comedies that deal with popular themes such as mistaken identity, the battle of the sexes, lovers' errors in judgment, and so on; romances that treat serious themes but in unrealistic, almost magical

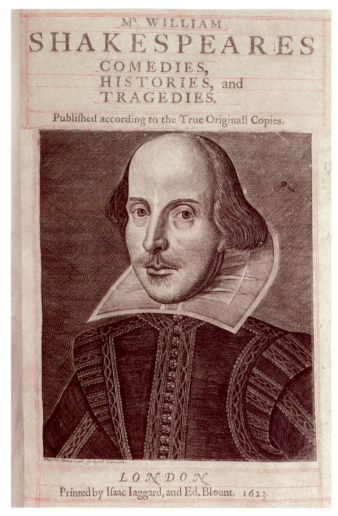

Fig. 19.11 Martin Droeshout, *William Shakespeare*, frontispiece of the first folio edition of his works, published in London. 1623. British Library, London. The first edition of the collected plays of Shakespeare was prepared by John Heminges and Henry Condell, both fellow actors at the Globe.

settings; and 11 tragedies. Fellow actors prepared the first edition of his collected plays and published them in 1623, after his death (Fig. **19.11**).

Hamlet (Fig. **19.12**), one of the tragedies, was perhaps his greatest achievement. It is a **revenge play**, constructed around a murder that must be avenged by the victim's relative, usually at the request of the murdered person's ghost. An Elizabethan audience would have recognized the plot as formulaic, but nothing about the play is standard fare. Hamlet himself, the Danish prince who must avenge the murder of his royal father, is one of the most complex and ambiguous personalities in the history of the theater. Early in the play, his father's ghost reveals to Hamlet that his uncle, Claudius, murdered his father to replace him as king and as husband to Hamlet's mother. The ghost orders Hamlet to avenge his murder, setting the play in motion. Hamlet alternately behaves like a raving madman and an intellectual of the most refined sensibility, at once deeply perceptive and blind to the most obvious truths. Even

in the company of friends, he is alone with himself, an intensely self-reflective soul tormented by the very act of self-reflection.

Consider Hamlet's famous soliloquy at the end of Act 2. A band of traveling actors has just performed for him some lines concerning the death of King Priam of Troy and the grief borne by his wife, Hecuba. Hamlet marvels at the players' ability to so emotionally identify with their roles (**Reading 19.11a**):

READING 19.11a

from William Shakespeare, *Hamlet*, Act 2, Scene 2 (1623)

O, what a rogue and peasant slave am I!
Is it not monstrous that this player here,
But in a fiction, in a dream of passion,
Could force his soul so to his own conceit
That from her working all his visage wann'd
Tears in his eyes, distraction in's aspect,
A broken voice, and his whole function suiting
With forms to his conceit? and all for nothing!
For Hecuba!
What's Hecuba to him, or he to Hecuba,
That he should weep for her? …

[The players are moved by their fiction, while he, Hamlet, burdened by the responsibility of avenging his father but unable to act, seems not moved at all:]

Yet I,
A dull and muddy-mettled[1] rascal, peak[2]
Like John-a-dreams, unpregnant of[3] my cause
And can say nothing—no, not for a king,
Upon whose property and most dear life
A damn'd defeat was made. …

[But even as Hamlet damns himself for procrastinating, he devises a plan of action to "catch the conscience of the king"—he will have a play performed before his uncle the king:]

… I'll have these players
Play something like the murder of my father
Before mine uncle: I'll observe his looks;
I'll tent him to the quick: if he but blench,
I know my course. The spirit that I have seen
May be the devil: and the devil hath power
To assume a pleasing shape; yea, and perhaps
Out of my weakness and my melancholy,
As he is very potent with such spirits,
Abuses me to damn me: I'll have grounds
More relative than this: the play's the thing
Wherein I'll catch the conscience of the king.

[1] **muddy-mettled:** dull-spirited.
[2] **peak:** mope.
[3] **unpregnant:** not quickened to action.

This is Shakespeare at his most dramatic. Written almost entirely in blank verse (unrhymed iambic pentameter)—a form that Marlowe first introduced in his tragedies and that became known as "Marlowe's mighty line"—the soliloquy

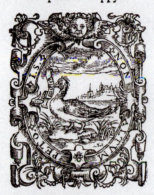

Fig. 19.12 *The Tragedy of Hamlet*, title page of the third quarto edition of the play, published in London. 1611. Courtesy of the Library of Congress. Hamlet was first performed in July 1602. Quarto editions are relatively inexpensive publications containing the text of a single play, as opposed to the more expensive and much larger First Folio of 1623 (see Fig. 19.11).

is alternately fast or slow, smooth or rough, the rhythm changing at almost every line with Hamlet's emotional twists and turns. By the time Hamlet finishes this soliloquy, with a rhymed couplet to round off the passage, Shakespeare has himself captured the conscience of his audience. Is it not a miracle, we ask ourselves, that this actor playing Hamlet "in a fiction, in a dream of passion, / Could force his soul so to his own conceit" that we are moved to complete identification with his plight?

In the next act, Shakespeare furthers the audience's identification with his play. In Scene 1, Hamlet rejects the love of Ophelia. This is the occasion of what may be his most famous soliloquy, the "To be or not to be" speech, which he delivers as Ophelia sits nearby, "pretending to read a book." The question that the speech raises is timeless. Is Hamlet playacting, pretending to be so tormented in order to convince Ophelia of his madness, or does he not

know that Ophelia is present, and is thus sincere in what he says? Such ambiguity goes to the very heart of our understanding of the play (**Reading 19.11b**):

READING 19.11b

from William Shakespeare, *Hamlet*, Act 3, Scene 1 (1623)

HAMLET To be, or not to be, that is the question:
  Whether 'tis nobler in the mind to suffer
  The slings and arrows of outrageous fortune,
  Or to take arms against a sea of troubles,
  And by opposing end them. To die, to sleep—
  No more—and by a sleep to say we end
  The heart-ache and the thousand natural shocks
  That flesh is heir to. 'Tis a consummation
  Devoutly to be wish'd. To die, to sleep;
  To sleep, perchance to dream. Ay, there's the rub,[1]
  For in that sleep of death what dreams may come
  When we have shuffled[2] off this mortal coil,[3]
  Must give us pause. There's the respect[4]
  That makes calamity of so long life.[5]
  For who would bear the whips and scorns of time,
  Th' oppressor's wrong, the proud man's contumely,[6]
  The pangs of despis'd[7] love, the law's delay,
  The insolence of office,[8] and the spurns[9]
  That patient merit of th' unworthy takes,
  When he himself might his quietus[10] make
  With a bare bodkin?[11] Who would fardels[12] bear,
  To grunt and sweat under a weary life,
  But that the dread of something after death,
  The undiscover'd country from whose bourn[13]
  No traveler returns, puzzles the will,
  And makes us rather bear those ills we have
  Than fly to others that we know not of?
  Thus conscience does make cowards of us all,
  And thus the native hue[14] of resolution
  Is sicklied o'er with the pale cast[15] of thought,
  And enterprises of great pitch[16] and moment[17]
  With this regard[18] their currents[19] turn awry,
  And lose the name of action.—Soft you now,
  The fair Ophelia. Nymph, in thy orisons[20]
  Be all my sins rememb'red.

[1] **rub** (literally, an obstacle in the game of bowls) [2] **shuffled** sloughed, cast [3] **coil** turmoil [4] **respect** consideration [5] **of . . . life** so long-lived [6] **contumely** insolent abuse [7] **despis'd** rejected [8] **office** officialdom [9] **spurns** insults [10] **quietus** acquittance; here, death [11] **bodkin** dagger [12] **fardels** burdens [13] **bourn** boundary [14] **native hue** natural color, complexion [15] **cast** shade of color [16] **pitch** height (as of a falcon's flight) [17] **moment** importance [18] **regard** respect, consideration [19] **currents** courses [20] **orisons** prayers

---

However, the audience understands that Hamlet's feigned madness—believed by all the characters in the play—is potentially more destructive than productive. In Scene 2, the players perform what has become known as "the play within the play." As Hamlet planned in the soliloquy at the end of Act 2, he means the play to move his uncle to such identification with the scene that he will reveal his own involvement in the murder of Hamlet's father. But the audience members recognize that they too must identify with the play they are watching. This is, after all, as Hamlet says at the beginning of the scene, "the purpose of playing, whose end, both at the first and now, was and is, to hold, as 'twere, the mirror up to nature. ..." The audience members understand, therefore, that they are looking at a reflection of themselves.

In all his contradiction and ambiguity, Hamlet is the most desired role and the most often performed character in the history of the English stage, because he lays himself so bare before us, like some open wound that refuses to heal. He demands our understanding, even as he resists it. In fact, Hamlet represents a new idea of character—no longer a unified and coherent being, but rather a conflicted and driven personality, as mysterious to itself as to others, and as unpredictable as its very dreams. Hamlet is, in this sense, the first modern person. He inaugurates a type who will become in future centuries increasingly recognizable as a version of ourselves.

Above all, Hamlet is an individual. He represents the logical outcome of the English taste for portraiture, with its humanist emphasis on individualism. But the questions he poses in his soliloquies reveal a first-person "I" new to the Western tradition in 1600, but totally recognizable to us today. Just as Montaigne (see Chapter 17), Shakespeare's contemporary, became increasingly convinced that he could never wholly know himself, creating for himself the motto *"Que sais-je?"* ("What do I know?"), Shakespeare's Hamlet recognizes that knowing anything fully and truly is at best difficult, and that knowing one's self is even more so. You can only take stabs at it—*essais*, as Montaigne called them. From 1600 onward, the human personality increasingly becomes the obsessive object of human study. In Shakespeare's Hamlet and Montaigne's first-person "I," Western culture inaugurates its tradition of self-examination and self-absorption.

THE ENGLISH IN VIRGINIA

What was unique about the English colonization of the Americas?

In one of his last plays, *The Tempest*, first performed in November 1611, Shakespeare created a work that many scholars find tempting to read as a parable of the colonial exploitation of the Americas. His chief protagonist, Prospero, once Duke of Milan, has been stranded on a remote island for 12 years with his daughter Miranda, the two having been left to die on a raft at sea by Prospero's jealous brother. Over the years, Prospero has assumed control of the island and its spirits and nymphs, including Ariel, the chief agent of Prospero's considerable magical powers, whom he has promised to one day free, and Caliban, his servant, described as a monster, a "thing of darkness ... as disproportion'd in his manners / As in his shape." Caliban

rankles at his servitude. Told that he should be grateful for having learned language, he replies:

> You taught me language; and my proft on't
> Is, I know how to curse: the red plague rid you
> For learning me your language!

It is easy enough, then, to see Caliban as a figure for the Native American (it seems likely that Shakespeare was reading a new English translation of Montaigne's essay "Of Cannibals" [see Reading 17.7 in Chapter 17] as he wrote the play), and Prospero as the embodiment of colonial overseer.

Whether Shakespeare intended this reading—or instead was interested only in exploring the faces of political power in more general terms—we can be certain that he was well aware of England's colonial aspirations. Faced with the prospect of an ever more powerful and increasingly wealthy Hispanic Catholic presence in the Americas, England sought to establish its own colonial foothold in the New World as well. In 1584, Sir Walter Raleigh (1552–1618) secured a charter from Queen Elizabeth giving him the right "to discover, search, find and view such remote heathen and barbarous lands, countries and territories, not actually possessed of any Christian Prince, nor inhabited by Christian people as to him, his heirs and assigns, to every or any of them shall seem good, and the same to have hold and occupy and enjoy, to him his heirs and assigns forever." America, north of Florida at least, was Raleigh's for the taking.

The Roanoke Colonies

An expedition led by two of Raleigh's lieutenants determined that the best place to establish such a colony was the Outer Banks of present-day North Carolina. From there, they believed, it would be possible to raid Spanish settlements to the south, as well as explore the as yet uncharted territories inland. To those ends, Raleigh dispatched an expedition of 108 men in the spring of 1585, which was composed almost entirely of soldiers who had fought to establish English rule in Ireland. In June, seven vessels led by Sir Richard Greenville landed on an island they called Roanoke, after the word for "money" in the language of the Algonquin peoples whom they found living in the larger region, which they named Virginia, after Queen Elizabeth, the "Virgin Queen."

The first expedition was short-lived. For one, Greenville's supply ship was grounded on a shoal off the Outer Banks, and almost all the company's supplies were lost. Greenville returned to England in order to resupply the colony. In his absence, Algonquian Indians did at first come to their aid, but relations quickly deteriorated and within a year, the desperate settlers sailed home on board a ship commanded by Sir Francis Drake (1540–96), who stopped at Roanoke on his way home from the Caribbean on a mission, also financed by Raleigh, to capture Spanish treasure ships

Undaunted, Raleigh organized a second expedition, this one to be headed by a member of the original 1585 expedition,

John White (ca. 1540–ca. 1593). White had returned from the 1585 expedition with watercolors that, in addition to recording the local flora and fauna of the region, chronicled the customs of the local Algonquian peoples as carefully as possible. In 1590, Theodore de Bry (1528–98), a Flemish engraver particularly dedicated to publishing accounts of the New World, issued *A Brief and True Report of the New Found Land of Virginia*, an account of the 1585 Roanoke expedition written by White's friend, the scientist Thomas Hariot (1560–1621). It was originally written in Latin, as a scientific text, and translated into English by Richard Hakluyt (1522/23–1616). Hakluyt was himself author of a lengthy memorandum personally delivered to Queen Elizabeth in 1584 in support of Raleigh's request for a charter entitled *A Particular Discourse concerninge the Greate Necessitie and Manifolde Commodyties That Are Like to Growe to This Realme of Englande by the Westerne Discoveries Lately Attempted*. He readily understood the value in creating popular interest in and enthusiasm for settling the New World, and he encouraged de Bry to include in Hariot's *Brief and True Report* illustrations based on White's watercolors (all of White's paintings survive, housed today in the British Museum).

White's bird's-eye view of the unenclosed Indian village of Secotan, on the Pamilico River, was probably done in mid-July 1585. It shows 13 houses, or *wigwams*, with barrel-shaped roofs and wooden frames covered with woven mats and sheets of birchbark (Fig. **19.13**). At the top, a path leads from water (a stream or pond) to the main group of houses, widening into a central path. To the right of the path and street are three cornfields each at a different stage of growth. At the bottom right, a path separates the lowest cornfield from the ceremonial area where Indians are dancing. Ten men and seven women are dancing in a circle of seven upright posts, the tops of which are carved in the form of human heads. Two figures stand between the posts in the foreground with clasped hands. In the middle of the circle a woman, viewed from the back, stands naked before a taller central pole, her arms clasping the necks of two other women. In his *Brief and True Report*, Hariot describes the scene (**Reading 19.12**):

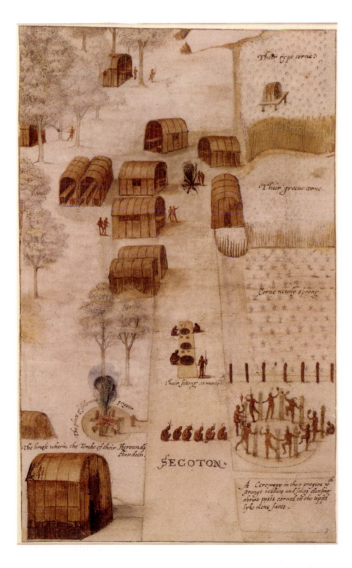

Fig. 19.13 John White, *The Village of Secotan*. ca. 1585. Watercolor on paper, 12¾" × 7¾". © The Trustees of the British Museum. Inscribed in dark brown ink, in the top right-hand corner, on the first field of maize are the words "Their rype corne"; below, on the second field, "Their greene corne"; on the third field, "Corne newly sprong."

> ### READING 19.12
>
> **from Thomas Hariot, *A Brief and True Report of the New Found Land of Virginia* (1590)**
>
> At a certain time in the year, a great and solemn feast is celebrated, at which all the inhabitants of the neighboring towns are collected, decorated in their outlandish fashions, and having on their shoulders the marks that designate the places of their nativity. A large area is enclosed by posts rudely carved with faces, around which they dance, sing and make the most uncouth gesticulations, while three of their most beautiful young women, with arms entwined, dance and leap around together in the centre. This takes place after sunset to avoid the heat; and, as one party becomes wearied, another succeeds, until they are ready to assemble at the feast.

Many of the Indians carry leafy branches of plants that, together with what Hariot describes as three of "their most beautiful young women" encircling the center post, suggests that the dance is some sort of fertility ritual.

It was very important to Raleigh that Hariot's *Brief and True Report* should emphasize such fertility and not discourage potential investors. Hariot's account is, by and large, a catalog of the country's wealth. If he had to admit that there was little or no gold to be found, he described the abundant variety of Virginia's flora and fauna and outlined their commercial potential—dense pine forests, rich soil, medicinal plants, and silk worms.

Jamestown

White's second expedition arrived at Roanoke in July 1587 with about 100 colonists, many of them families from Devon who had been promised 500 acres apiece in return for settling the new colony. But the expedition was woefully undersupplied, and on August 25, White returned to England in order to reprovision the colony for the winter. England's war with Spain, primarily a naval affair headed by Raleigh himself, left White unable to secure a relief expedition, and it was not until August 1590 that he returned to Roanoke. There he found no trace of any colonists, including his own daughter, Eleanor, her husband, Ananias Dare, and his granddaughter, Virginia Dare, who on August 18, 1587, had been the first child born of English parents in the New World.

The prospect of colonization seemed tenuous, until finally, in 1607, Captain John Smith (1580–1631) established the first successful British colony in Virginia at Jamestown on the James River, about 40 miles inland from the Atlantic Ocean and the entrance to Chesapeake Bay, both the settlement and the river named after Queen Elizabeth's successor in England, King James I. This expedition was financed by a group of investors from London that came to be known as the London Company of Virginia. In order to recruit settlers, they inaugurated what historian Richard Hofstadter has called "one of the first concerted and sustained advertising campaigns in the history of the modern world." Hakluyt, an original member of the London Company, published in 1609 a tract entitled *Virginia Richly Valued*, typical of the materials intended to promote the Company. Its purpose is summarized on the title page: "Wherein are truly observed the riches and fertilities of these parts, abounding with things necessary, pleasant, and profitable for the life of man."

If descriptions of the horticultural prospects of the New World were designed to seem appealing, it seemed equally important to downplay the hostilities of the Indians. The famous story of Pocahontas, daughter of Powhatan, the chief of the Algonquian-speaking Powhatan tribes of the lower Chesapeake region, saving Captain Smith's life was popularized in no small part to demonstrate the inherent goodness of the native peoples. If the story is, perhaps, apocryphal, and whatever her actual role in saving Smith's life when her father threatened him, it seems certain that Smith wanted to associate himself more closely with the young woman who epitomized in the eyes of many the successes of the Jamestown colony and its "civilizing" mission. In 1613, Pocahontas had been captured by the Jamestown colonists in order to pressure Powhatan to release a number of English prisoners and stolen weapons. Negotiations between Powhatan and the English proved fruitless, and over the course of the next year, Pocahontas was instructed in English and Christianity, baptized and christened Rebecca, and married to the settler John Rolfe, who in 1611 had begun to farm tobacco successfully, creating the first real cash crop export from the New World. Their only

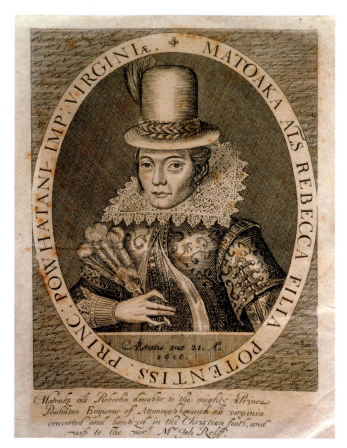

Fig. 19.14 Simon van de Passe, *Pocahontas*. 1616. Engraving, 6¾" × 4⅝". Private collection. No image of the era better underscores the belief that the indigenous peoples of the New World might be "civilized."

child, Thomas Rolfe, was born in 1615, and the marriage apparently soothed relations between the colonists and the Powhatans.

In 1616, John and Rebecca Rolfe travelled to England, where they were invited to attend a Twelfth Night masked ball given by King James and Queen Anne. (Contrary to popular belief, the Rolfes were not received at court.) Soon after, Pocahontas sat for a portrait by Simon van de Passe (Fig. **19.14**), commissioned by the London Company and quickly engraved so that it might be sold in the streets to attract new colonists and investors. Although she is dressed in English fashion, her high cheekbones, darkish skin, and proud demeanor announce her as an Indian princess, a fact that the inscription in the oval frame surrounding her affirms: "Matoaka als [also known as] Rebecca, daughter to the mighty prince, Powhatan, Emperor of Virginia." Not long after this portrait was completed, and just as she was about to return to Virginia, Pocahontas died, probably of some pulmonary disorder, and was buried at Gravesend on the south bank of the Thames, downstream from London. Rolfe returned home to attend to his business. By then, tobacco exports to England from Virginia totaled 20,000 pounds a year, and the success of the Virginia colony was thus assured, as was the English presence in North America.

The New Universe

In the last half of the sixteenth century, the Western conception of the universe began to change dramatically. First, in 1543, the Polish scholar Nicolaus Copernicus (1473–1543) published *On the Revolutions of the Heavenly Spheres*, which argued that Earth was not the center of the universe but, like the other planets, revolved around the Sun. This theory was considered heretical by the Church, which put the work on its Index of Prohibited Books in 1616. (It was not removed until 1835.) In the first decade of the seventeenth century, however, Johannes Kepler (1571–1630), a court mathematician and astronomer to the Holy Roman Emperor, proved that Earth and the other planets revolve in elliptical orbits around the Sun. When Kepler learned that the astronomer and mathematician Galileo Galilei (1564–1642) had perfected the telescope, a tool that made it possible to confirm much of Copernican theory, he obtained one for himself.

Thus, when two Netherlandish painters, Peter Paul Rubens (1577–1640) and Jan Brueghel the Elder (1568–1625), came together to paint a series of five paintings on the theme of the five senses in 1617 to 1618, they knew that the new universe of Copernicus, Kepler, and Galileo had to be addressed in their *Allegory of Sight* (Fig. **19.15**), the painting that many now consider the most splendid in the series.

At first look, this painting seems to be about the royal art collection, but its real subject is the nature of seeing. As she contemplates a painting of Christ healing the blind, Venus appears melancholy, as if she is suggesting that the concept of physical love that she and Cupid embody falls short of Christian spiritual love. Christ's healing gesture suggests the power of faith—that is, he restores "true vision." The monkey at the bottom center of the allegory holds a set of spectacles, an image of those who look but do not see. In this, Brueghel and Rubens convey the traditional moral and religious convictions of the Church. But the presence of scientific instruments in the painting—the giant globe, the telescope, the magnifying glass, the astrolabe, and others—transforms the work into a new allegory of seeing that would come to dominate thinking in the seventeenth century. Just as linear perspective in painting uses two dimensions to create the illusion of real, three-dimensional space, the visual world was seen as an expression of what might be called divine space. For the next three centuries, the Western imagination would increasingly imbue the physical world with suggestions of the divine. ■

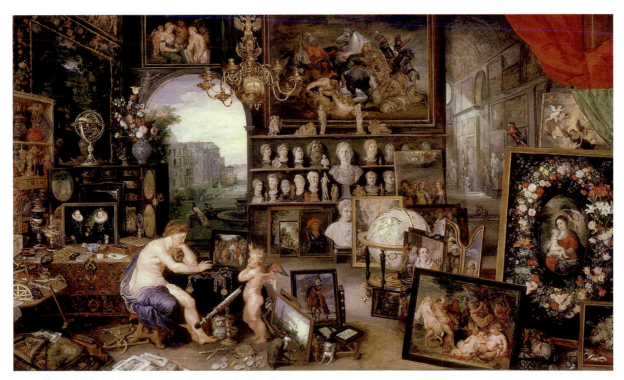

Fig. 19.15 Jan Brueghel the Elder and Peter Paul Rubens, *Allegory of Sight*, from *Allegories of the Five Senses*. ca. 1617–18. Oil on wood panel, 25⅝" × 43". Museo del Prado, Madrid.

View the Closer Look for the *Allegory of Sight* on **MyArtsLab**

19.1 Explain how Henry VIII transformed England.

In the sixteenth century, London would become one of the most rapidly growing cities in the world, due in no small part to Henry VIII's dissolution of the monasteries in 1536. Henry surrounded himself with humanist scholars, including Desiderius Erasmus and Thomas More. How does More's *Utopia* critique Henry's England? Portraiture was the chief form of visual art supported by Henry's court. How do you account for this taste? The chief portrait painter of the day was Hans Holbein. While Holbein's paintings evidence the meticulous realism characteristic of the Northern Renaissance, how do they reflect larger concerns?

Henry's reign was complicated by his unceasing desire to father a male heir and, as a consequence, his marriage to a succession of wives. These marriages forced him to break with the Church in Rome. Henry's three heirs—Edward, Mary, and Elizabeth—were variously Protestant or Catholic. What strains did his heirs' varying religious sympathies put on the court? How did Elizabeth finally secure England's central place in world affairs?

19.2 Outline the flourishing of the arts under the rule of Queen Elizabeth I.

England flourished under Elizabeth's rule, and the queen was a great supporter of the arts. How did portrait painting in her court differ stylistically from portrait painting under her father? How did Elizabeth's taste manifest itself in poetry as well? What are the characteristics of one of the primary poetic forms of Elizabethan England, the sonnet? Elizabeth was also an accomplished musician, whose favorite form was apparently the madrigal, hundreds of which were written by Thomas Morley. The publication of *The Book of Common Prayer* encouraged composers to write motets in English that came to be known as anthems, a form in which the composer Thomas Tallis excelled. Perhaps the greatest composer of the day was William Byrd. Although he excelled in almost every form of musical composition, what did he particularly encourage?

19.3 Characterize the Elizabethan stage and the contributions to it of both Marlowe and Shakespeare.

Perhaps the greatest artistic achievement of the Elizabethan age was its drama. Thousands of people flocked daily to the playhouses on the south bank of the Thames. Christopher Marlowe's *Tragical History of Dr. Faustus* introduced an important figure to the Elizabethan theater, the tragic hero who seeks the unattainable. But audiences were especially attracted to the plays of William Shakespeare, whose greatest achievement is, perhaps, the tragedy *Hamlet*. In what way is Hamlet unique in the early seventeenth century as a dramatic character?

19.4 Describe the unique features of the English colonization of the Americas.

Unwilling to cede control of the New World to the Spanish, Queen Elizabeth encouraged exploration and settlement of areas north of Spanish control. Unlike the Spanish, the English dispatched families intent on settling and making a new life in the New World. What was the primary motive for settlement? What were the obstacles that settlers faced?

✓ **Study** and **review** on **MyArtsLab**

READINGS

from Thomas More, *Utopia*, Book 2 (1516)

More's *Utopia* is the first description of an ideal society since Plato's *Republic*. It is narrated by a fictional traveler named Raphael Hythloday (whose surname means "dispenser of nonsense" in Greek), and it contrasts the contentious social life of More's contemporary English—and European—society to the tranquil, orderly social arrangements of Utopia itself. The following excerpts, which are just a sampling of Utopia's virtues, give a fair indication of Utopia's distinct difference from More's own world.

Agriculture is that which is so universally understood among them that no person, either man or woman, is ignorant of it; they are instructed in it from their childhood, partly by what they learn at school and partly by practice; they being led out often into the fields, about the town, where they not only see others at work, but are likewise exercised in it themselves. Besides agriculture, which is so common to them all, every man has some peculiar trade to which he applies himself, such as the manufacture of wool, or flax, masonry, smith's work, or carpenter's work; for there is no sort of trade that is not in great esteem among them. Throughout the island they wear the same sort of clothes without any other distinction, except what is necessary to distinguish the two sexes, and the married and unmarried. The fashion never alters; and as it is neither disagreeable nor uneasy, so it is suited to the climate, and calculated both for their summers and winters. ... [10]

[As] to their manner of living in society, the oldest man of every family, as has been already said, is its governor. Wives serve their husbands, and children their parents, and always the younger serves the elder. Every city is divided into four equal parts, and in the middle of each there is a marketplace: what is brought thither, and manufactured by the several families, is carried from thence to houses appointed for that purpose, in which all things of a sort are laid by themselves; and thither every father goes and takes whatsoever he or his family stand in need of, without either paying for it or leaving anything in exchange. ... [20]

They reckon up several sorts of pleasures, which they call true ones: some belong to the body and others to the mind. The pleasures of the mind lie in knowledge, and in that delight which the contemplation of truth carries with it; to which they add the joyful reflections on a well-spent life, and the assured hopes of a future happiness. They divide the pleasures of the body into two sorts; the one is that which gives our senses some real delight, and is performed, either by recruiting nature, and supplying those parts which feed the internal heat of life by eating and drinking; or when nature is eased of any surcharge that oppresses it; when we are relieved from sudden pain, or that which arises from satisfying the appetite which nature has wisely given to lead us to the propagation of the species. There is another kind of pleasure that arises neither from our receiving what the body requires nor its being relieved when overcharged, and yet by a secret, unseen virtue affects the senses, [30] [40]

raises the passions, and strikes the mind with generous impressions; this is the pleasure that arises from music. Another kind of bodily pleasure is that which results from an undisturbed and vigorous constitution of body, when life and active spirits seem to actuate every part. This lively health, when entirely free from all mixture of pain, of itself gives an inward pleasure, independent of all external objects of delight; and though this pleasure does not so powerfully affect us, nor act so strongly on the [50] senses as some of the others, yet it may be esteemed as the greatest of all pleasures, and almost all the Utopians reckon it the foundation and basis of all the other joys of life; since this alone makes the state of life easy and desirable; and when this is wanting, a man is really capable of no other pleasure. They look upon freedom from pain, if it does not rise from perfect health, to be a state of stupidity rather than of pleasure. ...

They take great pleasure in fools, and as it is thought a base and unbecoming thing to use them ill, so they do not think it amiss for people to divert themselves with their folly: and, in [60] their opinion, this is a great advantage to the fools themselves: for if men were so sullen and severe as not at all to please themselves with their ridiculous behavior and foolish sayings, which is all that they can do to recommend themselves to others, it could not be expected that they would be so well provided for, nor so tenderly used as they must otherwise be. If any man should reproach another for his being misshaped or imperfect in any part of his body, it would not at all be thought a reflection on the person so treated, but it would be accounted scandalous in him that had upbraided another with what he could not help. [70] It is thought a sign of a sluggish and sordid mind not to preserve carefully one's natural beauty; but it is likewise infamous among them to use paint. They all see that no beauty recommends a wife so much to her husband as the probity of her life, and her obedience: for as some few are caught and held only by beauty, so all are attracted by the other excellences which charm all the world. ...

READING CRITICALLY

Plato's ideal society in the *Republic* is presented as an attainable ideal, but More's *Utopia* is a fiction, and by implication unattainable. Why does More choose to make his ideal community a fiction?

Protestant Reformation. The Church recognized that its own excesses had fueled the Reformation, but the Holy Roman Emperor Charles V (r. 1519–58)—Maximilian II became emperor by virtue of marrying Charles's daughter, Maria—continued to feud with Francis I of France, thus stymying the Church's efforts to respond politically. Still, despite their ongoing conflict—financed, on the Holy Roman Emperor's side, by gold and silver from the newly discovered Americas—both monarchs understood the necessity of addressing the threat posed by the Protestant Reformation. They convinced the pope to convene the so-called Council of Trent in 1545. Its charge was to outline a path of reform for the Church itself. The Council called for a return to "simplicity, zeal toward God, and a contempt of vanities" in the lifestyles of its bishops. It believed the Church's art and music should reflect these values as well. In Italy, the Church initiated an Inquisition as a method of enforcing the strictures of the Counter-Reformation. In Spain, an Inquisition had been in place since 1478 as a tool to expel or convert all non-Christian Spaniards, especially Spanish Muslims and Jews, but also Catholic nuns and priests who practiced a brand of mysticism closely related to Jewish mystical tracts.

Even as the early Counter-Reformation would seek to impose a sense of restraint in all aspects of life, a more secular approach to art represented by the likes of Arcimboldo arose, originating in the High Renaissance's love for artistic genius and originality. Increasingly, the courts supported the production of works of art devoid of religious themes and without the restraint and decorum called for by Church reform. A clear division arose between the public face of the courts, which were almost uniformly aligned with the Church, and the tastes for the exotic and the inventive that those courts felt free to indulge in private. And in other lesser cultural centers, namely the princely courts of northern Italy, artists were free to pursue the spirit of originality and invention that had defined the High Renaissance, especially in nonreligious imagery. Inspired by the late work of Michelangelo, the style of painting and sculpture that developed in the courts of the Gonzaga in Mantua and the d'Este in Ferrara was notable for its freedom to experiment, its virtuosity and eccentricity, and its often frank sensuality.

We have come to call this style Mannerist, from the Italian word *maniera*, "style." Mannerism, in general, can be thought of as a style of refined elegance, reflecting the virtuosity and sophistication of its practitioners, often by means of an exaggeration and distortion of proportion that tests the boundaries of the beautiful and ideal. It resulted in an art almost the opposite of that called for by the Council of Trent, and it spawned an equally free and inventive literature. Eventually some artists managed to reconcile the aims of the Counter-Reformation and the inventiveness of Mannerism, creating a style that would pave the way for the Baroque era to come.

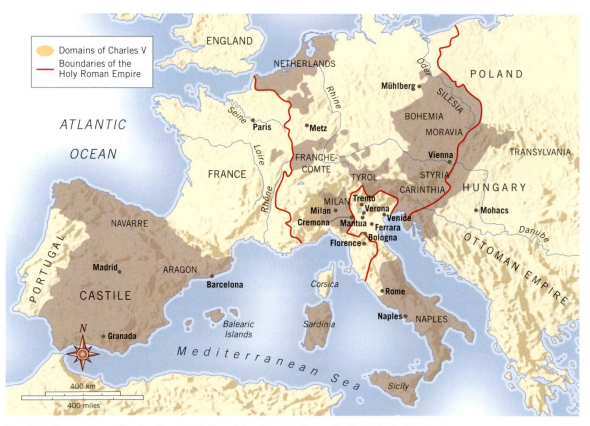

Map 20.1 The empire of Charles V. ca. 1521. The whole of the Holy Roman Empire in Charles V's time lies between the red lines, but Charles was in absolute control of the areas shaded in brown. In addition to the lands shown here, Charles also controlled almost all of the Americas.

THE COUNTER-REFORMATION

What was the Counter-Reformation and how did it address the arts?

In 1493, the year after Columbus arrived in America, Pope Alexander VI decreed that the New World was the property of the Church, which he chose to rent in its entirety to Spain (he was himself Spanish). Alexander's papal bull made clear that no other country could occupy any of these territories without the pope's permission and, by extension, his direct financial benefit. Thus, the subsequent colonization of North America by France and England was, from the Church's point of view, an act of piracy.

As King of Spain, Charles V was the direct beneficiary of the pope's pronouncements. From his point of view, the Americas served but one purpose—to provide funds for his continuing war against Francis I of France. The two monarchs had been at war since 1521 but never with any clear outcome for any significant period of time. The papacy needed both of them as allies in its campaign against the Protestant Reformation. But it was Charles V whose troops, to his embarrassment, had sacked Rome in 1527 and imprisoned Pope Clement VII (Giulio de' Medici), as a direct response to Clement's alliance with Francis I and Henry VIII of England.

The enmity between Charles V and Francis I went back to the election of Charles as Emperor of the Holy Roman Empire in 1521. When, after the death of Emperor Maximilian, Charles out of courtesy informed Francis that he intended to seek election as emperor, Francis had replied, "Sire, we are both courting the same lady." The pope backed Francis, but Charles secured a loan of 500,000 florins from a bank in Augsburg and literally bought the votes of the seven electors.

Charles's empire was immense. By heredity and marriage, it included the Netherlands, where he had been born (in Ghent), the Iberian peninsula, southern Italy, Milan, Austria and parts of present-day Germany, and the Franche-Comté (see brown areas in Map 20.1). To this was added the lands of the Holy Roman Empire (outlined in red in Map 20.1), including all of Germany, Switzerland, and more of Italy. Because of its vast size, Charles's territory was susceptible to attack from virtually all directions, as Suleiman the Magnificent, Emperor of the Ottoman Empire, demonstrated when, at Francis's request, he defeated and killed Charles's brother-in-law, Louis II of Hungary, in 1526. Thus embattled, Charles claimed to want peace so that the Church, and its Catholic kings, could turn their united attention to the threat of Protestantism. And finally, in 1544, Charles entered France from the Netherlands. Francis was sufficiently frightened, or sufficiently tired of the endless conflict, that he sued for peace. Together the two kings then turned to Pope Paul III and pressured him to call a general council to be held at Trento, in northern Italy, beginning December 3, 1545, to confront their common enemy, the Protestant challenge.

The Council of Trent

The resolution of the conflict between Charles and Francis marks a moment when historical urgency profoundly affected the direction of humanistic enterprise. The resulting Council of Trent was charged with reforming the Church. It met in three sessions, and owing to war, plague, and the political strategies of the papacy itself, it spanned the careers of four different popes over 18 years: 1545–47, 1551–52, and 1562–63. The Council concentrated on restoring internal Church discipline. It called a halt to the selling of Church offices and religious goods, a common practice used by clergy to pad their coffers. It required bishops, many of whom lived in Rome, to return to their dioceses, where, they were told, they needed to preach regularly, exert discipline over local religious practice, and be active among their parishioners. They were warned not to live ostentatiously:

> It is to be desired that those who undertake the office of bishop shall understand ... that they are called, not to their own convenience, not to riches or luxury, but to labors and cares, for the glory of God. ... Wherefore ... this Council not only orders that bishops be content with modest furniture and a frugal table and diet, but that they also give heed that in the rest of their manner of living and in their whole house there be nothing seen which is alien to this holy institution, and which does not manifest simplicity, zeal toward God, and a contempt of vanities.

The bishops were to maintain strict celibacy, which they had not been required to do before. And they were to construct a seminary in every diocese.

There is good reason to believe that the Council of Trent came to recognize, as Charles himself finally did, that there could be no military victory over Protestantism. Rather, if the Church were to be victorious, it had to win back the hearts and souls of the people themselves. So it did not give in to the Protestants on a single doctrinal point, reaffirming the role of good works in salvation, transubstantiation (in the Eucharist, the conversion of bread and wine into the body and blood of Christ), the Eucharist itself as a ritual embodying the true presence of Christ, clerical celibacy, the reality of purgatory, the veneration of saints and relics, and letters of indulgence. In other words, even as the Council enforced a new standard of discipline among its bishops, it strongly reinforced traditional Roman Catholic doctrine.

Catholic Reform of the Arts: Palestrina and the Music of the Early Counter-Reformation

The Council of Trent's injunction against luxury and its assertion of the principle of simple piety were directly translated to the arts. Contrary to many Protestant sects, the Council of Trent insisted on the use of religious imagery:

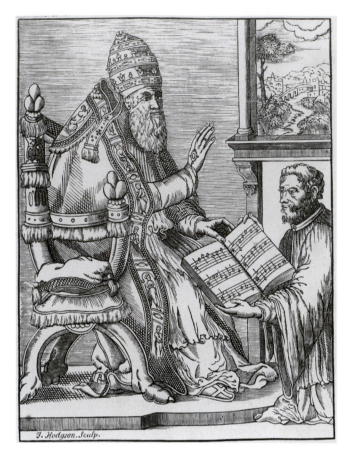

Fig. 20.2 Title page of Palestrina's *Missarum liber primus* ("First Book of Masses"). Published in Rome. 1554. The page shows Palestrina showing the work to Pope Julius III.

The images of Christ, of the Virgin Mother of God, and of other saints are to be placed and retained especially in churches ... [and] set before the eyes of the faithful so that they ... may fashion their own life and conduct in imitation of the saints and be moved to adore and love God and cultivate piety.

Subsequent treatises on art, written by clergy, called explicitly for direct treatment of subjects, unencumbered by anything "sensuous," from brushwork to light effects.

The Council of Trent's order for a visual art that would directly affect the souls of the people influenced the direction in which church music developed as well. The function of music in the liturgy, the Council insisted, was to serve the text, and so the text should be clear and intelligible to the congregation:

The whole plan of singing should be constituted not to give empty pleasure to the ear, but in such a way that the words be clearly understood by all, and thus the hearts of the listeners be drawn to the desire of heavenly harmonies. ... They shall also banish from church all music that contains, whether in the singing or in the organ playing, things that are lascivious or impure.

For some, polyphony (two or more voices of equal importance) constituted "lascivious or impure" music, and they argued that only the single line of monophonic plainchant should be performed in the church. The Council rejected this idea.

Legend has it that the Council rejected the replacement of polyphonic music by plainchant because of a particular, polyphonic mass, composed in 1567 by Giovanni Pierluigi da Palestrina (ca. 1525–94): *Missa Papae Marcelli*, or *Mass for Pope Marcellus*. The story is not true, but that it was widely believed for centuries testifies to the power of Palestrina's choral work. In his career, which included serving as choirmaster at the Capella Giulia in the Vatican for many years, Palestrina wrote 104 settings for the Mass, 375 motets, 80 hymns, and about 140 songs, both sacred and secular. He was the first composer of the sixteenth century to have his complete works published and was one of the most influential composers of his day (Fig. **20.2**).

The *Missa Papae Marcelli* is notable for the way it carries out the requirements of the Council of Trent. Its music is restrained so that the words, when sung by the choir, stand out in utter clarity, especially at the beginning of phrases. Although the voices in the Credo section enunciate each syllable of the text in chordal unison (usually thirds and sixths, or what we have come to recognize as consonant intervals), a constant interplay between **counterpoint**, in which voices imitate the main melody in succession, and **homophony**, in which the subordinate voices simply accompany the melody in unison, enlivens the music (track **20.1**). Likewise, Palestrina often plays one voice sustaining a single note per syllable against a voice engaged in **melisma**, or many notes per syllable. Above all, however, the intelligibility of the text is of paramount concern.

This quality is also audible in Palestrina's setting for *Super Flumina Babylonis*, or *By the Rivers of Babylon*, one of his most famous motets (track **20.2**). The **motet** was the most important form of polyphonic vocal music in the Middle Ages and Renaissance (see Chapter 14). From the Renaissance onward, it normally had a Latin sacred text and, like a *Missa*, was sung during Catholic service. The text of *Super Flumina Babylonis* is from Psalm 137 of the Bible and expresses the lamentation of the Jewish people:

By the rivers of Babylon, there we sat down
    and wept,
When we remembered you, O Zion.
On the willows, in the midst of everything,
    we hung up our harps.

The rhythm of each word matches up directly to the musical cadence. The accented syllable of each word is also usually set to a higher note, thus blending text and music with absolute clarity. In Palestrina's own words, the intention is to draw out "the vital impulse given to its words, according to their meaning." In keeping with the thinking of the Council of Trent, Palestrina's music serves to enliven—even glorify—the words, words that the Council believed every member of the congregation must be moved to understand and believe.

MICHELANGELO AND THE RISE OF MANNERISM

What new stylistic direction defines Michelangelo's late work?

The demand for clarity and directness that marks the art and music of the Counter-Reformation did not constrain so original an artist as Michelangelo, who introduced a different, more inventive direction in sixteenth-century art. Raphael had already arrived at a new style in the last paintings he executed for the Vatican before his death in 1520. He replaced the clarity, restraint, and order of his *School of Athens* (see Chapter 15, *Closer Look*, pages 512–513) with a more active, dynamic, even physically distorted realization of the human figure, probably in response to Michelangelo's own innovations in the same direction in the later frescoes for the Sistine Chapel ceiling—in the *Libyan Sibyl*, for instance, or the figures of Day and Night in the tomb of Giuliano de' Medici (see Figs. 15.12 and 15.18 in Chapter 15). This new proto-Mannerist style, reflecting the virtuosity and sophistication of its practitioners, manifests itself in architecture in Michelangelo's stairway for the Laurentian Library (see Fig. 15.19 in Chapter 15), which some believe to be among the style's earliest examples. In painting and sculpture, it resulted in distorted, artificial poses, mysterious or obscure settings, and, very often, elongated proportions. It is marked by the rejection of the Classicizing tendencies of the High Renaissance and by the artist's display of virtuosity through manipulations and distortions of the conventional figure.

Michelangelo's *Pietà*, one of the artist's last works, is a fully realized example of the new Mannerist artistic vocabulary (Fig. 20.3). The traditional *contrapposto* pose that evolved from Classical Greek sculpture in order to give a

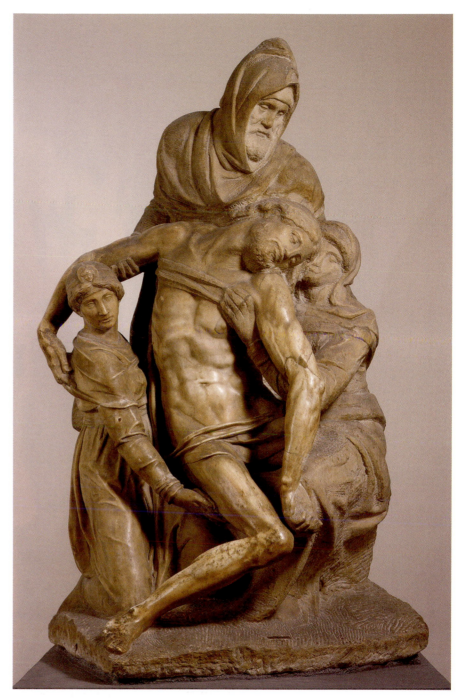

Fig. 20.3 Michelangelo, *Pietà*. 1547–53. Marble, height 89". Museo dell'Opera del Duomo, Florence. The female figure on the left was finished by Tiberio Calcagni, and the whole reconstructed by him, after Michelangelo smashed the sculpture upon discovering, after seven years of work, an imperfection in the marble that he had not previously detected.

static figure the illusion of potential movement is here exaggerated by the dynamic, spiral turn of the Christ's body as he falls to the ground. The result is what would become known as a **serpentine figure**, with no single predominant view. The right arm twists away from the body even as Christ's right leg seems to fold forward to the right at a 90-degree angle.

Michelangelo incorporated this serpentine pose somewhat less dramatically in his first commission in Rome

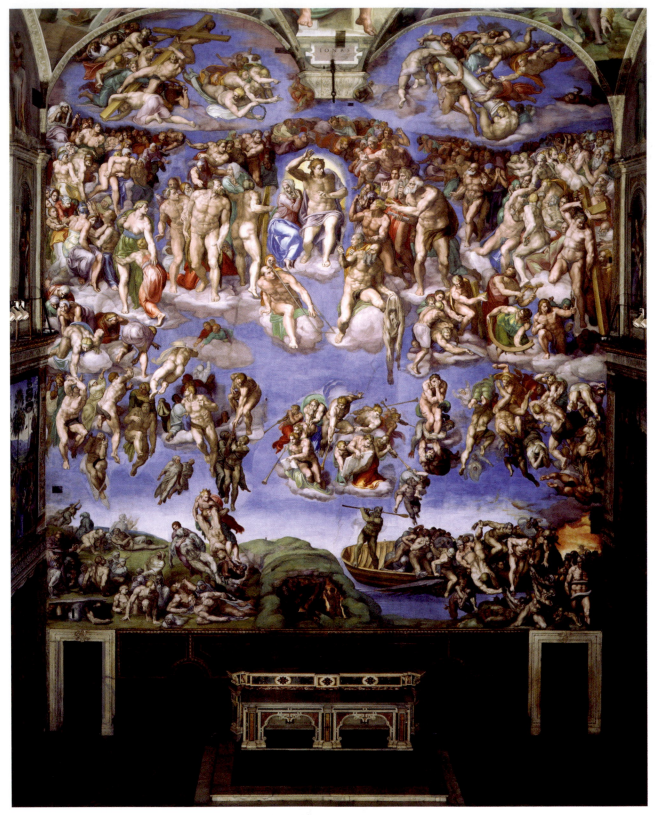

Fig. 20.4 Michelangelo, *Last Judgment.* **1534–41.** Fresco, 48' × 44'. Sistine Chapel, Vatican, Rome. Foto Musei Vaticani. Well to Christ's right, past the nude figure of John the Baptist, is a personification of the Church embracing a woman kneeling before her. The personification is bare-breasted to symbolize her ability to nourish the faithful. Balancing her, at the far right of the painting, a man places a large cross on the Sistine Chapel cornice, a symbolic representation of Christ's sacrifice. The pair, male and female, mirror Christ and Mary in the painting's center.

📖 **Read** the document related to Michelangelo at **MyArtsLab** after returning in 1534, a *Last Judgment* fresco for the altar wall of the Sistine Chapel (Fig. **20.4**). At the top center of the painting, Mary crouches beside Christ, turning her head away from her body toward the left-hand side of the composition, apparently absorbed in her own thoughts (Fig. **20.5**). Christ himself turns his attention to the saints and martyrs on the right-hand side of the composition, such as white-bearded Saint Peter holding gold and silver keys to heaven. Saint Bartholomew, who was martyred by being skinned alive, sits just below Christ's feet, holding in his right hand a knife, the instrument of his torture, and in his left hand his own flayed skin.

Many scholars believe that the face on the flayed skin is a self-portrait of Michelangelo, suggesting his sense of his own martyrdom under the unrelenting papal commissions of Pope Paul III. These figures, whose bodies were mutilated and maimed in their martyrdom, have been healed and restored as they rise to heaven. At the bottom of the painting, on the left, angels welcome souls ascending from the grave. At the right, demons drag the damned down into hell as Charon, the mythological boatman of the Classical world, ferries them across the River Styx. In the bottom center of the painting, directly behind the altar of the Sistine Chapel, is Hell's Mouth, and above it, angels trumpeting the arrival of the Last Judgment.

Michelangelo's *Last Judgment* almost immediately provoked controversy because of its presentation of religious figures nude. The poet Pietro Aretino sent him a letter in 1545 objecting to the fresco, a letter especially interesting when considered in the context of the Council of Trent, which was then in session (**Reading 20.1**):

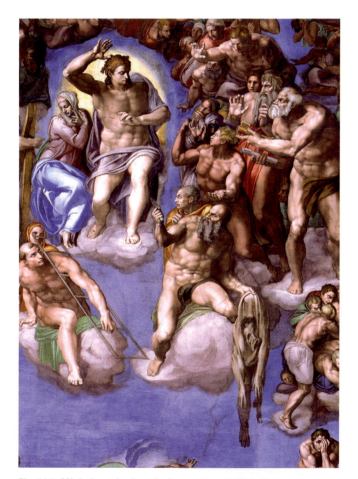

Fig. 20.5 Michelangelo, *Last Judgment,* **detail. 1534–41.** Fresco, 48' × 44'. Sistine Chapel, Vatican, Rome. Foto Musei Vaticani. Just below Mary's feet sits Saint Lawrence, holding the grill upon which he was roasted in 248 for refusing to turn over the treasures of the Church to the Roman emperor Valerian.

READING 20.1

from Pietro Aretino, Letter to Michelangelo (1545)

The pagans when they made statues I do not say of Diana who is clothed, but of naked Venus, made them cover with their hand the parts which should not be seen. And here there comes a Christian who, because he rates art higher than faith, deems a royal spectacle martyrs and virgins in improper attitudes, men dragged down by their genitals, things in front of which brothels would shut their eyes in order not to see them. Your art would be at home in some voluptuous *bagnio* [bathhouse], certainly not in the highest chapel in the world. … Restore it to good repute by turning the indecent parts of the damned to flames, and those of the blessed to sunbeams, or imitate the modesty of Florence, who hides your David's shame beneath some gilded leaves. And yet that statue is exposed upon a public square, not in a consecrated chapel.

When Michelangelo did not respond to this letter, Aretino published it. The letter underscores the growing tension between the developing Mannerist style and the aims of the Counter-Reformation. In fact, as long as Paul III remained pope, the *Last Judgment* stayed as Michelangelo had painted it. But with the election of Paul IV in 1555, the first new pope after Paul III had convened the Council of Trent in 1545, the painting fell into ever-increasing disfavor. Shortly after Michelangelo's death in 1564, Daniele da Volterra and others painted draperies over the genital areas of the fresco's nude figures, a feat for which they ignominiously earned the name *braghettoni,* "breeches-painters." Even when the painting was cleaned and restored in 1994, the Vatican chose to leave the draperies in place.

MANNERISM IN ART: A MATTER OF DECORUM

What are the stylistic characteristics of Mannerism?

As long as painting confined itself to depicting nonreligious subjects for nonreligious venues, it was more or less free to do as it pleased. Even the nudity of Michelangelo's Sistine Chapel figures would have been tolerable if painted in some less holy place. The Roman cardinal Cirillo Franco summed

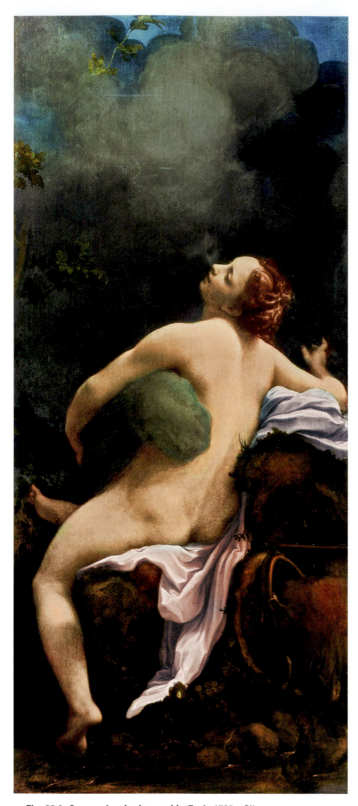

Fig. 20.6 Correggio, *Jupiter and Io*. Early 1530s. Oil on canvas, 69" × 29½". Kunsthistoriches Museum, Vienna. In the myth, Jupiter (Zeus) appears in a dream to Io, daughter of the king of Argos, and takes her to Lerna, a marsh and stream in the eastern Peloponnese, where he seduces her disguised as a cloud. The painting was created for the pleasure chamber of Federico Gonzaga in the Palazzo Ducale, Mantua.

up the general attitude in a letter: "I hold the painting and sculpture of Michelangelo to be a miracle of nature; but I would praise it so much more if, when he wants to show the supremacy of his art in all that posturing of naked limbs, and all those nudes … he did not paint it on the vault of the Pope's Chapel, but in a gallery, or some garden loggia." It was a matter of decorum, or propriety. What might be decorous and appropriate in a gallery or garden loggia was absolutely not so in a church.

Court Painting: Beyond the Church's Reach

In the private galleries of the princely courts throughout Europe, this more indecorous but highly inventive imagery thrived. Federico Gonzaga of Mantua, son of Isabella d'Este and nephew of Alphonso d'Este, commissioned a set of erotic paintings, perhaps intending to compete with the cycle decorating his uncle's palace at Ferrara. The indecorous embodiment of what the Council of Trent would label "the lascivious or impure," they were the work of the northern Italian artist Correggio (given name Antonio Allegri; ca. 1494–1534) and depicted the loves of Jupiter, or Zeus.

Jupiter and Io, painted in the early 1530s, is one of these (Fig. **20.6**). The painting illustrates Jupiter consummating his love for Io, a priestess of Hera (Jupiter's wife). Jupiter appears to Io in the guise of a cloud, his face barely visible behind her, kissing her lightly on the cheek. His bearlike arm embraces her as she abandons herself, quite visibly, to sensual pleasure. In addition to the unabashed sensuality of the presentation, the somewhat bizarre juxtaposition of Io's fully lit and well-defined body with Jupiter's dark and amorphous form is fully Mannerist in spirit.

This same theme occupied Titian in a series of paintings commissioned by Philip II of Spain in the late 1550s. Philip built a special room to house them in the Escorial (his palace complex near Madrid). In *The Rape of Europa*, Jupiter has assumed the form of a bull to abduct the nymph Europa as she adorns its horns with flowers (Fig. **20.7**). What most distinguishes the work is this Venetian artist's loose, sensual way of handling paint—a far cry from the crisp, even cold linearity of Correggio's Mannerist technique in the drapery beneath Io and in the porcelain-like quality of Io's skin. Titian's lush brushwork mirrors the sensuality of the image. And yet, in the way that Europa falls across the bull's back in a serpentine posture emphasized by the spiraling form of the red robe that flies from her hand, the painting demonstrates just how strongly Mannerist expression had entered the vocabulary of sixteenth-century painting as a whole. Like the Mannerists, the later Titian draws attention to his own virtuosity and skill, to the presence of his so-called **hand**, or stylistic signature through brushwork, in the composition. (The root of *maniera*, not coincidentally, is *mano*, "hand.")

The French court was as eager to look at sexually charged Mannerist paintings as its Spanish counterpart. In fact, in his later years, Francis I had an enormous taste for erotic art. Statesmen often catered to this taste in the form of gifts as a way to build alliances (see *Closer Look*, pages 672–673).

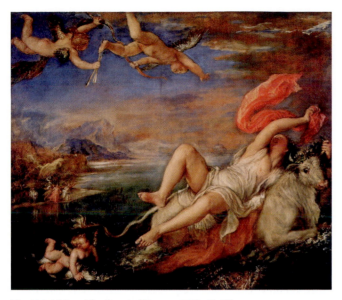

Fig. 20.7 Titian, *The Rape of Europa*. 1559–62. Oil on canvas, 5'9¼" × 7'8¼". Isabella Stewart Gardner Museum, Boston, MA. On the distant shore, Europa's maidservants gesture in vain at her abduction.

Mannerist Religious Painting

Even when Mannerists did find themselves working in a religious context, they tended to paint works designed to unsettle the viewer. When, for instance, Girolamo Francesco Maria Mazzola (1503–40), known as Parmigianino, was commissioned in 1535 to decorated a family chapel in the Church of Santa Maria dei Servi in his native Parma (where, not coincidentally, Correggio spent most of his career), the resulting Madonna and Child must have startled more than one viewer. Known as *The Madonna with the Long Neck* (Fig. 20.8), the painting seems, from the very first glance, oddly organized. How much space, for instance, is there between the Madonna and her attendants, compressed into the left three-quarters of the painting, and the figure of Saint Jerome reading a scroll in the distant, open space at the right? He appears to be standing just a short step below the Madonna's chair, but because Parmigianino has not accounted for the wide gap between the saint and the foreground group, the space in which he stands is visually almost totally incoherent. In fact, he must be standing far below her. We know that Saint Jerome's presence in the painting was a requirement of the commission—he was famous for his adoration of the Virgin, and Parmigianino had even painted a *Vision of Saint Jerome* in 1527, in which, oddly, the saint is sound asleep—but it is almost as if Parmigianino is scoffing at his patron's wishes, or at least acceding to them in an almost flippant way. The painting, it is worth noting, is over 7 feet high, and thus the miniature Saint Jerome contrasts even more dramatically with the greater-than-life-size Virgin who rises above him almost as if she is analogous in size to the column beside which he stands. Indeed, the Virgin's swanlike neck is a traditional conceit, found in medieval hymns, comparing her neck to

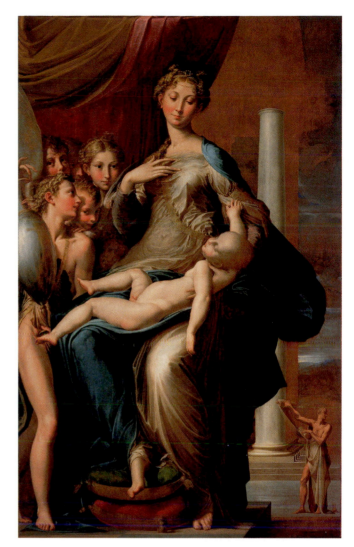

Fig. 20.8 Parmigianino, *The Madonna with the Long Neck*. ca. 1535. Oil on panel, 7'1" × 4'4". Galleria degli Uffizi, Florence. This work was begun in 1535, but the background space above Saint Jerome remained unfinished at Parmigianino's death in 1540.

The CONTINUING PRESENCE *of the* PAST

See John Ashbery's poem "Self-Portrait in a Convex Mirror," after Parmigianino's painting of the same name, at **MyArtsLab**

an ivory tower or column, a sort of vernacular expression of the Virgin as the allegorical representation of the Church.

But it is not only the spatial ambiguity of the painting that lends it such a sense of the unorthodox. The uncannily long-legged figure at the left inexplicably holds a long, oval amphora, as if he is offering it to the Virgin. It serves no real allegorical purpose. Rather, it defines the compositional principle upon which Parmigianino has organized his painting. Like the amphora, the Virgin's head is oval, and her entire body sweeps across the canvas forming the same oval shape. This oval is transected by the disproportionately long body of the Christ Child, who lies across the Virgin's lap in a sort of parody (or prefiguration,

Cosimo I de' Medici commissioned his Florentine-born court painter Agnolo Bronzino (b. Agnolo di Cosimo; 1503–72) to paint *Allegory with Venus and Cupid* as one of many gifts to Francis I of France. The king's taste for paintings of an erotic nature was well known. The painting was intended not only to appeal to his taste but also to demonstrate Florentine intellectual cleverness through an allegory that required unraveling. Here Venus (Aphrodite, to the Greeks, goddess of love and beauty) and her son, the adolescent Cupid (Eros, to the Greeks, god of love and sexual desire), engage in an incestuous embrace. The elaborate allegory is as fully Mannerist as the painting's complex and inventive poses. The governing theme of the painting is Luxuria (Sensual Indulgence). Exposure by Chronos (Time) and Oblivion (Forgetfulness) is the central action. The exact meaning of the figures behind the two illicit lovers is ambiguous. Works such as this decorated many of Francis I's palaces and chateaux, including the Chateau de Chambord.

Oblivion is imaged as a masklike empty shell, cut off behind the ears.

Pain, or perhaps the **"French Disease,"** the illness we know today as syphilis, which first appeared in epidemic proportions in Italy after the French invaded in 1494.

Luxuria, that is, **Sensual Indulgence**, is the governing theme of the painting. Its exposure by Chronos and Oblivion is the central action.

View the Closer Look for Bronzino's *Allegory with Venus and Cupid* on **MyArtsLab**

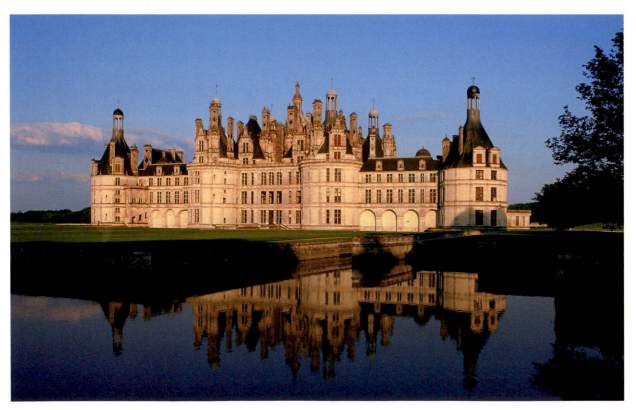

Chateau de Chambord, near Blois, France. 1519–47. Built by Francis I, Chambord is one of the finest examples of French Renaissance architecture, though the turret and pinnacles seem medieval. The chateau has 365 chimneys, a double spiral staircase, and a rooftop village, which housed servants and staff.

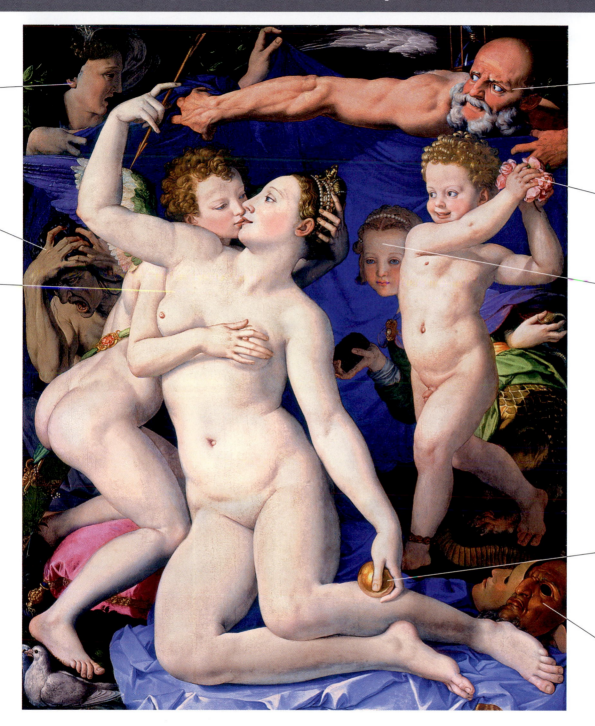

Chronos, or **Time**, with an hourglass on his back, draws a blue cloth behind Cupid and Venus to reveal the perverse behavior of mother and son.

Giuoco, or **Playfulness**, is about to throw rose petals over the central pair.

Pleasure, or perhaps **Fraud**, extends a honeycomb to the couple, but her body is that of a dragon whose tail curves below Giuoco's feet.

The **Golden Apple** was given to Venus by Paris when he judged her more beautiful than either Juno or Minerva. This decision supposedly initiated the Trojan War.

Deceit is represented as two masks.

Agnolo Bronzino, *Allegory with Venus and Cupid*. 1540s. Oil on panel, 61" × 56¼". National Gallery, London.

Something to Think About ...

How does Bronzino's use of color contribute to the meaning of the painting?

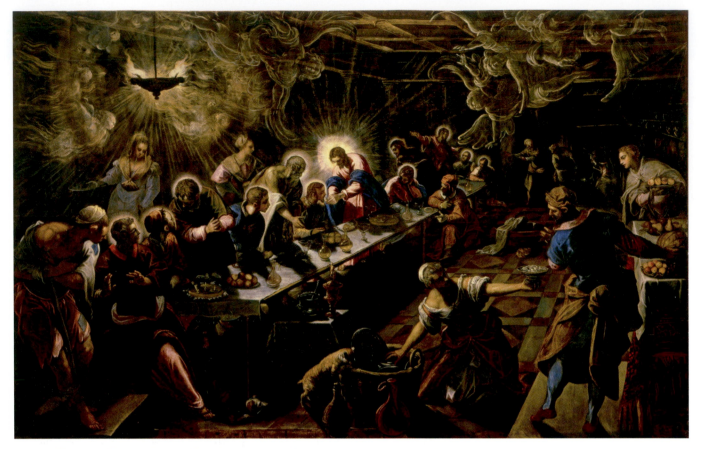

Fig. 20.9 Tintoretto, *The Last Supper.* **1592–94.** Oil on canvas, 12' × 18'8". Church of San Giorgio Maggiore, Venice. Notice how the smoke from the oil lamp seems to transform itself into angels, suggesting, as in the Eucharist, the transubstantiation of the natural world into the divine.

depending upon how one wants to read Parmigiano's intent) of the *Pietà* (see Fig. 15.3 in Chapter 15). In any event, the Virgin seems to withdraw from the child as if recognizing what will befall him. In one of the painting's oddest effects, Parmigianino has posed the Madonna so that, between her glance and the Christ Child's face, the folds of her blouse hang stiffly from a decidedly pointed nipple. Equally unsettling is the way that the Virgin's right foot seems to extend beyond the plane of the support into our own space, so that the gap between ourselves and the world of the painting mirrors the unaccounted-for space that lies between the Virgin and Saint Jerome.

The Last Supper (Fig. 20.9) by Jacopo Robusti (1518–94), known as Tintoretto, the "Little Dyer," because his father was a dyer in Venice, reinvents Leonardo's masterpiece (see Fig. 14.25 in Chapter 14). Instead of the frontal view of the scene that Leonardo gives us, Tintoretto's composition plunges in a dramatic diagonal to a vanishing point at the far right. The figures themselves are united in a continuous serpentine line that underscores their elongated features. There are two sources of light, the worldly flare of the oil lamp above the table, and the heavenly light that emanates from Christ himself as he offers bread and wine to an apostle, enacting what would become the Eucharist. The brushwork is quick and gestural, lending

the scene a sense of immediacy, as if it were sketched on the spot.

The most Mannerist element in the *Descent from the Cross* (Fig. 20.10) by Jacopo da Pontormo (1494–1557) is perhaps its color—pinks and baby blues bounded on the right by olive-green and yellow robes and on the left by a scarlet drapery. But, in addition, the crowd of figures in the painting seems to levitate upward around Christ's falling body, creating an odd tension around his death (and imminent Resurrection). Most odd of all is the figure in the foreground, holding Christ's legs on his shoulders. He wears a skin-tight pink blouse, shaded with a kind of transparent gray-green, and his upper body seems disproportionately large compared to his rather scrawny legs. Likewise his head seems too small for his body, as it turns toward us as if he is asking for help. It is worth suggesting that the unsettling aspects of the Mannerist style underscore the more unsettling aspects of religious faith.

The Rise of Women Artists in Northern Italy

In the last half of the sixteenth century, in the context of this widespread emphasis on inventiveness and originality, a number of women were encouraged to display their artistic virtuosity. In northern Italy, particularly, women seem on the painting. Directly above that, Sofonisba's face stares out at the viewer or, as the case may be, at her "actual" self, as Campi turns to look at her while he paints. This witty collapsing of the subject–object relationship (just who is subject to whose gaze?) is further amplified by the placement of Campi's hand directly over Anguissola's breast. (Compare the placement of Cupid's hand in Bronzino's *Allegory of Cupid and Venus*, in *Closer Look*, pages 672–673.) In other words, the painting implies intimacy even as it withholds it, a concept common in the poetry of the day and wholly fitting a young woman who served for 20 years (1559–80) as court painter and lady-in-waiting to Queen Elizabeth of Valois, wife of King Philip II of Spain. Above all, the painting embodies the spirit of inventiveness and originality (as well as the implicit sensuality) that distinguishes Mannerist art as a whole. It is perhaps not too much to suggest that the Mannerist belief in experimentation encouraged women artists to explore the possibilities suggested by their own talents.

Lavinia Fontana If there was one city in the sixteenth century where women were empowered to be artists, it was Bologna, perhaps not coincidentally the site of the oldest university in Europe, which by 1550 employed more than 80 professors. The University of Bologna admitted women to study. They could not pursue degrees in canon law or jurisprudence, but they could study history, literature, botany, and possibly astronomy. One of these was the painter Lavinia Fontana (1552–1614). The daughter of a painter,

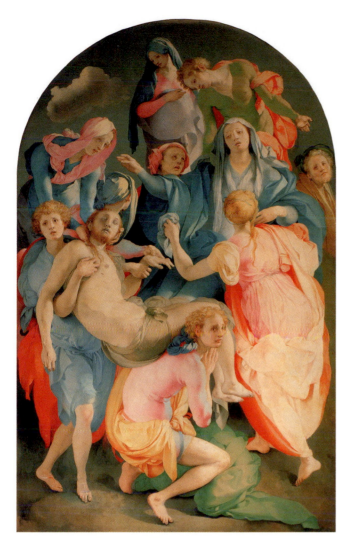

Fig. 20.10 Jacopo da Pontormo, *Descent from the Cross*. ca. 1525–28. Oil and tempera on wood panel, 10'3" × 6'4". Capponi Chapel, Church of Santa Felicità, Florence.

to have been better educated, and more likely to be artists, than women in the rest of Italy and Europe, perhaps due to the presence of powerful court ladies such as Isabella d'Este, Duchess of Mantua (see Chapter 15).

Sofonisba Anguissola One of the first truly important women painters of the Italian Renaissance was Sofonisba Anguissola (1527–1625), born in Cremona. Her father, a minor nobleman, made sure that all seven of his children, including his four daughters, received a humanist education, including training in art. Her father was so impressed by her talents that he wrote Michelangelo asking for his support, which in fact the older artist provided.

One of Anguissola's most interesting paintings is a portrait of her teacher, Bernardino Campi, painting a portrait of her (Fig. 20.11). It draws direct attention to the Mannerist *mano*, the "hand" of the artist. Anguissola's left hand, in the bottom center of the painting, holds a pair of gloves, a sign of her nobility. Directly above is Campi's hand, at work

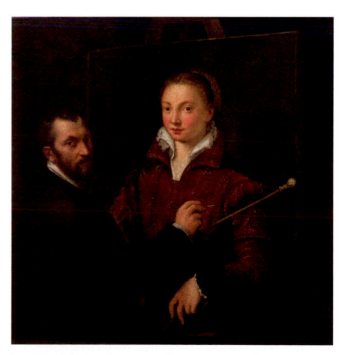

Fig. 20.11 Sofonisba Anguissola, *Bernardino Campi Painting Sofonisba Anguissola*. Late 1550s. Oil on canvas, 42½" × 43". Pinacoteca Nazionale, Siena. The stick with the cloth-covered end extending from Campi's right hand is a maulstick, a device used to steady the painter's hand. He holds the other end with his left hand and rests his painting hand upon it.

Mannerist Sculpture: Focus on Individual Genius

The belief that an artist's individual genius manifests itself in the virtuosity of the hand owes much to the influence of the Accademia del Disegno ("Academy of Design") in Florence, founded by Giorgio Vasari in 1562 under the patronage of Cosimo de' Medici. The Accademia emphasized history and theory, and Vasari's own *Lives of the Most Excellent Painters, Architects, and Sculptors*, published first in 1550 and then greatly expanded in a second edition in 1568, provided the historical framework. Vasari's *Lives* (see Chapter 14) focuses on individual creative genius, hardly surprising given the biographical framework of the text (see Reading 14.5 in Chapter 14).

Giovanni Bologna The practical result of Vasari's emphasis on individual genius was that the Accademia encouraged artists to develop their talents outside the constraints of tradition and convention. Genius, from Vasari's point of view, was most readily apparent in invention. And it was, in fact, simply to demonstrate his inventive skill that sculptor Giovanni Bologna (1529–1608) undertook to carve a triple *figura serpentinata* at the Accademia in 1579–83. Rising in a complex spiral to a height of nearly 13½ feet and lacking a single predominant view, Giovanni's larger-than-life-size masterpiece was simply a sculptural invention, without specific reference, let alone title (Fig. 20.13). But when Cosimo's son, Ferdinand I, decided to place it in the Loggia della Signoria, a focal point of Florentine life, and asked Giovanni to name it, the latter suggested that the woman might be Andromeda, wife of Perseus, a statue of whom already graced the Loggia della Signoria. Another member of the Academy, however, suggested the Sabines as a subject, and the sculpture has been known as *Rape of the Sabine Women* ever since. (According to legend, the founders of ancient Rome, unable to find wives among their neighbors, the Sabines, tricked the entire tribe into Rome for a festival and then took its women by force.) What mattered was not the piece's subject, however, but its sculptural genius in uniting three figures in a single successful spiral composition.

Benvenuto Cellini One of the most inventive sculptors of the day was not a member of Vasari's Accademia but a goldsmith by trade: Benvenuto Cellini (1500–71). It was his *Perseus* (Fig. 20.14) that was already in place under the left arch of the Loggia della Signoria when Giovanni Bologna's *Rape of the Sabine Women* was installed under the right arch in 1583. Cellini's figure holds the head of the slain Medusa, a monster so hideous that to look upon her meant death. Cosimo I commissioned the statue for the loggia as an emblem of the Medici's role in saving the city from tyranny, as inscriptions on the base affirm. Working in the tradition of Michelangelo's well-muscled *David* (see Fig. 14.30 in Chapter 14), Cellini adds a full-blown Mannerist sensuality. The force of the extended left arm, which raises the monster's severed head in triumph, counters the

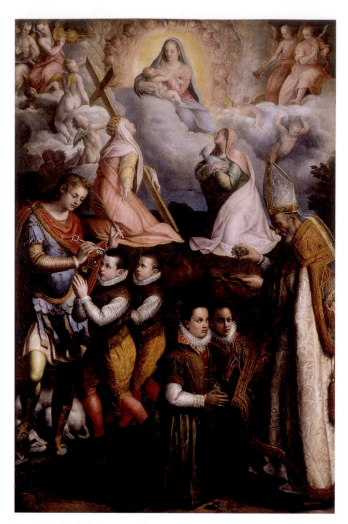

Fig. 20.12 Lavinia Fontana, *Consecration of the Virgin*. 1599. Oil on canvas, 9'2¼" × 6'2¼". Musée des Beaux-Arts, Marseille. Fontana's skill as a portraitist, evident in her treatment of the children here, helped to make her the most sought-after portrait artist in her native Bologna and, after 1604, portraitist to the court of Pope Paul V.

she achieved an international reputation by the end of the sixteenth century, painting more than 150 known works. The Spanish prelate in Rome commissioned her to paint her own self-portrait for his collection. It was meant to hang beside a self-portrait by Sofonisba Anguissola.

Among Fontana's greatest works is an altarpiece commissioned by the Gnetti family of Bologna, a *Consecration of the Virgin*. Instead of including its patrons, Fontana painted their children (Fig. 20.12). It is a fully Mannerist work. Note the elongated features of Saint Donnino, at the left, handing a key to the two boys; the expressive features of the children, each of whom seems occupied with his or her own individual thoughts; and, especially, the serpentine pose of the angel who holds the top of the cross. The Church had called for a high moral tone in religious art, and Fontana's altarpiece, with its emphasis on prayer and devotion and the familial continuity of the Church's flock, fulfilled that desire. Above all, especially in celebrating the piety of the children, it is a completely decorous work.

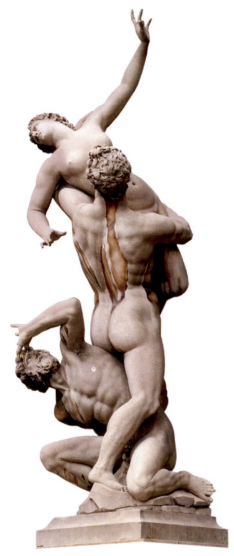

Fig. 20.13 Giovanni Bologna, *Rape of the Sabine Women*. 1579–83. Marble, height 13'5½". Loggia della Signoria, Florence. Giovanni was actually a Flemish-born artist named Jean de Boulogne who became better known by his Italian name after settling in Florence in 1557.

Classical *contrapposto* pose, with Perseus' weight entirely on the right foot pressing into Medusa's body.

Cellini was a notorious figure who led an openly bisexual life. He once gilded the body of an assistant and dressed up another as a young woman to accompany him to a party. He was imprisoned in 1557 for committing repeated acts of sodomy with another of his apprentices, who probably reported the offenses to authorities in retaliation for having been fired. Sentenced to four years in prison, and stripped of the privilege of ever holding public office, Cellini spent only a little over a month in jail before the sentence was reduced to confinement in his own house. There he began work on his *Life*, one of the first secular autobiographies ever written. It was published in 1728, over 150 years after his death. Publicly disgraced, Cellini clearly intended to use this work of literature to rescue his reputation, or at least to celebrate his audacity. The narrative is anything but tame:

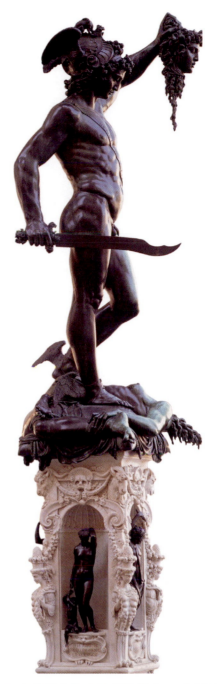

Fig. 20.14 Benvenuto Cellini, *Perseus*. 1545–54. Bronze, height 10'6". Loggia della Signoria, Florence. The sculpture depicts the moment when the slain Medusa's blood turns to coral as it pours from her body and neck, depicted in elaborate, twisting forms by Cellini.

sword fights, duels, murders, seduction scenes, quarrels, and gossip fill its pages. Interspersed are descriptions of the complex relationship between artist and patron in the sixteenth century, which makes the *Life* a very important document for those interested in cultural history. At one point, Cellini describes making the model for an intricately sculptural and inventive saltcellar (Fig. **20.15**) that was initially intended for the cardinal of Ferrara but was later executed for King Francis I, whose taste for Mannerist art, especially of an erotic nature, as noted, was great (**Reading 20.2**):

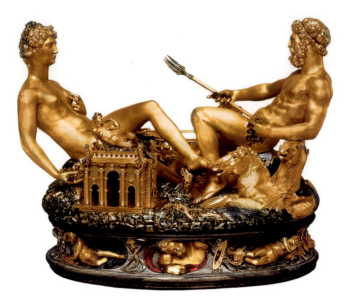

Fig. 20.15 Benvenuto Cellini, *Saltcellar of Francis I*. 1539–43. Gold with enamel, 9¼" × 13⅛". Kunsthistorisches Museum, Vienna. This is the only known surviving example of Cellini's extraordinary work as a goldsmith.

📖 **Read** a document on the *Saltcellar of Francis I* on **MyArtsLab**

While Cellini later changed the positions of the hands and what they were holding, the description, which must have been written some 20 years after the fact, is accurate. When the cardinal saw the model, he told Cellini: "Unless you make it for the King, to whom I mean to take you, I do not think that you will make it for another man alive." Subsequently, the two traveled to Francis I's royal residence and showed the model to the king, who quickly ordered the gold necessary for its completion. The erotic content of the *Saltcellar* was possible only because the work was a private commission destined for use at the king's own table, where public decorum was not an issue.

INQUISITION AND INNOVATION

What was the Inquisition and how did it affect the arts?

The liberty to invent is the hallmark of art and architecture throughout the middle years of the sixteenth century and the defining characteristic of Mannerist art. But if invention led to the kind of indecorous images produced in the courts of Europe, the Church could not tolerate it. Nor could it tolerate religious beliefs that did not strictly follow Church doctrine. Like Lavinia Fontana, artists working on religious subjects had to discover ways to blend their Mannerist style with properly decorous religious imagery. Muslims and Jews living in Catholic countries had to convert or be expelled. And Catholics inspired by a different kind of spirituality than the Church recognized were deemed a special threat and suffered greatly under repression or worse.

Art under the Italian Inquisition: Veronese

A clear example of the need to use invention decorously in art is provided by the fate of a *Last Supper*, now known as the *Feast in the House of Levi*, by the Venetian artist Paolo Veronese (1528–88). Veronese was born Paolo Cagliari and nicknamed after the city of his birth, Verona (Fig. **20.16**). As early as 1542, Pope Paul III had initiated a Roman **Inquisition**—an official inquiry into possible heresy—and in 1573, Veronese was called before the Inquisition to answer charges that his *Last Supper*, painted with life-size figures for a Dominican monastery in Venice, was heretical in its inappropriate treatment of the subject matter. His testimony before the tribunal illuminates the aesthetic and religious concerns of the era (**Reading 20.3**):

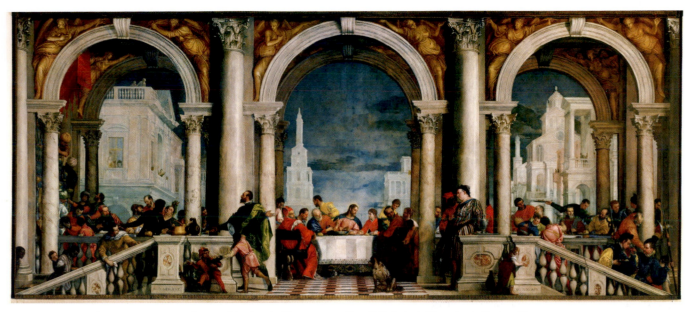

Fig. 20.16 Paolo Veronese, *Feast in the House of Levi*. 1573. Oil on canvas, 18' × 42'. Galleria dell'Accademia, Venice. After his testimony before the Inquisition, Veronese made it clear that his "new" source for the painting was the feast in the house of Levi by citing the biblical reference on the balustrade.

View the Closer Look for *Feast in the House of Levi* on **MyArtsLab**

INQUISITOR: In this Supper which you made for SS. Giovanni e Paolo, what is the significance of the man whose nose is bleeding?

VERONESE: I intended to represent a servant whose nose was bleeding because of some accident.

INQUISITOR: What is the significance of those armed men dressed as Germans, each with a halberd in his hand?

VERONESE: We painters take the same license the poets and the jesters take and I have represented these two halberdiers, one drinking and the other eating nearby on the stairs. They are placed there so that they might be of service because it seemed to me fitting, according to what I have been told, that the master of the house, who was great and rich, should have such servants.

INQUISITOR: And that man dressed as a buffoon with a parrot on his wrist, for what purpose did you paint him on that canvas?

VERONESE: For ornament, as is customary ...

INQUISITOR: Are not the decorations which you painters are accustomed to add to paintings or pictures supposed to be suitable and proper to the subject and the principal figures or are they for pleasure—simply what comes to your imagination without any discretion or judiciousness?

VERONESE: I paint pictures as I see fit and as well as my talent permits.

INQUISITOR: Does it seem fitting at the Last Supper of the Lord to paint buffoons, drunkards, Germans, dwarfs and similar vulgarities?

VERONESE: No, milords.

The tribunal concluded that Veronese should "improve and correct" the painting in three months' time or face penalties. But rather than change the painting, Veronese simply changed the painting's title to *Feast in the House of Levi*. This title refers to a biblical passage: "Levi gave a great banquet for him [Jesus] in his house, and a large crowd of tax collectors and others were at table with them" (Luke 5:29). Through this strategy Veronese could justify the artistic invention in his crowded scene.

The Spanish Inquisition

In Spain, the Church implemented the Inquisition in 1478, much earlier than in Italy, but not as a method of enforcing the strictures of the Counter-Reformation. Rather, it was used as a tool to expel or convert all non-Christian Spaniards. Its first target was the Muslims of Andalusia, the Islamic emirate in the south of Spain. In 1492, after the armies of Ferdinand and Isabella had finally succeeded in taking the Nasrid stronghold of Granada (see Chapter 9), the Church encouraged Muslims to convert by means of friendly persuasion, permitting them to retain the Mudéjar language and culture, and to use Arabic during religious services. By 1500, however, the clergy had begun to impose Christianity upon the Muslim population by force, systematically baptizing Muslims in mass ceremonies. Within the year, all Muslims were officially considered Christian—*moriscos*, they were called—and by royal decree in October 1501, a huge bonfire destroyed Arabic books in Granada, signaling the symbolic if not actual end of Muslim al-Andalus.

The second target of the Spanish Inquisition was Spaniards of Jewish origin who had converted to Christianity, known as *conversos*. Since 1480, the Inquisition had persecuted Jews whose conversion they deemed suspect and had executed scores of them on the charge of heresy. The fall of Granada inspired the inquisitors to bring about the conversion of all Jews. So on March 31, 1492, Ferdinand and Isabella issued an edict of expulsion, giving the Jews of Castile and Aragon until July 31 to accept baptism or leave the country. Over half the Jews of Spain chose to leave. (Over the course of the previous century, many thousands had already emigrated, as Spanish Christendom had become intolerant of their presence. In Barcelona, where more than 4,000 Jews had lived the century before, only 20 Jewish families remained in 1492.) The forcible conversion and expulsion of the *conversos* and *moriscos* reinforced the image of the Spanish monarchy as champions of Christianity, a role that both Charles V and Philip II would take very seriously.

The persecutions of the Inquisition were complicated further by the rise, in the sixteenth century, of a brand of religious mysticism that threatened the Church from within. The *alumbrados*, or "illuminated ones," nuns, monks, and priests lit by the Holy Spirit, practiced an extremely individualistic and private brand of faith, which led to accusations that they also claimed to have no need of the sacraments of the Church. The *alumbrados* were therefore susceptible to charges of heresy. Chief among them were the Carmelite nun Teresa of Ávila (1515–82) and the Carmelite friar Juan de la Cruz (1542–91), known as John of the Cross. Teresa was from a *converso* family that lived in Ávila, the medieval center of Jewish mystical thought. Dissatisfied with the worldliness that had crept into her Carmelite order, Teresa campaigned to reform it, founding the Discalced (or shoeless) Carmelites, dedicated to absolute poverty and the renunciation of all property. Between 1567 and 1576, she traveled across Spain, founding Discalced convents and a reform convent for Carmelite men. Juan de la Cruz was one of the first two members, and the two would become close friends. Juan's powers as a teacher, preacher, and poet served to strengthen the movement. Teresa's writings, including an autobiography and *The Way to Perfection*, both written before 1567, and *The Interior Castle*, written in 1577, all describe the ascent of the soul to union with the Holy Spirit in four basic stages. In the final of these stages, "devotion of ecstasy or rapture," consciousness of being in the body disappears and the spirit finds itself alternating between the ecstatic throes of a sweet, happy pain and a fearful, glowing fire.

In 1574, Teresa was denounced to the Inquisition as a restless wanderer who under the pretext of religion lived a life of dissipation. As a result, in 1576, she was confined in a convent. Juan de la Cruz suffered an even worse fate. Calced Carmelites arrested him in Toledo on the night of December 3, 1577. They held him in solitary confinement and lashed him before the community on a weekly basis until he escaped eight months later. Among the great works written following his escape is *The Dark Night of the Soul*, a book-length commentary on his eight-stanza poem "The

Dark Night" (see **Reading 20.4**, pages 683–684), itself an account of the author's mystical union with God.

The Counter-Reformation and Mannerism United: El Greco in Spain

The moral strictures of the Inquisition and the mysticism of the *alumbrados* are recognizable in the art of one of the most original sixteenth-century painters, El Greco, "The Greek" (born Domenico Theotokopulos; 1541–1614). He trained as an icon painter in his native Crete, in those days a Venetian possession. In 1567, he went to Venice, then three years later to Rome, and in 1576 to Spain, where he soon developed a style that wedded Mannerism with the elongated, iconic figures of his Byzantine training. He used painting to convey an intensely expressive spirituality.

Painted at the turn of the sixteenth century, El Greco's *Resurrection* is decorous to the extent that draperies carefully conceal all inappropriate nudity (Fig. 20.17). The poses of the writhing Roman soldiers who surround the vision of the triumphant Christ are as artificial and contrived as any in Mannerist art. The verticality of the composition, popular since the time of Correggio, mirrors the elongated anatomies of El Greco's figures. And yet, El Greco's style is unique, singular in the angularity of its draperies, in the drama of the representation, and in its overall composition. The Roman soldiers rise and fall in *figura serpentinata* poses around Christ like petals on a blossom, with Christ himself as the flower's stamen. If Christ's sexuality has been repressed, the effect of his presence on the soldiers, who swoon in near-hysterical ecstasy, is unmistakable. Above all, this painting celebrates raw physicality, even as it presents the greatest spiritual mystery of the Christian faith. Here the aspirations of the Counter-Reformation and the inventiveness of the Mannerist style are fully united, as they would come to be in the Baroque art of the seventeenth century.

Cervantes and the Picaresque Tradition

In the last half of the sixteenth century, a literary genre originated in Spain that celebrated inventiveness, particularly suited to Spanish taste, and had a strong effect on literary events in the seventeenth century. This was the **picaresque novel**, a genre of prose that narrates, in a realistic way, the adventures of a *picaro*, a roguish hero of low social rank living by his wits in a corrupt society. The first book to introduce the picaresque tradition in Spain was *Lazarillo de Tormes*, published anonymously in 1554. Raised by beggars and thieves, Lazarillo is a frankly common man, particularly bent on ridiculing and satirizing the Catholic Church and its officials. For that reason and probably because its hero was not highborn, the Spanish crown banned the book and listed it in the Index of Forbidden Books of the Inquisition. A much more complex *picaro* and undoubtedly the greatest hero of the picaresque tradition in Spanish literature is Don Quixote, the creation of novelist, poet, and playwright Miguel de Cervantes (1547–1616).

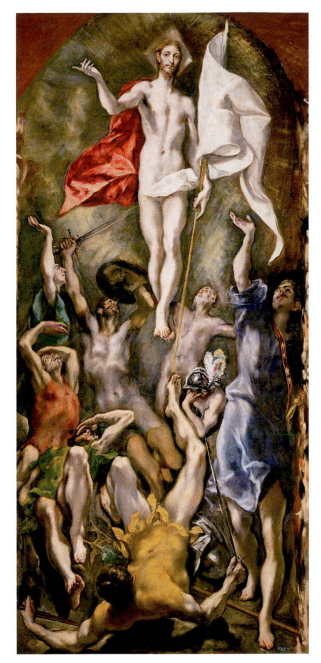

Fig. 20.17 El Greco, *Resurrection*. 1597–1604. Oil on canvas, 9'1¼" × 4'2". Museo del Prado, Madrid. The image was probably painted for the Colegio de Doña Maria, Madrid, and paired with a depiction of the Pentecost, the descent of the Holy Spirit upon the apostles on the seventh Sunday after Easter.

Cervantes was himself a hero in the army of Philip II at the Battle of Lepanto in 1569 (where Spain defeated the Turks, gaining control of the Mediterranean), a captive of Barbary pirates for five years (1575–80), a supplier of provisions for the ill-fated Spanish Armada (see Chapter 19), and several times imprisoned for debt. In 1605, when he was 58 years of age, he published *The Ingenious Hidalgo Don Quixote de la Mancha*. (A *hidalgo* is a member of the lower Spanish nobility, generally exempt from paying taxes but not necessarily owning any real property.) A second part

followed a decade later, a year before his death. The novel is more familiarly known today simply as *Don Quixote*.

Don Quixote is often considered the first great modern novel. It is set in La Mancha, a great arid plain southeast of Madrid. Into this landscape Cervantes places his two principal characters, Don Quixote and his servant Sancho Panza. Don Quixote is obsessed with the old stories of romance literature about questing knights and decides to become one himself. Cervantes presents him as a highly satiric recreation of the conquistadors, whose exploits in the Americas were, Cervantes understood, similarly inspired by a thirst for romantic adventuring. Don Quixote's enthusiasm and self-deception unintentionally produce comic results. Sancho Panza, on the other hand, is a down-to-earth realist who believes the Don to be a bit crazy but plays along and accompanies him as squire on his adventures, hoping to get rich. The two search for the Don's ideal—and imaginary—lady, Dulcinea. Sancho convinces the Don that she is a plain, poorly dressed peasant riding a donkey and that he cannot recognize her for the beauty he knows Dulcinea to be because his vision has been bewitched by an enchantress. In other scenes, the Don mistakes a common country inn for a castle, a herd of sheep for a pagan army at battle with Christian forces, and two windmills for battling giants sent by an evil enchanter. This last is his most famous adventure, and in it Don Quixote, ever the noble conquistador, proceeds to tilt at the two windmills with his lance (see **Reading 20.5**, pages 684–685).

All of these episodes are parables of the relation between illusion and reality, art and life. They anticipate the psychological complexities that will come to define the novel as a form. Don Quixote cannot reconcile his dreams with the realities of life itself, and his comic adventuring becomes his tragic fate. Above all, Don Quixote's adventures underscore both the marvelous possibilities that come from unleashing the imagination and the dangers of leaving the world behind.

Because in most of his adventures the Don attempts to apply the simple morality of a knight to situations in which more complex issues are at hand, the novel satirizes chivalric romances, a literary genre that had been popular for more than a century in both written and oral form. But in the prologue to his novel, Cervantes states other, related goals. He says that he wanted to give a picture of real life and manners, and to do so in clear language. This was a departure from chivalric fiction. *Don Quixote* is innovative in using everyday speech in dialogue (for which Cervantes was acclaimed by his contemporaries), creating vivid and complex portraits of both his main and subordinate characters, and presenting the narrative in a solemn style, free from affectation and in delicate juxtaposition with the comic scenes. The extent of Cervantes's achievement can be gauged, in part, by the fact that his picaresque hero so captured the imagination of his time and of future generations that he gave his name to the adjective *quixotic*, meaning "idealistic and impractical," and inspired the expression "tilting at windmills" to describe fighting illusory battles.

The Frenzy of Inspiration

Not long before the death of Lavinia Fontana in 1614, Bolognese medalist Felice Antonio Casoni struck a portrait medal in her honor. Fontana was, by then, a civic celebrity, and while on one side of the medal Casoni depicted her in profile, in a dignified, even matronly pose, on the reverse, he shows her in the act of painting, her hair extending behind her in a frenzy of curls, the very image of divine inspiration (Fig. **20.18**). Fontana holds in her left hand a maulstick (a rod used as a support or rest in order to steady the artist's brush), in her right a brush, a perfect representation of the Renaissance figure of *La Pittura*, the very art of painting itself.

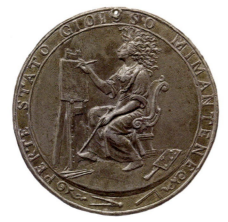

Fig. 20.18 Felice Maria Casoni, *Portrait Medal of Lavinia Fontana*. 1611. Diameter 2½". © The Trustees of the British Museum.

La Pittura is the feminine noun for "the picture" in Italian, and so it is hardly surprising that painting should be represented as a woman. Even Vasari represented *La Pittura* as a woman in his cycle of frescoes on the liberal arts in the main room of his own home in Arezzo in 1542. But it is surprising that a living woman artist would take on the symbolic figure's identity by the early years of the seventeenth century. Casoni's medal is testimony not only to Fontana's reputation as a painter, but also to a gradual shift in Western culture to the acceptance of women as meaningful contributors to the vitality of Western civilization.

Within 20 years, when new cultural currents were flowing through Europe, another Italian painter would paint herself as *La Pittura* (Fig. **20.19**). Her name was Artemesia Gentileschi (1593–1652/3), and like Fontana, she was the daughter of a respected painter. Though her hair is not nearly so unkempt as Fontana's in her medal, the curled strands that fall away to the side of her face are meant to suggest the same intensity of inspiration. Hanging from her neck is a pendant that symbolizes Imitation—or, from the Greek, ***mimesis***, the art of faithful representation. The

effects of light that modulate the color of her dress, with their contrast of the complementary colors red and green, demonstrate her skill as an artist. Above all, her intensity, her apparent obliviousness to the viewer's gaze—even though, as we know, she has designed the composition intentionally to create this effect—marks the greatest transformation represented by the painting.

Gentileschi's *La Pittura* depicts the moment of inspiration, the moment of the individual genius in command of all its resources, that writers like Vasari had argued was the very definition of sixteenth-century art. To find that moment in the hands of a woman, to recognize the audacity and sense of self-worth that allowed her to so depict herself, is to witness a moment that would not find its full expression until the twentieth century, when Gentileschi would serve as an inspiration for women struggling for recognition in the modern art world. ■

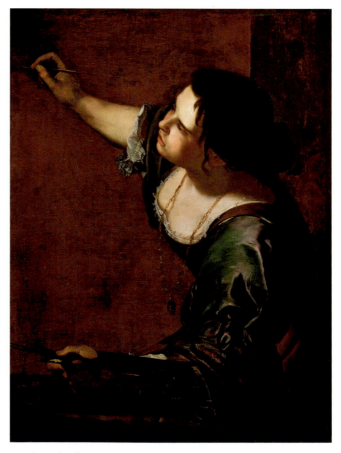

Fig. 20.19 Artemesia Gentileschi, *Self-Portrait as the Allegory of Painting*. 1630. Oil on canvas, 35¼" × 29". The Royal Collection.

🔍 **View** the Closer Look for *Self-Portrait as the Allegory of Painting* on **MyArtsLab**

20.1 Explain the rationale behind the Counter-Reformation and the Council of Trent's effect on the arts.

The Counter-Reformation was the Roman Catholic Church's conscious attempt to reform itself in reaction to the Protestant Reformation. To that end and under the urging of Charles V and Francis I, Pope Paul III convened the Council of Trent in 1545. What guiding principles did the Council adopt? How did these principles affect art and music?

20.2 Discuss the new stylistic directions introduced by Michelangelo in his late work.

The edicts of the Council of Trent did not constrain Michelangelo, who introduced a different direction in sixteenth-century art. With its virtuoso manipulations and distortions, his new style is already evident in the inventiveness of his design for the stairway of the Laurentian Library, and anticipates what has come to be called Mannerism. In what ways does his sculpture of the *Pietà*, or his painting of the *Last Judgment*, exaggerate the Classicizing tendencies of the Renaissance?

20.3 Define Mannerism and describe its stylistic features.

Many had found the nudity in Michelangelo's *Last Judgment* inappropriate for religious painting, but this lack of decorum was acceptable outside a religious context. In the private galleries of the princely courts throughout Europe, a more lascivious imagery thrived. How would you describe this less decorous Mannerist style? If words like "surprising," "odd," and "unorthodox" seem appropriate, how do they manifest themselves in more formal ways, in both painting and sculpture? How does the style manifest itself in religious painting? Why do invention and experimentation come to be so valued in Mannerist art? How did women artists respond to the possibilities offered by Mannerism?

20.4 Examine how the Inquisition affected the arts.

In the art of Veronese and El Greco, Mannerist inventiveness sought to accommodate itself to the more conventional aspirations of the Counter-Reformation and to the Roman Catholic Church's Inquisition in Italy and Spain, dedicated to rooting out heresy. How did Veronese accommodate the Inquisition? The Inquisition prosecuted the Spanish mystics Teresa of Ávila and Juan de la Cruz because of their intensely personalized faith. Nevertheless, both composed written accounts of their mystical unions with the divine. Finally, in what many consider the Western world's first great novel, *Don Quixote*, the writer Miguel de Cervantes captured the complexities of the era in a picaresque character whose imagination isolates him from reality. How would you define the picaresque?

✔ **Study** and **review** on **MyArtsLab**

READINGS

READING 20.4

from John of the Cross, *The Dark Night of the Soul*, "The Dark Night"

The Carmelite friar John of the Cross was canonized in 1726. *The Dark Night of the Soul* describes, in John's words, "the method followed by the soul in its journey upon the spiritual road to the attainment of the perfect union of love with God, to the extent that is possible in this life." One of the primary works of Spanish mysticism, the book consists almost entirely of a line-by-line, sometimes word-by-word, exposition of the poem that opens it and that is reproduced here, "The Dark Night."

1 One dark night,
fired with love's urgent longings
— ah, the sheer grace!—
I went out unseen,
my house being now all stilled.

2 In darkness, and secure,
by the secret ladder, disguised,
—ah, the sheer grace!—
in darkness and concealment,
my house being now all stilled.   10

3 On that glad night
in secret, for no one saw me,
nor did I look at anything
with no other light or guide
than the one that burned in my heart.

4 This guided me
more surely than the light of noon
to where he was awaiting me
—him I knew so well—
there in a place where no one appeared.   20

5 O guiding night!
O night more lovely than the dawn!
O night that has united
the Lover with his beloved,
transforming the beloved in her Lover.

6 Upon my flowering breast,
which I kept wholly for him alone,
there he lay sleeping,
and I caressing him
there in a breeze from the fanning cedars.   30

7 When the breeze blew from the turret,
as I parted his hair,
it wounded my neck
with its gentle hand,
suspending all my senses.

8 I abandoned and forgot myself,
laying my face on my Beloved;
all things ceased; I went out from myself,
leaving my cares
forgotten among the lilies.   40

READING CRITICALLY

This poem is part of a long tradition in Western literature in which spiritual love is metaphorically fused with physical love. What other instances of this have we so far encountered? Can you usefully compare this to one or two earlier works?

READING 20.5

from Miguel de Cervantes, *Don Quixote*, Part 1, Chapter 8 (1605)

No excerpt, let alone one so brief as the single chapter that follows, can begin to convey the complex emotional world of *Don Quixote*. The novel begins in the burlesque, almost slapstick mode embodied by the tilting-at-windmills episode included here but slowly turns into a moving story of two friends whose unfolding relationship reaches levels of profundity by the story's end. Tradition has it that Cervantes began his novel in prison in Seville in 1597, where he was serving time for shortages in his accounts. Whether true or not, soon after his release, he was hard at work on his novel, and Part 1 was published in 1605. It became an immediate best seller and was quickly translated into French, Italian, and other European languages. Cervantes had always planned a sequel, and by 1614 had written 59 chapters of it, when a pirated continuation appeared. This caused him to rush the work, in which he attacked the "false Quixote," into press. Part 2 also met with great success. The complete work amounts to what many consider the first great novel in Western literature.

Chapter 8

Of the good success which the valorous Don Quixote had in the dreadful and never-before-imagined adventure of the windmills, with other events worthy to be recorded.

As they were thus discoursing, they perceived some thirty or forty windmills that are in that plain; and as soon as Don Quixote espied them, he said to his squire:

"Fortune disposes our affairs better than we ourselves could have desired; look yonder, friend Sancho Panza, where you may discover somewhat more than thirty monstrous giants, with whom I intend to fight, and take away all their lives; with whose spoils we will begin to enrich ourselves; for it is lawful war, and doing God good service to take away so wicked a generation from off the face of the earth."   10

"What giants?" said Sancho Panza.

"Those you see yonder," answered his master, "with those long arms; for some of them are wont to have them almost of the length of two leagues."

"Consider, Sir," answered Sancho, "that those which appear yonder, are not giants, but windmills; and what seem to be arms are the sails, which, whirled about by the wind, make the millstone go."

"One may easily see," answered Don Quixote, "that you are not versed in the business of adventures: they are giants; and, if you are afraid, get aside and pray, whilst I engage with them in a fierce and unequal combat."

And so saying, he clapped spurs to Rosinante, without minding the cries his squire sent after him, assuring him that those he went to assault were without all doubt, windmills, and not giants. But he was so fully possessed that they were giants, that he neither heard the outcries of his squire Sancho, nor yet discerned what they were, though he was very near them, but went on, crying out aloud:

"Fly not, ye cowards and vile caitiffs; for it is a single knight who assaults you."

Now the wind rose a little, and the great sails began to move: which Don Quixote perceiving, he said:

"Well, though you should move more arms than the giant Briareus, you shall pay for it."

And so saying, and recommending himself devoutly to his lady Dulcinea, beseeching her to succour him in the present danger, being well covered with his buckler, and setting his lance in the rest, he rushed on as fast as Rosinante could gallop, and attacked the first mill before him; and running his lance into the sail, the wind whirled it about with so much violence that it broke the lance to shivers, dragging horse and rider after it, and tumbling them over and over on the plain, in very evil plight. Sancho Panza hastened to his assistance, as fast as his ass could carry him; and when he came up to him, he found him not able to stir; so violent was the blow he and Rosinante had received in falling.

"God save me," quoth Sancho, "did not I warn you to have a care of what you did, for that they were nothing but windmills; and nobody could mistake them, but one that had the like in his head."

"Peace, friend Sancho," answered Don Quixote; "for matters of war are, of all others, most subject to continual mutations. Now I verily believe, and it is most certainly so, that the sage Friston who stole away my chamber and books, has metamorphosed these giants into windmills on purpose to deprive me of the glory of vanquishing them, so great is the enmity he bears me; but when he has done his worst, his wicked arts will avail but little against the goodness of my sword."

"God grant it, as he can," answered Sancho Panza; and, helping him to rise, he mounted him again upon Rosinante, who was half shoulder-slipped.

And discoursing of the late adventure, they followed the road that led to the pass of Lápice; for there, Don Quixote said, they could not fail to meet with many and various adventures, it being a great thoroughfare; and yet he went on very melancholy for want of his lance; and, speaking of it to his squire, he said:

"I remember to have read that a certain Spanish knight, called Diego Perez de Vargas, having broken his sword in fight, tore off a huge branch or limb from an oak, and performed such wonders with it that day, and dashed out the brains of so many Moors, that he was surnamed Machuca; and from that day forward, he and his descendants bore the names of Vargas and Machuca. I tell you this because from the first oak or crabtree we meet, I mean to tear such another limb, at least as good as that; and I purpose and resolve to do such feats with it, that you shall deem yourself most fortunate in meriting to behold them;

and to be an eye-witness of things which can scarcely be believed."

"God's will be done," quoth Sancho: "I believe all just as you say, Sir: but, pray, set yourself upright in your saddle; for you seem to me to ride sideling, occasioned, doubtless, by your being so sorely bruised by the fall."

"It is certainly so," answered Don Quixote, "and if I do not complain of pain, it is because knights-errant are not allowed to complain of any wound whatever, though their entrails came out at it."

"If it be so, I have nothing to reply," answered Sancho; "but God knows I should be glad to hear your worship complain, when anything ails you. As for myself, I must complain of the least pain I feel, unless this business of not complaining be understood to extend to the squires of knights-errant."

Don Quixote could not forbear smiling at the simplicity of his squire, and told him he might complain whenever, and as much as he pleased, with or without cause, having never yet read anything to the contrary in the laws of chivalry.

Sancho put him in mind that it was time to dine. His master answered, that at present he had no need; but that he might eat whenever he thought fit. With this licence, Sancho adjusted himself the best he could upon his beast; and taking out what he carried in his wallet, he jogged on eating, behind his master, very leisurely, and now and then lifted the bottle to his mouth with so much relish, that the best-fed victualler of Malaga might have envied him. And whilst he went on in this manner, repeating his draughts, he thought no more of the promises his master had made him; nor did he think it any toil, but rather a recreation to go in quest of adventures, though never so perilous. In fine, they passed that night among some trees, and from one of them Don Quixote tore a withered branch, that might serve him in some sort for a lance, and fixed it to the iron head or spear of that which was broken. All that night Don Quixote slept not a wink, ruminating on his lady Dulcinea, in conformity to what he had read in his books where the knights are wont to pass many nights together, without closing their eyes, in forests and deserts, entertaining themselves with the remembrance of their mistresses. Not so did Sancho pass the night; whose stomach being full (and not of dandelion-water) he made but one sleep of it: and if his master had not roused him, neither the beams of the sun that darted full in his face, nor the melody of the birds, which in great numbers most cheerfully saluted the approach of the new day, could have awaked him. At this uprising he took a swig at his bottle, and found it much lighter than the evening before; which grieved his very heart, for he did not think they were in the way to remedy that defect very soon. Don Quixote would not break his fast; for, as it is said, he resolved to subsist upon savoury remembrances. … Lápice, which they discovered about three in the afternoon. …

READING CRITICALLY

How would you describe Don Quixote and Sancho Panza's relationship in this early episode from the novel?

INDEX

PHOTO CREDITS

Chapter 11

11.1 © Ian Griffiths/Robert Harding World Imagery/Corbis; **11.2** © Wolfgang Kaehler/Corbis; **11.4** © Jean-Pierre De Mann/Robert Harding World Imagery; **11.5** Photo: Galileo Picture Services LLC, NY; pages 370 and 371, © Corbis; **11.6** Rossi & Rossi; **11.7** © Keren Su/Corbis; **11.8** © Neil Grant/Alamy; **11.10** Andrew Gunners/Digital Vision/Getty Images; **11.11** Philip Baird/Anthroarcheart.org; **11.12** Photo: Bruce White. © 2013. Image © The Metropolitan Museum of Art/Art Resource/Scala, Florence; **11.13** © Sakamoto Photo Research Laboratory/Corbis. All Rights Reserved; **11.14** Courtesy of Japanese Art/Laurence King Publishing Ltd.; **11.15** The Tokugawa Reimeikai Foundation/DNP; **11.16** © 2013. Photo Art Resource/Scala, Florence; **11.18** © Dirk Bakker/The Bridgeman Art Library; **11.21** Image © The Metropolitan Museum of Art/Art Resource/Scala, Florence; **11.22** © Kazuyoshi Nomachi/HAGA/The Image Works; **11.23** Werner Forman Archive; **11.24** © Colin Haskins/Alamy; **11-25** Werner Forman Archive; **11.26** © Photo Scala, Florence; **11.27** © MJ Photography/Alamy; **11.28** Francesca Yorke © Dorling Kindersley; page 394 (CPP), © Enrique Chagoya. Photo: Ruben Guzman; **11.30** © Danny Lehman/Corbis; **11.31** The Art Archive/Gianni Dagli Orti; **11.32** Kate S. Buckingham Endowment, 1955.2281, The Art Institute of Chicago; **11.33** The Art Archive/Gianni Dagli Orti; **11.34** Dumbarton Oaks Research Library and Collections, Washington, D.C. Photograph by Justin Kerr; **11.35** © Richard Maschmeyer/Robert Harding World Imagery/Corbis; **11.36** The Art Archive/ Gianni Dagli Orti.

Chapter 12

12.1 © Adam Woolfitt/Corbis; **12.2** © Achim Bednorz, Köln; **12.4** © Achim Bednorz, Köln; **12.5** © Achim Bednorz, Köln; **12.6** Chartres Cathedral, Chartres, France/Peter Willi/The Bridgeman Art Library; **12.7** Sonia Halliday Photographs; **12.8** © Achim Bednorz, Köln; **12.9** © Achim Bednorz, Köln; page 412 (left), Sonia Halliday Photographs; page 412 (center), © Dorling Kindersley; page 413 (right), © Angelo Hornak; **12.10** John Bryson/Photo Researchers, Inc.; **12.12** © Stuart Black/Robert Harding World Imagery/Corbis; **12.13** © Angelo Hornak; **12.14** © Achim Bednorz, Köln; page 416 (CC), Photo By DEA/G. Dagli Orti/De Agostini/Getty Images; **12.15** © Achim Bednorz, Köln; **12.16** © Photo Scala, Florence; **12.17** Museo Civico, Bologna, Italy/Giraudon/The Bridgeman Art Library; **12.18** © The British Library Board. Harley MS 4425, f. 14v. All rights reserved/The British Library Board/The Bridgeman Art Library; **12.19** Erich Lessing/akg-images; **12.20** Sonia Halliday Photographs; **12.21** © Achim Bednorz, Köln; **12.22** © Réunion des Musées Nationaux–Grand Palais (domaine de Chantilly)/René-Gabriel Ojéda; **12.23** © Réunion des Musées Nationaux–Grand Palais (domaine de Chantilly)/René-Gabriel Ojéda; **12.24** © Réunion des Musées Nationaux–Grand Palais (domaine de Chantilly)/René-Gabriel Ojéda; **12.25** © Achim Bednorz, Köln; **12.26** © Photo Opera Metropolitana Siena/Scala, Florence; **12.27** © Sylvie Allouche/The Bridgeman Art Library; **12.28** © Photo Scala, Florence/Fondo Edifici di Culto – Min. dell'Interno; **12.29** Alinari Archives; page 428 (CC), Bibliothèque des Arts Decoratifs, Paris, France/Archives Charmet/The Bridgeman Art Library; **12.30** © Photo Scala, Florence; **12.31** Giraudon/The Bridgeman Art Library; **12.32** © Réunion des Musées Nationaux–Grand Palais (Musée du Louvre)/Martine Beck-Coppola; **12.33** © National Gallery, London/Scala, Florence.

Chapter 13

13.1 © Atlantide Phototravel/Corbis; **13.2** © Hideo Kurihara/Alamy; **13.3** © Quattrone, Florence; page 437 (CPP), Courtesy Ronald Feldman Fine Arts, New York/www.feldmangallery.com; **13.4** Alinari Archives; **13.5** © Quattrone, Florence; **13.6** © Photo Scala, Florence; page 441 (CC), Studio Kontos Photostock; **13.7** © Quattrone, Florence; **13.8** © Quattrone, Florence; page 444 (top), © Quattrone, Florence; page 444 (bottom), © Quattrone, Florence; page 445 © Quattrone, Florence; **13.9** The Art Archive/Duomo Florence/Alfredo Dagli Orti; **13.10** G.W. Scott-Giles; **13.11** G.W. Scott-Giles; **13.12** Image © The Metropolitan Museum of Art/Art Resource/Scala, Florence; **13.13** Erich Lessing/akg-images; **13.14** The Art Archive/Victoria and Albert Museum London/Eileen Tweedy; **13.16** Courtesy of the Library of Congress.

PART THREE

page 464: © Bildarchiv Preussischer Kulturbesitz/Photo Scala, Florence; page 465, timeline (top to bottom): © National Gallery, London/Scala, Florence; © Bildarchiv Preussischer Kulturbesitz/Photo Scala, Florence; Zigrossi Bracchetti/Vatican Musei/IKONA; © Quattrone, Florence; Image © The Metropolitan Museum of Art/Art Resource/Scala, Florence.

Chapter 14

14.1 Art Resource/Alinari; **14.2** © Arte & Immagini srl/Corbis; **14.3** Erich Lessing/akg-images; **14.4** Canali Photobank, Milan, Italy; **14.5** Erich Lessing/akg-images; **14.6** © Photo Scala, Florence; **14.7** © Photo Scala, Florence; **14.8** (left) © Quattrone, Florence; page 473 (CC), Bibliothèque des Arts Decoratifs, Paris, France/Archives Charmet/The Bridgeman Art Library; page 474–475, © Dorling Kindersley; page 475 (bottom right), © Topham/The Granger Collection, New York; **14.10** © Quattrone, Florence; **14.11** © Quattrone, Florence; **14.12** © Quattrone, Florence; **14.13** Canali Photobank, Milan, Italy; page 478 (CC), Photo By DEA/G. Dagli Orti/De Agostini/Getty Images; **14.14** © Quattrone, Florence; page 470 (CC, left), Erich Lessing/akg-images; page 470 (CC, right), akg-images/Nimatallah; **14.15** © Photo Scala, Florence – courtesy Ministero per i Beni e le Attività Culturali; **14.16** © Photo Scala, Florence; **14.17** © Achim Bednorz, Köln; page 482 (CC), Canali Photobank, Milan, Italy; **14.18** © Photo Scala, Florence; **14.19** © Quattrone, Florence; **14.20** © Quattrone, Florence; **14.21** © Quattrone, Florence; **14.22** © Photo Scala, Florence – courtesy Ministero per i Beni e le Attività Culturali; **14.23** © Quattrone, Florence; **14.24** The Royal Collection © 2011 Her Majesty Queen Elizabeth II/The Bridgeman Art Library; **14.25** © Quattrone, Florence; **14.26** © Quattrone, Florence; **14.27** Erich Lessing/akg-images; page 491 (CCP), © Julie Green; **14.28** © Réunion des Musées Nationaux–Grand Palais (Musée du Louvre)/Michel Urtado; **14.29** © Photo Scala, Florence – courtesy Ministero per i Beni e le Attività Culturali; **14.30** © Quattrone, Florence; **14.31** © Vincenzo Pirozzi, Rome, fotopirozzi@inwind.it.

Chapter 15

15.1 © Photo Scala, Florence – courtesy Ministero per i Beni e le Attività Culturali; **15.2** © Photo Scala, Florence; **15.3** © Araldo de Luca/Corbis; **15.4** © CAMERAPHOTO Arte, Venice; **15.5** © Vincenzo Pirozzi, Rome, fotopirozzi@inwind.it; page 505 (CPP), Photo by Brian Mengini; page 505 (CC), © Vincenzo Pirozzi, Rome, fotopirozzi@inwind.it; **15.7** Zigrossi Bracchetti/Vatican Musei/IKONA; **15.8** Foto Musei Vaticani; **15.10** Foto Musei Vaticani; **15.11** Image © The Metropolitan Museum of Art/Art Resource/Scala, Florence; **15-12** A. Bracchetti/P. Zigrossi/IKONA; **15.14** © 2013. Photo Scala, Florence; page 512, Vatican Museums, Rome, Italy; page 513, IAM/akg-images; **15.15** © Quattrone, Florence; **15.16** V&A Images/The Royal Collection, on loan from HM The Queen; **15.17** © 2013. Photo Scala, Florence; **15.18** © Quattrone, Florence; **15.19** © Photo Scala, Florence – courtesy Ministero per i Beni e le Attività Culturali; **15.20** ONB Vienna: Cod. 4809, fol. 1v–2r; **15.21** Cameraphoto Arte, Venice/Art Resource, NY; **15.22** Piero Codato/

TEXT CREDITS

Chapter 2

Reading 2.1, page 44: From "The Law Code of Hammurabi" from LAW COLLECTIONS FROM MESOPOTAMIA AND ASIA MINOR, 2/e, 1997 by Martha T. Roth, reprinted by permission of the Society of Biblical Literature. **Reading 2.2,** page 47: "The Blessing of Inanna" from MESOPOTAMIA: WRITING, REASONING, AND THE GODS by Jean Bottero, trans. by Zainab Bahrani and Marc Van De Mieroop. Copyright © 1992 by the University of Chicago. Reprinted by permission of The University of Chicago Press. **Reading 2.3,** page 63: From THE EPIC OF GILGAMESH, with an Introduction and Notes, trans. by Maureen Gallery Kovacs. Copyright © 1989 by the Board of Trustees of the Leland Stanford Jr. University. Used with the permission of Stanford University Press, www.sup.org. **Reading 2.3a–e,** pages 48–51: From THE EPIC OF GILGAMESH, with an Introduction and Notes, trans. by Maureen Gallery Kovacs. Copyright © 1989 by the Board of Trustees of the Leland Stanford Jr. University. Used with the permission of Stanford University Press, www.sup.org. **Reading 2.4,** pages 63–65: From The Hebrew Bible, Genesis 2–3, 6–7, from the NEW REVISED STANDARD VERSION BIBLE, copyright © 1989, Division of Christian Education of the National Council of the Churches of Christ in the United States of America. Used by permission. All rights reserved. **Reading 2.4a,** page 53: from the NEW REVISED STANDARD VERSION BIBLE, copyright © 1989, Division of Christian Education of the National Council of the Churches of Christ in the United States of America. Used by permission. All rights reserved. **Reading 2.4b,** page 54: From The Hebrew Bible, Song of Solomon 4:1–6, 7:13–14, from THE SONG OF SONGS: A NEW TRANSLATION AND COMMENTARY by Ariel Bloch and Chana Bloch. Copyright © 1995 by Ariel Bloch and Chana Bloch. Reprinted by permission of Georges Borchardt, Inc., on behalf of Ariel Bloch and Chana Bloch. **Reading 2.5,** page 60: From the "Hymn to Marduk" from MESOPOTAMIA: WRITING, REASONING, AND THE GODS by Jean Bottero, trans. by Zainab Bahrani and Marc Van De Mieroop. Copyright © 1992 by the University of Chicago. Reprinted by permission of The University of Chicago Press.

Chapter 3

Reading 3.1, page 71: "This It Is said of Ptah" from ANCIENT EGYPTIAN LITERATURE: VOLUME 1: THE OLD AND MIDDLE KINGDOMS by Miriam Lichtheim. Copyright © 2006 by the Regents of the University of California. Published by the University of California Press. Reproduced by permission of the publisher. **Reading 3.3,** page 88: From "Akhenaten's Hymn to the Sun" from ANCIENT EGYPTIAN LITERATURE: AN ANTHOLOGY, trans. by John L. Foster. Copyright © 2001. By permission of the University of Texas Press.

Chapter 4

Reading 4.1, page 128: "Patroclus Fights and Dies" from THE ILIAD by Homer, trans. by Robert Fagles, trans. copyright © 1990 by Robert Fagles. Used by permission of Viking Penguin, a division of Penguin Group (USA) LLC. **Reading 4.1a,** page 108: "Achilles and Priam" from THE ILIAD by Homer, trans. by Robert Fagles, trans. copyright © 1990 by Robert Fagles. Used by permission of Viking Penguin, a division of Penguin Group (USA) LLC. **Reading 4.2,** page 130:

Excerpt from Book 9 from THE ODYSSEY by Homer, trans. by Robert Fitzgerald. Copyright © 1961, 1963 by Robert Fitzgerald. Copyright renewed 1989 by Benedict R.C. Fitzgerald, on behalf of the Fitzgerald children. Reprinted by permission of Farrar, Straus and Giroux, LLC and the Estate of Robert Fitzgerald. **Reading 4.2a–b,** pages 108-109: Excerpts from Book 4 and Book 1 from THE ODYSSEY by Homer, trans. by Robert Fitzgerald. Copyright © 1961, 1963 by Robert Fitzgerald. Copyright renewed 1989 by Benedict R.C. Fitzgerald, on behalf of the Fitzgerald children. Reprinted by permission of Farrar, Straus and Giroux, LLC and the Estate of Robert Fitzgerald. **Reading 4.3,** page 112: "Autumn", from WORKS AND DAYS; THEOGONY by Hesiod, trans. by Stanley Lombardo. Copyright © 1993. Reprinted by permission of Hackett Publishing Company, Inc. All rights reserved. **Reading 4.6a–b,** page 124: 2 poems from SAPPHO: A NEW TRANSLATION by Mary Barnard. Copyright © 1986 by Mary Barnard. Published by the University of California Press. Reproduced by permission of the publisher.

Chapter 5

Reading 5.6, page 171: From THE SYMPOSIUM by Plato, trans. with an introduction and notes by Christopher Gill (Penguin Classics, 1999). Copyright © 1999 Christopher Gill. Reproduced by permission of Penguin Books Ltd. **Reading 5.7a,** page 153: From "Antigone", from THREE THEBAN PLAYS by Sophocles, trans. by Robert Fagles, copyright © 1982 by Robert Fagles. Used by permission of Viking Penguin, a division of Penguin Group (USA) LLC.

Chapter 6

Reading 6.1a, page 180: From THE AENEID OF VIRGIL: A VERSE TRANSLATION by Rolfe Humphries, ed. Brian Wilkie, 1/e, copyright © 1987. Printed and electronically reproduced by permission of Pearson Education, Inc., Upper Saddle River, New Jersey. **Reading 6.1b,** page 181: Excerpts from Book 8 from THE ODYSSEY by Homer, trans. by Robert Fitzgerald. Copyright © 1961, 1963 by Robert Fitzgerald. Copyright renewed 1989 by Benedict R.C. Fitzgerald, on behalf of the Fitzgerald children. Reprinted by permission of Farrar, Straus and Giroux, LLC and the Estate of Robert Fitzgerald. **Reading 6.1c,** page 181: From THE AENEID OF VIRGIL: A VERSE TRANSLATION by Rolfe Humphries, ed. Brian Wilkie, 1/e, copyright © 1987. Printed and electronically reproduced by permission of Pearson Education, Inc., Upper Saddle River, New Jersey. **Reading 6.6,** page 213: Poems 5 and 43 from THE POEMS OF CATULLUS, trans. with an introduction by Peter Whigham (Penguin Classics, 1966). Copyright © Penguin Books Ltd, 1966. Reproduced by permission of Penguin Books Ltd. **Reading 6.8,** page 213: From THE AENEID OF VIRGIL: A VERSE TRANSLATION by Rolfe Humphries, ed. Brian Wilkie, 1/e, copyright © 1987. Printed and electronically reproduced by permission of Pearson Education, Inc., Upper Saddle River, New Jersey. **Reading 6.9,** page 215: Reprinted by permission of the publishers and the Trustees of the Loeb Classical Library from HORACE: ODES AND EPODES, Loeb Classical Library, vol. 33, trans. by C.E. Bennett, Cambridge, Mass.: Harvard University Press, 1914. Copyright © 1927, 1968 by the President and Fellows of Harvard College. Loeb Classical Library® is a registered trademark of the President and Fellows of Harvard College.

Chapter 7

Reading 7.1, page 241: Poems from "The Book of Songs" trans. by Tony Barnstone and Chou Ping from LITERATURES OF ASIA, ed. by Tony Barnstone (Pearson Education 2003). Reprinted by permission of Tony Barnstone. **Reading 7.1a,** page 221: From THE BOOK OF SONGS, translated by Arthur Waley (Allen & Unwin, 1937). Copyright © by permission of The Arthur Waley Estate. **Reading 7.2,** page 222: "There are ways but the Way is uncharted" from THE WAY OF LIFE by Lao Tzu, trans. by Raymond B. Blakney, trans. copyright © 1955 by Raymond B. Blakney, renewed © 1983 by Charles Philip Blakney. Used by permission of Dutton Signet, a division of Penguin Group (USA) LLC, and the Estate of Raymond B. Blakney. **Reading 7.4,** page 228: Lines from Emperor Wu's "Heavenly Horses," trans. by Arthur Waley. Source: "Heavenly Horses of Ferghana" by Arthur Waley, p. 96, *History Today*, v. 5 # 2 (1955) 96-193. Copyright © 1955 by History Today. Reprinted by permission of the publisher. **Reading 7.5,** page 228: "Lament" by Liu Xijun, trans. by Tony Barnstone and Chou Ping, From LITERATURES OF ASIA, ed. by Tony Barnstone (Pearson Education 2003). Reprinted by permission of Tony Barnstone. **Reading 7.6,** page 228: "To Be a Woman" by Fu Xuan, trans. by Tony Barnstone and Willis Barnstone from LITERATURES OF ASIA, ed. by Tony Barnstone (Pearson Education 2003). Reprinted by permission of the translators. **Reading 7.7,** page 242: Excerpt from THE BHAGAVAD-GITA by Barbara Miller, trans. copyright © 1986 by Barbara Stoler Miller. Used by permission of Bantam Books, an imprint of The Random House Publishing Group, a division of Random House LLC. All rights reserved. Any third party use of this material, outside of this publication, is prohibited. Interested parties mus apply directly to Random House LLC for permission. **Reading 7.8,** page 244: Reprinted from THE DHAMMAPADA (1995) trans. by Ven. Ananda Maitreya, revised by Rose Kramer, with the permission of Parallax Press, Berkeley, California, www.parallax.org.

Chapter 8

Reading 8.2, page 252: From the Bible, Romans 5:1–11, from the NEW REVISED STANDARD VERSION BIBLE, copyright © 1989, Division of Christian Education of the National Council of the Churches of Christ in the United States of America. Used by permission. All rights reserved. **Reading 8.3,** page 254: From the Bible, Matthew 6:25–33, from the NEW REVISED STANDARD VERSION BIBLE, copyright © 1989, Division of Christian Education of the National Council of the Churches of Christ in the United States of America. Used by permission. All rights reserved. **Reading 8.5,** page 285: From AUGUSTINE: CONFESSIONS AND ENCHIRIDION, trans. and ed. by Albert C. Outler, copyright © 1955 SCM Press. Reproduced by permission of Westminster John Knox and Hymns Ancient & Modern Ltd. rights@hymnsam.co.uk. **Reading 8.5a,** page 266: From AUGUSTINE: CONFESSIONS AND ENCHIRIDION, trans. and ed. by Albert C. Outler, copyright © 1955 SCM Press. Reproduced by permission of Westminster John Knox and Hymns Ancient & Modern Ltd. rights@hymnsam.co.uk. **Reading 8.6,** page 286: From "Augustine's City of God." Reprinted by permission of the publishers and the Trustees of the Loeb Classical Library from AUGUSTINE: Vol. IV, Loeb Classical Library vol. 414, trans. by Philip Levine, Cambridge, Mass.: Harvard University Press. Copyright © 1966 by the President and Fellows of Harvard College. Loeb Classical Library® is a registered trademark of the President and Fellows of Harvard College. **Reading 8.6a,** page 267: From "Augustine's City of God." Reprinted by permission of the publishers and the Trustees of the Loeb Classical Library from AUGUSTINE: Vol. IV, Loeb Classical Library vol. 414, trans. by Philip Levine, Cambridge, Mass.: Harvard University Press. Copyright © 1966 by the President and Fellows of Harvard College. Loeb Classical Library® is a registered trademark of the President and Fellows of Harvard College.

Chapter 9

Reading 9.1, page 315: From Surah 47 from HOLY QUR'AN, trans. by M.H. Shakir (1982). Reprinted by permission of Tahrike Tarsile Qur'an, Inc. **Reading 9.1a,** page 292: From Surah 76 from HOLY QUR'AN, trans. by M.H. Shakir (1982). Reprinted by permission of Tahrike Tarsile Qur'an, Inc. **Reading 9.1b,** page 293: From Surah 5 from HOLY QUR'AN, trans. by M.H. Shakir (1982). Reprinted by permission of Tahrike Tarsile Qur'an, Inc. **Reading 9.4,** page 306: "My Heart Is in the East" by Judah Halevi, trans. by Willis Barnstone from LITERATURES OF THE MIDDLE EAST (Pearson Education 2003) is reprinted by permission of Willis Barnstone. **Reading 9.5,** page 310: From HAFT PAYKAR: A MEDIEVAL PERSIAN ROMANCE, trans. by Julie Scott Meisami (1995), 28 lines from "The Tale of the Black Princess" by permission of Oxford University Press. **Reading 9.6,** page 315: "The Tale of the Fisherman and the Genie," adapted text reprinted by permission of Emma Varesio. **Reading 9.8,** page 317: "Love's Body" and "Caring for My Lover" by Rumi, trans. by Tony Barnstone, Willis Barnstone, and Reza Baraheni, from LITERATURES OF THE MIDDLE EAST (Pearson 2003). Reprinted by permission of Tony Barnstone and Willis Barnstone. "The Clear Bead at the Center" by Rumi from OPEN SECRET: VERSIONS OF RUMI, trans. by John Moyne and Coleman Barks (1984) is reprinted by permission of Coleman Barks.

Chapter 10

Reading 10.1a–d, pages 323–325: From BEOWULF, trans. by Burton Raffel. Copyright © 1963, renewed © 1991 by Burton Raffel. Used by permission of Dutton Signet, a division of Penguin Group (USA) LLC, and Russell & Volkening as agents for the author. **Reading 10.2,** page 326: "Caedmon's Hymn," trans. by John C. Pope. Copyright © 1993, 1986, 1979, 1974, 1968, 1962 by W.W. Norton & Company, Inc. from THE NORTON ANTHOLOGY OF ENGLISH LITERATURE, 6th ed., Vol. 1, ed. by M.H. Abrams. Used by permission of W.W. Norton & Company, Inc. **Reading 10.3,** page 331: From SONG OF ROLAND, trans. by Patricia Terry, 2nd ed., © 1992. Reprinted by permission of Pearson Education, Inc., Upper Saddle River, NJ. **Reading 10.4,** page 357: Excerpts from HILDEGARD OF BINGEN: SCIVIAS, trans. by Columba Hart and Jane Bishop. Copyright © 1990 by the Abbey of Regina Laudis: Benedictine Congregation Regina Laudis of the Strict Observance, Inc. Paulist Press, Inc., New York/Mahwah, NJ. Reprinted by permission of Paulist Press, Inc. www.paulistpress.com. **Reading 10.7,** page 351: Bernard de Ventadour, from "The Skylark," trans. by W.D. Snodgrass from LARK IN THE MORNING: THE VERSES OF THE TROUBADOURS, ed. by Robert Kehew. Translations by Ezra Pound, W.D. Snodgrass, & Robert Kehew. Chicago: University of Chicago Press, 2005. Reprinted by permission of Kathleen Snodgrass. **Reading 10.8,** page 351: Comtessa de Dia's "Cruel are the Pains I've Suffered," trans. by Robert Kehew, from LARK IN THE MORNING: THE VERSES OF THE TROUBADORS, ed. by Robert Kehew, trans. by Ezra Pound, W.D. Snodgrass, and Robert Kehew. Copyright © 2005 by The University of Chicago. Reprinted by permission of the publisher. **Reading 10.9,** page 359: "Bisclavret (The Werewolf)" from THE LAIS OF MARIE DE FRANCE, trans. by Robert Hanning and Joan Ferrante, published by Baker Academic, a division of Baker Publishing Group, 1990. Used by permission.

Chapter 11

Reading 11.1, page 401: "Drinking Alone by Moonlight" by Li Bai, trans. by Willis Barnstone, Tony Barnstone, and Chou Ping, and "Dreaming of Li Bai" by Du Fu, trans. by Tony Barnstone and Chou Ping, from LITERATURES OF ASIA, ed. by Tony Barnstone (Pearson: 2003). Reprinted by permission of Willis Barnstone and Tony Barnstone. **Reading 11.1a,** page 366: "Summer Day in the Mountains" by Li Bai, trans. by Willis Barnstone, Tony Barnstone, and Chou Ping, and "Broken Lines" by Du Fu, trans. by Tony Barnstone and Chou Ping, from LITERATURES OF ASIA, ed. by Tony Barnstone (Pearson: 2003). Reprinted by permission of Willis Barnstone and Tony Barnstone. **Reading 11.3,** page 379: From DIARIES OF COURT LADIES OF OLD JAPAN, trans. by Annie Shepley Omori and Koch Doi (Houghton Mifflin: 1920). **Reading 11.4,** page 379: "This Perfectly Still" by Ki no Tomonori from ANTHOLOGY OF JAPANESE LITERATURE, comp. and ed. by Donald Keene, copyright © 1955 by Grove Press, Inc. Used by permission of Grove/Atlantic, Inc. and Penguin Books Ltd. **Reading 11.5,** pages 402–403: From "Hateful Things" from THE PILLOW BOOK OF SEI SHONAGON, trans. and ed. by Ivan Morris. Copyright © 1991 by Columbia University Press. Reprinted by permission of Columbia University Press and Oxford University Press (UK). Electronic rights for THE PILLOW BOOK OF SEI SHONAGON, tr. and ed. by Ivan Morris, copyright © 1967, 1991 by Ivan Morris. Reprinted by permission of Georges Borchardt, Inc., on behalf of the Estate of Ivan Morris. **Reading 11.5a,** page 379: "Elegant Things" from THE PILLOW BOOK OF SEI SHONAGON, trans. and ed. by Ivan Morris. Copyright © 1991 by Columbia University Press. Reprinted by permission of Columbia University Press and Oxford University Press (UK). Electronic rights for THE PILLOW BOOK OF SEI SHONAGON, tr. and ed. by Ivan Morris, copyright © 1967, 1991 by Ivan Morris. Reprinted by permission of Georges Borchardt, Inc., on behalf of the Estate of Ivan Morris. **Reading 11.7,** pages 395–396: From POPUL VUH, trans. by Ralph Nelson. Copyright © 1974, 1976 by Ralph Nelson. Reprinted by permission of Houghton Mifflin Harcourt Publishing Company. All rights reserved.

Chapter 13

Reading 13.1, pages 460–461: From THE DIVINE COMEDY by Dante Alighieri, trans. by John Ciardi. Copyright © 1954, 1957, 1959, 1960, 1961, 1965, 1967, 1970 by the Ciardi Family Publishing Trust. Used by permission of W.W. Norton & Company, Inc. **Reading 13.2,** page 448: From THE DIVINE COMEDY by Dante Alighieri, trans. by John Ciardi. Copyright © 1954, 1957, 1959, 1960, 1961, 1965, 1967, 1970 by the Ciardi Family Publishing Trust. Used by permission of W.W. Norton & Company, Inc. **Reading 13.3,** page 449: From THE DIVINE COMEDY by Dante Alighieri, trans. by John Ciardi. Copyright © 1954, 1957, 1959, 1960, 1961, 1965, 1967, 1970 by the Ciardi Family Publishing Trust. Used by permission of W.W. Norton & Company, Inc. **Reading 13.4,** pages 451–452: From THE DECAMERON OF GIOVANNI BOCCACCIO, trans. by Frances Winwar, copyright 1930 The Limited Editions Club, Inc.; renewed 1957. Used by permission. **Reading 13.6,** page 454: Excerpt from Sonnet 338, and Sonnet 134 from THE POETRY OF PETRARCH, trans. by David Young. Translation copyright © 2004 by David Young. Reprinted by permission of Farrar, Straus & Giroux, LLC. **Reading 13.7,** page 454: From "Prologue" from THE PORTABLE CHAUCER, ed. by Theodore Morrison, trans. by Theodore Morrison, trans. copyright © 1949, © 1975, renewed © 1977 by Theodore Morrison. Used by permission of Viking Penguin,

a division of Penguin Group (USA) LLC. **Reading 13.8,** page 463: From THE DECAMERON OF GIOVANNI BOCCACCIO, tr. Frances Winwar, copyright 1930 The Limited Editions Club, Inc.; renewed 1957. Used by permission.

Chapter 14

Reading 14.2, page 485: The poem "Triumph of Bacchus and Ariadne" from LORENZO DE MEDICI: SELECTED POEMS AND PROSE, trans. by Jon Thiem. Copyright © 1992 by The Pennsylvania State University. Reproduced by permission of Pennsylvania State University Press. **Reading 14.3,** page 485: From the book ORATION ON THE DIGNITY OF MAN by Pico della Mirandola, trans. by A. Robert Caponigri. Copyright © 1956. Published by Regnery Publishing, Inc. All rights reserved. Reprinted by special permission of Regnery Publishing, Inc., Washington, D.C.

Chapter 15

Reading 15.1, page 509: "Sonnet to John of Pistoia on the Sistine Ceiling" from COMPLETE POEMS AND SELECTED LETTERS OF MICHELANGELO by Creighton Gilbert. Copyright © 1980 by Creighton Gilbert. Published by Princeton University Press. Reprinted by permission of the Estate of Creighton Gilbert. **Reading 15.5,** pages 540–541: From THE NOBILITY AND EXCELLENCE OF WOMEN, AND THE DEFECTS AND VICES OF MEN by Lucrezia Marinella, ed. and trans. by Anne Dunhill. Copyright © 1999 by The University of Chicago. Reprinted by permission of the publisher. **Reading 15.5a,** page 530: From THE NOBILITY AND EXCELLENCE OF WOMEN, AND THE DEFECTS AND VICES OF MEN by Lucrezia Marinella, ed. and trans. by Anne Dunhill. Copyright © 1999 by The University of Chicago. Reprinted by permission of the publisher. **Reading 15.6,** pages 530–531: "Terze Rime, Capitolo 13" from POEMS AND SELECTED LETTERS BY VERONICA FRANCO, ed. and trans. by Ann Rosalind Jones and Margaret F. Rosenthal. Copyright © 1998 by The University of Chicago. Reprinted by permission of The University of Chicago Press.

Chapter 16

Reading 16.1, pages 566–567: From THE HEPTAMERON by Marguerite de Navarre, trans. with an introduction by P.A. Chilton (Penguin Classics, 1984). Copyright © 1984 P.A. Chilton. Reproduced by permission of Penguin Books Ltd.

Chapter 17

Reading 17.4, page 593: From THE REFORMATION WRITINGS OF MARTIN LUTHER, trans. by Bertram Lee-Woolf. Copyright © James Clarke & Co./The Lutterworth Press (2002). Reprinted by permission of the publisher. **Reading 17.6,** page 583: From Francois Rabelais, GARGANTUA AND PANTAGRUEL, Book 2, chapter 7 (1532–64), tr. Paul Brians from READING ABOUT THE WORLD, vol. 2, ed. by Paul Brians (Harcourt Custom Publishing, 1999). Reprinted by permission of Paul Brians. **Reading 17.7,** pages 594–595: From THE COMPLETE WORKS OF MONTAIGNE, trans. by Donald Frame. Copyright © 1948, 1953, 1958 by the Board of Trustees of the Leland Stanford Junior University, renewed 1970, 1975, 1986 by Donald Frame. Used with the permission of Stanford University Press. www.sup.org.

Chapter 18

Reading 18.1, page 631: From FLORENTINE CODEX: GENERAL HISTORY OF THE THINGS OF NEW SPAIN by Bernardino de Sahagun, trans. by Arthur J.O. Anderson and Charles E. Dibble (1970). Reprinted by permission of the University of Utah Press. **Reading 18.5,** pages 632–633: From "Semimaru" by Zeami Motokiyo from TWENTY PLAYS OF THE NO THEATRE by Donald Keene, trans. by Royall Tyler. Copyright © 1970 by Columbia University Press. Reprinted with permission of the publisher. **Reading 18.6,** page 626: "The One Mind Linking All Powers" by Zeami Motokiyo, from ANTHOLOGY OF JAPANESE LITERATURE, comp. and ed. by Donald Keene, copyright © 1955 by Grove Press, Inc. Used by permission of Grove/Atlantic, Inc. and Penguin Books Ltd.

Chapter 19

Reading 19.4, page 648: "On Monsieur's Departure" from THE POEMS OF QUEEN ELIZABETH I, ed. by Leicester Bradner. Copyright © 1964 by Brown University. Reprinted by permission of University Press of New England, Lebanon, NH.

Chapter 20

Reading 20.3, pages 678–679: From "The Trial of Veronese" from LITERARY SOURCES OF ART HISTORY by Elizabeth Gilmore Holt. Copyright © 1947 Princeton University Press; 1975 renewed by Princeton University Press. Reprinted by permission of Princeton University Press. **Reading 20.4,** pages 683–684: From THE COLLECTED WORKS OF ST. JOHN OF THE CROSS, tr. by Kieran Kavanaugh and Otilio Rodriguez. Copyright © 1964, 1979, 1991 by Washington Province of Discalced Carmelites ICS Publications 2131 Lincoln Road, NE, Washington, DC 20002-1199 USA. www.icspublications.org. **Reading 20.5,** Pages 684–685: DON QUIXOTE DE LA MANCHA by Miguel de Cervantes Saavedra, trans. by Charles Jarvis, ed. by E.C. Riley (Oxford World's Classics, 1992). Reprinted by permission of Oxford University Press (UK).